# Baseball America
# PROSPECT HANDBOOK
## 2007

### EDITORS
Jim Callis, Will Lingo, John Manuel

### ASSOCIATE EDITORS
Matt Eddy, Chris Kline

### CONTRIBUTING WRITERS
Andy Baggarly, Bill Ballew, Mike Berardino, J.J. Cooper, Matt Eddy, Aaron Fitt, Derrick Goold, Tom Haudricourt, Chris Kline, Alan Matthews, Matt Meyers, Jon Paul Morosi, John Perrotto, Tracy Ringolsby, Phil Rogers

### PHOTO EDITOR
Matt Meyers

### EDITORIAL ASSISTANT
Aaron Peeler

### DESIGN & PRODUCTION
Phillip Daquila, Drew McDaniel, Linwood Webb

### COVER PHOTOS
Philip Hughes by David Schofield; Delmon Young by Carl Kline; Homer Bailey by Sports On Film; Carlos Gonzalez by Larry Goren; Justin Morneau by Dan Arnold; Hanley Ramirez by Ken Babbitt; Roy Oswalt by Taylor Jones

### COVER DESIGN
Linwood Webb

## Baseball America

President/CEO: Catherine Silver
Vice President/Publisher: Lee Folger
Editors in Chief: Will Lingo, John Manuel
Executive Editor: Jim Callis
Design & Production Director: Phillip Daquila

Distributed by Simon & Schuster

ISBN-10: 1-932391-14-2     ISBN-13: 978-1-932391-14-5

■ Statistics compiled and provided by Major League Baseball Advanced Media.

## BaseballAmerica.com

# TABLE OF CONTENTS

Foreword by Dayton Moore                          5
Introduction                                      6
Profiling Prospects                               7
Explanation of Minor League Depth Charts          8
Staff Top 50s                                     9
Organization Rankings                            12

Arizona Diamondbacks                             14
Atlanta Braves                                   30
Baltimore Orioles                                46
Boston Red Sox                                   62
Chicago Cubs                                     78
Chicago White Sox                                94
Cincinnati Reds                                 110
Cleveland Indians                               126
Colorado Rockies                                142
Detroit Tigers                                  158
Florida Marlins                                 174
Houston Astros                                  190
Kansas City Royals                              206
Los Angeles Angels                              222
Los Angeles Dodgers                             238
Milwaukee Brewers                               254
Minnesota Twins                                 270
New York Mets                                   286
New York Yankees                                302
Oakland Athletics                               318
Philadelphia Phillies                           334
Pittsburgh Pirates                              350
St. Louis Cardinals                             366
San Diego Padres                                382
San Francisco Giants                            398
Seattle Mariners                                414
Tampa Bay Devil Rays                            430
Texas Rangers                                   446
Toronto Blue Jays                               462
Washington Nationals                            478

APPENDIX: Extra scouting reports                494
Scouting Dictionary                             495
2005, 2006 Signing Bonuses                      501
Minor League Top Prospects                      503
Index                                           506

# FOREWORD

Achieving long-term success is the primary goal of all 30 major league teams. Each organization's measure of success will be determined by the consistent production of their scouting and player-development departments.

Here in Kansas City, building from the top is not an option. Our energies, resources and vision will be focused on making good decisions about our current players as well as the players we are looking to acquire. Each decision we make will impact our future success.

I often give thought to that single, and very significant, decision that the Atlanta Braves made to acquire a Double-A pitcher by the name of John Smoltz in August 1987. That one move has helped change the course of the Braves and to this day is impacting them in a positive way.

As the Royals meet these challenges, our scouts must explore every talent pool and utilize all sources of information. Baseball America has been providing its readers with information and keen insight on baseball players for more than 25 years. The Prospect Handbook is a comprehensive guide with draft analysis and in-depth scouting summaries on every team's top 30 prospects.

We will continue to depend on the judgment and recommendations of our scouting staff. But, like so many fans, we will also turn to Baseball America's Prospect Handbook for additional perspective as we focus on returning a championship to Kansas City.

**Dayton Moore**
General Manager
Kansas City Royals

# INTRODUCTION

E very year, just before the Prospect Handbook goes out the door, a feeling comes over me that I like to call Prospect Handbook euphoria. The result of too much caffeine and not enough sleep? Perhaps. The realization that this massive undertaking is finally complete? Certainly. But more than anything else, it's the feeling that this book is the best of its kind—and in my opinion, it's not even close

We know you can find prospect rankings anywhere. We look at them too. But Baseball America's rankings have gained so much respect over the 25 years we've been around because so much work and care go into every list.

The people who wrote up each organization's rankings have talked to scouts, minor league managers, instructors, farm directors, scouting directors, and anyone else they can find with an educated opinion on the players in every farm system. And don't think we don't do statistical analysis, either. There's a reason you see all those numbers beneath each player's scouting report.

After a writer gathers all of his information and ranks his prospects, though, comes his toughest test: vetting his list with Jim Callis. Jim has strong, educated opinions on nearly every prospect you'll read about in this book, and he challenges at least a few rankings on every list.

Jim edits every organization (except the four he writes up himself), and then the writeups have stats and other complementary information added, and the pages are laid out, cut and proofed before they go to the printer. Just determining how many individuals have a hand in getting the Prospect Handbook into your hands each year is almost impossible.

One of the most important and underappreciated roles, though, is that of our production staff, which improves the look of the book every year. Go back through your collection of Prospect Handbooks and check out how much better the book is now than it was back in 2001. That's the result of hours of tweaking the design from year to year, and continual tinkering as the book goes from computer screen to printed page.

And this year the book has gotten on the page earlier than ever before. We hope you're reading the book even before spring training has started, giving you even more time to get ready for the season—and perhaps even for your big fantasy auction. Yes, we know the Prospect Handbook is your secret weapon for fantasy domination, but we promise not to tell anyone else.

Because the book went to press earlier this year, players are listed with the organizations they were with on Dec. 15. We know players like John Danks (and inevitably others) have changed organizations, but you can still find them with their old clubs by using the handy-dandy index in back. You'll also find scouting reports for 2006 Diamondbacks first-round pick Max Scherzer and Japanese import Kei Igawa of the Yankees on Page 494. And of course you can always visit BaseballAmerica.com for the most up-to-date prospect information anywhere.

Remember that for the purposes of this book, a prospect is anyone who is still rookie-eligible under Major League Baseball guidelines (no more than 50 innings pitched or 130 at-bats), without regard to service time.

You'll also find grades for each team's drafts from 2003-2005 in each organization section. The grades are based solely on the quality of the players signed, with no consideration given to whom they were traded for or how many first-round picks the club had or lost.

**Will Lingo**
Editor in Chief
Baseball America

# PROFILING PROSPECTS

mong all the scouting lingo you'll come across in this book, perhaps no terms are more telling and prevalent than "profile" and "projection."

When scouts evaluate a player, their main objective is to identify—or project—what the player's future role will be in the major leagues. Each organization has its own philosophy when it comes to grading players, so we talked to scouts from several teams to provide general guidelines.

The first thing to know is what scouts are looking for. In short, tools. These refer to the physical skills a player needs to be successful in the major leagues. For a position player, the five basic tools are hitting, hitting for power, fielding, arm strength and speed. For a pitcher, the tools are based on the pitches he throws. Each pitch is graded, as well as a pitcher's control, delivery and durability.

For most teams, the profiling system has gone through massive changes in recent years because of the offensive explosion in baseball. Where arm strength and defense used to be a must in the middle of the diamond, there has been an obvious swing toward finding players who can rake, regardless of their gloves. In the past, players like Jeff Kent and Chase Utley wouldn't have been accepted as second basemen, but now they are the standard for offensive-minded second basemen.

While more emphasis is placed on hitting—which also covers getting on base—fielding and speed are still at a premium up the middle. As teams sacrifice defense at the corner outfield slots, they look for a speedy center fielder to make up ground in the alleys. Most scouts prefer at least a 55 runner (on the 20-80 scouting scale; see chart)

at short and center field, but as power increases at those two positions, running comes down (see Michael Young, Jim Edmonds). Shortstops need range and at least average arm strength, and second basemen need to be quick on the pivot. Teams are more willing to put up with an immobile corner infielder if he can mash.

Arm strength is the one tool moving way down preference lists. For a catcher, it was always the No. 1 tool, but with fewer players stealing and the slide step helping to shut down running games, scouts are looking for more offensive production from the position. Receiving skills, including game-calling, blocking pitches and release times, can make up for the lack of a plus arm.

On the mound, it doesn't just come down to pure stuff. While a true No. 1 starter on a first-division team should have a couple of 70 or 80 pitches in his repertoire, like Johan Santana and Roy Oswalt, they also need to produce 250-plus innings, 35 starts and 15-plus wins.

player's overall future potential is also graded on the 20-80 scale, though some teams use a letter grade. This number is not just the sum of his tools, but rather a profiling system and a scout's ultimate opinion of the player.

**70-80 (A):** This category is reserved for the elite players in baseball. This player will be a perennial all-star, the best player at his position, one of the top five starters in the game or a frontline closer. Alex Rodriguez, Barry Bonds and Santana reside here.

**60-69 (B)** You'll find all-star-caliber players here: No. 2 starters on a championship club and first-division players. See Andy Pettitte, Miguel Tejada and David Wright.

**55-59 (C+)** The majority of first-division starters are found in this range, including quality No. 2 and 3 starters, frontline set-up men and second-tier closers.

**50-54 (C)** Solid-average everyday major leaguers. Most are not first-division regulars. This group also includes No. 4 and 5 starters.

**45-49 (D+)** Fringe everyday players, backups, some No. 5 starters, middle relievers, pinch-hitters and one-tool players.

**40-44 (D)** Up-and-down roster fillers, situational relievers and 25th players.

**38-39 (O)** Organizational players who provide depth for the minor leagues but are not considered future major leaguers.

**20-37 (NP)** Not a prospect.

## THE SCOUTING SCALE

When grading a player's tools, scouts use a standard 20-80 scale. When you read that a pitcher throws an above-average slider, it can be interpreted as a 60 pitch, or a plus pitch. Plus-plus is 70, or well-above-average, and so on. Scouts don't throw 80s around very freely. Here's what each grade means:

| | |
|---|---|
| 80 | Outstanding |
| 70 | Well-above-average |
| 60 | Above-average |
| 50 | Major league average |
| 40 | Below-average |
| 30 | Well-below-average |
| 20 | Poor |

# MINOR LEAGUE DEPTH CHART
## AN OVERVIEW

Another feature of the Prospect Handbook is a depth chart of every organization's minor league talent. This shows you at a glance what kind of talent a system has and provides even more prospects beyond the top 30. Each depth chart is accompanied by a quick take on a system's strengths and weaknesses, as well as where it ranks in baseball (see facing page for the complete list). The rankings are based on the quality and quanti-ty of talent in each system, with higher marks to clubs that have more high-ceiling prospects or a deep system. The best systems have both.

Players are usually listed on the depth charts where we think they'll ultimately end up. To help you better understand why players are slotted at particular positions, we show you here what scouts look for in the ideal candidate at each spot, with individual tools ranked in descending order.

| LF | CF | RF |
|---|---|---|
| Hitting | Fielding | Hitting |
| Power | Hitting | Power |
| Fielding | Speed | Arm Strength |
| Arm Strength | Power | Fielding |
| Speed | Arm Strength | Speed |

| 3B | SS | 2B | 1B |
|---|---|---|---|
| Hitting | Fielding | Hitting | Hitting |
| Power | Arm Strength | Fielding | Power |
| Fielding | Hitting | Power | Fielding |
| Arm Strength | Speed | Speed | Arm Strength |
| Speed | Power | Arm Strength | Speed |

| C |
|---|
| Fielding |
| Arm Strength |
| Hitting |
| Power |
| Speed |

| STARTING PITCHERS | | | |
|---|---|---|---|
| **No. 1 starter** | **No. 2 starter** | **No. 3 starter** | **No. 4-5 starters** |
| • Two plus pitches | • Two plus pitches | • One plus pitch | • Command of two major league pitches |
| • Average third pitch | • Average third pitch | • Two average pitches | • Average velocity |
| • Plus-plus command | • Average command | • Average command | • Consistent breaking ball |
| • Plus makeup | • Average makeup | • Average makeup | • Decent changeup |

| CLOSER |
|---|
| • One dominant pitch |
| • Second plus pitch |
| • Plus command |
| • Plus-plus makeup |

# TOP 50 PROSPECTS

**W**hile you may not regard him as a prospect in the purest sense of the word, Daisuke Matsuzaka is a rookie in the eyes of Major League Baseball. So he's eligible for inclusion in the Prospect Handbook and on our top 50 lists. And he's a pretty easy choice as the top prospect on all three of our lists. Who wouldn't want a potential ace, in the prime of his career, ready to step in to the big leagues right away?

After that, though, personal opinion takes the lists in different directions pretty quickly. It's from lists such as these that we begin to formulate our individual top 150 rankings, which are mashed together with lists from others in the creation of Baseball America's Top 100 Prospects. That list comes out during spring training, and we consider it the definitive guide to the best talent in the minor leagues.

**Yovani Gallardo**                                          *Brewers*

SPORTS ON FILM

The rules for these lists are the same for any prospect who appears in the handbook: rookie standards of no more than 130 at-bats or 50 innings in the major leagues. We do not consider service time in our eligibility requirements.

As with any prospect list, these rankings represent how each person regarded the top minor league talent in the game at a moment in time. Ask us again in a few months—or even tomorrow—how these prospects stack up, and you'll get a different answer.

## JIM CALLIS

1. Daisuke Matsuzaka, rhp, Red Sox
2. Alex Gordon, 3b, Royals
3. Delmon Young, of, Devil Rays
4. Brandon Wood, ss, Angels
5. Philip Hughes, rhp, Yankees
6. Homer Bailey, rhp, Reds
7. Jay Bruce, of, Reds
8. Cameron Maybin, of, Tigers
9. Justin Upton, of, Diamondbacks
10. Tim Lincecum, rhp, Giants
11. Andrew Miller, lhp, Tigers
12. Evan Longoria, 3b, Devil Rays
13. Yovani Gallardo, rhp, Brewers
14. Chris Young, of, Diamondbacks
15. Andrew McCutchen, of, Pirates
16. Andy LaRoche, 3b, Dodgers
17. Matt Garza, rhp, Twins
18. Reid Brignac, ss, Devil Rays
19. Troy Tulowitzki, ss, Rockies
20. Billy Butler, of, Royals
21. Carlos Gonzalez, of, Diamondbacks
22. Ian Stewart, 3b, Rockies
23. Ryan Braun, 3b, Brewers
24. Adam Jones, of, Mariners
25. Jose Tabata, of, Yankees
26. Fernando Martinez, of, Mets
27. Colby Rasmus, of, Cardinals
28. Clayton Kershaw, lhp, Dodgers
29. Scott Elbert, lhp, Dodgers
30. Adam Miller, rhp, Indians
31. Mike Pelfrey, rhp, Mets
32. Luke Hochevar, rhp, Royals
33. James Loney, 1b, Dodgers
34. Joey Votto, 1b, Reds
35. Nick Adenhart, rhp, Angels
36. Jacob McGee, lhp, Devil Rays
37. Jeff Niemann, rhp, Devil Rays
38. Jarrod Saltalamacchia, c, Braves
39. Jeff Clement, c, Mariners
40. Jacoby Ellsbury, of, Red Sox
41. Hunter Pence, of, Astros
42. Felix Pie, of, Cubs
43. Donald Veal, lhp, Cubs
44. Josh Fields, 3b, White Sox
45. Travis Snider, of, Blue Jays
46. Clay Buchholz, rhp, Red Sox
47. Adam Lind, of, Blue Jays
48. Jason Hirsh, rhp, Rockies
49. Dexter Fowler, of, Rockies
50. Travis Buck, of, Athletics

**Cameron Maybin**                                                                                          *Tigers*

## WILL LINGO

| | |
|---|---|
| 1. Daisuke Matsuzaka, rhp, Red Sox | 26. Miguel Montero, c, Diamondbacks |
| 2. Alex Gordon 3b, Royals | 27. Chris Volstad, rhp, Marlins |
| 3. Homer Bailey, rhp, Reds | 28. Jason Hirsh, rhp, Rockies |
| 4. Cameron Maybin, of, Tigers | 29. Jacoby Ellsbury, of, Red Sox |
| 5. Andrew McCutchen, of, Pirates | 30. Jose Tabata, of, Yankees |
| 6. Jay Bruce, of, Reds | 31. Billy Butler, of, Royals |
| 7. Delmon Young, of, Devil Rays | 32. Travis Buck, of, Athletics |
| 8. Justin Upton, of, Diamondbacks | 33. Adam Jones, of, Mariners |
| 9. Philip Hughes, rhp, Yankees | 34. Trevor Crowe, of, Indians |
| 10. Troy Tulowitzki, ss, Rockies | 35. Franklin Morales, lhp, Rockies |
| 11. Brandon Wood, ss, Angels | 36. Nick Adenhart, rhp, Angels |
| 12. Chris Young, of, Diamondbacks | 37. Hunter Pence, rhp, Astros |
| 13. Carlos Gonzalez, of, Diamondbacks | 38. Luke Hochevar, rhp, Royals |
| 14. Adam Miller, rhp, Indians | 39. Ryan Sweeney, of, White Sox |
| 15. Yovani Gallardo, rhp, Brewers | 40. Jarrod Saltalamacchia, c, Braves |
| 16. Mike Pelfrey, rhp, Mets | 41. Chuck Lofgren, lhp, Indians |
| 17. Tim Lincecum, rhp, Giants | 42. Bill Rowell, 3b, Orioles |
| 18. Evan Longoria, 3b, Devil Rays | 43. John Danks, lhp, Rangers |
| 19. Matt Garza, rhp, Twins | 44. Travis Snider, of, Blue Jays |
| 20. Colby Rasmus, of, Cardinals | 45. Jonathan Sanchez, lhp, Giants |
| 21. Reid Brignac, ss, Devil Rays | 46. Ryan Braun, 3b, Brewers |
| 22. Andrew Miller, lhp, Tigers | 47. Carlos Carrasco, rhp, Phillies |
| 23. Andy LaRoche, 3b, Dodgers | 48. Jaime Garcia, rhp, Cardinals |
| 24. Alberto Callaspo, 2b, Diamondbacks | 49. Elvis Andrus, ss, Braves |
| 25. Adam Lind, of, Blue Jays | 50. Clayton Kershaw, lhp, Dodgers |

# JOHN MANUEL

1. Daisuke Matsuzaka, rhp, Red Sox
2. Alex Gordon, 3b, Royals
3. Delmon Young, of, Devil Rays
4. Evan Longoria, 3b/ss, Devil Rays
5. Cameron Maybin, of, Tigers
6. Philip Hughes, rhp, Yankees
7. Homer Bailey, rhp, Reds
8. Brandon Wood, ss, Angels
9. Andrew Miller, lhp, Tigers
10. Andrew McCutchen, of, Pirates
11. Jay Bruce, of, Reds
12. Tim Lincecum, rhp, Giants
13. Fernando Martinez, of, Mets
14. Jose Tabata, of, Yankees
15. Reid Brignac, ss, Devil Rays
16. Justin Upton, of, Diamondbacks
17. Matt Garza, rhp, Twins
18. Yovani Gallardo, rhp, Brewers
19. Troy Tulowitzki, ss, Rockies
20. Chris Young, of, Diamondbacks
21. Clayton Kershaw, lhp, Dodgers
22. Carlos Gonzalez, of, Diamondbacks
23. Mike Pelfrey, rhp, Mets
24. Billy Butler, of, Royals
25. Adam Lind, of, Blue Jays
26. Adam Miller, rhp, Indians
27. Andy LaRoche, 3b, Dodgers
28. Ryan Braun, 3b, Brewers
29. Scott Elbert, lhp, Dodgers
30. Jeff Niemann, rhp, Devil Rays
31. Adam Jones, of, Mariners
32. Carlos Gomez, of, Mets
33. Carlos Carrasco, rhp, Phillies
34. Luke Hochevar, rhp, Royals
35. Jacoby Ellsbury, of, Red Sox
36. Nick Adenhart, rhp, Angels
37. Colby Rasmus, of, Cardinals
38. Franklin Morales, lhp, Rockies
39. Hunter Pence, of, Astros
40. Jonathan Sanchez, lhp, Giants
41. Chris Volstad, rhp, Marlins
42. Elvis Andrus, ss, Braves
43. Humberto Sanchez, rhp, Yankees
44. Troy Patton, lhp, Astros
45. Joey Votto, 1b, Reds
46. Glen Perkins, lhp, Twins
47. Jason Hirsh, rhp, Rockies
48. Travis Buck, of, Athletics
49. Jacob McGee, lhp, Devil Rays
50. Dexter Fowler, of, Rockies

**Reid Brignac** *Devil Rays*

**Andrew McCutchen** *Pirates*

# TALENT RANKINGS

| | | 2006 | 2005 | 2004 | 2003 | 2002 |
|---|---|---|---|---|---|---|
| 1 | **Tampa Bay Devil Rays** | 10 | 9 | 9 | 10 | 15 |

Really, with a major league club that never has won more than 70 games in a season, the Rays should have ranked No. 1 earlier in their history. Their parade of high draft picks should soon pay off now that they've been able to develop some pitching.

| | | 2006 | 2005 | 2004 | 2003 | 2002 |
|---|---|---|---|---|---|---|
| 2 | **Colorado Rockies** | 11 | 6 | 15 | 25 | 24 |

Again, a string of major league futility, combined with good scouting (and a strong Latin American program), produces an elite farm system. The Rockies don't have the Rays' sheer raw talent but seem better at bringing that talent out.

| | | 2006 | 2005 | 2004 | 2003 | 2002 |
|---|---|---|---|---|---|---|
| 3 | **Arizona Diamondbacks** | 1 | 13 | 13 | 21 | 23 |

No. 4 in the Handbook last year, Arizona jumped to No. 1 after signing Justin Upton. They fall back down a bit after graduating several potential studs, led by shortstop Stephen Drew, to the parent club.

| | | 2006 | 2005 | 2004 | 2003 | 2002 |
|---|---|---|---|---|---|---|
| 4 | **Los Angeles Angels** | 4 | 1 | 3 | 5 | 17 |

In the top five for a fifth consecutive season, the Angels have seen dividends from the likes of Howie Kendrick and Jered Weaver in the majors. More pitching is on the way, and Brandon Wood remains an elite prospect.

| | | 2006 | 2005 | 2004 | 2003 | 2002 |
|---|---|---|---|---|---|---|
| 5 | **Milwaukee Brewers** | 5 | 3 | 1 | 16 | 26 |

The Brewers join the Angels as regular residents in the top five, with their fourth straight season. And like the Rays and Rockies, the Brewers really should rank highly considering their last winning season was 1991.

| | | 2006 | 2005 | 2004 | 2003 | 2002 |
|---|---|---|---|---|---|---|
| 6 | **Los Angeles Dodgers** | 2 | 2 | 2 | 14 | 25 |

The best reason to drop in these rankings is by graduating impact players to the big leagues (ask the Marlins). The Dodgers weren't Organization of the Year for nothin', and they have two of the minors' top LHPs in Scott Elbert and Clayton Kershaw.

| | | 2006 | 2005 | 2004 | 2003 | 2002 |
|---|---|---|---|---|---|---|
| 7 | **New York Yankees** | 17 | 24 | 27 | 17 | 5 |

After four straight seasons as a second-tier farm system, the Yankees vault up the rankings thanks to their prodigious pitching depth and willingness to spend money in the draft. Philip Hughes and Jose Tabata are a terrific twosome at the top.

| | | 2006 | 2005 | 2004 | 2003 | 2002 |
|---|---|---|---|---|---|---|
| 8 | **Minnesota Twins** | 6 | 4 | 5 | 4 | 6 |

No team has had an above-average farm system longer than the Twins, in their sixth straight season ranking in our top 10. Though they've drafted a high school hitter first five times in the last six years, the Twins are pitcher-heavy.

| | | 2006 | 2005 | 2004 | 2003 | 2002 |
|---|---|---|---|---|---|---|
| 9 | **Boston Red Sox** | 8 | 21 | 23 | 27 | 28 |

The Red Sox lost plenty in trades (Hanley Ramirez, Anibal Sanchez) and graduation (Jon Lester, Jonathan Papelbon), but their top-flight draft class in 2006 improved their depth markedly and provided plenty of power arms.

| | | 2006 | 2005 | 2004 | 2003 | 2002 |
|---|---|---|---|---|---|---|
| 10 | **Cleveland Indians** | 9 | 7 | 6 | 1 | 20 |

The Indians' formula remains consistent. They have outstanding depth, keeping them around the top 10 even while remaking the big league club. The organization's strengths include lefthanded pitching and power relievers.

| | | 2006 | 2005 | 2004 | 2003 | 2002 |
|---|---|---|---|---|---|---|
| 11 | **Kansas City Royals** | 23 | 28 | 19 | 26 | 21 |

General manager Dayton Moore will emphasize development, and he wisely retained scouting director Deric Ladnier, who has hit on first-round picks such as Minor League Player of the Year Alex Gordon and Billy Butler.

| | | 2006 | 2005 | 2004 | 2003 | 2002 |
|---|---|---|---|---|---|---|
| 12 | **Cincinnati Reds** | 30 | 23 | 26 | 24 | 14 |

The biggest mover on the list from last year, the Reds have three players who would rank highly in any organization in Homer Bailey, Jay Bruce and Joey Votto. After that, well, it gets dicey thanks to a slew of 2006 trades.

| | | 2006 | 2005 | 2004 | 2003 | 2002 |
|---|---|---|---|---|---|---|
| 13 | **New York Mets** | 28 | 19 | 10 | 13 | 27 |

The Mets' top 10 ranks with any organization's, but the talent falls off quickly thereafter. General manager Omar Minaya's international emphasis has paid quick dividends with elite outfield prospect Fernando Martinez.

| | | 2006 | 2005 | 2004 | 2003 | 2002 |
|---|---|---|---|---|---|---|
| 14 | **Detroit Tigers** | 13 | 29 | 22 | 12 | 18 |

The most dynamic duo in the minors might just be Detroit's Cameron Maybin, a classic toolsy outfielder who performed in his debut, and 6-foot-6 lefthander Andrew Miller, who reached the majors in his pro debut.

| | | 2006 | 2005 | 2004 | 2003 | 2002 |
|---|---|---|---|---|---|---|
| 15 | **Florida Marlins** | 3 | 14 | 14 | 8 | 10 |

The Marlins set a record for most at-bats by rookies, and they had four rookie pitchers win 10 or more games in the big leagues. So it's no wonder that despite a nice group of pitchers in A-ball, the system had to drop a little.

| | 2006 | 2005 | 2004 | 2003 | 2002 |
|---|---|---|---|---|---|

**16 Atlanta Braves** — 7 — 5 — 4 — 2 — 7

The Braves' streak of National League division championships ended, and so did their streak of having one of the game's top-tier farm systems. Not only do the Braves lack their customary depth, but they also lack pitching depth.

**17 Baltimore Orioles** — 12 — 25 — 19 — 30 — 29

The Orioles wish they had the Braves' depth, but they'll have to settle for a system that's no longer a disaster. Scouting director Joe Jordan had another solid draft, adding an elite power bat (Bill Rowell) and an intriguing power arm (Pedro Beato).

**18 Chicago Cubs** — 15 — 10 — 7 — 3 — 1

The Cubs' farm system keeps sliding in concert with its major league win-loss record, and the Cubs haven't spent as wildly to keep pace in the minors. Top prospects such as Felix Pie and Donald Veal have tools but lack polish.

**19 Pittsburgh Pirates** — 19 — 18 — 11 — 18 — 22

Despite a streak of losing seasons that started in 1993, the Pirates have been unable to accumulate significant talent. Outfielder Andrew McCutchen and 2006 first-rounder Brad Lincoln highlight an otherwise tepid group.

**20 San Francisco Giants** — 18 — 17 — 24 — 11 — 12

It's probably not a good thing when a 16-year-old (Angel Villalona) is the No. 3 prospect in the system. The Giants gave away high draft picks as a matter of team policy for years, and the result is a system with more questions than answers.

**21 Philadelphia Phillies** — 22 — 20 — 21 — 7 — 11

The Phillies seem to be following the same plan of the Angels circa 2002. They have built a dynamic homegrown infield one piece at a time, and now are bringing the pitching along to supplement it.

**22 Houston Astros** — 20 — 22 — 29 — 23 — 3

The Astros' 2004 draft props up an otherwise uninspiring group that took a hit when Jason Hirsh was traded to the Rockies. Houston's Venezuelan pipeline hasn't completely dried up, but there are no Bob Abreus here either.

**23 St. Louis Cardinals** — 21 — 30 — 28 — 28 — 30

The reigning World Series champions have done just enough in the farm system to make trades to help the big league club. The system's track record going forward hinges on Jeff Luhnow, put in charge of scouting and player development.

**24 Seattle Mariners** — 27 — 11 — 12 — 9 — 2

GM Bill Bavasi likes to push his prospects, so the Mariners don't let their minor leaguers pile up big numbers. That approach seems ill-suited to an organization particularly heavy on international players.

**25 Toronto Blue Jays** — 25 — 15 — 8 — 6 — 13

The Jays are J.P. Ricciardi's franchise, and his stamp has been diminishing returns from a farm system that used to be one of the industry's best models. That won't matter if Ricciardi's big league moves help Toronto usurp the Yankees.

**26 Chicago White Sox** — 14 — 12 — 20 — 15 — 9

Few GMs have ever been more aggressive about trading their farm products than Kenny Williams, and it's hard to argue with the man who ended an 88-year World Series drought. Bet he'd like that Chris Young deal with the Diamondbacks back, though.

**27 Oakland Athletics** — 26 — 8 — 17 — 22 — 19

The constant winning in Oakland has taken its toll on the A's farm system, which also hasn't had as much success on the international front as it once did. Turning to high school pitchers in the draft could pay off, with patience.

**28 Texas Rangers** — 16 — 16 — 16 — 19 — 8

An organization's strength should not be failed starters who have become interesting middle relievers, but that's what the Rangers do best. No hitter in the system looks ready to step forward as a surefire big league regular.

**29 San Diego Padres** — 29 — 27 — 25 — 20 — 4

It's a five-year skid for the Padres on the scouting and player-development sides, now in their second year under the guidance of Grady Fuson. Agree or disagree with it, Fuson has a philosophy and the power to execute it.

**30 Washington Nationals** — 24 — 26 — 30 — 29 — 16

This really should come as no surprise considering the organization was under Major League Baseball ownership for four seasons. New ownership has committed publicly to revitalizing the franchise via scouting and player development.

# ARIZONA
# DIAMONDBACKS

BY **WILL LINGO**

You'd be hard-pressed to find an organization more excited following the completion of a season when it finished tied for last place. But that's the vibe coming from the Diamondbacks.

In part, that's because of what happened in Arizona last season. The team actually was on the fringes of playoff contention until Labor Day, and it finished in the top half of the National League in scoring, pitching and fielding. Brandon Webb solidified his status as an ace by winning the NL Cy Young Award, and the Diamondbacks solidified their commitment to him and Chad Tracy as franchise cornerstones by signing them to long-term extensions.

Arizona also worked in the first wave of its touted prospects into the big leagues. Conor Jackson took hold of the first-base job by putting up a .368 on-base percentage and 15 homers as a rookie. **Stephen Drew** seized the shortstop position with an .874 on-base plus slugging percentage in his first half-season in the big leagues. Outfielder Carlos Quentin had his moments, and Enrique Gonzalez and Tony Pena showed they're ready to contribute to the pitching staff.

And there's even more excitement about the talent on the way. Drew, Jackson and Quentin ranked as the top three prospects on this list a year ago, but the system remains loaded despite their graduations.

Outfielder Justin Upton, the No. 1 overall pick in the 2005 draft, takes over as the top prospect. His pro debut had its ups and downs, but his talent is undeniable. The Diamondbacks also have been successful adding talent in trades, with outfielder Chris Young and do-everything infielder Alberto Callaspo the most notable examples. And their successful Latin American program has produced outfielder Carlos Gonzalez and catcher Miguel Montero, who will be ready for the big leagues soon, and a younger generation of prospects behind them.

One of biggest keys to the steady flow of talent has been the successful drafts of former scouting director Mike Rizzo, who left to take a job as assistant general manager with the Nationals after another strong effort. The most promising member of the Class of '06, Missouri righthander Max Scherzer, isn't even on this prospect list because he had yet to sign. The Diamondbacks are expected to land him before spring training, and they found plenty of good arms behind him.

With its influx of talent, Arizona has had to say goodbye to a lot of veterans, including franchise icon Luis Gonzalez after the 2006 season. But while the Diamondbacks fondly remember a past that included the 2001 World Series title, they're focused on the future. The deferred salaries that weighed down the club's finances finally are coming off the books, and it's no accident the team unveiled a new logo and color scheme for the 2007 season.

The transformation of the Diamondbacks is well under way, and the outlook is bright.

## TOP 30 PROSPECTS

| | |
|---|---|
| 1. Justin Upton, of | 16. Cyle Hankerd, of |
| 2. Chris Young, of | 17. Chris Carter, 1b |
| 3. Carlos Gonzalez, of | 18. Chris Rahl, of |
| 4. Alberto Callaspo, 2b | 19. Brooks Brown, rhp |
| 5. Miguel Montero, c | 20. Brian Barden, inf |
| 6. Micah Owings, rhp | 21. Andrew Fie, 3b |
| 7. Mark Reynolds, inf | 22. Hector Ambriz, rhp |
| 8. Dustin Nippert, rhp | 23. Daniel Stange, rhp |
| 9. Tony Pena, rhp | 24. Danny Richar, 2b |
| 10. Ross Ohlendorf, rhp | 25. Pedro Ciriaco, ss |
| 11. Brett Anderson, lhp | 26. Dallas Buck, rhp |
| 12. Emilio Bonifacio, 2b | 27. Kyler Newby, rhp |
| 13. Alberto Gonzalez, ss | 28. Evan MacLane, lhp |
| 14. Gerardo Parra, of | 29. Leyson Septimo, of |
| 15. Greg Smith, lhp | 30. Matt Torra, rhp |

Photo credit: LARRY GOREN

# ORGANIZATION OVERVIEW

**General manager:** Josh Byrnes **Farm director:** A.J. Hinch. **Scouting director:** Tom Allison.

## 2006 PERFORMANCE

| Class | Team | League | W | L | PCT | Finish* | Manager | Affiliated |
|---|---|---|---|---|---|---|---|---|
| Majors | Arizona | National | 76 | 86 | .469 | 11th (16) | Bob Melvin | — |
| Triple-A | Tucson Sidewinders | Pacific Coast | 91 | 53 | .632 | +1st (16) | Chip Hale | 1998 |
| Double-A | *Mobile BayBears | Southern | 62 | 76 | .449 | 7th (10) | Gary Jones | 2005 |
| High A | †Lancaster Jethawks | California | 68 | 72 | .486 | 7th (10) | Brett Butler | 2001 |
| Low A | South Bend Silver Hawks | Midwest | 74 | 62 | .544 | 4th (14) | Mark Haley | 1997 |
| Short-season | Yakima Bears | Northwest | 28 | 48 | .368 | 7th (8) | Jay Gainer | 1999 |
| Rookie | Missoula Osprey | Pioneer | 42 | 34 | .553 | +3rd (8) | Hector De La Cruz | 1999 |
| **OVERALL 2006 MINOR LEAGUE RECORD** | | | 373 | 338 | .525 | 9th (30) | | |

*Finish in overall standings (No. of teams in league). +League champion. *Affiliate will be in Mobile (Southern) in 2007. †Affiliate will be in Visalia (California) in 2007.

## ORGANIZATION LEADERS

### BATTING
| | | |
|---|---|---|
| AVG | Parra, Gerardo, Missoula | .328 |
| R | Bonifacio, Emilio, Lancaster | 117 |
| H | Rahl, Chris, Lancaster | 195 |
| 2B | Rahl, Chris, Lancaster | 47 |
| 3B | Callaspo, Alberto, Tucson | 12 |
| HR | Reynolds, Mark, Lancaster/Tennessee | 35 |
| RBI | Reynolds, Mark, Lancaster/Tennessee | 112 |
| BB | Carter, Chris, Tucson | 79 |
| SO | Burgess, Brandon, Lancaster | 132 |
| SB | Bonifacio, Emilio, Lancaster | 61 |
| OBP | Quentin, Carlos, Tucson | .424 |
| SLG | Reynolds, Mark, Lancaster/Tennessee | .635 |

### PITCHING
| | | |
|---|---|---|
| W | Owings, Micah, Tennessee/Tucson | 16 |
| L | Schreppel, Ryan, South Bend | 13 |
| ERA | Dove, Shane, Yakima | 2.26 |
| G | Schultz, Mike, Tennessee/Tucson | 65 |
| SV | Elliott, Matt, Lancaster/Tennessee | 25 |
| IP | Ohlendorf, Ross, Tennessee/Tucson | 183 |
| BB | Cupps, Anthony, South Bend/Lancaster | 60 |
| SO | Nippert, Dustin, Tucson | 130 |
| | Owings, Micah, Tennessee/Tucson | 130 |
| AVG | Norberto, Jordan, Missoula | .216 |

## BEST TOOLS

| | |
|---|---|
| Best Hitter for Average | Justin Upton |
| Best Power Hitter | Mark Reynolds |
| Best Strike-Zone Discipline | Alberto Callaspo |
| Fastest Baserunner | Emilio Bonafacio |
| Best Athlete | Justin Upton |
| Best Fastball | Tony Pena |
| Best Curveball | Dustin Nippert |
| Best Slider | Tony Pena |
| Best Changeup | Greg Smith |
| Best Control | Ross Ohlendorf |
| Best Defensive Catcher | Miguel Montero |
| Best Defensive Infielder | Alberto Gonzalez |
| Best Infield Arm | Alberto Gonzalez |
| Best Defensive Outfielder | Chris Young |
| Best Outfield Arm | Carlos Gonzalez |

## PROJECTED 2010 LINEUP

| | |
|---|---|
| Catcher | Miguel Montero |
| First Base | Conor Jackson |
| Second Base | Alberto Callaspo |
| Third Base | Chad Tracy |
| Shortstop | Stephen Drew |
| Left Field | Carlos Quentin |
| Center Field | Chris Young |
| Right Field | Justin Upton |
| No. 1 Starter | Brandon Webb |

| | |
|---|---|
| No. 2 Starter | Micah Owings |
| No. 3 Starter | Dustin Nippert |
| No. 4 Starter | Doug Davis |
| No. 5 Starter | Ross Ohlendorf |
| Closer | Tony Pena |

## LAST YEAR'S TOP 20 PROSPECTS

1. Stephen Drew, ss
2. Conor Jackson, 1b
3. Carlos Quentin, of
4. Carlos Gonzalez, of
5. Dustin Nippert, rhp
6. Miguel Montero, c
7. Garrett Mock, rhp
8. Matt Torra, rhp
9. Micah Owings, rhp
10. Sergio Santos, ss
11. Chris Carter, 1b/of
12. Matt Green, rhp
13. Greg Smith, lhp
14. Tony Pena, rhp
15. Enrique Gonzalez, rhp
16. Jon Zeringue, of
17. Matt Chico, lhp
18. A.J. Shappi, rhp
19. Brian Barden, 3b/2b
20. Dan Uggla, inf

## TOP PROSPECTS OF THE DECADE

| Year | Player, Pos. | 2006 Org. |
|---|---|---|
| 1997 | Travis Lee, 1b | Devil Rays |
| 1998 | Travis Lee, 1b | Devil Rays |
| 1999 | Brad Penny, rhp | Dodgers |
| 2000 | John Patterson, rhp | Nationals |
| 2001 | Alex Cintron, ss | White Sox |
| 2002 | Luis Terrero, of | Orioles |
| 2003 | Scott Hairston, 2b | Diamondbacks |
| 2004 | Scott Hairston, 2b | Diamondbacks |
| 2005 | Carlos Quentin, of | Diamondbacks |
| 2006 | Stephen Drew, ss | Diamondbacks |

## TOP DRAFT PICKS OF THE DECADE

| Year | Player, Pos. | 2006 Org. |
|---|---|---|
| 1997 | Jack Cust, 1b | Padres |
| 1998 | Darryl Conyer, of (3rd round) | Out of baseball |
| 1999 | Corey Myers, ss | Angels |
| 2000 | Mike Schultz, rhp (2nd round) | Diamondbacks |
| 2001 | Jason Bulger, rhp | Angels |
| 2002 | Sergio Santos, ss | Blue Jays |
| 2003 | Conor Jackson, of | Diamondbacks |
| 2004 | Stephen Drew, ss | Diamondbacks |
| 2005 | Justin Upton, ss | Diamondbacks |
| 2006 | *Max Scherzer, rhp | None |

*Has not signed.

## ALL-TIME LARGEST BONUSES

| | |
|---|---|
| Travis Lee, 1996 | $10,000,000 |
| Justin Upton, 2005 | $6,100,000 |
| John Patterson, 1996 | $6,075,000 |
| Stephen Drew, 2004 | $4,000,000 |
| Byung-Hyun Kim, 1999 | $2,000,000 |
| Corey Myers, 1999 | $2,000,000 |
| Mike Gosling, 2001 | $2,000,000 |

# MINOR LEAGUE DEPTH CHART

## Arizona Diamondbacks

**Impact: A.** The Diamondbacks' top five prospects are all potential stars—led by outfielders Justin Upton, Chris Young and Carlos Gonzalez—and the rest of the top 10 has impact potential as well.

**Depth: A.** The pitching isn't as deep beyond the top five or six prospects, but among position players Arizona has legitimate prospects at every position and a ridiculous assortment of outfielders.

**Sleeper:** Bryant Thompson, rhp. He would have jumped onto the prospect lists of many organizations, but Thompson is a face in the crowd for the Diamondbacks. He's athletic with plus stuff and looked good in instructional league, so he could break out in 2007.

*Numbers in parentheses indicate prospect rankings.*

| LF | CF | RF |
|---|---|---|
| Cyle Hankerd (16) | Justin Upton (1) | Carlos Gonzalez (3) |
| Chris Rahl (18) | Chris Young (2) | Gerardo Parra (14) |
| Joey Side | Dave Krynzel | Leyson Septimo (29) |
| Brandon Burgess | Jereme Milons | Jon Zeringue |

| 3B | SS | 2B | 1B |
|---|---|---|---|
| Mark Reynolds (7) | Alberto Gonzalez (13) | Alberto Callaspo (4) | Chris Carter (17) |
| Brian Barden (20) | Pedro Ciriaco (25) | Emilio Bonafacio (12) | Jamie D'Antona |
| Andrew Fie (21) | | Danny Richar (24) | Cesar Nicolas |
| Agustin Murillo | | | |

| C |
|---|
| Miguel Montero (5) |
| Wilken Castillo |
| Josh Ford |
| John Hester |

| RHP | | LHP | |
|---|---|---|---|
| **Starters** | **Relievers** | **Starters** | **Relievers** |
| Micah Owings (6) | Tony Pena (9) | Brett Anderson (11) | Evan MacLane (28) |
| Dustin Nippert (8) | Brooks Brown (19) | Greg Smith (15) | Doug Slaten |
| Ross Ohlendorf (10) | Daniel Stange (23) | Ryan Schreppel | Bill Murphy |
| Hector Ambriz (22) | Kyler Newby (27) | Shane Dove | Doug Slaten |
| Dallas Buck (26) | Mike Schultz | Eddie Romero | |
| Matt Torra (30) | A.J. Shappi | Jordan Norberto | |
| Bryant Thompson | Osbek Castillo | | |
| Steven Jackson | Abe Woody | | |
| Matt Green | Matt Elliott | | |
| Daniel Fournier | Jason Neighborgall | | |
| Chase Christianson | | | |

## 2006 SIGNING BUDGET: $3.3 million

**Best Pro Debut:** OF Cyle Hankerd (3) was the Northwest League MVP and batting champ, and he was even more productive after a two-level jump to high Class A. Diamondbacks RHPs excelled in the Pioneer League, with Daniel Stange (7) topping the circuit with 13 saves and Tony Barnette (10) and Osbek Castillo (33) sharing the win lead with six each. Stange is the best prospect of that group and hit 98-99 mph in instructional league.

**Best Athlete:** RHP Dallas Buck (3) spent two years as a defensive back on Oregon State's football team. He gutted through his junior season with an elbow injury, playing a key role in the Beavers' College World Series championship, and may yet require Tommy John surgery. Among the position players, OF Joey Side (6) has all the tools except for home run power.

**Best Pure Hitter:** Hankerd, who showed he could hit with wood bats by winning MVP honors in the New England Collegiate League in the summer of 2005.

**Best Raw Power:** 1B Brad Miller (18) is a 6-foot-5, 230-pounder who owns Ball State's career record with 50 homers. Miller can hit a ball farther than anyone in this crop, but Hankerd may have more usable power.

**Fastest Runner:** OF Tyler Jones (19) used his plus-plus speed to steal 21 bases in 26 attempts as a pro.

**Best Defensive Player:** Side sticks out at any of the three outfield positions with his speed, breaks, routes and solid-average arm.

**Best Fastball:** RHP Max Scherzer (1) hadn't signed yet, but he's expected to eventually come to terms. He pitched in the mid-to upper 90s with Team USA in 2005, but his velocity was down as he battled biceps tendinitis last spring. In addition to Stange, whose fastball usually ranges from 90-96 mph when he's not working in relief, other hard throwers include RHPs Brooks Brown (1), Bryant Thompson (4) and Chase Christianson (8), all of whom top out at 94-95.

**Best Breaking Ball:** Scherzer's slider can be inconsistent, but he has flashed it at 87-88 mph, and the Diamondbacks envision it becoming a wipeout pitch.

**Most Intriguing Background:** LHP Brett Anderson's (2) father Frank is the head coach at Oklahoma State, where Brett committed before signing for $950,000. RHP Chad Beck (14) originally went to college on a football scholarship, and his brother Casey signed with the Braves as an eighth-round pick in June. Unsigned OF Riley Etchebarren's (39) uncle Andy caught in the majors and managed short-season Aberdeen in the Orioles' system this season.

**Closest To The Majors:** Scherzer. Anderson is polished for a high school pitcher, with some scouts saying he has the best command of any prep lefty in recent memory. He throws three pitches, including a plus changeup, for strikes.

**Best Late-Round Pick:** 3B Andrew Fie (12) is a mature high school hitter with some power potential. C Justin Brashear (44) also has pop and improved defensively by handling several quality pitchers at Mississippi.

**The One Who Got Away:** The Diamondbacks made a good if ultimately unsuccessful run at RHP Kendall Volz (50), a strongly built 6-foot-4, 220-pounder who has topped out at 94-95 mph. He's now at Baylor.

**Assessment:** Mike Rizzo's last draft as Arizona scouting director landed several quality arms to balance a system flush with bats. His first four picks (Scherzer, Brown, Anderson, Buck) were first-round talents, and Hankerd is an advanced college hitter in a draft that didn't feature many.

## 2005 BUDGET: $9.5 million

OF Justin Upton (1) was the right choice with the No. 1 overall pick. RHP Matt Torra (1) got hurt almost immediately, but RHP Micah Owings (3) and LHP Greg Smith (8) are keepers. **GRADE: A**

## 2004 BUDGET: $5.7 million

SS Stephen Drew (1) was worth the nearly yearlong wait it took to sign him. INF Mark Reynolds (16) emerged as a serious power threat last season. **GRADE: A**

## 2003 BUDGET: $4.2 million

The Diamondbacks wisely gambled on OF Carlos Quentin (1), even though he needed Tommy John surgery. Their earlier first-rounder, 1B Conor Jackson, also can hit in the middle of the order. **GRADE: A**

*Draft analysis by Jim Callis. Numbers in parentheses indicate draft rounds. Budgets are bonuses in first 10 rounds.*

# UPTON

OF

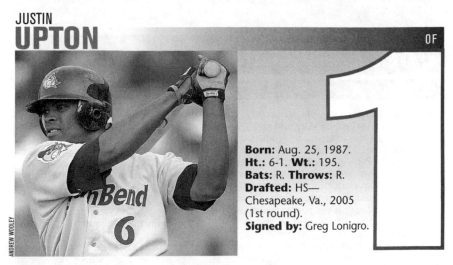

ANDREW WOOLEY

**Born:** Aug. 25, 1987.
**Ht.:** 6-1. **Wt.:** 195.
**Bats:** R. **Throws:** R.
**Drafted:** HS—
Chesapeake, Va., 2005
(1st round).
**Signed by:** Greg Lonigro.

1

Upton and his brother B.J. are the highest-drafted brothers in baseball history, with B.J. going second overall to the Devil Rays in 2002 and Justin doing him one better in 2005. He held out until January 2006 before finally signing for a then-draft-record $6.1 million bonus. Because of his last name and unbelievable tools, Justin has been on the scouting radar since he stood out at the 2002 Area Code Games—as a 14-year-old. He kept up his level of play throughout his prep career and was Baseball America's 2005 High School Player of the Year. While he played shortstop as an amateur, the Diamondbacks immediately moved him to center field to take advantage of his plus-plus speed and allow him to worry less about defense. The returns in his first pro season were mixed. While scouts loved his tools, they weren't as enthusiastic about his demeanor. He ranked as the No. 3 prospect in the low Class A Midwest League, behind Jay Bruce (Reds) and Cameron Maybin (Tigers), two other outfielders drafted in 2005's first round.

The term "five-tool prospect" somehow doesn't seem strong enough for Upton. He does everything exceptionally well and already has the body and composure of a big leaguer. If one thing stands out, however, it's his bat speed. He whips his bat through the hitting zone and has great leverage in his swing, which allows him to sting the ball like few players can and gives him plus power potential. His arm and speed are plenty good enough for center field, and though he was raw at the position he was taking better routes to balls by season's end. Even as he was learning, Diamondbacks officials say he "out-athletic-ed" the position early in the year.

Upton evokes comparisons to Ken Griffey Jr. in center field, but he didn't show Griffey's enthusiasm in his first season. Several managers and scouts in the MWL didn't like Upton's attitude and effort. They said he showed bad body language and often ran slowly to first, and they saw a few blowups in the dugout when he broke bats or got into arguments with his manager. The Diamondbacks, however, say they have no concerns about Upton's make-up and that he held his own on and off the field. From their perspective, he came to the MWL with a bullseye on his chest and was pitched like Albert Pujols from Opening Day, so it was natural that he occasionally got frustrated. At the plate, Arizona wants Upton to control the strike zone better and get into hitter's counts where he can be aggressive. At times he slides out to the front side a bit, but he has such tremendous bat speed that he just has to stay back and trust his swing. In the field, he still has to learn the nuances of playing the outfield, from learning how to charge the ball to hitting the cutoff man to becoming more of a field general.

The Diamondbacks say Upton has a strong desire to get to the big leagues quickly, and they have no plans to hold him back. They think the makeup questions will become little more than a footnote to his career as he matures. He'll open the season at the team's new high Class A Visalia affiliate and could put up huge numbers in the hitter-friendly California League.

| Year | Club (League) | Class | AVG | G | AB | R | H | 2B | 3B | HR | RBI | BB | SO | SB | OBP | SLG |
|------|---------------|-------|------|-----|-----|----|-----|----|----|----|-----|----|----|----|------|------|
| 2006 | South Bend (MWL) | A | .263 | 113 | 438 | 71 | 115 | 28 | 1 | 12 | 66 | 52 | 96 | 15 | .343 | .413 |
| **MINOR LEAGUE TOTALS** | | | .263 | 113 | 438 | 71 | 115 | 28 | 1 | 12 | 66 | 52 | 96 | 15 | .343 | .413 |

## 2 CHRIS YOUNG OF

**Born:** Sept. 5, 1983. **B-T:** R-R. **Ht.:** 6-2. **Wt.:** 180. **Drafted:** HS—Bellaire, Texas, 2001 (16th round). **Signed by:** Joe Butler/Paul Provas (White Sox).

The White Sox were the first team to steal Young, after he broke his left arm three days before the 2001 draft. But the Diamondbacks may be the ultimate winners after grabbing him in the Javier Vazquez deal before the 2006 season. Young missed the first three weeks of the season with a broken right wrist but made his major league debut by season's end. Arizona knew it was getting a good player in Young, but he turned out to be even better than expected. He quickly took to the organization's selective-aggression approach at the plate and dramatically cut down on his strikeouts while maintaining his power stroke. He's a great athlete, with well above-average speed that could make him a 30-30 man in the majors. He's a pure center fielder with a long stride that allows him to get to a lot of balls. The Diamondbacks have worked with Young to get more timing and rhythm in his swing so he can handle offspeed pitches better. His arm is his only tool that doesn't rate as a plus, but it's more than adequate. Arizona is loaded with talented young outfielders, but he's the best center fielder of the bunch and ready to take over in the majors.

| Year | Club (League) | Class | AVG | G | AB | R | H | 2B | 3B | HR | RBI | BB | SO | SB | OBP | SLG |
|------|---------------|-------|-----|---|----|---|---|----|----|----|-----|----|----|----|-----|-----|
| 2002 | White Sox (AZL) | R | .217 | 55 | 184 | 26 | 40 | 13 | 1 | 5 | 17 | 19 | 54 | 7 | .308 | .380 |
| 2003 | Bristol (Appy) | R | .290 | 64 | 238 | 47 | 69 | 18 | 3 | 7 | 28 | 23 | 40 | 21 | .357 | .479 |
| | Great Falls (Pio) | R | .176 | 10 | 34 | 5 | 6 | 3 | 0 | 0 | 0 | 1 | 10 | 0 | .200 | .265 |
| 2004 | Kannapolis (SAL) | A | .262 | 135 | 465 | 83 | 122 | 31 | 5 | 24 | 56 | 66 | 145 | 31 | .365 | .505 |
| 2005 | Birmingham (SL) | AA | .277 | 126 | 466 | 100 | 129 | 41 | 3 | 26 | 77 | 70 | 129 | 32 | .377 | .545 |
| 2006 | Tucson (PCL) | AAA | .276 | 100 | 402 | 78 | 111 | 32 | 4 | 21 | 77 | 52 | 71 | 17 | .363 | .532 |
| | Arizona (NL) | MLB | .243 | 30 | 70 | 10 | 17 | 4 | 0 | 2 | 10 | 6 | 12 | 2 | .308 | .386 |
| **MINOR LEAGUE TOTALS** | | | .267 | 490 | 1789 | 339 | 477 | 138 | 16 | 83 | 255 | 231 | 449 | 108 | .358 | .501 |
| **MAJOR LEAGUE TOTALS** | | | .243 | 30 | 70 | 10 | 17 | 4 | 0 | 2 | 10 | 6 | 12 | 2 | .308 | .386 |

## 3 CARLOS GONZALEZ OF

STEVE MOORE

**Born:** Oct. 17, 1985. **B-T:** L-L. **Ht.:** 6-1. **Wt.:** 180. **Signed:** Venezuela, 2002. **Signed by:** Miguel Nava.

Gonzalez followed up his 2005 MVP campaign in the Midwest League by again showing the all-around ability that gets scouts excited and allowed him to stand out among the crowd of prospects at the Futures Game. The Diamondbacks have an embarrassment of outfielders with all-around ability, and Gonzalez can hit with any of them. He has a quiet approach at the plate with good bat speed and quick hands, giving him above-average power. He became more confident last season. He's a prototype right fielder and has the best outfield arm in the organization. Gonzalez can get in home run mode and overswing, which slows down his bat, and he gets so anxious at the plate sometimes that he expands his strike zone. He didn't always hustle last season, but he apologized after an early-season benching and played hard the rest of the way. He has played center field during winter ball in Venezuela, but he'll probably slow down to a slightly below-average runner as he fills out and settle in right. He'll return to Double-A with the new affiliate in Mobile to open 2007.

| Year | Club (League) | Class | AVG | G | AB | R | H | 2B | 3B | HR | RBI | BB | SO | SB | OBP | SLG |
|------|---------------|-------|-----|---|----|---|---|----|----|----|-----|----|----|----|-----|-----|
| 2003 | Missoula (Pio) | R | .258 | 72 | 275 | 45 | 71 | 14 | 4 | 6 | 25 | 16 | 61 | 12 | .308 | .404 |
| 2004 | South Bend (MWL) | A | .275 | 14 | 51 | 5 | 14 | 4 | 0 | 1 | 8 | 1 | 13 | 0 | .288 | .412 |
| | Yakima (NWL) | A | .273 | 73 | 300 | 44 | 82 | 15 | 2 | 9 | 44 | 22 | 70 | 2 | .327 | .427 |
| 2005 | South Bend (MWL) | A | .307 | 129 | 515 | 91 | 158 | 28 | 6 | 18 | 92 | 48 | 86 | 7 | .371 | .489 |
| 2006 | Tennessee (SL) | AA | .213 | 18 | 61 | 11 | 13 | 6 | 0 | 2 | 5 | 7 | 12 | 1 | .294 | .410 |
| | Lancaster (Cal) | A | .300 | 104 | 403 | 82 | 121 | 35 | 4 | 21 | 94 | 30 | 104 | 15 | .356 | .563 |
| **MINOR LEAGUE TOTALS** | | | .286 | 410 | 1605 | 278 | 459 | 102 | 16 | 57 | 268 | 124 | 346 | 37 | .343 | .476 |

## 4 ALBERTO CALLASPO 2B

BILL MITCHELL

**Born:** April 19, 1983. **B-T:** B-R. **Ht.:** 5-11. **Wt.:** 173. **Signed:** Venezuela, 2001. **Signed by:** Carlos Porte/Amador Arias (Angels).

Faced with a logjam of middle infielders, the Angels dealt Callaspo to Arizona last February for righthander Jason Bulger. Callaspo was a do-everything player for a Triple-A Tucson team that was Baseball America's Minor League Team of the Year. He was the toughest full-season minor leaguer to strike out for the third year in a row, averaging 20.5 plate appearances per whiff. Callaspo has amazing plate coverage, but what's more impressive is his knowledge of the strike zone and knack for taking

borderline pitches. He can spray line drives all over the field. He has good speed and good actions at second base, and he can play almost anywhere on the field. He's a loosy-goosy player who brings energy to the ballpark each day. Callaspo doesn't have much power, so he has to get on base to maximize his value. He did a much better job of that last year. His lack of basestealing savvy keeps him from taking full advantage of his speed. While he's best at second base, Callaspo can also play shortstop, third base and the outfield. The Diamondbacks will look for him to make the big league team in a super-utility role out of spring training.

| Year | Club (League) | Class | AVG | G | AB | R | H | 2B | 3B | HR | RBI | BB | SO | SB | OBP | SLG |
|---|---|---|---|---|---|---|---|---|---|---|---|---|---|---|---|---|
| 2001 | Angels (DSL) | R | .356 | 66 | 275 | 55 | 98 | 11 | 4 | 2 | 39 | 22 | 16 | 14 | .403 | .447 |
| 2002 | Provo (Pio) | R | .338 | 70 | 299 | 70 | 101 | 16 | 10 | 3 | 60 | 17 | 14 | 13 | .374 | .488 |
| 2003 | Cedar Rapids (MWL) | A | .327 | 133 | 514 | 86 | 168 | 38 | 4 | 2 | 67 | 42 | 28 | 20 | .377 | .428 |
| 2004 | Arkansas (TL) | AA | .284 | 136 | 550 | 76 | 156 | 29 | 2 | 6 | 48 | 47 | 25 | 15 | .338 | .376 |
| 2005 | Arkansas (TL) | AA | .297 | 89 | 350 | 53 | 104 | 8 | 0 | 10 | 49 | 28 | 17 | 9 | .346 | .406 |
|  | Salt Lake (PCL) | AAA | .316 | 50 | 212 | 28 | 67 | 21 | 2 | 1 | 31 | 10 | 13 | 2 | .345 | .448 |
| 2006 | Tucson (PCL) | AAA | .337 | 114 | 490 | 93 | 165 | 24 | 12 | 7 | 68 | 56 | 27 | 8 | .404 | .478 |
|  | Arizona (NL) | MLB | .238 | 23 | 42 | 2 | 10 | 1 | 1 | 0 | 6 | 4 | 6 | 0 | .298 | .310 |
| MINOR LEAGUE TOTALS | | | .319 | 658 | 2690 | 461 | 859 | 147 | 34 | 31 | 362 | 222 | 140 | 81 | .370 | .434 |
| MAJOR LEAGUE TOTALS | | | .238 | 23 | 42 | 2 | 10 | 1 | 1 | 0 | 6 | 4 | 6 | 0 | .298 | .310 |

## ⑤ MIGUEL MONTERO  C

**Born:** July 9, 1983. **B-T:** L-R. **Ht.:** 5-11. **Wt.:** 190. **Signed:** Venezuela, 2001. **Signed by:** Junior Noboa.

The Diamondbacks showed their confidence in Montero's future by trading Johnny Estrada to the Brewers over the winter. While he didn't tear it up as he did the year before, Montero may have been more impressive in 2006 because he never struggled and proved himself as a catcher. He has a quick, short swing and uses the entire field, and he still has the power to jerk balls out of the park. He has an average arm and quick release. Montero loves to hit so much that, defensively, he was little more than a backstop a couple of seasons ago. But his work behind the plate has improved dramatically, both from a mechanical standpoint as well as the energy and leadership he brings. He will expand his zone at times, so he still can improve his understanding of the strike zone. Montero again played winter ball in Venezuela, which should further prepare him for the big leagues. He may share time with Chris Snyder to start the season, but Arizona expects him to take over the starting job for himself before too long.

| Year | Club (League) | Class | AVG | G | AB | R | H | 2B | 3B | HR | RBI | BB | SO | SB | OBP | SLG |
|---|---|---|---|---|---|---|---|---|---|---|---|---|---|---|---|---|
| 2001 | Diamondbacks (DSL) | R | .220 | 43 | 118 | 15 | 26 | 5 | 1 | 1 | 17 | 17 | 19 | 7 | .343 | .305 |
| 2002 | Missoula (Pio) | R | .263 | 50 | 152 | 21 | 40 | 10 | 1 | 3 | 14 | 17 | 26 | 2 | .343 | .401 |
| 2003 | Missoula (Pio) | R | .301 | 59 | 196 | 24 | 59 | 10 | 2 | 4 | 32 | 9 | 15 | 2 | .352 | .434 |
| 2004 | South Bend (MWL) | A | .263 | 115 | 403 | 47 | 106 | 22 | 2 | 11 | 59 | 36 | 74 | 8 | .330 | .409 |
| 2005 | Lancaster (Cal) | A | .349 | 85 | 355 | 73 | 124 | 24 | 1 | 24 | 82 | 26 | 52 | 1 | .403 | .625 |
|  | Tennessee (SL) | AA | .250 | 30 | 108 | 13 | 27 | 1 | 2 | 2 | 13 | 7 | 26 | 1 | .311 | .352 |
| 2006 | Tennessee (SL) | AA | .270 | 81 | 289 | 24 | 78 | 18 | 0 | 10 | 46 | 39 | 44 | 0 | .362 | .436 |
|  | Tucson (PCL) | AAA | .321 | 36 | 134 | 21 | 43 | 5 | 0 | 7 | 29 | 14 | 21 | 1 | .396 | .515 |
|  | Arizona (NL) | MLB | .250 | 6 | 16 | 0 | 4 | 1 | 0 | 0 | 3 | 1 | 3 | 0 | .294 | .313 |
| MINOR LEAGUE TOTALS | | | .287 | 499 | 1755 | 238 | 503 | 95 | 9 | 62 | 292 | 165 | 277 | 22 | .358 | .457 |
| MAJOR LEAGUE TOTALS | | | .250 | 6 | 16 | 0 | 4 | 1 | 0 | 0 | 3 | 1 | 3 | 0 | .294 | .313 |

## ⑥ MICAH OWINGS  RHP

**Born:** Sept. 28, 1982. **B-T:** R-R. **Ht.:** 6-5. **Wt.:** 220. **Drafted:** Tulane, 2005 (3rd round). **Signed by:** Mike Valarezo.

Owings was a second-round pick by the Rockies out of high school, but he went to Georgia Tech instead and was a two-way standout there. After the Cubs picked him in the 19th round as a draft-eligible sophomore in 2004, he again declined to sign and transferred to Tulane. Arizona landed him in 2005. He was pushed to Double-A in his first full season and excelled, winning a midseason promotion to Triple-A and going undefeated the rest of the way. He was the winning pitcher in the Triple-A championship game as Tucson defeated Toledo. After working out of the bullpen in his pro debut, Owings moved into the rotation and showed why so many people describe him as a warrior. While he threw 94-97 mph as a reliever, he paces himself as a starter and usually works at 88-92, though he has the extra velocity when he needs it. His mid-80s slider shows flashes of being a plus pitch. He does a lot of the intangible things good pitchers do, and he's a great athlete who fields his position well. He made a run at the national high school home run record and is still a good hitter. Arizona put Owings in the Double-A rotation to

work on his secondary pitches. While he didn't struggle, his slider and changeup still need to become more consistent. Owings is a big 24-year-old with strong makeup, so he'll move up once he shows he's ready. He'll likely open the season back in the Triple-A rotation.

| Year | Club (League) | Class | W | L | ERA | G | GS | CG | SV | IP | H | R | ER | HR | BB | SO | AVG |
|---|---|---|---|---|---|---|---|---|---|---|---|---|---|---|---|---|---|
| 2005 | Lancaster (Cal) | A | 1 | 1 | 2.45 | 16 | 0 | 0 | 0 | 22 | 17 | 6 | 6 | 0 | 4 | 30 | .221 |
| 2006 | Tennessee (SL) | AA | 6 | 2 | 2.91 | 12 | 12 | 0 | 0 | 74 | 66 | 24 | 24 | 4 | 17 | 69 | .246 |
| | Tucson (PCL) | AAA | 10 | 0 | 3.70 | 15 | 15 | 1 | 0 | 88 | 96 | 40 | 36 | 4 | 34 | 61 | .291 |
| **MINOR LEAGUE TOTALS** | | | 17 | 3 | 3.23 | 43 | 27 | 1 | 0 | 184 | 179 | 70 | 66 | 8 | 55 | 160 | .265 |

## 7 MARK REYNOLDS INF

BILL MITCHELL

**Born:** Aug. 3, 1983. **B-T:** R-R. **Ht.:** 6-1. **Wt.:** 200. **Drafted:** Virginia, 2004 (16th round). **Signed by:** Howard McCullough.

Reynolds played shortstop in a Virginia infield that also featured Ryan Zimmerman and Rockies prospect Joe Koshansky, but an injured wrist in his junior season dented his draft prospects. He broke out in 2006, hitting 31 homers between two stops before playing for Team USA in the Olympic qualifying tournament. He led that squad with four homers in just six games. Reynolds always had bat speed and power potential, and he finally has put together a consistent approach at the plate to tap into his ability. In the past he would show his strong hands in batting practice but float out on his front foot in games and sell out to pull the ball. Now he's staying back and is a threat to put a charge in the ball every time up. He's a versatile defender who played at first, second, third and the outfield last season. He's an average runner. While Reynolds can play a lot of positions, he'll never be a standout with the glove. His best spots are second and third base, and his ceiling is as a power-hitting second baseman in the Jeff Kent mold. The slow change in his approach illustrates how stubborn he can be. Reynolds will probably begin the season as the second baseman in Double-A, though he'll get time at other positions as well.

| Year | Club (League) | Class | AVG | G | AB | R | H | 2B | 3B | HR | RBI | BB | SO | SB | OBP | SLG |
|---|---|---|---|---|---|---|---|---|---|---|---|---|---|---|---|---|
| 2004 | South Bend (MWL) | A | .067 | 4 | 15 | 0 | 1 | 1 | 0 | 0 | 0 | 1 | 5 | 0 | .125 | .133 |
| | Yakima (NWL) | A | .274 | 64 | 234 | 58 | 64 | 19 | 1 | 12 | 41 | 25 | 65 | 4 | .372 | .517 |
| | Lancaster (Cal) | A | .083 | 4 | 12 | 1 | 1 | 0 | 0 | 0 | 1 | 0 | 4 | 0 | .083 | .083 |
| 2005 | South Bend (MWL) | A | .253 | 118 | 434 | 65 | 110 | 26 | 2 | 19 | 76 | 37 | 107 | 4 | .319 | .454 |
| 2006 | Tennessee (SL) | AA | .272 | 30 | 114 | 23 | 31 | 7 | 0 | 8 | 21 | 11 | 37 | 0 | .346 | .544 |
| | Lancaster (Cal) | A | .337 | 76 | 273 | 64 | 92 | 18 | 2 | 23 | 77 | 41 | 72 | 1 | .422 | .670 |
| **MINOR LEAGUE TOTALS** | | | .276 | 296 | 1082 | 211 | 299 | 71 | 5 | 62 | 216 | 115 | 290 | 9 | .356 | .523 |

## 8 DUSTIN NIPPERT RHP

**Born:** May 6, 1981. **B-T:** R-R. **Ht.:** 6-7. **Wt.:** 215. **Drafted:** West Virginia, 2002 (15th round). **Signed by:** Greg Lonigro.

After bouncing back from Tommy John surgery in June 2004 and taking the Southern League ERA crown in 2005, Nippert got off to a strong start last season, winning his first seven decisions to earn a big league callup. He got rocked in two starts with Arizona and didn't perform as well when he returned to Tucson, but the Diamondbacks were pleased that he completed 150 healthy innings. Nippert has top-of-the-rotation stuff, with a power fastball and power curveball. His fastball sits in the mid-90s and his curveball is a devastating pitch when he commands it. His changeup also has made progress, though it's a clear notch behind his other two pitches. The Diamondbacks are preaching patience with Nippert, mindful that a 6-foot-7 pitcher who missed a year will need extra development time. They're trying to establish more rhythm in his delivery so he can more consistently repeat his mechanics. He's also still learning about the art of pitching and that every fastball doesn't have to be 95 mph. Nippert will compete for a big league rotation spot in spring training, but he's not one of the top candidates. He has options remaining, so he'll probably go back to Triple-A with an eye toward contributing in 2008.

| Year | Club (League) | Class | W | L | ERA | G | GS | CG | SV | IP | H | R | ER | HR | BB | SO | AVG |
|---|---|---|---|---|---|---|---|---|---|---|---|---|---|---|---|---|---|---|
| 2002 | Missoula (Pio) | R | 4 | 2 | 1.65 | 17 | 11 | 0 | 0 | 55 | 42 | 12 | 10 | 2 | 9 | 77 | .208 |
| 2003 | South Bend (MWL) | A | 6 | 4 | 2.82 | 17 | 17 | 0 | 0 | 96 | 66 | 32 | 30 | 4 | 32 | 96 | .191 |
| 2004 | El Paso (TL) | AA | 2 | 5 | 3.64 | 14 | 14 | 0 | 0 | 72 | 77 | 45 | 29 | 0 | 40 | 73 | .273 |
| 2005 | Tennessee (SL) | AA | 8 | 3 | 2.36 | 18 | 18 | 3 | 0 | 118 | 95 | 33 | 31 | 4 | 42 | 97 | .225 |
| | Arizona (NL) | MLB | 1 | 0 | 5.52 | 3 | 3 | 0 | 0 | 15 | 10 | 9 | 9 | 1 | 13 | 11 | .185 |
| 2006 | Arizona (NL) | MLB | 0 | 2 | 11.70 | 2 | 2 | 0 | 0 | 10 | 15 | 13 | 13 | 5 | 7 | 9 | .349 |
| | Tucson (PCL) | AAA | 13 | 8 | 4.87 | 25 | 24 | 1 | 0 | 140 | 161 | 85 | 76 | 11 | 52 | 130 | .290 |
| **MINOR LEAGUE TOTALS** | | | 33 | 22 | 3.30 | 91 | 84 | 4 | 0 | 481 | 441 | 207 | 176 | 21 | 175 | 473 | .244 |
| **MAJOR LEAGUE TOTALS** | | | 1 | 2 | 8.03 | 5 | 5 | 0 | 0 | 24 | 25 | 22 | 22 | 6 | 20 | 20 | .258 |

## TONY PENA
**RHP**

**Born:** Jan. 9, 1982. **B-T:** R-R. **Ht.:** 6-1. **Wt.:** 220. **Signed:** Dominican Republic, 2002. **Signed by:** Junior Noboa.

While most of the players involved in the Dominican age scandal a few years ago have washed out of pro ball, Pena (formerly known as Adriano Rosario and believed to be five years younger) looks like he'll contribute in Arizona. After he missed most of the 2004 season and performed poorly as a starter in 2005, he took to a new role in the bullpen last season. With a mid-90s fastball and a slider that usually sits in the high 80s, Pena has a power repertoire well suited to bullpen work. His velocity and movement give him room for error with his pitches, and working in relief has allowed him to just let those pitches go and not worry so much about finesse. Refining his command in the strike zone will be the final step in Pena's development, as major league hitters punished him after he had been dominant in the minors. His changeup is inconsistent and average at best, but that's not much of a concern now that he's pitching in relief. Pena has missed time each of the past two springs because of visa issues, but if he comes to camp on time and in shape this year, he should win a job in the major league bullpen.

| Year | Club (League) | Class | W | L | ERA | G | GS | CG | SV | IP | H | R | ER | HR | BB | SO | AVG |
|------|---------------|-------|---|---|-----|---|----|----|----|----|----|----|----|----|----|----|-----|
| 2002 | Diamondbacks (DSL) | R | 3 | 1 | 2.05 | 10 | 10 | 1 | 0 | 57 | 41 | 16 | 13 | 0 | 7 | 57 | .193 |
| | Missoula (Pio) | R | 1 | 2 | 6.30 | 4 | 4 | 0 | 0 | 20 | 26 | 15 | 14 | 0 | 3 | 14 | .321 |
| 2003 | South Bend (MWL) | A | 9 | 5 | 2.86 | 27 | 27 | 0 | 0 | 160 | 149 | 69 | 51 | 3 | 30 | 119 | .247 |
| 2004 | El Paso (TL) | AA | 3 | 3 | 5.44 | 7 | 7 | 0 | 0 | 43 | 47 | 27 | 26 | 4 | 5 | 36 | .280 |
| | Diamondbacks (DSL) | R | 1 | 0 | 0.64 | 3 | 1 | 0 | 2 | 14 | 11 | 2 | 1 | 0 | 0 | 17 | .216 |
| 2005 | Tennessee (SL) | AA | 7 | 13 | 4.43 | 25 | 25 | 2 | 0 | 148 | 165 | 86 | 73 | 17 | 40 | 95 | .283 |
| 2006 | Tennessee (SL) | AA | 2 | 0 | 0.89 | 17 | 0 | 0 | 6 | 20 | 18 | 2 | 2 | 0 | 5 | 17 | .231 |
| | Tucson (PCL) | AAA | 3 | 1 | 1.71 | 24 | 0 | 0 | 7 | 26 | 17 | 6 | 5 | 1 | 2 | 21 | .183 |
| | Arizona (NL) | MLB | 3 | 4 | 5.58 | 25 | 0 | 0 | 1 | 31 | 36 | 21 | 19 | 6 | 8 | 21 | .290 |
| **MINOR LEAGUE TOTALS** | | | 29 | 25 | 3.41 | 117 | 74 | 3 | 15 | 488 | 474 | 223 | 185 | 25 | 92 | 376 | .253 |
| **MAJOR LEAGUE TOTALS** | | | 3 | 4 | 5.58 | 25 | 0 | 0 | 1 | 30 | 36 | 21 | 19 | 6 | 8 | 21 | .290 |

## ROSS OHLENDORF
**RHP**

**Born:** Aug. 8, 1982. **B-T:** R-R. **Ht.:** 6-4. **Wt.:** 235. **Drafted:** Princeton, 2004 (4th round). **Signed by:** Greg Lonigro.

Ohlendorf raised his draft profile by pitching Princeton to an NCAA regional playoff win against Virginia, but he didn't show his full potential as a pro until last season. Diamondbacks officials say he took the biggest leap forward in the organization. A big, physical presence on the mound, Ohlendorf has learned how to tone down his fastball to give him better sink and command. He now throws his power sinker anywhere from 89-94 mph. His changeup has become his second-best pitch, and his slider is average. He has developed a much better feel for pitching and now understands the importance of getting grounders and controlling his pitch count. While his secondary pitches have improved, he still needs to sharpen his slider to give him a more effective weapon against lefthanders. They hit .324 against him last season, compared with .236 for righthies. He's learning how to make in-game adjustments when things aren't going well. Arizona expected Ohlendorf's development to take time, and he has moved a little more quickly than expected. He'll open 2007 in the Triple-A rotation.

| Year | Club (League) | Class | W | L | ERA | G | GS | CG | SV | IP | H | R | ER | HR | BB | SO | AVG |
|------|---------------|-------|---|---|-----|---|----|----|----|----|----|----|----|----|----|----|-----|
| 2004 | Yakima (NWL) | A | 2 | 3 | 2.79 | 7 | 7 | 0 | 0 | 29 | 22 | 14 | 9 | 1 | 19 | 28 | .210 |
| 2005 | South Bend (MWL) | A | 11 | 10 | 4.53 | 27 | 26 | 1 | 0 | 157 | 181 | 97 | 79 | 10 | 48 | 144 | .286 |
| 2006 | Tennessee (SL) | AA | 10 | 8 | 3.29 | 27 | 27 | 4 | 0 | 178 | 180 | 70 | 65 | 13 | 29 | 125 | .271 |
| | Tucson (PCL) | AAA | 0 | 0 | 1.80 | 1 | 1 | 0 | 0 | 5 | 6 | 1 | 1 | 0 | 0 | 4 | .300 |
| **MINOR LEAGUE TOTALS** | | | 23 | 21 | 3.76 | 62 | 61 | 5 | 0 | 369 | 389 | 182 | 154 | 24 | 96 | 301 | .273 |

## BRETT ANDERSON
**LHP**

**Born:** Feb. 1, 1988. **B-T:** L-L. **Ht.:** 6-4. **Wt.:** 205. **Drafted:** HS—Stillwater, Okla., 2006 (2nd round). **Signed by:** Joe Robinson.

Anderson was regarded as a likely first-round pick going into the 2006 draft, but questions about his athleticism caused him to slide to the second round, where the Diamondbacks were happy to grab him. He signed for $950,000, too late to play during the summer, but stood out in instructional league in the fall. He's the son of Frank Anderson, long one of the most respected pitching coaches in college baseball before he became Oklahoma State's head coach. That's a big reason why he's so polished, with what scouts called the best command of any

high school lefty in recent memory. His development is far ahead that of most teenagers, and he has smooth, repeatable mechanics. He throws a fastball that touches 90 mph but usually sits in the high 80s, and he has a good feel for his plus changeup. He throws two breaking balls—a hard slider and a slow curveball—and the Diamondbacks will let him take both into his first season to see which works better. He has a good feel for pitching and competes hard. The biggest knock against Anderson is his soft body and lack of athleticism and agility. He had trouble fielding bunts and covering first base at times in high school. The Diamondbacks will work to improve that, but Anderson is just fine over the rubber and manipulates the baseball as well as any teenager. He'll open his first pro season at low Class A South Bend.

| Year | Club (League) | Class | W | L | ERA | G | GS | CG | SV | IP | H | R | ER | HR | BB | SO | AVG |
|------|---------------|-------|---|---|-----|---|----|----|----|----|---|---|----|----|----|----|-----|
| 2006 | Did not play—Signed 2007 contract | | | | | | | | | | | | | | | | |

## EMILIO BONIFACIO
2B

**Born:** April 23, 1985. **B-T:** B-R. **Ht.:** 5-11. **Wt.:** 180. **Signed:** Dominican Republic, 2001. **Signed by:** Junior Noboa.

Even with the wealth of position-player prospects in the organization, one Diamondbacks official called Bonifacio the most exciting player of all in the organization. After repeating low Class A in 2005, Bonifacio has made significant progress as a hitter and is now on the fast track. Of course, he's always on the fast track because his speed rates an 80 on the 20-80 scouting scale. When he makes like Luis Polonia from the left side and lays his bat on the ball as he's bolting from the box, Bonifacio has been timed at 3.6 seconds down the line to first. He has improved his basestealing approach, learning when to go and how to get good jumps rather than just trying to outrun the ball to second. He also has cut down on his swing and improved at working counts and fighting off tough pitches, though he still needs to understand the zone better and cut down on his strikeouts. He has good range and a solid arm on defense, but he needs to get more consistent and improve his footwork. Bonifacio brings so much energy to the park every day that the Diamondbacks are just trying to slow him down. If he continues to improve at the plate, he could be a prototype lead-off hitter. He'll get a good test by jumping to Double-A to start 2007.

| Year | Club (League) | Class | AVG | G | AB | R | H | 2B | 3B | HR | RBI | BB | SO | SB | OBP | SLG |
|------|---------------|-------|-----|---|----|---|---|----|----|----|-----|----|----|----|-----|-----|
| 2002 | Diamondbacks (DSL) | R | .300 | 68 | 227 | 60 | 68 | 9 | 5 | 1 | 15 | 51 | 55 | 51 | .428 | .396 |
| 2003 | Missoula (Pio) | R | .199 | 54 | 146 | 20 | 29 | 1 | 1 | 0 | 16 | 18 | 43 | 15 | .298 | .219 |
| 2004 | South Bend (MWL) | A | .260 | 120 | 411 | 59 | 107 | 9 | 6 | 1 | 37 | 25 | 122 | 40 | .306 | .319 |
| 2005 | South Bend (MWL) | A | .270 | 127 | 522 | 81 | 141 | 14 | 7 | 1 | 44 | 56 | 90 | 55 | .341 | .330 |
| 2006 | Lancaster (Cal) | A | .321 | 130 | 546 | 117 | 175 | 35 | 7 | 7 | 50 | 44 | 104 | 61 | .375 | .449 |
| **MINOR LEAGUE TOTALS** | | | .281 | 499 | 1852 | 337 | 520 | 68 | 26 | 10 | 162 | 194 | 414 | 222 | .352 | .362 |

## ALBERTO GONZALEZ
SS

**Born:** April 18, 1983. **B-T:** R-R. **Ht.:** 5-11. **Wt.:** 170. **Signed:** Venezuela, 2003. **Signed by:** Miguel Nava.

The Diamondbacks have rightly earned kudos in recent years for their successful drafts, but their Latin American scouting has been just as productive and is starting to produce big leaguers. Gonzalez has been viewed as a defensive master since signing out of Venezuela, but there were questions about his bat until the last two seasons. Now he looks like an everyday big league shortstop. Gonzalez is the best defensive player in the organization, regardless of position, and his pure shortstop actions rate an 80 on the 20-80 scouting scale. The Diamondbacks moved him to Triple-A for the PCL playoffs, an illustration of their confidence in his glove, and one team official said his defense had a noticeable effect on the pitchers he worked behind and on the other defenders in the infield. He has a strong arm and great range to both sides. At the plate, he has improved his approach and made some mechanical adjustments that allow him to use the whole field and stay inside the ball. He has developed good bat control and has the bat speed to hit the ball out of the park on occasion. If he continues to improve, he could be an ideal No. 2 hitter. He earned comparisons to Adam Everett for both his offense and defense. He'll open the season as Tucson's shortstop, but the long-term picture isn't clear because of Arizona's wealth of hitting prospects and young big leaguers.

| Year | Club (League) | Class | AVG | G | AB | R | H | 2B | 3B | HR | RBI | BB | SO | SB | OBP | SLG |
|------|---------------|-------|-----|---|----|---|---|----|----|----|-----|----|----|----|-----|-----|
| 2003 | Diamondbacks (DSL) | R | .283 | 58 | 205 | 38 | 58 | 13 | 2 | 1 | 18 | 19 | 10 | 15 | .363 | .380 |
| 2004 | South Bend (MWL) | A | .238 | 100 | 319 | 39 | 76 | 15 | 6 | 2 | 25 | 16 | 44 | 9 | .296 | .342 |
| 2005 | South Bend (MWL) | A | .318 | 95 | 352 | 60 | 112 | 21 | 7 | 1 | 42 | 20 | 42 | 12 | .359 | .426 |
| 2006 | Tennessee (SL) | AA | .290 | 129 | 434 | 67 | 126 | 20 | 3 | 6 | 50 | 37 | 42 | 5 | .356 | .392 |
| | Tucson (PCL) | AAA | .200 | 4 | 15 | 2 | 3 | 0 | 0 | 0 | 1 | 1 | 1 | 0 | .294 | .200 |
| **MINOR LEAGUE TOTALS** | | | .283 | 386 | 1325 | 206 | 375 | 69 | 18 | 10 | 136 | 93 | 139 | 41 | .343 | .385 |

## GERARDO PARRA
OF

**Born:** May 6, 1987. **B-T:** L-L. **Ht.:** 6-1. **Wt.:** 186. **Signed:** Venezuela, 2004. **Signed by:** Miguel Nava.

Parra made his domestic debut last season and impressed everyone who saw him, finishing among the Rookie-level Pioneer League batting and stolen-base leaders and rating as the league's No. 5 prospect and best outfield arm. More than one Diamondbacks official compared him with Carlos Gonzalez, and one said he's further along than Gonzalez at the same stage. Parra can do everything, but what impressed people the most was how well he handled the Pioneer League and made adjustments as a 19-year-old. He's a student of the game who always has a good plan at the plate, and he's great at centering the ball on the bat. He doesn't have a huge frame so he won't be a masher, but he'll certainly be a home run threat if only because of his bat speed. He has a cannon arm in right field, as well as good speed and great defensive instincts. Parra can still improve his plate discipline and handle inside pitches better, but there's not much to quibble with. On top of everything else, he has passion for the game and never takes an inning or an at-bat off. He'll make his full-season debut in low Class A this season.

| Year | Club (League) | Class | AVG | G | AB | R | H | 2B | 3B | HR | RBI | BB | SO | SB | OBP | SLG |
|---|---|---|---|---|---|---|---|---|---|---|---|---|---|---|---|---|
| 2005 | Diamondbacks (DSL) | R | .384 | 64 | 237 | 53 | 91 | 14 | 5 | 6 | 45 | 22 | 25 | 26 | .444 | .561 |
| 2006 | Missoula (Pio) | R | .328 | 69 | 271 | 46 | 89 | 18 | 4 | 4 | 43 | 25 | 30 | 23 | .386 | .469 |
| **MINOR LEAGUE TOTALS** | | | .354 | 133 | 508 | 99 | 180 | 32 | 9 | 10 | 88 | 47 | 55 | 49 | .413 | .512 |

## GREG SMITH
LHP

**Born:** Dec. 22, 1983. **B-T:** L-L. **Ht.:** 6-2. **Wt.:** 190. **Drafted:** Louisiana State, 2005 (6th round). **Signed by:** Matt Valarezo.

The Diamondbacks were happy to move their high Class A affiliation away from Lancaster, one of the best hitter's parks in the minor leagues. The park tended to inflate numbers for both hitters and pitchers, making it tough to judge either. Smith was one of the few pitchers who had the formula to succeed there, however, going 9-0 and even throwing two shutouts. He emerged at Louisiana State in 2005, putting together a 28⅔-inning scoreless streak, and has had consistent success as a pro. He completed his 2006 season with Team USA in the Olympic qualifying tournament. Smith has great touch and feel for his pitches, and his fastball touches 90 mph. His curveball is a potential strikeout pitch, and his changeup has the potential to be above-average, but he needs to improve the command of both. He has a good idea of how to set up hitters. Smith has one of the best pickoff moves in the minors, and basestealers were just 8-for-24 against him last season. He handled a two-level jump to high Class A in 2006, but he'll probably go back to Double-A to open this year.

| Year | Club (League) | Class | W | L | ERA | G | GS | CG | SV | IP | H | R | ER | HR | BB | SO | AVG |
|---|---|---|---|---|---|---|---|---|---|---|---|---|---|---|---|---|---|
| 2005 | Missoula (Pio) | R | 8 | 5 | 4.15 | 16 | 14 | 0 | 0 | 82 | 69 | 40 | 38 | 8 | 18 | 100 | .231 |
| 2006 | Lancaster (Cal) | A | 9 | 0 | 1.63 | 13 | 13 | 2 | 0 | 88 | 57 | 21 | 16 | 3 | 31 | 71 | .190 |
| | Tennessee (SL) | AA | 5 | 4 | 3.90 | 11 | 11 | 0 | 0 | 60 | 65 | 32 | 26 | 4 | 23 | 38 | .284 |
| **MINOR LEAGUE TOTALS** | | | 22 | 9 | 3.12 | 40 | 38 | 2 | 0 | 231 | 191 | 93 | 80 | 15 | 72 | 209 | .231 |

## CYLE HANKERD
OF

**Born:** Jan. 24, 1985. **B-T:** R-R. **Ht.:** 6-3. **Wt.:** 180. **Drafted:** Southern California, 2006 (3rd round). **Signed by:** Hal Kurtzman.

Hankerd has been on a roll over the past year and a half. After a pedestrian sophomore season at Southern California, he was MVP of the New England Collegiate League in the summer of 2005, then carried it over to his junior year. Arizona grabbed him in the third round, and he signed for $430,000 before winning the short-season Northwest League batting title (by 41 points) and MVP award. He had more hits than any other 2006 draft pick and was the only one to top 100. Hankerd is a pure hitter who can hit the ball with authority to all fields. He showed the ability to pull the ball early in the count or shorten up and go the opposite way with two strikes. He has a flat swing but puts good backspin on the ball, so he should hit 20-25 homers a year eventually. He has good makeup, good baseball instincts and a strong body. Hankerd's defense is nothing to get excited about, but he's adequate in left field. His arm is below average and he's a below-average runner. But it's his bat that will carry Hankerd. He was banged up and missed instructional league, and he'll probably open his first full season back in high Class A.

| Year | Club (League) | Class | AVG | G | AB | R | H | 2B | 3B | HR | RBI | BB | SO | SB | OBP | SLG |
|---|---|---|---|---|---|---|---|---|---|---|---|---|---|---|---|---|
| 2006 | Yakima (NWL) | A | .384 | 54 | 216 | 24 | 83 | 17 | 0 | 4 | 38 | 13 | 54 | 0 | .424 | .519 |
| | Lancaster (Cal) | A | .369 | 18 | 65 | 15 | 24 | 4 | 0 | 8 | 23 | 8 | 9 | 0 | .474 | .800 |
| **MINOR LEAGUE TOTALS** | | | .381 | 72 | 281 | 39 | 107 | 21 | 0 | 12 | 61 | 21 | 63 | 0 | .436 | .584 |

## CHRIS CARTER                                                    1B

**Born:** Sept. 16, 1982. **B-T:** L-L. **Ht.:** 6-0. **Wt.:** 195. **Drafted:** Stanford, 2004 (17th round). **Signed by:** Fred Costello.

Carter was a late-round bargain coming out of Stanford, where injuries and poor defense pushed him down the depth chart, and he has hit his way to prospect status. He has moved methodically through the organization and produced consistent results at the plate, and he finished ninth in the Pacific Coast League batting race in his first Triple-A experience. Carter has great bat speed along with outstanding knowledge of the strike zone, so he knows how to pick pitches he can punish and he does damage to them. He can hit the ball out to any part of the park and could bat in the middle of any batting order. His future is inextricably tied to his bat, however. He has been looking for a defensive position since he was in college, when a torn labrum and subsequent surgery cost him arm strength and needed development time in the outfield, and first base is the only option unless he moves to an American League organization. Carter has improved but remains a below-average defender, and he led PCL first basemen with 15 errors. He has a fringy arm and well below-average speed. Carter had a great spring in big league camp last year, and with a similar performance he could earn a bench job in Arizona in 2007. Otherwise he'll head back to Triple-A.

| Year | Club (League) | Class | AVG | G | AB | R | H | 2B | 3B | HR | RBI | BB | SO | SB | OBP | SLG |
|---|---|---|---|---|---|---|---|---|---|---|---|---|---|---|---|---|
| 2004 | Yakima (NWL) | A | .336 | 70 | 256 | 47 | 86 | 15 | 1 | 15 | 63 | 46 | 34 | 2 | .438 | .578 |
| 2005 | Lancaster (Cal) | A | .296 | 103 | 412 | 71 | 122 | 26 | 2 | 21 | 85 | 46 | 66 | 0 | .370 | .522 |
| | Tennessee (SL) | AA | .297 | 36 | 128 | 21 | 38 | 4 | 0 | 10 | 30 | 19 | 11 | 0 | .397 | .563 |
| 2006 | Tucson (PCL) | AAA | .301 | 136 | 509 | 87 | 153 | 30 | 3 | 19 | 97 | 78 | 69 | 10 | .395 | .483 |
| **MINOR LEAGUE TOTALS** | | | .306 | 345 | 1305 | 226 | 399 | 75 | 6 | 65 | 275 | 189 | 180 | 12 | .396 | .522 |

## CHRIS RAHL                                                      OF

**Born:** Dec. 5, 1983. **B-T:** R-R. **Ht.:** 6-0. **Wt.:** 185. **Drafted:** William & Mary, 2005 (5th round). **Signed by:** Greg Lonigro.

Rahl earned All-American honors in his sophomore season at William & Mary, but he pressed as a junior and fell to the Diamondbacks in the fifth round. He showed his ability in his first full season by winning the California League batting title and leading the league in hits, extra-base hits and total bases. He has a quick bat, controls the strike zone and has a good feel for the bat head. He drew a comparison with Paul Molitor for his quickness inside—it's hard to throw a fastball by him. He needs to improve his recognition of breaking balls and get less aggressive to cut down on his strikeouts. Playing in Lancaster probably boosted his power numbers, as he's regarded as more of a gap to gap hitter who could hit 10-15 home runs a year. He has good speed and a plus arm and plays mostly in center field, though some wonder if he could play there every day in the big leagues. That's the biggest knock on Rahl overall. He's a true baseball player with good makeup and no glaring weaknesses, but he also doesn't have an impact tool and might profile best as an extra outfielder. It's too early to pigeonhole him, though, and he'll go to Double-A to open 2007.

| Year | Club (League) | Class | AVG | G | AB | R | H | 2B | 3B | HR | RBI | BB | SO | SB | OBP | SLG |
|---|---|---|---|---|---|---|---|---|---|---|---|---|---|---|---|---|
| 2005 | Yakima (NWL) | A | .269 | 47 | 182 | 29 | 49 | 12 | 5 | 1 | 10 | 12 | 44 | 10 | .318 | .407 |
| 2006 | Lancaster (Cal) | A | .327 | 131 | 568 | 101 | 186 | 44 | 8 | 13 | 83 | 35 | 119 | 19 | .369 | .502 |
| **MINOR LEAGUE TOTALS** | | | .313 | 178 | 750 | 130 | 235 | 56 | 13 | 14 | 93 | 47 | 163 | 29 | .356 | .479 |

## BROOKS BROWN                                                    RHP

**Born:** June 20, 1985. **B-T:** L-R. **Ht.:** 6-3. **Wt.:** 205. **Drafted:** Georgia, 2006 (1st round supplemental). **Signed by:** Howard McCullough.

The second of 10 pitchers the Diamondbacks drafted in the first 10 rounds in 2006, Brown signed for $900,000 and got only limited work last summer after a heavy workload at Georgia. He was on low pitch counts and was used mostly in one- or two-inning stints. His Georgia career ended with a flourish after he adjusted his delivery in the Cape Cod League the summer before his junior season, and he helped the Bulldogs reach the College World Series with eight wins in 111 innings of work. Brown is a sinker/slider pitcher whose fastball has a nice downward plane and usually sits in the low 90s. His slider is above average at times, though he's not consistent enough with it, and his changeup has improved to be at least an average pitch. His athletic ability might be his greatest attribute, as he has good mechanics and should be durable. His stuff tended to fade during games in college, but the Diamondbacks will still try to use him as a starter because he has a good pitcher's frame and the potential for three legitimate major league pitches. He'll probably open the season in low Class A, though he could jump to high Class A with a good spring.

| Year | Club (League) | Class | W | L | ERA | G | GS | CG | SV | IP | H | R | ER | HR | BB | SO | AVG |
|------|---------------|-------|---|---|-----|---|----|----|----|----|---|---|----|----|----|----|-----|
| 2006 | Yakima (NWL) | A | 0 | 2 | 3.42 | 13 | 1 | 0 | 0 | 24 | 23 | 11 | 9 | 2 | 12 | 30 | .250 |
| **MINOR LEAGUE TOTALS** | | | 0 | 2 | 3.42 | 13 | 1 | 0 | 0 | 24 | 23 | 11 | 9 | 2 | 12 | 30 | .250 |

## BRIAN BARDEN

INF

**Born:** April 2, 1981. **B-T:** R-R. **Ht.:** 5-11. **Wt.:** 195. **Drafted:** Oregon State, 2002 (6th round). **Signed by:** Ed Gustafson.

Barden doesn't get much attention but keeps plugging away for the Diamondbacks and hitting enough that he's about to force his way into a big league job. He has added power to his offensive game and versatility to his defense in the last couple of seasons, making him a legitimate candidate for a utility job. Barden is the kind of player who just grinds out solid performances every day, and at the end of the year has produced good numbers. He has a nice line-drive stroke and is a good situational hitter, and his overall hitting approach has improved a little bit every year. On defense, his hands are as good as just about anyone in the organization. While third base is his best position, he played all four infield spots in Triple-A last season. He went to the Mexican Pacific League for winter ball and performed well as the starting third baseman for Hermosillo, priming him to compete for a bench job in spring training. In the right situation, he'll be a great role player for a big league team.

| Year | Club (League) | Class | AVG | G | AB | R | H | 2B | 3B | HR | RBI | BB | SO | SB | OBP | SLG |
|------|---------------|-------|-----|---|----|---|---|----|----|----|-----|----|----|----|-----|-----|
| 2002 | Yakima (NWL) | A | .333 | 4 | 15 | 5 | 5 | 1 | 0 | 0 | 2 | 1 | 1 | 0 | .412 | .400 |
| | Lancaster (Cal) | A | .335 | 64 | 269 | 58 | 90 | 19 | 1 | 8 | 46 | 16 | 63 | 3 | .370 | .502 |
| 2003 | El Paso (TL) | AA | .287 | 109 | 383 | 50 | 110 | 24 | 5 | 3 | 57 | 29 | 78 | 10 | .348 | .399 |
| 2004 | El Paso (TL) | AA | .303 | 48 | 195 | 33 | 59 | 10 | 6 | 3 | 28 | 10 | 48 | 1 | .335 | .462 |
| | Tucson (PCL) | AAA | .283 | 89 | 332 | 50 | 94 | 30 | 5 | 8 | 50 | 17 | 83 | 3 | .324 | .476 |
| 2005 | Tucson (PCL) | AAA | .307 | 135 | 518 | 78 | 159 | 36 | 5 | 15 | 85 | 38 | 111 | 14 | .363 | .483 |
| 2006 | Tucson (PCL) | AAA | .298 | 128 | 494 | 80 | 147 | 35 | 3 | 16 | 96 | 44 | 92 | 1 | .361 | .478 |
| **MINOR LEAGUE TOTALS** | | | .301 | 577 | 2206 | 354 | 664 | 155 | 25 | 53 | 364 | 155 | 476 | 32 | .353 | .466 |

## ANDREW FIE

3B

**Born:** Oct. 25, 1987. **B-T:** R-R. **Ht.:** 6-3. **Wt.:** 205. **Drafted:** HS—Jacksonville, Fla., 2006 (12th round). **Signed by:** Luke Wrenn.

It's rare for a player from Florida to slip under scouts' radar, but that's what the Diamondbacks think happened in Fie's case. He attended a small Christian school in north Florida that's off the beaten scouting path, so when he showed up at the Florida high school all-star game just before the 2006 draft, few people knew much about him other than Diamondbacks area scout Luke Wrenn. Wrenn quickly found allies in the Arizona scouting department when they saw a player with a good body who ran the 60-yard dash in 6.8 seconds and swung the bat well. The scouts had to sweat as Arizona waited until the 12th round to grab Fie, then signed him for $40,000. He's a youngster—he showed up at Rookie-level Missoula still wearing braces—but he held his own in the Pioneer League as an 18-year-old. Fie has a lot of rough edges, and he's raw at the plate, but he shows gap power already and the ball makes a loud sound off his bat. He'll have to improve his pitch recognition as well. He made 18 errors at third base but has the agility and arm to be at least an average defender there. Fie is a classic risk/reward high school player, but for $40,000 he could be quite a steal.

| Year | Club (League) | Class | AVG | G | AB | R | H | 2B | 3B | HR | RBI | BB | SO | SB | OBP | SLG |
|------|---------------|-------|-----|---|----|---|---|----|----|----|-----|----|----|----|-----|-----|
| 2006 | Missoula (Pio) | R | .259 | 67 | 255 | 33 | 66 | 23 | 2 | 6 | 31 | 21 | 81 | 8 | .318 | .435 |
| **MINOR LEAGUE TOTALS** | | | .259 | 67 | 255 | 33 | 66 | 23 | 2 | 6 | 31 | 21 | 81 | 8 | .318 | .435 |

## HECTOR AMBRIZ

RHP

**Born:** May 24, 1984. **B-T:** L-R. **Ht.:** 6-1. **Wt.:** 210. **Drafted:** UCLA, 2006 (5th round). **Signed by:** Hal Kurtzman.

Ambriz was a two-way star for UCLA after having shoulder surgery in 2004, batting cleanup and serving as the Bruins' Friday starter, but his pro future was always on the mound. After signing for $160,000 as a fifth-rounder, he emerged as the best pitching prospect at Missoula, working as a swingman and getting the save in the clinching game of the Pioneer League playoffs. While he had a controlled workload after pitching 113 innings for UCLA in the spring, Ambriz will work as a starter in 2007 because he has three pitches he can throw for strikes. His fastball sits in the low 90s and touches 95 mph at times, he has a splitter in the mid-80s that has the potential to be a plus pitch, and he made a lot of progress in tightening his curveball. He did a good job of keeping the ball down in his first summer, and scouts have been impressed with his feel for pitching and willingness to compete. His biggest weakness is a changeup that's still a ways off from being an effective pitch.

Health is also an issue; he had shoulder surgery as a freshman with the Bruins, and his body is such that he'll have to work hard to keep in shape. Ambriz will move into full-season ball at one of Arizona's Class A stops, and if he doesn't pan out as a starter he should be an effective reliever.

| Year | Club (League) | Class | W | L | ERA | G | GS | CG | SV | IP | H | R | ER | HR | BB | SO | AVG |
|------|---------------|-------|---|---|-----|---|----|----|----|----|---|---|----|----|----|----|-----|
| 2006 | Missoula (Pio) | R | 1 | 3 | 1.91 | 15 | 4 | 0 | 3 | 42 | 29 | 10 | 9 | 1 | 11 | 52 | .192 |
| **MINOR LEAGUE TOTALS** | | | 1 | 3 | 1.91 | 15 | 4 | 0 | 3 | 42 | 29 | 10 | 9 | 1 | 11 | 52 | .192 |

 ## DANIEL STANGE RHP

**Born:** Dec. 22, 1985. **B-T:** R-R. **Ht.:** 6-3. **Wt.:** 185. **Drafted:** UC Riverside, 2006 (7th round). **Signed by:** Mark Baca.

The Diamondbacks showed a definite affinity for big, strong, physical college pitchers under former scouting director Mike Rizzo, particularly in a 2006 draft designed to restock the system's pitching supply. Of that crop, Stange could be the most intriguing. He compiled 11 saves as UC Riverside's closer last spring, and the Diamondbacks took him in the seventh round and signed him for $115,000 because of his big body and bigger fastball. He led the Pioneer League with 13 saves while pitching at 90-96 mph, then followed that by hitting as high as 99 during instructional league, so he could move up fast. He also throws a good slider and average changeup, and all his pitches have good life. Stange has a violent delivery with a head jerk that precludes him from starting, but he seems better suited to a relief role anyway. He needs to establish more consistent fastball command and will have to improve his secondary pitches as he moves up. Stange will open the season as the closer in low Class A.

| Year | Club (League) | Class | W | L | ERA | G | GS | CG | SV | IP | H | R | ER | HR | BB | SO | AVG |
|------|---------------|-------|---|---|-----|---|----|----|----|----|---|---|----|----|----|----|-----|
| 2006 | Missoula (Pio) | R | 5 | 2 | 4.25 | 27 | 0 | 0 | 13 | 36 | 39 | 19 | 17 | 2 | 17 | 48 | .267 |
| **MINOR LEAGUE TOTALS** | | | 5 | 2 | 4.25 | 27 | 0 | 0 | 13 | 36 | 39 | 19 | 17 | 2 | 17 | 48 | .267 |

 ## DANNY RICHAR 2B

**Born:** June 9, 1983. **B-T:** L-R. **Ht.:** 6-0. **Wt.:** 170. **Signed:** Dominican Republic, 2001. **Signed by:** Junior Noboa.

Richar looked like a utility player in his first few seasons in the organization, but he kept getting bigger, stronger and better. He was the Double-A Southern League's all-star second baseman last year and was added to the 40-man roster after the season, though his performance tailed off late in the year as he got tired. He started working on his swing with hitting coach Damon Mashore in high Class A, and he has developed a good approach at the plate. He has a much better swing now and has even shown a little power in the last couple of seasons. He has also settled in at second base after working at shortstop and third base earlier in his career and has become a solid defender. He has an average arm and above-average speed. While Richar has become a solid player, he's not dynamic. He's a good bet to get to the big leagues, but the question is how much he'll hit when he gets there. Other teams have asked about him in trade talks, so his best value to the Diamondbacks might be as a bargaining chip. He'll open the season in Triple-A.

| Year | Club (League) | Class | AVG | G | AB | R | H | 2B | 3B | HR | RBI | BB | SO | SB | OBP | SLG |
|------|---------------|-------|-----|---|----|---|---|----|----|----|-----|----|----|----|-----|-----|
| 2002 | Lancaster (Cal) | A | .231 | 85 | 251 | 27 | 58 | 7 | 1 | 1 | 17 | 12 | 49 | 4 | .274 | .279 |
| | Yakima (NWL) | A | .227 | 25 | 88 | 7 | 20 | 5 | 1 | 0 | 9 | 6 | 21 | 0 | .274 | .307 |
| 2003 | Lancaster (Cal) | A | .304 | 123 | 405 | 51 | 123 | 19 | 9 | 1 | 42 | 14 | 70 | 6 | .331 | .402 |
| 2004 | El Paso (TL) | AA | .207 | 26 | 82 | 6 | 17 | 3 | 0 | 0 | 5 | 7 | 17 | 2 | .286 | .244 |
| | Lancaster (Cal) | A | .282 | 96 | 383 | 51 | 108 | 13 | 4 | 6 | 44 | 16 | 78 | 22 | .312 | .384 |
| 2005 | Lancaster (Cal) | A | .300 | 121 | 454 | 78 | 136 | 32 | 8 | 20 | 79 | 32 | 64 | 9 | .347 | .537 |
| 2006 | Tennessee (SL) | AA | .292 | 130 | 480 | 79 | 140 | 25 | 5 | 8 | 42 | 52 | 77 | 15 | .360 | .415 |
| **MINOR LEAGUE TOTALS** | | | .281 | 606 | 2143 | 299 | 602 | 104 | 28 | 36 | 238 | 139 | 376 | 58 | .327 | .406 |

 ## PEDRO CIRIACO SS

**Born:** Sept. 27, 1985. **B-T:** R-R. **Ht.:** 6-0. **Wt.:** 150. **Signed:** Dominican Republic, 2003. **Signed by:** Junior Noboa.

While he's moving steadily through the organization, Ciriaco is one of the rawest players in the Diamondbacks system and little more than a package of intriguing tools at this point. But those tools are very intriguing. Ciriaco has a strong arm, though he's still learning how to harness it. He has poor footwork on defense and led the minor leagues with 45 errors last season, but that was an improvement on the 34 he committed in a half-season a year earlier. He also is very athletic and is a plus runner, yet he has been caught on a third of his career basestealing attempts, including a 19-for-27 effort in 2006. At the plate, he has the bat speed and hand-eye coordination to hit but he's still learning a coherent approach. He'll chase just

about anything and gets himself out more often than pitchers do. Still, the Diamondbacks are developing a track record of not only discovering talent in Latin America but also developing it. They're trying to get Ciraco to slow himself down, and they may do the same thing by returning him to South Bend to start the season.

| Year | Club (League) | Class | AVG | G | AB | R | H | 2B | 3B | HR | RBI | BB | SO | SB | OBP | SLG |
|---|---|---|---|---|---|---|---|---|---|---|---|---|---|---|---|---|
| 2003 | Diamondbacks (DSL) | R | .231 | 57 | 221 | 40 | 51 | 10 | 2 | 0 | 16 | 16 | 34 | 14 | .290 | .294 |
| 2004 | Diamondbacks (DSL) | R | .349 | 67 | 252 | 45 | 88 | 11 | 4 | 1 | 18 | 19 | 33 | 29 | .401 | .437 |
| 2005 | Missoula (Pio) | R | .240 | 69 | 254 | 28 | 61 | 9 | 4 | 2 | 31 | 7 | 50 | 7 | .264 | .331 |
| 2006 | South Bend (MWL) | A | .264 | 128 | 550 | 77 | 145 | 15 | 5 | 2 | 32 | 32 | 96 | 19 | .308 | .320 |
| MINOR LEAGUE TOTALS | | | .270 | 321 | 1277 | 190 | 345 | 45 | 15 | 5 | 97 | 74 | 213 | 69 | .315 | .341 |

## DALLAS BUCK                                                          RHP

**Born:** Nov. 11, 1984. **B-T:** R-R. **Ht.:** 6-3. **Wt.:** 210. **Drafted:** Oregon State, 2006 (3rd round). **Signed by:** Ed Gustafson.

Buck had one of the more intriguing college careers a player can have. A former special-teams player on Oregon State's football team, he was regarded as a hard-throwing bad boy and was one of the top prospects for the 2006 draft heading into his junior season. While he got results, his fastball dropped into the mid-80s after sitting around 89-91 mph and touching 94 as a sophomore. He battled anyway, and he got the win in relief—two days after going six-plus innings as a starter—as Oregon State defeated North Carolina to win the College World Series. He finished the spring 13-3, 3.34 and solidified his reputation as a warrior. He signed with the Arizona at a below-market $250,000 for a third-rounder, after doctors discovered a partial tear of the ulnar collateral ligament in his right elbow. Buck elected to try rehab and weightlifting instead of having Tommy John surgery over the winter, and the Diamondbacks let him because they saw little downside. If he's not healthy in spring training, he'll have the operation. Either way, he would have missed the 2007 season. When healthy, Buck complements his sinking fastball with an average slider and changeup. He showed moxie and an improved feel for pitching when working without his best stuff last spring. The Diamondbacks will hope he's healthy in spring training, and if so he could open in high Class A. If not, he'll start his career in 2008.

| Year | Club (League) | Class | W | L | ERA | G | GS | CG | SV | IP | H | R | ER | HR | BB | SO | AVG |
|---|---|---|---|---|---|---|---|---|---|---|---|---|---|---|---|---|---|
| 2006 | Did not play—Signed 2007 contract | | | | | | | | | | | | | | | | |

## KYLER NEWBY                                                         RHP

**Born:** Feb. 22, 1985. **B-T:** R-R. **Ht.:** 6-4. **Wt.:** 225. **Drafted:** Mesa (Ariz.) CC, D/F 2004 (50th round). **Signed by:** Steve Kmetko.

Newby came close to being the Mr. Irrelevant of the 2004 draft, going to Arizona with the 15th pick of the 50th round. He was the ace of the Mesa (Ariz.) Community College staff but got little notice from scouts because of his below-average fastball velocity, and the Diamondbacks signed him as a draft-and-follow with no fanfare and moved him to the bullpen. Newby still doesn't throw hard, but he has had nothing but success during his pro career, including a 2.95 ERA and .227 opponent average in Hawaii Winter Baseball after the 2006 season. His fastball sits at 88-90 mph, but because of his deceptive delivery hitters don't pick it up. He throws a big curveball that can be a plus pitch, and is working on a changeup and splitter that he added to his repertoire at the Diamondbacks' suggestion. The splitter has been an effective weapon when Newby commands it. He has the frame that would suggest more velocity is possible, and he has followed a rigorous conditioning program from the organization to get stronger, but at this point the Diamondbacks are thinking velocity is overrated. Hitters are telling Newby that his pitches are plenty effective with their empty swings. Newby still has doubters, so he'll likely prove them wrong again in high Class A this season.

| Year | Club (League) | Class | W | L | ERA | G | GS | CG | SV | IP | H | R | ER | HR | BB | SO | AVG |
|---|---|---|---|---|---|---|---|---|---|---|---|---|---|---|---|---|---|
| 2005 | Yakima (NWL) | A | 1 | 0 | 2.18 | 24 | 0 | 0 | 2 | 41 | 25 | 12 | 10 | 1 | 14 | 66 | .172 |
| 2006 | South Bend (MWL) | A | 6 | 1 | 2.05 | 28 | 0 | 0 | 11 | 44 | 22 | 10 | 10 | 0 | 19 | 64 | .151 |
| MINOR LEAGUE TOTALS | | | 7 | 1 | 2.11 | 52 | 0 | 0 | 13 | 85 | 47 | 22 | 20 | 1 | 33 | 130 | .162 |

## EVAN MacLANE                                                        LHP

**Born:** Nov. 4, 1982. **B-T:** L-L. **Ht.:** 6-2. **Wt.:** 185. **Drafted:** Feather River (Calif.) CC, 2003 (25th round). **Signed by:** Chuck Hensley Jr. (Mets).

MacLane is the prototypical soft-tossing lefthander who succeeds with command and a great feel for pitching. He signed with the Mets for $7,500 and worked his way to Triple-A before coming to the Diamondbacks in the Shawn Green trade last August. Arizona added

him to the 40-man roster after the season. One Mets coach called MacLane "Kirk Reuter with a better curve," and his changeup is a plus pitch that usually comes in at the high 70s. His fastball usually runs in the mid-80s, and his curveball is an effective pitch because he commands it so well. MacLane is learning that he'll need to sharpen his fastball command to get hitters out at the highest levels. While he's generally a strike thrower, he needs to move the ball around in the zone better to keep hitters from putting good swings on it, which they did quite a bit in Triple-A. He's also learning that there's little point in dialing up his fastball to the high 80s because he still can't throw it by anyone. MacLane is likely to return to the Triple-A rotation, but he could win a spot in the Arizona with a great spring.

| Year | Club (League) | Class | W | L | ERA | G | GS | CG | SV | IP | H | R | ER | HR | BB | SO | AVG |
|------|---------------|-------|---|---|-----|---|----|----|----|----|---|---|----|----|----|----|-----|
| 2003 | Kingsport (Appy) | R | 4 | 1 | 2.88 | 14 | 6 | 0 | 0 | 56 | 59 | 20 | 18 | 4 | 8 | 57 | .271 |
| | Brooklyn (NYP) | A | 1 | 0 | 0.00 | 1 | 1 | 0 | 0 | 6 | 3 | 0 | 0 | 0 | 1 | 5 | .136 |
| 2004 | Capital City (SAL) | A | 5 | 2 | 2.39 | 14 | 10 | 0 | 0 | 68 | 57 | 21 | 18 | 9 | 10 | 66 | .228 |
| | Brooklyn (NYP) | A | 5 | 2 | 2.48 | 12 | 12 | 0 | 0 | 69 | 61 | 27 | 19 | 5 | 6 | 68 | .236 |
| 2005 | St. Lucie (FSL) | A | 8 | 5 | 3.20 | 19 | 19 | 1 | 0 | 112 | 96 | 51 | 40 | 14 | 15 | 92 | .224 |
| | Binghamton (EL) | AA | 3 | 2 | 4.14 | 9 | 9 | 1 | 0 | 59 | 63 | 31 | 27 | 7 | 9 | 48 | .266 |
| 2006 | Binghamton (EL) | AA | 3 | 1 | 4.64 | 6 | 6 | 0 | 0 | 33 | 34 | 17 | 17 | 4 | 2 | 25 | .266 |
| | Norfolk (IL) | AAA | 9 | 8 | 3.86 | 20 | 20 | 1 | 0 | 121 | 136 | 61 | 52 | 11 | 35 | 67 | .285 |
| | Tucson (PCL) | AAA | 1 | 0 | 3.38 | 2 | 1 | 0 | 0 | 8 | 10 | 3 | 3 | 1 | 1 | 4 | .323 |
| **MINOR LEAGUE TOTALS** | | | 39 | 21 | 3.28 | 97 | 84 | 3 | 0 | 532 | 519 | 231 | 194 | 55 | 87 | 432 | .253 |

## 29 LEYSON SEPTIMO OF

**Born:** July 7, 1985. **B-T:** L-L. **Ht.:** 6-0. **Wt.:** 150. **Signed:** Dominican Republic, 2003. **Signed by:** Junior Noboa.

While Gerardo Parra is regarded as potentially a more refined Carlos Gonzalez, Septimo is seen as a player with the same raw materials as Gonzalez who hasn't figured out how to put them together yet. Midwest League managers rated his outfield arm as the best in the league, and it's at the top of the scale. Diamondbacks officials say he could probably throw 95 mph off the mound. At the other end of the spectrum, his approach at the plate is unrefined and he has a big swing—a bad combination. He has a tendency to swing at everything, so the Diamondbacks are trying to get him to cut his swing down a bit and see more pitches. While he has some raw power, he'll be better off focusing on making contact for now. He's a good runner and has all the tools needed to play right field if his bat comes around. Septimo has a long way to go, but he'll benefit from the wealth of outfield talent in the organization. There's no need to rush him, so he can go back to low Class A where coaches and instructors will continue to polish this diamond in the rough.

| Year | Club (League) | Class | AVG | G | AB | R | H | 2B | 3B | HR | RBI | BB | SO | SB | OBP | SLG |
|------|---------------|-------|-----|---|----|---|---|----|----|----|-----|----|----|----|-----|-----|
| 2003 | Diamondbacks (DSL) | R | .214 | 52 | 182 | 20 | 39 | 10 | 3 | 0 | 21 | 23 | 57 | 1 | .319 | .302 |
| 2004 | Diamondbacks (DSL) | R | .276 | 63 | 221 | 29 | 61 | 9 | 3 | 2 | 25 | 14 | 41 | 8 | .335 | .371 |
| 2005 | Yakima (NWL) | A | .241 | 67 | 237 | 20 | 57 | 11 | 2 | 2 | 21 | 10 | 51 | 2 | .272 | .329 |
| 2006 | South Bend (MWL) | A | .251 | 132 | 529 | 79 | 133 | 22 | 5 | 6 | 51 | 36 | 112 | 10 | .310 | .346 |
| **MINOR LEAGUE TOTALS** | | | .248 | 314 | 1169 | 148 | 290 | 52 | 13 | 10 | 118 | 83 | 261 | 21 | .309 | .340 |

## 30 MATT TORRA RHP

**Born:** June 29, 1984. **B-T:** R-R. **Ht.:** 6-3. **Wt.:** 225. **Drafted:** Massachusetts, 2005 (1st round supplemental). **Signed by:** Matt Merullo.

Torra soared up draft boards in 2005 and became a supplemental first-round pick after leading NCAA Division I with a 1.14 ERA for a weak Massachusetts team. Almost immediately there were concerns about Torra's arm, however, and he was shut down after just 10 pro innings. It turned out he had a torn labrum in right shoulder, and he had surgery that September. He stayed in extended spring training and got back on the mound at the end of July. He also pitched in instructional league. He didn't look good, but the point was just to get him back on the field and get some healthy innings under his belt. When healthy, Torra features a 92-94 mph fastball and a power curve that can both be strikeout pitches, as well as good command. Aside from his health, Torra has a lot of refinement to do because he has never pitched against advanced competition. The biggest obstacle he faces now is learning to trust his arm again, and showing the confidence to unleash his fastball. Shoulder injuries can lay waste to pitching careers quickly, so this is a pivotal year for Torra to show he can recapture his best stuff.

| Year | Club (League) | Class | W | L | ERA | G | GS | CG | SV | IP | H | R | ER | HR | BB | SO | AVG |
|------|---------------|-------|---|---|-----|---|----|----|----|----|---|---|----|----|----|----|-----|
| 2005 | Yakima (NWL) | A | 0 | 1 | 1.80 | 5 | 2 | 0 | 0 | 10 | 11 | 3 | 2 | 1 | 4 | 10 | .297 |
| 2006 | South Bend (MWL) | A | 0 | 1 | 1.80 | 7 | 7 | 0 | 0 | 25 | 24 | 7 | 5 | 0 | 5 | 20 | .258 |
| **MINOR LEAGUE TOTALS** | | | 0 | 2 | 1.80 | 12 | 9 | 0 | 0 | 35 | 35 | 10 | 7 | 1 | 9 | 30 | .269 |

# ATLANTA
# BRAVES

BY **BILL BALLEW**

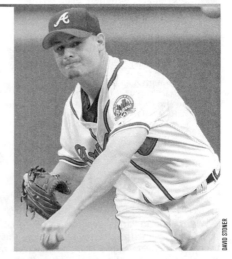

DAVID STONER

Since winning the first of their record 14 consecutive division championships in 1991, the Braves never have endured as much change as they have the last two seasons. And though that streak came to an end with a 79-83 third-place finish in 2006, Atlanta still has plenty of young talent that should allow it to contend in the future.

The Braves began their makeover in 2005, en route to perhaps the most surprising of their playoff berths. Atlanta used 18 rookies—12 of whom made their major league debuts—while Jeff Francoeur and Brian McCann already have established themselves as cornerstones the franchise will build around.

The influx of young talent continued in 2006, if to a less dramatic extent, with **Chuck James** the most significant rookie. But the year was more notable for the changes in the front office.

Assistant general manager in charge of baseball operations Dayton Moore long had been considered one of the game's top GM prospects and a possible successor to Atlanta GM John Schuerholz. After pulling out of the running for the Red Sox job last winter, Moore accepted the Royals' offer to run their franchise. He left right after the June draft, and by the end of the season he brought Braves farm director J.J. Picollo, international scouting supervisor Rene Francisco and minor league pitching coordinator Bill Fischer with him to Kansas City.

To help replace Moore and Picollo, Atlanta expanded the role of legendary scout Paul Snyder. Originally signed by the Milwaukee Braves as a player in 1957,

Snyder became scouting director in 1977 and helped build the franchise into a juggernaut. After overseeing both scouting and player development from 1996-1999, he took a step back and became a special assistant to Schuerholz in 2000. Now Snyder is supervising scouting and player development again, with protégé Roy Clark still in place as scouting director and former West Coast crosschecker Kurt Kemp the new farm director.

Though Time Warner is in the process of selling the club and has put some limitations on signing bonuses, Atlanta spent $6.8 million on the 2006 draft, the third-highest figure in baseball. The Braves snapped up four high school pitchers in the first three rounds and 11 hurlers in the first 10 rounds.

Atlanta also inked six draft-and-follows from 2005 in May—most notably righthander Tommy Hanson—and continued to make a splash on the international front. The Braves landed three Cubans in January, most significantly lefthander Francisley Bueno, and acquired Taiwanese righthander Chen-En Hung and Japanese catcher Ryohei Shimabukuro during the summer signing period.

The number of potential major league standouts doesn't compare with the Braves' recent past or the system's heyday in the early 1990s. Then again, very few organizations ever have been as productive.

## TOP 30 PROSPECTS

| | |
|---|---|
| 1. Jarrod Saltalamacchia, c | 16. Cory Rasmus, rhp |
| 2. Elvis Andrus, ss | 17. Tommy Hanson, rhp |
| 3. Matt Harrison, lhp | 18. Neftali Feliz, rhp |
| 4. Brandon Jones, of | 19. Jeff Locke, lhp |
| 5. Van Pope, 3b | 20. Chad Rodgers, lhp |
| 6. Eric Campbell, 3b | 21. Dan Smith, lhp |
| 7. Scott Thorman, 1b/of | 22. Brayan Pena, c |
| 8. Jo-Jo Reyes, lhp | 23. Jamie Romak, of |
| 9. Joey Devine, rhp | 24. Jamie Richmond, rhp |
| 10. Yunel Escobar, inf | 25. Chase Fontaine, ss |
| 11. Kala Kaaihue, 1b | 26. Clint Sammons, c |
| 12. Anthony Lerew, rhp | 27. Jordan Schafer, of |
| 13. Steve Evarts, lhp | 28. Kris Medlen, rhp |
| 14. Beau Jones, lhp | 29. Kevin Gunderson, lhp |
| 15. Jeff Lyman, rhp | 30. Cody Johnson, 1b |

# ORGANIZATION OVERVIEW

**General manager:** John Schuerholz. **Farm director:** Kurt Kemp. **Scouting director:** Roy Clark.

## 2006 PERFORMANCE

| Class | Team | League | W | L | Pct. | Finish* | Manager | Affiliated |
|---|---|---|---|---|---|---|---|---|
| Majors | Atlanta | National | 79 | 83 | .488 | 8th (16) | Bobby Cox | — |
| Triple-A | Richmond Braves | International | 57 | 86 | .399 | 14th (14) | Brian Snitker | 1966 |
| Double-A | Mississippi Braves | Southern | 58 | 80 | .420 | 10th (10) | Jeff Blauser | 2005 |
| High A | Myrtle Beach Pelicans | Carolina | 72 | 68 | .514 | 3rd (8) | Rocket Wheeler | 1999 |
| Low A | Rome Braves | South Atlantic | 71 | 68 | .511 | 8th (16) | Randy Ingle | 2003 |
| Rookie | Danville Braves | Appalachian | 40 | 27 | .597 | +2nd (10) | Paul Runge | 1993 |
| Rookie | GCL Braves | Gulf Coast | 23 | 27 | .460 | 8th (13) | Luis Ortiz | 1998 |
| **OVERALL 2006 MINOR LEAGUE RECORD** | | | 321 | 356 | .474 | 25th (30) | | |

*Finish in overall standings (No. of teams in league). +League champion

## ORGANIZATION LEADERS

### BATTING
| | | |
|---|---|---|
| AVG | Loadenthal, Carl, Mississippi/Myrtle Beach | .305 |
| R | Blanco, Gregor, Mississippi/Richmond | 99 |
| H | Blanco, Gregor, Mississippi/Richmond | 163 |
| 2B | Campbell, Eric, Rome | 33 |
| | Pope, Van, Myrtle Beach | 33 |
| 3B | Davis, Quentin, Rome | 8 |
| HR | Kaaihue, Kala, Rome/Myrtle Beach | 28 |
| RBI | Campbell, Eric, Rome | 84 |
| | Pope, Van, Myrtle Beach | 84 |
| BB | Blanco, Gregor, Mississippi/Richmond | 104 |
| SO | Kaaihue, Kala, Rome/Myrtle Beach | 123 |
| SB | Suero, Ovandy, Rome/Myrtle Beach | 53 |
| OBP | Fontaine, Robert, Danville | .411 |
| SLG | Kaaihue, Kala, Rome/Myrtle Beach | .540 |
| XBH | Campbell, Eric, Rome | 59 |

### PITCHING
| | | |
|---|---|---|
| W | Reyes, Jo-Jo, Rome/Myrtle Beach | 12 |
| L | Waters, Chris, Mississippi | 14 |
| ERA | Harrison, Matt, Myrtle Beach/Mississippi | 3.35 |
| G | Acosta, Manny, Mississippi/Richmond | 55 |
| SV | Schreiber, Zach, Myrtle Beach/Mississippi | 24 |
| IP | Harrison, Matt, Myrtle Beach/Mississippi | 159 |
| BB | Jones, Beau, Rome | 83 |
| SO | Reyes, Jo-Jo, Rome/Myrtle Beach | 142 |
| AVG | Reyes, Jo-Jo, Rome/Myrtle Beach | .223 |

## BEST TOOLS

| | |
|---|---|
| Best Hitter for Average | Jarrod Saltalamacchia |
| Best Power Hitter | Scott Thorman |
| Best Strike-Zone Discipline | Wes Timmons |
| Fastest Baserunner | Ovandy Suero |
| Best Athlete | Brandon Jones |
| Best Fastball | Neftali Feliz |
| Best Curveball | Cory Rasmus |
| Best Slider | Joey Devine |
| Best Changeup | Steve Evarts |
| Best Control | Matt Harrison |
| Best Defensive Catcher | Clint Sammons |
| Best Defensive Infielder | Van Pope |
| Best Infield Arm | Van Pope |
| Best Defensive Outfielder | Jordan Schafer |
| Best Outfield Arm | Jon Mark Owings |

## PROJECTED 2010 LINEUP

| | |
|---|---|
| Catcher | Brian McCann |
| First Base | Adam LaRoche |
| Second Base | Edgar Renteria |
| Third Base | Chipper Jones |
| Shortstop | Elvis Andrus |
| Left Field | Jarrod Saltalamacchia |
| Center Field | Andruw Jones |
| Right Field | Jeff Francoeur |
| No. 1 Starter | Tim Hudson |
| No. 2 Starter | Kyle Davies |
| No. 3 Starter | Matt Harrison |
| No. 4 Starter | Jo-Jo Reyes |
| No. 5 Starter | Chuck James |
| Closer | Rafael Soriano |

## LAST YEAR'S TOP 20 PROSPECTS

1. Jarrod Saltalamacchia, c
2. Elvis Andrus, ss
3. Yunel Escobar, ss
4. Anthony Lerew, rhp
5. Joey Devine, rhp
6. Chuck James, lhp
7. Brandon Jones, of
8. Eric Campbell, 3b
9. Beau Jones, lhp
10. Matt Harrison, lhp
11. Scott Thorman, 1b
12. Blaine Boyer, rhp
13. Macay McBride, lhp
14. James Parr, rhp
15. Brayan Pena, c
16. Van Pope, 3b
17. Martin Prado, 2b
18. Jake Stevens, lhp
19. Josh Burrus, of
20. Max Ramirez, c

## TOP PROSPECTS OF THE DECADE

| Year | Player, Pos. | 2006 Org. |
|---|---|---|
| 1997 | Andruw Jones, of | Braves |
| 1998 | Bruce Chen, lhp | Orioles |
| 1999 | Bruce Chen, lhp | Orioles |
| 2000 | Rafael Furcal, ss | Dodgers |
| 2001 | Wilson Betemit, ss | Dodgers |
| 2002 | Wilson Betemit, ss | Dodgers |
| 2003 | Adam Wainwright, rhp | Cardinals |
| 2004 | Andy Marte, 3b | Indians |
| 2005 | Jeff Francoeur, of | Braves |
| 2006 | Jarrod Saltalamacchia, c | Braves |

## TOP DRAFT PICKS OF THE DECADE

| Year | Player, Pos. | 2006 Org. |
|---|---|---|
| 1997 | Troy Cameron, ss | Out of baseball |
| 1998 | Matt Belisle, rhp (2nd round) | Reds |
| 1999 | Matt Butler, rhp (2nd round) | Out of baseball |
| 2000 | Adam Wainwright, rhp | Cardinals |
| 2001 | Macay McBride, lhp | Braves |
| 2002 | Jeff Francoeur, of | Braves |
| 2003 | Luis Atilano, rhp | Nationals |
| 2004 | Eric Campbell, 3b (2nd round) | Braves |
| 2005 | Joey Devine, rhp | Braves |
| 2006 | Cody Johnson, of | Braves |

## LARGEST BONUSES IN CLUB HISTORY

| | |
|---|---|
| Jeff Francoeur, 2002 | $2,200,000 |
| Matt Belisle, 1998 | $1,750,000 |
| Jung Bong, 1997 | $1,700,000 |
| Cody Johnson, 2006 | $1,375,000 |
| Macay McBride, 2001 | $1,340,000 |

# MINOR LEAGUE DEPTH CHART

## Atlanta Braves

**Impact: B.** In Saltalamacchia, Escobar and Harrison the Braves have top prospects at three premium positions.

**Depth: C.** After relying on farm system to carry 2005 run, the Braves are still lacking in reinforcements at upper levels.

**Sleeper:** Tommy Hanson, rhp. Showed in run through Appy League he's got the fastball command to move up this list.

*Numbers in parentheses indicate prospect rankings.*

| LF |
|---|
| Brandon Jones (4) |
| Carl Loadenthal |
| Onil Joseph |
| Josh Burrus |
| Bill McCarthy |
| Matt Young |
| Willie Cabrera |

| CF |
|---|
| Jordan Schafer (27) |
| Gregor Blanco |
| Ovandy Suero |

| RF |
|---|
| Jamie Romak (23) |
| Jon Mark Owings |
| Matt Esquivel |
| Steve Doetsch |

| 3B |
|---|
| Van Pope (5) |
| Wes Timmons |
| Adam Coe |
| Danny Brezeale |

| SS |
|---|
| Elvis Andrus (2) |
| Yunel Escobar (10) |
| Chase Fontaine (25) |
| T.J. Pena |
| Diory Hernandez |

| 2B |
|---|
| Eric Campbell (6) |
| Martin Prado |
| J.C. Holt |

| 1B |
|---|
| Scott Thorman (7) |
| Kala Kaaihue (11) |
| Cody Johnson (30) |
| James Jurries |

| C |
|---|
| Jarrod Saltalamacchia (1) |
| Brayan Pena (22) |
| Clint Sammons (26) |
| Philip Britton |

| RHP | |
|---|---|
| **Starters** | **Relievers** |
| Anthony Lerew (12) | Joey Devine (9) |
| Jeff Lyman (15) | Neftali Feliz (18) |
| Cory Rasmus (16) | Kris Medlen (28) |
| Tommy Hanson (17) | Kevin Barry |
| Jamie Richmond (24) | Charlie Morton |
| Dustin Evans | Ryan Basner |
| James Parr | |
| Mike Broadway | |
| Jairo Cuevas | |

| LHP | |
|---|---|
| **Starters** | **Relievers** |
| Matt Harrison (3) | Dan Smith (21) |
| Jo-Jo Reyes (8) | Kevin Gunderson (29) |
| Steve Evarts (13) | Will Startup |
| Beau Jones (14) | Lee Hyde |
| Jeff Locke (19) | |
| Chad Rodgers (20) | |
| Kelvin Villa | |
| Jonathan Venters | |
| Jake Stevens | |
| Brady Endl | |

## 2006 — SIGNING BUDGET: $6.2 million

**Best Pro Debut:** RHP Kris Medlen (10) had a 0.41 ERA, 10 saves and a 36-2 K-BB ratio in 22 innings. After getting worked hard as Oregon State's closer during a College World Series championship run, LHP Kevin Gunderson (5) went 4-0, 1.13 in low Class A. Appalachian League all-star SS Chase Fontaine (2) batted .296/.411/.412.

**Best Athlete:** Fontaine stands out most for his bat, but he also has slightly above-average speed and range to go with a plus arm. He may profile better at second base, where his athleticism would stand out more.

**Best Pure Hitter:** Fontaine has drawn comparisons to Chase Utley, though with less power. The Braves signed just four position players out of the draft but got three more as draft-and-follows from 2005. OF Willie Cabrera, who batted .308 with seven homers in his debut, has similar offensive potential to Fontaine.

**Best Raw Power:** Several teams questioned the ability of OF Cody Johnson (1) to make consistent contact, and he hit just .184 with one homer in Rookie ball. But when he gets a hold of a pitch, he can crush it out of any part of any ballpark. Power is also the best tool for 3B Adam Coe (7) and 1B Josh Morris (12).

**Fastest Runner:** Fontaine among the draftees, but he's not nearly as quick as draft-and-follow OF Cole Miles. Miles can cover 60 yards in 6.5 seconds and succeeded on 18 of his 20 pro steal attempts.

**Best Defensive Player:** Coe has a strong arm and good actions at the hot corner.

**Best Fastball:** The Braves have seen RHPs Cory Rasmus (1), Dustin Evans (2) and Ryne Reynoso (26) all touch 97, and RHP Deunte Heath (19) get up to 96. Rasmus throws in the mid-90s the most consistently.

**Best Breaking Ball:** Rasmus and RHP Mike Mehlich (11) both have power curveballs.

**Most Intriguing Background:** Rasmus' brother Colby was a Cardinals first-round pick in 2005 and is one of the game's better outfield prospects. Gunderson's uncle Eric pitched in the majors. RHP Casey Beck's (8) brother signed with the Diamondbacks as a 14th-rounder in June. Unsigned C J.B. Paxson (18) turned down a football scholarship from Purdue.

**Closest To The Majors:** Gunderson's stuff is unremarkable, but he has guts and command, and the Braves need lefthanded relief help. RHP Tim Gustafson (9) would have gone much earlier in the draft if not for shoulder soreness. Now healthy, he's capable of showing three plus pitches. Draft-and-follow RHP Tommy Hanson throws four pitches for strikes, including an 89-92 mph fastball that peaks at 94.

**Best Late-Round Pick:** Medlen, who doubled as an everyday shortstop at Santa Ana (Calif.) JC, has a 91-93 mph fastball and a good curveball. Reynoso was an outfielder who pitched just four innings at Boston College in the spring, but area scout Lonnie Goldberg saw him throw a bullpen and followed him in the New England Collegiate League during the summer.

**The One Who Got Away:** Atlanta lost just three players to four-year schools. The best was Paxson, who transferred from Juco World Series champion Walters State (Tenn.) to Western Kentucky.

**Assessment:** The Braves spent five of their first nine choices on polished lefthanders—Steve Evarts (1), Jeff Locke (2), Chad Rodgers (3), Lee Hyde (4) and Gunderson. Johnson was the riskiest pick in the entire first round, but the pitching depth and draft-and-follows should help compensate if he bombs.

## 2005 — BUDGET: $4.2 million

RHP Joey Devine (1) and LHP Beau Jones (1) took a step back in their first full seasons. They still have promise, as does INF Yunel Escobar (2). **GRADE: C**

## 2004 — BUDGET: $1.8 million

The Braves didn't have a first-rounder but grabbed slugging 3B Eric Campbell (2) with their top choice. 3B Van Pope (5) gives them another option at the hot corner. **GRADE: C**

## 2003 — BUDGET: $5.0 million

Despite an off year, Jarrod Saltalamacchia (1) is still one of the game's top catching prospects. Atlanta also found a pair of lefties in Jo-Jo Reyes (2) and Matt Harrison (3), plus a fine athlete in draft-and-follow OF Brandon Jones (24). **GRADE: B**

*Draft analysis by Jim Callis. Numbers in parentheses indicate draft rounds. Budgets are bonuses in first 10 rounds.*

# JARROD
# SALTALAMACCHIA

C

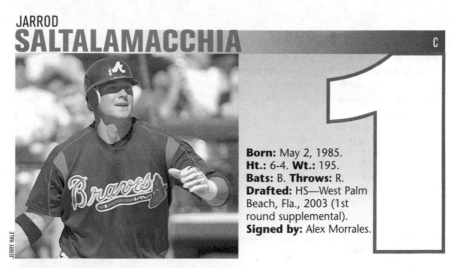

**Born:** May 2, 1985.
**Ht.:** 6-4. **Wt.:** 195.
**Bats:** B. **Throws:** R.
**Drafted:** HS—West Palm
Beach, Fla., 2003 (1st
round supplemental).
**Signed by:** Alex Morrales.

JERRY HALE

The 36th overall pick in the 2003 draft, Saltalamacchia built a reputation during high school as a big league hitter and has done little to disappoint. He established himself as the best all-around catching prospect in the minors with a breakout 2005 campaign. He rated as the top prospect in the high Class A Carolina League and starred for Team USA in an Olympic pre-qualifying tournament after the season. However, he followed up with his most difficult season as a pro. A lingering wrist injury and focus on improving his defense led to struggles at the plate during the first half of the year. Saltalamacchia batted just .197 with four homers in the first three months before going on the disabled list with an injury to his wrist. He bounced back by hitting .338 with five homers in his last 23 games before leaving Double-A Mississippi to rejoin Team USA for an Olympic qualifying tournament. Saltalamacchia helped the United States qualify for the 2008 Beijing Games and capped the event with a homer off Cuban closer Pedro Luis Lazo. He continued to rake in a brief stint in the Arizona Fall League, going 13-for-23 (.535) with three homers before hamstring problems shut him down.

Saltalamacchia's calling card is his ability to hit and drive the ball from both sides of the plate. He has one of the sweetest swings in the game from the left side, displaying natural loft that should produce solid home run numbers. Despite his troubles in 2006, the Braves have no concerns about his offense, especially with the way he regrouped at midseason. His walk rate continues to increase as he climbs the minor league ladder. Considered suspect defensively coming out of high school, Saltalamacchia has worked hard to get better. He spent the spring picking veteran Todd Pratt's brain to upgrade his game-calling ability, and he continues to get more comfortable working with pitchers. He has a strong arm and a release that has quickened considerably, enabling him to throw out 36 percent of basestealers in 2006. Saltalamacchia has shown increased maturity, particularly after getting married midway through the 2005 season. Always upbeat, he has a desire to learn and improve.

Consistency is the key to Saltalamacchia reaching the majors. He'll make more consistent contact once he displays more patience. In 2006, opponents noticed Saltalamacchia collapsing the back side of his swing from both sides of the plate. His righthanded swing is a little mechanical, though he was more productive from that side in 2006. He batted .262 against lefties, compared with .214 against righties. Defensively, he needs to continue to improve his footwork and to learn how to set up advanced hitters.

Brian McCann is one of the best young catchers in baseball, and while Saltamacchia is similarly gifted, there's room for only one of them behind the plate in Atlanta. For now, Saltalamacchia will continue to work at catcher, where he has the most value. If he doesn't begin the year at Triple-A Richmond, he should get there at some point in 2007. His bat should be ready for Atlanta by mid-2008, when the Braves may have to move him to first base or left field.

| Year | Club (League) | Class | AVG | G | AB | R | H | 2B | 3B | HR | RBI | BB | SO | SB | OBP | SLG |
|------|---------------|-------|-----|---|----|---|---|----|----|----|-----|----|----|----|-----|-----|
| 2003 | Braves (GCL) | R | .239 | 46 | 134 | 23 | 32 | 11 | 2 | 2 | 14 | 28 | 33 | 0 | .382 | .396 |
| 2004 | Rome (SAL) | A | .272 | 91 | 323 | 42 | 88 | 19 | 2 | 10 | 51 | 34 | 83 | 1 | .348 | .437 |
| 2005 | Myrtle Beach (CL) | A | .314 | 129 | 459 | 70 | 144 | 35 | 1 | 19 | 81 | 57 | 99 | 4 | .394 | .519 |
| 2006 | Mississippi (SL) | AA | .230 | 92 | 313 | 30 | 72 | 18 | 1 | 9 | 39 | 55 | 71 | 0 | .353 | .380 |
| **MINOR LEAGUE TOTALS** | | | .273 | 358 | 1229 | 165 | 336 | 83 | 6 | 40 | 185 | 174 | 286 | 5 | .370 | .448 |

## ② ELVIS ANDRUS SS

RICH ABEL

**Born:** Aug. 26, 1988. **B-T:** R-R. **Ht.:** 6-0. **Wt.:** 180. **Signed:** Venezuela, 2005. **Signed by:** Rolando Petit/Julian Perez.

The younger brother of Devil Rays minor league outfielder Erold Andrus, Elvis held his own in the low Class A South Atlantic League, showing no signs of being overwhelmed in a league with players who were on average four years older than him. Andrus has three plus tools and a chance to develop plus hitting ability and possibly power. His soft hands, impressive range and above-average arm strength make him a natural shortstop. Andrus employs a mature approach at the plate by using the entire field. His instincts and knowledge of the game far exceed his age. The Braves rave about his work ethic and enthusiasm, and he has become fluent in English in less than two years in the United States. Andrus is still raw in all phases of his offensive game. Plate discipline is his biggest weakness, and he also must improve his overall strength. Though he has plus speed, he's still learning to steal bases and was caught 15 times in 38 tries in 2006. The Braves feel no need to push Andrus more than a level at a time, but he's still well ahead of almost every player his age. He's headed to high Class A Myrtle Beach as an 18-year-old and could accelerate his timetable once he improves at the plate.

| Year | Club (League) | Class | AVG | G | AB | R | H | 2B | 3B | HR | RBI | BB | SO | SB | OBP | SLG |
|------|---------------|-------|-----|---|----|---|---|----|----|----|-----|----|----|----|-----|-----|
| 2005 | Braves (GCL) | R | .295 | 46 | 166 | 26 | 49 | 6 | 1 | 3 | 20 | 19 | 28 | 7 | .377 | .398 |
| | Danville (Appy) | R | .278 | 6 | 18 | 3 | 5 | 1 | 0 | 0 | 1 | 4 | 4 | 1 | .409 | .333 |
| 2006 | Rome (SAL) | A | .265 | 111 | 437 | 67 | 116 | 25 | 4 | 3 | 50 | 36 | 91 | 23 | .324 | .362 |
| **MINOR LEAGUE TOTALS** | | | .274 | 163 | 621 | 96 | 170 | 32 | 5 | 6 | 71 | 59 | 123 | 31 | .341 | .370 |

## ③ MATT HARRISON LHP

ROBERT GURGANUS

**Born:** Aug. 16, 1985. **B-T:** L-L. **Ht.:** 6-5. **Wt.:** 220. **Drafted:** HS—Stem, N.C., 2003 (3rd round). **Signed by:** Billy Best.

The Braves cited Harrison as their breakthrough pitcher of 2005, and he maintained his momentum in 2006. He led Atlanta farmhands in ERA, reached Double-A before he turned 21 and now ranks as the system's top mound prospect. It seems like every quality lefthanded pitching prospect must be likened to Tom Glavine, but that comparison seems more legitimate when applied to Harrison. He's adept at using both sides of the plate and altering the batter's eye level. He delivers a heavy fastball between 89-92 mph and does an excellent job of keeping it down in the zone. His above-average curveball breaks at times like a slider. Harrison also has a plus changeup that he uses at any time in the count. Harrison admits he gave Double-A hitters too much credit and wasn't aggressive enough following his midseason promotion. He needs to continue to learn how to mix his pitches in order to keep batters off balance. Harrison, who has No. 3 starter potential, could open 2007 in Triple-A, where he'd be knocking on the door to the big leagues.

| Year | Club (League) | Class | W | L | ERA | G | GS | CG | SV | IP | H | R | ER | HR | BB | SO | AVG |
|------|---------------|-------|---|---|-----|---|----|----|----|----|---|---|----|----|----|----|-----|
| 2003 | Braves (GCL) | R | 3 | 1 | 3.69 | 11 | 6 | 0 | 1 | 39 | 40 | 18 | 16 | 2 | 9 | 33 | .263 |
| 2004 | Danville (Appy) | R | 4 | 4 | 4.09 | 13 | 12 | 1 | 0 | 66 | 72 | 36 | 30 | 3 | 10 | 49 | .278 |
| 2005 | Rome (SAL) | A | 12 | 7 | 3.23 | 27 | 27 | 2 | 0 | 167 | 151 | 65 | 60 | 17 | 30 | 118 | .239 |
| 2006 | Myrtle Beach (CL) | A | 8 | 4 | 3.10 | 13 | 13 | 2 | 0 | 81 | 77 | 30 | 28 | 6 | 16 | 60 | .252 |
| | Mississippi (SL) | AA | 3 | 4 | 3.61 | 13 | 12 | 1 | 0 | 77 | 83 | 36 | 31 | 6 | 17 | 54 | .272 |
| **MINOR LEAGUE TOTALS** | | | 30 | 20 | 3.45 | 77 | 70 | 6 | 1 | 431 | 423 | 185 | 165 | 34 | 82 | 314 | .256 |

## ④ BRANDON JONES OF

**Born:** Dec. 10, 1983. **B-T:** L-R. **Ht.:** 6-2. **Wt.:** 195. **Drafted:** Tallahassee (Fla.) CC, D/F 2003 (24th round). **Signed by:** Al Goetz.

A baseball/basketball/football star in high school, Jones turned down the Royals as a sixth-rounder in 2002. The Braves aggressively pursue draft-and-follows, and that's how they signed him after taking him in the 24th round in 2003. He's the best all-around athlete in the system but has been sidelined by injuries in each of his two full seasons. Though he had just 20 extra-base hits at Myrtle Beach, managers rated Jones the best power prospect in the Carolina League. He makes hard contact and drives the ball into the gaps with his quick, line-drive swing. Jones possesses above-average wheels and could become a solid power-speed threat at the major league level. His plus range and strong arm enable him to play anywhere in the outfield. A broken left hand cost Jones two

months in 2005, and he missed the last three weeks of 2006 after having surgery to repair a labrum tear in his throwing shoulder. He needs game action to add some loft to his swing and improve his pitch recognition. He also can improve his routes on fly balls and his instincts as a basestealer. While he still needs to polish many aspects of his game, he continues to attract comparisons with Matt Lawton and could emerge as Atlanta's long-term answer in left field. Jones should be healthy for spring training and likely will open 2007 in Double-A.

| Year | Club (League) | Class | AVG | G | AB | R | H | 2B | 3B | HR | RBI | BB | SO | SB | OBP | SLG |
|------|---------------|-------|------|-----|------|-----|-----|-----|-----|-----|------|------|------|------|------|------|
| 2004 | Danville (Appy) | R | .297 | 57 | 209 | 35 | 62 | 6 | 5 | 3 | 33 | 23 | 33 | 4 | .366 | .416 |
| 2005 | Danville (Appy) | R | .286 | 2 | 7 | 0 | 2 | 0 | 0 | 0 | 1 | 1 | 0 | 0 | .375 | .286 |
| | Rome (SAL) | A | .308 | 43 | 156 | 37 | 48 | 12 | 3 | 8 | 27 | 29 | 29 | 4 | .423 | .577 |
| | Myrtle Beach (CL) | A | .350 | 17 | 60 | 7 | 21 | 4 | 0 | 0 | 5 | 9 | 9 | 0 | .437 | .417 |
| | Braves (GCL) | R | .125 | 2 | 8 | 0 | 1 | 0 | 0 | 0 | 2 | 0 | 2 | 0 | .125 | .125 |
| 2006 | Mississippi (SL) | AA | .273 | 48 | 176 | 18 | 48 | 9 | 3 | 7 | 25 | 15 | 38 | 4 | .326 | .477 |
| | Myrtle Beach (CL) | A | .257 | 59 | 226 | 27 | 58 | 10 | 3 | 7 | 35 | 25 | 49 | 11 | .329 | .420 |
| **MINOR LEAGUE TOTALS** | | | .285 | 228 | 842 | 124 | 240 | 41 | 14 | 25 | 128 | 102 | 160 | 23 | .363 | .456 |

## ⑤ VAN POPE                                              3B

**Born:** Feb. 26, 1984. **B-T:** R-R. **Ht.:** 6-0. **Wt.:** 200. **Drafted:** Meridian (Miss.) JC, 2004 (5th round). **Signed by:** Lonnie Goldberg.

Before the 2006 season the Braves thought Pope was on the verge of blossoming. They were right, as he more than doubled his previous career high in homers (seven) and earned Carolina League all-star recognition. He was a two-way star who threw in the low 90s in junior college, but Atlanta hasn't regretted making him a full-time third baseman. An aggressive hitter, Pope possesses above-average raw power. He worked deeper counts in 2006, waiting for a pitch to attack rather than swinging at what pitchers wanted him to chase. He has slightly above-average speed and runs the bases very well. Managers rated him as the best defensive infielder and strongest infield arm in the CL. He has soft hands, plays balls to both sides with ease and is adept at making plays on slow rollers. Pope has the athleticism and skill to be a Gold Glove third baseman, but some scouts question whether he'll refine his raw power enough to provide the pop wanted at the position. He must continue to do a better job at recognizing pitches he can drive. The Braves believe Pope will continue to make adjustments and accelerate his development at Double-A in 2007. He's the heir apparent to Chipper Jones at third base.

| Year | Club (League) | Class | AVG | G | AB | R | H | 2B | 3B | HR | RBI | BB | SO | SB | OBP | SLG |
|------|---------------|-------|------|-----|------|-----|-----|-----|-----|-----|------|------|------|------|------|------|
| 2004 | Danville (Appy) | R | .270 | 60 | 233 | 39 | 63 | 18 | 2 | 5 | 39 | 11 | 44 | 5 | .333 | .429 |
| 2005 | Rome (SAL) | A | .277 | 100 | 386 | 48 | 107 | 24 | 7 | 6 | 60 | 42 | 70 | 0 | .347 | .422 |
| | Myrtle Beach (CL) | A | .167 | 25 | 84 | 7 | 14 | 1 | 0 | 1 | 5 | 9 | 21 | 0 | .253 | .214 |
| 2006 | Myrtle Beach (CL) | A | .263 | 127 | 467 | 78 | 123 | 31 | 1 | 15 | 74 | 58 | 92 | 7 | .353 | .430 |
| **MINOR LEAGUE TOTALS** | | | .262 | 312 | 1170 | 172 | 307 | 74 | 10 | 27 | 178 | 120 | 227 | 12 | .340 | .412 |

## ⑥ ERIC CAMPBELL                                         3B

**Born:** Aug. 6, 1985. **B-T:** R-R. **Ht.:** 6-0. **Wt.:** 195. **Drafted:** HS—Owensville, Ind., 2004 (2nd round). **Signed by:** Sherard Clinkscales.

The co-MVP in the Rookie-level Appalachian League in 2005, Campbell led the South Atlantic League in homers for an encore. Atlanta's top pick in the 2004 draft, he overcame a midseason back injury to set single-season Rome records for homers and RBIs. Campbell is an aggressive hitter with above-average power from right-center to the left-field line. He's one of the most adept hitters at capitalizing on pitchers' mistakes in the system. He has soft hands and an accurate arm at third base. Though not particularly fleet afoot, he's an intelligent baserunner who can read pitchers. He succeeded on 18 of his 21 steal attempts in 2006. Campbell lacks ideal quickness and explosiveness. His power comes more from his natural strength than bat speed. His open stance can cause him to fly open on the front side of his swing, which limits his power to the right side. His plate discipline needs improvement. He also has to do a better job of controlling his emotions on the diamond. Drafted as a shortstop, Campbell has played third base the last two seasons and saw time at second base in Hawaii Winter Baseball. With Chipper Jones and Van Pope ahead of him, Campbell may have a better opportunity at second in the long run, but he'll stay at third base as he advances to high Class A.

| Year | Club (League) | Class | AVG | G | AB | R | H | 2B | 3B | HR | RBI | BB | SO | SB | OBP | SLG |
|------|---------------|-------|-----|---|----|---|---|----|----|----|-----|----|----|----|-----|-----|
| 2004 | Braves (GCL) | R | .251 | 56 | 211 | 30 | 53 | 7 | 0 | 7 | 29 | 15 | 47 | 3 | .306 | .384 |
| | Rome (SAL) | A | .136 | 7 | 22 | 0 | 3 | 0 | 0 | 0 | 1 | 2 | 7 | 0 | .240 | .136 |
| 2005 | Danville (Appy) | R | .313 | 66 | 262 | 77 | 82 | 26 | 2 | 18 | 64 | 28 | 64 | 15 | .383 | .634 |
| 2006 | Rome (SAL) | A | .296 | 116 | 449 | 83 | 133 | 27 | 3 | 22 | 77 | 23 | 68 | 18 | .335 | .517 |
| **MINOR LEAGUE TOTALS** | | | .287 | 245 | 944 | 190 | 271 | 60 | 5 | 47 | 171 | 68 | 186 | 36 | .340 | .511 |

## 7 SCOTT THORMAN 1B/OF

**Born:** Jan. 6, 1982. **B-T:** L-R. **Ht.:** 6-3. **Wt.:** 235. **Drafted:** HS—Cambridge, Ont., 2000 (1st round). **Signed by:** John Stewart/Jim Kane.

After developing slowly but steadily since being drafted out of Canada in 2000, Thorman finally became the hitter the Braves have long expected. Managers rated him the top power prospect in the Triple-A International League, and he was leading the circuit in RBIs before he was promoted to Atlanta in mid-June. Thorman has had tremendous raw power since he signed, but didn't show it consistently in games until 2006. He can produce tape-measure shots to all fields. He has shortened his swing in recent years and consequently has hit for a higher average. Clocked as high as 95 mph off the mound in high school, Thorman has a strong and accurate arm. He runs and moves well for his size. Thorman needs to refine his knowledge of the strike zone to maximize his production. He becomes too pull-conscious on occasion. Though he has worked hard on his defense, he'll never be a Gold Glove candidate. Hard on himself in the past, Thorman has learned to keep his temper in check but needs to maintain a more even keel at the major league level. Adam LaRoche is blocking Thorman at his natural position, but the Braves have an unsettled situation in left field. Thorman could win a regular job or platoon role if he performs well in spring training.

| Year | Club (League) | Class | AVG | G | AB | R | H | 2B | 3B | HR | RBI | BB | SO | SB | OBP | SLG |
|------|---------------|-------|-----|---|----|---|---|----|----|----|-----|----|----|----|-----|-----|
| 2000 | Braves (GCL) | R | .227 | 29 | 97 | 15 | 22 | 7 | 1 | 1 | 19 | 12 | 23 | 0 | .330 | .351 |
| 2001 | Did not play—Injured | | | | | | | | | | | | | | | |
| 2002 | Macon (SAL) | A | .294 | 127 | 470 | 57 | 138 | 38 | 3 | 16 | 82 | 51 | 83 | 2 | .367 | .489 |
| 2003 | Myrtle Beach (CL) | A | .243 | 124 | 445 | 44 | 108 | 26 | 2 | 12 | 56 | 42 | 79 | 0 | .311 | .391 |
| 2004 | Myrtle Beach (CL) | A | .299 | 43 | 154 | 20 | 46 | 11 | 1 | 4 | 29 | 12 | 19 | 1 | .358 | .461 |
| | Greenville (SL) | AA | .252 | 94 | 345 | 31 | 87 | 14 | 3 | 11 | 51 | 39 | 73 | 5 | .326 | .406 |
| 2005 | Mississippi (SL) | AA | .305 | 90 | 348 | 49 | 106 | 21 | 2 | 15 | 65 | 28 | 76 | 2 | .360 | .506 |
| | Richmond (IL) | AAA | .276 | 52 | 210 | 23 | 58 | 10 | 3 | 6 | 27 | 9 | 42 | 0 | .313 | .438 |
| 2006 | Richmond (IL) | AAA | .298 | 81 | 309 | 38 | 92 | 16 | 2 | 15 | 48 | 31 | 48 | 4 | .360 | .508 |
| | Atlanta (NL) | MLB | .234 | 55 | 128 | 13 | 30 | 11 | 0 | 5 | 14 | 5 | 21 | 1 | .263 | .438 |
| **MINOR LEAGUE TOTALS** | | | .276 | 640 | 2378 | 277 | 657 | 143 | 17 | 80 | 377 | 224 | 443 | 14 | .342 | .452 |
| **MAJOR LEAGUE TOTALS** | | | .234 | 55 | 128 | 13 | 30 | 11 | 0 | 5 | 14 | 5 | 21 | 1 | .263 | .438 |

## 8 JO-JO REYES LHP

**Born:** Nov. 20, 1984. **B-T:** L-L. **Ht.:** 6-2. **Wt.:** 230. **Drafted:** Riverside (Calif.) CC, 2003 (2nd round). **Signed by:** John Ramey.

The 43rd overall pick in the 2003 draft, Reyes had Tommy John surgery in 2004 and tore the anterior cruciate ligament in his knee after returning in 2005. Finally healthy in 2006, Reyes earned the starting nod in the South Atlantic League all-star game. Reyes is a thick-bodied left-hander who does a good job of keeping hitters off balance. His four-seam fastball sits in the low 90s and appears harder due to his deceptive delivery. He also has an overhand curveball and a solid changeup with good movement. He has an abundance of confidence and relishes being atop a rotation. Injuries have been the biggest roadblock to Reyes' progress. Because he never had built up his endurance, he ran out of gas while pitching 141 innings in 2006—67 more than his previous career high. Reyes body offers nothing in the way of projection, and he'll have to watch his weight. Reyes is back on track and will pitch in Double-A as a 22-year-old. He could become a No. 3 or 4 starter in the major leagues.

| Year | Club (League) | Class | W | L | ERA | G | GS | CG | SV | IP | H | R | ER | HR | BB | SO | AVG |
|------|---------------|-------|---|---|-----|---|----|----|----|----|---|---|----|----|----|----|-----|
| 2003 | Braves (GCL) | R | 5 | 3 | 2.56 | 11 | 10 | 0 | 0 | 46 | 34 | 16 | 13 | 1 | 14 | 55 | .205 |
| 2004 | Rome (SAL) | A | 2 | 4 | 5.33 | 15 | 14 | 1 | 0 | 74 | 84 | 49 | 44 | 10 | 25 | 71 | .290 |
| 2005 | Braves (GCL) | R | 0 | 1 | 1.69 | 3 | 2 | 0 | 0 | 5 | 6 | 2 | 1 | 0 | 1 | 6 | .273 |
| | Danville (Appy) | R | 3 | 0 | 3.53 | 9 | 8 | 0 | 0 | 43 | 37 | 18 | 17 | 3 | 6 | 27 | .228 |
| 2006 | Rome (SAL) | A | 8 | 1 | 2.99 | 13 | 13 | 1 | 0 | 75 | 62 | 26 | 25 | 5 | 25 | 84 | .225 |
| | Myrtle Beach (CL) | A | 4 | 4 | 4.11 | 14 | 14 | 0 | 0 | 66 | 52 | 36 | 30 | 0 | 36 | 58 | .220 |
| **MINOR LEAGUE TOTALS** | | | 22 | 13 | 3.78 | 65 | 61 | 2 | 0 | 310 | 275 | 147 | 130 | 19 | 107 | 301 | .239 |

## 9 JOEY DEVINE RHP

**Born:** Sept. 29, 1983. **B-T:** R-R. **Ht.:** 6-0. **Wt.:** 212. **Drafted:** North Carolina State, 2005 (1st round). **Signed by:** Billy Best.

Devine has endured a bumpy road since the Braves drafted him 27th overall in 2005. Pushed to Atlanta less than three months after signing, he became the first big leaguer to give up grand slams in his first two appearances, and he also served up an 18th-inning, Division Series-ending homer to Chris Burke. In 2006, a degenerative disc in his lower back sidelined him for most of the first half. Devine's main pitch is a sinker that sits at 92-94 mph and can touch 97. He also has a sidearm slider that starts out behind righthanders before cutting across the strike zone. He has excellent athleticism and the makeup to close games. Devine's ailing back caused his mechanics to become shaky, although Mississippi pitching coach Kent Willis helped correct some flaws in August. His inconsistent delivery has led to problems with his command, which must improve in order for him to succeed in the late innings. The addition of a consistent change-up would help him against lefthanders. Devine broke camp with Atlanta in 2006 and will have the opportunity to do so again in 2007. He could emerge as a closer down the road, but Bob Wickman will open 2007 in that role.

| Year | Club (League) | Class | W | L | ERA | G | GS | CG | SV | IP | H | R | ER | HR | BB | SO | AVG |
|---|---|---|---|---|---|---|---|---|---|---|---|---|---|---|---|---|---|
| 2005 | Myrtle Beach (CL) | A | 0 | 0 | 0.00 | 4 | 0 | 0 | 1 | 5 | 0 | 0 | 0 | 0 | 3 | 7 | .000 |
| | Mississippi (SL) | AA | 1 | 1 | 2.70 | 18 | 0 | 0 | 5 | 20 | 19 | 13 | 6 | 2 | 12 | 28 | .250 |
| | Richmond (IL) | AAA | 0 | 0 | 18.00 | 1 | 0 | 0 | 0 | 1 | 3 | 2 | 2 | 0 | 1 | 1 | .600 |
| | Atlanta (NL) | MLB | 0 | 1 | 12.60 | 5 | 0 | 0 | 0 | 5 | 6 | 7 | 7 | 2 | 5 | 3 | .286 |
| 2006 | Richmond (IL) | AAA | 0 | 0 | — | 1 | 0 | 0 | 0 | 0 | 1 | 1 | 1 | 0 | 1 | 0 | 1.000 |
| | Myrtle Beach (CL) | A | 1 | 3 | 5.89 | 13 | 2 | 0 | 0 | 18 | 13 | 12 | 12 | 1 | 11 | 28 | .203 |
| | Mississippi (SL) | AA | 2 | 0 | 0.82 | 6 | 0 | 0 | 0 | 11 | 2 | 1 | 1 | 1 | 4 | 20 | .065 |
| | Atlanta (NL) | MLB | 0 | 0 | 9.95 | 10 | 0 | 0 | 0 | 6 | 8 | 7 | 7 | 1 | 9 | 10 | .308 |
| **MINOR LEAGUE TOTALS** | | | 4 | 4 | 3.58 | 43 | 2 | 0 | 6 | 55 | 38 | 29 | 22 | 4 | 32 | 84 | .199 |
| **MAJOR LEAGUE TOTALS** | | | 0 | 1 | 11.12 | 15 | 0 | 0 | 0 | 11 | 14 | 14 | 14 | 3 | 14 | 13 | .298 |

## 10 YUNEL ESCOBAR INF

**Born:** Nov. 2, 1982. **B-T:** R-R. **Ht.:** 6-2. **Wt.:** 200. **Drafted:** Miami (no school), 2005 (2nd round). **Signed by:** Gregg Kilby.

A Cuban defector who was a childhood friend of Braves catcher Brayan Pena, Escobar went in the second round after becoming draft-eligible just a month before the 2005 draft. He spent his first full season in Double-A, shifting between second base, shortstop and third base as part of a three-man infield rotation with Luis Hernandez and Martin Prado. He represented Cuba in the Futures Game last summer. Escobar has solid tools across the board. His smooth swing produces line drives from gap to gap. Though aggressive at the plate, he has good plate discipline and pitch recognition. He has consistent hands and a strong arm that's a plus at any infield position. Escobar hasn't shown the ability to drive the ball that many scouts projected before the 2005 draft. His modest range could prevent him from playing shortstop in the majors. He has just average speed and is a tick below-average for a middle infielder. A year ago, Escobar figured to be in a tight battle with Elvis Andrus as the Braves' long-term answer at shortstop. Because second baseman Marcus Giles was non-tendered, Escobar's best shot will probably come at that position or as a utilityman. He's ready for Triple-A.

| Year | Club (League) | Class | AVG | G | AB | R | H | 2B | 3B | HR | RBI | BB | SO | SB | OBP | SLG |
|---|---|---|---|---|---|---|---|---|---|---|---|---|---|---|---|---|
| 2005 | Danville (Appy) | R | .400 | 8 | 30 | 9 | 12 | 2 | 1 | 2 | 8 | 5 | 4 | 0 | .472 | .733 |
| | Rome (SAL) | A | .313 | 48 | 198 | 30 | 62 | 13 | 3 | 4 | 19 | 14 | 30 | 0 | .358 | .470 |
| 2006 | Mississippi (SL) | AA | .264 | 121 | 428 | 55 | 113 | 21 | 4 | 2 | 45 | 59 | 77 | 7 | .361 | .346 |
| **MINOR LEAGUE TOTALS** | | | .285 | 177 | 656 | 94 | 187 | 36 | 8 | 8 | 72 | 78 | 111 | 7 | .365 | .401 |

## 11 KALA KAAIHUE 1B

**Born:** March 29, 1985. **B-T:** R-R. **Ht.:** 6-2. **Wt.:** 230. **Signed:** NDFA/South Mountain (Ariz.) CC, 2005. **Signed by:** Tom Battista/Lonnie Goldberg.

Kaaihue is part of a baseball family. Father Kala Sr. reached Triple-A in the Pirates system during the mid-1970s, and older brother Kila spent 2006 as a Double-A first baseman for the Royals. The Red Sox drafted Kala out of a Hawaii high school as a 22nd-round pick in 2003, but he opted to attend South Mountain (Ariz.) CC, out of where he signed with the Braves for $50,000 as a nondrafted free agent in 2005. Kaaihue had a strong pro debut and an even better first full season, leading the system in homers (28), RBIs (80) and slugging percentage

(.550). He topped the South Atlantic League in homers, RBIs and walks during the first half of the season. Promoted to high Class A in late June, Kaaihue struggled initially before redis-covering his power stroke. The only negative came on Aug. 18, when an errant pitch broke his left wrist and ended his season. Kaaihue draws comparisons to Andres Galarraga, both for his power and for his 6-foot-2, 230-pound build. He doesn't have to get all of a pitch to drive it out of the yard. Though his 115 strikeouts led all Braves farmhands last year, he com-pensates by drawing a lot of walks. He'll need to improve his pitch recognition, however. He's a below-average runner but has made a nice conversion from a high school catcher to a steady first baseman with quick reflexes. He should open 2007 in Double-A. Kaaihue is one of the system's best power prospects, but he'll have to contend with Adam LaRoche, Scott Thorman and possibly Jarrod Saltalamacchia to play at first base for the Braves.

| Year | Club (League) | Class | AVG | G | AB | R | H | 2B | 3B | HR | RBI | BB | SO | SB | OBP | SLG |
|------|---------------|-------|-----|---|----|---|---|----|----|----|-----|----|----|----|-----|-----|
| 2005 | Braves (GCL) | R | .283 | 40 | 127 | 18 | 36 | 8 | 2 | 6 | 22 | 15 | 38 | 0 | .358 | .520 |
| | Danville (Appy) | R | .438 | 5 | 16 | 4 | 7 | 3 | 0 | 2 | 3 | 0 | 5 | 0 | .438 | 1.000 |
| 2006 | Myrtle Beach (CL) | A | .223 | 53 | 188 | 37 | 42 | 8 | 0 | 13 | 31 | 30 | 49 | 0 | .342 | .473 |
| | Rome (SAL) | A | .329 | 67 | 228 | 44 | 75 | 16 | 2 | 15 | 49 | 52 | 66 | 3 | .458 | .614 |
| **MINOR LEAGUE TOTALS** | | | .286 | 165 | 559 | 103 | 160 | 35 | 4 | 36 | 105 | 97 | 158 | 3 | .397 | .556 |

## 12 ANTHONY LEREW                                                        RHP

**Born:** Oct. 28, 1982. **B-T:** L-R. **Ht.:** 6-3. **Wt.:** 220. **Drafted:** HS—Wellsville, Pa., 2001 (11th round). **Signed by:** J.J. Picollo.

A talented high school athlete who was more of a football prospect than a baseball stand-out, Lerew made rapid strides in 2004, when he added 5 mph to his fastball over the course of the season. He parlayed the increased velocity into 10 wins, a Futures Game selection and his first taste of the majors in 2005. Yet just as it appeared that Lerew was on the verge of breaking into the Atlanta rotation, he experience a difficult 2006 campaign that included a midseason demotion to Double-A. Lerew's problems stemmed from mechanical issues. Despite possessing a loose and easy arm action and maintaining his 92-95 mph fastball, he lost the feel for his solid changeup and slider. His command also suffered. While consistent mechanics and command remain his biggest needs, Lerew is the most athletic pitcher in the system, which bodes well for him figuring it out. He helps himself at the plate (career .302 average), can steal bases (three swipes in 14 trips to first base) and is an excellent fielder. If Lerew can make the necessary adjustments, he can bounce back from a dismal 2006 to be a middle-of-the-rotation starter or a setup man in the majors.

| Year | Club (League) | Class | W | L | ERA | G | GS | CG | SV | IP | H | R | ER | HR | BB | SO | AVG |
|------|---------------|-------|---|---|-----|---|----|----|----|----|---|---|----|----|----|----|-----|
| 2001 | Braves (GCL) | R | 1 | 2 | 2.92 | 12 | 7 | 0 | 0 | 49 | 43 | 25 | 16 | 3 | 14 | 40 | .228 |
| 2002 | Danville (Appy) | R | 8 | 3 | 1.73 | 14 | 14 | 0 | 0 | 83 | 60 | 23 | 16 | 2 | 25 | 75 | .205 |
| 2003 | Rome (SAL) | A | 7 | 6 | 2.38 | 25 | 25 | 0 | 0 | 144 | 112 | 45 | 38 | 7 | 43 | 127 | .215 |
| 2004 | Myrtle Beach (CL) | A | 8 | 9 | 3.75 | 27 | 27 | 0 | 0 | 144 | 145 | 75 | 60 | 12 | 46 | 125 | .271 |
| 2005 | Mississippi (SL) | AA | 6 | 2 | 3.93 | 14 | 14 | 1 | 0 | 76 | 70 | 34 | 33 | 6 | 32 | 64 | .246 |
| | Richmond (IL) | AAA | 4 | 4 | 3.48 | 13 | 13 | 0 | 0 | 72 | 63 | 34 | 28 | 9 | 23 | 53 | .232 |
| | Atlanta (NL) | MLB | 0 | 0 | 5.63 | 7 | 0 | 0 | 0 | 8 | 9 | 5 | 5 | 1 | 5 | 5 | .290 |
| 2006 | Mississippi (SL) | AA | 4 | 2 | 2.03 | 9 | 8 | 0 | 0 | 49 | 43 | 18 | 11 | 1 | 13 | 37 | .234 |
| | Richmond (IL) | AAA | 3 | 5 | 7.48 | 16 | 15 | 1 | 0 | 71 | 92 | 63 | 59 | 12 | 36 | 69 | .315 |
| | Atlanta (NL) | MLB | 0 | 0 | 22.50 | 1 | 0 | 0 | 0 | 2 | 5 | 5 | 5 | 0 | 3 | 1 | .455 |
| **MINOR LEAGUE TOTALS** | | | 41 | 33 | 3.42 | 130 | 123 | 2 | 0 | 688 | 628 | 317 | 261 | 52 | 232 | 590 | .245 |
| **MAJOR LEAGUE TOTALS** | | | 0 | 0 | 9.00 | 8 | 0 | 0 | 0 | 10 | 14 | 10 | 10 | 1 | 8 | 6 | .333 |

## 13 STEVE EVARTS                                                        LHP

**Born:** Oct. 13, 1987. **B-T:** L-L. **Ht.:** 6-3. **Wt.:** 180. **Drafted:** HS—Tampa, 2006 (1st round sup-plemental). **Signed by:** Gregg Kilby.

Evarts put together an impressive spring to emerge as the top high school southpaw in Florida last year. Taken by the Braves with the 43rd overall pick, he signed for $800,000 and made a seamless move to pro ball. He had the best combination of stuff and feel on a tal-ented Rookie-level Gulf Coast League pitching staff that featured five other members of this top 30 list. Evarts is a projection project with an immature, lanky build and a loose, lively arm. He throws strikes with his smooth mechanics and his ability to repeat his easy deliv-ery. He has an average fastball that sits consistently around 90 mph and touches 93 with plus life and late movement, particularly when he cuts it. His best pitch is a nasty change-up that breaks much like a screwball. Evarts throws the change with an unusual grip and will use it at any time in the count. It has the potential to carry him into the upper levels. His breaking ball is well below-average. He showed some promise in developing a hard slurve in the GCL and worked on a slider during instructional league. He was arrested in December in Tampa and charged with criminal mischief, a felony. Police said he damaged a

vehicle with a baseball bat, and the incident highlights questions scouts had about his makeup. Evarts needs innings, which he'll get as one of the younger starters in the South Atlantic League in 2007.

| Year | Club (League) | Class | W | L | ERA | G | GS | CG | SV | IP | H | R | ER | HR | BB | SO | AVG |
|---|---|---|---|---|---|---|---|---|---|---|---|---|---|---|---|---|---|
| 2006 | Braves (GCL) | R | 2 | 2 | 2.93 | 11 | 9 | 0 | 0 | 43 | 42 | 19 | 14 | 0 | 12 | 33 | .255 |
| MINOR LEAGUE TOTALS | | | 2 | 2 | 2.93 | 11 | 9 | 0 | 0 | 43 | 42 | 19 | 14 | 0 | 12 | 33 | .255 |

## 14 BEAU JONES                                                          LHP

**Born:** Aug. 26, 1986. **B-T:** L-L. **Ht.:** 6-1. **Wt.:** 205. **Drafted:** HS—Destrehan, La., 2005 (1st round supplemental). **Signed by:** Don Thomas.

The Braves considered taking Jones with their first pick in 2005 and were delighted to get him 14 selections later. After a strong debut, though, his control regressed in his first full season, and he wore down late in the year, allowing 32 earned runs in his final 32 innings. The good news was that his stuff remained promising. Jones has a low-90s fastball that reaches 95 and has nice movement. His curveball shows signs of becoming an out pitch with high-70s velocity and hard, sharp break. His changeup remains in the developmental stages, and he lacks confidence in it. He has an easy delivery and a determined approach that attracts comparisons to Kyle Davies. Jones has a lot of work to do, as he must make major strides with his control, command and changeup while becoming more consistent with his fastball and curve. Those will be his goals this year in high Class A.

| Year | Club (League) | Class | W | L | ERA | G | GS | CG | SV | IP | H | R | ER | HR | BB | SO | AVG |
|---|---|---|---|---|---|---|---|---|---|---|---|---|---|---|---|---|---|
| 2005 | Braves (GCL) | R | 3 | 2 | 3.86 | 8 | 7 | 0 | 0 | 35 | 25 | 15 | 15 | 0 | 16 | 41 | .212 |
| 2006 | Rome (SAL) | A | 5 | 5 | 5.61 | 25 | 22 | 0 | 1 | 111 | 125 | 79 | 69 | 8 | 83 | 101 | .286 |
| MINOR LEAGUE TOTALS | | | 8 | 7 | 5.19 | 33 | 29 | 0 | 1 | 146 | 150 | 94 | 84 | 8 | 99 | 142 | .270 |

## 15 JEFF LYMAN                                                          RHP

**Born:** Jan. 14, 1987. **B-T:** R-R. **Ht.:** 6-3. **Wt.:** 225. **Drafted:** HS—Monte Vista. Calif., 2005 (2nd round). **Signed by:** Nick Hostetler.

Like fellow 2005 draftee Beau Jones, Lyman had a strong Gulf Coast League debut before running into command difficulties in low Class A last year. He got off to a nice start prior to missing a month with back spasms. He was inconsistent upon his return in late June. Lyman throws strikes with his 92-95 mph fastball, and he can run his two-seamer in on hitters, making it difficult for them to center the ball. His secondary offerings are works in progress. He has a sharp curveball that can be effective, as well as a splitter that functions as a changeup. Lyman's mechanics aren't always fluid, which has led to difficulties with his command and control. The Braves love his intensity and believe his work ethic will allow him to iron out the rough spots in his game. He'll team up with Jones again this year in high Class A.

| Year | Club (League) | Class | W | L | ERA | G | GS | CG | SV | IP | H | R | ER | HR | BB | SO | AVG |
|---|---|---|---|---|---|---|---|---|---|---|---|---|---|---|---|---|---|
| 2005 | Braves (GCL) | R | 0 | 3 | 4.24 | 8 | 7 | 0 | 0 | 34 | 41 | 27 | 16 | 2 | 7 | 28 | .295 |
| 2006 | Braves (GCL) | R | 0 | 0 | 1.50 | 2 | 2 | 0 | 0 | 6 | 2 | 1 | 1 | 0 | 1 | 9 | .095 |
| | Rome (SAL) | A | 6 | 6 | 4.49 | 22 | 18 | 0 | 0 | 100 | 118 | 57 | 50 | 3 | 47 | 80 | .296 |
| MINOR LEAGUE TOTALS | | | 6 | 9 | 4.30 | 32 | 27 | 0 | 0 | 140 | 161 | 85 | 67 | 5 | 55 | 117 | .288 |

## 16 CORY RASMUS                                                         RHP

**Born:** Nov. 6, 1987. **B-T:** R-R. **Ht.:** 6-1. **Wt.:** 220. **Drafted:** HS—Seale, Ala., 2006 (1st round supplemental). **Signed by:** Al Goetz.

Before the Braves made Rasmus the 38th overall pick in 2006 and signed him for $900,000, he had a storied amateur career. He helped Russell County High (Seale, Ala.)—coached by his father Tony and featuring his older brother Colby (the Cardinals' No. 1 prospect)—win the 2005 national championship. Cory has a power arm and a deeper repertoire than most pitchers his age. He throws a 92-94 mph fastball that tops out at 97 and has decent life. His best pitch is a knee-buckling 11-to-5 curveball that seems to fall out of the sky and left many batters shaking their heads during instructional league. Rasmus also has an above-average changeup, a pitch that he has become so adept with that he sometimes relies on it too much instead of challenging hitters. He has a thick body that leaves little room for projection. His arm is quick and he has a good feel for pitching. As he moves up the ladder, Rasmus will have to smooth out his command and the mechanics of his full-effort delivery. He has the ability to be a No. 2 or 3 starter in the big leagues, though that's a long ways off. He'll open 2007 in low Class A.

| Year | Club (League) | Class | W | L | ERA | G | GS | CG | SV | IP | H | R | ER | HR | BB | SO | AVG |
|---|---|---|---|---|---|---|---|---|---|---|---|---|---|---|---|---|---|
| 2006 | Braves (GCL) | R | 0 | 0 | 8.59 | 3 | 1 | 0 | 0 | 7 | 7 | 7 | 7 | 0 | 5 | 3 | .280 |
| MINOR LEAGUE TOTALS | | | 0 | 0 | 8.59 | 3 | 1 | 0 | 0 | 7 | 7 | 7 | 7 | 0 | 5 | 3 | .280 |

## TOMMY HANSON

RHP

**Born:** Aug. 28, 1986. **B-T:** R-R. **Ht.:** 6-6. **Wt.:** 210. **Drafted:** Riverside (Calif.) CC, D/F 2005 (22nd round). **Signed by:** Mike Baker.

Hanson could prove to be the crown jewel of the seven draft-and-follow picks the Braves signed last May. After he went in the 22nd round of the 2005 draft, he ranked as the No. 1 prospect in the West Coast Collegiate League that summer and led California juco pitchers with 138 strikeouts in 101 innings. Signed away from an Arizona State commitment for $325,000, Hanson presents an imposing physical presence on the mound thanks to his 6-foot-6 frame. He throws the ball on a tough downhill plane to the plate. He's not overpowering but commands his 89-92 mph fastball with precision, leading to an impressive 56-9 K-BB ratio in his pro debut. His secondary pitches show promise, particularly after he worked extensively with Rookie-level Danville pitching coach Doug Henry on tightening the spin of his curveball and the depth of his changeup. As he continues to develop those pitches, Hanson will need to mix his three offerings instead of focusing on his fastball, as he did in his pro debut. Hanson will be part of a strong but young Rome rotation in 2007.

| Year | Club (League) | Class | W | L | ERA | G | GS | CG | SV | IP | H | R | ER | HR | BB | SO | AVG |
|------|---------------|-------|---|---|-----|---|----|----|----|----|----|----|----|----|----|----|-----|
| 2006 | Danville (Appy) | R | 4 | 1 | 2.09 | 13 | 8 | 0 | 0 | 52 | 42 | 15 | 12 | 2 | 9 | 56 | .218 |
| **MINOR LEAGUE TOTALS** | | | 4 | 1 | 2.09 | 13 | 8 | 0 | 0 | 52 | 42 | 15 | 12 | 2 | 9 | 56 | .218 |

## NEFTALI FELIZ

RHP

**Born:** May 2, 1988. **B-T:** R-R. **Ht.:** 6-3. **Wt.:** 180. **Signed:** Dominican Republic, 2005. **Signed by:** Julian Perez/Roberto Aquino.

Feliz shined as bright as any of the organization's young arms last summer in the Gulf Coast League, recording more than twice as many strikeouts as hits allowed. He has a lanky frame to grow into, along with a clean delivery that produces an effortless 90-93 mph fastball with late life. He reaches 96-97 with his heater and the ball jumps out of his hand. At this point, his fastball is his lone plus offering. Feliz has a sweeping low-80s slider that's sharp when he stays on top of it, but his changeup needs considerable work in order to become a usable pitch. His biggest challenge will be learning to harness his repertoire by pitching down in the strike zone more consistently and gaining better overall control. Feliz might have as much upside as any pitcher in the system. He doesn't turn 19 until May, so he could open 2007 in extended spring training before reporting to Danville.

| Year | Club (League) | Class | W | L | ERA | G | GS | CG | SV | IP | H | R | ER | HR | BB | SO | AVG |
|------|---------------|-------|---|---|-----|---|----|----|----|----|----|----|----|----|----|----|-----|
| 2005 | Braves (DSL) | R | 0 | 0 | 3.60 | 10 | 0 | 0 | 0 | 10 | 7 | 4 | 4 | 0 | 11 | 8 | .184 |
| 2006 | Braves (GCL) | R | 0 | 2 | 4.03 | 11 | 5 | 0 | 2 | 29 | 20 | 13 | 13 | 0 | 14 | 42 | .192 |
| **MINOR LEAGUE TOTALS** | | | 0 | 2 | 3.92 | 21 | 5 | 0 | 2 | 39 | 27 | 17 | 17 | 0 | 25 | 50 | .190 |

## JEFF LOCKE

LHP

**Born:** Nov. 20, 1987. **B-T:** L-L. **Ht.:** 6-2. **Wt.:** 180. **Drafted:** HS—Conway, N.H., 2006 (2nd round). **Signed by:** Lonnie Goldberg.

Locke has the potential to carry on the New Hampshire pitching tradition—the state has produced all-stars Chris Carpenter, Mike Flanagan and Bob Tewksbury—after pitching his way into the second round last June. He recovered from a rocky start to allow just one earned run over his final four outings and led the loaded GCL Braves in victories. Locke has good command of a lively fastball that he throws at 88-91 mph and touches 93. He turned his breaking ball, a slurvy pitch in the spring, into a true curveball by the end of instructional league. It projects as a plus pitch. His changeup is still a work in progress, but he has shown some touch for the offspeed pitch. Though Locke's delivery could use some smoothing out, his arm works easy and his command should be a strength. He's confident and relishes a challenge. His next one will come when he spends his first full season in low Class A.

| Year | Club (League) | Class | W | L | ERA | G | GS | CG | SV | IP | H | R | ER | HR | BB | SO | AVG |
|------|---------------|-------|---|---|-----|---|----|----|----|----|----|----|----|----|----|----|-----|
| 2006 | Braves (GCL) | R | 4 | 3 | 4.22 | 10 | 5 | 0 | 0 | 32 | 38 | 18 | 15 | 4 | 5 | 38 | .299 |
| **MINOR LEAGUE TOTALS** | | | 4 | 3 | 4.22 | 10 | 5 | 0 | 0 | 32 | 38 | 18 | 15 | 4 | 5 | 38 | .299 |

## CHAD RODGERS

LHP

**Born:** Nov. 23, 1987. **B-T:** L-L. **Ht.:** 6-3. **Wt.:** 185. **Drafted:** HS—Stow, Ohio, 2006 (3rd round). **Signed by:** Nick Hostetler.

Ohio's top pitching prospect in the 2006 draft, Rodgers went in the third round and passed up the chance to attend Kent State in order to turn pro for $385,000. He outperformed the other top high school lefties from Atlanta's 2006 draft class who were assigned

to the Gulf Coast League, supplemental first-rounder Steve Evarts and second-rounder Jeff Locke. Rodgers had a reputation for being very polished for a teenager, drawing comparisons to Jeremy Sowers, and he backed it up by filling the strike zone in his pro debut. He already throws 87-91 mph and should gain more velocity on his fastball as he fills out his slender, projectable frame. He has an advanced feel for mixing pitches and changing locations to keep hitters off balance. He throws two- and four-seam fastballs, a hard downer curveball and a changeup, all of which should be average or better pitches. Rodgers is well equipped to handle the jump to low Class A in 2007.

| Year | Club (League) | Class | W | L | ERA | G | GS | CG | SV | IP | H | R | ER | HR | BB | SO | AVG |
|------|---------------|-------|---|---|-----|---|----|----|----|----|---|---|----|----|----|----|-----|
| 2006 | Braves (GCL) | R | 3 | 2 | 2.31 | 11 | 5 | 0 | 1 | 39 | 31 | 14 | 10 | 1 | 13 | 30 | .217 |
| **MINOR LEAGUE TOTALS** | | | 3 | 2 | 2.31 | 11 | 5 | 0 | 1 | 39 | 31 | 14 | 10 | 1 | 13 | 30 | .217 |

 ## DAN SMITH
LHP

**Born:** Sept. 9, 1983. **B-T:** L-L. **Ht.:** 6-5. **Wt.:** 225. **Signed:** NDFA/Fort Myers, Fla., 2003. **Signed by:** Alex Morrales/George Martin.

Undrafted out of high school in 2002 and signed as a free agent in 2003, Smith quietly has made rapid progress. He reached Double-A in 2006 and posted a 1.63 ERA when the Braves moved him into the rotation on a full-time basis in August. Smith's fastball velocity has increased every season since he signed. His four-seamer sat in the low 90s last year, and he continued to throw it on a downhill angle to the plate. He also has a solid changeup with consistent fade. To continue to progress as a starter, Smith will have to improve the command and consistency of his breaking ball. If not, he still could serve as a reliever in the majors, though he performed better while pitching in the rotation in 2006. He'll receive a long look during spring training and should spend the year knocking on the door in Triple-A if he doesn't make the Braves.

| Year | Club (League) | Class | W | L | ERA | G | GS | CG | SV | IP | H | R | ER | HR | BB | SO | AVG |
|------|---------------|-------|---|---|-----|---|----|----|----|----|-----|-----|----|----|-----|-----|-----|
| 2003 | Danville (Appy) | R | 0 | 0 | 5.40 | 2 | 0 | 0 | 0 | 2 | 3 | 1 | 1 | 0 | 3 | 2 | .429 |
| | Braves (GCL) | R | 6 | 0 | 1.91 | 13 | 0 | 0 | 1 | 28 | 22 | 7 | 6 | 2 | 8 | 35 | .210 |
| 2004 | Rome (SAL) | A | 0 | 0 | 7.71 | 1 | 1 | 0 | 0 | 5 | 5 | 5 | 4 | 1 | 2 | 5 | .250 |
| | Danville (Appy) | R | 3 | 1 | 2.27 | 14 | 2 | 0 | 1 | 40 | 24 | 10 | 10 | 2 | 16 | 52 | .174 |
| 2005 | Rome (SAL) | A | 3 | 2 | 1.89 | 19 | 0 | 0 | 5 | 33 | 24 | 8 | 7 | 1 | 18 | 45 | .205 |
| | Myrtle Beach (CL) | A | 2 | 2 | 2.61 | 25 | 0 | 0 | 6 | 38 | 33 | 11 | 11 | 1 | 17 | 32 | .232 |
| 2006 | Myrtle Beach (CL) | A | 1 | 0 | 1.13 | 8 | 0 | 0 | 5 | 8 | 5 | 1 | 1 | 1 | 4 | 13 | .172 |
| | Mississippi (SL) | AA | 3 | 6 | 3.13 | 28 | 8 | 0 | 0 | 60 | 41 | 26 | 21 | 3 | 32 | 86 | .196 |
| **MINOR LEAGUE TOTALS** | | | 18 | 11 | 2.57 | 110 | 11 | 0 | 18 | 214 | 157 | 69 | 61 | 11 | 100 | 270 | .205 |

## BRAYAN PENA
C

**Born:** Jan. 7, 1982. **B-T:** B-R. **Ht.:** 5-11. **Wt.:** 220. **Signed:** Cuba, 2000. **Signed by:** Julian Perez/Rene Francisco.

For the second straight season, Pena was on call in Triple-A waiting for an emergency opportunity. He played sparingly for the Braves in May and June while Brian McCann was injured, and otherwise turned in his second straight strong season in Richmond. The switch-hitting Pena has a knack for centering the ball on the bat but possesses minimal power at the plate. He's known as "The Cuban Ichiro" for his bat control. Pena has the speed of a typical catcher, making him a liability on the bases, yet he has improved his mobility behind the plate. He does a good job of blocking balls in the dirt, and he has a quick release and makes accurate throws. He erased 29 percent of Triple-A basestealers last year. Though McCann has developed into one of the premier young backstops in the game and Jarrod Saltalamacchia is on his heels, the Braves believe Pena has shown enough to serve as their backup catcher. He'll get a chance to claim that role in 2007.

| Year | Club (League) | Class | AVG | G | AB | R | H | 2B | 3B | HR | RBI | BB | SO | SB | OBP | SLG |
|------|---------------|-------|-----|---|-----|-----|-----|----|----|----|-----|-----|-----|----|-----|-----|
| 2001 | Danville (Appy) | R | .370 | 64 | 235 | 39 | 87 | 16 | 2 | 1 | 33 | 31 | 30 | 3 | .440 | .468 |
| 2002 | Myrtle Beach (CL) | A | .211 | 6 | 19 | 3 | 4 | 1 | 0 | 0 | 1 | 3 | 4 | 0 | .318 | .263 |
| | Macon (SAL) | A | .229 | 81 | 271 | 26 | 62 | 10 | 0 | 3 | 25 | 22 | 37 | 0 | .290 | .299 |
| 2003 | Myrtle Beach (CL) | A | .294 | 82 | 286 | 24 | 84 | 14 | 1 | 2 | 27 | 11 | 28 | 2 | .320 | .371 |
| 2004 | Greenville (SL) | AA | .314 | 77 | 277 | 30 | 87 | 10 | 4 | 2 | 30 | 15 | 29 | 3 | .349 | .401 |
| 2005 | Richmond (IL) | AAA | .326 | 81 | 282 | 27 | 92 | 21 | 2 | 0 | 25 | 28 | 19 | 3 | .383 | .415 |
| | Atlanta (NL) | MLB | .179 | 18 | 39 | 2 | 7 | 2 | 0 | 0 | 4 | 1 | 7 | 0 | .200 | .231 |
| 2006 | Richmond (IL) | AAA | .302 | 87 | 325 | 32 | 98 | 18 | 1 | 1 | 33 | 21 | 28 | 6 | .342 | .372 |
| | Atlanta (NL) | MLB | .268 | 23 | 41 | 9 | 11 | 2 | 0 | 1 | 5 | 2 | 5 | 0 | .302 | .390 |
| **MINOR LEAGUE TOTALS** | | | .303 | 478 | 1695 | 181 | 514 | 90 | 10 | 9 | 174 | 131 | 175 | 17 | .352 | .384 |
| **MAJOR LEAGUE TOTALS** | | | .225 | 41 | 80 | 11 | 18 | 4 | 0 | 1 | 9 | 3 | 12 | 0 | .253 | .313 |

## JAMIE ROMAK OF

**Born:** Sept. 30, 1985. **B-T:** R-R. **Ht.:** 6-2. **Wt.:** 220. **Drafted:** HS—London, Ont., 2003 (4th round). **Signed by:** Lonnie Goldberg.

Romak attracted comparisons to fellow Canadian Scott Thorman last season with his development as one of the more impressive power hitters in the system. Like Thorman, Romak has come along slowly since being drafted. He spent three seasons in Rookie ball before placing second behind Eric Campbell at Rome in doubles, homers and RBIs in 2006. Romak followed that performance by consistently hitting the ball harder than anyone in the Braves' instructional league camp during the fall. He has a couple of plus tools: the pop in his bat from right-center to the left-field foul pole, and a strong arm suited for right field. His ability to make consistent contact will determine just how high he's able to climb. He needs to shorten his swing and close some holes. Originally signed as a third baseman, Romak is a lumbering defender with below-average speed. His overall defensive game could use some polish. Scheduled to open 2007 in high Class A, he has a chance to become an average big league corner outfielder who hits in the bottom half of the order.

| Year | Club (League) | Class | AVG | G | AB | R | H | 2B | 3B | HR | RBI | BB | SO | SB | OBP | SLG |
|------|---------------|-------|-----|---|----|---|---|----|----|----|-----|----|----|----|-----|-----|
| 2003 | Braves (GCL) | R | .176 | 19 | 51 | 5 | 9 | 2 | 0 | 0 | 4 | 9 | 10 | 0 | .300 | .216 |
| 2004 | Danville (Appy) | R | .190 | 48 | 158 | 25 | 30 | 5 | 1 | 5 | 22 | 14 | 56 | 1 | .287 | .329 |
| 2005 | Danville (Appy) | R | .274 | 34 | 124 | 25 | 34 | 10 | 1 | 7 | 27 | 14 | 38 | 2 | .368 | .540 |
| 2006 | Rome (SAL) | A | .247 | 108 | 348 | 55 | 86 | 26 | 2 | 16 | 68 | 59 | 102 | 3 | .369 | .471 |
| **MINOR LEAGUE TOTALS** | | | .233 | 209 | 681 | 110 | 159 | 43 | 4 | 28 | 121 | 96 | 206 | 6 | .345 | .432 |

## JAMIE RICHMOND RHP

**Born:** March 23, 1986. **B-T:** R-R. **Ht.:** 6-3. **Wt.:** 190. **Drafted:** Texarkana (Texas) JC, D/F 2004 (31st round). **Signed by:** Lonnie Goldberg.

Richmond joins Jamie Romak as a developing Canadian who could be on the verge of a breakthrough. With his command of three pitches and advanced feel for pitching, Richmond was the Appalachian League's 2006 pitcher of the year and ERA leader. He works both sides of the plate with a 90-91 mph fastball that features late cutting action, making it difficult for hitters to center the ball. He still has projection in his lanky frame and could add more velocity. His curveball and changeup are average pitches that he locates well, and he's not afraid to throw the curve when he's behind in the count. His 52-4 K-BB ratio was even more pronounced than teammate Tommy Hanson's. Some scouts label Richmond as a slinger, but he repeats his delivery well and pounds the strike zone. He'll move up to low Class A in 2007.

| Year | Club (League) | Class | W | L | ERA | G | GS | CG | SV | IP | H | R | ER | HR | BB | SO | AVG |
|------|---------------|-------|---|---|-----|---|----|----|----|-----|----|----|----|----|----|----|-----|
| 2005 | Braves (GCL) | R | 2 | 0 | 3.09 | 8 | 0 | 0 | 0 | 12 | 7 | 4 | 4 | 0 | 2 | 12 | .179 |
| 2006 | Danville (Appy) | R | 7 | 1 | 1.21 | 14 | 12 | 0 | 0 | 67 | 51 | 11 | 9 | 0 | 4 | 52 | .210 |
| **MINOR LEAGUE TOTALS** | | | 9 | 1 | 1.49 | 22 | 12 | 0 | 0 | 79 | 58 | 15 | 13 | 0 | 6 | 64 | .206 |

## CHASE FONTAINE SS

**Born:** Oct, 22, 1985. **B-T:** L-R. **Ht.:** 6-2. **Wt.:** 185. **Drafted:** Daytona Beach CC, 2006 (2nd round). **Signed by:** Gregg Kilby.

The sixth of six Braves picks in the first two rounds last June, Fontaine made the Appalachian League all-star team in his pro debut. His career path didn't always look so promising, however. A slump as a high school senior in 2004 caused him to go undrafted and head to Texas, but he transferred to Daytona Beach (Fla.) Community College before he ever took the field for the Longhorns. After the Rangers drafted him in the 18th round in 2005, he hit .407 with 10 homers and starred in the Florida state community college tournament this spring. Fontaine sought $500,000 as a draft-and-follow, and while the Rangers wouldn't meet his price, Atlanta did. He's a line-drive hitter who's aggressive at the plate. His bat does not have a lot of pop at this point, but some scouts believe he could develop power as he gets stronger and adds some loft to his swing. Though he has slightly above-average speed and a strong arm, Fontaine doesn't profile defensively as a shortstop. His stiff hands, mechanical actions and modest range should force him off shortstop, especially with superior defenders such as Elvis Andrus ahead of him in the system. Fontaine eventually will move to second base, but he'll stay at shortstop for now as he advances to low Class A.

| Year | Club (League) | Class | AVG | G | AB | R | H | 2B | 3B | HR | RBI | BB | SO | SB | OBP | SLG |
|------|---------------|-------|-----|---|----|---|---|----|----|----|-----|----|----|----|-----|-----|
| 2006 | Danville (Appy) | R | .296 | 60 | 199 | 42 | 59 | 11 | 0 | 4 | 25 | 37 | 45 | 4 | .411 | .412 |
| **MINOR LEAGUE TOTALS** | | | .296 | 60 | 199 | 42 | 59 | 11 | 0 | 4 | 25 | 37 | 45 | 4 | .411 | .412 |

## CLINT SAMMONS                                                        C
**Born:** May 15, 1983. **B-T:** R-R. **Ht.:** 6-0. **Wt.:** 195. **Drafted:** Georgia, 2004 (6th round). **Signed by:** Al Goetz.

After leading Georgia to a surprise third-place finish at the 2004 College World Series, Sammons has shown everything the Braves look for in a catcher. Rome's MVP in 2005, he batted .221 during the first three months of last season before starting to drive the ball more consistently and hitting .303 the rest of the way. His knowledge of the strike zone has improved significantly since he signed, and he has learned how to recognize and smash certain pitches into the gaps and over the wall. His eight homers doubled his total from his first two pro seasons. While Sammons has improved offensively, defense remains his forte. He has a strong arm and a quick release, enabling him to throw out 40 percent of basestealers in each of the last two seasons. He does a good job of blocking balls, working with pitchers and taking charge behind the plate. Atlanta projects Sammons as a borderline starter or a solid backup, though he won't relegate Brian McCann or Jarrod Saltalamacchia to the bench. Sammons will spend this year in Double-A.

| Year | Club (League) | Class | AVG | G | AB | R | H | 2B | 3B | HR | RBI | BB | SO | SB | OBP | SLG |
|------|---------------|-------|-----|---|----|---|---|----|----|----|-----|----|----|----|-----|-----|
| 2004 | Danville (Appy) | R | .288 | 40 | 132 | 19 | 38 | 7 | 2 | 0 | 17 | 18 | 26 | 5 | .368 | .371 |
| 2005 | Rome (SAL) | A | .286 | 121 | 427 | 60 | 122 | 29 | 0 | 4 | 62 | 55 | 66 | 4 | .368 | .382 |
| 2006 | Myrtle Beach (CL) | A | .258 | 103 | 360 | 36 | 93 | 21 | 0 | 8 | 56 | 32 | 65 | 4 | .323 | .383 |
| **MINOR LEAGUE TOTALS** | | | .275 | 264 | 919 | 115 | 253 | 57 | 2 | 12 | 135 | 105 | 157 | 13 | .351 | .381 |

 ## JORDAN SCHAFER                                                        OF
**Born:** Sept. 4, 1986. **B-T:** L-L. **Ht.:** 6-1. **Wt.:** 190. **Drafted:** HS—Winter Haven, Fla., 2005 (3rd round). **Signed by:** Gregg Kilby.

Schafer has been on the prospect radar since he played first base for his high school team as a 13-year-old, at which time Baseball America ranked him as the top player in the nation for his age group. By the time he graduated in 2005, he attracted serious consideration as a lefthanded pitcher, but his solid tools and desire to play every day led to his signing as a center fielder. Schafer's production to this point has been lackluster, but the Braves aren't concerned. He has a quick bat and should be more of a force once he gets stronger. He also needs to improve his plate discipline and pitch recognition. Schafer has good speed but needs to get better at reading pitchers because he has been caught in 15 of his 43 pro steal attempts. He has stood out the most in center field. Managers rated him the best defensive outfielder in the South Atlantic League last year, a credit to his instincts, quick first step and plus arm. Schafer's spring-training performance will determine whether he repeats low Class A or moves up to high Class A. A return trip to Rome wouldn't be considered a setback, but he needs to start making some positive strides at the plate.

| Year | Club (League) | Class | AVG | G | AB | R | H | 2B | 3B | HR | RBI | BB | SO | SB | OBP | SLG |
|------|---------------|-------|-----|---|----|---|---|----|----|----|-----|----|----|----|-----|-----|
| 2005 | Braves (GCL) | R | .203 | 49 | 182 | 18 | 37 | 12 | 3 | 3 | 19 | 13 | 49 | 13 | .256 | .352 |
| 2006 | Rome (SAL) | A | .240 | 114 | 388 | 49 | 93 | 15 | 7 | 8 | 60 | 28 | 95 | 15 | .293 | .376 |
| **MINOR LEAGUE TOTALS** | | | .228 | 163 | 570 | 67 | 130 | 27 | 10 | 11 | 79 | 41 | 144 | 28 | .281 | .368 |

 ## KRIS MEDLEN                                                          RHP
**Born:** Oct. 7, 1985. **B-T:** B-R. **Ht.:** 5-10. **Wt.:** 175. **Drafted:** Santa Ana (Calif.) JC, 2006 (10th round). **Signed by:** Tom Battista.

Drafted by the Devil Rays in the 37th round out of high school, Medlen spent time at El Camino (Calif.) Junior College before transferring to Southern California juco powerhouse Santa Ana. He also played shortstop for the Warriors, but the Braves took him in the 10th round last June as a pitcher. He signed quickly for $85,000 and wasted little time opening eyes in the organization, allowing only one earned run in 20 relief outings. He tied for third in the Appalachian League with 10 saves, then added another along with a victory in the postseason to help Danville win the championship. Though he's just 5-foot-10, Medlen has a quick arm and works at 91-93 mph with his fastball. He commands it well, setting up hitters for a sharp curveball that has the potential to become a major league out pitch. He's still honing his changeup but has displayed a good feel for the pitch. He throws with an easy arm action, repeats his compact delivery with consistency and isn't afraid to go right after hitters. Medlen has drawn comparisons to former all-star closer Jeff Montgomery because of his size and overall approach to the job. He could reach high Class A at some point in his first full season.

| Year | Club (League) | Class | W | L | ERA | G | GS | CG | SV | IP | H | R | ER | HR | BB | SO | AVG |
|------|---------------|-------|---|---|-----|---|----|----|----|----|---|---|----|----|----|----|-----|
| 2006 | Danville (Appy) | R | 1 | 0 | 0.41 | 20 | 0 | 0 | 10 | 22 | 14 | 2 | 1 | 0 | 2 | 36 | .175 |
| **MINOR LEAGUE TOTALS** | | | 1 | 0 | 0.41 | 20 | 0 | 0 | 10 | 22 | 14 | 2 | 1 | 0 | 2 | 36 | .175 |

## KEVIN GUNDERSON

LHP

**Born:** Sept. 16, 1984: **B-T:** R-L. **Ht.:** 5-10. **Wt.:** 165. **Drafted:** Oregon State, 2006 (6th round). **Signed by:** Tim Moore.

Gunderson was one of the heroes of Oregon State's 2006 College World Series championship. He earned a victory and three saves in Omaha, winning an elimination game with 5⅓ gutsy innings and coming back the next day to record the final two outs of the clincher. The NCAA Division I leader with 20 saves, he signed for $162,000 as a sixth-round pick. Gunderson doesn't have a high ceiling, but he has a huge heart and excellent command. Given those attributes and the Braves' need for lefthanded relievers, he could advance quickly to the majors—where his uncle Eric Gunderson carved out a 10-year career as a reliever. Kevin gets ahead of hitters by locating his 86-89 mph fastball, then tries to put them away with a slider that's effective against both lefties and righties. He can vary the break and velocity on his slider to keep hitters off balance. He also mixes in an occasional changeup. Gunderson keeps hitters uncomfortable with his low three-quarters arm angle and slingshot delivery. Though he's small, he's athletic and has proved resilient during his college career. He had every reason to be gassed during his pro debut, yet he handled low Class A with ease. Don't be surprised if he climbs to Double-A—or higher—in his first full season.

| Year | Club (League) | Class | W | L | ERA | G | GS | CG | SV | IP | H | R | ER | HR | BB | SO | AVG |
|------|---------------|-------|---|---|------|----|----|----|----|----|----|---|----|----|----|----|------|
| 2006 | Danville (Appy) | R | 0 | 0 | 0.00 | 1 | 0 | 0 | 0 | 1 | 0 | 0 | 0 | 0 | 0 | 0 | .000 |
|  | Rome (SAL) | A | 4 | 0 | 1.13 | 14 | 0 | 0 | 3 | 24 | 16 | 3 | 3 | 1 | 4 | 21 | .195 |
| **MINOR LEAGUE TOTALS** | | | 4 | 0 | 1.08 | 15 | 0 | 0 | 3 | 25 | 16 | 3 | 3 | 1 | 4 | 21 | .188 |

 ## CODY JOHNSON

1B

**Born:** August 18, 1988. **B-T:** L-R. **Ht.:** 6-4. **Wt.:** 195. **Drafted:** HS—Lynn Haven, Fla., 2006 (1st round). **Signed by:** Al Goetz.

It came as a mild surprise when Atlanta drafted Johnson in the first round with the 24th overall pick last June. He made a name for himself on the showcase circuit in the summer of 2005, highlighted by winning MVP honors at a pair of Perfect Game wood-bat tournament in Marietta, Ga. But his performance as a high school senior raised major questions about whether he'll make enough contact to be a productive hitter, and striking out 49 times in 114 pro at-bats did nothing to dispel them. Johnson earned a $1.375 million bonus, the fourth-highest in club history, on the basis of his power potential. He can hit majestic home runs to all fields, particularly when he gets his long arms extended. He struggles with pitch recognition, though, and some scouts are worried about a hitch in his swing. Johnson has solid speed, though he'll slow down as he fills out. And though he runs well, his lack of athleticism limits him defensively. He showed little agility in left field after signing and was a below-average defender at first base as an amateur. The Braves know Johnson is a work in progress and will move him slowly, but they think he has the work ethic and aptitude to make adjustments at the plate. He'll begin 2007 in extended spring training and report to Danville in June.

| Year | Club (League) | Class | AVG | G | AB | R | H | 2B | 3B | HR | RBI | BB | SO | SB | OBP | SLG |
|------|---------------|-------|------|----|-----|----|----|----|----|----|-----|----|----|----|------|------|
| 2006 | Braves (GCL) | R | .184 | 32 | 114 | 13 | 21 | 6 | 1 | 1 | 16 | 12 | 49 | 2 | .260 | .281 |
| **MINOR LEAGUE TOTALS** | | | .184 | 32 | 114 | 13 | 21 | 6 | 1 | 1 | 16 | 12 | 49 | 2 | .260 | .281 |

# BALTIMORE ORIOLES

BY **WILL LINGO**

Is it the best of times or worst of times in Baltimore?

The Orioles integrated four of the top five players from last year's prospect list into their big league roster in 2006, led by right fielder Nick Markakis, who hit .311 with 14 homers after the all-star break, and Chris Ray, who saved 33 games. That group didn't include righthander John Maine, who went to the Mets in the Kris Benson deal and rose to prominence during New York's playoff run.

Baltimore also had its second straight productive draft under scouting director Joe Jordan, adding more high-ceiling talent to the farm system, starting with new No. 1 prospect Bill Rowell. The Orioles also moved their Triple-A affiliation to Norfolk after four years in Ottawa, giving them perhaps the most attractive arrangement of affiliates in the game.

But there's also the small matter of a ninth straight losing season at the big league level, the worst stretch in team history. The Orioles finished in fourth place in the American League East for the eighth time in the last nine years, leading inevitably to the lowest attendance ever at Camden Yards. And the farm system still lacks depth, especially among position players, and had virtually no legitimate big league talent at the upper levels after the graduation of Markakis and friends. The meddling of owner Peter Angelos and his sons also continues to hamper the franchise. The Orioles sought deals for their most marketable asset—shortstop Miguel Tejada—only to have them vetoed by ownership.

MORRIS FOSTOFF

Manager Sam Perlozzo and pitching coach Leo Mazzone have stabilized things in the big league dugout, but they haven't produced improved results on the field yet. That's because the Orioles simply don't have enough good players at this point.

The pitching staff is young and shows promise, with 27-year-old lefthander **Erik Bedard** emerging as the team's ace and Daniel Cabrera, Adam Loewen and Hayden Penn trying to show they can be consistent winners. Ray has taken a stranglehold on the closer's job, and James Hoey shows promise as a set-up man.

It's harder to be optimistic about the team's hitters, though. Whether he's happy or not, Tejada was still the team's best offensive player again in 2006, leading the Orioles with 24 home runs and 100 RBIs. Ramon Hernandez was a good signing at catcher, Markakis should be a productive player for years and Corey Patterson benefited from his change of scenery. But the team lacks power, finishing 11th in the AL in both home runs and slugging percentage in 2006, and probably will have to go outside the organization if it wants to patch the holes quickly.

So it's no wonder Orioles fans remain frustrated. Though there are some reasons for optimism, the last decade has taught them all too well to be skeptical of whether the team can pull everything together.

## TOP 30 PROSPECTS

| | |
|---|---|
| 1. Bill Rowell, 3b | 16. Jason Berken, rhp |
| 2. Brandon Erbe, rhp | 17. Val Majewski, of/1b |
| 3. Nolan Reimold, of | 18. Marino Salas, rhp |
| 4. Pedro Beato, rhp | 19. Chris Vinyard, 1b |
| 5. Radhames Liz, rhp | 20. Adam Stern, of |
| 6. Garrett Olson, lhp | 21. Kurt Birkins, lhp |
| 7. Brandon Snyder, c | 22. Luis Hernandez, ss/2b |
| 8. James Hoey, rhp | 23. Beau Hale, rhp |
| 9. Jeff Fiorentino, of | 24. Pedro Florimon, ss |
| 10. Kieron Pope, of | 25. Chorye Spoone, rhp |
| 11. Ryan Adams, 2b | 26. J.R. House, c/1b |
| 12. Luis Lebron, rhp | 27. Anderson Garcia, rhp |
| 13. James Johnson, rhp | 28. Luis Montanez, of |
| 14. Zach Britton, lhp | 29. Brian Burres, lhp |
| 15. Sendy Rleal, rhp | 30. Adam Donachie, c |

# ORGANIZATION OVERVIEW

**General manager:** Mike Flanagan. **Farm director:** David Stockstill. **Scouting director:** Joe Jordan.

## 2006 PERFORMANCE

| Class | Team | League | W | L | PCT | Finish* | Manager | Affiliated |
|---|---|---|---|---|---|---|---|---|
| Majors | Baltimore | American | 70 | 92 | .432 | (12th) 14 | Sam Perlozzo | — |
| Triple-A | #Ottawa Lynx | International | 74 | 69 | .517 | 8th (14) | Dave Trembley | 2003 |
| Double-A | Bowie Baysox | Eastern | 67 | 74 | .475 | 8th (12) | Don Werner | 1993 |
| High A | Frederick Keys | Carolina | 61 | 77 | .442 | 8th (8) | Bien Figueroa | 1989 |
| Low A | Delmarva Shorebirds | South Atlantic | 64 | 73 | .467 | 12th (16) | Gary Kendall | 1997 |
| Short-season | Aberdeen IronBirds | New York-Penn | 41 | 34 | .547 | 5th (14) | Andy Etchebarren | 2002 |
| Rookie | Bluefield Orioles | Appalachian | 31 | 37 | .456 | 8th (10) | Gary Allenson | 1958 |
| **OVERALL 2006 MINOR LEAGUE RECORD** | | | 338 | 364 | .481 | 23rd (30) | | |

*Finish in overall standings (No. of teams in league). +League champion. #Affiliate will be in Norfolk (International) in 2007.

## ORGANIZATION LEADERS

### BATTING
| | | |
|---|---|---|
| AVG | Rowell, Billy, Bluefield/Aberdeen | .328 |
| R | Finan, Ryan, Delmarva | 87 |
| H | Keylor, Cory, Bowie | 131 |
| 2B | Reed, Keith, Ottawa | 35 |
| 3B | Rivas, Arturo, Delmarva/Frederick | 7 |
| HR | Fransz, Jason, Frederick | 24 |
| RBI | Fransz, Jason, Frederick | 84 |
| BB | Finan, Ryan, Delmarva | 91 |
| SO | Bass, Bryan, Frederick/Bowie | 172 |
| SB | Scott Jr., Lorenzo, Delmarva | 29 |
| OBP | Rowell, Billy, Bluefield/Aberdeen | .415 |
| SLG | Rowell, Billy, Bluefield/Aberdeen | .503 |
| XBH | Finan, Ryan, Delmarva | 52 |

### PITCHING
| | | |
|---|---|---|
| W | Johnson, Jim, Bowie | 13 |
| L | Finch, Brian, Bowie | 12 |
| | Hamblet, Reid, Delmarva | 12 |
| ERA | Moore, Jeffrey, Aberdeen | 2.41 |
| G | McCurdy, Nick, Ottawa/Bowie | 60 |
| SV | Hoey, Jim, Delmarva/Frederick/Bowie | 33 |
| IP | Olson, Garrett, Frederick/Bowie | 166 |
| BB | Spoone, Chorye, Delmarva | 80 |
| SO | Olson, Garrett, Frederick/Bowie | 162 |
| AVG | Ramirez, Luis, Frederick | .226 |

## BEST TOOLS

| | |
|---|---|
| Best Hitter for Average | Bill Rowell |
| Best Power Hitter | Nolan Reimold |
| Best Strike-Zone Discipline | Jeff Fiorentino |
| Fastest Baserunner | Jarod Rine |
| Best Athlete | Nolan Reimold |
| Best Fastball | Brandon Erbe |
| Best Curveball | Garrett Olson |
| Best Slider | James Hoey |
| Best Changeup | Garrett Olson |
| Best Control | Garrett Olson |
| Best Defensive Catcher | Adam Donachie |
| Best Defensive Infielder | Luis Hernandez |
| Best Infield Arm | Bryan Bass |
| Best Defensive Outfielder | Jeff Fiorentino |
| Best Outfield Arm | Arturo Rivas |

## PROJECTED 2010 LINEUP

| | |
|---|---|
| Catcher | Ramon Hernandez |
| First Base | Brandon Snyder |
| Second Base | Brian Roberts |
| Third Base | Bill Rowell |
| Shortstop | Miguel Tejada |
| Left Field | Nolan Reimold |
| Center Field | Corey Patterson |
| Right Field | Nick Markakis |

| | |
|---|---|
| Designated Hitter | Jay Gibbons |
| No. 1 Starter | Erik Bedard |
| No. 2 Starter | Adam Loewen |
| No. 3 Starter | Daniel Cabrera |
| No. 4 Starter | Hayden Penn |
| No. 5 Starter | Brandon Erbe |
| Closer | Chris Ray |

## LAST YEAR'S TOP 20 PROSPECTS

| | |
|---|---|
| 1. Nick Markakis, of | 11. Jeff Fiorentino, of |
| 2. Adam Loewen, lhp | 12. Radhames Liz, rhp |
| 3. Hayden Penn, rhp | 13. Sendy Rleal, rhp |
| 4. Nolan Reimold, of | 14. Brian Finch, rhp |
| 5. Chris Ray, rhp | 15. Dave Haenhel, lhp |
| 6. Garrett Olson, lhp | 16. John Maine, rhp |
| 7. Brandon Snyder, c | 17. Nate Spears, 2b |
| 8. J.J. Johnson, rhp | 18. Kieron Pope, of |
| 9. Brandon Erbe, rhp | 19. Chris Britton, rhp |
| 10. Val Majewski, of | 20. Ryan Keefer, rhp |

## TOP PROSPECTS OF THE DECADE

| Year | Player, Pos. | 2006 Org. |
|---|---|---|
| 1997 | Nerio Rodriguez, rhp | Pirates |
| 1998 | Ryan Minor, 3b | Out of baseball |
| 1999 | Matt Riley, lhp | Out of baseball |
| 2000 | Matt Riley, lhp | Out of baseball |
| 2001 | Keith Reed, of | Orioles |
| 2002 | Richard Stahl, lhp | Orioles |
| 2003 | Erik Bedard, lhp | Orioles |
| 2004 | Adam Loewen, lhp | Orioles |
| 2005 | Nick Markakis, of | Orioles |
| 2006 | Nick Markakis, of | Orioles |

## TOP DRAFT PICKS OF THE DECADE

| Year | Player, Pos. | 2006 Org. |
|---|---|---|
| 1997 | Jayson Werth, c | Dodgers |
| 1998 | Rick Elder, of | Out of baseball |
| 1999 | Mike Paradis, rhp | Out of baseball |
| 2000 | Beau Hale, rhp | Orioles |
| 2001 | Chris Smith, lhp | Out of baseball |
| 2002 | Adam Loewen, lhp | Orioles |
| 2003 | Nick Markakis, of | Orioles |
| 2004 | *Wade Townsend, rhp | Devil Rays |
| 2005 | Brandon Snyder, c | Orioles |
| 2006 | Bill Rowell, 3b | Orioles |

*Did not sign.

## LARGEST BONUSES IN CLUB HISTORY

| | |
|---|---|
| Adam Loewen, 2002 | $3,200,000 |
| Beau Hale, 2000 | $2,250,000 |
| Chris Smith, 2001 | $2,175,000 |
| Bill Rowell, 2006 | $2,100,000 |
| Darnell McDonald, 1997 | $1,900,000 |

# MINOR LEAGUE DEPTH CHART

## Baltimore Orioles

**Impact: B.** Losing Nick Markakis and Adam Loewen from last year's list really stings, but Rowell and Erbe offer similar promise.
**Depth: C.** Still waiting for top prospects to reach Double-A, but consecutive strong drafts have greatly increased the O's number of power arms and bats.
**Sleeper:** Jason Berken, rhp. The sixth rounder had Tommy John surgery at Clemson but has the stuff and knowledge of his craft to move quickly.

*Numbers in parentheses indicate prospect rankings.*

### LF
Kieron Pope (10)
Val Majewski (17)
David Cash
Jason Fransz

### CF
Jeff Fiorentino (9)
Adam Stern (20)
Jarod Rine
Arturo Rivas
Lorenzo Scott
Danny Figueroa

### RF
Nolan Reimold (3)
Luis Montanez (28)
Cory Keylor

### 3B
Bill Rowell (1)
Bryan Bass
Ryan Finan

### SS
Luis Hernandez (22)
Pedro Florimon (24)
Blake Davis
Tyler Henson

### 2B
Ryan Adams (11)
Paco Figueroa

### 1B
Brandon Snyder (7)
Chris Vineyard (19)
J.R. House (26)
Mark Fleisher

### C
Adam Donachie (30)
Eli Whiteside
Ryan Hubele

### RHP

| Starters | Relievers |
| --- | --- |
| Brandon Erbe (2) | James Hoey (8) |
| Pedro Beato (4) | Luis Lebron (12) |
| Radhames Liz (5) | Sendy Rleal (15) |
| James Johnson (13) | Marino Salas (18) |
| Jason Berken (16) | Beau Hale (23) |
| Chorye Spoone (25) | Anderson Garcia (27) |
| Brian Finch | Aaron Rakers |
| Ryan Keefer | Josh Faiola |
| Cory Morris | Brent Allar |
| Bob McCrory | |
| David Hernandez | |
| Ryan Stadanlick | |
| Ryan Ouellette | |

### LHP

| Starters | Relievers |
| --- | --- |
| Garrett Olson (6) | Kurt Birkins (21) |
| Zach Britton (14) | Dave Haehnel |
| Brian Burress (29) | Brett Bordes |
| | Scott Rice |
| | Brian Forystek |
| | Rommie Lewis |
| | Wilfredo Perez |

# DRAFT ANALYSIS

## 2006      SIGNING BUDGET: $5.0 million

**Best Pro Debut:** The first high school position player drafted, 3B Billy Rowell (1) met every expectation by hitting .328/ .415/.503. RHP Josh Faiola (24), who features a sinker/slider combo, bounced back after a subpar spring, and he posted a 0.97 ERA and 37 strikeouts in as many innings.

**Best Athlete:** INF Tyler Henson (5) quarterbacked his high school football team to a 14-0 record and an Oklahoma state title, and he pitched and won the state championship game for the baseball squad. He also started at point guard in basketball. On the diamond, he has plus speed, arm strength and shortstop actions, and there's also pop in his bat.

**Best Pure Hitter:** Rowell has a simple, fluid swing and drives the ball to the gaps. 2B Ryan Adams (2) was one of the best-hitting middle infielders in the draft and might have snuck into the supplemental first round had he not been bothered by severe hamstring problems.

**Best Raw Power:** Rowell has well-above-average raw power and the skill and know-how to translate it into home runs. Draft-and-follow 1B Chris Vinyard shared the New York-Penn League homer crown with eight.

**Fastest Runner:** Henson is a step quicker than OF David Cash (40).

**Best Defensive Player:** Blake Davis (4) is a steady shortstop with quick hands, feet and actions. He's also a solid line-drive hitter who can steal an occasional base.

**Best Fastball:** RHP Brent Allar (14) has the most pure arm strength, topping out at 96-97 mph, but didn't pitch much at Texas Christian in the spring because he couldn't find the strike zone. He made some progress with his control after signing but still has a ways to go. RHP Pedro Beato (1) is right behind him, pitching from 90-96 mph, and throws a lot more strikes. LHP Zach Britton (2) has more velo than most southpaws at 92-93 mph.

**Best Breaking Ball:** Beato had an 84-85 mph slider, but the Orioles wanted him to reduce his five-pitch repertoire and had him scrap it. His 78-82 mph curveball is a power breaker that grades out as well-above-average when it's on.

**Most Intriguing Background:** Cash's father Dave was an all-star second baseman and is Baltimore's first-base coach. 1B Anthony Martinez (11) began his college career as a quarterback at Virginia. OF Isaiah Stanback (45) accounted for 14 touchdowns in his first seven games as Washington's quarterback this fall before a foot injury ended his season. Baltimore still controls the rights to Stanback, who hasn't played baseball since high school, because he's a fifth-year senior.

**Closest To The Majors:** Brett Bordes (9), because he's a lefty reliever with a tough 88-91 mph sinker. Lefties went 2-for-47 (.043) against him in pro ball, with 15 whiffs and 27 grounders. Rowell will advance rapidly for a high school hitter.

**Best Late-Round Pick:** Cash, who hit much better in the Cape Cod League this summer than he did at Florida during the spring. Martinez is also interesting because he has power and good athleticism for a 6-foot-3, 240-pounder.

**The One Who Got Away:** The Orioles were willing to give draft-eligible sophomore lefthander Tony Watson (17) third- or fourth-round money, but he opted to return to Nebraska. He's still projectable at 6-foot-4 and 210 pounds, and currently works at 88-92 mph.

**Assessment:** Rowell and Beato have huge ceilings, a nice way to start any draft. Baltimore's focus on athletes was obvious, as the top five position players it signed all played shortstop as amateurs.

## 2005      BUDGET: $4.2 million

The Orioles started strong, as their first four picks were C Brandon Snyder (1), LHP Garrett Olson (1), OF Nolan Reimold (2) and RHP Brandon Erbe (3).     **GRADE: B**

## 2004      BUDGET: $1.3 million

Baltimore botched negotiations with RHP Wade Townsend (1) and didn't have a second-round pick. OF Jeff Fiorentino (3) is as good as this crop gets.     **GRADE: D**

## 2003      BUDGET: $4.0 million

Making Nick Markakis (1) a full-time hitter turned out to be a stroke of genius. RHP Chris Ray (3) quickly became the Orioles' closer.     **GRADE: B+**

*Draft analysis by Jim Callis. Numbers in parentheses indicate draft rounds. Budgets are bonuses in first 10 rounds.*

BILL
# ROWELL

3B

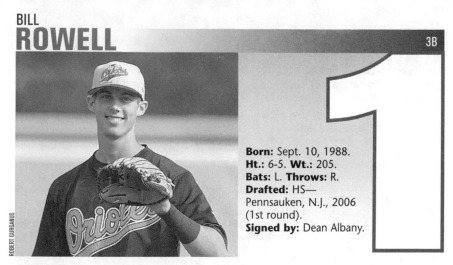

ROBERT GURGANUS

**Born:** Sept. 10, 1988.
**Ht.:** 6-5. **Wt.:** 205.
**Bats:** L. **Throws:** R.
**Drafted:** HS—
Pennsauken, N.J., 2006
(1st round).
**Signed by:** Dean Albany.

Rowell was a four-year starter in high school at Bishop Eustace Prep in New Jersey, and he first emerged on the national scene in the summer before his junior season. Aside from a few scouts' questions about whether he was a better hitter in batting practice than in games, his stock never wavered much, even as he saw few pitches to hit as a high school senior. He sealed the deal for the Orioles in a predraft workout at Camden Yards with an impressive round of batting practice. Baltimore made him the ninth overall pick and the first high school hitter selected in the 2006 draft, and he lived up to that billing at Rookie-level Bluefield before earning a promotion to short-season Aberdeen for the last few weeks of the season. Rowell signed with the Orioles for a $2.1 million bonus, the most the team ever has given to a hitter out of the draft, and instantly became the top prospect in a system low on bats.

Rowell is a big young man—he's still growing, and the Orioles think he could end up being about 6-foot-7—with a smooth, fluid swing that generates easy power. He has the bat speed to catch up to any pitch, and he can hit the ball out to any part of the park. He's a baseball junkie who spent hours honing his swing in a batting cage in his backyard, either taking turns pitching to his brother or hitting off a tee. All that work in the cage has resulted in an advanced hitter for his age, and Baltimore officials say they have rarely seen him mis-hit a ball. He also shows an ability to make adjustments, crushing lefthanders later in his pro debut after they made him look foolish early. He spreads out his stance to get better balance at the plate, and he sits low to reduce the size of his strike zone. Rowell was a short-stop in high school but moved to third base when he started his pro career. He committed 18 errors in 47 games at the hot corner, but showed enough potential that the Orioles will give him more time to learn the position. He's athletic for his size and works hard, but he's so big that he could end up at first base or in the outfield.

Though he's ahead of most players his age, Rowell still has a lot to learn about hitting. He stays back on breaking balls well but needs work on his pitch recognition. He's not as pull-happy as some young hitters, but the Orioles still want him to hit the ball the other way more consistently. Rowell's biggest challenge might be integrating himself into a professional team. He's so accustomed to working out on his own, with his own routines in his own cage, that he'll have to learn to be part of a larger group. And, perhaps not surprising for a player who has said he models his game after Barry Bonds, he has a considerable ego as well.

Rowell is exactly the kind of impact bat the Orioles desperately need in their big league lineup, so they'll move him up as soon as he shows he has mastered a level. His bat is good enough that defense is a secondary consideration. While he'll open 2007 as the third baseman at low Class A Delmarva, don't be surprised if he moves off that position and quickly shoots up through the system.

| Year | Club (League) | Class | AVG | G | AB | R | H | 2B | 3B | HR | RBI | BB | SO | SB | OBP | SLG |
|------|---------------|-------|------|----|-----|----|----|----|----|----|-----|----|----|----|------|------|
| 2006 | Bluefield (Appy) | R | .329 | 42 | 152 | 38 | 50 | 15 | 3 | 2 | 26 | 25 | 47 | 3 | .422 | .507 |
|      | Aberdeen (NYP) | A | .326 | 11 | 43 | 8 | 14 | 4 | 0 | 1 | 6 | 4 | 12 | 0 | .388 | .488 |
| **MINOR LEAGUE TOTALS** | | | .328 | 53 | 195 | 46 | 64 | 19 | 3 | 3 | 32 | 29 | 59 | 3 | .415 | .503 |

## BRANDON ERBE

RHP

**Born:** Dec. 25, 1987. **B-T:** R-R. **Ht.:** 6-4. **Wt.:** 180. **Drafted:** HS—Baltimore, 2005 (3rd round). **Signed by:** Ty Brown.

Erbe continues to look like a steal as a third-rounder who signed for $415,000 in 2005. The Orioles' only real goal for him in 2006 was to take his turn every fifth day, and he handled that with aplomb. He was limited to five innings or 85-90 pitches a start and was on an even tighter leash after he reached the 100-innings mark, but he still ranked fourth among starters in full-season leagues with 10.4 strikeouts per nine innings. Erbe works anywhere from 92-97 mph with his fastball, sitting around 94-95, and he can locate it on both sides of the plate. His slider is also a potential plus pitch when he commands it. Orioles officials have been impressed by his demeanor and mound presence, which is advanced for his age and has been compared to that of Jim Palmer. The Orioles worked with Erbe to resolve a hop in his delivery, as he tried to get maximum extension with his front foot, and they're happy with his mechanics now. His changeup is a quality pitch but still needs work. He prefers to work to the outer third of the plate, so he needs to show he can come inside as well. The Erbe blueprint is going exactly as planned so far. He'll play the entire 2007 season at 19, opening the year at high Class A Frederick.

| Year | Club (League) | Class | W | L | ERA | G | GS | CG | SV | IP | H | R | ER | HR | BB | SO | AVG |
|------|---------------|-------|---|---|------|----|----|----|----|-----|-----|----|----|----|----|-----|------|
| 2005 | Bluefield (Appy) | R | 1 | 1 | 3.09 | 11 | 3 | 0 | 1 | 23 | 8 | 10 | 8 | 1 | 10 | 48 | .103 |
|  | Aberdeen (NYP) | A | 1 | 1 | 7.71 | 3 | 1 | 0 | 0 | 7 | 6 | 6 | 6 | 0 | 4 | 9 | .261 |
| 2006 | Delmarva (SAL) | A | 5 | 9 | 3.22 | 28 | 27 | 0 | 0 | 115 | 88 | 47 | 41 | 2 | 47 | 133 | .217 |
| **MINOR LEAGUE TOTALS** | | | 7 | 11 | 3.41 | 42 | 31 | 0 | 1 | 145 | 102 | 63 | 55 | 3 | 61 | 190 | .202 |

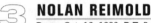

## NOLAN REIMOLD

OF

**Born:** Oct. 12, 1983. **B-T:** R-R. **Ht.:** 6-4. **Wt.:** 210. **Drafted:** Bowling Green State, 2005 (2nd round). **Signed by:** Marc Ziegler.

Reimold bashed his way into the second round of the draft with an NCAA Division I-best .770 slugging percentage and had a huge pro debut in 2005. He followed that with a solid season in 2006 in spite of nagging foot and back injuries that bothered him early in the year. From the moment he signed, Reimold became the organization's best power prospect. He improved his pitch selection and wasn't so pull-happy by the end of the 2006 season, finding balls to drive and not just making contact. He's learning that he can hit the fastball away out of the park, just as he can the fastball in. The Orioles say he's athletic enough to play anywhere in the outfield but profiles best as a right fielder. Scouts who aren't as high on Reimold say he'll end up at first base, and they question how much his power will play in the big leagues. He has hit just .255 in high Class A, and the pitching is only going to get tougher at higher levels. His back injury made him timid for a time in the middle of the season, but he looked fine by the end. Questions about Reimold's athleticism aren't as important as the development of his bat. It's unlikely he'll move Nick Markakis out of right field, but Baltimore is desperate for power and will find a place for him when his bat is ready. He'll open 2007 at Double-A Bowie.

| Year | Club (League) | Class | AVG | G | AB | R | H | 2B | 3B | HR | RBI | BB | SO | SB | OBP | SLG |
|------|---------------|-------|------|-----|-----|-----|-----|----|----|----|-----|-----|-----|----|------|------|
| 2005 | Aberdeen (NYP) | A | .294 | 50 | 180 | 33 | 53 | 15 | 2 | 9 | 30 | 29 | 44 | 2 | .392 | .550 |
|  | Frederick (CL) | A | .265 | 23 | 83 | 17 | 22 | 6 | 0 | 6 | 11 | 12 | 27 | 3 | .371 | .554 |
| 2006 | Frederick (CL) | A | .255 | 119 | 415 | 73 | 106 | 26 | 0 | 19 | 75 | 76 | 107 | 14 | .379 | .455 |
| **MINOR LEAGUE TOTALS** | | | .267 | 192 | 678 | 123 | 181 | 47 | 2 | 34 | 116 | 117 | 178 | 19 | .381 | .493 |

## PEDRO BEATO

RHP

**Born:** Oct. 27, 1986. **B-T:** R-R. **Ht.:** 6-5. **Wt.:** 210. **Drafted:** St. Petersburg (Fla.) JC, 2006 (1st round supplemental). **Signed by:** Nick Presto.

Beato first drew attention as a high school pitcher in Brooklyn, but Tommy John surgery in April 2004 dented his draft prospects. The Mets still took him as a draft-and-follow in the 17th round in 2005, but decided not to exceed Major League Baseball's recommendation of an $800,000 bonus last spring. The Orioles jumped on him with the 31st overall pick, signed him for $1 million and were encouraged by the returns from his first summer and instructional league. Beato came to instructional league bragging about adding a sixth pitch to his repertoire, but the Orioles want him to focus on three: his fastball, curveball and changeup. He works in the mid-90s and always leaned on his fastball most, showing an ability to locate it to either side of the

plate. His power curve is a well-above-average pitch at times. He's a strong competitor who brings an upbeat attitude to the park. His elbow is healthy and not a concern. The main reason Beato needs to focus on just a few pitches is to improve his location of all of them. He loves to pitch inside, but the Orioles want him to concentrate on commanding the fastball away better. He's athletic but is still working to repeat his delivery. With Erik Bedard and Adam Loewen having graduated to the big leagues, Beato is one of the Orioles' best pitching prospects, albeit at least a couple of years away from joining them. He could open his first full season in high Class A.

| Year | Club (League) | Class | W | L | ERA | G | GS | CG | SV | IP | H | R | ER | HR | BB | SO | AVG |
|------|---------------|-------|---|---|-----|---|----|----|----|----|---|---|----|----|----|----|-----|
| 2006 | Aberdeen (NYP) | A | 3 | 2 | 3.63 | 14 | 10 | 0 | 0 | 57 | 47 | 31 | 23 | 6 | 23 | 52 | .222 |
| **MINOR LEAGUE TOTALS** | | | 3 | 2 | 3.63 | 14 | 10 | 0 | 0 | 57 | 47 | 31 | 23 | 6 | 23 | 52 | .222 |

## ⑤ RADHAMES LIZ                                                     RHP

**Born:** Oct. 6, 1983. **B-T:** R-R. **Ht.:** 6-2. **Wt.:** 170. **Signed:** Dominican Republic, 2003. **Signed by:** Carlos Bernhardt.

Liz was the talk of the minors early in the 2006 season as he dominated at Frederick, including an April start when he struck out 13 in five innings in a combined no-hitter against Salem. He found out in Double-A that he still had a lot to learn about pitching, however. Liz throws his fastball with such life that there's a clicking sound when he throws it at its highest velocity—in the 94-97 mph range—as his thumb hits his index and middle fingers. His curveball is another plus pitch that he's still learning how to use. His changeup can be an average pitch when he doesn't try to throw it too slow. He likes to elevate his heater, but Double-A hitters showed Liz he needs to pitch down in the zone. He's also working on control and command of all his pitches. Liz doesn't like to get hit, and the Orioles are trying to teach him that contact on his terms is desirable. Liz' command questions and two dominant pitches make him a candidate to be a reliever, but Baltimore officials say his durability and potential three-pitch mix will keep him in a rotation until hitters tell them otherwise. He'll begin 2007 back in Double-A.

| Year | Club (League) | Class | W | L | ERA | G | GS | CG | SV | IP | H | R | ER | HR | BB | SO | AVG |
|------|---------------|-------|---|---|-----|---|----|----|----|----|---|---|----|----|----|----|-----|
| 2003 | Orioles (DSL) | R | 2 | 2 | 3.18 | 9 | 7 | 1 | 0 | 45 | 40 | 16 | 16 | 1 | 12 | 43 | .233 |
| 2004 | Orioles (DSL) | R | 8 | 4 | 2.62 | 15 | 14 | 2 | 0 | 82 | 53 | 32 | 24 | 2 | 28 | 109 | .177 |
| 2005 | Aberdeen (NYP) | A | 5 | 4 | 1.77 | 11 | 11 | 0 | 0 | 56 | 36 | 14 | 11 | 1 | 19 | 82 | .188 |
| | Delmarva (SAL) | A | 2 | 3 | 4.46 | 10 | 10 | 0 | 0 | 38 | 33 | 23 | 19 | 2 | 23 | 55 | .231 |
| 2006 | Frederick (CL) | A | 6 | 5 | 2.82 | 16 | 16 | 0 | 0 | 83 | 57 | 32 | 26 | 8 | 44 | 95 | .196 |
| | Bowie (EL) | AA | 3 | 1 | 5.36 | 10 | 10 | 0 | 0 | 50 | 55 | 31 | 30 | 9 | 31 | 54 | .281 |
| **MINOR LEAGUE TOTALS** | | | 26 | 19 | 3.19 | 71 | 68 | 3 | 0 | 355 | 274 | 148 | 126 | 23 | 157 | 438 | .212 |

## ⑥ GARRETT OLSON                                                    LHP

**Born:** Oct. 18, 1983. **B-T:** R-L. **Ht.:** 6-1. **Wt.:** 200. **Drafted:** Cal Poly, 2005 (1st round supplemental). **Signed by:** Gil Kubski.

If you're looking for the safest bet in this system to pitch in the big leagues, Olson is it. He jumped to high Class A in his pro debut in 2005, then made it to Double-A halfway through his first full season. The Orioles said the quality of his pitches improved at Bowie, as he seemed to pitch to the level of his competition. Olson has a well-rounded package of pitches, works efficiently and has a desire to learn and improve unmatched by anyone in the organization. He threw his fastball at 88-91 mph early in the season but worked at 89-93 later, complementing it with a hard breaking ball. His changeup has improved significantly, though he still needs to command it better. The Orioles say Olson was too fine with his pitches early in 2006, though he got more confident and was more willing to pitch to contact later. Some scouts doubt the quality of his stuff and say he'll end up as a lefty reliever. There are those in the organization who would like Olson to get a shot at the Baltimore rotation in spring training, though he'll likely open the season at Triple-A Norfolk. Assuming his changeup continues to come along, he has the stuff and work ethic to pitch in the middle of a rotation.

| Year | Club (League) | Class | W | L | ERA | G | GS | CG | SV | IP | H | R | ER | HR | BB | SO | AVG |
|------|---------------|-------|---|---|-----|---|----|----|----|----|---|---|----|----|----|----|-----|
| 2005 | Aberdeen (NYP) | A | 2 | 1 | 1.58 | 11 | 6 | 0 | 1 | 40 | 22 | 7 | 7 | 1 | 13 | 40 | .164 |
| | Frederick (CL) | A | 0 | 0 | 3.14 | 3 | 3 | 0 | 0 | 14 | 10 | 5 | 5 | 0 | 7 | 19 | .192 |
| 2006 | Frederick (CL) | A | 4 | 4 | 2.77 | 14 | 14 | 0 | 0 | 81 | 81 | 32 | 25 | 7 | 19 | 77 | .266 |
| | Bowie (EL) | AA | 6 | 5 | 3.42 | 14 | 14 | 0 | 0 | 84 | 78 | 33 | 32 | 5 | 31 | 85 | .249 |
| **MINOR LEAGUE TOTALS** | | | 12 | 10 | 2.82 | 42 | 37 | 0 | 1 | 220 | 191 | 77 | 69 | 13 | 70 | 221 | .238 |

## ⑦ BRANDON SNYDER

C

**Born:** Nov. 23, 1986. **B-T:** R-R. **Ht.:** 6-2. **Wt.:** 205. **Drafted:** HS—Centreville, Va., 2005 (1st round). **Signed by:** Ty Brown.

The 13th overall pick in the 2005 draft, Snyder had a lost first full season. He performed poorly at Delmarva—where he dislocated his right shoulder while swinging—and Aberdeen before having surgery to repair a tear in his left rotator cuff in August. Snyder is regarded as a potential impact bat, with a smooth swing, good approach and the ability to use the whole field. He also showed power potential when fully healthy in 2005. He's athletic and played several positions in high school before working as a catcher as a pro. Becoming a big league catcher is a longshot for Snyder, who threw out just 22 percent of basestealers in 2006 and still has much to grasp behind the plate. He'll likely move to an infield corner, putting more pressure on him to fulfill his potential with the bat. First base is probably his next destination because it's less demanding and Bill Rowell is at third base. Getting Snyder healthy is the Orioles' only concern right now. His offensive production will determine his ultimate value, and they just want to get his bat going. He'll go to Delmarva when he's healthy enough to play.

| Year | Club (League) | Class | AVG | G | AB | R | H | 2B | 3B | HR | RBI | BB | SO | SB | OBP | SLG |
|------|---------------|-------|-----|---|----|----|----|----|----|----|-----|----|----|----|-----|-----|
| 2005 | Bluefield (Appy) | R | .271 | 44 | 144 | 26 | 39 | 8 | 0 | 8 | 35 | 28 | 36 | 7 | .380 | .493 |
| | Aberdeen (NYP) | A | .393 | 8 | 28 | 4 | 11 | 2 | 0 | 0 | 6 | 2 | 7 | 0 | .419 | .464 |
| 2006 | Delmarva (SAL) | A | .194 | 38 | 144 | 12 | 28 | 12 | 0 | 3 | 20 | 9 | 55 | 0 | .237 | .340 |
| | Aberdeen (NYP) | A | .234 | 34 | 124 | 14 | 29 | 8 | 1 | 1 | 11 | 5 | 43 | 2 | .267 | .339 |
| **MINOR LEAGUE TOTALS** | | | .243 | 124 | 440 | 56 | 107 | 30 | 1 | 12 | 66 | 44 | 141 | 9 | .308 | .398 |

## ⑧ JAMES HOEY

RHP

**Born:** Dec. 30, 1982. **B-T:** R-R. **Ht.:** 6-6. **Wt.:** 200. **Drafted:** Rider, 2003 (13th round). **Signed by:** Jim Howard.

Hoey had a promising debut at Bluefield in 2003, but he made just two appearances in 2004 before going down with an elbow strain that eventually required Tommy John surgery. He worked back into shape in 2005 and was at full strength in 2006, jumping through three levels and reaching the big leagues as a reliever. During his rehabilitation, Hoey smoothed out his mechanics and tapped into the full strength of his arm, and in 2006 he consistently worked at 96-97 mph. In an August appearance with Bowie, he touched 100 six times. He also showed a good slider most of the season. Getting knocked around in the big leagues reinforced Hoey's need to improve his command, though he also may have been tired. His slider also wasn't sharp in the majors, and he tends to get on the side of it at times. Hoey has the frame to be a starter, but with his success in 2006 he'll remain a reliever. With a good spring, he should return to the big league bullpen.

| Year | Club (League) | Class | W | L | ERA | G | GS | CG | SV | IP | H | R | ER | HR | BB | SO | AVG |
|------|---------------|-------|---|---|-----|---|----|----|----|----|----|----|----|----|----|----|-----|
| 2003 | Bluefield (Appy) | R | 2 | 3 | 2.79 | 11 | 8 | 0 | 0 | 42 | 33 | 19 | 13 | 3 | 19 | 20 | .219 |
| 2004 | Aberdeen (NYP) | A | 0 | 1 | 9.45 | 2 | 2 | 0 | 0 | 7 | 12 | 8 | 7 | 1 | 1 | 6 | .375 |
| 2005 | Aberdeen (NYP) | A | 1 | 1 | 4.80 | 9 | 0 | 0 | 0 | 15 | 11 | 10 | 8 | 1 | 10 | 15 | .216 |
| 2006 | Delmarva (SAL) | A | 2 | 1 | 2.54 | 27 | 0 | 0 | 18 | 28 | 17 | 8 | 8 | 2 | 10 | 46 | .175 |
| | Frederick (CL) | A | 0 | 0 | 0.64 | 14 | 0 | 0 | 11 | 14 | 13 | 3 | 1 | 0 | 5 | 16 | .228 |
| | Bowie (EL) | AA | 0 | 0 | 4.00 | 8 | 0 | 0 | 4 | 9 | 9 | 5 | 4 | 1 | 3 | 11 | .243 |
| | Baltimore (AL) | MLB | 0 | 1 | 10.24 | 12 | 0 | 0 | 0 | 10 | 14 | 11 | 11 | 1 | 5 | 6 | .359 |
| **MINOR LEAGUE TOTALS** | | | 5 | 6 | 3.21 | 71 | 10 | 0 | 33 | 115 | 95 | 53 | 41 | 8 | 48 | 114 | .224 |
| **MAJOR LEAGUE TOTALS** | | | 0 | 1 | 10.24 | 12 | 0 | 0 | 0 | 9 | 14 | 11 | 11 | 1 | 5 | 6 | .359 |

## ⑨ JEFF FIORENTINO

OF

**Born:** April 14, 1983. **B-T:** L-R. **Ht.:** 6-1. **Wt.:** 185. **Drafted:** Florida Atlantic, 2004 (3rd round). **Signed by:** Nick Presto.

The numbers show a pedestrian 2006 season, but they don't show two nagging injuries—a sprained ankle, followed by a strained hamstring—that short-circuited Fiorentino for most of the first half. Healthy by the end of the year, he hit .376 with four home runs in August. He's a do-everything player who brings energy to the ballpark every day, runs well and can play anywhere in the outfield. He has an unorthodox approach, putting his upper half over the plate, but he has good hand-eye coordination and gets himself into position to hit for power when the ball enters the hitting zone. He's a good situational hitter who should have enough power to hit 15-20 homers a year. While he does everything pretty well, Fiorentino doesn't have one overwhelming tool. He

also needs to be more consistent with his pitch selection, as he wavers between being too patient and too aggressive. In a perfect world, Fiorentino would be a fourth outfielder who could fill in at all three positions and provide a lefthanded bat with some pop. The Orioles will give him a chance to be more than that, and he'll probably start 2007 in Triple-A.

| Year | Club (League) | Class | AVG | G | AB | R | H | 2B | 3B | HR | RBI | BB | SO | SB | OBP | SLG |
|------|---------------|-------|-----|---|----|---|---|----|----|----|-----|----|----|----|-----|-----|
| 2004 | Aberdeen (NYP) | A | .348 | 14 | 46 | 9 | 16 | 7 | 1 | 2 | 12 | 9 | 4 | 3 | .474 | .674 |
| | Delmarva (SAL) | A | .302 | 49 | 179 | 40 | 54 | 15 | 2 | 10 | 36 | 20 | 50 | 2 | .379 | .575 |
| 2005 | Baltimore (AL) | MLB | .250 | 13 | 44 | 7 | 11 | 2 | 0 | 1 | 5 | 2 | 10 | 1 | .277 | .364 |
| | Frederick (CL) | A | .286 | 103 | 413 | 70 | 118 | 18 | 4 | 22 | 66 | 34 | 90 | 12 | .346 | .508 |
| 2006 | Bowie (EL) | AA | .275 | 104 | 385 | 63 | 106 | 14 | 0 | 13 | 62 | 53 | 58 | 9 | .365 | .413 |
| | Baltimore (AL) | MLB | .256 | 19 | 39 | 8 | 10 | 2 | 0 | 0 | 7 | 7 | 3 | 1 | .375 | .308 |
| **MINOR LEAGUE TOTALS** | | | .287 | 270 | 1023 | 182 | 294 | 54 | 7 | 47 | 176 | 116 | 202 | 26 | .365 | .492 |
| **MAJOR LEAGUE TOTALS** | | | .253 | 32 | 83 | 15 | 21 | 4 | 0 | 1 | 12 | 9 | 13 | 2 | .326 | .337 |

## 10   KIERON POPE   OF

**Born:** Oct. 3, 1986. **B-T:** R-R. **Ht.:** 6-1. **Wt.:** 195. **Drafted:** HS—Gay, Ga., 2005 (4th round). **Signed by:** Dave Jennings.

Pope gave up football midway through his high school career to focus on baseball, though his inexperience still shows on the diamond. He made a strong impression in his second tour through the Appalachian League in 2006, but an August stint at Aberdeen showed that he still has a lot of work to do. Pope's raw power is the best in the organization, and when he gets hold of the ball he can drive it out to any part of the ballpark. His other tools are fairly average across the board. He should be a fine left fielder, and he's a smart player who's anxious to learn and get better. Pope came into pro ball with a metal-bat swing and a bad approach, but his talent allowed him to get away with them as an amateur. Baltimore has remade his stroke and worked on his pitch recognition, and he has made strides. However, he may never hit for much of an average. It will probably be three or four seasons before the Orioles know what they have in Pope, but they're encouraged by his work ethic and power potential. They'll keep giving him instruction and at-bats, and he'll make his full-season debut in low Class A this spring.

| Year | Club (League) | Class | AVG | G | AB | R | H | 2B | 3B | HR | RBI | BB | SO | SB | OBP | SLG |
|------|---------------|-------|-----|---|----|---|---|----|----|----|-----|----|----|----|-----|-----|
| 2005 | Bluefield (Appy) | R | .228 | 41 | 149 | 23 | 34 | 3 | 1 | 5 | 22 | 8 | 62 | 5 | .297 | .362 |
| 2006 | Bluefield (Appy) | R | .341 | 37 | 135 | 20 | 46 | 16 | 1 | 5 | 29 | 10 | 36 | 4 | .411 | .585 |
| | Aberdeen (NYP) | A | .107 | 20 | 75 | 9 | 8 | 0 | 0 | 0 | 7 | 2 | 33 | 1 | .160 | .107 |
| **MINOR LEAGUE TOTALS** | | | .245 | 98 | 359 | 52 | 88 | 19 | 2 | 10 | 58 | 20 | 131 | 10 | .312 | .393 |

## 11   RYAN ADAMS   2B

**Born:** April 21, 1987. **B-T:** R-R. **Ht.:** 6-0. **Wt.:** 185. **Drafted:** HS—New Orleans, 2006 (2nd round). **Signed by:** Mike Tullier.

Adams led New Orleans' Jesuit High to the Louisiana 5-A state championship in 2005, and after the school was turned upside down by Hurricane Katrina, he returned last spring and got the team back to the state semifinals. He was regarded as a potential first-round talent, but repeated hamstring problems caused scouts to doubt his durability. The Orioles were able to get him in the second round and sign him for $675,000. His hamstrings bothered him again in August. Adams' bat is his best tool. He has a nice swing and a mature approach, showing a willingness to go the other way that's not common among younger hitters. He also stays on breaking balls better than most players his age and shows good patience at the plate. He's not a masher but should have gap power as he matures, and he has good hand-eye coordination after playing a lot of ping-pong growing up. The Orioles drafted five players who were high school shortstops, so they moved Adams to second base. That's a better fit for him anyway because of his range and his arm. With his approach and athleticism, Adams can be an offensive second baseman who can hit at the top of an order, but he'll have to prove he can stay healthy. He could open 2007 in low Class A.

| Year | Club (League) | Class | AVG | G | AB | R | H | 2B | 3B | HR | RBI | BB | SO | SB | OBP | SLG |
|------|---------------|-------|-----|---|----|---|---|----|----|----|-----|----|----|----|-----|-----|
| 2006 | Bluefield (Appy) | R | .256 | 34 | 133 | 24 | 34 | 8 | 1 | 2 | 7 | 19 | 32 | 2 | .361 | .376 |
| | Aberdeen (NYP) | A | .316 | 6 | 19 | 2 | 6 | 3 | 0 | 1 | 5 | 4 | 7 | 0 | .458 | .632 |
| **MINOR LEAGUE TOTALS** | | | .263 | 40 | 152 | 26 | 40 | 11 | 1 | 3 | 12 | 23 | 39 | 2 | .374 | .408 |

## 12   LUIS LEBRON   RHP

**Born:** March 13, 1985. **B-T:** R-R. **Ht.:** 6-1. **Wt.:** 170. **Signed:** Dominican Republic, 2004. **Signed by:** Carlos Bernhardt.

Lebron made his U.S. debut in 2005 at Bluefield, but in seven starts there the Orioles found he usually hit a wall after about 50 pitches, losing velocity and command. He always

had expressed a preference for pitching at the end of games, so Baltimore moved him to the bullpen last year and watched him blossom. He throws his fastball at 94-96 mph, touching 97-98, and the pitch has good life. He also has an average slider. He has no changeup to speak of at this point, and the Orioles think he could get to the big leagues quickly if he could add one—though it isn't essential for success out of the bullpen. Lebron has been able to get outs with his fastball so far, and he'll need to develop his slider into a strikeout pitch rather than trying to blow every hitter away to continue moving up. He'll open 2007 in low Class A and could move fast if he continues to show dominant stuff out of the bullpen.

| Year | Club (League) | Class | W | L | ERA | G | GS | CG | SV | IP | H | R | ER | HR | BB | SO | AVG |
|------|---------------|-------|---|---|-----|---|----|----|----|----|----|----|----|----|----|----|-----|
| 2005 | Bluefield (Appy) | R | 2 | 4 | 11.16 | 14 | 7 | 0 | 0 | 25 | 34 | 37 | 31 | 2 | 22 | 45 | .318 |
| 2006 | Delmarva (SAL) | A | 1 | 0 | 27.00 | 2 | 0 | 0 | 0 | 1 | 3 | 4 | 4 | 1 | 1 | 1 | .500 |
| | Aberdeen (NYP) | A | 0 | 2 | 1.17 | 32 | 0 | 0 | 20 | 31 | 17 | 6 | 4 | 2 | 15 | 46 | .163 |
| **MINOR LEAGUE TOTALS** | | | 3 | 6 | 6.16 | 48 | 7 | 0 | 20 | 57 | 54 | 47 | 39 | 5 | 38 | 92 | .249 |

## 13 JAMES JOHNSON                                    RHP

**Born:** June 27, 1983. **B-T:** R-R. **Ht.:** 6-5. **Wt.:** 224. **Drafted:** HS—Endicott, N.Y., 2001 (5th round). **Signed by:** Jim Howard.

After establishing himself as a prospect in 2005, Johnson took a step back in 2006, though he did make his major league debut in an emergency start in July. Orioles officials thought he pitched better after his brief big league experience, despite getting touched for eight runs in three innings, because he got to see firsthand what it takes to get major leaguers out. Johnson has three pitches that can be average or better. His fastball ranges from 88-92 mph with average life, and he maintains the same velocity from Opening Day through the end of the season. He also throws a 12-to-6 curveball and a straight changeup. He's a big, strong, durable pitcher who doesn't back down from batters. To get big league hitters out, Johnson needs to improve his command in the strike zone and learn how to throw off the plate at times. His curveball command was inconsistent in 2006 because he tried to create too much break on the pitch. He'll compete for a spot in the Triple-A rotation in spring training.

| Year | Club (League) | Class | W | L | ERA | G | GS | CG | SV | IP | H | R | ER | HR | BB | SO | AVG |
|------|---------------|-------|---|---|-----|---|----|----|----|----|----|----|----|----|----|----|-----|
| 2001 | Orioles (GCL) | R | 0 | 1 | 3.86 | 7 | 4 | 0 | 0 | 19 | 17 | 10 | 8 | 3 | 7 | 19 | .239 |
| 2002 | Bluefield (Appy) | R | 4 | 2 | 4.37 | 11 | 9 | 0 | 0 | 56 | 52 | 36 | 27 | 5 | 16 | 36 | .250 |
| 2003 | Bluefield (Appy) | R | 3 | 2 | 3.68 | 11 | 11 | 0 | 0 | 51 | 62 | 24 | 21 | 2 | 18 | 46 | .291 |
| 2004 | Delmarva (SAL) | A | 8 | 7 | 3.29 | 20 | 17 | 0 | 0 | 107 | 97 | 44 | 39 | 9 | 30 | 93 | .246 |
| 2005 | Frederick (CL) | A | 12 | 9 | 3.49 | 28 | 27 | 2 | 1 | 160 | 139 | 77 | 62 | 11 | 64 | 168 | .231 |
| | Bowie (EL) | AA | 0 | 0 | 0.00 | 1 | 1 | 0 | 0 | 7 | 3 | 0 | 0 | 0 | 2 | 6 | .136 |
| 2006 | Bowie (EL) | AA | 13 | 6 | 4.44 | 27 | 26 | 0 | 0 | 156 | 165 | 80 | 77 | 13 | 57 | 124 | .274 |
| | Baltimore (AL) | MLB | 0 | 1 | 24.00 | 1 | 1 | 0 | 0 | 3 | 9 | 8 | 8 | 1 | 3 | 0 | .563 |
| **MINOR LEAGUE TOTALS** | | | 40 | 27 | 3.79 | 105 | 95 | 2 | 1 | 555 | 535 | 271 | 234 | 43 | 194 | 492 | .253 |
| **MAJOR LEAGUE TOTALS** | | | 0 | 1 | 24.00 | 1 | 1 | 0 | 0 | 3 | 9 | 8 | 8 | 1 | 3 | 0 | .563 |

## 14 ZACH BRITTON                                    LHP

**Born:** Dec. 22, 1987. **B-T:** L-L. **Ht.:** 6-2. **Wt.:** 180. **Drafted:** HS—Weatherford, Texas, 2006 (3rd round). **Signed by:** Jim Richardson.

Britton looked like a solid recruit for Texas A&M heading into his senior year of high school, but his velocity jumped as did his performance. The Orioles grabbed him in the third round and he signed for $435,000. The Orioles kept him on tight pitch counts during his pro debut. Britton pitched in the high 80s as a high school junior, and he jumped up to 92-93 mph as a senior before tailing off late in the spring. He pitched at 86-90 mph in Bluefield, but he should get back to 88-93 as his athletic frame matures. He showed that kind of velocity in instructional league. Britton didn't need to use his breaking ball or changeup much in high school, so they still need work. He has thrown both a slider and curveball, and the Orioles will have him focus on the curve. It's a good pitch, though he needs to find a consistent release point with it. Baltimore has been most impressed by his mound presence and understanding of the game. He'll open 2007 in the low Class A rotation.

| Year | Club (League) | Class | W | L | ERA | G | GS | CG | SV | IP | H | R | ER | HR | BB | SO | AVG |
|------|---------------|-------|---|---|-----|---|----|----|----|----|----|----|----|----|----|----|-----|
| 2006 | Bluefield (Appy) | R | 0 | 4 | 5.29 | 11 | 11 | 0 | 0 | 34 | 35 | 22 | 20 | 4 | 20 | 21 | .271 |
| **MINOR LEAGUE TOTALS** | | | 0 | 4 | 5.29 | 11 | 11 | 0 | 0 | 34 | 35 | 22 | 20 | 4 | 20 | 21 | .271 |

## 15 SENDY RLEAL                                    RHP

**Born:** June 21, 1980. **B-T:** R-R. **Ht.:** 6-1. **Wt.:** 180. **Signed:** Dominican Republic, 1999. **Signed by:** Carlos Bernhardt.

Rleal was known to few outside the organization when he was added to the 40-man roster after the 2005 season because he had been handled carefully while filling out his frame and battling minor injuries. He won a spot in the big league bullpen to open 2006 and gave

up no runs in his first four appearances, but struggled after that and went back to Triple-A Ottawa in mid-July before returning to Baltimore in September. Rleal has a legitimate power stuff, with a 93-95 mph fastball that touches 97 and a hard slider. To be consistently effective in the majors, he'll have to maintain the sharpness of his pitches as well as his command. He tired quickly in several outings, and he tended to get sloppy with his mechanics. He also needs to maintain his composure when things get tight. The Orioles asked Rleal to focus on better work habits and attention to detail, in the hopes he can claim a role as a set-up man for Chris Ray in spring training.

| Year | Club (League) | Class | W | L | ERA | G | GS | CG | SV | IP | H | R | ER | HR | BB | SO | AVG |
|---|---|---|---|---|---|---|---|---|---|---|---|---|---|---|---|---|---|
| 1999 | Orioles (DSL) | R | 4 | 3 | 3.47 | 9 | 9 | 0 | 0 | 47 | 43 | 24 | 18 | 3 | 20 | 43 | .243 |
| 2000 | Bluefield (Appy) | R | 6 | 2 | 3.39 | 13 | 12 | 0 | 0 | 61 | 61 | 26 | 23 | 5 | 25 | 55 | .268 |
| | Delmarva (SAL) | A | 0 | 1 | 10.80 | 1 | 1 | 0 | 0 | 3 | 3 | 5 | 4 | 0 | 3 | 4 | .214 |
| 2001 | Delmarva (SAL) | A | 3 | 6 | 3.57 | 20 | 20 | 1 | 0 | 103 | 79 | 50 | 41 | 9 | 27 | 83 | .207 |
| 2002 | Delmarva (SAL) | A | 1 | 0 | 6.10 | 28 | 1 | 0 | 1 | 41 | 53 | 28 | 28 | 4 | 15 | 34 | .317 |
| 2003 | Frederick (CL) | A | 3 | 5 | 3.16 | 44 | 0 | 0 | 11 | 57 | 35 | 20 | 20 | 8 | 23 | 59 | .177 |
| 2004 | Bowie (EL) | AA | 4 | 0 | 2.66 | 39 | 0 | 0 | 3 | 47 | 41 | 16 | 14 | 7 | 12 | 60 | .227 |
| 2005 | Bowie (EL) | AA | 4 | 4 | 2.04 | 56 | 0 | 0 | 16 | 71 | 46 | 19 | 16 | 4 | 18 | 75 | .187 |
| 2006 | Baltimore (AL) | MLB | 1 | 1 | 4.44 | 42 | 0 | 0 | 0 | 47 | 48 | 25 | 23 | 10 | 23 | 19 | .274 |
| | Ottawa (IL) | AAA | 2 | 2 | 6.65 | 19 | 0 | 0 | 0 | 23 | 29 | 18 | 17 | 4 | 5 | 14 | .315 |
| **MINOR LEAGUE TOTALS** | | | 27 | 23 | 3.59 | 229 | 43 | 1 | 31 | 454 | 390 | 206 | 181 | 44 | 148 | 427 | .232 |
| **MAJOR LEAGUE TOTALS** | | | 1 | 1 | 4.44 | 42 | 0 | 0 | 0 | 47 | 48 | 25 | 23 | 10 | 23 | 19 | .274 |

## 16 JASON BERKEN                                         RHP

**Born:** Nov. 27, 1983. **B-T:** R-R. **Ht.:** 6-0. **Wt.:** 195. **Drafted:** Clemson, 2006 (6th round). **Signed by:** Dominic Viola.

Berken became the No. 1 starter at Clemson as a sophomore in 2004, but his career took a detour when he had Tommy John surgery and missed all of 2005. He returned to action in 2006 and helped the Tigers reach the College World Series. He showed inconsistent velocity, but the Orioles took him in the sixth round, signed him for $155,000 and were pleased with the results in Berken's first full summer back in action. He showed better control and feel for his pitches than the typical player returning from surgery, but his velocity still isn't back to its previous 94 mph peak. He sat at 88-92 last summer. His changeup is the best of his secondary pitches, which also include a curveball and slider. Baltimore probably will have him focus on the curve. Berken is a leader who was voted as one of Clemson's captains in 2005 even though he couldn't play, and his feel for pitching is another strength. He proved his durability last season, and now the Orioles hope his stuff will improve a tick in 2007. He'll likely open in low Class A, and he could move up quickly if he performs well.

| Year | Club (League) | Class | W | L | ERA | G | GS | CG | SV | IP | H | R | ER | HR | BB | SO | AVG |
|---|---|---|---|---|---|---|---|---|---|---|---|---|---|---|---|---|---|
| 2006 | Aberdeen (NYP) | A | 1 | 4 | 2.80 | 9 | 8 | 0 | 0 | 45 | 39 | 20 | 14 | 4 | 5 | 46 | .234 |
| **MINOR LEAGUE TOTALS** | | | 1 | 4 | 2.80 | 9 | 8 | 0 | 0 | 45 | 39 | 20 | 14 | 4 | 5 | 46 | .234 |

## 17 VAL MAJEWSKI                                         OF/1B

**Born:** June 19, 1981. **B-T:** L-L. **Ht.:** 6-2. **Wt.:** 215. **Drafted:** Rutgers, 2002 (3rd round). **Signed by:** Jim Howard.

Majewski was on the verge of battling for a big league job when he tore the labrum in his left shoulder and missed all of the 2005 season following surgery. He stayed healthy through 2006 and knocked most of the rust off his swing, and he went from hitting .204 at the end of June to .260 by the end of the season. Majewski's bat is his best tool when he's healthy, and he's still recovering his complex yet fluid swing on a consistent basis. He was viewed as an ideal right fielder before the injury, but he spent some time in left and at first base (as well as DH) in 2006. In case his arm doesn't allow him to stay in the outfield, he did a good job at first base, though he doesn't fit the power profile there. His increased versatility could make Majewski a useful bench player if he doesn't hit enough to win an everyday job. The Orioles will throw out his 2006 performance and let him come to big league spring training to compete for a job, though he'll likely return to Triple-A to begin the season.

| Year | Club (League) | Class | AVG | G | AB | R | H | 2B | 3B | HR | RBI | BB | SO | SB | OBP | SLG |
|---|---|---|---|---|---|---|---|---|---|---|---|---|---|---|---|---|
| 2002 | Aberdeen (NYP) | A | .300 | 31 | 110 | 22 | 33 | 7 | 4 | 1 | 15 | 13 | 14 | 8 | .376 | .464 |
| | Delmarva (SAL) | A | .118 | 7 | 17 | 2 | 2 | 0 | 0 | 1 | 3 | 1 | 1 | 0 | .158 | .294 |
| 2003 | Delmarva (SAL) | A | .303 | 56 | 208 | 38 | 63 | 15 | 8 | 7 | 48 | 28 | 20 | 10 | .383 | .553 |
| | Orioles (GCL) | R | .333 | 1 | 3 | 0 | 1 | 0 | 0 | 0 | 0 | 1 | 0 | 0 | .500 | .333 |
| | Aberdeen (NYP) | A | .375 | 4 | 16 | 2 | 6 | 2 | 2 | 0 | 3 | 1 | 2 | 1 | .412 | .750 |
| | Frederick (CL) | A | .289 | 41 | 159 | 15 | 46 | 18 | 1 | 5 | 20 | 7 | 23 | 0 | .321 | .509 |
| 2004 | Bowie (EL) | AA | .307 | 112 | 433 | 71 | 133 | 24 | 5 | 15 | 80 | 33 | 68 | 14 | .359 | .490 |
| | Baltimore (AL) | MLB | .154 | 9 | 13 | 3 | 2 | 1 | 0 | 0 | 1 | 0 | 1 | 0 | .154 | .231 |
| 2005 | Did not play—Injured | | | | | | | | | | | | | | | |

| 2006 | Ottawa (IL) | AAA | .260 | 99 | 323 | 44 | 84 | 15 | 6 | 4 | 39 | 37 | 72 | 7 | .344 | .381 |
| **MINOR LEAGUE TOTALS** | | | .290 | 351 | 1269 | 194 | 368 | 81 | 26 | 33 | 208 | 121 | 200 | 40 | .355 | .473 |
| **MAJOR LEAGUE TOTALS** | | | .154 | 9 | 13 | 3 | 2 | 1 | 0 | 0 | 1 | 0 | 1 | 0 | .154 | .231 |

## 18 MARINO SALAS                                                        RHP

**Born:** Feb. 2, 1981. **B-T:** R-R. **Ht.:** 6-0. **Wt.:** 188. **Signed:** Dominican Republic, 1998. **Signed by:** Carlos Bernhardt.

The Orioles are exceedingly patient with their Dominican pitchers, and the approach is paying dividends with Salas, who didn't make it out of short-season ball until his seventh season in the system. He served as Bowie's closer in 2006 and thrived in the role, and he impressed in instructional league as well. Salas has boosted his fastball to 93-95 mph, and he also has a plus slider. He showed an ability to get both lefthanders and righthanders out in 2006 after struggling against lefties in previous seasons. He still needs to improve his fastball command and keep the ball out of the middle of the plate. He also needs to maintain his concentration and his mechanics. When he gets sloppy, he gets in trouble, but that's happening less often as he matures. Salas continues to make good progress and will be in the big league mix during spring training, though he's likely to open the year in Triple-A.

| Year | Club (League) | Class | W | L | ERA | G | GS | CG | SV | IP | H | R | ER | HR | BB | SO | AVG |
|------|---------------|-------|---|---|-----|---|----|----|----|----|---|---|----|----|----|----|-----|
| 1998 | Orioles (DSL) | R | 3 | 3 | 4.15 | 21 | 0 | 0 | 3 | 43 | 47 | 26 | 20 | 4 | 28 | 25 | .280 |
| 1999 | Orioles (DSL) | R | 8 | 2 | 2.87 | 23 | 0 | 0 | 2 | 47 | 46 | 23 | 15 | 5 | 24 | 43 | .249 |
| 2000 | Orioles (DSL) | R | 3 | 3 | 4.30 | 23 | 0 | 0 | 6 | 38 | 39 | 25 | 18 | 8 | 18 | 31 | .264 |
| 2001 | Orioles (GCL) | R | 1 | 5 | 4.82 | 15 | 0 | 0 | 6 | 19 | 21 | 12 | 10 | 0 | 13 | 10 | .288 |
| 2002 | Bluefield (Appy) | R | 3 | 0 | 5.40 | 27 | 0 | 0 | 0 | 37 | 44 | 31 | 22 | 6 | 21 | 34 | .291 |
| 2003 | Bluefield (Appy) | R | 1 | 2 | 4.89 | 23 | 0 | 0 | 0 | 35 | 36 | 22 | 19 | 1 | 9 | 27 | .271 |
| 2004 | Delmarva (SAL) | A | 2 | 4 | 2.15 | 40 | 0 | 0 | 13 | 50 | 51 | 15 | 12 | 5 | 17 | 46 | .252 |
| 2005 | Frederick (CL) | A | 4 | 2 | 3.63 | 50 | 0 | 0 | 16 | 62 | 54 | 32 | 25 | 7 | 28 | 63 | .233 |
| 2006 | Bowie (EL) | AA | 2 | 6 | 2.92 | 44 | 0 | 0 | 19 | 49 | 39 | 16 | 16 | 3 | 16 | 46 | .215 |
| **MINOR LEAGUE TOTALS** | | | 27 | 27 | 3.72 | 266 | 0 | 0 | 65 | 380 | 377 | 202 | 157 | 39 | 174 | 325 | .256 |

## 19 CHRIS VINYARD                                                        1B

**Born:** Dec. 15, 1985. **B-T:** R-R. **Ht.:** 6-4. **Wt.:** 230. **Drafted:** Chandler-Gilbert (Ariz.) CC, D/F 2005 (38th round). **Signed by:** Bill Bliss/John Gillette.

Vinyard grew up in San Diego playing more basketball than baseball, but he shifted his focus when his family moved to Arizona while he was in high school. The Orioles took him as a 38th-round draft-and-follow in 2005, and he signed for $90,000 last May. He led the short-season New York-Penn League with 26 doubles (an Aberdeen franchise record), eight home runs and 36 extra-base hits, and he won the home run derby at the league's all-star game. Vinyard is a big, strong man with a nice, short swing and the bat speed to produce legitimate plus raw power. He's not just an all-or-nothing slugger, as he's willing to use the whole field. The big question about Vinyard is where he'll play. He's a righthanded first baseman who's average at best defensively, and his big body and lack of athleticism make a trial in the outfield unlikely. He's a below-average runner. Vinyard also struggled against quality breaking stuff late in the summer, though the Orioles expect him to make adjustments. He'll move up to low Class A and try to prove he can slug his way to the big leagues.

| Year | Club (League) | Class | AVG | G | AB | R | H | 2B | 3B | HR | RBI | BB | SO | SB | OBP | SLG |
|------|---------------|-------|-----|---|----|---|---|----|----|----|-----|----|----|----|-----|-----|
| 2006 | Aberdeen (NYP) | A | .284 | 73 | 264 | 40 | 75 | 26 | 2 | 8 | 47 | 28 | 62 | 0 | .366 | .489 |
| **MINOR LEAGUE TOTALS** | | | .284 | 73 | 264 | 40 | 75 | 26 | 2 | 8 | 47 | 28 | 62 | 0 | .366 | .489 |

## 20 ADAM STERN                                                        OF

**Born:** Feb. 12, 1980. **B-T:** L-R. **Ht.:** 5-11. **Wt.:** 180. **Drafted:** Nebraska, 2001 (3rd round). **Signed by:** Tyrone Brooks (Braves).

The Orioles system has improved significantly in the past couple of years, but depth is still an issue, particularly among hitters at the upper levels. So Baltimore was happy to get a potential big leaguer, albeit a complementary one, when they traded Javy Lopez to the Red Sox last August. The Red Sox got Stern from the Braves in the 2004 major league Rule 5 draft after he emerged as a prospect by accentuating his plus speed and strong center-field defense (including a solid arm) and shortening his line-drive swing. While spending most of 2005 with Boston to satisfy the Rule 5 guidelines, he got just 96 at-bats, and the rust showed at the plate last season. Stern isn't going to hit for much power, so he needs to make better contact and get on base more often. He'll compete for a job as an extra outfielder in Baltimore this spring, and that's the role he best fits into in the long term as well.

| Year | Club (League) | Class | AVG | G | AB | R | H | 2B | 3B | HR | RBI | BB | SO | SB | OBP | SLG |
|------|---------------|-------|-----|---|----|---|---|----|----|----|-----|----|----|----|-----|-----|
| 2001 | Jamestown (NYP) | A | .307 | 21 | 75 | 20 | 23 | 4 | 2 | 0 | 11 | 15 | 11 | 9 | .413 | .413 |
| 2002 | Myrtle Beach (CL) | A | .253 | 119 | 462 | 65 | 117 | 22 | 10 | 3 | 47 | 27 | 89 | 40 | .298 | .364 |

| Year | Club (League) | Class | AVG | G | AB | R | H | 2B | 3B | HR | RBI | BB | SO | SB | OBP | SLG |
|------|---------------|-------|-----|---|-----|---|-----|----|----|----|-----|----|-----|----|-----|-----|
| 2003 | Braves (GCL) | R | .345 | 7 | 29 | 6 | 10 | 1 | 0 | 1 | 6 | 6 | 3 | 2 | .457 | .483 |
|  | Myrtle Beach (CL) | A | .194 | 28 | 103 | 11 | 20 | 2 | 0 | 0 | 6 | 13 | 21 | 7 | .282 | .214 |
| 2004 | Greenville (SL) | AA | .322 | 102 | 394 | 64 | 127 | 26 | 6 | 8 | 47 | 35 | 58 | 27 | .378 | .480 |
| 2005 | Pawtucket (IL) | AAA | .321 | 20 | 81 | 16 | 26 | 8 | 0 | 2 | 14 | 8 | 10 | 3 | .385 | .494 |
|  | Boston (AL) | MLB | .133 | 36 | 15 | 4 | 2 | 0 | 0 | 1 | 2 | 0 | 4 | 1 | .188 | .333 |
| 2006 | Boston (AL) | MLB | .150 | 10 | 20 | 3 | 3 | 1 | 0 | 0 | 4 | 0 | 4 | 1 | .190 | .200 |
|  | Pawtucket (IL) | AAA | .258 | 93 | 392 | 59 | 101 | 21 | 3 | 8 | 34 | 23 | 78 | 23 | .300 | .388 |
| **MINOR LEAGUE TOTALS** | | | .276 | 390 | 1536 | 241 | 424 | 84 | 21 | 22 | 165 | 127 | 270 | 111 | .332 | .401 |
| **MAJOR LEAGUE TOTALS** | | | .143 | 46 | 35 | 7 | 5 | 1 | 0 | 1 | 6 | 0 | 8 | 2 | .189 | .257 |

## 21  KURT BIRKINS                                                    LHP

**Born:** Aug. 11, 1980. **B-T:** L-L. **Ht.:** 6-2. **Wt.:** 188. **Drafted:** Los Angeles Pierce JC, D/F 2000 (33rd round). **Signed by:** Gil Kubski.

Birkins had never attracted much attention until minor league spring training last year, when the Orioles thought he might be able to help the organization as a lefty specialist. That opportunity came sooner than expected, after just five starts in Triple-A, and Birkins performed well until his elbow started bothering him. He developed inflammation in the elbow because of a nerve problem, and he was shut down for more than a month before getting some work at the end of the minor league season and in instructional league. Birkins's curveball is his best pitch. He also has an 88-90 mph fastball and an an adequate changeup, though he won't use the latter pitch as much out of the bullpen. He'll need to refine his command to keep big league hitters off balance. Birkins is expected to be healthy for spring training, so he'll compete for a big league job.

| Year | Club (League) | Class | W | L | ERA | G | GS | CG | SV | IP | H | R | ER | HR | BB | SO | AVG |
|------|---------------|-------|---|---|------|---|----|----|----|----|----|----|----|----|----|----|-----|
| 2001 | Orioles (GCL) | R | 2 | 1 | 2.05 | 5 | 4 | 0 | 0 | 22 | 13 | 5 | 5 | 2 | 3 | 24 | .167 |
|  | Bluefield (Appy) | R | 4 | 1 | 2.92 | 6 | 6 | 0 | 0 | 37 | 28 | 14 | 12 | 2 | 5 | 42 | .206 |
| 2002 | Delmarva (SAL) | A | 9 | 7 | 3.51 | 27 | 25 | 3 | 0 | 144 | 140 | 66 | 56 | 10 | 46 | 102 | .257 |
| 2003 | Frederick (CL) | A | 8 | 11 | 4.70 | 25 | 25 | 0 | 0 | 126 | 152 | 82 | 66 | 10 | 40 | 79 | .297 |
| 2004 | Frederick (CL) | A | 5 | 2 | 4.50 | 27 | 6 | 0 | 2 | 68 | 70 | 36 | 34 | 9 | 22 | 55 | .269 |
| 2005 | Bowie (EL) | AA | 7 | 11 | 3.91 | 26 | 24 | 0 | 0 | 129 | 134 | 69 | 56 | 8 | 42 | 114 | .270 |
| 2006 | Ottawa (IL) | AAA | 1 | 3 | 3.20 | 5 | 5 | 0 | 0 | 25 | 20 | 10 | 9 | 2 | 11 | 19 | .225 |
|  | Baltimore (AL) | MLB | 5 | 2 | 4.94 | 35 | 0 | 0 | 0 | 31 | 25 | 19 | 17 | 4 | 16 | 27 | .221 |
|  | Frederick (CL) | A | 0 | 0 | 0.00 | 1 | 0 | 0 | 0 | 1 | 0 | 0 | 0 | 0 | 1 | 1 | .000 |
|  | Aberdeen (NYP) | A | 1 | 1 | 3.38 | 2 | 0 | 0 | 0 | 3 | 3 | 1 | 1 | 0 | 0 | 2 | .375 |
|  | Bowie (EL) | AA | 0 | 1 | 9.00 | 2 | 0 | 0 | 0 | 4 | 5 | 4 | 4 | 2 | 1 | 5 | .313 |
| **MINOR LEAGUE TOTALS** | | | 37 | 38 | 3.91 | 126 | 95 | 3 | 2 | 559 | 565 | 287 | 243 | 45 | 171 | 443 | .264 |
| **MAJOR LEAGUE TOTALS** | | | 5 | 2 | 4.94 | 35 | 0 | 0 | 0 | 31 | 25 | 19 | 17 | 4 | 16 | 27 | .221 |

## 22  LUIS HERNANDEZ                                                SS/2B

**Born:** June 26, 1984. **B-T:** B-R. **Ht.:** 5-10. **Wt.:** 140. **Signed:** Venezuela, 2000. **Signed by:** Rolando Petit/Julian Perez (Braves).

The signing of Hernandez as a minor league free agent—not to mention his addition to the 40-man roster—is another sign the Orioles are looking to supplement their stock of position players at the upper levels. The Braves let him go after he showed little progress with the bat in the last two seasons. Defense has always been his calling card, and Hernandez instantly becomes one of the slickest defenders in the Baltimore system. He has quick, soft hands with above-average range and a strong arm that would make him a legitimate big league shortstop. Hernandez will need to get a lot stronger and improve his offensive approach. Advanced pitchers have been able to keep him off balance with breaking stuff, and he's often tentative at the plate. He has just average speed, so he won't be a basestealer. Hernandez still will open the season as a 22-year-old in Triple-A, so he has upside.

| Year | Club (League) | Class | AVG | G | AB | R | H | 2B | 3B | HR | RBI | BB | SO | SB | OBP | SLG |
|------|---------------|-------|-----|---|-----|---|-----|----|----|----|-----|----|-----|----|-----|-----|
| 2001 | Braves (DSL) | R | .209 | 68 | 253 | 39 | 53 | 8 | 4 | 1 | 18 | 23 | 33 | 24 | .287 | .285 |
| 2002 | Braves (GCL) | R | .254 | 53 | 201 | 34 | 51 | 8 | 4 | 0 | 20 | 19 | 29 | 11 | .330 | .333 |
| 2003 | Rome (SAL) | A | .231 | 111 | 337 | 27 | 78 | 4 | 1 | 2 | 25 | 24 | 42 | 7 | .287 | .267 |
| 2004 | Myrtle Beach (CL) | A | .271 | 117 | 402 | 49 | 109 | 23 | 4 | 6 | 45 | 16 | 70 | 8 | .306 | .393 |
| 2005 | Braves (GCL) | R | .250 | 1 | 4 | 1 | 1 | 0 | 0 | 1 | 1 | 0 | 2 | 0 | .250 | 1.000 |
|  | Mississippi (SL) | AA | .243 | 122 | 415 | 47 | 101 | 12 | 5 | 2 | 32 | 41 | 56 | 5 | .315 | .311 |
| 2006 | Mississippi (SL) | AA | .268 | 104 | 380 | 39 | 102 | 12 | 4 | 1 | 29 | 20 | 46 | 4 | .308 | .329 |
|  | Richmond (IL) | AAA | .192 | 19 | 73 | 3 | 14 | 4 | 0 | 1 | 5 | 0 | 8 | 0 | .192 | .288 |
| **MINOR LEAGUE TOTALS** | | | .246 | 595 | 2065 | 239 | 509 | 71 | 22 | 14 | 175 | 143 | 286 | 59 | .301 | .323 |

## 23  BEAU HALE                                                        RHP

**Born:** Dec. 1, 1978. **B-T:** R-R. **Ht.:** 6-2. **Wt.:** 205. **Drafted:** Texas, 2000 (1st round). **Signed by:** Deron Rombach.

The Orioles spent the 14th overall pick and $2.25 million on Hale in 2000, but it wasn't long before his career was derailed by shoulder injuries. He missed the entire 2003 season

after labrum surgery and needed another operation in 2004, keeping him out for another year. In 2006 he again showed the stuff that made him a premium draft pick. Baltimore considers him one of the most inspirational stories in the minors, as he worked diligently to rehab his shoulder and smooth out his mechanics. Hale's fastball got back to 88-92 mph and touched 93-94 with sink last year, and he also showed a good slider and control. His change-up lags behind his other two pitches. The Orioles always have liked his makeup, and the determination he showed in coming back from so many injuries has them convinced he can be a major league pitcher. He still needs to refine his command, and while his fastball has bounced back, he didn't dominate hitters last season. He could open the season back in Double-A, but Hale will be in Triple-A at some point and could earn a September callup.

| Year | Club (League) | Class | W | L | ERA | G | GS | CG | SV | IP | H | R | ER | HR | BB | SO | AVG |
|------|---------------|-------|---|---|-----|---|----|----|----|----|---|---|----|----|----|----|-----|
| 2001 | Frederick (CL) | A | 1 | 2 | 1.32 | 5 | 5 | 1 | 0 | 34 | 30 | 8 | 5 | 1 | 4 | 30 | .236 |
| | Bowie (EL) | AA | 1 | 5 | 5.11 | 12 | 12 | 0 | 0 | 62 | 74 | 39 | 35 | 8 | 15 | 40 | .306 |
| 2002 | Frederick (CL) | A | 8 | 8 | 5.02 | 22 | 22 | 0 | 0 | 131 | 157 | 83 | 73 | 8 | 27 | 79 | .297 |
| | Bowie (EL) | AA | 2 | 0 | 0.84 | 2 | 2 | 0 | 0 | 11 | 11 | 2 | 1 | 0 | 3 | 6 | .256 |
| 2003 | Did not play—Injured | | | | | | | | | | | | | | | | |
| 2004 | Did not play—Injured | | | | | | | | | | | | | | | | |
| 2005 | Frederick (CL) | A | 1 | 2 | 5.23 | 22 | 5 | 0 | 0 | 53 | 51 | 34 | 31 | 7 | 23 | 48 | .256 |
| 2006 | Frederick (CL) | A | 2 | 0 | 3.80 | 12 | 1 | 0 | 1 | 21 | 28 | 14 | 9 | 1 | 5 | 20 | .304 |
| | Bowie (EL) | AA | 4 | 6 | 3.22 | 19 | 12 | 0 | 0 | 95 | 85 | 40 | 34 | 8 | 20 | 65 | .237 |
| **MINOR LEAGUE TOTALS** | | | 19 | 23 | 4.16 | 94 | 59 | 1 | 1 | 407 | 436 | 220 | 188 | 33 | 97 | 288 | .274 |

 ## 24  PEDRO FLORIMON SS

**Born:** Dec. 10, 1986. **B-T:** B-L. **Ht.:** 6-2. **Wt.:** 180. **Signed:** Dominican Republic, 2004. **Signed by:** Carlos Bernhardt.

Florimon made his U.S. debut in 2006 after two seasons when he batted around the Mendoza line in the Rookie-level Dominican Summer League. Baltimore likes his swing, but he has a raw approach and will need a lot of at-bats to become a serviceable offensive player. He switch-hits now but scouts aren't convinced he can hit righthanded, so he may just focus on the left side. He also hasn't proven he can handle quality breaking balls, and he needs to add strength to his tall, slender frame. Scouts do get excited with his defensive ability, featuring great actions, good range and a plus-plus arm. He needs to get more consistent, and that should come with time. Some scouts have questioned his work ethic, and one said he's the kind of player who looks slick at first before you see the holes in his game. But another compared him to Tony Fernandez because of his hands and quick wrists. It will be up to Florimon to prove who's right, beginning this season in low Class A.

| Year | Club (League) | Class | AVG | G | AB | R | H | 2B | 3B | HR | RBI | BB | SO | SB | OBP | SLG |
|------|---------------|-------|-----|---|----|---|---|----|----|----|-----|----|----|----|-----|-----|
| 2004 | Orioles (DSL) | R | .204 | 52 | 167 | 33 | 34 | 5 | 5 | 0 | 19 | 34 | 59 | 17 | .351 | .293 |
| 2005 | Orioles (DSL) | R | .200 | 63 | 175 | 35 | 34 | 4 | 2 | 0 | 8 | 41 | 55 | 19 | .387 | .247 |
| 2006 | Bluefield (Appy) | R | .333 | 33 | 120 | 23 | 40 | 6 | 1 | 1 | 8 | 28 | 29 | 7 | .456 | .425 |
| | Aberdeen (NYP) | A | .248 | 26 | 105 | 13 | 26 | 4 | 1 | 0 | 5 | 13 | 26 | 0 | .336 | .305 |
| **MINOR LEAGUE TOTALS** | | | .238 | 174 | 562 | 104 | 134 | 19 | 9 | 1 | 40 | 116 | 169 | 43 | .383 | .310 |

## 25  CHORYE SPOONE RHP

**Born:** Sept. 16, 1985. **B-T:** R-R. **Ht.:** 6-1. **Wt.:** 215. **Drafted:** Catonsville (Md.) CC, 2005 (8th round). **Signed by:** Ty Brown.

The Orioles jumped on Spoone, a local Baltimore product, after the Padres were unable to sign him as a draft-and-follow before the 2005 draft. They've been excited by his live arm but still aren't quite sure what to make of him. Once club official said everything about him is immature. Spoone's fastball sits at 93-95 mph and touches 96, and his curveball is a big breaker that looks good when he commands it. He was introduced to a changeup last season and the early results were promising. But Spoone also struggled with his control, and his lack of experience shows in his approach and his demeanor on the mound. For now he'll keep starting, but Spoone's stuff and mentality might be more suited to a relief role. Right now the only plan is to move him up another level and get him more innings to see where Spoone's arm can take him. It's too early to plan for anything more.

| Year | Club (League) | Class | W | L | ERA | G | GS | CG | SV | IP | H | R | ER | HR | BB | SO | AVG |
|------|---------------|-------|---|---|-----|---|----|----|----|----|---|---|----|----|----|----|-----|
| 2005 | Bluefield (Appy) | R | 2 | 5 | 8.03 | 15 | 3 | 0 | 0 | 25 | 27 | 25 | 22 | 3 | 13 | 27 | .273 |
| 2006 | Delmarva (SAL) | A | 7 | 9 | 3.56 | 26 | 25 | 0 | 0 | 129 | 118 | 72 | 51 | 5 | 80 | 90 | .241 |
| **MINOR LEAGUE TOTALS** | | | 9 | 14 | 4.28 | 41 | 28 | 0 | 0 | 154 | 145 | 97 | 73 | 8 | 93 | 117 | .247 |

 ## 26  J.R. HOUSE C/1B

**Born:** Nov. 11, 1979. **B-T:** R-R. **Ht.:** 5-10. **Wt.:** 200. **Drafted:** HS—Daytona Beach, Fla., 1999 (5th round). **Signed by:** Rob Sidwell (Pirates).

Just when it looked like House's once-promising baseball career finally had died, it gained

new life in 2006. House was regarded as one of the best catching prospects in the minors after hitting .348 in 2000, but injuries kept him from building on that season. He left baseball and tried to resurrect his football career in 2005. House had set since-broken national passing records in high school, and he joined the West Virginia program. After falling down the depth chart, however, House decided to give baseball another try with the Astros last year. He showed his old hitting ability in the minors and appeared in four big league games, but Houston took him off its 40-man roster, allowing the Orioles to sign him as a minor league free agent. House's bat has always been his calling card, and he can drive the ball to all parts of the park. The Orioles also like his work ethic. He's a better athlete than most catchers but still a below-average runner. House's defensive skills behind the plate never were his strong suit, and Baltimore will keep him at first base to keep him healthy. He likely will open the season in Triple-A, but the Orioles are desperate for power bats and wouldn't hesitate to give him a shot if he gets off to a good start.

| Year | Club (League) | Class | AVG | G | AB | R | H | 2B | 3B | HR | RBI | BB | SO | SB | OBP | SLG |
|---|---|---|---|---|---|---|---|---|---|---|---|---|---|---|---|---|
| 1999 | Pirates (GCL) | R | .327 | 33 | 113 | 13 | 37 | 9 | 3 | 5 | 23 | 11 | 23 | 1 | .394 | .593 |
| | Williamsport (NYP) | A | .300 | 26 | 100 | 11 | 30 | 6 | 0 | 1 | 13 | 9 | 21 | 0 | .358 | .390 |
| | Hickory (SAL) | A | .273 | 4 | 11 | 1 | 3 | 0 | 0 | 0 | 0 | 0 | 3 | 0 | .273 | .273 |
| 2000 | Hickory (SAL) | A | .348 | 110 | 420 | 78 | 146 | 29 | 1 | 23 | 90 | 46 | 91 | 1 | .414 | .586 |
| 2001 | Altoona (EL) | AA | .258 | 112 | 426 | 51 | 110 | 25 | 1 | 11 | 56 | 37 | 103 | 1 | .323 | .399 |
| 2002 | Altoona (EL) | AA | .264 | 30 | 91 | 9 | 24 | 6 | 0 | 2 | 11 | 13 | 21 | 0 | .349 | .396 |
| | Pirates (GCL) | R | .313 | 5 | 16 | 3 | 5 | 2 | 0 | 1 | 2 | 3 | 1 | 0 | .421 | .625 |
| 2003 | Pirates (GCL) | R | .400 | 20 | 65 | 16 | 26 | 9 | 0 | 4 | 23 | 12 | 5 | 0 | .476 | .723 |
| | Altoona (EL) | AA | .333 | 20 | 63 | 12 | 21 | 6 | 0 | 2 | 11 | 5 | 11 | 0 | .382 | .524 |
| | Pittsburgh (NL) | MLB | 1.000 | 1 | 1 | 0 | 1 | 0 | 0 | 0 | 0 | 0 | 0 | 0 | 1.000 | 1.000 |
| 2004 | Nashville (PCL) | AAA | .288 | 92 | 309 | 38 | 89 | 21 | 1 | 15 | 49 | 23 | 72 | 1 | .344 | .508 |
| | Pittsburgh (NL) | MLB | .111 | 5 | 9 | 1 | 1 | 1 | 0 | 0 | 0 | 0 | 0 | 2 | 0 | .111 | .222 |
| 2005 | Did not play | | | | | | | | | | | | | | | |
| 2006 | Corpus Christi (TL) | AA | .325 | 97 | 379 | 58 | 123 | 23 | 2 | 10 | 69 | 32 | 44 | 2 | .376 | .475 |
| | Round Rock (PCL) | AAA | .412 | 31 | 114 | 25 | 47 | 15 | 0 | 5 | 36 | 9 | 15 | 0 | .445 | .675 |
| | Houston (NL) | MLB | .000 | 4 | 9 | 0 | 0 | 0 | 0 | 0 | 0 | 0 | 0 | 2 | 0 | .000 | .000 |
| **MINOR LEAGUE TOTALS** | | | .314 | 580 | 2107 | 315 | 661 | 151 | 8 | 79 | 383 | 200 | 410 | 6 | .375 | .505 |
| **MAJOR LEAGUE TOTALS** | | | .105 | 10 | 19 | 1 | 2 | 1 | 0 | 0 | 0 | 0 | 0 | 4 | 0 | .105 | .158 |

## ANDERSON GARCIA                                                          RHP

**Born:** March 23, 1981. **B-T:** R-R. **Ht.:** 6-2. **Wt.:** 170. **Signed:** Dominican Republic, 2001. **Signed by:** Victor Mata (Yankees).

The Orioles claimed Garcia off waivers from the Mets in August, and he made a good impression in just a couple of weeks of action. Originally signed by the Yankees, he was traded to the Mets in a 2003 deadline deal for Armando Benitez. Garcia's 2006 season got off to a late start because of visa problems in the Dominican Republic, so the Orioles just had him pitch an inning or two every two to three days to get him regular work. He showed them a fastball that ranged from 93-96 mph as well as a good slider, and his command was much better than it had been in the Mets system. He has a maximum-effort delivery that is much more suited to short outings, and his fastball is much more effective in that role as well. Garcia will compete for a big league bullpen job in spring training.

| Year | Club (League) | Class | W | L | ERA | G | GS | CG | SV | IP | H | R | ER | HR | BB | SO | AVG |
|---|---|---|---|---|---|---|---|---|---|---|---|---|---|---|---|---|---|
| 2001 | Yankees (DSL) | R | 2 | 3 | 3.15 | 14 | 8 | 0 | 1 | 66 | 52 | 29 | 23 | 3 | 25 | 49 | .217 |
| | Staten Island (NYP) | A | 0 | 1 | 5.79 | 1 | 1 | 0 | 0 | 5 | 7 | 3 | 3 | 0 | 1 | 1 | .368 |
| 2002 | Yankees (GCL) | R | 4 | 1 | 2.30 | 11 | 9 | 1 | 0 | 59 | 43 | 22 | 15 | 1 | 22 | 41 | .204 |
| 2003 | Battle Creek (MWL) | A | 3 | 6 | 3.32 | 16 | 11 | 1 | 0 | 76 | 57 | 35 | 28 | 2 | 36 | 62 | .208 |
| | Capital City (SAL) | A | 0 | 1 | 4.26 | 5 | 2 | 0 | 0 | 13 | 10 | 6 | 6 | 1 | 2 | 12 | .217 |
| 2004 | Capital City (SAL) | A | 9 | 2 | 4.71 | 35 | 5 | 0 | 2 | 84 | 92 | 57 | 44 | 7 | 47 | 75 | .272 |
| 2005 | St. Lucie (FSL) | A | 2 | 2 | 2.70 | 16 | 0 | 0 | 3 | 27 | 21 | 9 | 8 | 2 | 9 | 20 | .212 |
| | Binghamton (EL) | AA | 4 | 2 | 4.97 | 30 | 1 | 0 | 5 | 51 | 59 | 32 | 28 | 8 | 20 | 41 | .299 |
| 2006 | Binghamton (EL) | AA | 1 | 1 | 1.29 | 11 | 0 | 0 | 1 | 21 | 21 | 5 | 3 | 0 | 6 | 17 | .266 |
| | Norfolk (IL) | AAA | 1 | 4 | 6.32 | 20 | 0 | 0 | 0 | 31 | 35 | 25 | 22 | 4 | 14 | 18 | .287 |
| | Mets (GCL) | R | 0 | 0 | 3.00 | 2 | 0 | 0 | 0 | 3 | 0 | 1 | 1 | 0 | 2 | 3 | .000 |
| | Bowie (EL) | AA | 2 | 1 | 2.16 | 4 | 0 | 0 | 0 | 8 | 6 | 2 | 2 | 0 | 0 | 8 | .200 |
| | Ottawa (IL) | AAA | 0 | 0 | 2.70 | 5 | 1 | 0 | 0 | 7 | 4 | 2 | 2 | 0 | 3 | 3 | .174 |
| **MINOR LEAGUE TOTALS** | | | 28 | 24 | 3.71 | 170 | 38 | 2 | 12 | 449 | 407 | 228 | 185 | 28 | 187 | 350 | .241 |

## LUIS MONTANEZ                                                            OF

**Born:** Dec. 15, 1981. **B-T:** R-R. **Ht.:** 6-2. **Wt.:** 180. **Drafted:** HS—Miami, 2000 (1st round). **Signed by:** Mike Soper (Cubs).

The third overall pick in the 2000 draft, Montanez may have as much upside as any of the Orioles' veteran acquisitions. He was drafted as a shortstop but his defensive problems seemed to affect him at the plate, so he went back to short-season ball and moved to the

outfield in 2004. The move gave his career a boost and he reached Triple-A last season. The Orioles think his swing and power potential give him a chance to contribute in the big leagues. He adds needed athleticism and has handled all three outfield positions, though he's best suited to a corner, and he could even play back in the infield in a pinch. He has average speed. Montanez was invited to big league spring training and could serve Baltimore in a utility role, but he'll likely open the season in Triple-A.

| Year | Club (League) | Class | AVG | G | AB | R | H | 2B | 3B | HR | RBI | BB | SO | SB | OBP | SLG |
|------|---------------|-------|-----|---|----|---|---|----|----|----|-----|----|----|----|-----|-----|
| 2000 | Cubs (AZL) | R | .344 | 50 | 192 | 50 | 66 | 16 | 7 | 2 | 37 | 25 | 42 | 11 | .438 | .531 |
| | Lansing (MWL) | A | .138 | 8 | 29 | 2 | 4 | 1 | 0 | 0 | 0 | 3 | 6 | 0 | .219 | .172 |
| 2001 | Lansing (MWL) | A | .255 | 124 | 499 | 70 | 127 | 33 | 6 | 5 | 54 | 34 | 121 | 20 | .316 | .375 |
| 2002 | Daytona (FSL) | A | .265 | 124 | 487 | 69 | 129 | 21 | 5 | 4 | 59 | 44 | 89 | 14 | .333 | .353 |
| 2003 | Daytona (FSL) | A | .253 | 126 | 486 | 51 | 123 | 18 | 3 | 5 | 38 | 33 | 89 | 11 | .305 | .333 |
| 2004 | Daytona (FSL) | A | .215 | 21 | 79 | 8 | 17 | 4 | 2 | 1 | 7 | 7 | 16 | 2 | .292 | .354 |
| | Boise (NWL) | A | .297 | 72 | 266 | 47 | 79 | 15 | 7 | 8 | 48 | 35 | 53 | 5 | .381 | .496 |
| 2005 | Peoria (MWL) | A | .305 | 82 | 315 | 54 | 96 | 28 | 2 | 12 | 48 | 32 | 46 | 10 | .384 | .521 |
| | West Tenn (SL) | AA | .268 | 45 | 153 | 20 | 41 | 9 | 1 | 2 | 14 | 12 | 21 | 0 | .325 | .379 |
| 2006 | West Tenn (SL) | AA | .369 | 38 | 141 | 24 | 52 | 11 | 0 | 2 | 25 | 15 | 26 | 5 | .438 | .489 |
| | Iowa (PCL) | AAA | .224 | 82 | 245 | 23 | 55 | 12 | 0 | 8 | 31 | 17 | 44 | 0 | .281 | .371 |
| **MINOR LEAGUE TOTALS** | | | .273 | 772 | 2892 | 418 | 789 | 168 | 33 | 49 | 361 | 257 | 553 | 78 | .341 | .405 |

## 29 BRIAN BURRES                                                                                    LHP

**Born:** April 8, 1981. **B-T:** L-L. **Ht.:** 6-1. **Wt.:** 182. **Drafted:** Mount Hood (Ore.) CC, D/F 2000 (31st round). **Signed by:** John Shafer (Giants).

Burres emerged in the Giants system in 2004 but followed with a mediocre year in Double-A, and when he was optioned off the 40-man after the 2005 season, the Orioles claimed him. He spent all of 2006 in Triple-A, leading Ottawa in wins and strikeouts, then made his major league debut in September. His fastball was a tick faster last season, sitting at 87-88 mph rather than the mid-80s, and it still showed good sink and movement. His slider and change-up were effective as well, and he showed better command and was more consistent from start to start. Because of his thin frame, Burres still doesn't have his best stuff in every outing, however. Burres isn't the kind of pitcher teams build a rotation around, but he has usable stuff and should be able to throw strikes in the big leagues. He'll probably go back to Triple-A and wait for an opening on the big league staff.

| Year | Club (League) | Class | W | L | ERA | G | GS | CG | SV | IP | H | R | ER | HR | BB | SO | AVG |
|------|---------------|-------|---|---|-----|---|----|----|----|----|---|---|----|----|----|----|-----|
| 2001 | Salem-Keizer (NWL) | A | 3 | 1 | 3.10 | 14 | 6 | 0 | 1 | 41 | 43 | 20 | 14 | 2 | 11 | 38 | .274 |
| 2002 | Hagerstown (SAL) | A | 5 | 10 | 4.75 | 32 | 16 | 0 | 1 | 119 | 114 | 78 | 63 | 15 | 53 | 119 | .252 |
| 2003 | San Jose (Cal) | A | 3 | 3 | 3.86 | 39 | 0 | 0 | 1 | 61 | 55 | 33 | 26 | 4 | 36 | 64 | .239 |
| 2004 | San Jose (Cal) | A | 12 | 1 | 2.84 | 36 | 15 | 0 | 0 | 124 | 115 | 49 | 39 | 10 | 30 | 114 | .249 |
| 2005 | Norwich (EL) | AA | 9 | 6 | 4.20 | 26 | 24 | 0 | 0 | 129 | 130 | 66 | 60 | 13 | 57 | 105 | .264 |
| 2006 | Ottawa (IL) | AAA | 10 | 6 | 3.76 | 26 | 26 | 1 | 0 | 139 | 133 | 63 | 58 | 14 | 57 | 110 | .255 |
| | Baltimore (AL) | MLB | 0 | 0 | 2.25 | 11 | 0 | 0 | 0 | 8 | 6 | 2 | 2 | 1 | 1 | 6 | .200 |
| **MINOR LEAGUE TOTALS** | | | 42 | 27 | 3.82 | 173 | 87 | 1 | 3 | 612 | 590 | 309 | 260 | 58 | 244 | 550 | .255 |
| **MAJOR LEAGUE TOTALS** | | | 0 | 0 | 2.25 | 11 | 0 | 0 | 0 | 8 | 6 | 2 | 2 | 1 | 1 | 6 | .200 |

## 30 ADAM DONACHIE                                                                                    C

**Born:** March 3, 1984. **B-T:** R-R. **Ht.:** 6-1. **Wt.:** 215. **Drafted:** HS—Orlando, 2002 (2nd round). **Signed by:** Cliff Pastornicky (Royals).

The Orioles selected righthander Alfredo Simon in the major league Rule 5 draft, then sent him to the Phillies for fellow Rule 5 choice Donachie and cash. Donachie has to stay on Baltimore's major league roster, or else he'll have to clear waivers and be offered back to the Royals. Whether he'll be able to hit enough to stick remains a huge question. A former switch-hitter, Donachie has exclusively righthanded since 2004. He's at his best when he stays with a gap-to-gap approach and has good extension in his swing. He does draw a good amount of his walks. Donachie is a defensive standout, however. He has a lightning-quick exchange with a strong, accurate arm and threw out 45 percent of basestealers last season. He's a below-average runner. He has recovered fully from a skull fracture in 2004, when teammate Kila Kaaihue hit him in the head with a bat while swinging in the on-deck circle.

| Year | Club (League) | Class | AVG | G | AB | R | H | 2B | 3B | HR | RBI | BB | SO | SB | OBP | SLG |
|------|---------------|-------|-----|---|----|---|---|----|----|----|-----|----|----|----|-----|-----|
| 2002 | Royals (GCL) | R | .206 | 21 | 68 | 7 | 14 | 3 | 0 | 0 | 3 | 9 | 12 | 0 | .304 | .250 |
| 2003 | Royals 2 (AZL) | R | .444 | 2 | 9 | 3 | 4 | 1 | 0 | 0 | 0 | 1 | 4 | 0 | .500 | .556 |
| | Royals 1 (AZL) | R | .222 | 20 | 63 | 8 | 14 | 3 | 1 | 0 | 7 | 9 | 12 | 0 | .338 | .302 |
| 2004 | Burlington (MWL) | A | .189 | 67 | 228 | 17 | 43 | 7 | 0 | 1 | 21 | 21 | 41 | 5 | .261 | .232 |
| 2005 | High Desert (Cal) | A | .294 | 95 | 347 | 64 | 102 | 24 | 0 | 12 | 48 | 43 | 78 | 1 | .375 | .467 |
| 2006 | High Desert (Cal) | A | .271 | 62 | 210 | 32 | 57 | 12 | 0 | 6 | 21 | 31 | 46 | 0 | .365 | .414 |
| | Wichita (TL) | AA | .191 | 29 | 94 | 21 | 18 | 5 | 0 | 2 | 10 | 19 | 20 | 0 | .325 | .309 |
| **MINOR LEAGUE TOTALS** | | | .247 | 296 | 1019 | 152 | 252 | 55 | 1 | 21 | 110 | 133 | 213 | 6 | .337 | .365 |

# BOSTON
# RED SOX

## BY JIM CALLIS

No team had a more turbulent offseason and 2006 season than Boston. Shortly after the White Sox swept them out of the 2005 playoffs, the Red Sox were reeling from a more unexpected loss. Theo Epstein, the first general manager in franchise history to build three straight playoff clubs, abruptly resigned on Halloween.

Boston interviewed several candidates before promoting farm director Ben Cherington and assistant to the GM Jed Hoyer to replace Epstein on Dec. 12. Team president Larry Lucchino maintained that Epstein was still welcome back—and Epstein took him up on it by returning as GM on Jan. 19. The Red Sox managed to retain most of their young front-office executives despite the uncertainty during Epstein's absence, though assistant GM Josh Byrnes took Arizona's GM job before Epstein stepped down.

The Red Sox also spent the offseason reshaping their club. They traded four prospects, including shortstop Hanley Ramirez and righthander Anibal Sanchez, to get Josh Beckett from the Marlins. They pulled the plug on Edgar Renteria, shipping him to the Braves for third-base prospect Andy Marte. When they lost Johnny Damon to the Yankees, the Sox used Marte as the centerpiece of a four-piece package to get Coco Crisp from the Indians.

Through July, Boston seemed destined for a fourth straight postseason appearance. But injuries and the implosion of the pitching staff contributed to a 9-21 August that took the Red Sox from a game ahead to eight behind the Yankees. They finished 86-76 and

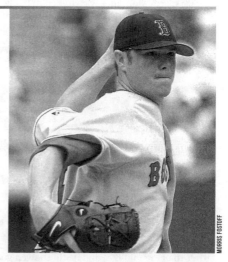

MORRIS FISTOFF

in third place, their worst standing in the American League East since 1997.

Boston's farm system also went through a significant makeover. Baseball America assessed the organization's talent as the eighth-best in the game entering the year, and that came after Top 100 Prospects Marte, Ramirez and Sanchez had departed. The Red Sox held onto Jonathan Papelbon, who became an all-star closer, and **Jon Lester**, who went 7-2 in 15 starts before being diagnosed with a treatable form of a blood cancer in his back.

Red Sox affiliates won championships in the Double-A Eastern League and Rookie-level Gulf Coast League, the system's first dual titles since 1979. But all of the trades (catcher Kelly Shoppach and reliever Cla Meredith also left town) and promotions thinned out the depth at the upper levels of the minors. The majority of the system's most attractive prospects are now products of Jason McLeod's two drafts as scouting director. BA appraised the Red Sox' 2006 draft crop as the best in the game, and they spent a club-record $8.5 million on the draft—a pittance compared to their foray into the Japanese market during the offseason. Boston bid $51.1 million for the rights to righthander Daisuke Matsuzaka, then signed him to a six-year, $52 million contract. He became the Sox' top prospect and should emerge as their No. 1 starter.

## TOP 30 PROSPECTS

| | |
|---|---|
| 1. Daisuke Matsuzaka, rhp | 16. Jed Lowrie, ss |
| 2. Jacoby Ellsbury, of | 17. Ryan Kalish, of |
| 3. Clay Buchholz, rhp | 18. Felix Doubront, lhp |
| 4. Michael Bowden, rhp | 19. Caleb Clay, rhp |
| 5. Daniel Bard, rhp | 20. Engel Beltre, of |
| 6. Lars Anderson, 1b | 21. Oscar Tejada, ss |
| 7. Dustin Pedroia, ss/2b | 22. Hideki Okajima, lhp |
| 8. Bryce Cox, rhp | 23. Devern Hansack, rhp |
| 9. Craig Hansen, rhp | 24. Jon Egan, c |
| 10. Kris Johnson, lhp | 25. Aaron Bates, 1b |
| 11. Jason Place, of | 26. Edgar Martinez, rhp |
| 12. George Kottaras, c | 27. Ty Weeden, c/1b |
| 13. Justin Masterson, rhp | 28. Chad Spann, 3b |
| 14. Brandon Moss, of | 29. Kris Negron, ss/3b |
| 15. David Murphy, of | 30. Jeff Natale, 2b |

# ORGANIZATION OVERVIEW

**General manager:** Theo Epstein. **Farm director:** Mike Hazen. **Scouting director:** Jason McLeod.

## 2006 PERFORMANCE

| Class | Team | League | W | L | PCT | Finish* | Manager | Affiliated |
|---|---|---|---|---|---|---|---|---|
| Majors | Boston | American | 86 | 76 | .531 | 8th (14) | Terry Francona | — |
| Triple-A | Pawtucket Red Sox | International | 69 | 75 | .479 | 10th (14) | Ron Johnson | 1973 |
| Double-A | Portland Sea Dogs | Eastern | 72 | 67 | .518 | +4th (12) | Todd Claus | 2003 |
| High A | #Wilmington Blue Rocks | Carolina | 67 | 71 | .486 | 4th (8) | Chad Epperson | 2005 |
| Low A | Greenville Bombers | South Atlantic | 67 | 73 | .479 | 11th (16) | Ivan DeJesus | 2005 |
| Short-season | Lowell Spinners | New York-Penn | 39 | 36 | .520 | 9th (14) | Bruce Crabbe | 1996 |
| Rookie | GCL Red Sox | Gulf Coast | 35 | 19 | .648 | +1st (12) | Dave Tomlin | 1993 |

**OVERALL 2006 MINOR LEAGUE RECORD** 349 341 .506 13th (30)

*Finish in overall standings (No. of teams in league). +League champion. #Affiliate will be in Lancaster (California) in 2007.

## ORGANIZATION LEADERS

### BATTING
| | | |
|---|---|---|
| AVG | Pedroia, Dustin, Pawtucket | .305 |
| R | Johnson, Jay, Portland/Greenville/Wilmington | 86 |
| H | Ellsbury, Jacoby, Wilmington/Portland | 149 |
| 2B | Murphy, David, Portland/Pawtucket | 40 |
| 3B | Ellsbury, Jacoby, Wilmington/Portland | 10 |
| HR | Bailey, Jeff, Pawtucket | 22 |
| RBI | Natale, Jeff, Greenville/Wilmington | 87 |
| BB | Natale, Jeff, Greenville/Wilmington | 103 |
| SO | Hall, Michael, Wilmington/Greenville | 151 |
| SB | Ellsbury, Jacoby, Wilmington/Portland | 45 |
| OBP | Natale, Jeff, Greenville/Wilmington | .446 |
| SLG | Bailey, Jeff, Pawtucket | .489 |
| XBH | Murphy, David, Portland/Pawtucket | 57 |

### PITCHING
| | | |
|---|---|---|
| W | Jackson, Kyle, Wilmington/Portland | 12 |
| L | Galvez, Gary, Wilmington | 10 |
| | Hottovy, Thomas, Wilmington/Portland | 10 |
| ERA | Rodriguez, Jorge, GCL Red Sox | 2.35 |
| G | Hertzler, Barry, Pawtucket/Portland | 57 |
| SV | James, Michael, Wilmington | 25 |
| IP | Hottovy, Thomas, Wilmington/Portland | 163 |
| BB | Vaquedano, Jose, Wilmington/Portland | 73 |
| SO | Buchholz, Clay, Greenville/Wilmington | 140 |
| AVG | Doubront, Felix, GCL Red Sox/Lowell | .207 |

## BEST TOOLS

| | |
|---|---|
| Best Hitter for Average | Jacoby Ellsbury |
| Best Power Hitter | Lars Anderson |
| Best Strike-Zone Discipline | Jeff Natale |
| Fastest Baserunner | Jacoby Ellsbury |
| Best Athlete | Jacoby Ellsbury |
| Best Fastball | Daniel Bard |
| Best Curveball | Clay Buchholz |
| Best Slider | Bryce Cox |
| Best Changeup | Ryan Phillips |
| Best Control | Michael Bowden |
| Best Defensive Catcher | Mark Wagner |
| Best Defensive Infielder | Argenis Diaz |
| Best Infield Arm | Oscar Tejada |
| Best Defensive Outfielder | Jacoby Ellsbury |
| Best Outfield Arm | Chris Durbin |

## PROJECTED 2010 LINEUP

| | |
|---|---|
| Catcher | George Kottaras |
| First Base | Lars Anderson |
| Second Base | Dustin Pedroia |
| Third Base | Kevin Youkilis |
| Shortstop | Julio Lugo |
| Left Field | Manny Ramirez |
| Center Field | Jacoby Ellsbury |
| Right Field | Jason Place |

| | |
|---|---|
| Designated Hitter | David Ortiz |
| No. 1 Starter | Daisuke Matsuzaka |
| No. 2 Starter | Jonathan Papelbon |
| No. 3 Starter | Josh Beckett |
| No. 4 Starter | Jon Lester |
| No. 5 Starter | Clay Buchholz |
| Closer | Bryce Cox |

## LAST YEAR'S TOP 20 PROSPECTS

| | |
|---|---|
| 1. Andy Marte, 3b | 11. Michael Bowden, rhp |
| 2. Jon Lester, lhp | 12. David Murphy, of |
| 3. Jonathan Papelbon, rhp | 13. Luis Soto, of |
| 4. Craig Hansen, rhp | 14. Brandon Moss, of |
| 5. Dustin Pedroia, 2b/ss | 15. Edgar Martinez rhp |
| 6. Jacoby Ellsbury, of | 16. David Pauley, rhp |
| 7. Kelly Shoppach, c | 17. Ian Bladergroen, 1b |
| 8. Manny Delcarmen, rhp | 18. Christian Lara, ss |
| 9. Jed Lowrie, ss | 19. Jeff Corsaletti, of |
| 10. Clay Buchholz, rhp | 20. Cla Meredith, rhp |

## TOP PROSPECTS OF THE DECADE

| Year | Player, Pos. | 2006 Org. |
|---|---|---|
| 1997 | Nomar Garciaparra, ss | Dodgers |
| 1998 | Brian Rose, rhp | Out of baseball |
| 1999 | Dernell Stenson, of | Deceased |
| 2000 | Steve Lomasney, c | Twins |
| 2001 | Dernell Stenson, of/1b | Deceased |
| 2002 | Seung Song, rhp | Royals |
| 2003 | Hanley Ramirez, ss | Marlins |
| 2004 | Hanley Ramirez, ss | Marlins |
| 2005 | Hanley Ramirez, ss | Marlins |
| 2006 | Andy Marte, 3b | Indians |

## TOP DRAFT PICKS OF THE DECADE

| Year | Player, Pos. | 2006 Org. |
|---|---|---|
| 1997 | John Curtice, lhp | Out of baseball |
| 1998 | Adam Everett, ss | Astros |
| 1999 | Rick Asadoorian, of | Reds |
| 2000 | Phil Dumatrait, lhp | Reds |
| 2001 | Kelly Shoppach, c (2nd round) | Indians |
| 2002 | Jon Lester, lhp (2nd round) | Red Sox |
| 2003 | David Murphy, of | Red Sox |
| 2004 | Dustin Pedroia, ss (2nd round) | Red Sox |
| 2005 | Jacoby Ellsbury, of | Red Sox |
| 2006 | Jason Place, of | Red Sox |

## ALL-TIME LARGEST BONUSES

| | |
|---|---|
| Daisuke Matsuzaka, 2006 | $2,000,000 |
| Risk Asadoorian, 1999 | $1,725,500 |
| Adam Everett, 1998 | $1,725,000 |
| Mike Rozier, 2004 | $1,575,000 |
| Daniel Bard, 2006 | $1,550,000 |

# MINOR LEAGUE DEPTH CHART

## Boston Red Sox

**Impact: A.** Daisuke Matsuzaka earns this grade himself, but Boston also added impact talent in the 2006 draft.
**Depth: C.** At the upper levels, Boston's talent has thinned.
**Sleeper:** Devern Hansack, rhp. From Nicaraguan lobsterman to Red Sox closer? Only in America.

*Numbers in parentheses indicate prospect rankings.*

### LF
Jeff Corsaletti
Carlos Fernandez

### CF
Jacoby Ellsbury (2)
Jason Place (11)
David Murphy (15)
Ryan Kalish (17)
Engel Beltre (20)
Reid Engel
Josh Reddick

### RF
Brandon Moss (14)
Zach Daeges
Chris Turner
Luis Soto

### 3B
Chad Spann (28)
Andrew Pinckney

### SS
Oscar Tejada (22)
Kris Negron (29)
Argenis Diaz
Christian Lara

### 2B
Dustin Pedroia (7)
Jed Lowrie (16)
Jeff Natale (30)
Chih-Hsien Chiang

### 1B
Lars Anderson (6)
Aaron Bates (25)
Michael Jones

### C
George Kottaras (12)
Jon Egan (24)
Ty Weeden (27)
Mark Wagner

### RHP

| Starters | Relievers |
| --- | --- |
| Daisuke Matsuzaka (1) | Bryce Cox (8) |
| Clay Buchholz (3) | Craig Hansen (9) |
| Michael Bowden (4) | Devern Hansack (23) |
| Daniel Bard (5) | Edgar Martinez (26) |
| Justin Masterson (13) | Kyle Jackson |
| Caleb Clay (19) | Beau Vaughan |
| David Pauley | Josh Papelbon |
| Charlie Zink | |
| Jordan Craft | |
| Chris Smith | |
| Chris Jones | |

### LHP

| Starters | Relievers |
| --- | --- |
| Kris Johnson (10) | Hideki Okajima (21) |
| Felix Doubront (18) | Hunter Jones |
| Kason Gabbard | Dustin Richardson |
| Ryan Phillips | Craig Breslow |
| Tommy Hottovy | Tim Cox |
| Andrew Dobies | Abe Alvarez |
| Michael Rozier | |

## 2006    SIGNING BUDGET: $6.8 million

**Best Pro Debut:** LHP Kris Johnson (1) and RHPs Justin Masterson (2) and Bryce Cox (3) all posted sub-1.00 ERAs. Masterson had a 33-2 K-BB ratio in 32 innings, while Cox did most of his dominating in high Class A. Submarining RHP Josh Papelbon (48) had a 1.86 ERA, 13 saves and a 36-6 K-BB ratio in 29 innings.

**Best Athlete:** OF Ryan Kalish (9) had the opportunity to play quarterback at Virginia. OF Jason Place (1) offers the best combination of power and speed. SS/3B Kris Negron (7) does the best job of translating his athleticism to the diamond at this point.

**Best Pure Hitter:** Kalish has a pretty left-handed stroke. Boston originally took OF Josh Reddick (17) as a draft-and-follow, then signed him after he homered and doubled against Team USA in summer competition.

**Best Raw Power:** Balls just explode off the bat of 1B Lars Anderson (18), who led California high schoolers with 15 homers in the spring. C/1B Ty Weeden (16) showed tremendous power to all fields at the 2005 Area Code Games. Place also has well-above-average power potential. The Red Sox wanted to add power to their system, and they spent $2.545 million to sign this trio.

**Fastest Runner:** Negron and Kalish have plus speed. Draft-and-follow OF Matt Sheely is faster than both of them.

**Best Defensive Player:** Boston believes Negron can stay at shortstop, and he has the tools and actions to do well at second or third base if needed.

**Best Fastball:** RHP Daniel Bard (1) usually pitched from 93-96 mph in college, and when he reported to instructional league after signing late he had one sequence where he threw 99, 100 and 99 again. Cox works at 93-94 mph and tops out at 96-97 with tremendous run and sink. RHP Jordan Craft (13) occasionally touches 96, while RHP Caleb Clay (1), an outfielder before 2006, and Masterson both can reach 94.

**Best Breaking Ball:** Cox' mid-80s slider has so much lateral break that catchers struggle to hold onto it.

**Most Intriguing Background:** If not for his baseball responsibilities, LHP Dustin Richardson (5) would have made Texas Tech's basketball team as a walk-on in ESPN's reality show "Knight School." Papelbon's older brother Jonathan is Boston's all-star closer, and his twin Jeremy signed with the Cubs as a 19th-rounder. Unsigned RHP Kyle Snider's (10) brother Brian was an Athletics first-rounder who played in Double-A last year, while Weeden's brother Brandon pitches in the Royals system. RHP Richie Lentz' (19) dad Mike was the No. 2 overall pick in the June 1975 draft.

**Closest To The Majors:** Cox, because of his stuff and his role as a reliever.

**Best Late-Round Pick:** Anderson, then Weeden. In the non-big-money division, it would be Reddick and Craft.

**The One Who Got Away:** Boston still controls the rights to prime draft-and-follows Snider and LHP Brandon Belt (11). The Red Sox never got close financially to signing slugging 1B Matt LaPorta (14), who returned to Florida for his senior year.

**Assessment:** After depleting their system through callups and trades, the Red Sox took a big step toward restocking it with this draft. They addressed their biggest shortcoming (home run power) while also adding athletes and power arms.

## 2005    BUDGET: $6.2 million

They spent a lot of money, and a year later, the Red Sox are thrilled with their five first-rounders: OF Jacoby Ellsbury; RHPs Craig Hansen, Clay Buchholz and Michael Bowden; and SS Jed Lowrie. Unsigned SS Pedro Alvarez (14) could become the top pick in the 2008 draft.    **GRADE: B+**

## 2004    BUDGET: $1.8 million

Boston's top pick, SS/2B Dustin Pedroia (2), should become a big league regular this season. RHP Cla Meredith (6) could have helped a beleaguered Sox bullpen if he hadn't been traded to the Padres.    **GRADE: C+**

## 2003    BUDGET: $5.1 million

RHP Jonathan Papelbon (4) became an all-star closer in his first full major league season and could move into the rotation. OF David Murphy (1) looks like a role player, while OF Matt Murton (1) was used in the Orlando Cabrera trade that helped Boston win the 2004 World Series.    **GRADE: A**

*Draft analysis by Jim Callis. Numbers in parentheses indicate draft rounds. Budgets are bonuses in first 10 rounds.*

# DAISUKE
# MATSUZAKA

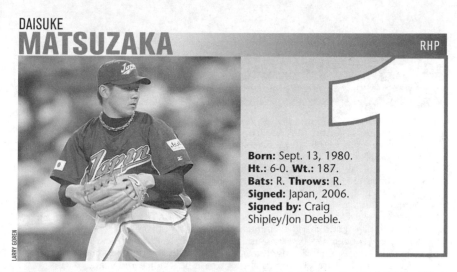

**Born:** Sept. 13, 1980.
**Ht.:** 6-0. **Wt.:** 187.
**Bats:** R. **Throws:** R.
**Signed:** Japan, 2006.
**Signed by:** Craig
Shipley/Jon Deeble.

LARRY GOREN

The Red Sox shook up major leagues on two continents when they bid $51.1 million for Matsuzaka's rights after Japan's Seibu Lions made him available through the posting process in November. Seibu had expected to receive $30 million, but Boston coveted him after scouting him for years. The initial investment made more sense when he signed a six-year, $52 million contract. The total cost of $103.1 million over six seasons is in line with the going rate for a frontline starter, and that's exactly what Matsuzaka is. He first attracted notice in Japan's national high school tournament in 1998, throwing 250 pitches to win a 17-inning quarterfinal, saving the semifinal and tossing a no-hitter to win the championship game. In two Olympics, he has posted a 2.30 ERA and 45 strikeouts in 43 innings. Matsuzaka pitched a five-hitter against a team of all-stars from the U.S. in 2004, and he won MVP honors and all three of his starts while leading Japan to the championship of the inaugural World Baseball Classic last spring.

About the worst thing any scout will say about Matsuzaka is that he might be a No. 2 starter rather than a No. 1. There's disagreement about whether the number of quality pitches he possesses is five or six or seven. His best is a forkball that dives at the plate. He usually pitches in the low 90s with his two-seam fastball, and he can dial up the velocity with a four-seamer. He finished an 11-inning win last season with a 97 mph heater. Matsuzaka also can make hitters look silly with a 12-to-6 curveball, a hard slider and a changeup that has screwball action. All six of those pitches grade as plus pitches at times, and some as plus-plus. There's talk that he throws the mystical gyroball, a breaking pitch with double spin, but he denies it. Matsuzaka also has command and control of his pitches, as well as a feel for setting up hitters. There are no doubts about his mental toughness, as he has been in the spotlight since he was in high school and has pitched well on big stage after big stage.

Matsuzaka has pitched more stressful innings than most 26-year-olds and often worked on five days' rest in Japan, so there are questions about how he'll hold up in the United States. But he has a strong frame and is efficient with his pitches, and the only arm problem he ever had in Japan was a sore elbow that knocked him out for a month in 2002, when he missed most of the second half with a thigh injury. He likes to work up in the strike zone with his fastball, which can be dangerous, but he mixes pitches and locations well.

Pitching in the American League East will be the ultimate test for Matsuzaka, and he's physically and mentally equipped for the challenge. Boston probably will ease the pressure by starting him toward the back of the rotation, but he should emerge as the top pitcher by season's end. With him, Jonathan Papelbon and Josh Beckett, the Red Sox have an enviable trio of 26-year-old starters they can build a staff around.

| Year | Club (League) | Class | W | L | ERA | G | GS | CG | SV | IP | H | R | ER | HR | BB | SO | AVG |
|------|---------------|-------|---|---|-----|---|----|----|----|----|---|---|----|----|----|----|-----|
| 1999 | Seibu (PL) | JAP | 16 | 5 | 2.60 | 25 | 24 | 6 | 0 | 180 | 124 | 55 | 52 | 14 | 87 | 151 | .197 |
| 2000 | Seibu (PL) | JAP | 14 | 7 | 3.97 | 27 | 24 | 6 | 1 | 168 | 132 | 85 | 74 | 12 | 95 | 144 | .219 |
| 2001 | Seibu (PL) | JAP | 15 | 15 | 3.60 | 33 | 32 | 12 | 0 | 240 | 184 | 104 | 96 | 27 | 117 | 214 | .214 |
| 2002 | Seibu (PL) | JAP | 6 | 2 | 3.68 | 14 | 11 | 2 | 0 | 73 | 60 | 30 | 30 | 13 | 15 | 78 | .221 |
| 2003 | Seibu (PL) | JAP | 16 | 7 | 2.83 | 29 | 27 | 8 | 0 | 194 | 165 | 71 | 61 | 13 | 63 | 215 | .230 |
| 2004 | Seibu (PL) | JAP | 10 | 6 | 2.90 | 23 | 19 | 10 | 0 | 146 | 127 | 50 | 47 | 7 | 42 | 127 | .236 |
| 2005 | Seibu (PL) | JAP | 14 | 13 | 2.30 | 28 | 28 | 15 | 0 | 215 | 172 | 63 | 55 | 13 | 49 | 226 | .216 |
| 2006 | Seibu (PL) | JAP | 17 | 5 | 2.13 | 25 | 25 | 13 | 0 | 186 | 138 | 50 | 44 | 13 | 34 | 200 | .206 |
| **JAPANESE TOTALS** | | | 108 | 60 | 2.95 | 204 | 190 | 72 | 1 | 1403 | 1102 | 508 | 459 | 112 | 502 | 1355 | .217 |

## 2 JACOBY ELLSBURY OF

**Born:** Sept. 11, 1983. **B-T:** L-L. **Ht.:** 6-1. **Wt.:** 185. **Drafted:** Oregon State, 2005 (1st round). **Signed by:** John Booher

Ellsbury had done nothing to disappoint the Red Sox since they targeted him with the 23rd overall pick in the 2005 draft and signed him for $1.4 million. In his first full season, managers rated him both the best and fastest baserunner and the top defensive outfielder in the high Class A Carolina League. He performed even better following a promotion to Double-A Portland. Boston officials shy away from making the comparison, but Ellsbury can be the leadoff hitter and center field the team missed after letting Johnny Damon leave for the Yankees. He makes consistent hard line-drive contact with ease, thanks to a sound stroke and outstanding hand-eye coordination. He has hit just eight homers in 146 pro games, but there's some uppercut in his swing and strength in his frame that should allow him to produce at least 10-15 homers a year. Ellsbury has plus-plus speed that makes him an asset on the bases and in center field. He gets good jumps and takes efficient routes in center, enhancing his range. Ellsbury's lone below-average tool is his arm strength, but he compensates somewhat by getting to balls and unloading quickly. He has the on-base ability, speed and explosiveness to be an elite basestealer, but he was caught 17 times in 2006, showing that he can do a better job of reading pitchers and situations. Ellsbury should open 2007 at Triple-A Pawtucket and likely will be starting for the Red Sox by Opening Day 2008.

| Year | Club (League) | Class | AVG | G | AB | R | H | 2B | 3B | HR | RBI | BB | SO | SB | OBP | SLG |
|------|---------------|-------|-----|---|----|----|----|----|----|----|-----|----|----|----|-----|-----|
| 2005 | Lowell (NYP) | A | .317 | 35 | 139 | 28 | 44 | 3 | 5 | 1 | 19 | 24 | 20 | 23 | .418 | .432 |
| 2006 | Portland (EL) | AA | .308 | 50 | 198 | 29 | 61 | 10 | 3 | 3 | 19 | 24 | 25 | 16 | .387 | .434 |
| | Wilmington (CL) | A | .299 | 61 | 244 | 35 | 73 | 7 | 5 | 4 | 32 | 25 | 28 | 25 | .379 | .418 |
| **MINOR LEAGUE TOTALS** | | | .306 | 146 | 581 | 92 | 178 | 20 | 13 | 8 | 70 | 73 | 73 | 64 | .391 | .427 |

## 3 CLAY BUCHHOLZ RHP

**Born:** Aug. 14, 1984. **B-T:** L-R. **Ht.:** 6-3. **Wt.:** 190. **Drafted:** Angelina (Texas) JC, 2005 (1st round supplemental). **Signed by:** Jim Robinson.

Buchholz was Boston's minor league pitcher of the year in 2006, his first full pro season and just his second as a full-time pitcher. He began his college career as a seldom-used infielder at McNeese State before transferring to Angelina (Texas) Junior College, where he was a two-way star. Energized by a late-season promotion to high Class A Wilmington, Buchholz dominated and pitched at 95-97 mph during the playoffs. His fastball sat at 90-93 for most of the season, and while it's a plus pitch, at times it's only his fourth-best offering. When he gets ahead in the count, he buries hitters with his secondary pitches. He has the best curveball in the system, a 12-to-6 hammer, and he can throw a hard slider. Some scouts think his changeup is his best offering. Relatively inexperienced on the mound, he still is learning the nuances of pitching. Improved fastball command and overall consistency are Buchholz' biggest needs. Some clubs passed on him in the 2005 draft because he was arrested in April 2004 and charged with stealing laptop computers from a middle school, but the Red Sox say it was a one-time incident and don't worry about his makeup. Buchholz is a possible No. 1 starter. Boston will bring him along conservatively, so he'll probably open 2007 at the club's new high Class A Lancaster affiliate.

| Year | Club (League) | Class | W | L | ERA | G | GS | CG | SV | IP | H | R | ER | HR | BB | SO | AVG |
|------|---------------|-------|---|---|-----|---|----|----|----|----|----|----|----|----|----|-----|-----|
| 2005 | Lowell (NYP) | A | 0 | 1 | 2.61 | 15 | 15 | 0 | 0 | 41 | 34 | 15 | 12 | 2 | 9 | 45 | .219 |
| 2006 | Greenville (SAL) | A | 9 | 4 | 2.62 | 21 | 21 | 0 | 0 | 103 | 78 | 34 | 30 | 10 | 29 | 117 | .211 |
| | Wilmington (CL) | A | 2 | 0 | 1.13 | 3 | 3 | 0 | 0 | 16 | 10 | 4 | 2 | 0 | 4 | 23 | .182 |
| **MINOR LEAGUE TOTALS** | | | 11 | 5 | 2.47 | 39 | 39 | 0 | 0 | 160 | 122 | 53 | 44 | 12 | 42 | 185 | .211 |

## 4 MICHAEL BOWDEN RHP

**Born:** Sept. 9, 1986. **B-T:** R-R. **Ht.:** 6-3. **Wt.:** 215. **Drafted:** HS—Aurora, Ill., 2005 (1st round supplemental). **Signed by:** Danny Haas

Chosen five picks after Clay Buchholz in the 2005 draft, Bowden pitched with him at two Class A stops in 2006 and showed a similar build, athleticism and stuff. He's not as spectacular as Buchholz, but Bowden has more natural feel for pitching and had an impressive first full season. Bowden sets hitters up and puts them away with his fastball-curveball combination. His two-plane curve is his best pitch, though his low-90s fastball isn't far behind, and he has the best command in the sys-

tem. Working from a high arm slot, he throws everything downhill. Bowden would have gone higher in the draft if not for his unorthodox delivery, which is long in back and short in front, resembling that of former all-star Ken Hill. The Red Sox had him checked out and found no cause for concern. His main focus on the mound is his changeup, which has some promise, and he may add a slider to give him a pitch with lateral break. Boston has handled Bowden carefully because of his youth but envisions him as a workhorse No. 2 or 3 starter in time. He'll spend most of 2007 in high Class A and has a big league ETA of mid-2009.

| Year | Club (League) | Class | W | L | ERA | G | GS | CG | SV | IP | H | R | ER | HR | BB | SO | AVG |
|------|---------------|-------|---|---|-----|---|----|----|----|----|----|----|----|----|----|----|-----|
| 2005 | Red Sox (GCL) | R | 1 | 0 | 0.00 | 4 | 2 | 0 | 0 | 6 | 4 | 0 | 0 | 0 | 4 | 10 | .190 |
| 2006 | Greenville (SAL) | A | 9 | 6 | 3.51 | 24 | 24 | 0 | 0 | 108 | 91 | 50 | 42 | 9 | 31 | 118 | .224 |
| | Wilmington (CL) | A | 0 | 0 | 9.00 | 1 | 1 | 0 | 0 | 5 | 9 | 5 | 5 | 0 | 1 | 3 | .391 |
| **MINOR LEAGUE TOTALS** | | | 10 | 6 | 3.56 | 29 | 27 | 0 | 0 | 119 | 104 | 55 | 47 | 9 | 36 | 131 | .231 |

## 5 DANIEL BARD

RHP

**Born:** June 25, 1985. **B-T:** R-R. **Ht.:** 6-4. **Wt.:** 202. **Drafted:** North Carolina, 2006 (1st round). **Signed by:** Jeff Zona.

Lefthander Andrew Miller was the consensus top prospect in the 2006 draft, and his North Carolina teammate Bard is capable of being just as overpowering. They ranked as the top two prospects in the Cape Cod League in 2005 and pitched the Tar Heels to within a win of a national title in 2006. Both dropped slightly in the draft because of signability, with Bard going 28th overall and agreeing to a $1.55 million bonus. When Bard reported to instructional league, he touched 100 mph on multiple occasions and pitched at 95-98 mph with his fastball. His heater's combination of velocity and heavy life chews up wood bats, and he dials it up with no effort. His fastball is so good that command and secondary pitches will be less important to him than they are for other pitchers—but he does need to improve both. He'll flash a plus slider but it's inconsistent, and he's still developing feel for a changeup. Bard is a product of a major college program yet still very much a project. The Red Sox will try to turn him into a frontline starter, but with his fastball alone he could be an effective reliever.

| Year | Club (League) | Class | W | L | ERA | G | GS | CG | SV | IP | H | R | ER | HR | BB | SO | AVG |
|------|---------------|-------|---|---|-----|---|----|----|----|----|----|----|----|----|----|----|-----|
| 2006 | Did not play—Signed 2007 contract | | | | | | | | | | | | | | | | |

## 6 LARS ANDERSON

1B

**Born:** Sept. 25, 1987. **B-T:** L-L. **Ht.:** 6-5. **Wt.:** 190. **Drafted:** HS—Carmichael, Calif., 2006 (18th round). **Signed by:** Blair Henry.

Power hitters were the biggest need in the farm system, and the Red Sox hope they addressed that in the draft. The best in the crop is Anderson, who led California high schoolers with 15 homers last spring. A supplemental first-round talent, he fell to the 18th round because of his price tag and signed for $825,000. Anderson doesn't just have tape-measure power, but he generates it with ease. One scout compared him to Carlos Delgado for his ability to flip the barrel at the ball and have it explode off his bat. There's room for more strength on his 6-foot-5 frame, and for a power hitter he has a short swing and good approach. He sees the ball well and uses the opposite field already. He's a solid athlete. Anderson has to work on his defense, though he has the hands and footwork to become at least an average first baseman. Once he fills out, he'll be a below-average runner but shouldn't be a baseclogger. Anderson could make his pro debut in low Class A Greenville as a 19-year-old. The Sox can't wait to see what he does in game action.

| Year | Club (League) | Class | AVG | G | AB | R | H | 2B | 3B | HR | RBI | BB | SO | SB | OBP | SLG |
|------|---------------|-------|-----|---|----|---|---|----|----|----|-----|----|----|----|-----|-----|
| 2006 | Did not play—Signed 2007 contract | | | | | | | | | | | | | | | |

## 7 DUSTIN PEDROIA

SS/2B

**Born:** Aug. 17, 1983. **B-T:** R-R. **Ht.:** 5-9. **Wt.:** 180. **Drafted:** Arizona State, 2004 (2nd round). **Signed by:** Dan Madsen.

Since he was Boston's top pick (second round) in 2004, Pedroia consistently has hit .300 and stayed at shortstop in spite of scouts' belief he'll have to eventually move to second base. He continually draws David Eckstein comparisons, though he has more pop and less speed than the World Series MVP does. Pedroia has some of the best hand-eye coordination in baseball. That allows him to make consistent contact while swinging from his heels, which in turn gives him gap power. He led the Triple-

A International League by averaging just one strikeout per 18.3 plate appearances, and he fanned just seven times in 89 big league at-bats. His instincts make him an effective defender and baserunner. Surehanded, he has made just 17 errors in 301 pro games. Pedroia is undersized and needs to get stronger so he can avoid the nagging injuries (wrist and shoulder) that have bothered him the last two years. His speed, range and arm strength are all below-average, but that hasn't stopped him yet. The Red Sox signed free agent Julio Lugo to start at shortstop, but they also let Mark Loretta depart, leaving an opening at second base. That's the best fit for Pedroia, the frontrunner to claim the starting job there.

| Year | Club (League) | Class | AVG | G | AB | R | H | 2B | 3B | HR | RBI | BB | SO | SB | OBP | SLG |
|---|---|---|---|---|---|---|---|---|---|---|---|---|---|---|---|---|
| 2004 | Augusta (SAL) | A | .400 | 12 | 50 | 11 | 20 | 5 | 0 | 1 | 5 | 6 | 3 | 2 | .474 | .560 |
| | Sarasota (FSL) | A | .336 | 30 | 107 | 23 | 36 | 8 | 3 | 2 | 14 | 13 | 4 | 0 | .417 | .523 |
| 2005 | Portland (EL) | AA | .324 | 66 | 256 | 39 | 83 | 19 | 2 | 8 | 40 | 34 | 26 | 7 | .409 | .508 |
| | Pawtucket (IL) | AAA | .255 | 51 | 204 | 39 | 52 | 9 | 1 | 5 | 24 | 24 | 17 | 1 | .356 | .382 |
| 2006 | Pawtucket (IL) | AAA | .305 | 111 | 423 | 55 | 129 | 30 | 3 | 5 | 50 | 48 | 27 | 1 | .384 | .426 |
| | Boston (AL) | MLB | .191 | 31 | 89 | 5 | 17 | 4 | 0 | 2 | 7 | 7 | 7 | 0 | .258 | .303 |
| **MINOR LEAGUE TOTALS** | | | .308 | 270 | 1040 | 167 | 320 | 71 | 9 | 21 | 133 | 125 | 77 | 11 | .392 | .454 |
| **MAJOR LEAGUE TOTALS** | | | .191 | 31 | 89 | 5 | 17 | 4 | 0 | 2 | 7 | 7 | 7 | 0 | .258 | .303 |

## 8 BRYCE COX                                       RHP

**Born:** Aug. 10, 1984. **B-T:** R-R. **Ht.:** 6-4. **Wt.:** 200. **Drafted:** Rice, 2006 (3rd round). **Signed by:** Jim Robinson.

More of a third baseman at Paris (Texas) Junior College, Cox had major command issues after transferring to Rice. Then a shortened delivery suddenly clicked for him, and he posted a 0.32 ERA and a 36-4 K-BB ratio over his final 28 innings. After signing for $250,000 as a college senior, he was nearly as dominant in his pro debut. Cox' wipeout slider features so much lateral break that the Owls' Danny Lehmann, one of college baseball's top receivers, struggled to hang on to it. The Red Sox knew Cox had a 92-93 mph fastball that could touch 96, but they were surprised by how much riding life and sink the pitch has. He's working on a changeup for lefthanders, but they didn't give him much trouble in his debut, going 7-for-43 (.163) with one extra-base hit (a double). The Red Sox rushed relievers from the previous two drafts, and both Cla Meredith and Craig Hansen suffered for it. They'll try to take it slow with Cox and may start him back in high Class A. If he keeps pitching like this, though, he could reach Boston by the end of 2007.

| Year | Club (League) | Class | W | L | ERA | G | GS | CG | SV | IP | H | R | ER | HR | BB | SO | AVG |
|---|---|---|---|---|---|---|---|---|---|---|---|---|---|---|---|---|---|
| 2006 | Lowell (NYP) | A | 0 | 1 | 1.59 | 3 | 0 | 0 | 0 | 6 | 6 | 2 | 1 | 0 | 2 | 3 | .261 |
| | Wilmington (CL) | A | 2 | 0 | 0.74 | 13 | 0 | 0 | 0 | 24 | 14 | 4 | 2 | 0 | 9 | 25 | .165 |
| **MINOR LEAGUE TOTALS** | | | 2 | 1 | 0.90 | 16 | 0 | 0 | 0 | 30 | 20 | 6 | 3 | 0 | 11 | 28 | .185 |

## 9 CRAIG HANSEN                                   RHP

**Born:** Nov. 15, 1983. **B-T:** R-R. **Ht.:** 6-5. **Wt.:** 185. **Drafted:** St. John's, 2005 (1st round). **Signed by:** Ray Fagnant.

Hansen fell to the 26th overall pick in 2005 because of signability issues, then signed a four-year, $4.4 million big league contract and made his major league debut in September. The Red Sox tried to get him more minor league time in 2006 but needed him in June—and the results weren't pretty. Hansen can light up a radar gun, pitching from 93-98 mph with good boring action on his fastball. His slider was the best breaking ball in the 2005 draft, but it hasn't been the same pitch since he got to the majors. Hansen is throwing with more effort and a lower arm slot than he did in college. That has hurt his fastball command, which has led to him falling behind in counts and relying too much on his slider. He needs to solve big league lefthanders, who have hit .344 against him, either by getting back to where he was at St. John's or coming up with a changeup. More than anything, Hansen needs time to catch his breath in Triple-A. The Red Sox continue to believe he has the stuff and mentality to be their future closer.

| Year | Club (League) | Class | W | L | ERA | G | GS | CG | SV | IP | H | R | ER | HR | BB | SO | AVG |
|---|---|---|---|---|---|---|---|---|---|---|---|---|---|---|---|---|---|
| 2005 | Red Sox (GCL) | R | 1 | 0 | 0.00 | 2 | 1 | 0 | 0 | 3 | 2 | 0 | 0 | 0 | 0 | 4 | .182 |
| | Portland (EL) | AA | 0 | 0 | 0.00 | 8 | 0 | 0 | 1 | 10 | 9 | 0 | 0 | 0 | 1 | 10 | .243 |
| | Boston (AL) | MLB | 0 | 0 | 6.00 | 4 | 0 | 0 | 0 | 3 | 6 | 2 | 2 | 1 | 1 | 3 | .429 |
| 2006 | Portland (EL) | AA | 1 | 0 | 0.82 | 5 | 0 | 0 | 0 | 11 | 4 | 1 | 1 | 0 | 4 | 12 | .105 |
| | Pawtucket (IL) | AAA | 1 | 2 | 2.75 | 14 | 4 | 0 | 0 | 36 | 31 | 14 | 11 | 0 | 19 | 26 | .238 |
| | Boston (AL) | MLB | 2 | 2 | 6.63 | 38 | 0 | 0 | 0 | 38 | 46 | 32 | 28 | 5 | 15 | 30 | .305 |
| **MINOR LEAGUE TOTALS** | | | 3 | 2 | 1.81 | 29 | 5 | 0 | 1 | 60 | 46 | 15 | 12 | 0 | 24 | 52 | .213 |
| **MAJOR LEAGUE TOTALS** | | | 2 | 2 | 6.59 | 42 | 0 | 0 | 0 | 41 | 52 | 34 | 30 | 6 | 16 | 33 | .315 |

## KRIS JOHNSON                                      LHP

**Born:** Oct. 14, 1984. **B-T:** L-L. **Ht.:** 6-3. **Wt.:** 185. **Drafted:** Wichita State, 2006 (1st round supplemental). **Signed by:** Ernie Jacobs.

The Red Sox considered taking Johnson with the No. 28 pick in 2006 that they spent on Bard, and were glad to get him 12 selections later. He returned to the mound just 10 months after Tommy John surgery in April 2005. Johnson is an athletic lefthander who throws three solid-average pitches for strikes. The life on his 88-93 mph fastball makes it a swing-and-miss pitch, and he backs it up with a hard curveball and a changeup. His delivery is both sound and deceptive, and he repeats it well. Boston is making minor tweaks to get Johnson to throw on more of a downhill plane so he'll be less prone to getting under and flattening out his pitches. His delivery got out of whack late in the college season, causing him to slide slightly in the draft. His command and curveball aren't all the way back to where they were before his surgery, but should be next year. He has had no setbacks with his elbow. The Red Sox kept Johnson on a tight pitch count in his debut, but will turn him loose in 2007 with his elbow reconstruction two years behind him. He may jump to hitter-friendly Lancaster, which will be a good test of his stuff and savvy.

| Year | Club (League) | Class | W | L | ERA | G | GS | CG | SV | IP | H | R | ER | HR | BB | SO | AVG |
|------|---------------|-------|---|---|-----|---|----|----|----|----|---|---|----|----|----|----|-----|
| 2006 | Lowell (NYP) | A | 0 | 2 | 0.88 | 14 | 13 | 0 | 0 | 31 | 25 | 7 | 3 | 0 | 7 | 27 | .229 |
| **MINOR LEAGUE TOTALS** | | | 0 | 2 | 0.88 | 14 | 13 | 0 | 0 | 31 | 25 | 7 | 3 | 0 | 7 | 27 | .229 |

## JASON PLACE                                         OF

**Born:** May 8, 1988. **B-T:** R-R. **Ht.:** 6-3. **Wt.:** 205. **Drafted:** HS—Piedmont, S.C., 2006 (1st round). **Signed by:** Rob English.

The Red Sox used their top 2006 draft pick on Place, a high-ceilinged but raw high schooler—exactly the type of player they've avoided during most of Theo Epstein's tenure as general manager. Place signed for $1.3 million and was just starting to hit his stride in the Rookie-level Gulf Coast League when he was beaned, sidelining him for most of the final two weeks. Place repeatedly evokes Jeff Francoeur comparisons because of his aggressive approach and raw power. His tremendous bat speed allows him to drive the ball to all fields. He's an above-average runner and exceeded expectations defensively, showing the instincts, range and routes to possibly stay in center field. He has a plus arm that will fit easily in right if he moves there. Some clubs backed off Place in the draft because of concerns about his long-term ability to hit. He has a funny load, starting his hands in the middle of his body and circling them back into position. The Red Sox like his swing and his bat speed, and they think he'll be able to adjust. He can get overaggressive and pull-happy at the plate, which also diminishes his chances of making contact. Place returned to action and worked on his hitting mechanics in instructional league. It will take him time to adjust to each level, starting at low Class A in 2007, but his upside could well be worth the wait.

| Year | Club (League) | Class | AVG | G | AB | R | H | 2B | 3B | HR | RBI | BB | SO | SB | OBP | SLG |
|------|---------------|-------|-----|---|----|---|---|----|----|----|-----|----|----|----|-----|-----|
| 2006 | Red Sox (GCL) | R | .292 | 33 | 113 | 14 | 33 | 3 | 1 | 4 | 21 | 17 | 35 | 3 | .386 | .442 |
| **MINOR LEAGUE TOTALS** | | | .292 | 33 | 113 | 14 | 33 | 3 | 1 | 4 | 21 | 17 | 35 | 3 | .386 | .442 |

## GEORGE KOTTARAS                                      C

**Born:** May 16, 1983. **B-T:** L-R. **Ht.:** 6-0. **Wt.:** 185. **Drafted:** Connors State (Okla.) JC, D/F 2002 (20th round). **Signed by:** Lane Decker (Padres).

The Red Sox usually are trading prospects for veterans during the season, but their plunge out of contention last August led them to deal David Wells to the Padres for Kottaras. Since signing for $375,000 as a draft-and-follow in 2003, he has made steady progress toward the majors. A Canadian who played for the 2004 Greek Olympic team, Kottaras is much more advanced offensively than defensively at this point. He generates solid power with a quiet approach and simple swing, and he controls the strike zone well. He's more athletic and runs better than most catchers. While Kottaras has work to do on his catch-and-throw skills as well as his game-calling, Boston believes he just needs fine-tuning rather than a complete overhaul. He has enough arm strength and hands to get the job done, and he spent a lot of time in instructional league and the Arizona Fall League working with field coordinator Rob Leary on his defense. Kottaras projects as a lefthanded-hitting catcher who will provide offense and fringy to average defense. In order to become a regular, he'll have to add strength so he can hold up over a full season. The Red Sox re-signed Doug Mirabelli to back up Jason Varitek, a positive move for Kottaras' development. He'll be best served by getting regular at-bats in Triple-A for at least half a season.

| Year | Club (League) | Class | AVG | G | AB | R | H | 2B | 3B | HR | RBI | BB | SO | SB | OBP | SLG |
|------|---------------|-------|-----|---|----|---|---|----|----|----|-----|----|----|----|-----|-----|
| 2003 | Idaho Falls (Pio) | R | .259 | 42 | 143 | 27 | 37 | 8 | 1 | 7 | 24 | 19 | 36 | 1 | .348 | .476 |
| 2004 | Fort Wayne (MWL) | A | .310 | 78 | 271 | 40 | 84 | 18 | 1 | 7 | 46 | 51 | 41 | 0 | .415 | .461 |
| 2005 | Lake Elsinore (Cal) | A | .303 | 91 | 337 | 54 | 102 | 29 | 0 | 9 | 50 | 50 | 60 | 2 | .390 | .469 |
|  | Mobile (SL) | AA | .287 | 29 | 101 | 16 | 29 | 7 | 0 | 2 | 15 | 19 | 23 | 0 | .397 | .416 |
| 2006 | Mobile (SL) | AA | .276 | 78 | 257 | 40 | 71 | 19 | 1 | 8 | 33 | 50 | 68 | 0 | .394 | .451 |
|  | Portland (PCL) | AAA | .210 | 33 | 119 | 14 | 25 | 10 | 1 | 2 | 17 | 12 | 30 | 0 | .286 | .361 |
| **MINOR LEAGUE TOTALS** | | | .283 | 351 | 1228 | 191 | 348 | 91 | 4 | 35 | 185 | 201 | 258 | 3 | .383 | .450 |

## 13 JUSTIN MASTERSON
RHP

**Born:** March 22, 1985. **B-T:** R-R. **Ht.:** 6-6. **Wt.:** 245. **Drafted:** San Diego State, 2006 (2nd round). **Signed by:** Dan Madsen.

Masterson was a second-round pick in 2006 after being anonymous a year earlier. He was primarily a catcher until his junior year in high school and spent his first two seasons in college at NAIA Bethel (Ind.). He gained notoriety in the Cape Cod League in the summer of 2005, when scouts fell in love with his huge frame and hard sinker/slider combination. After he signed for $510,000, the Red Sox kept Masterson in the bullpen and on short pitch counts because he logged 116 innings in the spring at San Diego State. He excelled in that role, just as he did on the Cape. Masterson throws from a low three-quarters angle that generates so much life on his pitches that he can be tough to catch. His out pitch is an 89-92 mph fastball that touches 94 and is more notable for its heavy sink and his ability to command it. He put up eye-popping numbers in his debut, including a 0.85 ERA, 33-2 K-BB ratio and 45-16 ground-fly ratio. His slider is a decent pitch with promise, though Boston had him scrap it in instructional league to focus on his changeup. He showed good feel for the changeup, and the Sox think he can develop three pitches and will use him as a starter until he shows a need to do otherwise. If he returns to the bullpen, he has the out pitch and poise to be a set-up man and possibly a closer. Rotation spots could be in short supply at Lancaster, so Masterson may open his first full season in low Class A.

| Year | Club (League) | Class | W | L | ERA | G | GS | CG | SV | IP | H | R | ER | HR | BB | SO | AVG |
|------|---------------|-------|---|---|-----|---|----|----|----|----|---|---|----|----|----|----|-----|
| 2006 | Lowell (NYP) | A | 3 | 1 | 0.85 | 14 | 0 | 0 | 0 | 32 | 20 | 4 | 3 | 0 | 2 | 33 | .174 |
| **MINOR LEAGUE TOTALS** | | | 3 | 1 | 0.85 | 14 | 0 | 0 | 0 | 32 | 20 | 4 | 3 | 0 | 2 | 33 | .174 |

## 14 BRANDON MOSS
OF

**Born:** Sept. 16, 1983. **B-T:** L-R. **Ht.:** 6-0. **Wt.:** 195. **Drafted:** HS—Monroe, Ga., 2002 (8th round). **Signed by:** Rob English.

The low Class A South Atlantic League MVP and batting champ in 2004, Moss has spent the last two years in Double-A in search of offensive consistency. He can fall into extended cold periods and began 2006 by hitting .221 with three homers in the first two months. He's also capable of carrying a team when he heats up, and he batted .324 with nine homers over the final three months. He was the Eastern League playoff MVP, batting .361 with five homers in nine games as Portland won the championship. Moss has a quick bat and strong hands, so he can drive the ball from left-center to right field. He led the EL in doubles and the Red Sox think he could hit 20-25 homers in a big league park that plays to his strengths, though Fenway Park doesn't fit that description. He cut down on his strikeouts in his second tour of Double-A and improved defensively in right field, where he has one of the better outfield arms in the system. He's a slightly below-average runner. Despite repeating a level, Moss will play in Triple-A at age 23 and could push for an everyday job in Boston in 2008.

| Year | Club (League) | Class | AVG | G | AB | R | H | 2B | 3B | HR | RBI | BB | SO | SB | OBP | SLG |
|------|---------------|-------|-----|---|----|---|---|----|----|----|-----|----|----|----|-----|-----|
| 2002 | Red Sox (GCL) | R | .204 | 42 | 113 | 10 | 23 | 6 | 2 | 0 | 6 | 13 | 40 | 1 | .295 | .292 |
| 2003 | Lowell (NYP) | A | .237 | 65 | 228 | 29 | 54 | 15 | 4 | 7 | 34 | 15 | 53 | 7 | .290 | .430 |
| 2004 | Augusta (SAL) | A | .339 | 109 | 433 | 66 | 147 | 25 | 6 | 13 | 101 | 46 | 75 | 19 | .402 | .515 |
|  | Sarasota (FSL) | A | .422 | 23 | 83 | 16 | 35 | 2 | 1 | 2 | 10 | 7 | 15 | 2 | .462 | .542 |
| 2005 | Portland (EL) | AA | .268 | 135 | 503 | 87 | 135 | 31 | 4 | 16 | 61 | 53 | 129 | 6 | .337 | .441 |
| 2006 | Portland (EL) | AA | .285 | 133 | 508 | 76 | 145 | 36 | 3 | 12 | 83 | 56 | 108 | 8 | .357 | .439 |
| **MINOR LEAGUE TOTALS** | | | .289 | 507 | 1868 | 284 | 539 | 115 | 20 | 50 | 295 | 190 | 420 | 43 | .355 | .452 |

## 15 DAVID MURPHY
OF

**Born:** Oct. 18, 1981. **B-T:** L-L. **Ht.:** 6-4. **Wt.:** 192. **Drafted:** Baylor, 2003 (1st round). **Signed by:** Jim Robinson.

When the Red Sox made Murphy the 17th overall pick in the 2003 draft, they hoped he'd be ready to take over in center field when Johnny Damon's contract expired two years later. That didn't come to fruition, though Murphy did make his big league debut in 2006, highlighted by a homer off Jaret Wright. Whether he becomes a major league regular probably will depend on how much he can tap into his raw power. Murphy is capable of driving balls

400-450 feet in batting practice, but in games he uses an easy, level swing designed more for contact and doesn't attack the ball. If he adds loft and gets more aggressive, he could hit 20-plus homers annually. Murphy has come further with his defense in pro ball after playing right field in college. He has shown he can handle center field, where his average speed plays up thanks to his instincts and positioning. He could wind up as a tweener, however, because his bat fits better in center while his defense is more suited for right. The Red Sox had all but finalized a deal with J.D. Drew, which would close off the possibility that Murphy would platoon with Wily Mo Pena in right field. He'll try to help Boston as a useful reserve instead.

| Year | Club (League) | Class | AVG | G | AB | R | H | 2B | 3B | HR | RBI | BB | SO | SB | OBP | SLG |
|---|---|---|---|---|---|---|---|---|---|---|---|---|---|---|---|---|
| 2003 | Lowell (NYP) | A | .346 | 21 | 78 | 13 | 27 | 4 | 0 | 0 | 13 | 16 | 9 | 4 | .453 | .397 |
| | Sarasota (FSL) | A | .242 | 45 | 153 | 18 | 37 | 5 | 1 | 1 | 18 | 20 | 33 | 6 | .329 | .307 |
| 2004 | Red Sox (GCL) | R | .278 | 5 | 18 | 3 | 5 | 1 | 0 | 0 | 1 | 1 | 2 | 1 | .316 | .333 |
| | Sarasota (FSL) | A | .261 | 73 | 272 | 35 | 71 | 11 | 0 | 4 | 38 | 25 | 46 | 3 | .323 | .346 |
| 2005 | Portland (EL) | AA | .275 | 135 | 484 | 71 | 133 | 25 | 4 | 14 | 75 | 46 | 83 | 13 | .337 | .430 |
| 2006 | Pawtucket (IL) | AAA | .267 | 84 | 318 | 45 | 85 | 23 | 5 | 8 | 44 | 45 | 53 | 3 | .355 | .447 |
| | Portland (EL) | AA | .273 | 42 | 172 | 22 | 47 | 17 | 1 | 3 | 25 | 11 | 29 | 4 | .315 | .436 |
| | Boston (AL) | MLB | .227 | 20 | 22 | 4 | 5 | 1 | 0 | 1 | 2 | 4 | 4 | 0 | .346 | .409 |
| **MINOR LEAGUE TOTALS** | | | .271 | 405 | 1495 | 207 | 405 | 86 | 11 | 30 | 214 | 164 | 255 | 34 | .342 | .403 |
| **MAJOR LEAGUE TOTALS** | | | .227 | 20 | 22 | 4 | 5 | 1 | 0 | 1 | 2 | 4 | 4 | 0 | .346 | .409 |

## 16 JED LOWRIE                                                            SS

**Born:** April 17, 1984. **B-T:** B-R. **Ht.:** 6-0. **Wt.:** 180. **Drafted:** Stanford, 2005 (1st round supplemental). **Signed by:** Nakia Hill.

Lowrie had the best pro debut among Boston's 2005 draftees and showed a better righthanded swing and shortstop defense than the Red Sox expected. His first full pro season didn't go as well. He was hitting just .227 when a high ankle sprain on May 1 sidelined him for five weeks, and he didn't regain his 2005 form until mid-August. Lowrie pressed and lost confidence when he began the year in a slump, and it was worrisome that it took him so long to recover. He continued to produce similar numbers from both sides of the plate, so it wasn't a matter of his righty stroke regressing. Wilmington's Frawley Stadium is a tough hitter's park that muted his power, but Lowrie has double-digit home run pop. He'll need to do a better job of maintaining his strength through the six-month grind of pro ball. He has the hands and arm to stay at shortstop, but his speed is just average and he doesn't have the quickness and range to stay there. He committed 25 errors in 88 games at short last year despite a reputation for being fundamentally sound. Boston knows he can handle second base due to his experience there at Stanford. He'll probably move up to Double-A in 2007, when he'll try to erase doubts about whether he profiles as a regular on a contender.

| Year | Club (League) | Class | AVG | G | AB | R | H | 2B | 3B | HR | RBI | BB | SO | SB | OBP | SLG |
|---|---|---|---|---|---|---|---|---|---|---|---|---|---|---|---|---|
| 2005 | Lowell (NYP) | A | .328 | 53 | 201 | 36 | 66 | 12 | 0 | 4 | 32 | 34 | 30 | 7 | .429 | .448 |
| 2006 | Wilmington (CL) | A | .262 | 97 | 374 | 43 | 98 | 21 | 6 | 3 | 50 | 54 | 65 | 2 | .352 | .374 |
| **MINOR LEAGUE TOTALS** | | | .285 | 150 | 575 | 79 | 164 | 33 | 6 | 7 | 82 | 88 | 95 | 9 | .379 | .400 |

## 17 RYAN KALISH                                                          OF

**Born:** March 28, 1988. **B-T:** L-L. **Ht.:** 6-1. **Wt.:** 205. **Drafted:** HS—Red Bank, N.J., 2006 (9th round). **Signed by:** Ray Fagnant.

Kalish fell to the ninth round in June because of signability questions, but when he learned Boston had selected him right before he received his high school diploma, he quickly swapped his mortarboard for a Sox cap. Kalish agreed to terms for $600,000. He was a three-sport star in high school who had a baseball scholarship to Virginia. Boston is confident that Kalish will hit, because he has a good set-up and a sweet lefthanded strokie. He didn't swing and miss at a single pitch as a high school senior. His numbers in his pro debut were lackluster, but he was coming off a long layoff and most of his at-bats came in the New York-Penn League against more experienced pitchers. Kalish has some pull power, but he doesn't have a lot of leverage in his swing and is more liable to drive the ball in the gaps. He's a plus runner who has the range to play center field and the arm strength to throw out runners from right. He's a high-energy player who loves to be on the diamond. The Red Sox showed that they're not shy about challenging Kalish when they sent him to the NY-P, and they also had him spend time in their Dominican instructional league to broaden his horizons. They could test him again in 2007 by sending him to low Class A.

| Year | Club (League) | Class | AVG | G | AB | R | H | 2B | 3B | HR | RBI | BB | SO | SB | OBP | SLG |
|---|---|---|---|---|---|---|---|---|---|---|---|---|---|---|---|---|
| 2006 | Red Sox (GCL) | R | .300 | 6 | 20 | 6 | 6 | 2 | 0 | 1 | 2 | 1 | 2 | 0 | .333 | .550 |
| | Lowell (NYP) | A | .200 | 11 | 35 | 8 | 7 | 0 | 1 | 0 | 4 | 2 | 14 | 2 | .275 | .257 |
| **MINOR LEAGUE TOTALS** | | | .236 | 17 | 55 | 14 | 13 | 2 | 1 | 1 | 6 | 3 | 16 | 2 | .295 | .364 |

## 18 FELIX DOUBRONT
LHP

**Born:** Oct. 23, 1987. **B-T:** L-L. **Ht.:** 6-2. **Wt.:** 166. **Signed:** Venezuela, 2004. **Signed by:** Miguel Garcia.

Signed for $150,000, Doubront broke into pro ball by going 7-1, 0.97 in the Rookie-level Venezuelan Summer League and winning the organization's minor league Latin pitcher of the year award in 2005. He continued to succeed in his stateside debut last season, capping it by winning two starts in the New York-Penn League as an 18-year-old. Doubront has the best arm action in the system. His arm works so clean and easy that he can pound both sides of the plate with his fastball better than most teenagers. Doubront's fastball ranges from 86-91 mph, and he likes to throw his two-seamer to get grounders so much that the Red Sox have to remind him to use his four-seamer to dial up velocity. Like his fastball command, his changeup is advanced for his age. His curveball is his third pitch, but there's some power to it and it should become a solid-average offering once he tightens it. Doubront didn't miss a lot of bats in 2006, when he led the Gulf Coast League in both opponent average and home runs allowed, but should become more of a strikeout pitcher as his body and his stuff mature. He's ready for low Class A and could reach Boston by the end of 2009.

| Year | Club (League) | Class | W | L | ERA | G | GS | CG | SV | IP | H | R | ER | HR | BB | SO | AVG |
|------|---------------|-------|---|---|-----|---|----|----|----|----|---|---|----|----|----|----|-----|
| 2005 | Red Sox (VSL) | R | 7 | 1 | 0.97 | 13 | 13 | 0 | 0 | 65 | 32 | 11 | 7 | 0 | 29 | 58 | .152 |
| 2006 | Red Sox (GCL) | R | 2 | 3 | 2.52 | 11 | 11 | 0 | 0 | 54 | 41 | 17 | 15 | 6 | 13 | 36 | .212 |
|  | Lowell (NYP) | A | 2 | 0 | 4.91 | 2 | 2 | 0 | 0 | 11 | 7 | 6 | 6 | 1 | 3 | 7 | .179 |
| **MINOR LEAGUE TOTALS** | | | 11 | 4 | 1.95 | 26 | 26 | 0 | 0 | 129 | 80 | 34 | 28 | 7 | 45 | 101 | .181 |

## 19 CALEB CLAY
RHP

**Born:** Feb. 15, 1988. **B-T:** R-R. **Ht.:** 6-2. **Wt.:** 180. **Drafted:** HS—Cullman, Ala., 2006 (1st round supplemental). **Signed by:** Danny Watkins.

Clay was such an obscure prospect at the outset of 2006 that he wasn't even on Boston's draft follow list, but teams quickly flocked to see him once he moved from center field to the mound and started throwing low-90s fastballs. In the Alabama 5-A playoffs, he struck out 10 and hit three homers in a second-round doubleheader. Clay signed for $775,000 two days after Boston drafted him but didn't pitch during the summer because of his heavy workload during the spring. Clay's fastball comes out of his hand easily and features late, heavy life. While he has a fresh arm, he's also raw as a pitcher. He didn't have much of a between-starts routine or know much about a shoulder-strengthening program before he got into pro ball. His mechanics graded out well, though he doesn't always repeat his delivery. He can fly open and drop his shoulder, which elevates and flattens out his pitches. Clay's secondary pitches are promising yet unrefined. He used both a curveball and slider as an amateur, and likely will stick with the slider as a pro. His changeup, control and command are still inconsistent. The Red Sox will be patient with him, which means he'll probably open 2007 in extended spring training before making his pro debut.

| Year | Club (League) | Class | W | L | ERA | G | GS | CG | SV | IP | H | R | ER | HR | BB | SO | AVG |
|------|---------------|-------|---|---|-----|---|----|----|----|----|---|---|----|----|----|----|-----|
| 2006 | Did not play—Signed 2007 contract | | | | | | | | | | | | | | | | |

## 20 ENGEL BELTRE
OF

**Born:** Nov. 1, 1989. **B-T:** L-L. **Ht.:** 6-1. **Wt.:** 165. **Signed:** Dominican Republic, 2006. **Signed by:** Pablo Lantigua.

Besides all the talent they signed out of the 2006 draft, the Red Sox also are excited about a pair of Dominicans they landed for a combined $1.125 million during the summer: Beltre and shortstop Oscar Tejada. Said one international scouting director of Beltre, who signed for $600,000: "Beltre to me is a young Barry Bonds—all five tools. He can do it all. He's going to be terrifying when he fills into that body." Barry Bonds comparisons are hyperbole at this point for a 17-year-old who has yet to get a pro plate appearance, though another scout likened him to Darryl Strawberry. Beltre's most enticing tool is his power potential. He has a solid swing with natural loft, and his hands whip the bat through the strike zone. He also has more plate discipline than most young Latin American players. Beltre has above-average speed and arm strength. If he doesn't stick in center field, he still profiles well in right field. He spent some of his youth in New York, so he speaks English and is comfortable in the United States. He's years from the majors and needs a lot of physical maturity, but the Red Sox can't wait to see what Beltre does in the Gulf Coast League this summer.

| Year | Club (League) | Class | AVG | G | AB | R | H | 2B | 3B | HR | RBI | BB | SO | SB | OBP | SLG |
|------|---------------|-------|-----|---|----|---|---|----|----|----|-----|----|----|----|-----|-----|
| 2006 | Did not play—Signed 2007 contract | | | | | | | | | | | | | | | |

## HIDEKI OKAJIMA
LHP

**Born:** Dec. 25, 1975. **B-T:** L-L. **Ht.:** 6-1. **Wt.:** 195. **Signed:** Japan, 2006. **Signed by:** Craig Shipley/Jon Deeble.

The Red Sox' quest for relievers took them to Japan, where they signed Okajima with far less fanfare than surrounded Daisuke Matsuzaka. Because he had nine years of service time, Okajima was a free agent who didn't have to be posted. He signed a two-year contract with annual salaries of $1.25 million and a $1.75 million club option for 2009. Other clubs offered more money, but he signed with the Sox in part because they were the first team to show interest. Okajima is a versatile pitcher who served as a starter, middle reliever, set-up man and closer in Japan, where he was a key cog in Japan Series championship teams in 2000, '02 and '06. His best pitch is an overhand curveball that's tough on lefties. He doesn't throw hard, operating in the mid- to high 80s and topping out at 91, but his fastball is effective because he can locate it to both sides of the plate. He keeps righties honest by throwing two versions of a splitter, one for strikes and another as a chase pitch. His command has improved in the last two years as he has done a better job of keeping his focus on the plate during his delivery. Boston lacked reliable southpaw relievers for most of last season, and the organization believes Okajima can serve as more than a situational lefty. At the least, he'll help ease Matsuzaka's transition to the United States.

| Year | Club (League) | Class | W | L | ERA | G | GS | CG | SV | IP | H | R | ER | HR | BB | SO | AVG |
|------|---------------|-------|---|---|-----|---|----|----|----|-----|-----|-----|-----|----|-----|-----|------|
| 1995 | Yomiuri (CL) | JAP | 0 | 0 | 1.80 | 1 | 1 | 0 | 0 | 5 | 5 | 1 | 1 | 0 | 2 | 9 | .278 |
| 1996 | Yomiuri (CL) | JAP | 1 | 0 | 0.71 | 5 | 1 | 0 | 0 | 13 | 13 | 2 | 1 | 0 | 9 | 8 | .260 |
| 1997 | Yomiuri (CL) | JAP | 4 | 9 | 3.46 | 25 | 21 | 2 | 0 | 109 | 92 | 47 | 42 | 7 | 59 | 102 | .229 |
| 1998 | Yomiuri (CL) | JAP | 3 | 6 | 4.33 | 14 | 12 | 0 | 0 | 62 | 61 | 31 | 30 | 7 | 32 | 54 | .263 |
| 1999 | Yomiuri (CL) | JAP | 4 | 1 | 2.97 | 37 | 3 | 0 | 0 | 70 | 42 | 25 | 23 | 6 | 28 | 77 | .173 |
| 2000 | Yomiuri (CL) | JAP | 5 | 4 | 3.11 | 56 | 0 | 0 | 7 | 72 | 53 | 26 | 25 | 4 | 31 | 102 | .203 |
| 2001 | Yomiuri (CL) | JAP | 2 | 1 | 2.76 | 58 | 0 | 0 | 25 | 62 | 62 | 21 | 19 | 5 | 39 | 70 | .271 |
| 2002 | Yomiuri (CL) | JAP | 6 | 3 | 3.40 | 52 | 0 | 0 | 0 | 56 | 42 | 21 | 21 | 8 | 22 | 58 | .211 |
| 2003 | Yomiuri (CL) | JAP | 2 | 3 | 4.89 | 41 | 0 | 0 | 0 | 39 | 45 | 22 | 21 | 6 | 20 | 29 | .296 |
| 2004 | Yomiuri (CL) | JAP | 4 | 3 | 3.09 | 53 | 0 | 0 | 5 | 47 | 33 | 16 | 16 | 5 | 20 | 53 | .193 |
| 2005 | Yomiuri (CL) | JAP | 1 | 0 | 4.75 | 42 | 0 | 0 | 0 | 53 | 55 | 31 | 28 | 10 | 19 | 56 | .271 |
| 2006 | Hokkaido (PL) | JAP | 2 | 2 | 2.14 | 55 | 0 | 0 | 4 | 55 | 46 | 14 | 13 | 5 | 14 | 63 | .230 |
| **JAPANESE TOTALS** | | | 34 | 32 | 3.36 | 439 | 38 | 2 | 41 | 642 | 549 | 257 | 240 | 63 | 295 | 681 | .233 |

## OSCAR TEJADA
SS

**Born:** Dec. 12, 1989. **B-T:** R-R. **Ht.:** 6-1. **Wt.:** 170. **Signed:** Dominican Republic, 2006. **Signed by:** Luis Scheker.

Tejada, who signed for $525,000, also drew praise from the same scouting director who compared Engel Beltre to Barry Bonds: "Tejada is Alfonso Soriano with better hands. And he just rakes." Tejada is similar to Soriano in that he has a wiry build and loads of righthanded power potential—though he's also years from realizing it. Tejada runs well, albeit not as well as Soriano, but he's a better defender. He has strong hands and his bat flies through the hitting zone. He also has an aptitude for contact, so he may produce for both power and average. Tejada's arm rated as big league average when he was 14, and it already ranks as the strongest in the Red Sox system. He also has good range and reliable hands. He's not as polished and doesn't speak English as well as Beltre, but Tejada does have some aptitude for the language. He'll get a chance to make the Gulf Coast League roster in 2007.

| Year | Club (League) | Class | AVG | G | AB | R | H | 2B | 3B | HR | RBI | BB | SO | SB | OBP | SLG |
|------|---------------|-------|-----|---|----|----|----|----|----|----|-----|----|----|----|-----|-----|
| 2006 | Did not play—Signed 2007 contract | | | | | | | | | | | | | | | |

## DEVERN HANSACK
RHP

**Born:** Feb. 5, 1978. **B-T:** R-R. **Ht.:** 6-2. **Wt.:** 180. **Signed:** Nicaragua, 1999. **Signed by:** Andres Reiner (Astros).

Hansack signed with the Astros in 1999 and advanced to low Class A before being released in spring training five years later. Houston had discovered that he was more than four years older than originally believed, but they cut him for undisclosed off-field reasons. He spent two years as a lobster fisherman in his native Nicaragua until Red Sox vice president of international scouting Craig Shipley spotted him pitching at the 2005 World Cup in the Netherlands. Hansack signed as a minor league free agent and spent most of the first half of 2006 as a reliever in Double-A. He pitched himself into Portland's rotation and won the game that clinched the Eastern League championship. Hansack's season got even better, when he was promoted to Boston to make two starts. On the final day of the season, he twirled a five-inning no-hitter against the Orioles. Hansack's fastball sits at 90-92 mph and peaks at 94, and he gets swings and misses with his slider. He likes to vary his arm angles in a manner remi-

niscent of Orlando Hernandez, making him deceptive. He pitched nearly year-round in Nicaragua during his two-year layoff from pro ball, a testament to the resiliency of his arm. He's a fearless competitor who appreciates his second chance and has addressed his off-field issues. Hansack's changeup is a fringy third pitch that he was reluctant to use in the minors, though he seemed to trust it more in the majors. Not only will he come to big league camp in 2007, there's a chance that he could fill Boston's void at closer. More likely, he'll contribute as a middle reliever and spot starter.

| Year | Club (League) | Class | W | L | ERA | G | GS | CG | SV | IP | H | R | ER | HR | BB | SO | AVG |
|------|---------------|-------|---|---|-----|---|----|----|----|----|---|---|----|----|----|----|-----|
| 2000 | Venoco (VSL) | R | 1 | 2 | 2.67 | 8 | 4 | 1 | 2 | 27 | 14 | 9 | 8 | 0 | 6 | 20 | .154 |
| 2001 | Venoco (VSL) | R | 2 | 3 | 4.98 | 13 | 0 | 0 | 2 | 22 | 23 | 14 | 12 | 0 | 8 | 13 | — |
| 2002 | Tri-City (NYP) | A | 3 | 4 | 3.60 | 12 | 10 | 0 | 0 | 50 | 44 | 21 | 20 | 6 | 17 | 37 | .240 |
| 2003 | Lexington (SAL) | A | 10 | 6 | 4.52 | 22 | 16 | 0 | 0 | 92 | 100 | 53 | 46 | 10 | 32 | 76 | .279 |
| 2004 | Did not play | | | | | | | | | | | | | | | | |
| 2005 | Did not play | | | | | | | | | | | | | | | | |
| 2006 | Portland (EL) | AA | 8 | 7 | 3.26 | 31 | 18 | 0 | 1 | 132 | 122 | 55 | 48 | 14 | 36 | 124 | .242 |
| | Boston (AL) | MLB | 1 | 1 | 2.70 | 2 | 2 | 1 | 0 | 10 | 6 | 3 | 3 | 2 | 1 | 8 | .171 |
| **MINOR LEAGUE TOTALS** | | | 24 | 22 | 3.74 | 86 | 48 | 1 | 5 | 323 | 303 | 152 | 134 | 30 | 99 | 270 | .266 |
| **MAJOR LEAGUE TOTALS** | | | 1 | 1 | 2.70 | 2 | 2 | 1 | 0 | 10 | 6 | 3 | 3 | 2 | 1 | 8 | .171 |

## 24 JON EGAN C

**Born:** Oct. 12, 1986. **B-T:** R-R. **Ht.:** 6-4. **Wt.:** 210. **Drafted:** HS—Hephzibah, Ga., 2005 (2nd round). **Signed by:** Rob English.

Drafted primarily for his power potential, Egan looked sluggish and tentative at the plate in 2005. Things got worse in September, when police arrested him for driving while intoxicated and found traces of cocaine in his wallet. The Red Sox say it was an isolated incident, and he entered a counseling program and apologized to his instructional league teammates. Egan looked like an entirely different hitter in 2006. He possesses raw power similar to Lars Anderson's, and it was more evident once he stopped taking so many hittable pitches. He looked much more comfortable against pro pitching and did a better job of keeping his strength through the summer. When Egan was coming out of high school, some clubs viewed him as a masher who would have to move to first base, but his defense has been a pleasant surprise. Though he's 6-foot-4 and 210 pounds, he moves well behind the plate and has better receiving skills than anticipated. He has a strong arm but his big frame hampers his release and his pop times (mitt to glove at second base) are a mediocre 2-2.15 seconds. He still threw out 33 percent of basestealers last year. After two seasons in Rookie and short-season leagues, Egan is ready for low Class A in 2007.

| Year | Club (League) | Class | AVG | G | AB | R | H | 2B | 3B | HR | RBI | BB | SO | SB | OBP | SLG |
|------|---------------|-------|-----|---|----|---|---|----|----|----|-----|----|----|----|-----|-----|
| 2005 | Red Sox (GCL) | R | .222 | 35 | 126 | 19 | 28 | 6 | 0 | 1 | 15 | 21 | 29 | 0 | .340 | .294 |
| 2006 | Red Sox (GCL) | R | .339 | 37 | 127 | 22 | 43 | 10 | 3 | 4 | 19 | 13 | 36 | 0 | .400 | .559 |
| | Lowell (NYP) | A | .083 | 4 | 12 | 2 | 1 | 1 | 0 | 0 | 1 | 1 | 5 | 0 | .214 | .167 |
| **MINOR LEAGUE TOTALS** | | | .272 | 76 | 265 | 43 | 72 | 17 | 3 | 5 | 35 | 35 | 70 | 0 | .362 | .415 |

## 25 AARON BATES 1B

**Born:** March 10, 1984. **B-T:** R-R. **Ht.:** 6-4. **Wt.:** 232. **Drafted:** North Carolina State, 2006 (3rd round). **Signed by:** Jeff Zona.

The Marlins couldn't sign Bates as an eighth-rounder in 2005, when he was a draft-eligible sophomore and won the home run derby at the Cape Cod League all-star game. One of several hitters targeted by the Red Sox as they looked to add power in the 2006 draft, he got a $440,000 bonus as a third-rounder. Bates is a polished hitter with an advanced approach, a quick bat and excellent plate coverage. He uses the entire field and has the raw power to hit the ball out of any part of the park. He has produced more for average because he has a level stroke, but the home runs should come if he can add loft. He used to have a high leg kick that lengthened his swing and worried some scouts, but he has modified it after approaching the Red Sox about it toward the end of his pro debut. Bates looked tired late in the summer, which affected his approach, so he'll need to work on his conditioning. He's a below-average runner. He has the work ethic and desire to be at least an average defender and presents a big target at first base. He spent most of his first pro summer in low Class A, so he'll probably go to Lancaster, where he could thrive at hitter-friendly Clear Channel Stadium.

| Year | Club (League) | Class | AVG | G | AB | R | H | 2B | 3B | HR | RBI | BB | SO | SB | OBP | SLG |
|------|---------------|-------|-----|---|----|---|---|----|----|----|-----|----|----|----|-----|-----|
| 2006 | Greenville (SAL) | A | .270 | 43 | 152 | 13 | 41 | 7 | 0 | 4 | 16 | 17 | 26 | 0 | .351 | .395 |
| | Lowell (NYP) | A | .360 | 27 | 100 | 17 | 36 | 8 | 0 | 3 | 14 | 9 | 21 | 2 | .436 | .530 |
| **MINOR LEAGUE TOTALS** | | | .306 | 70 | 252 | 30 | 77 | 15 | 0 | 7 | 30 | 26 | 47 | 2 | .385 | .448 |

## 26 EDGAR MARTINEZ
RHP

**Born:** Oct. 23, 1981. **B-T:** R-R. **Ht.:** 6-0. **Wt.:** 222. **Signed:** Venezuela, 1998. **Signed by:** Levy Ochoa.

The Red Sox decided in mid-2004 that Martinez' arm strength gave him a better chance of making it to the majors on the mound, and he has progressed quickly for a pitcher who spent most of his first six years in pro ball as a catcher. But his development slowed last year, and while Boston had plenty of bullpen holes, Martinez stayed in Double-A for the entire season. Lackadaisical conditioning was the biggest culprit, as he resembled former Boston folk hero Rich Garces by packing a lot more than his listed 222 pounds on a 6-foot frame. Because he wasn't in good shape, Martinez lost 2-3 mph off his fastball, pitching at 91-92 and touching 94. His secondary pitches still lack consistency, though his slider is an average pitch at times. He hasn't shown much feel for a changeup. Martinez still had success in Double-A working mainly with a plus fastball because of his command and deception. He's headed for Triple-A, and if he can do a better job of preparing physically and develop a reliable slider, he'll get the call to Boston.

| Year | Club (League) | Class | AVG | G | AB | R | H | 2B | 3B | HR | RBI | BB | SO | SB | OBP | SLG |
|------|---------------|-------|-----|---|----|---|---|----|----|----|-----|----|----|----|-----|-----|
| 1999 | Red Sox (GCL) | R | .239 | 33 | 113 | 12 | 27 | 3 | 0 | 1 | 20 | 9 | 13 | 1 | .292 | .301 |
| 2000 | Augusta (SAL) | A | .100 | 16 | 50 | 4 | 5 | 1 | 0 | 1 | 4 | 3 | 13 | 0 | .180 | .167 |
| | Red Sox (GCL) | R | .168 | 35 | 119 | 12 | 20 | 3 | 0 | 3 | 14 | 5 | 23 | 0 | .269 | .225 |
| 2001 | Lowell (NYP) | A | .320 | 49 | 175 | 21 | 56 | 12 | 2 | 3 | 25 | 10 | 23 | 1 | .463 | .370 |
| 2002 | Augusta (SAL) | A | .249 | 77 | 265 | 30 | 66 | 13 | 1 | 2 | 29 | 19 | 34 | 1 | .328 | .314 |
| 2003 | Sarasota (FSL) | A | .201 | 66 | 199 | 17 | 40 | 6 | 0 | 0 | 11 | 13 | 24 | 6 | .231 | .263 |
| 2004 | Portland (EL) | AA | .163 | 53 | 141 | 9 | 23 | 3 | 0 | 1 | 10 | 3 | 20 | 0 | .206 | .207 |
| **MINOR LEAGUE TOTALS** | | | .223 | 329 | 1062 | 105 | 237 | 41 | 3 | 11 | 113 | 62 | 150 | 9 | .298 | .282 |

| Year | Club (League) | Class | W | L | ERA | G | GS | CG | SV | IP | H | R | ER | HR | BB | SO | AVG |
|------|---------------|-------|---|---|-----|---|----|----|----|----|---|---|----|----|----|----|-----|
| 2004 | Augusta (SAL) | A | 0 | 0 | 0.90 | 9 | 0 | 0 | 0 | 10 | 8 | 1 | 1 | 0 | 4 | 5 | .211 |
| 2005 | Wilmington (CAR) | A | 1 | 1 | 2.10 | 28 | 0 | 0 | 7 | 34 | 20 | 10 | 8 | 3 | 12 | 46 | .167 |
| 2005 | Portland (EAS) | AA | 0 | 0 | 1.50 | 15 | 0 | 0 | 1 | 18 | 12 | 3 | 3 | 0 | 8 | 13 | .190 |
| 2006 | Portland (EAS) | AA | 5 | 3 | 2.61 | 49 | 0 | 0 | 12 | 69 | 51 | 23 | 20 | 9 | 18 | 59 | .205 |
| **MINOR LEAGUE TOTALS** | | | 6 | 4 | 2.19 | 101 | 0 | 0 | 20 | 131 | 91 | 37 | 32 | 12 | 42 | 123 | .194 |

## 27 TY WEEDEN
C/1B

**Born:** Sept. 26, 1987. **B-T:** R-R. **Ht.:** 6-2. **Wt.:** 220. **Drafted:** HS—Edmond, Okla., 2006 (16th round). **Signed by:** Ernie Jacobs.

Weeden would have gone in the first five rounds of the 2006 draft has clubs been convinced that he definitely could stay at catcher and would turn down a scholarship from Arkansas. As part of their efforts to add raw power to the system, the Red Sox took him in the 16th round and signed him for $420,000. His older brother Brandon was the Yankees' first pick (second round) in the 2002 draft and was part of the Kevin Brown trade with the Dodgers. Ty first made a name for himself at the 2005 Area Code Games, where he put on one of the best shows in batting practice. Weeden has a lot of work to do behind the plate, but Boston was pleasantly surprised by his arm strength and the life in his lower half when they saw him in instructional league. He did throw 90-92 off the mound in high school. He'll need to get stronger and lose weight, but he has agility and even shows fringe-average speed coming out of the batter's box. If Weeden has to move to first base, his big righthanded power still would allow him to project as a regular. He'll compete for a spot in low Class A, but Jonathan Egan figures to be the starting catcher in Greenville to open 2007.

| Year | Club (League) | Class | AVG | G | AB | R | H | 2B | 3B | HR | RBI | BB | SO | SB | OBP | SLG |
|------|---------------|-------|-----|---|----|---|---|----|----|----|-----|----|----|----|-----|-----|
| 2006 | Did not play—Signed 2007 contract | | | | | | | | | | | | | | | |

## 28 CHAD SPANN
3B

**Born:** Oct. 25, 1983. **B-T:** R-R. **Ht.:** 6-1. **Wt.:** 195. **Drafted:** HS—Buena Vista, Ga., 2002 (5th round). **Signed by:** Rob English.

Spann became a forgotten man in the Red Sox system after a knee injury in 2004 and a lost year at the plate in 2005. He reclaimed his prospect status last year despite having his season come to an end Aug. 2 because of a high ankle sprain in his left leg. Spann used good pitch recognition and a line-drive approach to finish fifth in the Eastern League in hitting. He also showed more power than he ever had as a pro, but there still are questions as to whether he'll have even average pop as a big leaguer. His strike-zone discipline has slipped measurably the last two years as he has tried to drive the ball more. Spann's speed and defense are below-average, though he has worked hard to improve his arm strength and first-step quickness. If he can't cut it at the hot corner, the only other option would be first

base, where his bat wouldn't profile. Ticketed for Triple-A, Spann doesn't profile as a regular on a contender like the Red Sox and he's more apt to help them as trade bait.

| Year | Club (League) | Class | AVG | G | AB | R | H | 2B | 3B | HR | RBI | BB | SO | SB | OBP | SLG |
|---|---|---|---|---|---|---|---|---|---|---|---|---|---|---|---|---|
| 2002 | Red Sox (GCL) | R | .222 | 57 | 203 | 20 | 45 | 8 | 3 | 6 | 28 | 12 | 37 | 1 | .271 | .379 |
| 2003 | Augusta (SAL) | A | .312 | 116 | 414 | 55 | 129 | 21 | 3 | 5 | 63 | 40 | 64 | 9 | .379 | .413 |
| 2004 | Red Sox (GCL) | R | .333 | 7 | 24 | 3 | 8 | 2 | 0 | 0 | 4 | 2 | 1 | 0 | .385 | .417 |
| | Sarasota (FSL) | A | .248 | 61 | 214 | 26 | 53 | 9 | 0 | 4 | 22 | 9 | 53 | 6 | .286 | .346 |
| 2005 | Wilmington (CL) | A | .248 | 111 | 400 | 55 | 99 | 23 | 4 | 13 | 48 | 39 | 106 | 1 | .322 | .423 |
| | Portland (EL) | AA | .207 | 9 | 29 | 1 | 6 | 2 | 0 | 0 | 1 | 3 | 8 | 1 | .281 | .276 |
| 2006 | Portland (EL) | AA | .294 | 99 | 360 | 53 | 106 | 28 | 3 | 10 | 50 | 29 | 85 | 3 | .361 | .472 |
| MINOR LEAGUE TOTALS | | | .271 | 460 | 1644 | 213 | 446 | 93 | 13 | 38 | 216 | 134 | 354 | 21 | .335 | .413 |

## 29 KRIS NEGRON                                    SS/3B

**Born:** Feb. 1, 1986. **B-T:** R-R. **Ht.:** 6-0. **Wt.:** 180. **Drafted:** Cosumnes River (Calif.) JC, 2006 (7th round). **Signed by:** Blair Henry.

Negron became an organization favorite in his first summer in pro ball. Team officials rave about his energy, leadership and work ethic, and he has the physical ability to make it to the majors. He went to UC Davis out of high school, but redshirted in 2005 and had academic difficulties that led him to transfer to Cosumnes River (Calif.) Junior College in 2006. He became a seventh-round pick and signed for $105,000. Negron doesn't have the prettiest swing in the world, but it's short and effective. He already has shown the ability to make adjustments. After making weak contact at the outset of his pro debut, he was working counts and hitting hard line drives following a promotion to short-season Lowell and throughout instructional league. Negron has plus speed and the instincts to steal bases, succeeding in 15 of 16 pro attempts. Some scouts have questioned whether he has the arm strength to remain at shortstop, but the Red Sox say he does. They played him some at third base because he was on the same Gulf Coast League club as Argenis Diaz, the best defensive infielder in the system. Negron has the tools and actions to be a good second or third baseman if needed, and the athleticism to play the outfield. He'll play shortstop this year in low Class A.

| Year | Club (League) | Class | AVG | G | AB | R | H | 2B | 3B | HR | RBI | BB | SO | SB | OBP | SLG |
|---|---|---|---|---|---|---|---|---|---|---|---|---|---|---|---|---|
| 2006 | Red Sox (GCL) | R | .261 | 41 | 142 | 19 | 37 | 6 | 2 | 2 | 16 | 12 | 20 | 10 | .340 | .373 |
| | Lowell (NYP) | A | .393 | 9 | 28 | 8 | 11 | 2 | 1 | 0 | 5 | 4 | 2 | 5 | .485 | .536 |
| MINOR LEAGUE TOTALS | | | .282 | 50 | 170 | 27 | 48 | 8 | 3 | 2 | 21 | 16 | 22 | 15 | .365 | .400 |

## 30 JEFF NATALE                                    2B

**Born:** Aug. 24, 1982. **B-T:** R-R. **Ht.:** 5-9. **Wt.:** 180. **Drafted:** Trinity (Conn.), 2005 (32nd round). **Signed by:** Ray Fagnant.

Natale played two sports at NCAA Division III Trinity (Conn.), where he never batted less than .412 in four years of baseball and scored 31 goals in three seasons as a hockey forward. He hit .368 in his pro debut and was Boston's 2006 minor league offensive player of the year after topping the system in hits (136), RBIs (87), walks (103), on-base percentage (.446) and OPS (.915). Natale has tremendous hand-eye coordination and plate discipline. Using a short stroke, he consistently gets the barrel to the ball and rarely swings at bad pitches. He works counts and has no fear of hitting with two strikes. He has good pop for his size, especially to left field, and the Red Sox think he could hit 15 homers annually in the majors. If there's a knock on his offensive game, it's that he could wait a little better on breaking balls. Despite his two-sport background, Natale is limited athletically. He's a below-average runner and looks rough at second base. His hands, range and footwork are subpar, and though he has worked hard on his defense, he faces a move to left field if he doesn't show significant improvement. If that happens, he likely would rate as no more than a reserve. Natale should earn a spot at Portland in 2007.

| Year | Club (League) | Class | AVG | G | AB | R | H | 2B | 3B | HR | RBI | BB | SO | SB | OBP | SLG |
|---|---|---|---|---|---|---|---|---|---|---|---|---|---|---|---|---|
| 2005 | Lowell (NYP) | A | .488 | 12 | 41 | 9 | 20 | 5 | 0 | 0 | 9 | 3 | 3 | 2 | .522 | .610 |
| | Greenville (SAL) | A | .338 | 47 | 160 | 35 | 54 | 19 | 4 | 2 | 35 | 28 | 14 | 1 | .463 | .544 |
| 2006 | Greenville (SAL) | A | .343 | 50 | 175 | 38 | 60 | 10 | 0 | 10 | 41 | 41 | 20 | 2 | .487 | .571 |
| | Wilmington (CL) | A | .278 | 82 | 273 | 46 | 76 | 13 | 0 | 7 | 46 | 62 | 54 | 1 | .419 | .403 |
| MINOR LEAGUE TOTALS | | | .324 | 191 | 649 | 128 | 210 | 47 | 4 | 19 | 131 | 134 | 91 | 6 | .454 | .496 |

# CHICAGO
# CUBS

BY JIM CALLIS

The Cubs expected to contend in 2006, and that they did—for the No. 1 overall pick in the 2007 draft. They finished at 66-96, their second-worst in the last 25 years.

Chicago was cruising at the start of the season, going 9-5 though April 19, when Derrek Lee broke two bones in his right wrist in a collision at first base. By the time he returned to the lineup on June 25, the club was 28-45. But citing Lee's injury as the reason for team's disastrous performance would be a gross oversimplification. The Cubs had problems that would have undermined them even had Lee stayed healthy—the same problems that have plagued them since they got within five outs of reaching the World Series in 2003.

Mark Prior and Kerry Wood combined for 32 wins that season, but they have just 30 in the three seasons since. Yet Chicago continued to bank on a full return to health for both, optimism at its worst. With Prior and Wood able to make just 13 starts in 2006, the club trotted out a succession of rookies in their place. **Rich Hill** proved to be one of the better young lefthanders in baseball, but Angel Guzman, Carlos Marmol and Sean Marshall got rocked.

The pitching staff finished next to last in the National League in runs allowed, mirroring its rank in runs scored. Chicago has posted on-base percentages below the league average since Jim Hendry became general manager in July 2002, yet its three newcomers in the lineup last season were rookie Ronnie Cedeno, free agent Jacques Jones and trade acquisition Juan Pierre.

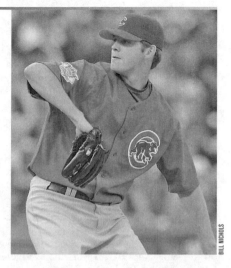

None is known for on-base ability, and the Cubs plunged to last in the league in OBP.

The team's performance cost manager Dusty Baker his job, and club president Andy MacPhail resigned at the end of the regular season. Senior vice president of marketing and broadcasting John McDonough replaced MacPhail, and Hendry hired Lou Piniella to succeed Baker. Piniella won't tolerate losing, and speculation is that the Tribune Co., which may be considering selling the team, won't either.

With that pressure to win and a farm system thinned out by injuries, trades and attrition, Chicago plunged headlong into the free-agent market this offseason. The first move was to re-sign Aramis Ramirez for five years and $75 million, a deal quickly trumped by the eight years and $136 million given to Alfonso Soriano. All told, the Cubs committed $294.6 million to nine free agents, and they'll cross the nine-figure payroll threshold for the first time.

In an attempt to revive the system, Chicago also outspent every team in the 2006 draft. Despite not having second- through fourth-round picks, the Cubs shelled out $11.6 million in bonuses. If they succeed in luring Jeff Samardzija away from football, he'll get a record $7.25 million. They also gave Chris Huseby $1.3 million, though he barely pitched during the spring while recovering from Tommy John surgery.

## TOP 30 PROSPECTS

1. Felix Pie, of
2. Donald Veal, lhp
3. Tyler Colvin, of
4. Jeff Samardzija, rhp
5. Sean Gallagher, rhp
6. Eric Patterson, 2b
7. Scott Moore, 3b
8. Ryan Harvey, of
9. Chris Huseby, rhp
10. Mark Pawelek, lhp
11. Juan Mateo, rhp
12. Brian Dopirak, 1b
13. Jae-Kuk Ryu, rhp
14. Mark Reed, c
15. Drew Rundle, of
16. Rocky Cherry, rhp
17. Geovany Soto, c
18. Billy Petrick, rhp
19. Dylan Johnston, ss
20. Josh Lansford, 3b
21. Sammy Baez, ss
22. Chris Robinson, c
23. Mark Holliman, rhp
24. Jake Fox, c
25. Larry Suarez, rhp
26. Rocky Roquet, rhp
27. Sam Fuld, of
28. Scott Taylor, rhp
29. Mitch Atkins, rhp
30. Mike Fontenot, 2b

# ORGANIZATION OVERVIEW

**General manager:** Jim Hendry. **Farm director:** Oneri Fleita. **Scouting director:** Tim Wilken

## 2006 PERFORMANCE

| Class | Team | League | W | L | PCT | Finish* | Manager | Affiliated |
|---|---|---|---|---|---|---|---|---|
| Majors | Chicago | National | 66 | 96 | .407 | 16th (16) | Dusty Baker | — |
| Triple-A | Iowa Cubs | Pacific Coast | 76 | 68 | .528 | 6th (16) | Bobby Dickerson | 1981 |
| Double-A | #West Tenn Diamond Jaxx | Southern | 70 | 69 | .504 | 5th (10) | Bill Plummer | 2006 |
| High A | Daytona Cubs | Florida State | 71 | 66 | .518 | 5th (12) | Don Buford | 1993 |
| Low A | Peoria Chiefs | Midwest | 75 | 64 | .540 | 5th (14) | Jody Davis | 2005 |
| Short-season | Boise Hawks | Northwest | 44 | 32 | .579 | 2nd (8) | Steve McFarland | 2001 |
| Rookie | AZL Cubs | Arizona | 21 | 34 | .382 | 7th (9) | Carmelo Martinez | 1997 |
| **OVERALL 2006 MINOR LEAGUE RECORD** | | | 362 | 329 | .524 | 10th (30) | | |

*Finish in overall standings (No. of teams in league). +League champion. #Affiliate will be in Tennessee (Southern) in 2007.

## ORGANIZATION LEADERS

### BATTING
| | | |
|---|---|---|
| AVG | Norwood, Ryan, Peoria | .307 |
| R | Patterson, Eric, West Tenn/Iowa | 95 |
| H | Walker, Christopher, West Tenn | 168 |
| 2B | Three tied at | 35 |
| 3B | Patterson, Eric, West Tenn/Iowa | 11 |
| | Walker, Christopher, West Tenn | 11 |
| HR | Restovich, Michael, Iowa | 27 |
| RBI | Fox, Jacob, Daytona/West Tenn | 94 |
| BB | Chirinos, Robinson, Peoria | 70 |
| SO | Moore, Scott, West Tenn/Iowa | 139 |
| SB | Walker, Christopher, West Tenn | 61 |
| OBP | Craig, Matt, Daytona | .384 |
| SLG | Restovich, Michael, Iowa | .560 |
| XBH | Restovich, Michael, Iowa | 60 |

### PITCHING
| | | |
|---|---|---|
| W | Atkins, Mitch, Peoria | 13 |
| | Walrond, Les, Iowa | 13 |
| L | Brownlie, Robert, Iowa/West Tenn | 14 |
| ERA | Veal, Donald, Peoria/Daytona | 2.16 |
| G | Rapada, Clay, West Tenn/Iowa | 69 |
| SV | Campusano, Edward, Peoria/West Tenn | 25 |
| IP | Gallagher, Sean, Daytona/West Tenn | 165 |
| BB | Veal, Donald, Peoria/Daytona | 82 |
| SO | Veal, Donald, Peoria/Daytona | 174 |
| AVG | Veal, Donald, Peoria/Daytona | .175 |

## BEST TOOLS

| | |
|---|---|
| Best Hitter for Average | Tyler Colvin |
| Best Power Hitter | Ryan Harvey |
| Best Strike-Zone Discipline | Sam Fuld |
| Fastest Baserunner | Chris Walker |
| Best Athlete | Felix Pie |
| Best Fastball | Jeff Samardzija |
| Best Curveball | Donald Veal |
| Best Slider | Rocky Cherry |
| Best Changeup | Billy Muldowney |
| Best Control | Scott Taylor |
| Best Defensive Catcher | Jake Muyco |
| Best Defensive Infielder | Josh Lansford |
| Best Infield Arm | Josh Lansford |
| Best Defensive Outfielder | Felix Pie |
| Best Outfield Arm | Ryan Harvey |

## PROJECTED 2010 LINEUP

| | |
|---|---|
| Catcher | Michael Barrett |
| First Base | Derrek Lee |
| Second Base | Eric Patterson |
| Third Base | Aramis Ramirez |
| Shortstop | Ronny Cedeno |
| Left Field | Alfonso Soriano |
| Center Field | Felix Pie |

| | |
|---|---|
| Right Field | Tyler Colvin |
| No. 1 Starter | Carlos Zambrano |
| No. 2 Starter | Mark Prior |
| No. 3 Starter | Donald Veal |
| No. 4 Starter | Ted Lilly |
| No. 5 Starter | Sean Gallagher |
| Closer | Jeff Samardzija |

## TOP PROSPECTS OF THE DECADE

| Year | Player, Pos. | 2006 Org. |
|---|---|---|
| 1997 | Kerry Wood, rhp | Cubs |
| 1998 | Kerry Wood, rhp | Cubs |
| 1999 | Corey Patterson, of | Orioles |
| 2000 | Corey Patterson, of | Orioles |
| 2001 | Corey Patterson, of | Orioles |
| 2002 | Mark Prior, rhp | Cubs |
| 2003 | Hee Seop Choi, 1b | Red Sox |
| 2004 | Angel Guzman, rhp | Cubs |
| 2005 | Brian Dopirak, 1b | Cubs |
| 2006 | Felix Pie, of | Cubs |

## TOP DRAFT PICKS OF THE DECADE

| Year | Player, Pos. | 2006 Org. |
|---|---|---|
| 1997 | Jon Garland, rhp | White Sox |
| 1998 | Corey Patterson, of | Orioles |
| 1999 | Ben Christensen, rhp | Out of baseball |
| 2000 | Luis Montanez, ss | Cubs |
| 2001 | Mark Prior, rhp | Cubs |
| 2002 | Bobby Brownlie, rhp | Cubs |
| 2003 | Ryan Harvey, of | Cubs |
| 2004 | Grant Johnson, rhp (2nd round) | Cubs |
| 2005 | Mark Pawelek, lhp | Cubs |
| 2006 | Tyler Colvin, of | Cubs |

## LAST YEAR'S TOP 20 PROSPECTS

1. Felix Pie, of
2. Mark Pawelek, lhp
3. Ronny Cedeno, ss
4. Angel Guzman, rhp
5. Rich Hill, lhp
6. Sean Marshall, lhp
7. Ryan Harvey, of
8. Brian Dopirak, 1b
9. Eric Patterson, 2b
10. Carlos Marmol, rhp
11. Donald Veal, lhp
12. Sean Gallagher, rhp
13. Scott Moore, 3b
14. Jae-Kuk Ryu, rhp
15. Brandon Sing, 1b/of
16. Geovany Soto, c
17. Grant Johnson, rhp
18. Billy Petrick, rhp
19. Mark Reed, c
20. Michael Phelps, rhp

## ALL-TIME LARGEST BONUSES

| | |
|---|---|
| Jeff Samardzija, 2006 | $7,250,000 |
| Mark Prior, 2001 | $4,000,000 |
| Corey Patterson, 1998 | $3,700,000 |
| Luis Montanez, 2000 | $2,750,000 |
| Bobby Brownlie, 2002 | $2,500,000 |

# MINOR LEAGUE DEPTH CHART

## Chicago Cubs

**Impact: C.** Other than Sean Gallagher and Donald Veal, the pitching inventory is either young or flawed, and plenty of projection is needed to see most of the top hitters as regulars.

**Depth: C.** The Cubs still have star talent on the farm, if it develops. The organization's recent development record doesn't leave room for optimism, though.

**Sleeper:** Miguel Cuevas, rhp. The Dominican righty fell to the 36th round (after attending Los Angeles Pierce Junior College) due to visa concerns, but he's a 6-foot-8 monster who's flashed a 92-93 mph fastball.

*Numbers in parentheses indicate prospect rankings.*

| LF |
| --- |
| Jesus Valdez |

| CF |
| --- |
| Felix Pie (1) |
| Sam Fuld (27) |
| Buck Coats |
| Chris Walker |
| Matt Camp |

| RF |
| --- |
| Tyler Colvin (3) |
| Ryan Harvey (8) |
| Drew Rundle (15) |
| Alfred Joseph |
| Miguel Negron |

| 3B |
| --- |
| Scott Moore (7) |
| Josh Lansford (20) |
| Casey McGehee |

| SS |
| --- |
| Dylan Johnston (19) |
| Sammy Baez (21) |
| Jonathan Mota |

| 2B |
| --- |
| Eric Patterson (6) |
| Mike Fontenot (30) |
| Robinson Chirinos |
| Steven Clevenger |

| 1B |
| --- |
| Brian Dopirak (12) |
| Russ Canzler |
| Ryan Norwood |

| C |
| --- |
| Mark Reed (14) |
| Geovany Soto (17) |
| Chris Robinson (22) |
| Jake Fox (24) |
| Jake Muyco |
| Matt Canepa |

| RHP | |
| --- | --- |
| **Starters** | **Relievers** |
| Jeff Samardzija (5) | Juan Mateo (11) |
| Sean Gallagher (6) | Rocky Cherry (16) |
| Chris Huseby (9) | Rocky Roquet (26) |
| Jae-Kuk Ryu (13) | Mitch Atkins (29) |
| Billy Petrick (18) | Jose Ceda |
| Mark Holliman (23) | Jon Hunton |
| Larry Suarez (25) | Michael Phelps |
| Scott Taylor (28) | Michael Cooper |
| Justin Berg | Miguel Cuevas |
| Randy Wells | Matt Avery |
| Adam Harben | Rafael Dolis |
| Jake Renshaw | Julio Castillo |

| LHP | |
| --- | --- |
| **Starters** | **Relievers** |
| Donald Veal (2) | Clay Rapada |
| Mark Pawelek (10) | Tim Layden |
| Chris Shaver | Jeremy Papelbon |
| Ryan O'Malley | Carmen Pignatiello |
| | Scott Koerber |

# DRAFT ANALYSIS

## 2006
SIGNING BUDGET: $9.3 million

**Best Pro Debut:** OF Tyler Colvin (1) was a surprise as the 13th overall pick, then went out and hit .268 with 11 homers and 12 steals to earn top-prospect recognition in the Northwest League. RHP Jeremy Papelbon (19) made the NWL all-star team after going 4-0, 1.83 with 50 strikeouts in 44 innings. OF Matt Camp (13) batted .289 with 22 steals and an NWL-high 87 hits, and looked good at second base in instructional league.

**Best Athlete:** RHP Jeff Samardzija (5) is an all-America wide receiver who set Notre Dame records for receptions (77) and touchdown catches (15) in 2005 and has definite NFL potential. If he sticks with baseball, he'll collect a record $7.25 million bonus; if he walks, the Cubs are out only $250,000 at this point. In terms of baseball athleticism, Colvin has a chance to develop plus tools across the board. OF Drew Rundle (14) has similar tools.

**Best Pure Hitter:** Colvin, with Rundle and OF Cliff Andersen (9) right behind him.

**Best Raw Power:** Both Colvin and Rundle have nice loft in their swings. Colvin has more projection remaining than most college juniors, as he didn't turn 21 until September and is still growing into his 6-foot-3, 190-pound frame.

**Fastest Runner:** Andersen runs the 60-yard dash in 60 seconds and is a good all-around athlete.

**Best Defensive Player:** 3B Josh Lansford (6) has plus-plus arm strength, plus range and surprising agility for a 6-foot-2, 220-pounder. He can get a little pull-happy, but he can do damage at the plate as well.

**Best Fastball:** Samardzija has touched 99 mph a couple of times and usually pitches at 91-94 mph. If he turns to baseball full-time, he's expected to throw in the mid- to upper 90s with regularity. RHP Chris Huseby (11) barely pitched in the spring while coming back from 2005 Tommy John surgery, but showed enough to get a $1.3 million bonus. He throws 90-95 mph with good life. Fifth-year senior sign Rocky Roquet and fellow RHPs Michael Cooper (26) and Miguel Cuevas (36) can pitch into the mid-90s.

**Best Breaking Ball:** Either Huseby's or RHP Billy Muldowney's (8) curveball, both of which need more consistency. There's more power to Huseby's hook.

**Most Intriguing Background:** Lansford's father Carney won an American League batting title; his uncles Jody and Phil were for-

mer first-round picks; and his brother Jared was a second-round choice by the Athletics in 2005. Papelbon's twin brother Josh signed with the Red Sox as a 48th-rounder in June, and their older brother Jonathan is an all-star with Boston. Cubs scouting director Tim Wilken drafted SS Matt Matulia's (24) brother John in 2005, while with the Devil Rays.

**Closest To The Majors:** There's a lot of upside but may not be a fast-track player in this draft. Pitching could come together quickly for Samardzija, but he still needs work on his delivery and secondary pitches and has yet to commit to baseball full-time. Colvin needs at least two years in the minors before he'll be a finished product.

**Best Late-Round Pick:** Huseby and Rundle. Cooper and Cuevas required much smaller investments.

**The One Who Got Away:** The Cubs lost the rights to just four players, the best of whom is offensive-minded Clemson 3B Marquez Smith (35).

**Assessment:** The Cubs gave up their second- through fourth-round picks as free-agent compensation, but they made up for it with Samardzija, Huseby and Rundle. Wilken's drafts have the best track record among current scouting directors, and this was a typical Wilken effort with power pitchers and multi-tooled position players.

## 2005
BUDGET: $3.8 million

Few lefties have arms to match Mark Pawelek (1) and Donald Veal (2), though they have rough edges to smooth out. **GRADE: B**

## 2004
BUDGET: $2.8 million

The Cubs had no first-rounder and their top choice, RHP Grant Johnson (2), has been a $1.26 million bust. RHP Shawn Gallagher (12) and 2B Eric Patterson (8) are left to salvage this draft class. **GRADE: C+**

## 2003
BUDGET: $3.9 million

OF Ryan Harvey (1) is a high-risk, high-reward player whose future is still unclear. LHP Sean Marshall (6) was a nice find, but signing RHP Tim Lincecum (48) would have been even nicer. **GRADE: C**

*Draft analysis by Jim Callis. Numbers in parentheses indicate draft rounds. Budgets are bonuses in first 10 rounds.*

BASEBALL AMERICA 2007 PROSPECT HANDBOOK • 81

# FELIX
## PIE

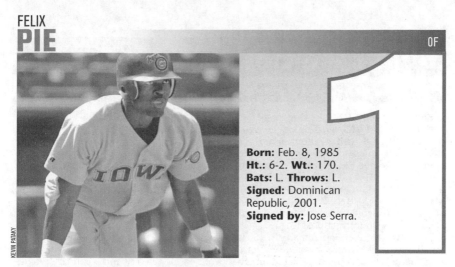

KEVIN PATAKY

**Born:** Feb. 8, 1985
**Ht.:** 6-2. **Wt.:** 170.
**Bats:** L. **Throws:** L.
**Signed:** Dominican Republic, 2001.
**Signed by:** Jose Serra.

The best thing that may happen to Pie was hurting his right ankle sliding into a base in June 2005. The resulting bone bruise kept him out for the rest of the season, and ended the Cubs' plans to promote him when they tired of Corey Patterson in July. Unsure whether Pie would be ready to jump to Chicago after missing most of 2005, they traded for Juan Pierre in the offseason. So instead of being rushed as Patterson was, Pie got a full year of development at Triple-A Iowa in 2006. He wasn't ready for the majors, hitting just .248 with seven homers in the first three months. He adjusted and batted .322 with eight homers in the final two months, reaffirming that he's by far the Cubs' best position prospect. Success has followed Pie throughout the minors, as he has appeared in two Futures Games and won championships with each of the first four clubs he played with.

The best athlete in the system, Pie has tools reminiscent of Carlos Beltran's. He's a power-hitting center fielder with basestealing ability. His bat is so quick that he can make hard contact against any pitch he can reach, even out of the strike zone. Though he always has been one of the youngest regulars in his leagues, he consistently has hit for average. In the last two years, Pie has started to incorporate his legs more into his swing and to turn on more pitches, allowing him to realize more of his power potential. He has well above-average speed, making him dangerous on the bases and able to run down most balls in center field. His arm is strong enough for right field, and he led Triple-A Pacific Coast League outfielders with 18 assists last year. In addition to his physical skills, the Cubs also like his makeup. They like how he turned his season around last year, and they say it's no coincidence that his teams have won consistently.

Pie still needs to refine his instincts in all phases of the game. He doesn't control the strike zone, resulting in few walks and too many outs on balls he shouldn't chase. Chicago had him bat at the top of the Triple-A lineup to have him work on his plate discipline, with only moderate success. For all his speed, Pie was caught stealing 11 times in 28 tries in 2006 and has succeeded on just 63 percent of his attempts as a pro. Though he's the system's best defensive outfielder, he'll occasionally take erratic routes.

Though the Cubs seemingly filled their outfield by signing Alfonso Soriano to a $136 million contract, they'd prefer to trade Jacque Jones and play Soriano in right. That would leave center open for Pie, who would offer a lefty bat in a predominantly righthanded lineup. If Chicago can't deal Jones, more development in Triple-A wouldn't hurt, as Pie showed by hitting a soft .216 through 125 at-bats in the Dominican Winter League. He'll make his major league debut at age 22, though it may be a few years before he can become an offensive force.

| Year | Club (League) | Class | AVG | G | AB | R | H | 2B | 3B | HR | RBI | BB | SO | SB | OBP | SLG |
|------|---------------|-------|------|-----|------|-----|-----|-----|----|----|-----|-----|-----|----|------|------|
| 2002 | Cubs (AZL) | R | .321 | 55 | 218 | 42 | 70 | 16 | 13 | 4 | 37 | 21 | 47 | 17 | .385 | .569 |
| | Boise (NWL) | A | .125 | 2 | 8 | 1 | 1 | 1 | 0 | 0 | 1 | 1 | 1 | 0 | .222 | .250 |
| 2003 | Lansing (MWL) | A | .285 | 124 | 505 | 72 | 144 | 22 | 9 | 4 | 47 | 41 | 98 | 19 | .346 | .388 |
| 2004 | Daytona (FSL) | A | .301 | 106 | 415 | 79 | 125 | 17 | 10 | 8 | 47 | 39 | 113 | 32 | .364 | .448 |
| 2005 | West Tenn (SL) | AA | .304 | 59 | 240 | 41 | 73 | 17 | 5 | 11 | 25 | 16 | 53 | 13 | .349 | .554 |
| 2006 | Iowa (PCL) | AAA | .283 | 141 | 559 | 78 | 158 | 33 | 8 | 15 | 57 | 46 | 126 | 17 | .341 | .451 |
| **MINOR LEAGUE TOTALS** | | | .294 | 487 | 1945 | 313 | 571 | 106 | 45 | 42 | 214 | 164 | 438 | 98 | .353 | .459 |

## ② DONALD VEAL

LHP

**Born:** Sept. 18, 1984. **B-T:** L-L. **Ht.:** 6-4. **Wt.:** 215. **Drafted:** Pima (Ariz.) CC, 2005 (2nd round). **Signed by:** Steve McFarland.

After signing him for $530,000 as a second-rounder in 2005, the Cubs kept Veal on short pitch counts because he was worn out from a heavy workload at Pima (Ariz.) CC. When they turned him loose last year, he led minor league starters in opponent batting average (.175) and shared Chicago's minor league player of the year award with Rich Hill. Hitters can't square up the ball well against Veal because he has quality stuff and hides it with an unorthodox delivery. He has a 92-93 mph fastball that tops out at 95, and he likes to bust hitters inside with a four-seamer and then paint the outside corner with a two-seamer. His 74-79 mph curveball has tight rotation and is a strikeout pitch when it's on. His changeup is a solid third pitch. He has long arms and operates with a big leg kick and a high three-quarters slot, and his pitches get on top of hitters before they're ready. Veal's delivery is complicated, so command becomes an issue. He locates his fastball where he wants, but he won't be able to do the same with his secondary pitches until he starts using them more often. His inconsistent curveball can get loopy at times. He'll open 2007 at the Chicago's new Double-A Tennessee affiliate. Though the Cubs have signed free agents Ted Lilly and Jason Marquis, Veal has the electric arm to push his way into the big league rotation by the end of the year if he improves the consistency of his secondary pitches. He's a possible No. 2 starter in the future.

| Year | Club (League) | Class | W | L | ERA | G | GS | CG | SV | IP | H | R | ER | HR | BB | SO | AVG |
|------|---------------|-------|---|---|-----|---|----|----|----|----|---|---|----|----|----|----|-----|
| 2005 | Cubs (AZL) | R | 0 | 1 | 5.06 | 4 | 3 | 0 | 0 | 11 | 8 | 6 | 6 | 2 | 5 | 14 | .205 |
| | Boise (NWL) | A | 1 | 2 | 2.48 | 7 | 6 | 0 | 0 | 29 | 18 | 11 | 8 | 2 | 15 | 34 | .180 |
| 2006 | Peoria (MWL) | A | 5 | 3 | 2.69 | 14 | 14 | 0 | 0 | 74 | 45 | 26 | 22 | 4 | 40 | 86 | .179 |
| | Daytona (FSL) | A | 6 | 2 | 1.67 | 14 | 14 | 0 | 0 | 81 | 46 | 18 | 15 | 3 | 42 | 88 | .170 |
| **MINOR LEAGUE TOTALS** | | | 12 | 8 | 2.37 | 39 | 37 | 0 | 0 | 194 | 117 | 61 | 51 | 11 | 102 | 222 | .177 |

## ③ TYLER COLVIN

OF

**Born:** Sept. 5, 1985. **B-T:** L-L. **Ht.:** 6-3. **Wt.:** 190. **Drafted:** Clemson, 2006 (1st round). **Signed by:** Antonio Grissom.

Colvin was the biggest surprise of the first round of the 2006 draft, going 13th overall after not receiving a lot of hype at Clemson. He led the Tigers to the College World Series, then signed for $1.475 million. He ranked as the short-season Northwest League's No. 1 prospect in his pro debut. There's more projection remaining for Colvin than with most college draftees because of his gangly frame and age; he didn't turn 21 until the end of the season. He's the best pure hitter in the system and should develop plus power as he gets stronger, as he has quick hands and drives the ball to all fields. The Cubs believe his solid-average speed could improve as he matures physically. He also plays fine defense, with the range for center field and the arm for right. Colvin tried to do too much at the start of his pro career, leading to an immediate 8-for-46 slump. He learned to just let the game come to him, and made a similar adjustment at the plate. Rather than trying to muscle up for power against righthanders, he has started to let the ball travel deeper and trust his hands. He'll need to tighten his strike zone and lay off high fastballs. While Colvin's upside, which draws comparisons to Steve Finley and Shawn Green, excites Chicago, he'll need time to develop. He could open his first full pro season at low Class A Peoria, though he should be able to handle high Class A Daytona.

| Year | Club (League) | Class | AVG | G | AB | R | H | 2B | 3B | HR | RBI | BB | SO | SB | OBP | SLG |
|------|---------------|-------|-----|---|----|---|---|----|----|----|-----|----|----|----|-----|-----|
| 2006 | Boise (NWL) | A | .268 | 64 | 265 | 50 | 71 | 12 | 6 | 11 | 53 | 17 | 55 | 12 | .313 | .483 |
| **MINOR LEAGUE TOTALS** | | | .268 | 64 | 265 | 50 | 71 | 12 | 6 | 11 | 53 | 17 | 55 | 12 | .313 | .483 |

## ④ JEFF SAMARDZIJA

RHP

**Born:** Jan. 23, 1985. **B-T:** R-R. **Ht.:** 6-5. **Wt.:** 218. **Drafted:** Notre Dame, 2006 (5th round). **Signed by:** Stan Zielinski.

Samardzija is the most accomplished wide receiver in Notre Dame history, owning school records for single-season and career catches, receiving yards and receiving touchdowns. He also has a big-time arm that would have made him a first-round pick in baseball if not for his football commitment. The Cubs didn't have second- through fourth-round picks in the 2006 draft, and they compensated by taking Samardzija in the fifth. They drew Major League Baseball's ire by signing him to a record

$7.25 million bonus, though the payments are spread over five years and they'll be out just $250,000 in up-front money if he leaves for the NFL this spring. Samardzija usually pitches at 91-94 mph with his fastball, but he has touched 99 and Chicago thinks he'll operate in the mid-90s if he focuses on baseball and cleans up his mechanics. His low-80s slider is inconsistent, but it presently grades as average and has plus potential. He's a phenomenal athlete who proved coachable and able to make quick adjustments in his first summer of pro ball. The biggest concern is that Samardzija will bolt for the NFL, though his football draft stock seems to be dropping. Because football has been his priority, he's still raw in baseball. He'll open up early in his delivery and sling the ball, costing him deception and flattening his pitches. He rarely has used his changeup, a below-average pitch. Samardzija's dream would be to play both sports, though that's difficult to imagine. The NFL draft is in April, and he projects as a second-round pick. If he stays with baseball, he'd start the season at one of the Cubs' Class A stops. They think he'll move quickly if they hang onto him, with one club official comparing him to John Smoltz.

| Year | Club (League) | Class | W | L | ERA | G | GS | CG | SV | IP | H | R | ER | HR | BB | SO | AVG |
|------|---------------|-------|---|---|-----|---|----|----|----|----|---|---|----|----|----|----|-----|
| 2006 | Boise (NWL) | A | 1 | 1 | 2.37 | 5 | 5 | 0 | 0 | 19 | 18 | 5 | 5 | 1 | 6 | 13 | .247 |
| | Peoria (MWL) | A | 0 | 1 | 3.27 | 2 | 2 | 0 | 0 | 11 | 6 | 5 | 4 | 1 | 6 | 4 | .167 |
| **MINOR LEAGUE TOTALS** | | | 1 | 2 | 2.70 | 7 | 7 | 0 | 0 | 30 | 24 | 10 | 9 | 2 | 12 | 17 | .220 |

## 5 SEAN GALLAGHER                                        RHP

**Born:** Dec. 30, 1985. **B-T:** R-R. **Ht.:** 6-1. **Wt.:** 210. **Drafted:** HS—Fort Lauderdale, Fla., 2004 (12th round). **Signed by:** Rolando Pino.

Gallagher was considered a tough sign if he didn't go in the first three rounds of the 2004 draft, but area scout Rolando Pino stayed on him and got a deal done in the 12th round. He won 14 games in low Class A as a teenager in 2005, then motored through two levels last year as his stuff improved. The biggest key to pitching is fastball command, and Gallagher can put his heater where he wants in the strike zone. It also surged from 88-90 mph in 2005 to 90-94 last year while retaining its boring life. His curveball remains his best pitch, and he has improved his changeup. He's built for durability and has the mindset that he should win every time he takes the mound. When he got to Double-A, Gallagher overthrew and lost the edge off his control and command. He sometimes leaves his pitches up when he doesn't finish his delivery. His changeup still needs fine-tuning. He'll have to watch the weight on his stocky frame, but he's athletic for his size and pays attention to his conditioning. Gallagher has developed faster than anticipated and has a ceiling of a No. 3 starter. He'll begin 2007 with a few starts in Double-A, but he'll move up to Triple-A by midseason and could make his big league debut in September.

| Year | Club (League) | Class | W | L | ERA | G | GS | CG | SV | IP | H | R | ER | HR | BB | SO | AVG |
|------|---------------|-------|----|----|-----|----|----|----|----|-----|-----|-----|-----|----|-----|-----|-----|
| 2004 | Cubs (AZL) | R | 1 | 2 | 3.12 | 10 | 9 | 0 | 0 | 35 | 38 | 19 | 12 | 0 | 11 | 44 | .275 |
| 2005 | Peoria (MWL) | A | 14 | 5 | 2.71 | 26 | 26 | 0 | 0 | 146 | 107 | 53 | 44 | 10 | 55 | 139 | .206 |
| | Daytona (FSL) | A | 0 | 0 | 1.80 | 1 | 1 | 0 | 0 | 5 | 6 | 1 | 1 | 1 | 0 | 7 | .286 |
| 2006 | Daytona (FSL) | A | 4 | 0 | 2.30 | 13 | 13 | 0 | 0 | 78 | 75 | 24 | 20 | 5 | 21 | 80 | .260 |
| | West Tenn (SL) | AA | 7 | 5 | 2.71 | 15 | 15 | 0 | 0 | 86 | 74 | 30 | 26 | 4 | 55 | 91 | .239 |
| **MINOR LEAGUE TOTALS** | | | 26 | 12 | 2.65 | 65 | 64 | 0 | 0 | 350 | 300 | 127 | 103 | 20 | 142 | 361 | .235 |

## 6 ERIC PATTERSON                                        2B

**Born:** April 8, 1983. **B-T:** L-R. **Ht.:** 5-11. **Wt.:** 170. **Drafted:** Georgia Tech, 2004 (8th round). **Signed by:** Sam Hughes.

His older brother Corey may have played his way out of Chicago, but Eric is firmly in the club's plans. An eighth-round pick who signed for fourth-round money ($300,000) in 2004, he won the low Class A Midwest League batting title in his first pro season and reached Triple-A in his second. He led the Arizona Fall League with 15 steals and batted .345. Manager rated him the best baserunner in the Southern League last year, as Patterson has plus speed and good instincts. He hits for a solid average and has surprising pop for his size. Scouts see him as a less explosive version of Delino DeShields. There are a lot of questions about whether Patterson can play second base in the major leagues. He has made improvements but still has a long way to go. He relies on his speed rather than reading balls off the bat, and he doesn't have great range to his right. His plate discipline is just fair and he sometimes gets caught up in trying to hitting homers, compromising his ability to get on base and use his speed. Though he'll remain at second base for now, Patterson spent some time in center field during instructional league and could become a super utilityman along the lines of Chone Figgins or Ryan Freel. The free-

agent signing of Mark DeRosa will buy Patterson at least a half-season in Triple-A, but he's still the Cubs' second baseman of the future.

| Year | Club (League) | Class | AVG | G | AB | R | H | 2B | 3B | HR | RBI | BB | SO | SB | OBP | SLG |
|------|---------------|-------|-----|---|----|---|---|----|----|----|-----|----|----|----|-----|-----|
| 2005 | Peoria (MWL) | A | .333 | 110 | 432 | 90 | 144 | 26 | 11 | 13 | 71 | 53 | 94 | 40 | .405 | .535 |
| | West Tenn (SL) | AA | .200 | 9 | 30 | 5 | 6 | 2 | 0 | 0 | 2 | 6 | 7 | 3 | .324 | .267 |
| 2006 | West Tenn (SL) | AA | .263 | 121 | 441 | 66 | 116 | 22 | 9 | 8 | 48 | 46 | 89 | 38 | .330 | .408 |
| | Iowa (PCL) | AAA | .358 | 17 | 67 | 14 | 24 | 1 | 1 | 2 | 12 | 6 | 9 | 8 | .395 | .493 |
| **MINOR LEAGUE TOTALS** | | | .299 | 257 | 970 | 175 | 290 | 51 | 21 | 23 | 133 | 111 | 199 | 89 | .368 | .466 |

## ⑦ SCOTT MOORE 3B

**Born:** Nov. 17, 1983. **B-T:** L-R. **Ht.:** 6-2. **Wt.:** 180. **Drafted:** HS—Long Beach, 2002 (1st round). **Signed by:** Rob Wilfong (Tigers).

A change of scenery was apparently just what Moore needed. He struggled after the Tigers made him the eighth overall pick in the 2002 draft, but he has hit 44 homers in two seasons since coming to the Cubs in a February 2005 trade for Kyle Farnsworth. Moore's power grades as a 55 on the 20-80 scouting scale and plays to all fields. After leading the high Class A Florida State League in errors the previous two years, he was much steadier in 2006 and managers rated him the best defensive third baseman in the Double-A Southern League. He has average speed and runs the bases well. Until he cuts down on his swing and his strikeouts, Moore won't hit for a high average. He's not as pull-crazy as he used to be, but he'll still chase breaking balls. Most of his errors still come on throws, though he has improved his accuracy and footwork. With Aramis Ramirez locked up for the next five years, Moore is blocked at third base with the Cubs. He saw time at first base, left field and even shortstop in the Arizona Fall League, and will move around the diamond this year in Triple-A. He has the ceiling of a lefthanded David Bell, but Moore ultimately will serve Chicago as a versatile reserve or as trade bait.

| Year | Club (League) | Class | AVG | G | AB | R | H | 2B | 3B | HR | RBI | BB | SO | SB | OBP | SLG |
|------|---------------|-------|-----|---|----|---|---|----|----|----|-----|----|----|----|-----|-----|
| 2002 | Tigers (GCL) | R | .293 | 40 | 133 | 18 | 39 | 6 | 2 | 4 | 25 | 10 | 31 | 1 | .349 | .459 |
| 2003 | West Michigan (MWL) | A | .239 | 107 | 372 | 40 | 89 | 16 | 6 | 6 | 45 | 41 | 110 | 2 | .325 | .363 |
| 2004 | Lakeland (FSL) | A | .223 | 118 | 391 | 52 | 87 | 13 | 4 | 14 | 56 | 49 | 125 | 2 | .322 | .384 |
| 2005 | Daytona (FSL) | A | .281 | 128 | 466 | 77 | 131 | 31 | 2 | 20 | 82 | 55 | 134 | 22 | .358 | .485 |
| 2006 | West Tenn (SL) | AA | .276 | 132 | 463 | 52 | 128 | 28 | 0 | 22 | 75 | 55 | 126 | 12 | .360 | .479 |
| | Iowa (PCL) | AAA | .250 | 1 | 4 | 1 | 1 | 1 | 0 | 0 | 0 | 0 | 1 | 0 | .250 | .500 |
| | Chicago (NL) | MLB | .263 | 16 | 38 | 6 | 10 | 2 | 0 | 2 | 5 | 2 | 10 | 0 | .317 | .474 |
| **MINOR LEAGUE TOTALS** | | | .260 | 526 | 1829 | 240 | 475 | 95 | 14 | 66 | 283 | 210 | 527 | 39 | .343 | .435 |
| **MAJOR LEAGUE TOTALS** | | | .263 | 16 | 38 | 6 | 10 | 2 | 0 | 2 | 5 | 2 | 10 | 0 | .317 | .474 |

## ⑧ RYAN HARVEY OF

**Born:** Aug. 30, 1984. **B-T:** R-R. **Ht.:** 6-5. **Wt.:** 220. **Drafted:** HS—Dunedin, Fla., 2003 (1st round). **Signed by:** Rolando Pino.

Four years after making Harvey the fifth overall pick in the 2003 draft, the Cubs still don't know what they have him. Few players in the minors can hit a ball as far or look as silly on a strikeout as he can. He hit just .203 with seven homers in his first 68 games last year, then .320 with 13 longballs in his last 54, including a four-homer outburst on July 28. With his natural strength and leverage, Harvey is a threat to go deep at any time in any park against any pitcher. A right fielder, he threw 90-93 mph off the mound in high school and has accuracy to go with his arm strength. A good athlete for his size, he runs well once he gets going. Harvey still uses the same one-plane swing he had in high school, and he could work harder to make changes. His approach also leaves a lot to be desired, as he chases too many pitches. Pitchers can bust him inside, and when he looks that way, he's easy prey for soft stuff on the outer half. Did Harvey figure things out in the second half of 2006, or did he just ride an extended hot streak? The Cubs don't know for sure, but they're anxious to see how he performs this year in Double-A.

| Year | Club (League) | Class | AVG | G | AB | R | H | 2B | 3B | HR | RBI | BB | SO | SB | OBP | SLG |
|------|---------------|-------|-----|---|----|---|---|----|----|----|-----|----|----|----|-----|-----|
| 2003 | Cubs (AZL) | R | .235 | 14 | 51 | 9 | 12 | 3 | 2 | 1 | 7 | 6 | 21 | 0 | .339 | .431 |
| 2004 | Cubs (AZL) | R | .400 | 2 | 10 | 1 | 4 | 3 | 0 | 0 | 5 | 0 | 4 | 0 | .400 | .700 |
| | Boise (NWL) | A | .264 | 58 | 231 | 42 | 61 | 8 | 0 | 14 | 43 | 20 | 78 | 2 | .327 | .481 |
| 2005 | Peoria (MWL) | A | .257 | 117 | 467 | 71 | 120 | 30 | 2 | 24 | 100 | 24 | 137 | 8 | .302 | .484 |
| 2006 | Daytona (FSL) | A | .248 | 122 | 475 | 64 | 118 | 25 | 1 | 20 | 84 | 25 | 125 | 7 | .290 | .432 |
| **MINOR LEAGUE TOTALS** | | | .255 | 313 | 1234 | 187 | 315 | 69 | 5 | 59 | 239 | 75 | 365 | 17 | .305 | .463 |

## 9 CHRIS HUSEBY RHP

**Born:** Jan. 11, 1988. **B-T:** R-R. **Ht.:** 6-7. **Wt.:** 220. **Drafted:** HS—Stuart, Fla., 2006 (11th round). **Signed by:** Rolando Pino.

Huseby had pitched for the U.S. youth national team and was establishing himself as an early-round prospect for the 2006 draft when he blew out his elbow as a high school junior in March 2005. After recovering from Tommy John surgery, the Auburn recruit pitched just a handful of innings last spring. But led by area scout Rolando Pino, the Cubs saw enough in his limited action and a workout to give him a $1.3 million bonus last June, a record for an 11th-rounder. Huseby has intimidating size and a chance for three plus pitches. He was throwing 90-95 mph 15 months removed from Tommy John surgery, and there's more projection remaining in his frame. He also has a power curveball and a promising changeup. He's athletic and has a sound delivery, so throwing strikes shouldn't be an issue. Because he has efficient mechanics and works hard at staying in shape, Chicago isn't worried about further arm problems. Like most pitchers coming back from elbow reconstruction, Huseby will need  more time to build up his endurance and regain his feel for his secondary pitches. His changeup is promising but still in the developmental stages. The Cubs will do their best to take care of Huseby's valuable right arm. Rather than send him to the cold weather of the Midwest League in April, they'll probably keep him in extended spring training and ship him to Boise in June.

| Year | Club (League) | Class | W | L | ERA | G | GS | CG | SV | IP | H | R | ER | HR | BB | SO | AVG |
|---|---|---|---|---|---|---|---|---|---|---|---|---|---|---|---|---|---|
| 2006 | Cubs (AZL) | R | 0 | 2 | 5.19 | 6 | 6 | 0 | 0 | 17 | 21 | 10 | 10 | 1 | 6 | 14 | .296 |
| **MINOR LEAGUE TOTALS** | | | 0 | 2 | 5.19 | 6 | 6 | 0 | 0 | 17 | 21 | 10 | 10 | 1 | 6 | 14 | .296 |

## 10 MARK PAWELEK LHP

**Born:** Aug. 18, 1986. **B-T:** L-L. **Ht.:** 6-3. **Wt.:** 190. **Drafted:** HS—Springville, Utah, 2005 (1st round). **Signed by:** John Bartsch.

Pawelek surpassed Bruce Hurst as the highest-drafted Utah high schooler ever, going 20th overall in 2005 and signing for $1.75 million. Rated the No. 1 prospect in the Rookie-level Arizona League in his pro debut, he showed up at his first spring training unprepared mentally or physically. The Cubs sent him a wakeup call by scrapping a planned assignment to low Class A and keeping him in extended spring training. Pawelek has a chance for three solid-average pitches. He pitched at 88-92 mph and touched 95 with his fastball during the summer. Chicago had him scrap his slider and splitter to concentrate on his curveball and changeup, and his secondary pitches are improving. A year ago, scouts thought Pawelek had a chance for three plus pitches. Even when he got into shape, he didn't show his previous arm speed and didn't work at 92-95 mph like he had in 2005. He has an awkward delivery that's  long in back and leaves him slinging his pitches. If he can't clean that up, shoulder problems could be in his future. The Cubs believe Pawelek learned his lesson and expect him to be in better throwing shape when he arrives in 2007. Ticketed for low Class A, he still has promise even if his ceiling has diminished.

| Year | Club (League) | Class | W | L | ERA | G | GS | CG | SV | IP | H | R | ER | HR | BB | SO | AVG |
|---|---|---|---|---|---|---|---|---|---|---|---|---|---|---|---|---|---|
| 2005 | Cubs (AZL) | R | 0 | 3 | 2.72 | 14 | 13 | 0 | 0 | 43 | 25 | 18 | 13 | 0 | 21 | 56 | .170 |
| | Boise (NWL) | A | 0 | 0 | 0.00 | 1 | 1 | 0 | 0 | 3 | 6 | 1 | 0 | 0 | 1 | 4 | .462 |
| 2006 | Boise (NWL) | A | 3 | 5 | 2.51 | 15 | 12 | 0 | 0 | 61 | 54 | 24 | 17 | 1 | 23 | 52 | .232 |
| **MINOR LEAGUE TOTALS** | | | 3 | 8 | 2.52 | 30 | 26 | 0 | 0 | 107 | 85 | 43 | 30 | 1 | 45 | 112 | .216 |

## 11 JUAN MATEO RHP

**Born:** Dec. 17, 1982. **B-T:** R-R. **Ht.:** 6-2. **Wt.:** 180. **Signed:** Dominican Republic, 2002. **Signed by:** Jose Serra.

Chicago almost lost Mateo when St. Louis took Mateo in the major league Rule 5 draft at the 2005 Winter Meetings. But he showed up in Cardinals camp out of shape last spring, and the Cubs gladly took him back for half the $50,000 draft price after he cleared waivers. It didn't take long for him to get into condition, as he pitched well in Double-A and spent the last two months of the season in Chicago's rotation. Managers rated Mateo's fastball the best in the Southern League last summer. It has good velocity at 90-95 mph, and it's also notable for its life and his command of the pitch. He also throws a slider and a changeup, but they're just borderline average at their best right now. He always has done a good job of throwing strikes and he showed little fear in his stint in the majors. Because he doesn't have a deep repertoire, he may well wind up back in the bullpen, where he spent most of his first four years in pro ball. After signing Ted Lilly and Jason Marquis, the Cubs believe they've

filled the holes that riddled their rotation in 2006, so Mateo probably will serve in long relief if he makes the big league club.

| Year | Club (League) | Class | W | L | ERA | G | GS | CG | SV | IP | H | R | ER | HR | BB | SO | AVG |
|------|--------------|-------|---|---|-----|---|----|----|----|----|---|---|----|----|----|----|-----|
| 2002 | Cubs (DSL) | R | 3 | 0 | 3.18 | 11 | 4 | 0 | 3 | 28 | 24 | 15 | 10 | 1 | 10 | 22 | .214 |
| 2003 | Cubs (AZL) | R | 4 | 1 | 4.46 | 18 | 0 | 0 | 2 | 36 | 42 | 25 | 18 | 2 | 14 | 35 | .288 |
| 2004 | Lansing (MWL) | A | 4 | 1 | 3.28 | 53 | 1 | 0 | 9 | 74 | 61 | 28 | 27 | 3 | 19 | 60 | .216 |
| 2005 | Daytona (FSL) | A | 10 | 5 | 3.21 | 32 | 16 | 1 | 2 | 109 | 99 | 47 | 39 | 9 | 27 | 123 | .240 |
| 2006 | West Tenn (SL) | AA | 7 | 4 | 2.82 | 18 | 17 | 0 | 0 | 93 | 78 | 32 | 29 | 6 | 26 | 70 | .229 |
| | Chicago (NL) | MLB | 1 | 3 | 5.32 | 11 | 10 | 0 | 0 | 46 | 51 | 31 | 27 | 6 | 23 | 35 | .288 |
| **MINOR LEAGUE TOTALS** | | | 28 | 11 | 3.25 | 132 | 38 | 1 | 16 | 341 | 304 | 147 | 123 | 21 | 96 | 310 | .235 |
| **MAJOR LEAGUE TOTALS** | | | 1 | 3 | 5.32 | 11 | 10 | 0 | 0 | 45 | 51 | 31 | 27 | 6 | 23 | 35 | .288 |

## 12  BRIAN DOPIRAK                                                     1B

**Born:** Dec. 20, 1983. **B-T:** R-R. **Ht.:** 6-4. **Wt.:** 230. **Drafted:** HS—Dunedin, Fla., 2002 (2nd round). **Signed by:** Tom Shafer.

Dopirak is one of several Cubs who attended Dunedin (Fla.) High, along with general manager Jim Hendry, scouting director Tim Wilken and fellow slugger Ryan Harvey. Dopirak was the Paul Bunyan of the Midwest League in 2004, winning the MVP award and the home run crown, and he ranked No. 1 on this list. But nothing has gone right for him since. He got off to a slow start in high Class A the following season, panicked trying to get out of his slump and messed up his swing. He seemed to be putting the pieces back together last spring when he hit .355 in big league camp, but disaster struck on Opening Day. Dopirak broke the metatarsal bone in his left foot while running the bases, requiring surgery that sidelined him for two months. When he returned in June he never got his timing back, and he hit just one homer in 52 games before he needed another operation to correct further problems with his foot. When he's going well, Dopirak generates tremendous power with a short stroke. When he's not hitting home runs, he brings little else to the table. He doesn't control the strike zone and sells out for power, so he doesn't hit for average. He's a well below-average runner and a subpar defender at first base, though he works at his defense. Chicago hopes he can regain his confidence and his 2004 form when he returns to Double-A this year.

| Year | Club (League) | Class | AVG | G | AB | R | H | 2B | 3B | HR | RBI | BB | SO | SB | OBP | SLG |
|------|--------------|-------|-----|---|----|---|---|----|----|----|-----|----|----|----|-----|-----|
| 2002 | Cubs (AZL) | R | .253 | 21 | 79 | 10 | 20 | 4 | 0 | 0 | 6 | 6 | 23 | 0 | .306 | .304 |
| 2003 | Boise (NWL) | A | .240 | 52 | 192 | 25 | 46 | 4 | 0 | 13 | 37 | 24 | 58 | 0 | .330 | .464 |
| | Lansing (MWL) | A | .269 | 19 | 78 | 8 | 21 | 3 | 0 | 2 | 10 | 2 | 22 | 0 | .305 | .385 |
| 2004 | Lansing (MWL) | A | .307 | 137 | 541 | 94 | 166 | 38 | 0 | 39 | 120 | 48 | 123 | 4 | .363 | .593 |
| 2005 | Daytona (FSL) | A | .235 | 132 | 507 | 53 | 119 | 26 | 0 | 16 | 76 | 37 | 107 | 1 | .289 | .381 |
| 2006 | West Tenn (SL) | AA | .257 | 52 | 179 | 16 | 46 | 12 | 0 | 1 | 23 | 16 | 41 | 0 | .322 | .341 |
| **MINOR LEAGUE TOTALS** | | | .265 | 413 | 1576 | 206 | 418 | 87 | 0 | 71 | 272 | 133 | 374 | 5 | .325 | .456 |

## 13  JAE-KUK RYU                                                       RHP

**Born:** May 30, 1983. **B-T:** R-R. **Ht.:** 6-3. **Wt.:** 220. **Signed:** Korea, 2001. **Signed by:** Leon Lee.

Ryu rode a roller coaster to the majors, finally arriving in Chicago last May. He signed for $1.6 million out of Korea in 2001 and made national headlines two years later when he killed an osprey by knocking it off its perch at Daytona's Jackie Robinson Ballpark with a thrown baseball. He came down with elbow tendinitis in 2004, limiting him to 30 innings. Ryu has lost velocity since, dropping from 92-93 mph to 88-89, but has found success by mixing four pitches. His best offering is his changeup, and he also throws a slider and curveball. Ryu stands out more for his command than his pure stuff. He was so conscious of not issuing walks when he got to the big leagues that he went too far in the other direction, laying the ball over the plate. Not surprisingly, he got hammered, and the Cubs hope he learned that he has to change speeds and live on the corners of the plate. He doesn't have the same ceiling he once did, but he still could become a back-of-the-rotation starter. As with Juan Mateo, Ryu probably is looking at a middle-relief role if he makes the Chicago staff this season.

| Year | Club (League) | Class | W | L | ERA | G | GS | CG | SV | IP | H | R | ER | HR | BB | SO | AVG |
|------|--------------|-------|---|---|-----|---|----|----|----|----|---|---|----|----|----|----|-----|
| 2001 | Cubs (AZL) | R | 1 | 0 | 0.61 | 4 | 3 | 0 | 0 | 15 | 11 | 2 | 1 | 0 | 5 | 20 | .196 |
| 2002 | Boise (NWL) | A | 6 | 1 | 3.57 | 10 | 10 | 0 | 0 | 53 | 45 | 28 | 21 | 1 | 25 | 56 | .223 |
| | Lansing (MWL) | A | 1 | 2 | 7.11 | 5 | 4 | 0 | 0 | 19 | 26 | 16 | 15 | 1 | 8 | 21 | .333 |
| 2003 | Daytona (FSL) | A | 0 | 1 | 3.05 | 4 | 4 | 0 | 0 | 21 | 14 | 14 | 7 | 1 | 11 | 22 | .187 |
| | Lansing (MWL) | A | 6 | 1 | 1.75 | 11 | 11 | 0 | 0 | 72 | 59 | 19 | 14 | 2 | 19 | 57 | .225 |
| | West Tenn (SL) | AA | 2 | 5 | 5.43 | 11 | 11 | 1 | 0 | 58 | 63 | 37 | 35 | 3 | 25 | 45 | .280 |
| 2004 | Cubs (AZL) | R | 0 | 0 | 4.50 | 2 | 2 | 0 | 0 | 4 | 4 | 2 | 2 | 1 | 0 | 5 | .250 |
| | Boise (NWL) | A | 0 | 2 | 2.57 | 5 | 0 | 0 | 0 | 7 | 7 | 3 | 2 | 0 | 5 | 7 | .250 |
| | West Tenn (SL) | AA | 1 | 0 | 2.95 | 14 | 0 | 0 | 0 | 18 | 22 | 8 | 6 | 0 | 10 | 19 | .286 |
| | Iowa (PCL) | AAA | 0 | 0 | 40.50 | 1 | 0 | 0 | 0 | 1 | 2 | 4 | 3 | 1 | 1 | 0 | .500 |

| Year | Club (League) | Class | | | | | | | | | | | | | | | |
|---|---|---|---|---|---|---|---|---|---|---|---|---|---|---|---|---|---|
| 2005 | West Tenn (SL) | AA | 11 | 8 | 3.34 | 27 | 27 | 1 | 0 | 170 | 154 | 67 | 63 | 12 | 49 | 133 | .246 |
| 2006 | Iowa (PCL) | AAA | 8 | 8 | 3.23 | 24 | 23 | 1 | 0 | 139 | 123 | 54 | 50 | 12 | 51 | 114 | .237 |
| | Chicago (NL) | MLB | 0 | 1 | 8.40 | 10 | 1 | 0 | 0 | 15 | 23 | 14 | 14 | 7 | 6 | 17 | .348 |
| **MINOR LEAGUE TOTALS** | | | 36 | 28 | 3.42 | 118 | 95 | 3 | 0 | 576 | 530 | 254 | 219 | 34 | 209 | 499 | .244 |
| **MAJOR LEAGUE TOTALS** | | | 0 | 1 | 8.40 | 10 | 1 | 0 | 0 | 15 | 23 | 14 | 14 | 7 | 6 | 17 | .348 |

## 14 MARK REED                                                                 C

**Born:** April 13, 1986. **B-T:** L-R. **Ht.:** 5-11. **Wt.:** 175. **Drafted:** HS—LaVerne, Calif., 2004 (2nd round). **Signed by:** Jim Crawford.

Like his older brother Jeremy, who has struggled in the majors with the Mariners, Reed hasn't hit as expected the last two years. When the Cubs took him in the second round in 2004, they thought he'd be an offense-first catcher, and they still think he can. Reed has a short, smooth lefthanded swing that should allow him to be productive, and he hit .312 in the first three months of last season. But he faded horribly, batting .167 with no home runs the rest of the way because he wore down physically and his approach deteriorated. He lacks discipline and tries to hit homers, lengthening his stroke and swinging through pitches. Reed is more athletic and runs better than most catchers. He has encouraged Chicago with his progress behind the plate. He has fringy arm strength but makes accurate throws, which helped him nail 42 percent of basestealers in 2006. His receiving skills are good enough and he moves well behind the plate. The Cubs continue to compare his total package to that of Greg Zaun. Reed will have to get stronger and get his bat going to fit that profile, and that will be his main task this year in high Class A.

| Year | Club (League) | Class | AVG | G | AB | R | H | 2B | 3B | HR | RBI | BB | SO | SB | OBP | SLG |
|---|---|---|---|---|---|---|---|---|---|---|---|---|---|---|---|---|
| 2004 | Cubs (AZL) | R | .351 | 10 | 37 | 5 | 13 | 5 | 1 | 1 | 7 | 4 | 8 | 0 | .429 | .622 |
| 2005 | Peoria (MWL) | A | .135 | 14 | 52 | 2 | 7 | 1 | 1 | 0 | 6 | 1 | 12 | 0 | .167 | .192 |
| | Boise (NWL) | A | .250 | 55 | 184 | 32 | 46 | 10 | 0 | 4 | 18 | 15 | 53 | 7 | .310 | .370 |
| 2006 | Peoria (MWL) | A | .252 | 101 | 349 | 47 | 88 | 12 | 0 | 2 | 30 | 26 | 82 | 14 | .313 | .304 |
| **MINOR LEAGUE TOTALS** | | | .248 | 180 | 622 | 86 | 154 | 28 | 2 | 7 | 61 | 46 | 155 | 21 | .308 | .333 |

## 15 DREW RUNDLE                                                              OF

**Born:** Nov. 5, 1987. **B-T:** L-L. **Ht.:** 6-4. **Wt.:** 180. **Drafted:** HS—Bend, Ore., 2006 (14th round). **Signed by:** John Bartsch.

The Cubs surrendered their second- through fourth-round picks in the 2006 draft as free-agent compensation, but they made up for it by spending heavily on Jeff Samardzija, Chris Huseby and Rundle. Chicago took Rundle in the 14th round after he scared off clubs with his commitment to Arizona, then signed him for $500,000, the equivalent of late second-round money. He struck out in 24 of his first 47 pro at-bats before making adjustments and finishing his debut on a positive note. Rundle entered the spring as a possible first-round pick, but his stock dropped after he spread out his stance. He was trying to improve his plate coverage but succeeded only in diminishing his power, as he wasn't strong enough to make his new swing work. After his brutal start in Rookie ball, the Cubs got him to close his stance and shorten his swing. They think he's a younger and slightly less athletic version of their 2006 first-round pick, Tyler Colvin. The ball carries well of Rundle's bat, though he still needs to improve his plate discipline. He has average speed and arm strength, making him fit best in right field. He'll move up to Boise in 2007.

| Year | Club (League) | Class | AVG | G | AB | R | H | 2B | 3B | HR | RBI | BB | SO | SB | OBP | SLG |
|---|---|---|---|---|---|---|---|---|---|---|---|---|---|---|---|---|
| 2006 | Cubs (AZL) | R | .230 | 37 | 126 | 22 | 29 | 9 | 3 | 1 | 15 | 20 | 49 | 3 | .376 | .373 |
| **MINOR LEAGUE TOTALS** | | | .230 | 37 | 126 | 22 | 29 | 9 | 3 | 1 | 15 | 20 | 49 | 3 | .376 | .373 |

## 16 ROCKY CHERRY                                                             RHP

**Born:** Aug. 19, 1979. **B-T:** R-R. **Ht.:** 6-5. **Wt.:** 225. **Drafted:** Oklahoma, 2002 (14th round). **Signed by:** Brian Milner.

Cherry has been healthy for just 3 1/2 months over the last two seasons, but the Cubs protected him on their 40-man roster this offseason because they were certain they'd lose him in the major league Rule 5 draft if they didn't. He made just three starts in 2005 before needing surgery to reconstruct his elbow, which had bothered him since his college days at Oklahoma. He developed a bone spur in the middle finger of his pitching hand early last season, and pitched through it until it dislodged in mid-July, requiring a minor operation. Chicago had moved him to the bullpen to ease his return from Tommy John surgery, and Cherry was lights out for much of 2006. He threw a heavy 92-93 mph sinker that topped out at 95, and he backed it up with a plus slider that rates as the best in the system. He also owns a usable changeup that he didn't need much while working in relief. Cherry has good control, so all he needs to do in Triple-A is make his slider a little more consistent. Then he'll

be ready to help the Cubs.

| Year | Club (League) | Class | W | L | ERA | G | GS | CG | SV | IP | H | R | ER | HR | BB | SO | AVG |
|------|---------------|-------|---|---|-----|---|----|----|----|----|---|---|----|----|----|----|-----|
| 2003 | Boise (NWL) | A | 5 | 2 | 2.17 | 10 | 10 | 0 | 0 | 54 | 36 | 21 | 13 | 1 | 18 | 55 | .180 |
| | Lansing (MWL) | A | 2 | 0 | 2.76 | 8 | 4 | 0 | 0 | 29 | 23 | 10 | 9 | 1 | 7 | 18 | .217 |
| 2004 | Daytona (FSL) | A | 5 | 10 | 5.20 | 27 | 22 | 1 | 0 | 125 | 138 | 79 | 72 | 16 | 46 | 104 | .286 |
| 2005 | West Tenn (SL) | AA | 0 | 0 | 2.89 | 3 | 3 | 0 | 0 | 9 | 8 | 5 | 3 | 0 | 4 | 9 | .229 |
| 2006 | West Tenn (SL) | AA | 4 | 1 | 2.22 | 31 | 0 | 0 | 2 | 49 | 43 | 14 | 12 | 3 | 14 | 50 | .246 |
| | Iowa (PCL) | AAA | 1 | 0 | 10.12 | 2 | 0 | 0 | 0 | 3 | 3 | 3 | 3 | 0 | 1 | 2 | .273 |
| **MINOR LEAGUE TOTALS** | | | 17 | 13 | 3.75 | 81 | 39 | 1 | 2 | 269 | 251 | 132 | 112 | 21 | 90 | 238 | .249 |

## 17  GEOVANY SOTO                                                      C

**Born:** Jan. 20, 1983. **B-T:** R-R. **Ht.:** 6-1. **Wt.:** 230. **Drafted:** HS—Rio Piedras, P.R., 2001 (11th round). **Signed by:** Jose Trujillo.

Soto got the chance to make an impression early in the Cactus League season. With the Cubs' two big league catcher, Michael Barrett and Henry Blanco, off at the World Baseball Classic, Soto got into the lineup and hit .333. When the regular season started, he returned to Triple-A and replicated his 2005 performance there. Despite lacking a standout tool, he might be the most well-rounded of the system's catching prospects. He has enough bat-handling ability and strength to project as a .260 hitter with double-digit homers if he played regularly in the majors. He shows patience at the plate and draws his share of walks. He's a below-average runner but agile for a catcher. Soto's arm is his best tool, though he threw out just 29 percent of basestealers in Triple-A last year. He's a solid receiver and blocks balls well. Soto profiles more as a backup than as a regular, but he doesn't have much of an opportunity in Chicago after Blanco re-signed for two years and $5.25 million in that role. Soto looks destined for a third straight season in Iowa.

| Year | Club (League) | Class | AVG | G | AB | R | H | 2B | 3B | HR | RBI | BB | SO | SB | OBP | SLG |
|------|---------------|-------|-----|---|----|---|---|----|----|----|----|----|----|----|-----|-----|
| 2001 | Cubs (AZL) | R | .260 | 41 | 150 | 18 | 39 | 16 | 0 | 1 | 20 | 15 | 33 | 1 | .339 | .387 |
| 2002 | Cubs (AZL) | R | .269 | 44 | 156 | 24 | 42 | 10 | 2 | 3 | 24 | 13 | 35 | 0 | .333 | .417 |
| | Boise (NWL) | A | .400 | 1 | 5 | 1 | 2 | 0 | 0 | 0 | 0 | 0 | 1 | 0 | .400 | .400 |
| 2003 | Daytona (FSL) | A | .242 | 89 | 297 | 26 | 72 | 12 | 2 | 2 | 38 | 31 | 58 | 0 | .313 | .316 |
| 2004 | West Tenn (SL) | AA | .271 | 104 | 332 | 47 | 90 | 16 | 0 | 9 | 48 | 40 | 71 | 1 | .355 | .401 |
| 2005 | Iowa (PCL) | AAA | .253 | 91 | 292 | 30 | 74 | 14 | 0 | 4 | 39 | 48 | 77 | 0 | .357 | .342 |
| | Chicago (NL) | MLB | .000 | 1 | 1 | 0 | 0 | 0 | 0 | 0 | 0 | 0 | 0 | 0 | .000 | .000 |
| 2006 | Iowa (PCL) | AAA | .272 | 108 | 342 | 34 | 93 | 21 | 0 | 6 | 38 | 41 | 74 | 0 | .353 | .386 |
| | Chicago (NL) | MLB | .200 | 11 | 25 | 1 | 5 | 1 | 0 | 0 | 2 | 0 | 5 | 0 | .231 | .240 |
| **MINOR LEAGUE TOTALS** | | | .262 | 478 | 1574 | 180 | 412 | 89 | 4 | 25 | 207 | 188 | 349 | 2 | .344 | .371 |
| **MAJOR LEAGUE TOTALS** | | | .192 | 12 | 26 | 1 | 5 | 1 | 0 | 0 | 2 | 0 | 5 | 0 | .222 | .231 |

## 18  BILLY PETRICK                                                    RHP

**Born:** April 29, 1984. **B-T:** R-R. **Ht.:** 6-6. **Wt.:** 220. **Drafted:** HS—Morris, Ill., 2002 (3rd round). **Signed by:** Bob Hale.

Petrick was one of the Cubs' top pitching prospects until he hurt his shoulder in May 2005. Doctors discovered a small tear in his labrum, which was repaired with arthroscopic surgery. Sidelined for a year, he returned to the mound in the second half of 2006 and showed that he still had his trademark 91-92 mph heavy sinker. The pitch is so difficult to lift that he has given up just 10 homers in 332 pro innings. The key for Petrick will be developing his secondary pitches. He threw a curveball early in his pro career before scrapping it in favor of a slider. He's still working on throwing his changeup with the same arm speed as his fastball. Petrick's strike-throwing ability hasn't diminished. Nor has his aggressive mentality that's fitting for a once-promising football prospect who could have gone to Washington State as a long snapper. He'll open 2007 with his third stint in high Class A, and the Cubs would love to see him complete his first full season since 2004.

| Year | Club (League) | Class | W | L | ERA | G | GS | CG | SV | IP | H | R | ER | HR | BB | SO | AVG |
|------|---------------|-------|---|---|-----|---|----|----|----|----|---|---|----|----|----|----|-----|
| 2002 | Cubs (AZL) | R | 2 | 1 | 1.71 | 6 | 6 | 0 | 0 | 32 | 21 | 8 | 6 | 0 | 6 | 35 | .189 |
| 2003 | Boise (NWL) | A | 2 | 5 | 4.76 | 14 | 14 | 0 | 0 | 64 | 60 | 49 | 34 | 4 | 27 | 64 | .241 |
| 2004 | Lansing (MWL) | A | 13 | 7 | 3.50 | 26 | 24 | 0 | 0 | 147 | 149 | 66 | 57 | 3 | 43 | 113 | .276 |
| 2005 | Daytona (FSL) | A | 1 | 4 | 5.59 | 9 | 9 | 0 | 0 | 37 | 39 | 23 | 23 | 0 | 19 | 25 | .275 |
| 2006 | Boise (NWL) | A | 5 | 0 | 2.23 | 7 | 7 | 0 | 0 | 36 | 37 | 10 | 9 | 0 | 12 | 28 | .268 |
| | Daytona (FSL) | A | 1 | 2 | 6.06 | 3 | 3 | 0 | 0 | 16 | 24 | 11 | 11 | 3 | 2 | 9 | .343 |
| **MINOR LEAGUE TOTALS** | | | 24 | 19 | 3.79 | 65 | 63 | 0 | 0 | 332 | 330 | 167 | 140 | 10 | 109 | 274 | .264 |

## 19  DYLAN JOHNSTON                                                   SS

**Born:** March 25, 1987. **B-T:** L-R. **Ht.:** 6-0. **Wt.:** 180. **Drafted:** HS—Chandler, Ariz., 2005 (4th round). **Signed by:** Steve McFarland.

Johnston starred as a high schooler in Arizona, leading Chandler's Hamilton High to state

5-A titles in 2003 and 2004 and a runner-up finish in 2005. Less than a year later, the Cubs gave him an at-bat in big league camp, and he responded with a long homer off future Hall of Famer Trevor Hoffman. Johnston is still raw and years removed from being ready for the majors, but his bomb hinted at his upside. He has a quick bat and above-average potential. Chicago widened his setup and raised his hands in his stance when he immediately struggled in this 2005 pro debut, and he has further adjustments to make. He strikes out too much and will have to tone down his approach. He needs a lot of minor league at-bats, and he lost valuable development time when he severely sprained his ankle sliding into a base last July. He also had problems with a bone bruise in the webbing of his thumb after the Cubs tried to get him to grip the bat more toward his fingertips. Johnston has average speed and range. His strong arm and quick release allow him to make plays at shortstop, though he could outgrow the position as he fills out. Chicago thought enough of him to send him to low Class A as a 19-year-old, and he'll return there in 2007.

| Year | Club (League) | Class | AVG | G | AB | R | H | 2B | 3B | HR | RBI | BB | SO | SB | OBP | SLG |
|------|---------------|-------|------|----|-----|----|----|----|----|----|-----|----|----|----|------|------|
| 2005 | Cubs (AZL) | R | .182 | 13 | 44 | 4 | 8 | 2 | 0 | 0 | 5 | 6 | 24 | 0 | .280 | .227 |
| 2006 | Peoria (MWL) | A | .200 | 58 | 190 | 22 | 38 | 7 | 3 | 0 | 11 | 26 | 60 | 8 | .306 | .268 |
| **MINOR LEAGUE TOTALS** | | | .197 | 71 | 234 | 26 | 46 | 9 | 3 | 0 | 16 | 32 | 84 | 8 | .301 | .261 |

## 20  JOSH LANSFORD                                       3B

**Born:** July 3, 1984. **B-T:** R-R. **Ht.:** 6-2. **Wt.:** 220. **Drafted:** Cal Poly, 2006 (6th round). **Signed by:** Steve Fuller.

Big-money signees Tyler Colvin, Jeff Samardzija and Chris Huseby attracted most of the attention given to the Cubs' 2006 draft crop, but the team is also enthused about Lansford, a relative bargain at $155,000 in the sixth round. He comes from a baseball family, as his father Carney won an American League batting title, his uncles Jody and Phil were both first-round picks and his brother Jared went in the second round to the Athletics in 2005. At Cal Poly, Lansford was inconsistent offensively in 2005 and defensively in 2006, dropping his draft stock a bit. He has a quick bat and good power, though he gets too pull-happy and flies open too early in his swing at times. His stroke is long but he makes reasonable contact. Lansford is a potential Gold Glove defender. He has plus-plus arm strength, and he unloads the ball quickly and accurately. He has tremendous agility for his size and good range to his right. His speed is slightly below average, yet he's not a liability on the bases. He hyperextended his left elbow on a swing in August but he was able to return before the end of the season. Lansford will advance to low Class A in 2007 and should be a candidate for a midseason promotion.

| Year | Club (League) | Class | AVG | G | AB | R | H | 2B | 3B | HR | RBI | BB | SO | SB | OBP | SLG |
|------|---------------|-------|------|----|-----|----|----|----|----|----|-----|----|----|----|------|------|
| 2006 | Boise (NWL) | A | .255 | 62 | 235 | 32 | 60 | 7 | 1 | 5 | 35 | 24 | 43 | 4 | .333 | .357 |
| **MINOR LEAGUE TOTALS** | | | .255 | 62 | 235 | 32 | 60 | 7 | 1 | 5 | 35 | 24 | 43 | 4 | .333 | .357 |

## 21  SAMMY BAEZ                                          SS

**Born:** Dec. 10, 1984. **B-T:** R-R. **Ht.:** 6-3. **Wt.:** 175. **Signed:** Dominican Republic, 2004. **Signed by:** Jose Serra.

Baez has an intriguing toolset for a middle infielder, though he didn't get to show it off much last season before going down with a shoulder injury that required surgery. After being an easy out in his pro debut in the Arizona League in 2005, he made much more consistent line-drive contact against more advanced Northwest League pitchers last summer. His 6-foot-3 frame still lacks strength, and he could develop solid power once he matures physically. If he provides any offense, Baez will be a big leaguer because the rest of his tools are above-average. He has plus-plus speed, though he's still figuring out how to steal bases. Defensively, his hands, range and arm are all plusses, and he should be able to stay at shortstop even after he fills out. Baez didn't sign until after he turned 20, an unusually late start for a Dominican player. As a result, the Cubs will advance him as quickly as he can cope with, which likely means an assignment to low Class A in 2007.

| Year | Club (League) | Class | AVG | G | AB | R | H | 2B | 3B | HR | RBI | BB | SO | SB | OBP | SLG |
|------|---------------|-------|------|----|-----|----|----|----|----|----|-----|----|----|----|------|------|
| 2005 | Cubs (AZL) | R | .213 | 41 | 150 | 13 | 32 | 4 | 1 | 0 | 10 | 5 | 26 | 3 | .242 | .253 |
| 2006 | Boise (NWL) | A | .310 | 19 | 71 | 8 | 22 | 3 | 1 | 0 | 10 | 1 | 9 | 9 | .342 | .380 |
| **MINOR LEAGUE TOTALS** | | | .244 | 60 | 221 | 21 | 54 | 7 | 2 | 0 | 20 | 6 | 35 | 12 | .275 | .294 |

## 22  CHRIS ROBINSON                                      C

**Born:** May 12, 1984. **B-T:** R-R. **Ht.:** 6-0. **Wt.:** 200. **Drafted:** Illinois, 2005 (3rd round). **Signed by:** Marty Miller (Tigers).

Just getting rid of Neifi Perez last August would have helped the Cubs, because his inabil-

ity to get on base harmed their offense for two years. But they also received Robinson, who adds to their stable of decent if not overwhelming catching prospects. A third-round pick in 2005 after leading Illinois to the Big Ten Conference regular-season title, he signed for $422,000. Robinson has a line-drive approach and gap power, and he may produce just enough offense to cut it as a regular in the big leagues. He won't drive many balls out of the park, so he'd be better off focusing on getting on base by showing more patience. He does a good job behind the plate, with plus arm strength (belied by his 26 percent success rate throwing out basestealers last year) and average receiving skills. A strong leader, he runs a pitching staff well. Like most catchers, he's a below-average runner. Robinson is ready for Double-A but may have to share time behind the plate in Tennessee with Jake Fox expected to return to that level.

| Year | Club (League) | Class | AVG | G | AB | R | H | 2B | 3B | HR | RBI | BB | SO | SB | OBP | SLG |
|------|---------------|-------|-----|---|----|---|---|----|----|----|-----|----|----|----|-----|-----|
| 2005 | Oneonta (NYP) | A | .154 | 4 | 13 | 2 | 2 | 0 | 0 | 0 | 1 | 1 | 3 | 0 | .200 | .154 |
|  | West Michigan (MWL) | A | .257 | 41 | 148 | 16 | 38 | 8 | 1 | 2 | 18 | 15 | 39 | 0 | .329 | .365 |
| 2006 | Lakeland (FSL) | A | .286 | 95 | 322 | 30 | 92 | 22 | 0 | 1 | 47 | 25 | 73 | 6 | .335 | .363 |
|  | Daytona (FSL) | A | .356 | 12 | 45 | 2 | 16 | 2 | 0 | 2 | 12 | 1 | 16 | 1 | .383 | .533 |
| **MINOR LEAGUE TOTALS** |  |  | .280 | 152 | 528 | 50 | 148 | 32 | 1 | 5 | 78 | 42 | 131 | 7 | .334 | .373 |

## 23 MARK HOLLIMAN RHP

**Born:** Sept. 19, 1983. **B-T:** R-R. **Ht.:** 6-0. **Wt.:** 195. **Drafted:** Mississippi, 2005 (3rd round). **Signed by:** Bob Rossi.

Holliman faced a tough decision to sign in 2005 and spent most of the summer making up his mind. Mississippi had fallen one game short of the College World Series, while he came up one strikeout shy of the school's career record held by former big leaguer Jeff Calhoun. He agreed to a $385,000 bonus that August but didn't make his pro debut until 2006. The Cubs had a number of young arms for their low Class A rotation and they knew Holliman was mentally tough, so they sent him to high Class A to begin his career. He competed well with average stuff. After showing a 90-92 mph fastball in college, he worked more at 88-91 last season. He uses both a curveball and a slider, and his curve shows signs of becoming a plus pitch. He also has a changeup that helped him deal with lefties (.237 average, .329 slugging) more effectively than righties (.244 average, .390 slugging) in 2006. Holliman isn't tall but does a good job of keeping his pitches down in the zone. Headed for Double-A, he profiles as a back-of-rotation starter.

| Year | Club (League) | Class | W | L | ERA | G | GS | CG | SV | IP | H | R | ER | HR | BB | SO | AVG |
|------|---------------|-------|---|---|-----|---|----|----|----|----|---|---|----|----|----|----|-----|
| 2006 | Daytona (FSL) | A | 8 | 11 | 4.38 | 26 | 26 | 0 | 0 | 144 | 129 | 76 | 70 | 12 | 58 | 121 | .241 |
| **MINOR LEAGUE TOTALS** |  |  | 8 | 11 | 4.38 | 26 | 26 | 0 | 0 | 144 | 129 | 76 | 70 | 12 | 58 | 121 | .241 |

## 24 JAKE FOX C

**Born:** July 20, 1982. **B-T:** R-R. **Ht.:** 6-0. **Wt.:** 210. **Drafted:** Michigan, 2003 (3rd round). **Signed by:** Stan Zielinski.

Trying to address a shortage in their system, the Cubs drafted nine catchers in 2003, starting with Fox in the third round. He's easily the best hitter among their current catching prospects, but also the weakest defender. Fox generates power with a short stroke. He hit a career-high 21 homers in 2006, and scouts credited him with doing a better job of using the whole field. However, he did most of his damage while repeating high Class A and wasn't nearly as dangerous after a promotion to Double-A, where his plate discipline deteriorated. Fox has to hit, because he's adequate at best behind the plate. He has some arm strength, but his footwork and transfer from mitt to hand don't work well. He threw out 30 percent of basestealers last year. He has more problems as a receiver, much of which can be attributed to a lack of concentration. He tied for the Southern League lead with 14 passed balls in just 43 games as a catcher. His game-calling skills also leave something to be desired. He works on his defense but doesn't have much to show for his efforts. He's a below-average runner but not a baseclogger like many catchers are. Both he and Chris Robinson will be stationed in Double-A this year, so Fox may also see time in the outfield and on the infield corners. The best-case scenario is that he becomes Chris Hoiles.

| Year | Club (League) | Class | AVG | G | AB | R | H | 2B | 3B | HR | RBI | BB | SO | SB | OBP | SLG |
|------|---------------|-------|-----|---|----|---|---|----|----|----|-----|----|----|----|-----|-----|
| 2003 | Cubs (AZL) | R | .240 | 15 | 50 | 4 | 12 | 5 | 0 | 1 | 6 | 5 | 14 | 0 | .321 | .400 |
|  | Lansing (MWL) | A | .260 | 29 | 100 | 13 | 26 | 8 | 0 | 5 | 12 | 8 | 19 | 0 | .330 | .490 |
| 2004 | Lansing (MWL) | A | .287 | 97 | 366 | 49 | 105 | 19 | 3 | 14 | 55 | 17 | 75 | 2 | .331 | .470 |
| 2005 | Daytona (FSL) | A | .281 | 83 | 270 | 37 | 76 | 20 | 0 | 9 | 40 | 26 | 48 | 5 | .357 | .456 |
| 2006 | Daytona (FSL) | A | .313 | 66 | 249 | 45 | 78 | 15 | 1 | 16 | 61 | 27 | 49 | 4 | .383 | .574 |
|  | West Tenn (SL) | AA | .269 | 55 | 193 | 20 | 52 | 17 | 0 | 5 | 25 | 9 | 44 | 0 | .304 | .435 |
| **MINOR LEAGUE TOTALS** |  |  | .284 | 345 | 1228 | 168 | 349 | 84 | 4 | 50 | 199 | 92 | 249 | 11 | .343 | .481 |

## LARRY SUAREZ                                                    RHP

**Born:** Dec. 20, 1989. **B-T:** R-R. **Ht.:** 6-5. **Wt.:** 240. **Signed:** Venezuela, 2006. **Signed by:** Hector Ortega.

In an attempt to beef up their system, the Cubs not only spent heavily on the draft but also made a large investment on the international front in 2006. They landed Suarez, the top pitcher available in Venezuela last summer, for $850,000. He first attracted attention when he touched 91 mph as a 15-year-old, and now he consistently throws his fastball at 88-92 mph. He already shows good command of his fastball and an effective changeup. He doesn't have much of a breaking ball at this point. Because he has a big build and is from Venezuela, he's compared to Carlos Zambrano, though he lacks Zambrano's athleticism. Suarez' weight already is getting away from him a little bit, and he'll have to monitor it carefully. Chicago worked on improving his conditioning during instructional league, but those efforts were hampered when he came down with a minor back strain. He'll likely make his pro debut in the Arizona League in June.

| Year | Club (League) | Class | W | L | ERA | G | GS | CG | SV | IP | H | R | ER | HR | BB | SO | AVG |
|------|---------------|-------|---|---|-----|---|----|----|----|----|---|---|----|----|----|----|-----|
| 2006 | Did not play—Signed 2007 contract | | | | | | | | | | | | | | | | |

## ROCKY ROQUET                                                   RHP

**Born:** Nov. 6, 1982. **B-T:** R-R. **Ht.:** 6-2. **Wt.:** 210. **Signed:** NDFA/Cal Poly, 2006. **Signed by:** Steve Fuller.

Roquet began his college career as an outfielder at Florida State, redshirting as a freshman when he became a full-time pitcher in his second semester. He later transferred to Santa Ana (Calif.) JC, Northeast Texas CC and finally Cal Poly, from where he signed as a fifth-year senior free agent before the 2006 draft. Roquet has two plus pitches, a fastball that runs from 91-97 mph and a hard slider. He has a strong frame that bodes well for his durability, as does his ability to throw strikes and keep his pitch counts down. Used primarily as a reliever in college, he doesn't have much experience with a changeup. Roquet gets hit when he opens up too soon his delivery, allowing hitters a better look at the ball and reducing the quality of his stuff. The Cubs moved him to the hitter's side of the rubber and were pleased with the early results. He lost three weeks in his pro debut when he stepped on a baseball while running and twisted his ankle. Roquet will be 24 this season, so Chicago will want to accelerate his development. He could open his first full season in high Class A.

| Year | Club (League) | Class | W | L | ERA | G | GS | CG | SV | IP | H | R | ER | HR | BB | SO | AVG |
|------|---------------|-------|---|---|-----|---|----|----|----|----|---|---|----|----|----|----|-----|
| 2006 | Boise (NWL) | A | 0 | 0 | 5.49 | 19 | 0 | 0 | 3 | 20 | 21 | 13 | 12 | 1 | 5 | 31 | .273 |
| **MINOR LEAGUE TOTALS** | | | 0 | 0 | 5.49 | 19 | 0 | 0 | 3 | 20 | 21 | 13 | 12 | 1 | 5 | 31 | .273 |

## SAM FULD                                                        OF

**Born:** Nov. 20, 1981. **B-T:** L-L. **Ht.:** 5-10. **Wt.:** 180. **Drafted:** Stanford, 2004 (10th round). **Signed by:** Steve Hinton.

Fuld starred for four seasons at Stanford, setting the College World Series record for career hits (24) and graduating with an economics degree. The Cubs drafted him in the 24th round in 2003 and again in the 10th round the following year, when they landed him for $25,000 as a senior sign. He partially tore the rotator cuff and labrum in his throwing shoulder in one of his final games for the Cardinal, so Fuld didn't make his pro debut until 2005. He reinjured his shoulder again that year, jamming it on a headfirst slide. A bulging disc in his back cost him two weeks in the middle of 2006, and his season ended with a hip injury in late July. To top it off, he had surgery to repair a sports hernia in November. When healthy, Fuld has put up consistent numbers in two years in Class A. He has the best strike-zone discipline in the system, which led to a 17-game hitting streak and a 33-game on-base streak in 2006. He doesn't have much pop, but he stings line drives all over the field. He's has slightly above-average speed and basestealing savvy, succeeding on 22 of 25 attempts last year. He gets good breaks and plays a solid center field, though his arm is below average. Fuld could crack the major league as a platoon or reserve outfielder, but he'll have to stay healthy to do so. He's ready for Double-A this year.

| Year | Club (League) | Class | AVG | G | AB | R | H | 2B | 3B | HR | RBI | BB | SO | SB | OBP | SLG |
|------|---------------|-------|-----|---|----|---|---|----|----|----|-----|----|----|----|-----|-----|
| 2005 | Peoria (MWL) | A | .300 | 125 | 443 | 82 | 133 | 32 | 6 | 5 | 37 | 50 | 44 | 18 | .377 | .433 |
| 2006 | Daytona (FSL) | A | .300 | 89 | 353 | 63 | 106 | 19 | 6 | 4 | 40 | 40 | 54 | 22 | .378 | .422 |
| **MINOR LEAGUE TOTALS** | | | .300 | 214 | 796 | 145 | 239 | 51 | 12 | 9 | 77 | 90 | 98 | 40 | .378 | .428 |

## 28  SCOTT TAYLOR                                                        RHP

**Born:** Dec. 28, 1986. **B-T:** R-R. **Ht.:** 6-3. **Wt.:** 240. **Drafted:** HS—Richmond, Va., 2005 (5th round). **Signed by:** Billy Swoope.

A fifth-round pick out of a Virginia high school in 2005, Taylor began his first full pro season in extended spring training but was summoned to the Peoria rotation in late April. When he gave up just five earned runs over his first four starts, he claimed a starting job on a full-time basis. He earned Peoria's lone playoff victory with seven shutout innings. Though he's 6-foot-3 and 240 pounds, he's more about control than power. Taylor throws strikes better than anyone in the system and needed just 99 pitches to throw a nine-inning complete game in August. He can be around the zone too much, however, surrendering too many hits after getting ahead in the count. His best pitch is a 91-93 mph fastball with boring action. Taylor needs to improve the rest of his repertoire, which includes a curveball, slider and changeup, in order to do a better job of putting hitters away. He'll have to watch his thick frame, though he's a better athlete than he looks. He'll move up to high Class A this year.

| Year | Club (League) | Class | W | L | ERA | G | GS | CG | SV | IP | H | R | ER | HR | BB | SO | AVG |
|---|---|---|---|---|---|---|---|---|---|---|---|---|---|---|---|---|---|
| 2005 | Cubs (AZL) | R | 0 | 3 | 6.89 | 6 | 6 | 0 | 0 | 16 | 21 | 14 | 12 | 0 | 7 | 13 | .313 |
| | Boise (NWL) | A | 0 | 0 | 5.63 | 2 | 2 | 0 | 0 | 8 | 7 | 5 | 5 | 0 | 2 | 7 | .233 |
| 2006 | Peoria (MWL) | A | 8 | 8 | 3.39 | 23 | 22 | 1 | 0 | 141 | 145 | 61 | 53 | 8 | 28 | 71 | .268 |
| **MINOR LEAGUE TOTALS** | | | 8 | 11 | 3.83 | 31 | 30 | 1 | 0 | 164 | 173 | 80 | 70 | 8 | 37 | 91 | .271 |

## 29  MITCH ATKINS                                                        RHP

**Born:** Oct. 1, 1985. **B-T:** R-R. **Ht.:** 6-3. **Wt.:** 230. **Drafted:** HS—Browns Summit, N.C., 2004 (7th round). **Signed by:** Billy Swoope.

Atkins is similar to Scott Taylor, his teammate at Peoria last season. Both are stocky righthanders signed out of high school who have live sinkers and are working on the rest of their game. In his first taste of full-season ball, Atkins led Cubs farmhands in victories and ranked second to Donald Veal in ERA in 2006. He also finished strong, going 7-2, 2.08 over his final 10 regular-season starts before losing a 2-0 heartbreaker in the playoffs. Atkins goes after hitters with a 91-92 mph fastball. His three-quarters delivery gives him sink on his heater but makes it hard for him to stay on top of his slurvy breaking ball. He shows feel for a changeup, though it's not consistently reliable at this point. Because Atkins lacks a second solid pitch and plus command, he may wind up in the bullpen down the road. He'll pitch alongside Taylor again in 2007, this time in the Daytona rotation.

| Year | Club (League) | Class | W | L | ERA | G | GS | CG | SV | IP | H | R | ER | HR | BB | SO | AVG |
|---|---|---|---|---|---|---|---|---|---|---|---|---|---|---|---|---|---|
| 2004 | Cubs (AZL) | R | 2 | 2 | 7.89 | 10 | 8 | 0 | 0 | 30 | 42 | 33 | 26 | 0 | 14 | 20 | .333 |
| 2005 | Boise (NWL) | A | 3 | 6 | 5.03 | 15 | 15 | 0 | 0 | 73 | 85 | 45 | 41 | 8 | 30 | 59 | .291 |
| 2006 | Peoria (MWL) | A | 13 | 4 | 2.41 | 25 | 25 | 0 | 0 | 138 | 110 | 47 | 37 | 10 | 53 | 127 | .217 |
| **MINOR LEAGUE TOTALS** | | | 18 | 12 | 3.88 | 50 | 48 | 0 | 0 | 241 | 237 | 125 | 104 | 18 | 97 | 206 | .256 |

## 30  MIKE FONTENOT                                                        2B

**Born:** June 9, 1980. **B-T:** L-R. **Ht.:** 5-8. **Wt.:** 160. **Drafted:** Louisiana State, 2001 (1st round). **Signed by:** Mike Tullier (Orioles).

Fontenot was considered a better prospect than double-play partner Ryan Theriot when they were helping Louisiana State win the 2000 College World Series. While Theriot carved out a big league role for himself in 2006, Fontenot has become more of an afterthought. He has offensive ability that shouldn't be ignored, however. He hits for average, draws walks and has occasional power. Fontenot doesn't stand out athletically, and that's what hurts him. He's an average runner but isn't a basestealing threat and has just adequate range. Defensively, he's limited to second base because of his below-average arm. The Cubs tried to make him a utilityman in 2005, but it didn't take. If he got a chance in the majors, Fontenot could be a lesser version of another former LSU second baseman, Todd Walker, providing less pop but better defense. However, that opportunity probably won't come with the Cubs, who left him exposed to the Rule 5 draft but kept him when he wasn't selected.

| Year | Club (League) | Class | AVG | G | AB | R | H | 2B | 3B | HR | RBI | BB | SO | SB | OBP | SLG |
|---|---|---|---|---|---|---|---|---|---|---|---|---|---|---|---|---|
| 2002 | Frederick (CL) | A | .264 | 122 | 481 | 61 | 127 | 16 | 4 | 8 | 53 | 42 | 117 | 13 | .333 | .364 |
| 2003 | Bowie (EL) | AA | .325 | 126 | 449 | 63 | 146 | 24 | 5 | 12 | 66 | 50 | 89 | 16 | .399 | .481 |
| 2004 | Ottawa (IL) | AAA | .279 | 136 | 524 | 73 | 146 | 30 | 10 | 8 | 49 | 48 | 111 | 14 | .346 | .420 |
| 2005 | Iowa (PCL) | AAA | .272 | 111 | 379 | 60 | 103 | 22 | 10 | 6 | 39 | 59 | 77 | 3 | .377 | .430 |
| | Chicago (NL) | MLB | .000 | 7 | 2 | 4 | 0 | 0 | 0 | 0 | 0 | 2 | 0 | 0 | .600 | .000 |
| 2006 | Iowa (PCL) | AAA | .296 | 111 | 362 | 54 | 107 | 28 | 2 | 8 | 36 | 47 | 64 | 5 | .375 | .450 |
| **MINOR LEAGUE TOTALS** | | | .287 | 606 | 2195 | 311 | 629 | 120 | 31 | 42 | 243 | 246 | 458 | 51 | .364 | .427 |
| **MAJOR LEAGUE TOTALS** | | | .000 | 7 | 2 | 4 | 0 | 0 | 0 | 0 | 0 | 2 | 0 | 0 | .600 | .000 |

# CHICAGO
# WHITE SOX

BY **PHIL ROGERS**

General manager Ken Williams, the architect of the White Sox' World Series championship in 2005, likes to say he enjoyed that success for about 24 hours before getting to work on a repeat. He appeared to strengthen the roster with a series of offseason moves funded by a significant increase in payroll, including the additions of Jim Thome and Javier Vazquez, but Chicago ultimately fell short of returning to the playoffs.

A pitching staff built around a veteran rotation couldn't duplicate its 2005 performance, with the staff ERA climbing from 3.61 to 4.61. The lineup picked up the pace early, helping the White Sox to a 56-29 start, but wore down late in the season. A 33-36 second half caused Chicago to slide into third place in the deep American League Central, missing the postseason despite delivering back-to-back 90-win seasons for the first time since the Sox had three straight from 1963-65.

While going backward in the standings, the White Sox flexed some new muscle in the Chicago market. They filled U.S. Cellular Field with regularity, drawing a record 2.96 million fans, nearly as many as the crosstown rival Cubs. Ratings showed that more people followed the Sox on television than the Cubs.

Williams has helped change the outlook of his franchise with his aggressive approach, almost always joining the pursuit of high-profile players on the market. He doesn't mind trading prospects for proven talent and hasn't seen many of his deals come back to bite him. The Vazquez trade could be an exception, as he sent promising center fielder Chris Young to the Diamondbacks. Trying to improve a thin bullpen, Williams sent two pitching prospects, lefthander Tyler Lumsden and righthander Daniel Cortes, to the Royals for Mike MacDougal in July. The White Sox eventually may suffer for draining so much talent away from the farm system. Their big league club was older than all of its AL Central rivals except for the Tigers in 2006.

Chicago did break in some young players last season, with Brian Anderson taking over in center field, **Bobby Jenks** saving 41 games in his first full year and Brandon McCarthy serving in middle relief while awaiting an opening in the rotation. Most of the system's top prospects are at the upper levels, led by outfielder Ryan Sweeney and third baseman Josh Fields, who starred in Triple-A and are ready for jobs with the Sox.

But at the lower levels, there's an alarming lack of talent. The bottom three clubs in Chicago's system combined for a .333 winning percentage. The White Sox have leaned toward safer, more easily projected prospects in recent drafts, leading to a shortage of high-ceiling talent. They also haven't been productive at mining international talent, prompting manager Ozzie Guillen to prod Williams for an increased effort at finding players from Latin America, particularly Guillen's native Venezuela.

## TOP 30 PROSPECTS

1. Ryan Sweeney, of
2. Josh Fields, 3b
3. Gio Gonzalez, lhp
4. Lance Broadway, rhp
5. Kyle McCulloch, rhp
6. Charlie Haeger, rhp
7. Aaron Cunningham, of
8. Adam Russell, rhp
9. Lucas Harrell, rhp
10. Matt Long, rhp
11. Chris Carter, 1b
12. Heath Phillips, lhp
13. Jerry Owens, of
14. Ray Liotta, lhp
15. Oneli Perez, rhp
16. Jack Egbert, rhp
17. Justin Edwards, lhp
18. Boone Logan, lhp
19. Robert Valido, ss
20. Pedro Lopez, ss/2b
21. John Shelby Jr., 2b/ss
22. Dewon Day, rhp
23. Chris Stewart, c
24. Anderson Gomes, of
25. Francisco Hernandez, c
26. Sean Tracey, rhp
27. Brian Omogrosso, rhp
28. Paulo Orlando, of
29. Wes Whisler, lhp
30. Ricardo Nanita, of

# ORGANIZATION OVERVIEW

**General manager:** Kenny Williams. **Farm director:** Alan Regier. **Scouting director:** Duane Shaffer.

## 2006 PERFORMANCE

| Class | Team | League | W | L | PCT | Finish* | Manager | Affiliated |
|---|---|---|---|---|---|---|---|---|
| Majors | Chicago | American | 90 | 72 | .556 | 5th (14) | Ozzie Guillen | — |
| Triple-A | Charlotte Knights | International | 79 | 62 | .560 | 2nd (14) | Razor Shines | 1999 |
| Double-A | Birmingham Barons | Southern | 59 | 81 | .421 | 9th (10) | Chris Cron | 1986 |
| High A | Winston-Salem Warthogs | Carolina | 66 | 72 | .478 | 5th (8) | Rafael Santana | 1997 |
| Low A | Kannapolis Intimidators | South Atlantic | 42 | 94 | .309 | 16th (16) | Omer Munoz | 2001 |
| Rookie | Great Falls White Sox | Pioneer | 28 | 48 | .368 | 7th (8) | Bobby Tolan | 2003 |
| Rookie | Bristol Sox | Appalachian | 22 | 42 | .344 | 10th (10) | Nick Leyva | 1995 |
| **OVERALL 2006 MINOR LEAGUE RECORD** | | | 296 | 399 | .426 | 29th (30) | | |

*Finish in overall standings (No. of teams in league). +League champion

## ORGANIZATION LEADERS

### BATTING
| | | |
|---|---|---|
| AVG | Fields, Josh, Charlotte | .305 |
| R | Fields, Josh, Charlotte | 86 |
| H | Velandia, Jorge, Charlotte | 153 |
| TB | Fields, Josh, Charlotte | 246 |
| 2B | Mercedes, Victor, Winston-Salem | 35 |
| 3B | Orlando, Paulo, Kannapolis | 10 |
| HR | Kelly, Christopher, Winston-Salem | 20 |
| RBI | Kelly, Christopher, Winston-Salem | 77 |
| | Sweeney, Ryan, Charlotte | 77 |
| BB | Cook, David, Winston-Salem | 77 |
| SO | Fields, Josh, Charlotte | 147 |
| SB | Owens, Jerry, Charlotte | 42 |
| OBP | Young, Ernie, Charlotte | 405 |
| SLG | Carter, Christopher, Kannapolis/Great Falls | .522 |
| XBH | Fields, Josh, Charlotte | 56 |

### PITCHING
| | | |
|---|---|---|
| W | Haeger, Charlie, Charlotte | 14 |
| | Redding, Tim, Charlotte | 14 |
| L | Rote, Ryan, Kannapolis/Great Falls | 15 |
| ERA | Egbert, Jack, Winston-Salem/Birmingham | 2.67 |
| G | Wassermann, Ehren, Birmingham | 68 |
| CG | Redding, Tim, Charlotte | 5 |
| SV | Wassermann, Ehren, Birmingham | 22 |
| IP | Redding, Tim, Charlotte | 207 |
| BB | Randolph, Stephen, Charlotte | 118 |
| SO | Randolph, Stephen, Charlotte | 155 |
| SO | Redding, Tim, Charlotte | 155 |
| AVG | Haeger, Charlie, Charlotte | 231 |

## BEST TOOLS

| | |
|---|---|
| Best Hitter for Average | Ryan Sweeney |
| Best Power Hitter | Josh Fields |
| Best Strike-Zone Discipline | Ricardo Nanita |
| Fastest Baserunner | Paulo Orlando |
| Best Athlete | Jerry Owens |
| Best Fastball | Adam Russell |
| Best Curveball | Gio Gonzalez |
| Best Slider | Kanekoa Texeira |
| Best Changeup | Kyle McCulloch |
| Best Control | Heath Phillips |
| Best Defensive Catcher | Chris Stewart |
| Best Defensive Infielder | Robert Valido |
| Best Infield Arm | Angel Gonzalez |
| Best Defensive Outfielder | Ryan Sweeney |
| Best Outfield Arm | Christian Marrero |

## PROJECTED 2010 LINEUP

| | |
|---|---|
| Catcher | A.J. Pierzynski |
| First Base | Josh Fields |
| Second Base | Tadahito Iguchi |
| Third Base | Joe Crede |
| Shortstop | Juan Uribe |

| | |
|---|---|
| Left Field | Jermaine Dye |
| Center Field | Brian Anderson |
| Right Field | Ryan Sweeney |
| Designated Hitter | Paul Konerko |
| No. 1 Starter | Mark Buehrle |
| No. 2 Starter | Brandon McCarthy |
| No. 3 Starter | Gio Gonzalez |
| No. 4 Starter | Jon Garland |
| No. 5 Starter | Lance Broadway |
| Closer | Bobby Jenks |

## LAST YEAR'S TOP 20 PROSPECTS

| | |
|---|---|
| 1. Bobby Jenks, rhp | 11. Sean Tracey, rhp |
| 2. Chris Young, of | 12. Casey Rogowski, 1b |
| 3. Brian Anderson, of | 13. Brandon Allen, 1b |
| 4. Ryan Sweeney, of | 14. Charlie Haeger, rhp |
| 5. Josh Fields, 3b | 15. Chris Getz, 2b/ss |
| 6. Jerry Owens, of | 16. Jeff Bajenaru, rhp |
| 7. Robert Valido, ss | 17. Aaron Cunningham, of |
| 8. Ray Liotta, lhp | 18. Tyler Lumsden, lhp |
| 9. Lance Broadway, rhp | 19. Chris Stewart, c |
| 10. Francisco Hernandez, c | 20. Pedro Lopez, ss/2b |

## TOP PROSPECTS OF THE DECADE

| Year | Player, Pos. | 2006 Org. |
|---|---|---|
| 1997 | Mike Cameron, of | Padres |
| 1998 | Mike Caruso, ss | Out of baseball |
| 1999 | Carlos Lee, 3b | Rangers |
| 2000 | Kip Wells, rhp | Rangers |
| 2001 | Jon Rauch, rhp | Nationals |
| 2002 | Joe Borchard, of | Marlins |
| 2003 | Joe Borchard, of | Marlins |
| 2004 | Joe Borchard, of | Marlins |
| 2005 | Brian Anderson, of | White Sox |
| 2006 | Bobby Jenks, rhp | White Sox |

## TOP DRAFT PICKS OF THE DECADE

| Year | Player, Pos. | 2006 Org. |
|---|---|---|
| 1997 | Jason Dellaero, ss | Out of baseball |
| 1998 | Kip Wells, rhp | Rangers |
| 1999 | Jason Stumm, rhp | Out of baseball |
| 2000 | Joe Borchard, of | Marlins |
| 2001 | Kris Honel, rhp | White Sox |
| 2002 | Royce Ring, lhp | Mets |
| 2003 | Brian Anderson, of | White Sox |
| 2004 | Josh Fields, 3b | White Sox |
| 2005 | Lance Broadway, rhp | White Sox |
| 2006 | Kyle McCulloch, rhp | White Sox |

## LARGEST BONUSES IN CLUB HISTORY

| | |
|---|---|
| Joe Borchard, 2000 | $5,300,000 |
| Jason Stumm, 1999 | $1,750,000 |
| Royce Ring, 2002 | $1,600,000 |
| Brian Anderson, 2003 | $1,600,000 |
| Lance Broadway, 2005 | $1,570,000 |

# MINOR LEAGUE DEPTH CHART

## Chicago White Sox

**Impact: B.** Sweeney and Fields are solid, but have questions about power and contact, respectively. Severe lack of power arms at upper levels offers few immediate options.
**Depth: D.** Picking low in the draft hasn't helped, but neither has conservative drafting strategy. Very good Triple-A Charlotte team could provide solid complementary players, like Haeger, Gonzalez, Stewart, Owens and Rogowski.
**Sleeper:** Dewon Day, rhp. A late addition to the 40-man roster, Day's improved fastball command and ridiculous slider impressed everybody in the AFL.

*Numbers in parentheses indicate prospect rankings.*

| LF | CF | RF |
|---|---|---|
| Aaron Cunningham (7) | Jerry Owens (13) | Ryan Sweeney (1) |
| Paulo Orlando (28) | Anderson Gomes (24) | Sean Smith |
| Ricardo Nanita (30) | Kent Gerst | David Cook |
| Thomas Collaro | Michael Myers | Stefan Gartrell |
| Archie Gilbert | | Sal Sanchez |
| Daron Roberts | | Lee Cruz |

| 3B | SS | 2B | 1B |
|---|---|---|---|
| Josh Fields (2) | Robert Valido (19) | Pedro Lopez (20) | Chris Carter (11) |
| Micah Schnurstein | Javier Castillo | John Shelby (21) | Casey Rogowski |
| Adam Ricks | | Andy Gonzalez | Brandon Allen |
| | | Chris Getz | Josh Hansen |
| | | Jose De los Santos | Chris Kelly |

| C |
|---|
| Chris Stewart (23) |
| Francisco Hernandez (25) |
| Donny Lucy |
| Gustavo Molina |
| Raymundo Tavares |
| Matt Inouye |
| Tyler Reves |

| RHP | | LHP | |
|---|---|---|---|
| **Starters** | **Relievers** | **Starters** | **Relievers** |
| Lance Broadway (4) | Adam Russell (8) | Gio Gonzalez (3) | Boone Logan (18) |
| Kyle McCulloch (5) | Matt Long (10) | Heath Phillips (12) | Wes Whisler (29) |
| Charlie Haeger (6) | Oneli Perez (15) | Ray Liotta (14) | Paulino Reynoso |
| Lucas Harrell (9) | Dewon Day (22) | Justin Edwards (17) | Clayton Richard |
| Jack Egbert (16) | Brian Omogrosso (27) | Corwin Malone | Carlos Vasquez |
| Sean Tracey (26) | Edwardo Sierra | Noe Rodriguez | Ryan Wing |
| Ricky Brooks | Jason Rice | Ryan Rodriguez | Alex Woodson |
| Derek Rodriguez | Kaneoka Texeira | Garrett Johnson | |
| Carlos Torres | Fernando Hernandez Jr. | | |
| | Matt Zaleski | | |
| | Ehren Wasserman | | |
| | Kris Honel | | |

## 2006     SIGNING BUDGET: $2.3 million

**Best Pro Debut:** After leading NCAA Division II with 26 homers and 97 RBIs and winning D-II player-of-the-year and College World Series MVP awards, OF Lee Cruz (10) batted .301 with five homers in pro ball. RHP Kyle McCulloch (1) posted a solid 3.12 ERA and reached high Class A. OF Stefan Gartrell (21) hit .301 with a .438 on-base percentage.

**Best Athlete:** 2B/SS John Shelby (5) has slightly above-average power and speed, while Gartrell is solid in both areas. Shelby also showed marked defensive improvement in pro ball.

**Best Pure Hitter:** Cruz. He played second base in instructional league, and if he can stay there his bat would be all the more valuable.

**Best Raw Power:** White Sox scouting director Duane Shaffer saw DH/C Tyler Reves (4) hit a ball over a four-lane road that runs behind Arizona State's Packard Stadium, the longest ball he's seen hit in 27 years scouting there. If Reves is going to find a position, first base is more likely than catcher.

**Fastest Runner:** OF Kent Gerst (8) was one of the fastest players at the 2005 Area Code Games. He can run the 60-yard dash in 6.4-6.5 seconds. He's still raw on the basepaths, however, as he was caught in seven of his 11 pro steal attempts.

**Best Defensive Player:** C Matt Inouye (21) receives well, calls a good game and knows how to run a pitching staff. His arm rates just a 45 on the 20-80 scouting scale, but his quick release allows it to play as at least average.

**Best Fastball:** RHP Matt Long (2), the first college senior drafted in 2006, sits at 92-94 mph and peaks at 96. As he puts his 2004 Tommy John surgery further behind him, he could add a little velocity. Another Tommy John survivor, RHP Brian Omogrosso (6) had the operation in 2005 and hit 96 mph early this spring. He spent most of the year pitching at 90-92 with good sink.

**Best Breaking Ball:** RHP Kanekoa Texeira (22) has the best slider in the White Sox system, not just their draft crop. Long's hard curveball can be devastating, but he doesn't always throw it for strikes. McCulloch's changeup is the best secondary pitch in Chicago's draft crop.

**Most Intriguing Background:** For the second time in three years, the White Sox drafted a son of GM Ken Williams, this time taking (but not signing) 2B Kyle (47). Shelby's father John played in the majors and is the Pirates' first-base coach. RHP Justin Cassel's (7) brother Matt is a backup quarterback on the New England Patriots. RHP Kanekoa Texeira (22) is a cousin of Phillies outfielder Shane Victorino. Unsigned RHP Mike Bolsenbroek (41) has pitched for several Dutch youth and junior national teams.

**Closest To The Majors:** McCulloch likely will open 2007 in Double-A. Long could beat him to Chicago if he gets back on track quickly.

**Best Late-Round Pick:** Cruz.

**The One Who Got Away:** The White Sox loved 3B Chris Duffy's (9) lefthanded power, but couldn't quite get a deal completed by his mid-July deadline, so he went to Central Florida. They weren't as close to landing Evansville-bound RHP Wade Kapteyn (20).

**Assessment:** For the second straight year, Chicago spent its first-rounder on a polished college righthander with average stuff, following Lance Broadway with McCulloch. The White Sox system is starting to flag a bit, so they need Long and hitters such as Reves, Shelby and Cruz to live up to their projections.

## 2005     BUDGET: $2.7 million

RHP Lance Broadway (1) is almost ready for the majors. OF Aaron Cunningham (6) and 1B Chris Carter (15) may have more upside but are much further away. **GRADE: C**

## 2004     BUDGET: $6.3 million

The White Sox grabbed three quality first-rounders in 3B Josh Fields and LHPs Gio Gonzalez and Tyler Lumsden, though they traded the two southpaws (and later reacquired Gonzalez). **GRADE: B**

## 2003     BUDGET: $3.8 million

Chicago stocked up its outfield with Brian Anderson (1) and Ryan Sweeney (2). But the Sox failed to sign LHP Donald Veal (12) and 3B Wes Hodges (13). **GRADE: B**

*Draft analysis by Jim Callis. Numbers in parentheses indicate draft rounds. Budgets are bonuses in first 10 rounds.*

# SWEENEY

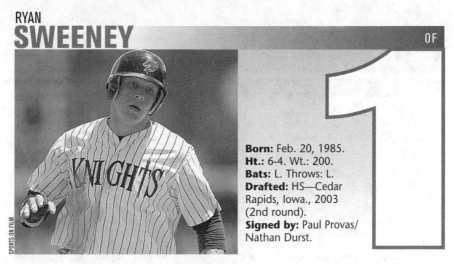

**Born:** Feb. 20, 1985.
**Ht.:** 6-4. **Wt.:** 200.
**Bats:** L. Throws: L.
**Drafted:** HS—Cedar
Rapids, Iowa., 2003
(2nd round).
**Signed by:** Paul Provas/
Nathan Durst.

SPORTS ON FILM

There's no doubt that Ryan Sweeney loves baseball. That's the only way you can grow up in Iowa and get this far, this fast as a baseball prospect. High school baseball isn't even played during the school year, making it tough for players to get scouted. But Sweeney starred on the showcase circuit, and the only thing teams wondered about was whether he was a better prospect as a lefthanded pitcher or as an outfielder. He had a chance to become the first Iowa high schooler ever drafted in the first round, but just missed. The White Sox selected him in the second round in 2003, signing him for $785,000. Chicago needed an extra outfielder in big league camp the following spring, and when he hit .367 he jumped on the fast track. He began his first full season at high Class A Winston-Salem as a 19-year-old. He consistently has been one of the youngest players in his leagues and made his major league debut in September, just three years removed from high school.

Sweeney has an advanced approach at the plate for his age. He has a technically sound swing that has evoked comparisons to that of Harold Baines. He's willing to go with a pitch, giving him the ability to spray doubles from gap to gap. Getting pushed through the minors forced Sweeney to learn to make adjustments against pitchers with much more experience than he had. He totaled just eight homers in his first two full pro seasons—including just one longball in Double-A in 2005, when he played through a wrist injury—but his power started to blossom in 2006. An excellent athlete, Sweeney is a good baserunner but may not steal more than 5-10 bases a season. A right fielder for most of his career, he got a shot to play center in 2006. Sweeney quickly showed he has the instincts and ability to play anywhere in the outfield, and he covers ground well for a big man. The arm strength that once made him a coveted pitching prospect translates into a plus in the outfield.

Sweeney still needs to develop his power if he's to hit 20-plus homers on an annual basis in the majors; 10 of his career-high 13 homers came at Triple-A Charlotte's cozy Knights Stadium. He didn't manage a single extra-base hit in 35 at-bats with the White Sox. He's still learning to pull the ball with loft on a consistent basis. Once he learns to stay back better on pitches, he should drive more balls because he won't be out on his front foot. While Sweeney makes good contact, he could stand to work more counts.

Brian Anderson batted just .225 with eight homers as a rookie, and manager Ozzie Guillen said Chicago's center-field job will be open to competition in spring training. Sweeney went one round later than Anderson in the 2003 draft but has more potential at the plate. He's the White Sox' No. 3 hitter of the future. Sweeney fits better defensively on a corner, and he could wind up playing there for the Sox this year if Scott Podsednik is moved. He'll only be 22, so it won't be a disappointment if Sweeney returns for a second season at Charlotte.

| Year | Club (League) | Class | AVG | G | AB | R | H | 2B | 3B | HR | RBI | BB | SO | SB | OBP | SLG |
|------|---------------|-------|------|-----|------|-----|-----|----|----|----|-----|-----|-----|----|------|------|
| 2003 | Bristol (Appy) | R | .313 | 19 | 67 | 11 | 21 | 3 | 0 | 2 | 5 | 7 | 10 | 3 | .387 | .448 |
| | Great Falls (Pio) | R | .353 | 10 | 34 | 0 | 12 | 2 | 0 | 0 | 4 | 2 | 3 | 0 | .389 | .412 |
| 2004 | Winston-Salem (CL) | A | .283 | 134 | 515 | 71 | 146 | 22 | 3 | 7 | 66 | 40 | 65 | 8 | .342 | .379 |
| 2005 | Birmingham (SL) | AA | .298 | 113 | 429 | 64 | 128 | 22 | 3 | 1 | 47 | 35 | 53 | 6 | .357 | .371 |
| 2006 | Charlotte (IL) | AAA | .296 | 118 | 449 | 64 | 133 | 25 | 3 | 13 | 70 | 35 | 73 | 7 | .350 | .452 |
| | Chicago (AL) | MLB | .229 | 18 | 35 | 1 | 8 | 0 | 0 | 0 | 5 | 0 | 7 | 0 | .229 | .229 |
| **MINOR LEAGUE TOTALS** | | | .295 | 394 | 1494 | 210 | 440 | 74 | 9 | 23 | 192 | 119 | 204 | 24 | .352 | .402 |
| **MAJOR LEAGUE TOTALS** | | | .229 | 18 | 35 | 1 | 8 | 0 | 0 | 0 | 5 | 0 | 7 | 0 | .229 | .229 |

## JOSH FIELDS 3B

**Born:** Dec. 14, 1982. **B-T:** R-R. **Ht.:** 6-1. **Wt.:** 215. **Drafted:** Oklahoma State, 2004 (1st round). **Signed by:** Alex Slattery/Nathan Durst.

For some organizations, a bust the magnitude of Joe Borchard would have scared them away from two-sport players. But the White Sox went the quarterback/slugger route again four years later by taking Fields 18th overall and signing him for $1.55 million. Fields had a big year in 2006, making his big league debut. He has made great strides since concentrating on baseball. He generates impressive bat speed from a solid right-handed stroke, and he easily set career highs in average and homers in 2006. He's a plus baserunner with the speed to steal some bases, and he also has an above-average arm. He was raw defensively when he entered pro ball but has improved his footwork and throwing accuracy to become a sound third baseman. When Fields gets overaggressive, his swing gets long and he's prone to strikeouts. He could need time to adjust to big league breaking pitches. He might not hit for a high average, though if he hits 25-30 homers a year that will be fine with the White Sox. Joe Crede doesn't become a free agent for two more years, so Fields has no clear path to a regular job. They hoped he'd become a left-field candidate by playing there in Venezuelan winter ball, but he came home early. There's nothing left for Fields to prove in Triple-A, so a trade may be in order for him or Crede.

| Year | Club (League) | Class | AVG | G | AB | R | H | 2B | 3B | HR | RBI | BB | SO | SB | OBP | SLG |
|------|---------------|-------|-----|---|----|----|-----|----|----|----|-----|----|-----|----|------|------|
| 2004 | Winston-Salem (CL) | A | .285 | 66 | 256 | 36 | 73 | 12 | 4 | 7 | 39 | 18 | 74 | 0 | .333 | .445 |
| 2005 | Birmingham (SL) | AA | .252 | 134 | 477 | 76 | 120 | 27 | 0 | 16 | 79 | 55 | 142 | 7 | .341 | .409 |
| 2006 | Charlotte (IL) | AAA | .305 | 124 | 462 | 85 | 141 | 32 | 4 | 19 | 70 | 54 | 136 | 28 | .379 | .515 |
| | Chicago (AL) | MLB | .150 | 11 | 20 | 4 | 3 | 2 | 0 | 1 | 2 | 5 | 8 | 0 | .320 | .400 |
| **MINOR LEAGUE TOTALS** | | | .279 | 324 | 1195 | 197 | 334 | 71 | 8 | 42 | 188 | 127 | 352 | 35 | .354 | .458 |
| **MAJOR LEAGUE TOTALS** | | | .150 | 11 | 20 | 4 | 3 | 2 | 0 | 1 | 2 | 5 | 8 | 0 | .320 | .400 |

## GIO GONZALEZ LHP

**Born:** Sept. 19, 1985. **B-T:** R-L. **Ht.:** 6-0. **Wt.:** 190. **Drafted:** HS—Miami, 2004 (1st round supplemental). **Signed by:** Jose Ortega.

The White Sox signed Gonzalez for $850,000 as the 38th overall pick in the 2004 draft, then packaged him with Aaron Rowand and minor league lefty Daniel Haigwood in the Jim Thome trade following the 2005 season. They brought him back from the Phillies 13 months later, along with Gavin Floyd, for Freddy Garcia. Gonzalez spent 2006 in Double-A as a 20-year-old, holding his own despite erratic command at times. He has a fundamentally sound delivery that he repeats well, creating effortless 92-95 mph velocity with his fastball. His low-80s hammer curveball always has been his go-to pitch, and he'll use it in any count. He located his changeup better in 2006, and it shows flashes of being a third plus pitch. Though there were questions about his durability, he pitched a career-high 155 innings and added 16 more in the Arizona Fall League. Gonzalez will need better command with his fastball and more consistency with his changeup to succeed at higher levels. He fell behind in the count early and often in Double-A, leading to too many homers and walks. Gonzales has all the makings of a legitimate No. 2 starter, but they have no reason to rush him. He'll likely return to Double-A.

| Year | Club (League) | Class | W | L | ERA | G | GS | CG | SV | IP | H | R | ER | HR | BB | SO | AVG |
|------|---------------|-------|---|---|-----|---|----|----|----|----|----|----|----|----|----|-----|------|
| 2004 | Bristol (Appy) | R | 1 | 2 | 2.25 | 7 | 6 | 0 | 0 | 24 | 17 | 8 | 6 | 0 | 8 | 36 | .207 |
| | Kannapolis (SAL) | A | 1 | 1 | 3.03 | 6 | 6 | 0 | 0 | 33 | 30 | 13 | 11 | 1 | 13 | 27 | .229 |
| 2005 | Kannapolis (SAL) | A | 5 | 3 | 1.87 | 11 | 10 | 0 | 0 | 58 | 36 | 16 | 12 | 3 | 22 | 84 | .175 |
| | Winston-Salem (CL) | A | 8 | 3 | 3.56 | 13 | 13 | 0 | 0 | 73 | 61 | 33 | 29 | 5 | 25 | 79 | .228 |
| 2006 | Reading (EL) | AA | 7 | 12 | 4.66 | 27 | 27 | 0 | 0 | 155 | 140 | 88 | 80 | 24 | 81 | 166 | .239 |
| **MINOR LEAGUE TOTALS** | | | 22 | 21 | 3.63 | 64 | 62 | 0 | 0 | 342 | 284 | 158 | 138 | 33 | 149 | 392 | .223 |

## LANCE BROADWAY RHP

**Born:** Aug. 20, 1983. **B-T:** R-R. **Ht.:** 6-2. **Wt.:** 210. **Drafted:** Texas Christian, 2005 (1st round). **Signed by:** Keith Staab.

Undrafted out of high school in Texas, Broadway started his college career at Dallas Baptist before transferring to Texas Christian and becoming an All-American in 2005. He spent his first full pro season at Double-A Birmingham before moving up for the International League playoffs. Broadway knows how to pitch. He pounds the strike zone with a collection of pitches, the best of which is a spike curveball that some scouts rate as a plus-plus offering. He sets up his curve with an 89-92 mph fast-

ball. He has made progress with the arm speed on his changeup, making it more effective. He's a physical specimen who had no trouble adjusting to a pro workload. Because he has just an average fastball, Broadway has less margin for error. His mechanics got out of sync in midseason, and he got hit hard when he left heaters up in the strike zone. He'll need a more consistent changeup to get big league lefthanders out. Given their veteran rotation, Chicago has no need to rush Broadway. He'll almost certainly start 2007 in Triple-A and profiles as an innings-eating starter. General manager Kenny Williams isn't afraid to deal prospects, and the White Sox' pitching depth makes Broadway one of their best trade chips.

| Year | Club (League) | Class | W | L | ERA | G | GS | CG | SV | IP | H | R | ER | HR | BB | SO | AVG |
|---|---|---|---|---|---|---|---|---|---|---|---|---|---|---|---|---|---|
| 2005 | Winston-Salem (CL) | A | 1 | 3 | 4.58 | 11 | 11 | 0 | 0 | 55 | 68 | 31 | 28 | 4 | 20 | 58 | .306 |
| 2006 | Birmingham (SL) | AA | 8 | 8 | 2.74 | 25 | 25 | 2 | 0 | 154 | 160 | 59 | 47 | 10 | 40 | 111 | .269 |
| | Charlotte (IL) | AAA | 0 | 0 | 3.00 | 1 | 1 | 0 | 0 | 6 | 5 | 2 | 2 | 0 | 1 | 6 | .217 |
| **MINOR LEAGUE TOTALS** | | | 9 | 11 | 3.22 | 37 | 37 | 2 | 0 | 215 | 233 | 92 | 77 | 14 | 61 | 175 | .277 |

## 5 KYLE McCULLOCH                                                     RHP

BILL MITCHELL

**Born:** March 20, 1985. **B-T:** R-R. **Ht.:** 6-3. **Wt.:** 185. **Drafted:** Texas, 2006 (1st round). **Signed by:** Keith Staab.

Known more as a shortstop in high school, McCulloch became a full-time pitcher at Texas. He went 27-11 in three years with the Longhorns and won the clinching game of the 2005 College World Series. The 29th overall pick last June, he signed for $1.05 million. McCulloch's plus changeup rates as the system's best. He gets good natural movement on his 88-92 mph fastball, and his curveball is consistently effective. He has tremendous poise and challenges hitters even on days when he lacks his best stuff. He's polished, athletic and durable. McCulloch's velocity stayed in the upper 80s last year more than it had in the past, perhaps because he didn't work off his fastball enough. He won't overpower advanced hitters, and he'll have to walk a fine line while setting them up for his changeup. There's little difference between McCulloch and Lance Broadway. Broadway opened his first full season in Double-A and McCulloch likely will do the same. They could team up as mid-rotation starters for the White Sox by mid-2008.

| Year | Club (League) | Class | W | L | ERA | G | GS | CG | SV | IP | H | R | ER | HR | BB | SO | AVG |
|---|---|---|---|---|---|---|---|---|---|---|---|---|---|---|---|---|---|
| 2006 | Great Falls (Pio) | R | 1 | 1 | 1.61 | 6 | 5 | 0 | 0 | 22 | 19 | 15 | 4 | 1 | 7 | 27 | .213 |
| | Winston-Salem (CL) | A | 2 | 5 | 4.08 | 7 | 7 | 0 | 0 | 35 | 37 | 20 | 16 | 4 | 17 | 21 | .266 |
| **MINOR LEAGUE TOTALS** | | | 3 | 6 | 3.12 | 13 | 12 | 0 | 0 | 58 | 56 | 35 | 20 | 5 | 24 | 48 | .246 |

## 6 CHARLIE HAEGER                                                     RHP

**Born:** Sept. 19, 1983. **B-T:** R-R. **Ht.:** 6-1. **Wt.:** 200. **Drafted:** HS—Plymouth, Mich., 2001 (25th round). **Signed by:** Ken Stauffer/Nathan Durst.

Haeger spent two years in Rookie ball with a fringe-average fastball before leaving the White Sox in 2003. He reinvented himself as a knuckleballer, then blitzed through the minors to Chicago in 2006. On the way, he led the International League in wins. Charlie Hough says Haeger has the best knuckleball he's seen since Tim Wakefield arrived in the big leagues. It dances like a good knuckler should and Haeger has learned to trust it in any situation. He has a mid-80s fastball and a decent curve, but he'll throw his knuckler 70-80 percent of the time when it's on. He's an excellent pupil who has developed a rapport with Hough and Wakefield. The knuckler can give catchers fits, and A.J. Pierzynski committed three passed balls in Haeger's big league debut. It's a fickle pitch that sometimes moves so much he can't throw it for strikes. Chicago doesn't have a rotation opening for Haeger, which could leave him in a bind. Though he was effective out of the bullpen in September, it's hard for a contender to trust a knuckleballer in critical relief situations. He may make the White Sox in 2007 but probably will be kept on a short leash.

| Year | Club (League) | Class | W | L | ERA | G | GS | CG | SV | IP | H | R | ER | HR | BB | SO | AVG |
|---|---|---|---|---|---|---|---|---|---|---|---|---|---|---|---|---|---|
| 2001 | White Sox (AZL) | R | 0 | 3 | 6.39 | 13 | 4 | 0 | 0 | 31 | 44 | 29 | 22 | 2 | 17 | 17 | .336 |
| 2002 | White Sox (AZL) | R | 1 | 4 | 4.17 | 25 | 0 | 0 | 6 | 41 | 46 | 25 | 19 | 2 | 13 | 24 | .295 |
| 2003 | Did not play | | | | | | | | | | | | | | | | |
| 2004 | Bristol (Appy) | R | 1 | 6 | 5.18 | 10 | 10 | 0 | 0 | 57 | 70 | 41 | 33 | 6 | 22 | 23 | .303 |
| | Kannapolis (SAL) | A | 1 | 3 | 2.01 | 5 | 5 | 0 | 0 | 31 | 31 | 17 | 7 | 0 | 12 | 21 | .270 |
| 2005 | Winston-Salem (CL) | A | 8 | 2 | 3.20 | 14 | 13 | 0 | 0 | 82 | 82 | 33 | 29 | 3 | 40 | 64 | .267 |
| | Birmingham (SL) | AA | 6 | 3 | 3.78 | 13 | 13 | 3 | 0 | 86 | 84 | 43 | 36 | 1 | 45 | 48 | .263 |
| 2006 | Charlotte (IL) | AAA | 14 | 6 | 3.07 | 26 | 25 | 2 | 0 | 170 | 143 | 71 | 58 | 9 | 78 | 130 | .231 |
| | Chicago (AL) | MLB | 1 | 1 | 3.44 | 7 | 1 | 0 | 1 | 18 | 12 | 10 | 7 | 0 | 13 | 19 | .182 |
| **MINOR LEAGUE TOTALS** | | | 31 | 27 | 3.69 | 106 | 70 | 5 | 6 | 498 | 500 | 259 | 204 | 23 | 227 | 327 | .266 |
| **MAJOR LEAGUE TOTALS** | | | 1 | 1 | 3.44 | 7 | 1 | 0 | 1 | 18 | 12 | 10 | 7 | 0 | 13 | 19 | .182 |

## 7 AARON CUNNINGHAM OF

**Born:** April 24, 1986. **B-T:** R-R. **Ht.:** 5-11. **Wt.:** 195. **Drafted:** Everett (Wash.) CC, 2005 (6th round). **Signed by:** Joe Butler/Adam Virchis.

Undrafted out of high school and unknown when he arrived at Everett (Wash.) Community College, Cunningham tore the cover off the ball as scouts flocked to see his teammates, pitchers Zach Simons and J.T. Zink. He has batted .301 since signing as a sixth-rounder. A muscular, compact athlete, Cunningham produces above-average bat speed and drives the ball to all fields. He stepped up his power production in 2006, and the White Sox believe there's more to come. He crowds the plate and handles the bat well. He has above-average speed and arm strength. Cunningham is a born hitter but still a bit green in other facets of his game. He must work better counts and curb his aggressiveness at the plate. He doesn't get good jumps and probably won't be a basestealer at higher levels. He's going to be a left fielder because his jumps, throwing mechanics and accuracy all need work. Easily Chicago's best position prospect in the lower minors, Cunningham is at least a couple of seasons away from being ready for the majors. He should start 2007 in high Class A and could hit his way to Double-A with a strong spring and fast start.

| Year | Club (League) | Class | AVG | G | AB | R | H | 2B | 3B | HR | RBI | BB | SO | SB | OBP | SLG |
|------|---------------|-------|-----|---|----|---|---|----|----|----|-----|----|----|----|-----|-----|
| 2005 | Bristol (Appy) | R | .315 | 56 | 222 | 41 | 70 | 10 | 2 | 5 | 25 | 16 | 45 | 6 | .392 | .446 |
| | Kannapolis (SAL) | A | .115 | 10 | 26 | 7 | 3 | 0 | 0 | 0 | 2 | 3 | 7 | 1 | .207 | .115 |
| 2006 | Kannapolis (SAL) | A | .305 | 95 | 341 | 58 | 104 | 26 | 3 | 11 | 41 | 34 | 72 | 19 | .386 | .496 |
| **MINOR LEAGUE TOTALS** | | | .301 | 161 | 589 | 106 | 177 | 36 | 5 | 16 | 68 | 53 | 124 | 26 | .381 | .460 |

## 8 ADAM RUSSELL RHP

**Born:** April 14, 1983. **B-T:** R-R. **Ht.:** 6-8. **Wt.:** 250. **Drafted:** Ohio, 2004 (6th round). **Signed by:** Larry Grefer/Nathan Durst.

Russell had little success at Ohio, going 6-11, 6.28 in three seasons, but made a late push and became a sixth-round pick. He has fared much better in pro ball since finding a reliable breaking ball, and he spent the second half of 2006 in Double-A. Russell's size presents an intimidating presence on the mound, and he has learned to use it to his advantage. He throws on a downhill plane from a high slot, and he reaches the mid-90s with his lively fastball on his best days. He'll alter his arm slot and drop down to give batters a different look with his fastball and slider. He has gained confidence in throwing four-seam fastballs at the top of the strike zone after establishing his heater in the lower half. Russell's changeup and curveball are still works in progress, and he doesn't dominate hitters because they don't have to respect his offspeed stuff. He tends to overthrow when things aren't going well. Entering 2006, the White Sox were excited about Russell's potential as a reliever, but now they believe he can be a starter. He still needs to flesh out his repertoire, and he probably will head back to Double-A to start 2007.

| Year | Club (League) | Class | W | L | ERA | G | GS | CG | SV | IP | H | R | ER | HR | BB | SO | AVG |
|------|---------------|-------|---|---|-----|---|----|----|----|----|---|---|----|----|----|----|-----|
| 2004 | Great Falls (Pio) | R | 4 | 0 | 2.37 | 15 | 4 | 0 | 0 | 38 | 31 | 11 | 10 | 2 | 18 | 33 | .228 |
| | Kannapolis (SAL) | A | 0 | 2 | 9.00 | 2 | 2 | 0 | 0 | 10 | 18 | 11 | 10 | 3 | 7 | 3 | .409 |
| 2005 | Kannapolis (SAL) | A | 9 | 7 | 3.78 | 24 | 24 | 0 | 0 | 126 | 116 | 61 | 53 | 10 | 55 | 82 | .246 |
| 2006 | Winston-Salem (CL) | A | 7 | 3 | 2.66 | 17 | 17 | 0 | 0 | 95 | 80 | 35 | 28 | 5 | 39 | 61 | .235 |
| | Birmingham (SL) | AA | 3 | 3 | 4.75 | 10 | 10 | 0 | 0 | 55 | 59 | 33 | 29 | 5 | 19 | 47 | .269 |
| **MINOR LEAGUE TOTALS** | | | 23 | 15 | 3.61 | 68 | 57 | 0 | 0 | 324 | 304 | 151 | 130 | 25 | 138 | 226 | .251 |

## 9 LUCAS HARRELL RHP

**Born:** June 3, 1985. **B-T:** B-R. **Ht.:** 6-2. **Wt.:** 200. **Drafted:** HS—Ozark, Mo., 2004 (4th round). **Signed by:** Alex Slattery/Nathan Durst.

Harrell was part of a banner crop of Missouri high school talent in 2004, and he led Ozark High to the state title. Considered a bit of a project as a fourth-rounder, Harrell nevertheless reached Double-A last year. Harrell goes after hitters with a low-90s fastball. He has sacrificed some velocity for command and life, and he induces a lot of groundballs with the sinking action on his two-seamer. His changeup is much improved and might be his best pitch. He's a good athlete who also played basketball in high school. His 2006 season ended early because he strained a trapezius muscle, but it's not expected to hamper his development. Harrell continues to work on developing an effective slider, and his control is still far from polished. Harrell will open 2007 in Double-A. He's on schedule to be ready for the big leagues in 2009, when the veteran White Sox rotation finally may have openings.

| Year | Club (League) | Class | W | L | ERA | G | GS | CG | SV | IP | H | R | ER | HR | BB | SO | AVG |
|---|---|---|---|---|---|---|---|---|---|---|---|---|---|---|---|---|---|
| 2004 | Bristol (Appy) | R | 3 | 5 | 5.59 | 13 | 9 | 0 | 0 | 48 | 53 | 39 | 30 | 5 | 32 | 33 | .282 |
| 2005 | Kannapolis (SAL) | A | 7 | 11 | 3.65 | 26 | 26 | 0 | 0 | 133 | 128 | 86 | 54 | 8 | 71 | 85 | .248 |
| 2006 | Winston-Salem (CL) | A | 7 | 2 | 2.45 | 17 | 17 | 0 | 0 | 92 | 58 | 29 | 25 | 3 | 44 | 70 | .182 |
| 2006 | Birmingham (SL) | AA | 0 | 2 | 10.24 | 3 | 3 | 0 | 0 | 10 | 12 | 12 | 11 | 1 | 14 | 4 | .316 |
| **MINOR LEAGUE TOTALS** | | | 17 | 20 | 3.82 | 59 | 55 | 0 | 0 | 283 | 251 | 166 | 120 | 17 | 161 | 192 | .237 |

## 10 MATT LONG
RHP

BILL MITCHELL

**Born:** Feb. 23, 1984. **B-T:** R-R. **Ht.:** 6-6. **Wt.:** 200. **Drafted:** Miami (Ohio), 2006 (2nd round). **Signed by:** Mike Shirley/Keith Staab.

Healthy once again after having Tommy John surgery in 2004, Long made the right move when he turned down the Dodgers as a 35th-rounder out of high school and the Giants as a 34th-rounder in 2005. The White Sox made him a second-round pick last June and signed him for $330,000. Long has a great build and has added strength in recent years. His fastball is his primary weapon, and it sat at 92-94 mph and peaked at 96 last spring. He usually pitched at 91 mph after signing, but Chicago expects more velocity when he's fresh in 2007. He has a tight curveball that became more consistent after the Sox worked to tighten his delivery in instructional league. He is a hard worker who put in the time to come back from surgery. Long lacks command with his curveball and his changeup. Chicago wants him to focus on his changeup and may use him as a starter in his first full pro season. He's raw for his age because he didn't get many innings against high-level competition in college. But he could move quickly, especially if he stays in a bullpen role. How well he masters his offspeed stuff will determine his long-term role.

| Year | Club (League) | Class | W | L | ERA | G | GS | CG | SV | IP | H | R | ER | HR | BB | SO | AVG |
|---|---|---|---|---|---|---|---|---|---|---|---|---|---|---|---|---|---|
| 2006 | Kannapolis (SAL) | A | 3 | 5 | 8.02 | 22 | 0 | 0 | 1 | 34 | 51 | 37 | 30 | 5 | 13 | 20 | .345 |
| **MINOR LEAGUE TOTALS** | | | 3 | 5 | 8.02 | 22 | 0 | 0 | 1 | 34 | 51 | 37 | 30 | 5 | 13 | 20 | .345 |

## 11 CHRIS CARTER
1B

**Born:** Dec. 18, 1986. **B-T:** R-R. **Ht.:** 6-4. **Wt.:** 210. **Drafted:** HS—Las Vegas, 2005 (15th round). **Signed by:** George Kachigian/Joe Butler.

Carter's bat has launched him from 15th-round high school draftee to prospect in less than two years. The White Sox hoped he could spend 2006 at low Class A Kannapolis, but he returned to extended spring training after a bumpy start. He led the Rookie-level Pioneer League in homers, extra-base hits (37) and total bases (143). While the rest of his game is pedestrian, Carter's power is impossible to overlook. He swings hard and can drive good fastballs and hanging curveballs. He's a pull hitter but has the strength to hit the ball out to the opposite field as well. He has a decent eye at the plate and is willing to take a walk when pitchers start nibbling, as they often do against him. Carter's power comes with a tradeoff—lots of strikeouts. His bat will have to carry him because he's a below-average runner, defender and thrower. Drafted as a third baseman, he moved to first base full-time in 2006. He's prone to errors because he lacks soft hands, and he'll need a lot more work fielding grounders and taking throws. Carter will return to Kannapolis, and he's probably three to five years away from Chicago.

| Year | Club (League) | Class | AVG | G | AB | R | H | 2B | 3B | HR | RBI | BB | SO | SB | OBP | SLG |
|---|---|---|---|---|---|---|---|---|---|---|---|---|---|---|---|---|
| 2005 | Bristol (Appy) | R | .283 | 65 | 233 | 33 | 66 | 17 | 0 | 10 | 37 | 17 | 64 | 2 | .350 | .485 |
| 2006 | Kannapolis (SAL) | A | .130 | 13 | 46 | 4 | 6 | 3 | 0 | 1 | 5 | 5 | 17 | 0 | .231 | .261 |
| | Great Falls (Pio) | R | .299 | 69 | 251 | 37 | 75 | 21 | 1 | 15 | 59 | 34 | 70 | 4 | .398 | .570 |
| **MINOR LEAGUE TOTALS** | | | .277 | 147 | 530 | 74 | 147 | 41 | 1 | 26 | 101 | 56 | 151 | 6 | .363 | .506 |

## 12 HEATH PHILLIPS
LHP

**Born:** March 24, 1982. **B-T:** L-L. **Ht.:** 6-3. **Wt.:** 205. **Drafted:** Lake City (Fla.) CC (10th round). **Signed by:** Larry Grefer/Doug Laumann.

Phillips has been White Sox property since 2000, and they still don't know what they have in him. That's because the presence of five veteran starters plus Brandon McCarthy left no reason for Chicago to give him a big league audition in 2006, when he was the International League's pitcher of the year and beat both Canada and the Dominican Republic for Team USA in the Olympic qualifying tournament. He has earned 46 victories in the minors but gets overlooked because of underwhelming stuff. Some in the organization connsider him Mark Buehrle Lite, as he offers a similar collection of pitches but not quite as much velocity. Phillips relies on location and changing speeds. His closest thing to an out pitch is his changeup, though hitters can look for it because they know he can't blow

them away with heat. He hits his spots with an 86-88 mph fastball and also has a cutter and a serviceable curveball. Like a young Buehrle, he works fast and takes advantage of baserunners who stray too far from first. Phillips led all IL pitchers with 16 basestealers caught on his watch, and the Sox credited him with a total of 20 pickoffs. He gets in trouble when he tries to muscle up with his fastball, causing it to straighten out. Phillips has nothing left to prove in Triple-A, but the White Sox don't have much of an opportunity for him either.

| Year | Club (League) | Class | W | L | ERA | G | GS | CG | SV | IP | H | R | ER | HR | BB | SO | AVG |
|------|---------------|-------|---|---|-----|---|----|----|----|----|---|---|----|----|----|----|-----|
| 2001 | Kannapolis (SAL) | A | 2 | 7 | 3.64 | 14 | 12 | 1 | 0 | 72 | 74 | 36 | 29 | 1 | 18 | 54 | .276 |
| 2002 | Winston-Salem (CL) | A | 6 | 16 | 3.52 | 28 | 28 | 5 | 0 | 179 | 184 | 82 | 70 | 17 | 50 | 112 | .268 |
| 2003 | Kannapolis (SAL) | A | 2 | 0 | 1.71 | 3 | 3 | 0 | 0 | 21 | 13 | 4 | 4 | 1 | 5 | 11 | .178 |
| | Birmingham (SL) | AA | 0 | 1 | 10.50 | 1 | 1 | 0 | 0 | 6 | 14 | 8 | 7 | 1 | 1 | 5 | .467 |
| | Winston-Salem (CL) | A | 2 | 7 | 3.58 | 13 | 13 | 0 | 0 | 75 | 84 | 37 | 30 | 6 | 7 | 51 | .289 |
| 2004 | Birmingham (SL) | AA | 12 | 10 | 4.02 | 27 | 26 | 0 | 0 | 154 | 179 | 78 | 69 | 12 | 36 | 107 | .302 |
| 2005 | Charlotte (IL) | AAA | 0 | 3 | 8.31 | 5 | 5 | 0 | 0 | 22 | 29 | 22 | 20 | 10 | 13 | 16 | .333 |
| | Birmingham (SL) | AA | 9 | 5 | 4.07 | 22 | 21 | 2 | 0 | 135 | 161 | 64 | 61 | 12 | 30 | 78 | .308 |
| 2006 | Charlotte (IL) | AAA | 13 | 5 | 2.96 | 25 | 24 | 2 | 0 | 155 | 152 | 62 | 51 | 12 | 39 | 102 | .263 |
| **MINOR LEAGUE TOTALS** | | | 46 | 54 | 3.75 | 138 | 133 | 10 | 0 | 819 | 890 | 393 | 341 | 72 | 199 | 536 | .285 |

## 13 JERRY OWENS                                                          OF

**Born:** Feb. 16, 1981. **B-T:** L-L. **Ht.:** 6-3. **Wt.:** 195. **Drafted:** The Masters (Calif.), 2003 (2nd round). **Signed by:** Tony Arango (Expos).

Owens appeared to take a major step forward as a hitter in 2005, winning the Southern League batting title and hitting .356 in Venezuelan winter ball. But general manager Ken Williams was upset when Owens returned early from Venezuela, and the negative tone carried over to 2006. Owens was disappointing in big league game and never got going in Triple-A. He earned a September callup, though only because he's the White Sox' lone true stolen-base threat in the upper minors. A former wide receiver at UCLA who was acquired from the Nationals in a February 2005 trade for Alex Escobar, Owens is a tremendous athlete, but he's going to have to kick his bat back into gear. He's a contact hitter who controls the strike zone, and he knows his role is to get on base so he can use his blazing speed. He struggles to drive the ball, however, and while he has flashes of power, Triple-A pitchers overpowered him too much. He covers plenty of ground in center field, though his arm is below average. Owens faces a critical season of development in Triple-A this year. If he can't make adjustments at the plate, he won't be more than an extra outfielder in the majors.

| Year | Club (League) | Class | AVG | G | AB | R | H | 2B | 3B | HR | RBI | BB | SO | SB | OBP | SLG |
|------|---------------|-------|-----|---|----|---|---|----|----|----|-----|----|----|----|-----|-----|
| 2003 | Vermont (NYP) | A | .125 | 2 | 8 | 0 | 1 | 0 | 0 | 0 | 0 | 0 | 2 | 1 | .125 | .125 |
| 2004 | Savannah (SAL) | A | .292 | 108 | 418 | 69 | 122 | 17 | 2 | 1 | 37 | 46 | 59 | 30 | .365 | .349 |
| 2005 | Birmingham (SL) | AA | .331 | 130 | 522 | 99 | 173 | 21 | 6 | 2 | 52 | 52 | 72 | 38 | .393 | .406 |
| 2006 | Charlotte (IL) | AAA | .262 | 112 | 439 | 75 | 115 | 15 | 5 | 4 | 48 | 45 | 61 | 40 | .330 | .346 |
| | Chicago (AL) | MLB | .333 | 12 | 9 | 4 | 3 | 1 | 0 | 0 | 0 | 0 | 2 | 1 | .333 | .444 |
| **MINOR LEAGUE TOTALS** | | | .296 | 352 | 1387 | 243 | 411 | 53 | 13 | 7 | 137 | 143 | 194 | 109 | .363 | .368 |
| **MAJOR LEAGUE TOTALS** | | | .333 | 12 | 9 | 4 | 3 | 1 | 0 | 0 | 0 | 0 | 2 | 1 | .333 | .444 |

## 14 RAY LIOTTA                                                          LHP

**Born:** April 3, 1983. **B-T:** L-L. **Ht.:** 6-3. **Wt.:** 220. **Drafted:** Gulf Coast (Fla.) CC, 2004 (2nd round). **Signed by:** Warren Hughes.

A New Orleans native, Liotta had won consecutive ERA titles in his first two seasons as a pro. But he wasn't the same in 2006, which the White Sox attribute to his conditioning and preparation understandably suffering as he focused on helping his family get back on its feet after Hurricane Katrina. A nonroster invitee, Liotta wasn't sharp when he reported to big league camp and made no impact. He opened the year in Double-A but ended it back in high Class A, where he regressed after dominating there the season before. Liotta's trademark pitch has been a 12-to-6 curveball with tight downward action, but it wasn't as effective in 2006. Neither was his fastball, down to 86-88 mph from it's usual 89-92. His changeup always has been his third pitch and still needs more work. When Liotta tried to overthrow last year, his problems only increased. The White Sox want him to tighten his delivery but mostly hope his life will be less chaotic, allowing him to regain the focus he had in his first two seasons. Assuming all goes well this spring, he could open 2007 in Double-A.

| Year | Club (League) | Class | W | L | ERA | G | GS | CG | SV | IP | H | R | ER | HR | BB | SO | AVG |
|------|---------------|-------|---|---|-----|---|----|----|----|----|---|---|----|----|----|----|-----|
| 2004 | Great Falls (Pio) | R | 5 | 1 | 2.54 | 14 | 11 | 0 | 0 | 64 | 59 | 27 | 18 | 1 | 28 | 65 | .250 |
| 2005 | Kannapolis (SAL) | A | 8 | 3 | 2.26 | 20 | 20 | 1 | 0 | 115 | 108 | 39 | 29 | 5 | 35 | 107 | .252 |
| | Winston-Salem (CL) | A | 6 | 2 | 1.45 | 8 | 8 | 0 | 0 | 50 | 46 | 11 | 8 | 1 | 16 | 37 | .254 |
| 2006 | Birmingham (SL) | AA | 3 | 8 | 4.93 | 18 | 18 | 0 | 0 | 97 | 109 | 57 | 53 | 3 | 46 | 52 | .290 |
| | Winston-Salem (CL) | A | 1 | 6 | 8.08 | 10 | 9 | 0 | 0 | 42 | 62 | 49 | 38 | 5 | 19 | 30 | .354 |
| **MINOR LEAGUE TOTALS** | | | 23 | 20 | 3.57 | 70 | 66 | 1 | 0 | 368 | 384 | 183 | 146 | 15 | 144 | 291 | .275 |

**ONELI PEREZ** RHP

**Born:** May 26, 1983. **B-T:** R-R. **Ht.:** 6-2. **Wt.:** 187. **Signed:** Dominican Republic, 2001. **Signed by:** Ronquito Garcia (Padres).

The White Sox have produced few players from Latin America in recent years, with Carlos Lee and Magglio Ordonez their last real success stories. Perez is the type of find who could get their Latin operations moving in the right direction. Originally signed by the Padres in 2001, he was released three years later and picked up by Chicago at the recommendation of Denny Gonzalez. Perez has developed nicely after joining the Sox and put himself on the map with a huge 2006, posting a combined 0.81 ERA at three levels and finishing strong in Double-A. Perez' formula is simple. He attacks the strike zone with a low-90s fastball from a low three-quarters angle. He works ahead in the count, challenging hitters. His secondary pitches are works in progress, but his fastball/slider combination could be enough for a big league career. If he doesn't tire from his winter workload, he could earn a late-season look in Chicago this season and push for a permanent spot in 2008.

| Year | Club (League) | Class | W | L | ERA | G | GS | CG | SV | IP | H | R | ER | HR | BB | SO | AVG |
|------|---------------|-------|---|---|-----|---|----|----|----|----|---|---|----|----|----|----|-----|
| 2003 | Padres (DSL) | R | 3 | 0 | 1.77 | 15 | 0 | 0 | 3 | 41 | 33 | 11 | 8 | 0 | 7 | 33 | .213 |
| 2004 | White Sox (DSL) | R | 7 | 5 | 2.08 | 20 | 1 | 1 | 5 | 65 | 53 | 17 | 15 | 1 | 17 | 52 | .227 |
| 2005 | Kannapolis (SAL) | A | 4 | 2 | 3.71 | 36 | 2 | 0 | 2 | 80 | 84 | 41 | 33 | 7 | 32 | 62 | .265 |
| 2006 | Kannapolis (SAL) | A | 3 | 1 | 0.99 | 30 | 0 | 0 | 8 | 36 | 23 | 5 | 4 | 1 | 8 | 42 | .172 |
| | Winston-Salem (CL) | A | 1 | 0 | 0.72 | 17 | 0 | 0 | 0 | 25 | 17 | 5 | 2 | 1 | 5 | 29 | .181 |
| | Birmingham (SL) | AA | 0 | 1 | 0.55 | 7 | 0 | 0 | 1 | 16 | 6 | 1 | 1 | 1 | 6 | 20 | .115 |
| **MINOR LEAGUE TOTALS** | | | 18 | 9 | 2.15 | 125 | 3 | 1 | 19 | 263 | 216 | 80 | 63 | 11 | 75 | 238 | .219 |

**JACK EGBERT** RHP

**Born:** May 12, 1983. **B-T:** L-R. **Ht.:** 6-3. **Wt.:** 205. **Drafted:** Rutgers, 2004 (13th round). **Signed by:** John Tumminia/Chuck Fox.

A plus changeup, the willingness to challenge hitters inside and durability have allowed Egbert to climb the ladder after signing as a 13th-round pick. He reached Double-A in his second full pro season, allowing just two earned runs in four starts. Egbert gets a lot of movement on his 88-92 mph fastball and has improved his curveball. Not only has his curve gotten better, but he also trusts it enough to throw it in any count. He throws strikes, works fast and gets a lot of groundballs when he's in a groove. He gave up just two homers in 162 innings last year. There are games where his fastball sits at just 87-88 mph, but Egbert has shown the ability to compete without his best stuff. The White Sox had concerns about his commitment early in his pro career, but he has erased those. Though he doesn't have the stuff to be a front-of-the-rotation guy, Egbert will get big league consideration in the near future if he stays on course.

| Year | Club (League) | Class | W | L | ERA | G | GS | CG | SV | IP | H | R | ER | HR | BB | SO | AVG |
|------|---------------|-------|---|---|-----|---|----|----|----|----|---|---|----|----|----|----|-----|
| 2004 | Great Falls (Pio) | R | 4 | 1 | 3.38 | 17 | 9 | 0 | 0 | 59 | 51 | 25 | 22 | 2 | 33 | 52 | .244 |
| 2005 | Kannapolis (SAL) | A | 10 | 5 | 3.12 | 30 | 24 | 4 | 0 | 147 | 127 | 66 | 51 | 5 | 48 | 107 | .236 |
| 2006 | Winston-Salem (CL) | A | 9 | 8 | 2.94 | 25 | 25 | 0 | 0 | 141 | 131 | 57 | 46 | 2 | 46 | 120 | .246 |
| | Birmingham (SL) | AA | 0 | 2 | 0.86 | 4 | 4 | 0 | 0 | 21 | 17 | 4 | 2 | 0 | 8 | 24 | .215 |
| **MINOR LEAGUE TOTALS** | | | 23 | 16 | 2.96 | 76 | 62 | 4 | 0 | 367 | 326 | 152 | 121 | 9 | 135 | 303 | .240 |

**JUSTIN EDWARDS** LHP

**Born:** Sept. 7, 1987. **B-T:** L-L. **Ht.:** 5-11. **Wt.:** 170. **Drafted:** HS—Orlando, 2006 (3rd round). **Signed by:** Jaymie Bane.

Edwards is a product of one of the nation's top youth programs, Chet Lemon's Juice, which the former big league all-star runs out of Sanford, Fla. Though he was drafted out of high school, he fits the White Sox' preference for polished pitchers over raw, high-ceiling gambles. Edwards turned down a scholarship from Georgia to sign for $310,000 after Chicago took him in the third round last June. While he displays an advanced feel for pitching, Edwards sometimes took his lumps while facing older hitters in the Rookie-level Appalachian League. He kept his poise throughout, prompting compliments about his maturity and approach. Edwards' fastball touched the low-90s during the summer showcase tour in 2005, but he settled in at 86-89 mph last year. It's still an effective pitch without plus velocity because it has nice life. His changeup and curveball have a chance to develop into plus pitches, and his smooth, repeatable delivery gives him good control. He's not big, so he's not very projectable and will have to work to keep the ball down in the zone. Edwards will spend his first full season in low Class A.

| Year | Club (League) | Class | W | L | ERA | G | GS | CG | SV | IP | H | R | ER | HR | BB | SO | AVG |
|------|---------------|-------|---|---|-----|---|----|----|----|----|---|---|----|----|----|----|-----|
| 2006 | Bristol (Appy) | R | 3 | 7 | 5.30 | 12 | 12 | 0 | 0 | 53 | 69 | 39 | 31 | 6 | 21 | 42 | .319 |
| **MINOR LEAGUE TOTALS** | | | 3 | 7 | 5.30 | 12 | 12 | 0 | 0 | 53 | 69 | 39 | 31 | 6 | 21 | 42 | .319 |

## 18 BOONE LOGAN
LHP

**Born:** Aug. 13, 1984. **B-T:** R-L. **Ht.:** 6-5. **Wt.:** 200. **Drafted:** Temple (Texas) JC, D/F 2002 (20th round). **Signed by:** Paul Provas/Keith Staab.

Logan spent almost all of his first three pro seasons floundering at Rookie-level Great Falls before last year. Great Falls pitching coach Curt Hasler suggested he drop down to a low-three-quarters arm slot in 2005, a move that worked wonders. Logan got a chance to pitch in an intrasquad game last spring, making an impression on manager Ozzie Guillen when he struck out Jim Thome and Rob Mackowiak. Guillen put Logan into the wide-open competition to fill the lefty vacancy left by Damaso Marte in the bullpen, and he seized the moment and opened the season with the defending World Series champs. Logan's 2006 was really a tale of two seasons, as he looked tentative and not as sharp in the majors but dominated in Triple-A. His fastball sat mostly in the high 80s and he had trouble throwing his slider for strikes with Chicago, but he pitched in the 90s, topped out at 94 and had a devastating breaking ball at Charlotte. He gets deception and surprising command from his low arm slot. He's still very raw and can be exploited by teams that bunt and steal bases. Logan needs a lot of work to stay on top of his game, one reason he wasn't as effective in the majors. He returned home early from Venezuela winter ball after experiencing shoulder stiffness, but should be 100 percent for spring training. After trading Neal Cotts to the Cubs, the White Sox will give Logan the chance to win a full-time job as a lefty reliever.

| Year | Club (League) | Class | W | L | ERA | G | GS | CG | SV | IP | H | R | ER | HR | BB | SO | AVG |
|------|---------------|-------|---|---|-----|---|----|----|----|----|---|---|----|----|----|----|-----|
| 2003 | Great Falls (Pio) | R | 3 | 3 | 6.58 | 16 | 14 | 0 | 0 | 67 | 76 | 60 | 49 | 4 | 31 | 48 | .279 |
| 2004 | Great Falls (Pio) | R | 3 | 7 | 5.60 | 18 | 9 | 0 | 1 | 64 | 74 | 48 | 40 | 7 | 31 | 48 | .287 |
| 2005 | Great Falls (Pio) | R | 1 | 1 | 3.31 | 21 | 0 | 0 | 2 | 35 | 34 | 15 | 13 | 1 | 4 | 29 | .258 |
| | Winston-Salem (CL) | A | 0 | 0 | 5.06 | 4 | 0 | 0 | 0 | 5 | 7 | 3 | 3 | 2 | 4 | 5 | .318 |
| 2006 | Charlotte (IL) | AAA | 3 | 1 | 3.38 | 38 | 0 | 0 | 11 | 43 | 35 | 18 | 16 | 1 | 12 | 57 | .222 |
| | Chicago (AL) | MLB | 0 | 0 | 8.31 | 21 | 0 | 0 | 1 | 17 | 21 | 18 | 16 | 2 | 15 | 15 | .288 |
| **MINOR LEAGUE TOTALS** | | | 10 | 12 | 5.07 | 97 | 23 | 0 | 14 | 215 | 226 | 144 | 121 | 15 | 82 | 187 | .268 |
| **MAJOR LEAGUE TOTALS** | | | 0 | 0 | 8.31 | 21 | 0 | 0 | 1 | 17 | 21 | 18 | 16 | 2 | 15 | 15 | .288 |

## 19 ROBERT VALIDO
SS

**Born:** May 16, 1985. **B-T:** R-R. **Ht.:** 6-2. **Wt.:** 180. **Drafted:** HS—Miami, 2003 (4th round). **Signed by:** Jose Ortega.

Valido headed into 2006 with everything going for him. He ranked No. 7 on this list after hitting .288 with 52 steals in high Class A and turning in a strong performance in the Arizona Fall League. He remained on track to become the White Sox' first homegrown regular at shortstop since Bucky Dent and saw regular time in big league camp last spring as an understudy to Juan Uribe. But once the regular season started, Valido couldn't solve Double-A pitching and missed most of the last three months with hand and wrist injuries. He was a fourth-round pick out of high school, primarily because of his defensive prowess. He has plus range to both sides, hands and arm strength, and some scouts project him as a future Gold Glover. Valido had exceeded offensive expectations before 2006, but Southern League pitchers took advantage of his lack of patience. He makes consistent contact but he has to do a much better job of getting on base so he can use his above-average speed. He lacks power and must focus on working counts, drawing walks and hitting the ball on the ground. Valido drew a 15-game suspension in May 2005 after testing positive for performance-enhancing drugs, which he blamed on an over-the-counter supplement. He should be healthy in 2007, but he'll still have to prove he can hit advanced pitching.

| Year | Club (League) | Class | AVG | G | AB | R | H | 2B | 3B | HR | RBI | BB | SO | SB | OBP | SLG |
|------|---------------|-------|-----|---|----|---|---|----|----|----|-----|----|----|----|-----|-----|
| 2003 | Bristol (Appy) | R | .307 | 58 | 215 | 39 | 66 | 15 | 2 | 6 | 31 | 17 | 28 | 17 | .364 | .479 |
| 2004 | Kannapolis (SAL) | A | .252 | 122 | 456 | 65 | 115 | 25 | 0 | 4 | 43 | 35 | 59 | 28 | .313 | .333 |
| 2005 | Winston-Salem (CL) | A | .288 | 119 | 513 | 86 | 148 | 28 | 7 | 8 | 59 | 21 | 64 | 52 | .320 | .417 |
| 2006 | Birmingham (SL) | AA | .208 | 45 | 168 | 15 | 35 | 9 | 3 | 1 | 11 | 13 | 24 | 8 | .269 | .315 |
| | Winston-Salem (CL) | A | .222 | 9 | 36 | 5 | 8 | 1 | 1 | 1 | 5 | 3 | 3 | 0 | .282 | .389 |
| **MINOR LEAGUE TOTALS** | | | .268 | 353 | 1388 | 210 | 372 | 78 | 13 | 20 | 149 | 89 | 178 | 105 | .317 | .386 |

## 20 PEDRO LOPEZ
SS/2B

**Born:** April 28, 1984. **B-T:** R-R. **Ht.:** 6-1. **Wt.:** 160. **Signed:** Dominican Republic, 2000. **Signed by:** Denny Gonzalez.

Lopez played so well in big league camp in 2005 that it proved to be his undoing. The White Sox jumped him to Triple-A to open that season and to Chicago in May. In over his head, he had his worst year at the plate and didn't improve much after a demotion to Double-A. Lopez got back on track in 2006, hitting .300 with 10 homers—just one less than his total in five previous pro seasons. He seems to be getting stronger and has stopped chas-

ing as many pitches. He'll never draw a lot of walks because he's still aggressive and makes contact easily, but it one again looks like he can hit for average with decent power. He's just an average runner, so he won't be a basestealer. Defensively, Lopez has the range to get to balls at shortstop but lacks the arm to make plays in the hole. He has soft hands and may fit better at second base. His long-term role is probably as a utilityman, and he'll probably start his third straight season in Triple-A.

| Year | Club (League) | Class | AVG | G | AB | R | H | 2B | 3B | HR | RBI | BB | SO | SB | OBP | SLG |
|---|---|---|---|---|---|---|---|---|---|---|---|---|---|---|---|---|
| 2001 | AZL White Sox (AZL) | R | .312 | 50 | 199 | 26 | 62 | 11 | 3 | 1 | 19 | 16 | 24 | 12 | .359 | .412 |
| 2002 | Bristol (Appy) | R | .319 | 63 | 260 | 42 | 83 | 11 | 0 | 0 | 35 | 20 | 27 | 22 | .370 | .362 |
| 2003 | Kannapolis (SAL) | A | .264 | 109 | 390 | 40 | 103 | 23 | 0 | 0 | 33 | 26 | 43 | 24 | .314 | .323 |
| | Winston-Salem (CL) | A | .231 | 4 | 13 | 1 | 3 | 0 | 0 | 0 | 0 | 1 | 0 | 0 | .286 | .231 |
| 2004 | Winston-Salem (CL) | A | .288 | 111 | 430 | 62 | 124 | 13 | 0 | 4 | 35 | 23 | 35 | 12 | .328 | .347 |
| | Birmingham (SL) | AA | .217 | 7 | 23 | 3 | 5 | 0 | 1 | 0 | 0 | 5 | 2 | 2 | .379 | .304 |
| 2005 | Chicago (AL) | MLB | .286 | 2 | 7 | 1 | 2 | 0 | 0 | 0 | 2 | 0 | 1 | 0 | .286 | .286 |
| | Charlotte (IL) | AAA | .202 | 55 | 188 | 14 | 38 | 6 | 0 | 3 | 17 | 7 | 24 | 1 | .236 | .282 |
| | Birmingham (SL) | AA | .238 | 68 | 239 | 26 | 57 | 7 | 1 | 3 | 24 | 13 | 29 | 0 | .287 | .314 |
| 2006 | Birmingham (SL) | AA | .322 | 65 | 258 | 30 | 83 | 15 | 2 | 5 | 34 | 16 | 32 | 3 | .358 | .453 |
| | Charlotte (IL) | AAA | .274 | 59 | 208 | 32 | 57 | 12 | 0 | 5 | 24 | 11 | 28 | 4 | .320 | .404 |
| **MINOR LEAGUE TOTALS** | | | .279 | 591 | 2208 | 276 | 615 | 98 | 7 | 21 | 221 | 138 | 244 | 80 | .324 | .358 |
| **MAJOR LEAGUE TOTALS** | | | .286 | 2 | 7 | 1 | 2 | 0 | 0 | 0 | 2 | 0 | 1 | 0 | .286 | .286 |

## 21  JOHN SHELBY JR.                                                   2B/SS

**Born:** Aug. 6, 1985. **B-T:** R-R. **Ht.:** 5-10. **Wt.:** 185. **Drafted:** Kentucky, 2006 (5th round). **Signed by:** Mike Shirley

The son of the former major league outfielder and current Pirates first-base coach of the same name, Shelby has made major strides after going undrafted out of high school. He emerged as a sophomore at Kentucky, hitting .344 with 10 home runs, and helped lead the Wildcats to their first-ever Southeastern Conference regular-season title in 2006 by batting .291 with 18 homers and 12 steals. Shelby continued to show slightly above-average power and speed in his pro debut. He has very good bat speed but suspect plate discipline. He was overanxious at times in Rookie ball, chasing curveballs out of the strike zone, and also has a little bit of an uppercut in his swing. Given his background, it's no surprise he has excellent instincts. A versatile athlete, Shelby saw time at second base and shortstop in pro ball and also played some outfield in college. Second base is his best fit, and his hands and body control improved there during 2006. He has an average arm. With a strong spring, Shelby could advance to high Class A for his first full pro season.

| Year | Club (League) | Class | AVG | G | AB | R | H | 2B | 3B | HR | RBI | BB | SO | SB | OBP | SLG |
|---|---|---|---|---|---|---|---|---|---|---|---|---|---|---|---|---|
| 2006 | Great Falls (Pio) | R | .272 | 66 | 250 | 37 | 68 | 12 | 3 | 8 | 36 | 18 | 55 | 8 | .332 | .440 |
| **MINOR LEAGUE TOTALS** | | | .272 | 66 | 250 | 37 | 68 | 12 | 3 | 8 | 36 | 18 | 55 | 8 | .332 | .440 |

## 22  DEWON DAY                                                              RHP

**Born:** Sept. 29, 1980. **B-T:** R-R. **Ht.:** 6-4. **Wt.:** 210. **Drafted:** Southern, D/F 2002 (26th round). **Signed by:** Jaymie Bane (Blue Jays).

A two-way player in college at Jackson State and Southern, Day pitched sparingly in 2002 because of tightness and a pinched nerve in his arm. The Blue Jays took him in the 26th round anyway and signed him the following spring as a fifth-year senior draft-and-follow. He never got past low Class A in three years in the Toronto system, in part because of Tommy John surgery in 2004. The White Sox grabbed him with the last pick in the Double-A phase of the Rule 5 draft at the 2005 Winter Meetings, on the recommendation of scout Jaymie Bane—who had signed him for the Jays. Day opened a lot of the eyes in 2006, both during the regular season and in the Arizona Fall League. He has two above-average pitches, a 90-96 mph fastball and an 85-88 mph slider with impressive tilt and depth. He's a very disciplined athlete and meshed well with Winston-Salem pitching coach J.R. Perdew, who helped him improve his mechanics. Day still can be wild at times but he's tough to hit when he's on. Though he's old for a prospect at 26, his arm could warrant a look in Chicago before 2007 is over. Double-A will be the next step for now.

| Year | Club (League) | Class | W | L | ERA | G | GS | CG | SV | IP | H | R | ER | HR | BB | SO | AVG |
|---|---|---|---|---|---|---|---|---|---|---|---|---|---|---|---|---|---|
| 2003 | Pulaski (Appy) | R | 2 | 0 | 1.80 | 26 | 0 | 0 | 12 | 30 | 21 | 8 | 6 | 0 | 9 | 26 | .184 |
| | Auburn (NYP) | A | 0 | 0 | 0.00 | 2 | 0 | 0 | 0 | 1 | 1 | 0 | 0 | 0 | 0 | 1 | .200 |
| 2004 | Auburn (NYP) | A | 0 | 3 | 1.50 | 27 | 0 | 0 | 8 | 24 | 24 | 8 | 4 | 0 | 10 | 28 | .250 |
| 2005 | Auburn (NYP) | A | 0 | 0 | 3.00 | 3 | 0 | 0 | 0 | 3 | 4 | 2 | 1 | 0 | 3 | 4 | .286 |
| | Lansing (MID) | A | 0 | 0 | 4.05 | 9 | 0 | 0 | 0 | 13 | 15 | 6 | 6 | 2 | 9 | 14 | .300 |
| 2006 | Winston-Salem (CL) | A | 1 | 4 | 3.40 | 40 | 0 | 0 | 8 | 48 | 40 | 23 | 18 | 3 | 21 | 63 | .222 |
| **MINOR LEAGUE TOTALS** | | | 3 | 7 | 2.64 | 107 | 0 | 0 | 28 | 119 | 105 | 47 | 35 | 5 | 52 | 136 | .229 |

## CHRIS STEWART                                                             C

**Born:** Feb. 19, 1982. **B-T:** R-R. **Ht.:** 6-4. **Wt.:** 205. **Drafted:** Riverside (Calif.) CC, 2001 (12th round). **Signed by:** Mark Salas/Joe Butler.

Perseverance has been the key for Stewart, who developed quietly since signing as a 12th-round pick in 2001. He's the best defensive catcher in the system, and the White Sox credit his role in the development for pitchers as varied as fireballer Bobby Jenks and knuckleballer Charlie Haeger. He enhances average arm strength with a quick release and accuracy, allowing him to led the Southern League in catching basestealers (52 percent) in 2005 and rank second in the International League (49 percent) last year. He's solid in all phases of catching and pitchers enjoy working to him. Stewart's bat is question mark and probably will limit him to a backup role. He hit a career-high 11 homers in 2005 but has totaled eight longballs in his other four pro seasons. The gains he made at the plate in Double-A didn't extend to Triple-A. He makes contact but his lack of bat speed forces him to be a guess hitter. He doesn't hit for average, draw walks or offer more than marginal power. He's also a below-average runner though not as much of a baseclogger as most catchers. Stewart's defense could make him a valuable reserve, but the signing of free agent Toby Hall hurts his chances of opening the season in Chicago.

| Year | Club (League) | Class | AVG | G | AB | R | H | 2B | 3B | HR | RBI | BB | SO | SB | OBP | SLG |
|------|---------------|-------|-----|---|----|---|---|----|----|----|-----|----|----|----|-----|-----|
| 2002 | Bristol (Appy) | R | .278 | 42 | 158 | 25 | 44 | 9 | 0 | 1 | 12 | 14 | 23 | 0 | .350 | .354 |
| 2003 | Winston-Salem (CL) | A | .207 | 76 | 217 | 18 | 45 | 8 | 2 | 2 | 27 | 27 | 29 | 1 | .294 | .290 |
| 2004 | Charlotte (IL) | AAA | .071 | 5 | 14 | 1 | 1 | 1 | 0 | 0 | 1 | 1 | 3 | 0 | .188 | .143 |
|      | Birmingham (SL) | AA | .231 | 83 | 260 | 26 | 60 | 11 | 2 | 1 | 17 | 22 | 59 | 2 | .299 | .300 |
| 2005 | Birmingham (SL) | AA | .286 | 95 | 311 | 39 | 89 | 21 | 0 | 11 | 51 | 24 | 37 | 3 | .341 | .460 |
| 2006 | Charlotte (IL) | AAA | .265 | 89 | 272 | 40 | 72 | 17 | 3 | 4 | 28 | 15 | 35 | 3 | .314 | .393 |
|      | Chicago (AL) | MLB | .000 | 6 | 8 | 0 | 0 | 0 | 0 | 0 | 0 | 0 | 2 | 0 | .000 | .000 |
| **MINOR LEAGUE TOTALS** | | | .252 | 390 | 1232 | 149 | 311 | 67 | 7 | 19 | 136 | 103 | 186 | 9 | .317 | .364 |
| **MAJOR LEAGUE TOTALS** | | | .000 | 6 | 8 | 0 | 0 | 0 | 0 | 0 | 0 | 0 | 2 | 0 | .000 | .000 |

## ANDERSON GOMES                                                            OF

**Born:** March 12, 1985. **B-T:** R-R. **Ht.:** 6-1. **Wt.:** 185. **Signed:** Brazil, 2005. **Signed by:** Ray Poitevint.

Gomes oozes tools. He signed with Japan's Fukuoka Daiei Hawks as a 16-year-old righthander with a live arm. He spent three years in Fukuoka's minor league system until he blew out his elbow and had Tommy John surgery. After he was released he returned to Brazil and became an outfielder. Like countryman Paulo Orlando, Gomes was a star sprinter in Brazil, but it was his bat potential that sold White Sox international scout Ray Poitevint, who signed him for the equivalent of third-round money. Chicago farm director Dave Wilder compares Gomes to Alfonso Soriano when the Yankees signed Soriano out of the Japanese minor leagues. Though Gomes made the Futures Game in his U.S. debut, it was mostly a disappointment. He wasn't able to handle high Class A and didn't improve much after a demotion. Though the ball jumps off Gomes' bat, he had difficulty making consistent contact. He has plus speed but lacks baserunning and basestealing instincts. He did look good defensively, with enough range for center field and enough arm for right. The White Sox will be patient with Gomes, who will get another shot at the Carolina League in 2007. Chicago has few players with higher ceilings or longer odds of reaching them.

| Year | Club (League) | Class | AVG | G | AB | R | H | 2B | 3B | HR | RBI | BB | SO | SB | OBP | SLG |
|------|---------------|-------|-----|---|----|---|---|----|----|----|-----|----|----|----|-----|-----|
| 2006 | Kannapolis (SAL) | A | .250 | 80 | 288 | 37 | 72 | 11 | 3 | 7 | 30 | 24 | 67 | 10 | .312 | .382 |
|      | Winston-Salem (CL) | A | .205 | 34 | 112 | 14 | 23 | 6 | 2 | 2 | 12 | 11 | 30 | 2 | .291 | .348 |
| **MINOR LEAGUE TOTALS** | | | .238 | 114 | 400 | 51 | 95 | 17 | 5 | 9 | 42 | 35 | 97 | 12 | .306 | .373 |

## FRANCISCO HERNANDEZ                                                        C

**Born:** Feb. 4, 1986. **B-T:** B-R. **Ht.:** 5-9. **Wt.:** 160. **Signed:** Dominican Republic, 2002. **Signed by:** Denny Gonzalez/Miguel Ibarra.

Hernandez has mastered Rookie ball, hitting .323 over three seasons, but has struggled with the jump to full-season ball, hitting .241 in two stints in low Class A. He's a contact hitter with gap power who has been overmatched at times against quality breaking pitches. Despite his bat control, he needs to be more selective. His value as a switch-hitter is muted by his ongoing struggles from the right side of the plate, where he hit .196 with one extra-base hit in 97 at-bats last year, and he may become a full-time lefty swinger in the future. Hernandez hasn't gain upper-body strength as quickly as the White Sox would have liked. Like most catchers, he's a below-average runner. On defense, his calling card is a plus arm and a quick release. He threw out 33 percent of basestealers in 2006. His receiving isn't as advanced as his throwing. He sometimes takes his troubles at the plate with him onto the

field, impacting his ability to work with pitchers. Patience will be required with his development, and he faces a critical season to show he can hit more advanced pitching.

| Year | Club (League) | Class | W | L | ERA | G | GS | CG | SV | IP | H | R | ER | HR | BB | SO | AVG |
|---|---|---|---|---|---|---|---|---|---|---|---|---|---|---|---|---|---|
| 2003 | Great Falls (Pio) | R | 1 | 3 | 2.70 | 24 | 0 | 0 | 7 | 23 | 23 | 10 | 7 | 0 | 10 | 14 | .261 |
| 2004 | Kannapolis (SAL) | A | 3 | 3 | 2.98 | 28 | 0 | 0 | 4 | 45 | 43 | 20 | 15 | 2 | 16 | 59 | .240 |
| | Winston-Salem (CL) | A | 0 | 0 | 0.00 | 2 | 0 | 0 | 0 | 2 | 1 | 0 | 0 | 0 | 1 | 1 | .143 |
| 2005 | Monterrey (MEX) | AAA | 2 | 2 | 5.28 | 6 | 6 | 0 | 0 | 31 | 33 | 18 | 18 | 2 | 16 | 10 | .300 |
| | Aguascalientes (MEX) | AAA | 2 | 1 | 5.82 | 16 | 4 | 0 | 0 | 39 | 51 | 28 | 25 | 9 | 20 | 19 | .317 |
| | Winston-Salem (CL) | A | 4 | 1 | 5.14 | 45 | 0 | 0 | 1 | 70 | 83 | 44 | 40 | 6 | 30 | 59 | .303 |
| 2006 | Winston-Salem (CL) | A | 7 | 5 | 1.93 | 57 | 0 | 0 | 13 | 65 | 50 | 24 | 14 | 4 | 32 | 81 | .207 |
| **MINOR LEAGUE TOTALS** | | | 15 | 12 | 3.32 | 156 | 0 | 0 | 25 | 206 | 200 | 98 | 76 | 12 | 89 | 214 | .253 |

## SEAN TRACEY
RHP

**Born:** Nov. 14, 1980. **B-T:** L-R. **Ht.:** 6-3. **Wt.:** 210. **Drafted:** UC Irvine, 2002 (8th round). **Signed by:** Joe Butler/Matt Hattabaugh.

Tracey unwittingly was thrust into the national spotlight in June, shortly after his first big league callup. After A.J. Pierzynski was hit by two pitches in a game against the Rangers, manager Ozzie Guillen ordered Tracey to drill Hank Blalock. When Tracey missed Blalock with two inside pitches before inducing a groundout, Guillen pulled him from the game and berated him in front of teammates and television cameras. Tracey was demoted afterward, though he showed impressive resolve by pitching his way back to Chicago in September. The irony is that Tracey never has been adverse to throwing inside, as he has hit 80 batters in four full seasons in the minors. The question with Tracey isn't his toughness but his stuff. He threw in the mid-90s in 2004 but has dropped into the low 90s the last two years. He never has fully developed his secondary pitches, shown consistent control or command, or learned to change speeds effectively. It's hard to succeed with one reliable pitch that's less than overpowering. Groomed as a starter for most of his career, Tracey more fits the profile of a reliever. He'll get a look in spring training but still has several refinements to make.

| Year | Club (League) | Class | W | L | ERA | G | GS | CG | SV | IP | H | R | ER | HR | BB | SO | AVG |
|---|---|---|---|---|---|---|---|---|---|---|---|---|---|---|---|---|---|
| 2002 | Bristol (Appy) | R | 5 | 2 | 3.02 | 13 | 12 | 0 | 0 | 66 | 57 | 27 | 22 | 4 | 19 | 50 | .241 |
| 2003 | Kannapolis (SAL) | A | 2 | 7 | 9.50 | 14 | 9 | 0 | 0 | 42 | 51 | 54 | 44 | 4 | 46 | 28 | .305 |
| | Great Falls (Pio) | R | 8 | 5 | 3.69 | 16 | 12 | 1 | 0 | 93 | 90 | 45 | 38 | 5 | 22 | 74 | .259 |
| 2004 | Winston-Salem (CL) | A | 9 | 8 | 2.73 | 27 | 27 | 0 | 0 | 148 | 108 | 60 | 45 | 5 | 69 | 130 | .213 |
| 2005 | Birmingham (SL) | AA | 14 | 6 | 4.07 | 28 | 28 | 2 | 0 | 164 | 154 | 80 | 74 | 13 | 76 | 106 | .257 |
| 2006 | Charlotte (IL) | AAA | 8 | 9 | 4.30 | 29 | 20 | 1 | 0 | 130 | 111 | 67 | 62 | 17 | 76 | 102 | .238 |
| | Chicago (AL) | MLB | 0 | 0 | 3.38 | 7 | 0 | 0 | 0 | 8 | 4 | 3 | 3 | 2 | 5 | 3 | .143 |
| **MINOR LEAGUE TOTALS** | | | 46 | 37 | 4.00 | 127 | 108 | 4 | 0 | 642 | 571 | 333 | 285 | 48 | 308 | 490 | .245 |
| **MAJOR LEAGUE TOTALS** | | | 0 | 0 | 3.38 | 7 | 0 | 0 | 0 | 8 | 4 | 3 | 3 | 2 | 5 | 3 | .143 |

## BRIAN OMOGROSSO
RHP

**Born:** April 26, 1984. **B-T:** R-R. **Ht.:** 6-3. **Wt.:** 230. **Drafted:** Indiana State, 2006 (6th round). **Signed by:** Mike Shirley

Omogrosso intrigued scouts by throwing 92-95 mph with a plus slider as an Indiana State sophomore in 2004, but his draft hopes were quashed by Tommy John surgery in 2005. He bounced back last year to touch 96 mph early in the spring and pitch at 92-93. He also dropped his arm slot from low three-quarters to sidearm, improving the sink on his fastball. The White Sox took him in the sixth round in June and signed him for $105,000. As is typical of pitchers coming back from elbow reconstruction, his secondary pitches and control have lagged behind his velocity. His slider has been inconsistent, and his new arm angle makes it tougher to stay on top of the pitch. Omogrosso was able to go straight to low Class A, reinforcing the White Sox' belief that he can move quickly one he's healthy. He figures begin his first full pro season in high Class A, possibly as a closer.

| Year | Club (League) | Class | W | L | ERA | G | GS | CG | SV | IP | H | R | ER | HR | BB | SO | AVG |
|---|---|---|---|---|---|---|---|---|---|---|---|---|---|---|---|---|---|
| 2006 | Kannapolis (SAL) | A | 1 | 2 | 3.19 | 22 | 0 | 0 | 2 | 37 | 27 | 14 | 13 | 2 | 13 | 23 | .209 |
| **MINOR LEAGUE TOTALS** | | | 1 | 2 | 3.19 | 22 | 0 | 0 | 2 | 37 | 27 | 14 | 13 | 2 | 13 | 23 | .209 |

## PAULO ORLANDO
OF

**Born:** Nov. 1, 1985. **B-T:** R-R. **Ht.:** 6-3. **Wt.:** 184. **Signed:** Brazil, 2005. **Signed by:** Orlando Santana

Signed out of a tryout camp in Brazil two years ago, Orlando was challenged with a full-season assignment last year. He showed remarkable maturity to weather ups and downs as a leadoff hitter and center fielder in low Class A. Orlando's quickness was the first thing that caught scouts' eyes—no surprise, considering he was a sprinter on the Brazilian national team. He's an electric runner but is still learning how to read pitchers and get good jumps.

To make the most of his speed, Orlando is going to need a lot more polish at the plate. He struck out nearly eight times for every walk he drew in 2006. He chased low breaking balls and high fastballs, and he seems to get anxious with runners in scoring position. He batted .306 in April, but low Class A pitchers realized they didn't have to throw him strikes, and he hit just .254 afterward. Orlando has a lean body but drives the ball well enough and has enough speed to take the occasional extra base.He's a graceful center fielder with a decent arm. Because he has so much to learn, Orlando almost certainly will return to Kannapolis in 2007.

| Year | Club (League) | Class | AVG | G | AB | R | H | 2B | 3B | HR | RBI | BB | SO | SB | OBP | SLG |
|---|---|---|---|---|---|---|---|---|---|---|---|---|---|---|---|---|
| 2006 | Kannapolis (SAL) | A | .262 | 116 | 470 | 71 | 123 | 23 | 10 | 6 | 31 | 18 | 143 | 29 | .305 | .391 |
| **MINOR LEAGUE TOTALS** | | | .262 | 116 | 470 | 71 | 123 | 23 | 10 | 6 | 31 | 18 | 143 | 29 | .305 | .391 |

## 29 WES WHISLER

LHP

**Born:** April 7, 1983. **B-T:** L-L. **Ht.:** 6-5. **Wt.:** 240. **Drafted:** UCLA, 2004 (2nd round). **Signed by:** Rick Ingalls/Matt Hattabaugh.

Drafted in the 41st round by the Cubs out of high school, Whisler opted instead for UCLA. He led the Pacific-10 Conference with 18 homers as a freshman and ranked as the top prospect in the Cape Cod League in 2002. But he changed his swing and approach and regressed at the plate. He emerged a better prospect as a pitcher, though he never dominated on the mound. The White Sox still gambled on his 6-foot-5 strong athletic frame in the second round of the 2004 draft, and they even let him DH some in his pro debut. Whisler has spent most of his three pro seasons in high Class A, and he finally took a step forward last year after working with Winston-Salem pitching coach J. R. Perdew to close his delivery. Whisler remains a work in progress, but his refined mechanics helped both his command in the strike zone as well as his deception. His best pitch is his sinker that clocks in the low-90s, often forcing hitters to pound the ball on the ground. He allowed just five homers in 163 innings last year. He still needs to improve his secondary pitches, the best of which is his slider, and learn to do a better job of changing speeds. Whisler doesn't miss many bats and doesn't have a quality breaking ball for left-on-left matchups, so his ceiling and future role will be limited if he can't develop a deeper repertoire. Because the White Sox have a logjam of starters in the majors and in Triple-A, he could begin 2007 back in Double-A.

| Year | Club (League) | Class | W | L | ERA | G | GS | CG | SV | IP | H | R | ER | HR | BB | SO | AVG |
|---|---|---|---|---|---|---|---|---|---|---|---|---|---|---|---|---|---|---|
| 2004 | Kannapolis (SAL) | A | 4 | 1 | 3.38 | 10 | 7 | 0 | 0 | 45 | 52 | 29 | 17 | 2 | 11 | 28 | .292 |
| | Winston-Salem (CL) | A | 2 | 1 | 3.38 | 5 | 5 | 0 | 0 | 27 | 17 | 10 | 10 | 3 | 7 | 13 | .183 |
| 2005 | Winston-Salem (CL) | A | 4 | 9 | 6.73 | 26 | 21 | 1 | 1 | 112 | 153 | 93 | 84 | 10 | 42 | 79 | .325 |
| 2006 | Winston-Salem (CL) | A | 10 | 7 | 2.97 | 20 | 20 | 1 | 0 | 118 | 112 | 52 | 39 | 0 | 44 | 57 | .250 |
| | Birmingham (SL) | AA | 2 | 3 | 4.43 | 7 | 7 | 0 | 0 | 45 | 50 | 28 | 22 | 5 | 15 | 28 | .284 |
| **MINOR LEAGUE TOTALS** | | | 22 | 21 | 4.46 | 68 | 60 | 2 | 1 | 347 | 384 | 212 | 172 | 20 | 119 | 205 | .281 |

## 30 RICARDO NANITA

OF

**Born:** June 12, 1981. **B-T:** L-L. **Ht.:** 6-0. **Wt.:** 202. **Drafted:** Florida International, 2003 (14th round). **Signed by:** Jose Ortega.

Nanita came out hitting as a pro, batting .384 and setting a since-broken Pioneer League record with a 30-game hitting streak in his 2003 debut. Since then, only injuries have stopped him. A broken hamate bone at the end of that season hampered his swing for much of 2004, and he missed most of the final month last year with a sprained ankle. Nanita has advanced to Double-A while continuing to show the ability to get on base. He's a very disciplined hitter with a professional approach. He has a knack for fighting off tough pitches to extend an at-bat. He's tough to strike out and bunts well. His lack of power makes it difficult to project him as a regular. He runs well but isn't a basestealing threat. An adequate defender with an average arm, he played all three outfield positions in 2006 and fits best in left field. Nanita is ready for Triple-A but could return to Double-A if Ryan Sweeney and Jerry Owens fail to win big league jobs.

| Year | Club (League) | Class | AVG | G | AB | R | H | 2B | 3B | HR | RBI | BB | SO | SB | OBP | SLG |
|---|---|---|---|---|---|---|---|---|---|---|---|---|---|---|---|---|
| 2003 | Great Falls (Pio) | R | .384 | 47 | 185 | 38 | 71 | 7 | 4 | 5 | 37 | 17 | 28 | 11 | .445 | .546 |
| 2004 | Kannapolis (SAL) | A | .316 | 61 | 225 | 32 | 71 | 12 | 2 | 1 | 31 | 26 | 32 | 5 | .391 | .400 |
| | Winston-Salem (CL) | A | .241 | 55 | 187 | 21 | 45 | 8 | 1 | 2 | 28 | 23 | 46 | 7 | .327 | .326 |
| 2005 | Winston-Salem (CL) | A | .292 | 120 | 415 | 73 | 121 | 36 | 2 | 9 | 54 | 61 | 53 | 14 | .392 | .453 |
| 2006 | Birmingham (SL) | AA | .286 | 106 | 364 | 48 | 104 | 14 | 3 | 8 | 42 | 51 | 56 | 11 | .372 | .407 |
| **MINOR LEAGUE TOTALS** | | | .299 | 389 | 1376 | 212 | 412 | 77 | 12 | 25 | 192 | 178 | 215 | 48 | .385 | .427 |

# CINCINNATI
# REDS

BY **J.J. COOPER**

The final result wasn't what they wanted, but the 2006 season gave Cincinnati fans a feeling they were unaccustomed to: hope.

The Reds stayed in the thick of the National League Central and wild card play-off races until September. And the farm system features their best group of impact prospects since Adam Dunn and Austin Kearns arrived in Cincinnati.

Cincinnati fans can thank new ownership for lifting much of the doom and gloom that had hung over the team. The group, led by Bob Castellini, took over just before spring training. Castellini quickly fired general manager Dan O'Brien and replaced him with longtime Twins assistant GM Wayne Krivsky.

Hired in early February, Krivsky had little time to remake the team, but he didn't let the late start get in the way. Within two months he had made a trio of deals that improved the Reds. He added an all-star starter (**Bronson Arroyo**) by trading from his outfield surplus (Wily Mo Pena). Krivsky picked up two regulars, Brandon Phillips and David Ross, for even less.

Not every move Krivsky made paid off. The midseason eight-player swap that sent Kearns, Felipe Lopez and Ryan Wagner to Washington for Bill Bray, Gary Majewski, Royce Clayton, Brendan Harris and Daryl Thompson was supposed to bulk up a sagging bullpen. The plan fell apart when Majewski was sidelined with shoulder problems, and the Reds later filed a grievance saying the Nationals weren't forthcoming about his health.

Cincinnati's offense collapsed in September, but even an 80-82 finish—the franchise's sixth straight losing year—couldn't dim all the optimism. First-year farm director Johnny Almaraz quickly scrapped O'Brien policies such as the tandem-starter system and a requirement that hitters take at least one pitch before they swung.

Several of the Reds' top prospects seemed energized by the change. Righthander Homer Bailey had a breakthrough season as his performance caught up to his exceptional stuff, while first baseman Joey Votto bounced back from a bad 2005 season to finish among the Double-A Southern League leaders in nearly every category. The Reds also managed to get through the season without any significant injuries to their top pitching prospects, a problem that had plagued the system for years.

In his first draft as Reds scouting director, Chris Buckley brought in a number of polished college draftees. Players such as outfielder Drew Stubbs (first round), righthander Sean Watson (second) and shortstop Chris Valaika (third) helped to bulk up the bottom levels of the system.

The team did suffer some turmoil after the season, as Almaraz and special assistant to the GM Larry Barton Jr. both resigned in December. Both had said they were unhappy at being left out of discussions between Krivsky and other lieutenants.

## TOP 30 PROSPECTS

| | |
|---|---|
| 1. Homer Bailey, rhp | 16. Phil Dumatrait, lhp |
| 2. Jay Bruce, of | 17. Tyler Pelland, lhp |
| 3. Joey Votto, 1b | 18. Daryl Thompson, rhp |
| 4. Johnny Cueto, rhp | 19. Camilo Vazquez, lhp |
| 5. Drew Stubbs, of | 20. David Shafer, rhp |
| 6. Travis Wood, lhp | 21. Miguel Perez, c |
| 7. Sean Watson, rhp | 22. Jon Coutlangus, lhp |
| 8. Milton Loo, ss | 23. Jordan Smith, rhp |
| 9. Paul Janish, ss | 24. Justin Reed, of |
| 10. Chris Valaika, ss | 25. Brad Salmon, rhp |
| 11. Cody Strait, of | 26. Juan Francisco, 3b |
| 12. Sam LeCure, rhp | 27. Norris Hopper, of |
| 13. Josh Ravin, rhp | 28. Rafael Gonzalez, rhp |
| 14. James Avery, rhp | 29. B.J. Szymanski, of |
| 15. Chris Dickerson, of | 30. Josh Hamilton, of |

# ORGANIZATION OVERVIEW

**General manager:** Wayne Krivsky. **Farm director:** Johnny Almaraz. **Scouting director:** Chris Buckley.

## 2006 PERFORMANCE

| Class | Team | League | W | L | PCT | Finish* | Manager | Affiliated |
|-------|------|--------|---|---|-----|---------|---------|-----------|
| Majors | Cincinnati | National | 80 | 82 | .494 | 7th (16) | Jerry Narron | — |
| Triple-A | Louisville RiverBats | International | 75 | 68 | .524 | 6th (14) | Rick Sweet | 2000 |
| Double-A | Chattanooga Lookouts | Southern | 81 | 59 | .579 | 2nd (10) | Jayhawk Owens | 1988 |
| High A | Sarasota Reds | Florida State | 66 | 73 | .475 | 10th (12) | Donnie Scott | 2005 |
| Low A | Dayton Dragons | Midwest | 67 | 73 | .479 | 9th (14) | Buddy Bailey | 2000 |
| Rookie | Billings Mustangs | Pioneer | 51 | 25 | .671 | 1st (8) | Rick Burleson | 1974 |
| Rookie | GCL Reds | Gulf Coast | 18 | 34 | .346 | 13th (13) | Luis Aguayo | 1999 |
| **OVERALL 2006 MINOR LEAGUE RECORD** | | | 358 | 332 | .519 | 11th (30) | | |

*Finish in overall standings (No. of teams in league). +League champion

## ORGANIZATION LEADERS

### BATTING
| | | |
|---|---|---|
| AVG | Dorn, Daniel, Billings | .354 |
| R | Strait, Cody, Sarasota/Louisville | 99 |
| H | Votto, Joey, Chattanooga | 165 |
| TB | Votto, Joey, Chattanooga | 284 |
| 2B | Votto, Joey, Chattanooga | 46 |
| 3B | Anderson, Drew, Sarasota/Chattanooga | 12 |
| HR | Votto, Joey, Chattanooga | 23 |
| RBI | Strait, Cody, Sarasota/Louisville | 87 |
| BB | Votto, Joey, Chattanooga | 79 |
| SO | Szymanski, Brandon, Dayton | 191 |
| SB | Strait, Cody, Sarasota/Louisville | 56 |
| OBP | Dorn, Daniel, Billings | .457 |
| SLG | Dorn, Daniel, Billings | .573 |
| XBH | Votto, Joey, Chattanooga | 71 |

### PITCHING
| | | |
|---|---|---|
| W | Cueto, Johnny, Dayton/Sarasota | 15 |
| L | Lecure, Sam, Sarasota | 12 |
| ERA | Bailey, Homer, Sarasota/Chattanooga | 2.47 |
| G | Chiasson, Scott, Louisville | 60 |
| CG | Cueto, Johnny, Dayton/Sarasota | 3 |
| SV | Chiasson, Scott, Louisville | 29 |
| IP | Hall, Josh, Louisville/Chattanooga | 152 |
| BB | Pelland, Tyler, Chattanooga | 93 |
| SO | Bailey, Homer, Sarasota/Chattanooga | 156 |
| AVG | Bailey, Homer, Sarasota/Chattanooga | .198 |

## BEST TOOLS

| | |
|---|---|
| Best Hitter for Average | Jay Bruce |
| Best Power Hitter | Joey Votto |
| Best Strike-Zone Discipline | Joey Votto |
| Fastest Baserunner | Chris Dickerson |
| Best Athlete | Chris Dickerson |
| Best Fastball | Homer Bailey |
| Best Curveball | Homer Baley |
| Best Slider | David Shafer |
| Best Changeup | Travis Wood |
| Best Control | Johnny Cueto |
| Best Defensive Catcher | Miguel Perez |
| Best Defensive Infielder | Paul Janish |
| Best Infield Arm | Juan Francisco |
| Best Defensive Outfielder | Chris Dickerson |
| Best Outfield Arm | Jerry Gil |

## PROJECTED 2010 LINEUP

| | |
|---|---|
| Catcher | Miguel Perez |
| First Base | Joey Votto |
| Second Base | Brandon Phillips |
| Third Base | Edwin Encarnacion |
| Shortstop | Milton Loo |
| Left Field | Adam Dunn |
| Center Field | Drew Stubbs |

| | |
|---|---|
| Right Field | Jay Bruce |
| No. 1 Starter | Homer Bailey |
| No. 2 Starter | Aaron Harang |
| No. 3 Starter | Bronson Arroyo |
| No. 4 Starter | Johnny Cueto |
| No. 5 Starter | Travis Wood |
| Closer | Sean Watson |

## LAST YEAR'S TOP 20 PROSPECTS

1. Homer Bailey, rhp
2. Jay Bruce, of
3. Travis Wood, lhp
4. B.J. Szymanski, of
5. Chris Denorfia, of
6. Rafael Gonzalez, rhp
7. Miguel Perez, c
8. Tyler Pelland, lhp
9. Joey Votto, 1b
10. Travis Chick, rhp
11. William Bergolla, 2b/ss
12. Philip Dumatrait, lhp
13. Zach Ward, rhp
14. Paul Janish, ss
15. Adam Rosales, ss
16. Richie Gardner, rhp
17. Thomas Pauly, rhp
18. Brandon Roberts, of
19. Chris Dickerson, of
20. Philippe Valiquette, lhp

## TOP PROSPECTS OF THE DECADE

| Year | Player, Pos. | 2006 Org. |
|------|-------------|-----------|
| 1997 | Aaron Boone, 3b | Indians |
| 1998 | Damian Jackson, ss/2b | Nationals |
| 1999 | Rob Bell, rhp | Indians |
| 2000 | Gookie Dawkins, ss | Pirates |
| 2001 | Austin Kearns, of | Nationals |
| 2002 | Austin Kearns, of | Nationals |
| 2003 | Chris Gruler, rhp | Reds |
| 2004 | Ryan Wagner, rhp | Nationals |
| 2005 | Homer Bailey, rhp | Reds |
| 2006 | Homer Bailey, rhp | Reds |

## TOP DRAFT PICKS OF THE DECADE

| Year | Player, Pos. | 2006 Org. |
|------|-------------|-----------|
| 1997 | Brandon Larson, 3b | Nationals |
| 1998 | Austin Kearns, of | Nationals |
| 1999 | Ty Howington, lhp | Out of baseball |
| 2000 | David Espinosa, ss | Tigers |
| 2001 | *Jeremy Sowers, lhp | Indians |
| 2002 | Chris Gruler, rhp | Reds |
| 2003 | Ryan Wagner, rhp | Nationals |
| 2004 | Homer Bailey, rhp | Reds |
| 2005 | Jay Bruce, of | Reds |
| 2006 | Drew Stubbs, of | Reds |

*Did not sign.

## ALL-TIME LARGEST BONUSES

| | |
|---|---|
| Chris Gruler, 2002 | $2,500,000 |
| Homer Bailey, 2004 | $2,300,000 |
| Drew Stubbs, 2006 | $2,000,000 |
| Austin Kearns, 1998 | $1,950,000 |
| Jay Bruce, 2005 | $1,800,000 |

# MINOR LEAGUE DEPTH CHART

## Cincinnati Reds

**Impact: A.** Homer Bailey could be the best pitcher in the minors, and Jay Bruce and Joey Votto both look like big league regulars.

**Depth: D.** The Reds have had some productive drafts the last three years, but trades to stay in the 2006 playoff hunt thinned the system again.

**Sleeper:** Justin Turner, ss/2b. Former Cal State Fullerton four-year starter doesn't have overwhelming tools but grinds and grinds and grinds.

*Numbers in parentheses indicate prospect rankings.*

### LF
Norris Hopper (27)
Danny Dorn

### CF
Drew Stubbs (5)
Chris Dickerson (25)
B.J. Szymanski (29)
Jerry Gil
Keltavious Jones

### RF
Jay Bruce (2)
Cody Strait (11)
Justin Reed (24)
Josh Hamilton (30)
Javon Moran

### 3B
Juan Francisco (26)
Michael Jones

### SS
Milton Loo (8)
Paul Janish (9)
Chris Valaika (10)
Adam Rosales
Angel Cabrera

### 2B
Brendan Harris
Drew Anderson
Justin Turner
Michael Griffin

### 1B
Joey Votto (3)
Logan Parker
Jesse Gutierrez
Tonys Gutierrez

### C
Miguel Perez (21)
Craig Tatum
John Purdom
Justin Tordi

### RHP

| Starters | Relievers |
|---|---|
| Homer Bailey (1) | David Shafer (20) |
| Johnny Cueto (4) | Brad Salmon (25) |
| Sean Watson (7) | Calvin Medlock |
| Sam LeCure (12) | Jose Rojas |
| Josh Ravin (13) | Carlos Guevara |
| James Avery (14) | Terrell Young |
| Jordan Smith (23) | Derrick Lutz |
| Daryl Thompson (18) | Bo Lanier |
| Rafael Gonzalez (28) | Thomas Pauly |
| Carlos Fisher | |
| Steve Kelly | |
| Richie Gardner | |

### LHP

| Starters | Relievers |
|---|---|
| Travis Wood (6) | Jon Coutlangus (22) |
| Phil Dumatrait (16) | Philippe Valiquette |
| Tyler Pelland (17) | Jamie Arneson |
| Camilo Vazquez (19) | Jan Granado |

# DRAFT ANALYSIS

## 2006

SIGNING BUDGET: $3.9 million

**Best Pro Debut:** SS Chris Valaika (3) won the Pioneer League MVP award, set a league mark with a 32-game hitting streak and batted .324/.387/.520 with eight homers and 60 RBIs. OF Danny Dorn (32) batted .354/.457/.573 and paced the Pioneer League in hitting and slugging percentage. RHP Jordan Smith (6), who went 6-3, 3.01, and 2B Justin Turner (7), who hit .338/.411/.511, were PL all-stars.

**Best Athlete:** The top college athlete in the draft, OF Drew Stubbs (1) plays Gold Glove-caliber defense in center, has well above-average speed, plus power and average arm strength. The only question is whether he'll make enough consistent contact to hit for average, and he didn't answer it by batting .252 in his debut. OF Justin Reed (4) had a football scholarship to Mississippi but signed with the Reds. SS Milton Loo, one of the game's prime draft-and-follows from 2005, is another quality athlete.

**Best Pure Hitter:** Valaika's quick hands help him at the plate and allow him to compensate for fringe-average range at shortstop. Loo's best tool is his bat, and he hit .372 before an elbow injury ended his debut after 14 games.

**Best Raw Power:** Since Texas' Disch-Falk Field opened in 1975, Stubbs is just one of four players who has twice cleared the 20-foot batting eye that stands 400 feet away from the plate. 1B Logan Parker (12) is a 6-foot-4, 220-pounder who hit .329 with nine homers in his first taste of pro ball.

**Fastest Runner:** Despite battling turf toe, Stubbs swiped 19 bases in 23 pro attempts. Reed has plus speed, as does Loo.

**Best Defensive Player:** Stubbs. Turner is the best infielder and probably could get by at shortstop even with his fringy arm.

**Best Fastball:** RHP Josh Ravin (5) had a tired arm in the spring but recovered to throw 94-96 mph in the summer. RHP Sean Watson is just behind him at 92-95 mph. Smith touched 96 mph at the CC of Southern Nevada and worked at 90-93 in pro ball. RHPs Jeremy Burchette (9) and Josh Roenicke (10) can reach 94.

**Best Breaking Ball:** Watson's 82-85 mph knuckle-curve. He joined Todd Helton as the only pitchers to reach double digits in saves at Tennessee.

**Most Intriguing Background:** OF Carson Kainer (14) didn't sign immediately, instead preparing for a kidney transplant in September. He then came to terms at the end of October. His uncle Don pitched briefly in the majors. C Tyler Hauschild (28) is the great-great-grandson of Hall of Famer Carl Hubbell. RHP Travis Webb (8) is a cousin of longtime NBA guard Craig Ehlo. Stubbs' brother Clint turned down a 49th-round offer from the Rangers and decided to follow in Drew's footsteps at Texas. Roenicke's father Gary and uncle Ron played in the big leagues, as did unsigned OF Jason Chapman's (44) dad Kelvin.

**Closest To The Majors:** Watson.

**Best Late-Round Pick:** Dorn and RHP Derrik Lutz (19). Lutz starred in the Cape Cod League in 2005 but fell prey to elbow tendinitis this spring. When healthy, he has a 90-92 mph sinker and an effective slider.

**The One Who Got Away:** The Reds couldn't lock up draft-eligible sophomore SS Ryan Wehrle (18), who improved significantly and drew comparisons to Michael Cuddyer in his second season at Nebraska.

**Assessment:** To a large extent, how well Stubbs hits will determine the success of the draft. However, early returns indicate that that scouting director Chris Buckley's first draft with Cincinnati could be one of its deeper efforts in years.

## 2005 — BUDGET: $3.8 million

OF Jay Bruce (1) led a deep crop that also features LHP Travis Wood (2), RHPs Sam LeCure (4) and James Avery (5) and draft-and-follow SS Milton Loo (9). The Reds already have used RHPs Zach Ward (3) and Abe Woody (31) and OF Brandon Roberts (7) as trade fodder. **GRADE: B+**

## 2004 — BUDGET: $4.7 million

If the 2004 draft were staged again, RHP Homer Bailey (1) wouldn't fall to Cincinnati at No. 7. SS Paul Janish (5) came on with the bat last season. **GRADE: B+**

## 2003 — BUDGET: $3.1 million

Injuries waylaid RHPs Ryan Wagner (1), Thomas Pauly (2) and Richie Gardner (6), leaving OF Chris Dickerson (16) as the Reds' best hope from this class. **GRADE: F**

*Draft analysis by Jim Callis. Numbers in parentheses indicate draft rounds. Budgets are bonuses in first 10 rounds.*

# HOMER
# BAILEY

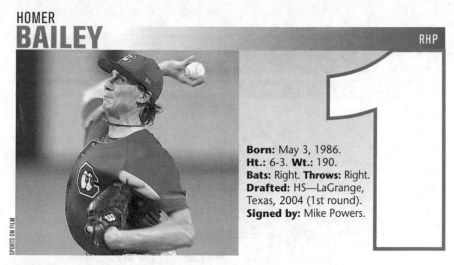

SPORTS ON FILM

**Born:** May 3, 1986.
**Ht.:** 6-3. **Wt.:** 190.
**Bats:** Right. **Throws:** Right.
**Drafted:** HS—LaGrange, Texas, 2004 (1st round).
**Signed by:** Mike Powers.

Bailey finally got his training wheels taken off in 2006, and he seemed to enjoy the freedom. Shackled to a 75-pitch limit in a tandem-starter system under previous general manager Dan O'Brien, he handled an increased workload with aplomb in 2006. He was allowed to work six innings in an outing 11 times, compared to just once the year before. The longer starts forced Bailey to rely more on his secondary stuff. The seventh overall pick in 2004, when he was also Baseball America's High School Player of the Year, he pitched the best baseball of his pro career following a midseason promotion to Double-A Chattanooga. While Bailey impressed scouts and prospect-watchers all season, he popped up on the national radar with a Joel Zumayaesque inning at the Futures Game. Bailey threw 20 pitches, topping out at 98 mph and not dipping under 92. He has good secondary pitches, but decided to challenge hitters with his heat at the prospect all-star game.

Bailey's stuff is as good as anyone's in the minors. He has an athletic frame and a free and easy motion that makes it seem like he's just playing catch even when he's lighting up the radar gun. His fastball sits at 92-96 mph and touches 98. Because of its late life, his heater seems to have an extra gear, exploding on hitters just before it reaches the plate. He has learned to work the bottom of the zone. His curveball is also a plus pitch. He can throw a 12-to-6 hammer or a slower, loopier version with 11-to-5 break. It's effective both as a knee-buckler for righthanders and as a backdoor pitch that sneaks over against lefties. While it will always be his third best offering, Bailey's changeup has improved and shows some potential. He throws it with good arm speed, generating some deception and a little sink. He has good control for a power pitcher. He also has impressed the Reds with his competitive nature.

Finding weaknesses in Bailey's pitching is nitpicking at best. He needs to continue to refine his changeup and sharpen the command of his fastball, though he already works both sides of the plate well. He has just started working on hitting and bunting in preparation for his role as a National League starter, but he's a good athlete and already looks comfortable with the bat. He can quicken his delivery to the plate and hold runners better, but he did show improvement in those facets in 2006.

The Reds resisted the temptation to call Bailey up in September, when he might have given their rotation a boost or bolstered their bullpen. They're not going to be able to hold off too much longer, and he could win a spot in the Cincinnati rotation during spring training. It's more likely that he'll head to Triple-A Louisville for some final polish before a midseason callup. In time, he should become a true No. 1 starter.

| Year | Club (League) | Class | W | L | ERA | G | GS | CG | SV | IP | H | R | ER | HR | BB | SO | AVG |
|------|---------------|-------|---|---|-----|---|----|----|----|----|---|---|----|----|----|----|-----|
| 2004 | Reds (GCL) | R | 0 | 1 | 4.38 | 6 | 3 | 0 | 0 | 12 | 14 | 7 | 6 | 0 | 3 | 9 | .275 |
| 2005 | Dayton (MWL) | A | 8 | 4 | 4.43 | 28 | 21 | 0 | 0 | 104 | 89 | 64 | 51 | 5 | 62 | 125 | .232 |
| 2006 | Sarasota (FSL) | A | 3 | 5 | 3.31 | 13 | 13 | 0 | 0 | 71 | 49 | 35 | 26 | 6 | 22 | 79 | .189 |
| | Chattanooga (SL) | AA | 7 | 1 | 1.59 | 13 | 13 | 0 | 0 | 68 | 50 | 13 | 12 | 1 | 28 | 77 | .208 |
| **MINOR LEAGUE TOTALS** | | | 18 | 11 | 3.36 | 60 | 50 | 0 | 0 | 255 | 202 | 119 | 95 | 12 | 115 | 290 | .217 |

## JAY BRUCE OF

**Born:** April 3, 1987. **B-T:** L-L. **Ht.:** 6-2. **Wt.:** 206. **Drafted:** HS—Beaumont, Texas, 2005 (1st round). **Signed by:** Brian Wilson.

The low Class A Midwest League was loaded with outfielders last year—including fellow 2005 first-round picks Cameron Maybin, Colby Rasmus and Justin Upton—but it was Bruce who ranked as the circuit's No. 1 prospect. The youngest player in the MWL all-star game, he came away with the MVP award, and led the league in doubles and extra-base hits (63). Bruce quickly has established himself as the best hitting prospect in the system and one of the best in the minors. He has quick hands and a smooth swing path that allow him to keep the bat in the strike zone for quite a while. Scouts were impressed that he could turn on 95-mph fastballs with his plus bat speed, and he also knows how to go the other way if pitchers try to work the outside corner. He projects to be an above-average hitter with above-average power. In the outfield, Bruce gets good jumps to go with his slightly above-average speed. He can handle center field, though most scouts expect he'll end up as a strong-armed right fielded once he fills out. He can show more plate discipline, but the Reds will happily live with some strikeouts if Bruce continues to pound the ball. A pulled quadriceps muscle helped lead to a late-season slump. The Reds took a cautious approach with Bruce in 2006, letting him remain in low Class A all season even as he dominated. He'll likely begin this year at high Class A Sarasota, but he could start to move quickly and reach Cincinnati at some point in 2008.

| Year | Club (League) | Class | AVG | G | AB | R | H | 2B | 3B | HR | RBI | BB | SO | SB | OBP | SLG |
|------|---------------|-------|-----|---|----|---|---|----|----|----|-----|----|----|----|-----|-----|
| 2005 | Reds (GCL) | R | .270 | 37 | 122 | 29 | 33 | 9 | 2 | 5 | 25 | 11 | 31 | 4 | .331 | .500 |
|  | Billings (Pio) | R | .257 | 17 | 70 | 16 | 18 | 2 | 0 | 4 | 13 | 11 | 22 | 2 | .358 | .457 |
| 2006 | Dayton (MWL) | A | .291 | 117 | 444 | 69 | 129 | 42 | 5 | 16 | 81 | 44 | 106 | 19 | .355 | .516 |
| **MINOR LEAGUE TOTALS** | | | .283 | 171 | 636 | 114 | 180 | 53 | 7 | 25 | 119 | 66 | 159 | 25 | .351 | .506 |

## JOEY VOTTO 1B

**Born:** Sept. 10, 1983. **B-T:** L-L. **Ht.:** 6-3. **Wt.:** 200. **Drafted:** HS—Toronto, 2002 (2nd round). **Signed by:** John Castleberry.

Votto bounced back from a difficult 2005 season to emerge as the Double-A Southern League's MVP last year. He led the SL in batting, on-base percentage and slugging, as well as runs, hits, total bases (278), extra-base hits (70), doubles and walks. Votto has the ability to drive the ball to all fields, especially to left-center when he's locked in. His hands are quick enough that he can punish pitchers if they try to bust him inside. A hard worker, Votto devoted time to his baserunning and stole 24 bases in 31 tries last year despite average speed. A catcher when he signed, Votto still is a little raw at first base. He sometimes goes too far into the hole on balls, leaving him out of position. He also can improve his footwork and throwing accuracy. Like many young left-handed hitters, he struggles against southpaws. Votto is the Reds' first baseman of the future—and that future could begin as soon as this year. He'll head to Triple-A and be in line for a September callup, though he could accelerate that timetable with a strong start.

| Year | Club (League) | Class | AVG | G | AB | R | H | 2B | 3B | HR | RBI | BB | SO | SB | OBP | SLG |
|------|---------------|-------|-----|---|----|---|---|----|----|----|-----|----|----|----|-----|-----|
| 2002 | Reds (GCL) | R | .269 | 50 | 175 | 29 | 47 | 13 | 3 | 9 | 33 | 21 | 45 | 7 | .342 | .531 |
| 2003 | Dayton (MWL) | A | .231 | 60 | 195 | 19 | 45 | 8 | 0 | 1 | 20 | 34 | 64 | 2 | .348 | .287 |
|  | Billings (Pio) | R | .317 | 70 | 240 | 47 | 76 | 17 | 3 | 6 | 38 | 56 | 80 | 4 | .452 | .488 |
| 2004 | Dayton (MWL) | A | .302 | 111 | 391 | 60 | 118 | 26 | 2 | 14 | 72 | 79 | 110 | 9 | .419 | .486 |
|  | Potomac (CL) | A | .298 | 24 | 84 | 11 | 25 | 7 | 0 | 5 | 20 | 11 | 21 | 1 | .385 | .560 |
| 2005 | Sarasota (FSL) | A | .256 | 124 | 464 | 64 | 119 | 23 | 2 | 17 | 83 | 52 | 122 | 4 | .330 | .425 |
| 2006 | Chattanooga (SL) | AA | .319 | 136 | 508 | 85 | 162 | 46 | 2 | 22 | 77 | 78 | 109 | 24 | .408 | .547 |
| **MINOR LEAGUE TOTALS** | | | .288 | 575 | 2057 | 315 | 592 | 140 | 12 | 74 | 343 | 331 | 551 | 51 | .386 | .475 |

## JOHNNY CUETO RHP

**Born:** Feb. 15, 1986. **B-T:** R-R. **Ht.:** 5-10. **Wt.:** 192. **Signed:** Dominican Republic, 2004. **Signed by:** Johnny Almaraz.

Cueto was the first player the Reds signed in the Dominican after revitalizing their nearly dormant Latin American scouting program. In his first extended taste of full-season ball, he went 15-3, 3.00 and allowed just one run in his final 30 innings in high Class A. The 5-foot-10, 192-pounder doesn't look like he has a big arm, but Cueto throws a 92-94 mph fastball that touches 96 mph. He does so with a relatively free and easy high three-quarters delivery, and he commands his heat to both

sides of the plate. During spring training, former Reds ace Mario Soto taught Cueto a changeup that quickly became a major league average pitch with tailing life. He also throws a slider that overmatches hitters at times. Cueto's size doesn't lend itself to durability, but Cincinnati believes he'll be able to remain a starter. He has long arms that give him good leverage, so he doesn't wear himself out by throwing hard. He needs to get more consistent with his secondary pitches. While he likes to challenge hitters up in the zone, that won't work as well at higher levels. He could open 2007 in Double-A at age 21.

| Year | Club (League) | Class | W | L | ERA | G | GS | CG | SV | IP | H | R | ER | HR | BB | SO | AVG |
|------|---------------|-------|---|---|-----|---|----|----|----|-----|-----|-----|----|----|----|-----|------|
| 2004 | Reds (DSL) | R | 3 | 6 | 2.58 | 18 | 10 | 0 | 0 | 77 | 66 | 35 | 22 | 2 | 26 | 69 | .222 |
| 2005 | Reds (GCL) | R | 2 | 2 | 5.02 | 13 | 6 | 0 | 1 | 43 | 49 | 31 | 24 | 2 | 8 | 38 | .285 |
| | Sarasota (FSL) | A | 0 | 1 | 3.00 | 2 | 1 | 0 | 0 | 6 | 5 | 2 | 2 | 0 | 2 | 6 | .217 |
| 2006 | Dayton (MWL) | A | 8 | 1 | 2.59 | 14 | 14 | 2 | 0 | 76 | 52 | 22 | 22 | 5 | 15 | 82 | .191 |
| | Sarasota (FSL) | A | 7 | 2 | 3.50 | 12 | 12 | 1 | 0 | 62 | 48 | 25 | 24 | 6 | 23 | 61 | .214 |
| **MINOR LEAGUE TOTALS** | | | 20 | 12 | 3.21 | 59 | 43 | 3 | 1 | 264 | 220 | 115 | 94 | 15 | 74 | 256 | .223 |

## 5 DREW STUBBS OF

**Born:** Oct. 4, 1984. **B-T:** R-R. **Ht.:** 6-4. **Wt.:** 200. **Drafted:** Texas, 2006 (1st round). **Signed by:** Brian Wilson.

A borderline first-round talent with questionable signability coming out high school in 2003, Stubbs was set to sign for $900,000 as a third-rounder until the commissioner's office talked Astros owner Drayton McLane out of the deal. Stubbs starred in three years at Texas, winning the 2005 College World Series and the 2006 Big 12 Conference co-player of the year award. He signed for $2 million after the Reds took him eighth overall in June. His younger brother Clint turned down a 49th-round offer from the Rangers to follow his brother's footsteps with the Longhorns. Stubbs has evoked comparisons to Dale Murphy as a tall speedster with plus power, speed and Gold Glove ability in center field. He has light-tower power and is a 70 runner on the 20-to-80 scale, clocking in at 4.1 seconds from the right side of the plate to first base. He has an average arm. Since high school, there have been concerns that Stubbs' long swing would lead to strikeouts and extended slumps. He struggles at times to make contact, and a smart pitcher can take advantage of his difficulties with breaking balls. He was hobbled by turf toe in his pro debut but played through it and is healthy now. Stubbs probably always will strike out a lot, but he could develop into a Mike Cameron/Torii Hunter type, which would more than satisfy the Reds. They'll be patient with him, which means he'll start 2007 at low Class A Dayton.

| Year | Club (League) | Class | AVG | G | AB | R | H | 2B | 3B | HR | RBI | BB | SO | SB | OBP | SLG |
|------|---------------|-------|-----|---|----|---|---|----|----|----|-----|----|----|----|-----|-----|
| 2006 | Billings (Pio) | R | .252 | 56 | 210 | 39 | 53 | 7 | 3 | 6 | 24 | 32 | 64 | 19 | .368 | .400 |
| **MINOR LEAGUE TOTALS** | | | .252 | 56 | 210 | 39 | 53 | 7 | 3 | 6 | 24 | 32 | 64 | 19 | .368 | .400 |

## 6 TRAVIS WOOD LHP

**Born:** Feb. 6, 1987. **B-T:** R-L. **Ht.:** 6-0. **Wt.:** 165. **Drafted:** HS—Alexander, Ark., 2005 (2nd round). **Signed by:** Mike Keenan.

Wood became a rare find as an Arkansas high school pitcher with some polish. The Reds were intrigued enough to draft him in 2005's second round and entice him from his college commitment to Arkansas with a $600,000 bonus. He handled low Class A well as a teenager last year. Wood boasts the system's top changeup, and it's one of the best in the minors. It's nearly impossible to discern that it's not a fastball coming out of his hand, and it has good sink right before it crosses the plate. He also has the confidence to throw it in any count, and his overall approach is extremely advanced for his age. He regularly topped out at 93-94 mph with his fastball as a high school senior and in his debut, though he pitched at 87-91 in 2006. He's a good athlete who repeats his delivery well and throws strikes. After two years of trying, Wood still is seeking a consistent curveball. There's some effort to his delivery and he doesn't have the biggest frame, so Cincinnati will have to watch him closely. He needs to add some strength. The curve will be the key ingredient in Wood becoming a No. 3 or 4 starter. He'll focus on his breaking ball this year in high Class A.

| Year | Club (League) | Class | W | L | ERA | G | GS | CG | SV | IP | H | R | ER | HR | BB | SO | AVG |
|------|---------------|-------|---|---|-----|---|----|----|----|-----|-----|----|----|----|----|-----|------|
| 2005 | Reds (GCL) | R | 0 | 0 | 0.75 | 8 | 7 | 0 | 0 | 24 | 13 | 3 | 2 | 0 | 7 | 45 | .157 |
| | Billings (Pio) | R | 2 | 0 | 1.82 | 6 | 4 | 0 | 0 | 25 | 15 | 6 | 5 | 0 | 13 | 22 | .174 |
| 2006 | Dayton (MWL) | A | 10 | 5 | 3.66 | 27 | 27 | 0 | 0 | 140 | 108 | 65 | 57 | 14 | 56 | 133 | .215 |
| **MINOR LEAGUE TOTALS** | | | 12 | 5 | 3.05 | 41 | 38 | 0 | 0 | 189 | 136 | 74 | 64 | 14 | 76 | 200 | .203 |

## 7 SEAN WATSON
RHP

**Born:** July 24, 1985. **B-T:** R-R. **Ht.:** 6-3. **Wt.:** 215. **Drafted:** Tennessee, 2006 (2nd round). **Signed by:** Perry Smith.

Watson teamed with fellow Reds 2006 draftee Chris Valaika on the U.S. national team that won the 2001 World Youth Championships in Mexico. At Tennessee, Watson began his career as a member of the weekend rotation but shifted to the closer's role as a sophomore. He and Todd Helton are the only Volunteers to record 10 saves in a season. Watson has two plus offerings. He has a 92-93 mph fastball that touches 95, and he pairs it with an 82-85 mph knuckle-curve that's a true out pitch. It's a hard tumbler with tilt and depth. He goes after hitters with an aggressive approach that serves him well in a closer's role. Watson's mechanics are inconsistent, so his pitches are as well. He sometimes struggles to locate his fastball, which is why he got hammered in low Class A. He'll need to come up with a changeup if he's going to be a starter, and his slider needs improvement as well. With two above-average pitches, a tough mindset and some effort to his delivery, Watson has strengths and weaknesses that seem to point him to a future in the bullpen. For now, however, the Reds will let him build up innings and refine his arsenal as a starter. He'll probably return to low Class A to open 2007.

| Year | Club (League) | Class | W | L | ERA | G | GS | CG | SV | IP | H | R | ER | HR | BB | SO | AVG |
|------|---------------|-------|---|---|-----|---|----|----|----|----|---|---|----|----|----|----|-----|
| 2006 | Billings (Pio) | R | 0 | 0 | 1.52 | 7 | 4 | 0 | 1 | 24 | 16 | 7 | 4 | 0 | 5 | 19 | .190 |
|      | Dayton (MWL) | A | 1 | 2 | 8.59 | 10 | 0 | 0 | 0 | 15 | 22 | 14 | 14 | 2 | 5 | 16 | .349 |
| **MINOR LEAGUE TOTALS** | | | 1 | 2 | 4.23 | 17 | 4 | 0 | 1 | 38 | 38 | 21 | 18 | 2 | 10 | 35 | .259 |

## 8 MILTON LOO
SS

**Born:** April 2, 1986. **B-T:** R-R. **Ht.:** 6-1. **Wt.:** 185. **Drafted:** Yavapai (Ariz.) CC, D/F 2005 (9th round) **Signed by:** Jeff Morris/Tom Wheeler.

BILL MITCHELL

The Reds had to draft Loo twice and wait for his Yavapai (Ariz.) CC team to finish up at the 2006 Junior College World Series before they could sign him as a draft-and-follow for $200,000. He hit three homers and stole home at the Juco World Series, where Yavapai finished second. He barely played after turning pro because of lingering elbow pain. Loo is a tremendous athlete who flashes five-tool potential. He has good life in his bat, allowing him to hit for average and giving him power potential. He's also a plus runner with the actions, hands and arm strength to play almost anywhere on the diamond. Loo's biggest hurdle is proving that he can stay healthy. He was able to participate in instructional league, but he also missed time in 2005 with ankle and thumb injuries. While his swing and frame project power, he has yet to show he can drive the ball with a wood bat. Though he eventually may move to third base or center field, the Reds want to keep Loo at shortstop for now. They also need to play 2006 third-rounder Chris Valaika at short, so they may push Valaika to Sarasota and put Loo at Dayton.

| Year | Club (League) | Class | AVG | G | AB | R | H | 2B | 3B | HR | RBI | BB | SO | SB | OBP | SLG |
|------|---------------|-------|-----|---|----|---|---|----|----|----|-----|----|----|----|-----|-----|
| 2006 | Reds (GCL) | R | .372 | 14 | 43 | 10 | 16 | 6 | 0 | 1 | 7 | 1 | 5 | 0 | .413 | .581 |
| **MINOR LEAGUE TOTALS** | | | .372 | 14 | 43 | 10 | 16 | 6 | 0 | 1 | 7 | 1 | 5 | 0 | .413 | .581 |

## 9 PAUL JANISH
SS

**Born:** Oct. 12, 1982. **B-T:** R-R. **Ht.:** 6-2. **Wt.:** 180. **Drafted:** Rice, 2004 (5th round). **Signed by:** Mike Powers.

STEVE MOORE

A member of Rice's 2003 College World Series champions, Janish was just starting to get his bat going in pro ball in 2005 when he blew out his throwing elbow and needed Tommy John surgery. He picked up where he left off when he returned last year, hitting .304 with 14 homers while reaching Double-A. Janish is a major league caliber shortstop. His range and quickness are average but play up because he's an expert at positioning and has nearly flawless footwork, soft hands and a plus arm. He has made strides at the plate, learning to use the entire field and to drive the ball for occasional power. He always has controlled the strike zone well. He's a natural leader who inspires his teammates. Janish will go as far as his bat allows him. He may not do much more than make contact and likely always will be a bottom-of-the-order hitter, but that should be sufficient considering his defense. Set to return to Double-A, where he finished 2006, Janish once again will need to prove that his bat can handle the jump to a higher level. The Reds need a long-term shortstop, and they suddenly have three candidates in Janish and 2006 signees Milton Loo and Chris Valaika.

| Year | Club (League) | Class | AVG | G | AB | R | H | 2B | 3B | HR | RBI | BB | SO | SB | OBP | SLG |
|---|---|---|---|---|---|---|---|---|---|---|---|---|---|---|---|---|
| 2004 | Billings (Pio) | R | .263 | 66 | 205 | 39 | 54 | 11 | 0 | 2 | 22 | 45 | 45 | 7 | .406 | .346 |
| 2005 | Dayton (MWL) | A | .245 | 55 | 208 | 30 | 51 | 10 | 2 | 5 | 29 | 29 | 38 | 5 | .346 | .385 |
| 2006 | Sarasota (FSL) | A | .278 | 91 | 335 | 53 | 93 | 17 | 2 | 9 | 55 | 38 | 39 | 8 | .355 | .421 |
| | Chattanooga (SL) | AA | .267 | 4 | 15 | 1 | 4 | 1 | 0 | 0 | 2 | 1 | 5 | 0 | .313 | .333 |
| | Dayton (MWL) | A | .398 | 26 | 98 | 19 | 39 | 6 | 0 | 5 | 18 | 7 | 10 | 0 | .435 | .612 |
| **MINOR LEAGUE TOTALS** | | | .280 | 242 | 861 | 142 | 241 | 45 | 4 | 21 | 126 | 120 | 137 | 20 | .374 | .415 |

## 10 CHRIS VALAIKA                                SS

**Born:** Aug. 14, 1985. **B-T:** R-R. **Ht.:** 6-0. **Wt.:** 195. **Drafted:** UC Santa Barbara, 2006 (3rd round). **Signed by:** Rex de la Nunez.

Valaika has extensive experience with USA Baseball, playing on national youth, junior and college teams. He was a Freshman All-American in 2004, but missed most of his sophomore season with a torn anterior-cruciate ligament in his right knee. He had a brilliant pro debut after signing for $437,500 as a third-round pick, setting a Pioneer League record with a 32-game hitting streak and winning league MVP honors. Valaika uses quick hands and a short stroke to spray liners to all fields. His bat was his calling card coming out of college, and he showed even more hitting ability than expected with a dominant debut. Some Pioneer League managers compared him to Bobby Crosby as an offensive shortstop. Valaika also has advanced pitch recognition and gap power. Defensively, he offers a strong arm and good hands. Valaikia's below-average speed limits his range at shortstop, and one day he may end up sliding over to second base but the Reds will leave him at shortstop until he plays his way off the position. Milton Loo needs to play shortstop in low Class A so Valaika will likely jump to high Class A.

| Year | Club (League) | Class | AVG | G | AB | R | H | 2B | 3B | HR | RBI | BB | SO | SB | OBP | SLG |
|---|---|---|---|---|---|---|---|---|---|---|---|---|---|---|---|---|
| 2006 | Billings (Pio) | R | .324 | 70 | 275 | 58 | 89 | 22 | 4 | 8 | 60 | 24 | 61 | 2 | .387 | .520 |
| **MINOR LEAGUE TOTALS** | | | .324 | 70 | 275 | 58 | 89 | 22 | 4 | 8 | 60 | 24 | 61 | 2 | .387 | .520 |

## 11 CODY STRAIT                                OF

**Born:** May 28, 1983. **B-T:** R-R. **Ht.:** 6-1. **Wt.:** 181. **Drafted:** Evansville, 2004 (12th round). **Signed by:** Paul Pierson.

Beaumont, Texas, has been very good to the Reds. Jay Bruce, the team's top outfield prospect, and Strait both grew up in the southeast Texas town. A University of Evansville product, Strait is proof that basestealers can be made. He possesses 55 speed on the 20-80 scouting scale and has worked hard on getting good jumps, which allowed him to steal 50 bags last season to tie for the high Class A Florida State League lead. He also has tick above-average power, as he also tied for top honors in the FSL with 57 extra-base hits. He's a plus defender in right field, with a strong throwing arm that ranks with the best in the organization, and is adequate in center. Though strikeouts have been a problem for Strait, he trimmed his strikeout rate compared to 2005, and scouts in the Arizona Fall League were impressed with his improved two-strike approach. The hit tool is Strait's biggest problem. He projects to be a below-average hitter unless he can shorten his swing and tone down the aggressiveness that sometimes leaves him chasing pitches out of the zone. Some scouts don't see a lot of projection left in Strait—he already has a very muscular build. Strait is headed to Double-A in 2007.

| Year | Club (League) | Class | AVG | G | AB | R | H | 2B | 3B | HR | RBI | BB | SO | SB | OBP | SLG |
|---|---|---|---|---|---|---|---|---|---|---|---|---|---|---|---|---|
| 2004 | Billings (Pio) | R | .388 | 12 | 49 | 10 | 19 | 1 | 3 | 2 | 11 | 1 | 14 | 3 | .434 | .653 |
| | Dayton (MWL) | A | .209 | 56 | 220 | 15 | 46 | 10 | 2 | 0 | 13 | 13 | 81 | 3 | .266 | .273 |
| 2005 | Dayton (MWL) | A | .266 | 116 | 413 | 63 | 110 | 16 | 4 | 14 | 60 | 38 | 102 | 25 | .349 | .426 |
| 2006 | Sarasota (FSL) | A | .258 | 131 | 489 | 85 | 126 | 36 | 4 | 17 | 74 | 36 | 108 | 50 | .325 | .452 |
| | Louisville (IL) | AAA | .100 | 3 | 10 | 2 | 1 | 0 | 1 | 0 | 1 | 2 | 0 | 0 | .250 | .300 |
| **MINOR LEAGUE TOTALS** | | | .256 | 318 | 1181 | 175 | 302 | 63 | 14 | 33 | 159 | 90 | 305 | 81 | .326 | .417 |

## 12 SAM LeCURE                                RHP

**Born:** May 4, 1984. **B-T:** R-R. **Ht.:** 6-1. **Wt.:** 195. **Drafted:** Texas, 2005 (4th round). **Signed by:** Brian Wilson.

The Reds were able to get LeCure in the fourth round because he had to sit out the 2005 season at Texas because he was academically ineligible. They've been impressed with his feel for pitching and his makeup, which led them to send LeCure straight to high Class A in his first pro season. LeCure struggled a bit at first, but once he settled down he proved unhittable at times, stringing together a stretch of three straight scoreless starts in July, spanning 16 innings. LeCure's biggest strength is his refined approach. He has a clean delivery and the ability to pound the zone. He has three solid pitches, though none stands out as a plus

pitch. He sits at 90-91 mph with his fastball, throwing up occasional 92s and 93s, and he also throws an average slider and an average changeup. He commands his fastball to both sides of the plate and does a good job of busting hitters inside. He throws his slider and changeup at any point in the count. At 6-foot-1, 190 pounds, LeCure lacks physical projection, and what the Reds see in his stuff now is what they'll get. He'll head to Double-A with a chance to prove his average stuff works against more advanced hitters.

| Year | Club (League) | Class | W | L | ERA | G | GS | CG | SV | IP | H | R | ER | HR | BB | SO | AVG |
|---|---|---|---|---|---|---|---|---|---|---|---|---|---|---|---|---|---|
| 2005 | Billings (Pio) | R | 5 | 1 | 3.27 | 13 | 6 | 0 | 0 | 41 | 43 | 18 | 15 | 2 | 15 | 44 | .272 |
| 2006 | Sarasota (FSL) | A | 7 | 12 | 3.43 | 27 | 27 | 0 | 0 | 142 | 130 | 63 | 54 | 12 | 46 | 115 | .243 |
| **MINOR LEAGUE TOTALS** | | | 12 | 13 | 3.39 | 40 | 33 | 0 | 0 | 183 | 173 | 81 | 69 | 14 | 61 | 159 | .250 |

## 13 JOSH RAVIN                                                                RHP

**Born:** Jan. 21, 1988. **B-T:** R-R. **Ht.:** 6-4. **Wt.:** 195. **Drafted:** HS—Chatsworth, Calif., 2006 (5th round). **Signed by:** Rex de la Nunez.

Ravin has been on scouts' radar for years as a member of Chatsworth (Calif.) High program that won back-to-back national championships in 2003 and 2004. But during his senior season in 2006 his velocity dropped to 89-91 as he was sidelined for a month with a tired arm. The Reds stuck with him, and after they signed him for $200,000, they found they were getting a better arm than he had shown in high school. Ravin sat at 90-94 mph and touched 96 with heavy life in the Gulf Coast League. He has a free and easy high three-quarters delivery with a durable pitcher's body that still has some projection, with a large frame and sloping shoulders. While his delivery is clean, like many young pitchers he doesn't always repeat it. His curveball and changeup are advanced for his age, but still have to be refined as he heads to full-season ball. He needs to learn to rely on them more. Expect to see him near the front of the Dayton rotation in 2007.

| Year | Club (League) | Class | W | L | ERA | G | GS | CG | SV | IP | H | R | ER | HR | BB | SO | AVG |
|---|---|---|---|---|---|---|---|---|---|---|---|---|---|---|---|---|---|
| 2006 | Reds (GCL) | R | 0 | 1 | 4.29 | 7 | 6 | 0 | 0 | 21 | 21 | 13 | 10 | 0 | 10 | 22 | .266 |
| | Billings (Pio) | R | 0 | 0 | 3.52 | 4 | 4 | 0 | 0 | 15 | 10 | 7 | 6 | 1 | 13 | 18 | .189 |
| **MINOR LEAGUE TOTALS** | | | 0 | 1 | 3.96 | 11 | 10 | 0 | 0 | 36 | 31 | 20 | 16 | 1 | 23 | 40 | .235 |

## 14 JAMES AVERY                                                              RHP

**Born:** June 10, 1984. **B-T:** R-R. **Ht.:** 6-1. **Wt.:** 210. **Drafted:** Niagara, 2005 (5th round). **Signed by:** Jason Baker.

The Reds have never been afraid to scout Canadians, but unlike most Canadian prospects, Avery was a relatively refined product when drafted. He had been taken by the Twins in the 29th round in 2002 out of high school, but chose to sign with Niagara. Pitching at Niagara and two summers in the Cape Cod League helped add polish. Like Sam LeCure, the Reds sent Avery to high Class A in his first full pro season, and like LeCure he got better as the season went along. Avery was hit around in the first half of the season, but bounced back to go 2-1, 1.91 in 33 innings (allowing 33 hits, nine walks and 25 strikeouts) in his final five starts. The Reds were impressed enough to give him a one-start cameo in Triple-A. Avery throws a 88-92 mph fastball with a clean three-quarters delivery. He has an improving 12-to-6 curveball and an average changeup. He relied more on his curveball in 2006, which has developed into an average pitch. He doesn't blow away hitters, as evidenced by his 5.8 strikeouts per nine innings, which could be a concern as he climbs the ladder, but he's likely earned a promotion to Double-A for 2007.

| Year | Club (League) | Class | W | L | ERA | G | GS | CG | SV | IP | H | R | ER | HR | BB | SO | AVG |
|---|---|---|---|---|---|---|---|---|---|---|---|---|---|---|---|---|---|
| 2005 | Reds (GCL) | R | 0 | 1 | 2.12 | 6 | 5 | 0 | 0 | 17 | 16 | 7 | 4 | 0 | 3 | 18 | .239 |
| | Dayton (MWL) | A | 1 | 1 | 3.94 | 5 | 2 | 0 | 0 | 16 | 17 | 8 | 7 | 1 | 6 | 8 | .274 |
| 2006 | Louisville (IL) | AAA | 0 | 0 | 9.00 | 1 | 1 | 0 | 0 | 4 | 5 | 4 | 4 | 1 | 2 | 1 | .333 |
| | Sarasota (FSL) | A | 8 | 8 | 4.43 | 26 | 26 | 1 | 0 | 130 | 136 | 73 | 64 | 14 | 48 | 86 | .274 |
| **MINOR LEAGUE TOTALS** | | | 9 | 10 | 4.26 | 38 | 34 | 1 | 0 | 167 | 174 | 92 | 79 | 16 | 59 | 113 | .271 |

## 15 CHRIS DICKERSON                                                          OF

**Born:** April 10, 1982. **B-T:** L-L. **Ht.:** 6-4. **Wt.:** 212. **Drafted:** Nevada, 2003 (16th round). **Signed by:** Keith Chapman.

Whether you want to focus on the positives or the negatives, Chris Dickerson provides plenty to mull over. If you're looking for negatives, Dickerson doesn't hit for average, strikes out too much and has made little progress in improving those drawbacks over his four-year pro career. He doesn't recognize pitches well and is overaggressive at times with an uppercut swing that gets too long. He can't handle lefthanders, who have limited him to a .204 average with 89 strikeouts in 245 at-bats the last two seasons. But on the plus side, Dickerson is the best athlete in the system, and he managed to play the entire season despite a nagging

injury in his non-throwing shoulder. He plays an exceptional center field. He reads the ball off the bat well and his plus speed (4.0-4.1 seconds from the left side of the plate to first base) allows him to track down balls to the gaps and over his head. He has an accurate, average throwing arm and he's a threat to steal on the basepaths. And he did show progress at the plate—he hit .273 with a .515 slugging percentage over the final three months of the season, and slugged .487 overall against righthanders—which was enough to convince the Reds to add him to their 40-man roster. If Chris Denorfia and Norris Hooper end up in Cincinnati, Dickerson will play center field in Triple-A this year.

| Year | Club (League) | Class | AVG | G | AB | R | H | 2B | 3B | HR | RBI | BB | SO | SB | OBP | SLG |
|------|---------------|-------|-----|---|----|---|---|----|----|----|-----|----|----|----|-----|-----|
| 2003 | Billings (Pio) | R | .244 | 58 | 201 | 36 | 49 | 6 | 4 | 6 | 38 | 39 | 66 | 9 | .376 | .403 |
| 2004 | Dayton (MWL) | A | .303 | 84 | 314 | 50 | 95 | 15 | 3 | 4 | 34 | 51 | 92 | 27 | .410 | .408 |
| | Potomac (CL) | A | .200 | 15 | 45 | 5 | 9 | 2 | 0 | 0 | 5 | 7 | 14 | 3 | .321 | .244 |
| 2005 | Sarasota (FSL) | A | .236 | 119 | 436 | 68 | 103 | 17 | 7 | 11 | 43 | 53 | 124 | 19 | .325 | .383 |
| 2006 | Chattanooga (SL) | AA | .242 | 115 | 389 | 65 | 94 | 21 | 7 | 12 | 48 | 65 | 129 | 21 | .355 | .424 |
| **MINOR LEAGUE TOTALS** | | | .253 | 391 | 1385 | 224 | 350 | 61 | 21 | 33 | 168 | 215 | 425 | 79 | .360 | .399 |

## 16 PHIL DUMATRAIT LHP

**Born:** July 12, 1981. **B-T:** R-L. **Ht.:** 6-2. **Wt.:** 170. **Drafted:** Bakersfield (Calif.) JC, 2000 (1st round). **Signed by:** Ed Roebuck (Red Sox).

Dumatrait joined fellow southpaw Tyler Pelland as the Reds' bounty in the 2003 Scott Williamson trade with the Red Sox. And like Pelland, his development has been slow. Dumatrait missed the 2004 season because of Tommy John surgery, but has shown few ill effects from the injury over the last two seasons. Dumatrait has an average 88-91 mph fastball, a changeup that's a tick below average and a slurvy breaking ball. Dumatrait doesn't repeat his delivery particularly well. He struggles with flying open with his front shoulder, which causes him to leave the ball up in the zone. Unlike Pelland, the sum of the parts is actually a little better than it would appear because Dumatrait has a feel for pitching. He'll get a shot to earn the No. 5 starter job in Cincinnati in 2007, competing with Matt Belisle and Elizardo Ramirez. Otherwise, he'll head back to Triple-A to refine his delivery.

| Year | Club (League) | Class | W | L | ERA | G | GS | CG | SV | IP | H | R | ER | HR | BB | SO | AVG |
|------|---------------|-------|---|---|-----|---|----|----|----|----|---|---|----|----|----|----|-----|
| 2000 | Red Sox (GCL) | R | 0 | 1 | 1.65 | 6 | 6 | 0 | 0 | 16 | 10 | 6 | 3 | 0 | 12 | 12 | .172 |
| 2001 | Red Sox (GCL) | R | 3 | 0 | 2.76 | 8 | 8 | 0 | 0 | 33 | 27 | 10 | 10 | 0 | 9 | 33 | .229 |
| | Lowell (NYP) | A | 1 | 1 | 3.48 | 2 | 2 | 0 | 0 | 10 | 9 | 4 | 4 | 0 | 4 | 15 | .225 |
| 2002 | Augusta (SAL) | A | 8 | 5 | 2.77 | 22 | 22 | 1 | 0 | 120 | 109 | 44 | 37 | 5 | 47 | 108 | .249 |
| | Sarasota (FSL) | A | 0 | 2 | 3.86 | 4 | 4 | 0 | 0 | 14 | 10 | 9 | 6 | 0 | 15 | 16 | .192 |
| 2003 | Sarasota (FSL) | A | 7 | 5 | 3.02 | 21 | 20 | 0 | 1 | 104 | 74 | 41 | 35 | 4 | 59 | 74 | .204 |
| | Potomac (CL) | A | 4 | 1 | 3.35 | 7 | 7 | 1 | 0 | 38 | 36 | 17 | 14 | 2 | 14 | 32 | .248 |
| 2004 | Did not play—Injured | | | | | | | | | | | | | | | | |
| 2005 | Sarasota (FSL) | A | 0 | 0 | 2.70 | 3 | 2 | 0 | 0 | 10 | 8 | 4 | 3 | 0 | 3 | 13 | .211 |
| | Chattanooga (SL) | AA | 4 | 12 | 3.17 | 24 | 24 | 0 | 0 | 128 | 115 | 58 | 45 | 4 | 70 | 101 | .245 |
| 2006 | Chattanooga (SL) | AA | 3 | 4 | 3.62 | 10 | 10 | 0 | 0 | 50 | 39 | 24 | 20 | 4 | 22 | 45 | .218 |
| | Louisville (IL) | AAA | 5 | 7 | 4.72 | 16 | 15 | 1 | 0 | 88 | 104 | 49 | 46 | 10 | 36 | 58 | .301 |
| **MINOR LEAGUE TOTALS** | | | 35 | 38 | 3.29 | 123 | 120 | 3 | 1 | 611 | 541 | 266 | 223 | 29 | 291 | 507 | .241 |

## 17 TYLER PELLAND LHP

**Born:** Oct. 9, 1983. **B-T:** R-L. **Ht.:** 5-11. **Wt.:** 203. **Drafted:** HS—Bristol, Vt., 2002 (9th round). **Signed by:** Ray Fagnant (Red Sox).

The Reds have patiently waited for Pelland to prove to be the payoff from the 2003 Scott Williamson deal, but the Vermont native has struggled with inconsistency. The sum of Pelland's stuff has proven to be less than expected. He throws a 92-93 mph four-seamer and a two-seamer that shows good, if inconsistent, life. He'll spin off a plus curveball though his feel for the pitch comes and goes, and he also throws a below-average changeup. He doesn't trust his stuff, which leads to him nibbling. He gets behind in the count and his lack of a secondary pitch he can trust leads to too many walks. He walked three or more batters in 22 of his 28 starts. He also has had trouble fielding his position. His 3.99 ERA is somewhat misleading, as he gave up 15 unearned runs. At some point, Pelland may have to move to the pen if he can't cut down on his walks, but the Reds continue to exercise patience.

| Year | Club (League) | Class | W | L | ERA | G | GS | CG | SV | IP | H | R | ER | HR | BB | SO | AVG |
|------|---------------|-------|---|---|-----|---|----|----|----|----|---|---|----|----|----|----|-----|
| 2003 | Red Sox (GCL) | R | 3 | 4 | 1.62 | 11 | 8 | 0 | 0 | 39 | 26 | 12 | 7 | 0 | 18 | 34 | .186 |
| 2003 | Reds (GCL) | R | 0 | 0 | 0.00 | 1 | 1 | 0 | 0 | 3 | 3 | 0 | 0 | 0 | 0 | 1 | .273 |
| 2004 | Dayton (MWL) | A | 1 | 7 | 8.66 | 14 | 10 | 0 | 0 | 45 | 66 | 49 | 43 | 6 | 20 | 38 | .328 |
| | Billings (Pio) | R | 9 | 3 | 3.42 | 18 | 12 | 0 | 0 | 74 | 67 | 36 | 28 | 3 | 39 | 82 | .248 |
| 2005 | Sarasota (FSL) | A | 5 | 8 | 4.05 | 30 | 15 | 0 | 0 | 102 | 103 | 52 | 46 | 5 | 63 | 103 | .270 |
| 2006 | Chattanooga (SL) | AA | 9 | 5 | 3.99 | 28 | 28 | 0 | 0 | 142 | 144 | 78 | 63 | 11 | 89 | 107 | .275 |
| **MINOR LEAGUE TOTALS** | | | 27 | 27 | 4.16 | 102 | 74 | 0 | 0 | 404 | 409 | 227 | 187 | 25 | 229 | 365 | .268 |

## 18 DARYL THOMPSON RHP

**Born:** Nov. 2, 1985. **B-T:** R-R. **Ht.:** 6-1. **Wt.:** 170. **Drafted:** HS—Mechanicsville, Md., 2003 (8th round). **Signed by:** Alex Smith (Expos).

If he fully recovers from a torn labrum, Thompson could quickly become one of the Reds' top pitching prospects. Part of the eight-player trade that sent Austin Kearns and Felipe Lopez to the Nationals for relief help last summer, Thompson had a 92-94 mph fastball before he got hurt. He also had an average changeup and an average curveball that shows good rotation and has some potential to be a plus pitch. But Thompson has been sidelined for nearly a year after shoulder surgery, and the success rate on labrum repairs is sketchy. The Reds were very cautious with Thompson after acquiring him. They sent him to the Gulf Coast League for some very limited work. He had his fastball back up to 92 mph at instructional league and he once again showed the ability to work both sides of the plate with it. Thompson needs to show that he can maintain his velocity deeper into games, and the Nationals had some worries about his professionalism, largely because they felt he could eat better and get into a little bit better shape. After missing nearly a year and a half of development because of the shoulder injury, the Reds will continue to be cautious with Thompson, but they hope he can kick-start his development in high Class A.

| Year | Club (League) | Class | W | L | ERA | G | GS | CG | SV | IP | H | R | ER | HR | BB | SO | AVG |
|------|---------------|-------|---|---|-----|---|----|----|----|----|---|---|----|----|----|----|-----|
| 2003 | Expos (GCL) | R | 1 | 2 | 2.15 | 12 | 10 | 0 | 0 | 46 | 49 | 16 | 11 | 1 | 11 | 18 | .288 |
| 2004 | Savannah (SAL) | A | 4 | 9 | 5.08 | 25 | 21 | 0 | 0 | 103 | 117 | 66 | 58 | 13 | 30 | 79 | .296 |
| 2005 | Savannah (SAL) | A | 2 | 3 | 3.35 | 11 | 11 | 0 | 0 | 54 | 46 | 23 | 20 | 3 | 24 | 48 | .232 |
| 2006 | Vermont (NYP) | A | 0 | 1 | 6.75 | 4 | 4 | 0 | 0 | 7 | 5 | 5 | 5 | 0 | 5 | 8 | .200 |
| | Reds (GCL) | R | 0 | 0 | 2.57 | 5 | 4 | 0 | 0 | 14 | 10 | 4 | 4 | 1 | 4 | 16 | .222 |
| **MINOR LEAGUE TOTALS** | | | 7 | 15 | 3.96 | 57 | 50 | 0 | 0 | 223 | 227 | 114 | 98 | 18 | 74 | 169 | .273 |

## 19 CAMILO VAZQUEZ LHP

**Born:** Oct. 3, 1983. **B-T:** L-L. **Ht.:** 5-11. **Wt.:** 199. **Drafted:** HS—Hialeah, Fla., 2002 (4th round). **Signed by:** Greg Zunino.

It's been a long climb for Vasquez, a Cuban native who emigrated legally to the U.S. in 1999. After arriving in Florida, Vazquez quickly became the ace lefty on back-to-back state champions at Hialeah (Fla.) High, and he also was one of the best hitters in the state. Since signing it's been a slow climb through the minors. He missed almost the entire 2004 season after Tommy John surgery and struggled in his low Class A debut in 2005, when he missed time with an eye infection. Vasquez started to put things together last year and earned a promotion to Double-A. He features an 89-91 mph fastball with late movement. His best pitch is an above-average 12-to-6 curveball that's effective against both lefties and righties. His straight changeup is a tick below average. He still needs to sharpen his command, but he's showing signs of developing into a serviceable back-of-the-rotation starter.

| Year | Club (League) | Class | W | L | ERA | G | GS | CG | SV | IP | H | R | ER | HR | BB | SO | AVG |
|------|---------------|-------|---|---|-----|---|----|----|----|----|---|---|----|----|----|----|-----|
| 2003 | Dayton (MWL) | A | 1 | 4 | 5.93 | 13 | 11 | 0 | 0 | 44 | 54 | 37 | 29 | 6 | 28 | 47 | .297 |
| | Billings (Pio) | R | 2 | 3 | 3.03 | 9 | 8 | 0 | 0 | 36 | 35 | 20 | 12 | 2 | 15 | 33 | .255 |
| 2004 | Reds (GCL) | R | 0 | 2 | 12.27 | 3 | 3 | 0 | 0 | 4 | 5 | 5 | 5 | 0 | 2 | 6 | .313 |
| | Billings (Pio) | R | 1 | 0 | 0.00 | 2 | 0 | 0 | 0 | 3 | 1 | 0 | 0 | 0 | 3 | 6 | .111 |
| 2005 | Dayton (MWL) | A | 4 | 4 | 5.18 | 29 | 18 | 0 | 0 | 99 | 91 | 63 | 57 | 10 | 62 | 88 | .243 |
| 2006 | Sarasota (FSL) | A | 4 | 5 | 4.00 | 16 | 15 | 0 | 0 | 83 | 84 | 42 | 37 | 10 | 32 | 79 | .261 |
| | Chattanooga (SL) | AA | 3 | 5 | 4.33 | 11 | 11 | 0 | 0 | 60 | 66 | 39 | 29 | 6 | 25 | 56 | .283 |
| **MINOR LEAGUE TOTALS** | | | 15 | 23 | 4.63 | 83 | 66 | 0 | 0 | 329 | 336 | 206 | 169 | 34 | 167 | 315 | .264 |

## 20 DAVID SHAFER RHP

**Born:** March 7, 1982. **B-T:** R-R. **Ht.:** 6-2. **Wt.:** 191. **Drafted:** Central Arizona JC, D/F 2001 (32nd round). **Signed by:** Mark Corey.

Shafer has worked his way out of the organizational player tag to put himself in position to compete for a job in the Reds bullpen. Shafer was nearly unhittable during the first half of the season, when he was being used exclusively as a one-inning closer. At the end of June he had a 1.37 ERA with 25 saves in 26 innings. But over the second half of the season, the Reds worked him in longer stints of two innings to prepare him for eventual use as a setup man in the majors. He wasn't as dominant in longer outings, but the Reds believe it will help him when he reaches Cincinnati. Shafer works off a fastball/slider combo, using an 88-92 mph fastball and an average slider that he commands well. His overall command is above average, which allows him to challenge hitters. He started using his changeup more once he was stretched out though it's not an average pitch yet. Shafer has a loose arm and has gotten stronger and added velocity as a pro. He has worked himself into the position to compete for a spot in the Reds bullpen, and if he doesn't win a job, he'll head to Triple-A.

| Year | Club (League) | Class | W | L | ERA | G | GS | CG | SV | IP | H | R | ER | HR | BB | SO | AVG |
|------|---------------|-------|---|---|-----|---|----|----|----|-----|-----|-----|-----|-----|-----|-----|-----|
| ~~~~ | Reds (GCL) | R | 1 | 0 | 1.29 | 3 | 0 | 0 | 1 | 7 | 3 | 2 | 1 | 0 | 2 | 7 | .125 |
| | Billings (Pio) | R | 5 | 2 | 1.72 | 19 | 0 | 0 | 4 | 31 | 30 | 14 | 6 | 0 | 11 | 30 | .242 |
| 2003 | Billings (Pio) | R | 0 | 3 | 3.04 | 25 | 0 | 0 | 13 | 24 | 25 | 13 | 8 | 1 | 3 | 32 | .253 |
| 2004 | Dayton (MWL) | A | 5 | 3 | 2.92 | 31 | 7 | 0 | 5 | 77 | 60 | 32 | 25 | 8 | 16 | 84 | .216 |
| | Potomac (CL) | A | 0 | 0 | 0.00 | 3 | 0 | 0 | 3 | 4 | 5 | 0 | 0 | 0 | 0 | 5 | .278 |
| 2005 | Sarasota (FSL) | A | 1 | 0 | 0.00 | 10 | 0 | 0 | 5 | 14 | 9 | 0 | 0 | 0 | 2 | 18 | .188 |
| | Chattanooga (SL) | AA | 1 | 6 | 4.08 | 34 | 0 | 0 | 6 | 40 | 31 | 21 | 18 | 3 | 24 | 41 | .217 |
| 2006 | Chattanooga (SL) | AA | 1 | 2 | 2.36 | 44 | 0 | 0 | 26 | 50 | 37 | 14 | 13 | 2 | 16 | 52 | .204 |
| **MINOR LEAGUE TOTALS** | | | 14 | 16 | 2.59 | 169 | 7 | 0 | 63 | 246 | 200 | 96 | 71 | 14 | 74 | 269 | .219 |

## 21  MIGUEL PEREZ                                     C

**Born:** Sept. 25, 1983. **B-T:** R-R. **Ht.:** 6-3. **Wt.:** 190. **Signed:** Venezuela, 2000. **Signed by:** Jorge Oquendo.

Perez is ready to catch at the major league level right now, as he shows off a plus-plus arm and above-average receiving skills. He blocks balls in the dirt well, frames pitches and controls the running game. He threw out 41 percent of basestealers last year, and he throws behind runners aggressively, though he found his success rate at picking off runners dropped against the more experienced Double-A baserunners. His bat is significantly behind his defense, which could leave him stalled in the high minors. Perez has some raw power that comes out in batting practice, but he's been unable to convert it into production, as evidenced by his .326 career slugging percentage. At his best, Perez waits back and hits to the other field. He gets into ruts where he presses too much trying to pull the ball. Pitchers have also found they can get him to chase pitches out of the zone. Perez still has a long ways to go with the bat to prove he can be more than a fill-in. With the signing of Chad Moeller, Perez could end up back in Double-A to work on his hitting. The Reds dropped him from the 40-man roster in December, but quickly re-signed him to a minor league deal.

| Year | Club (League) | Class | AVG | G | AB | R | H | 2B | 3B | HR | RBI | BB | SO | SB | OBP | SLG |
|------|---------------|-------|-----|---|----|---|---|----|----|----|-----|----|----|----|-----|-----|
| 2001 | Cagua (VSL) | R | .331 | 48 | 163 | 20 | 54 | 3 | 1 | 0 | 19 | 12 | 33 | 6 | .377 | .362 |
| 2002 | Cagua (VSL) | R | .213 | 34 | 108 | 14 | 23 | 4 | 0 | 2 | 18 | 9 | 23 | 1 | .320 | .306 |
| | Reds (GCL) | R | .360 | 26 | 86 | 12 | 31 | 1 | 0 | 0 | 11 | 2 | 9 | 3 | .396 | .372 |
| 2003 | Dayton (MWL) | A | .172 | 20 | 58 | 3 | 10 | 0 | 0 | 0 | 3 | 4 | 19 | 1 | .273 | .172 |
| | Billings (Pio) | R | .339 | 60 | 227 | 46 | 77 | 11 | 2 | 1 | 25 | 18 | 27 | 1 | .410 | .419 |
| 2004 | Dayton (MWL) | A | .237 | 74 | 249 | 22 | 59 | 7 | 0 | 1 | 22 | 16 | 62 | 2 | .309 | .277 |
| | Potomac (CL) | A | .232 | 18 | 69 | 7 | 16 | 2 | 0 | 0 | 5 | 1 | 12 | 1 | .239 | .261 |
| 2005 | Sarasota (FSL) | A | .268 | 80 | 291 | 36 | 78 | 11 | 0 | 4 | 33 | 16 | 63 | 7 | .305 | .347 |
| | Louisville (IL) | AAA | .208 | 21 | 72 | 5 | 15 | 3 | 0 | 1 | 5 | 5 | 19 | 0 | .275 | .292 |
| | Cincinnati (NL) | MLB | .000 | 2 | 3 | 0 | 0 | 0 | 0 | 0 | 0 | 0 | 1 | 0 | .000 | .000 |
| 2006 | Chattanooga (SL) | AA | .241 | 111 | 394 | 33 | 95 | 16 | 0 | 3 | 33 | 19 | 88 | 5 | .290 | .305 |
| **MINOR LEAGUE TOTALS** | | | .267 | 492 | 1717 | 198 | 458 | 58 | 3 | 12 | 174 | 102 | 355 | 27 | .324 | .325 |
| **MAJOR LEAGUE TOTALS** | | | .000 | 2 | 3 | 0 | 0 | 0 | 0 | 0 | 0 | 0 | 1 | 0 | .000 | .000 |

## 22  JON COUTLANGUS                                   LHP

**Born:** Oct. 21, 1980 **B-T:** L-L. **Ht.:** 6-1. **Wt.:** 180. **Drafted:** South Carolina, 2003 (19th round). **Signed by:** Dick Tidrow (Giants).

The Giants drafted Coutlangus as an outfielder, but player-development chief Dick Tidrow always hoped to move him to the mound. After he batted .194 in low Class A in 2004, Tidrow got his wish. Coutlangus quickly showed a feel for pitching, even though he hadn't done it since high school. As a good natural athlete, he repeats his delivery well. The Reds claimed him off waivers when the Giants dropped him from their 40-man roster to add non-roster invitee Jamey Wright to the major league roster. He quickly proved to be a nice pickup: he features an 87-91 mph fastball that plays up a little bit because of his funky delivery that makes it hard for hitters to pick up the ball. Coutlangus profiles as a lefty who can be more then a specialist as he's also effective against righthanders thanks to a cutter that he can bust in on their hands. He also throws a sweeping slider that could be a plus pitch because he commands it so well. He occasionally throws a below-average changeup as well. Coutlangus was one of the surprises of the Arizona Fall League, where he impressed with his feel for pitching. He's ticketed for Triple-A, but he's not far away from helping out the Reds bullpen.

| Year | Club (League) | Class | W | L | ERA | G | GS | CG | SV | IP | H | R | ER | HR | BB | SO | AVG |
|------|---------------|-------|---|---|-----|---|----|----|----|----|-----|----|----|----|----|-----|-----|
| 2004 | Giants (AZL) | R | 0 | 0 | 0.00 | 1 | 0 | 0 | 0 | 1 | 1 | 0 | 0 | 0 | 0 | 0 | .250 |
| 2005 | San Jose (Cal) | A | 4 | 0 | 3.04 | 50 | 0 | 0 | 3 | 77 | 64 | 27 | 26 | 3 | 29 | 79 | .234 |
| 2006 | Chattanooga (SL) | AA | 1 | 3 | 2.86 | 49 | 0 | 0 | 9 | 63 | 40 | 24 | 20 | 0 | 32 | 56 | .185 |
| | Louisville (IL) | AAA | 0 | 0 | 0.00 | 2 | 0 | 0 | 0 | 3 | 2 | 0 | 0 | 0 | 1 | 2 | .222 |
| **MINOR LEAGUE TOTALS** | | | 5 | 3 | 2.88 | 102 | 0 | 0 | 12 | 144 | 107 | 51 | 46 | 3 | 62 | 137 | .213 |

## JORDAN SMITH
RHP

**Born:** Feb. 4, 1986. **B-T:** R-R. **Ht.:** 6-4. **Wt.:** 210. **Drafted:** CC of Southern Nevada, 2006 (5th round). **Signed by:** Jeff Morris.

Smith was a catcher/first baseman when he began his college career at Salt Lake CC, but it quickly became apparent that his arm was more promising than his bat and he moved to the mound midway through his freshman season. He transferred to the CC of Southern Nevada to get more innings as his new club's closer. He showed a plus fastball, a durable, projectable pitcher's frame and enough athleticism and durability to intrigue scouts, whose only disappointment was how infrequently Smith pitched. For a converted position player, Smith has shown some natural feel for pitching and he has a smooth free and easy delivery. The Reds, who signed him for $152,500, believe he has potential as a starter even though right now his fastball is the only pitch he's truly comfortable with throwing. Smith's fastball sits at 90-93 mph, touching 96 with some good natural movement. Smith had thrown a little harder in college, but the Reds told him to worry less about velocity and more about repeating his delivery without overthrowing. His hard curve and changeup are significantly behind his fastball, but his curve has some potential. Smith is rawer than most 20-year-old pitchers so expect the Reds to be patient. He'll open 2007 in low Class A.

| Year | Club (League) | Class | W | L | ERA | G | GS | CG | SV | IP | H | R | ER | HR | BB | SO | AVG |
|---|---|---|---|---|---|---|---|---|---|---|---|---|---|---|---|---|---|
| 2006 | Billings (Pio) | R | 6 | 3 | 3.01 | 14 | 14 | 0 | 0 | 69 | 58 | 29 | 23 | 3 | 20 | 49 | .227 |
| **MINOR LEAGUE TOTALS** | | | 6 | 3 | 3.01 | 14 | 14 | 0 | 0 | 69 | 58 | 29 | 23 | 3 | 20 | 49 | .227 |

## JUSTIN REED
OF

**Born:** Nov. 29, 1987. **B-T:** L-R. **Ht.:** 5-11. **Wt.:** 179. **Drafted:** HS—Hillcrest, Miss., 2006 (4th round). **Signed by:** Jerry Flowers.

Mississippi doesn't produce many star high school baseball players, but Reed established his credentials as he made it to the final cut for the junior national team. He turned down a baseball scholarship from Mississippi to turn pro for $287,000. Reed's best asset is his speed. He's a 60 runner on the 20-80 scouting scale and profiles as a top-of-the-order hitter. He has a relatively short swing, which fits his profile, as he projects as having only gap power. His arm is a tick below-average, but should be playable for center field, where Reed fits best. The Gulf Coast League chewed up Reed and spit him out, as he hit only .150 over his final 40 at-bats. The Reds aren't especially concerned, as there are plenty of examples of high school players struggling in the complex league. He is a long ways away, and could use another year of short-season ball unless he stars in spring training.

| Year | Club (League) | Class | AVG | G | AB | R | H | 2B | 3B | HR | RBI | BB | SO | SB | OBP | SLG |
|---|---|---|---|---|---|---|---|---|---|---|---|---|---|---|---|---|
| 2006 | Reds (GCL) | R | .180 | 44 | 161 | 17 | 29 | 2 | 6 | 1 | 16 | 19 | 45 | 6 | .271 | .286 |
| **MINOR LEAGUE TOTALS** | | | .180 | 44 | 161 | 17 | 29 | 2 | 6 | 1 | 16 | 19 | 45 | 6 | .271 | .286 |

## BRAD SALMON
RHP

**Born:** Jan. 3, 1980. **B-T:** L-R. **Ht.:** 6-3. **Wt.:** 232. **Drafted:** Jefferson Davis (Ala.) CC, 1999 (21st round). **Signed by:** Bob Filotei.

Salmon has been in the system long enough that he was around before the Reds traded for Ken Griffey Jr. He was added to the 40-man roster for the first time in November. His upside is very limited, as he's a 27-year-old with eight years of pro experience. But after a solid season at the upper levels, Salmon has a chance to help the Reds bullpen this season thanks to a 93-95 mph sinking fastball. Salmon does a good job of keeping his fastball down in the zone, giving up plenty of ground balls and few homers. His out pitch is a hard slider that's effective if inconsistent. As you would expect from a minor league vet, Salmon doesn't rattle easily, and his newfound confidence could pay off with a spot in the Reds bullpen.

| Year | Club (League) | Class | W | L | ERA | G | GS | CG | SV | IP | H | R | ER | HR | BB | SO | AVG |
|---|---|---|---|---|---|---|---|---|---|---|---|---|---|---|---|---|---|---|
| 1999 | Billings (Pio) | R | 2 | 2 | 7.48 | 16 | 6 | 0 | 1 | 49 | 67 | 46 | 41 | 2 | 19 | 43 | .322 |
| 2000 | Clinton (MWL) | A | 7 | 5 | 4.29 | 22 | 22 | 1 | 0 | 124 | 134 | 71 | 59 | 4 | 46 | 119 | .278 |
| 2001 | Mudville (Cal) | A | 5 | 8 | 4.06 | 33 | 18 | 1 | 0 | 135 | 132 | 75 | 61 | 10 | 51 | 110 | .253 |
| 2002 | Dayton (MWL) | A | 12 | 9 | 4.46 | 29 | 27 | 1 | 0 | 159 | 165 | 94 | 79 | 9 | 48 | 117 | .261 |
| 2003 | Potomac (CL) | A | 3 | 2 | 4.56 | 32 | 1 | 0 | 1 | 49 | 55 | 27 | 25 | 4 | 18 | 53 | .284 |
| | Chattanooga (SL) | AA | 4 | 0 | 5.11 | 10 | 1 | 0 | 1 | 25 | 27 | 14 | 14 | 2 | 9 | 21 | .278 |
| 2004 | Potomac (CL) | A | 1 | 0 | 0.54 | 5 | 1 | 0 | 0 | 17 | 12 | 1 | 1 | 0 | 3 | 16 | .194 |
| | Chattanooga (SL) | AA | 4 | 2 | 4.27 | 39 | 1 | 0 | 3 | 65 | 68 | 35 | 31 | 3 | 22 | 53 | .262 |
| 2005 | Louisville (IL) | AAA | 0 | 0 | 3.31 | 9 | 0 | 0 | 0 | 16 | 14 | 6 | 6 | 2 | 5 | 8 | .226 |
| | Chattanooga (SL) | AA | 3 | 8 | 3.34 | 38 | 0 | 0 | 4 | 73 | 66 | 31 | 27 | 3 | 31 | 71 | .247 |
| 2006 | Chattanooga (SL) | AA | 2 | 1 | 2.70 | 16 | 0 | 0 | 2 | 23 | 18 | 7 | 7 | 0 | 16 | 24 | .214 |
| | Louisville (IL) | AAA | 5 | 1 | 2.34 | 39 | 0 | 0 | 3 | 58 | 36 | 18 | 15 | 3 | 27 | 72 | .184 |
| **MINOR LEAGUE TOTALS** | | | 48 | 38 | 4.15 | 288 | 77 | 3 | 15 | 794 | 794 | 425 | 366 | 42 | 295 | 707 | .259 |

## 26 JUAN FRANCISCO
3B

**Born:** June 24, 1987. **B-T:** L-R. **Ht.:** 6-4. **Wt.:** 218. **Signed:** Dominican Republic, 2004. **Signed by:** Juan Peralta.

The Reds' minor league depth at third base is pretty thin, which isn't much of a concern since Edwin Encarnacion has the job locked up for the next several years. Just about the time that Encarnacion nears free agency, Francisco could be ready to replace him. Francisco has a plus arm that's strong and accurate and good athleticism at third base. For a 19-year-old in his first season in the U.S., Francisco showed a very advanced approach at the plate with a smooth lefty swing and strong hands that allow scouts to project him to hit for plus power. He shows the ability to drive outside pitches to the opposite field and shows solid pitch recognition. His bat is his best tool, but his defense could also be above average. His only present below-average tool is his speed. He's a long ways away from the majors, but he already has a solid frame. He should be one of the cornerstones of the Dayton team in 2007.

| Year | Club (League) | Class | AVG | G | AB | R | H | 2B | 3B | HR | RBI | BB | SO | SB | OBP | SLG |
|------|---------------|-------|-----|---|----|---|---|----|----|----|-----|----|----|----|-----|-----|
| 2006 | Reds (GCL) | R | .280 | 45 | 182 | 24 | 51 | 14 | 0 | 3 | 30 | 6 | 35 | 2 | .305 | .407 |
| | Billings (Pio) | R | .333 | 9 | 36 | 6 | 12 | 3 | 0 | 0 | 2 | 0 | 8 | 2 | .333 | .417 |
| **MINOR LEAGUE TOTALS** | | | .289 | 54 | 218 | 30 | 63 | 17 | 0 | 3 | 32 | 6 | 43 | 4 | .310 | .408 |

## 27 NORRIS HOPPER
OF

**Born:** March 24, 1979. **B-T:** R-R. **Ht.:** 5-10. **Wt.:** 198. **Drafted:** HS—Shelby, N.C., 1998 (8th round). **Signed by:** Balos Davis (Royals).

Hopper has proven to be a nice find for the Reds, who signed him as a six-year minor league free agent before the 2005 season. Hopper lacks power, with just three homers in nine minor league seasons. After three years in Double-A he excelled in his Triple-A debut winning the International League batting title by 39 points. Hopper will probably not be more than a fourth outfielder, but he can be pretty valuable in that role. He's able to play all three outfield positions with a tick above-average defense and an average arm. Adding to his versatility, he can play second base in a pinch. He's a 60 runner on the 20-80 scouting scale and also is a plus contact hitter with the ability to center the ball and spray hits to all fields. He doesn't walk much, but he also doesn't strike out. The Reds expect Hopper to compete for a backup job in Cincinnati during spring training.

| Year | Club (League) | Class | AVG | G | AB | R | H | 2B | 3B | HR | RBI | BB | SO | SB | OBP | SLG |
|------|---------------|-------|-----|---|----|---|---|----|----|----|-----|----|----|----|-----|-----|
| 1998 | Royals (GCL) | R | .308 | 40 | 133 | 19 | 41 | 2 | 1 | 0 | 11 | 13 | 12 | 11 | .365 | .338 |
| 1999 | Royals (GCL) | R | .257 | 46 | 179 | 33 | 46 | 3 | 2 | 0 | 13 | 19 | 20 | 22 | .322 | .296 |
| | Charleston, W.Va. (SAL) | A | .500 | 5 | 22 | 3 | 11 | 0 | 2 | 0 | 2 | 0 | 1 | 1 | .500 | .682 |
| 2000 | Charleston, W.Va. (SAL) | A | .280 | 116 | 454 | 70 | 127 | 20 | 6 | 0 | 29 | 51 | 55 | 24 | .357 | .350 |
| 2001 | Wilmington (CL) | A | .247 | 110 | 389 | 38 | 96 | 6 | 2 | 1 | 38 | 32 | 60 | 16 | .312 | .280 |
| 2002 | Wilmington (CL) | A | .272 | 125 | 514 | 78 | 140 | 12 | 3 | 1 | 46 | 31 | 55 | 22 | .323 | .313 |
| 2003 | Wichita (TL) | AA | .300 | 115 | 424 | 56 | 127 | 14 | 2 | 0 | 40 | 27 | 58 | 24 | .346 | .342 |
| 2004 | Wichita (TL) | AA | .278 | 98 | 363 | 48 | 101 | 5 | 3 | 0 | 40 | 33 | 44 | 17 | .345 | .309 |
| 2005 | Chattanooga (SL) | AA | .310 | 116 | 451 | 70 | 140 | 15 | 4 | 1 | 37 | 27 | 38 | 25 | .354 | .368 |
| 2006 | Chattanooga (SL) | AA | .283 | 13 | 46 | 7 | 13 | 2 | 1 | 0 | 10 | 6 | 3 | 3 | .365 | .370 |
| | Louisville (IL) | AAA | .347 | 98 | 383 | 47 | 133 | 11 | 3 | 0 | 26 | 20 | 25 | 25 | .378 | .392 |
| | Cincinnati (NL) | MLB | .359 | 21 | 39 | 6 | 14 | 1 | 0 | 1 | 5 | 6 | 4 | 2 | .435 | .462 |
| **MINOR LEAGUE TOTALS** | | | .290 | 882 | 3358 | 469 | 975 | 90 | 29 | 3 | 292 | 259 | 371 | 190 | .345 | .337 |
| **MAJOR LEAGUE TOTALS** | | | .359 | 21 | 39 | 6 | 14 | 1 | 0 | 1 | 5 | 6 | 4 | 2 | .435 | .462 |

## 28 RAFAEL GONZALEZ
RHP

**Born:** March 21, 1986. **B-T:** R-R. **Ht.:** 6-1. **Wt.:** 232. **Drafted:** HS—New York, 2004 (4th round). **Signed by:** Jason Baker.

When it comes to pure stuff, Gonzalez had a chance to be only a notch or two behind Homer Bailey as far as Reds starters. But while Bailey has gotten better and better each year, refining his command and improving his fastball and curveball, Gonzalez has to have the Reds wondering if the light bulb will ever turn on. Gonzalez showed up out of shape again this season, which has sapped a little from his fastball—it used to sit at 92-94, touching 97 mph, but it was more consistently 88-93 in 2006. Some scouts saw him sit at 92-94, while others saw only an average fastball combined with poor command. He also has the makings of a plus curveball but lacks consistency, largely because he struggles to repeat his delivery. After three seasons, Gonzalez has yet to prove he can succeed in low Class A. If he ever dedicates himself to being a pro, works himself into shape and focuses on becoming more consistent, he could move quickly, but up to now, he's not shown the willingness to pay the price greatness requires. Gonzalez will pitch this season as a 21-year-old, so a return to low Class A shouldn't stunt his development.

| Year | Club (League) | Class | W | L | ERA | G | GS | CG | SV | IP | H | R | ER | HR | BB | SO | AVG |
|------|---------------|-------|---|---|-----|---|----|----|----|----|----|---|----|----|----|----|-----|
| 2004 | Reds (GCL) | R | 1 | 6 | 4.20 | 12 | 8 | 0 | 0 | 41 | 38 | 25 | 19 | 3 | 18 | 32 | .259 |
| 2005 | Billings (Pio) | R | 3 | 0 | 3.43 | 11 | 6 | 0 | 1 | 42 | 36 | 18 | 16 | 7 | 23 | 37 | .234 |
|  | Dayton (MWL) | A | 3 | 5 | 9.35 | 10 | 5 | 0 | 0 | 26 | 24 | 29 | 27 | 5 | 24 | 22 | .250 |
| 2006 | Billings (Pio) | R | 1 | 1 | 2.40 | 3 | 3 | 0 | 0 | 15 | 12 | 6 | 4 | 3 | 2 | 6 | .222 |
|  | Reds (GCL) | R | 0 | 1 | 15.00 | 1 | 1 | 0 | 0 | 3 | 6 | 5 | 5 | 0 | 2 | 0 | .500 |
|  | Dayton (MWL) | A | 2 | 4 | 5.22 | 9 | 9 | 0 | 0 | 40 | 32 | 25 | 23 | 7 | 25 | 33 | .221 |
| **MINOR LEAGUE TOTALS** | | | 10 | 17 | 5.09 | 46 | 32 | 0 | 1 | 166 | 148 | 108 | 94 | 25 | 94 | 130 | .243 |

## 29 B.J. SZYMANSKI OF

**Born:** Oct. 1, 1982. **B-T:** B-R. **Ht.:** 6-5. **Wt.:** 215. **Drafted:** Princeton, 2004 (2nd round). **Signed by:** Mike Misuraca.

The book on Szymanski coming into the season was that he needed to prove that he could stay healthy after two injury-prone pro seasons. Szymanski was healthy in 2006, but that was about the only good news in a very difficult season for the former Princeton football star. He'll have to cut down on the strikeouts to have any chance of making the majors. He led the minors with 191 whiffs—one every 2.5 at-bats—in his second year in low Class A. His aggressive approach leaves him an easy mark for offspeed offerings, as he's struggled with pitch recognition. His lefthanded swing isn't as smooth and natural as his stroke from the right side, which explains his large splits (.302 against lefties, .216 against righties). The Reds will keep giving Szymanski chances because of his great athleticism, plus raw power, plus speed and above-average defense in center. He hasn't really earned a promotion to high Class A, but it's hard to imagine the Reds sending him back to Dayton for a third straight season.

| Year | Club (League) | Class | AVG | G | AB | R | H | 2B | 3B | HR | RBI | BB | SO | SB | OBP | SLG |
|------|---------------|-------|-----|---|----|---|---|----|----|----|-----|----|----|----|-----|-----|
| 2004 | Billings (Pio) | R | .259 | 22 | 81 | 13 | 21 | 4 | 2 | 3 | 17 | 9 | 26 | 2 | .330 | .469 |
| 2005 | Dayton (MWL) | A | .262 | 50 | 191 | 32 | 50 | 8 | 1 | 10 | 26 | 21 | 57 | 7 | .332 | .471 |
| 2006 | Dayton (MWL) | A | .239 | 128 | 482 | 68 | 115 | 31 | 3 | 16 | 59 | 46 | 191 | 22 | .309 | .415 |
| **MINOR LEAGUE TOTALS** | | | .247 | 200 | 754 | 113 | 186 | 43 | 6 | 29 | 102 | 76 | 274 | 31 | .317 | .435 |

## 30 JOSH HAMILTON OF

**Born:** May 21, 1981. **B-T:** L-L. **Ht.:** 6-4. **Wt.:** 205. **Drafted:** HS—Raleigh, N.C., 1999 (1st round). **Signed by:** Mark McKnight (Devil Rays).

The Reds electrified the major league Rule 5 draft at the Winter Meetings, paying the Cubs to move up into their slot and take Hamilton with the third overall pick in the draft. Cincinnati felt it needed to move up the board to select Hamilton before the Marlins could choose Hamilton with the sixth selection. For the Reds, selecting Hamilton is a low-risk throw at the dart board. In his brief stint in the New York-Penn league and during instructional league Hamilton showed that he still possesses the stellar raw tools that made him the No. 1 overall pick by the Devil Rays in the 1999 draft. He has above-average raw power that he showed off by putting on batting-practice shows again in 2006. He has exceptional arm strength in right field and he can still play all three outfield positions. He doesn't run as well as he did as a teenager, but he's still a plus runner. He has recovered from minor knee surgery that sidelined him during the New York-Penn League season. As Hamilton himself explained, his problems never have revolved around the baseball field. He was suspended for substance abuse for more than three years and will continue to be tested three times a week. The Reds believe that they can provide the support system Hamilton will need to succeed. Hamilton's baseball skills are undeniably rusty, but he'll have a legitimate chance to make the Reds if he shows signs of being able to harness the tools that once made him the No. 1 prospect in all of baseball—back when Homer Bailey was getting ready to enter high school. Cincinnati will have to keep him on its active roster all season, or else put him on waivers before offering him back to Tampa Bay for half his $50,000 draft price. The Reds face the same situation with their other big league Rule 5 pick, former Athletics righthanded reliever Jared Burton.

| Year | Club (League) | Class | AVG | G | AB | R | H | 2B | 3B | HR | RBI | BB | SO | SB | OBP | SLG |
|------|---------------|-------|-----|---|----|---|---|----|----|----|-----|----|----|----|-----|-----|
| 1999 | Princeton (Appy) | R | .347 | 56 | 236 | 49 | 82 | 20 | 4 | 10 | 48 | 13 | 43 | 17 | .378 | .593 |
|  | Hudson Valley (NYP) | A | .194 | 16 | 72 | 7 | 14 | 3 | 0 | 0 | 7 | 1 | 14 | 1 | .213 | .236 |
| 2000 | Charleston, S.C. (SAL) | A | .302 | 96 | 391 | 62 | 118 | 23 | 3 | 13 | 61 | 27 | 71 | 14 | .348 | .476 |
| 2001 | Orlando (SL) | AA | .180 | 23 | 89 | 5 | 16 | 5 | 0 | 0 | 4 | 5 | 22 | 2 | .221 | .236 |
|  | Charleston, S.C. (SAL) | A | .364 | 4 | 11 | 3 | 4 | 1 | 0 | 1 | 2 | 2 | 3 | 0 | .462 | .727 |
| 2002 | Bakersfield (CAL) | A | .303 | 56 | 211 | 32 | 64 | 14 | 1 | 9 | 44 | 20 | 46 | 10 | .359 | .507 |
| 2003 | Did not play—On restricted list | | | | | | | | | | | | | | | |
| 2004 | Did not play—On restricted list | | | | | | | | | | | | | | | |
| 2005 | Did not play—On restricted list | | | | | | | | | | | | | | | |
| 2006 | Hudson Valley (NYP) | A | .260 | 15 | 50 | 7 | 13 | 3 | 1 | 0 | 5 | 5 | 11 | 0 | .327 | .360 |
| **MINOR LEAGUE TOTALS** | | | .293 | 266 | 1060 | 165 | 311 | 69 | 9 | 33 | 171 | 73 | 210 | 44 | .338 | .469 |

# CLEVELAND
# INDIANS
## BY CHRIS KLINE

LARRY GOREN

After making over an older, overpaid roster in 2002, general manager Mark Shapiro and his rebuilding plan reaped rewards right on schedule. The Indians won 93 games and just missed the playoffs in 2005, with a promise of better things to come.

Instead, Cleveland stumbled. The Tribe went 13-12 in the season's first month and never got back into the American League Central race. The Indians dropped to 78 victories and fourth place in the division, 18 games behind the Twins.

The major step backward was mostly the result of inconsistency on the mound, particularly in the bullpen. Rookie Jeremy Sowers replaced Jason Johnson in the rotation and showed promise, but two other farm system products, Fausto Carmona and Fernando Cabrera, failed to shore up the bullpen. Cabrera went 3-3, 5.34 and couldn't convert any of his four save opportunities.

The Indians' handling of Carmona was curious at best and highlighted their big league pitching problems. Carmona opened the season as the No. 1 starter at Triple-A Buffalo, then earned a spot in the Cleveland rotation before moving to the bullpen. After the Indians traded closer Bob Wickman to the Braves, they briefly anointed Carmona closer before using him in middle relief. When Carmona struggled mightily with 1-9, 5.64 numbers, he headed back to Buffalo as a starter and resurfaced in the Tribe rotation at the end of the year.

Though the club has the nucleus of a strong rotation in C.C. Sabathia, Jake Westbrook, Cliff Lee and Sowers, the bullpen still needs an overhaul and 35-year-old free-agent signee Joe Borowski is just a Band-Aid solution at closer.

Offense wasn't an issue, as the Indians plated 870 runs and in fact outscored their opponents by 88. **Grady Sizemore** came into his own as an elite center fielder, while Travis Hafner continued to establish himself as one of the game's most dangerous mashers.

One positive the Indians took out of a disappointing year was getting a look at several position players later in the season, giving Ryan Garko, Franklin Gutierrez, Joe Inglett, Kevin Kouzmanoff and Andy Marte a chance to contribute. Kouzmanoff showed enough to be used as the primary chip to acquire Josh Barfield in a November trade with the Padres. Cleveland also added position-player talent when it fell out of the race, dealing Ben Broussard, Eduardo Perez and Wickman to get shortstop Asdrubal Cabrera, outfielder Shin-Soo Choo and catcher Max Ramirez.

Down on the farm, Kinston won the high Class A Carolina League title behind strong pitching, and Akron came within one game of winning its second straight Double-A Eastern League championship. The Indians spent most of their early draft picks in June on college players with solid if not spectacular ceilings, starting with polished lefthander David Huff in the supplemental first round.

## TOP 30 PROSPECTS

| | |
|---|---|
| 1. Adam Miller, rhp | 16. Matt McBride, c |
| 2. Chuck Lofgren, lhp | 17. Brian Slocum, rhp |
| 3. Trevor Crowe, of | 18. Edward Mujica, rhp |
| 4. Tony Sipp, lhp | 19. Kelly Shoppach, c |
| 5. Brian Barton, of | 20. Wyatt Toregas, c |
| 6. John Drennen, of | 21. Max Ramirez, c |
| 7. Scott Lewis, lhp | 22. Aaron Laffey, lhp |
| 8. Brad Snyder, of | 23. Josh Rodriguez, ss |
| 9. Wes Hodges, 3b | 24. Jordan Brown, of |
| 10. David Huff, lhp | 25. Jensen Lewis, rhp |
| 11. Rafael Perez, lhp | 26. Jose Constanza, of |
| 12. Sung-Wei Tseng, rhp | 27. Tom Mastny, rhp |
| 13. J.D. Martin, rhp | 28. Frank Herrmann, rhp |
| 14. Juan Lara, lhp | 29. Stephen Wright, rhp |
| 15. Asdrubal Cabrera, ss | 30. Stephen Head, 1b |

# ORGANIZATION OVERVIEW

**General manager:** Mark Shapiro. **Farm director:** John Farrell. **Scouting director:** John Mirabelli.

## 2006 PERFORMANCE

| Class | Team | League | W | L | PCT | Finish* | Manager | Affiliated |
|---|---|---|---|---|---|---|---|---|
| Majors | Cleveland | American | 78 | 84 | .481 | 11th (14) | Eric Wedge | — |
| Triple-A | Buffalo Bisons | International | 73 | 68 | .518 | 7th (14) | Torey Lovullo | 1995 |
| Double-A | Akron Aeros | Eastern | 87 | 55 | .613 | 1st (12) | Tim Bogar | 1997 |
| High A | Kinston Indians | Carolina | 85 | 54 | .612 | +1st (8) | Mike Sarbaugh | 1987 |
| Low A | Lake County Captains | South Atlantic | 64 | 74 | .464 | 13th (16) | Lee May | 2003 |
| Short-season | Mahoning Valley Scrappers | New York-Penn | 40 | 36 | .526 | 7th (14) | Rouglas Odor | 1999 |
| Rookie | #Burlington Indians | Appalachian | 34 | 33 | .507 | 4th (10) | Kevin Higgins | 1986 |
| Rookie | GCL Indians | Gulf Coast | 21 | 29 | .420 | 11th (13) | Chris Tremie | 2006 |
| **OVERALL 2006 MINOR LEAGUE RECORD** | | | 404 | 349 | .537 | 5th (30) | | |

*Finish in overall standings (No. of teams in league). +League champion. #Indians won't operate in Appalachian League in 2007.

## ORGANIZATION LEADERS

### BATTING
| | | |
|---|---|---|
| AVG | Kouzmanoff, Kevin, Akron/Buffalo | .379 |
| R | Francisco, Ben, Buffalo | 91 |
| H | Francisco, Ben, Buffalo | 161 |
| 2B | Francisco, Ben, Buffalo | 35 |
| 3B | Constanza, Jose, Lake County/Kinston | 9 |
| HR | Goleski, Ryan, Kinston/Akron | 27 |
| RBI | Goleski, Ryan, Kinston/Akron | 106 |
| BB | Crowe, Trevor, Kinston/Lake County/Akron | 76 |
| SO | Snyder, Brad, Akron | 158 |
| SB | Crowe, Trevor, Kinston/Lake County/Akron | 47 |
| OBP | Kouzmanoff, Kevin, Akron/Buffalo | .437 |
| SLG | Kouzmanoff, Kevin, Akron/Buffalo | .656 |
| XBH | Francisco, Ben, Buffalo | 59 |

### PITCHING
| | | |
|---|---|---|
| W | Lofgren, Chuck, Kinston | 17 |
| L | Vargas, Albert, Lake County | 14 |
| #ERA | Lewis, Scott, Kinston | 1.48 |
| G | Collins, Kyle, Akron/Kinston | 60 |
| SV | Davis, Matt, Lake County/Akron | 27 |
| IP | Smith, Sean, Kinston/Akron | 169 |
| BB | Ness, Joe, Kinston | 55 |
| SO | Miller, Adam, Buffalo/Akron | 161 |
| AVG | Tomlin, Josh, Mahoning Valley | .196 |

## BEST TOOLS

| | |
|---|---|
| Best Hitter for Average | Trevor Crowe |
| Best Power Hitter | Brad Snyder |
| Best Strike-Zone Discipline | Trevor Crowe |
| Fastest Baserunner | Jose Constanza |
| Best Athlete | Brian Barton |
| Best Fastball | Adam Miller |
| Best Curveball | Scott Lewis |
| Best Slider | Adam Miller |
| Best Changeup | Sean Smith |
| Best Control | Scott Lewis |
| Best Defensive Catcher | Wyatt Toregas |
| Best Defensive Infielder | Asdrubal Cabrera |
| Best Infield Arm | Asdrubal Cabrera |
| Best Defensive Outfielder | Jonathan Van Every |
| Best Outfield Arm | Brad Snyder |

## PROJECTED 2010 LINEUP

| | |
|---|---|
| Catcher | Matt McBride |
| First Base | Victor Martinez |
| Second Base | Josh Barfield |
| Third Base | Andy Marte |
| Shortstop | Jhonny Peralta |
| Left Field | Trevor Crowe |
| Center Field | Grady Sizemore |
| Right Field | Shin-Soo Choo |

| | |
|---|---|
| Designated Hitter | Travis Hafner |
| No. 1 Starter | C.C. Sabathia |
| No. 2 Starter | Adam Miller |
| No. 3 Starter | Jeremy Sowers |
| No. 4 Starter | Cliff Lee |
| No. 5 Starter | Jake Westbrook |
| Closer | Tony Sipp |

## LAST YEAR'S TOP 20 PROSPECTS

1. Adam Miller, rhp
2. Jeremy Sowers, lhp
3. Brad Snyder, of
4. Fausto Carmona, rhp
5. Ryan Garko, 1b/c
6. Franklin Gutierrez, of
7. Fernando Cabrera, rhp
8. Trevor Crowe, of
9. Stephen Head, 1b
10. Michael Aubrey, 1b
11. Chuck Lofgren, lhp
12. John Drennen, of
13. Rafael Perez, lhp
14. Tony Sipp, lhp
15. Andrew Brown, rhp
16. Nick Pesco, rhp
17. Cody Bunkelman, rhp
18. J.D. Martin, rhp
19. Jensen Lewis, rhp
20. Edward Mujica, rhp

## TOP PROSPECTS OF THE DECADE

| Year | Player, Pos. | 2006 Org. |
|---|---|---|
| 1997 | Bartolo Colon, rhp | Angels |
| 1998 | Sean Casey, 1b | Tigers |
| 1999 | Russell Branyan, 3b | Padres |
| 2000 | C.C. Sabathia, lhp | Indians |
| 2001 | C.C. Sabathia, lhp | Indians |
| 2002 | Corey Smith, 3b | White Sox |
| 2003 | Brandon Phillips, ss/2b | Reds |
| 2004 | Grady Sizemore, of | Indians |
| 2005 | Adam Miller, rhp | Indians |
| 2006 | Adam Miller, rhp | Indians |

## TOP DRAFT PICKS OF THE DECADE

| Year | Player, Pos. | 2006 Org. |
|---|---|---|
| 1997 | Tim Drew, rhp | Out of baseball |
| 1998 | C.C. Sabathia, lhp | Indians |
| 1999 | Will Hartley, c (2nd round) | Out of baseball |
| 2000 | Corey Smith, 3b | White Sox |
| 2001 | Dan Denham, rhp | Indians |
| 2002 | Jeremy Guthrie, rhp | Indians |
| 2003 | Michael Aubrey, 1b | Indians |
| 2004 | Jeremy Sowers, lhp | Indians |
| 2005 | Trevor Crowe, of | Indians |
| 2006 | David Huff, lhp | Indians |

## ALL-TIME LARGEST BONUSES

| | |
|---|---|
| Danys Baez, 1999 | $4,500,000 |
| Jeremy Guthrie, 2002 | $3,000,000 |
| Jeremy Sowers, 2004 | $2,475,000 |
| Michael Aubrey, 2003 | $2,010,000 |
| Dan Denham, 2001 | $1,860,000 |

# MINOR LEAGUE DEPTH CHART

## Cleveland Indians

**Impact: B.** The only reason the Tribe doesn't grade lower is because of the role the bullpen depth will play in the majors this season. But after Miller, Crowe and Lofgren, there are no blue-chippers.

**Depth: B.** They aren't as deep as they used to be, but the Indians continue to stockpile players with average, everyday ceilings in the majors.

**Sleeper:** Shawn Nottingham, lhp. The other half the Tribe received in the Ben Broussard deal, Nottingham pitched just four innings at Kinston. He's an aggressive lefthander who works in the low 90s with his fastball and throws his curveball and changeup for strikes.

*Numbers in parentheses indicate prospect rankings.*

### LF
Trevor Crowe (3)
John Drennen (6)
Jordan Brown (24)
Roman Pena
Jason Cooper
Mike Butia

### CF
Brian Barton (5)
Ben Francisco

### RF
Brad Snyder (8)
Jose Constanza (26)
Jonathan Van Every

### 3B
Wes Hodges (9)

### SS
Asdrubal Cabrera (15)
Josh Rodriguez (23)
Brian Finegan
Ivan Ochoa

### 2B
Adam Davis
Argenis Reyes

### 1B
Jordan Brown (24)
Stephen Head (30)
Ryan Mulhern
Michael Aubrey

### C
Matt McBride (16)
Kelly Shoppach (19)
Wyatt Toregas (20)
Max Ramirez (21)
Javi Herrera

### RHP

| Starters | Relievers |
| --- | --- |
| Adam Miller (1) | Juan Lara (14) |
| Sung-Wei Tseng (12) | Edward Mujica (18) |
| J.D. Martin (13) | Jensen Lewis (25) |
| Brian Slocum (17) | Tom Mastny (27) |
| Frank Herrmann (28) | Neil Wagner |
| Steven Wright (29) | Kyle Collins |
| Chris Archer | Dan Denham |
| Sean Smith | Travis Foley |
| Jeremy Guthrie | Cody Bunkelman |
| Nick Pesco | Michael Finocchi |
| Hyang-Nam Choi | |

### LHP

| Starters | Relievers |
| --- | --- |
| Chuck Lofgren (2) | Tony Sipp (4) |
| Scott Lewis (7) | Rafael Perez (11) |
| David Huff (10) | Juan Lara (14) |
| Aaron Laffey (22) | Shawn Nottingham |
| Ryan Morris | Reid Santos |
| Ryan Edell | Brandt Sanders |
| John Gaub | |

# DRAFT ANALYSIS

**Best Pro Debut:** RHP Josh Tomlin (19) used his sinker-slider combination to go 8-2, 2.09 with 69 strikeouts in 77 innings. The Indians give C Matt McBride (2) extra credit for hitting .272 with four homers while rehabbing a shoulder injury he suffered in college.

**Best Athlete:** 2B/SS Adam Davis (3) has above-average speed to go with solid range and arm strength, and he's a switch-hitter who can play just about anywhere on the diamond. The key will be to get his bat going again, as he slumped all spring at Florida and hit .213 in his debut. RHP Chris Archer (5) is very athletic for a pitcher, which helped Cleveland rework his mechanics in instructional league after he went 0-3, 7.71 in Rookie ball.

**Best Pure Hitter:** 3B Wes Hodges (2) recovered his swing and batting stroke once he got over a stress fracture in his left leg that was diagnosed late in the spring.

**Best Raw Power:** C Robbie Alcombrack (7) won the home run derby at the 2005 Aflac Game. 1B Chris Nash (24) is a 6-foot-3, 230-pound hulk who may have enough athleticism to play an outfield corner.

**Fastest Runner:** OF Stephen Douglas (16) covers 60 yards in 6.6 seconds.

**Best Defensive Player:** Davis should develop into an above-average second baseman.

**Best Fastball:** RHP Dan Frega (12) has the best pure arm strength, reaching 94 mph more consistently than the other Indians draftees, but his control and command are far from refined. RHPs Steven Wright (2), Austin Creps (6) and Kyle Harper (17) all touched 94 this spring. They all missed the summer recovering from maladies, as Wright had mononucleosis, Creps had knee surgery and Harper had Tommy John surgery.

**Best Breaking Ball:** Thanks to his curveball, RHP Mike Eisenberg (8) led NCAA Division III in wins (13) and strikeouts (138 in 115 innings) and shared MVP honors as Marietta (Ohio) won the D-III College World Series. LHP Ryan Morris (4) and Archer also have promising curves.

**Most Intriguing Background:** RHP Paolo Espino (10) pitched a scoreless inning for Panama at the World Baseball Classic. Unsigned RHP Greg Pryor's (26) uncle Greg played in the major leagues.

**Closest To The Majors:** LHP David Huff (1) could follow a path similar to the one Jeremy Sowers did, going from the first round of the draft to Cleveland in two years. Huff had one of the top changeups in the draft, throws strikes and is lefthanded.

**Best Late-Round Pick:** The Indians took gambles on several injured pitchers, among them Harper, LHP John Gaub (21) and RHP Vinnie Pestano (20), who was challenging for the NCAA Division I lead in saves until he injured his elbow and needed Tommy John surgery. Total cost: $410,000, far less than what they would have commanded if healthy.

**The One Who Got Away:** Cleveland also went after RHP Brant Rustich (13), who projected as an early-round pick before he was sidelined by an inflamed tendon in his middle pitching finger. He returned to UCLA.

**Assessment:** It's hard to judge this draft based on early performance, because several of the Indians' key signees have yet to make their debuts. Huff and Hodges could be very good values for where Cleveland got them, and McBride was the best all-around college catcher in the draft.

## 2005      BUDGET: $4.9 million

OFs Trevor Crowe (1) and John Drennen (1) continue to show promise, but 1B Stephen Head (2) took a severe downturn in 2006. Not signing RHP Tim Lincecum (42) turned out to be a grave mistake. **GRADE: C+**

## 2004      BUDGET: $4.9 million

LHP Jeremy Sowers (1) already is winning games in the majors. Three more lefties are on the way to Cleveland: minor league ERA leader Scott Lewis (3), Chuck Lofgren (4) and Tony Sipp (45). **GRADE: B+**

## 2003      BUDGET: $6.0 million

RHP Adam Miller (1) returned to health last year, and OF Brad Snyder (1) continues to progress. A third first-rounder, 1B Michael Aubrey, just can't stay healthy. 1B Ryan Garko (3) and since-traded 3B Kevin Kouzmanoff (6) have exceeded expectations. **GRADE: A**

*Draft analysis by Jim Callis. Numbers in parentheses indicate draft rounds. Budgets are bonuses in first 10 rounds.*

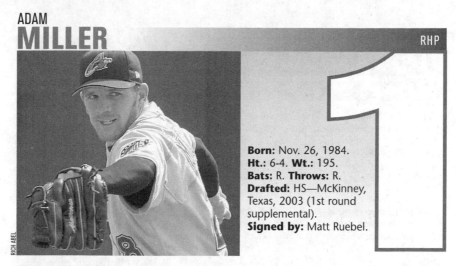

# ADAM
# MILLER

RHP

**Born:** Nov. 26, 1984.
**Ht.:** 6-4. **Wt.:** 195.
**Bats:** R. **Throws:** R.
**Drafted:** HS—McKinney, Texas, 2003 (1st round supplemental).
**Signed by:** Matt Ruebel.

RICH ABEL

**M**iller spent 2005 essentially on a season-long rehab stint after straining an elbow ligament while long-tossing in spring training. He pitched just 71 innings and ended the year at high Class A Kinston, the same place he had lit up radar guns to the tune of 101 mph in the Carolina League playoffs in 2004. After regaining command of his slider and slowly working a changeup back into his repertoire, Miller climbed back on track in 2006 at Double-A Akron. Though he was inconsistent during the season's first two months, he finished stronger than he ever had, winning six consecutive starts through July and August, including three straight 11-strikeout performances, the last of which was Miller's first-ever nine-inning complete game. He led the organization in strikeouts and topped the Eastern League in wins, while ranking second in ERA and third in strikeouts. He stayed healthy throughout, tossing a career-high 171 innings (including the playoffs).

Miller has blossomed into a potential frontline starter by becoming a more complete pitcher. The velocity on his four-seam fastball returned to 93-95 mph and he hit 98 in his final four starts, including the EL playoffs. He has added a two-seamer to change speeds on his fastball more effectively, and his changeup has emerged as a go-to pitch with good depth and late action. But Miller's best pitch remains his slider. It's back to where it was in 2004, with tilt, devastating late break and power. He throws his slider at 87-88 mph. Miller finally has come to grips with the fact that velocity isn't everything, and his ability to consistently command his offspeed stuff has him back on the fast track again. The further Miller gets away from injury, the stronger he's become. His delivery is free and easy, so there's no reason his health should be an issue down the road. He has excellent makeup, and he learned more about attacking lefthanders this season from Akron pitching coach Scott Radinsky. Miller dominated lefties, as they hit just .198 against him with twice as many groundouts as flyouts.

Though his changeup grew leaps and bounds in 2006, Miller still is learning when and how to use it. His mechanics with the pitch are solid, but he still tends to want to blow hitters away with his fastball or slider. He also can do a better job of locating it. While Miller works quickly to home plate, he still needs to refine his pickoff move to hold runners more effectively. He sometimes rushes his delivery, leading to erratic command of his fastball up in the zone. Intimidating on the mound, he can let his emotions get the better of him at times in pressure situations.

There isn't much left for Miller to prove in the minors. He'll battle for a big league rotation spot out of spring training, but likely will start the year at Triple-A Buffalo under manager Torey Lovullo and pitching coach Greg Hibbard—the same duo who brought him along during his breakout year in 2004. It's only a matter of time before Miller makes an impact in the major leagues.

| Year | Club (League) | Class | W | L | ERA | G | GS | CG | SV | IP | H | R | ER | HR | BB | SO | AVG |
|---|---|---|---|---|---|---|---|---|---|---|---|---|---|---|---|---|---|
| 2003 | Burlington (Appy) | R | 0 | 4 | 4.96 | 10 | 10 | 0 | 0 | 33 | 30 | 20 | 18 | 2 | 9 | 23 | .250 |
| 2004 | Lake County (SAL) | A | 7 | 4 | 3.36 | 19 | 19 | 1 | 0 | 91 | 79 | 39 | 34 | 7 | 28 | 106 | .240 |
| | Kinston (CL) | A | 3 | 2 | 2.08 | 8 | 8 | 0 | 0 | 43 | 29 | 17 | 10 | 1 | 12 | 46 | .193 |
| 2005 | Mahoning Valley (NYP) | A | 0 | 0 | 5.06 | 3 | 3 | 0 | 0 | 11 | 17 | 6 | 6 | 0 | 4 | 6 | .405 |
| | Kinston (CL) | A | 2 | 4 | 4.83 | 12 | 12 | 0 | 0 | 60 | 76 | 43 | 32 | 5 | 17 | 45 | .318 |
| 2006 | Buffalo (IL) | AAA | 0 | 0 | 5.79 | 1 | 1 | 0 | 0 | 5 | 4 | 3 | 3 | 0 | 3 | 4 | .235 |
| | Akron (EL) | AA | 15 | 6 | 2.75 | 26 | 24 | 1 | 0 | 154 | 129 | 56 | 47 | 9 | 43 | 157 | .226 |
| **MINOR LEAGUE TOTALS** | | | 27 | 20 | 3.41 | 79 | 77 | 2 | 0 | 396 | 364 | 184 | 150 | 24 | 116 | 387 | .248 |

## 2 CHUCK LOFGREN LHP

CARL KLINE

**Born:** Jan. 29, 1986. **B-T:** L-L. **Ht.:** 6-4. **Wt.:** 200. **Drafted:** HS—San Mateo, Calif., 2004 (4th round). **Signed by:** Don Lyle.

Several clubs liked Lofgren's bat better than his arm in the 2004 draft, but the Indians' decision to make him a full-time pitcher can't be second-guessed. He emerged as one of the top lefthanders in the minors in 2006, tying for the minor league lead in wins and ranking second in the Carolina League in both ERA and strikeouts. Lofgren has more velocity than most lefthanders with a fastball that sits at 89-93 mph and tops out at 95. His changeup serves as an out pitch, because he throws it with good arm action and can locate it to both sides of the plate. He also features a spike curveball in the mid-70s, and he has added a slider that has good depth. He has outstanding mound presence. Lofgren only started using the slider at midseason, so he needs to continue to develop it. While his delivery is clean with a quick, easy arm action, he rushes at times in his lower half and needs to keep his hips from opening up too early to stay on a direct line to home plate. This flaw at times costs him control. Lofgren took one of the largest leaps developmentally among Tribe farmhands in 2006. With a young big league rotation, though, the Indians see no reason to rush him, so he'll likely spend 2007 in Double-A.

| Year | Club (League) | Class | W | L | ERA | G | GS | CG | SV | IP | H | R | ER | HR | BB | SO | AVG |
|---|---|---|---|---|---|---|---|---|---|---|---|---|---|---|---|---|---|
| 2004 | Burlington (Appy) | R | 0 | 0 | 6.04 | 9 | 9 | 0 | 0 | 22 | 25 | 16 | 15 | 4 | 13 | 23 | .294 |
| 2005 | Lake County (SAL) | A | 5 | 5 | 2.81 | 18 | 18 | 0 | 0 | 93 | 73 | 31 | 29 | 6 | 43 | 89 | .218 |
| 2006 | Kinston (CL) | A | 17 | 5 | 2.32 | 25 | 25 | 1 | 0 | 140 | 108 | 51 | 36 | 5 | 54 | 125 | .217 |
| **MINOR LEAGUE TOTALS** | | | 22 | 10 | 2.82 | 52 | 52 | 1 | 0 | 255 | 206 | 98 | 80 | 15 | 110 | 237 | .224 |

## 3 TREVOR CROWE OF

CARL KLINE

**Born:** Nov. 17, 1983. **B-T:** B-R. **Ht.:** 6-0. **Wt.:** 200. **Drafted:** Arizona, 2005 (1st round). **Signed by:** Joe Graham.

One of the best athletes in the system, Crowe was hitting .329 in high Class A before going down with an oblique injury. After he got healthy, he went to Double-A Akron and tried to move from the outfield to second base, where he played some in high school and college. The conversion didn't take, and the Indians gave up on it after instructional league. A switch-hitter with quick, strong hands, Crowe hits with gap power to all fields. An above-average runner, Crowe takes advantage of his speed by taking walks and stealing bases efficiently. He shows enough range and arm strength to stay in center field, though he won't push Grady Sizemore to a corner. A better hitter from the left side, Crowe needs to work on keeping his hands inside the ball when hitting righthanded. His power is probably average at best. While he's an above-average defender, he lacks first-step quickness at times and could get better jumps. Crowe profiles best as the 2005 version of Coco Crisp—a speedy, high-on-base left fielder who hits 10-15 homers annually. He'll start 2007 at Triple-A and could quickly get the call to Cleveland.

| Year | Club (League) | Class | AVG | G | AB | R | H | 2B | 3B | HR | RBI | BB | SO | SB | OBP | SLG |
|---|---|---|---|---|---|---|---|---|---|---|---|---|---|---|---|---|
| 2005 | Mahoning Valley (NYP) | A | .255 | 12 | 51 | 9 | 13 | 2 | 1 | 1 | 6 | 6 | 8 | 4 | .345 | .392 |
| | Lake County (SAL) | A | .258 | 44 | 178 | 18 | 46 | 8 | 2 | 0 | 23 | 18 | 25 | 7 | .327 | .326 |
| | Akron (EL) | AA | .100 | 3 | 10 | 1 | 1 | 0 | 0 | 0 | 0 | 0 | 3 | 0 | .100 | .100 |
| 2006 | Akron (EL) | AA | .234 | 39 | 154 | 20 | 36 | 7 | 2 | 1 | 13 | 20 | 24 | 16 | .318 | .325 |
| | Kinston (CL) | A | .329 | 60 | 219 | 51 | 72 | 15 | 2 | 4 | 31 | 48 | 46 | 29 | .449 | .470 |
| | Lake County (SAL) | A | .000 | 2 | 5 | 0 | 0 | 0 | 0 | 0 | 0 | 0 | 1 | 0 | .000 | .000 |
| **MINOR LEAGUE TOTALS** | | | .272 | 160 | 617 | 99 | 168 | 32 | 7 | 6 | 73 | 92 | 107 | 56 | .367 | .376 |

## 4 TONY SIPP LHP

STEVE MOORE

**Born:** July 12, 1983. **B-T:** L-L. **Ht.:** 6-0. **Wt.:** 185. **Drafted:** Clemson, 2004 (45th round). **Signed by:** Tim Moore.

The Indians drafted Sipp, a center fielder/pitcher in junior college and at Clemson, in the 45th round and gave him $130,000 after he had a strong summer in the Cape Cod League. That deal now looks like a steal after Sipp cruised his way through Double-A after moving to the bullpen full-time. Sipp has good deception and extension toward home plate that makes his 89-93 mph fastball explode on hitters. His secondary stuff took a major step forward in 2006, as his slider showed much better depth and tilt, and his changeup emerged as a weapon against lefties and righties alike. He's controls the running game well, giving up just one steal in eight tries in 2006. While Sipp has little trouble throwing strikes, his command can be an issue at times. Though he's athletic, he

doesn't field his position as well as he could. Sipp no longer looks like just a lefty specialist. The development of his secondary pitches has some Tribe officials thinking he's a closer in the mold of Eddie Guardado. The signing of free agent Joe Borowski will allow Sipp to apprentice before he's asked to finish games.

| Year | Club (League) | Class | W | L | ERA | G | GS | CG | SV | IP | H | R | ER | HR | BB | SO | AVG |
|------|---------------|-------|---|---|-----|---|----|----|----|----|---|---|----|----|----|----|-----|
| 2004 | Mahoning Valley (NYP) | A | 3 | 1 | 3.16 | 10 | 10 | 0 | 0 | 43 | 33 | 23 | 15 | 5 | 13 | 74 | .212 |
| 2005 | Lake County (SAL) | A | 4 | 1 | 2.22 | 13 | 12 | 0 | 0 | 69 | 47 | 19 | 17 | 5 | 19 | 71 | .196 |
| 2005 | Kinston (CL) | A | 2 | 2 | 2.66 | 22 | 5 | 0 | 2 | 47 | 34 | 19 | 14 | 4 | 23 | 59 | .205 |
| 2006 | Akron (EL) | AA | 4 | 2 | 3.13 | 29 | 4 | 0 | 3 | 60 | 44 | 23 | 21 | 2 | 21 | 80 | .201 |
| **MINOR LEAGUE TOTALS** | | | 13 | 6 | 2.75 | 74 | 31 | 0 | 5 | 219 | 158 | 84 | 67 | 16 | 76 | 284 | .202 |

## ⑤ BRIAN BARTON                                                    OF

ROBERT GURGANUS

**Born:** April 25, 1982. **B-T:** R-R. **Ht.:** 6-3. **Wt.:** 190. **Signed:** Miami, NDFA 2004. **Signed by:** Jorge Diaz.

Barton scared off most teams before the 2004 draft because of his academic background, but the Indians were able to sign him as a nondrafted free agent after seeing him in the Cape Cod League. An aerospace engineering major at Miami who interned at Boeing, he turned pro for $100,000 with an additional $100,000 in college funds. In his second year as a pro, Barton made adjustments that allowed him to take more advantage of his natural power and speed. He got the load in his swing started earlier and worked hard to recognize offspeed pitches. His good instincts on the bases allow him to read pitchers, and he succeeded on 41 of 49 steal attempts. His plus speed also plays well in center field. Not only is he intelligent, he's mentally tough. Barton has trouble with balls in on his hands and his swing gets too long at times. He struggled against lefthanders after being promoted to Double-A, hitting just .219. Indians officials tried to move him back off the plate so he could better control the inner half. At 24, he's older than most prospects who haven't gotten past Double-A. Barton's power/speed combination makes him a potentially elite talent despite his age. He'll compete for a Triple-A job in a crowded outfield picture during spring training.

| Year | Club (League) | Class | AVG | G | AB | R | H | 2B | 3B | HR | RBI | BB | SO | SB | OBP | SLG |
|------|---------------|-------|-----|---|----|---|---|----|----|----|-----|----|----|----|-----|-----|
| 2005 | Lake County (SAL) | A | .414 | 35 | 133 | 31 | 55 | 14 | 1 | 4 | 32 | 18 | 21 | 7 | .506 | .624 |
| | Kinston (CL) | A | .274 | 64 | 223 | 42 | 61 | 15 | 6 | 3 | 32 | 34 | 57 | 13 | .404 | .435 |
| 2006 | Akron (EL) | AA | .351 | 42 | 151 | 32 | 53 | 5 | 0 | 6 | 26 | 13 | 26 | 15 | .415 | .503 |
| | Kinston (CL) | A | .308 | 82 | 295 | 56 | 91 | 16 | 3 | 13 | 57 | 39 | 83 | 26 | .410 | .515 |
| **MINOR LEAGUE TOTALS** | | | .324 | 223 | 802 | 161 | 260 | 50 | 10 | 26 | 147 | 104 | 187 | 61 | .425 | .509 |

## ⑥ JOHN DRENNEN                                                    OF

MIKE JANES

**Born:** Aug. 26, 1986. **B-T:** L-L. **Ht.:** 5-11. **Wt.:** 185. **Drafted:** HS—San Diego, 2005 (1st round supplemental). **Signed by:** Jason Smith.

One of the best pure hitters in the 2005 draft, Drennen batted just .238 in his pro debut but didn't disappoint in his first full season. He garnered national headlines after homering against Roger Clemens in the Rocket's first minor league tuneup start in June. After Drennen was promoted to high Class A, he found it hard to avoid the spotlight as the subject of an upcoming documentary on his rise through the minors. While undersized, Drennen uses his compact build to his advantage by getting good leverage in his fundamentally sound, repeatable swing. He has above-average power, and as he showed against Clemens, he can turn on good fastballs. His other tools all play about average, and once underway he runs a tick better than that. Drennen will have to get stronger, as he wore down during his first full season and started only once in the Carolina League playoffs. He can get pull-oriented, so Tribe officials sat him down before the season and pointed to Grady Sizemore's five homers in two years at Class A to remind Drennen to use the whole field now and let his power develop naturally. Though he has played mostly center field, his fringy range there means he'll probably wind up in left. He has a below-average arm. Drennen likely will return to high Class A for the first half of 2007.

| Year | Club (League) | Class | AVG | G | AB | R | H | 2B | 3B | HR | RBI | BB | SO | SB | OBP | SLG |
|------|---------------|-------|-----|---|----|---|---|----|----|----|-----|----|----|----|-----|-----|
| 2005 | Burlington (Appy) | R | .238 | 51 | 168 | 24 | 40 | 7 | 1 | 8 | 29 | 18 | 37 | 6 | .325 | .435 |
| 2006 | Kinston (CL) | A | .239 | 31 | 113 | 15 | 27 | 6 | 2 | 0 | 8 | 12 | 21 | 2 | .328 | .327 |
| | Lake County (SAL) | A | .321 | 67 | 240 | 33 | 77 | 12 | 3 | 6 | 30 | 31 | 52 | 6 | .409 | .471 |
| **MINOR LEAGUE TOTALS** | | | .276 | 149 | 521 | 72 | 144 | 25 | 6 | 14 | 67 | 61 | 110 | 14 | .365 | .428 |

## 7 SCOTT LEWIS
LHP

**Born:** Sept. 26, 1983. **B-T:** B-L. **Ht.:** 6-0. **Wt.:** 190. **Drafted:** Ohio State, 2004 (3rd round). **Signed by:** Bob Mayer.

Lewis struck out 16 and 20 in consecutive starts as an Ohio State sophomore in 2003 and looked like a future first-round pick. But he needed Tommy John surgery late that spring and fell to the third round in 2004. More medical concerns popped up the following year, when he was shut down with biceps tendinitis. Kept on a 60-75 pitch limit throughout 2006, he led the minors in ERA. Lewis' delivery is effortless and extremely deceptive, which helps his 84-88 mph fastball jump on hitters. His curveball rates as the best in the system with true 12-to-6 movement. Lewis' changeup is solid-average, and all of his stuff plays up because of deception and ability to locate his pitches. It remains to be seen how Lewis' below-average velocity will work against more advanced hitters. While his delivery is relatively simple, he sometimes gets out of whack and needs to stay on a direct line to home plate. He throws somewhat across his body, and he has worked on staying more compact with his stride. Lewis bounced back well after all of his starts, and the Indians will increase his pitch limit to 100 in 2007. He'll start the year in Double-A and could move quickly if healthy.

| Year | Club (League) | Class | W | L | ERA | G | GS | CG | SV | IP | H | R | ER | HR | BB | SO | AVG |
|------|---------------|-------|---|---|-----|---|----|----|----|----|---|---|----|----|----|----|-----|
| 2004 | Mahoning Valley (NYP) | A | 0 | 2 | 5.06 | 3 | 3 | 0 | 0 | 5 | 5 | 3 | 3 | 0 | 1 | 13 | .250 |
| 2005 | Mahoning Valley (NYP) | A | 0 | 1 | 4.60 | 7 | 6 | 0 | 0 | 16 | 13 | 8 | 8 | 2 | 6 | 24 | .224 |
| 2006 | Kinston (CL) | A | 3 | 3 | 1.48 | 27 | 26 | 0 | 0 | 116 | 84 | 24 | 19 | 3 | 28 | 123 | .203 |
| **MINOR LEAGUE TOTALS** | | | 3 | 6 | 1.98 | 37 | 35 | 0 | 0 | 137 | 102 | 35 | 30 | 5 | 35 | 160 | .207 |

## 8 BRAD SNYDER
OF

**Born:** May 25, 1982. **B-T:** L-L. **Ht.:** 6-3. **Wt.:** 200. **Drafted:** Ball State, 2003 (1st round). **Signed by:** Bob Mayer/Chuck Ricci.

Snyder led Akron to within a game of the Eastern League title in 2006, topping the Aeros in homers and RBIs. The Indians batted him second and even leadoff, trying to give him more experience working deep counts and taking pitches, but he still ranked 10th in the minors in strikeouts. Like Brian Barton, Snyder has an intriguing power/speed combination. He has a wide base of tools, plus bat speed and above-average arm strength. While he still struck out a lot, his plate discipline did improve as he set a career high in walks. His inability to make consistent contact mutes Snyder's impressive tools, and he'll probably never hit for much of an average. His main task coming into 2006 was to improve his two-strike approach, and while club officials commend his effort, he didn't make progress. Snyder hit .314 with nine of his 18 homers in August, but he still struck out in bunches. He'll compete with trade acquisition Shin-Soo Choo to be Cleveland's right fielder, and the Tribe may have to live with Snyder's whiffs for the tradeoff of his power and speed.

| Year | Club (League) | Class | AVG | G | AB | R | H | 2B | 3B | HR | RBI | BB | SO | SB | OBP | SLG |
|------|---------------|-------|-----|---|----|---|---|----|----|----|-----|----|----|----|-----|-----|
| 2003 | Mahoning Valley (NYP) | A | .284 | 62 | 225 | 52 | 64 | 11 | 6 | 6 | 31 | 41 | 82 | 14 | .393 | .467 |
| 2004 | Lake County (SAL) | A | .280 | 79 | 304 | 52 | 85 | 15 | 5 | 10 | 54 | 48 | 78 | 11 | .382 | .461 |
| | Kinston (CL) | A | .355 | 29 | 110 | 20 | 39 | 7 | 1 | 6 | 21 | 13 | 28 | 4 | .424 | .600 |
| 2005 | Kinston (CL) | A | .278 | 58 | 209 | 36 | 58 | 10 | 2 | 6 | 28 | 24 | 64 | 12 | .365 | .431 |
| | Akron (EL) | AA | .280 | 75 | 304 | 56 | 85 | 21 | 5 | 16 | 54 | 25 | 94 | 5 | .345 | .539 |
| 2006 | Akron (EL) | AA | .270 | 135 | 523 | 86 | 141 | 28 | 5 | 18 | 72 | 62 | 158 | 20 | .351 | .446 |
| **MINOR LEAGUE TOTALS** | | | .282 | 438 | 1675 | 302 | 472 | 92 | 24 | 62 | 260 | 213 | 504 | 66 | .368 | .476 |

## 9 WES HODGES
3B

**Born:** Sept. 14, 1984. **B-T:** R-R. **Ht.:** 6-1. **Wt.:** 205. **Drafted:** Georgia Tech, 2006 (2nd round). **Signed by:** Jerry Jordan.

A natural self-starter, Hodges taught himself to bat lefthanded after a wrist injury as a high school senior and still hit .430. A 13th-round pick by the White Sox in 2003, he opted to go to Georgia Tech and became a three-year starter. Hodges' stock slipped in 2006 due to a mysterious leg injury, finally diagnosed in late May as an early stress fracture. The Indians were able to nab him in the second round and signed him for $1 million. Hodges has advanced plate discipline and shows good power with a fluid line-drive stroke. His excellent hand-eye coordination aids his above-average bat speed, as he's able to make consistent contact with pitches all over the strike zone. He has

soft hands and above-average arm strength. Though he seemed like a shoo-in first-rounder heading into last spring, the injury killed Hodges' range and cost him defensively. The Indians believe he'll have plenty of range for third base and more life in his lower half when he's 100 percent, though he's a below-average runner.  With Andy Marte ahead of him, Hodges has time to get healthy and develop. His bat could force the issue, though, and Hodges may start at and definitely should reach high Class A in his pro debut.

| Year | Club (League) | Class | AVG | G | AB | R | H | 2B | 3B | HR | RBI | BB | SO | SB | OBP | SLG |
|------|---------------|-------|-----|---|----|---|---|----|----|----|-----|----|----|----|-----|-----|
| 2006 | Did not play—Signed 2007 contract | | | | | | | | | | | | | | | |

## 10  DAVID HUFF                                    LHP

**Born:** Aug. 22, 1984. **B-T:** L-L. **Ht.:** 6-2. **Wt.:** 210. **Drafted:** UCLA, 2006 (1st round supplemental). **Signed by:** Vince Sagisi.

Huff spent his college career at three schools, going from UC Irvine to Cypress (Calif.) JC to UCLA. A 19th-round pick of the Phillies in 2005, he turned down a reported $500,000 after a solid summer in the Cape Cod League. That decision paid off, as he got $900,000 as Cleveland's top pick in the 2006 draft. Tribe officials compare Huff to Jeremy Sowers for his ability to command and control his entire arsenal. Another thing the two lefties have in common is fringe-average fastball velocity, as Huff works in the high 80s and tops out at 91. His top pitch is his changeup, which may have been the best changeup in the '06 draft. He uses the same arm action as with his fastball, and it has plus late sink. He has excellent balance in his delivery and creates good deception with his arm angle, especially against lefthanders. Huff also throws a slurvy breaking ball, but it lacks consistent depth and tilt. Without a solid breaker, he has no obvious pitch to combat left-handers. Huff will start his first full season in high Class A. He could move quickly, just as Sowers did, if he adapts well to the pro game and sharpens his breaking ball.

| Year | Club (League) | Class | W | L | ERA | G | GS | CG | SV | IP | H | R | ER | HR | BB | SO | AVG |
|------|---------------|-------|---|---|-----|---|----|----|----|----|---|---|----|----|----|----|-----|
| 2006 | Mahoning Valley (NYP) | A | 0 | 1 | 5.87 | 4 | 4 | 0 | 0 | 8 | 9 | 5 | 5 | 0 | 7 | 8 | .300 |
| **MINOR LEAGUE TOTALS** | | | 0 | 1 | 5.87 | 4 | 4 | 0 | 0 | 8 | 9 | 5 | 5 | 0 | 7 | 8 | .300 |

## 11  RAFAEL PEREZ                                  LHP

**Born:** May 15, 1982. **B-T:** L-L. **Ht.:** 6-3. **Wt.:** 180. **Signed:** Dominican Republic, 2002. **Signed by:** Rene Gayo.

The Indians lacked a dependable lefthanded reliever in 2006, and they gave Perez a chance to fill that role. He acquitted himself well for the most part, but Cleveland eventually returned him to the minors and will try to develop him as a starter. He has flip-flopped between the two roles for the last two seasons. Formerly known as Hanlet Ramirez, Perez has electric stuff. He wasn't overpowering in the majors because he lacked command of his four-seam fastball. When he's on, he can run his four-seamer up to 96 mph, achieve run with his two-seamer and back both versions of his heater up with a put-away slider. It's a late break-er that arrives at 85-87 mph. Perez also has feel for a workable changeup, and the Indians believe it will allow him to eventually become part of their big league rotation. Perez lives in the lower half of the zone, making him a groundball machine. He'll begin 2007 back in Triple-A, where he pitched well out of the bullpen last year.

| Year | Club (League) | Class | W | L | ERA | G | GS | CG | SV | IP | H | R | ER | HR | BB | SO | AVG |
|------|---------------|-------|---|---|------|----|----|----|----|-----|-----|-----|-----|----|-----|-----|------|
| 2002 | Cleveland W (DSL) | R | 7 | 1 | 0.96 | 13 | 13 | 1 | 0 | 75 | 58 | 14 | 8 | 3 | 16 | 81 | .208 |
| 2003 | Burlington (Appy) | R | 9 | 3 | 1.70 | 13 | 12 | 0 | 0 | 69 | 56 | 23 | 13 | 1 | 16 | 63 | .220 |
| 2004 | Lake County (SAL) | A | 7 | 6 | 4.85 | 23 | 22 | 0 | 0 | 115 | 121 | 75 | 62 | 9 | 47 | 99 | .277 |
| | Kinston (CL) | A | 0 | 0 | 11.57 | 1 | 1 | 0 | 0 | 5 | 10 | 6 | 6 | 1 | 2 | 3 | .435 |
| 2005 | Kinston (CL) | A | 8 | 5 | 3.36 | 14 | 14 | 0 | 0 | 78 | 54 | 33 | 29 | 6 | 32 | 48 | .194 |
| | Akron (EL) | AA | 4 | 3 | 1.76 | 15 | 8 | 0 | 1 | 67 | 53 | 22 | 13 | 5 | 12 | 46 | .215 |
| 2006 | Akron (EL) | AA | 4 | 5 | 2.81 | 12 | 12 | 1 | 0 | 67 | 53 | 25 | 21 | 3 | 22 | 53 | .218 |
| | Buffalo (IL) | AAA | 0 | 3 | 2.63 | 13 | 0 | 0 | 0 | 27 | 20 | 11 | 8 | 0 | 8 | 33 | .202 |
| | Cleveland (AL) | MLB | 0 | 0 | 4.38 | 18 | 0 | 0 | 0 | 12 | 10 | 6 | 6 | 2 | 6 | 15 | .204 |
| **MINOR LEAGUE TOTALS** | | | 39 | 26 | 2.86 | 104 | 82 | 2 | 1 | 503 | 425 | 209 | 160 | 28 | 155 | 426 | .228 |
| **MAJOR LEAGUE TOTALS** | | | 0 | 0 | 4.38 | 18 | 0 | 0 | 0 | 12 | 10 | 6 | 6 | 2 | 6 | 15 | .204 |

## 12  SUNG-WEI TSENG                               RHP

**Born:** Dec. 28, 1985. **B-T:** R-R. **Ht.:** 5-11. **Wt.:** 180. **Signed:** Taiwan, 2006. **Signed by:** Jason Lee.

The Indians got active in the Pacific Rim in July, signing Australian shortstop Jason Smit for $350,000 and Tseng for $300,000. Taiwan's top amateur pitcher, Tseng ranked as the fourth-best prospect in the summer Alaska League in 2005. He pitched in the World Baseball

Classic, allowing two earned runs on three hits in just two-thirds of an inning, and finished the year by pitching in the Intercontinental Cup. Taiwan, the host nation, worked him hard, pitching him a team-high 14 innings over four games in nine days. Tseng earned a victory in relief against Cuba. Tseng pounds the bottom of the zone with a 90-93 mph fastball that touches 95. He's aggressive, and has good control of his fastball, slider and splitter. His splitter might be his biggest asset, featuring tight, downward spiral with explosion straight down in the strike zone at home plate. His slider has consistent shape and depth, though he tends to get around it at times. Still just 21, Tseng repeats his compact delivery well. He should make his pro debut in the low Class A Lake County rotation this year.

| Year | Club (League) | Class | W | L | ERA | G | GS | CG | SV | IP | H | R | ER | HR | BB | SO | AVG |
|------|---------------|-------|---|---|-----|---|----|----|----|----|---|---|----|----|----|----|-----|

Did Not Play—Signed 2007 Contract

## 13  J.D. MARTIN
RHP

**Born:** Jan. 2, 1983. **B-T:** R-R. **Ht.:** 6-4. **Wt.:** 190. **Drafted:** HS—Ridgecrest, Calif., 2001 (1st round supplemental). **Signed by:** Jason Smith.

Martin was one of three high school pitchers the Indians took in the first and supplemental first rounds of the 2001 draft, and despite a now-lengthy medical history, he represents Cleveland's best hope among the trio. Dan Denham has had little success in the upper minors, while the Tribe failed to sign Alan Horne, who's now in the Yankees system. Martin was shut down in 2003 with a strained elbow ligament and initially avoided surgery, but he needed to have his elbow reconstructed after opening 2005 with a dominant 10-start stretch in Double-A. Martin didn't return until mid-June 2006, and when he did, several club officials said he was more of a complete pitcher than he was before he had Tommy John surgery. Martin jumped to Kinston for its Carolina League stretch run, piggybacking starts with lefthander Scott Lewis and helping the K-Tribe to their second championship in three years. He made two more appearances out of the pen in the Eastern League playoffs, allowing just two hits and striking out six in six innings. Martin's fastball velocity is back in the 90-91 mph range. While many pitchers have control issues when they return from Tommy John surgery, Martin showed excellent command of his cutter, 12-to-6 curveball, slider and changeup in his return. The Indians attribute Martin's resurgence to the better body awareness he learned during his rehab. Martin will be monitored closely in his return to Double-A this year and could move quickly if he proves healthy.

| Year | Club (League) | Class | W | L | ERA | G | GS | CG | SV | IP | H | R | ER | HR | BB | SO | AVG |
|------|---------------|-------|---|---|-----|---|----|----|----|----|---|---|----|----|----|----|-----|
| 2001 | Burlington (Appy) | R | 5 | 1 | 1.38 | 10 | 10 | 0 | 0 | 46 | 26 | 9 | 7 | 3 | 11 | 72 | .164 |
| 2002 | Columbus (SAL) | A | 14 | 5 | 3.90 | 27 | 26 | 0 | 0 | 138 | 141 | 76 | 60 | 12 | 46 | 131 | .266 |
| 2003 | Kinston (CL) | A | 5 | 3 | 4.27 | 16 | 16 | 0 | 0 | 86 | 95 | 50 | 41 | 7 | 30 | 57 | .281 |
| 2004 | Buffalo (IL) | AAA | 0 | 0 | 10.80 | 1 | 1 | 0 | 0 | 5 | 9 | 6 | 6 | 1 | 2 | 2 | .375 |
|  | Kinston (CL) | A | 11 | 10 | 4.39 | 25 | 25 | 2 | 0 | 148 | 139 | 75 | 72 | 15 | 41 | 98 | .258 |
| 2005 | Akron (EL) | AA | 3 | 1 | 2.38 | 10 | 10 | 0 | 0 | 57 | 42 | 17 | 15 | 3 | 8 | 63 | .201 |
| 2006 | Mahoning Valley (NYP) | A | 0 | 1 | 1.50 | 6 | 6 | 0 | 0 | 18 | 11 | 3 | 3 | 1 | 1 | 13 | .169 |
|  | Lake County (SAL) | A | 0 | 1 | 4.20 | 5 | 5 | 0 | 0 | 15 | 13 | 7 | 7 | 2 | 3 | 16 | .241 |
|  | Kinston (CL) | A | 1 | 0 | 0.00 | 3 | 2 | 0 | 0 | 11 | 6 | 0 | 0 | 0 | 1 | 11 | .154 |
| **MINOR LEAGUE TOTALS** | | | 39 | 22 | 3.62 | 103 | 101 | 2 | 0 | 524 | 482 | 243 | 211 | 44 | 143 | 463 | .246 |

## 14  JUAN LARA
LHP

**Born:** Jan. 26, 1981. **B-T:** R-L. **Ht.:** 6-2. **Wt.:** 190. **Signed:** Dominican Republic, 1999. **Signed by:** Rene Gayo/Josue Herrera/Claudio Brito.

One of the more interesting development stories in the system, Lara signed out of the Dominican Republic for $10,000 as a 17-year-old in 1999. He spent three seasons in the Rookie-level Dominican Summer League and didn't make his U.S. debut until 2002. He spent his first two years in the States as a starter before moving to the bullpen full-time in 2004, when he also reached full-season ball for good. Lara is a resilient and durable, repeating his delivery well and topping out at 94 mph with his fastball. He sits at 90-92 with his heater, and he throws a wipeout 83-84 mph slider from a three-quarters angle. Some Tribe officials believe he can be more than a lefty specialist, as his changeup emerged as a legitimate weapon against righthanders in Double-A. If Lara continues to command his changeup, he could earn a setup spot in Cleveland's bullpen in 2007. If not, he still could be valuable in left-on-left matchups.

| Year | Club (League) | Class | W | L | ERA | G | GS | CG | SV | IP | H | R | ER | HR | BB | SO | AVG |
|------|---------------|-------|---|---|-----|---|----|----|----|----|---|---|----|----|----|----|-----|
| 1999 | Cleveland (DSL) | R | 1 | 0 | 4.05 | 4 | 0 | 0 | 0 | 7 | 7 | 3 | 3 | 1 | 4 | 3 | .280 |
| 2000 | Cleveland (DSL) | R | 4 | 1 | 3.31 | 12 | 10 | 0 | 1 | 54 | 58 | 29 | 20 | 1 | 15 | 51 | .269 |
| 2001 | Cleveland (DSL) | R | 3 | 5 | 1.80 | 13 | 12 | 0 | 0 | 65 | 57 | 28 | 13 | 0 | 10 | 49 | .230 |
| 2002 | Burlington (Appy) | R | 2 | 6 | 4.98 | 14 | 14 | 0 | 0 | 65 | 67 | 42 | 36 | 4 | 28 | 50 | .275 |

| | | | | | | | | | | | | | | | | | |
|---|---|---|---|---|---|---|---|---|---|---|---|---|---|---|---|---|---|
| 2003 | Lake County (SAL) | A | 1 | 4 | 5.00 | 16 | 3 | 0 | 1 | 45 | 51 | 31 | 25 | 7 | 26 | 37 | .279 |
| | Mahoning Valley (NYP) | A | 3 | 3 | 3.50 | 12 | 12 | 0 | 0 | 62 | 54 | 29 | 24 | 4 | 18 | 54 | .235 |
| 2004 | Kinston (CL) | A | 4 | 3 | 5.66 | 35 | 8 | 0 | 1 | 84 | 106 | 60 | 53 | 6 | 38 | 74 | .308 |
| 2005 | Kinston (CL) | A | 0 | 1 | 4.04 | 26 | 0 | 0 | 0 | 42 | 40 | 22 | 19 | 4 | 15 | 46 | .244 |
| | Akron (EL) | AA | 1 | 2 | 4.56 | 18 | 0 | 0 | 5 | 24 | 27 | 15 | 12 | 1 | 14 | 16 | .290 |
| 2006 | Akron (EL) | AA | 4 | 2 | 2.70 | 40 | 0 | 0 | 7 | 47 | 32 | 14 | 14 | 2 | 21 | 48 | .189 |
| | Buffalo (IL) | AAA | 1 | 1 | 3.00 | 13 | 0 | 0 | 1 | 15 | 17 | 6 | 5 | 1 | 3 | 15 | .279 |
| | Cleveland (AL) | MLB | 0 | 0 | 1.80 | 9 | 0 | 0 | 0 | 5 | 4 | 2 | 1 | 0 | 1 | 2 | .222 |
| **MINOR LEAGUE TOTALS** | | | 24 | 28 | 3.96 | 203 | 59 | 0 | 16 | 510 | 516 | 279 | 224 | 31 | 192 | 443 | .261 |
| **MAJOR LEAGUE TOTALS** | | | 0 | 0 | 1.80 | 9 | 0 | 0 | 0 | 5 | 4 | 2 | 1 | 0 | 1 | 2 | .222 |

## 15 ASDRUBAL CABRERA                                   SS

**Born:** Nov. 13, 1985. **B-T:** B-R. **Ht.:** 6-0. **Wt.:** 170. **Signed:** Venezuela, 2002. **Signed by:** Emilio Carrasquel (Mariners).

The Indians expected to contend in 2006, and when they didn't, they made a pair of profitable midseason deals with the Mariners. Cleveland sent its first-base platoon of Ben Broussard and Eduardo Perez to Seattle in exchange for Cabrera (who came over straight up for Perez), right fielder Shin-Soo Choo and lefty Shawn Nottingham. The Mariners moved Cabrera quickly, promoting him to Triple-A in 2005—his first year in full-season ball. He stayed at that level as a 20-year-old in 2006 and batted just .249—37 points below his previous career average. Cabrera won't be an offensive force, but he's a switch-hitter with some bat control and a whole-field approach. His speed is just average, and he doesn't have standout ability in terms of power, basestealing or on-base ability. Defense is Cabrera's forte. His soft hands and above-average arm are his biggest assets. He's stationary in his setup, lacks first-step quickness and has long actions, leaving him with fringe-average range at shortstop and in line to possibly move to second base down the road. Though the Tribe has questions about its middle infield, Cabrera needs to repeat Triple-A this year.

| Year | Club (League) | Class | AVG | G | AB | R | H | 2B | 3B | HR | RBI | BB | SO | SB | OBP | SLG |
|---|---|---|---|---|---|---|---|---|---|---|---|---|---|---|---|---|
| 2003 | Aguirre (VSL) | R | .283 | 55 | 198 | 31 | 56 | 12 | 4 | 0 | 29 | 16 | 31 | 5 | .367 | .384 |
| 2004 | Everett (NWL) | A | .272 | 63 | 239 | 44 | 65 | 16 | 3 | 5 | 41 | 21 | 43 | 7 | .330 | .427 |
| 2005 | Wisconsin (MID) | A | .318 | 51 | 192 | 26 | 61 | 12 | 3 | 4 | 30 | 30 | 32 | 2 | .407 | .474 |
| | Inland Empire (CAL) | A | .284 | 55 | 225 | 31 | 64 | 15 | 6 | 1 | 26 | 15 | 47 | 3 | .325 | .418 |
| | Tacoma (PCL) | AAA | .217 | 6 | 23 | 4 | 5 | 0 | 1 | 0 | 3 | 1 | 4 | 0 | .250 | .304 |
| 2006 | Buffalo (IL) | AAA | .263 | 52 | 190 | 26 | 50 | 11 | 0 | 1 | 14 | 8 | 39 | 5 | .295 | .337 |
| | Tacoma (PCL) | AAA | .236 | 60 | 203 | 27 | 48 | 12 | 2 | 3 | 22 | 24 | 51 | 7 | .323 | .360 |
| **MINOR LEAGUE TOTALS** | | | .275 | 342 | 1270 | 189 | 349 | 78 | 19 | 14 | 165 | 115 | 247 | 29 | .340 | .399 |

## 16 MATT McBRIDE                                   C

**Born:** May 23, 1985. **B-T:** R-R. **Ht.:** 6-3. **Wt.:** 205. **Drafted:** Lehigh, 2006 (2nd round supplemental). **Signed by:** Brent Urcheck.

The Indians' catching depth improved greatly in 2006, as they drafted McBride, traded for Kelly Shoppach and Max Ramirez and saw significant improvement from their previous top in-house candidate, Wyatt Toregas. After bouncing back from some tightness in his shoulder, the athletic McBride climbed draft boards last spring. He won Patriot League MVP honors after capturing the conference triple crown with .417-12-61 numbers. A supplemental second-round pick, he signed for $445,000. McBride has a strong work ethic and his makeup is off the charts. His father George spent time before or after every practice at Lehigh throwing him batting practice for an extra hour. That continued when McBride returned home from short-season Mahoning Valley for five days before reporting to instructional league. He produces above-average power with natural leverage and loft to his swing. He also makes good contact and controls the strike zone, which should enable him to hit for average. He's more athletic and runs better than most catchers. While McBride has solid-average arm strength, he needs to improve as a receiver and refine his game-calling skills. There's no question McBride bolsters the improved contingent at catcher in the system, but he has a long way to go to add defensive polish. He'll start his first full season in low Class A.

| Year | Club (League) | Class | AVG | G | AB | R | H | 2B | 3B | HR | RBI | BB | SO | SB | OBP | SLG |
|---|---|---|---|---|---|---|---|---|---|---|---|---|---|---|---|---|
| 2006 | Mahoning Valley (NYP) | A | .272 | 52 | 184 | 24 | 50 | 12 | 0 | 4 | 31 | 16 | 22 | 5 | .355 | .402 |
| **MINOR LEAGUE TOTALS** | | | .272 | 52 | 184 | 24 | 50 | 12 | 0 | 4 | 31 | 16 | 22 | 5 | .355 | .402 |

## 17 BRIAN SLOCUM                                   RHP

**Born:** March 27, 1981. **B-T:** R-R. **Ht.:** 6-4. **Wt.:** 200. **Drafted:** Villanova, 2002 (2nd round). **Signed by:** Phil Rossi.

Slocum quickly became one of the system's top righthanders after signing as a second-round pick in 2002, but inconsistency and his inability made him appear to be nothing

more than organizational fodder. He got back on track in the Arizona Fall League after the 2005 season, flourishing in the bullpen and attacking hitters aggressively. Slocum continued to have success in Triple-A last year, though he was hit hard in the majors. Still, 2006 was a breakthrough for him, as Slocum made adjustments and saw his overall arsenal improve. His fastball jumped to 91-94 mph and at times touched 96. He also showed a better feel for his low-80 slurvy breaking ball. He also has a workable changeup, though he needs to add depth and be more consistent with his release point if he's going to stick in the rotation for good. He had difficulty in the big leagues because he nibbled and worked too methodically while worrying too much about pacing himself and trying to keep hitters off balance. He'll probably start 2007 in the Triple-A rotation.

| Year | Club (League) | Class | W | L | ERA | G | GS | CG | SV | IP | H | R | ER | HR | BB | SO | AVG |
|------|---------------|-------|---|---|-----|---|----|----|----|-----|-----|-----|-----|----|-----|-----|------|
| 2002 | Mahoning Valley (NYP) | A | 5 | 2 | 2.60 | 11 | 11 | 0 | 0 | 55 | 47 | 19 | 16 | 1 | 14 | 48 | .230 |
| 2003 | Kinston (CL) | A | 6 | 7 | 4.46 | 22 | 21 | 0 | 1 | 107 | 112 | 61 | 53 | 7 | 41 | 66 | .266 |
| 2004 | Kinston (CL) | A | 15 | 6 | 4.33 | 25 | 25 | 2 | 0 | 135 | 136 | 66 | 65 | 13 | 41 | 102 | .267 |
| 2005 | Akron (EL) | AA | 7 | 5 | 4.40 | 21 | 18 | 1 | 0 | 102 | 98 | 52 | 50 | 9 | 36 | 95 | .255 |
| 2006 | Buffalo (IL) | AAA | 6 | 3 | 3.35 | 27 | 15 | 0 | 1 | 94 | 78 | 42 | 35 | 5 | 37 | 91 | .227 |
|  | Cleveland (AL) | MLB | 0 | 0 | 5.60 | 8 | 2 | 0 | 0 | 18 | 27 | 11 | 11 | 3 | 9 | 11 | .360 |
| **MINOR LEAGUE TOTALS** | | | 39 | 23 | 3.99 | 106 | 90 | 3 | 2 | 494 | 471 | 240 | 219 | 35 | 169 | 402 | .253 |
| **MAJOR LEAGUE TOTALS** | | | 0 | 0 | 5.60 | 8 | 2 | 0 | 0 | 17 | 27 | 11 | 11 | 3 | 9 | 11 | .360 |

## 18   EDWARD MUJICA              RHP

**Born:** May 10, 1984. **B-T:** R-R. **Ht.:** 6-2. **Wt.:** 220. **Signed:** Venezuela, 2001. **Signed by:** Rene Gayo/Luis Aponte.

Another of former international scouting director Rene Gayo's finds, Mujica signed for $30,000 in 2001. He strained his elbow during his debut in the Rookie-level Venezuelan Summer League, but it didn't cost him much development time. Used primarily as a starter during his first two years in the United States, he took off after becoming a full-time closer in 2005. He hasn't posted an ERA higher than 2.95 at any of his stops since—including 10 appearances with Cleveland in 2006. He didn't allow an earned run until June 24 last year, a span of 38⅔ innings. Mujica works quickly and aggressively, pounding the strike zone with a 92-95 mph fastball. He's still fine-tuning his secondary pitches, however. His 86-87 mph slider regressed in 2006, as he had trouble finding a consistent release point, leading it to flatten out. He has added a splitter that has the makings of a plus pitch, but it still needs work. With the Indians rebuilding their bullpen, Mujica could play a significant role in 2007 if he finds better command of his complementary pitches.

| Year | Club (League) | Class | W | L | ERA | G | GS | CG | SV | IP | H | R | ER | HR | BB | SO | AVG |
|------|---------------|-------|---|---|-----|---|----|----|----|-----|-----|-----|-----|----|-----|-----|------|
| 2002 | San Felipe (VSL) | R | 2 | 0 | 1.78 | 10 | 5 | 0 | 1 | 30 | 22 | 7 | 6 | 0 | 5 | 18 | .202 |
| 2003 | Burlington (Appy) | R | 2 | 6 | 4.37 | 14 | 10 | 0 | 0 | 56 | 57 | 31 | 27 | 3 | 20 | 41 | .275 |
| 2004 | Lake County (SAL) | A | 7 | 7 | 4.65 | 26 | 19 | 1 | 2 | 124 | 130 | 77 | 64 | 18 | 32 | 89 | .278 |
| 2005 | Kinston (CL) | A | 1 | 0 | 2.08 | 25 | 0 | 0 | 14 | 26 | 17 | 6 | 6 | 3 | 2 | 32 | .183 |
|  | Akron (EL) | AA | 2 | 1 | 2.88 | 27 | 0 | 0 | 10 | 34 | 36 | 11 | 11 | 2 | 5 | 33 | .273 |
| 2006 | Akron (EL) | AA | 1 | 0 | 0.00 | 12 | 0 | 0 | 8 | 19 | 11 | 1 | 0 | 0 | 9 | 17 | .169 |
|  | Buffalo (IL) | AAA | 3 | 1 | 2.48 | 22 | 0 | 0 | 5 | 33 | 31 | 10 | 9 | 1 | 5 | 29 | .258 |
|  | Cleveland (AL) | MLB | 0 | 1 | 2.95 | 10 | 0 | 0 | 0 | 18 | 25 | 6 | 6 | 1 | 0 | 12 | .333 |
| **MINOR LEAGUE TOTALS** | | | 18 | 15 | 3.44 | 136 | 34 | 1 | 40 | 322 | 304 | 143 | 123 | 27 | 78 | 259 | .255 |
| **MAJOR LEAGUE TOTALS** | | | 0 | 1 | 2.95 | 10 | 0 | 0 | 0 | 18 | 25 | 6 | 6 | 1 | 0 | 12 | .333 |

## 19   KELLY SHOPPACH              C

**Born:** April 29, 1980. **B-T:** R-R. **Ht.:** 6-1. **Wt.:** 210. **Drafted:** Baylor, 2001 (2nd round). **Signed by:** Jim Robinson (Red Sox).

The Red Sox made Shoppach their top pick (second round) in the 2001 draft and always thought highly of him. But he was eternally blocked by Jason Varitek, so Boston included him in a trade for Coco Crisp in January 2006. Shoppach immediately became the most polished defensive catcher in the Indians system. However, he hasn't found a clear shot at big league playing time in Cleveland. Victor Martinez is an all-star catcher, and Shoppach spent most of last season in the majors but got just 110 at-bats. He has slightly above-average, pull-side power and adjusted his approach in 2006, shortening his stroke and making more consistent contact. But he'll still get stiff and muscular with his swing and strike out in bunches, so he'll never hit for a high average. Shoppach is more well-rounded behind the plate. He controls the running game, is a solid receiver and has excellent leadership skills. Martinez has struggled behind the plate, so Shoppach's catching skills and righthanded pop could earn him more playing time in Cleveland this year.

| Year | Club (League) | Class | AVG | G | AB | R | H | 2B | 3B | HR | RBI | BB | SO | SB | OBP | SLG |
|------|---------------|-------|-----|---|----|---|---|----|----|----|-----|----|----|----|-----|-----|
| 2002 | Sarasota (FSL) | A | .271 | 116 | 414 | 54 | 112 | 35 | 1 | 10 | 66 | 59 | 112 | 2 | .369 | .432 |

| Year | Club (League) | Class | AVG | G | AB | R | H | 2B | 3B | HR | RBI | BB | SO | SB | OBP | SLG |
|---|---|---|---|---|---|---|---|---|---|---|---|---|---|---|---|---|
| 2003 | Portland (EL) | AA | .282 | 92 | 340 | 45 | 96 | 30 | 2 | 12 | 60 | 35 | 83 | 0 | .353 | .488 |
| 2004 | Pawtucket (IL) | AAA | .233 | 113 | 399 | 62 | 93 | 25 | 0 | 22 | 64 | 46 | 138 | 0 | .320 | .461 |
| 2005 | Pawtucket (IL) | AAA | .253 | 102 | 371 | 60 | 94 | 16 | 0 | 26 | 75 | 46 | 116 | 0 | .352 | .507 |
| | Boston (AL) | MLB | .000 | 9 | 15 | 1 | 0 | 0 | 0 | 0 | 0 | 0 | 7 | 0 | .063 | .000 |
| 2006 | Buffalo (IL) | AAA | .282 | 21 | 78 | 11 | 22 | 8 | 0 | 4 | 9 | 6 | 25 | 0 | .356 | .538 |
| | Cleveland (AL) | MLB | .245 | 41 | 110 | 7 | 27 | 6 | 0 | 3 | 16 | 8 | 45 | 0 | .297 | .382 |
| **MINOR LEAGUE TOTALS** | | | .260 | 444 | 1602 | 232 | 417 | 114 | 3 | 74 | 274 | 192 | 474 | 2 | .349 | .474 |
| **MAJOR LEAGUE TOTALS** | | | .216 | 50 | 125 | 8 | 27 | 6 | 0 | 3 | 16 | 8 | 52 | 0 | .269 | .336 |

## 20 WYATT TOREGAS — C

**Born:** Dec. 2, 1982. **B-T:** R-R. **Ht.:** 5-11. **Wt.:** 200. **Drafted:** Virginia Tech, 2004 (24th round). **Signed by:** Bob Mayer.

Toregas was one of the system's most improved players last year, vaulting himself from an afterthought to the top of the catcher depth chart when Kelly Shoppach was promoted to the big leagues in June. Toregas had a solid pro debut with the bat in 2004, then took a step backward offensively in 2005 as he honed his game-calling and receiving skills. He was the complete package in 2006, hitting for average and power with tremendous improvement defensively, and the Indians now believe that he has a higher ceiling than Shoppach. Toregas has a line-drive stroke and uses the whole field effectively, showing good opposite-field pop. He can become pull-oriented and his swing can get too long at times. His speed is well below-average. Toregas has solid catch-and-throw skills. With a strong, accurate arm and a quick release, he posts consistent 1.85 pop times to second base. He led the Carolina League by throwing out 48 percent of basestealers last year and erased 38 percent after his promotion to Double-A. Toregas' bat cooled off after he got to Akron, so while he'll get a long look in big league camp, he'll probably open 2007 in the minors.

| Year | Club (League) | Class | AVG | G | AB | R | H | 2B | 3B | HR | RBI | BB | SO | SB | OBP | SLG |
|---|---|---|---|---|---|---|---|---|---|---|---|---|---|---|---|---|
| 2004 | Mahoning Valley (NYP) | A | .294 | 59 | 214 | 38 | 63 | 18 | 1 | 7 | 48 | 11 | 26 | 1 | .338 | .486 |
| 2005 | Lake County (SAL) | A | .231 | 104 | 411 | 57 | 95 | 22 | 0 | 5 | 42 | 37 | 76 | 0 | .302 | .321 |
| 2006 | Akron (EL) | AA | .258 | 48 | 163 | 21 | 42 | 10 | 0 | 4 | 29 | 14 | 33 | 1 | .319 | .393 |
| | Kinston (CL) | A | .336 | 44 | 146 | 25 | 49 | 14 | 0 | 4 | 23 | 20 | 28 | 0 | .418 | .514 |
| **MINOR LEAGUE TOTALS** | | | .267 | 255 | 934 | 141 | 249 | 64 | 1 | 20 | 142 | 82 | 163 | 2 | .332 | .401 |

## 21 MAX RAMIREZ — C

**Born:** Oct. 11, 1984. **B-T:** R-R. **Ht.:** 6-0. **Wt.:** 175. **Signed:** Venezuela, 2002. **Signed by:** Rolando Petit (Braves).

The Indians dealt Bob Wickman to the Braves for Ramirez in June, further improving their depth at catcher—though there are questions about his ability to stay behind the plate in the long term. Signed as a third baseman, Ramirez moved behind the plate in 2005, when he was named co-MVP in the Rookie-level Appalachian League. Though he has an average arm, he threw out just 28 percent of basestealers last year. Ramirez lacks quick feet, slowing down his release. He's a below-average receiver. He actually saw more time at DH than catcher in 2006, going behind the plate for just 57 of his 117 games. Ramirez' bat will have to carry him. He has a line-drive stroke that produces gap power, and he uses the entire field well. He has above-average plate discipline and pitch recognition, and he does a good job of sitting back on breaking balls. Some club officials believe his ceiling could be as a utility player along the lines of Olmedo Saenz, with the ability to play both infield corners and serve as a third catcher.

| Year | Club (League) | Class | AVG | G | AB | R | H | 2B | 3B | HR | RBI | BB | SO | SB | OBP | SLG |
|---|---|---|---|---|---|---|---|---|---|---|---|---|---|---|---|---|
| 2003 | Braves (DSL) | R | .305 | 52 | 177 | 27 | 54 | 16 | 1 | 5 | 43 | 20 | 27 | 5 | .386 | .492 |
| 2004 | Braves (GCL) | R | .275 | 57 | 204 | 20 | 56 | 16 | 1 | 8 | 35 | 19 | 50 | 1 | .339 | .480 |
| 2005 | Danville (Appy) | R | .347 | 63 | 239 | 45 | 83 | 19 | 0 | 8 | 47 | 31 | 41 | 1 | .424 | .527 |
| 2006 | Lake County (SAL) | A | .307 | 37 | 127 | 19 | 39 | 6 | 1 | 4 | 26 | 30 | 27 | 0 | .435 | .465 |
| | Rome (SAL) | A | .285 | 80 | 267 | 50 | 76 | 17 | 0 | 9 | 37 | 54 | 72 | 2 | .408 | .449 |
| **MINOR LEAGUE TOTALS** | | | .304 | 289 | 1014 | 161 | 308 | 74 | 3 | 34 | 188 | 154 | 217 | 9 | .398 | .483 |

## 22 AARON LAFFEY — LHP

**Born:** April 15, 1985. **B-T:** L-L. **Ht.:** 6-0. **Wt.:** 180. **Drafted:** HS—Allegany, Md., 2003 (16th round). **Signed by:** Bob Mayer.

Laffey didn't allow an earned run in 44 innings as a high school senior, but he had a commitment to Virginia Tech and area scouts perceived that he wouldn't sign if he didn't go in the top 75 picks. The Indians took a flier on him in the 16th round (468th overall) and signed him for $363,000. Laffey was on the fast track after his debut at Rookie-level Burlington, where he was more overpowering than more heralded teammates Adam Miller, Rafael Perez and Nick Pesco. But Laffey struggled the next two seasons, particularly with the command of his secondary pitches, before bouncing back in 2006. When he's on, Laffey is

a groundball machine. He had a 2.4-1 ground-fly ratio last year, working mostly with an 86-89 mph sinker and an improving slider. He's still trying to find a consistent release point with his slider. Laffey's changeup is also a work in progress. He has a feel for it, but needs to find a comfortable grip in order to command it more effectively. If Laffey can harness his changeup, he could remain in the rotation. If not, he'll be a bullpen lefty. He could open the season in the Triple-A rotation as a 21-year-old.

| Year | Club (League) | Class | W | L | ERA | G | GS | CG | SV | IP | H | R | ER | HR | BB | SO | AVG |
|------|---------------|-------|---|---|-----|---|----|----|----|----|---|---|----|----|----|----|-----|
| 2003 | Burlington (Appy) | R | 3 | 1 | 2.91 | 9 | 4 | 0 | 0 | 34 | 22 | 13 | 11 | 0 | 15 | 46 | .183 |
| 2004 | Lake County (SAL) | A | 3 | 7 | 6.53 | 19 | 15 | 0 | 1 | 73 | 79 | 58 | 53 | 6 | 44 | 67 | .274 |
| | Mahoning Valley (NYP) | A | 3 | 1 | 1.24 | 8 | 8 | 0 | 0 | 44 | 38 | 15 | 6 | 1 | 10 | 30 | .229 |
| 2005 | Lake County (SAL) | A | 7 | 7 | 3.22 | 25 | 23 | 1 | 1 | 142 | 123 | 62 | 51 | 5 | 52 | 69 | .239 |
| | Akron (EL) | AA | 1 | 0 | 3.60 | 1 | 1 | 0 | 0 | 5 | 8 | 2 | 2 | 0 | 2 | 6 | .364 |
| 2006 | Kinston (CL) | A | 4 | 1 | 2.18 | 10 | 4 | 1 | 1 | 41 | 38 | 16 | 10 | 0 | 6 | 24 | .241 |
| | Akron (EL) | AA | 8 | 3 | 3.53 | 19 | 19 | 0 | 0 | 112 | 121 | 50 | 44 | 9 | 33 | 61 | .286 |
| **MINOR LEAGUE TOTALS** | | | 29 | 20 | 3.53 | 91 | 74 | 2 | 3 | 452 | 429 | 216 | 177 | 21 | 162 | 303 | .254 |

## 23 JOSH RODRIGUEZ
SS

**Born:** Dec. 18, 1984. **B-T:** R-R. **Ht.:** 6-0. **Wt.:** 180. **Drafted:** Rice, 2006 (2nd round). **Signed by:** Les Pajari.

Rodriguez entered 2006 as one of the best college shortstop prospects in the draft, but elbow problems limited him to DH early on. When he returned to the field, sophomore Brian Friday had claimed the shortstop job, so Rodriguez moved to third base for an Owls team that finished third at the College World Series. After he signed for $625,000 as a second-round pick, the Indians kept him at shortstop and will keep him there as long as possible. Area scouts were skeptical that his slightly below-average speed would not allow him to play anything more than second or third base. Rodriguez gets good plate coverage and has natural leverage in his compact swing. He has a penchant for drawing walks in college, though he didn't control the strike zone as well in his pro debut. Some club officials liken Rodriguez to John Valentin, with the ability to play anywhere on the infield while producing righthanded power. Rodriguez has enough arm to play shortstop, but his actions are long at times and he lacks first-step explosion going into the hole for balls. He'll likely start his first full season in high Class A.

| Year | Club (League) | Class | AVG | G | AB | R | H | 2B | 3B | HR | RBI | BB | SO | SB | OBP | SLG |
|------|---------------|-------|-----|---|----|---|---|----|----|----|-----|----|----|----|-----|-----|
| 2006 | Mahoning Valley (NYP) | A | .268 | 45 | 157 | 26 | 42 | 11 | 4 | 4 | 24 | 14 | 33 | 2 | .337 | .465 |
| **MINOR LEAGUE TOTALS** | | | .268 | 45 | 157 | 26 | 42 | 11 | 4 | 4 | 24 | 14 | 33 | 2 | .337 | .465 |

## 24 JORDAN BROWN
OF

**Born:** Dec. 18, 1983. **B-T:** L-L. **Ht.:** 6-0. **Wt.:** 205. **Drafted:** Arizona, 2005 (4th round). **Signed by:** Joe Graham.

Brown went undrafted in high school but improved his stock each season at Arizona, drawing comparisons to Wally Joyner for his aggressive approach and solid lefthanded bat. He finished third in the 2004 Cape Cod League batting race at .318, and led the Pacific-10 Conference with 80 RBIs in 2005, when the Indians made him a fourth-round pick. He played in the Kinston outfield with Wildcats teammate Trevor Crowe in 2006 and came into his own after Crowe left for Double-A. Brown batted .316 with eight homers over the final two months en route to leading the Carolina League in RBIs and total bases (222) and winning MVP honors. He has plenty of natural strength, though he doesn't hit for a corresponding amount of power because he has just average bat speed and gets too pull conscious. He's very disciplined and may wind up hitting for average, getting on base and providing doubles rather than becoming a true home run threat. More of a first baseman in college, Brown has earned kudos from the Indians for moving to left field and doing an adequate job there. His speed is below-average and his arm is ordinary, but he manages to get the job done. Brown may not have the home run power teams want in a left fielder, so he projects as more of a reserve at this point. He'll move up to Double-A in 2007.

| Year | Club (League) | Class | AVG | G | AB | R | H | 2B | 3B | HR | RBI | BB | SO | SB | OBP | SLG |
|------|---------------|-------|-----|---|----|---|---|----|----|----|-----|----|----|----|-----|-----|
| 2005 | Mahoning Valley (NYP) | A | .253 | 19 | 75 | 15 | 19 | 1 | 0 | 3 | 7 | 3 | 7 | 2 | .291 | .387 |
| 2006 | Kinston (CL) | A | .290 | 125 | 473 | 71 | 137 | 26 | 7 | 15 | 87 | 51 | 59 | 4 | .362 | .469 |
| **MINOR LEAGUE TOTALS** | | | .285 | 144 | 548 | 86 | 156 | 27 | 7 | 18 | 94 | 54 | 66 | 6 | .352 | .458 |

## 25 JENSEN LEWIS
RHP

**Born:** Sept. 26, 1983. **B-T:** R-R. **Ht.:** 6-0. **Wt.:** 180. **Drafted:** Vanderbilt, 2005 (3rd round). **Signed by:** Scott Barnsby.

Lewis was drafted twice by the Tribe, first in the 33rd round out of high school in 2002

and then in the third round after he spent three years at Vanderbilt. He saw his fastball spike slightly into the low 90s in his pro debut that sat comfortably at his previous 88-91 mph last season. He does a good job of changing speeds with his fastball and of locating it all over the strike zone. Lewis' changeup is among the best in the organization, with good depth and fade, and he throws it with the same easy arm action as his fastball. He struggled with the command of his slider early in 2006 and wound up scrapping it altogether. He replaced it with a looping curveball, which gives him another look and helps him expand the zone vertically. Though he's mechanically sound, Lewis tends to rush his delivery. When he does, his arm drags and he loses leverage, leaving pitches up in the zone. Used as a starter over his first two seasons, Lewis is expected to move to the bullpen in Double-A this year.

| Year | Club (League) | Class | W | L | ERA | G | GS | CG | SV | IP | H | R | ER | HR | BB | SO | AVG |
|------|---------------|-------|---|---|-----|---|----|----|----|----|----|----|----|----|----|----|-----|
| 2005 | Mahoning Valley (NYP) | A | 4 | 2 | 3.20 | 13 | 11 | 0 | 0 | 59 | 58 | 24 | 21 | 6 | 11 | 59 | .253 |
| 2006 | Kinston (CL) | A | 7 | 6 | 3.99 | 21 | 20 | 0 | 0 | 108 | 110 | 59 | 48 | 11 | 29 | 94 | .261 |
| | Akron (EL) | AA | 1 | 2 | 3.89 | 7 | 7 | 0 | 0 | 39 | 41 | 21 | 17 | 4 | 12 | 44 | .270 |
| **MINOR LEAGUE TOTALS** | | | 12 | 10 | 3.75 | 41 | 38 | 0 | 0 | 207 | 209 | 104 | 86 | 21 | 52 | 197 | .261 |

## 26 JOSE CONSTANZA                                                          OF

**Born:** Sept. 1, 1983. **B-T:** B-L. **Ht.:** 5-9. **Wt.:** 160. **Signed:** Dominican Republic, 2003. **Signed by:** Rene Gayo/Josue Herrera.

The Indians thought Constanza was 16 when they nearly signed him in 2003 for $40,000. When they discovered that he was actually three years older, they got him for $5,000. A switch-hitter with a short, compact stroke from both sides of the plate, Constanza commands the strike zone well, working deep counts and seldom giving at-bats away. His best tool is his plus speed, and he swiped 39 bases in 47 attempts last year. Scouts who saw him in the Carolina League compared him to former big league outfielder Luis Polonia for his slap-and-run approach. Constanza needs to sharpen up his bunting skills, though he has a knack for finding a hole in the defense and getting on base. While he played mostly right field in 2006, he has fringe-average arm strength and likely will wind up in left field. Though he's quick, he hasn't shown the instincts to play regularly in center field. Constanza profiles as a fourth outfielder and will advance to Double-A this season.

| Year | Club (League) | Class | AVG | G | AB | R | H | 2B | 3B | HR | RBI | BB | SO | SB | OBP | SLG |
|------|---------------|-------|-----|---|----|---|---|----|----|----|-----|----|----|----|-----|-----|
| 2003 | Indians (DSL) | R | .318 | 64 | 239 | 42 | 76 | 9 | 5 | 1 | 32 | 31 | 25 | 16 | .396 | .410 |
| 2004 | Indians (DSL) | R | .444 | 64 | 259 | 72 | 115 | 12 | 19 | 1 | 40 | 22 | 19 | 37 | .486 | .649 |
| 2005 | Lake County (SAL) | A | .236 | 23 | 72 | 9 | 17 | 0 | 0 | 0 | 4 | 15 | 13 | 2 | .368 | .236 |
| | Mahoning Valley (NYP) | A | .263 | 64 | 270 | 30 | 71 | 5 | 5 | 0 | 20 | 28 | 39 | 24 | .340 | .319 |
| 2006 | Kinston (CL) | A | .327 | 76 | 275 | 55 | 90 | 15 | 6 | 1 | 27 | 42 | 50 | 20 | .419 | .436 |
| | Lake County (SAL) | A | .277 | 44 | 159 | 31 | 44 | 5 | 3 | 1 | 9 | 30 | 30 | 19 | .395 | .365 |
| **MINOR LEAGUE TOTALS** | | | .324 | 335 | 1274 | 239 | 413 | 46 | 38 | 4 | 132 | 168 | 176 | 118 | .405 | .429 |

## 27 TOM MASTNY                                                              RHP

**Born:** Feb. 4, 1981. **B-T:** R-R. **Ht.:** 6-6. **Wt.:** 220. **Drafted:** Furman, 2003 (11th round). **Signed by:** Charles Aliano (Blue Jays).

The best pitcher in Furman history, Mastny led NCAA Division I with a 1.09 ERA and was the Southern Conference pitcher of the year in 2003. Because his stuff is fringy, he lasted until the 11th round of the draft and signed with the Blue Jays for $8,000. He led the short-season New York-Penn League in victories in his pro debut and topped the low Class A South Atlantic League in ERA during his first full season. The player to be named later in a trade for John McDonald, Mastny switched to the bullpen after joining the Indians system. Mastny is all about deception and control. He has great feel for all of his pitches, starting with a sneaky fastball that tops out at 91 mph. It has good late sink and he can locate it wherever he wants in the strike zone. He relies on his 10-to-6 curveball too much, making it less effective. While he has solid arm speed and average fade to his changeup, he doesn't locate it down in the zone consistently. While Mastny doesn't fit the closer profile, he should find a role in the Cleveland bullpen this season.

| Year | Club (League) | Class | W | L | ERA | G | GS | CG | SV | IP | H | R | ER | HR | BB | SO | AVG |
|------|---------------|-------|---|---|-----|---|----|----|----|----|----|----|----|----|----|----|-----|
| 2003 | Auburn (NYP) | A | 8 | 0 | 2.26 | 14 | 14 | 0 | 0 | 64 | 56 | 19 | 16 | 1 | 12 | 68 | .237 |
| 2004 | Charleston, W.Va. (SAL) | A | 10 | 3 | 2.17 | 27 | 27 | 0 | 0 | 149 | 123 | 44 | 36 | 4 | 41 | 141 | .230 |
| 2005 | Kinston (CL) | A | 7 | 3 | 2.35 | 29 | 11 | 0 | 2 | 88 | 78 | 28 | 23 | 4 | 26 | 94 | .237 |
| | Akron (EL) | AA | 1 | 1 | 2.18 | 5 | 3 | 0 | 0 | 21 | 18 | 7 | 5 | 0 | 5 | 18 | .225 |
| 2006 | Akron (EL) | AA | 0 | 1 | 1.09 | 12 | 1 | 0 | 1 | 25 | 15 | 5 | 3 | 0 | 8 | 30 | .169 |
| | Buffalo (IL) | AAA | 2 | 1 | 2.61 | 24 | 0 | 0 | 0 | 38 | 25 | 11 | 11 | 0 | 16 | 46 | .184 |
| | Cleveland (AL) | MLB | 0 | 1 | 5.51 | 15 | 0 | 0 | 5 | 16 | 17 | 10 | 10 | 1 | 8 | 14 | .279 |
| **MINOR LEAGUE TOTALS** | | | 28 | 9 | 2.20 | 111 | 56 | 0 | 3 | 384 | 315 | 114 | 94 | 9 | 108 | 397 | .224 |
| **MAJOR LEAGUE TOTALS** | | | 0 | 1 | 5.51 | 15 | 0 | 0 | 5 | 16 | 17 | 10 | 10 | 1 | 8 | 14 | .279 |

## 28 FRANK HERRMANN

RHP

**Born:** May 30, 1984. **B-T:** L-R. **Ht.:** 6-4. **Wt.:** 220. **Signed:** NDFA/Harvard, 2005. **Signed by:** Phil Rossi.

Passed over in the 2005 draft in part because he had elbow tendinitis, Herrmann got healthy that summer in the Hawaii Collegiate Baseball League. After he showed a low-90s fastball, the Indians swayed him away from returning to Harvard with a $35,000 bonus and a promise to pay for the last two semesters of his Ivy League education. Herrmann pitched just 99 innings over two seasons with the Crimson while also serving as the third-string quarterback on their football team. He came into his first full season with a drop-and-drive delivery that he didn't repeat well and had to be revamped with the help of Lake County pitching coach Ruben Niebla. Niebla got him to work on staying taller in his mechanics and scrapped both his slider and curveball, minimizing his pitch selection to keep things simple. Herrmann took off as a result, featuring a power sinker, a slurvy breaking ball and a feel for a changeup. Herrmann pitches at 89-91 with his fastball, touching 94 occasionally. His breaking ball is still in the developmental stages, but at times it's tight with late, two-plane break. He made strides with his changeup, which emerged as a weapon late in the season. He'll move into the high Class A rotation this year.

| Year | Club (League) | Class | W | L | ERA | G | GS | CG | SV | IP | H | R | ER | HR | BB | SO | AVG |
|------|---------------|-------|---|---|-----|---|----|----|----|----|---|---|----|----|----|----|-----|
| 2006 | Lake County (SAL) | A | 4 | 6 | 3.90 | 26 | 26 | 0 | 0 | 122 | 122 | 61 | 53 | 8 | 47 | 89 | .261 |
| **MINOR LEAGUE TOTALS** | | | 4 | 6 | 3.90 | 26 | 26 | 0 | 0 | 122 | 122 | 61 | 53 | 8 | 47 | 89 | .261 |

## 29 STEPHEN WRIGHT

RHP

**Born:** Aug. 30, 1984. **B-T:** R-R. **Ht.:** 6-2. **Wt.:** 205. **Drafted:** Hawaii, 2006 (2nd round). **Signed by:** Don Lyle

Wright earned a $630,000 bonus as a second-round pick after leading Hawaii to its first NCAA regional playoff appearance since 1993, going 11-2, 2.30. He also stood out as a closer in the Cape Cod League in 2005, tying for the lead with 12 saves. The Indians plan on initially trying him as a starter, though he wasn't able to take the mound until instructional league. He missed the entire summer with mononucleosis, which also knocked him out of the NCAA playoffs. He wasn't at his best when he returned in instructional league, as his command was below-average. Wright's fastball sits at 88-90 mph when he starts, though he touched 94 during the spring and hit it more regularly working out of the bullpen. His heater lacks life and he tends to elevate it in the strike zone. His slider is his best pitch, with good tilt and depth when he's on. He also throws a changeup and a curveball, and both need work. He probably will make his pro debut in low Class A this year.

| Year | Club (League) | Class | W | L | ERA | G | GS | CG | SV | IP | H | R | ER | HR | BB | SO | AVG |
|------|---------------|-------|---|---|-----|---|----|----|----|----|---|---|----|----|----|----|-----|
| 2006 | Did not play—Signed 2007 contract | | | | | | | | | | | | | | | | |

## 30 STEPHEN HEAD

1B

**Born:** Jan. 13, 1984. **B-T:** L-L. **Ht.:** 6-3. **Wt.:** 220. **Drafted:** Mississippi, 2005 (2nd round). **Signed by:** Scott Barnsby.

Head was better known on the mound than at first base during his amateur career, setting the career save mark at Mississippi. Projected as an early first-rounder in 2005, he fell to the Tribe in the second round after concerns about his ceiling emerged. There were no such concerns during his pro debut, after he hit six homers in 10 games at Mahoning Valley and later held his own in high Class A. But Head took a major step backward in a return trip to Kinston last season, showing only flashes of power and an inability to make adjustments on the fly. Head's swing has tendency to get long through the zone and he struggles with pitches on the outer half. He has the ability to turn on inside pitches or mistakes left up in the zone, but he hasn't shown much beyond pure pull power. He's a below-average runner but a plus defender with good range, soft hands and footwork around the bag. With Michael Aubrey's status uncertain because of injuries, Head was seen as Cleveland's first baseman of the future entering 2006. But now there are a lot of questions about him, and he'll try to answer them in his third stint in high Class A this year.

| Year | Club (League) | Class | AVG | G | AB | R | H | 2B | 3B | HR | RBI | BB | SO | SB | OBP | SLG |
|------|---------------|-------|-----|---|----|---|---|----|----|----|-----|----|----|----|-----|-----|
| 2005 | Mahoning Valley (NYP) | A | .432 | 10 | 37 | 11 | 16 | 4 | 0 | 6 | 14 | 8 | 5 | 0 | .533 | 1.027 |
| | Kinston (CL) | A | .286 | 47 | 203 | 31 | 58 | 15 | 0 | 4 | 36 | 8 | 33 | 4 | .310 | .419 |
| 2006 | Kinston (CL) | A | .235 | 130 | 477 | 65 | 112 | 26 | 0 | 14 | 73 | 54 | 73 | 2 | .319 | .377 |
| **MINOR LEAGUE TOTALS** | | | .259 | 187 | 717 | 107 | 186 | 45 | 0 | 24 | 123 | 70 | 111 | 6 | .328 | .423 |

# COLORADO
# ROCKIES

BY **TRACY RINGOLSBY**

Few teams have broken as many quality young players into the big leagues the last two years as the Rockies. Garrett Atkins, Clint Barmes, Brad Hawpe and Cory Sullivan all have become regulars in a predominantly homegrown lineup, while Jeff Francis has become the leader of the rotation.

Even with all that talent flowing to Colorado, the farm system remains one of the deepest in baseball. By the end of last season, shortstop Troy Tulowitzki, catcher **Chris Iannetta** and outfielder Jeff Baker also were playing regularly. Hard-throwing Manny Corpas was serving in middle relief, while 22-year-olds Ubaldo Jimenez and Juan Morillo made pitching cameos. Many members of that second group will graduate to full-time status in the majors in 2007, as will offseason trade acquisition Jason Hirsh. There's another wave coming behind them, and then even more depth in the lower levels of the system.

The Rockies haven't placed higher than fourth in the National League West since 1997. Years of losing have rewarded them with high first-round picks, and scouting director Bill Schmidt, who started running the team's drafts in 2000, has cashed them in for the likes of Francis (2002), Ian Stewart (2003) and Tulowitzki (2005).

Colorado's scouts also have done fine work in later rounds, nabbing Dexter Fowler (14th), Iannetta (fourth), Jeff Baker (fourth) and Joe Koshansky (sixth). Fowler and Baker were tough signs, while Iannetta and Koshansky have proven better than the consensus opinion at draft time.

The Rockies have made tremendous strides in the foreign market. The franchise's original general manager, Bob Gebhard, wasn't comfortable making a strong move into Latin American and wouldn't make the financial commitment to be a major player in Asia. But in 1999, Gebhard's final year as GM, ownership hired legendary scout Gary Hughes. Not only did Hughes impress upon ownership the importance of the Latin market, but he also moved Rolando Fernandez into the club's Latin operations department.

With guidance from scouting director Bill Schmidt and vice president of baseball operations Bill Geivett, Fernandez has turned the Rockies into a legitimate Latin presence. They don't shell out the signing bonuses of the big-market teams, but they have done an impressive job of finding arms. They're also starting to develop some middle infielders.

"What our guys have done is find good bodies, live arms, good projections," GM Dan O'Dowd says. "The heart and soul of this has been the work of Rolando and the guys he has brought in to work with him, like Felix Feliz (in the Dominican) and Francisco Cartaya (Venezuela)."

Their efforts will be crucial, as the Rockies' division rivals include the Diamondbacks and Dodgers, who also are loaded with young talent. But with the system continuing to deliver quality players to the majors, Colorado should return to contention soon.

## TOP 30 PROSPECTS

1. Troy Tulowitzki, ss
2. Franklin Morales, lhp
3. Jason Hirsh, rhp
4. Dexter Fowler, of
5. Ian Stewart, 3b
6. Ubaldo Jimenez, rhp
7. Greg Reynolds, rhp
8. Chris Iannetta, c
9. Jeff Baker, of
10. Chaz Roe, rhp
11. Manny Corpas, rhp
12. Juan Morillo, rhp
13. Joe Koshansky, 1b
14. Jonathan Herrera, ss
15. Hector Gomez, ss/3b
16. Seth Smith, of
17. Samuel Deduno, rhp
18. Shane Lindsay, rhp
19. Chris Nelson, ss
20. Brandon Hynick, rhp
21. Aneury Rodriguez, rhp
22. Corey Wimberly, 2b
23. Ching-Lung Lo, rhp
24. Darren Clarke, rhp
25. Alvin Colina, c
26. Matt Miller, of
27. Eric Young Jr., 2b
28. Pedro Strop, rhp
29. Andrew Johnston, rhp
30. David Christensen, of

# ORGANIZATION OVERVIEW

**General manager:** Dan O'Dowd. **Farm director:** Marc Gustafson. **Scouting director:** Bill Schmidt.

## 2006 PERFORMANCE

| Class | Team | League | W | L | PCT | Finish* | Manager | Affiliated |
|---|---|---|---|---|---|---|---|---|
| Majors | Colorado | National | 76 | 86 | .469 | 12th (16) | Clint Hurdle | — |
| Triple-A | Colorado Springs Sky Sox | Pacific Coast | 66 | 77 | .465 | 13th (16) | Tom Runnells | 1993 |
| Double-A | Tulsa Drillers | Texas | 75 | 64 | .540 | 4th (8) | Stu Cole | 2003 |
| High A | Modesto Nuts | California | 66 | 74 | .471 | 8th (10) | Chad Kreuter | 2005 |
| Low A | Asheville Tourists | South Atlantic | 74 | 63 | .540 | 6th (16) | Joe Mikulik | 1994 |
| Short-season | Tri-City Dust Devils | Northwest | 38 | 38 | .500 | 5th (8) | Fred Ocasio | 2001 |
| Rookie | Casper Rockies | Pioneer | 27 | 49 | .355 | 8th (8) | Paul Carey | 2001 |
| **OVERALL 2006 MINOR LEAGUE RECORD** | | | 346 | 365 | .487 | 21st (30) | | |

*Finish in overall standings (No. of teams in league). +League champion

## ORGANIZATION LEADERS

### BATTING
| | | |
|---|---|---|
| AVG | Rivera, Carlos, Colorado Springs | .325 |
| | Wimberly, Corey, Modesto | .325 |
| R | Garner, Cole, Asheville | 105 |
| H | Young Jr., Eric, Asheville | 164 |
| 2B | Smith, Seth, Tulsa | 46 |
| 3B | Three players tied at | 9 |
| HR | Koshansky, Joseph, Tulsa | 33 |
| RBI | Koshansky, Joseph, Tulsa | 116 |
| BB | Young Jr., Eric, Asheville | 72 |
| SO | Nelson, Justin, Modesto | 156 |
| SB | Young Jr., Eric, Asheville | 97 |
| OBP | Wimberly, Corey, Modesto | .404 |
| SLG | Koshansky, Joseph, Tulsa | .510 |
| XBH | Smith, Seth, Tulsa | 65 |

### PITCHING
| | | |
|---|---|---|
| W | Jimenez, Ubaldo, Tulsa/Colorado Springs | 14 |
| L | Esposito, Mike, Colorado Springs | 13 |
| ERA | Hynick, Brandon, Casper/Tri-City | 2.41 |
| G | Newman, Joshua, Tulsa | 68 |
| CG | Kaiser, Marc, Tulsa | 4 |
| SV | Field, Nate, Colorado Springs | 25 |
| | Johnston, Andrew, Asheville | 25 |
| IP | Kaiser, Marc, Tulsa | 165 |
| BB | Deduno, Samuel, Modesto | 92 |
| SO | Morales, Franklin, Modesto | 179 |
| AVG | Sullivan, Joshua, Tri-City | .188 |

## BEST TOOLS

| | |
|---|---|
| Best Hitter for Average | Ian Stewart |
| Best Power Hitter | Joe Koshansky |
| Best Strike-Zone Discipline | Chris Iannetta |
| Fastest Baserunner | Cory Wimberly |
| Best Athlete | Dexter Fowler |
| Best Fastball | Juan Morillo |
| Best Curveball | Franklin Morales |
| Best Slider | Darren Clarke |
| Best Changeup | Ubaldo Jimenez |
| Best Control | Brandon Hynick |
| Best Defensive Catcher | Chris Iannetta |
| Best Defensive Infielder | Jonathan Herrera |
| Best Infield Arm | Troy Tulowitzki |
| Best Defensive Outfielder | Sean Barker |
| Best Outfield Arm | Sean Barker |

## PROJECTED 2010 LINEUP

| | |
|---|---|
| Catcher | Chris Iannetta |
| First Base | Todd Helton |
| Second Base | Jonathan Herrera |
| Third Base | Garrett Atkins |
| Shortstop | Troy Tulowitzki |
| Left Field | Matt Holliday |

| | |
|---|---|
| Center Field | Dexter Fowler |
| Right Field | Ian Stewart |
| No. 1 Starter | Franklin Morales |
| No. 2 Starter | Jeff Francis |
| No. 3 Starter | Jason Hirsh |
| No. 4 Starter | Greg Reynolds |
| No. 5 Starter | Aaron Cook |
| Closer | Ubaldo Jimenez |

## LAST YEAR'S TOP 20 PROSPECTS

1. Ian Stewart, 3b
2. Troy Tulowitzki, ss
3. Franklin Morales, lhp
4. Chaz Roe, rhp
5. Ubaldo Jimenez, rhp
6. Chris Iannetta, c
7. Juan Morillo, rhp
8. Ryan Shealy, 1b
9. Chris Nelson, ss
10. Dexter Fowler, of
11. Omar Quintanilla, ss/2b
12. Matt Macri, ss
13. Shane Lindsay, rhp
14. Jeff Baker, 3b
15. Seth Smith, of
16. Jim Miller, rhp
17. Jeff Salazar, of
18. Samuel Deduno, rhp
19. Joe Koshansky, 1b
20. Ryan Spilborghs, of

## TOP PROSPECTS OF THE DECADE

| Year | Player, Pos. | 2006 Org. |
|---|---|---|
| 1997 | Todd Helton, 1b | Rockies |
| 1998 | Todd Helton, 1b | Rockies |
| 1999 | Choo Freeman, of | Rockies |
| 2000 | Choo Freeman, of | Rockies |
| 2001 | Chin-Hui Tsao, rhp | Rockies |
| 2002 | Chin-Hui Tsao, rhp | Rockies |
| 2003 | Aaron Cook, rhp | Rockies |
| 2004 | Chin-Hui Tsao, rhp | Rockies |
| 2005 | Ian Stewart, 3b | Rockies |
| 2006 | Ian Stewart, 3b | Rockies |

## TOP DRAFT PICKS OF THE DECADE

| Year | Player, Pos. | 2006 Org. |
|---|---|---|
| 1997 | Mark Mangum, rhp | Out of baseball |
| 1998 | Choo Freeman, of | Rockies |
| 1999 | Jason Jennings, rhp | Rockies |
| 2000 | *Matt Harrington, rhp | Fort Worth (Am. Assoc.) |
| 2001 | Jayson Nix, ss | Rockies |
| 2002 | Jeff Francis, lhp | Rockies |
| 2003 | Ian Stewart, 3b | Rockies |
| 2004 | Chris Nelson, 3b | Rockies |
| 2005 | Troy Tulowitzki, ss | Rockies |
| 2006 | Greg Reynolds, rhp | Rockies |

*Did not sign.

## ALL-TIME LARGEST BONUSES

| | |
|---|---|
| Greg Reynolds, 2006 | $3,250,000 |
| Jason Young, 2000 | $2,750,000 |
| Troy Tulowitzki, 2005 | $2,300,000 |
| Chin-Hui Tsao, 1999 | $2,200,000 |
| Chris Nelson, 2004 | $2,150,000 |

# MINOR LEAGUE DEPTH CHART

## Colorado Rockies

**Impact: A.** The Rockies expect shortstop Troy Tulowitzki and Chris Iannetta to leave imprints on the big league club this season, with impact bats Ian Stewart, Dexter Fowler and Joe Koshansky not far behind.

**Depth: B.** The Rockies have quietly built one of the deepest farm systems through scouting director Bill Schmidt's drafts, Rolando Fernandez' ability to procure talent on the international market and continuity in the player-development staff.

**Sleeper:** Esmil Rogers, rhp. Signed as an infielder out of the Dominican Republic in 2003, Rogers moved to the mound last season and finished with less than impressive numbers. But the 21-year-old has power stuff, featuring a 93-95 mph fastball, plus curveball and a good feel for a changeup.

*Numbers in parentheses indicate prospect rankings.*

| LF | CF | RF |
|---|---|---|
| Seth Smith (16) | Dexter Fowler (4) | Jeff Baker (9) |
| Matt Miller (26) | Chris Nelson (19) | David Christensen (30) |
| Cole Garner | Jeff Salazar | Kevin Clark |
| Joe Gaetti | Jordan Czarniecki | Sean Barker |

| 3B | SS | 2B | 1B |
|---|---|---|---|
| Ian Stewart (5) | Troy Tulowitzki (1) | Cory Wimberly (22) | Joe Koshansky (13) |
| Matt Macri | Jonathan Herrera (14) | Eric Young, Jr. (27) | Jeff Kindell |
| Phillip Cuadrado | Hector Gomez (15) | Jayson Nix | Christian Colonel |
|  | Chris Nelson (19) |  |  |
|  | Shane Lowe |  |  |
|  | Helder Velasquez |  |  |
|  | Carlos Martinez |  |  |
|  | Daniel Mayoral |  |  |
|  | Jason Van Kooten |  |  |

| C |
|---|
| Chris Iannetta (8) |
| Alvin Colina (25) |
| Neil Wilson |
| Michael McKenry |

| RHP | | LHP | |
|---|---|---|---|
| **Starters** | **Relievers** | **Starters** | **Relievers** |
| Jason Hirsh (3) | Manny Corpas (11) | Franklin Morales (2) | Josh Newman |
| Ubaldo Jimenez (6) | Darren Clarke (24) | Keith Weiser | Chad Bailey |
| Greg Reynolds (7) | Pedro Strop (28) | Brandon Durden | Thomas Baumgardner |
| Chaz Roe (10) | Andrew Johnston (29) | Xavier Cedeno | Devin Collis |
| Juan Morillo (12) | Craig Baker | Kelvin Guzman |  |
| Samuel Deduno (17) | Alberto Arias |  |  |
| Shane Lindsay (18) | Jim Miller |  |  |
| Brandon Hynick (20) | Judd Songster |  |  |
| Aneury Rodriguez (21) | Stephen Register |  |  |
| Ching-Lung Lo (23) | Ryan Speier |  |  |
| Josh Sullivan | Jason Burch |  |  |
| Ryan Matheus |  |  |  |
| David Arnold |  |  |  |
| Emmanuel Ulloa |  |  |  |

# DRAFT ANALYSIS

## 2006 SIGNING BUDGET: $5.4 million

**Best Pro Debut:** RHP Brandon Hynick (8) was named Pioneer League pitcher of the year after going 4-3, 2.41 with a 79-9 K-BB ratio in 71 innings. RHP Will Harris (9) was primarily a position player at Louisiana State and pitched just 22 innings in four years. He had no trouble become a full-time pitcher in pro ball, posting a 1.16 ERA and 42-9 K-BB ratio in 31 innings. LHP Tommy Baumgardner (28) showed more velocity than expected, hitting as high as 92 mph, and had a 1.04 ERA with 33 strikeouts in 26 innings.

**Best Athlete:** OF David Christensen (2) and SSs Helder Velazquez (5) and Shane Lowe (29) are all high school athletes who will need time for their bodies and skills to mature. OF/2B Anthony Jackson (16) reminds the Rockies of Quinton McCracken.

**Best Pure Hitter:** Christensen or Velazquez. Christensen has more work to do with his swing after hitting .198 with 93 strikeouts in 207 pro at-bats.

**Best Raw Power:** Christensen has the bat speed and strength to develop above-average pop.

**Fastest Runner:** Velazquez and Jackson have plus speed.

**Best Defensive Player:** Velazquez has the tools and actions to be a standout shortstop. He just needs to add a lot of strength to his 6-foot-3, 165-pound frame.

**Best Fastball:** RHP Greg Reynolds (1) has a 90-94 mph fastball that he can locate with uncanny precision for a pitcher of his size and relative pro inexperience. He does a better job of getting easy outs than missing bats, but that approach has worked for him so far and draws comparisons to Aaron Cook's. Harris can touch 95 mph, while Hynick works from 90-93.

**Best Breaking Ball:** Hynick has a below-average curveball until Casper pitching coach Mark Thompson helped him tighten it into a plus pitch. Reynolds has a curve that's at least solid-average and sometimes plus.

**Most Intriguing Background:** Unsigned 2B Zach Helton's (37) cousin Todd is the best player in franchise history. Harris' brother Clay signed with the Phillies as a ninth-round pick in 2005. Draft-and-follow SS Zack Murry (19) is playing for his father Steve at Neosho County (Kan.) CC. The Rockies usually like to take a football player as part of their draft effort, and this year they popped Southern Mississippi wide receiver Damion Carter (46). Carter, who hasn't played baseball in four years of college, turned down the chance to sign as an outfielder.

**Closest To The Majors:** Reynolds handled the hitter-friendly high Class A California League and will begin 2007 in Double-A. A mid-2008 ETA in Colorado seems reasonable.

**Best Late-Round Pick:** Lowe and Baumgardner.

**The One Who Got Away:** OF/LHP Aaron Miller (11) would have gone no later than the second round if not for his $1.3 million price tag. The Rockies couldn't make a deal work, so he became part of college baseball's best recruiting class at Baylor. OF Curtis Dupart (31) was a pitcher before 2006, when he showed classic right-field tools. He's now at Georgia Tech.

**Assessment:** The Rockies considered choosing Evan Longoria with the No. 2 overall selection, but after taking infielders with their first-round picks the last three years, they opted for an arm in Reynolds. Most of their pitching selections had strong debuts, while many of their position players struggled.

## 2005 BUDGET: $6.0 million

The Rockies never expected to get SS Troy Tulowitzki (1) with the seventh overall pick, and RHP Chaz Roe (1) has a big-time curveball. **GRADE: B+**

## 2004 BUDGET: $4.0 million

Colorado's haul included a possible all-star in OF Dexter Fowler (14) and projected regulars in C Chris Iannetta (4) and 1B Joe Koshansky (6). But their top pick, SS Chris Nelson (1), has moved slowly through the system to this point. **GRADE: B+**

## 2003 BUDGET: $4.0 million

3B Ian Stewart (1) has slowed down but remains one of the game's best young hitting prospects. The Rockies didn't get much beyond him, however. **GRADE: B**

*Draft analysis by Jim Callis. Numbers in parentheses indicate draft rounds. Budgets are bonuses in first 10 rounds.*

# TROY
# TULOWITZKI

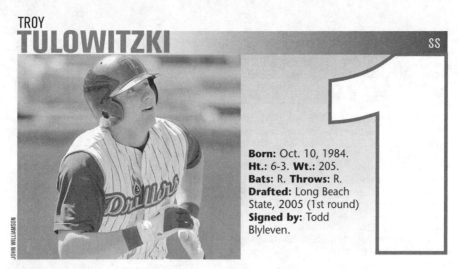

**Born:** Oct. 10, 1984.
**Ht.:** 6-3. **Wt.:** 205.
**Bats:** R. **Throws:** R.
**Drafted:** Long Beach
State, 2005 (1st round)
**Signed by:** Todd
Blyleven.

JOHN WILLIAMSON

Tulowitzki was in the big leagues 14 months after he was drafted, the quickest climb of any position player in Rockies history. He's part of an impressive trio of first-round shortstops to come out of Long Beach State this decade, sandwiched between Bobby Crosby (Athletics, 2001) and Evan Longoria (Devil Rays, 2006). Tulowitzki followed Crosby at shortstop for the 49ers and starred for three seasons. He missed 20 games with a broken hamate bone in his wrist during his draft year of 2005, though that didn't turn off scouts. The Rockies were both surprised and delighted to find him available with the seventh overall pick and signed him for $2.3 million. Another injury, this time a torn quadriceps, abbreviated his pro debut but he was back at full strength in 2006.

Tulowitzki has inner confidence that allowed him to open his first full pro season at Double-A Tulsa and finish it in the big leagues, never looking overmatched. He has legitimate power, but what's most impressive is he understands the need to use entire field and can drive the ball to right-center as easily as left-center. Tulowitzki spent most of his time in Double-A leading off. The Rockies don't envision him doing that in the majors, but it was a way to have him see more pitches and develop his plate discipline. He accomplished both goals. He has average speed and good baserunning instincts. He'll steal or take an extra base if the opportunity presents itself. At shortstop, Tulowitzki has one of the strongest and most accurate arms in the game. He has no fear defensively.

At times, Tulowitzki can get too aggressive at the plate. He'll chase fastballs up in the zone and breaking balls in the dirt, though he improved as 2006 wore on. Most of the work he needs to do center around his defense. Like most infielders out of Long Beach State, he has a tendency to circle around grounders, which gives runners an extra step. He's also trying to improve his ability to make plays to his backhand. Tulowitzki has learned that pure arm strength isn't enough to make difficult plays in the majors, and he's trying to position himself better and get rid of the ball quicker. Given his size, he'll always have to work a little extra to maintain his agility.

Tulowitzki skipped Triple-A and assumed the everyday shortstop job with the Rockies in the final weeks of the regular season. He built off a solid September in the big leagues by being named the top prospect in the Arizona Fall League. Now he's ready to establish himself as a big leaguer for good. Colorado will protect him by initially batting him toward the bottom of the order, but is counting on him evolving into a middle-of-the-lineup run producer. He also has the clubhouse mentality that will allow him to emerge as a leader on and off the field.

| Year | Club (League) | Class | AVG | G | AB | R | H | 2B | 3B | HR | RBI | BB | SO | SB | OBP | SLG |
|------|---------------|-------|------|-----|-----|----|-----|----|----|----|-----|----|----|----|------|------|
| 2005 | Modesto (Cal) | A | .266 | 22 | 94 | 17 | 25 | 6 | 0 | 4 | 14 | 9 | 18 | 1 | .343 | .457 |
| 2006 | Tulsa (TL) | AA | .291 | 104 | 423 | 75 | 123 | 34 | 2 | 13 | 61 | 46 | 71 | 6 | .370 | .473 |
| | Colorado (NL) | MLB | .240 | 25 | 96 | 15 | 23 | 2 | 0 | 1 | 6 | 10 | 25 | 3 | .318 | .292 |
| **MINOR LEAGUE TOTALS** | | | .286 | 126 | 517 | 92 | 148 | 40 | 2 | 17 | 75 | 55 | 89 | 7 | .365 | .470 |
| **MAJOR LEAGUE TOTALS** | | | .240 | 25 | 96 | 15 | 23 | 2 | 0 | 1 | 6 | 10 | 25 | 3 | .318 | .292 |

## FRANKLIN MORALES

LHP

**Born:** Jan. 24, 1986. **B-T:** L-L. **Ht.:** 6-3. **Wt.:** 180. **Signed:** Venezuela, 2002. **Signed by:** Francisco Cartaya.

Since posting a 7.62 ERA in his U.S. debut in 2004, Morales has made major strides in each of the last two seasons. He ranked as the top pitching prospect in the high Class A California League last year, when he led the circuit in ERA and strikeouts. A legitimate lefty power pitcher, Morales can blow hitters away with a 94-95 mph fastball or a hard-biting curveball. He does a good job of maintaining his arm speed with his changeup and throwing it for strikes. He's still growing, and his stuff has taken off as he has added three inches in height in the last three years. Morales still hasn't learned how to repeat his mechanics effectively, in part because he's still filling out. As a result, his control and command waver. So does his concentration, which doesn't help. He tends to rush and overthrow when he gets into a jam. His changeup is still a work in progress. Morales has all the ingredients to be a top-of-the-rotation starter. He'll make the move to Double-A in 2007 and figures to reach Coors Field by season's end. He'll stick in the majors as soon as he shows the ability to consistently throw strikes.

| Year | Club (League) | Class | W | L | ERA | G | GS | CG | SV | IP | H | R | ER | HR | BB | SO | AVG |
|---|---|---|---|---|---|---|---|---|---|---|---|---|---|---|---|---|---|
| 2003 | Colorado (DSL) | R | 9 | 3 | 2.18 | 13 | 13 | 0 | 0 | 78 | 58 | 24 | 19 | 0 | 34 | 69 | .211 |
| 2004 | Casper (Pio) | R | 6 | 4 | 7.62 | 15 | 15 | 1 | 0 | 65 | 92 | 61 | 55 | 8 | 39 | 82 | .338 |
| 2005 | Asheville (SAL) | A | 8 | 4 | 3.08 | 21 | 15 | 0 | 1 | 96 | 73 | 40 | 33 | 6 | 48 | 108 | .214 |
| 2006 | Modesto (Cal) | A | 10 | 9 | 3.68 | 27 | 26 | 0 | 0 | 154 | 126 | 77 | 63 | 9 | 89 | 179 | .223 |
| **MINOR LEAGUE TOTALS** | | | 33 | 20 | 3.89 | 76 | 69 | 1 | 1 | 394 | 349 | 202 | 170 | 23 | 210 | 438 | .240 |

## JASON HIRSH

RHP

**Born:** Feb. 20, 1982. **B-T:** R-R. **Ht.:** 6-8. **Wt.:** 245. **Drafted:** California Lutheran, 2003 (2nd round). **Signed by:** Mel Nelson.

The Rockies added a lot of youth and saved a lot of money when they traded Jason Jennings to the Astros in December for Hirsh, Willy Taveras and Taylor Buchholz. Hirsh was the pitcher of the year in the Double-A Texas League in 2005 and the Triple-A Pacific Coast League in 2006. Last year, he started the Futures Game, went 46⅔ innings without giving up an earned run in June and July and won his last 12 PCL decisions before making his big league debut. Hirsh not only is intimidating at 6-foot-8 and 245 pounds, but he's also athletic for his size. He's more about polish than power, going after hitters with a 91-93 mph fastball, a late-breaking slider and an effective changeup he'll throw in any count. He has made huge strides with his slider and his ability to change speeds since signing in 2003. Hirsh likes to get a little more velocity by going to a four-seam fastball. While he's confident, Hirsh tends to try to re-invent himself every time he reaches a new level. If he just pitches to his capabilities, he'll be fine. Both Hirsh and Buchholz could open 2007 in Colorado's rotation. Hirsh should develop into a No. 3 starter in time.

| Year | Club (League) | Class | W | L | ERA | G | GS | CG | SV | IP | H | R | ER | HR | BB | SO | AVG |
|---|---|---|---|---|---|---|---|---|---|---|---|---|---|---|---|---|---|
| 2003 | Tri-City (NYP) | A | 3 | 1 | 1.95 | 10 | 8 | 0 | 0 | 32 | 22 | 10 | 7 | 0 | 7 | 33 | .190 |
| 2004 | Salem (CL) | A | 11 | 7 | 4.01 | 26 | 23 | 0 | 0 | 130 | 128 | 66 | 58 | 8 | 57 | 96 | .269 |
| 2005 | Corpus Christi (TL) | AA | 13 | 8 | 2.87 | 29 | 29 | 1 | 0 | 172 | 137 | 63 | 55 | 12 | 42 | 165 | .218 |
| 2006 | Round Rock (PCL) | AAA | 13 | 2 | 2.10 | 23 | 23 | 1 | 0 | 137 | 94 | 37 | 32 | 5 | 51 | 118 | .193 |
| | Houston (NL) | MLB | 3 | 4 | 6.04 | 9 | 9 | 0 | 0 | 45 | 48 | 32 | 30 | 11 | 22 | 29 | .267 |
| **MINOR LEAGUE TOTALS** | | | 40 | 18 | 2.90 | 88 | 83 | 2 | 0 | 472 | 381 | 176 | 152 | 25 | 157 | 412 | .223 |
| **MAJOR LEAGUE TOTALS** | | | 3 | 4 | 6.04 | 9 | 9 | 0 | 0 | 44 | 48 | 32 | 30 | 11 | 22 | 29 | .267 |

## DEXTER FOWLER

OF

**Born:** March 22, 1986. **B-T:** B-R. **Ht.:** 6-5. **Wt.:** 187. **Drafted:** HS—Alpharetta, Ga., 2004 (14th round). **Signed by:** Damon Iannelli.

Fowler had offers to play basketball at Harvard and baseball at Miami but elected to pursue baseball full-time when the Rockies gave him a $925,000 bonus in the 14th round. Colorado came up with the money after trading Larry Walker to clear salary. A legitimate five-tool prospect with great makeup, Fowler learned to switch-hit at Rookie-level Casper in 2005. A natural righty, he has made progress with his lefthanded swing and homers from each side of the plate on Opening Day in 2006. He has an athletic build and projects to add strength as he matures. His speed is well-above-average. Fowler evokes former Gold Glover Devon White for his defensive skills in center field, as he seems to glide in the gaps with his long strides. His average arm features good carry and accu-

racy. Still adapting to switch-hitting, he'll pull off the ball too often and lengthen his swing from the left side. He has stolen bases on pure speed but was caught 23 times last year, and he'll have to improve his awareness and his leads at higher levels. Ticketed for high Class A Modesto in 2007, Fowler could break into the major leagues in 2008 if everything clicks.

| Year | Club (League) | Class | AVG | G | AB | R | H | 2B | 3B | HR | RBI | BB | SO | SB | OBP | SLG |
|------|---------------|-------|-----|---|----|---|---|----|----|----|-----|----|----|----|-----|-----|
| 2005 | Casper (Pio) | R | .273 | 62 | 220 | 43 | 60 | 10 | 4 | 4 | 23 | 27 | 73 | 18 | .357 | .409 |
| 2006 | Asheville (SAL) | A | .296 | 99 | 405 | 92 | 120 | 31 | 6 | 8 | 46 | 43 | 79 | 43 | .373 | .462 |
| **MINOR LEAGUE TOTALS** | | | .288 | 161 | 625 | 135 | 180 | 41 | 10 | 12 | 69 | 70 | 152 | 61 | .367 | .443 |

## ⑤ IAN STEWART                                              3B

STEVE MOORE

**Born:** April 5, 1985. **B-T:** L-R. **Ht.:** 6-3. **Wt.:** 215. **Drafted:** HS—Garden Grove, Calif., 2003 (1st round). **Signed by:** Todd Blyleven.

The first high school position player ever selected by the Rockies in the first round, Stewart went 10th overall in 2003 and ranked No. 1 on this list in each of the last two years. He battled injuries in 2005 and posted the worst numbers of his pro career in Double-A in 2006. There's legitimate power in Stewart's bat. He hit just 10 homers last year, but his 41 doubles showed how he can drive the ball. He has a quick bat and has excellent plate coverage when he stays in sync. He has average speed but is an excellent baserunner. His strong arm is his best defensive attribute. Last year, Stewart got carried away trying to jerk pitches. He lost his timing mechanism with his open stance and turned so quickly that he couldn't square up the ball on the bat. He also started to guess with pitchers and wound up getting overpowered by fastballs when he was looking for something offspeed. He has to get back to trusting his reflexes. This is a big year for Stewart. He should open at Triple-A Colorado Springs, though he could find himself back in Double-A to start the season. The biggest question is where he'll play. Garrett Atkins took hold of third base in Colorado last season, so Stewart could move to an outfield corner down the road.

| Year | Club (League) | Class | AVG | G | AB | R | H | 2B | 3B | HR | RBI | BB | SO | SB | OBP | SLG |
|------|---------------|-------|-----|---|----|---|---|----|----|----|-----|----|----|----|-----|-----|
| 2003 | Casper (Pio) | R | .317 | 57 | 224 | 40 | 71 | 14 | 5 | 10 | 43 | 29 | 54 | 4 | .401 | .558 |
| 2004 | Asheville (SAL) | A | .319 | 131 | 505 | 92 | 161 | 31 | 9 | 30 | 101 | 66 | 112 | 19 | .398 | .594 |
| 2005 | Modesto (Cal) | A | .274 | 112 | 435 | 83 | 119 | 32 | 7 | 17 | 86 | 52 | 113 | 2 | .353 | .497 |
| 2006 | Tulsa (TL) | AA | .268 | 120 | 462 | 75 | 124 | 41 | 7 | 10 | 71 | 50 | 103 | 3 | .351 | .452 |
| **MINOR LEAGUE TOTALS** | | | .292 | 420 | 1626 | 290 | 475 | 118 | 28 | 67 | 301 | 197 | 382 | 28 | .373 | .523 |

## ⑥ UBALDO JIMENEZ                                          RHP

STEVE MOORE

**Born:** Jan. 22, 1984. **B-T:** R-R. **Ht.:** 6-4. **Wt.:** 200. **Signed:** Dominican Republic, 2001. **Signed by:** Rolando Fernandez.

The Rockies overhauled Jimenez' mechanics last spring, and he adapted quickly. He toned down a hitch in his arm action, which tipped off his pitches and created concerns about stress on his arm. He dominated Double-A and pitched well in the thin air of Colorado Springs. Jimenez has a four-pitch repertoire built around a 96-97 mph fastball that has reached triple digits. He has a plus changeup that has become more deceptive thanks to his new arm action, and he also throws a slider and an overhand curveball. He improved his command and his ability to set up hitters. Jimenez went down with the beginnings of a stress fracture in his shoulder in 2004, and scouts still worry that his mechanics will hurt his durability. But he hasn't missed a start in the last two years. His curveball has good spin but can be inconsistent. Jimenez figures to return to Triple-A to open 2007, and he could move into the big league rotation as soon as midseason. His profile also would fit in the closer's role, which could save some wear and tear on his arm.

| Year | Club (League) | Class | W | L | ERA | G | GS | CG | SV | IP | H | R | ER | HR | BB | SO | AVG |
|------|---------------|-------|---|---|-----|---|----|----|----|----|---|---|----|----|----|----|-----|
| 2001 | Colorado (DSL) | R | 2 | 5 | 4.88 | 13 | 13 | 0 | 0 | 48 | 41 | 36 | 26 | 1 | 44 | 36 | .225 |
| 2002 | Casper (Pio) | R | 3 | 5 | 6.53 | 14 | 14 | 0 | 0 | 62 | 72 | 46 | 45 | 6 | 29 | 65 | .288 |
|  | Colorado (DSL) | R | 2 | 0 | 0.00 | 3 | 3 | 0 | 0 | 18 | 10 | 1 | 0 | 0 | 6 | 25 | .152 |
| 2003 | Asheville (SAL) | A | 10 | 6 | 3.46 | 27 | 27 | 0 | 0 | 154 | 129 | 67 | 59 | 11 | 67 | 138 | .230 |
|  | Visalia (Cal) | A | 1 | 0 | 0.00 | 1 | 0 | 0 | 0 | 5 | 3 | 0 | 0 | 0 | 1 | 7 | .176 |
| 2004 | Visalia (Cal) | A | 4 | 1 | 2.23 | 9 | 9 | 1 | 0 | 44 | 29 | 15 | 11 | 1 | 12 | 61 | .184 |
| 2005 | Modesto (Cal) | A | 5 | 3 | 3.98 | 14 | 14 | 0 | 0 | 72 | 61 | 35 | 32 | 5 | 40 | 78 | .232 |
|  | Tulsa (TL) | AA | 2 | 5 | 5.43 | 12 | 11 | 0 | 0 | 63 | 58 | 40 | 38 | 12 | 31 | 53 | .243 |
| 2006 | Tulsa (TL) | AA | 9 | 2 | 2.45 | 13 | 13 | 1 | 0 | 73 | 49 | 21 | 20 | 2 | 40 | 86 | .194 |
|  | Colorado Springs (PCL) | AAA | 5 | 2 | 5.06 | 13 | 13 | 0 | 0 | 78 | 74 | 49 | 44 | 7 | 43 | 64 | .252 |
|  | Colorado (NL) | MLB | 0 | 0 | 3.52 | 2 | 1 | 0 | 0 | 8 | 5 | 4 | 3 | 1 | 3 | 3 | .185 |
| **MINOR LEAGUE TOTALS** | | | 43 | 29 | 4.00 | 119 | 117 | 2 | 0 | 618 | 526 | 310 | 275 | 45 | 313 | 613 | .230 |
| **MAJOR LEAGUE TOTALS** | | | 0 | 0 | 3.52 | 2 | 1 | 0 | 0 | 7 | 5 | 4 | 3 | 1 | 3 | 3 | .185 |

## 7 GREG REYNOLDS RHP

**Born:** July 3, 1985. **B-T:** R-R. **Ht.:** 6-7. **Wt.:** 225. **Drafted:** Stanford, 2006 (1st round). **Signed by:** Gary Wilson.

Coming out of high school, Reynolds had offers to play quarterback at Division I-A college programs. His decision to stick with baseball paid off, as he received a $3.25 million bonus as the No. 2 overall pick in 2006. Reynolds maintained his 90-94 mph velocity on his fastball and the command of his solid-average curveball and changeup throughout his pro debut. He throws strikes with ease because he repeats his clean, athletic delivery so well. He doesn't try to overpower hitters, getting easy outs and keeping his pitch counts down. He competes well. Though he has the stuff to do so, Reynolds doesn't manage to miss many bats, which could become an issue at higher levels, especially in Colorado. He had no problems in the hitter's havens of the California League, however. In the past, he fell into ruts where he wasn't aggressive with his fastball, though that was less of an issue in 2006. Reynolds figures to move into the Double-A rotation at the start of this season. His experience and mound savvy give him a chance to move quickly, with a shot at the big league rotation in 2008.

| Year | Club (League) | Class | W | L | ERA | G | GS | CG | SV | IP | H | R | ER | HR | BB | SO | AVG |
|------|---------------|-------|---|---|-----|---|----|----|----|----|----|----|----|----|----|----|-----|
| 2006 | Modesto (Cal) | A | 2 | 1 | 3.33 | 11 | 11 | 0 | 0 | 49 | 51 | 22 | 18 | 1 | 14 | 29 | .271 |
| **MINOR LEAGUE TOTALS** | | | 2 | 1 | 3.33 | 11 | 11 | 0 | 0 | 49 | 51 | 22 | 18 | 1 | 14 | 29 | .271 |

## 8 CHRIS IANNETTA C

**Born:** April 8, 1983. **B-T:** R-R. **Ht.:** 5-11. **Wt.:** 195. **Drafted:** North Carolina, 2004 (4th round). **Signed by:** Jay Matthews.

Part of a long line of big league catchers produced by North Carolina, Iannetta reached the majors last August, barely two years after signing as an unheralded fourth-round pick. He set career highs with a .336 average and 14 homers in the minors. Iannetta has quality at-bat after quality at-bat, working counts and forcing pitchers to throw him strikes. He should be able to hit for average with decent pop in the majors. As a catcher, he has a strong arm and reliable receiving skills. He does a nice job of running a pitching staff. Though he's equipped to shut down the running game, Iannetta erased just 27 percent of basestealers in 2006. He has to get more consistent with his throws. Like most catchers, he's a below-average runner. Iannetta's late-season performance convinced the Rockies that he's ready to stay in the majors. He'll be their primary catcher in 2007 and should develop into a solid regular.

| Year | Club (League) | Class | AVG | G | AB | R | H | 2B | 3B | HR | RBI | BB | SO | SB | OBP | SLG |
|------|---------------|-------|-----|---|----|---|---|----|----|----|-----|----|----|----|-----|-----|
| 2004 | Asheville (SAL) | A | .314 | 36 | 121 | 23 | 38 | 5 | 1 | 5 | 17 | 27 | 29 | 0 | .454 | .496 |
| 2005 | Modesto (Cal) | A | .276 | 74 | 261 | 51 | 72 | 17 | 3 | 11 | 58 | 45 | 61 | 1 | .381 | .490 |
| | Tulsa (TL) | AA | .233 | 19 | 60 | 7 | 14 | 3 | 1 | 2 | 11 | 8 | 15 | 0 | .329 | .417 |
| 2006 | Tulsa (TL) | AA | .321 | 44 | 156 | 38 | 50 | 10 | 2 | 11 | 26 | 24 | 26 | 1 | .418 | .622 |
| | Colorado Springs (PCL) | AAA | .351 | 47 | 151 | 23 | 53 | 12 | 1 | 3 | 22 | 24 | 29 | 0 | .447 | .503 |
| | Colorado (NL) | MLB | .260 | 21 | 77 | 12 | 20 | 4 | 0 | 2 | 10 | 13 | 17 | 0 | .370 | .390 |
| **MINOR LEAGUE TOTALS** | | | .303 | 220 | 749 | 142 | 227 | 47 | 8 | 32 | 134 | 128 | 160 | 2 | .410 | .515 |
| **MAJOR LEAGUE TOTALS** | | | .260 | 21 | 77 | 12 | 20 | 4 | 0 | 2 | 10 | 13 | 17 | 0 | .370 | .390 |

## 9 JEFF BAKER OF

**Born:** June 21, 1981. **B-T:** R-R. **Ht.:** 6-2. **Wt.:** 220. **Drafted:** Clemson, 2002 (4th round). **Signed by:** Jay Matthews.

Signability and a poor history with wood bats dropped him to the fourth round of the 2002 draft, but he received a $2 million big league contact and has hit .306 in pro ball. Baker will go as far as his bat carries him. He has legitimate power and the ability to drive the ball to the opposite field. His professional approach at the plate allows him to stay on breaking balls. He has the arm strength and enough speed and athleticism to become a solid outfielder. Baker's development has been slowed by injuries, as he repeatedly missed time in his first three pro seasons with wrist and thumb ailments. Last year marked the first time he topped 400 at-bats in pro ball, and he finally achieved the success Colorado expected. He has always struck out frequently, which will be a tradeoff for his production. He's still learning the nuances of playing the outfield. The Rockies will find a place for Baker, because he provides a valuable righthanded bat and the versatility to play at any of the infield and outfield corners. If he stays healthy, his bat will earn him more playing time.

| Year | Club (League) | Class | AVG | G | AB | R | H | 2B | 3B | HR | RBI | BB | SO | SB | OBP | SLG |
|------|---------------|-------|-----|---|----|---|---|----|----|----|-----|----|----|----|-----|-----|
| 2003 | Asheville (SAL) | A | .289 | 70 | 263 | 44 | 76 | 17 | 0 | 11 | 44 | 30 | 79 | 4 | .377 | .479 |
| 2004 | Visalia (Cal) | A | .330 | 72 | 267 | 60 | 88 | 23 | 1 | 11 | 64 | 47 | 70 | 1 | .439 | .547 |
|  | Tulsa (TL) | AA | .297 | 24 | 91 | 10 | 27 | 5 | 1 | 4 | 20 | 7 | 22 | 1 | .343 | .505 |
| 2005 | Colorado (NL) | MLB | .211 | 12 | 38 | 6 | 8 | 4 | 0 | 1 | 4 | 5 | 12 | 0 | .302 | .395 |
|  | Colorado Springs (PCL) | AAA | .303 | 61 | 228 | 40 | 69 | 16 | 1 | 10 | 41 | 16 | 44 | 3 | .348 | .513 |
| 2006 | Colorado Springs (PCL) | AAA | .305 | 128 | 482 | 71 | 147 | 30 | 4 | 20 | 108 | 46 | 110 | 7 | .369 | .508 |
|  | Colorado (NL) | MLB | .368 | 18 | 57 | 13 | 21 | 7 | 2 | 5 | 21 | 1 | 14 | 2 | .379 | .825 |
| **MINOR LEAGUE TOTALS** | | | .306 | 355 | 1331 | 225 | 407 | 91 | 7 | 56 | 277 | 146 | 325 | 16 | .380 | .511 |
| **MAJOR LEAGUE TOTALS** | | | .305 | 30 | 95 | 19 | 29 | 11 | 2 | 6 | 25 | 6 | 26 | 2 | .347 | .653 |

## 10 CHAZ ROE RHP

BILL MITCHELL

**Born:** Oct. 9, 1986. **B-T:** R-R. **Ht.:** 6-5. **Wt.:** 180. **Drafted:** HS—Lexington, Ky., 2005 (1st round supplemental). **Signed by:** Scott Corman.

Roe had a chance to follow his father's lead and play quarterback at Kentucky, but he opted to turn pro when the Rockies took him 32nd overall in 2005 and gave him a $1.025 million bonus. He opened last year in extended spring because Colorado doesn't have an extensive track record of developing high school pitchers and wanted to monitor his workload. Roe's fastball has good life in the low 90s and tops out at 95, with the chance to add more consistent velocity as his body continues to fill out. His curveball is a definite plus pitch with good biting action. A loose-bodied athlete, he has a tall build that allows him to get a good downward angle in his delivery. Roe tends to rush his delivery out of the stretch. He shows signs of a decent changeup but still is working on making it more consistent. He can get lazy at times with his curveball. Roe is slated for a full season in high Class A. The Rockies will move him slowly, though he could be in the big leagues as a starter by late 2009.

| Year | Club (League) | Class | W | L | ERA | G | GS | CG | SV | IP | H | R | ER | HR | BB | SO | AVG |
|------|---------------|-------|---|---|-----|---|----|----|----|----|---|---|----|----|----|----|-----|
| 2005 | Casper (Pio) | R | 5 | 2 | 4.17 | 12 | 12 | 0 | 0 | 50 | 31 | 25 | 23 | 2 | 36 | 55 | .175 |
| 2006 | Asheville (SAL) | A | 7 | 4 | 4.06 | 19 | 19 | 0 | 0 | 100 | 105 | 54 | 45 | 4 | 47 | 80 | .273 |
| **MINOR LEAGUE TOTALS** | | | 12 | 6 | 4.10 | 31 | 31 | 0 | 0 | 149 | 136 | 79 | 68 | 6 | 83 | 135 | .242 |

## 11 MANNY CORPAS RHP

**Born:** Dec. 3, 1982. **B-T:** R-R. **Ht.:** 6-3. **Wt.:** 170 **Signed:** Panama, 1999. **Signed by:** Tim Ireland.

In his seventh pro season, Corpas was added to the 40-man roster and finally advanced past the Class A level. Penciled into a middle relief role in Double-A to start the season, Corpas stepped in when closer Jim Miller was sidelined with strained left oblique muscle, and he dominated. He earned a brief promotion to Triple-A before joining the big league staff. Corpas, who pitched for Panama in the World Baseball Classic, enjoys the challenge of the later innings. His fastball registers 92-95 mph from a loose, whippy low three-quarters slot creating good movement. Corpas keeps hitters honest with his slider, and he'll throw it at any time in the count but has to stay on top of the ball from his release point to prevent it from flattening out. His changeup has improved, and he'll flash an effective one with late bottom-out action at the plate. After lefties hit .394 off him in 2005, he limited them to an .096 average in his Double-A stint, a promising sign that his changeup has made strides. Corpas' dominant effort should keep him in the mix to contribute in relief.

| Year | Club (League) | Class | W | L | ERA | G | GS | CG | SV | IP | H | R | ER | HR | BB | SO | AVG |
|------|---------------|-------|---|---|-----|---|----|----|----|----|---|---|----|----|----|----|-----|
| 2000 | Rockies (VSL) | R | 0 | 1 | 15.43 | 1 | 0 | 0 | 0 | 2 | 5 | 4 | 4 | 0 | 0 | 3 | .385 |
| 2001 | Rockies (DSL) | R | 2 | 1 | 2.24 | 15 | 5 | 0 | 2 | 56 | 56 | 23 | 14 | 0 | 17 | 41 | .248 |
| 2002 | Casper (Pio) | R | 2 | 4 | 5.73 | 29 | 0 | 0 | 2 | 33 | 37 | 24 | 21 | 4 | 18 | 42 | .274 |
| 2003 | Tri-City (NWL) | A | 5 | 6 | 5.79 | 15 | 15 | 0 | 0 | 84 | 98 | 61 | 54 | 7 | 22 | 47 | .292 |
| 2004 | Asheville (SAL) | A | 2 | 3 | 3.05 | 43 | 0 | 0 | 3 | 44 | 48 | 20 | 15 | 3 | 13 | 52 | .267 |
| 2005 | Modesto (Cal) | A | 3 | 2 | 3.78 | 47 | 0 | 0 | 2 | 69 | 83 | 33 | 29 | 2 | 14 | 52 | .299 |
| 2006 | Tulsa (TL) | AA | 2 | 1 | 0.98 | 34 | 0 | 0 | 19 | 37 | 22 | 7 | 4 | 0 | 4 | 35 | .177 |
|  | Colorado Springs (PCL) | AAA | 0 | 0 | 1.04 | 8 | 0 | 0 | 0 | 9 | 5 | 1 | 1 | 1 | 2 | 7 | .167 |
|  | Colorado (NL) | MLB | 1 | 2 | 3.62 | 35 | 0 | 0 | 0 | 32 | 36 | 13 | 13 | 3 | 8 | 27 | .286 |
| **MINOR LEAGUE TOTALS** | | | 16 | 17 | 3.82 | 192 | 20 | 0 | 28 | 334 | 354 | 173 | 142 | 17 | 90 | 279 | .268 |
| **MAJOR LEAGUE TOTALS** | | | 1 | 2 | 3.62 | 35 | 0 | 0 | 0 | 32 | 36 | 13 | 13 | 3 | 8 | 27 | .286 |

## 12 JUAN MORILLO RHP

**Born:** Nov. 5, 1983. **B-T:** R-R. **Ht.:** 6-3. **Wt.:** 190. **Signed:** Dominican Republic, 2001. **Signed by:** Rolando Fernandez.

The Rockies continue to be patient with Morillo in the hopes that he'll harness his overpowering arsenal. The White Sox reportedly clocked him at 104 mph in 2004, and he can

average 98 and hold that velocity deep into starts. He's starting to learn the value of sacrificing a little velocity for the sake of command, though his control and command still leave a lot to be desired. His slider and changeup remain inconsistent, but the latter shows signs of becoming a plus pitch. Morillo has an extremely resilient arm, and his profile might fit best in the bullpen, perhaps even as a closer. For now, though, Colorado will keep him in the rotation. He'll pitch 2007 in Triple-A.

| Year | Club (League) | Class | W | L | ERA | G | GS | CG | SV | IP | H | R | ER | HR | BB | SO | AVG |
|------|---------------|-------|---|---|-----|---|----|----|----|-----|-----|-----|-----|----|-----|-----|------|
| 2001 | Colorado (DSL) | R | 2 | 4 | 6.81 | 14 | 7 | 0 | 0 | 36 | 35 | 31 | 27 | 1 | 38 | 20 | .248 |
| 2002 | Colorado (DSL) | R | 1 | 5 | 4.75 | 14 | 11 | 0 | 0 | 55 | 49 | 44 | 29 | 1 | 33 | 43 | .230 |
| 2003 | Casper (Pio) | R | 1 | 6 | 5.91 | 15 | 15 | 0 | 0 | 64 | 85 | 73 | 42 | 6 | 40 | 44 | .318 |
| 2004 | Tri-City (NWL) | A | 3 | 2 | 2.98 | 14 | 14 | 0 | 0 | 66 | 56 | 34 | 22 | 0 | 41 | 73 | .226 |
| 2005 | Asheville (SAL) | A | 1 | 3 | 4.54 | 7 | 7 | 0 | 0 | 34 | 40 | 24 | 17 | 2 | 13 | 43 | .290 |
| | Modesto (Cal) | A | 6 | 5 | 4.41 | 20 | 20 | 0 | 0 | 112 | 107 | 69 | 55 | 10 | 65 | 101 | .258 |
| 2006 | Tulsa (TL) | AA | 12 | 8 | 4.62 | 27 | 27 | 1 | 0 | 140 | 128 | 82 | 72 | 13 | 80 | 132 | .248 |
| | Colorado (NL) | MLB | 0 | 0 | 15.75 | 1 | 1 | 0 | 0 | 4 | 8 | 7 | 7 | 3 | 3 | 4 | .421 |
| **MINOR LEAGUE TOTALS** | | | 26 | 33 | 4.68 | 111 | 101 | 1 | 0 | 507 | 500 | 357 | 264 | 33 | 310 | 456 | .258 |
| **MAJOR LEAGUE TOTALS** | | | 0 | 0 | 15.75 | 1 | 1 | 0 | 0 | 4 | 8 | 7 | 7 | 3 | 3 | 4 | .421 |

## 13 JOE KOSHANSKY                                                1B

**Born:** May 26, 1982. **B-T:** L-L. **Ht.:** 6-4. **Wt.:** 225. **Drafted:** Virginia, 2004 (6th round). **Signed by:** Jay Matthews.

Hitting cleanup and starting as a pitcher on Sundays for Virginia, Koshansky went undrafted after his junior season, but scouts began to take him more seriously after his strong summer in the Valley League. The Atlantic Coast Conference player of the year as a senior in 2004—when he hit 16 homers while going 8-3 on the mound—he still lasted until the sixth round. He's led the organization in home runs in each of the last two years. At the plate, Koshansky gets in trouble when he tries to guess instead of just focusing on getting a good swing on the ball. Offspeed pitches can be a struggle because like many power hitters who have strength but not overwhelming bat speed, he often gears up for the fastball. He doesn't have to gear up to pull the ball, though, because he has natural power from gap to gap, with a fluid stroke. He plays a quality first base and moves very well for his size. He says he can play the outfield, but he's a well-below-average runner and that would be a challenge. Helton's presence and massive contract remain a daunting obstacle, but with Ryan Shealy traded to the Royals, at least a path to Triple-A has opened up.

| Year | Club (League) | Class | AVG | G | AB | R | H | 2B | 3B | HR | RBI | BB | SO | SB | OBP | SLG |
|------|---------------|-------|-----|---|----|---|---|----|----|----|-----|----|----|----|-----|-----|
| 2004 | Tri-City (NWL) | A | .234 | 66 | 239 | 41 | 56 | 18 | 0 | 12 | 43 | 31 | 84 | 1 | .330 | .460 |
| 2005 | Asheville (SAL) | A | .291 | 120 | 453 | 92 | 132 | 31 | 1 | 36 | 103 | 53 | 122 | 6 | .373 | .603 |
| | Tulsa (TL) | AA | .267 | 12 | 45 | 5 | 12 | 3 | 0 | 2 | 12 | 2 | 15 | 0 | .292 | .467 |
| 2006 | Tulsa (TL) | AA | .284 | 132 | 500 | 84 | 142 | 28 | 0 | 31 | 109 | 64 | 134 | 3 | .371 | .526 |
| **MINOR LEAGUE TOTALS** | | | .276 | 330 | 1237 | 222 | 342 | 80 | 1 | 81 | 267 | 150 | 355 | 10 | .361 | .539 |

## 14 JONATHAN HERRERA                                            SS

**Born:** Nov. 3, 1984. **B-T:** B-R. **Ht.:** 5-9. **Wt.:** 160. **Signed:** Venezuela, 2002. **Signed by:** Francisco Cartaya.

Herrera served a 15-game suspension in 2005 for violating MLB's policy on performance-enhancing substances. He bounced back, hit his way out of low Class A and spent the rest of that season in high Class A. In a return trip last year, Herrera showed enough that the Rockies added him to the 40-man roster. Managers rated him the top defensive shortstop in the California League. Herrera has dazzling defensive skills with plus range, arm strength and a quick release. He's not a burner, but he runs above-average and knows how to use his speed on the bases. He emerged as a legitimate leadoff candidate in high Class A. He began taking pitches and incorporated bunting in his offensive game. He led the organization with 24 bunt base hits. He also worked counts deep and went the other way. Herrera has modest power but has to be careful not to try and hit home runs. He's naturally righthanded and has more power from that side of the plate, but stays inside on the ball better from the left side. Herrera will jump to Double-A in 2007.

| Year | Club (League) | Class | AVG | G | AB | R | H | 2B | 3B | HR | RBI | BB | SO | SB | OBP | SLG |
|------|---------------|-------|-----|---|----|---|---|----|----|----|-----|----|----|----|-----|-----|
| 2002 | Colorado (DSL) | R | .300 | 61 | 230 | 39 | 69 | 10 | 2 | 0 | 22 | 25 | 27 | 23 | .371 | .361 |
| 2003 | Casper (Pio) | R | .308 | 39 | 159 | 27 | 49 | 7 | 1 | 1 | 25 | 10 | 25 | 12 | .355 | .384 |
| 2004 | Asheville (SAL) | A | .279 | 95 | 380 | 71 | 106 | 20 | 2 | 6 | 35 | 26 | 80 | 21 | .335 | .389 |
| 2005 | Asheville (SAL) | A | .310 | 19 | 87 | 17 | 27 | 2 | 0 | 0 | 5 | 8 | 11 | 6 | .384 | .333 |
| | Modesto (Cal) | A | .258 | 73 | 310 | 48 | 80 | 9 | 4 | 2 | 30 | 23 | 52 | 9 | .315 | .332 |
| 2006 | Modesto (Cal) | A | .310 | 127 | 487 | 87 | 151 | 20 | 8 | 7 | 77 | 58 | 67 | 34 | .382 | .427 |
| **MINOR LEAGUE TOTALS** | | | .292 | 414 | 1653 | 289 | 482 | 68 | 17 | 16 | 194 | 150 | 262 | 105 | .355 | .382 |

## 15  HECTOR GOMEZ
SS/3B

**Born:** March 5, 1988. **B-T:** R-R. **Ht.:** 6-1. **Wt.:** 157. **Signed:** Dominican Republic, 2004. **Signed by:** Felix Feliz.

Gomez brings back memories of the days when his hometown, San Pedro de Marcoris, was churning out quality big league shortstops on a regular basis. He's a quality defensive middle infielder with ample range, soft hands and a live, accurate arm. He spent the season as one of the youngest regulars in the Rookie-level Pioneer League (where he ranked as the No. 3 prospect), and at 157 pounds, he has plenty of room to grow into his 6-foot-1 frame. He'll need to get stronger to handle the grind as he prepares for his first full-season assignment. Gomez is a pure shortstop, but could be an offensive asset at second base, and played nearly half of his games at third base last year. He has a tendency to chase bad breaking balls and is a first-pitch fastball hitter, especially when he gets anxious. That, however, is something that experience can clear up. He knows how to use his hands in hitting and will hit the ball to all fields. He'll get his first taste of full-season ball this season in low Class A.

| Year | Club (League) | Class | AVG | G | AB | R | H | 2B | 3B | HR | RBI | BB | SO | SB | OBP | SLG |
|------|---------------|-------|-----|---|-----|----|-----|----|----|----|-----|----|----|----|------|------|
| 2005 | Rockies (DSL) | R | .335 | 67 | 242 | 49 | 81 | 16 | 1 | 6 | 43 | 24 | 38 | 15 | .423 | .483 |
| 2006 | Tri-City (NWL) | A | .244 | 12 | 45 | 4 | 11 | 3 | 0 | 0 | 6 | 0 | 14 | 0 | .255 | .311 |
| | Casper (Pio) | R | .327 | 50 | 202 | 24 | 66 | 9 | 4 | 5 | 35 | 11 | 26 | 5 | .364 | .485 |
| **MINOR LEAGUE TOTALS** | | | .323 | 129 | 489 | 77 | 158 | 28 | 5 | 11 | 84 | 35 | 78 | 20 | .385 | .468 |

## 16  SETH SMITH
OF

**Born:** Sept. 30, 1982. **B-T:** L-L. **Ht.:** 6-3. **Wt.:** 215. **Drafted:** Mississippi, 2004 (2nd round). **Signed by:** Damon Iannelli.

Smith was the backup at quarterback to Eli Manning for three seasons at Mississippi but never took a snap and knew his future was in baseball. Others, however, had doubts until last season. Smith finally showed an energy that scouts were concerned didn't exist. He grasped the need to play hard all the time and to treat the game as a business. Lasik surgery also was the key for Smith, who got rid of the contacts and glasses that he was never comfortable wearing. He has a pure hitter's swing and should get better as a hitter at the higher levels when pitchers are more around the plate. He has the power to hit the ball out of the park and has been a doubles machine in his pro career, tying for the minor league lead in 2006 and hitting 91 the past two seasons. Last year, he began to show more over-the-fence juice, but he stays inside the ball well and focuses on driving the ball to the gaps. He's a solid outfielder who could play some center field, but doesn't have the speed to play out there regularly in a big outfield. He's ready for his first Triple-A assignment, and Colorado Springs is the perfect venue to turn some of his doubles into home runs.

| Year | Club (League) | Class | AVG | G | AB | R | H | 2B | 3B | HR | RBI | BB | SO | SB | OBP | SLG |
|------|---------------|-------|-----|---|-----|----|-----|----|----|----|-----|----|-----|----|------|------|
| 2004 | Casper (Pio) | R | .369 | 56 | 233 | 46 | 86 | 21 | 3 | 9 | 61 | 25 | 47 | 9 | .427 | .601 |
| | Tri-City (NWL) | A | .259 | 9 | 27 | 6 | 7 | 1 | 1 | 2 | 5 | 1 | 3 | 0 | .276 | .593 |
| 2005 | Modesto (Cal) | A | .300 | 129 | 533 | 87 | 160 | 45 | 6 | 9 | 72 | 44 | 115 | 5 | .353 | .458 |
| 2006 | Tulsa (TL) | AA | .294 | 130 | 524 | 79 | 154 | 46 | 4 | 15 | 71 | 51 | 74 | 4 | .361 | .483 |
| **MINOR LEAGUE TOTALS** | | | .309 | 324 | 1317 | 218 | 407 | 113 | 14 | 35 | 209 | 121 | 239 | 18 | .368 | .496 |

## 17  SAMUEL DEDUNO
RHP

**Born:** July 2, 1983. **B-T:** R-R. **Ht.:** 6-1. **Wt.:** 170. **Signed:** Dominican Republic, 2003. **Signed by:** Felix Feliz.

Deduno was the Pioneer League pitcher of the year in 2005, his first season in the United States. He's a legitimate strikeout pitcher but is challenged to throw strikes at times. He topped the Cal League in walks last season and led the minors with 34 wild pitches, and his control was really an issue in the second half. After walking 36 in 76 first-half innings, including just five in four June starts, he issued 56 free passes in his final 70 innings. He tends to lose his release point and subsequently his feel for the strike zone. Deduno doesn't overpower hitters. His fastball is a steady 91-92 mph but has excellent sinking action. He uses a power curveball, which has earned 70 grades from some scouts, as his strikeout pitch. Deduno shows signs of developing a changeup but isn't comfortable throwing the pitch. A good athlete, Deduno has quick feet that help him hold runners. He will get another year in high Class A while he tries to gain consistency in his mechanics. He projects as a middle reliever.

| Year | Club (League) | Class | W | L | ERA | G | GS | CG | SV | IP | H | R | ER | HR | BB | SO | AVG |
|------|---------------|-------|---|---|------|----|----|----|----|-----|-----|-----|-----|----|-----|-----|------|
| 2003 | Colorado (DSL) | R | 3 | 4 | 2.47 | 12 | 12 | 0 | 0 | 69 | 53 | 26 | 19 | 1 | 26 | 61 | .202 |
| 2004 | Casper (Pio) | R | 6 | 4 | 3.18 | 15 | 15 | 0 | 0 | 76 | 62 | 40 | 27 | 3 | 32 | 118 | .219 |
| 2005 | Asheville (SAL) | A | 8 | 8 | 5.62 | 20 | 20 | 1 | 0 | 90 | 82 | 67 | 56 | 9 | 65 | 110 | .248 |
| 2006 | Modesto (Cal) | A | 5 | 8 | 4.80 | 27 | 26 | 0 | 0 | 146 | 121 | 88 | 78 | 3 | 92 | 167 | .222 |
| **MINOR LEAGUE TOTALS** | | | 22 | 24 | 4.24 | 74 | 73 | 1 | 0 | 382 | 318 | 221 | 180 | 16 | 215 | 456 | .224 |

## 18 SHANE LINDSAY
RHP

**Born:** Jan. 25, 1985. **B-T:** R-R. **Ht.:** 6-1. **Wt.:** 205. **Signed:** Australia, 2003. **Signed by:** Phil Allen.

After being named the No. 1 prospect in the short-season Northwest League in 2005, Lindsay found out he had a partially torn labrum. After rest and rehabilitation, he opened last year in extended spring training before returning to Tri-City. The second time around, he was equally as overpowering and rated as the top pitching prospect in the league. After an impressive tour of low Class A late in the year, Lindsay again had his labrum injury flare up, and this time he had surgery. He won't return to the mound until the mid-2007 at the earliest. Lindsay also has scoliosis, a curvature of the spine. It gives him a body tilt that keeps his right shoulder back, a good angle for pitching, but the long-range ramifications create concern. When he's right, his stuff is special. Lindsay's fastball will sit on 95-96 mph and comes out of a high overhand delivery. His power curveball is a put-away pitch and his changeup is a work in progress. Lindsay's prospect status hinges on his health. Until he pitches a full season—which won't be until at least 2008—the Rockies can't count on him.

| Year | Club (League) | Class | W | L | ERA | G | GS | CG | SV | IP | H | R | ER | HR | BB | SO | AVG |
|------|---------------|-------|---|---|-----|---|----|----|----|----|---|---|----|----|----|----|-----|
| 2004 | Casper (Pio) | R | 1 | 1 | 6.75 | 17 | 0 | 0 | 0 | 21 | 22 | 24 | 16 | 1 | 19 | 31 | .256 |
| 2005 | Tri-City (NWL) | A | 6 | 1 | 1.89 | 13 | 13 | 0 | 0 | 67 | 37 | 21 | 14 | 1 | 34 | 107 | .163 |
| 2006 | Tri-City (NWL) | A | 2 | 2 | 2.79 | 6 | 5 | 0 | 0 | 29 | 18 | 10 | 9 | 0 | 17 | 48 | .176 |
| | Asheville (SAL) | A | 2 | 1 | 2.67 | 7 | 7 | 0 | 0 | 34 | 26 | 15 | 10 | 2 | 27 | 43 | .211 |
| **MINOR LEAGUE TOTALS** | | | 11 | 5 | 2.93 | 43 | 25 | 0 | 0 | 151 | 103 | 70 | 49 | 4 | 97 | 229 | .191 |

## 19 CHRIS NELSON
SS

**Born:** Sept. 3, 1985. **B-T:** T-R. **Ht.:** 5-11. **Wt.:** 185. **Drafted:** HS—Decatur, Ga., 2004 (1st round). **Signed by:** Damon Iannelli.

Despite having Tommy John surgery prior to his senior season of high school, Nelson managed to go in the top 10 picks of the 2004 draft because of his athleticism and offensive potential. He has had a rough initiation into pro ball, and still has some maturing to do. Nelson has allowed his offensive struggles impact his game. He lost his focus at times defensively and led the low Class A South Atlantic League with 41 errors. What he hasn't lost is the package of tools that made him the ninth-overall pick in the 2004 draft. He has plus speed and will be a good baserunner. He has quick hands that give him a chance to be an impact offensive player once he stops overanalyzing everything. In repeating the SAL, Nelson showed encouraging signs at the plate, hitting 38 doubles and four more home runs than he had in his first year and a half. He has raw power and can drive the ball to all fields. He likely will wind up in center field or at second base, but he has the raw tools to be a shortstop. He gets caught in between on whether to charge, and can be overaggressive with his throws. Nelson should earn an assignment to high Class A this season.

| Year | Club (League) | Class | AVG | G | AB | R | H | 2B | 3B | HR | RBI | BB | SO | SB | OBP | SLG |
|------|---------------|-------|-----|---|----|---|---|----|----|----|-----|----|----|----|-----|-----|
| 2004 | Casper (Pio) | R | .347 | 38 | 147 | 36 | 51 | 6 | 3 | 4 | 20 | 20 | 42 | 6 | .432 | .510 |
| 2005 | Asheville (SAL) | A | .241 | 79 | 315 | 51 | 76 | 13 | 3 | 3 | 38 | 25 | 88 | 7 | .304 | .330 |
| 2006 | Asheville (SAL) | A | .260 | 118 | 466 | 69 | 121 | 38 | 1 | 11 | 76 | 32 | 101 | 14 | .313 | .416 |
| **MINOR LEAGUE TOTALS** | | | .267 | 235 | 928 | 156 | 248 | 57 | 7 | 18 | 134 | 77 | 231 | 27 | .329 | .402 |

## 20 BRANDON HYNICK
RHP

**Born:** Mar. 7, 1985. **B-T:** R-R. **Ht.:** 6-3. **Wt.:** 205. **Drafted:** Birmingham-Southern, 2006 (8th round). **Signed by:** Damon Iannelli

Hynick earned all-Big South Conference recognition as a pitcher and as first baseman last spring. After having an appendectomy, he still managed to lead Birmingham-Southern with 15 home runs and 100 innings pitched. Then he was the Pioneer League pitcher of the year in his pro debut after signing for $90,000 as an eighth-rounder. Hynick is a strike-thrower with a fastball that sits at 90-93 mph and has some sink. Club officials believe he'll throw even harder with more consistency with more experience, as he learns to integrate his lower half into his delivery more. He complements his fastball with a quality changeup and a improved curveball. Hynick also throws a split-finger fastball that has been his out pitch, but he's expected to put that aside to hone the command of his other secondary stuff. His mechanics improved at Casper thanks to work with pitching coach Mark Thompson, who got Hynick to break his hands sooner in his delivery, leading to better balance. His curveball took a step forward when Thompson improved Hynick's extension and got him to release the curve out in front of his body, increasing both its depth and deception. He had two impressive outings in the Northwest League and could jump to high Class A with a strong spring training.

| Year | Club (League) | Class | W | L | ERA | G | GS | CG | SV | IP | H | R | ER | HR | BB | SO | AVG |
|---|---|---|---|---|---|---|---|---|---|---|---|---|---|---|---|---|---|
| 2006 | Casper (Pio) | R | 4 | 3 | 2.39 | 12 | 12 | 0 | 0 | 64 | 55 | 23 | 17 | 3 | 8 | 70 | .227 |
| | Tri-City (NWL) | A | 0 | 0 | 2.57 | 2 | 1 | 0 | 0 | 7 | 5 | 2 | 2 | 0 | 1 | 9 | .208 |
| **MINOR LEAGUE TOTALS** | | | 4 | 3 | 2.41 | 14 | 13 | 0 | 0 | 71 | 60 | 25 | 19 | 3 | 9 | 79 | .226 |

## ANEURY RODRIGUEZ — RHP

**Born:** Dec. 13, 1987. **B-T:** R-R. **Ht.:** 6-3. **Wt.:** 180. **Signed:** Dominican Republic 2005. **Signed by:** Felix Feliz.

As a 17-year-old in 2005 Rodriguez went directly to Casper, skipping the Dominican Summer League altogether, and held his own. He was able to build off that in the college-oriented Northwest League in 2006. He'll likely advance to low Class A this year, and is poised for a breakout season. He's still growing into his body, which creates the expectation that he's only going to get stronger and throw harder. His huge hands are another indication of his potential size. He already has a fastball that sits in the low-90s, at times touching 93. He throws both a changeup and a curveball with some true power potential, and has been surprisingly adept with his changeup considering his youth. The Rockies have worked to get Rodriguez throwing more downhill to take advantage of his height. At times, he over-strides and leaves his stuff up in the strike zone. He shows all the makings of being a starting pitcher. More than anything, he hasn't been intimidated by his surrounding, playing against older players in a foreign country. The Rockies expect his projection will start paying off with production sooner than later.

| Year | Club (League) | Class | W | L | ERA | G | GS | CG | SV | IP | H | R | ER | HR | BB | SO | AVG |
|---|---|---|---|---|---|---|---|---|---|---|---|---|---|---|---|---|---|
| 2005 | Casper (Pio) | R | 3 | 4 | 7.55 | 15 | 15 | 0 | 0 | 62 | 77 | 54 | 52 | 7 | 26 | 47 | .309 |
| 2006 | Tri-City (NWL) | A | 4 | 4 | 4.14 | 15 | 15 | 1 | 0 | 76 | 78 | 42 | 35 | 2 | 30 | 69 | .261 |
| **MINOR LEAGUE TOTALS** | | | 7 | 8 | 5.67 | 30 | 30 | 1 | 0 | 138 | 155 | 96 | 87 | 9 | 56 | 116 | .283 |

## COREY WIMBERLY — 2B

**Born:** Oct. 26, 1983. **B-T:** B-R. **Ht.:** 5-8. **Wt.:** 180. **Drafted:** Alcorn State, 2005 (6th round). **Signed by:** Damon Iannelli.

Drafted as a redshirt sophomore (he had a broken wrist that cost him his first season), Wimberly was the first player from Alcorn State to be taken in the draft since 1991. Some in the organization say Wimberly stands a full two inches below his listed height. After leading the nation in hitting with a .462 average as a sophomore, Wimberly was an all-star and won another batting title in his 2005 debut with Casper. He jumped over Chris Nelson to high Class A last year and finished fourth in the California League in batting. He's a burner on the bases and knows how to use his 80 speed. Wimberly swiped 50 bases last year and continues to prompt comparisons to Chone Figgins, whom the Rockies drafted in 1997. He can get himself in trouble from the right side trying to hit for power, but as a lefthanded hitter he slaps at the ball and runs. He has quieted his approach and does a better job of rotating his hips, keeping his head steady and his hands back. Still, he has little present power and never projects to hit for even average pop. Wimberly is a tick below-average defensively but has accepted the challenge of getting better. He's learning to use his range and needs to adjust his near-sidearm throwing motion. Wimberly has played some center field and third base and could wind up as a utilityman, like Figgins. He'll play in Double-A this year.

| Year | Club (League) | Class | AVG | G | AB | R | H | 2B | 3B | HR | RBI | BB | SO | SB | OBP | SLG |
|---|---|---|---|---|---|---|---|---|---|---|---|---|---|---|---|---|
| 2005 | Casper (Pio) | R | .381 | 67 | 281 | 58 | 107 | 10 | 0 | 1 | 22 | 18 | 27 | 36 | .427 | .427 |
| 2006 | Modesto (Cal) | A | .325 | 87 | 342 | 72 | 111 | 6 | 4 | 2 | 24 | 30 | 42 | 50 | .404 | .383 |
| **MINOR LEAGUE TOTALS** | | | .350 | 154 | 623 | 130 | 218 | 16 | 4 | 3 | 46 | 48 | 69 | 86 | .414 | .403 |

## CHING-LUNG LO — RHP

**Born:** Aug., 20, 1985. **B-T:** R-R. **Ht.:** 6-6. **Wt.:** 210. **Signed:** Taiwan, 2001. **Signed by:** Kent Blasingame.

After watching Lo's slow development for four years in the lower levels, the Rockies finally decided to allow him to return to his natural approach to pitching last year. They quit trying to create more of a downhill plane in his delivery, allowing him to use the Asian pitching style of leaning on his back leg. It doesn't produce the arm angle the Rockies want, but his body responded to the return of his natural arm slot. They also allowed him to put the forkball back in his assortment. Lo made big strides during the fall in Hawaii Winter Baseball, where his performance was uneven but his stuff improved. Working again with pitching coach Butch Hughes, who had him in high Class A during the summer, Lo was pitching at 92-93 mph with his fastball in Hawaii, several ticks below his peak when he signed for $1.4 million as a 16-year-old, but better than where he was at the end of the 2005 season when he tired and was sitting in the upper 80s. He showed a regained confidence

when he was able to use his forkball instead of a straight changeup as his primary secondary pitch. He has some looping action in his slurvy slider, but Hughes has helped clean up that pitch, too. Lo figures to move to Double-A this year.

| Year | Club (League) | Class | W | L | ERA | G | GS | CG | SV | IP | H | R | ER | HR | BB | SO | AVG |
|------|---------------|-------|---|---|-----|---|----|----|----|----|---|---|----|----|----|----|-----|
| 2002 | Casper (Pio) | R | 2 | 4 | 3.20 | 14 | 9 | 0 | 0 | 45 | 44 | 22 | 16 | 3 | 22 | 21 | .246 |
| 2003 | Tri-City (NWL) | A | 3 | 7 | 2.85 | 14 | 14 | 0 | 0 | 76 | 66 | 27 | 24 | 1 | 27 | 48 | .237 |
| 2004 | Asheville (SAL) | A | 4 | 3 | 5.05 | 17 | 9 | 0 | 1 | 62 | 70 | 49 | 35 | 9 | 30 | 49 | .293 |
| 2005 | Asheville (SAL) | A | 7 | 9 | 5.65 | 24 | 24 | 1 | 0 | 121 | 148 | 90 | 76 | 23 | 38 | 91 | .303 |
| 2006 | Modesto (Cal) | A | 10 | 5 | 5.39 | 27 | 25 | 0 | 0 | 155 | 179 | 108 | 93 | 14 | 54 | 128 | .285 |
| **MINOR LEAGUE TOTALS** | | | 26 | 28 | 4.78 | 96 | 81 | 1 | 1 | 459 | 507 | 296 | 244 | 50 | 171 | 337 | .280 |

## DARREN CLARKE RHP

**Born:** Mar. 18, 1981. **B-T:** R-R. **Ht.:** 6-8. **Wt.:** 230. **Drafted:** South Florida CC, D/F 2000 (35th round). **Signed by:** John Cedarburg.

Clarke was dominating in high Class A last season, earning a spot in the California League-Carolina League all-star game roster. He was on the verge of jumping to Triple-A when he was sidelined by a strained right lat muscle. Staying healthy has been the biggest challenge for Clarke, who has intimidating size on the mound. He had reconstructive right elbow surgery in 2004, and had his 2005 season cut short because of a right elbow strain. The good news is the problems in 2006 had nothing to do with the elbow. With his height and a downhill delivery, Clarke's 98 mph fastball gets on hitters in a hurry. He has a hard slurve for a breaking pitch that is effective because hitters are so focused on the fastball. He also gained depth on it by adjusting his release point, moving it further from his head. The positive from his three-year battle with health problems has been the effort he put into a conditioning program, which allowed him to shed more than 40 pounds. The Rockies feel strongly enough about Clarke that they protected him on the 40-man roster in the offseason. He'll advance past Class A for the first time in 2007.

| Year | Club (League) | Class | W | L | ERA | G | GS | CG | SV | IP | H | R | ER | HR | BB | SO | AVG |
|------|---------------|-------|---|---|-----|---|----|----|----|----|---|---|----|----|----|----|-----|
| 2001 | Casper (Pio) | R | 3 | 6 | 6.02 | 14 | 14 | 0 | 0 | 55 | 76 | 47 | 37 | 3 | 33 | 42 | .336 |
| 2002 | Tri-City (NWL) | A | 4 | 3 | 6.98 | 12 | 9 | 0 | 0 | 40 | 51 | 34 | 31 | 3 | 19 | 38 | .305 |
| 2003 | Asheville (SAL) | A | 8 | 6 | 3.83 | 27 | 25 | 1 | 0 | 157 | 155 | 80 | 67 | 22 | 59 | 107 | .259 |
| 2004 | Visalia (Cal) | A | 1 | 3 | 7.39 | 8 | 7 | 0 | 0 | 35 | 54 | 35 | 29 | 6 | 16 | 27 | .342 |
| 2005 | Tri-City (NWL) | A | 0 | 0 | 0.64 | 12 | 0 | 0 | 3 | 14 | 9 | 1 | 1 | 0 | 2 | 18 | .184 |
|  | Modesto (Cal) | A | 0 | 0 | 9.00 | 5 | 0 | 0 | 0 | 6 | 13 | 8 | 6 | 2 | 3 | 4 | .433 |
| 2006 | Modesto (Cal) | A | 1 | 1 | 1.35 | 25 | 0 | 0 | 5 | 27 | 13 | 5 | 4 | 1 | 7 | 37 | .140 |
| **MINOR LEAGUE TOTALS** | | | 17 | 19 | 4.71 | 103 | 55 | 1 | 8 | 335 | 371 | 210 | 175 | 37 | 139 | 273 | .281 |

## ALVIN COLINA C

**Born:** Dec. 26, 1981. **B-T:** R-R. **Ht.:** 6-3. **Wt.:** 220. **Signed:** Venezuela, 1998. **Signed by:** Jorge Posada.

Colina made a quick recovery from mid-2005 surgery to repair a torn anterior-cruciate ligament in his left knee, and opened last season in Double-A, sharing time with Chris Iannetta before assuming regular duties when Iannetta was promoted. Colina has big-time power when he uses his hands and hips. He needs to discipline his game, both at the plate and behind it. Colina is a solid receiver, but can run into trouble in his pitch selection, not always staying in sync with his pitcher. He has a strong arm and threw out 40 percent of basestealers, but his receiving lags behind due to lazy fundamentals. He's going to have to learn to play through nicks and bruises to become an everyday catcher. Unless Iannetta stumbles, Colina will get a chance to be the starting catcher in Triple-A to open this season, and he'll be just an injury away from Coors Field, so he needs to make some quick adjustments and get his focus on the grind. Ultimately, Colina profiles best as Iannetta's backup.

| Year | Club (League) | Class | AVG | G | AB | R | H | 2B | 3B | HR | RBI | BB | SO | SB | OBP | SLG |
|------|---------------|-------|-----|---|----|---|---|----|----|----|-----|----|----|----|-----|-----|
| 1999 | Universidad (VSL) | R | .186 | 34 | 86 | 10 | 16 | 1 | 0 | 1 | 9 | 21 | 22 | 1 | .364 | .233 |
| 2000 | AZL Rockies (AZL) | R | .352 | 35 | 122 | 25 | 43 | 7 | 1 | 4 | 28 | 9 | 26 | 2 | .417 | .525 |
| 2001 | Tri-City (NWL) | A | .213 | 47 | 164 | 12 | 35 | 10 | 0 | 5 | 17 | 12 | 50 | 0 | .283 | .366 |
| 2002 | Asheville (SAL) | A | .236 | 59 | 212 | 22 | 50 | 8 | 0 | 7 | 36 | 20 | 57 | 1 | .312 | .373 |
| 2003 | Asheville (SAL) | A | .266 | 72 | 256 | 26 | 68 | 20 | 1 | 4 | 23 | 20 | 53 | 5 | .329 | .398 |
| 2004 | Visalia (Cal) | A | .251 | 95 | 334 | 43 | 84 | 23 | 0 | 11 | 47 | 24 | 81 | 0 | .312 | .419 |
| 2005 | Modesto (Cal) | A | .265 | 9 | 34 | 2 | 9 | 3 | 0 | 0 | 3 | 3 | 14 | 0 | .324 | .353 |
|  | Tulsa (TL) | AA | .256 | 59 | 207 | 23 | 53 | 5 | 0 | 9 | 35 | 20 | 42 | 0 | .330 | .411 |
| 2006 | Tulsa (TL) | AA | .254 | 92 | 323 | 45 | 82 | 14 | 1 | 12 | 46 | 23 | 77 | 3 | .314 | .415 |
|  | Colorado (NL) | MLB | .200 | 2 | 5 | 0 | 1 | 0 | 0 | 0 | 1 | 0 | 1 | 0 | .200 | .200 |
| **MINOR LEAGUE TOTALS** | | | .253 | 502 | 1738 | 208 | 440 | 91 | 3 | 53 | 244 | 152 | 422 | 12 | .325 | .400 |
| **MAJOR LEAGUE TOTALS** | | | .200 | 2 | 5 | 0 | 1 | 0 | 0 | 0 | 1 | 0 | 1 | 0 | .200 | .200 |

## MATT MILLER
**OF**

**Born:** Dec. 26, 1982. **B-T:** R-R. **Ht.:** 6-2. **Wt.:** 210. **Drafted:** Texas State, 2004 (13th round). **Signed by:** Jeff Edwards.

Miller dislocated his shoulder in 2004 when he ran into the wall while playing for Tri-City, and aggravated it again in the Arizona Fall League last year. In between, he earned MVP honors in the South Atlantic League in 2005. Before the latest injury, Miller had taken a major step forward in his development. He was hitting .322 with four home runs in 59 AFL at-bats, which would have been a nice cap on a fine season that covered three levels. Miller began letting the ball come to him instead of getting started too quickly and improved his plate discipline, nearly doubling his walk rate of '05. He has legitimate power when he stays balanced, keeps his hands back and waits on his pitch. He has trouble with the ball up and in, trying to come over the top and smother it. While his bat is his best tool, Miller has some polish to his all-around game. He played a lot of center field in high Class A and made strides defensively, but he's better suited for one of the corners, most likely left field because of a below-average but accurate arm. He's a step below average as a runner, but he won't clog the bases. Miller heads back to Double-A, this time to start the season.

| Year | Club (League) | Class | AVG | G | AB | R | H | 2B | 3B | HR | RBI | BB | SO | SB | OBP | SLG |
|---|---|---|---|---|---|---|---|---|---|---|---|---|---|---|---|---|
| 2004 | Tri-City (NWL) | A | .269 | 43 | 167 | 17 | 45 | 8 | 0 | 8 | 25 | 13 | 18 | 0 | .337 | .461 |
| 2005 | Asheville (SAL) | A | .331 | 127 | 508 | 79 | 168 | 34 | 0 | 30 | 100 | 26 | 71 | 9 | .375 | .575 |
| | Modesto (Cal) | A | .400 | 1 | 5 | 0 | 2 | 0 | 0 | 0 | 1 | 0 | 0 | 0 | .400 | .400 |
| 2006 | Modesto (Cal) | A | .323 | 92 | 368 | 52 | 119 | 20 | 2 | 12 | 77 | 31 | 37 | 4 | .381 | .486 |
| | Tulsa (TL) | AA | .229 | 27 | 83 | 14 | 19 | 1 | 1 | 1 | 7 | 11 | 13 | 1 | .330 | .301 |
| | Colorado Springs (PCL) | AAA | .333 | 8 | 24 | 2 | 8 | 0 | 0 | 0 | 3 | 3 | 6 | 0 | .393 | .333 |
| **MINOR LEAGUE TOTALS** | | | .313 | 298 | 1155 | 164 | 361 | 63 | 3 | 51 | 213 | 84 | 145 | 14 | .369 | .505 |

## ERIC YOUNG JR.
**2B**

**Born:** May 25, 1985. **B-T:** B-R. **Ht.:** 5-10. **Wt.:** 180. **Drafted:** Chandler-Gilbert (Ariz.) CC, D/F 2003 (30th round). **Signed by:** Mike Garlatti.

Young is a cult figure in Colorado and hasn't even advanced above low Class A. His dad was the Rockies original second baseman, and put himself into franchise history when he homered in the first at-bat by a Rockies player in Denver. His son, who signed in 2004 as a draft-and-follow, is opening eyes quicker than dad did, leading the minor leagues in stolen bases last season. He improved his stock with a solid turn in Hawaii Winter Baseball, hitting .287 to rank sixth in the league. He has game-changing speed and aggressiveness; the defense gets uncomfortable and pitchers can press to throw strikes. Young, who is at top speed after his first two explosive steps, is just starting to learn to read pitchers' moves and had the green light to run at will in 2006, leading to 31 caught stealings, also tops in the minors. Young's raw physical ability makes him a prospect, but so do his outstanding work habits. Young has improved at hitting the ball to the opposite field and has focused on the small game. A natural righthanded hitter, he has more power from that side and has improved with his lefty approach. He can struggle defensively at times but works to get better. He has trouble with the backhand play and has a below-average arm, but his commitment to improvement is evident by the fact he had only five second-half errors last season, and they were all throwing errors. With Cory Wimberly ahead of him, Young figures to move one step at a time and join Nelson again as a double-play tandem, this time in high Class A.

| Year | Club (League) | Class | AVG | G | AB | R | H | 2B | 3B | HR | RBI | BB | SO | SB | OBP | SLG |
|---|---|---|---|---|---|---|---|---|---|---|---|---|---|---|---|---|
| 2004 | Casper (Pio) | R | .264 | 23 | 87 | 20 | 23 | 5 | 1 | 0 | 7 | 20 | 13 | 14 | .407 | .345 |
| 2005 | Casper (Pio) | R | .301 | 63 | 219 | 48 | 66 | 7 | 7 | 3 | 25 | 35 | 52 | 25 | .404 | .438 |
| 2006 | Asheville (SAL) | A | .295 | 128 | 482 | 92 | 142 | 28 | 6 | 5 | 49 | 67 | 75 | 87 | .391 | .409 |
| **MINOR LEAGUE TOTALS** | | | .293 | 214 | 788 | 160 | 231 | 40 | 14 | 8 | 81 | 122 | 140 | 126 | .397 | .410 |

## PEDRO STROP
**RHP**

**Born:** June 13, 1985. **B-T:** R-R. **Ht.:** 6-1. **Wt.:** 170. **Signed:** Dominican Republic, 2002. **Signed by:** Rolando Fernandez/Felix Feliz.

Originally signed as a shortstop for $50,000, Strop (pronounced Strope) batted just .236 in 753 at-bats and never made it above low Class A in four years. The Rockies finally tired of his struggles with the bat before last season, converting him to the mound. When they left him off their 40-man roster this offseason, several clubs targeted Strop in the major league Rule 5 draft because of his power arm, but there were no takers based on his limited pitching experience. He produces easy velocity with a quick arm action, dialing his fastball up to 93-95 mph with good late life. He also flashes a plus slider, though he doesn't command it consistently. His slider sits in the low 80s, and he needs to stay on top of it more to

maintain its tilt and depth. Strop's mechanics are still somewhat raw, but the Rockies consider the flaws in his delivery to be correctable. He won't be rushed and will open 2007 in low Class A.

| Year | Club (League) | Class | AVG | G | AB | R | H | 2B | 3B | HR | RBI | BB | SO | SB | OBP | SLG |
|------|---------------|-------|------|-----|-----|----|-----|----|----|----|-----|----|-----|----|------|------|
| 2002 | Colorado (DSL) | R | .227 | 60 | 194 | 28 | 44 | 9 | 3 | 0 | 20 | 12 | 32 | 6 | .304 | .286 |
| 2003 | Casper (Pio) | R | .172 | 40 | 128 | 13 | 22 | 4 | 1 | 1 | 11 | 15 | 43 | 1 | .242 | .284 |
| 2004 | Tri-City (NWL) | A | .200 | 55 | 190 | 20 | 38 | 6 | 1 | 3 | 20 | 17 | 64 | 2 | .289 | .286 |
| 2005 | Asheville (SAL) | A | .167 | 4 | 12 | 2 | 2 | 0 | 0 | 0 | 0 | 0 | 6 | 0 | .167 | .167 |
| | Tri-City (NWL) | A | .236 | 62 | 229 | 26 | 54 | 11 | 2 | 3 | 25 | 6 | 86 | 7 | .341 | .261 |
| **MINOR LEAGUE TOTALS** | | | .212 | 221 | 753 | 89 | 160 | 30 | 7 | 7 | 76 | 50 | 231 | 16 | .299 | .277 |

| Year | Club (League) | Class | W | L | ERA | G | GS | CG | SV | IP | H | R | ER | HR | BB | SO | AVG |
|------|---------------|-------|---|---|------|----|----|----|----|----|----|----|----|----|----|----|------|
| 2006 | Casper (Pio) | R | 1 | 0 | 2.08 | 11 | 0 | 0 | 0 | 13 | 9 | 3 | 3 | 1 | 2 | 22 | .188 |
| | Asheville (SAL) | A | 2 | 1 | 4.73 | 11 | 0 | 0 | 0 | 13 | 10 | 7 | 7 | 3 | 5 | 13 | .213 |
| **MINOR LEAGUE TOTALS** | | | 3 | 1 | 3.42 | 22 | 0 | 0 | 0 | 26 | 19 | 10 | 10 | 4 | 7 | 35 | .200 |

## 29 ANDREW JOHNSTON                                                    RHP

**Born:** April 20, 1984. **B-T:** R-R. **Ht.:** 6-5. **Wt.:** 205. **Drafted:** Missouri, 2005 (9th round). **Signed by:** Mike Germann.

After tying a Pioneer League saves record in his debut, Johnston had a difficult 2006, but he impressed the Rockies with his mental toughness. First, his season was delayed because of the death of his mother, who suffered from cancer. He wound up in extended spring training and didn't join Asheville until mid-May. Then, in his first two appearances, he gave up game-deciding home runs. Johnston, however, bounced back strong, and finished second in the South Atlantic League in saves while giving up just two more homers the rest of the year. Johnston comes at hitters with a three-quarter delivery, adding some deception to a heavy sinking fastball that is consistently clocked at 92-93 mph. His slider can be a decent pitch, but he still leaves it over the plate too often. He doesn't have an offspeed pitch, but gets so many groundballs with his sinker (81-27 ground-fly ratio), he may not need one. He's a consistent strike-thrower and isn't afraid to pitch inside to righthanders. He's a good athlete, who can field his position, limiting opponents ability to bunt on him. Filling in for the injured Shane Lindsay, Johnston made up for lost time with a stint in Hawaii Winter Baseball and dominated, throwing 19 innings without giving up a home run or walk. He did give up two runs in the league championship game, though. Johnston has enough fastball command to handle a jump to Double-A.

| Year | Club (League) | Class | W | L | ERA | G | GS | CG | SV | IP | H | R | ER | HR | BB | SO | AVG |
|------|---------------|-------|---|---|------|----|----|----|----|----|----|----|----|----|----|----|------|
| 2005 | Casper (Pio) | R | 1 | 2 | 1.06 | 30 | 0 | 0 | 18 | 34 | 22 | 10 | 4 | 0 | 7 | 24 | .171 |
| 2006 | Asheville (SAL) | A | 0 | 3 | 2.84 | 45 | 0 | 0 | 25 | 44 | 43 | 21 | 14 | 5 | 5 | 23 | .246 |
| **MINOR LEAGUE TOTALS** | | | 1 | 5 | 2.07 | 75 | 0 | 0 | 43 | 78 | 65 | 31 | 18 | 5 | 12 | 47 | .214 |

## 30 DAVID CHRISTENSEN                                                   OF

**Born:** Feb. 11, 1988. **B-T:** R-R. **Ht.:** 6-1. **Wt.:** 195. **Drafted:** HS—Parkland, Fla., 2006 (2nd round). **Signed by:** John Cedarburg.

Christensen had college options, committing to Miami and also receiving offers from Stanford and Georgia Tech. He still signed relatively quickly for $750,000, lower than his expected bonus demands of $1 million. Christensen is a toolsy player with potential to be a complete player but also showed his youth and inexperience with his struggles in pro ball. His Pioneer League-leading 93 strikeouts in 207 at-bats seems like a misprint, and he had streaks of 14 and 15 consecutive games with a strikeout. He has tremendous bat speed and power potential to all fields, but has to learn to make his swing more compact. Christensen can be overly aggressive, particularly having trouble with the breaking ball, and has to recognize pitches better. Christensen is a slightly above-average runner and should be an asset on the bases as he gains experience, though his aggressiveness got the best of him in this area as well. He shows potential to be a respectable outfielder with refinement of his routes and has an impressive throwing arm. Christensen's tools project him as an everyday right fielder, but that's a lot of projection. He needs to gain confidence and likely will begin this season in extended spring training.

| Year | Club (League) | Class | AVG | G | AB | R | H | 2B | 3B | HR | RBI | BB | SO | SB | OBP | SLG |
|------|---------------|-------|------|----|-----|----|----|----|----|----|-----|----|----|----|------|------|
| 2006 | Casper (Pio) | R | .198 | 58 | 207 | 26 | 41 | 11 | 2 | 5 | 20 | 22 | 93 | 2 | .279 | .343 |
| **MINOR LEAGUE TOTALS** | | | .198 | 58 | 207 | 26 | 41 | 11 | 2 | 5 | 20 | 22 | 93 | 2 | .279 | .343 |

# DETROIT
# TIGERS

BY **JON PAUL MOROSI** (DETROIT FREE PRESS)

MICHAEL WALBY

At the close of spring training, many in the industry believed the Tigers would be an improved team in 2006. And they were right.

Few, however, could have forecast what came next. Guided by manager Jim Leyland, Detroit had the best record in baseball for a significant portion of the season, finished with the franchise's first winning mark since 1993 and reached the postseason for the first time in nearly two decades.

The Tigers' 95 wins concluded the greatest three-year improvement (52 games) for a 100-loss team in the modern era. Then Detroit scored an American League Division Series upset against the Yankees and swept Oakland in the AL Championship Series to earn its first pennant since 1984. A five-game loss to the Cardinals in the World Series couldn't put much of a damper on the year.

The explanation for the runaway success was the same cause for the springtime optimism: power pitching.

The Tigers' top prospects on this list a year ago, righthanders Justin Verlander and **Joel Zumaya**, were two of the best rookies in baseball. Verlander won 17 games and Baseball America's Rookie of the Year award. Zumaya became a Detroit rock star, routinely hitting 101 mph on the Comerica Park radar gun in his first year as a reliever.

Jeremy Bonderman is a four-year veteran but still just 23, and he won 14 games and lowered his ERA for a third straight year. Zach Miner joined the rotation when Mike Maroth (elbow surgery) went on the disabled list and won seven of his first nine decisions.

The Tigers were elated to add Andrew Miller with the sixth pick in last June's draft. A power lefthander, Miller was the draft's consensus top talent but fell because of signability. He signed by early August, joined the big league bullpen later that month and finished the regular season in the majors. He'll return to the minors to begin 2007 and could progress as quickly as Verlander.

Pitching depth throughout the organization helped Tigers affiliates combine for a .537 winning percentage in the minor leagues and win championships in the Triple-A International and low Class A Midwest leagues. It also allowed Detroit to add more sock to its lineup. The Tigers got Gary Sheffield from the Yankees in exchange for three righthanders who didn't work an inning in the majors in 2006: Humberto Sanchez and promising relievers Kevin Whelan and Anthony Claggett.

But the forecast for the system's position players is less certain—except, of course, for outfielder Cameron Maybin. He's among the best prospects in baseball and could be Detroit's regular center fielder by 2008. But three key Tigers—shortstop Carlos Guillen, third baseman Brandon Inge and catcher Ivan Rodriguez—could be free agents at the end of 2007, and there are no obvious successors. Detroit's top three farm clubs led their respective hitting leagues in strikeouts, and like the big league roster, their position prospects lack patience and power.

## TOP 30 PROSPECTS

| | |
|---|---|
| 1. Cameron Maybin, of | 16. Brennan Boesch, of |
| 2. Andrew Miller, lhp | 17. Edward Campusano, lhp |
| 3. Brent Clevlen, of | 18. Mike Rabelo, c |
| 4. Jair Jurrjens, rhp | 19. P.J. Finigan, rhp |
| 5. Jordan Tata, rhp | 20. Ronnie Bourquin, 3b |
| 6. Eulogio de la Cruz, rhp | 21. Jeff Frazier, of |
| 7. Gorkys Hernandez, of | 22. Burke Badenhop, rhp |
| 8. Dallas Trahern, rhp | 23. Matt Joyce, of |
| 9. Jeff Larish, 1b | 24. Virgil Vasquez, rhp |
| 10. Scott Sizemore, ss/2b | 25. Jonah Nickerson, rhp |
| 11. Kody Kirkland, 3b | 26. Preston Larrison, rhp |
| 12. Sendy Vasquez, rhp | 27. Ryan Raburn, of/2b |
| 13. Wilkin Ramirez, 3b | 28. Audy Ciriaco, ss |
| 14. Tony Giarratano, ss | 29. Clete Thomas, of |
| 15. Michael Hollimon, ss | 30. Kyle Sleeth, rhp |

# ORGANIZATION OVERVIEW

**General manager:** Dave Dombrowski. **Farm director:** Dan Lunetta **Scouting director:** David Chadd.

## 2006 PERFORMANCE

| Class | Team | League | W | L | PCT | Finish* | Manager | Affiliated |
|---|---|---|---|---|---|---|---|---|
| Majors | Detroit | American | 95 | 67 | .586 | +3rd (14) | Jim Leyland | — |
| Triple-A | Toledo Mud Hens | International | 76 | 66 | .535 | 5th (14) | Larry Parrish | 1987 |
| Double-A | Erie Sea Wolves | Eastern | 60 | 81 | .426 | 12th (12) | Duffy Dyer | 2001 |
| High A | Lakeland Tigers | Florida State | 68 | 68 | .500 | 6th (12) | Mike Rojas | 1967 |
| Low A | West Mich. Whitecaps | Midwest | 89 | 48 | .650 | +1st (14) | Matt Walbeck | 1997 |
| Short-season | Oneonta Tigers | New York-Penn | 40 | 34 | .541 | 6th (14) | Tom Brookens | 1999 |
| Rookie | GCL Tigers | Gulf Coast | 32 | 18 | .640 | 2nd (13) | Kevin Bradshaw | 1995 |
| **OVERALL 2006 MINOR LEAGUE RECORD** | | | 365 | 315 | .537 | 4th (30) | | |

*Finish in overall standings (No. of teams in league). +League champion

## ORGANIZATION LEADERS

### BATTING
| | | |
|---|---|---|
| AVG | Hernandez, Gorkys, GCL Tigers | .327 |
| | Sizemore, Scott, Oneonta | .327 |
| R | Ludwick, Ryan, Toledo | 81 |
| H | Phelps, Josh, Toledo | 143 |
| 2B | Larish, Jeffrey, Lakeland | 34 |
| | Ludwick, Ryan, Toledo | 34 |
| 3B | Hollimon, Michael, West Michigan | 13 |
| HR | Ludwick, Ryan, Toledo | 28 |
| RBI | Phelps, Josh, Toledo | 90 |
| BB | Airoso, Kurt, Erie | 81 |
| | Larish, Jeffrey, Lakeland | 81 |
| SO | Kirkland, Kody, Toledo/Erie | 184 |
| SB | Thomas, Clete, Lakeland | 34 |
| OBP | Carlson, Christopher, GCL Tigers | .402 |
| SLG | Carlson, Christopher, GCL Tigers | .588 |
| XBH | Ludwick, Ryan, Toledo | 64 |

### PITCHING
| | | |
|---|---|---|
| W | Badenhop, Burke, West Michigan | 14 |
| L | Bumstead, Nathan, Erie | 14 |
| ERA | Martinez, Cristhian, Lakeland/GCL/Oneonta | 2.56 |
| G | Gardner, Lee, Toledo | 58 |
| SV | Gardner, Lee, Toledo | 30 |
| IP | Durbin, Chad, Toledo | 185 |
| BB | Bumstead, Nathan, Erie | 79 |
| SO | Durbin, Chad, Toledo | 149 |
| AVG | Sanchez, Humberto, Erie/Toledo | .220 |

## BEST TOOLS

| | |
|---|---|
| Best Hitter for Average | Cameron Maybin |
| Best Power Hitter | Jeff Larish |
| Best Strike-Zone Discipline | Jeff Larish |
| Fastest Baserunner | Cameron Maybin |
| Best Athlete | Cameron Maybin |
| Best Fastball | Eulogio de la Cruz |
| Best Curveball | Eulogio de la Cruz |
| Best Slider | Andrew Miller |
| Best Changeup | Preston Larrison |
| Best Control | Jair Jurrjens |
| Best Defensive Catcher | Jeff Kunkel |
| Best Defensive Infielder | Tony Giarratano |
| Best Infield Arm | Kody Kirkland |
| Best Defensive Outfielder | Cameron Maybin |
| Best Outfield Arm | Brent Clevlen |

## PROJECTED 2010 LINEUP

| | |
|---|---|
| Catcher | Brandon Inge |
| First Base | Jeff Larish |
| Second Base | Placido Polanco |
| Third Base | Kody Kirkland |
| Shortstop | Carlos Guillen |
| Left Field | Curtis Granderson |
| Center Field | Cameron Maybin |
| Right Field | Brent Clevlen |
| Designated Hitter | Magglio Ordonez |
| No. 1 Starter | Justin Verlander |
| No. 2 Starter | Andrew Miller |
| No. 3 Starter | Jeremy Bonderman |
| No. 4 Starter | Nate Robertson |
| No. 5 Starter | Jair Jurrjens |
| Closer | Joel Zumaya |

## LAST YEAR'S TOP 20 PROSPECTS

1. Justin Verlander, rhp
2. Joel Zumaya, rhp
3. Cameron Maybin, of
4. Brent Clevlen, of
5. Wilkin Ramirez, 3b
6. Humberto Sanchez, rhp
7. Jordan Tata, rhp
8. Tony Giarratano, ss
9. Jeff Larish, 1b
10. Kevin Whelan, rhp
11. Kody Kirkland, 3b
12. Jeff Frazier, of
13. Dallas Trahern, rhp
14. Clete Thomas, of
15. Eulogio de la Cruz, rhp
16. Jair Jurrjens, rhp
17. Juan Francia, 2b
18. Ryan Raburn, 2b
19. Donald Kelly, 3b/ss
20. Kyle Sleeth, rhp

## TOP PROSPECTS OF THE DECADE

| Year | Player, Pos. | 2006 Org. |
|---|---|---|
| 1997 | Mike Drumright, rhp | Out of baseball |
| 1998 | Juan Encarnacion, of | Cardinals |
| 1999 | Gabe Kapler, of | Red Sox |
| 2000 | Eric Munson, 1b/c | Astros |
| 2001 | Brandon Inge, c | Tigers |
| 2002 | Nate Cornejo, rhp | White Sox |
| 2003 | Jeremy Bonderman, rhp | Tigers |
| 2004 | Kyle Sleeth, rhp | Tigers |
| 2005 | Curtis Granderson, of | Tigers |
| 2006 | Justin Verlander, rhp | Tigers |

## TOP DRAFT PICKS OF THE DECADE

| Year | Player, Pos. | 2006 Org. |
|---|---|---|
| 1997 | Matt Anderson, rhp | Giants |
| 1998 | Jeff Weaver, rhp | Cardinals |
| 1999 | Eric Munson, 1b/c | Astros |
| 2000 | Matt Wheatland, rhp | San Diego (Golden) |
| 2001 | Kenny Baugh, rhp | Padres |
| 2002 | Scott Moore, ss | Cubs |
| 2003 | Kyle Sleeth, rhp | Tigers |
| 2004 | Justin Verlander, rhp | Tigers |
| 2005 | Cameron Maybin, rhp | Tigers |
| 2006 | Andrew Miller, lhp | Tigers |

## LARGEST BONUSES IN CLUB HISTORY

| | |
|---|---|
| Andrew Miller, 2006 | $3,550,000 |
| Eric Munson, 1999 | $3,500,000 |
| Kyle Sleeth, 2003 | $3,350,000 |
| Justin Verlander, 2004 | $3,120,000 |
| Cameron Maybin, 2005 | $2,650,000 |

# MINOR LEAGUE DEPTH CHART

## Detroit Tigers

**Impact: A.** It's hard to beat Maybin and Miller at the top of the system. There's a significant drop-off thereafter, but that one-two punch is formidable.

**Depth: D.** The Gary Sheffield deal significantly diminished Detroit's pitching reserves, and 2006 provided more questions than answers among position players.

**Sleeper:** Matt Joyce, of. He's a bit older, but he showed power and plate discipline flanking Maybin in West Michigan, and he has athleticism as well.

*Numbers in parentheses indicate prospect rankings.*

| LF | CF | RF |
|---|---|---|
| Jeff Frazier (21) | Cameron Maybin (1) | Brent Clevlen (3) |
| Ryan Raburn (27) | Gorkys Hernandez (7) | Brennan Boesch (16) |
| David Espinosa | Clete Thomas (29) | Matt Joyce (23) |
| Michael Hernandez | Vince Blue | Victor Mendez |
| Justin Justice | Deik Scram | |

| 3B | SS | 2B | 1B |
|---|---|---|---|
| Kody Kirkland (11) | Tony Giarratano (14) | Scott Sizemore (10) | Jeff Larish (9) |
| Wilkin Ramirez (13) | Michael Hollimon (15) | Jack Hannahan | Ryan Strieby |
| Ronald Bourquin (20) | Audy Ciriaco (28) | Will Rhymes | Christopher Carlson |
| | Brent Dlugach | Gilberto Mejia | Kelly Hunt |

| C |
|---|
| Mike Rabelo (18) |
| Jordan Newton |
| Jeff Kunkel |
| Dusty Ryan |
| Joe Bowen |

| RHP | | LHP | |
|---|---|---|---|
| **Starters** | **Relievers** | **Starters** | **Relievers** |
| Jair Jurrjens (4) | P.J. Finigan (19) | Andrew Miller (2) | Edward Campusano (17) |
| Jordan Tata (5) | Preston Larrison (26) | Luke French | Corey Hamman |
| Eulogio de la Cruz (6) | Brett Jensen | Christopher Cody | Duane Below |
| Dallas Trahern (8) | Orlando Perdomo | Ramon Garcia | Ian Ostlund |
| Sendy Vasquez (12) | Ricky Steik | Erik Averill | Tony Peralta |
| Burke Badenhop (22) | | | |
| Virgil Vasquez (24) | | | |
| Jonah Nickerson (25) | | | |
| Kyle Sleeth (30) | | | |
| Nate Bumstead | | | |
| Andrew Kown | | | |
| Josh Rainwater | | | |
| Kevin Ardoin | | | |

# DRAFT ANALYSIS

**Best Pro Debut:** OF Brennan Boesch (3) topped the New York-Penn League with 54 RBIs, while SS Scott Sizemore (5) paced the NY-P with 49 runs and 96 hits. Sidearming RHP Brett Jensen (17) had a 0.67 ERA, 17 saves and a 31-5 K-BB ratio in 27 innings. LHP Paul Hammond (35) posted a 0.81 ERA and made it to high Class A, mainly by throwing strikes.

**Best Athlete:** Surprisingly, Oneonta manager Tom Brookens tabbed a catcher (Jordan Newton [6]) as the best athlete on his club, which received most of Detroit's draft picks. Newton was recruited to play strong safety by college football programs and has plus speed, arm strength and power potential.

**Best Pure Hitter:** Sizemore hit .303 in the Cape Cod League last summer and .327 in his pro debut. As a bonus, the Tigers drafted him as a second baseman but played him at short based on need, and he more than held his own defensively. 3B Ronnie Bourquin's (2) bat is his best tool, and he won the Big Ten Conference batting title with a .416 average.

**Best Raw Power:** 1B Ryan Strieby (4), who's 6-foot-6 and 235 pounds, has more pure pop than Boesch, a physical specimen himself at 6-foot-5 and 185 pounds.

**Fastest Runner:** OFs Deik Scram (18) and Mike Sullivan (31) are above-average runners.

**Best Defensive Player:** Sullivan has the range for center field, though he played right field in the GCL in deference to stud prospect Gorkys Hernandez. Draft-and-follow C Jeff Kunkel has impressive catch-and-throw skills.

**Best Fastball:** LHP Andrew Miller (1) throws 93-95 mph with ease, and the Tigers have seen him peak at 98. RHP Angel Castro (13), a 23-year-old Domincan, has a low-90s fastball. Assigned to the bottom rung of professional baseball (the Dominican Summer League) because of visa issues, he blew away teenagers to the tune of a 1.39 ERA, .167 opponent average and 71 strikeouts in 58 innings.

**Best Breaking Ball:** Miller's tight mid-80s slider.

**Most Intriguing Background:** RHP Jonah Nickerson (7) was MVP of the College World Series. OF Lance Durham's (45) father Leon was a big league all-star, while C Ben Petralli's (17) dad Geno played in the majors. Neither signed. C Adrian Casanova's (40) father Rolando is a Tigers area scout and a former assistant coach at Florida International, where Adrian spent the first three years of his college career.

**Closest To The Majors:** Miller became the first player from the 2006 draft to reach the big leagues, showing quality stuff but walking 10 in as many innings. Detroit was considering adding him to its World Series roster, which would make him the first player to participate in the College World Series and World Series in the same year. Nickerson's guts and command of four pitches will hasten his development.

**Best Late-Round Pick:** Jensen and Carlson.

**The One Who Got Away:** RHP Casey Weathers (25), a converted outfielder who has touched 95 mph, returned to Vanderbilt after failing to reach accord with the Tigers.

**Assessment:** Getting Miller, the consensus best prospect in the draft, at No. 6 is a coup that ranks with landing Cameron Maybin at No. 10 in 2005. Without an agreement in place, the Tigers didn't let Miller's excessive bonus demands scare them off and signed him for market value, a guaranteed $5.45 million big league contract.

OF Cameron Maybin (1) looks like a future superstar. 1B Jeff Larish has pop in his bat, while RHPs Kevin Whelan (4) and Anthony Claggett (11) were pieces in the offseason Gary Sheffield trade. **GRADE: A**

RHP Justin Verlander (1) was Baseball America's 2006 Rookie of the Year. Beyond him, RHP Dallas Trahern (34) has some upside. **GRADE: A**

The Tigers changed RHP Kyle Sleeth's (1) mechanics—and he quickly blew out his elbow. SS Tony Giarratano (3) and RHP Jordan Tata (16) have picked up the slack for this group. **GRADE: C**

*Draft analysis by Jim Callis. Numbers in parentheses indicate draft rounds. Budgets are bonuses in first 10 rounds.*

# CAMERON
# MAYBIN

3B

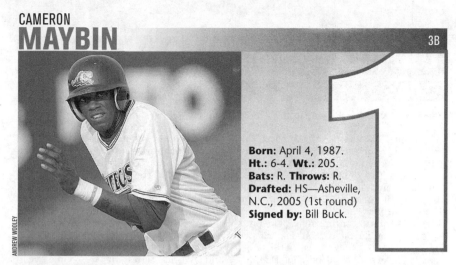

ANDREW WOOLEY

**Born:** April 4, 1987.
**Ht.:** 6-4. **Wt.:** 205.
**Bats:** R. **Throws:** R.
**Drafted:** HS—Asheville,
N.C., 2005 (1st round)
**Signed by:** Bill Buck.

Baseball America's third-rated prospect for the 2005 draft, Maybin fell to the Tigers at No. 10 because other teams preferred college players or had questions about his signability. BA's 2004 Youth Player of the Year after leading the Midland Redskins to the Connie Mack World Series title, Maybin missed his first pro summer while negotiating a $2.65 million bonus. From a standpoint of both development and performance, Detroit couldn't have asked for a better 2006 debut. Maybin nearly led the low Class A Midwest League in hitting despite competing against players who were often two or three years older. He played for a league champion West Michigan team, batting .343 with six extra-base hits in nine postseason games, including a pair of clutch triples that turned around the final series. Maybin also played for the U.S. team in the Futures Game and was the second-youngest player in the game, behind the Yankees' Jose Tabata. There were distractions and setbacks, too. Maybin missed a month early in the season with a bruise on his right index finger. Later, he was charged with underage possession of alcohol (a misdemeanor), but the incident didn't appear to suggest any more serious issues. By all accounts, the Tigers believe Maybin to have great character in addition to tremendous talent.

Maybin has all the tools and, all the more impressive, those tools are well developed at his young age. Managers rated him the MWL's best and fastest baserunner and its most exciting player, and he also drew votes as the top hitting prospect and best defensive out-fielder. Though he was considered somewhat raw and played in a tough hitter's park, Maybin hit .304 in his debut, showing more ability to make adjustments and awareness of the strike zone than expected. He has exceptional bat speed and raw power, so he'll be a home run threat as well. Seven of his nine longballs came in the season's last two months. He runs extremely well, both on the bases and in center field, and he succeeded on 27 of his 34 steal attempts. Maybin has a strong arm, and though he should have no difficulty staying in center, he also profiles well for right field. His overall ability has drawn comparisons to that of Mike Cameron and Torii Hunter. Maybin can be an elite player, with the potential to hit somewhere at the top or in the middle of the order.

Maybin has few shortcomings. The most apparent is that he strikes out too often, a common trait among Tigers farmhands. He had nearly as many whiffs as he had hits in his debut, and he can take some ugly swings when he's fooled at the plate. But he's also very gifted and advanced for a 19-year-old, and his plate discipline should improve with experience. He has lost some time to hamstring problems in 2005 instructional league and to the finger injury in his debut, but his long-term health isn't a worry.

After the trade deadline passed, Tigers general manager Dave Dombrowski declared, "I wouldn't trade Cameron Maybin straight up for Alfonso Soriano. That's how much we like him." Manager Jim Leyland later concurred and called Maybin a special talent. He'll likely start 2007 in Double-A Erie, and he could push his way to Detroit by the end of the season. Curtis Granderson played capably in center field in 2006 and starred in the postseason, so either he or Maybin eventually will have to move to a corner.

| Year | Club (League) | Class | AVG | G | AB | R | H | 2B | 3B | HR | RBI | BB | SO | SB | OBP | SLG |
|------|---------------|-------|-----|---|----|---|---|----|----|----|-----|----|----|----|-----|-----|
| 2006 | West Michigan (MWL) | A | .304 | 101 | 385 | 59 | 117 | 20 | 6 | 9 | 69 | 50 | 116 | 27 | .387 | .457 |
| **MINOR LEAGUE TOTALS** | | | .304 | 101 | 385 | 59 | 117 | 20 | 6 | 9 | 69 | 50 | 116 | 27 | .387 | .457 |

## 2 ANDREW MILLER LHP

**Born:** May 21, 1985. **B-T:** R-L. **Ht.:** 6-6. **Wt.:** 210. **Drafted:** North Carolina, 2006 (first round). **Signed by:** Grant Brittain.

The 2006 draft's consensus top talent and Baseball America's College Player of the Year, Miller slid to Detroit at No. 6 because of signability. By early August, the sides agreed on a major league contract with a $3.55 million bonus and $5.45 million guarantee. After five innings at high Class A Lakeland, Miller made his big league debut at Yankee Stadium later that month. His season included two other thrills: his North Carolina team went to the College World Series finals, and he was on the mound in Kansas City when the Tigers clinched their first postseason berth in 19 years. Few lefthanders can match Miller's combination of size and stuff, and he projects as a frontline starter. He throws 93-95 with little effort and tops out at 98. His mid-80s slider already qualifies as a major league out pitch. He has dominated against wood bats, earning top-prospect honors in the Cape Cod League in both 2004 and 2005. Miller doesn't have much of a changeup and may need one against big league righthanders. He has preferred to dial his two-seam fastball down to the low to mid-80s. His command faded at times during his stint with the Tigers. Most scouts' concerns about him center on his arm action, as he has a slight wrap in the back of his delivery that hampers his command. Though he pitched in relief for the Tigers, Miller's future clearly is in the rotation. He'll head to Double-A as a starter and could be back in Detroit by the end of the season.

| Year | Club (League) | Class | W | L | ERA | G | GS | CG | SV | IP | H | R | ER | HR | BB | SO | AVG |
|------|---------------|-------|---|---|------|---|----|----|----|----|---|---|----|----|----|----|------|
| 2006 | Lakeland (FSL) | A | 0 | 0 | 0.00 | 3 | 0 | 0 | 0 | 5 | 2 | 0 | 0 | 0 | 1 | 9 | .118 |
|      | Detroit (AL) | MLB | 0 | 1 | 6.10 | 8 | 0 | 0 | 0 | 10 | 8 | 9 | 7 | 0 | 10 | 6 | .205 |
| **MINOR LEAGUE TOTALS** | | | 0 | 0 | 0.00 | 3 | 0 | 0 | 0 | 5 | 2 | 0 | 0 | 0 | 1 | 9 | .118 |
| **MAJOR LEAGUE TOTALS** | | | 0 | 1 | 6.10 | 8 | 0 | 0 | 0 | 10 | 8 | 9 | 7 | 0 | 10 | 6 | .205 |

## 3 BRENT CLEVLEN OF

**Born:** Oct. 27, 1983. **B-T:** R-R. **Ht.:** 6-2. **Wt.:** 190. **Drafted:** HS—Cedar Park, Texas, 2002 (2nd round). **Signed by:** Tim Grieve.

The 2005 high Class A Florida State League MVP, Clevlen batted just .230 in Double-A but stood out in two late stints with Detroit. He attributed the difference in his performance to better lighting in the majors. A natural athlete, Clevlen has above-average power and arm strength. He has the speed and instincts to handle center field, though he fits better in right field. Clevlen's defensive ability impressed Tigers manager Jim Leyland during his major league stint. Double-A pitchers learned quickly that Clevlen will chase pitches out of the zone, both up and away, so he saw few good pitches to hit and struck out often. He probably won't ever hit for a high average, but he'll need to have better command of the strike zone in order to sustain success in the big leagues. Though he has slightly above-average speed, he's not much of a basestealing threat. Clevlen could see time in Detroit again, though it's more likely that he'll at least begin 2007 in the minors with an eye toward improving his plate discipline.

| Year | Club (League) | Class | AVG | G | AB | R | H | 2B | 3B | HR | RBI | BB | SO | SB | OBP | SLG |
|------|---------------|-------|------|-----|------|-----|-----|----|----|----|-----|-----|-----|----|------|------|
| 2002 | Tigers (GCL) | R | .330 | 28 | 103 | 14 | 34 | 2 | 3 | 3 | 21 | 8 | 24 | 2 | .372 | .495 |
| 2003 | West Michigan (MWL) | A | .260 | 138 | 481 | 67 | 125 | 22 | 7 | 12 | 63 | 72 | 111 | 6 | .359 | .410 |
| 2004 | Lakeland (FSL) | A | .224 | 117 | 420 | 49 | 94 | 23 | 6 | 6 | 50 | 44 | 127 | 1 | .300 | .350 |
| 2005 | Lakeland (FSL) | A | .302 | 130 | 494 | 77 | 149 | 28 | 4 | 18 | 102 | 65 | 118 | 14 | .387 | .484 |
| 2006 | Erie (EL) | AA | .230 | 109 | 395 | 47 | 91 | 17 | 0 | 11 | 45 | 47 | 138 | 6 | .313 | .357 |
|      | Detroit (AL) | MLB | .282 | 31 | 39 | 9 | 11 | 1 | 2 | 3 | 6 | 2 | 15 | 0 | .317 | .641 |
| **MINOR LEAGUE TOTALS** | | | .260 | 522 | 1893 | 254 | 493 | 92 | 20 | 50 | 281 | 236 | 518 | 30 | .345 | .409 |
| **MAJOR LEAGUE TOTALS** | | | .282 | 31 | 39 | 9 | 11 | 1 | 2 | 3 | 6 | 2 | 15 | 0 | .317 | .641 |

## 4 JAIR JURRJENS RHP

**Born:** Jan. 29, 1986. **B-T:** R-R. **Ht.:** 6-1. **Wt.:** 190. **Signed:** Curacao, 2003. **Signed by:** Greg Smith.

Jurrjens ended 2006 with a much higher profile than he had at the beginning of the year, after pitching in the World Baseball Classic and reaching Double-A at age 20. Jurrjens also was involved in an automobile accident, which caused him to go almost two weeks between starts in late July. The Tigers thought Jurrjens might make a No. 4 starter coming into 2006, but they've revised their hopes upward. He works in the low 90s with the ability to add and subtract from his fastball, which has good life

and reaches 97 mph. He has terrific control, especially considering his age. His curveball and changeup improved throughout the season, and now grade out as at least average. Jurrjens has just one plus pitch and both his curve and change still need polish. His youth is occasionally evident on the mound. He ended the season on the disabled list with right shoulder spasms. The Tigers exercised caution and scrapped plans for him to participate in the Arizona Fall League. Jurrjens probably won't be ready for the majors until 2008, but if he performs well at Triple-A Toledo he could get a late-season callup. Though the Tigers don't expect his shoulder to be an issue, there's a chance they could start him back in Double-A.

| Year | Club (League) | Class | W | L | ERA | G | GS | CG | SV | IP | H | R | ER | HR | BB | SO | AVG |
|---|---|---|---|---|---|---|---|---|---|---|---|---|---|---|---|---|---|
| 2003 | Tigers (GCL) | R | 2 | 1 | 3.21 | 7 | 2 | 0 | 0 | 28 | 33 | 16 | 10 | 3 | 3 | 20 | .292 |
| 2004 | Tigers (GCL) | R | 4 | 2 | 2.27 | 6 | 6 | 2 | 0 | 40 | 25 | 16 | 10 | 2 | 10 | 39 | .171 |
|  | Oneonta (NYP) | A | 1 | 5 | 5.31 | 7 | 7 | 0 | 0 | 39 | 50 | 25 | 23 | 0 | 10 | 31 | .311 |
| 2005 | West Michigan (MWL) | A | 12 | 6 | 3.41 | 26 | 26 | 0 | 0 | 143 | 132 | 62 | 54 | 5 | 36 | 108 | .246 |
| 2006 | Lakeland (FSL) | A | 5 | 0 | 2.08 | 12 | 12 | 0 | 0 | 74 | 53 | 23 | 17 | 4 | 10 | 59 | .198 |
|  | Erie (EL) | AA | 4 | 3 | 3.36 | 12 | 12 | 0 | 0 | 67 | 71 | 30 | 25 | 7 | 21 | 53 | .277 |
| **MINOR LEAGUE TOTALS** |  |  | 28 | 17 | 3.21 | 70 | 65 | 2 | 0 | 390 | 364 | 172 | 139 | 21 | 90 | 310 | .246 |

## 5 JORDAN TATA                                             RHP

**Born:** Sept. 20, 1981. **B-T:** R-R. **Ht.:** 6-6. **Wt.:** 220. **Drafted:** Sam Houston State, 2003 (16th round). **Signed by:** Tim Grieve.

Tata hadn't pitched above Class A, but he made the Opening Day bullpen after an injury to closer Todd Jones in Detroit's final exhibition game. Tata looked comfortable in Detroit before returning to the minors in May. He rejoined the Tigers in September. Tata's fastball, usually clocked from 89-93 mph, has natural cutting action. He also throws a good knuckle-curve. A good athlete who was a two-way player at Sam Houston State, he has a nice frame and sound delivery that allow him to throw strikes. He's not overpowering, so Tata must to refine his repertoire in order to be a big league starter. The Tigers have worked with him on developing a sinker, and he also could use a better changeup to use against lefthanders. Tigers manager Jim Leyland says Tata's future appears to be as a starter, but the Tigers don't have any obvious openings and plenty of internal competition for any vacancy that arises. Tata may have to start in Triple-A or relieve in the majors for most of 2007.

| Year | Club (League) | Class | W | L | ERA | G | GS | CG | SV | IP | H | R | ER | HR | BB | SO | AVG |
|---|---|---|---|---|---|---|---|---|---|---|---|---|---|---|---|---|---|
| 2003 | Oneonta (NYP) | A | 4 | 3 | 2.58 | 16 | 12 | 0 | 1 | 73 | 64 | 32 | 21 | 1 | 20 | 60 | .236 |
| 2004 | West Michigan (MWL) | A | 8 | 11 | 3.35 | 28 | 28 | 1 | 0 | 166 | 167 | 77 | 62 | 7 | 68 | 116 | .272 |
| 2005 | Lakeland (FSL) | A | 13 | 2 | 2.79 | 25 | 25 | 2 | 0 | 155 | 138 | 55 | 48 | 12 | 41 | 134 | .239 |
| 2006 | Toledo (IL) | AAA | 10 | 6 | 3.84 | 21 | 21 | 1 | 0 | 122 | 117 | 58 | 52 | 11 | 49 | 86 | .252 |
|  | Detroit (AL) | MLB | 0 | 0 | 6.14 | 8 | 0 | 0 | 0 | 15 | 14 | 11 | 10 | 1 | 7 | 6 | .250 |
| **MINOR LEAGUE TOTALS** |  |  | 35 | 22 | 3.19 | 90 | 86 | 4 | 1 | 517 | 486 | 222 | 183 | 31 | 178 | 396 | .252 |
| **MAJOR LEAGUE TOTALS** |  |  | 0 | 0 | 6.14 | 8 | 0 | 0 | 0 | 14 | 14 | 11 | 10 | 1 | 7 | 6 | .250 |

## 6 EULOGIO DE LA CRUZ                                      RHP

**Born:** March 12, 1984. **B-T:** R-R. **Ht.:** 5-11. **Wt.:** 177. **Signed:** Dominican Republic, 2001. **Signed by:** Ramon Pena.

Though he's short and stocky, de la Cruz has one of the biggest fastballs in the organization. He shuttled between starting and relieving in Double-A in 2006, and he was able to harness his energy more when he was in the rotation. He earned a promotion to Toledo for the Triple-A playoffs. At its best, his fastball compares favorably to those of Justin Verlander or Joel Zumaya. De la Cruz usually pitches in the mid- to high 90s and has reached 100 mph. His hard curveball is a genuine knee-buckler. Issues with control and command have put de la Cruz behind other young pitchers in the system, though he improved in those areas as a starter. His long-term role is in question because he was more effective as a reliever in 2005. His changeup can throw hitters off balance when they try to sit on his power stuff, but he doesn't have much confidence in the pitch. De la Cruz should be in Toledo this season and reach the big leagues in 2008. Though there's room in the bullpen, the Tigers may not want to jeopardize the progress he has made as a starter.

| Year | Club (League) | Class | W | L | ERA | G | GS | CG | SV | IP | H | R | ER | HR | BB | SO | AVG |
|---|---|---|---|---|---|---|---|---|---|---|---|---|---|---|---|---|---|
| 2002 | Tigers (GCL) | R | 1 | 1 | 2.63 | 20 | 0 | 0 | 1 | 38 | 40 | 24 | 11 | 0 | 21 | 46 | .260 |
|  | Oneonta (NYP) | A | 0 | 0 | 23.14 | 2 | 0 | 0 | 0 | 2 | 7 | 8 | 6 | 0 | 4 | 4 | .500 |
| 2003 | Tigers (GCL) | R | 2 | 2 | 2.59 | 22 | 0 | 0 | 7 | 24 | 18 | 10 | 7 | 0 | 15 | 30 | .205 |
|  | Oneonta (NYP) | A | 0 | 0 | 10.80 | 2 | 0 | 0 | 0 | 3 | 6 | 4 | 4 | 0 | 1 | 4 | .400 |
| 2004 | West Michigan (MWL) | A | 2 | 4 | 3.83 | 54 | 0 | 0 | 17 | 54 | 51 | 30 | 23 | 2 | 33 | 44 | .239 |

| Year | Club | Class | W | L | ERA | G | GS | CG | SV | IP | H | R | ER | HR | BB | SO | AVG |
|---|---|---|---|---|---|---|---|---|---|---|---|---|---|---|---|---|---|
| 2005 | Erie (EL) | AA | 0 | 1 | 16.20 | 1 | 0 | 0 | 0 | 2 | 2 | 3 | 3 | 0 | 4 | 0 | .286 |
| | Lakeland (FSL) | A | 4 | 3 | 3.39 | 40 | 10 | 0 | 5 | 96 | 66 | 46 | 36 | 5 | 36 | 97 | .191 |
| 2006 | Erie (EL) | AA | 5 | 6 | 3.43 | 38 | 12 | 0 | 2 | 105 | 103 | 46 | 40 | 3 | 45 | 87 | .258 |
| | Toledo (IL) | AAA | 0 | 0 | 11.57 | 1 | 1 | 0 | 0 | 2 | 4 | 3 | 3 | 1 | 2 | 3 | .333 |
| **MINOR LEAGUE TOTALS** | | | 14 | 17 | 3.67 | 180 | 23 | 0 | 32 | 326 | 297 | 174 | 133 | 11 | 161 | 315 | .238 |

## 7 GORKYS HERNANDEZ OF

**Born:** Sept. 7, 1987. **B-T:** R-R. **Ht.:** 6-0. **Wt.:** 175. **Signed:** Venezuela, 2005. **Signed by:** Ramon Pena.

After hitting .265 in the Rookie-level Venezuelan Summer League in 2005, Hernandez had a spectacular U.S. debut. Though he didn't turn 19 until after the Rookie-level Gulf Coast League schedule concluded, he topped the circuit in hitting, runs and hits while finishing second in steals and total bases (95). Well-above-average speed is Hernandez' best tool but far from his only one. He's a natural leadoff hitter with a gap-to-gap stroke. His raw power and arm strength are solid, and he gets very good jumps and covers significant real estate in center field. He showed off his basestealing prowess by swiping 20 in 24 tries in the GCL. As with many young players, Hernandez' biggest weakness is his plate discipline. He's advanced for his age but still needs more polish and experience in most phases of his game. He needs to get stronger and fill out his skinny frame, which should come with time. The only position player in the system with more upside is Cameron Maybin. Hernandez may follow the same path and play in low Class A as a 19-year-old. He could become a special prospect if he continues to mature.

| Year | Club (League) | Class | AVG | G | AB | R | H | 2B | 3B | HR | RBI | BB | SO | SB | OBP | SLG |
|---|---|---|---|---|---|---|---|---|---|---|---|---|---|---|---|---|
| 2005 | Tigers (VSL) | R | .265 | 63 | 211 | 44 | 56 | 10 | 0 | 4 | 19 | 30 | 38 | 10 | .377 | .370 |
| 2006 | Tigers (GCL) | R | .327 | 50 | 205 | 41 | 67 | 9 | 2 | 5 | 23 | 10 | 27 | 20 | .356 | .463 |
| **MINOR LEAGUE TOTALS** | | | .296 | 113 | 416 | 85 | 123 | 19 | 2 | 9 | 42 | 40 | 65 | 30 | .368 | .416 |

## 8 DALLAS TRAHERN RHP

**Born:** Nov. 29, 1985. **B-T:** R-R. **Ht.:** 6-3. **Wt.:** 190. **Drafted:** HS—Owasso, Okla., 2004 (34th round). **Signed by:** Steve Taylor.

Trahern was headed to Oklahoma out of high school, but when the Sooners fired pitching coach Ray Hayward, he changed his mind. Trahern signed for $160,000 as a 34th-round pick and has made steady progress. He has had tough luck, ranking in the top 10 in each of his Class A leagues in ERA and losses the last two years. Trahen's best pitch is a low-90s sinker that he throws for strikes. Hitters have trouble lifting it, as evidenced by his 3.3 ground/fly ratio in high Class A. His slider is an average pitch that he also keeps down in the zone to get ground balls. A two-way star on an Oklahoma 6-A state championship team, he's athletic and repeats his delivery well. He hasn't shown the ability to get hitters to consistently swing and miss, averaging just 4.8 strikeouts per nine innings as a pro. Trahern will throw a four-seamer with more velocity up in the zone but does so infrequently. His changeup needs more work after lefthanders hit .289 against him in 2006. The consistency of his sinker and quality of his makeup bode well for Trahern's chances to reach the majors. He'll probably spend much of 2007 in Double-A.

| Year | Club (League) | Class | W | L | ERA | G | GS | CG | SV | IP | H | R | ER | HR | BB | SO | AVG |
|---|---|---|---|---|---|---|---|---|---|---|---|---|---|---|---|---|---|---|
| 2004 | Tigers (GCL) | R | 1 | 2 | 0.59 | 7 | 6 | 0 | 0 | 31 | 22 | 8 | 2 | 1 | 7 | 24 | .198 |
| 2005 | West Michigan (MWL) | A | 7 | 11 | 3.58 | 26 | 26 | 2 | 0 | 156 | 158 | 78 | 62 | 9 | 50 | 66 | .265 |
| 2006 | Lakeland (FSL) | A | 6 | 11 | 3.30 | 25 | 25 | 4 | 0 | 145 | 129 | 66 | 53 | 9 | 41 | 86 | .238 |
| **MINOR LEAGUE TOTALS** | | | 14 | 24 | 3.18 | 58 | 57 | 6 | 0 | 331 | 309 | 152 | 117 | 19 | 98 | 176 | .248 |

## 9 JEFF LARISH 1B

**Born:** Oct. 11, 1982. **B-T:** L-R. **Ht.:** 6-2. **Wt.:** 200. **Drafted:** Arizona State, 2005 (5th round). **Signed by:** Brian Reid.

Expected to be one of the first college hitters drafted in 2004, Larish slumped instead and turned down a $650,000 offer from the Dodgers in the 13th round. He finished fourth in NCAA Division I with 23 homers (including a College World Series-record tying three in one game) in 2005 before signing for $220,000 as a fifth-rounder. He ranked third in the Florida State League in both extra-base hits (54) and walks in his first full season. Larish has strength and leverage in his swing, enabling him to hit the ball out of any part of the park. He's also patient at the plate, willing to take a walk if a pitcher won't give him something he can drive. For a first baseman, he has good athleticism

and arm strength. Larish's swing can get long and he can get too pull-conscious. As with many hitters on Detroit's current roster, strikeouts and a lower average will be the tradeoff for his power. He has trouble with changeups away and sliders at his back toe. He's a below-average runner. The Tigers re-signed Sean Casey to a one-year deal, but they have no long-term solution at first. Larish could fill that hole in 2008, but for now he's headed to Double-A.

| Year | Club (League) | Class | AVG | G | AB | R | H | 2B | 3B | HR | RBI | BB | SO | SB | OBP | SLG |
|---|---|---|---|---|---|---|---|---|---|---|---|---|---|---|---|---|
| 2005 | Tigers (GCL) | R | .222 | 6 | 18 | 1 | 4 | 1 | 0 | 0 | 4 | 4 | 5 | 0 | .375 | .278 |
| | Oneonta (NYP) | A | .297 | 18 | 64 | 16 | 19 | 3 | 0 | 6 | 13 | 13 | 6 | 0 | .430 | .625 |
| 2006 | Lakeland (FSL) | A | .258 | 135 | 457 | 76 | 118 | 34 | 2 | 18 | 65 | 81 | 101 | 9 | .379 | .460 |
| **MINOR LEAGUE TOTALS** | | | .262 | 159 | 539 | 93 | 141 | 38 | 2 | 24 | 82 | 98 | 112 | 9 | .385 | .473 |

## 10 SCOTT SIZEMORE SS/2B

MIKE JAMES

**Born:** Jan. 4, 1985. **B-T:** R-R. **Ht.:** 6-0. **Wt.:** 185. **Drafted:** Virginia Commonwealth, 2006 (5th round). **Signed by:** Bill Buck.

Sizemore has had more success with wood bats than metal. He hit .303 in the Cape Cod League in 2005 and .327 in his pro debut—but just .300 at Virginia Commonwealth in between. That slump dropped him to the fifth round last June, but the Tigers were glad to sign him for $197,500 after a strong workout at Comerica Park. Sizemore, who led the short-season New York-Penn League in runs and hits, projects as an offensive second baseman in the mold of Mark Loretta. He's at his best when he uses a short swing and a gap approach, and he went back to that after trying too much to hit for power last spring. He has average speed and arm strength. Though he played surprisingly well at shortstop when the Tigers needed him there at Oneonta, Sizemore is more likely an adequate second baseman who needs to improve his footwork and range. Some scouts have projected him defensively as a third baseman, which would put more pressure on his bat. Sizemore's strong summer makes him the system's top middle-infield prospect for now. He may open 2007 in low Class A with a chance for a promotion at midseason.

| Year | Club (League) | Class | AVG | G | AB | R | H | 2B | 3B | HR | RBI | BB | SO | SB | OBP | SLG |
|---|---|---|---|---|---|---|---|---|---|---|---|---|---|---|---|---|
| 2006 | Oneonta (NYP) | A | .327 | 70 | 294 | 49 | 96 | 15 | 4 | 3 | 37 | 32 | 47 | 7 | .394 | .435 |
| **MINOR LEAGUE TOTALS** | | | .327 | 70 | 294 | 49 | 96 | 15 | 4 | 3 | 37 | 32 | 47 | 7 | .394 | .435 |

## 11 KODY KIRKLAND 3B

**Born:** June 9, 1983. **B-T:** R-R. **Ht.:** 6-4. **Wt.:** 200. **Drafted:** JC of Southern Idaho, D/F 2001 (30th round). **Signed by:** Kevin Clouser (Pirates).

Scouts are divided on Kirkland. They either love his athleticism or doubt whether he'll ever be able to refine his impressive tools to become a major league regular. Acquired in the trade that sent Randall Simon to the Pirates in November 2002, Kirkland has raw power, a strong arm and a high ceiling. But he strikes out too much and has hit just .239 in full-season leagues. His swing has holes, but its length allows him to pulverize breaking pitches low in the zone. He chases pitches and is particularly susceptible to high, hard stuff. Kirkland runs well for his size. Defensively, he has the arm for third base and shows good range at times. However, his hands are somewhat stiff and he's prone to errors. Kirkland is facing a critical season in 2007. He'll return to Double-A, and if he's truly a legitimate prospect, he should crush pitchers on his second tour of the Eastern League.

| Year | Club (League) | Class | AVG | G | AB | R | H | 2B | 3B | HR | RBI | BB | SO | SB | OBP | SLG |
|---|---|---|---|---|---|---|---|---|---|---|---|---|---|---|---|---|
| 2002 | Pirates (GCL) | R | .306 | 46 | 157 | 22 | 48 | 10 | 2 | 0 | 18 | 14 | 39 | 2 | .373 | .395 |
| 2003 | Oneonta (NYP) | A | .303 | 67 | 254 | 46 | 77 | 15 | 11 | 4 | 49 | 25 | 60 | 14 | .390 | .496 |
| 2004 | West Michigan (MWL) | A | .236 | 129 | 496 | 50 | 117 | 30 | 11 | 10 | 61 | 15 | 149 | 6 | .276 | .401 |
| 2005 | Lakeland (FSL) | A | .266 | 125 | 443 | 78 | 118 | 24 | 9 | 16 | 65 | 36 | 102 | 12 | .342 | .470 |
| 2006 | Erie (EL) | AA | .217 | 119 | 428 | 61 | 93 | 25 | 5 | 22 | 65 | 26 | 157 | 9 | .290 | .453 |
| | Toledo (IL) | AAA | .176 | 4 | 17 | 1 | 3 | 2 | 0 | 0 | 1 | 0 | 10 | 0 | .176 | .294 |
| **MINOR LEAGUE TOTALS** | | | .254 | 490 | 1795 | 258 | 456 | 106 | 38 | 52 | 259 | 116 | 517 | 43 | .321 | .442 |

## 12 SENDY VASQUEZ RHP

**Born:** Aug. 10, 1982. **B-T:** B-R. **Ht.:** 6-1. **Wt.:** 160. **Signed:** Dominican Republic, 2003. **Signed by:** Ramon Pena.

Vasquez played a major role in West Michigan's Midwest League championship, winning his last 10 regular-season decisions and two more in the playoffs. He has a live, electric fastball that sits at 90-94 mph and tops out at 96. He throws with a bullwhip motion that can be tough for hitters to pick up. He's aggressive and wild in the strike zone. Though he was old for low Class A, Vasquez is still unpolished. His career got off to a late start because he was nearly 21 when he signed out of the Dominican Republic. His changeup and tight slid-

er are in the early stages of their development, though he showed an increased ability to command them late in the season. The Tigers will continue to move him one level at a time, though he could see Double-A at some point in 2007.

| Year | Club (League) | Class | W | L | ERA | G | GS | CG | SV | IP | H | R | ER | HR | BB | SO | AVG |
|------|---------------|-------|---|---|------|----|----|----|----|-----|-----|-----|-----|----|-----|-----|------|
| 2003 | Tigers (GCL) | R | 2 | 2 | 7.47 | 11 | 1 | 0 | 0 | 16 | 18 | 13 | 13 | 0 | 11 | 12 | .290 |
| | Tigers (DSL) | R | 0 | 0 | 3.21 | 4 | 2 | 0 | 1 | 14 | 7 | 7 | 5 | 1 | 10 | 14 | .152 |
| 2004 | Tigers (GCL) | R | 2 | 2 | 5.46 | 17 | 2 | 0 | 3 | 28 | 29 | 19 | 17 | 0 | 21 | 32 | .266 |
| 2005 | Oneonta (NYP) | A | 7 | 0 | 3.63 | 15 | 11 | 0 | 0 | 67 | 53 | 30 | 27 | 4 | 34 | 60 | .218 |
| 2006 | West Michigan (MWL) | A | 13 | 6 | 2.97 | 26 | 26 | 0 | 0 | 142 | 129 | 64 | 47 | 7 | 49 | 112 | .240 |
| **MINOR LEAGUE TOTALS** | | | 24 | 10 | 3.67 | 73 | 42 | 0 | 4 | 267 | 236 | 133 | 109 | 12 | 125 | 230 | .236 |

## WILKIN RAMIREZ                                                                      3B

**Born:** Oct. 25, 1985. **B-T:** R-R. **Ht.:** 6-2. **Wt.:** 190. **Signed:** Dominican Republic, 2003. **Signed by:** Ramon Pena.

Ramirez' tools have never been in doubt. His health, however, has been a constant issue. Ramirez missed the 2004 season after surgery to repair a torn labrum, spent much of 2005 as a DH, and then played just 66 games last year. He got into one game after June, when a foul ball caused a deep bruise and severe swelling in his shin. Even before the injury, though, Ramirez wasn't having the season Detroit had hoped for. Though he has one of the highest ceilings in the system, his poor plate discipline undermines his offensive potential. He has excellent bat speed and the ability to drive the ball out of any part of any park, but that won't matter much if he chases pitches and can't make consistent contact. His speed and arm strength are both above-average, giving him the tools to play in the outfield if he continues to struggle at third base. He has a career .857 fielding percentage at the hot corner, where he made 22 errors in 65 games in 2006. Ramirez probably will repeat high Class A this year, with a focus on remaining healthy and improving his hitting approach.

| Year | Club (League) | Class | AVG | G | AB | R | H | 2B | 3B | HR | RBI | BB | SO | SB | OBP | SLG |
|------|---------------|-------|------|-----|-----|-----|-----|----|----|----|-----|----|-----|----|------|------|
| 2003 | Tigers (GCL) | R | .275 | 54 | 200 | 34 | 55 | 6 | 7 | 5 | 35 | 13 | 51 | 6 | .321 | .450 |
| 2004 | Did not play—Injured | | | | | | | | | | | | | | | |
| 2005 | West Michigan (MWL) | A | .262 | 131 | 493 | 69 | 129 | 21 | 2 | 16 | 65 | 35 | 143 | 21 | .317 | .410 |
| 2006 | Lakeland (FSL) | A | .225 | 66 | 249 | 31 | 56 | 10 | 4 | 8 | 33 | 10 | 69 | 8 | .259 | .394 |
| **MINOR LEAGUE TOTALS** | | | .255 | 251 | 942 | 134 | 240 | 37 | 13 | 29 | 133 | 58 | 263 | 35 | .303 | .414 |

## TONY GIARRATANO                                                                     SS

**Born:** Nov. 29, 1982. **B-T:** B-R. **Ht.:** 6-0. **Wt.:** 180. **Drafted:** Tulane, 2003 (3rd round). **Signed by:** Steve Taylor.

For the third time in four pro seasons, Giarratano couldn't stay healthy. He got hot in June, injured his wrist, came back and lasted five games before suffering a season-ending tear of the anterior-cruciate ligament in his right knee. He had surgery and probably won't be ready for the start of spring training. He also had shoulder trouble that necessitated postseason surgery in 2004 and hamstring troubles in 2005. At his best, Giarratano is a smooth, athletic defender with a good arm. His biggest asset is an ability to save runs with his glove, and he also can run and hit for average. Prior to the knee injury, he had big league range and profiled as an everyday shortstop. He hits well from both sides of the plate and fits in the No. 2 hole or the bottom third of a major league lineup. He doesn't have much power, but he has a short stroke, hits line drives and uses the entire field. He also plays with an energy and enthusiasm that the Tigers love. The surgery's toll on his athleticism is unclear for the time being, and he may have to spend a third season in Double-A.

| Year | Club (League) | Class | AVG | G | AB | R | H | 2B | 3B | HR | RBI | BB | SO | SB | OBP | SLG |
|------|---------------|-------|------|-----|------|-----|-----|----|----|----|-----|-----|-----|----|------|------|
| 2003 | Oneonta (NYP) | A | .328 | 47 | 189 | 31 | 62 | 11 | 4 | 3 | 27 | 12 | 22 | 9 | .369 | .476 |
| 2004 | West Michigan (MWL) | A | .285 | 43 | 165 | 20 | 47 | 6 | 1 | 1 | 13 | 25 | 21 | 11 | .383 | .352 |
| | Lakeland (FSL) | A | .376 | 53 | 202 | 30 | 76 | 11 | 0 | 5 | 16 | 16 | 38 | 14 | .421 | .505 |
| 2005 | Detroit (AL) | MLB | .143 | 15 | 42 | 4 | 6 | 0 | 0 | 1 | 4 | 5 | 7 | 1 | .234 | .214 |
| | Erie (EL) | AA | .266 | 89 | 346 | 40 | 92 | 22 | 3 | 3 | 32 | 32 | 75 | 12 | .334 | .373 |
| 2006 | Erie (EL) | AA | .283 | 67 | 269 | 35 | 76 | 19 | 5 | 0 | 19 | 22 | 45 | 16 | .340 | .390 |
| **MINOR LEAGUE TOTALS** | | | .301 | 299 | 1171 | 156 | 353 | 69 | 13 | 12 | 116 | 107 | 202 | 62 | .363 | .413 |
| **MAJOR LEAGUE TOTALS** | | | .143 | 15 | 42 | 4 | 6 | 0 | 0 | 1 | 4 | 5 | 7 | 1 | .234 | .214 |

## MICHAEL HOLLIMON                                                                    SS

**Born:** June 14, 1982. **B-T:** B-R. **Ht.:** 6-1. **Wt.:** 185. **Drafted:** Oral Roberts, 2005 (16th round). **Signed by:** Steve Taylor.

Though he has been old for his leagues in two years as a pro, Hollimon has a chance to hit his way to the big leagues. A potential first-round pick out of high school, he went undrafted because he reportedly wanted a $2 million bonus. After a lackluster three years at Texas,

he transferred to Oral Roberts and had a solid senior season, signing with the Tigers for $5,000 as a 16th-rounder. Hollimon topped the Midwest League in triples and ranked in the top five in walks, extra-base hits, total bases and slugging last season. West Michigan manager Matt Walbeck was so impressed with Hollimon's makeup that he named him as the team's captain. He repeats his swing well from both sides of the plate, though he's much more effective hitting lefthanded. The tradeoff for Hollimon's power and patience is strikeouts, as he has fanned 200 times in 200 pro games. He's an adequate defender at shortstop, though not as good as Tony Giarratano, who could be his double-play partner if Hollimon skips a level and goes to Double-A. In that case, Hollimon would move to second base, a better fit for his range and arm strength. In the long run, he could wind up as an offensive-minded utilityman. He'll be 25 this year, so the Tigers will try to accelerate his development.

| Year | Club (League) | Class | AVG | G | AB | R | H | 2B | 3B | HR | RBI | BB | SO | SB | OBP | SLG |
|------|---------------|-------|-----|---|----|---|---|----|----|----|-----|----|----|----|-----|-----|
| 2005 | Oneonta (NYP) | A | .275 | 72 | 255 | 66 | 70 | 13 | 10 | 13 | 53 | 50 | 76 | 8 | .391 | .557 |
| 2006 | West Michigan (MWL) | A | .278 | 128 | 449 | 69 | 125 | 29 | 13 | 15 | 54 | 77 | 124 | 19 | .386 | .501 |
| MINOR LEAGUE TOTALS | | | .277 | 200 | 704 | 135 | 195 | 42 | 23 | 28 | 107 | 127 | 200 | 27 | .388 | .521 |

##  BRENNAN BOESCH OF

**Born:** April 12, 1985. **B-T:** L-L. **Ht.:** 6-5. **Wt.:** 185. **Drafted:** California, 2006 (3rd round). **Signed by:** Scott Cerny.

Boesch entered 2006 as a candidate to go in the first round of the draft, but an inconsistent junior season dropped him to the third round, where the Tigers signed him for $445,000. He was steadier in his pro debut, leading Oneonta in homers and the New York-Penn League in RBIs. The key for Boesch is maintaining a sound stroke. He shows plus bat speed and catches up to good fastballs at times, and a longer, slower swing at others. If he can load his hands better and generate more power, he could become a 20-25 homer threat without sacrificing his ability to hit for average. Boesch's other tools aren't overwhelming, so his ceiling might be no higher than a productive fourth outfielder. He has average speed that plays better in the outfield than on the bases, and a slightly above-average arm. He played mostly right field at Oneonta but also logged time in center field. Boesch has good baseball instincts and could flourish with the proper instruction and developmental plan. He'll open his first full season at one of Detroit's Class A affiliates.

| Year | Club (League) | Class | AVG | G | AB | R | H | 2B | 3B | HR | RBI | BB | SO | SB | OBP | SLG |
|------|---------------|-------|-----|---|----|---|---|----|----|----|-----|----|----|----|-----|-----|
| 2006 | Oneonta (NYP) | A | .291 | 70 | 292 | 27 | 85 | 15 | 6 | 5 | 54 | 21 | 42 | 3 | .344 | .435 |
| MINOR LEAGUE TOTALS | | | .291 | 70 | 292 | 27 | 85 | 15 | 6 | 5 | 54 | 21 | 42 | 3 | .344 | .435 |

## 17 EDWARD CAMPUSANO LHP

**Born:** July 14, 1982. **B-T:** L-L. **Ht.:** 6-4. **Wt.:** 175. **Signed:** Dominican Republic, 2001. **Signed by:** Jose Serra (Cubs).

In 2006, the Tigers received contributions from three players they had acquired through the major league Rule 5 draft: Wil Ledezma, Chris Shelton and Chris Spurling. The club went the Rule 5 route again in December, paying the Brewers to select Campusano on its behalf. He'll get a chance to replace departed lefty reliever Jamie Walker, who signed as a free agent with the Orioles. Managers rated Campusano the best relief prospect in the Midwest League last season, and he had no problem jumping to Double-A in late June. He has better stuff than most lefties, with a lively 92-93 mph fastball and a knockout 82-85 mph slider. He showed some feel for a changeup in 2006, and his command also improved. The Cubs didn't protect Campusano because he hasn't been able to stay healthy. He set a career high last year with 55 innings, but he didn't pitch after Aug. 12 because of elbow soreness. He has had shoulder problems in the past as well. While his long, loose body gives him some funk to his delivery, it hasn't given him any durability. To retain Campusano, the Tigers have to keep him on their big league roster all season or send him through waivers and offer him back to the Cubs. His elbow woes may allow Detroit to stash him on the disabled list, but Campusano still must spend 90 days on the active roster in 2007.

| Year | Club (League) | Class | W | L | ERA | G | GS | CG | SV | IP | H | R | ER | HR | BB | SO | AVG |
|------|---------------|-------|---|---|-----|---|----|----|----|-----|-----|-----|----|----|----|-----|-----|
| 2002 | Cubs (DSL) | R | 1 | 3 | 3.63 | 10 | 4 | 0 | 0 | 35 | 34 | 26 | 14 | 5 | 10 | 42 | .243 |
| 2003 | Cubs (AZL) | R | 1 | 1 | 4.91 | 6 | 3 | 0 | 0 | 22 | 30 | 12 | 12 | 0 | 9 | 14 | .323 |
| | Cubs (DSL) | R | 1 | 0 | 1.31 | 6 | 5 | 0 | 0 | 21 | 17 | 9 | 3 | 1 | 5 | 21 | .218 |
| 2004 | Lansing (MWL) | A | 2 | 1 | 4.76 | 9 | 1 | 0 | 0 | 17 | 19 | 9 | 9 | 3 | 7 | 17 | .264 |
| | Boise (NWL) | A | 0 | 5 | 5.29 | 14 | 5 | 0 | 0 | 34 | 37 | 29 | 20 | 5 | 15 | 24 | .270 |
| 2005 | Peoria (MWL) | A | 2 | 2 | 2.63 | 19 | 0 | 0 | 1 | 27 | 25 | 11 | 8 | 0 | 14 | 23 | .240 |
| | Cubs (AZL) | R | 0 | 0 | 0.00 | 1 | 1 | 0 | 0 | 2 | 1 | 0 | 0 | 0 | 0 | 2 | .125 |
| 2006 | Peoria (MWL) | A | 0 | 0 | 1.21 | 26 | 0 | 0 | 21 | 30 | 16 | 5 | 4 | 0 | 9 | 47 | .152 |
| | West Tenn (SL) | AA | 2 | 1 | 1.75 | 18 | 0 | 0 | 4 | 26 | 22 | 6 | 5 | 2 | 8 | 34 | .227 |
| MINOR LEAGUE TOTALS | | | 9 | 13 | 3.17 | 109 | 19 | 0 | 26 | 213 | 201 | 107 | 75 | 16 | 77 | 224 | .241 |

## MIKE RABELO                                                           C

**Born:** Jan. 17, 1980. **B-T:** B-R. **Ht.:** 6-1. **Wt.:** 200. **Drafted:** Tampa, 2001 (4th round). **Signed by:** Steve Nichols.

The late-season trade of 2005 third-round pick Chris Robinson to the Cubs left Rabelo as Detroit's only legitimate catching prospect. Rabelo has shown significant improvement over the last two seasons and had a breakthrough year with the bat in 2006. He had a solid season at Double-A, earned a promotion to Triple-A and finished the year with the Tigers as a September callup. He has all the hallmarks of a late-blooming catcher. Rabelo only began switch-hitting during his final season of college baseball, after he struggled to hit sliders from righthanders. Now his ability to hit from either side of the plate is helping his big league marketability. He doesn't have a lot of power but he showed a more respectable amount last year. Much of his value comes from being an athletic catcher who calls a good game, throws well and blocks balls. He threw out 39 percent of basestealers last year. He also has experience catching the Tigers' young power pitchers, many of whom are in the big leagues or will be soon, which should ease his transition to the majors. He projects as a big league backup, but he may not get that chance in Detroit soon. The Tigers signed Vance Wilson to a two-year extension, so it's likely that Rabelo will return to Triple-A in 2007.

| Year | Club (League) | Class | AVG | G | AB | R | H | 2B | 3B | HR | RBI | BB | SO | SB | OBP | SLG |
|------|---------------|-------|-----|---|-----|---|-----|----|----|----|-----|----|----|----|------|------|
| 2001 | Oneonta (NYP) | A | .325 | 53 | 194 | 27 | 63 | 4 | 2 | 0 | 32 | 23 | 45 | 1 | .405 | .366 |
| 2002 | West Michigan (MWL) | A | .195 | 123 | 410 | 42 | 80 | 13 | 1 | 2 | 41 | 42 | 91 | 3 | .281 | .246 |
| 2003 | West Michigan (MWL) | A | .274 | 123 | 394 | 41 | 108 | 16 | 0 | 5 | 40 | 31 | 62 | 9 | .328 | .353 |
| 2004 | Erie (EL) | AA | .100 | 5 | 20 | 0 | 2 | 0 | 0 | 0 | 2 | 1 | 4 | 0 | .182 | .100 |
|  | Lakeland (FSL) | A | .287 | 92 | 327 | 36 | 94 | 20 | 2 | 0 | 38 | 25 | 56 | 3 | .349 | .361 |
| 2005 | Erie (EL) | AA | .273 | 77 | 282 | 33 | 77 | 18 | 1 | 2 | 26 | 18 | 42 | 0 | .334 | .365 |
| 2006 | Erie (EL) | AA | .277 | 62 | 213 | 31 | 59 | 13 | 1 | 6 | 28 | 19 | 38 | 2 | .361 | .432 |
|  | Toledo (IL) | AAA | .270 | 38 | 137 | 19 | 37 | 12 | 0 | 3 | 22 | 11 | 33 | 1 | .333 | .423 |
|  | Detroit (AL) | MLB | .000 | 1 | 1 | 0 | 0 | 0 | 0 | 0 | 0 | 0 | 1 | 0 | .000 | .000 |
| **MINOR LEAGUE TOTALS** |  |  | .263 | 573 | 1977 | 229 | 520 | 96 | 7 | 18 | 229 | 170 | 371 | 19 | .333 | .346 |
| **MAJOR LEAGUE TOTALS** |  |  | .000 | 1 | 1 | 0 | 0 | 0 | 0 | 0 | 0 | 0 | 1 | 0 | .000 | .000 |

## P.J. FINIGAN                                                        RHP

**Born:** Sept. 30, 1982. **B-T:** R-R. **Ht.:** 6-0. **Wt.:** 185. **Drafted:** Southern Illinois, 2005 (7th round). **Signed by:** Marty Miller.

A two-way star who won the Missouri Valley Conference batting title with a .388 average in 2005, his draft year, Finigan has flourished as a full-time pitcher in pro ball. He reached Double-A at the end of his first full season, throwing harder at the finish than he did at the start. Finigan came down with a tired arm at the end of his pro debut and pitched in the high 80s in early 2006. As the year progressed, he righted his mechanics and got stronger. His fastball sat at its usual 91-92 mph, jumping occasionally to 93-94. His best pitch is a plus slider, and he'll mix in some changeups. Finigan isn't a strikeout pitcher, but he avoids hard contract and gets groundballs. He has a good feel for pitching and is a tough competitor. Though he'll return to Double-A at the outset of 2007, he could join Detroit's bullpen in the near future.

| Year | Club (League) | Class | W | L | ERA | G | GS | CG | SV | IP | H | R | ER | HR | BB | SO | AVG |
|------|---------------|-------|---|---|------|----|----|----|----|-----|-----|----|----|----|----|----|------|
| 2005 | West Michigan (MWL) | A | 2 | 2 | 2.39 | 25 | 0 | 0 | 4 | 38 | 35 | 11 | 10 | 0 | 7 | 32 | .243 |
| 2006 | Lakeland (FSL) | A | 9 | 2 | 3.16 | 33 | 2 | 0 | 0 | 63 | 55 | 24 | 22 | 2 | 21 | 36 | .234 |
|  | Erie (EL) | AA | 0 | 2 | 5.00 | 11 | 3 | 0 | 1 | 27 | 27 | 15 | 15 | 4 | 7 | 16 | .257 |
| **MINOR LEAGUE TOTALS** |  |  | 11 | 6 | 3.32 | 69 | 5 | 0 | 5 | 127 | 117 | 50 | 47 | 6 | 35 | 84 | .242 |

## RONNIE BOURQUIN                                                       3B

**Born:** April 29, 1985. **B-T:** L-R. **Ht.:** 6-3. **Wt.:** 205. **Drafted:** Ohio State, 2006 (2nd round). **Signed by:** Tom Osowski.

The Tigers were full of surprises on draft day in 2006. In the first round, they had consensus top prospect Andrew Miller fall to them in the second round. In the second round, they grabbed Bourquin, who had projected as a fourth- to eighth-rounder. Detroit loved his tools and grit so much that it decided not to wait, signing him for $690,000. The 2006 Big Ten player of the year, Bourquin led the conference in hitting (.416), hits (91), RBIs (66), total bases (134), on-base percentage (.492) and slugging (.612). He followed that up with a solid debut during which he walked as much as he struck out. He handles lefthanders and righthanders equally well. It's unclear how much power Bourquin will develop, though he does drive the ball well during batting practice. A good athlete for his size, he runs OK and has a strong arm. He must improve defensively, however, as his sluggish footwork leads to

errors. With Kody Kirkland and Wilkin Ramirez stalling ahead of him, Bourquin could pass them on the Tigers' third-base depth chart with a strong first full season. He'll open 2007 at one of their Class A affiliates.

| Year | Club (League) | Class | AVG | G | AB | R | H | 2B | 3B | HR | RBI | BB | SO | SB | OBP | SLG |
|------|---------------|-------|------|----|-----|----|----|----|----|----|-----|----|----|----|------|------|
| 2006 | Oneonta (NYP) | A | .266 | 67 | 252 | 37 | 67 | 13 | 1 | 2 | 24 | 46 | 46 | 3 | .391 | .349 |
| **MINOR LEAGUE TOTALS** | | | .266 | 67 | 252 | 37 | 67 | 13 | 1 | 2 | 24 | 46 | 46 | 3 | .391 | .349 |

## 21 JEFF FRAZIER OF

**Born:** Aug. 10, 1982. **B-T:** R-R. **Ht.:** 6-3. **Wt.:** 195. **Drafted:** Rutgers, 2004 (3rd round). **Signed by:** Derrick Ross.

Frazier is one of three baseball brothers in his family. Older brother Charlie spent six years in the Marlins organization as an outfielder. Younger brother Todd, who followed Jeff to Rutgers, is a potential first-round pick for the 2007 draft. Todd was the star of the Toms River (N.J.) team that won the 1998 Little League World Series, while Jeff played in the 1995 event. He slumped after a strong start in high Class A last year, prompting questions as to whether his good baseball sense and durability will do enough to augment his modest tools. Frazier makes reasonably consistent contact and drives in runs, but he also doesn't show much power or draw many walks. He does have a long, lean frame and should have more pop once he gets stronger. Frazier has a solid arm but his so-so speed and range make him a better fit in right field. The Tigers have no shortage of righthanded-hitting outfield prospects—Cameron Maybin, Brent Clevlen and Gorkys Hernandez rank well ahead of him—so Frazier could use a breakout year in Double-A to solidify his status.

| Year | Club (League) | Class | AVG | G | AB | R | H | 2B | 3B | HR | RBI | BB | SO | SB | OBP | SLG |
|------|---------------|-------|------|-----|------|-----|-----|----|----|----|-----|----|-----|----|------|------|
| 2004 | Oneonta (NYP) | A | .304 | 20 | 79 | 15 | 24 | 5 | 1 | 1 | 13 | 9 | 11 | 2 | .387 | .430 |
| 2005 | West Michigan (MWL) | A | .287 | 137 | 537 | 79 | 154 | 45 | 4 | 12 | 81 | 46 | 86 | 16 | .349 | .453 |
| 2006 | Lakeland (FSL) | A | .228 | 135 | 526 | 61 | 120 | 21 | 1 | 13 | 73 | 37 | 88 | 12 | .279 | .346 |
| **MINOR LEAGUE TOTALS** | | | .261 | 292 | 1142 | 155 | 298 | 71 | 6 | 26 | 167 | 92 | 185 | 30 | .320 | .402 |

## 22 BURKE BADENHOP RHP

**Born:** Feb. 8, 1983. **B-T:** R-R. **Ht.:** 6-5. **Wt.:** 220. **Drafted:** Bowling Green State, 2005 (19th round). **Signed by:** Tom Osowski.

A 19th-round pick in 2005, Badenhop had a good pro debut at short-season Oneonta in 2005 and emerged as a genuine prospect with a surprise, standout season in low Class A. He led the Midwest League in victories and ranked second in innings, helping West Michigan win the championship. Afterward, the Tigers honored him with their minor league pitcher of the year award. He's a product of Perrysburg, Ohio, as is Detroit manager Jim Leyland. Though Badenhop is 6-foot-5 and 220 pounds, he's more about polish than power. His high-80s sinker doesn't miss a lot of bats, but he uses his frame to drive it down in the strike zone and get ground balls. He can reach back and hit 92 mph with a four-seamer, but mostly pitches off his sinker with his slider and changeup, two solid if unspectacular pitchers. Badenhop gets ahead of hitters and isn't afraid to pitch inside. He's durable and his ceiling is as an innings-eater at the back of a rotation. Because he signed as a college senior he has been older than most of his competition, so the Tigers may try to push him in 2007. He'll open in high Class A with a chance to reach Double-A if he continues to pitch well.

| Year | Club (League) | Class | W | L | ERA | G | GS | CG | SV | IP | H | R | ER | HR | BB | SO | AVG |
|------|---------------|-------|----|----|------|----|----|----|----|-----|-----|----|----|----|----|-----|------|
| 2005 | Oneonta (NYP) | A | 6 | 4 | 2.92 | 14 | 14 | 1 | 0 | 77 | 69 | 32 | 25 | 0 | 26 | 55 | .238 |
| 2006 | West Michigan (MWL) | A | 14 | 3 | 2.84 | 27 | 27 | 3 | 0 | 171 | 170 | 59 | 54 | 6 | 31 | 124 | .260 |
| **MINOR LEAGUE TOTALS** | | | 20 | 7 | 2.87 | 41 | 41 | 4 | 0 | 248 | 239 | 91 | 79 | 6 | 57 | 179 | .253 |

## 23 MATT JOYCE OF

**Born:** Aug. 3, 1984. **B-T:** L-R. **Ht.:** 6-2. **Wt.:** 185. **Drafted:** Florida Southern, 2005 (12th round). **Signed by:** Steve Nichols.

Joyce isn't an attention-grabber, but he gets the most out of his average tools. He was the leading run producer on the Midwest League champion West Michigan club. The Tigers first noticed him when he homered against them in a scrimmage while with Florida Southern, which is based right down the street from the club's Lakeland spring-training base. Joyce has a good approach at the plate, with quiet swing mechanics and good plate discipline. He controls the strike zone and uses the entire field, and he has more power than his 2006 numbers indicate. Like most of the Whitecaps, he was hurt by pitcher-friendly Fifth Third Ballpark, where he hit just .238 with four homers. He can get pull-conscious at times. Joyce has average speed, a strong arm and good range for a right fielder. He and Brennan Boesch

are the only lefthanded-hitting corner outfielders of note in the organization. Joyce will advance to high Class A this year.

| Year | Club (League) | Class | AVG | G | AB | R | H | 2B | 3B | HR | RBI | BB | SO | SB | OBP | SLG |
|------|---------------|-------|-----|---|----|---|---|----|----|----|-----|----|----|----|-----|-----|
| 2005 | Oneonta (NYP) | A | .332 | 65 | 247 | 51 | 82 | 10 | 4 | 4 | 46 | 28 | 29 | 9 | .394 | .453 |
| 2006 | West Michigan (MWL) | A | .258 | 122 | 465 | 75 | 120 | 30 | 5 | 11 | 86 | 56 | 70 | 5 | .338 | .415 |
| **MINOR LEAGUE TOTALS** | | | .284 | 187 | 712 | 126 | 202 | 40 | 9 | 15 | 132 | 84 | 99 | 14 | .358 | .428 |

## 24 VIRGIL VASQUEZ
RHP

**Born:** June 7, 1982. **B-T:** R-R. **Ht.:** 6-3. **Wt.:** 205. **Drafted:** UC Santa Barbara, 2003 (7th round). **Signed by:** Tom Hinkle.

Vasquez boosted his stock with an impressive Arizona Fall League performance. Though he nearly led the Eastern League in innings pitch, he showed he had plenty left in his tank by topping the AFL in ERA (2.81), finishing the season with 24 consecutive scoreless innings and winning the clinching game in the playoffs. The Tigers made him the last player added to their 40-man roster in November. Vasquez' ceiling isn't terribly high and his stuff is just average, but his command and durability could make him a back-of-the-rotation starter in the majors. His high-80s sinker and slider are his two best pitches, and he tops out at 93 mph at times, even late in the season. He also throws a curveball and changeup. Vasquez is vulnerable when he doesn't keep his pitches down, and he surrendered 21 homers in 2006. Improving his changeup would help him against lefthanders, who batted .288 and slugged .434 against him. While Vasquez has had consistent success as a starter, he may find it difficult to crack a Toledo rotation that should include several of the organization's top pitching prospects.

| Year | Club (League) | Class | W | L | ERA | G | GS | CG | SV | IP | H | R | ER | HR | BB | SO | AVG |
|------|---------------|-------|---|---|-----|---|----|----|----|----|---|---|----|----|----|----|-----|
| 2003 | Oneonta (NYP) | A | 3 | 4 | 6.92 | 11 | 11 | 0 | 0 | 53 | 76 | 43 | 41 | 5 | 10 | 35 | .328 |
| 2004 | West Michigan (MWL) | A | 14 | 6 | 3.64 | 27 | 27 | 0 | 0 | 168 | 156 | 73 | 68 | 14 | 34 | 120 | .252 |
| 2005 | Lakeland (FSL) | A | 4 | 1 | 4.21 | 8 | 8 | 1 | 0 | 47 | 52 | 23 | 22 | 6 | 7 | 31 | .289 |
| | Erie (EL) | AA | 2 | 8 | 5.27 | 15 | 15 | 0 | 0 | 84 | 93 | 59 | 49 | 10 | 14 | 53 | .281 |
| 2006 | Erie (EL) | AA | 7 | 12 | 3.73 | 27 | 27 | 3 | 0 | 174 | 174 | 79 | 72 | 21 | 50 | 129 | .265 |
| **MINOR LEAGUE TOTALS** | | | 30 | 31 | 4.31 | 88 | 88 | 4 | 0 | 526 | 551 | 277 | 252 | 56 | 115 | 368 | .273 |

## 25 JONAH NICKERSON
RHP

**Born:** March 9, 1985. **B-T:** R-R. **Ht.:** 6-0. **Wt.:** 210. **Drafted:** Oregon State, 2006 (7th round). **Signed by:** Brian Reid.

Nickerson threw 323 pitches in an eight-day span during the College World Series, earning Most Outstanding Player honors as Oregon State defeated Andrew Miller's North Carolina team for the national title. After the Beavers lost their CWS opener, Nickerson beat Georgia while allowing two runs in seven innings and then put them in the final round by defeating Rice with 7 2/3 shutout innings on two days' rest. In the CWS finale, he got a no-decision after allowing just two unearned runs in 6 2/3 frames. Because of that workload and the 137 innings he totaled in the spring, the Tigers kept a close watch on his workload after signing him for $150,000 as a seventh-round pick. Nickerson's competitive makeup and his command overshadow his pure stuff. At his best, he has an 89-91 mph sinker, though he pitched in the mid-80s toward the end of his college season and in his pro debut. His curveball is his No. 2 pitch, and he also throws a cutter and changeup. He knows how to set up hitters and refuses to give in to them. Nickerson likely will reach high Class A at some point in his first pro season.

| Year | Club (League) | Class | W | L | ERA | G | GS | CG | SV | IP | H | R | ER | HR | BB | SO | AVG |
|------|---------------|-------|---|---|-----|---|----|----|----|----|---|---|----|----|----|----|-----|
| 2006 | Oneonta (NYP) | A | 0 | 0 | 2.77 | 5 | 0 | 0 | 2 | 13 | 8 | 4 | 4 | 1 | 4 | 12 | .190 |
| **MINOR LEAGUE TOTALS** | | | 0 | 0 | 2.77 | 5 | 0 | 0 | 2 | 13 | 8 | 4 | 4 | 1 | 4 | 12 | .190 |

## 26 PRESTON LARRISON
RHP

**Born:** Nov. 19, 1980. **B-T:** R-R. **Ht.:** 6-4. **Wt.:** 235. **Drafted:** Evansville, 2001 (2nd round). **Signed by:** Harold Zonder.

Larrison pitched well in his first two pro seasons, ranking right behind Jeremy Bonderman as the top prospect in the system. His progression has been mostly disappointing ever since. He has gone 19-32 in the last four seasons, had Tommy John surgery in August 2004 and dropped his last eight decisions and spent time on the disabled list with forearm stiffness in 2006. He did excel after two late-season callups to pitch relief in Triple-A, which may be his calling. As a starter, Larrison never came up with an effective breaking ball, allowing hitters to sit on his sinker and changeup. Both are quality pitches, but they arrive on the same plane and he gets in trouble when his sinker flattens out. Working out of the bullpen, he threw in the mid-90s after showing more average velocity

as a starter. Whatever his role, Larrison needs to do a better job of repeating his delivery so he can throw more strikes as well as more quality strikes. In turn, that would help him miss more bats. He hasn't fared well under pressure in the past, failing to live up to first-round draft expectations in college and pressing when he got close to making the Tigers. Detroit thinks highly enough of Larrison that they kept him on the 40-man roster throughout the 2006 season and sent him to the Arizona Fall League afterward. He most likely will open the year back in the Triple-A bullpen, and he has to distinguish himself in an organization that has rafts of righthanded pitching.

| Year | Club (League) | Class | W | L | ERA | G | GS | CG | SV | IP | H | R | ER | HR | BB | SO | AVG |
|------|---------------|-------|---|---|-----|---|----|----|----|----|---|---|----|----|----|----|-----|
| 2001 | Oneonta (NYP) | A | 1 | 3 | 2.47 | 10 | 8 | 0 | 0 | 47 | 37 | 22 | 13 | 1 | 21 | 50 | .208 |
| 2002 | Lakeland (FSL) | A | 10 | 5 | 2.39 | 21 | 19 | 3 | 0 | 120 | 86 | 39 | 32 | 6 | 45 | 92 | .200 |
| 2003 | Toledo (IL) | AAA | 0 | 1 | 3.38 | 1 | 1 | 0 | 0 | 5 | 3 | 3 | 2 | 1 | 2 | 3 | .158 |
|  | Erie (EL) | AA | 4 | 12 | 5.61 | 24 | 24 | 0 | 0 | 127 | 161 | 89 | 79 | 10 | 59 | 53 | .322 |
| 2004 | Erie (EL) | AA | 5 | 4 | 3.05 | 20 | 20 | 0 | 0 | 118 | 122 | 54 | 40 | 12 | 36 | 59 | .265 |
| 2005 | Lakeland (FSL) | A | 1 | 2 | 4.70 | 9 | 9 | 0 | 0 | 38 | 48 | 22 | 20 | 0 | 12 | 25 | .318 |
|  | Erie (EL) | AA | 4 | 3 | 5.23 | 7 | 7 | 0 | 0 | 33 | 38 | 21 | 19 | 3 | 9 | 11 | .290 |
| 2006 | Erie (EL) | AA | 4 | 10 | 3.92 | 26 | 15 | 1 | 1 | 106 | 108 | 48 | 46 | 10 | 40 | 48 | .272 |
|  | Toledo (IL) | AAA | 1 | 0 | 1.74 | 6 | 0 | 0 | 0 | 10 | 12 | 3 | 2 | 1 | 5 | 3 | .324 |
| **MINOR LEAGUE TOTALS** | | | 30 | 40 | 3.77 | 124 | 103 | 4 | 1 | 605 | 615 | 301 | 253 | 44 | 229 | 344 | .267 |

# 27  RYAN RABURN                                                    OF/2B

**Born:** April 17, 1981. **B-T:** R-R. **Ht.:** 6-0. **Wt.:** 185. **Drafted:** South Florida CC, 2001 (5th round). **Signed by:** Steve Nichols.

Raburn has hit 39 homers in Triple-A during the last seasons, but it's unclear whether he can play well enough defensively to find a role in the major leagues. Signed as a third baseman in 2001, he moved to second base in 2004 and played mostly in left field last year. The Tigers needed an extra bat several times in 2006, but opted for other outfielders such as prospect Brent Clevlen and journeyman Alexis Gomez over Raburn. The younger brother of Devil Rays minor league utilityman Johnny Raburn, Ryan has natural power. He looks to drive the ball at the expense of making contact, so he piles up strikeouts and hits only for a decent average. He's a below-average runner and lost some athleticism when he dislocated a hip in an all-terrain vehicle accident that cost him most of the 2002 season. Raburn has some arm strength but doesn't have a lot of range in the outfield. Still, that's a better fit for him than second base, where he lacks the actions to get the job done. Barring a trade, he may be looking at a third straight year at Triple-A.

| Year | Club (League) | Class | AVG | G | AB | R | H | 2B | 3B | HR | RBI | BB | SO | SB | OBP | SLG |
|------|---------------|-------|-----|---|----|---|---|----|----|----|-----|----|----|----|-----|-----|
| 2001 | Tigers (GCL) | R | .155 | 19 | 58 | 4 | 9 | 2 | 0 | 1 | 5 | 9 | 19 | 2 | .300 | .241 |
|  | Oneonta (NYP) | A | .363 | 44 | 171 | 25 | 62 | 17 | 8 | 8 | 42 | 17 | 42 | 1 | .418 | .696 |
| 2002 | Tigers (GCL) | R | .300 | 8 | 30 | 4 | 9 | 3 | 1 | 1 | 5 | 3 | 7 | 0 | .364 | .567 |
|  | West Michigan (MWL) | A | .220 | 40 | 150 | 27 | 33 | 10 | 1 | 6 | 28 | 16 | 46 | 0 | .306 | .420 |
| 2003 | West Michigan (MWL) | A | .351 | 16 | 57 | 14 | 20 | 7 | 0 | 3 | 12 | 6 | 14 | 1 | .431 | .632 |
|  | Lakeland (FSL) | A | .222 | 95 | 325 | 52 | 72 | 14 | 3 | 12 | 56 | 45 | 89 | 2 | .332 | .394 |
| 2004 | Lakeland (FSL) | A | .273 | 3 | 11 | 1 | 3 | 1 | 0 | 1 | 3 | 1 | 6 | 0 | .333 | .636 |
|  | Erie (EL) | AA | .301 | 98 | 366 | 66 | 110 | 29 | 4 | 16 | 63 | 47 | 96 | 3 | .390 | .533 |
|  | Detroit (AL) | MLB | .138 | 12 | 29 | 4 | 4 | 1 | 0 | 0 | 1 | 2 | 15 | 1 | .194 | .172 |
| 2005 | Toledo (IL) | AAA | .253 | 130 | 471 | 62 | 119 | 22 | 4 | 19 | 64 | 45 | 109 | 8 | .323 | .437 |
| 2006 | Toledo (IL) | AAA | .275 | 118 | 451 | 68 | 124 | 29 | 4 | 20 | 79 | 51 | 120 | 16 | .352 | .490 |
| **MINOR LEAGUE TOTALS** | | | .268 | 571 | 2090 | 323 | 561 | 134 | 25 | 87 | 357 | 240 | 548 | 33 | .352 | .481 |
| **MAJOR LEAGUE TOTALS** | | | .138 | 12 | 29 | 4 | 4 | 1 | 0 | 0 | 1 | 2 | 15 | 1 | .194 | .172 |

# 28  AUDY CIRIACO                                                        SS

**Born:** June 16, 1987. **B-T:** R-R. **Ht.:** 6-3. **Wt.:** 195. **Signed:** Dominican Republic, 2005. **Signed by:** Ramon Pena.

The Tigers like Ciriaco's tools. He's an intriguing yet unpolished athlete, with a long frame, strong arm, athletic actions and a high ceiling. Signed for $175,000 at age 17, he went straight from the Dominican Republic to extended spring training and then the Gulf Coast League. He repeated the GCL last season and didn't do as well offensively in his encore. Ciriaco has a quick bat and some strength, but he'll have to make adjustments to handle breaking pitches in order to realize his power potential. He made some modest gains in terms of plate discipline last year, which was encouraging. He's quick but doesn't projects to steal many bases. Defensively, Ciriaco has the range, hands and arm to stay at shortstop despite his size. He was more consistent defensively in his second season in the United States. He'll make the jump to low Class A this year, where he'll be one of the youngest players in the Midwest League.

| Year | Club (League) | Class | AVG | G | AB | R | H | 2B | 3B | HR | RBI | BB | SO | SB | OBP | SLG |
|---|---|---|---|---|---|---|---|---|---|---|---|---|---|---|---|---|
| 2005 | Tigers (GCL) | R | .250 | 40 | 152 | 20 | 38 | 3 | 4 | 5 | 23 | 10 | 46 | 5 | .299 | .421 |
| 2006 | Tigers (GCL) | R | .217 | 50 | 175 | 26 | 38 | 7 | 1 | 4 | 19 | 9 | 30 | 9 | .258 | .337 |
| **MINOR LEAGUE TOTALS** | | | .232 | 90 | 327 | 46 | 76 | 10 | 5 | 9 | 42 | 19 | 76 | 14 | .277 | .376 |

## 29 CLETE THOMAS OF

**Born:** Nov. 14, 1983. **B-T:** L-R. **Ht.:** 5-11. **Wt.:** 195. **Drafted:** Auburn, 2005 (6th round). **Signed by:** Jerome Cochran.

The Tigers have moved Thomas quickly since signing him as a sixth-round pick in 2005. He spent most of his pro debut in low Class A, and all of his first full season in high Class A. His all-around tools led Detroit to believe Thomas could handle being on the fast track, but he struck out in droves, struggled mightily against lefthanders (.217 with one homer) and didn't hit for much power. The Tigers have tried to improve the load in his swing to give him more pop, but his slashing style may not be conducive to more than average power. Thomas stands out most right now for his pure speed and terrific baserunning instincts, which enabled him to rank fourth in the Florida State League in stolen bases. He's a plus defender in center field with quality range and a strong arm. But the presence of Curtis Granderson and Cameron Maybin in the organization will make it difficult for Thomas to make the Tigers as a center fielder. His bat doesn't profile well on the corners, either. If Maybin goes to Double-A, it's possible that Thomas could repeat high Class A.

| Year | Club (League) | Class | AVG | G | AB | R | H | 2B | 3B | HR | RBI | BB | SO | SB | OBP | SLG |
|---|---|---|---|---|---|---|---|---|---|---|---|---|---|---|---|---|
| 2005 | Oneonta (NYP) | A | .386 | 18 | 70 | 19 | 27 | 5 | 1 | 1 | 14 | 12 | 11 | 9 | .488 | .529 |
| | West Michigan (MWL) | A | .284 | 51 | 194 | 39 | 55 | 8 | 5 | 0 | 11 | 21 | 37 | 11 | .356 | .376 |
| 2006 | Lakeland (FSL) | A | .257 | 132 | 529 | 67 | 136 | 30 | 5 | 6 | 40 | 56 | 127 | 34 | .333 | .367 |
| **MINOR LEAGUE TOTALS** | | | .275 | 201 | 793 | 125 | 218 | 43 | 11 | 7 | 65 | 89 | 175 | 54 | .353 | .383 |

## 30 KYLE SLEETH RHP

**Born:** Dec. 20, 1981. **B-T:** R-R. **Ht.:** 6-5. **Wt.:** 205. **Drafted:** Wake Forest, 2003 (1st round). **Signed by:** Bill Buck.

Sleeth is one year older and was a Tigers first-round pick one year before Justin Verlander. Yet while Verlander was Baseball America's 2006 Rookie of the Year, Sleeth was posting an 11.90 ERA in high Class A while coming back from Tommy John surgery. The No. 3 overall choice in 2003, Sleeth won an NCAA record-tying 26 straight decisions at Wake Forest and signed for $3.35 million. When he struggled in Double-A in his first pro season, the Tigers tried to modify his crossfire delivery. His stuff wasn't as crisp and he eventually blew out his elbow. In college, Sleeth had a mid-90s fastball to go with two quality breaking pitches. After the surgery that knocked him out for the entire 2005 season, he's still trying to regain that velocity, and his command and secondary pitches are even further behind. His mechanics have been adjusted further and now more closely resemble how he threw at Wake Forest. Sleeth made some progress but was still inconsistent in instructional league, and Detroit will try a different approach in 2007. He'll operate out of the bullpen on shorter pitch counts at the beginning of the year, with a return to the rotation and a promotion to Double-A possible if things go well. The Tigers have kept him on their 40-man roster but he'll have to earn that spot in 2007.

| Year | Club (League) | Class | W | L | ERA | G | GS | CG | SV | IP | H | R | ER | HR | BB | SO | AVG |
|---|---|---|---|---|---|---|---|---|---|---|---|---|---|---|---|---|---|
| 2004 | Lakeland (FSL) | A | 4 | 4 | 3.79 | 10 | 10 | 1 | 0 | 59 | 53 | 29 | 25 | 3 | 18 | 60 | .241 |
| | Erie (EL) | AA | 4 | 4 | 6.30 | 13 | 13 | 0 | 0 | 80 | 93 | 58 | 56 | 14 | 34 | 57 | .303 |
| 2005 | Did not play—Injured | | | | | | | | | | | | | | | | |
| 2006 | Tigers (GCL) | R | 1 | 0 | 3.63 | 5 | 4 | 0 | 1 | 17 | 22 | 9 | 7 | 0 | 3 | 17 | .319 |
| | Lakeland (FSL) | A | 1 | 4 | 11.90 | 8 | 7 | 0 | 0 | 20 | 23 | 27 | 26 | 2 | 21 | 7 | .291 |
| **MINOR LEAGUE TOTALS** | | | 10 | 12 | 5.82 | 36 | 34 | 1 | 1 | 176 | 191 | 123 | 114 | 19 | 76 | 141 | .283 |

# FLORIDA
# MARLINS

BY **MIKE BERARDINO**

GEORGE GOJKOVICH

The eternal push for a new South Florida stadium remains in limbo, but the Marlins continue to operate the baseball side with impressive skill. After blowing up a team that won the 2003 World Series and contended for the postseason the following two years, they exceeded all expectations by winning 78 games in 2006 with the game's youngest and least expensive club.

Many of the key pieces acquired in Florida's fire sale after the 2005 season already are making an impact in the big leagues. The Marlins set a record for rookie at-bats (3,694), with **Hanley Ramirez** (the key to the Josh Beckett trade with the Red Sox) winning National League rookie of the year honors and Dan Uggla (a Rule 5 steal) finishing third. Mike Jacobs (part of the Carlos Delgado deal with the Mets) slugged 20 homers. Florida also broke in two homegrown outfielders, Jeremy Hermida and Josh Willingham.

On the mound, the Marlins featured the first rookie foursome to each reach 10 victories each with the homegrown Josh Johnson and Scott Olsen, Anibal Sanchez (part of the Beckett trade) and Ricky Nolasco (included in the Juan Pierre deal with the Cubs). Sanchez threw the majors' only no-hitter in September against the Diamondbacks.

While Florida was introducing fresh faces in the majors, it also was adding new talent. For the fourth straight year, the Marlins used their top draft pick on a pitcher. The Jeff Allison (2003) mistake aside, the strategy has worked well for them. Lefty swingman Taylor Tankersley (2004) made his way to the majors last June and worked his way

into a prominent setup role. Chris Volstad (2005), the leader of the all-prospect rotation at low Class A Greensboro, rates as the system's top prospect after his first full season in pro ball. Right behind him is Brett Sinkbeil (2006), who joined Volstad at Greensboro a month after the draft.

Besides targeting pitching in the draft, general manager Larry Beinfest did the same when he was shedding salaries. He acquired 11 young arms in the fire sale, with Sergio Mitre, Yusmeiro Petit and Renyel Pinto and also pitching in the majors in 2006.

Not surprisingly, pitchers claim seven of the top eight spots on the Marlins Top 10 Prospects. Position talent in general is down throughout the system, with first baseman/catcher Gaby Sanchez considered on the fast track. While the Marlins figure to have baseball's youngest roster again in 2007, they still need long-term answers at catcher and center field.

Their minor league affiliates combined for one of the worst records in the game, 316-363 (.465). Only the Rookie-level Gulf Coast League entry posted a winning record. While disappointing, the performance was understandable considering most of Florida's best prospects were in the majors.

On the international front, the Marlins hired Albert Gonzalez from the Royals to be their coordinator of Latin American scouting and player development.

## TOP 30 PROSPECTS

1. Chris Volstad, rhp
2. Brett Sinkbeil, rhp
3. Gaby Hernandez, rhp
4. Sean West, lhp
5. Gaby Sanchez, 1b/c
6. Taylor Tankersley, lhp
7. Aaron Thompson, lhp
8. Ryan Tucker, rhp
9. Chris Coghlan, 3b/2b
10. Kris Harvey, of
11. Renyel Pinto, lhp
12. Jose Garcia, rhp
13. Rick Vanden Hurk, rhp
14. Henry Owens, rhp
15. Yusmeiro Petit, rhp
16. Jesus Delgado, rhp
17. Harvey Garcia, rhp
18. Matt Lindstrom, rhp
19. Tom Hickman, of
20. Robert Andino, ss
21. Brett Carroll, of
22. Kyle Winters, rhp
23. John Raynor, of
24. Brett Hayes, c
25. Jacob Marceaux, rhp
26. Jose Campusano, of
27. Greg Burns, of
28. Jason Stokes, 1b
29. Brad McCann, 1b
30. Todd Doolittle, rhp

# ORGANIZATION OVERVIEW

**General manager:** Larry Beinfest. **Farm director:** Brian Chattin. **Scouting director:** Jim Fleming.

## 2006 PERFORMANCE

| Class | Team | League | W | L | PCT | Finish* | Manager | Affiliated |
|---|---|---|---|---|---|---|---|---|
| Majors | Florida | National | 78 | 84 | .481 | 9th (16) | Joe Girardi | — |
| Triple-A | Albuquerque Isotopes | Pacific Coast | 70 | 72 | .493 | 10th (16) | Dean Treanor | 2003 |
| Double-A | Carolina Mudcats | Southern | 61 | 79 | .436 | 8th (10) | Luis Dorante | 2003 |
| High A | Jupiter Hammerheads | Florida State | 55 | 80 | .407 | 11th (12) | Tim Cossins | 2002 |
| Low A | Greensboro Grasshoppers | South Atlantic | 68 | 69 | .496 | 9th (16) | Brandon Hyde | 2003 |
| Short-season | Jamestown Jammers | New York-Penn | 33 | 39 | .458 | 11th (14) | Bo Porter | 2002 |
| Rookie | GCL Marlins | Gulf Coast | 29 | 24 | .547 | 5th (11) | Edwin Rodriguez | 1992 |
| **OVERALL 2006 MINOR LEAGUE RECORD** | | | 316 | 363 | .465 | 26th (30) | | |

*Finish in overall standings (No. of teams in league). +League champion

## ORGANIZATION LEADERS

### BATTING
| | | |
|---|---|---|
| AVG | Kinkade, Mike, Albuquerque | .328 |
| R | Andino, Robert, Albuquerque | 70 |
| H | Gonzalez, Edgar V., Jupiter/Carolina/Alb. | 154 |
| 2B | Mitchell, Lee, Carolina | 37 |
| 3B | Reed, Eric, Albuquerque | 9 |
| HR | Carroll, Brett, Jupiter/Carolina | 20 |
| RBI | Wood, Jason, Albuquerque | 77 |
| BB | Sanchez, Gabriel, Greensboro/GCL/Jupiter | 67 |
| SO | Brinkley, Dante, Jupiter | 139 |
| | Mitchell, Lee, Carolina | 139 |
| SB | Campusano, Jose, Carolina | 37 |
| OBP | Sanchez, Gabriel, Greensboro/GCL/Jupiter | 424 |
| SLG | Sanchez, Gabriel, Greensboro/GCL/Jupiter | .523 |
| XBH | Carroll, Brett, Jupiter/Carolina | 55 |

### PITCHING
| | | |
|---|---|---|
| W | Garcia, Jose, Jupiter/Albuquerque/Carolina | 12 |
| L | Tucker, Ryan, Greensboro | 13 |
| ERA | Winters, Kyle, Jamestown | 2.45 |
| G | Yourkin, Matt, Carolina/Albuquerque | 61 |
| SV | Clontz, Brad, Albuquerque | 23 |
| IP | Mildren, Paul, Carolina | 167 |
| BB | Bostick II, Adam, Carolina/Albuquerque | 85 |
| SO | Garcia, Jose, Jupiter/Albuquerque/Carolina | 161 |
| AVG | Winters, Kyle, Jamestown | .194 |

## BEST TOOLS

| | |
|---|---|
| Best Hitter for Average | Gaby Sanchez |
| Best Power Hitter | Gaby Sanchez |
| Best Strike-Zone Discipline | Gaby Sanchez |
| Fastest Baserunner | Jose Campusano |
| Best Athlete | Greg Burns |
| Best Fastball | Ryan Tucker |
| Best Curveball | Gaby Hernandez |
| Best Slider | Brett Sinkbeil |
| Best Changeup | Jose Garcia |
| Best Control | Chris Volstad |
| Best Defensive Catcher | Brett Hayes |
| Best Defensive Infielder | Robert Andino |
| Best Infield Arm | Robert Andino |
| Best Defensive Outfielder | Eric Reed |
| Best Outfield Arm | Brett Carroll |

## PROJECTED 2010 LINEUP

| | |
|---|---|
| Catcher | Brett Hayes |
| First Base | Mike Jacobs |
| Second Base | Dan Uggla |
| Third Base | Miguel Cabrera |
| Shortstop | Hanley Ramirez |
| Left Field | Josh Willingham |
| Center Field | Tom Hickman |

| | |
|---|---|
| Right Field | Jeremy Hermida |
| No. 1 Starter | Dontrelle Willis |
| No. 2 Starter | Anibal Sanchez |
| No. 3 Starter | Scott Olsen |
| No. 4 Starter | Josh Johnson |
| No. 5 Starter | Chris Volstad |
| Closer | Brett Sinkbeil |

## LAST YEAR'S TOP 20 PROSPECTS

| | |
|---|---|
| 1. Jeremy Hermida, of | 11. Josh Willingham, c/1b |
| 2. Hanley Ramirez, ss | 12. Mike Jacobs, 1b |
| 3. Anibal Sanchez, rhp | 13. Renyel Pinto, lhp |
| 4. Scott Olsen, lhp | 14. Taylor Tankersley, lhp |
| 5. Yusmeiro Petit, rhp | 15. Kris Harvey, 3b/of |
| 6. Josh Johnson, rhp | 16. Ryan Tucker, rhp |
| 7. Chris Volstad, rhp | 17. Robert Andino, ss |
| 8. Ricky Nolasco, rhp | 18. Eric Reed, of |
| 9. Gaby Hernandez, rhp | 19. Jason Stokes, 1b |
| 10. Aaron Thompson, lhp | 20. Sean West, lhp |

## TOP PROSPECTS OF THE DECADE

| Year | Player, Pos. | 2006 Org. |
|---|---|---|
| 1997 | Felix Heredia, lhp | Monterrey (Mexican) |
| 1998 | Mark Kotsay, of | Athletics |
| 1999 | A.J. Burnett, rhp | Blue Jays |
| 2000 | A.J. Burnett, rhp | Blue Jays |
| 2001 | Josh Beckett, rhp | Red Sox |
| 2002 | Josh Beckett, rhp | Red Sox |
| 2003 | Miguel Cabrera, 3b | Marlins |
| 2004 | Jeremy Hermida, of | Marlins |
| 2005 | Jeremy Hermida, of | Marlins |
| 2006 | Jeremy Hermida, of | Marlins |

## TOP DRAFT PICKS OF THE DECADE

| Year | Player, Pos. | 2006 Org. |
|---|---|---|
| 1997 | Aaron Akin, rhp | Out of baseball |
| 1998 | Chip Ambres, of | Royals |
| 1999 | Josh Beckett, rhp | Red Sox |
| 2000 | Adrian Gonzalez, 1b | Padres |
| 2001 | Garrett Berger, rhp (2nd round) | Out of baseball |
| 2002 | Jeremy Hermida, of | Marlins |
| 2003 | Jeff Allison, rhp | Marlins |
| 2004 | Taylor Tankersley, lhp | Marlins |
| 2005 | Chris Volstad, rhp | Marlins |
| 2006 | Brett Sinkbeil, rhp | Marlins |

## LARGEST BONUSES IN CLUB HISTORY

| | |
|---|---|
| Josh Beckett, 1999 | $3,625,000 |
| Adrian Gonzalez, 2000 | $3,000,000 |
| Livan Hernandez, 1996 | $2,500,000 |
| Jason Stokes, 2000 | $2,027,000 |
| Jeremy Hermida, 2002 | $2,012,500 |

# MINOR LEAGUE DEPTH CHART

## Florida Marlins

**Impact: A.** There isn't much in terms of position players, but the Marlins' talent on the mound rivals that of any other organization.

**Depth: D.** The majority of the players Florida received in the 2005 fire sale have already graduated to the big leagues, leaving the system much thinner than it was last year.

**Sleeper:** J.T. Restko, of. Like Brad McCann, both players struggled in high Class A last year, but Restko still has upside with above-average speed and some power.

*Numbers in parentheses indicate prospect rankings.*

| LF |
|---|
| Jose Campusano (26) |
| J.T. Restko |

| CF |
|---|
| Tom Hickman (19) |
| John Raynor (23) |
| Greg Burns (27) |
| Eric Reed |
| Alejandro De Aza |
| Jai Miller |

| RF |
|---|
| Kris Harvey (10) |
| Brett Carroll (21) |
| Scott Cousins |

| 3B |
|---|
| Grant Psomas (9) |
| Jonathan Fulton |
| Lee Mitchell |
| Jake Blackwood |
| Ketnold Noel |

| SS |
|---|
| Robert Andino (20) |
| Augustin Septimo |
| Rex Rundgren |
| James Guerrero |

| 2B |
|---|
| Chris Coghlan (9) |
| Brian Cleveland |
| Carlos Piste |

| 1B |
|---|
| Gaby Sanchez (5) |
| Jason Stokes (28) |
| Brad McCann (29) |
| Logan Morrison |

| C |
|---|
| Brett Hayes (24) |
| Brad Davis |
| Andy Jenkins |

| RHP | |
|---|---|
| **Starters** | **Relievers** |
| Chris Volstad (1) | Henry Owens (14) |
| Brett Sinkbeil (2) | Jesus Delgado (16) |
| Gaby Hernandez (3) | Harvey Garcia (17) |
| Ryan Tucker (8) | Matt Lindstrom (18) |
| Jose Garcia (12) | Todd Doolittle (30) |
| Rick Vanden Hurk (13) | Scott Tyler |
| Yusmeiro Petit (15) | Scott Nestor |
| Kyle Winters (22) | Kurk Koehler |
| Jacob Marceaux (25) | Rodolfo Encarnacion |
| Hector Correa | |

| LHP | |
|---|---|
| **Starters** | **Relievers** |
| Sean West (4) | Taylor Tankersley (6) |
| Aaron Thompson (7) | Matt Yourkin |
| Renyel Pinto (11) | |
| Paul Mildren | |
| Graham Taylor | |

# DRAFT ANALYSIS

## 2006         SIGNING BUDGET: $4.6 million

**Best Pro Debut:** RHP Brett Sinkbeil (1) made a complete recovery from a strained oblique during his college season to go 3-1, 3.65 with 54 strikeouts in 62 innings while advancing to low Class A. RHP Hector Correa (4) posted a 1.76 ERA and 36 strikeouts in 41 innings.

**Best Athlete:** OF John Raynor's (9) best tool is plus-plus speed, but he also plays quality defense, hits for average and for some pop and has a decent arm. OF Scott Cousins (3) will flash all five tools, and many teams liked him more as a pitcher until late in his college career. The Marlins see him as a Mark Kotsay type, maybe with more power.

**Best Pure Hitter:** 3B Chris Coghlan (1) won the 2005 Cape Cod League batting title with a .346 average and hit .297 in his pro debut. He covers the plate, makes consistent contact and uses the entire field. At this point, he's more advanced than high school OF Tom Hickman (2).

**Best Raw Power:** Hickman over Raynor. Draft-and-follow 1B Logan Morrison has more power than either of them.

**Fastest Runner:** Raynor can run a 6.4-second 60-yard dash. He stole 42 bases in 46 tries at UNC Wilmington in the spring, then had the same success rate (21 for 23) in the pros.

**Best Defensive Player:** Torre Langley (3) was one of the best defensive catchers in the draft. The Marlins quieted his set-up a little, but they didn't have to mess with his well-above-average arm and his aggressiveness. There are concerns about his size (5-foot-8, 170 pounds) and bat, and he hit .179 in his pro debut. Hickman has the instincts and arm to be a good outfielder and may be able to stay in center.

**Best Fastball:** Sinkbeil has a sweet combination of velocity (91-95 mph), sink and command, and he could throw harder if he adds more strength to his 6-foot-4, 190-pound frame. Correa and RHPs Don Czyz (7), Jay Buente (14) and Jordan Davis (19) all have touched 95.

**Best Breaking Ball:** Sinkbeil gets strikeouts with a hard breaker that features slider velocity and curveball movement.

**Most Intriguing:** Czyz' brother Nick pitched with him at Kansas and should be a decent prospect for 2008.

**Closest To The Majors:** Sinkbeil could be ready by 2008. The Marlins are trying to expedite Coghlan's timetable by getting him to pull more pitches for power and by moving him to second base, where less pop is required. And Buente could provide bullpen help in a hurry with his sinker/splitter combo.

**Best Late-Round Pick:** Buente. Florida hopes outfielder Hunter Mense (17) can recover after going from Team USA's college national team the previous summer to nose-diving out of Missouri's lineup last spring. He tried to hit for power and messed up his swing, and the early returns (a homerless .255 debut) are mixed.

**The One Who Got Away:** Florida has lost the rights to just one player, RHP T.J. Forrest (44), now at Louisiana State. Forrest was the best high school arm in Louisiana and touched 92 mph before Tommy John surgery in the spring.

**Assessment:** The Marlins were delighted to get Sinkbeil at No. 19, which would not have been possible had he been at full strength all spring. After spending five first-round picks on arms in pitchers in 2005, Florida looked for athletes after snagging Sinkbeil.

## 2005       BUDGET: $7.7 million

The Marlins spent all five of their first-rounders on pitchers, and a year later RHPs Chris Volstad and Ryan Tucker and LHPs Aaron Thompson and Sean West are still looking good. Only RHP Jacob Marceaux has already fizzled. OF Kris Harvey (2) and 1B/C Gaby Sanchez (4) have intriguing bats. **GRADE: B+**

## 2004       BUDGET: $3.0 million

LHP Jason Vargas (2) shot to the majors, then faded just as quickly and was traded to the Mets. LHP Taylor Tankersley (1) will stick around for a while longer. **GRADE: C**

## 2003       BUDGET: $3.9 million

Getting RHP Jason Allison (1) at No. 16 looked like a coup, but Florida had no idea that he had extensive drug problems. RHP Logan Kensing (2) has seen some major league duty. **GRADE: F**

*Draft analysis by Jim Callis. Numbers in parentheses indicate draft rounds. Budgets are bonuses in first 10 rounds.*

## CHRIS VOLSTAD

RHP

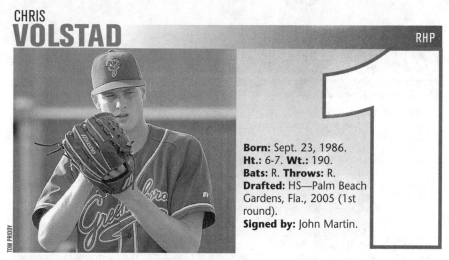

TOM PRIDDY

**Born:** Sept. 23, 1986.
**Ht.:** 6-7. **Wt.:** 190.
**Bats:** R. **Throws:** R.
**Drafted:** HS—Palm Beach Gardens, Fla., 2005 (1st round).
**Signed by:** John Martin.

V olstad started generating buzz at the Area Code Games in the summer before his high school senior season. The Marlins, who sponsored his Area Code team, had at least one scout at all but two of his 13 senior starts. He might not have gotten to them with the 16th overall pick in 2005 had he not struggled with his control in his final outing, a loss in the Florida state playoffs. But when he did, there was no doubt the Marlins would take him. He was the perfect choice to headline what became a five-man rotation of young arms taken in the first and supplemental first-rounds of the 2005 draft: Aaron Thompson, Jacob Marceaux, Ryan Tucker and Sean West. The first prep pitcher selected in that draft, Volstad quickly signed for $1.6 million and wasted little time proving his worth. He rated as the top pitching prospect in both the Rookie-level Gulf Coast and short-season New York-Penn leagues in his debut. In his first full season, he followed up by ranking as the second-best mound prospect in the low Class A South Atlantic League. He overcame a rough May (1-4, 5.94) to allow two earned runs or fewer in 13 of his final 15 starts.

A certified strike thrower, Volstad works his fastball effectively at 89-92 mph and touches 94 mph. His two-seamer has heavy sink, producing a 2.3 groundout-flyout ratio in 2006, and he has started to elevate his four-seamer to get overzealous hitters to chase balls out of the zone. He can throw his 80-82 mph curve for strikes and is doing a better job of varying speeds on it and burying it when necessary. He has a solid changeup for his experience level with the potential to make that a plus pitch as well. Volstad grew to his current 6-foot-7 height as a high school junior and credits his basketball background with improving his footwork and agility. That coordination leads to his uncanny control. The ability to mix it up in the lane couldn't have hurt his aggressiveness either. Volstad has strong makeup and good intelligence, both in a baseball and general sense, and takes coaching well. He's constantly poised on the mound, where he looks the same whether he's working on a no-hitter or one mistake from hitting the showers.

If anything, Volstad has a tendency to be around the plate too much. That allows hitters to dig in and led to his struggles in May. He has averaged just 6.4 strikeouts per nine innings his first two seasons, another sign that he has been too hittable considering the quality of his stuff. Some non-believers say he might wind up as little more than a middle-of-the-rotation workhorse who won't blow hitters away. Volstad still needs to add muscle and grow into his frame, especially in the lower half. Though he's well coordinated, his long frame always will make it a challenge for him to maintain his delivery.

Having avoided any major hiccups so far, Volstad will head to high Class A Jupiter along with several other members of the Class of '05. Like the Grasshoppers had in 2005, the Hammerheads likely will have a rotation comprised solely of first-rounders. With a talented young rotation already in the majors, the Marlins can afford to proceed cautiously with Volstad. He still could arrive for good by the end of 2008.

| Year | Club (League) | Class | W | L | ERA | G | GS | CG | SV | IP | H | R | ER | HR | BB | SO | AVG |
|------|---------------|-------|---|---|------|----|----|----|----|-----|-----|-----|----|----|----|-----|------|
| 2005 | Marlins (GCL) | R | 1 | 1 | 2.33 | 6 | 6 | 0 | 0 | 27 | 25 | 14 | 7 | 1 | 4 | 26 | .243 |
| | Jamestown (NYP) | A | 3 | 2 | 2.13 | 7 | 7 | 0 | 0 | 38 | 43 | 19 | 9 | 0 | 11 | 29 | .279 |
| 2006 | Greensboro (SAL) | A | 11 | 8 | 3.08 | 26 | 26 | 0 | 0 | 152 | 161 | 73 | 52 | 12 | 36 | 99 | .275 |
| **MINOR LEAGUE TOTALS** | | | 15 | 11 | 2.82 | 39 | 39 | 0 | 0 | 217 | 229 | 106 | 68 | 13 | 51 | 154 | .272 |

## 2 BRETT SINKBEIL
RHP

**Born:** Dec. 26, 1984. **B-T:** R-R. **Ht.:** 6-2. **Wt.:** 170. **Drafted:** Missouri State, 2006 (1st round). **Signed by:** Ryan Wardinsky.

Sinkbeil established himself as a possible first-round pick in the Cape Cod League in the summer of 2005 and backed that up with a strong spring at Missouri State. The only hurdle he had to overcome was proving was healthy after missing three weeks with a strained oblique. The Padres and Phillies showed some interest just ahead of the Marlins, who took him 19th overall and quickly signed him for $1.525 million. Sinkbeil's fastball sits at 89-93 mph and tops out at 95 mph, showing late life that often overwhelmed New York-Penn League hitters. His tight slider is a legitimate out pitch and he feels confident throwing it in any count. He throws strikes with both pitches. Driven and focused, he tries to pattern himself after Roger Clemens in terms of work ethic and preparation. He packed on 35 pounds of muscle in three years at Missouri State. His changeup was weak in college and still needs work. Sinkbeil has yet to find a comfortable grip and match the same arm speed of his fastball. If he can't, he'll be a reliever down the road. Though he's a strong competitor, some wish he would be a little more outgoing. After holding his own at low Class A Greensboro late in the summer, Sinkbeil might return there to begin his first full pro season. However, it won't be long before he joins the Class of '05 in high Class A. He projects as a solid No. 3 starter, possibly a No. 2, and could be ready in 2008.

| Year | Club (League) | Class | W | L | ERA | G | GS | CG | SV | IP | H | R | ER | HR | BB | SO | AVG |
|------|---------------|-------|---|---|-----|---|----|----|----|----|----|----|----|----|----|----|-----|
| 2006 | Jamestown (NYP) | A | 2 | 0 | 1.23 | 5 | 5 | 0 | 0 | 22 | 14 | 4 | 3 | 1 | 8 | 22 | .192 |
| | Greensboro (SAL) | A | 1 | 1 | 4.99 | 8 | 8 | 0 | 0 | 40 | 45 | 22 | 22 | 5 | 14 | 32 | .290 |
| **MINOR LEAGUE TOTALS** | | | 3 | 1 | 3.65 | 13 | 13 | 0 | 0 | 62 | 59 | 26 | 25 | 6 | 22 | 54 | .259 |

## 3 GABY HERNANDEZ
RHP

**Born:** May 21, 1986. **B-T:** R-R. **Ht.:** 6-3. **Wt.:** 210. **Drafted:** HS—Miami, 2004 (3rd round). **Signed by:** Joe Salermo (Mets).

Yusmeiro Petit was supposed to be the best arm the Marlins got in the twin deals that sent Carlos Delgado and Paul LoDuca to the Mets, but it's now clear that Hernandez is better. One of the youngest players in the high Class A Florida State League for the second straight year, he continued to build on a solid track record despite a minor toe injury that slowed him in the early going. Hernandez' fastball sits at 90-92 mph with good run and he'll pop his four-seamer at 94 mph. His changeup is average to maybe a tick above. Not afraid to work inside, he hit 13 batters in 2006, though most of those were on wayward curveballs. He has a tremendous work ethic and the ability to turn things up a notch with runners on base. Though it continues to make progress, Hernandez' slow curve is average at best. He may junk it and go with a slider in 2007. His overall command must improve. He's his own harshest critic, and his perfectionism works to his detriment at times. Hernandez will make the jump to Double-A Carolina as a 20-year-old. He projects as a No. 3 or No. 4 starter in the majors, but he must improve his breaking ball to get there.

| Year | Club (League) | Class | W | L | ERA | G | GS | CG | SV | IP | H | R | ER | HR | BB | SO | AVG |
|------|---------------|-------|---|---|-----|---|----|----|----|----|----|----|----|----|----|----|-----|
| 2004 | Mets (GCL) | R | 3 | 3 | 1.09 | 10 | 9 | 2 | 0 | 50 | 25 | 10 | 6 | 1 | 12 | 58 | .151 |
| | Brooklyn (NYP) | A | 1 | 0 | 0.00 | 1 | 0 | 0 | 0 | 3 | 2 | 0 | 0 | 0 | 6 | .200 |
| 2005 | Hagerstown (SAL) | A | 6 | 1 | 2.43 | 18 | 18 | 1 | 0 | 93 | 59 | 29 | 25 | 4 | 30 | 99 | .179 |
| | St. Lucie (FSL) | A | 2 | 5 | 5.74 | 10 | 10 | 0 | 0 | 42 | 48 | 28 | 27 | 1 | 10 | 32 | .298 |
| 2006 | Jupiter (FSL) | A | 9 | 7 | 3.68 | 21 | 20 | 0 | 0 | 120 | 120 | 60 | 49 | 7 | 35 | 115 | .259 |
| **MINOR LEAGUE TOTALS** | | | 21 | 16 | 3.13 | 60 | 57 | 3 | 0 | 308 | 254 | 127 | 107 | 13 | 87 | 310 | .225 |

## 4 SEAN WEST
LHP

**Born:** June 15, 1986. **B-T:** L-L. **Ht.:** 6-8. **Wt.:** 200. **Drafted:** HS—Shreveport, La., 2005 (1st round supplemental). **Signed by:** Ryan Fox.

Signed for $775,000 out of high school, West has wasted little time showing he belonged among those five pitchers the Marlins took in the top 44 picks in 2005. He pitched six shutout innings in his first 2006 start then spent a month on the disabled list with nagging shoulder pain. When he returned, he didn't give up more than two earned runs in his next six starts and later ripped off a five-game winning streak. West comes right at hitters from a three-quarters arm slot with a tailing fastball that sits at 90-93 mph and touches 96. He has two different sliders, one fairly tight and the other a big breaker. His changeup is a plus pitch at times. West needs to use his change-

up more. His shoulder woes were chalked up to the rigors of his first pro spring training. His off-center personality has at times interfered with his between-starts work, which contributed to a late-season fade. While at times he uses his emotions to his benefit, he must avoid showing up opponents on the mound. West will be part of an all-first-rounder rotation in high Class A in 2007. He's more polished than most lefthanders his age and has bigger stuff than most lefthanders, period. He's definitely on the fast track now.

| Year | Club (League) | Class | W | L | ERA | G | GS | CG | SV | IP | H | R | ER | HR | BB | SO | AVG |
|------|---------------|-------|---|---|-----|---|----|----|----|-----|-----|----|----|----|----|-----|------|
| 2005 | Marlins (GCL) | R | 2 | 3 | 2.35 | 9 | 8 | 0 | 0 | 38 | 33 | 12 | 10 | 2 | 7 | 40 | .229 |
| | Jamestown (NYP) | A | 0 | 2 | 5.73 | 3 | 3 | 0 | 0 | 11 | 17 | 7 | 7 | 1 | 5 | 14 | .362 |
| 2006 | Greensboro (SAL) | A | 8 | 5 | 3.74 | 21 | 21 | 0 | 0 | 120 | 115 | 55 | 50 | 13 | 40 | 102 | .255 |
| **MINOR LEAGUE TOTALS** | | | 10 | 10 | 3.55 | 33 | 32 | 0 | 0 | 170 | 165 | 74 | 67 | 16 | 52 | 156 | .257 |

## 5 GABY SANCHEZ
1B/C

**Born:** Sept. 2, 1983. **B-T:** R-R. **Ht.:** 6-2. **Wt.:** 225. **Drafted:** Miami, 2005 (4th round). **Signed by:** John Martin.

After a suspension cost him his junior year at Miami, Sanchez signed with the Marlins for $250,000 as a fourth-round pick in 2005. East Coast scouting supervisor Mike Cadahia vouched for a player he had known for years. Sanchez won the New York-Penn League batting title in his pro debut and played well in 2006 until nagging finger and foot injuries slowed him down. Sanchez has tremendous plate discipline and an advanced approach to hitting. He has plus raw power, makes quick adjustments and knows how to set pitchers up. Minor hitting coordinator John Mallee eliminated some of his extraneous pre-swing hand movement and also got him to stop pulling off the ball. Sanchez has shown versatility, flashing potential behind the plate and at first base in addition to his natural position at third. He has a strong, accurate arm. Though his footwork is sound, Sanchez never will be more than an average defender. His body could use more definition and his range is barely passable at first or third base. Because of his suspension and injuries, he has played the equivalent of just one season in the last two years. After holding his own in the Arizona Fall League, Sanchez figures to open 2007 back in high Class A. He will play mostly at first base, which should expedite getting him into the big league lineup.

| Year | Club (League) | Class | AVG | G | AB | R | H | 2B | 3B | HR | RBI | BB | SO | SB | OBP | SLG |
|------|---------------|-------|-----|---|----|---|---|----|----|----|-----|----|----|----|-----|-----|
| 2005 | Jamestown (NYP) | A | .355 | 62 | 234 | 34 | 83 | 16 | 0 | 5 | 42 | 16 | 24 | 11 | .401 | .487 |
| 2006 | Marlins (GCL) | R | .333 | 3 | 6 | 1 | 2 | 1 | 0 | 0 | 3 | 5 | 0 | 0 | .636 | .500 |
| | Jupiter (FSL) | A | .182 | 16 | 55 | 13 | 10 | 3 | 1 | 1 | 7 | 12 | 12 | 1 | .324 | .327 |
| | Greensboro (SAL) | A | .317 | 55 | 189 | 43 | 60 | 12 | 0 | 14 | 40 | 39 | 20 | 6 | .447 | .603 |
| **MINOR LEAGUE TOTALS** | | | .320 | 136 | 484 | 91 | 155 | 32 | 1 | 20 | 92 | 72 | 56 | 18 | .415 | .514 |

## 6 TAYLOR TANKERSLEY
LHP

**Born:** March 7, 1983. **B-T:** L-L. **Ht.:** 6-1. **Wt.:** 220. **Drafted:** Alabama, 2004 (1st round). **Signed by:** Dave Dangler.

Tankersley is the son of a nuclear physicist and the grandson of a former big league pitcher. Earl Tankersley taught his grandson the importance of pitching inside, and the lessons paid off with a $1.3 million bonus in 2004 and an early June callup to the majors in 2006. A bulldog with a quick wit and baseball savvy, Tankersley pounds the strike zone with an 88-92 mph fastball and knows how to move it around to good purpose. His low three-quarters arm slot makes him particularly nasty on lefthanders, and he's effective against righthanders as well. He uses a slurvy breaking ball that has good depth and will drop a changeup in on righties to keep them honest. His stuff isn't overpowering, so Tankersley must be precise with his location and pitch selection. He missed two months in 2005 with shoulder tendinitis but has been resilient since making the permanent move to the bullpen. With closer Joe Borowski departing as a free agent, Tankersley appears to be first in line to finish games for the 2007 Marlins. He has the tenacity and the versatility of a young Mike Stanton and could enjoy a similarly lengthy career.

| Year | Club (League) | Class | W | L | ERA | G | GS | CG | SV | IP | H | R | ER | HR | BB | SO | AVG |
|------|---------------|-------|---|---|-----|---|----|----|----|-----|-----|----|----|----|----|-----|------|
| 2004 | Jamestown (NYP) | A | 1 | 1 | 3.38 | 6 | 6 | 0 | 0 | 27 | 21 | 14 | 10 | 2 | 8 | 32 | .210 |
| 2005 | Greensboro (SAL) | A | 2 | 7 | 5.18 | 12 | 12 | 0 | 0 | 66 | 74 | 45 | 38 | 12 | 25 | 63 | .279 |
| | Jupiter (FSL) | A | 1 | 0 | 3.38 | 4 | 4 | 1 | 0 | 24 | 21 | 10 | 9 | 1 | 9 | 19 | .247 |
| 2006 | Carolina (SL) | AA | 4 | 1 | 0.95 | 22 | 0 | 0 | 6 | 28 | 11 | 4 | 3 | 0 | 14 | 40 | .125 |
| | Florida (NL) | MLB | 2 | 1 | 2.85 | 49 | 0 | 0 | 3 | 41 | 33 | 14 | 13 | 4 | 26 | 46 | .228 |
| **MINOR LEAGUE TOTALS** | | | 8 | 9 | 3.72 | 44 | 22 | 1 | 6 | 145 | 127 | 73 | 60 | 15 | 56 | 154 | .236 |
| **MAJOR LEAGUE TOTALS** | | | 2 | 1 | 2.85 | 49 | 0 | 0 | 3 | 41 | 33 | 14 | 13 | 4 | 26 | 46 | .228 |

## 7 AARON THOMPSON　LHP

**Born:** Feb. 28, 1987. **B-T:** L-L. **Ht.:** 6-3. **Wt.:** 195. **Drafted:** HS—Houston, 2005 (1st round). **Signed by:** Dennis Cardoza.

Thompson was considered a tough sign after committing to Texas A&M. The Aggies made his decision easier when they fired their coaching staff, and he turned pro for $1.225 million as part of the Marlins' 2005 draft. He has known former Marlin Kevin Millar since he was five, when Thompson's grandparents served as Millar's host family at Lamar University. Millar used to do cannonballs off the grandparents' roof into their swimming pool. As so many finesse lefties have been through the years, Thompson often draws comparisons to Tom Glavine. Thompson pitches at 88-90 mph with his fastball and also has an out-pitch slider, potential plus curveball and solid-average changeup. He holds runners well, thinks his way through a lineup and demonstrates good savvy. On some nights, Thompson's fastball is a little short, but he could add more velocity as his body matures. He did touch 92 mph in high school. He could tighten up his curve, use his changeup a little more and polish his overall command. After handing low Class A with three other members of the Class of '05, Thompson will head to high Class A with them. He may be close to his ceiling but that shouldn't keep him from pushing for a big-league rotation spot as early as midseason 2008.

| Year | Club (League) | Class | W | L | ERA | G | GS | CG | SV | IP | H | R | ER | HR | BB | SO | AVG |
|------|---------------|-------|---|---|-----|---|----|----|----|----|---|---|----|----|----|----|-----|
| 2005 | Marlins (GCL) | R | 2 | 4 | 4.50 | 8 | 8 | 0 | 0 | 32 | 42 | 20 | 16 | 1 | 10 | 41 | .316 |
| | Jamestown (NYP) | A | 1 | 2 | 3.10 | 5 | 5 | 0 | 0 | 20 | 25 | 13 | 7 | 1 | 10 | 17 | .301 |
| 2006 | Greensboro (SAL) | A | 8 | 8 | 3.63 | 24 | 24 | 0 | 0 | 134 | 139 | 68 | 54 | 12 | 35 | 114 | .270 |
| **MINOR LEAGUE TOTALS** | | | 11 | 14 | 3.72 | 37 | 37 | 0 | 0 | 186 | 206 | 101 | 77 | 14 | 55 | 172 | .282 |

## 8 RYAN TUCKER　RHP

**Born:** Dec. 6, 1986. **B-T:** R-R. **Ht.:** 6-2. **Wt.:** 190. **Drafted:** HS—Temple City, Calif., 2005 (1st round supplemental). **Signed by:** John Cole.

Tucker came on strong as a prep senior in 2005, wowing scouts with his big fastball. The Cardinals were among several clubs that thought about taking him in the first round, but he fell to the Marlins at No. 34 and signed for $975,000. He hasn't had as much success as the other members of the Class of 2005, but he may have the highest ceiling. Tucker's fastball remains his calling card, showing late life and the potential to dominate hitters. He pitches at 92-94 mph and touched 98 mph in his first full pro season. His changeup really took off at midseason, helping him post eight straight quality starts. He's a good athlete with a fluid delivery. He has an intense personality and shows no fear on the mound. His breaking stuff needs work. The Marlins took away Tucker's curveball and weren't too impressed with his slider, so they gave him a cutter instead. He began tinkering with it at a fall 2005 minicamp, then broke it out for game use in mid-2006. Tucker will continue to start as he climbs the ladder, though his fastball profiles him as future closer material. Despite middling results in low Class A, he should move up to high Class A along with his fellow 2005 first-rounders.

| Year | Club (League) | Class | W | L | ERA | G | GS | CG | SV | IP | H | R | ER | HR | BB | SO | AVG |
|------|---------------|-------|---|---|-----|---|----|----|----|----|---|---|----|----|----|----|-----|
| 2005 | Marlins (GCL) | R | 3 | 3 | 3.69 | 8 | 7 | 0 | 0 | 32 | 35 | 13 | 13 | 0 | 16 | 23 | .315 |
| | Jamestown (NYP) | A | 1 | 1 | 8.36 | 4 | 4 | 0 | 0 | 14 | 21 | 14 | 13 | 3 | 8 | 18 | .323 |
| 2006 | Greensboro (SAL) | A | 7 | 13 | 5.00 | 25 | 25 | 2 | 0 | 131 | 123 | 86 | 73 | 14 | 67 | 133 | .246 |
| **MINOR LEAGUE TOTALS** | | | 11 | 17 | 5.03 | 37 | 36 | 2 | 0 | 177 | 179 | 113 | 99 | 17 | 91 | 174 | .264 |

## 9 CHRIS COGHLAN　3B/2B

**Born:** June 18, 1985. **B-T:** L-R. **Ht.:** 6-1. **Wt.:** 190. **Drafted:** Mississippi, 2006 (1st round supplemental). **Signed by:** Mark Willoughby.

Though he never hit more than six homers in any of his three seasons at Mississippi, Coghlan boosted his stock by winning the 2005 Cape Cod League batting title with a .346 average. Taken with the 36th overall pick last June, he held out for seven weeks before signing for $950,000. He played with Tyler Jennings, the son of Marlins personnel chief Dan Jennings, at a Tampa-area high school. Coghlan's inside-out stroke allows him to spray line drives to all fields. He shows strong plate discipline, some gap power and a great desire to improve. A third baseman for most of his college career, he moved to second base during fall minicamp and took to the switch. With the help of infield coordinator Ed Romero, Coghlan moved well around the bag and showed solid range.

After signing, Coghlan had a little trouble with inside fastballs but worked with hitting coordinator John Mallee on pulling more balls. He doesn't have true third-base power, so moving to second base would help him profile better as a regular. Despite his experience at the hot corner, his arm is average at best. Coghlan earns comparisons to Bill Mueller for his ability to make solid contact and his overall gritty play. He should open his first full pro season in low Class A, where Greensboro's cozy First Horizon Park should help his power numbers spike.

| Year | Club (League) | Class | AVG | G | AB | R | H | 2B | 3B | HR | RBI | BB | SO | SB | OBP | SLG |
|------|---------------|-------|-----|---|----|---|---|----|----|----|-----|----|----|----|-----|-----|
| 2006 | Marlins (GCL) | R | .286 | 2 | 7 | 2 | 2 | 0 | 0 | 0 | 3 | 0 | 1 | 0 | .286 | .286 |
| | Jamestown (NYP) | A | .298 | 28 | 94 | 14 | 28 | 5 | 1 | 0 | 12 | 13 | 9 | 5 | .373 | .372 |
| **MINOR LEAGUE TOTALS** | | | .297 | 30 | 101 | 16 | 30 | 5 | 1 | 0 | 15 | 13 | 10 | 5 | .368 | .366 |

## 10 KRIS HARVEY
OF

STEVE MOORE

**Born:** Jan. 5, 1984. **B-T:** R-R. **Ht.:** 6-2. **Wt.:** 195. **Drafted:** Clemson, 2005 (2nd round). **Signed by:** Joel Matthews.

The son of Bryan Harvey, a former all-star and the first closer in Marlins history, Kris touched 97 mph with his fastball at Clemson. A two-way star for the Tigers, he finished second in NCAA Division I with 25 homers in 2005 before signing for $575,000 as a second-round pick. He missed nearly half of his first full pro season with a strained oblique muscle. He has easy power and the ability to punish hanging breaking balls, though some scouts believe he should lay off more of the latter. Quality fastballs are no problem for Harvey, who has excellent bat speed and loose wrists. He looks comfortable and effective in right field, showing a strong and accurate arm. His speed and athleticism are solid, and his makeup is strong. Harvey has 142 strikeouts in 630 pro at-bats, and he may not make enough consistent contact to hit for a high average. He could stand to reshape his 6-foot-2 frame, adding 10-15 pounds of muscle. His value would have been enhanced if he had been able to stay at third base, but Florida scrapped that plan after his 2005 debut. Harvey could return to low Class A in 2007 in an effort to get his bat going again. He faces roadblocks in the form of Jeremy Hermida, who has staked a claim to right field, and Josh Willingham, who smacked 25 homers in his first year as Florida's left fielder.

| Year | Club (League) | Class | AVG | G | AB | R | H | 2B | 3B | HR | RBI | BB | SO | SB | OBP | SLG |
|------|---------------|-------|-----|---|----|---|---|----|----|----|-----|----|----|----|-----|-----|
| 2005 | Jamestown (NYP) | A | .300 | 65 | 263 | 34 | 79 | 14 | 3 | 9 | 38 | 9 | 60 | 4 | .320 | .479 |
| 2006 | Greensboro (SAL) | A | .245 | 96 | 367 | 46 | 90 | 18 | 2 | 15 | 60 | 24 | 82 | 9 | .291 | .428 |
| **MINOR LEAGUE TOTALS** | | | .268 | 161 | 630 | 80 | 169 | 32 | 5 | 24 | 98 | 33 | 142 | 13 | .303 | .449 |

## 11 RENYEL PINTO
LHP

**Born:** July 8, 1982. **B-T:** L-L. **Ht.:** 6-4. **Wt.:** 195. **Signed:** Venezuela, 1999. **Signed by:** Alberto Rondon (Cubs).

Acquired from the Cubs in the Juan Pierre deal, big league pitching coach Rick Kranitz knows Pinto well from their time in that organization. If he ever harnesses his physical gifts, he could have a long career. For now the trouble seems to be determining whether he should be a starter or a reliever. He worked in the former role exclusively at Triple-A Albuquerque, but the Marlins used him only in long relief in the majors, where he was promoted three separate times last year. A big-bodied slinger with a 91-93 mph fastball, Pinto handled lefties and righties equally well. Pinto has a putaway slider against lefties and an underrated changeup he needs to use more. Command remains a problem, but he did strike out more than a batter per inning at both levels. He does a good job of holding runners but sometimes gets into trouble by being too quick to the plate. The Marlins would like to see him be more aggressive in general as he reprises his role in the big league bullpen.

| Year | Club (League) | Class | W | L | ERA | G | GS | CG | SV | IP | H | R | ER | HR | BB | SO | AVG |
|------|---------------|-------|---|---|-----|---|----|----|----|----|---|---|----|----|----|----|-----|
| 1999 | Cubs (DSL) | R | 4 | 5 | 4.38 | 13 | 13 | 1 | 0 | 64 | 70 | 35 | 31 | 5 | 22 | 62 | .289 |
| 2000 | Cubs (AZL) | R | 0 | 2 | 6.30 | 9 | 4 | 0 | 0 | 30 | 42 | 29 | 21 | 3 | 16 | 23 | .326 |
| 2001 | Lansing (MWL) | A | 4 | 8 | 5.22 | 20 | 20 | 1 | 0 | 88 | 94 | 64 | 51 | 9 | 44 | 69 | .278 |
| 2002 | Daytona (FSL) | A | 3 | 3 | 5.51 | 7 | 7 | 0 | 0 | 33 | 45 | 23 | 20 | 5 | 11 | 24 | .338 |
| | Lansing (MWL) | A | 7 | 5 | 3.31 | 17 | 16 | 0 | 0 | 98 | 79 | 39 | 36 | 9 | 28 | 92 | .221 |
| 2003 | Daytona (FSL) | A | 3 | 8 | 3.22 | 20 | 19 | 0 | 0 | 115 | 91 | 47 | 41 | 4 | 45 | 104 | .221 |
| 2004 | West Tenn (SL) | AA | 11 | 8 | 2.92 | 25 | 25 | 0 | 0 | 142 | 107 | 50 | 46 | 10 | 72 | 179 | .216 |
| | Iowa (PCL) | AAA | 1 | 1 | 7.71 | 2 | 2 | 0 | 0 | 9 | 9 | 9 | 8 | 2 | 8 | 9 | .257 |
| 2005 | Iowa (PCL) | AAA | 1 | 2 | 9.53 | 6 | 6 | 0 | 0 | 23 | 31 | 30 | 24 | 3 | 24 | 24 | .348 |
| | West Tenn (SL) | AA | 10 | 3 | 2.71 | 22 | 21 | 1 | 0 | 130 | 101 | 43 | 39 | 3 | 58 | 123 | .223 |
| 2006 | Albuquerque (PCL) | AAA | 8 | 2 | 3.40 | 18 | 18 | 1 | 0 | 95 | 82 | 40 | 36 | 8 | 47 | 96 | .232 |
| | Florida (NL) | MLB | 0 | 0 | 3.03 | 27 | 0 | 0 | 1 | 30 | 20 | 12 | 10 | 3 | 27 | 36 | .190 |
| **MINOR LEAGUE TOTALS** | | | 52 | 47 | 3.85 | 159 | 151 | 4 | 0 | 826 | 751 | 409 | 353 | 61 | 375 | 805 | .247 |
| **MAJOR LEAGUE TOTALS** | | | 0 | 0 | 3.03 | 27 | 0 | 0 | 1 | 29 | 20 | 12 | 10 | 3 | 27 | 36 | .190 |

## JOSE GARCIA                                                    RHP

**Born:** Jan. 7, 1985. **B-T:** R-R. **Ht.:** 5-11. **Wt.:** 165. **Signed:** Dominican Republic, 2001. **Signed by:** Cesar Santiago.

Garcia continued to gain momentum for the second straight year after opening his career with three seasons in the Rookie-level Dominican Summer League. He was the only Marlins farmhand selected to the Futures Game—where he gave up a two-run homer to the Royals' Billy Butler—and he saw action at four different levels, including a September callup to the majors. His fastball sits at 88-90 mph and touches 92 mph. He has an advanced feel for pitching, knows how to change speeds and eye levels and shows the makings of four plus pitches. His swing-and-miss changeup has good action and might be the best in the system. His slider is ahead of his curve. He learned how to keep hitters honest by coming inside more with his fastball. He's a good fielder and holds runners well. Popular with teammates, Garcia has an easygoing personality, good energy and enjoys being on the mound, where he works fast and aggressively. His smallish frame could land him in the bullpen down the road, but his wide repertoire should keep him in a starting role for now. He'll open the season in the Triple-A rotation.

| Year | Club (League) | Class | W | L | ERA | G | GS | CG | SV | IP | H | R | ER | HR | BB | SO | AVG |
|------|---------------|-------|---|---|-----|---|----|----|----|----|---|---|----|----|----|----|-----|
| 2002 | Marlins (DSL) | R | 3 | 2 | 1.16 | 15 | 1 | 0 | 3 | 39 | 25 | 18 | 5 | 0 | 13 | 42 | .179 |
| 2003 | Marlins (DSL) | R | 2 | 6 | 2.83 | 12 | 12 | 2 | 0 | 70 | 78 | 37 | 22 | 3 | 14 | 87 | .284 |
| 2004 | Marlins (DSL) | R | 5 | 3 | 1.43 | 14 | 10 | 0 | 0 | 69 | 43 | 16 | 11 | 2 | 10 | 84 | .176 |
| 2005 | Greensboro (SAL) | A | 3 | 0 | 1.27 | 5 | 4 | 0 | 0 | 28 | 11 | 5 | 4 | 1 | 4 | 39 | .115 |
|  | Marlins (GCL) | R | 0 | 0 | 0.00 | 1 | 1 | 0 | 0 | 2 | 1 | 0 | 0 | 0 | 1 | 3 | .167 |
|  | Jupiter (FSL) | A | 0 | 0 | 18.00 | 1 | 1 | 0 | 0 | 2 | 2 | 4 | 4 | 0 | 2 | 0 | .286 |
| 2006 | Jupiter (FSL) | A | 6 | 2 | 1.87 | 12 | 11 | 1 | 0 | 77 | 60 | 31 | 16 | 3 | 16 | 69 | .210 |
|  | Albuquerque (PCL) | AAA | 0 | 1 | 11.25 | 1 | 1 | 0 | 0 | 4 | 5 | 5 | 5 | 0 | 4 | 5 | .294 |
|  | Carolina (SL) | AA | 6 | 7 | 3.40 | 14 | 14 | 0 | 0 | 85 | 78 | 37 | 32 | 10 | 25 | 87 | .242 |
|  | Florida (NL) | MLB | 0 | 0 | 4.91 | 5 | 0 | 0 | 0 | 11 | 10 | 6 | 6 | 1 | 5 | 8 | .233 |
| **MINOR LEAGUE TOTALS** | | | 25 | 21 | 2.37 | 75 | 55 | 3 | 3 | 376 | 303 | 153 | 99 | 19 | 89 | 416 | .218 |
| **MAJOR LEAGUE TOTALS** | | | 0 | 0 | 4.91 | 5 | 0 | 0 | 0 | 11 | 10 | 6 | 6 | 1 | 5 | 8 | .233 |

## RICK VANDEN HURK                                               RHP

**Born:** May 22, 1985. **B-T:** R-R. **Ht.:** 6-5. **Wt.:** 195. **Signed:** Netherlands, 2002. **Signed by:** Fred Ferreira.

Signed at 17 out of the Marlins' Dutch academy, Vanden Hurk was one of the better European signs for former international scouting supervisor Fred Ferreira. A converted catcher, he has been pitching for just four years but shows more polish than you would expect—especially considering he had Tommy John surgery in 2005. He's also one of the hardest workers in the system and shows great makeup. He came back late in 2006 from his elbow surgery and showed no ill effects. He pitched at 90-92 mph and topped out at 94 with late life. He babies his slow curveball at times, but has shown the ability to throw it harder and sharper. His changeup is coming along, and he has picked up a cutter as well. Smart and coachable, he has a long, loose frame and an easy motion that creates deception. Mound time is Vanden Hurk's biggest need because he still lapses into bad habits mechanically, such as throwing across his body. He was sent to Hawaii Winter Baseball for more innings and projects as back-of-the-rotation starter in the majors. After pitching just 54 innings over the past two seasons, Vanden Hurk will try to carry a full workload this season, which he could open back in high Class A.

| Year | Club (League) | Class | W | L | ERA | G | GS | CG | SV | IP | H | R | ER | HR | BB | SO | AVG |
|------|---------------|-------|---|---|-----|---|----|----|----|----|---|---|----|----|----|----|-----|
| 2003 | Marlins (GCL) | R | 2 | 6 | 5.35 | 11 | 10 | 0 | 0 | 39 | 49 | 30 | 23 | 2 | 20 | 30 | .308 |
| 2004 | Jupiter (FSL) | A | 2 | 3 | 3.26 | 14 | 14 | 0 | 0 | 58 | 54 | 22 | 21 | 2 | 31 | 43 | .260 |
| 2005 | Greensboro (SAL) | A | 1 | 2 | 2.45 | 4 | 4 | 1 | 0 | 22 | 17 | 7 | 6 | 1 | 11 | 26 | .218 |
|  | Jupiter (FSL) | A | 0 | 1 | 4.05 | 2 | 2 | 0 | 0 | 7 | 7 | 4 | 3 | 0 | 0 | 6 | .259 |
| 2006 | Marlins (GCL) | R | 0 | 0 | 1.20 | 5 | 5 | 0 | 0 | 15 | 4 | 2 | 2 | 0 | 8 | 26 | .085 |
|  | Jupiter (FSL) | A | 0 | 0 | 2.70 | 3 | 3 | 0 | 0 | 10 | 5 | 4 | 3 | 1 | 6 | 15 | .147 |
| **MINOR LEAGUE TOTALS** | | | 5 | 12 | 3.47 | 39 | 38 | 1 | 0 | 150 | 136 | 69 | 58 | 6 | 76 | 146 | .246 |

## HENRY OWENS                                                    RHP

**Born:** April 23, 1979. **B-T:** R-R. **Ht.:** 6-3. **Wt.:** 230. **Signed:** NDFA/ Barry (Fla.), 2001. **Signed by:** Delvy Santiago (Pirates).

A backup catcher in college, Owens decided to delay his plan of going to medical school to give pitching a shot as a pro. He never got past Class A with the Pirates, so the Mets nabbed him in Triple-A phase of the 2004 Rule 5 draft and added him to their 40-man roster after the 2005 season. He came to Florida with righthander Matt Lindstrom after the 2006 season in a deal that sent lefthanders Jason Vargas and Adam Bostick to New York.

Though he missed three weeks of 2006 due to elbow tenderness, he was impressive enough that he earned a spot on Team USA's Olympic qualifying team. He had three saves in the tournament, including the win over Cuba, and was effective over the winter in the Dominican League as well. Owens dominated Double-A on the strength of his lively 94 mph fastball that touches 96. His velocity plays up because he hides the ball well behind a funky delivery and has a short, quick arm action. He falls off to the first-base side of the mound in his finish, but his command is still solid. He has made major strides with his slider, a two-plane breaker that he throws at 83-84 mph. Owens is also adding a split-finger fastball to his repertoire. Though he was roughed up in his brief big league exposure, Owens has shown the ability to make hitters miss at the upper levels of the minors. He should win a spot in the Marlins bullpen in spring training.

| Year | Club (League) | Class | W | L | ERA | G | GS | CG | SV | IP | H | R | ER | HR | BB | SO | AVG |
|------|---------------|-------|---|---|-----|---|----|----|----|----|---|---|----|----|----|----|-----|
| 2001 | Pirates (GCL) | R | 1 | 0 | 1.29 | 6 | 0 | 0 | 1 | 7 | 5 | 1 | 1 | 0 | 2 | 8 | .192 |
| 2002 | Williamsport (NYP) | A | 0 | 3 | 2.62 | 23 | 0 | 0 | 7 | 45 | 26 | 18 | 13 | 4 | 16 | 63 | .166 |
| 2003 | Hickory (SAL) | A | 2 | 1 | 2.91 | 22 | 0 | 0 | 9 | 34 | 21 | 14 | 11 | 1 | 17 | 52 | .176 |
| | Lynchburg (CL) | A | 1 | 2 | 2.45 | 13 | 0 | 0 | 5 | 15 | 9 | 6 | 4 | 0 | 11 | 21 | .176 |
| 2004 | Lynchburg (CL) | A | 3 | 4 | 4.28 | 39 | 0 | 0 | 4 | 55 | 46 | 26 | 26 | 4 | 26 | 49 | .219 |
| 2005 | St. Lucie (FSL) | A | 2 | 5 | 3.15 | 38 | 1 | 0 | 4 | 54 | 49 | 29 | 19 | 2 | 24 | 74 | .233 |
| 2006 | New York (NL) | MLB | 0 | 0 | 9.00 | 3 | 0 | 0 | 0 | 4 | 4 | 4 | 4 | 0 | 4 | 2 | .286 |
| | Binghamton (EL) | AA | 2 | 2 | 1.58 | 37 | 0 | 0 | 20 | 40 | 19 | 9 | 7 | 1 | 10 | 74 | .137 |
| **MINOR LEAGUE TOTALS** | | | 11 | 17 | 2.92 | 178 | 1 | 0 | 50 | 249 | 175 | 103 | 81 | 12 | 106 | 341 | .192 |
| **MAJOR LEAGUE TOTALS** | | | 0 | 0 | 9.00 | 3 | 0 | 0 | 0 | 4 | 4 | 4 | 4 | 0 | 4 | 2 | .286 |

## 15 YUSMEIRO PETIT                                              RHP

**Born:** Nov. 22, 1984. **B-T:** R-R. **Ht.:** 6-0. **Wt.:** 180. **Signed:** Venezuela, 2001. **Signed by:** Gregorio Machado (Mets).

Acquired from the Mets along with Mike Jacobs in the November 2005 deal that sent Carlos Delgado to Flushing, Petit was supposed to contend for a spot in the Marlins rotation by midseason. Instead it was Anibal Sanchez who blasted his way to fame with a September no-hitter, while Petit bounced back and forth between Triple-A and the big leagues. Petit's fastball velocity fluctuated to an alarming degree, dipping into the mid-80s during a woeful spring training and settling into the 89-91 mph range later in the year. He has a plus change, but his curve and slider were not the weapons they had been with the Mets. He was decent against Triple-A hitters but struggled mightily in the majors, where he was limited to one start in 15 appearances. His ERA was the highest in the majors for any of the 460 pitchers to work at least 21 innings. The deception that was his hallmark never seemed to materialize. With the Marlins rotation seemingly set, Petit could be used as a trade chip or head back to Triple-A to work out his problems.

| Year | Club (League) | Class | W | L | ERA | G | GS | CG | SV | IP | H | R | ER | HR | BB | SO | AVG |
|------|---------------|-------|---|---|-----|---|----|----|----|----|---|---|----|----|----|----|-----|
| 2002 | Mets (VSL) | R | 3 | 5 | 2.43 | 12 | 11 | 0 | 0 | 56 | 53 | 25 | 15 | 1 | 16 | 62 | .252 |
| 2003 | Kingsport (Appy) | R | 3 | 3 | 2.32 | 12 | 12 | 0 | 0 | 62 | 47 | 19 | 16 | 2 | 8 | 65 | .219 |
| | Brooklyn (NYP) | A | 1 | 0 | 2.19 | 2 | 2 | 0 | 0 | 12 | 5 | 3 | 3 | 0 | 2 | 20 | .119 |
| 2004 | Capital City (SAL) | A | 9 | 2 | 2.39 | 15 | 15 | 0 | 0 | 83 | 47 | 29 | 22 | 8 | 22 | 122 | .162 |
| | St. Lucie (FSL) | A | 2 | 3 | 1.22 | 9 | 9 | 1 | 0 | 44 | 27 | 9 | 6 | 0 | 14 | 62 | .174 |
| | Binghamton (EL) | AA | 1 | 1 | 4.50 | 2 | 2 | 0 | 0 | 12 | 10 | 6 | 6 | 0 | 5 | 16 | .233 |
| 2005 | Binghamton (EL) | AA | 9 | 3 | 2.91 | 21 | 21 | 2 | 0 | 118 | 90 | 41 | 38 | 15 | 18 | 130 | .209 |
| | Norfolk (IL) | AAA | 0 | 3 | 9.20 | 3 | 3 | 0 | 0 | 15 | 24 | 16 | 15 | 5 | 6 | 14 | .375 |
| 2006 | Albuquerque (PCL) | AAA | 4 | 6 | 4.28 | 17 | 17 | 0 | 0 | 97 | 101 | 53 | 46 | 14 | 20 | 68 | .268 |
| | Florida (NL) | MLB | 1 | 1 | 9.57 | 15 | 1 | 0 | 0 | 26 | 46 | 28 | 28 | 7 | 9 | 20 | .390 |
| **MINOR LEAGUE TOTALS** | | | 32 | 26 | 3.02 | 93 | 92 | 3 | 0 | 498 | 404 | 201 | 167 | 45 | 111 | 559 | .221 |
| **MAJOR LEAGUE TOTALS** | | | 1 | 1 | 9.57 | 15 | 1 | 0 | 0 | 26 | 46 | 28 | 28 | 7 | 9 | 20 | .390 |

## 16 JESUS DELGADO                                              RHP

**Born:** April 19, 1984. **B-T:** R-R. **Ht.:** 6-0. **Wt.:** 170. **Signed:** Venezuela, 2001. **Signed by:** Ben Cherington (Red Sox).

Hanley Ramirez and Anibal Sanchez weren't the only pieces the Marlins got from the Red Sox in the Josh Beckett/Mike Lowell deal. They also received a pair of righty relievers who spent 2006 in high Class A: Harvey Garcia and Delgado. A Tommy John survivor who already missed two seasons earlier in his career, Delgado suffered through another injury-marred campaign. This time it was a pulled muscle under his armpit that caused him to miss the bulk of the second half. He still showed the potential for three plus pitches: a 92-93 mph fastball that touched 95, a hard curve that came in at 78-82 mph, and a devastating change-up he didn't use nearly enough. A former outfielder, Delgado made a quick conversion to the mound after the Red Sox signed him. His makeup is good and his work ethic is strong. His mix of pitches makes him a candidate to start, but the Marlins rotation depth probably

means he'll stay in the bullpen. If he can stay healthy, he projects as a useful option in the middle innings. For now he'll move up to Double-A.

| Year | Club (League) | Class | W | L | ERA | G | GS | CG | SV | IP | H | R | ER | HR | BB | SO | AVG |
|------|---------------|-------|---|---|-----|---|----|----|----|----|----|----|----|----|----|----|-----|
| 2001 | Red Sox (DSL) | R | 0 | 2 | 5.34 | 10 | 8 | 0 | 0 | 32 | 31 | 25 | 19 | 1 | 14 | 19 | .240 |
| 2002 | Did not play—Injured | | | | | | | | | | | | | | | | |
| 2003 | Did not play—Injured | | | | | | | | | | | | | | | | |
| 2004 | Red Sox (GCL) | R | 0 | 0 | 10.80 | 1 | 0 | 0 | 0 | 2 | 4 | 2 | 2 | 0 | 0 | 2 | .500 |
| | Augusta (SAL) | A | 1 | 5 | 5.22 | 21 | 16 | 0 | 0 | 59 | 61 | 40 | 34 | 10 | 26 | 34 | .275 |
| 2005 | Greenville (SAL) | A | 7 | 3 | 3.50 | 33 | 0 | 0 | 2 | 72 | 57 | 30 | 28 | 3 | 39 | 69 | .215 |
| 2006 | Jupiter (FSL) | A | 2 | 4 | 2.58 | 28 | 0 | 0 | 0 | 38 | 33 | 19 | 11 | 0 | 18 | 40 | .231 |
| **MINOR LEAGUE TOTALS** | | | 10 | 14 | 4.17 | 93 | 24 | 0 | 2 | 203 | 186 | 116 | 94 | 14 | 97 | 164 | .243 |

## 17 HARVEY GARCIA                                           RHP

**Born:** March 16, 1984. **B-T:** R-R. **Ht.:** 6-2. **Wt.:** 170. **Signed:** Venezuela, 2000. **Signed by:** Louie Eljaua/Miguel Garcia.

Released by the new Marlins regime shortly after it took over in 2002, Garcia followed signing scouts Louie Eljaua and Miguel Garcia to the Red Sox. Three years later he came back to Florida as a throw-in to complete the sprawling Josh Beckett deal with Boston. Garcia emerged as the primary closer at Jupiter in 2006, touching 97 mph with his fastball and pitching at 93-95. Demonstrative on the mound, some saw a little bit of Pascual Perez in him. Others said he resembled a young Mariano Rivera in his lean, broad-shouldered, projectable physique. Garcia has the makings of a solid changeup but didn't use it much, in part because he still throws it too hard. He relied instead on a slurvy breaking ball to get hitters off his heater. His velocity tailed off near season's end and his command remains a question. He also struggled to maintain his confidence when things went against him, leading some to deduce his animated behavior was really a front. Always willing to take the ball, he projects as a set-up man more so than a closer. He'll take the next step to Double-A in 2007.

| Year | Club (League) | Class | W | L | ERA | G | GS | CG | SV | IP | H | R | ER | HR | BB | SO | AVG |
|------|---------------|-------|---|---|-----|---|----|----|----|----|----|----|----|----|----|----|-----|
| 2001 | Marlins (VSL) | R | 2 | 2 | 3.58 | 12 | 4 | 0 | 0 | 33 | 36 | 20 | 13 | 0 | 18 | 23 | -- |
| 2002 | Marlins (VSL) | R | 0 | 2 | 6.08 | 4 | 3 | 0 | 0 | 13 | 16 | 11 | 9 | 3 | 8 | 12 | .320 |
| | Red Sox (VSL) | R | 2 | 3 | 2.68 | 9 | 7 | 0 | 0 | 40 | 32 | 15 | 12 | 0 | 14 | 31 | .221 |
| 2003 | Red Sox (GCL) | R | 3 | 0 | 1.89 | 9 | 8 | 0 | 0 | 33 | 21 | 11 | 7 | 2 | 12 | 32 | .179 |
| | Red Sox (DSL) | R | 0 | 2 | 1.20 | 3 | 3 | 0 | 0 | 15 | 10 | 4 | 2 | 0 | 3 | 10 | .172 |
| 2004 | Lowell (NYP) | A | 4 | 6 | 5.16 | 14 | 14 | 0 | 0 | 61 | 61 | 40 | 35 | 8 | 30 | 54 | .268 |
| 2005 | Greenville (SAL) | A | 3 | 5 | 2.01 | 32 | 0 | 0 | 6 | 45 | 49 | 18 | 10 | 3 | 18 | 54 | .275 |
| 2006 | Jupiter (FSL) | A | 0 | 7 | 2.92 | 55 | 0 | 0 | 21 | 65 | 54 | 27 | 21 | 5 | 32 | 83 | .221 |
| **MINOR LEAGUE TOTALS** | | | 14 | 27 | 3.22 | 138 | 39 | 0 | 27 | 305 | 279 | 146 | 109 | 21 | 135 | 299 | .274 |

## 18 MATT LINDSTROM                                         RHP

**Born:** Feb. 11, 1980. **B-T:** R-R. **Ht.:** 6-4. **Wt.:** 205. **Drafted:** Ricks (Idaho) JC, 2002 (10th round). **Signed by:** Jim Reeves (Mets).

Lindstrom spent two years on a Mormon mission in Sweden before returning to the United States in 2001 to pitch at Ricks (Idaho) Junior College with his brother Rob. He first gained attention as a pro with his impressive velocity in the Arizona Fall League in 2004, and he finally put up big strikeout numbers in 2006. He played in the Futures Game and stood out even among the best pitching prospects in the game with his triple-digit velocity. The Mets included him a four-pitcher swap with the Marlins in December. With a fastball that sits at 94-97 mph and has touched 101, Lindstrom throws as hard as anyone in the minors, and his command vastly improved last season. His fastball is relatively straight, though, and he has been working on various grips and finger pressures to increase movement. His slider has emerged as his second-best pitch. He throws it at 83-86 mph, but he has a tendency to get under it. He also toys with a changeup and a curveball, but now that he is strictly a reliever it's unlikely he'll need them much. Lindstrom does need to improve his pitch selection and the way he attacks hitters. His performance has improved significantly since switching exclusively to relief in 2005, and he should win a spot in the Florida bullpen in spring training.

| Year | Club (League) | Class | W | L | ERA | G | GS | CG | SV | IP | H | R | ER | HR | BB | SO | AVG |
|------|---------------|-------|---|---|-----|---|----|----|----|----|----|----|----|----|----|----|-----|
| 2002 | Kingsport (Appy) | R | 0 | 6 | 4.84 | 12 | 11 | 0 | 0 | 48 | 56 | 45 | 26 | 6 | 21 | 39 | .280 |
| 2003 | Capital City (SAL) | A | 2 | 3 | 2.86 | 12 | 11 | 0 | 0 | 57 | 46 | 21 | 18 | 2 | 33 | 50 | .228 |
| | Brooklyn (NYP) | A | 7 | 3 | 3.44 | 14 | 14 | 0 | 0 | 65 | 61 | 28 | 25 | 2 | 27 | 52 | .250 |
| 2004 | St. Lucie (FSL) | A | 5 | 5 | 3.73 | 14 | 14 | 1 | 0 | 80 | 83 | 44 | 33 | 5 | 20 | 50 | .282 |
| | Capital City (SAL) | A | 3 | 2 | 3.21 | 13 | 12 | 0 | 0 | 56 | 47 | 26 | 20 | 3 | 10 | 64 | .230 |
| 2005 | Binghamton (EL) | AA | 2 | 5 | 5.40 | 35 | 10 | 0 | 0 | 73 | 90 | 61 | 44 | 11 | 55 | 58 | .302 |
| 2006 | St. Lucie (FSL) | A | 1 | 0 | 2.50 | 11 | 0 | 0 | 2 | 18 | 14 | 7 | 5 | 2 | 7 | 16 | .212 |
| | Binghamton (EL) | AA | 2 | 4 | 3.76 | 35 | 0 | 0 | 11 | 41 | 42 | 19 | 17 | 2 | 14 | 54 | .266 |
| **MINOR LEAGUE TOTALS** | | | 22 | 28 | 3.86 | 146 | 72 | 1 | 13 | 438 | 439 | 251 | 188 | 33 | 187 | 383 | .264 |

## 19 TOM HICKMAN                                                        OF

**Born:** April 18, 1988. **B-T:** L-L. **Ht.:** 6-1. **Wt.:** 180. **Drafted:** HS--Lindale, Ga., 2006 (2nd round). **Signed by:** Brian Bridges.

The Marlins were calling Hickman "Baby Hermida" after his strong debut in the Gulf Coast League. Like their former No. 1 prospect and current right fielder, Hickman is a Georgia high school product with an excellent idea of the strike zone. He also shares some of the same mechanical and physical characteristics of Hermida, though Hickman is smaller. A pre-draft mystery because of shoulder stiffness that limited his playing time as a senior, Hickman signed for $575,000. A third-team high school All-American, Hickman may have cost himself a higher draft slot by playing basketball his senior year. Though he's just an average runner, he will stay in center field for now. He gets good jumps and takes good routes. With quiet confidence and great makeup, he seems to thrive under pressure. He projects as a No. 2 hitter because he sees a lot of pitches and can handle the bat. As he adds bulk, his gap power should increase. He'll open his first full season in low Class A.

| Year | Club (League) | Class | AVG | G | AB | R | H | 2B | 3B | HR | RBI | BB | SO | SB | OBP | SLG |
|------|--------------|-------|-----|---|-----|----|----|----|----|----|-----|----|----|----|------|------|
| 2006 | Marlins (GCL) | R | .263 | 50 | 175 | 28 | 46 | 12 | 4 | 2 | 20 | 30 | 43 | 4 | .377 | .411 |
| **MINOR LEAGUE TOTALS** | | | .263 | 50 | 175 | 28 | 46 | 12 | 4 | 2 | 20 | 30 | 43 | 4 | .377 | .411 |

## 20 ROBERT ANDINO                                                     SS

**Born:** April 25, 1984. **B-T:** R-R. **Ht.:** 6-0. **Wt.:** 170. **Drafted:** HS--Miami, 2002 (2nd round). **Signed by:** John Martin.

In some ways the train has already left the station for Andino, who saw both middle-infield slots filled last spring by rookies Hanley Ramirez and Dan Uggla, now Marlins cornerstones. Signed for $750,000 out of a Miami high school, Andino contines to play exemplary defense and he got a little better with the bat last year. He is blessed with soft hands, quick feet and smooth actions, though he sometimes gets a little lazy on his throws. His attitude was horrendous at the Arizona Fall League after 2005, but he showed a much greater desire to play last year. He also did a better job of taking breaking balls to the opposite field and stayed on pitches much better in general. He continues to struggle as a basestealer and is an average runner at best. Some believe he could make the move to center field, but he has yet to see any action out there. While he probably won't be pushing Hanley Ramirez or Dan Uggla to the bench, Andino may be ready to stick in the majors as a utilityman.

| Year | Club (League) | Class | AVG | G | AB | R | H | 2B | 3B | HR | RBI | BB | SO | SB | OBP | SLG |
|------|--------------|-------|-----|---|-----|----|-----|----|----|----|-----|-----|-----|----|------|------|
| 2002 | Marlins (GCL) | R | .259 | 9 | 27 | 2 | 7 | 0 | 0 | 0 | 2 | 5 | 6 | 3 | .364 | .259 |
| | Jamestown (NYP) | A | .167 | 9 | 36 | 2 | 6 | 1 | 1 | 0 | 3 | 1 | 9 | 1 | .189 | .250 |
| 2003 | Greensboro (SAL) | A | .188 | 119 | 416 | 45 | 78 | 17 | 2 | 2 | 27 | 46 | 128 | 6 | .266 | .252 |
| 2004 | Greensboro (SAL) | A | .281 | 76 | 295 | 27 | 83 | 10 | 1 | 8 | 46 | 18 | 83 | 9 | .321 | .403 |
| | Jupiter (FSL) | A | .281 | 49 | 196 | 18 | 55 | 7 | 2 | 0 | 15 | 7 | 43 | 6 | .304 | .337 |
| 2005 | Carolina (SL) | AA | .269 | 127 | 516 | 63 | 139 | 30 | 0 | 5 | 48 | 37 | 111 | 22 | .324 | .357 |
| | Florida (NL) | MLB | .159 | 17 | 44 | 4 | 7 | 4 | 0 | 0 | 1 | 5 | 8 | 1 | .245 | .250 |
| 2006 | Albuquerque (PCL) | AAA | .255 | 120 | 498 | 70 | 127 | 18 | 6 | 8 | 46 | 33 | 100 | 13 | .303 | .363 |
| | Florida (NL) | MLB | .167 | 11 | 24 | 0 | 4 | 1 | 0 | 0 | 2 | 1 | 6 | 1 | .185 | .208 |
| **MINOR LEAGUE TOTALS** | | | .249 | 509 | 1984 | 227 | 495 | 83 | 12 | 23 | 187 | 147 | 480 | 60 | .302 | .338 |
| **MAJOR LEAGUE TOTALS** | | | .162 | 28 | 68 | 4 | 11 | 5 | 0 | 0 | 3 | 6 | 14 | 2 | .224 | .235 |

## 21 BRETT CARROLL                                                    OF

**Born:** Oct. 3, 1982. **B-T:** R-R. **Ht.:** 6-0. **Wt.:** 190. **Drafted:** Middle Tennessee State, 2004 (10th round). **Signed by:** Brian Bridges.

Carroll took a big step forward in 2006, making it to Double-A for the second half on the basis of a power stroke, cannon arm and energetic playing style. He still strikes out too much, but at least he began to walk more last season. Carroll was able to carry that more patient approach into the Arizona Fall League, where he hit .284. Strong for his size, he projects as a 20- to 25-homer threat in the majors if he can polish his command of the zone. In right field, his athleticism allows him to make highlight plays in the Eric Byrnes mold. He isn't afraid to bang into walls, and his 70 throwing arm (on the 20-80 scouting scale) is fast becoming the stuff of legend. Carroll should make it to Triple-A at some point this year and might get his first taste of the majors.

| Year | Club (League) | Class | AVG | G | AB | R | H | 2B | 3B | HR | RBI | BB | SO | SB | OBP | SLG |
|------|--------------|-------|-----|----|------|----|-----|----|---|----|-----|----|-----|----|------|------|
| 2004 | Jamestown (NYP) | A | .251 | 60 | 211 | 27 | 53 | 16 | 1 | 6 | 28 | 15 | 57 | 1 | .321 | .422 |
| 2005 | Greensboro (SAL) | A | .243 | 118 | 412 | 57 | 100 | 28 | 1 | 18 | 54 | 17 | 108 | 10 | .296 | .447 |
| 2006 | Jupiter (FSL) | A | .241 | 59 | 216 | 31 | 52 | 12 | 1 | 8 | 30 | 18 | 48 | 9 | .324 | .417 |
| | Carolina (SL) | AA | .231 | 74 | 251 | 29 | 58 | 15 | 3 | 9 | 30 | 18 | 62 | 4 | .303 | .422 |
| **MINOR LEAGUE TOTALS** | | | .241 | 311 | 1090 | 144 | 263 | 71 | 6 | 41 | 142 | 68 | 275 | 24 | .308 | .430 |

## KYLE WINTERS
RHP

**Born:** April 22, 1987. **B-T:** R-R. **Ht.:** 6-4. **Wt.:** 190. **Drafted:** HS--Arvada, Colo., 2005 (5th round). **Signed by:** Scott Stanley.

It's easy for a righthanded starter to get lost in the shuffle considering the Marlins' depth in that area, but Winters is doing his part to stay on the radar. Unbeaten as a high school senior with 81 strikeouts in 51 innings, he was a University of New Mexico signee who slipped to the fifth round and signed for $166,000. His Colorado roots mean he's still relatively raw, but his lean, projectable frame has prompted comparisons to a young Roy Halladay or Brandon McCarthy. Winters' fastball ranges from 89-92 mph with good life and the potential to add a little velocity as he gains strength. He can command his slurvy breaking ball, which makes it a tick above average, and his changeup is coming along. Among Marlins insiders, Winters evokes memories of a young Josh Johnson in terms of his ability to pitch downhill and create leverage. Their quiet personalities are similar, too. Winters' makeup is excellent and he accepts coaching well. He should go to low Class A in 2007.

| Year | Club (League) | Class | W | L | ERA | G | GS | CG | SV | IP | H | R | ER | HR | BB | SO | AVG |
|------|---------------|-------|---|---|-----|---|----|----|----|----|---|---|----|----|----|----|-----|
| 2005 | Marlins (GCL) | R | 0 | 4 | 3.64 | 11 | 10 | 0 | 0 | 42 | 37 | 26 | 17 | 4 | 12 | 33 | .237 |
| 2006 | Jamestown (NYP) | A | 6 | 6 | 2.45 | 15 | 15 | 0 | 0 | 88 | 63 | 31 | 24 | 2 | 15 | 60 | .194 |
| **MINOR LEAGUE TOTALS** | | | 6 | 10 | 2.83 | 26 | 25 | 0 | 0 | 130 | 100 | 57 | 41 | 6 | 27 | 93 | .208 |

## JOHN RAYNOR
OF

**Born:** Jan. 14, 1984. **B-T:** R-R. **Ht.:** 6-2. **Wt.:** 185. **Drafted:** UNC Wilmington, 2006 (9th round). **Signed by:** Joel Matthews.

A 12th-round pick of the Orioles as a junior in the 2005 draft, Raynor declined to sign and returned to UNC Wilmington to complete his biology degree. He boosted his stock a bit on the field, batting .370 with 12 home runs and 42 steals, and the Marlins took him in the ninth round, four rounds after another UNC Wilmington product, catcher Chris Hatcher. Raynor received a bonus of just $17,500 as a senior with no bargaining leverage. Already among the fastest players in the system, he beat the blazing Greg Burns in a 60-yard match race at minicamp and has been timed at 6.4 seconds in the 60-yard dash. But he's no speedy slap hitter. With a muscular physique some compare to that of Marlins left fielder Josh Willingham, Raynor shows gap power as well. He worked with hitting coordinator John Mallee to add a leg kick at the plate, and the change helped him stop jumping at pitches. He projects to hit 10-15 homers a year. He shows strong makeup, a great work ethic and the ability to use his speed on the basepaths. He was caught stealing just twice in 23 attempts in his debut after going 42 for 46 as a senior. His arm is below-average, but for now it shouldn't keep him from playing center field, where his intelligence and instincts combine with his speed to make him a plus defender. After performing well at short-season Jamestown in the pro debut, Raynor could jump to high Class A to open 2007.

| Year | Club (League) | Class | AVG | G | AB | R | H | 2B | 3B | HR | RBI | BB | SO | SB | OBP | SLG |
|------|---------------|-------|-----|---|----|---|---|----|----|----|-----|----|----|----|-----|-----|
| 2006 | Jamestown (NYP) | A | .286 | 54 | 199 | 36 | 57 | 8 | 4 | 4 | 21 | 17 | 51 | 21 | .356 | .427 |
| **MINOR LEAGUE TOTALS** | | | .286 | 54 | 199 | 36 | 57 | 8 | 4 | 4 | 21 | 17 | 51 | 21 | .356 | .427 |

## BRETT HAYES
C

**Born:** Feb. 13, 1984. **B-T:** R-R. **Ht.:** 6-1. **Wt.:** 200. **Drafted:** Nevada, 2005 (2nd round supplemental). **Signed by:** John Hughes.

Hayes loves to play and has the bloodlines to prove it. His father Tim was drafted by the Royals and his great-grandfather Tim Hayes played in the Indians organization. Signed for $450,000, Hayes has struggled with injuries as a pro. His first season was hampered by a broken left thumb, and year two included a broken hamate bone and a stress fracture in his shin. When healthy he has been impressive. Hayes has great versatility and athletic ability and played seven positions for USA Baseball's college national team in 2004. While his body evokes comparisons to Craig Biggio and Mike Lieberthal, his bat projects as more in the Brad Ausmus or Jason Kendall mold. His catch-and-throw skills are evident, as he regularly gets the ball down to second base in 1.9 seconds when challenged. An intelligent and savvy player, he has good leadership skills and shows the ability to handle a pitching staff. In a system without much in the way of catching prospects, Hayes is already the best. He'll open the season in high Class A and could move quickly if he can stay healthy.

| Year | Club (League) | Class | AVG | G | AB | R | H | 2B | 3B | HR | RBI | BB | SO | SB | OBP | SLG |
|------|---------------|-------|-----|---|----|---|---|----|----|----|-----|----|----|----|-----|-----|
| 2005 | Marlins (GCL) | R | .417 | 3 | 12 | 2 | 5 | 1 | 0 | 0 | 2 | 0 | 2 | 0 | .417 | .500 |
| | Jamestown (NYP) | A | .239 | 36 | 117 | 11 | 28 | 6 | 1 | 1 | 12 | 12 | 21 | 3 | .313 | .333 |
| 2006 | Greensboro (SAL) | A | .245 | 82 | 278 | 39 | 68 | 13 | 1 | 9 | 38 | 29 | 61 | 4 | .321 | .396 |
| **MINOR LEAGUE TOTALS** | | | .248 | 121 | 407 | 52 | 101 | 20 | 2 | 10 | 52 | 41 | 84 | 7 | .321 | .381 |

## JACOB MARCEAUX

RHP

**Born:** Feb. 14, 1984. **B-T:** R-R. **Ht.:** 6-1. **Wt.:** 195. **Drafted:** McNeese State, 2005 (1st round). **Signed by:** Dennis Cardoza.

While scouting director Stan Meek hit on four of the five arms he took in the first and sandwich rounds in 2005, Marceaux—the only college arm of the bunch—has disappointed to this point. He was the highest draft pick ever out of McNeese State and signed for a $1 million bonus, but blisters and nagging injuries plagued him much of his first full season. He first had a problem near his shoulder blade early in the year, and later he took a line drive off his ankle and missed time. His repertoire includes an 88-92 mph fastball with good life that he can cut and sink, a hard overhand curve with 12-to-6 break, a decent slider and a developing changeup that at times was his best offspeed offering. The blisters, which were particularly nasty and developed near the fingernail on his right middle finger, limited his use of the slider. Marceaux also tends to be hard on himself and often has a tough time repeating his delivery. As a result, some believe he is best suited for relief work. He may go back to high Class A to open 2007, but he should reach Double-A at some point.

| Year | Club (League) | Class | W | L | ERA | G | GS | CG | SV | IP | H | R | ER | HR | BB | SO | AVG |
|---|---|---|---|---|---|---|---|---|---|---|---|---|---|---|---|---|---|
| 2005 | Jamestown (NYP) | A | 3 | 5 | 5.55 | 10 | 10 | 0 | 0 | 47 | 56 | 33 | 29 | 5 | 13 | 32 | .287 |
| | Greensboro (SAL) | A | 0 | 3 | 12.36 | 5 | 5 | 0 | 0 | 20 | 40 | 32 | 27 | 4 | 9 | 12 | .426 |
| 2006 | Jupiter (FSL) | A | 4 | 11 | 3.99 | 22 | 22 | 1 | 0 | 117 | 115 | 65 | 52 | 8 | 49 | 80 | .254 |
| **MINOR LEAGUE TOTALS** | | | 7 | 19 | 5.28 | 37 | 37 | 1 | 0 | 184 | 211 | 130 | 108 | 17 | 71 | 124 | .285 |

## JOSE CAMPUSANO

OF

**Born:** Dec. 19, 1983. **B-T:** B-R. **Ht.:** 5-11. **Wt.:** 165. **Signed:** Dominican Republic, 2003. **Signed by:** Fred Ferreira/Jesus Campos.

The Marlins signed Campusano as an infielder, but his progress toward Florida is now taking place in the outfield. He began the year in center in Double-A but soon moved to left as the more polished Alejandro de Aza took over. Speed remains Campusano's greatest tool, rating an 80 on the 20-80 scouting scale, but he must show the ability to make it more usable. He had great trouble judging fly balls off the bat. His jumps and routes were poor. At the plate, he has worked daily on his bunting with Mudcats hitting coach Paul Sanigorski, but the light hasn't flipped on yet. He has learned to drive the ball at times from the left side but mostly slaps at it. He is a hard worker with good makeup, and though he's thin, he has wiry strength and could develop gap power as he progresses. Campusano loves to play and in 2004 stayed with his Gulf Coast League team rather than return home for his father's funeral. He'll battle for a spot in the Triple-A outfield in spring training.

| Year | Club (League) | Class | AVG | G | AB | R | H | 2B | 3B | HR | RBI | BB | SO | SB | OBP | SLG |
|---|---|---|---|---|---|---|---|---|---|---|---|---|---|---|---|---|
| 2003 | Marlins (DSL) | R | .244 | 57 | 205 | 30 | 50 | 9 | 4 | 0 | 12 | 33 | 43 | 27 | .366 | .327 |
| 2004 | Marlins (GCL) | R | .255 | 59 | 196 | 24 | 50 | 8 | 4 | 1 | 16 | 10 | 38 | 11 | .319 | .352 |
| 2005 | Jupiter (FSL) | A | .277 | 89 | 300 | 37 | 83 | 9 | 3 | 0 | 32 | 9 | 67 | 13 | .305 | .327 |
| 2006 | Carolina (SL) | AA | .285 | 99 | 337 | 41 | 96 | 14 | 1 | 1 | 15 | 15 | 78 | 37 | .330 | .341 |
| **MINOR LEAGUE TOTALS** | | | .269 | 304 | 1038 | 132 | 279 | 40 | 12 | 2 | 75 | 67 | 226 | 88 | .329 | .336 |

## GREG BURNS

OF

**Born:** Nov. 7, 1986. **B-T:** R-R. **Ht.:** 6-2. **Wt.:** 185. **Drafted:** HS--West Covina, Calif., 2004 (3rd round). **Signed by:** Robby Corsaro.

How coachable is Burns? Enough to take the suggestion of assistant general manager Jim Fleming that he could cure his problem of striding too far into the plate by placing a 4-by-4 piece of wood at his feet during cage work. Suddenly Burns was packing additional lumber for road trips and ignoring the ribbing of teammates. The teaching aid helped Burns salvage what a disappointing year with a strong August. He missed three weeks during the first half, after he jammed him thumb while sliding, and he often appeared overmatched at the plate. But his improved approach turned things around. Burns' all-around athleticism, especially his 3.9-second speed to first base, will always allow him to catch up in a hurry. His strong hands gives him some power. He has a flat swing and understands his role. Bunting remains a challenge even though he dropped 100 bunts a day during early work at home. Burns is a plus defender because of his range and closing speed. His arm is average despite an unusual throwing motion. He will try to carry his late surge to 2007 in high Class A.

| Year | Club (League) | Class | AVG | G | AB | R | H | 2B | 3B | HR | RBI | BB | SO | SB | OBP | SLG |
|---|---|---|---|---|---|---|---|---|---|---|---|---|---|---|---|---|
| 2004 | Marlins (GCL) | R | .243 | 42 | 136 | 28 | 33 | 5 | 4 | 0 | 7 | 26 | 48 | 7 | .372 | .338 |
| 2005 | Jamestown (NYP) | A | .257 | 65 | 241 | 43 | 62 | 5 | 2 | 1 | 11 | 39 | 84 | 17 | .366 | .307 |
| 2006 | Greensboro (SAL) | A | .231 | 105 | 342 | 44 | 79 | 13 | 8 | 2 | 23 | 38 | 109 | 20 | .307 | .333 |
| **MINOR LEAGUE TOTALS** | | | .242 | 212 | 719 | 115 | 174 | 23 | 14 | 3 | 41 | 103 | 241 | 44 | .340 | .325 |

## JASON STOKES                                                        1B

**Born:** Jan. 23, 1982. **B-T:** R-R. **Ht.:** 6-4. **Wt.:** 225. **Drafted:** HS--Coppell, Texas, 2000 (2nd round). **Signed by:** Bob Laurie.

Was it really way back in 2002 when Stokes made his one and only trip to the Futures Game? Signed for a $2.027 million bonus in 2000, Stokes hit 27 home runs in low Class A in 2002 and seemed destined to mash in the big leagues within a few seasons. Still armed with some of the best raw power in the system, the big Texan just hasn't been able to stay on the field enough to make use of it. In 2006, back and left shoulder injuries limited him to just 65 games at Triple-A. Toss in the thumb and wrist problems that plagued him the previous year, and Stokes has totaled just 78 games the past two seasons. No wonder the Marlins insisted on Mike Jacobs from the Mets as a replacement at first base when they traded Carlos Delgado. Perhaps it was because of rust, but Stokes wasn't nearly the threat at the plate last year when he did manage to play. He runs well for his size, but his fielding strides have leveled off. His power, such a rare commodity, means Stokes will keep getting chances.

| Year | Club (League) | Class | AVG | G | AB | R | H | 2B | 3B | HR | RBI | BB | SO | SB | OBP | SLG |
|------|---------------|-------|-----|---|----|---|---|----|----|----|-----|----|----|----|-----|-----|
| 2001 | Utica (NYP) | A | .231 | 35 | 130 | 12 | 30 | 2 | 1 | 6 | 19 | 11 | 48 | 0 | .299 | .400 |
| 2002 | Kane County (MWL) | A | .341 | 97 | 349 | 73 | 119 | 25 | 0 | 27 | 75 | 47 | 96 | 1 | .421 | .645 |
| 2003 | Jupiter (FSL) | A | .258 | 121 | 462 | 67 | 119 | 31 | 3 | 17 | 89 | 36 | 135 | 6 | .312 | .448 |
| 2004 | Marlins (GCL) | R | .250 | 3 | 8 | 1 | 2 | 1 | 0 | 1 | 1 | 1 | 3 | 0 | .333 | .750 |
|      | Carolina (SL) | AA | .272 | 106 | 394 | 66 | 107 | 26 | 0 | 23 | 78 | 42 | 121 | 5 | .345 | .513 |
| 2005 | Albuquerque (PCL) | AAA | .283 | 13 | 46 | 12 | 13 | 1 | 1 | 5 | 15 | 3 | 16 | 2 | .340 | .674 |
| 2006 | Marlins (GCL) | R | 1.000 | 1 | 3 | 1 | 3 | 1 | 0 | 1 | 2 | 0 | 0 | 0 | 1.000 | 2.333 |
|      | Albuquerque (PCL) | AAA | .257 | 65 | 237 | 39 | 61 | 13 | 2 | 7 | 34 | 35 | 85 | 2 | .350 | .418 |
| **MINOR LEAGUE TOTALS** | | | .279 | 441 | 1629 | 271 | 454 | 100 | 7 | 87 | 313 | 175 | 504 | 16 | .351 | .509 |

## BRAD McCANN                                                         1B

**Born:** Dec. 9, 1982. **B-T:** R-R. **Ht.:** 6-3. **Wt.:** 190. **Drafted:** Clemson, 2004 (6th round). **Signed by:** Joel Matthews.

After earning Marlins minor league player of the year honors in 2005, McCann suffered through a maddening season in high Class A in 2006. Seemingly psyched out by the larger parks of the Florida State League, McCann's line-drive stroke and ability to hit mistakes didn't yield nearly the same results they had in the cozier parks of the South Atlantic League. He wasn't overmatched by FSL pitching as much as he took too many hittable strikes and always seemed to be working out of a hole. His stroke and power potential still suggest he can hit with power to all fields. McCann's concentration lagged in the field, where he seemed to take his offensive struggles with him. A college third baseman who is 14 months older than his all-star brother Brian, the Braves catcher, he continues to work with roving infield coordinator Ed Romero in an effort to become a serviceable first baseman. His lackluster performance will likely force McCann to go back to high Class A to open the season.

| Year | Club (League) | Class | AVG | G | AB | R | H | 2B | 3B | HR | RBI | BB | SO | SB | OBP | SLG |
|------|---------------|-------|-----|---|----|---|---|----|----|----|-----|----|----|----|-----|-----|
| 2004 | Jamestown (NYP) | A | .287 | 28 | 108 | 16 | 31 | 6 | 2 | 3 | 13 | 7 | 15 | 0 | .339 | .463 |
| 2005 | Greensboro (SAL) | A | .295 | 123 | 478 | 67 | 141 | 35 | 2 | 28 | 106 | 37 | 97 | 1 | .355 | .552 |
| 2006 | Jupiter (FSL) | A | .231 | 121 | 458 | 47 | 106 | 23 | 0 | 12 | 40 | 32 | 108 | 3 | .288 | .360 |
| **MINOR LEAGUE TOTALS** | | | .266 | 272 | 1044 | 130 | 278 | 64 | 4 | 43 | 159 | 76 | 220 | 4 | .324 | .459 |

## TODD DOOLITTLE                                                      RHP

**Born:** Nov. 1, 1982. **B-T:** R-R. **Ht.:** 5-10. **Wt.:** 175. **Signed:** NDFA/Mississippi State, 2005. **Signed by:** Dave Dangler.

Undrafted and undersized, Doolittle has earned comparisons to another former Mississippi State Bulldog, Jeff Brantley. Doolittle goes right at hitters with a straight 88-91 mph fastball that touches 93. He complements his heater with a plus 12-to-6 curveball he throws at two different speeds, as well as a little slider he'll mix in for effect. Doolittle hides the ball well, shows a good feel for pitching and has tremendous confidence. That combination enables him to get tons of strikeouts up in the zone, much to the amazement of the Marlins. In two pro seasons, he has averaged 11.5 strikeouts per nine innings, so he must be doing something right. His lack of pedigree will force Doolittle to prove himself each year, but that just seems to drive him even more. After a strong finish in high Class A to end 2006, he could open this season in Double-A.

| Year | Club (League) | Class | W | L | ERA | G | GS | CG | SV | IP | H | R | ER | HR | BB | SO | AVG |
|------|---------------|-------|---|---|-----|---|----|----|----|----|---|---|----|----|----|----|-----|
| 2005 | Jamestown (NYP) | A | 4 | 5 | 4.03 | 22 | 3 | 0 | 2 | 58 | 61 | 36 | 26 | 4 | 20 | 71 | .263 |
| 2006 | Greensboro (SAL) | A | 4 | 1 | 1.37 | 30 | 2 | 0 | 2 | 59 | 36 | 11 | 9 | 1 | 21 | 79 | .176 |
|      | Jupiter (FSL) | A | 3 | 1 | 0.84 | 16 | 0 | 0 | 0 | 21 | 12 | 2 | 2 | 0 | 7 | 26 | .160 |
| **MINOR LEAGUE TOTALS** | | | 11 | 7 | 2.41 | 68 | 5 | 0 | 4 | 138 | 109 | 49 | 37 | 5 | 48 | 176 | .213 |

# HOUSTON
# ASTROS
## BY JIM CALLIS

After recovering from a 61-62 start in 2004 and a 15-30 beginning in 2005 to win the National League wild card in both years and reach the World Series in the latter season, the Astros couldn't execute a similar comeback in 2006. They nearly pulled off their biggest miracle to date, however.

Houston dug itself a 49-56 hole, and then trailed the Cardinals by 8½ games in the NL  Central with 12 to play. The Astros swept four games from St. Louis and went on a 10-2 run that left them just a game short of the eventual World Series champions. They now have now posted six consecutive winning seasons, capturing one division title and two wild cards during that span while missing the playoffs by a single win on two other occasions. The increased cost of that success has been staggering.

When Minute Maid Park opened in 2000, the Astros ranked 16th in baseball with a payroll of $66.4 million. At that point, they were known for trading players such as Carl Everett and Mike Hampton when they got expensive. They built a deep farm system with thrifty draft picks, emphasizing draft-and-follows and college senior signs, and by dominating the Venezuela talent market.

It's a different story now. Houston was Baseball America's Organization of the Year in 2001, when we ranked their minor league talent the third-best in the game. The Astros system hasn't rated higher than 20th since—it currently checks in at No. 22—so owner **Drayton McLane** has opened his wallet to sustain the winning. Local product Andy Pettitte received a three-year, $31.5

million contract to come home after the 2003 season, and his buddy Roger Clemens collected more than $40 million during the same span. Jeff Bagwell, Lance Berkman, Richard Hidalgo, Jeff Kent and Roy Oswalt have received eight-figure salaries as well.

Houston's payroll soared to $107.7 million in 2006, trailing only the game's financial giants: the Yankees, Red Sox and Mets. The Astros continued to spend this offseason, giving Carlos Lee a six-year, $100 million deal in an attempt to bolster an offense that ranked 11th in the NL last year.

Because Houston hasn't drafted as well and has faced stiffer competition in Venezuela in recent years, the system hasn't been able to feed the big league club as it once did. While the top four home run hitters (Berkman, Morgan Ensberg, Craig Biggio, Jason Lane), leading winner (Oswalt) and closer (Brad Lidge) in 2006 were all homegrown products, precious little new blood has arrived on the scene.

Not only have the Astros paid dearly for veteran help, but they've also sacrificed young talent. They traded righthander Mitch Talbot and shortstop Ben Zobrist to the Devil Rays for Aubrey Huff last July. Righty Jason Hirsh was the club's top pitching prospect until Houston packaged him with 24-year-old center fielder Willy Taveras and 25-year-old righty Taylor Buchholz to get Jason Jennings from the Rockies in December.

## TOP 30 PROSPECTS

| | |
|---|---|
| 1. Hunter Pence, of | 16. Josh Anderson, of |
| 2. Troy Patton, lhp | 17. Chance Douglass, rhp |
| 3. Matt Albers, rhp | 18. Lou Santangelo, c |
| 4. Jimmy Barthmaier, rhp | 19. Josh Flores, of |
| 5. Juan Gutierrez, rhp | 20. Jordan Parraz, of |
| 6. J.R. Towles, c | 21. Lincoln Holdzkom, rhp |
| 7. Paul Estrada, rhp | 22. Bud Norris, rhp |
| 8. Felipe Paulino, rhp | 23. Tommy Manzella, ss |
| 9. Max Sapp, c | 24. Chris Johnson, 3b |
| 10. Chad Reineke, rhp | 25. Koby Clemens, 3b |
| 11. Sergio Perez, rhp | 26. Sergio Severino, lhp |
| 12. Chris Sampson, rhp | 27. Hector Gimenez, c |
| 13. Eli Iorg, of | 28. Ronald Ramirez, ss/2b |
| 14. Brian Bogusevic, lhp | 29. Mike Rodriguez, of |
| 15. Brooks Conrad, 2b/3b | 30. Chris Salamida, lhp |

# ORGANIZATION OVERVIEW

**General manager:** Tim Purpura. **Farm director:** Ricky Bennett. **Scouting director:** Paul Ricciarini.

## 2006 PERFORMANCE

| Class | Team | League | W | L | PCT | Finish* | Manager | Affiliated |
|---|---|---|---|---|---|---|---|---|
| Majors | Houston | National | 82 | 80 | .506 | 6th (16) | Phil Garner | — |
| Triple-A | Round Rock Express | Pacific Coast | 85 | 59 | .590 | 2nd (16) | Jackie Moore | 2005 |
| Double-A | Corpus Christi Hooks | Texas | 76 | 63 | .547 | +3rd (8) | Dave Clark | 2005 |
| High A | Salem Avalanche | Carolina | 76 | 61 | .555 | 2nd (8) | Jim Pankovits | 2003 |
| Low A | Lexington Legends | South Atlantic | 75 | 63 | .543 | 5th (16) | Jack Lind | 2001 |
| Short-season | Tri-City ValleyCats | New York-Penn | 43 | 31 | .581 | 9th (14) | Gregg Langbehn | 2001 |
| Rookie | Greeneville Astros | Appalachian | 34 | 33 | .507 | 5th (10) | Ivan DeJesus | 2004 |

**OVERALL 2006 MINOR LEAGUE RECORD** 389 310 .557 2nd (30)
*Finish in overall standings (No. of teams in league). +League champion

## ORGANIZATION LEADERS

### BATTING
| | | |
|---|---|---|
| AVG | House, J.R., Corpus Christi/Round Rock | .345 |
| R | Pence, Hunter, Corpus Christi | 107 |
| H | Anderson, Josh, Corpus Christi | 173 |
| 2B | Caraballo, Francisco, Salem | 40 |
| | Conrad, Brooks, Round Rock | 40 |
| | Sellers, Neil, Salem | 40 |
| 3B | Conrad, Brooks, Round Rock | 15 |
| HR | Pence, Hunter, Corpus Christi | 31 |
| RBI | Pence, Hunter, Corpus Christi | 106 |
| BB | Sheldon, Ole, Lexington/Salem | 74 |
| SO | Jimerson, Charlton, Round Rock | 183 |
| SB | Anderson, Josh, Corpus Christi | 43 |
| OBP | Zobrist, Ben, Corpus Christi/Durham | .434 |
| SLG | Pence, Hunter, Corpus Christi | .537 |
| XBH | Conrad, Brooks, Round Rock | 79 |

### PITCHING
| | | |
|---|---|---|
| W | Fairchild, Thomas, Lexington/Salem | 14 |
| L | Patton, Troy, Salem/Corpus Christi | 12 |
| ERA | Salamida, Christopher, Tri-City | 1.06 |
| G | Estrada, Paul, Corpus Christi | 56 |
| SV | Escobar, Rodrigo, Salem | 17 |
| IP | Fairchild, Thomas, Lexington/Salem | 173 |
| BB | Barthmaier, James, Salem | 67 |
| SO | Patton, Troy, Salem/Corpus Christi | 148 |
| AVG | Salamida, Christopher, Tri-City | .189 |

## BEST TOOLS

| | |
|---|---|
| Best Hitter for Average | Hunter Pence |
| Best Power Hitter | Hunter Pence |
| Best Strike-Zone Discipline | Mike Rodriguez |
| Fastest Baserunner | Josh Flores |
| Best Athlete | Charlton Jimerson |
| Best Fastball | Felipe Paulino |
| Best Curveball | Paul Estrada |
| Best Slider | Chad Reineke |
| Best Changeup | Chance Douglass |
| Best Control | Chris Sampson |
| Best Defensive Catcher | J.R. Towles |
| Best Defensive Infielder | Tommy Manzella |
| Best Infield Arm | Tommy Manzella |
| Best Defensive Outfielder | Charlton Jimerson |
| Best Outfield Arm | Charlton Jimerson |

## PROJECTED 2010 LINEUP

| | |
|---|---|
| Catcher | J.R. Towles |
| First Base | Lance Berkman |
| Second Base | Chris Burke |
| Third Base | Morgan Ensberg |
| Shortstop | Adam Everett |
| Left Field | Carlos Lee |
| Center Field | Hunter Pence |

| | |
|---|---|
| Right Field | Luke Scott |
| No. 1 Starter | Roy Oswalt |
| No. 2 Starter | Troy Patton |
| No. 3 Starter | Jason Jennings |
| No. 4 Starter | Fernando Nieve |
| No. 5 Starter | Matt Albers |
| Closer | Brad Lidge |

## LAST YEAR'S TOP 20 PROSPECTS

1. Jason Hirsh, rhp
2. Troy Patton, lhp
3. Fernando Nieve, rhp
4. Jimmy Barthmaier, rhp
5. Eli Iorg, of
6. Hunter Pence, of
7. Felipe Paulino, rhp
8. Juan Gutierrez, rhp
9. Brian Bogusevic, lhp
10. Josh Flores, of
11. J.R. Towles, c
12. Matt Albers, rhp
13. Josh Anderson, of
14. Taylor Buchholz, rhp
15. Luke Scott, of
16. Ben Zobrist, ss
17. Chance Douglass, rhp
18. Koby Clemens, 3b
19. Mitch Einertson, of
20. Ryan Mitchell, rhp

## TOP PROSPECTS OF THE DECADE

| Year | Player, Pos. | 2006 Org. |
|---|---|---|
| 1997 | Richard Hidalgo, of | Yankees |
| 1998 | Richard Hidalgo, of | Yankees |
| 1999 | Lance Berkman, of | Astros |
| 2000 | Wilfredo Rodriguez, lhp | San Angelo (United) |
| 2001 | Roy Oswalt, rhp | Astros |
| 2002 | Carlos Hernandez, lhp | Astros |
| 2003 | John Buck, c | Royals |
| 2004 | Taylor Buchholz, rhp | Astros |
| 2005 | Chris Burke, 2b | Astros |
| 2006 | Jason Hirsh, rhp | Astros |

## TOP DRAFT PICKS OF THE DECADE

| Year | Player, Pos. | 2006 Org. |
|---|---|---|
| 1997 | Lance Berkman, 1b | Astros |
| 1998 | Brad Lidge, rhp | Astros |
| 1999 | Mike Rosamond, of | Braves |
| 2000 | Robert Stiehl, rhp | Astros |
| 2001 | Chris Burke, ss | Astros |
| 2002 | Derick Grigsby, rhp | Out of baseball |
| 2003 | Jason Hirsh, rhp (2nd round) | Astros |
| 2004 | Hunter Pence, of (2nd round) | Astros |
| 2005 | Brian Bogusevic, lhp | Astros |
| 2006 | Max Sapp, c | Astros |

## ALL-TIME LARGEST BONUSES

| | |
|---|---|
| Chris Burke, 2001 | $2,125,000 |
| Max Sapp, 2006 | $1,400,000 |
| Brian Bogusevic, 2005 | $1,375,000 |
| Robert Stiehl, 2000 | $1,250,000 |
| Derick Grigsby, 2002 | $1,125,000 |

# MINOR LEAGUE DEPTH CHART

## Houston Astros

**Impact: D.** Even top prospect Hunter Pence doesn't look like a future star, and the players behind him either have limited upside or significant holes in their games.

**Depth: C.** The Astros have a good number of pitchers, both lefthanded and righthanded, who have succeeded at the upper levels of the minors. But depth is another area of their farm system that has been hurt by unsuccessful drafts and significant trades.

**Sleeper:** Bud Norris, rhp. Norris didn't get much attention at Cal Poly, but he has a very good arm and could turn out to be a nice reliever.

*Numbers in parentheses indicate prospect rankings.*

| LF | CF | RF |
|---|---|---|
| (None) | Josh Anderson (16)<br>Josh Flores (19)<br>Mike Rodriguez (29)<br>Nick Moresi<br>Charlton Jimerson | Hunter Pence (1)<br>Eli Iorg (13)<br>Jordan Parraz (20)<br>Mitch Einertson |

| 3B | SS | 2B | 1B |
|---|---|---|---|
| Chris Johnson (24)<br>Koby Clemens (25) | Tommy Manzella (23)<br>Ronald Ramirez (28)<br>Edwin Maysonet<br>Wladimir Sutil | Brooks Conrad (15)<br>Jonny Ash<br>Drew Sutton | Mark Saccomanno |

### C
J.R. Towles (6)
Max Sapp (9)
Lou Santangelo(18)
Hector Gimenez (27)
Ralph Henriquez

### RHP

| Starters | Relievers |
|---|---|
| Matt Albers (3) | Paul Estrada (7) |
| Jimmy Barthmaier (4) | Felipe Paulino (8) |
| Juan Gutierrez (5) | Chad Reineke (10) |
| Sergio Perez (11) | Lincoln Holdzkom (21) |
| Chris Sampson (12) | Bud Norris (22) |
| Chance Douglass (17) | Samuel Gervacio |
| Jared Gothreaux | German Melendez |
| Tip Fairchild | Casey Hudspeth |
| Ronnie Martinez | |
| Ryan Mitchell | |

### LHP

| Starters | Relievers |
|---|---|
| Troy Patton (2) | Sergio Severino (26) |
| Brian Bogusevic (14) | Victor Garate |
| Chris Salamida (30) | Phil Barzilla |
| Mark McLemore | Jeff Wigdahl |
| Polin Trinidad | |

# DRAFT ANALYSIS

## 2006 SIGNING BUDGET: $3.1 million

**Best Pro Debut:** LHP Chris Salamida (13) led the New-York Penn League with 10 wins and a 1.06 ERA. He has a sneaky 89-91 mph fastball, a deceptive low-three-quarters delivery and a plus changeup at times.

**Best Athlete:** OF Nick Moresi's (3) junior season at Fresno State and his pro debut were marred by wrist problems that hampered his ability at the plate. He's a legitimate center fielder with speed and gap power. He needs to get healthier and stronger.

**Best Pure Hitter:** C Max Sapp (1) hit just .229 in the NY-P, but he was young for the league at 18 and got pushed there because the organization had a hole there and thought he could handle the challenge mentally. He'll sell out for power at times, but he makes consistently hard contact.

**Best Raw Power:** 3B Chris Johnson (4) has the most present power, but Sapp could catch him with more experience.

**Fastest Runner:** The Astros are on the lookout for speed but didn't sign any burners. Moresi is an above-average runner.

**Best Defensive Player:** Moresi catches up to balls with ease in center field. There were questions about Sapp's ability to stay behind the plate, but he began to answer them in a positive way by losing weight to increase his agility. He does have arm strength and led the NY-P by throwing out 72 percent of basestealers.

**Best Fastball:** RHP Sergio Perez (2) touched 97 mph pitching in relief this summer but usually sits at 92-93 mph as a starter, a role to which he'll return in 2007. He achieves good life on his fastball, though his command of the pitch can waver. RHP Bud Norris (6) pitches in the mid-90s more consistently and likely will stay in the bullpen.

**Best Breaking Ball:** For power and bite, Norris' curveball. For feel and command, Perez' slider.

**Most Intriguing Background:** Salamida grew up five minutes from Tri-City's Bruno Stadium, where he went 4-1, 1.10 in seven starts. LHP John Wiedenbauer's (24) father Tom is Houston's field coordinator, 1B Cirilo Cruz' (27) uncle Jose is the club's first-base coach and C Johnathan Moore's (36) dad Jackie is the Astros' Triple-A manager. Tom Wiedenbauer and Jose Cruz also played in the majors. So did Johnson's dad Ron (the Red Sox Triple-A Pawtucket manager) and SS Trent Henderson's (37) father Dave. SS Joey Wong (46) is playing at Oregon State, where his dad Dave is a volunteer assistant. Wiedenbauer, Moore and Henderson also didn't sign.

**Closest To The Majors:** Perez could skip a level once he adjusts to starting again and improves his command. As a catcher, Sapp could advance faster than most high schoolers if everything comes together for him.

**Best Late-Round Pick:** Salamida.

**The One Who Got Away:** The Astros really wanted to add SS Mark Sobolewski's (20) bat, but owner Drayton McLane wouldn't let them exceed slot money and he went to Florida. Houston wasn't as close to reaching an accord with RHP Nathan Karns (10), who pitched at 92-95 mph early in the spring. He's at North Carolina State.

**Assessment:** The Astros are counting on Sapp, Moresi and Johnson proving that their lackluster debuts were flukes. If not, the system will still be short on position players. Perez quickly has become an organization favorite.

## 2005 BUDGET: $4.1 million

LHP Brian Bogusevic (1) and OF Eli Iorg (1) have struggled in pro ball, though they did show improvement late in 2006. Signing 3B Koby Clemens (8) spurred his father Roger to return for another season. **GRADE: D**

## 2004 BUDGET: $2.2 million

Who needs a first-round pick? OF Hunter Pence (2), Houston's top choice, and LHP Troy Patton (9) have emerged as the system's top two prospects. Since-traded SS Ben Zobrist (6), RHP Chad Reineke (13) and C J.R. Towles (20) were astute late-round finds. **GRADE: A**

## 2003 BUDGET: $1.5 million

Again without a first-rounder, the Astros still scored with their top pick, RHP Jason Hirsh (2), and included him in the offseason Jason Jennings deal. RHP Jimmy Barthmaier also has a quality arm. Houston was set to sign OF Drew Stubbs (3) before MLB talked owner Drayton McLane out of it. **GRADE: B**

*Draft analysis by Jim Callis. Numbers in parentheses indicate draft rounds. Budgets are bonuses in first 10 rounds.*

# HUNTER
# PENCE

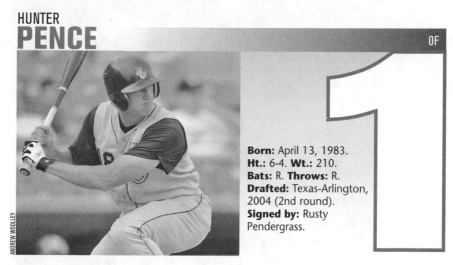

ANDREW WOOLLEY

**Born:** April 13, 1983.
**Ht.:** 6-4. **Wt.:** 210.
**Bats:** R. **Throws:** R.
**Drafted:** Texas-Arlington,
2004 (2nd round).
**Signed by:** Rusty
Pendergrass.

Pence was the Southland Conference player of the year and batting champ (.395) in 2004, but he wasn't a premium draft prospect because he looked gangly and awkward and used an unorthodox set-up at the plate. Higher on him than most clubs, the Astros made him their top pick, taking him in the second round (64th overall) and signing him for $575,000. He has gotten better as he has moved up the ladder, slowed only by a strained left quadriceps in the second half of 2005. Managers rated him the most exciting player in the Double-A Texas League last year, and Pence batted .387 with a team-high nine RBIs in the playoffs, leading Corpus Christi to a championship. Pence batted .339 in the Arizona Fall League before the Astros suspended him following a drunken-driving charge in late October.

Pence doesn't do anything pretty but he does most things well. His approach at the plate is anything but textbook, as he chokes up on the bat and has a hitch in his swing. There were concerns that advanced pitchers might be able to pound him inside, but he put that notion to rest in Double-A. Pence has quick hands, terrific bat speed and plenty of strength, so he has no problem catching up to any fastball. He tinkered with his load last year, lifting his back elbow and turning his right wrist slightly so he could impart more backspin on balls. That improved his ability to drive pitches, which he does to all fields. Pence isn't the most fluid runner, but he has above-average speed and an aggressive nature on the basepaths. He stole 17 bases in 21 tries in 2006 after going just 12-for-22 over his first three pro seasons. When he entered pro ball, he had a below-average arm that figured to limit him to left field. But he since has improved his throwing mechanics, accuracy and arm strength. While his arm action still looks funky, he had 13 assists last year while spending most of his time in right field. He also saw extended action in center down the stretch. He brings a high-energy mindset to the ballpark every day.

While Pence has solid plate discipline, he also has a bad habit of chasing sliders off the plate. He uses an open stance and sets up away from the plate, so he sometimes has trouble covering the outside corner. Houston believes he can get the job done in center field, though scouts from outside the organization knock him for taking less than optimal routes to balls. The Astros praise his makeup and believe his embarrassment over the DUI charge last fall will mean it was just a one-time mistake.

Houston would like to give Pence a couple of months at Triple-A Round Rock, but those plans may change after incumbent center fielder Willy Taveras went to the Rockies in December's Jason Jennings trade. Chris Burke is the favorite to replace Taveras, but Pence has a better arm and arguably better instincts in center. The long-term plan is for Burke to succeed Craig Biggio at second base, creating an outfield opening, but Pence could force the issue in 2007.

| Year | Club (League) | Class | AVG | G | AB | R | H | 2B | 3B | HR | RBI | BB | SO | SB | OBP | SLG |
|------|---------------|-------|-----|---|----|---|---|----|----|----|-----|----|----|----|-----|-----|
| 2004 | Tri-City (NYP) | A | .296 | 51 | 199 | 36 | 59 | 18 | 1 | 8 | 37 | 23 | 30 | 3 | .369 | .518 |
| 2005 | Lexington (SAL) | A | .338 | 80 | 302 | 59 | 102 | 14 | 3 | 25 | 60 | 38 | 53 | 8 | .413 | .652 |
| | Salem (CL) | A | .305 | 41 | 151 | 24 | 46 | 8 | 1 | 6 | 30 | 18 | 37 | 1 | .374 | .490 |
| 2006 | Corpus Christi (TL) | AA | .283 | 136 | 523 | 97 | 148 | 31 | 8 | 28 | 95 | 60 | 109 | 17 | .357 | .533 |
| **MINOR LEAGUE TOTALS** | | | .302 | 308 | 1175 | 216 | 355 | 71 | 13 | 67 | 222 | 139 | 229 | 29 | .376 | .556 |

## 2 TROY PATTON
LHP

**Born:** Sept. 3, 1985. **B-T:** B-L. **Ht.:** 6-1. **Wt.:** 185. **Drafted:** HS—Magnolia, Texas, 2004 (9th round). **Signed by:** Rusty Pendergrass.

After the commissioner's office talked owner Drayton McLane out of signing 2003 third-round pick Drew Stubbs for $900,000, MLB didn't bat an eye when the Astros Patton (also set to attend the University of Texas) the same amount as a ninth-rounder a year later. Patton is a lefthander with stuff, savvy and moxie. He runs his fastball from 89-94 mph, generates exceptional life at times and easily gets inside on righthanders with it. His changeup improved significantly last year and has nice fade. His hard curveball was his top pitch in high school but now ranks as his third pitch. He's athletic and repeats his compact delivery well. Patton likes to drop down when he throws his curve, making it difficult to stay on top of the pitch and alerting hitters that it's coming. He had minor shoulder fatigue in each of the last two seasons, resulting in diminished mechanics and command. For someone who can command the outside corner, he pounds the inner half too much. Once he adds strength and consistency, Patton will be ready for the big leagues and could grow into a No. 2 starter. He'll probably open 2007 in Triple-A.

| Year | Club (League) | Class | W | L | ERA | G | GS | CG | SV | IP | H | R | ER | HR | BB | SO | AVG |
|---|---|---|---|---|---|---|---|---|---|---|---|---|---|---|---|---|---|
| 2004 | Greeneville (Appy) | R | 2 | 2 | 1.93 | 6 | 6 | 0 | 0 | 28 | 23 | 8 | 6 | 1 | 5 | 32 | .225 |
| 2005 | Lexington (SAL) | A | 5 | 2 | 1.94 | 15 | 15 | 0 | 0 | 79 | 59 | 24 | 17 | 3 | 20 | 94 | .211 |
| | Salem (CL) | A | 1 | 4 | 2.63 | 10 | 9 | 0 | 0 | 41 | 34 | 12 | 12 | 2 | 8 | 38 | .227 |
| 2006 | Salem (CL) | A | 7 | 7 | 2.93 | 19 | 19 | 1 | 0 | 101 | 92 | 49 | 33 | 4 | 37 | 102 | .240 |
| | Corpus Christi (TL) | AA | 2 | 5 | 4.37 | 8 | 8 | 0 | 0 | 45 | 48 | 26 | 22 | 6 | 13 | 37 | .271 |
| **MINOR LEAGUE TOTALS** | | | 17 | 20 | 2.75 | 58 | 57 | 1 | 0 | 294 | 256 | 119 | 90 | 16 | 83 | 303 | .234 |

## 3 MATT ALBERS
RHP

**Born:** Jan. 20, 1983. **B-T:** L-R. **Ht.:** 6-0. **Wt.:** 215. **Drafted:** San Jacinto (Texas) JC, D/F 2001 (23rd round). **Signed by:** Rusty Pendergrass.

A local product who played at a suburban Houston high school and nearby San Jacinto (Texas) Junior College, Albers has had one of the system's best arms since signing as a draft-and-follow in 2002. But he showed newfound dedication in 2006, when he was the Texas League pitcher of the year, led the circuit in ERA and made his big league debut. Albers' 91-94 mph two-seam fastball runs in on righthanders and away from lefties, and it chews up bats. He also can hit 97 mph with a four-seamer when needed. He uses a hard breaking ball with slider velocity and curveball break, and it's a solid-average pitch. He does a good job of repeating his windmill delivery, so his command should continue to improve. Albers' changeup is making progress but he needs to trust it more. He sometimes rushes his mechanics and gets under his pitches, losing life and leaving them up in the zone. He had problems with alcohol earlier in his career but has put that behind him. Ticketed for Triple-A at the start of the season, Albers has a ceiling as a good No. 3 starter and could help solidify the back of Houston's rotation later in the year.

| Year | Club (League) | Class | W | L | ERA | G | GS | CG | SV | IP | H | R | ER | HR | BB | SO | AVG |
|---|---|---|---|---|---|---|---|---|---|---|---|---|---|---|---|---|---|
| 2002 | Martinsville (Appy) | R | 2 | 3 | 5.13 | 13 | 13 | 0 | 0 | 60 | 61 | 38 | 34 | 2 | 38 | 72 | .274 |
| 2003 | Tri-City (NYP) | A | 5 | 4 | 2.92 | 15 | 14 | 0 | 0 | 86 | 69 | 37 | 28 | 1 | 25 | 94 | .214 |
| 2004 | Lexington (SAL) | A | 8 | 3 | 3.31 | 22 | 21 | 0 | 0 | 111 | 95 | 51 | 41 | 3 | 57 | 140 | .237 |
| 2005 | Salem (CL) | A | 8 | 12 | 4.66 | 28 | 27 | 0 | 0 | 149 | 161 | 86 | 77 | 15 | 62 | 146 | .278 |
| 2006 | Corpus Christi (TL) | AA | 10 | 2 | 2.17 | 19 | 19 | 0 | 0 | 116 | 96 | 40 | 28 | 4 | 47 | 95 | .223 |
| | Houston (NL) | MLB | 0 | 2 | 6.00 | 4 | 2 | 0 | 0 | 15 | 17 | 10 | 10 | 1 | 7 | 11 | .298 |
| | Round Rock (PCL) | AAA | 2 | 1 | 3.96 | 4 | 4 | 0 | 0 | 25 | 24 | 11 | 11 | 2 | 10 | 26 | .253 |
| **MINOR LEAGUE TOTALS** | | | 35 | 25 | 3.60 | 101 | 98 | 0 | 0 | 547 | 506 | 263 | 219 | 27 | 239 | 573 | .247 |
| **MAJOR LEAGUE TOTALS** | | | 0 | 2 | 6.00 | 4 | 2 | 0 | 0 | 15 | 17 | 10 | 10 | 1 | 7 | 11 | .298 |

## 4 JIMMY BARTHMAIER
RHP

**Born:** Jan. 6, 1984. **B-T:** R-R. **Ht.:** 6-4. **Wt.:** 210. **Drafted:** HS—Roswell, Ga., 2003 (13th round). **Signed by:** Ellis Dungan.

A highly recruited quarterback in high school, Barthmaier signed for a 13th-round record $750,000 in 2003. He had less polish and more ceiling than any starter in a talented Salem rotation last season—leading the high Class A Carolina League in both strikeouts and walks—and he finished on a 7-1, 1.82 tear. Barthmaier has life on his fastballs, pitching at 91-93 mph with his two-seamer and reaching 96 with his four-seamer. That sets up a curveball that managers rated the best in the Carolina League. Barthmaier made progress with his changeup and his control in the second half of 2006. Strong and ath-

letic, he has missed just one start in four years of pro ball—and that was because of an ankle injury. He battles inconsistency with all his pitches and his command. He overthrows his fastball and loses movement, hangs some curveballs and still fights the feel for his change-up. His arm action is long and there's effort to his delivery. Showing more maturity and improving his preparation would be a big help. Barthmaier could make a dynamic closer, which would allow him to focus on his fastball and curve while not worrying about pacing himself. For now, he'll remain a starter and go to Double-A.

| Year | Club (League) | Class | W | L | ERA | G | GS | CG | SV | IP | H | R | ER | HR | BB | SO | AVG |
|------|---------------|-------|---|---|-----|---|----|----|----|----|---|---|----|----|----|----|-----|
| 2003 | Martinsville (Appy) | R | 1 | 1 | 2.49 | 8 | 3 | 0 | 0 | 22 | 19 | 9 | 6 | 0 | 7 | 18 | .226 |
| 2004 | Greeneville (Appy) | R | 4 | 3 | 3.78 | 13 | 13 | 0 | 0 | 69 | 70 | 32 | 29 | 3 | 22 | 65 | .262 |
| 2005 | Lexington (SAL) | A | 11 | 6 | 2.27 | 25 | 25 | 0 | 0 | 135 | 108 | 41 | 34 | 3 | 55 | 142 | .220 |
| | Salem (CL) | A | 1 | 0 | 1.50 | 1 | 0 | 0 | 0 | 6 | 4 | 4 | 1 | 1 | 1 | 6 | .167 |
| 2006 | Salem (CL) | A | 11 | 8 | 3.62 | 27 | 27 | 0 | 0 | 147 | 137 | 64 | 59 | 6 | 67 | 134 | .252 |
| **MINOR LEAGUE TOTALS** | | | 28 | 18 | 3.07 | 74 | 68 | 0 | 0 | 378 | 338 | 150 | 129 | 13 | 152 | 365 | .240 |

## 5 JUAN GUTIERREZ RHP

**Born:** July 14, 1983. **B-T:** R-R. **Ht.:** 6-3. **Wt.:** 200. **Signed:** Venezuela, 2000. **Signed by:** Andres Reiner/Pablo Torrealba/Rafael Lara.

The Astros had to protect Gutierrez on their 40-man roster before he got to full-season ball, and they haven't regretted the decision. He missed six weeks last year with a tender elbow, but returned and did not allow a run in his last four regular-season starts. He won both his playoff outings and was Corpus Christi's Game One starter. Gutierrez has lit up radar guns from years and attacks hitters with a 92-95 sinker. Though he was reluctant to use his secondary pitches against more advanced hitters, his curve-ball and changeup are solid. One scout liked his changeup more than his fastball, which is saying something. If Gutierrez had his way, he'd still try to blow the ball by most hitters, so he needs to keep mixing pitches and changing speeds. His command is improving but still requires work. He hasn't had arm problems in the past, but Houston will watch him closely after his elbow issues cropped up. All three of his pitches show at least flashes of being out pitches, giving Gutierrez the highest ceiling among the system's pitchers. Destined for Triple-A at the start of 2007, he could help Houston as a starter or reliever in the second half.

| Year | Club (League) | Class | W | L | ERA | G | GS | CG | SV | IP | H | R | ER | HR | BB | SO | AVG |
|------|---------------|-------|---|---|-----|---|----|----|----|----|---|---|----|----|----|----|-----|
| 2001 | Astros (VSL) | R | 1 | 0 | 1.78 | 10 | 3 | 0 | 4 | 25 | 23 | 8 | 5 | 0 | 8 | 17 | — |
| 2002 | Astros (VSL) | R | 3 | 2 | 2.13 | 13 | 7 | 0 | 1 | 38 | 35 | 14 | 9 | 0 | 12 | 28 | .252 |
| 2003 | Martinsville (Appy) | R | 1 | 2 | 4.76 | 16 | 3 | 0 | 2 | 34 | 42 | 22 | 18 | 2 | 13 | 30 | .302 |
| 2004 | Greeneville (Appy) | R | 8 | 2 | 3.70 | 13 | 13 | 0 | 0 | 66 | 74 | 31 | 27 | 4 | 30 | 59 | .294 |
| 2005 | Lexington (SAL) | A | 9 | 5 | 3.21 | 22 | 21 | 1 | 0 | 121 | 106 | 55 | 43 | 10 | 43 | 100 | .239 |
| | Salem (CL) | A | 1 | 1 | 3.00 | 3 | 2 | 0 | 0 | 12 | 10 | 4 | 4 | 1 | 8 | 9 | .233 |
| 2006 | Corpus Christi (TL) | AA | 8 | 4 | 3.04 | 20 | 20 | 0 | 0 | 104 | 94 | 39 | 35 | 10 | 34 | 106 | .237 |
| **MINOR LEAGUE TOTALS** | | | 31 | 16 | 3.18 | 97 | 69 | 1 | 7 | 399 | 384 | 173 | 141 | 27 | 148 | 349 | .255 |

## 6 J.R. TOWLES C

**Born:** Feb. 11, 1984. **B-T:** R-R. **Ht.:** 6-2. **Wt.:** 195. **Drafted:** North Central Texas JC, 2004 (20th round). **Signed by:** Pat Murphy.

Towles' five-tool ability at catcher excites the Astros, but they wish they could see more of it. After finger surgery in 2004, he came back slowly the following year, and he was bothered by tendinitis in his right knee during the second half of 2006. He has played in just 165 games in 2½ pro seasons. Towles handles the bat well and has good pitch recognition. He has added 20 pounds of muscle and developed pull power since turning pro. More athletic than most catchers, he runs well and can steal a base when the opportunity presents itself. Managers rated him the best defensive catcher in the low Class A South Atlantic League last year, when he showed consistent 1.95-second pop times and solid receiving skills. He also calls a good game. None of his injuries has been serious or chronic, but Towles has lost valuable development time. He struggles against quality breaking balls, and he just needs experience to polish his overall game. Add it all up, and Towles could be Jason Kendall with more power and better receiving skills. Houston would love to see him stay healthy enough to catch 110-120 games this year in high Class A.

| Year | Club (League) | Class | AVG | G | AB | R | H | 2B | 3B | HR | RBI | BB | SO | SB | OBP | SLG |
|------|---------------|-------|-----|---|----|---|---|----|----|----|-----|----|----|----|-----|-----|
| 2004 | Greeneville (Appy) | R | .243 | 39 | 111 | 17 | 27 | 6 | 0 | 0 | 8 | 12 | 23 | 4 | .370 | .297 |
| 2005 | Lexington (SAL) | A | .346 | 45 | 162 | 35 | 56 | 14 | 2 | 5 | 23 | 16 | 29 | 11 | .436 | .549 |
| 2006 | Lexington (SAL) | A | .317 | 81 | 284 | 39 | 90 | 19 | 2 | 12 | 55 | 21 | 46 | 13 | .382 | .525 |
| **MINOR LEAGUE TOTALS** | | | .311 | 165 | 557 | 91 | 173 | 39 | 4 | 17 | 86 | 49 | 98 | 28 | .395 | .487 |

## 7 PAUL ESTRADA RHP

BILL MITCHELL

**Born:** Sept. 10, 1982. **B-T:** R-R. **Ht.:** 6-1. **Wt.:** 220. **Signed:** Venezuela, 1999. **Signed by:** Andres Reiner.

After Estrada didn't get to low Class A until his sixth pro season, the Astros decided to skip him a level to Double-A in 2006. He responded by nearly leading the Texas League in strikeouts while working out of the bullpen. He led minor league relievers by averaging 13.6 whiffs per nine innings. Estrada has one of the minors' best curveballs, as his looks like a power knuckler before breaking straight down. He also can get strike-outs with his 83-86 mph splitter, and he achieves a lot of sink and arm-side run with his 92-94 mph fastball. With so much to worry about, hitters take a lot of ugly swings against him. A lot of Estrada's strikeouts come on curveballs out of the zone and splitters in the dirt, and that approach might not work as well against more discerning hit-ters. Houston has to keep leaning on him to throw his fastball. His stuff isn't as sharp when he pitches on consecutive days. Texas League observers were convinced Estrada could have helped the Astros as a set-up man at the end of last season. They'll be more conservative and start him in Triple-A this year, though he should be one of their first in-season callups.

| Year | Club (League) | Class | W | L | ERA | G | GS | CG | SV | IP | H | R | ER | HR | BB | SO | AVG |
|------|---------------|-------|---|---|-----|---|----|----|----|----|---|---|----|----|----|----|-----|
| 2000 | Astros (VSL) | R | 1 | 0 | 7.14 | 16 | 1 | 0 | 0 | 29 | 38 | 33 | 23 | 1 | 28 | 27 | .311 |
| 2001 | Astros (VSL) | R | 2 | 2 | 4.20 | 14 | 9 | 0 | 3 | 41 | 35 | 24 | 19 | 0 | 29 | 50 | — |
| 2002 | Martinsville (Appy) | R | 2 | 2 | 11.65 | 14 | 6 | 0 | 0 | 32 | 45 | 45 | 41 | 2 | 36 | 42 | .326 |
| 2003 | Martinsville (Appy) | R | 1 | 0 | 5.48 | 12 | 1 | 0 | 1 | 21 | 19 | 17 | 13 | 2 | 22 | 25 | .235 |
| 2004 | Tri-City (NYP) | A | 5 | 1 | 2.81 | 23 | 0 | 0 | 8 | 42 | 26 | 13 | 13 | 4 | 17 | 56 | .172 |
| 2005 | Lexington (SAL) | A | 6 | 7 | 2.69 | 46 | 3 | 0 | 3 | 90 | 65 | 31 | 27 | 6 | 34 | 94 | .202 |
| 2006 | Corpus Christi (TL) | AA | 8 | 5 | 3.05 | 56 | 0 | 0 | 15 | 89 | 61 | 33 | 30 | 10 | 37 | 134 | .191 |
| **MINOR LEAGUE TOTALS** | | | 25 | 17 | 4.35 | 181 | 20 | 0 | 30 | 343 | 289 | 196 | 166 | 25 | 203 | 428 | .224 |

## 8 FELIPE PAULINO RHP

**Born:** Oct. 5, 1983. **B-T:** R-R. **Ht.:** 6-2. **Wt.:** 180. **Signed:** Venezuela, 2001. **Signed by:** Andres Reiner/Omar Lopez.

Paulino has the best pure arm strength among the Astros' starting pitching prospects. They've clocked him as high as 100 mph, while other clubs have seen him hit 102. Paulino usually works at 93-96 mph with his heavy fastball and drives it down in the strike zone with a straight-over-the-top delivery. He changed his curveball grip two years ago and now has a hard 80-85 mph downer that's a plus-plus pitch when it's really on. Still raw after five years as a pro, Paulino doesn't command much beyond his fastball. His shoulder flies open and he falls toward first base in his delivery, making it diffi-cult to stay on top of his curveball and to locate his work-in-progress changeup. He started working on a slider last August. He's a shaky fielder who led high Class A Carolina League pitchers with seven errors in just 21 chances last year. Though Houston will continue to groom Paulino as a starter in Double-A this season, it's easy to envision him as a late-inning reliever. In that role, he could rely more on his fastball and not worry about his changeup.

| Year | Club (League) | Class | W | L | ERA | G | GS | CG | SV | IP | H | R | ER | HR | BB | SO | AVG |
|------|---------------|-------|---|---|-----|---|----|----|----|----|---|---|----|----|----|----|-----|
| 2002 | Astros (VSL) | R | 0 | 0 | 1.29 | 4 | 0 | 0 | 0 | 7 | 4 | 1 | 1 | 1 | 6 | 4 | .182 |
| 2003 | Astros (VSL) | R | 1 | 0 | 5.59 | 5 | 0 | 0 | 0 | 10 | 6 | 6 | 6 | 0 | 12 | 13 | .194 |
| | Martinsville (Appy) | R | 2 | 2 | 5.61 | 16 | 0 | 0 | 1 | 26 | 23 | 20 | 16 | 0 | 19 | 27 | .235 |
| 2004 | Greeneville (Appy) | R | 1 | 3 | 7.59 | 10 | 10 | 0 | 0 | 32 | 30 | 30 | 27 | 4 | 22 | 37 | .246 |
| 2005 | Tri-City (NYP) | A | 2 | 2 | 3.82 | 13 | 2 | 0 | 1 | 31 | 21 | 15 | 13 | 2 | 11 | 34 | .189 |
| | Lexington (SAL) | A | 1 | 1 | 1.85 | 7 | 5 | 0 | 0 | 24 | 21 | 8 | 5 | 2 | 6 | 30 | .233 |
| 2006 | Salem (CL) | A | 9 | 7 | 4.35 | 27 | 26 | 0 | 0 | 126 | 119 | 67 | 61 | 13 | 59 | 91 | .250 |
| **MINOR LEAGUE TOTALS** | | | 16 | 15 | 4.54 | 82 | 43 | 0 | 2 | 256 | 224 | 147 | 129 | 22 | 135 | 236 | .236 |

## 9 MAX SAPP C

BILL MITCHELL

**Born:** Feb. 21, 1988. **B-T:** L-R. **Ht.:** 6-2. **Wt.:** 220. **Drafted:** HS—Orlando, 2006 (1st round). **Signed by:** John Bunnell.

The Astros planned on taking a college pitcher with the No. 23 choice in the 2006 draft, but when all the arms they liked went off the board, they took Sapp. Signed for $1.4 million, he went to short-season Tri-City because 2005 second-rounder Ralph Henriquez needed to repeat Rookie ball. Sapp held his own as the youngest regular in the New-York Penn League before battling elbow tendinitis late in the summer. He went in the first round because of his bat. He has a strong frame and plus power. Reducing a high leg kick that he used as a trigger improved his timing and gives him a bet-

ter chance to hit for average. He has a good approach for a young player, including a willingness to draw walks. His arm strength is his best defensive tool, and he led NY-P catchers by throwing out 42 percent of basestealers. Some clubs worried that Sapp wouldn't be able to remain behind the plate, but he sold the Astros by promising to commit to it. Thick and barrel-chested, he has lost weight and started doing Pilates to improve his agility. His receiving still needs work, especially on pitches out of the zone. He's a below-average runner. Sapp has enough bat to get the job done at first base, but Houston is confident he'll stay at catcher. He'll move up to low Class A Lexington this year at age 19.

| Year | Club (League) | Class | AVG | G | AB | R | H | 2B | 3B | HR | RBI | BB | SO | SB | OBP | SLG |
|------|---------------|-------|-----|---|----|---|---|----|----|----|-----|----|----|----|-----|-----|
| 2006 | Tri-City (NYP) | A | .229 | 50 | 166 | 20 | 38 | 9 | 0 | 1 | 20 | 22 | 37 | 0 | .317 | .301 |
| **MINOR LEAGUE TOTALS** | | | .229 | 50 | 166 | 20 | 38 | 9 | 0 | 1 | 20 | 22 | 37 | 0 | .317 | .301 |

##  CHAD REINEKE                                           RHP

CARL KLINE

**Born:** April 9, 1982. **B-T:** R-R. **Ht.:** 6-6. **Wt.:** 210. **Drafted:** Miami (Ohio), 2004 (13th round). **Signed by:** Nick Venuto.

The Astros have a knack for finding college seniors, with Eric Bruntlett, Morgan Ensberg, Jason Lane and Chad Qualls all contributing to their 2006 club. Next in line is Reineke, who has alternated between starting and relieving in pro ball and pitched better in the latter role once he reached Double-A last year. Reineke uses his 6-foot-6 frame to deliver his pitches on a steep plane, and yet his 93-95 mph fastball seems to climb on hitters. His hard slider has late sweep and is a strikeout pitch at its best. His delivery was much improved in 2006, with less effort and better balance. He's comfortable pitching out of the bullpen with the game on the line. Reineke is more effective in relief because he doesn't have to worry about his changeup. It shows good dive at times, but it's inconsistent and he's reluctant to throw it. His fastball has velocity but only sporadic life, so he'll need to keep it down against big leaguers. If Houston wants to continue trying Reineke as a starter, he'll return to Double-A. If he's going to stay in the bullpen, he could move up to Triple-A. Either way, he could make his major league debut late in 2007.

| Year | Club (League) | Class | W | L | ERA | G | GS | CG | SV | IP | H | R | ER | HR | BB | SO | AVG |
|------|---------------|-------|---|---|-----|---|----|----|----|----|---|---|----|----|----|----|-----|
| 2004 | Tri-City (NYP) | A | 1 | 2 | 2.45 | 23 | 0 | 0 | 3 | 37 | 27 | 13 | 10 | 0 | 23 | 52 | .197 |
| 2005 | Lexington (SAL) | A | 10 | 8 | 3.52 | 42 | 11 | 0 | 4 | 102 | 84 | 46 | 40 | 5 | 49 | 108 | .230 |
| 2006 | Salem (CL) | A | 6 | 5 | 2.98 | 17 | 17 | 1 | 0 | 100 | 82 | 42 | 33 | 5 | 29 | 87 | .220 |
|      | Corpus Christi (TL) | AA | 1 | 3 | 3.05 | 15 | 4 | 0 | 0 | 44 | 33 | 17 | 15 | 3 | 26 | 45 | .209 |
| **MINOR LEAGUE TOTALS** | | | 18 | 18 | 3.12 | 97 | 32 | 1 | 7 | 283 | 226 | 118 | 98 | 13 | 127 | 292 | .219 |

## SERGIO PEREZ                                           RHP

**Born:** Dec. 5, 1984. **B-T:** R-R. **Ht.:** 6-3. **Wt.:** 230. **Drafted:** Tampa, 2006 (2nd round). **Signed by:** John Bunnell.

If Max Sapp had been gone when it came time for the Astros' first-round choice last June, their backup plan was to take Perez. Instead, they got him 44 picks later in the second round and signed him for $550,000. Perez starred at Tampa, throwing the Spartans' first no-hitter in a decade and helping them win the Division II College World Series. He earned a win as a starter in the semifinal and a save in the finale. After his long college season, Houston eased him into pro ball as a reliever in low Class A. Though he wasn't comfortable coming out of the bullpen, Perez showed a lively 92-93 mph fastball that topped out at 97 and good feel for his hard slider. He struggles at times to repeat his delivery, which includes violent arm action. The Astros plan on developing him as a starter, and he'll need to develop a usable changeup to flourish in that role. He could return to Lexington to begin his first full season, but he has the stuff to skip a level at some point.

| Year | Club (League) | Class | W | L | ERA | G | GS | CG | SV | IP | H | R | ER | HR | BB | SO | AVG |
|------|---------------|-------|---|---|-----|---|----|----|----|----|---|---|----|----|----|----|-----|
| 2006 | Lexington (SAL) | A | 3 | 0 | 2.20 | 11 | 0 | 0 | 0 | 16 | 9 | 6 | 4 | 0 | 8 | 21 | .153 |
| **MINOR LEAGUE TOTALS** | | | 3 | 0 | 2.20 | 11 | 0 | 0 | 0 | 16 | 9 | 6 | 4 | 0 | 8 | 21 | .153 |

## CHRIS SAMPSON                                           RHP

**Born:** May 23, 1978. **B-T:** R-R. **Ht.:** 6-1. **Wt.:** 190. **Drafted:** Texas Tech, 1999 (8th round). **Signed by:** Ralph Bratton.

Originally drafted by Houston as a shortstop, Sampson retired after hitting .239 in his pro debut. He drifted into coaching at Collin County (Texas) Community College, where he threw batting practice and began to wonder if he might have potential on the mound. He contacted the Astros and was re-signed in January 2003. From the day he returned, Sampson has shown amazing command and feel. His stuff doesn't leave him much margin for error, so he just doesn't make many mistakes. He led Triple-A Pacific Coast League starters in fewest

unintentional walks (1.1) and baserunners (9.4) per nine innings, and he threw 67 percent of his pitches for strikes in the majors last season. Sampson's best pitch is his 87-92 mph sinker, followed by his slider. He also has an 11-to-5 curveball and a changeup, and he has come up with a promising splitter. He has plus command to both sides of the plate and he's unflappable. He likes to back lefthanders off the plate by throwing his slider down and in to them, and he could come up with a four-seam fastball to go up and in against righties. As would be expected given his background, Sampson hits better than most pitchers. He batted .391 in Triple-A last year, including a 5-for-15 (.333) performance as a pinch-hitter. He handled every role Houston threw at him in the majors, allowing just one earned run in three starts and pitching well out of the bullpen. He should make the Opening Day roster in 2007 and projects as either an effective No. 5 starter or as a set-up man.

| Year | Club (League) | Class | AVG | G | AB | R | H | 2B | 3B | HR | RBI | BB | SO | SB | OBP | SLG |
|---|---|---|---|---|---|---|---|---|---|---|---|---|---|---|---|---|
| 1999 | Auburn (NYP) | A | .239 | 51 | 159 | 23 | 38 | 7 | 3 | 1 | 19 | 22 | 49 | 21 | .333 | .340 |
| 2000 | Did not play | | | | | | | | | | | | | | | |
| 2001 | Did not play | | | | | | | | | | | | | | | |
| 2002 | Did not play | | | | | | | | | | | | | | | |
| 2005 | Corpus Christi (TL) | AA | .100 | 36 | 10 | 1 | 1 | 0 | 0 | 0 | 0 | 0 | 4 | 0 | .100 | .100 |
| 2006 | Round Rock (PCL) | AAA | .391 | 44 | 46 | 9 | 18 | 2 | 0 | 0 | 7 | 1 | 12 | 1 | .404 | .435 |
| | Houston (NL) | MLB | .000 | 12 | 5 | 0 | 0 | 0 | 0 | 0 | 0 | 0 | 2 | 0 | .000 | .000 |
| **MINOR LEAGUE TOTALS** | | | .265 | 186 | 215 | 33 | 57 | 9 | 3 | 1 | 26 | 23 | 65 | 22 | .338 | .349 |
| **MAJOR LEAGUE TOTALS** | | MLB | .000 | 12 | 5 | 0 | 0 | 0 | 0 | 0 | 0 | 0 | 2 | 0 | .000 | .000 |

| Year | Club (League) | Class | W | L | ERA | G | GS | CG | SV | IP | H | R | ER | HR | BB | SO | AVG |
|---|---|---|---|---|---|---|---|---|---|---|---|---|---|---|---|---|---|
| 2003 | Lexington (SAL) | A | 4 | 3 | 1.39 | 22 | 14 | 0 | 1 | 84 | 66 | 17 | 13 | 2 | 14 | 66 | .212 |
| | Salem (CL) | A | 1 | 1 | 5.91 | 9 | 0 | 0 | 1 | 11 | 14 | 8 | 7 | 0 | 5 | 6 | .326 |
| 2004 | Salem (CL) | A | 7 | 11 | 3.80 | 27 | 27 | 2 | 0 | 152 | 170 | 72 | 64 | 8 | 26 | 101 | .295 |
| | Round Rock (TL) | AA | 0 | 0 | 0.00 | 1 | 0 | 0 | 0 | 2 | 3 | 0 | 0 | 0 | 0 | 1 | .333 |
| 2005 | Corpus Christi (TL) | AA | 4 | 12 | 3.12 | 32 | 19 | 2 | 4 | 150 | 147 | 67 | 52 | 11 | 19 | 92 | .256 |
| 2006 | Round Rock (PCL) | AAA | 12 | 3 | 2.51 | 27 | 18 | 2 | 4 | 126 | 110 | 48 | 35 | 12 | 14 | 68 | .234 |
| | Houston (NL) | MLB | 2 | 1 | 2.12 | 12 | 3 | 0 | 0 | 34 | 25 | 10 | 8 | 3 | 5 | 15 | .205 |
| **MINOR LEAGUE TOTALS** | | | 28 | 30 | 2.94 | 118 | 78 | 6 | 10 | 524 | 510 | 212 | 171 | 33 | 78 | 334 | .257 |
| **MAJOR LEAGUE TOTALS** | | | 2 | 1 | 2.12 | 12 | 3 | 0 | 0 | 34 | 25 | 10 | 8 | 3 | 5 | 15 | .205 |

## 13  ELI IORG                                                          OF

**Born:** March 14, 1983. **B-T:** R-R. **Ht.:** 6-3. **Wt.:** 200. **Drafted:** Tennessee, 2005 (1st round supplemental). **Signed by:** Mike Rosamond.

Iorg has an extended baseball family, as his father Garth and uncle Dane played in the majors, older brother Isaac played in the Braves system, and younger brother Cale will be drafted once he returns from a two-year Mormon mission. Eli spent 2003 on a mission to Argentina, which is why he was a 22-year-old junior when the Astros made him the 38th overall pick in 2005 and signed for $950,000. He has been slow to get untracked in pro ball. A stress fracture in his right foot lingering from college abbreviated his pro debut, and his swing got out of whack in his first full season. Perhaps because he was disappointed to be assigned to low Class A, Iorg tried to hit homers and pressed too hard at the plate. Houston tried to stress a more disciplined approach, with only moderate success. He has plus raw power and slightly above-average speed, so he could be a 20-20 man in the majors. He needs better pitch recognition, however, which would help him stop chasing breaking balls in the dirt. Iorg has solid range and a strong arm in right field, but he needs to do a better job of hitting the cutoff man. He also can get too aggressive on the bases. He'll begin 2007 in high Class A, though the Astros would like to get him to Double-A before season's end.

| Year | Club (League) | Class | AVG | G | AB | R | H | 2B | 3B | HR | RBI | BB | SO | SB | OBP | SLG |
|---|---|---|---|---|---|---|---|---|---|---|---|---|---|---|---|---|---|
| 2005 | Greeneville (Appy) | R | .333 | 35 | 138 | 36 | 46 | 7 | 2 | 7 | 34 | 9 | 27 | 12 | .391 | .565 |
| 2006 | Lexington (SAL) | A | .256 | 125 | 469 | 68 | 120 | 32 | 4 | 15 | 85 | 33 | 119 | 42 | .313 | .437 |
| **MINOR LEAGUE TOTALS** | | | .273 | 160 | 607 | 104 | 166 | 39 | 6 | 22 | 119 | 42 | 146 | 54 | .331 | .466 |

## 14  BRIAN BOGUSEVIC                                                  LHP

**Born:** Feb. 18, 1984. **B-T:** L-L. **Ht.:** 6-3. **Wt.:** 215. **Drafted:** Tulane, 2005 (1st round). **Signed by:** Mike Rosamond.

A two-way star at Tulane, Bogusevic led the Green Wave to the 2005 College World Series by going 13-3, 3.25 and batting .328 as a right fielder. Though he offered plus hitting ability, raw power and speed, the Astros went with the conventional wisdom and took Bogusevic as a pitcher, signing him for $1.375 million. They're still waiting to see the pitcher they thought they were drafting. Bogusevic was worn out in his pro debut after a long college season, but he didn't look any better for most of 2006. After he hit rock bottom by allowing eight runs (including three homers) without recording an out on May 4, doctors diagnosed elbow tendinitis and Houston shut him down for seven weeks. Upon his return, he seemed

to get back on track. His fastball was back at 88-92 mph and his slider regained its sharpness. He also flashed a solid changeup. Bogusevic posted a 3.43 ERA over his final 11 starts and finally earned his first pro victories. When things weren't going well for him, he let the pressure of being a first-round pick get to him. He rushed his delivery and battled his mechanics, leaving his pitches up in the zone. Including a 2004 stint in the Cape Cod League, he has tired in each of the last three summers and must get stronger to handle the grind of pro ball. He also has to do a better job of holding runners after surrendering 13 steals in 14 attempts in 2006. The Astros also have worked with him to lower his arm angle to a true three-quarters slot. There's some thought that he'd hold up better as a reliever, but he'll stay in the rotation this year in high Class A.

| Year | Club (League) | Class | W | L | ERA | G | GS | CG | SV | IP | H | R | ER | HR | BB | SO | AVG |
|------|---------------|-------|---|---|-----|---|----|----|----|----|---|---|----|----|----|----|-----|
| 2005 | Tri-City (NYP) | A | 0 | 2 | 7.59 | 13 | 0 | 0 | 3 | 21 | 30 | 20 | 18 | 2 | 9 | 17 | .316 |
| 2006 | Lexington (SAL) | A | 2 | 5 | 4.73 | 17 | 17 | 0 | 0 | 70 | 76 | 44 | 37 | 6 | 24 | 60 | .274 |
| | Tri-City (NYP) | A | 0 | 0 | 4.09 | 3 | 3 | 0 | 0 | 11 | 10 | 8 | 5 | 1 | 5 | 6 | .233 |
| **MINOR LEAGUE TOTALS** | | | 2 | 7 | 5.26 | 33 | 20 | 0 | 3 | 103 | 116 | 72 | 60 | 9 | 38 | 83 | .280 |

# 15  BROOKS CONRAD                                                           2B/3B

**Born:** Jan. 16, 1980. **B-T:** B-R. **Ht.:** 5-11. **Wt.:** 190. **Drafted:** Arizona State, 2001 (8th round). **Signed by:** Andrew Cotner.

Snubbed for a spot on Houston's 40-man roster after the 2004 and 2005 seasons, Conrad came out and did what he always does in 2006. He brought high energy to the ballpark every day and continued to overachieve. He had the best season of his career, leading the minors with 79 extra-base hits and topping the Pacific Coast League in runs, triples and total bases (284). Conrad has always shown offensive ability, with a short stroke, gap (and sometimes home run) power, an eye for drawing a fair amount of walks, and the savvy and enough speed to steal an occasional base. He did strike out more than ever, a tradeoff for his added power production, but he continued to work counts. More important for his career, Conrad displayed increased versatility last year. His arm, range and throwing accuracy all rate as 40 or 45 on the 20-80 scouting scale, limiting him even at second base. But his arm responded to a throwing program and he was able to play a passable third base. He also saw time at all three outfield positions in the Arizona Fall League, where he hit .359 as a replacement for Hunter Pence. Conrad can be David Eckstein with less polish and more power. He won that 40-man spot this offseason, though he still faces a challenge to make the big league club in spring training.

| Year | Club (League) | Class | AVG | G | AB | R | H | 2B | 3B | HR | RBI | BB | SO | SB | OBP | SLG |
|------|---------------|-------|-----|---|----|---|---|----|----|----|-----|----|----|----|-----|-----|
| 2001 | Pittsfield (NYP) | A | .280 | 65 | 232 | 41 | 65 | 16 | 5 | 4 | 39 | 26 | 52 | 14 | .375 | .444 |
| 2002 | Michigan (MWL) | A | .287 | 133 | 499 | 94 | 143 | 25 | 14 | 14 | 94 | 62 | 102 | 18 | .368 | .477 |
| 2003 | Lexington (SAL) | A | .186 | 38 | 140 | 20 | 26 | 5 | 2 | 3 | 11 | 17 | 25 | 7 | .288 | .314 |
| | Salem (CL) | A | .284 | 99 | 345 | 50 | 98 | 24 | 3 | 11 | 61 | 42 | 60 | 4 | .369 | .467 |
| 2004 | Round Rock (TL) | AA | .290 | 129 | 480 | 84 | 139 | 38 | 6 | 13 | 83 | 63 | 105 | 8 | .365 | .475 |
| 2005 | Round Rock (PCL) | AAA | .263 | 113 | 418 | 84 | 110 | 22 | 3 | 12 | 57 | 52 | 104 | 12 | .347 | .481 |
| | Corpus Christi (TL) | AA | .234 | 22 | 77 | 13 | 18 | 6 | 1 | 2 | 11 | 16 | 15 | 8 | .372 | .416 |
| 2006 | Round Rock (PCL) | AAA | .267 | 138 | 532 | 100 | 142 | 40 | 15 | 24 | 94 | 54 | 135 | 15 | .334 | .534 |
| **MINOR LEAGUE TOTALS** | | | .272 | 737 | 2723 | 486 | 741 | 176 | 49 | 92 | 450 | 332 | 598 | 86 | .355 | .474 |

# 16  JOSH ANDERSON                                                               OF

**Born:** Aug. 10, 1982. **B-T:** L-R. **Ht.:** 6-2. **Wt.:** 195. **Drafted:** Eastern Kentucky, 2003 (4th round). **Signed by:** Nick Venuto.

Anderson led the minors in steals in 2004 and the Texas League in each of the last two years, but he's still trying to prove he can do more than run wild on the bases. He repeated Double-A and put up essentially the same numbers as the season before. Managers rated Anderson the Texas League's best and fastest baserunner, and his speed rates at least a 70 on the 20-80 scouting scale. He also uses his quickness well in center field, where he did a better job reading fly balls last year. The key for Anderson will be producing at the plate. He's a slightly below-average hitter—his speed allows him to beat out infield hits and pump up his average—with well-below-average power, so he must focus on getting on base. But his plate discipline has regressed during his two years in Double-A, and his bunting needs work as well. Anderson tried to get his hands in position earlier in 2006, which would allow him to fend off inside fastballs better, but the results weren't noticeable. His biggest improvement came against lefthanders, as he hit .354 off them after they held him to a .210 average in 2005. He has a playable, accurate arm and did a better job of hitting the cutoff man last year. He's similar to Willy Taveras, who was traded to the Rockies in December. But Anderson is a lesser defender, and he'll play in Triple-A this year rather than take over for Taveras.

| Year | Club (League) | Class | AVG | G | AB | R | H | 2B | 3B | HR | RBI | BB | SO | SB | OBP | SLG |
|------|---------------|-------|-----|---|-----|----|-----|----|----|----|-----|-----|-----|-----|------|------|
| 2003 | Tri-City (NYP) | A | .286 | 74 | 297 | 44 | 85 | 11 | 4 | 3 | 30 | 16 | 53 | 26 | .339 | .380 |
| 2004 | Lexington (SAL) | A | .324 | 73 | 299 | 69 | 97 | 12 | 3 | 4 | 31 | 33 | 47 | 47 | .402 | .425 |
| | Salem (CL) | A | .268 | 66 | 280 | 45 | 75 | 13 | 6 | 2 | 21 | 13 | 53 | 31 | .314 | .379 |
| 2005 | Corpus Christi (TL) | AA | .282 | 127 | 524 | 67 | 148 | 16 | 9 | 1 | 26 | 29 | 80 | 50 | .329 | .353 |
| 2006 | Corpus Christi (TL) | AA | .308 | 130 | 561 | 83 | 173 | 26 | 4 | 3 | 50 | 27 | 73 | 43 | .349 | .385 |
| **MINOR LEAGUE TOTALS** | | | .295 | 470 | 1961 | 308 | 578 | 78 | 26 | 13 | 158 | 118 | 306 | 197 | .346 | .381 |

##  CHANCE DOUGLASS
RHP

**Born:** Feb. 24, 1984. **B-T:** R-R. **Ht.:** 6-1. **Wt.:** 200. **Drafted:** HS—Amarillo, Texas, 2002 (12th round). **Signed by:** Rusty Pendergrass.

Douglass signed for an above-slot $225,000 as a 12th-rounder in 2002, then did little to justify the bonus in his first three pro seasons. He broke through by leading the Carolina League in ERA in 2005, then was a solid starter on Corpus Christi's championship team. He won both his Texas League playoff starts, striking out 19 in 12 innings. Douglass is a lesser version of Chris Sampson, relying on command of average stuff. He now has the best changeup in the system after refining it over the last two years. He sits at 87-88 mph and tops out at 92 mph with his sinker, and he also mixes in a curveball and slider. Both of his breaking balls have their moments. Douglass does a good job of throwing strikes and working inside, but he sometimes catches too much of the plate. He needs to improve his conditioning and athleticism. Douglass has a ceiling as a workhorse back-of-the-rotation starter, and he'll work toward that goal in Triple-A this year.

| Year | Club (League) | Class | W | L | ERA | G | GS | CG | SV | IP | H | R | ER | HR | BB | SO | AVG |
|------|---------------|-------|---|---|-----|---|----|----|----|-----|-----|-----|-----|----|-----|-----|------|
| 2002 | Martinsville (Appy) | R | 2 | 1 | 3.65 | 12 | 9 | 0 | 0 | 44 | 45 | 19 | 18 | 4 | 23 | 34 | .269 |
| 2003 | Martinsville (Appy) | R | 5 | 1 | 2.34 | 10 | 10 | 0 | 0 | 58 | 50 | 17 | 15 | 1 | 10 | 48 | .242 |
| 2004 | Lexington (SAL) | A | 9 | 10 | 5.33 | 29 | 24 | 0 | 0 | 137 | 156 | 99 | 81 | 18 | 73 | 106 | .298 |
| 2005 | Salem (CL) | A | 12 | 9 | 2.90 | 27 | 27 | 1 | 0 | 168 | 157 | 59 | 54 | 7 | 44 | 128 | .249 |
| 2006 | Corpus Christi (TL) | AA | 7 | 8 | 3.52 | 28 | 26 | 2 | 0 | 161 | 144 | 67 | 63 | 13 | 56 | 102 | .241 |
| **MINOR LEAGUE TOTALS** | | | 35 | 29 | 3.66 | 106 | 96 | 3 | 0 | 567 | 552 | 261 | 231 | 43 | 206 | 418 | .260 |

## LOU SANTANGELO
C

**Born:** March 16, 1983. **B-T:** R-R. **Ht.:** 6-1. **Wt.:** 200. **Drafted:** Clemson, 2004 (4th round). **Signed by:** Brian Keegan.

Few Astros farmhands can hit a fastball farther than Santangelo, but he's still seeking offensive consistency after three years in pro ball. He never managed to hit .300 with metal bats in college at Seton Hall and Clemson, and he matched his career average by hitting .241 in high Class A last year as a 23-year-old. Santangelo doesn't recognize offspeed and breaking pitches well, so they give him fits and he has trouble making contact. Nevertheless, he has averaged a homer for every 20 pro at-bats and tantalized Houston with a three-homer game on July 22. That he's also a catcher makes Santangelo all the more intriguing. Fully recovered from a labrum tear that truncated his 2005 season, he has a strong arm and threw out 42 percent of basestealers last year. His receiving skills aren't as advanced, but he did move better behind the plate in 2006 than he had in the past. He's a below-average runner but not bad for a backstop. Santangelo will advance to Double-A this year and could have a future as a platoon catcher in the majors.

| Year | Club (League) | Class | AVG | G | AB | R | H | 2B | 3B | HR | RBI | BB | SO | SB | OBP | SLG |
|------|---------------|-------|-----|---|-----|----|-----|----|----|----|-----|-----|-----|-----|------|------|
| 2004 | Tri-City (NYP) | A | .201 | 47 | 164 | 28 | 33 | 5 | 2 | 6 | 20 | 21 | 58 | 2 | .299 | .366 |
| 2005 | Lexington (SAL) | A | .268 | 70 | 239 | 43 | 64 | 14 | 2 | 14 | 39 | 24 | 86 | 4 | .336 | .519 |
| 2006 | Salem (CL) | A | .241 | 98 | 357 | 48 | 86 | 19 | 5 | 18 | 57 | 36 | 112 | 0 | .310 | .473 |
| **MINOR LEAGUE TOTALS** | | | .241 | 215 | 760 | 119 | 183 | 38 | 9 | 38 | 116 | 81 | 256 | 6 | .316 | .464 |

## JOSH FLORES
OF

**Born:** Nov. 18, 1985. **B-T:** R-R. **Ht.:** 6-0. **Wt.:** 195. **Drafted:** Triton (Ill.) JC, 2005 (4th round). **Signed by:** Kevin Stein.

Flores won the national juco batting title with a .519 average in 2005, turning down six-figure offers from the Braves both before and afterward. His gamble paid off, as the Astros gave him $217,500 as a fourth-rounder that June. After an encouraging pro debut, he struggled to adjust to the speed of the game in low Class A in 2006. Flores stood on top of the plate and tried to pull everything, failing to stay back and protect the outer third of the plate. He does have power, but he'll have to tighten his strike zone and adjust his approach. His best tool is his speed, which ranks as the best in the system, just ahead of Josh Anderson. Flores swiped bases at an 82 percent success rate last year, but he needs to be more aggressive and run more. A shortstop before turning pro, he's still learning in center field. He's good on balls hit directly in front of or behind him, but struggles to take efficient routes on

drives in the gaps. His arm is average. Houston believes he has the makeup to succeed, and thus feels confident he can handle a jump to high Class A in 2007.

| Year | Club (League) | Class | AVG | G | AB | R | H | 2B | 3B | HR | RBI | BB | SO | SB | OBP | SLG |
|------|---------------|-------|-----|---|----|---|---|----|----|----|-----|----|----|----|-----|-----|
| 2005 | Greeneville (Appy) | R | .335 | 59 | 248 | 49 | 83 | 12 | 5 | 8 | 25 | 16 | 57 | 20 | .384 | .520 |
|      | Lexington (SAL) | A | .278 | 5 | 18 | 1 | 5 | 2 | 0 | 0 | 1 | 1 | 4 | 4 | .316 | .389 |
| 2006 | Lexington (SAL) | A | .253 | 125 | 475 | 81 | 120 | 19 | 2 | 11 | 35 | 33 | 107 | 28 | .313 | .371 |
| **MINOR LEAGUE TOTALS** | | | .281 | 189 | 741 | 131 | 208 | 33 | 7 | 19 | 61 | 50 | 168 | 52 | .337 | .421 |

## 20 JORDAN PARRAZ OF

**Born:** Oct. 8, 1984. **B-T:** R-R. **Ht.:** 6-3. **Wt.:** 220. **Drafted:** CC of Southern Nevada, 2004 (3rd round). **Signed by:** Doug Deutsch.

After the Phillies drafted him as a pitcher in the sixth round in 2003, Parraz opted to attend junior college. He hit 96 mph with his fastball but lost his spot in the rotation because of poor command. He also hit .359 with wood bats as an outfielder, and the Astros took him in 2004 for his bat. Parraz was inconsistent and played out of control during his first two lackluster years in pro ball before breaking out in 2006. Perhaps because he heard whispers that Houston might return him to the mound, a move he didn't want to make, Parraz toned down his game and played more under control. In his second tour of the New York-Penn League, he led the circuit in batting, slugging and on-base percentage. He showed a more consistent swing, allowing him to make better use of his average power and slightly above-average speed. Parraz runs well for his size and has seen time in center field, though he fits best in right. He reads balls off the bat better on the corners, and he obviously has enough arm strength. He still plays with reckless abandon, but he's also beginning to figure pro ball out. Parraz is finally ready for low Class A in his fourth pro season.

| Year | Club (League) | Class | AVG | G | AB | R | H | 2B | 3B | HR | RBI | BB | SO | SB | OBP | SLG |
|------|---------------|-------|-----|---|----|---|---|----|----|----|-----|----|----|----|-----|-----|
| 2004 | Greeneville (Appy) | R | .244 | 53 | 180 | 35 | 44 | 6 | 5 | 4 | 21 | 24 | 44 | 8 | .349 | .400 |
| 2005 | Tri-City (NYP) | A | .262 | 71 | 282 | 31 | 74 | 11 | 2 | 5 | 35 | 12 | 45 | 17 | .310 | .369 |
| 2006 | Tri-City (NYP) | A | .336 | 70 | 253 | 46 | 85 | 18 | 2 | 6 | 38 | 33 | 44 | 23 | .421 | .494 |
| **MINOR LEAGUE TOTALS** | | | .284 | 194 | 715 | 112 | 203 | 35 | 9 | 15 | 94 | 69 | 133 | 48 | .361 | .421 |

## 21 LINCOLN HOLDZKOM RHP

**Born:** March 23, 1982. **B-T:** R-R. **Ht.:** 6-4. **Wt.:** 240. **Drafted:** Arizona Western CC, 2002 (7th round). **Signed by:** David Finley (Marlins).

Holdzkom's father Christopher was a well-known pianist in the late 1960s, and he started his son on the piano at age 2. Lincoln played the piano on "The Tonight Show" with Johnny Carson when he was 6 and later contributed a song to the "Forrest Gump" soundtrack. He shares baseball in common with his brother John, a 6-foot-7 righthander who signed with the Mets as a fourth-round pick last June. Holdzkom had a chance to go early in the 2001 draft, but after he was kicked off the team at Arizona Western he lasted until the Marlins took him in the seventh round. He blew out his elbow in 2004, when he missed the entire year following Tommy John surgery. Florida brought him back slowly in 2005, then sent him to the Cubs in a deal for Todd Wellemeyer at the end of spring training last March. Holdzkom came down with shoulder problems that cost him two months last summer, so Chicago thought it could leave him unprotected for the major league Rule 5 draft. But after he touched 95 mph with his fastball in the Arizona Fall League, the Astros pounced. Holdzkom usually works at 91-93 with his fastball and backs it up with a hard slurve. He has yet to allow a home run in 206 pro innings. After six years in pro ball, he's still a project. He has to prove he can stay healthy, throw consistent strikes and maintain his stuff for more than an inning at a time. Makeup questions also have dogged him in the past. But if Holdzkom can harness his electric arm, he can help Houston's bullpen. The Astros have to keep him on their major league roster throughout 2007. If not, they have to pass him through waivers and offer him back to the Cubs for half his $50,000 draft price.

| Year | Club (League) | Class | W | L | ERA | G | GS | CG | SV | IP | H | R | ER | HR | BB | SO | AVG |
|------|---------------|-------|---|---|-----|---|----|----|----|----|---|---|----|----|----|----|-----|
| 2001 | Marlins (GCL) | R | 1 | 3 | 2.49 | 12 | 7 | 0 | 2 | 43 | 26 | 18 | 12 | 0 | 27 | 4 | .176 |
| 2002 | Kane County (MWL) | A | 1 | 5 | 2.53 | 30 | 0 | 0 | 11 | 32 | 21 | 11 | 9 | 0 | 29 | 42 | .181 |
| 2003 | Greensboro (SAL) | A | 1 | 4 | 2.84 | 43 | 0 | 0 | 4 | 57 | 36 | 24 | 18 | 0 | 27 | 74 | .182 |
|      | Jupiter (FSL) | A | 0 | 2 | 3.07 | 13 | 0 | 0 | 2 | 15 | 9 | 6 | 5 | 0 | 7 | 20 | .167 |
| 2004 | Did not play—Injured | | | | | | | | | | | | | | | | |
| 2005 | Marlins (GCL) | R | 0 | 0 | 2.25 | 3 | 0 | 0 | 0 | 4 | 5 | 3 | 1 | 0 | 1 | 6 | .313 |
|      | Jupiter (FSL) | A | 0 | 1 | 5.79 | 9 | 0 | 0 | 1 | 9 | 7 | 6 | 6 | 0 | 5 | 9 | .206 |
| 2006 | West Tenn (SL) | AA | 0 | 0 | 1.95 | 18 | 0 | 0 | 0 | 32 | 25 | 7 | 7 | 0 | 10 | 27 | .221 |
|      | Cubs (AZL) | R | 0 | 0 | 2.08 | 5 | 1 | 0 | 0 | 9 | 11 | 4 | 2 | 0 | 3 | 10 | .324 |
|      | Daytona (FSL) | A | 0 | 0 | 0.00 | 2 | 0 | 0 | 0 | 5 | 3 | 0 | 0 | 0 | 2 | 6 | .167 |
| **MINOR LEAGUE TOTALS** | | | 5 | 18 | 2.62 | 135 | 8 | 0 | 20 | 206 | 143 | 79 | 60 | 0 | 111 | 237 | .196 |

## BUD NORRIS
RHP

**Born:** March 2, 1985. **B-T:** R-R. **Ht.:** 6-0. **Wt.:** 195. **Drafted:** Cal Poly, 2006 (6th round). **Signed by:** Dennis Twombley.

Norris began his career at Cal Poly as a two-way player before focusing on pitching as a sophomore and emerging as the Mustangs' No. 1 starter as a junior last spring. He eased into pro ball as a reliever and spent the summer throwing his four-seam fastball by New York-Penn League hitters. Norris pitched at 90-93 mph as a starter during the spring, and his velocity rose to the mid-90s and topped out at 97 when he worked out of the bullpen. His heater has late hop at the end, making it difficult for hitters to square up. His No. 2 pitch is a power curveball with 12-to-6 break, though he doesn't command it effectively. The Astros will start Norris this year in low Class A to give him the innings to polish his repertoire. He needs to do a better job of working all four quadrants of the strike zone. He throws his changeup too hard and it doesn't have enough separation from his fastball. In the long term, Norris' stuff and bulldog attitude will probably fit best in the bullpen.

| Year | Club (League) | Class | W | L | ERA | G | GS | CG | SV | IP | H | R | ER | HR | BB | SO | AVG |
|------|---------------|-------|---|---|-----|---|----|----|----|----|---|---|----|----|----|----|-----|
| 2006 | Tri-City (NYP) | A | 2 | 0 | 3.79 | 15 | 3 | 0 | 2 | 38 | 28 | 20 | 16 | 1 | 13 | 46 | .200 |
| **MINOR LEAGUE TOTALS** | | | 2 | 0 | 3.79 | 15 | 3 | 0 | 2 | 38 | 28 | 20 | 16 | 1 | 13 | 46 | .200 |

## TOMMY MANZELLA
SS

**Born:** April 16, 1983. **B-T:** R-R. **Ht.:** 6-2. **Wt.:** 190. **Drafted:** Tulane, 2005 (3rd round). **Signed by:** Mike Rosamond.

Manzella hasn't had anything come easy to him since he turned pro in 2005. Hurricane Katrina destroyed his family's home in Chalmette, La., during his debut. He also had a tough time adjusting to wood bats and had elbow problems that required arthroscopic surgery. In 2006, he went down twice during the season with ankle problems, and had to leave Hawaii Winter Baseball early when doctor diagnosed the injury as a hairline stress fracture. The Astros would love to see what Manzella can do when healthy, as he has the best all-around package of tools among their shortstop prospects. He is cutting down a swing better tailored for metal bats, and with further adjustments he could hit for a decent average. He also has gap power and enough speed to steal an occasional base. Where Manzella really stands out is with his glove. Managers rated him the best defensive shortstop in the South Atlantic League last year. He has solid range, a strong arm and fine instincts. Manzella's upside is as a stronger version of Adam Everett. He'll head to high Class A in 2007, with a good chance at a midseason promotion if all goes well.

| Year | Club (League) | Class | AVG | G | AB | R | H | 2B | 3B | HR | RBI | BB | SO | SB | OBP | SLG |
|------|---------------|-------|-----|---|----|---|---|----|----|----|-----|----|----|----|-----|-----|
| 2005 | Tri-City (NYP) | A | .232 | 53 | 220 | 24 | 51 | 6 | 4 | 0 | 18 | 9 | 39 | 5 | .260 | .295 |
| 2006 | Lexington (SAL) | A | .275 | 99 | 338 | 50 | 93 | 22 | 1 | 7 | 43 | 33 | 80 | 16 | .340 | .408 |
| **MINOR LEAGUE TOTALS** | | | .258 | 152 | 558 | 74 | 144 | 28 | 5 | 7 | 61 | 42 | 119 | 21 | .310 | .364 |

## CHRIS JOHNSON
3B

**Born:** Oct. 1, 1984. **B-T:** R-R. **Ht.:** 6-3. **Wt.:** 220. **Drafted:** Stetson, 2006 (4th round). **Signed by:** John Bunnell.

The son of former big leaguer and current Red Sox Triple-A manager Ron Johnson, Chris turned down Boston as a 37th-round pick in 2003 and opted to attend Stetson instead. After redshirting in his first year, Johnson set a school record with a career .379 batting average. When he signed for $242,500 as a fourth-round pick in June, he immediately became the system's top corner-infield prospect. Johnson has more raw power than most Houston farmhands and can drive the ball to all fields. He tried to do too much in his pro debut, hampering his own pop when he lost control of the strike zone. After playing mostly first base in college, Johnson shifted to third base in pro ball. He runs and moves well for his size, has enough arm for the hot corner and made just three errors in 49 games there. His lower half has gotten thicker, however, and some scouts believe he'll wind up back at first base. Houston expects significant improvement with the bat in low Class A this year.

| Year | Club (League) | Class | AVG | G | AB | R | H | 2B | 3B | HR | RBI | BB | SO | SB | OBP | SLG |
|------|---------------|-------|-----|---|----|---|---|----|----|----|-----|----|----|----|-----|-----|
| 2006 | Tri-City (NYP) | A | .212 | 60 | 222 | 18 | 47 | 7 | 1 | 1 | 29 | 11 | 35 | 7 | .251 | .266 |
| **MINOR LEAGUE TOTALS** | | | .212 | 60 | 222 | 18 | 47 | 7 | 1 | 1 | 29 | 11 | 35 | 7 | .251 | .266 |

## KOBY CLEMENS
3B

**Born:** Dec. 4, 1986. **B-T:** R-R. **Ht.:** 5-11. **Wt.:** 193. **Drafted:** HS—Houston, 2005 (8th round). **Signed by:** Rusty Pendergrass.

Clemens already has made a significant contribution to the Astros, as his presence in the organization helped persuade his father Roger to pitch at least one more season for the club

in 2006. When Roger made his first tuneup start at Lexington on June 6, Koby was his third baseman and backed him with an RBI double. He's also a natural leader who's looked up to by many of his teammates. Houston believes Clemens can help them with his on-field performance as well. He missed five weeks after dislocating his left pinky diving into a base in late April, and he never got going in low Class A. He does have a sound swing and raw power, and the Astros think his ability to make adjustments will get him back on track. Clemens has below-average speed, range and athleticism, but he has worked hard to make himself into a third baseman. He gladly accepted an assignment to Hawaii Winter Baseball, where he focused on his defense. He showed a low-90s fastball as a high school senior, so he has more than enough arm for the hot corner, but if his body gets any thicker he could face a move to first base. Houston could challenge him with a move to high Class A in 2007.

| Year | Club (League) | Class | AVG | G | AB | R | H | 2B | 3B | HR | RBI | BB | SO | SB | OBP | SLG |
|------|---------------|-------|-----|---|-----|----|-----|----|----|----|-----|----|----|----|------|------|
| 2005 | Greeneville (Appy) | R | .297 | 33 | 111 | 14 | 33 | 8 | 0 | 4 | 17 | 18 | 26 | 4 | .398 | .477 |
|  | Tri-City (NYP) | A | .281 | 9 | 32 | 3 | 9 | 1 | 2 | 0 | 6 | 4 | 5 | 1 | .361 | .438 |
| 2006 | Lexington (SAL) | A | .229 | 91 | 306 | 40 | 70 | 19 | 1 | 5 | 39 | 32 | 67 | 2 | .313 | .346 |
| MINOR LEAGUE TOTALS |  |  | .249 | 133 | 449 | 57 | 112 | 28 | 3 | 9 | 62 | 54 | 98 | 7 | .338 | .385 |

## 26 SERGIO SEVERINO
LHP

**Born:** Sept. 1, 1984. **B-T:** L-L. **Ht.:** 5-11. **Wt.:** 155. **Signed:** Dominican Republic, 2003. **Signed by:** Adriano Rodriguez/Julio Linares.

As with many of their Latin American prospects, the Astros have brought Severino along slowly, keeping him in Rookie leagues for four straight years. Last season was his most impressive yet, as he led the Appalachian League in strikeouts, whiffs per nine innings (11.9) and even caught-stealing percentage (60 percent). At this point, Severino is a small, lean lefty with a quick arm that delivers explosive 92-93 mph fastballs. He scrapped his curveball last year in favor of a slider that can be tough to hit, but he doesn't always throw it for strikes. His changeup and mechanics are similarly inconsistent, and his maximum-effort approach doesn't lend itself to working deep into games. Severino's profile screams reliever, but Houston likely will continue using him as a starter to maximize his innings. At 22, he'll finally get his first opportunity in low Class A.

| Year | Club (League) | Class | W | L | ERA | G | GS | CG | SV | IP | H | R | ER | HR | BB | SO | AVG |
|------|---------------|-------|---|---|------|----|----|----|----|-----|-----|-----|----|----|-----|-----|------|
| 2003 | Astros (DSL) | R | 3 | 1 | 1.67 | 14 | 10 | 0 | 1 | 54 | 35 | 18 | 10 | 0 | 33 | 85 | .176 |
| 2004 | Astros (DSL) | R | 5 | 3 | 2.63 | 15 | 15 | 1 | 0 | 75 | 45 | 32 | 22 | 0 | 34 | 105 | .169 |
| 2005 | Greeneville (Appy) | R | 3 | 5 | 4.67 | 13 | 13 | 0 | 0 | 62 | 47 | 35 | 32 | 3 | 36 | 69 | .210 |
| 2006 | Greeneville (Appy) | R | 6 | 3 | 2.90 | 13 | 13 | 0 | 0 | 68 | 50 | 24 | 22 | 4 | 27 | 90 | .204 |
| MINOR LEAGUE TOTALS |  |  | 17 | 12 | 2.98 | 55 | 51 | 1 | 1 | 259 | 177 | 109 | 86 | 7 | 130 | 349 | .189 |

## 27 HECTOR GIMENEZ
C

**Born:** Sept. 28, 1982. **B-T:** B-R. **Ht.:** 5-10. **Wt.:** 210. **Signed:** Venezuela, 1999. **Signed by:** Andres Reiner.

When John Buck went to the Royals in the Carlos Beltran trade in June 2004, Gimenez was left as the best catcher in the Houston system. But J.R. Towles, Max Sapp and Lou Santangelo since have eclipsed him as prospects, and Humberto Quintero has made an inroads on the Astros' backup job. A switch-hitter, Gimenez is much better from the left side. He hits for average and has home run pop, but he doesn't stand out in either regard because his bat speed and plate discipline are fringy. Sanchez is more of a defensive player who has a strong arm and a quick release. He's aggressive at picking off runners and threw out 36 percent of Triple-A basestealers last year. He has made significant improvements with his English and his game-calling since signing as a 16-year-old Venezuela. He's a well-below-average runner. Gimenez has seen time at first base and even taken grounders at third in an attempt to increase his versatility. He did make his big league debut last September, but his chances of making much of a contribution in Houston have diminished. He seems to wear down mentally and physically over the course of a season, which doesn't help his case.

| Year | Club (League) | Class | AVG | G | AB | R | H | 2B | 3B | HR | RBI | BB | SO | SB | OBP | SLG |
|------|---------------|-------|-----|----|-----|-----|-----|----|----|----|-----|-----|-----|----|------|------|
| 2000 | Astros (VSL) | R | .297 | 34 | 91 | 9 | 27 | 8 | 0 | 1 | 13 | 12 | 21 | 0 | .396 | .418 |
| 2001 | Astros (VSL) | R | .278 | 42 | 144 | 27 | 40 | 12 | 3 | 5 | 34 | 26 | 30 | 4 | .388 | .507 |
| 2002 | Lexington (SAL) | A | .263 | 85 | 297 | 41 | 78 | 16 | 1 | 11 | 42 | 25 | 78 | 2 | .320 | .434 |
| 2003 | Salem (CL) | A | .247 | 109 | 381 | 41 | 94 | 17 | 1 | 7 | 54 | 29 | 75 | 2 | .304 | .352 |
| 2004 | Round Rock (TL) | AA | .245 | 97 | 331 | 38 | 81 | 16 | 3 | 6 | 46 | 18 | 64 | 2 | .284 | .366 |
| 2005 | Corpus Christi (TL) | AA | .273 | 121 | 454 | 47 | 124 | 19 | 1 | 12 | 58 | 32 | 88 | 2 | .322 | .399 |
| 2006 | Round Rock (PCL) | AAA | .273 | 76 | 275 | 31 | 75 | 8 | 0 | 8 | 37 | 24 | 42 | 2 | .331 | .389 |
|  | Houston (NL) | MLB | .000 | 2 | 2 | 0 | 0 | 0 | 0 | 0 | 0 | 0 | 1 | 0 | .000 | .000 |
| MINOR LEAGUE TOTALS |  |  | .263 | 564 | 1973 | 234 | 519 | 96 | 9 | 50 | 284 | 166 | 398 | 14 | .322 | .397 |
| MAJOR LEAGUE TOTALS |  |  | .000 | 2 | 2 | 0 | 0 | 0 | 0 | 0 | 0 | 0 | 1 | 0 | .000 | .000 |

## 28 RONALD RAMIREZ
SS/2B

**Born:** Jan. 30, 1986. **B-T:** R-R. **Ht.:** 6-0. **Wt.:** 149. **Signed:** Colombia, 2003. **Signed by:** Andres Reiner/Guillermo Ramirez.

Ramirez made a successful U.S. debut in 2006 and was the MVP at Rookie-level Greeneville and an Appalachian League all-star. Though he weighs just 149 pounds, he has surprising pop for his size and pitchers can't knock the bat out of his hands. His plate discipline still leaves something to be desired, but he does a good job of using the entire field. If he gets stronger, he could be an asset on offense as he moves up the system. He's an average runner. Ramirez is a legitimate middle infielder but may not be able to stay at shortstop. He has good body control and nice range to his left, but his footwork needs improvement and his arm grades as just a 45 on the 20-80 scouting scale. The Astros haven't given up on him at shortstop yet and believe that his arm may improve. They appreciate his bubbly personality and love for the game. Ramirez had a three-game cameo in low Class A at the end of last season and will return there in 2007.

| Year | Club (League) | Class | AVG | G | AB | R | H | 2B | 3B | HR | RBI | BB | SO | SB | OBP | SLG |
|------|---------------|-------|-----|---|-----|-----|-----|----|----|----|-----|----|-----|----|------|------|
| 2003 | Astros (VSL) | R | .202 | 56 | 198 | 30 | 40 | 12 | 1 | 0 | 16 | 17 | 40 | 8 | .278 | .273 |
| 2004 | Astros 1 (VSL) | R | .276 | 59 | 203 | 36 | 56 | 14 | 1 | 1 | 28 | 28 | 22 | 15 | .358 | .369 |
| 2005 | Astros 1 (VSL) | R | .267 | 46 | 172 | 22 | 46 | 10 | 2 | 3 | 29 | 9 | 18 | 5 | .312 | .401 |
| 2006 | Greeneville (Appy) | R | .314 | 57 | 229 | 23 | 72 | 20 | 2 | 3 | 33 | 11 | 42 | 7 | .349 | .459 |
| | Lexington (SAL) | A | .200 | 3 | 10 | 0 | 2 | 0 | 0 | 0 | 0 | 0 | 4 | 0 | .200 | .200 |
| **MINOR LEAGUE TOTALS** | | | .266 | 221 | 812 | 111 | 216 | 56 | 6 | 7 | 106 | 65 | 126 | 35 | .324 | .376 |

## 29 MIKE RODRIGUEZ
OF

**Born:** Oct. 15, 1980. **B-T:** L-L. **Ht.:** 5-10. **Wt.:** 180. **Drafted:** Miami, 2001 (2nd round). **Signed by:** Chuck Carlson.

Rodriguez played on College World Series championship teams at Miami in 1999 and 2001, ranking second in NCAA Division I with 53 steals (in 55 attempts) for the latter club. The Astros thought they were getting a catalyst who could wreak havoc when they made him a second-round pick in 2001. Instead, he has proven to be an above-average runner and not a burner, and he hasn't made a huge impact on the bases. He's a poor man's version of Josh Anderson, albeit with the best plate discipline in the system. Rodriguez has a sound swing and puts the ball in play. Getting stronger would make him more of a threat at the plate. He's also a solid center fielder who takes good routes, especially on balls hit in front of him. He has an average arm and a quick release. Rodriguez has been bothered by shoulder problems throughout his career, and he had to leave the Arizona Fall League early to have surgery to clean up his labrum. Added to the 40-man roster for the first time in the off-season, he'll get a look as an extra outfielder this spring.

| Year | Club (League) | Class | AVG | G | AB | R | H | 2B | 3B | HR | RBI | BB | SO | SB | OBP | SLG |
|------|---------------|-------|-----|---|-----|-----|-----|----|----|----|-----|----|-----|-----|------|------|
| 2001 | Pittsfield (NYP) | A | .318 | 47 | 157 | 38 | 50 | 14 | 4 | 0 | 14 | 33 | 30 | 13 | .443 | .459 |
| 2002 | Michigan (MWL) | A | .253 | 133 | 499 | 94 | 126 | 23 | 4 | 4 | 46 | 65 | 85 | 35 | .338 | .339 |
| 2003 | Salem (CL) | A | .278 | 113 | 443 | 78 | 123 | 22 | 8 | 5 | 42 | 50 | 50 | 23 | .356 | .397 |
| 2004 | Round Rock (TL) | AA | .267 | 105 | 397 | 59 | 106 | 23 | 5 | 4 | 53 | 39 | 55 | 16 | .331 | .380 |
| 2005 | Corpus Christi (TL) | AA | .281 | 116 | 392 | 51 | 110 | 16 | 9 | 5 | 50 | 47 | 50 | 25 | .359 | .406 |
| 2006 | Round Rock (PCL) | AAA | .276 | 113 | 439 | 70 | 121 | 16 | 7 | 6 | 38 | 51 | 55 | 28 | .352 | .385 |
| **MINOR LEAGUE TOTALS** | | | .273 | 627 | 2327 | 390 | 636 | 114 | 37 | 24 | 243 | 285 | 325 | 140 | .354 | .385 |

## 30 CHRIS SALAMIDA
LHP

**Born:** May 7, 1984. **B-T:** L-L. **Ht.:** 6-0. **Wt.:** 180. **Drafted:** Oneonta State (N.Y.), 2006 (13th round). **Signed by:** Mike Maggart.

Salamida was a 13th-round find by area scout Mike Maggart, who previously stole Wade Miller and Tim Redding for the Astros. Signed for $20,000, Salamida headed to Tri-City, based just five minutes from where he grew up, and became the New York-Penn League's most dominant pitcher, leading the circuit in wins, ERA and opponent average. A two-way player at Division III Oneonta State, Salamida is a good athlete who repeats his low three-quarters delivery well. His arm angle makes his 89-91 mph fastball seem quicker, as does a changeup that rates as a plus pitch at times. His slider needs the most refinement, and he doesn't consistently stay on top of the pitch. He likes to cross up hitters by pitching backward. Houston compares his competitive drive to Mark Buehrle's, and thinks Salamida could become a No. 5 starter or a middle reliever. If the Astros don't send him to high Class A to begin 2007, he should get there by the end of the year.

| Year | Club (League) | Class | W | L | ERA | G | GS | CG | SV | IP | H | R | ER | HR | BB | SO | AVG |
|------|---------------|-------|---|---|-----|---|----|----|----|----|----|----|----|----|----|----|------|
| 2006 | Tri-City (NYP) | A | 10 | 1 | 1.06 | 14 | 14 | 0 | 0 | 68 | 44 | 12 | 8 | 2 | 23 | 53 | .189 |
| **MINOR LEAGUE TOTALS** | | | 10 | 1 | 1.06 | 14 | 14 | 0 | 0 | 68 | 44 | 12 | 8 | 2 | 23 | 53 | .189 |

# KANSAS CITY
# ROYALS

BY **MATT MEYERS**

LARRY GOREN

During the 1970s and 1980s, the Royals could stake a claim to being baseball's model franchise. Not coincidentally, their demise corresponded with John Schuerholz leaving his general manager post to take the same job with the Braves for the 1991 season. Now the Royals hope some of that karma will come back their way.

Kansas City went to the Atlanta well in search of the cure for its problems, hiring Dayton Moore to replace Allard Baird as general manager in May. Moore had been with the Braves since 1997 and was an integral part of the best player-development system of the past decade. Now the Royals are banking on Moore being able to turn the Braves Way into the new Royals Way.

In his first few months on the job, Moore wasn't subtle in his attempt to bring the Atlanta model with him to Kansas City. Among his first orders of business were bringing on J.J. Picollo as farm director and Rene Francisco as director of international scouting, after working closely with both while with the Braves. With the addition of Francisco, the Royals plan to beef up their scouting in Latin America after it was limited by financial constraints in recent years. They're set to open up a new academy in the Dominican Republic in 2007.

The other change based on Atlanta's model is the addition of a seventh minor league affiliate, with a new club in the Rookie-level Appalachian League. The Braves carried at least seven and sometimes eight from 1986-2001 before trimming costs.

"Adding another Rookie league club is another opportunity for players to develop, especially pitchers," Moore said. "We felt a strong need to build depth with pitching. If you have 20 pitching prospects, you might get four or five to the big leagues."

Depth of pitching is still a weakness for Royals system, but they are addressing it. Just before Moore took over, they selected Luke Hochevar with the No. 1 overall pick in the draft. Moore pulled off a series of trades that added promising young arms such as lefthander Tyler Lumsden and righthanders Blake Johnson, Julio Pimentel, Joselo Diaz and Daniel Cortes.

As for position players, the Royals have arguably the best 1-2 prospect punch in third baseman Alex Gordon, Baseball America's 2006 Minor League Player of the Year, and outfielder **Billy Butler**. Both have bats that will play anywhere and are almost major league-ready. The only question is where they'll play. Gordon is a natural third baseman, but Mark Teahen developed into a solid everyday player in 2006, so one of them will have to move to the outfield. Long viewed as a DH in waiting, Butler will get the chance to establish himself as a right fielder. With only one winning season in their last 14, having too many talented players at a position is a new problem for the Royals, one they're not complaining about. With Moore on board and a vision for the future, there's cause for hope in Kansas City.

## TOP 30 PROSPECTS

1. Alex Gordon, 3b
2. Luke Hochevar, rhp
3. Billy Butler, of
4. Chris Lubanski, of
5. Tyler Lumsden, lhp
6. Mitch Maier, of
7. Brian Bannister, rhp
8. Justin Huber, of/1b
9. Billy Buckner, rhp
10. Brent Fisher, lhp
11. Jeff Bianchi, ss
12. Ryan Braun, rhp
13. Joakim Soria, rhp
14. Blake Wood, rhp
15. Erik Cordier, rhp
16. Jason Taylor, 3b
17. Blake Johnson, rhp
18. Julio Pimentel, rhp
19. Carlos Rosa, rhp
20. Luis Cota, rhp
21. Derrick Robinson, of
22. Chris Nicoll, rhp
23. Jarod Plummer, rhp
24. Danny Christensen, lhp
25. Angel Sanchez, ss
26. Kurt Mertins, 2b
27. Chris McConnell, ss
28. Joe Dickerson, of
29. Jason Godin, rhp
30. Daniel Cortes, rhp

# ORGANIZATION OVERVIEW

**General manager:** Dayton Moore. **Farm director:** J.J. Picollo. **Scouting director:** Deric Ladnier.

## 2006 PERFORMANCE

| Class | Team | League | W | L | PCT | Finish* | Manager | Affiliated |
|-------|------|--------|---|---|-----|---------|---------|------------|
| Majors | Kansas City | American | 62 | 100 | .383 | 13th (14) | Buddy Bell | — |
| Triple-A | Omaha Royals | Pacific Coast | 53 | 91 | .368 | 16th (16) | Mike Jirschele | 1969 |
| Double-A | Wichita Wranglers | Texas | 77 | 62 | .554 | 2nd (8) | Frank White | 1995 |
| High A | #High Desert Mavericks | California | 73 | 67 | .521 | 4th (10) | Jeff Carter | 2007 |
| Low A | Burlington Bees | Midwest | 64 | 73 | .467 | 11th (14) | Jim Gabella | 2001 |
| Rookie | Idaho Falls Chukars | Pioneer | 40 | 36 | .526 | 4th (8) | Brian Rupp | 2004 |
| Rookie | AZL Royals | Arizona | 36 | 20 | .643 | 2nd (9) | Lloyd Simmons | 2003 |
| **OVERALL 2006 MINOR LEAGUE RECORD** | | | 343 | 349 | .496 | 17th (30) | | |

*Finish in overall standings (No. of teams in league). #Affiliate will move to Burlington (Carolina) in 2007. Royals will operate seven affiliates in 2007, adding an Appalachian League team in Burlington, N.C.

## ORGANIZATION LEADERS

### BATTING
| | | |
|---|---|---|
| AVG | Mertins, Kurt, Idaho Falls | .342 |
| R | Gordon, Alex, Wichita | 111 |
| H | Maier, Mitch, Wichita | 183 |
| TB | Gordon, Alex, Wichita | 286 |
| 2B | Gordon, Alex, Wichita | 39 |
| 3B | Lubanski, Chris, Wichita | 11 |
| HR | Gordon, Alex, Wichita | 29 |
| RBI | Gordon, Alex, Wichita | 101 |
| BB | Johnson, Joshua, Burlington | 93 |
| SO | Senreiso, Juan, Wichita/High Desert | 122 |
| SB | Lisson, Mario, Burlington | 41 |
| OBP | Doscher, Nicholas, AZL Royals | .462 |
| SLG | Gordon, Alex, Wichita | .588 |
| XBH | Gordon, Alex, Wichita | 69 |

### PITCHING
| | | |
|---|---|---|
| W | Plummer, Jarod, High Desert/Wichita | 13 |
| L | Cota, Luis, High Desert | 11 |
| | Middleton, Kyle, Wichita/Omaha | 11 |
| ERA | Fisher, Brent, AZL Royals/Idaho Falls | 2.12 |
| G | DeHoyos, Gabe, High Desert/Wichita | 58 |
| CG | Bernero, Adam, Scranton/WB/Omaha | 2 |
| SV | DeHoyos, Gabe, High Desert/Wichita | 20 |
| IP | Buckner, Billy, High Desert/Wichita | 166 |
| BB | Buckner, Billy, High Desert/Wichita | 86 |
| SO | Nicoll, Christopher, Burlington/High Desert | 166 |
| AVG | Fisher, Brent, AZL Royals/Idaho Falls | 169 |

## BEST TOOLS

| | |
|---|---|
| Best Hitter for Average | Billy Butler |
| Best Power Hitter | Alex Gordon |
| Best Strike-Zone Discipline | Alex Gordon |
| Fastest Baserunner | Derrick Robinson |
| Best Athlete | Derrick Robinson |
| Best Fastball | Erik Cordier |
| Best Curveball | Luke Hochevar |
| Best Slider | Carlos Rosa |
| Best Changeup | Danny Christensen |
| Best Control | Chris Nicoll |
| Best Defensive Catcher | Matt Tupman |
| Best Defensive Infielder | Angel Sanchez |
| Best Infield Arm | Angel Sanchez |
| Best Defensive Outfielder | Mitch Maier |
| Best Outfield Arm | Jose Duarte |

## PROJECTED 2010 LINEUP

| | |
|---|---|
| Catcher | John Buck |
| First Base | Ryan Shealy |
| Second Base | Esteban German |
| Third Base | Alex Gordon |
| Shortstop | Jeff Bianchi |
| Left Field | Chris Lubanski |
| Center Field | David DeJesus |
| Right Field | Mark Teahen |
| Designated Hitter | Billy Butler |
| No. 1 Starter | Luke Hochevar |
| No. 2 Starter | Gil Meche |
| No. 3 Starter | Zack Greinke |
| No. 4 Starter | Tyler Lumsden |
| No. 5 Starter | Billy Buckner |
| Closer | Ryan Braun |

## LAST YEAR'S TOP 20 PROSPECTS

1. Alex Gordon, 3b
2. Billy Butler, of
3. Justin Huber, 1b
4. Chris Lubanski, of
5. Jeff Bianchi, ss
6. Luis Cota, rhp
7. Chris McConnell, ss
8. Mitch Maier, of
9. Donnie Murphy, 2b
10. Shane Costa, of
11. Billy Buckner, rhp
12. Brian Bass, rhp
13. Adam Donachie, c
14. Angel Sanchez, ss
15. Danny Christensen, lhp
16. Erik Cordier, rhp
17. Joe Dickerson, of
18. Jose Duarte, of
19. Chris Nicoll, rhp
20. Kila Kaaihue, 1b

## TOP PROSPECTS OF THE DECADE

| Year | Player, Pos. | 2006 Org. |
|------|--------------|-----------|
| 1997 | Glendon Rusch, lhp | Cubs |
| 1998 | Dee Brown, of | Royals |
| 1999 | Carlos Beltran, of | Mets |
| 2000 | Dee Brown, of | Royals |
| 2001 | Chris George, lhp | Marlins |
| 2002 | Angel Berroa, ss | Royals |
| 2003 | Zack Greinke, rhp | Royals |
| 2004 | Zack Greinke, rhp | Royals |
| 2005 | Billy Butler, of | Royals |
| 2006 | Alex Gordon, 3b | Royals |

## TOP DRAFT PICKS OF THE DECADE

| Year | Player, Pos. | 2006 Org. |
|------|--------------|-----------|
| 1997 | Dan Reichert, rhp | Nashua (Can-Am) |
| 1998 | Jeff Austin, rhp | Out of baseball |
| 1999 | Kyle Snyder, rhp | Red Sox |
| 2000 | Mike Stodolka, lhp | Royals |
| 2001 | Colt Griffin, rhp | Royals |
| 2002 | Zack Greinke, rhp | Royals |
| 2003 | Chris Lubanski, of | Royals |
| 2004 | Billy Butler, of | Royals |
| 2005 | Alex Gordon, 3b | Royals |
| 2006 | Luke Hochevar, rhp | Royals |

## ALL-TIME LARGEST BONUSES

| | |
|---|---|
| Alex Gordon, 2005 | $4,000,000 |
| Luke Hochevar, 2006 | $3,500,000 |
| Jeff Austin, 1998 | $2,700,000 |
| Mike Stodolka, 2000 | $2,500,000 |
| Zack Greinke, 2002 | $2,475,000 |

# MINOR LEAGUE DEPTH CHART

## Kansas City Royals

**Impact: A.** With Gordon, Hochevar and Butler, they might have the best top three in the minors. All three should be impact big leaguers.

**Depth: C.** Beyond the top three, there is not much in the way of high-ceiling talent. Their strength is a number of solid righthanders who profile as middle to back of the rotation starters.

**Sleeper:** Jarod Plummer, rhp. His 4.05 ERA was inflated by the Cal League and he was dominant in Hawaii Winter Baseball. The disappearing splitter is his strikeout pitch.

*Numbers in parentheses indicate prospect rankings.*

| LF | CF | RF |
|---|---|---|
| Chris Lubanski (4) | Mitch Maier (6) | Billy Butler (3) |
| Joe Dickerson (28) | Derrick Robinson (21) | Nick Van Stratten |
| Brett Bigler | Jarrod Dyson | O.D. Gonzalez |
| | Jose Duarte | |

| 3B | SS | 2B | 1B |
|---|---|---|---|
| Alex Gordon (1) | Jeff Bianchi (11) | Kurt Mertins (26) | Justin Huber (8) |
| Jason Taylor (16) | Angel Sanchez (25) | Marc Maddox | Miguel Vega |
| Mario Lisson | Chris McConnell (27) | Josh Johnson | Mike Stodolka |
| | Irving Falu | | |

| C |
|---|
| Kiel Thibault |
| Matt Morizio |

| RHP | | LHP | |
|---|---|---|---|
| **Starters** | **Relievers** | **Starters** | **Relievers** |
| Luke Hochevar (2) | Ryan Braun (12) | Tyler Lumsden (5) | Gilbert de la Vara |
| Billy Buckner (9) | Joakim Soria (13) | Brent Fisher (10) | Rowdy Hardy |
| Brian Bannister (7) | Jarod Plummer (23) | Danny Christensen (24) | |
| Blake Wood (14) | Leo Nunez | Everett Teaford | |
| Erik Cordier (15) | Cody Smith | Matt Campbell | |
| Blake Johnson (17) | Matt Kniginyzky | | |
| Julio Pimentel (18) | | | |
| Carlos Rosa (19) | | | |
| Luis Cota (20) | | | |
| Chris Nicoll (22) | | | |
| Jason Godin (29) | | | |
| Daniel Cortes (30) | | | |
| Brian Bass | | | |
| Harold Mozingo | | | |
| Josh Cribb | | | |
| Tyler Chambliss | | | |

## 2006
SIGNING BUDGET: $6.3 million

**Best Pro Debut:** RHP Aaron Hartsock (23) went 6-2, 2.91 with 43 strikeouts in 46 innings, leading the Pioneer League in wins. Kurt Mertins (13) and Marc Maddox (9) shared the second-base job at Idaho Falls and finished among the PL batting leaders at .342 and .336, with Mertins also stealing 26 bases.

**Best Athlete:** OF Derrick Robinson (4) was a top cornerback recruit headed to play at Florida before signing for $850,000, easily the highest bonus in his round. The Royals landed several quality athletes, among them 3B Jason Taylor (2); OFs Brett Bigler (7), Nick Francis (15) and Jarrod Dyson (50); and 2B Tyrone Wilson (16). Taylor's athleticism drew comparisons to that of fellow Virginia high school product Justin Upton, the No. 1 overall pick in 2005.

**Best Pure Hitter:** Taylor's balance, approach and strike-zone judgment are advanced for an 18-year-old.

**Best Raw Power:** Maddox has the most present pop, but Francis has more power potential and is just learning how to use it.

**Fastest Runner:** Robinson ran a 6.19-second 60-yard dash at a summer showcase in June 2005. He's still learning as a basestealer after getting caught in 14 of 34 pro attempts. Dyson, a find for first-year area scout Brian Rhees, is just as fast. Bigler and Wilson are plus-plus runners, while OF Nick Van Stratten (10) and Mertins have above-average speed.

**Best Defensive Player:** Robinson still needs work on taking better routes to balls, but he has the speed to become a plus defender in center field.

**Best Fastball:** After sitting out for the better part of a year, RHP Luke Hochevar (1) returned to throw a 92-95 mph fastball that topped out at 97 in independent and pro ball. Better yet, he has above-average life and command to go with his velocity.

**Best Breaking Ball:** Though some teams considered Hochevar's slider more advanced than his curveball, the Royals have had him focus on his curve. It may be his second-best breaking ball, but it's also the best in this draft crop.

**Most Intriguing Background:** C Matt Morizio's (17) father Michael is the president of a company that developed the ScoutAdvisor information system used by 13 big league clubs, including all four League Championship Series participants.

RHP Brad Boxberger's (20) dad Rod was a first-round pick and MVP of the College World Series in 1978.

**Closest To The Majors:** Hochevar finished the season pitching in the Double-A Texas League playoffs, and he could open 2007 in Triple-A. RHP Blake Wood (3) could move quickly as well. After ironing out his mechanics and recovering from shin splints that plagued him at Georgia Tech, he threw 93-95 mph during the summer.

**Best Late-Round Pick:** Mertins and Francis.

**The One Who Got Away:** RHPs Jeff Inman (19) and Boxberger (20) are now Pacfic-10 Conference rivals at Stanford and Southern California. Both pitch in the low 90s at times, with Inman possessing better velocity and Boxberger owning a superior breaking ball.

**Assessment:** By taking Hochevar first overall, the Royals dispelled the notion they'd try to save money, just as they did the year before with No. 2 overall choice Alex Gordon. Hochevar is the perfect fit for an organization that lacked pitching.

## 2005
BUDGET: $6.0 million

Kansas City made the right call at No. 2 with 3B Alex Gordon (1), the only player ever to win both Baseball America's College and Minor League Player of the Year awards. SS Jeff Bianchi (2) has looked good when he has been healthy. **GRADE: A**

## 2004
BUDGET: $5.8 million

The Royals surprised a lot of teams by grabbing OF Billy Butler (1) with the 14th overall choice, but they have no regrets. They traded LHP J.P. Howell (1), while LHP Matt Campbell (1) and RHP Erik Cordier (2) got hurt. **GRADE: B+**

## 2003
BUDGET: $5.6 million

Kansas City didn't find any cornerstones, but did land depth with OFs Chris Lubanski (1), Mitch Maier (1) and Shane Costa (2) and RHP Ryan Braun (6). Draft-and-follow RHP Luis Cota (10) has yet to live up to his $1.05 million bonus. **GRADE: C**

*Draft analysis by Jim Callis. Numbers in parentheses indicate draft rounds. Budgets are bonuses in first 10 rounds.*

# ALEX
# GORDON

3B

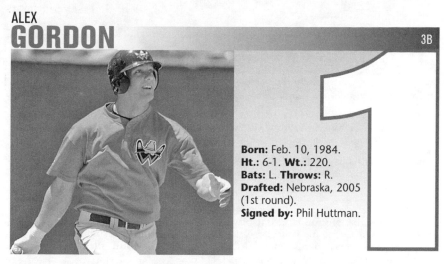

**Born:** Feb. 10, 1984.
**Ht.:** 6-1. **Wt.:** 220.
**Bats:** L. **Throws:** R.
**Drafted:** Nebraska, 2005
(1st round).
**Signed by:** Phil Huttman.

Since the Royals made him the No. 2 overall pick in the 2005 draft, Gordon has done nothing to make the Royals think twice about their club-record $4 million bonus investment. He pulled off an unprecedented feat by winning Baseball America's College Player of the Year Award and Minor League Player of the Year awards in consecutive seasons, capturing the latter honor in his pro debut. Gordon is accustomed to accumulating hardware, as he was a two-time Big 12 Conference player of the year at Nebraska and was the offensive MVP when Team USA won a gold medal at the 2004 World University Championships. After signing late in 2005, he played in the Arizona Fall League, his only pro experience before he led the Double-A Texas League in slugging (.588), finished second in on-base percentage (.427) and ranked fourth in batting (.325). A native of Lincoln, Neb., Gordon grew up as a Royals fan, and his brother Brett was named for Hall of Famer George Brett, the greatest player in franchise history. Gordon may one day make a run at that title.

There's little that Gordon can't do offensively. He has a smooth stroke with impressive bat speed and is able to generate power to all fields. In college he was able to wait longer on pitches because of the metal bat, but he quickly learned how to get his load started earlier with wood. That allowed his power to emerge quickly as the season progressed and he hit 19 home runs in the final two months. He finds ways to get hits even when his swing isn't at its best, further evidence of his knack for centering the ball on the barrel of the bat. He has a strong concept of the strike zone and is willing to draw walks. An average runner with terrific instincts, Gordon is an efficient basestealer. He succeeded on 22 of his 25 attempts in 2006. Defensively, he has proven to be more athletic at third base than Kansas City expected. He has above-average arm strength.

Gordon has had a habit of tinkering with his swing going back to his days at Nebraska, as well as a tendency to open up that causes a slight uppercut. The Royals are trying to get him to focus on keeping his swing on a slight downward plane to generate more backspin and loft. Gordon has the most room to improve defensively. He was mechanical and a little stiff as third baseman coming out of college, but he has made significant improvement. While he still needs to get lighter on his feet, there's no reason he shouldn't be at least an average defender.

With incumbent Royals third baseman Mark Teahen coming off a solid season, either he or Gordon could end up switching positions. Possible destinations for Gordon include the outfield corners or first base, and he provides enough offense to play anywhere. Because his bat is nearly major league-ready, he'll get a look with big club this spring and could make the Royals' Opening Day roster. Teahen's shoulder surgery could enhance Gordon's chances of breaking camp with Kansas City. Even if Gordon opens the year at Triple-A Omaha, he'll surely make his way to the majors to stay at some point in 2007.

| Year | Club (League) | Class | AVG | G | AB | R | H | 2B | 3B | HR | RBI | BB | SO | SB | OBP | SLG |
|------|---------------|-------|-----|---|----|---|---|----|----|----|-----|----|----|----|-----|-----|
| 2006 | Wichita (TL) | AA | .325 | 130 | 486 | 111 | 158 | 39 | 1 | 29 | 101 | 72 | 113 | 22 | .427 | .588 |
| **MINOR LEAGUE TOTALS** | | | .325 | 130 | 486 | 111 | 158 | 39 | 1 | 29 | 101 | 72 | 113 | 22 | .427 | .588 |

## 2 LUKE HOCHEVAR                                                   RHP

**Born:** Sept. 15, 1983. **B-T:** R-R. **Ht.:** 6-5. **Wt.:** 205. **Drafted:** Fort Worth (American Association), 2006 (1st round). **Signed by:** Phil Huffman and Gerald Turner.

A candidate to go No. 1 in the 2005 draft, Hochevar dropped to the Dodgers at No. 40 because of signability. Negotiations took a strange turn that September, when he switched agents and agreed to a $2.98 million bonus, then switched back to Scott Boras and declined to sign. After a sharp stint in the independent American Association, he did go No. 1 to the Royals in June. Hochevar got a $3.5 million bonus and $5.25 million guarantee as part of the first major league contract the Royals have given to a draft pick since Bo Jackson in 1986. Hochevar features a lively four-seam fastball that sits at 92-93 mph and touches 95. He complements his fastball with a plus-plus late-breaking curveball that he can throw for strikes or bury for strikeouts. He worked more with a slider in college, but the Royals wanted him to focus on his curve and have been pleased with the results. His changeup is a usable third pitch, and he has good overall command of his entire arsenal. Because of his tendency to land on his heel, Hochevar's fastball command can be inconsistent. His changeup can use further improvement. He signed late, so he has just 38 pro innings under his belt at age 23. The Royals sent him to the Arizona Fall League to get more experience, but he left early with shoulder fatigue. Hochevar's shoulder problem isn't considered serious, and he could earn a spot in Kansas City's Opening Day rotation with a strong spring training. More likely, he'll begin the season at Double-A Wichita, where he finished 2006 in the Texas League playoffs, and make his big league debut later in the year.

| Year | Club (League) | Class | W | L | ERA | G | GS | CG | SV | IP | H | R | ER | HR | BB | SO | AVG |
|------|---------------|-------|---|---|-----|---|----|----|----|-----|---|---|----|----|----|----|-----|
| 2006 | Burlington (MWL) | A | 0 | 1 | 1.17 | 4 | 4 | 0 | 0 | 15 | 8 | 3 | 2 | 2 | 2 | 16 | .148 |
| **MINOR LEAGUE TOTALS** | | | 0 | 1 | 1.17 | 4 | 4 | 0 | 0 | 15 | 8 | 3 | 2 | 2 | 2 | 16 | .148 |

## 3 BILLY BUTLER                                                    OF

**Born:** April 18, 1986. **B-T:** R-R. **Ht.:** 6-2. **Wt.:** 225. **Drafted:** HS— Jacksonville, 2004 (1st round). **Signed by:** Cliff Pastornicky.

In 2004, Butler and Eric Hurley (Rangers) made Jacksonville Wolfson the fifth high school ever to produce two first-rounders in the same draft. Somewhat of a surprise selection at No. 14, Butler has justified the pick by hitting .344/.417/.564 as a pro. He won the Texas League batting title and the Futures Game MVP award in 2006, and capped the year by hitting .313 while helping Team USA qualify for the 2008 Olympics. With excellent bat speed, balance and a cerebral approach, Butler has no real weakness as a hitter. He has great plate coverage and will hit the ball where it is pitched. He has the best raw power in the system and is still learning how to turn on inside pitches. He's content to go the other way, particularly with runners on base. While there are no questions about his bat, Butler's defense is another story. Drafted as a third baseman, he since has moved to the outfield. His arm is strong enough for right field, but his speed is below average and his routes and footwork need plenty of work. There are no doubts that Butler has the bat to be an all-star, but his lack of defensive skills might mean his future is as a DH. He desperately wants to prove he can play the outfield and the Royals will give him every chance to do so in Triple-A this year. His bat could force him to Kansas City by midseason.

| Year | Club (League) | Class | AVG | G | AB | R | H | 2B | 3B | HR | RBI | BB | SO | SB | OBP | SLG |
|------|---------------|-------|-----|---|----|---|---|----|----|----|-----|----|----|----|-----|-----|
| 2004 | Idaho Falls (Pio) | R | .373 | 74 | 260 | 74 | 97 | 22 | 3 | 10 | 68 | 57 | 63 | 5 | .488 | .596 |
| 2005 | High Desert (Cal) | A | .348 | 92 | 379 | 70 | 132 | 30 | 2 | 25 | 91 | 42 | 80 | 0 | .419 | .636 |
| | Wichita (TL) | AA | .313 | 29 | 112 | 14 | 35 | 9 | 0 | 5 | 19 | 7 | 18 | 0 | .353 | .527 |
| 2006 | Wichita (TL) | AA | .331 | 119 | 477 | 82 | 158 | 33 | 1 | 15 | 96 | 41 | 67 | 1 | .388 | .499 |
| **MINOR LEAGUE TOTALS** | | | .344 | 314 | 1228 | 240 | 422 | 94 | 6 | 55 | 274 | 147 | 228 | 6 | .417 | .564 |

## 4 CHRIS LUBANSKI                                                  OF

**Born:** March 24, 1985. **B-T:** L-L. **Ht.:** 6-3. **Wt.:** 206. **Drafted:** HS— Schwenksville, Pa., 2003 (1st round). **Signed by:** Sean Rooney.

Always among the youngest players in his league, Lubanski has shown the ability to make adjustments as the season progresses as evidenced by a career-long trend of second-half surges. The fifth overall pick in the 2003 draft had a .704 on-base plus slugging percentage before the 2006 all-star break, compared to a .978 OPS afterward. Though he has filled out since being drafted, Lubanski is still very athletic. He has plus speed and a smooth stroke with leverage that bodes well for power. His plate

discipline and pitch recognition continue to improve, and he led the Texas League in walks in 2006. He has good range in the outfield. Though he runs well, Lubanski isn't the speedster he was billed as coming out of high school. He's not adept at stealing bases and is tentative in the outfield. His routes, jumps and arm are all fringy, making him a left fielder rather than a center fielder. He sometimes misses hittable pitches when he gets them. He hit just .225 against lefthanders in 2006 because he lunges too often and needs to trust his hands more. Lubanski looked like a possible first-round bust by mid-2005, but he has turned his career around, and the Royals see him as their long-term answer in left field. He'll probably spend most of 2007 in Triple-A.

| Year | Club (League) | Class | AVG | G | AB | R | H | 2B | 3B | HR | RBI | BB | SO | SB | OBP | SLG |
|------|---------------|-------|-----|---|----|---|---|----|----|----|-----|----|----|----|-----|-----|
| 2003 | Royals 1 (AZL) | R | .326 | 53 | 221 | 41 | 72 | 4 | 6 | 4 | 27 | 18 | 50 | 9 | .382 | .452 |
| 2004 | Burlington (MWL) | A | .275 | 127 | 483 | 64 | 133 | 26 | 7 | 9 | 56 | 43 | 104 | 16 | .336 | .414 |
| 2005 | High Desert (Cal) | A | .301 | 126 | 531 | 91 | 160 | 38 | 6 | 28 | 116 | 38 | 131 | 14 | .349 | .554 |
| 2006 | Wichita (TL) | AA | .282 | 137 | 524 | 93 | 148 | 34 | 11 | 15 | 70 | 72 | 112 | 11 | .369 | .475 |
| **MINOR LEAGUE TOTALS** | | | .292 | 443 | 1759 | 289 | 513 | 102 | 30 | 56 | 269 | 171 | 397 | 50 | .356 | .479 |

## TYLER LUMSDEN

LHP

**Born:** May 9, 1983. **B-T:** R-L. **Ht.:** 6-4. **Wt.:** 205. **Drafted:** Clemson, 2004 (1st round supplemental). **Signed by:** Nick Hostetler (White Sox).

In his first summer as Royals general manager, Dayton Moore made it a goal to acquire as many pitching prospects as possible. The best he got was Lumsden, who came from the White Sox along with righthander Daniel Cortes in exchange for Mike MacDougal. A supplemental first-round pick in 2004, Lumsden missed all of 2005 following arthroscopic surgery to remove bone chips in his elbow. Lumsden had no physical problems and showed three quality pitches in 2006. His fastball sits at 90-93 mph and tops out at 95. He also features a hard 12-to-6 curveball and a solid changeup. His delivery is sound and balanced. Lumsden sometimes has trouble repeating his mechanics, landing too hard on his front foot and throwing across his body. When that happens, he gets under his pitches and leaves them up in the strike zone. That's why he was more hittable than a southpaw with three legitimate pitches should have been in 2006. Developing pitchers has been problematic for the Royals, who have far more openings on their big league staff than the White Sox did. Lumsden's elbow problems appear behind him, and he could grab a spot in Kansas City's rotation with a strong spring training. More likely, he'll head to Triple-A for a few starts.

| Year | Club (League) | Class | W | L | ERA | G | GS | CG | SV | IP | H | R | ER | HR | BB | SO | AVG |
|------|---------------|-------|---|---|-----|---|----|----|----|----|---|---|----|----|----|----|-----|
| 2004 | Winston-Salem (CL) | A | 3 | 1 | 4.12 | 15 | 3 | 0 | 0 | 39 | 45 | 25 | 18 | 2 | 20 | 31 | .280 |
| 2005 | Did not play—Injured | | | | | | | | | | | | | | | | |
| 2006 | Birmingham (SL) | AA | 9 | 4 | 2.69 | 20 | 20 | 0 | 0 | 124 | 114 | 47 | 37 | 9 | 40 | 72 | .252 |
| | Wichita (TL) | AA | 2 | 1 | 3.06 | 7 | 6 | 0 | 0 | 35 | 35 | 12 | 12 | 3 | 20 | 24 | .276 |
| **MINOR LEAGUE TOTALS** | | | 14 | 6 | 3.04 | 42 | 29 | 0 | 0 | 198 | 194 | 84 | 67 | 14 | 80 | 127 | .262 |

## MITCH MAIER

OF

**Born:** June 30, 1982. **B-T:** L-R. **Ht.:** 6-2. **Wt.:** 210. **Drafted:** Toledo, 2003 (1st round). **Signed by:** Jason Bryans.

Maier prompts more divided opinion than perhaps any player in the system. Some see him as an everyday center fielder, while others think he's a fourth outfielder. He was part of an all-first-rounder outfield in Wichita, flanked by Billy Butler and Chris Lubanski. A catcher in college, Maier first moved to third base as a pro. He was the leader of a star-studded Wichita club and earns high praise for his work ethic. He has shortened his swing and improved his rhythm and balance. He stays tough against lefthanders and posted an .888 OPS against them in 2006. He has average speed and arm strength, and his good instincts allow him to play center. Though Maier is a well-rounded player, none of his tools jump out. His swing still gets long with an uppercut at times, and he needs to continue refining his approach at the plate. He profiles better for the top rather than for the middle of a batting order, and thus could stand to draw more walks. Maier's defense has improved and his chances of being an everyday player have increased now that he has proven he can play center. His makeup and all-around tools should make him at least a big league reserve. He'll get the opportunity to make the Royals in spring training.

| Year | Club (League) | Class | AVG | G | AB | R | H | 2B | 3B | HR | RBI | BB | SO | SB | OBP | SLG |
|------|---------------|-------|-----|---|----|---|---|----|----|----|-----|----|----|----|-----|-----|
| 2003 | AZL Royals 1 (AZL) | R | .350 | 51 | 203 | 41 | 71 | 14 | 6 | 2 | 45 | 18 | 25 | 7 | .403 | .507 |
| 2004 | Burlington (MWL) | A | .300 | 82 | 317 | 41 | 95 | 24 | 3 | 4 | 36 | 27 | 51 | 34 | .354 | .432 |

| 2004 | Wilmington (CL) | A | .264 | 51 | 174 | 25 | 46 | 9 | 2 | 3 | 17 | 15 | 29 | 9 | .326 | .391 |
| 2005 | High Desert (Cal) | A | .336 | 50 | 211 | 42 | 71 | 26 | 1 | 8 | 32 | 12 | 43 | 6 | .370 | .583 |
| | Wichita (TL) | AA | .255 | 80 | 322 | 55 | 82 | 21 | 5 | 7 | 49 | 15 | 47 | 10 | .289 | .416 |
| 2006 | Wichita (TL) | AA | .306 | 138 | 543 | 95 | 166 | 35 | 7 | 14 | 92 | 41 | 96 | 13 | .357 | .473 |
| | Kansas City (AL) | MLB | .154 | 5 | 13 | 3 | 2 | 0 | 0 | 0 | 0 | 2 | 4 | 0 | .267 | .154 |
| **MINOR LEAGUE TOTALS** | | | .300 | 452 | 1770 | 299 | 531 | 129 | 24 | 38 | 271 | 128 | 291 | 79 | .348 | .464 |
| **MAJOR LEAGUE TOTALS** | | | .154 | 5 | 13 | 3 | 2 | 0 | 0 | 0 | 0 | 2 | 4 | 0 | .267 | .154 |

## 7 BRIAN BANNISTER RHP

STEVE MOORE

**Born:** Feb. 28, 1981. **B-T:** R-R. **Ht.:** 6-2. **Wt.:** 200. **Drafted:** Southern California, 2003 (7th round). **Signed by:** Steve Leavitt (Mets).

Bannister's father Floyd was the No. 1 overall pick in the June 1976 draft and won 134 games in the majors, while his brother Brett signed with the Mariners as a 19th-rounder in 2005. An unheralded seventh-round pick in 2003, Brian won 15 games in a breakthrough 2005 minor league season and opened last year in the Mets rotation. He hurt a hamstring running the bases in late April and pitched just once in the next three months. In December, the Royals shipped closer Ambiorix Burgos to New York for Bannister. They're polar opposites on the mound, as Burgos has overpowering stuff but is very raw, while Bannister is underwhelming but very polished. Though he had more walks than strikeouts in his brief big league exposure, his strengths are his above-average command his feel for pitching. His most effective pitch is his 85-87 mph cutter. His fastball sits at 89-91 mph, and while his curveball has nasty bite, he doesn't throw it for strikes. He used his rehab time to focus on his changeup, which had always been fringy. Bannister projects as a decent back-of-the-rotation starter, and he should make Kansas City's Opening Day roster in 2007.

| Year | Club (League) | Class | W | L | ERA | G | GS | CG | SV | IP | H | R | ER | HR | BB | SO | AVG |
|------|--------------|-------|---|---|-----|---|----|----|----|----|---|---|----|----|----|----|-----|
| 2003 | Brooklyn (NYP) | A | 4 | 1 | 2.15 | 12 | 9 | 0 | 1 | 46 | 27 | 12 | 11 | 0 | 18 | 42 | .173 |
| 2004 | St. Lucie (FSL) | A | 5 | 7 | 4.24 | 20 | 20 | 0 | 0 | 110 | 111 | 63 | 52 | 6 | 27 | 106 | .270 |
| | Binghamton (EL) | AA | 3 | 3 | 4.06 | 8 | 8 | 0 | 0 | 44 | 45 | 23 | 20 | 2 | 17 | 28 | .283 |
| 2005 | Binghamton (EL) | AA | 9 | 4 | 2.56 | 18 | 18 | 1 | 0 | 109 | 91 | 36 | 31 | 11 | 27 | 94 | .232 |
| | Norfolk (IL) | AAA | 4 | 1 | 3.18 | 8 | 8 | 0 | 0 | 45 | 48 | 19 | 16 | 0 | 13 | 48 | .270 |
| 2006 | St. Lucie (FSL) | A | 1 | 0 | 1.50 | 2 | 2 | 0 | 0 | 12 | 10 | 4 | 2 | 0 | 4 | 9 | .233 |
| | Norfolk (IL) | AAA | 3 | 3 | 3.86 | 6 | 6 | 1 | 0 | 30 | 34 | 15 | 13 | 4 | 5 | 24 | .279 |
| | New York (NL) | MLB | 2 | 1 | 4.26 | 8 | 6 | 0 | 0 | 38 | 34 | 18 | 18 | 4 | 22 | 19 | .239 |
| **MINOR LEAGUE TOTALS** | | | 29 | 19 | 3.28 | 74 | 71 | 2 | 1 | 397 | 366 | 172 | 145 | 23 | 111 | 351 | .250 |
| **MAJOR LEAGUE TOTALS** | | | 2 | 1 | 4.26 | 8 | 6 | 0 | 0 | 38 | 34 | 18 | 18 | 4 | 22 | 19 | .239 |

## 8 JUSTIN HUBER OF/1B

**Born:** July 1, 1982. **B-T:** R-R. **Ht.:** 6-2. **Wt.:** 200. **Signed:** Australia, 2000. **Signed by:** Fred Mazzuca/Omar Minaya (Mets).

Huber has been on the prospect radar for so long that he has appeared in three Futures Games, winning MVP honors in 2005. A catcher in the Mets system before coming to the Royals in a three-team deal for Kris Benson in 2004, he moved to first base after switching organizations. Passed by 2006 trade acquisition Ryan Shealy at that position, Huber is now getting time in the outfield. He surprisingly didn't get a September callup and spent the month back home in Australia. Huber stays inside the ball well and can spray line drives all over the field. He has a good knowledge of the strike zone and could hit 15-20 homers per season. He has solid arm strength and more athleticism than most former catchers. Huber has yet to prove he has the power to warrant everyday play at first base or an outfield corner. His athleticism hasn't translated well to his defense, where he lacks instincts. He was a shaky receiver and is now an adequate first baseman and a raw outfielder. His speed is slightly below average. With Shealy at first and a multitude of outfield candidates, Huber's chances of becoming a regular with Kansas City are diminishing. He doesn't have much to gain from a third stint in Triple-A, so a trade could be possible.

| Year | Club (League) | Class | AVG | G | AB | R | H | 2B | 3B | HR | RBI | BB | SO | SB | OBP | SLG |
|------|--------------|-------|-----|---|----|---|---|----|----|----|-----|----|----|----|-----|-----|
| 2001 | St. Lucie (FSL) | A | .000 | 2 | 6 | 0 | 0 | 0 | 0 | 0 | 0 | 0 | 2 | 0 | .000 | .000 |
| | Kingsport (Appy) | R | .314 | 47 | 159 | 24 | 50 | 11 | 1 | 7 | 31 | 17 | 42 | 4 | .415 | .528 |
| 2001 | Brooklyn (NYP) | A | .000 | 3 | 9 | 0 | 0 | 0 | 0 | 0 | 0 | 0 | 4 | 0 | .000 | .000 |
| 2002 | St. Lucie (FSL) | A | .270 | 28 | 100 | 15 | 27 | 2 | 1 | 3 | 15 | 11 | 18 | 0 | .370 | .400 |
| | Columbia (SAL) | A | .291 | 95 | 330 | 49 | 96 | 22 | 2 | 11 | 78 | 45 | 81 | 1 | .408 | .470 |
| 2003 | St. Lucie (FSL) | A | .284 | 50 | 183 | 26 | 52 | 15 | 0 | 9 | 36 | 17 | 30 | 1 | .370 | .514 |
| | Binghamton (EL) | AA | .264 | 55 | 193 | 16 | 51 | 13 | 0 | 6 | 36 | 19 | 54 | 0 | .350 | .425 |
| 2004 | St. Lucie (FSL) | A | .245 | 14 | 49 | 10 | 12 | 2 | 0 | 2 | 8 | 5 | 8 | 1 | .327 | .408 |
| | Binghamton (EL) | AA | .271 | 70 | 236 | 44 | 64 | 16 | 1 | 11 | 33 | 46 | 57 | 2 | .414 | .487 |

| Year | Club (League) | Class | AVG | G | AB | R | H | 2B | 3B | HR | RBI | BB | SO | SB | OBP | SLG |
|---|---|---|---|---|---|---|---|---|---|---|---|---|---|---|---|---|
| 2004 | Norfolk (IL) | AAA | .313 | 5 | 16 | 3 | 5 | 2 | 0 | 0 | 3 | 3 | 3 | 0 | .421 | .438 |
| 2005 | Wichita (TL) | AA | .343 | 88 | 335 | 68 | 115 | 22 | 3 | 16 | 74 | 51 | 70 | 7 | .432 | .570 |
| | Omaha (PCL) | AAA | .274 | 32 | 113 | 19 | 31 | 6 | 1 | 7 | 23 | 16 | 33 | 3 | .374 | .531 |
| | Kansas City (AL) | MLB | .218 | 25 | 78 | 6 | 17 | 3 | 0 | 0 | 6 | 5 | 20 | 0 | .271 | .256 |
| 2006 | Kansas City (AL) | MLB | .200 | 5 | 10 | 1 | 2 | 1 | 0 | 0 | 1 | 1 | 4 | 1 | .273 | .300 |
| | Omaha (PCL) | AAA | .278 | 100 | 352 | 47 | 98 | 22 | 2 | 15 | 44 | 40 | 94 | 2 | .358 | .480 |
| **MINOR LEAGUE TOTALS** | | | .289 | 589 | 2081 | 321 | 601 | 133 | 11 | 87 | 381 | 270 | 496 | 21 | .389 | .489 |
| **MAJOR LEAGUE TOTALS** | | | .216 | 30 | 88 | 7 | 19 | 4 | 0 | 0 | 7 | 6 | 24 | 1 | .271 | .261 |

## 9 BILLY BUCKNER RHP

STEVE MOORE

**Born:** Aug. 27, 1983. **B-T:** R-R. **Ht.:** 6-2. **Wt.:** 210. **Drafted:** South Carolina, 2004 (2nd round). **Signed by:** Spencer Graham.

Lefthander Matt Campbell, a 2004 first-rounder, hasn't pitched since tearing his labrum in mid-2005. But his former college teammate Buckner, a second-rounder in 2004, has acquitted himself quite well. He allowed only one run in his final 21 innings in 2006, including a playoff victory. His father (not the former big league batting champion of the same name) taught Buckner how to throw a knuckle-curve as a kid. It has a devastating 12-to-6 spike and is a strikeout pitch. His fastball sits in the low 90s with natural sink that creates groundballs. Buckner needs better command across the board. He refuses to give in to hitters and walks too many hitters in an attempt to be too fine. The Royals don't want to take away his aggressive nature, but they would like him to do a better job of channeling his emotions while trusting his fastball more. His changeup can be an average pitch but needs more work. Kansas City sees him as a reliable starter with some upside if he can improve his command. He is set to begin 2007 in Triple-A Omaha.

| Year | Club (League) | Class | W | L | ERA | G | GS | CG | SV | IP | H | R | ER | HR | BB | SO | AVG |
|---|---|---|---|---|---|---|---|---|---|---|---|---|---|---|---|---|---|
| 2004 | Idaho Falls (Pio) | R | 2 | 1 | 3.30 | 7 | 5 | 0 | 0 | 30 | 36 | 14 | 11 | 4 | 4 | 37 | .303 |
| 2005 | Burlington (MWL) | A | 3 | 7 | 3.88 | 11 | 11 | 0 | 0 | 60 | 66 | 36 | 26 | 9 | 17 | 60 | .268 |
| | High Desert (Cal) | A | 5 | 6 | 5.36 | 17 | 17 | 0 | 0 | 94 | 105 | 65 | 56 | 10 | 46 | 92 | .285 |
| 2006 | High Desert (Cal) | A | 7 | 1 | 3.90 | 16 | 16 | 0 | 0 | 90 | 92 | 44 | 39 | 6 | 47 | 85 | .271 |
| | Wichita (TL) | AA | 5 | 3 | 4.64 | 13 | 13 | 0 | 0 | 76 | 78 | 40 | 39 | 7 | 39 | 63 | .265 |
| **MINOR LEAGUE TOTALS** | | | 22 | 18 | 4.40 | 64 | 62 | 0 | 0 | 350 | 377 | 199 | 171 | 36 | 153 | 337 | .276 |

## 10 BRENT FISHER LHP

BILL MITCHELL

**Born:** Aug. 6, 1987. **B-T:** L-L. **Ht.:** 6-2. **Wt.:** 190. **Drafted:** HS—Goodyear, Ariz., 2005 (7th round). **Signed by:** Mike Brown.

Fisher did not draw much attention as an amateur because his fastball wasn't overpowering, but he has done nothing but dominate as a pro. He repeated the Rookie-level Arizona League in 2006 and easily won the strikeout crown. He led all starters in short-season leagues in whiffs per nine innings (13.3) and finished second in opponent average (.169). Because of the remarkable deception on his 88-91 mph fastball, Fisher's Rookie-level Idaho Falls teammates took to calling it the "Invisi-ball." He gets swings and misses with his fastball by hiding it behind a compact arm action. He also throw a curveball that he can spot for strikes and backdoor righthanders with. Fisher has a feel for a changeup, but he doesn't throw it often because he has been able to dominate Rookie ball with just his fastball and curve. The Royals want him to throw the change more as he'll need it at higher levels. His fringe-average velocity may not play as well against more advanced hitters. Still just 19, Fisher offers plenty of projection and could add velocity. He'll head to low Class A Burlington in 2007 and offers as much upside of any pitcher in the lower levels of the system.

| Year | Club (League) | Class | W | L | ERA | G | GS | CG | SV | IP | H | R | ER | HR | BB | SO | AVG |
|---|---|---|---|---|---|---|---|---|---|---|---|---|---|---|---|---|---|
| 2005 | Royals (AZL) | R | 5 | 2 | 3.04 | 13 | 8 | 0 | 1 | 50 | 48 | 20 | 17 | 2 | 13 | 69 | .249 |
| 2006 | Royals (AZL) | R | 3 | 1 | 2.11 | 14 | 14 | 0 | 0 | 68 | 41 | 18 | 16 | 2 | 19 | 98 | .171 |
| | Idaho Falls (Pio) | R | 0 | 0 | 2.25 | 1 | 0 | 0 | 1 | 4 | 2 | 1 | 1 | 1 | 0 | 9 | .143 |
| **MINOR LEAGUE TOTALS** | | | 8 | 3 | 2.49 | 28 | 22 | 0 | 2 | 123 | 91 | 39 | 34 | 5 | 32 | 176 | .204 |

## 11 JEFF BIANCHI SS

**Born:** Oct. 5, 1986. **B-T:** R-R. **Ht.:** 6-0. **Wt.:** 175. **Drafted:** HS—Lampeter, Pa., 2005 (2nd round). **Signed by:** Sean Rooney.

No player has caused more frustration in the system then Bianchi, who has hit .414 but hasn't gotten past the Arizona League because he has been plagued by injuries since signing as a second-rounder in 2005. He caught the Royals' eye when they viewed a Major League Scouting Bureau video that one scout said displayed the best hitting approach he ever had seen from a high school player. But his pro debut was shortened by a lower back strain and his 2006 sea-

son ended early when he required surgery on the labrum in his right shoulder. Bianchi has a short, quick swing that allows him to use the entire field while showing average power. He works counts and doesn't chase bad pitches. His best pure tool is his well above-average speed, and he profiles as a leadoff hitter. Bianchi's shoulder operation might lead to a future switch to second base because his arm already was a question at shortstop, but he has the hands and feet to stay in the middle infield. The Royals see some Michael Young in Bianchi and are anxious to find out what he can do with a full-season assignment to low Class A this year.

| Year | Club (League) | Class | AVG | G | AB | R | H | 2B | 3B | HR | RBI | BB | SO | SB | OBP | SLG |
|------|---------------|-------|-----|---|-----|----|----|----|----|----|-----|----|----|----|------|------|
| 2005 | Royals (AZL) | R | .408 | 28 | 98 | 29 | 40 | 7 | 4 | 6 | 30 | 16 | 22 | 5 | .484 | .745 |
| 2006 | Royals (AZL) | R | .429 | 12 | 42 | 13 | 18 | 4 | 0 | 2 | 6 | 9 | 3 | 1 | .537 | .667 |
| **MINOR LEAGUE TOTALS** | | | .414 | 40 | 140 | 42 | 58 | 11 | 4 | 8 | 36 | 25 | 25 | 6 | .500 | .721 |

## 12 RYAN BRAUN                                                        RHP

**Born:** July 29, 1980. **B-T:** R-R. **Ht.:** 6-1. **Wt.:** 215. **Drafted:** Nevada-Las Vegas, 2003 (6th round). **Signed by:** Mike Brown.

In an attempt to save money in the 2003 draft, the Royals drafted college seniors in rounds five through nine and signed them for $1,000 each. Braun has turned out to be the most promising of the bunch. The power reliever features a fastball that he can dial up to 96 mph to go with an 88-90 mph slider and an 85-87 mph curveball. His curve is more of a strikeout pitch than his slider because of its greater velocity differential from his fastball. He also has a changeup that he throws infrequently. Braun got knocked around in his big league debut last year, when he learned that major leaguers aren't going to be intimidated by sheer power. He'll have to improve his control and command in order to succeed at the highest level after relying mostly on throwing the ball by minor leaguers. Braun had Tommy John surgery in college in 1998 and missed most of the 2005 season following shoulder surgery, but was healthy throughout last season. He operates with a maximum-effort delivery, not the best prescription for throwing quality strikes and staying healthy.

| Year | Club (League) | Class | W | L | ERA | G | GS | CG | SV | IP | H | R | ER | HR | BB | SO | AVG |
|------|---------------|-------|---|---|------|----|----|----|----|-----|-----|----|----|----|----|-----|------|
| 2003 | Royals 1 (AZL) | R | 0 | 0 | 2.95 | 18 | 0 | 0 | 3 | 21 | 15 | 9 | 7 | 0 | 10 | 25 | .185 |
| 2004 | Wilmington (CL) | A | 2 | 3 | 2.21 | 51 | 0 | 0 | 23 | 57 | 48 | 25 | 14 | 2 | 25 | 58 | .219 |
| 2005 | Wichita (TL) | AA | 0 | 1 | 17.36 | 6 | 0 | 0 | 0 | 5 | 15 | 10 | 9 | 0 | 7 | 1 | .536 |
| | High Desert (Cal) | A | 1 | 0 | 4.50 | 2 | 0 | 0 | 0 | 4 | 3 | 2 | 2 | 0 | 2 | 6 | .214 |
| 2006 | Wichita (TL) | AA | 1 | 6 | 2.21 | 26 | 0 | 0 | 10 | 41 | 30 | 11 | 10 | 2 | 16 | 58 | .204 |
| | Omaha (PCL) | AAA | 0 | 2 | 2.16 | 17 | 0 | 0 | 3 | 25 | 23 | 9 | 6 | 0 | 13 | 22 | .247 |
| | Kansas City (AL) | MLB | 0 | 1 | 6.75 | 9 | 0 | 0 | 0 | 11 | 13 | 8 | 8 | 2 | 3 | 6 | .317 |
| **MINOR LEAGUE TOTALS** | | | 4 | 12 | 2.83 | 120 | 0 | 0 | 39 | 153 | 134 | 66 | 48 | 4 | 73 | 170 | .230 |
| **MAJOR LEAGUE TOTALS** | | | 0 | 1 | 6.75 | 9 | 0 | 0 | 0 | 10 | 13 | 8 | 8 | 2 | 3 | 6 | .317 |

## 13 JOAKIM SORIA                                                     RHP

**Born:** May 18, 1984. **B-T:** R-R. **Ht.:** 6-3. **Wt.:** 185. **Signed:** Mexico, 2001. **Signed by:** Mike Brito (Dodgers).

Several teams were interested in trading up to get Soria in the major league Rule 5 draft at the 2006 Winter Meetings, but the Royals held onto the No. 2 overall pick and claimed him for themselves. Having pitched just 16⅔ innings in the United States since the Dodgers signed him as a 17-year-old in 2001, he was tough to evaluate. He missed all of 2003 recovering from Tommy John surgery, got released in 2004 and spent most of the last two seasons pitching in the Mexican League. The Padres bought his contract from the Mexico City Red Devils in December 2005, then loaned him back to the club in 2006. Soria generated buzz by going 8-0, 2.02 in the winter Mexican Pacific League before the Rule 5 draft. He works off an 89-93 mph fastball with late movement, and he can locate it to both sides of the plate. He also flashes a plus changeup and keeps both pitches down in the strike zone. His curveball is average, though he'll sometimes fly open in his mechanics and leaves it up. Soria, who threw a perfect game in his first outing after Kansas City selected him, has to stay on the major league roster throughout 2007, or else clear waivers and be offered back to San Diego for half his $50,000 draft price. That shouldn't be an issue, and he should stick with the Royals as a swingman.

| Year | Club (League) | Class | W | L | ERA | G | GS | CG | SV | IP | H | R | ER | HR | BB | SO | AVG |
|------|---------------|-------|---|---|------|----|----|----|----|-----|-----|----|----|----|----|-----|------|
| 2002 | Dodgers (DSL) | R | 3 | 2 | 2.01 | 9 | 8 | 0 | 0 | 45 | 38 | 15 | 10 | 0 | 7 | 62 | .216 |
| | Dodgers (GCL) | R | 0 | 0 | 3.60 | 4 | 0 | 0 | 0 | 5 | 6 | 2 | 2 | 0 | 0 | 6 | .286 |
| 2003 | Did not play—Injured | | | | | | | | | | | | | | | | |
| 2004 | Dodgers (DSL) | R | 0 | 0 | 1.69 | 4 | 0 | 0 | 1 | 5 | 3 | 1 | 1 | 0 | 5 | 4 | .158 |
| 2005 | Mexico (Mex) | AAA | 5 | 0 | 4.48 | 30 | 5 | 0 | 0 | 66 | 75 | 34 | 33 | 7 | 31 | 60 | .288 |
| 2006 | Mexico (Mex) | AAA | 0 | 0 | 3.89 | 39 | 0 | 0 | 15 | 37 | 37 | 16 | 16 | 2 | 11 | 30 | .255 |
| | Fort Wayne (MWL) | A | 1 | 0 | 2.31 | 7 | 0 | 0 | 0 | 12 | 5 | 3 | 3 | 1 | 2 | 11 | .132 |
| **MINOR LEAGUE TOTALS** | | | 9 | 2 | 3.44 | 93 | 13 | 0 | 16 | 170 | 164 | 71 | 64 | 10 | 56 | 173 | .249 |

## 14 BLAKE WOOD RHP

**Born:** Aug. 8, 1985. **B-T:** R-R. **Ht.:** 6-4. **Wt.:** 225. **Drafted:** Georgia Tech, 2006 (3rd round). **Signed by:** Spencer Graham.

Wood went 10-1, 3.13 as a Georgia Tech sophomore before slumping to an 11-4, 4.79 mark as a junior last spring. The Royals thought he was better than a third-round talent and gladly took him there and signed him for $460,000. Once he recovered from shin splints that bothered him in college and made some progress with his delivery, Wood threw his lively fastball at 93-95 mph in his pro debut. He also has a changeup with good action down in the strike zone. Wood's biggest problem is inconsistent mechanics. He'll lower his arm slot while landing on a stiff front side, causing his pitches to stay up in the zone as he flies off the mound in his finish. It also leads to his curveball flattening out. Wood went to instructional league with a focus on improving his direction to the plate and incorporating his lower half more. The Royals love his arm strength and raw stuff and see a lot of upside once he smoothes out his delivery. A good spring training could mean he skips low Class A.

| Year | Club (League) | Class | W | L | ERA | G | GS | CG | SV | IP | H | R | ER | HR | BB | SO | AVG |
|------|---------------|-------|---|---|-----|---|----|----|----|----|---|---|----|----|----|----|-----|
| 2006 | Idaho Falls (Pio) | R | 3 | 1 | 4.50 | 12 | 12 | 0 | 0 | 52 | 50 | 28 | 26 | 1 | 15 | 46 | .258 |
| **MINOR LEAGUE TOTALS** | | | 3 | 1 | 4.50 | 12 | 12 | 0 | 0 | 52 | 50 | 28 | 26 | 1 | 15 | 46 | .258 |

## 15 ERIK CORDIER RHP

**Born:** Feb. 25, 1986. **B-T:** R-R. **Ht.:** 6-3. **Wt.:** 214. **Drafted:** HS—Sturgeon Bay, Wis., 2004 (2nd round). **Signed by:** Phil Huttman.

The highest drafted player out of Wisconsin since the Angels selected Jarrod Washburn 31st overall in 1995, Cordier missed 2005 while recovering from knee surgery. He came back strong in mid-June before elbow problems shut him down again two months later. The Royals hoped he could avoid surgery, but he had Tommy John in the fall. Cordier's fastball, which sits at 92-95 mph and tops out at 98, is the best in the system. It has good arm-side run and he can pound it in on righthanders to get groundballs. He also has advanced feel for a plus changeup. Though he'll flash a plus breaking ball, Cordier's release point varies and often leaves him with a slurve. He's still trying to figure out if he should throw a curveball or a slider. The Royals prefer their pitchers first try to develop a curve, so he likely will go that route. With his latest surgery, his health is an obvious concern and has limited him to 87 innings in 2½ pro seasons. Patience will be required as he comes back from surgery, but his arm strength is rare and the Royals think his upside rivals Hochevar's because of his potential for three plus pitches. He won't pitch again until 2008.

| Year | Club (League) | Class | W | L | ERA | G | GS | CG | SV | IP | H | R | ER | HR | BB | SO | AVG |
|------|---------------|-------|---|---|-----|---|----|----|----|----|---|---|----|----|----|----|-----|
| 2004 | Royals (AZL) | R | 2 | 4 | 5.19 | 11 | 11 | 0 | 0 | 35 | 38 | 27 | 20 | 1 | 21 | 22 | .279 |
| 2005 | Did not play—Injured | | | | | | | | | | | | | | | | |
| 2006 | Idaho Falls (Pio) | R | 1 | 0 | 3.38 | 3 | 3 | 0 | 0 | 16 | 11 | 6 | 6 | 0 | 3 | 19 | .186 |
| | Burlington (MWL) | A | 3 | 1 | 2.70 | 7 | 7 | 0 | 0 | 37 | 27 | 17 | 11 | 3 | 14 | 23 | .203 |
| **MINOR LEAGUE TOTALS** | | | 6 | 5 | 3.81 | 21 | 21 | 0 | 0 | 87 | 76 | 50 | 37 | 4 | 38 | 64 | .232 |

## 16 JASON TAYLOR 3B

**Born:** Jan. 14, 1988. **B-T:** R-R. **Ht.:** 6-0. **Wt.:** 210. **Drafted:** HS—Virginia Beach, 2006 (2nd round). **Signed by:** Steve Connelly.

No one was more surprised that he was a second-round pick last June than Taylor himself. Given the impression he would last until at least the fifth round, he was hanging out with friends when he got a telephone call telling him he was the first pick of the second round. He turned down Clemson to sign with the Royals for $762,500. He lost the chance for some exposure when a broken arm kept him out of most of the summer showcases, but he did hit .316 for the U.S. junior national team. Some scouts likened his athleticism to that of Justin Upton, a fellow Virginia high school product and the No. 1 overall pick in 2005. Taylor has good hand-eye coordination and can drive the ball to all fields. He shows plus raw power but has more of a line-drive stroke. He should hit more homers as he learns to incorporate his lower half into his swing more often. His approach and plate discipline are well beyond those of most teenagers, though he's still learning to adjust to the better off-speed pitches he'll see in pro ball. A shortstop in high school, Taylor lacked the range to play there as a pro and moved to third base. He arm and hands are both above average, and he runs well. Because he's now at the hot corner, more will be expected of his bat. He'll be tested in low Class A this year.

| Year | Club (League) | Class | AVG | G | AB | R | H | 2B | 3B | HR | RBI | BB | SO | SB | OBP | SLG |
|------|---------------|-------|-----|---|----|---|---|----|----|----|-----|----|----|----|-----|-----|
| 2006 | Royals (AZL) | R | .258 | 46 | 151 | 27 | 39 | 8 | 1 | 0 | 22 | 26 | 30 | 7 | .374 | .325 |
| **MINOR LEAGUE TOTALS** | | | .258 | 46 | 151 | 27 | 39 | 8 | 1 | 0 | 22 | 26 | 30 | 7 | .374 | .325 |

## 17 BLAKE JOHNSON RHP

**Born:** June 14, 1985. **B-T:** R-R. **Ht.:** 6-3. **Wt.:** 185. **Drafted:** HS—Baton Rouge, 2004 (2nd round). **Signed by:** Clarence Johns (Dodgers).

Johnson established himself as a potential first-round pick with a dominant performance at the 2003 Area Code Games, but he slumped as a high school senior and went to the Dodgers in the second round in 2004. He has had an up-and-down pro career, struggling in his pro debut, having a fine first full season and then getting knocked around in two high Class A leagues last year. Los Angeles traded him, Odalis Perez and Julio Pimentel to acquire Elmer Dessens last July. Johnson has a lean, wiry frame and gets good downward plane on an average 89-92 mph fastball that he throws for strikes, albeit without pinpoint command. He uses it to set up a mid-70s curveball that has good downward bite and serves as his out pitch. He also features a developing changeup with nice action. Johnson is very laid back but shows some aggressiveness when he gets into jams. Kansas City wants to see him come out of his shell and show more ferocity. His command is average but he has clean mechanics, so it should improve with experience. Johnson pitched in two hitter-friendly home parks in 2006, so his performance wasn't as rough as his statistics might suggest. Nevertheless, he may have to repeat high Class A at the Royals' new Wilmington affiliate.

| Year | Club (League) | Class | W | L | ERA | G | GS | CG | SV | IP | H | R | ER | HR | BB | SO | AVG |
|------|---------------|-------|---|---|-----|---|----|----|----|----|---|---|----|----|----|----|-----|
| 2004 | Ogden (Pio) | R | 3 | 3 | 6.47 | 13 | 12 | 0 | 0 | 57 | 73 | 46 | 41 | 5 | 19 | 57 | .324 |
| 2005 | Columbus (SAL) | A | 9 | 4 | 3.33 | 24 | 17 | 1 | 0 | 100 | 83 | 47 | 37 | 4 | 36 | 88 | .226 |
| 2006 | Vero Beach (FSL) | A | 4 | 5 | 4.92 | 20 | 18 | 0 | 0 | 106 | 121 | 70 | 58 | 11 | 19 | 73 | .285 |
| | High Desert (Cal) | A | 1 | 1 | 5.73 | 3 | 2 | 0 | 0 | 11 | 15 | 7 | 7 | 1 | 0 | 9 | .319 |
| **MINOR LEAGUE TOTALS** | | | 17 | 13 | 4.70 | 60 | 49 | 1 | 0 | 274 | 292 | 170 | 143 | 21 | 74 | 227 | .275 |

## 18 JULIO PIMENTEL RHP

**Born:** Dec. 14, 1985. **B-T:** R-R. **Ht.:** 6-1. **Wt.:** 185. **Signed:** Dominican Republic, 2003. **Signed by:** Pablo Peguero/Angel Santana (Dodgers).

Another piece of the Elmer Dessens deal, Pimentel originally signed as an outfielder. He wasn't hitting well at the Dodgers' Dominican academy, so they put him on the mound and he quickly took to the conversion. With a lean, athletic frame, Pimentel pitches at 91-92 mph with his fastball and touches 95. He also features a hard breaking ball that he throws at 83-84 mph. It's a curveball-slider hybrid with short, tight break. His changeup sits at 85-86 mph and is a little on the hard side relative to his fastball, but it bottoms out nicely. Command is his biggest shortcoming. Pimentel has a tendency to land on the outside of his left foot, and will spin off to the first-base side of his mound. The Royals are trying to get him to land on his toe consistently, which will improve the command of all of his pitches. His inconsistent mechanics may limit him to the bullpen, and Los Angeles moved him there last May. He continued in relief after the trade, but Kansas City believes he still has a chance to be a starter. He'll open 2007 in the Double-A rotation.

| Year | Club (League) | Class | W | L | ERA | G | GS | CG | SV | IP | H | R | ER | HR | BB | SO | AVG |
|------|---------------|-------|---|---|-----|---|----|----|----|----|---|---|----|----|----|----|-----|
| 2003 | Dodgers (DSL) | R | 1 | 1 | 4.09 | 8 | 3 | 0 | 0 | 22 | 17 | 12 | 10 | 1 | 13 | 24 | .221 |
| 2004 | Columbus (SAL) | A | 10 | 8 | 3.48 | 23 | 23 | 2 | 0 | 111 | 106 | 56 | 43 | 14 | 47 | 102 | .260 |
| 2005 | Vero Beach (FSL) | A | 8 | 10 | 5.08 | 26 | 24 | 1 | 0 | 124 | 149 | 79 | 70 | 9 | 43 | 105 | .305 |
| 2006 | Vero Beach (FSL) | A | 3 | 8 | 5.69 | 30 | 9 | 0 | 2 | 74 | 85 | 56 | 47 | 4 | 45 | 77 | .290 |
| | High Desert (Cal) | A | 2 | 1 | 3.18 | 12 | 0 | 0 | 2 | 23 | 21 | 8 | 8 | 3 | 10 | 26 | .244 |
| **MINOR LEAGUE TOTALS** | | | 24 | 28 | 4.52 | 99 | 59 | 3 | 4 | 354 | 378 | 211 | 178 | 31 | 158 | 334 | .280 |

## 19 CARLOS ROSA RHP

**Born:** Sept. 21, 1984. **B-T:** R-R. **Ht.:** 6-1. **Wt.:** 185. **Signed:** Dominican Republic, 2001. **Signed by:** Luis Silverio.

Rosa missed all of 2005 recovering from Tommy John surgery, but rebounded to finish fourth in the low Class A Midwest League in ERA and win the organization's minor league pitcher of the year award. Rosa features a lively fastball with late arm-side run that sits at 92 mph. He never was comfortable with a conventional circle changeup before his elbow reconstruction, so the Royals taught him a fosh changeup that's now his second-best pitch. He maintains his fastball arm speed when he throws the fosh, which arrives at 84-85 mph and has excellent late sink. His slider is a fringy third pitch. Under new general manager Dayton Moore, Kansas City now emphasizes curveballs over sliders, but pitchers like Rosa who used a slider as their only breaking pitch were allowed to continue doing so. The Royals have also smoothed out his delivery since surgery and have him landing on his toe, as opposed to his heel, and that has improved all of his offerings. Rosa will take the next step up to high Class A this year.

| Year | Club (League) | Class | W | L | ERA | G | GS | CG | SV | IP | H | R | ER | HR | BB | SO | AVG |
|------|---------------|-------|---|---|-----|---|----|----|----|----|---|---|----|----|----|----|-----|
| 2002 | Royals (GCL) | R | 0 | 4 | 6.19 | 10 | 9 | 0 | 0 | 32 | 52 | 32 | 22 | 3 | 12 | 11 | .361 |
| | Kansas City (DSL) | R | 1 | 0 | 1.80 | 1 | 1 | 0 | 0 | 5 | 3 | 1 | 1 | 0 | 0 | 2 | .167 |
| 2003 | Royals 1 (AZL) | R | 5 | 3 | 3.63 | 15 | 11 | 0 | 0 | 69 | 79 | 36 | 28 | 4 | 18 | 54 | .288 |
| 2004 | Royals (AZL) | R | 0 | 0 | 4.91 | 4 | 4 | 0 | 0 | 11 | 14 | 6 | 6 | 1 | 9 | 8 | .326 |
| | Burlington (MWL) | A | 0 | 5 | 4.67 | 8 | 8 | 0 | 0 | 35 | 41 | 24 | 18 | 1 | 17 | 23 | .297 |
| 2005 | Did not play—Inujured | | | | | | | | | | | | | | | | |
| 2006 | Burlington (MWL) | A | 8 | 6 | 2.53 | 24 | 24 | 1 | 0 | 139 | 121 | 50 | 39 | 6 | 54 | 102 | .239 |
| | High Desert (Cal) | A | 0 | 1 | 7.15 | 3 | 3 | 0 | 0 | 11 | 20 | 12 | 9 | 1 | 4 | 13 | .392 |
| **MINOR LEAGUE TOTALS** | | | 14 | 19 | 3.67 | 65 | 60 | 1 | 0 | 302 | 330 | 161 | 123 | 16 | 114 | 213 | .281 |

## LUIS COTA

RHP

**Born:** Aug. 18, 1985. **B-T:** R-R. **Ht.:** 6-2. **Wt.:** 200. **Drafted:** South Mountain (Ariz.) CC, D/F 2003 (10th round). **Signed by:** Mike Brown.

Cota played mostly shortstop in high school and the Royals took a chance on his arm strength in the 10th round in 2003. The move paid off as he was named Arizona's junior college player of the year the following spring and signed as a draft-and-follow for $1.05 million, a record for a 10th-rounder. Cota has gone just 12-20, 5.52 as a pro and had a career-worst 7.09 ERA last year. While high Class A High Desert and the California League as a whole are extremely hitter-friendly, that can't be blamed for all of his struggles. His command is erratic and he leaves too many balls up in the zone. Cota does have strikeout stuff and just needs to learn how to harness it. He possesses one of the best arms in the system as his fastball touches 95 mph and he sits at 91-92 mph with ease. His slider came on as the season progressed but is still too erratic. It's a mid-80s breaker with slight downward bite when he stays on top of it. While the slider has more potential, he currently gets more out of his changeup because he keeps it down in the zone. Cota's ceiling is as high as any pitcher's in the system. Because the Royals have shifted their high Class A affiliate from High Desert to Wilmington, which favors pitchers, he'll likely repeat the level in 2007.

| Year | Club (League) | Class | W | L | ERA | G | GS | CG | SV | IP | H | R | ER | HR | BB | SO | AVG |
|------|---------------|-------|---|---|-----|---|----|----|----|----|---|---|----|----|----|----|-----|
| 2004 | Idaho Falls (Pio) | R | 2 | 1 | 5.81 | 14 | 12 | 0 | 0 | 48 | 61 | 37 | 31 | 5 | 21 | 40 | .313 |
| 2005 | Burlington (MWL) | A | 5 | 8 | 4.01 | 26 | 26 | 0 | 0 | 148 | 143 | 75 | 66 | 10 | 63 | 137 | .253 |
| 2006 | High Desert (Cal) | A | 5 | 11 | 7.09 | 27 | 26 | 0 | 0 | 132 | 153 | 113 | 104 | 19 | 63 | 126 | .290 |
| **MINOR LEAGUE TOTALS** | | | 12 | 20 | 5.52 | 67 | 64 | 0 | 0 | 328 | 357 | 225 | 201 | 34 | 147 | 303 | .277 |

## DERRICK ROBINSON

OF

**Born:** Sept. 28, 1987. **B-T:** B-L. **Ht.:** 5-11. **Wt.:** 170. **Drafted:** HS—Gainesville, Fla., 2006 (4th round). **Signed by:** Cliff Pastornicky.

Robinson had scouts salivating in the summer of 2005, when he was clocked running a 6.19-second 60-yard dash on the showcase circuit. Though he committed to Florida as a cornerback in football, he told scouts he wanted to play baseball and signed with the Royals for $850,000, easily the highest bonus in the fourth round last year. Robinson's rare speed plays better on defense than on the bases at this point. He easily tracks balls and has nifty instincts in center field, but he was caught in 14 of his 34 steal attempts as a pro. Opponents knew he planned on running nearly every time he reached base in order to work on his basestealing skills, which made it tough to run. The question mark with Robinson is his bat. A natural righthanded hitter, he struggled horribly from the left side in his pro debut, hitting just .194 with 52 strikeouts in 134 at-bats. He has some strength and bat speed, but he needs a smoother stroke and better plate discipline. His speed will be wasted if he can't consistently make contact and get on base. His arm is below average. Robinson's is a project and Kansas City will be patient in trying to mold him into a leadoff hitter. He likely will open 2007 in low Class A.

| Year | Club (League) | Class | AVG | G | AB | R | H | 2B | 3B | HR | RBI | BB | SO | SB | OBP | SLG |
|------|---------------|-------|-----|---|----|---|---|----|----|----|-----|----|----|----|-----|-----|
| 2006 | Royals (AZL) | R | .233 | 54 | 176 | 25 | 41 | 6 | 3 | 1 | 24 | 24 | 55 | 20 | .335 | .318 |
| **MINOR LEAGUE TOTALS** | | | .233 | 54 | 176 | 25 | 41 | 6 | 3 | 1 | 24 | 24 | 55 | 20 | .335 | .318 |

## CHRIS NICOLL

RHP

**Born:** Oct. 30, 1983. **B-T:** R-R. **Ht.:** 6-2. **Wt.:** 190. **Drafted:** UC Irvine, 2005 (3rd round). **Signed by:** John Ramey.

The Royals may have hit on back-to-back college righthanders in the third round, taking Nicoll in 2005 and Blake Wood last year. Kansas City liked Nicoll's strong performance in the Cape Cod League in 2004 and at UC Irvine the following spring, and it has carried over into pro ball. Prior to last season Nicoll didn't have a standout pitch, but his slider has improved drastically and is now his best offering. He throws it with short, tight rotation at around 83 mph, though he has yet to master full command of it. Kansas City has moved him from the first-base side of the rubber to the third-base side to improve the angle on his slider against

righthanders. His darting fastball sits at 88-90 mph and he locates it well on both sides of the plate. Nicoll tends to pitch too much off of his slider and also needs to incorporate his change-up more. He earned a late-season promotion to high Class A and could begin 2007 there.

| Year | Club (League) | Class | W | L | ERA | G | GS | CG | SV | IP | H | R | ER | HR | BB | SO | AVG |
|------|---------------|-------|---|---|-----|---|----|----|----|-----|-----|----|----|----|----|-----|------|
| 2005 | Idaho Falls (Pio) | R | 0 | 3 | 3.62 | 7 | 7 | 0 | 0 | 27 | 26 | 14 | 11 | 4 | 9 | 34 | .250 |
| 2006 | Burlington (MWL) | A | 4 | 9 | 2.82 | 23 | 23 | 0 | 0 | 134 | 105 | 49 | 42 | 13 | 40 | 140 | .210 |
| | High Desert (Cal) | A | 2 | 0 | 4.86 | 3 | 3 | 0 | 0 | 17 | 17 | 11 | 9 | 3 | 6 | 26 | .258 |
| **MINOR LEAGUE TOTALS** | | | 6 | 12 | 3.13 | 33 | 33 | 0 | 0 | 178 | 148 | 74 | 62 | 20 | 55 | 200 | .221 |

## JAROD PLUMMER                                     RHP

**Born:** Jan. 27, 1984. **B-T:** R-R. **Ht.:** 6-5. **Wt.:** 200. **Drafted:** HS—South Garland, Texas, 2002 (26th round). **Signed by:** Mike Leuzinger (Dodgers).

Acquired from the Dodgers for shortstop Wilson Valdez in March, Plummer quietly put together on of the best seasons by any pitcher in the system. The organization's High Desert pitcher of the year, he reached double figures in both wins and saves as a swingman. Plummer's strong suit is his ability to command his 88-92 mph fastball, which looks deceptively fast because of his slightly unorthodox delivery. His arm action is long in back but whiplike coming forward, and it throws hitters off without affecting his ability to throw strikes. Plummer pitches mostly off of his fastball. He picks up some strikeouts by burying his 80-82 splitter in the dirt once he gets ahead in the count. His curveball, a big, looping breaker that he throws in the mid-70s, is mostly for show. Plummer spent the offseason in the Hawaiian Winter League and will open in Double-A this year. His fastball command should allow him to reach the big leagues if he can get a little more out of his secondary stuff.

| Year | Club (League) | Class | W | L | ERA | G | GS | CG | SV | IP | H | R | ER | HR | BB | SO | AVG |
|------|---------------|-------|---|---|-----|---|----|----|----|-----|-----|-----|-----|----|----|-----|------|
| 2002 | Dodgers (GCL) | R | 2 | 2 | 2.94 | 16 | 2 | 0 | 0 | 34 | 28 | 17 | 11 | 0 | 7 | 41 | .220 |
| | Great Falls (Pio) | R | 1 | 0 | 0.00 | 1 | 0 | 0 | 0 | 2 | 1 | 0 | 0 | 0 | 1 | 1 | .125 |
| 2003 | Dodgers (GCL) | R | 0 | 0 | 2.25 | 2 | 2 | 0 | 0 | 4 | 3 | 2 | 1 | 0 | 1 | 4 | .200 |
| | South Georgia (SAL) | A | 1 | 2 | 4.34 | 9 | 0 | 0 | 2 | 19 | 12 | 10 | 9 | 2 | 10 | 21 | .188 |
| 2004 | Columbus (SAL) | A | 2 | 1 | 2.45 | 4 | 4 | 0 | 0 | 22 | 13 | 8 | 6 | 4 | 5 | 23 | .167 |
| | Vero Beach (FSL) | A | 4 | 4 | 3.86 | 11 | 11 | 0 | 0 | 63 | 65 | 29 | 27 | 8 | 14 | 49 | .270 |
| 2005 | Dodgers (GCL) | R | 0 | 0 | 4.50 | 1 | 1 | 0 | 0 | 4 | 4 | 2 | 2 | 0 | 0 | 2 | .267 |
| | Columbus (SAL) | A | 3 | 2 | 4.14 | 9 | 8 | 0 | 0 | 54 | 52 | 27 | 25 | 5 | 6 | 49 | .244 |
| | Vero Beach (FSL) | A | 1 | 1 | 3.20 | 9 | 1 | 0 | 0 | 25 | 22 | 9 | 9 | 1 | 7 | 23 | .239 |
| 2006 | High Desert (Cal) | A | 11 | 5 | 4.05 | 39 | 6 | 0 | 10 | 96 | 92 | 50 | 43 | 11 | 20 | 114 | .249 |
| | Wichita (TL) | AA | 1 | 0 | 0.00 | 1 | 0 | 0 | 0 | 2 | 1 | 0 | 0 | 0 | 2 | 3 | .143 |
| **MINOR LEAGUE TOTALS** | | | 26 | 17 | 3.69 | 102 | 35 | 0 | 12 | 325 | 293 | 154 | 133 | 31 | 73 | 330 | .238 |

## DANNY CHRISTENSEN                                  LHP

**Born:** Aug. 10, 1983. **B-T:** L-L. **Ht.:** 6-1. **Wt.:** 205. **Drafted:** HS—Brooklyn, 2002 (4th round). **Signed by:** Steve Connelly.

Christensen came out of Brooklyn's Xaverian High, the same school as Rich Aurilia and Orioles 2006 supplemental first-rounder Pedro Beato. He showed up in spring training out of shape for his first full pro season in 2003 and went 1-12, then made just one start in 2004 before needing Tommy John surgery. Christensen has put himself back on the prospect map the last two years. Though not overpowering, he succeeds with an excellent feel for pitching and above-average command of an 85-89 mph fastball. He wasn't afraid to attack the strike zone despite the favorable hitting conditions he faced at High Desert and in the California League. He also flashes an average curveball and a plus changeup that's effective against righthanders with it's down-and-away life. Command is typically the last thing that comes back after Tommy John surgery, and Christensen still is working on locating his secondary pitches. That will be key for him, as his fastball velocity offers little margin for error. After surviving High Desert, he'll begin this season in Double-A.

| Year | Club (League) | Class | W | L | ERA | G | GS | CG | SV | IP | H | R | ER | HR | BB | SO | AVG |
|------|---------------|-------|---|---|-----|---|----|----|----|-----|-----|-----|-----|----|-----|-----|------|
| 2002 | Royals (GCL) | R | 1 | 3 | 3.10 | 7 | 6 | 0 | 0 | 29 | 20 | 13 | 10 | 2 | 14 | 28 | .196 |
| | Spokane (NWL) | A | 2 | 0 | 1.10 | 6 | 6 | 0 | 0 | 33 | 24 | 6 | 4 | 3 | 14 | 23 | .198 |
| 2003 | Burlington (MWL) | A | 1 | 12 | 5.92 | 17 | 16 | 0 | 0 | 79 | 83 | 62 | 52 | 11 | 31 | 46 | .269 |
| | Royals 1 (AZL) | R | 0 | 0 | 2.25 | 4 | 2 | 0 | 0 | 12 | 8 | 4 | 3 | 0 | 5 | 12 | .178 |
| 2004 | Burlington (MWL) | A | 0 | 1 | 15.00 | 1 | 1 | 0 | 0 | 3 | 6 | 8 | 5 | 0 | 3 | 2 | .353 |
| 2005 | Burlington (MWL) | A | 3 | 7 | 3.54 | 26 | 21 | 0 | 1 | 109 | 100 | 54 | 43 | 9 | 53 | 110 | .238 |
| 2006 | High Desert (Cal) | A | 6 | 6 | 4.89 | 28 | 28 | 1 | 0 | 162 | 175 | 94 | 88 | 23 | 58 | 153 | .285 |
| **MINOR LEAGUE TOTALS** | | | 13 | 29 | 4.32 | 89 | 80 | 1 | 1 | 427 | 416 | 241 | 205 | 48 | 178 | 374 | .256 |

## 25  ANGEL SANCHEZ                                                    SS

**Born:** Sept. 20, 1983. **B-T:** R-R. **Ht.:** 6-2. **Wt.:** 185. **Drafted:** HS—La Piedras, P.R., 2001 (11th round). **Signed by:** Johnny Ramos.

Sanchez has been a grinder, slowly working his way up the ladder. He repeated both the Rookie-level Gulf Coast League and the low Class A Midwest League in his first four seasons. Helped by the hitting environment at High Desert, he put together his best season in 2005, and he proved it wasn't a total fluke last year. The Royals always have liked Sanchez' ability to put the bat on the ball and his situational hitting skills. Though he makes good contact, he doesn't hit for much power and doesn't have exceptional on-base ability. Despite above-average speed, he was thrown out in nine of his 17 steal attempts last year. If Sanchez makes it to the big leagues, his glove will be his ticket. He's an excellent shortstop who can make both routine and spectacular plays. With a strong arm, he can effortlessly make throws from the hole without taking an extra step. Sanchez will move up to Triple-A in 2007.

| Year | Club (League) | Class | AVG | G | AB | R | H | 2B | 3B | HR | RBI | BB | SO | SB | OBP | SLG |
|---|---|---|---|---|---|---|---|---|---|---|---|---|---|---|---|---|
| 2001 | Royals (GCL) | R | .242 | 30 | 95 | 10 | 23 | 4 | 0 | 0 | 6 | 6 | 28 | 3 | .287 | .284 |
| 2002 | Royals (GCL) | R | .251 | 49 | 175 | 21 | 44 | 4 | 0 | 0 | 12 | 10 | 24 | 9 | .302 | .274 |
| 2003 | Burlington (MWL) | A | .270 | 106 | 408 | 54 | 110 | 8 | 1 | 2 | 35 | 28 | 52 | 14 | .321 | .309 |
| 2004 | Burlington (MWL) | A | .252 | 90 | 337 | 34 | 85 | 12 | 1 | 2 | 24 | 15 | 47 | 16 | .300 | .312 |
| 2005 | High Desert (Cal) | A | .313 | 133 | 585 | 102 | 183 | 33 | 4 | 5 | 70 | 39 | 54 | 10 | .356 | .409 |
| 2006 | Wichita (TL) | AA | .282 | 133 | 542 | 105 | 153 | 24 | 1 | 4 | 57 | 44 | 63 | 8 | .339 | .352 |
| | Kansas City (AL) | MLB | .222 | 8 | 27 | 2 | 6 | 0 | 0 | 0 | 1 | 0 | 4 | 0 | .214 | .222 |
| **MINOR LEAGUE TOTALS** | | | .279 | 541 | 2142 | 326 | 598 | 85 | 7 | 13 | 204 | 142 | 268 | 60 | .329 | .344 |
| **MAJOR LEAGUE TOTALS** | | | .222 | 8 | 27 | 2 | 6 | 0 | 0 | 0 | 1 | 0 | 4 | 0 | .214 | .222 |

## 26  KURT MERTINS                                                    2B

**Born:** April 22, 1986. **B-T:** R-R. **Ht.:** 6-0. **Wt.:** 175. **Drafted:** JC of the Desert (Calif.), 2006 (13th round). **Signed by:** John Ramey.

Undrafted before 2006, Mertins created buzz among scouts when he got a chance to play shortstop at the JC of the Desert (Calif.). He hit .387, went 37-for-42 stealing bases and showed some arm strength. After signing for $35,000 as a 13th-round pick, he maintained that pace in his pro debut, batting .342 and succeeding on 26 of 30 steal attempts. Mertins stays inside the ball well and while he's not a slap hitter, he has a little man's approach. The power he does have is mostly to the gaps, though he has the bat speed to turn on mistakes. A savvy basestealer, he has above-average speed but isn't a burner. Mertins has a lean frame and should add strength as he gets older, but that also could come at the expense of some speed. He played second base and DHed in his debut, but the Royals may give him the chance to play shortstop this year. There's also talk of skipping him a level and sending him to high Class A.

| Year | Club (League) | Class | AVG | G | AB | R | H | 2B | 3B | HR | RBI | BB | SO | SB | OBP | SLG |
|---|---|---|---|---|---|---|---|---|---|---|---|---|---|---|---|---|
| 2006 | Idaho Falls (Pio) | R | .342 | 61 | 225 | 46 | 77 | 11 | 3 | 1 | 26 | 18 | 39 | 26 | .397 | .431 |
| **MINOR LEAGUE TOTALS** | | | .342 | 61 | 225 | 46 | 77 | 11 | 3 | 1 | 26 | 18 | 39 | 26 | .397 | .431 |

## 27  CHRIS McCONNELL                                                 SS

**Born:** Dec. 18, 1985. **B-T:** R-R. **Ht.:** 5-11. **Wt.:** 170. **Drafted:** HS—Franklinville, N.J., 2004 (9th round). **Signed by:** Sean Rooney.

The Royals thought they had a ninth-round steal when McConnell hit .333 and showed good gap power through his first two seasons, but he took an enormous step backwards with the bat in 2006. He struggled early in the year in low Class A, stopped trusting his swing and his approach disintegrated. He would chase a curve in the dirt and then stare at a fastball right over the plate for strike three. McConnell has an unorthodox swing with a low crouch and a high back elbow, and it remains to be seen whether that will work above Rookie ball. Kansas City was impressed that his problems at the plate didn't carry over into the field. McConnell is a plus defender with quick feet, good hands and an above-average arm, though he is also a little unorthodox in the field as well. He's a slightly above-average runner who's still honing his instincts on the bases. McConnell rallied to post decent numbers after a demotion to Idaho Falls, so his season was not a total loss. The Royals will try and keep him and Jeff Bianchi separated so they can both play shortstop, but both need to advance to low Class A this year. They may split time between second base and short together at Burlington this year.

| Year | Club (League) | Class | AVG | G | AB | R | H | 2B | 3B | HR | RBI | BB | SO | SB | OBP | SLG |
|---|---|---|---|---|---|---|---|---|---|---|---|---|---|---|---|---|
| 2004 | AZL Royals (AZL) | R | .339 | 37 | 124 | 22 | 42 | 5 | 0 | 3 | 11 | 17 | 19 | 8 | .420 | .452 |
| 2005 | Idaho Falls (Pio) | R | .331 | 70 | 275 | 56 | 91 | 17 | 8 | 6 | 39 | 31 | 34 | 7 | .403 | .516 |
| 2006 | Burlington (MWL) | A | .172 | 69 | 239 | 23 | 41 | 4 | 0 | 1 | 18 | 17 | 47 | 8 | .254 | .201 |

| | | | | | | | | | | | | | | | |
|---|---|---|---|---|---|---|---|---|---|---|---|---|---|---|---|
| Idaho Falls (Pio) | R | .262 | 47 | 183 | 25 | 48 | 8 | 4 | 4 | 35 | 15 | 35 | 8 | .320 | .415 |
| **MINOR LEAGUE TOTALS** | | .270 | 223 | 821 | 126 | 222 | 34 | 12 | 14 | 103 | 80 | 135 | 31 | .345 | .392 |

## 28 JOE DICKERSON                                                                    OF

**Born:** Oct. 3, 1986. **B-T:** L-L. **Ht.:** 6-1. **Wt.:** 190. **Drafted:** HS—Yorba Linda, Calif., 2005 (4th round). **Signed by:** John Ramey.

Dickerson led the Arizona League in RBIs and triples in his 2005 pro debut, and he posted similar numbers in his encore last year one step up in the Rookie-level Pioneer League. He uses a short, quick stroke to generate pull-side power. He consistently makes hard contact with pitches on the inner half, but his plate coverage needs to improve because pitchers at higher levels will exploit his hole on the outer half. Dickerson shows the ability to close that hole during soft-toss and batting practice, but it's still an issue during games. Though he has above-average speed, he's still learning to steal bases and has been nailed in 20 of his 38 pro attempts. Dickerson is solid in center field because he gets good reads and breaks, but there are concerns that he lacks the athleticism to stay there. As he adds strength to his frame, he may not be able to maintain his current range. If that happens, his fringe-average arm would limit him to left field. After two years of Rookie ball, Dickerson is ready to prove himself in low Class A.

| Year | Club (League) | Class | AVG | G | AB | R | H | 2B | 3B | HR | RBI | BB | SO | SB | OBP | SLG |
|---|---|---|---|---|---|---|---|---|---|---|---|---|---|---|---|---|
| 2005 | Royals (AZL) | R | .294 | 56 | 214 | 27 | 63 | 12 | 9 | 4 | 40 | 27 | 46 | 9 | .371 | .491 |
| 2006 | Idaho Falls (Pio) | R | .281 | 63 | 242 | 36 | 68 | 14 | 3 | 7 | 38 | 19 | 34 | 9 | .338 | .450 |
| **MINOR LEAGUE TOTALS** | | | .287 | 119 | 456 | 63 | 131 | 26 | 12 | 11 | 78 | 46 | 80 | 18 | .354 | .469 |

## 29 JASON GODIN                                                                    RHP

**Born:** Sept. 23, 1984. **B-T:** R-R. **Ht.:** 6-4. **Wt.:** 177. **Drafted:** Old Dominion, 2006 (5th round). **Signed by:** Steve Connelly.

Godin had back surgery in November 2004, missed all of 2005 and returned with no ill effects last spring. He had 146 strikeouts in 115 innings to lead the Colonial Athletic Association, following in the footsteps of Harold Mozingo (drafted one round after Godin by the Royals in June) and Justin Verlander. A fifth-rounder, Godin turned pro for $210,000. His best pitch is a 12-to-6 curveball that sits at 79-80 mph. He can throw the curve for strikes or bury it in the dirt when he's ahead in the count. He throws his 88-91 mph fastball on a good downhill plane and commands it well. He added a slider when he returned at Old Dominion, but probably will scrap it per the new organization philosophy that prefers the curveball. He rarely threw a changeup before he signed but quickly made strides with it as a pro. After he logged 115 innings in college, the Royals shut Godin down after just 22 pro innings. They put him on a program to add muscle mass and weight in hopes of increasing his durability. If he has a strong spring, he could skip a level and go to high Class A.

| Year | Club (League) | Class | W | L | ERA | G | GS | CG | SV | IP | H | R | ER | HR | BB | SO | AVG |
|---|---|---|---|---|---|---|---|---|---|---|---|---|---|---|---|---|---|
| 2006 | Idaho Falls (Pio) | R | 0 | 1 | 2.49 | 6 | 4 | 0 | 0 | 22 | 23 | 6 | 6 | 2 | 8 | 18 | .288 |
| **MINOR LEAGUE TOTALS** | | | 0 | 1 | 2.49 | 6 | 4 | 0 | 0 | 22 | 23 | 6 | 6 | 2 | 8 | 18 | .288 |

## 30 DANIEL CORTES                                                                    RHP

**Born:** March 4, 1987. **B-T:** R-R. **Ht.:** 6-5. **Wt.:** 205. **Drafted:** HS—Pomona, Calif., 2005 (7th round). **Signed by:** Dan Ontiveros (White Sox).

Acquired from the White Sox along with Tyler Lumsden in exchange for Mike MacDougal last July, Cortes offers more projection than most pitchers in the Royals system but is still very raw. He committed to San Diego State out of high school, but a three-inch growth spurt as a senior added 5 mph of velocity and earned him a $115,000 signing bonus as a seventh-rounder. Cortes operates at 87-92 mph with his fastball but once he fills out his lean frame he should add more velocity. The Royals took away his slider and moved him to the third-base side of the rubber when they acquired him. Though his ERA ballooned to 6.69 after the trade, they were pleased with the progress of his curveball, an 82-83 mph bender with hard 12-to-6 break. Though Cortes has an outstanding pitcher's frame, he uses too much effort in his delivery and tries to hard to light up radar guns. He lands on his heel too often and his pitches have a tendency to fade to the right when he does. He needs to improve his changeup and command. He's certainly a work in progress, but Cortes' upside is significant. He might have to repeat low Class A to start 2007.

| Year | Club (League) | Class | W | L | ERA | G | GS | CG | SV | IP | H | R | ER | HR | BB | SO | AVG |
|---|---|---|---|---|---|---|---|---|---|---|---|---|---|---|---|---|---|
| 2005 | Bristol (Appy) | R | 1 | 4 | 5.17 | 15 | 7 | 0 | 0 | 38 | 44 | 23 | 22 | 2 | 13 | 38 | .289 |
| 2006 | Kannapolis (SAL) | A | 3 | 9 | 4.01 | 20 | 19 | 0 | 0 | 108 | 109 | 61 | 48 | 6 | 38 | 96 | .260 |
| | Burlington (MWL) | A | 1 | 2 | 6.69 | 7 | 7 | 0 | 0 | 35 | 40 | 27 | 26 | 7 | 17 | 30 | .284 |
| **MINOR LEAGUE TOTALS** | | | 5 | 15 | 4.77 | 42 | 33 | 0 | 0 | 181 | 193 | 111 | 96 | 15 | 68 | 164 | .271 |

# LOS ANGELES
# ANGELS

BY **ALAN MATTHEWS**

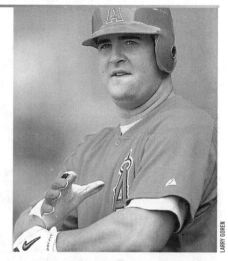

For the better part of the new millennium, the Angels have accrued talent as effectively as any organization in baseball. In 2006, the masses were to finally find out just how good Los Angeles' well-decorated farm system was.

General manager Bill Stoneman tested the trade waters prior to the season but ultimately elected to employ an Opening Day roster rife with promise, if also inexperience. Youngsters Casey Kotchman, Dallas McPherson and Ervin Santana were expected to settle into regular roles, as were rookies Jeff Mathis, Kendry Morales, Joe Saunders and Jered Weaver. If a middle-infield spot opened up, Erick Aybar, Howie Kendrick and Brandon Wood were ready to do the same.

Seven weeks into the season, the Angels were 17-28 and their hopes for a third consecutive American League West title were slipping away quickly. Kotchman (mononucleosis) and McPherson (oblique) missed most of the season, while Mathis was batting .103 when he was demoted in early May. The veterans weren't pulling their weight either and the defense was abominable. Reigning AL Cy Young award winner Bartolo Colon went down with what eventually would be diagnosed as a partially torn rotator cuff.

The year was shaping up as a disaster, but Los Angeles pulled out of it. Weaver—replacing his older brother Jeff—stepped into the rotation and won his first seven starts, going 9-0 before recording a loss. Kendrick, **Mike Napoli** (who homered in his first major league at-bat), Santana and

Saunders made significant contributions down the stretch. The Angels finished with 89 victories, four behind division champion Oakland.

Los Angeles will be in shape to contend once again in 2007, and Stoneman bolstered the lineup by committing five years and $50 million to Gary Matthews, who should improve the Angels' defensive efficiency.

The Angels face a position crunch they've long anticipated. Incumbent shortstop Orlando Cabrera is under contract through 2008, and thoughts of trying Aybar, a pure shortstop, in center field ended with Matthews' signing. Furthermore, the organization's top prospect (Wood) also plays shortstop.

The system is still strong but not as deep as it has been in recent years. Five of its top 11 prospects from a year ago (Kendrick, Weaver, Morales, Saunders and Napoli) have graduated to the majors, and a sixth (Alberto Callaspo) was traded for middle relief help. Nick Adenhart, Stephen Marek and Sean O'Sullivan all made progress in the minors and have impact potential on the mound, but are all at least two years away from contributing. International scouting supervisor Clay Daniel and Pacific Rim scout Charlie Kim worked together to bring Korean righthander Young-Il Jung into the fold in September, and he too could be a frontline starter down the road.

## TOP 30 PROSPECTS

| | |
|---|---|
| 1. Brandon Wood, ss | 16. Matt Sweeney, 1b |
| 2. Nick Adenhart, rhp | 17. Jeremy Haynes, rhp |
| 3. Erick Aybar, ss | 18. Terry Evans, of |
| 4. Young-Il Jung, rhp | 19. Bobby Wilson, c |
| 5. Stephen Marek, rhp | 20. Ryan Mount, 2b |
| 6. Hank Conger, c | 21. Trevor Bell, rhp |
| 7. Jeff Mathis, c | 22. Rafael Rodriguez, rhp |
| 8. Sean Rodriguez, 2b | 23. Nick Green, rhp |
| 9. Sean O'Sullivan, rhp | 24. Chris Resop, rhp |
| 10. Tommy Mendoza, rhp | 25. Richard Aldridge, rhp |
| 11. Kenneth Herndon, rhp | 26. Tommy Murphy, of |
| 12. Peter Bourjos, of | 27. Reggie Willits, of |
| 13. Jose Arredondo, rhp | 28. Barret Browning, lhp |
| 14. P.J. Phillips, 3b/ss | 29. Mark Trumbo, 1b |
| 15. Hainley Statia, ss | 30. Phil Seibel, lhp |

# ORGANIZATION OVERVIEW

**General manager:** Bill Stoneman. **Farm director:** Tony Reagins. **Scouting director:** Eddie Bane.

## 2006 PERFORMANCE

| Class | Team | League | W | L | PCT | Finish* | Manager | Affiliated |
|---|---|---|---|---|---|---|---|---|
| Majors | Los Angeles | American | 89 | 73 | .549 | 6th (14) | Mike Scioscia | — |
| Triple-A | Salt Lake Bees | Pacific Coast | 81 | 63 | .563 | 3rd (16) | Brian Harper | 2001 |
| Double-A | Arkansas Travelers | Texas | 51 | 87 | .370 | 8th (8) | Tyrone Boykin | 2001 |
| High A | Rancho Cuca. Quakes | California | 63 | 77 | .450 | 9th (10) | Bobby Mitchell | 2001 |
| Low A | Cedar Rapids Kernels | Midwest | 65 | 74 | .468 | 10th (14) | Bobby Magallanes | 1993 |
| Rookie | Orem Owlz | Pioneer | 45 | 31 | .592 | 2nd (8) | Tom Kotchman | 2001 |
| Rookie | AZL Angels | Arizona | 34 | 21 | .618 | 3rd (9) | Brian Harper | 2001 |
| **OVERALL 2006 MINOR LEAGUE RECORD** | | | 339 | 353 | .490 | 20th (30) | | |

*Finish in overall standings (No. of teams in league). +League champion

## ORGANIZATION LEADERS

### BATTING
| | | |
|---|---|---|
| AVG | Pettit, Chris, Orem | .336 |
| R | Rodriguez, Sean, Rancho Cuca./Ark./S.L. | 94 |
| H | Eylward, Mike, Arkansas/Salt Lake | 166 |
| 2B | Brown, Matt, Arkansas | 44 |
| 3B | Reilly, Patrick, Cedar Rapids/Rancho Cuca. | 11 |
| HR | Rodriguez, Sean, Rancho Cuca./Ark./S.L. | 29 |
| RBI | Eylward, Mike, Arkansas/Salt Lake | 88 |
| BB | Willits, Reggie, Salt Lake | 77 |
| SO | Renz, Jordan, Cedar Rapids | 178 |
| SB | Coon, Brad, Cedar Rapids | 57 |
| OBP | Willits, Reggie, Salt Lake | .448 |
| SLG | Pettit, Chris, Orem | .566 |
| XBH | Wood, Brandon, Arkansas | 71 |

### PITCHING
| | | |
|---|---|---|
| W | Adenhart, Nick, Cedar Rapids/Rancho Cuca. | 15 |
| L | Hunter, Christopher, Arkansas | 14 |
| ERA | Veras, Nicholas, AZL Angels | 1.35 |
| G | Wilhite, Matt, Salt Lake | 61 |
| SV | Aldridge, Richard, C. Rapids/Rancho Cuca. | 25 |
| IP | Mosebach, Bobby, C. Rapids/Rancho Cuca. | 182 |
| BB | Torres, Joe, Rancho Cucamonga | 75 |
| SO | Arredondo, Jose, Rancho Cucamonga/Ark. | 163 |
| AVG | Veras, Nicholas, AZL Angels | .210 |

## BEST TOOLS

| | |
|---|---|
| Best Hitter for Average | Erick Aybar |
| Best Power Hitter | Brandon Wood |
| Best Strike-Zone Discipline | Reggie Willits |
| Fastest Baserunner | Peter Bourjos |
| Best Athlete | P.J. Phillips |
| Best Fastball | Jose Arredondo |
| Best Curveball | Nick Adenhart |
| Best Slider | Richard Aldridge |
| Best Changeup | Nick Green |
| Best Control | Sean O'Sullivan |
| Best Defensive Catcher | Jeff Mathis |
| Best Defensive Infielder | Erick Aybar |
| Best Infield Arm | Erick Aybar |
| Best Defensive Outfielder | Tommy Murphy |
| Best Outfield Arm | Tommy Murphy |

## PROJECTED 2010 LINEUP

| | |
|---|---|
| Catcher | Hank Conger |
| First Base | Casey Kotchman |
| Second Base | Howie Kendrick |
| Third Base | Brandon Wood |
| Shortstop | Erick Aybar |
| Left Field | Juan Rivera |
| Center Field | Gary Matthews Jr. |
| Right Field | Vladimir Guerrero |

| | |
|---|---|
| Designated Hitter | Kendry Morales |
| No. 1 Starter | Nick Adenhart |
| No. 2 Starter | Jered Weaver |
| No. 3 Starter | John Lackey |
| No. 4 Starter | Ervin Santana |
| No. 5 Starter | Young-Il Jung |
| Closer | Francisco Rodriguez |

## LAST YEAR'S TOP 20 PROSPECTS

| | |
|---|---|
| 1. Brandon Wood, ss | 11. Mike Napoli, c |
| 2. Howie Kendrick, 2b | 12. Mark Trumbo, 1b |
| 3. Erick Aybar, ss | 13. Trevor Bell, rhp |
| 4. Jeff Mathis, c | 14. P.J. Phillips, ss/3b |
| 5. Jered Weaver, rhp | 15. Steven Shell, rhp |
| 6. Nick Adenhart, rhp | 16. Hainley Statia, ss |
| 7. Kendry Morales, 1b | 17. Jose Arredondo, rhp |
| 8. Alberto Callaspo, 2b | 18. Stephen Marek, rhp |
| 9. Joe Saunders, lhp | 19. Nick Gorneault, of |
| 10. Tommy Mendoza, rhp | 20. Tommy Murphy, of |

## TOP PROSPECTS OF THE DECADE

| Year | Player, Pos. | 2006 Org. |
|---|---|---|
| 1997 | Jarrod Washburn, lhp | Mariners |
| 1998 | Troy Glaus, 3b | Blue Jays |
| 1999 | Ramon Ortiz, rhp | Nationals |
| 2000 | Ramon Ortiz, rhp | Nationals |
| 2001 | Joe Torres, lhp | Angels |
| 2002 | Casey Kotchman, 1b | Angels |
| 2003 | Francisco Rodriguez, rhp | Angels |
| 2004 | Casey Kotchman, 1b | Angels |
| 2005 | Casey Kotchman, 1b | Angels |
| 2006 | Brandon Wood, ss | Angels |

## TOP DRAFT PICKS OF THE DECADE

| Year | Player, Pos. | 2006 Org. |
|---|---|---|
| 1997 | Troy Glaus, 3b | Blue Jays |
| 1998 | Seth Etherton, rhp | Royals |
| 1999 | John Lackey, rhp (2nd round) | Angels |
| 2000 | Joe Torres, lhp | Angels |
| 2001 | Casey Kotchman, 1b | Angels |
| 2002 | Joe Saunders, lhp | Angels |
| 2003 | Brandon Wood, ss | Angels |
| 2004 | Jered Weaver, rhp | Angels |
| 2005 | Trevor Bell, rhp | Angels |
| 2006 | Hank Conger, c | Angels |

## LARGEST BONUSES IN CLUB HISTORY

| | |
|---|---|
| Jered Weaver, 2004 | $4,000,000 |
| Kendry Morales, 2004 | $3,000,000 |
| Troy Glaus, 1997 | $2,250,000 |
| Joe Torres, 2000 | $2,080,000 |
| Casey Kotchman, 2001 | $2,075,000 |

# MINOR LEAGUE DEPTH CHART

## Los Angeles Angels

**Impact: B.** Adenhart, Jung and Marek won't be ready to contribute to the big league team for at least two years, but all could become frontline starters.
**Depth: B.** Aggressive drafts have elicited plenty of prospects down the line.
**Sleeper:** Bobby Mosebach, rhp. Another junior college find, Mosebach has feel for three pitches and solid-average command.

*Numbers in parentheses indicate prospect rankings.*

| LF | CF | RF |
|---|---|---|
| Aaron Peel | Peter Bourjos (12) | Tommy Murphy (26) |
| Tyler Johnson | Terry Evans (18) | Nick Gorneault |
| Andrew Toussaint | Reggie Willits (27) | Norberto Ortiz |
| | Brad Coon | |
| | Jerome Moore | |
| | Stantrel Smith | |

| 3B | SS | 2B | 1B |
|---|---|---|---|
| P.J. Phillips (14) | Brandon Wood (1) | Sean Rodriguez (8) | Mark Sweeney (16) |
| Matt Brown | Erick Aybar (3) | Ryan Mount (20) | Mark Trumbo (29) |
| Freddy Sandoval | Hainley Statia (15) | Tadd Brewer | Michael Collins |
| | Wilberto Ortiz | | Baltazar Lopez |

| C |
|---|
| Hank Conger (6) |
| Jeff Mathis (7) |
| Bobby Wilson (19) |
| Ben Johnson |
| Jordan Renz |

| RHP | | LHP | |
|---|---|---|---|
| **Starters** | **Relievers** | **Starters** | **Relievers** |
| Nick Adenhart (2) | Tommy Mendoza (10) | Gustavo Espinosa | Barret Browning (28) |
| Young-Il Jung (4) | Jose Arredondo (13) | Nate Boman | Phil Seibel (30) |
| Stephen Marek (5) | Trevor Bell (21) | Robert Fish | Leonardo Calderon |
| Sean O'Sullivan (9) | Rafael Rodriguez (22) | | Blake Holler |
| Kenneth Herndon (11) | Chris Resop (24) | | |
| Jeremy Haynes (17) | Richard Aldridge (25) | | |
| Nick Green (23) | Steven Shell | | |
| Bobby Mosebach | Von Sterzbach | | |
| Dustin Moseley | Felipe Arredondo | | |
| Bobby Cassevah | Richard Thompson | | |
| | Anthony Ortega | | |
| | Brok Butcher | | |
| | Marcus Gwyn | | |
| | Warner Madrigal | | |
| | Kevin Lynch | | |

# DRAFT ANALYSIS

## 2006

SIGNING BUDGET: $2.4 million

**Best Pro Debut:** C Hank Conger (1) batted .319/.382/.522 before breaking the hamate bone in his right wrist, and ranked as the No. 1 prospect in the Arizona League. 1B Matt Sweeney (8) hit .341/.431/.576 to earn all-star honors in the AZL, while OF Chris Pettit (19) batted .336/.445/.566 with a league-high 25 doubles to do the same in the Pioneer League.

**Best Athlete:** OF Clay Fuller (4). He has good bloodlines, as his brothers Cody and Lance and father Kenny all played football at Texas Tech—and Clay can outrun all of them.

**Best Pure Hitter:** Conger was drafted for his bat, though his catching is also improving and he should be able to stay behind the plate. He didn't receive as much predraft hype as Conger did, but Sweeney is nearly as gifted.

**Best Raw Power:** Conger has well-above-average power from both sides of the plate, more as a lefty. He also makes very good contact for a slugger.

**Fastest Runner:** Fuller has plus-plus speed and stole 15 bases in 19 tries during his 46-game pro debut.

**Best Defensive Player:** Fuller, once he adds a little more polish in center field. 2B Tadd Brewer (17) was the best defensive infielder signed by the Angels.

**Best Fastball:** Of the players the Angels signed out of the 2006 draft, it's RHP David Herndon (5), who pitches at 90-93 mph and tops out at 95. They still control the rights to RHP Jordan Walden (12), who has hit 99 mph in the past and currently is at San Jacinto (Texas) JC.

**Best Breaking Ball:** LHP Chris Armstrong's (14) curveball. He would have gone higher in the draft had he not been committed strongly to Oklahoma State.

**Most Intriguing Background:** Fuller was just one of several prominent two-sport athletes drafted by the Angels. The most notable is OF Jarrad Page (7), who had an impressive Angel Stadium workout before signing with the NFL's Kansas City Chiefs as a hard-hitting safety. RHP Jake Locker (40) was arguably the best athlete in the 2006 draft class, but he too turned down baseball and is now a quarterback at Washington. RHP Scott Carroll (16), a former Purdue and Missouri State quarterback, might have signed if he hadn't been shut down while pitching in the Cape Cod League. Unsigned 6-foot-8 RHP Jon Plefka (47) is a forward on the Texas Tech basketball team.

**Closest To The Majors:** LHP Nate Boman (9) sat out the spring recovering from labrum surgery, but returned to show solid stuff and polish in the Cape Cod League. He's the most advanced player in Los Angeles' high school-heavy draft.

**Best Late-Round Pick:** LHP Barret Browning (28) and Armstrong. Browing's stuff improved after the Angels cleaned up his delivery. He could be an answer as a situational lefty sooner than later.

**The One Who Got Away:** Locker, though the Angels knew he was virtually unsignable. They expected to land hard-hitting OF Russ Moldenhauer (3) and met his $425,000 asking price, but he opted to attend Texas.

**Assessment:** Conger becomes one of the game's best catching prospects and added to an organization strength. Not having a second-round pick and failing to sign their third-rounder hurt, though the blow was lessened by landing prime draft-and-follow Sean O'Sullivan.

## 2005 BUDGET: $3.4 million

They're all a long ways from the majors, but the Angels scooped up several interesting prospects in RHP Trevor Bell (1), SS Ryan Mount (2), 3B/SS P.J. Phillips (2), draft-and-follow RHP Sean O'Sullivan (3), RHP Tommy Mendoza (5) and OF Peter Bourjos (10). **GRADE: C+**

## 2004 BUDGET: $4.7 million

RHP Jered Weaver (1) was spectacular as a rookie last year. RHP Nick Adenhart (14), who blew out his elbow just before the draft, has made a full recovery and may be better than Weaver. And draft-and-follow RHP Stephen Marek (40) has nearly as much as talent. **GRADE: A**

## 2003 BUDGET: $3.2 million

The Angels did an excellent job of projecting SS Brandon Wood's (1) power. SS Sean Rodriguez (3) and OF Reggie Willits (7) should be useful role players. **GRADE: B+**

*Draft analysis by Jim Callis. Numbers in parentheses indicate draft rounds. Budgets are bonuses in first 10 rounds.*

# BRANDON
# WOOD

SS

**Born:** March 2, 1985.
**Ht.:** 6-3. **Wt.:** 185.
**Bats:** R. **Throws:** R.
**Drafted:** HS—Scottsdale,
Ariz., 2003 (1st round).
**Signed by:** Jeff Scholzen.

BILL MITCHELL

A n undersized, overachieving high school underclassman, Wood was thought of mostly as a defense-first shortstop until his senior year at Horizon High (Scottsdale, Ariz.) in 2003. He started filling out his frame and fulfilling his potential, and passed up a scholarship from Texas to sign as a first-round pick for $1.3 million. Wood contended for Minor League Player of the Year honors in 2005, slamming 58 homers between the minors, the Arizona Fall League and Team USA. He led the minors in doubles (53), homers (an Angels minor league record 43), total bases (370) and extra-base hits (101). Wood proved it was no fluke in 2006, topping the Double-A Texas League with 71 extra-base hits and again coming through for Team USA. At an Olympic qualifying tournament in Cuba, he crushed an eighth-inning tiebreaking homer off closer Pedro Luis Lazo for the first win by a U.S. pro team against Cuba since Ben Sheets shut down the Cubans to win Olympic gold in 2000.

Wood's bat speed, power and fundamentally sound defensive package have prompted comparisons to Cal Ripken. He profiles as a middle-of-the-order run producer and perennial all-star. Wood has an aggressive approach with a leveraged swing that produces well above-average power to all fields. Whether or not he'll remain at shortstop is predicated on the Angels' needs, but he's a solid defender capable of playing shortstop everyday in the big leagues. His range is average, his hands are soft and his arm is a plus. He's adept at making accurate throws on the run and shows proper footwork turning double plays. His defensive skills would play well at third base, his most likely destination if he moves, and he definitely has the bat to profile at the hot corner. Wood is lauded for his instincts in all phases of the game, as well as his makeup. He's an average runner.

Wood ranked among the TL leaders in several offensive categories, including finishing first in strikeouts with the highest total of his career. His uppercut swing path won't allow him to make contact often enough to contend for batting titles, and he could post modest averages his first few years in the majors. Wood could reduce his empty swings by fine-tuning his approach. He occasionally tries to do too much with pitcher's pitches, when letting them go by or simply putting them in play would be more effective. Like many young power hitters, Wood will chase balls above his hands and occasionally pulls off pitches on the outer half. When behind in the count, he could shorten his swing.

Wood should open 2007 at Triple-A Salt Lake but is close to being ready to contribute in Los Angeles. The Angels already have two superior defensive shortstops in Orlando Cabrera, who's signed through 2008, and Erick Aybar, who's still trying to crack the big league lineup. They also have no clear frontrunner to start at third base, though it's unlikely they'd have Wood learn the position on the job in the majors. He could slide over to the hot corner at Salt Lake if Aybar doesn't make the big league club.

| Year | Club (League) | Class | AVG | G | AB | R | H | 2B | 3B | HR | RBI | BB | SO | SB | OBP | SLG |
|------|---------------|-------|-----|---|----|---|---|----|----|----|-----|----|----|----|-----|-----|
| 2003 | Angels (AZL) | R | .308 | 19 | 78 | 14 | 24 | 8 | 2 | 0 | 13 | 4 | 15 | 3 | .349 | .462 |
| | Provo (Pio) | R | .278 | 42 | 162 | 25 | 45 | 13 | 2 | 5 | 31 | 16 | 48 | 1 | .348 | .475 |
| 2004 | Cedar Rapids (MWL) | A | .251 | 125 | 478 | 65 | 120 | 30 | 5 | 11 | 64 | 46 | 117 | 21 | .322 | .404 |
| 2005 | Rancho Cucamonga (Cal) | A | .321 | 130 | 536 | 109 | 172 | 51 | 4 | 43 | 115 | 48 | 128 | 7 | .383 | .672 |
| | Salt Lake (PCL) | AAA | .316 | 4 | 19 | 1 | 6 | 2 | 1 | 0 | 1 | 0 | 6 | 0 | .316 | .526 |
| 2006 | Arkansas (TL) | AA | .276 | 118 | 453 | 74 | 125 | 42 | 4 | 25 | 83 | 54 | 149 | 19 | .355 | .552 |
| **MINOR LEAGUE TOTALS** | | | .285 | 438 | 1726 | 288 | 492 | 146 | 18 | 84 | 307 | 168 | 463 | 51 | .353 | .537 |

## 2 NICK ADENHART RHP

**Born:** Aug. 24, 1986. **B-T:** R-R. **Ht.:** 6-4. **Wt.:** 190. **Drafted:** HS—Williamsport, Md., 2004 (14th round). **Signed by:** Dan Radcliff.

Though he was just 19 and pitching for the first time above Rookie ball, Adenhart reinforced sentiment that he has made a full recovery from Tommy John surgery. He blew out his elbow his senior year, then signed for $710,000 after the Angels took a 14th-round flier on him. He earned an invitation to the Futures Game and a spot on the U.S. Olympic qualifying team. Adenhart has above-average command of three plus pitches. His fastball has life at 93-95 mph and comes out of his hand easily. His deceptive 81-84 mph circle changeup is ahead of his breaking ball, though his 75-76 mph curveball has tight spin with 11-to-5 shape. He's aggressive, works ahead in the count and pitches to both sides of the plate. Adenhart tends to overthrow his curve, leading to inconsistent control of the pitch. His delivery is generally smooth, though his lead leg is stiff and he could do a better job of maintaining his high-three-quarters release point. Adenhart profiles as a future No. 2 starter. He should climb to Double-A Arkansas sometime in 2007.

| Year | Club (League) | Class | W | L | ERA | G | GS | CG | SV | IP | H | R | ER | HR | BB | SO | AVG |
|------|---------------|-------|---|---|-----|---|----|----|----|-----|-----|----|----|----|----|-----|------|
| 2005 | Angels (AZL) | R | 2 | 3 | 3.68 | 13 | 12 | 1 | 0 | 44 | 39 | 26 | 18 | 0 | 24 | 52 | .245 |
| | Orem (Pio) | R | 1 | 0 | 0.00 | 1 | 1 | 0 | 0 | 6 | 3 | 1 | 0 | 0 | 0 | 7 | .143 |
| 2006 | Cedar Rapids (MWL) | A | 10 | 2 | 1.95 | 16 | 16 | 1 | 0 | 106 | 84 | 33 | 23 | 2 | 26 | 99 | .215 |
| | Rancho Cucamonga (Cal) | A | 5 | 2 | 3.78 | 9 | 9 | 0 | 0 | 52 | 51 | 23 | 22 | 1 | 16 | 46 | .258 |
| **MINOR LEAGUE TOTALS** | | | 18 | 7 | 2.72 | 39 | 38 | 2 | 0 | 208 | 177 | 83 | 63 | 3 | 66 | 204 | .230 |

## 3 ERICK AYBAR SS

**Born:** Jan. 14, 1984. **B-T:** B-R. **Ht.:** 5-11. **Wt.:** 170. **Signed:** Dominican Republic, 2002. **Signed by:** Leo Perez/Clay Daniel.

Aybar made his major league debut last May and was used primarily as a defensive replacement before returning to Triple-A. Aybar was included in trade offers for Miguel Tejada and Carlos Lee in July, which may have precipitated his lackluster finish. Much is made of Aybar's free-swinging approach at the plate, but he makes consistent hard contact and is a confident, efficient hitter. He has above-average bat speed and could wind up batting second in a contending lineup. His glove, arm and speed are also plus tools. He has true shortstop actions with above-average range and outstanding instincts, all of which underscore his penchant for making the electrifying play. Aybar doesn't work deep counts or walk very often. He's no power threat, though he can drive balls from gap to gap. He's careless at times in the field and on the bases. A switch-hitter, he's more comfortable and centers the ball more regularly from the left side. He's ready for big league playing time, but is blocked by Orlando Cabrera. He probably faces another year in Triple-A, unless Los Angeles decides to cash him in as a trade chip.

| Year | Club (League) | Class | AVG | G | AB | R | H | 2B | 3B | HR | RBI | BB | SO | SB | OBP | SLG |
|------|---------------|-------|-----|---|----|---|---|----|----|----|-----|----|----|----|-----|-----|
| 2002 | Provo (Pio) | R | .326 | 67 | 273 | 64 | 89 | 15 | 6 | 4 | 29 | 21 | 43 | 15 | .395 | .469 |
| 2003 | Cedar Rapids (MWL) | A | .308 | 125 | 496 | 83 | 153 | 30 | 10 | 6 | 57 | 17 | 54 | 32 | .346 | .446 |
| 2004 | Rancho Cucamonga (Cal) | A | .330 | 136 | 573 | 102 | 189 | 25 | 11 | 6 | 65 | 26 | 66 | 51 | .370 | .485 |
| 2005 | Arkansas (TL) | AA | .303 | 134 | 535 | 101 | 162 | 29 | 10 | 9 | 54 | 29 | 51 | 49 | .350 | .445 |
| 2006 | Salt Lake (PCL) | AAA | .283 | 81 | 339 | 63 | 96 | 20 | 3 | 6 | 45 | 21 | 36 | 32 | .327 | .413 |
| | Los Angeles (AL) | MLB | .250 | 34 | 40 | 5 | 10 | 1 | 1 | 0 | 2 | 0 | 8 | 1 | .250 | .325 |
| **MINOR LEAGUE TOTALS** | | | .311 | 543 | 2216 | 413 | 689 | 119 | 40 | 39 | 250 | 114 | 250 | 179 | .356 | .454 |
| **MAJOR LEAGUE TOTALS** | | | .250 | 34 | 40 | 5 | 10 | 1 | 1 | 0 | 2 | 0 | 8 | 1 | .250 | .325 |

## 4 YOUNG-IL JUNG RHP

**Born:** Nov. 16, 1988. **B-T:** R-R. **Ht.:** 6-2. **Wt.:** 190. **Signed:** Korea, 2006. **Signed By:** Charlie Kim/Clay Daniel.

Rarely does a Korean player sign with a major league team out of high school, but Jung did for $1 million last August. Charlie Kim, the Angels' part-time scout in Korea, forged a relationship with Jung and his family, and international scouting supervisor Clay Daniel endorsed the signing. Jung's mature, thick frame and clean delivery belie his age. Newly appointed minor league pitching coordinator Kernan Ronan simplified Jung's repertoire during instructional league, and he'll work with a fastball, slider and straight changeup after ditching his splitter and curve. He has feel for all three pitches. His 89-92 mph fastball is heavy with occasional late run. He maintains his arm speed when throwing his 82 mph changeup with good sinking action. Jung's slider sits

between 83-85 mph with short, late tilt. He's poised, and Los Angeles lauds his effort to learn English and establish rapport with teammates. Jung's body doesn't lend considerable room for growth. His frame and drop-and-drive delivery could make it tough for him to generate downward plane. His command is below-average, especially of his slider. Jung is polished for his age and offers the promise of a No. 2 or 3 starter. His performance during spring training will predicate his assignment, and he could see time at low Class A in his debut season.

| Year | Club (League) | Class | W | L | ERA | G | GS | CG | SV | IP | H | R | ER | HR | BB | SO | AVG |
|------|---------------|-------|---|---|-----|---|----|----|----|----|---|---|----|----|----|----|-----|
| 2006 | Did not play—Signed 2007 contract | | | | | | | | | | | | | | | | |

## 5 STEPHEN MAREK

RHP

BILL MITCHELL

**Born:** Sept. 3, 1983. **B-T:** L-R. **Ht.:** 6-2. **Wt.:** 220. **Drafted:** San Jacinto (Texas) JC, D/F 2004 (40th round). **Signed by:** Chad McDonald.

Signed for $800,000 as a draft-and-follow prior to the 2005 draft, Marek provided a potent complement to Nick Adenhart atop the Cedar Rapids rotation. He led the Midwest League in ERA. Armed with a three-pitch arsenal, Marek pounds the zone with powerful stuff. His 88-93 mph fastball has late life and has touched 96-98 in the past. His curveball has sharp break at 78-82 mph. His changeup is hard and heavy, with action that resembles a splitter. He made strides in his command and pitches with a dogged demeanor. A junior college reliever without much experience, Marek has some work to do on his delivery. It isn't effortless, and he could improve his balance over the rubber. He tends to miss up in the zone with his fastball. Marek projects as a No. 3 or 4 starter, and should climb to Double-A in 2007.

| Year | Club (League) | Class | W | L | ERA | G | GS | CG | SV | IP | H | R | ER | HR | BB | SO | AVG |
|------|---------------|-------|----|---|------|----|----|----|----|-----|-----|----|----|----|----|-----|------|
| 2005 | Orem (Pio) | R | 1 | 3 | 4.50 | 15 | 14 | 0 | 0 | 66 | 74 | 37 | 33 | 7 | 25 | 55 | .292 |
| 2006 | Cedar Rapids (MWL) | A | 10 | 2 | 1.96 | 19 | 19 | 1 | 0 | 119 | 95 | 27 | 26 | 8 | 24 | 100 | .216 |
| | Rancho Cucamonga (Cal) | A | 2 | 3 | 3.94 | 6 | 6 | 0 | 0 | 32 | 26 | 14 | 14 | 4 | 13 | 33 | .230 |
| **MINOR LEAGUE TOTALS** | | | 13 | 8 | 3.02 | 40 | 39 | 1 | 0 | 217 | 195 | 78 | 73 | 19 | 62 | 188 | .242 |

## 6 HANK CONGER

C

BILL MITCHELL

**Born:** Jan. 29, 1988. **B-T:** B-R. **Ht.:** 6-0. **Wt.:** 205. **Drafted:** HS—Huntington Beach, Calif., 2006 (1st round). **Signed by:** Bobby DeJardin.

Conger was tabbed as a future star when he slugged 34 home runs for an Ocean View, Calif., team that fell one win shy of the 2000 Little League World Series. A second-generation Korean, his given name is Hyun and his grandfather, who lived in Atlanta, nicknamed him after Hall of Famer Hank Aaron. Conger signed for $1.35 million and rated as the No. 1 prospect in the Arizona League, though his debut there ended after 19 games when he broke the hamate bone in his right hand. He has an aggressive approach with plus power from both sides of the plate. He's also an intelligent hitter who makes consistent hard contact. He has well-above-average arm strength and championship-caliber makeup. There have been questions about whether Conger will stay behind the plate, as he's not light on his feet. But early returns were positive, as his hands and receiving skills are playable, and he blocks adequately. He has an uppercut swing and tends to try to muscle balls out of the park rather than let his hands and leveraged stroke do the work. He's a well-below-average runner. Whether he arrives in the big leagues behind the plate, at an infield corner or as a DH will determine his ultimate value.

| Year | Club (League) | Class | AVG | G | AB | R | H | 2B | 3B | HR | RBI | BB | SO | SB | OBP | SLG |
|------|---------------|-------|------|----|----|----|----|----|----|----|-----|----|----|----|------|------|
| 2006 | Angels (AZL) | R | .319 | 19 | 69 | 11 | 22 | 3 | 4 | 1 | 11 | 7 | 11 | 1 | .382 | .522 |
| **MINOR LEAGUE TOTALS** | | | .319 | 19 | 69 | 11 | 22 | 3 | 4 | 1 | 11 | 7 | 11 | 1 | .382 | .522 |

## 7 JEFF MATHIS

C

**Born:** March 31, 1983. **B-T:** R-R. **Ht.:** 6-0. **Wt.:** 180. **Drafted:** HS—Marianna, Fla., 2001 (1st round supplemental). **Signed by:** Tom Kotchman.

The Angels didn't expect considerable offensive production out of Mathis when they broke camp with him penciled in as a platoon partner for Jose Molina, but manager Mike Scioscia lost patience when Mathis carried his offensive struggles behind the plate. He was sent down to Triple-A, Mike Napoli got his shot and thrived, and Mathis wasn't called up again until September. Managers rated Mathis the best defensive catcher in the Triple-A Pacific Coast League. He's agile, blocks and receives well, owns a solid-average arm and calls a good game. He has shown 15-20 homer

power potential in the past, though his power regressed in 2006. Mathis took a step backward at the plate in 2006. His bat speed was just fringe-average, his plate discipline declined and his swing got long. He reduced his propensity chase pitches, but has additional room for improvement. Despite outstanding makeup, he didn't handle adversity well in Los Angeles and put too much pressure on himself. He's a below-average runner, albeit with good instincts. Mathis still could reach his ceiling of a dependable, everyday backstop provided he improves his contact at the plate. He has a better all-around game than Molina and Napoli, who will be his main competition in spring training.

| Year | Club (League) | Class | AVG | G | AB | R | H | 2B | 3B | HR | RBI | BB | SO | SB | OBP | SLG |
|------|---------------|-------|-----|---|----|---|---|----|----|----|-----|----|----|----|-----|-----|
| 2001 | Angels (AZL) | R | .304 | 7 | 23 | 1 | 7 | 1 | 0 | 0 | 3 | 2 | 4 | 0 | .346 | .348 |
| | Provo (Pio) | R | .299 | 22 | 77 | 14 | 23 | 6 | 3 | 0 | 18 | 11 | 13 | 1 | .387 | .455 |
| 2002 | Cedar Rapids (MWL) | A | .287 | 128 | 491 | 75 | 141 | 41 | 3 | 10 | 73 | 40 | 75 | 7 | .346 | .444 |
| 2003 | Rancho Cucamonga (Cal) | A | .323 | 97 | 378 | 73 | 122 | 28 | 3 | 11 | 54 | 35 | 74 | 5 | .384 | .500 |
| | Arkansas (TL) | AA | .284 | 24 | 95 | 19 | 27 | 11 | 0 | 2 | 14 | 12 | 16 | 1 | .364 | .463 |
| 2004 | Arkansas (TL) | AA | .227 | 117 | 432 | 57 | 98 | 24 | 3 | 14 | 55 | 49 | 102 | 2 | .310 | .394 |
| 2005 | Salt Lake (PCL) | AAA | .276 | 112 | 427 | 78 | 118 | 26 | 3 | 21 | 73 | 42 | 85 | 4 | .340 | .499 |
| | Los Angeles (AL) | MLB | .333 | 5 | 3 | 1 | 1 | 0 | 0 | 0 | 0 | 0 | 1 | 0 | .333 | .333 |
| 2006 | Salt Lake (PCL) | AAA | .289 | 99 | 384 | 62 | 111 | 33 | 3 | 5 | 45 | 26 | 75 | 3 | .333 | .430 |
| | Los Angeles (AL) | MLB | .145 | 23 | 55 | 9 | 8 | 2 | 0 | 2 | 6 | 7 | 14 | 0 | .238 | .291 |
| **MINOR LEAGUE TOTALS** | | | .280 | 606 | 2307 | 379 | 647 | 170 | 18 | 63 | 335 | 217 | 444 | 23 | .344 | .452 |
| **MAJOR LEAGUE TOTALS** | | | .155 | 28 | 58 | 10 | 9 | 2 | 0 | 2 | 6 | 7 | 15 | 0 | .242 | .293 |

## 8 SEAN RODRIGUEZ                                                 2B

STEVE MOORE

**Born:** April 26, 1985. **B-T:** R-R. **Ht.:** 6-0. **Wt.:** 195. **Drafted:** HS—Miami, 2003 (3rd round). **Signed by:** Mike Silvestri.

Rodriguez' bat speed stood out among a thin crop of East Coast prep hitters in 2003 when he signed for $400,000. Rodriguez hit a career-high 29 homers while playing almost solely at shortstop for the first time as a pro. He led the minors in total bases (291) and was the Angels' organization player of the year in 2006. The son of Marlins minor league coach Johnny Rodriguez, he honed his swing as a kid after watching his dad throw batting practice to Alex Rodriguez (no relation). Sean's days of emulating A-Rod are over, as he has overhauled his approach at the plate. He has all but eliminated his leg kick and is more upright in his setup. It's a little unorthodox, but it improved his balance. He still shows plus bat speed with above-average power to all fields. He's an instinctual player with soft hands and plus arm strength. Rodriguez chases pitches out of the zone too often and set a career high for strikeouts in 2006. He has a feel for hitting, though he may not be as good as his numbers suggest—he hit .342 with 16 homers in 61 games at the launching pad that is Rancho Cucamonga's Epicenter. His thick frame and below-average speed eventually will move him off shortstop, probably to second base. Ticketed for Double-A in 2007, Rodriguez could become an everyday big leaguer who hits .270 with 20 homers. He has played second base, third base and the outfield, so at worst he should become an offensive-minded utilityman.

| Year | Club (League) | Class | AVG | G | AB | R | H | 2B | 3B | HR | RBI | BB | SO | SB | OBP | SLG |
|------|---------------|-------|-----|---|----|---|---|----|----|----|-----|----|----|----|-----|-----|
| 2003 | Angels (AZL) | R | .269 | 54 | 216 | 30 | 58 | 8 | 5 | 2 | 25 | 14 | 37 | 11 | .332 | .380 |
| 2004 | Cedar Rapids (MWL) | A | .250 | 57 | 196 | 35 | 49 | 8 | 4 | 4 | 17 | 18 | 54 | 14 | .333 | .393 |
| | Provo (Pio) | R | .338 | 64 | 225 | 64 | 76 | 14 | 4 | 10 | 55 | 51 | 62 | 9 | .486 | .569 |
| 2005 | Cedar Rapids (MWL) | A | .250 | 124 | 448 | 86 | 112 | 29 | 3 | 14 | 45 | 78 | 85 | 27 | .371 | .422 |
| 2006 | Arkansas (TL) | AA | .354 | 18 | 65 | 16 | 23 | 5 | 0 | 5 | 9 | 11 | 18 | 0 | .462 | .662 |
| | Rancho Cucamonga (Cal) | A | .301 | 116 | 455 | 78 | 137 | 29 | 5 | 24 | 77 | 47 | 124 | 15 | .377 | .545 |
| | Salt Lake (PCL) | AAA | .000 | 1 | 2 | 0 | 0 | 0 | 0 | 0 | 0 | 0 | 2 | 0 | .000 | .000 |
| **MINOR LEAGUE TOTALS** | | | .283 | 434 | 1607 | 309 | 455 | 93 | 21 | 59 | 228 | 219 | 382 | 76 | .384 | .477 |

## 9 SEAN O'SULLIVAN                                               RHP

BILL MITCHELL

**Born:** Sept. 1, 1987. **B-T:** R-R. **Ht.:** 6-1. **Wt.:** 220. **Drafted:** Grossmont (Calif.) JC, D/F 2005 (3rd round). **Signed by:** Tim Corcoran.

Baseball America recognized O'Sullivan as the best 12-year-old in the nation in 2000. A candidate to be the first high school pitcher drafted in 2005, he saw his velocity and draft stock slip that spring. He went in the third round and spent a season at Grossmont (Calif.) JC before signing as a draft-and-follow for $500,000—roughly what Los Angeles offered him after the draft. He led the Pioneer League in ERA during his debut. While his calling card as an amateur was low- to mid-90s heat, O'Sullivan's upside now lies in his feel for pitching rather than his arm strength. He can spot his 88-91

mph fastball, curveball, slider and changeup to all four quadrants of the strike zone. He adds and subtracts off his fastball, toys with a two-seamer and mixes his stuff well. O'Sullivan's loss of velocity is curious. Some Angels officials believe he'll regain the fastball he had as an underclassman, but his thick, mature body—which draws comparisons to Chris Bosio—has earned him the nickname "Nacho" and doesn't lend projection. His breaking pitches are effective but lack significant bite. His overall stuff doesn't grade out as more than average, so his command will be paramount against more advanced hitters. O'Sullivan showed stamina and poise in his first taste of pro ball, and his cerebral approach could carry him quickly through the minors. He'll likely open 2007 in low Class A.

| Year | Club (League) | Class | W | L | ERA | G | GS | CG | SV | IP | H | R | ER | HR | BB | SO | AVG |
|------|---------------|-------|---|---|-----|---|----|----|----|-----|----|----|----|----|----|----|-----|
| 2006 | Orem (Pio) | R | 4 | 0 | 2.14 | 14 | 14 | 0 | 0 | 71 | 65 | 23 | 17 | 2 | 7 | 55 | .239 |
| MINOR LEAGUE TOTALS | | | 4 | 0 | 2.14 | 14 | 14 | 0 | 0 | 71 | 65 | 23 | 17 | 2 | 7 | 55 | .239 |

## 10 TOMMY MENDOZA                                         RHP

**Born:** Aug. 18, 1987. **B-T:** R-R. **Ht.:** 6-2. **Wt.:** 185. **Drafted:** HS— Miami, 2005 (4th round). **Signed by:** Mike Silvestri.

Mendoza set the bar high in his 2005 debut, dominating the Arizona League and throwing 10 shutout innings without a walk in high Class A. He tried to blow the ball by Midwest League hitters at the outset of the 2006 season, which led to a 2-5, 5.81 record in his first 10 starts. Once he learned he had to pitch rather than just throw hard, he went 10-1, 3.57 the rest of the way—all the more impressive considering he was the second-youngest starter in the MWL. Mendoza's lone plus pitch is a lively 89-94 mph fastball that can touch 96. It's heavy and he has learned how to add and subtract velocity from it. He'll cut his fastball and also mixes in a two-seamer. His fastball command is solid-average. His 72-76 mph curveball is average at times but is inconsistent, often morphing into a slurve, and he doesn't spot it effectively. His changeup also is below-average at this point. He needs to make mechanical adjustments, such as staying over the rubber longer, to improve his command and stuff. Mendoza should at least develop into a reliever. If his stuff tightens and his command improves, he could become a No. 3-5 starter. He's ready for high Class A at age 19.

| Year | Club (League) | Class | W | L | ERA | G | GS | CG | SV | IP | H | R | ER | HR | BB | SO | AVG |
|------|---------------|-------|----|---|------|----|----|----|----|-----|-----|----|----|----|----|-----|------|
| 2005 | Angels (AZL) | R | 3 | 3 | 1.55 | 13 | 4 | 0 | 0 | 52 | 42 | 14 | 9 | 1 | 13 | 56 | .221 |
| | Rancho Cucamonga (Cal) | A | 1 | 0 | 0.00 | 2 | 1 | 0 | 1 | 10 | 4 | 0 | 0 | 0 | 0 | 12 | .121 |
| 2006 | Cedar Rapids (MWL) | A | 11 | 6 | 4.17 | 27 | 27 | 1 | 0 | 171 | 169 | 83 | 79 | 15 | 32 | 134 | .261 |
| MINOR LEAGUE TOTALS | | | 15 | 9 | 3.40 | 42 | 32 | 1 | 1 | 233 | 215 | 97 | 88 | 16 | 45 | 202 | .247 |

## 11 KENNETH HERNDON                                       RHP

**Born:** Sept. 4, 1985. **B-T:** R-R. **Ht.:** 6-5. **Wt.:** 200. **Drafted:** Gulf Coast (Fla.) CC, 2006 (5th round). **Signed by:** Tom Kotchman.

Major League Baseball not only has clamped down on bonuses in the first 10 rounds of the draft, but it also has tried to keep the cost of draft-and-follows down as well. The Twins wanted to sign Herndon, their 23rd-round pick in 2005, after he spent the spring at Gulf Coast (Fla.) CC. But they acceded to MLB's wishes and didn't fork over the bonus they knew he'd get when he re-entered the draft. The Angels jumped on him in the fifth round and quickly signed him for $157,500. Herndon's bread and butter is a hard, heavy sinker that he throws at 90-93 mph, topping out at 95. Herndon achieves maximum extension in his delivery, which produces the life on his pitches. His durable, 6-foot-5 frame allows him to pitch downhill. He used both a curveball and a slider as an amateur, but scrapped his curve after signing. His slider is a fringe-average offering that occasionally shows sharp, late tilt. His changeup is an average, usable third offering. He has solid-average command. Herndon struggled against lefthanders in junior college and at Orem, where they batted .271 against him (compared to .214 by righties). A potential workhorse No. 4 starter in the big leagues, Herndon likely will begin 2007 in low Class A.

| Year | Club (League) | Class | W | L | ERA | G | GS | CG | SV | IP | H | R | ER | HR | BB | SO | AVG |
|------|---------------|-------|---|---|------|----|----|----|----|----|----|----|----|----|----|----|------|
| 2006 | Orem (Pio) | R | 5 | 2 | 2.21 | 14 | 14 | 0 | 0 | 69 | 65 | 25 | 17 | 6 | 10 | 36 | .242 |
| MINOR LEAGUE TOTALS | | | 5 | 2 | 2.21 | 14 | 14 | 0 | 0 | 69 | 65 | 25 | 17 | 6 | 10 | 36 | .242 |

## 12 PETER BOURJOS                                          OF

**Born:** March 31, 1987. **B-T:** R-R. **Ht.:** 6-1. **Wt.:** 175. **Drafted:** HS—Scottsdale, Ariz., 2005 (10th round). **Signed by:** John Gracio.

The Angels grew fond of Bourjos' tools during his senior season in high school, and took

him in the 10th round of the 2005 draft and signed him for $325,000, the equivalent of late third-round money. His father Chris played 24 games as an outfielder for the 1980 Giants and scouts for the Brewers. Peter made his pro debut in 2006, turning in a solid performance and standing out with his speed and defense. Longtime manager and scout Tom Kotchman went as far as to proclaim him the best defensive center fielder he had coached since Devon White. Bourjos is an easy, graceful runner with good instincts that are evident in his reads and routes. He has average arm strength. His approach at the plate is crude. He has above-average bat speed and average raw power, but his swing is loopy and he tends to work around the ball. He has a rudimentary feel for the strike zone, and he needs to improve his bunting and pitch selection. He also will have to refine his basestealing skills. He'll continue to develop level by level, spending 2007 in low Class A.

| Year | Club (League) | Class | AVG | G | AB | R | H | 2B | 3B | HR | RBI | BB | SO | SB | OBP | SLG |
|------|---------------|-------|-----|---|----|---|---|----|----|----|-----|----|----|----|-----|-----|
| 2006 | Orem (Pio) | R | .292 | 65 | 250 | 42 | 73 | 16 | 7 | 5 | 28 | 22 | 67 | 13 | .354 | .472 |
| **MINOR LEAGUE TOTALS** | | | .292 | 65 | 250 | 42 | 73 | 16 | 7 | 5 | 28 | 22 | 67 | 13 | .354 | .472 |

## 13  JOSE ARREDONDO                                                    RHP

**Born:** March 30, 1984. **B-T:** R-R. **Ht.:** 6-0. **Wt.:** 170. **Signed:** Dominican Republic, 2002. **Signed by:** Leo Perez.

Converted from shortstop to pitcher in 2004, Arredondo earned a spot on the Angels' 40-man roster after the 2005 season even though he had pitched just five innings above Rookie ball. He opened 2006 in high Class A, wowing scouts and performing remarkably well considering his lack of experience. Managers rated Arredondo's fastball the best in the Cal League, and he dials it up to 97 mph, pitching at 93-94. He's raw and has little feel for pitching, usually resorting to trying to throw his fastball by hitters—a recipe for disaster because it arrives on a level plane. Arredondo has a difficult time creating movement on his pitches. He cuts his delivery off, losing extension upon release, which causes his stuff to flatten out. He has average control. He throws a splitter and slider, which are both fringe-average, inconsistent offerings. He has been durable since converting but best fits the profile of a reliever. He was removed after two innings of a start in May because Rancho Cucamonga manager Bobby Mitchell said Arredondo had lost interest, and the Angels hope he matures, especially in his approach to pitching. He'll return to Arkansas in 2007.

| Year | Club (League) | Class | W | L | ERA | G | GS | CG | SV | IP | H | R | ER | HR | BB | SO | AVG |
|------|---------------|-------|---|---|-----|---|----|----|----|----|---|---|----|----|----|----|-----|
| 2004 | Angels (AZL) | R | 0 | 0 | 2.92 | 8 | 0 | 0 | 1 | 12 | 14 | 10 | 4 | 1 | 4 | 14 | .280 |
| 2005 | Arkansas (TL) | AA | 0 | 0 | 3.38 | 5 | 0 | 0 | 0 | 5 | 5 | 2 | 2 | 0 | 4 | 4 | .278 |
|  | Orem (Pio) | R | 5 | 0 | 4.19 | 15 | 13 | 0 | 0 | 69 | 76 | 34 | 32 | 4 | 20 | 60 | .285 |
| 2006 | Rancho Cucamonga (Cal) | A | 5 | 6 | 2.30 | 15 | 15 | 0 | 0 | 90 | 62 | 28 | 23 | 4 | 35 | 115 | .198 |
|  | Arkansas (TL) | AA | 2 | 3 | 6.53 | 11 | 11 | 1 | 0 | 61 | 80 | 47 | 44 | 8 | 22 | 48 | .317 |
| **MINOR LEAGUE TOTALS** | | | 12 | 9 | 3.99 | 54 | 39 | 1 | 1 | 237 | 237 | 121 | 105 | 17 | 85 | 241 | .263 |

## 14  P.J. PHILLIPS                                                    3B/SS

**Born:** Sept. 23, 1986. **B-T:** R-R. **Ht.:** 6-3. **Wt.:** 170. **Drafted:** HS—Stone Mountain, Ga., 2005 (2nd round). **Signed by:** Chris McAlpin.

Phillips' older brother Brandon emerged as the Reds' second baseman this year, and his younger sister Porsha is a freshman guard at Louisiana State. P.J. signed for $505,000 and remains a high-ceiling, unrefined prospect. Following a solid debut in 2005, Phillips struggled considerably last year. Though he has seen time at shortstop, Phillips fits the third-base profile. He has an easy, quick swing and when he connects, he can drive balls out to all parts of the park. His stroke, while long at times, has outstanding leverage. He has plus arm strength, throws accurately from different angles and displays body control on slow rollers. He's an average runner with long, even strides. Poor pitch recognition keeps Phillips' hitting tools from translating to games consistently. His plan vacillates from at-bat to at-bat, and he needs to improve his focus and attitude in order to overcome his deficiencies. His baserunning and defense are raw. His hands are fine, but he doesn't trust them and must improve his footwork and fielding mechanics. The Angels will have to be patient with Phillips, who can become an everyday player with well-above-average power if he closes the holes in his game presently. He may require more than 2,000 minor league at-bats before he's ready for a major league role. He should get his first full-season assignment in 2007, though there's an outside chance he begins the season in extended spring training.

| Year | Club (League) | Class | AVG | G | AB | R | H | 2B | 3B | HR | RBI | BB | SO | SB | OBP | SLG |
|------|---------------|-------|-----|---|----|---|---|----|----|----|-----|----|----|----|-----|-----|
| 2005 | Angels (AZL) | R | .291 | 49 | 182 | 25 | 53 | 6 | 6 | 1 | 24 | 9 | 53 | 13 | .328 | .407 |
| 2006 | Orem (Pio) | R | .240 | 69 | 263 | 36 | 63 | 12 | 1 | 6 | 27 | 20 | 75 | 11 | .298 | .361 |
| **MINOR LEAGUE TOTALS** | | | .261 | 118 | 445 | 61 | 116 | 18 | 7 | 7 | 51 | 29 | 128 | 24 | .310 | .380 |

## 15 HAINLEY STATIA SS

**Born:** Jan. 19, 1986. **B-T:** B-R. **Ht.:** 5-11. **Wt.:** 162. **Drafted:** HS—Lake Worth, Fla., 2004 (9th round). **Signed by:** Mike Silvestri.

Florida-based scout Mike Silvestri noticed Statia after the rangy teenager moved from his native Curacao to South Florida for his senior year in high school. Statia received a $90,000 bonus, and has progressed steadily. He speaks four languages—Dutch, English, Papiamento and Spanish—which is handy in the clubhouse. A knee injury nagged him last year. Statia is a wiry, athletic and instinctual middle infielder with plus defensive skills. He's surehanded and confident around the bag and has good actions and range. His arm is above-average. He makes consistent contact from both sides of the plate, though he lacks the strength and bat speed of an impact hitter. He works counts well, with a feel for the strike zone and has valuable situational-hitting ability. Statia's most significant shortcoming is his below-average speed, though he's better under way. He got a taste of high Class A in each of his first two seasons—breaking into pro ball there after baseball's visa shortage delayed his debut—and should have no problem handling that level full-time in 2007.

| Year | Club (League) | Class | AVG | G | AB | R | H | 2B | 3B | HR | RBI | BB | SO | SB | OBP | SLG |
|------|---------------|-------|-----|---|----|----|----|----|----|----|-----|----|----|----|-----|-----|
| 2005 | Rancho Cucamonga (Cal) | A | .245 | 23 | 106 | 12 | 26 | 2 | 0 | 1 | 8 | 5 | 13 | 6 | .286 | .292 |
| | Orem (Pio) | R | .300 | 68 | 277 | 44 | 83 | 17 | 6 | 2 | 41 | 23 | 40 | 12 | .360 | .426 |
| 2006 | Cedar Rapids (MWL) | A | .297 | 111 | 417 | 68 | 124 | 31 | 1 | 1 | 38 | 52 | 54 | 23 | .379 | .384 |
| | Rancho Cucamonga (Cal) | A | .300 | 18 | 60 | 8 | 18 | 2 | 1 | 0 | 8 | 8 | 7 | 1 | .386 | .367 |
| **MINOR LEAGUE TOTALS** | | | .292 | 220 | 860 | 132 | 251 | 52 | 8 | 4 | 95 | 88 | 114 | 42 | .363 | .385 |

## 16 MATT SWEENEY 1B

**Born:** April 14, 1988. **B-T:** L-R. **Ht.:** 6-3. **Wt.:** 212. **Drafted:** HS—Rockville, Md., 2006 (8th round). **Signed by:** Dan Radcliff.

Late-round steals typically are accompanied by generous signing bonuses, but when the Angels drafted Sweeney in the eighth round last June, they signed him for $75,000. He earned little attention in suburban Washington D.C. and had committed to Potomac State (W.Va.) JC, but area scout Dan Radcliff and East Coast crosschecker Marc Russo (now a major league scout) loved Sweeney's swing. A standout football star, as well, Sweeney lost 30 pounds before his senior season. Sweeney has plus bat speed and leverage to his swing, which he repeats well. He has a knack for squaring up the ball, is selective and has strong pitch recognition skills. He split time between catcher and DH in high school, but he likely will wind up at first base. He's heavy-footed and somewhat stiff defensively, with hard hands. He has solid-average arm strength. His uncle works for the NFL's Washington Redskins, and Sweeney worked with 'Skins receiver James Thrash on his agility. He's a below-average runner but goes first to third adequately. He should spend 2007 at Orem, though his bat could earn him a promotion to low Class A at some point during the year.

| Year | Club (League) | Class | AVG | G | AB | R | H | 2B | 3B | HR | RBI | BB | SO | SB | OBP | SLG |
|------|---------------|-------|-----|---|----|----|----|----|----|----|-----|----|----|----|-----|-----|
| 2006 | Angels (AZL) | R | .341 | 44 | 170 | 38 | 58 | 11 | 7 | 5 | 39 | 23 | 27 | 4 | .431 | .576 |
| | Orem (Pio) | R | .167 | 2 | 6 | 0 | 1 | 0 | 0 | 0 | 0 | 0 | 2 | 0 | .286 | .167 |
| **MINOR LEAGUE TOTALS** | | | .335 | 46 | 176 | 38 | 59 | 11 | 7 | 5 | 39 | 23 | 29 | 4 | .426 | .563 |

## 17 JEREMY HAYNES RHP

**Born:** May 28, 1986. **B-T:** R-R. **Ht.:** 6-2. **Wt.:** 180. **Drafted:** Tallahassee (Fla.) CC, D/F 2005 (37th round). **Signed by:** Tom Kotchman.

A teammate of Brewers outfield prospect Lorenzo Cain at Madison County (Fla.) High and Tallahassee (Fla.) CC, Haynes signed for $100,000 as a draft-and-follow last spring. He spent time in junior college as a center fielder, with his arm strength and athleticism his best attributes. The Angels decided to put those tools to use full-time on the mound, and he flashed a pair of plus pitches in his debut. He has prompted comparisons to Tom Gordon, though he's taller and thicker than Gordon was at the same age. Haynes' lively fastball sits in the low 90s and touches 95. He's aggressive and pitches off his fastball, which features plus sink at times. His out pitch is a hard curveball that has occasional two-plane break at 76-82 mph. His changeup is below-average, and he has a tendency to slow his arm on his offspeed stuff. Haynes is raw, but began repeating his delivery when he returned to the full windup he employed in junior college. He works deep in counts and often misses up in the zone, but with a fresh, live arm and strong makeup, he has a high ceiling. He should open 2007 at low Class A.

| Year | Club (League) | Class | W | L | ERA | G | GS | CG | SV | IP | H | R | ER | HR | BB | SO | AVG |
|------|---------------|-------|---|---|-----|---|----|----|----|----|---|---|----|----|----|----|-----|
| 2006 | Orem (Pio) | R | 3 | 1 | 2.76 | 16 | 14 | 0 | 1 | 59 | 46 | 21 | 18 | 5 | 41 | 68 | .217 |
| **MINOR LEAGUE TOTALS** | | | 3 | 1 | 2.76 | 16 | 14 | 0 | 1 | 59 | 46 | 21 | 18 | 5 | 41 | 68 | .217 |

## TERRY EVANS
OF

**Born:** Jan. 19, 1982. **B-T:** R-R. **Ht.:** 6-4. **Wt.:** 211. **Drafted:** Middle Georgia JC, D/F 2001 (47th round). **Signed by:** Roger Smith (Cardinals).

Trading the ineffective Jeff Weaver to the Cardinals last July served two purposes for the Angels. It opened a spot in the rotation for Jeff's brother Jered, and it landed Evans, who continued a breakout season after switching organizations. Evans had batted just .239 with 40 homers in 398 games before 2006, when he hit .309 with 33 longballs and 37 steals. A devout Christian, he said his improved mental approach enabled him to turn the corner. One Texas League scout called him a poor man's Dale Murphy, as Evans does everything well. For the first time in his career he displayed above-average power that translated to games. His approach improved significantly and he did a better job of laying off chase pitches, though he remains a free swinger and is especially vulnerable to breaking balls. He likes to drive the ball to right field and also can pull pitches out of the park on occasion. His power comes more from his strength rather than pure bat speed. He could better incorporate his lower half into his swing. Capable of playing all three outfield positions, he's an adequate defensive center fielder with average speed. He has a slightly-above-average arm. The Angels weren't sure what they were getting when they picked up Evans, but they're encouraged by the early returns and will send him to Triple-A in 2007.

| Year | Club (League) | Class | AVG | G | AB | R | H | 2B | 3B | HR | RBI | BB | SO | SB | OBP | SLG |
|------|---------------|-------|-----|---|----|---|---|----|----|----|-----|----|----|----|-----|-----|
| 2002 | Johnson City (Appy) | R | .287 | 60 | 230 | 42 | 66 | 22 | 2 | 7 | 41 | 29 | 67 | 17 | .364 | .491 |
| 2003 | Peoria (MWL) | A | .246 | 104 | 382 | 35 | 94 | 28 | 1 | 10 | 41 | 19 | 86 | 13 | .286 | .403 |
| 2004 | Peoria (MWL) | A | .222 | 101 | 365 | 48 | 81 | 21 | 1 | 13 | 59 | 35 | 105 | 8 | .301 | .392 |
| | Palm Beach (FSL) | A | .224 | 19 | 58 | 7 | 13 | 4 | 0 | 2 | 7 | 4 | 16 | 1 | .281 | .397 |
| 2005 | Palm Beach (FSL) | A | .221 | 114 | 385 | 34 | 85 | 16 | 1 | 8 | 47 | 29 | 110 | 12 | .285 | .330 |
| 2006 | Arkansas (TL) | AA | .309 | 52 | 188 | 48 | 58 | 9 | 2 | 11 | 22 | 18 | 56 | 11 | .385 | .553 |
| | Palm Beach (FSL) | A | .311 | 60 | 238 | 43 | 74 | 10 | 1 | 15 | 45 | 20 | 50 | 21 | .373 | .550 |
| | Springfield (TL) | AA | .307 | 21 | 75 | 13 | 23 | 4 | 0 | 7 | 20 | 3 | 21 | 5 | .369 | .640 |
| **MINOR LEAGUE TOTALS** | | | .257 | 531 | 1921 | 270 | 494 | 114 | 8 | 73 | 282 | 157 | 511 | 88 | .322 | .439 |

## BOBBY WILSON
C

**Born:** April 8, 1983. **B-T:** R-R. **Ht.:** 6-0. **Wt.:** 205. **Drafted:** St. Petersburg (Fla.) CC, D/F 2002 (48th round). **Signed by:** Tom Kotchman.

The draft-and-follow process was good to the Angels, especially in Florida, where longtime area scout Tom Kotchman mines the junior colleges resourcefully. He had a distinct advantage in the evaluation of Wilson, who played with his son Casey on Seminole (Fla.) High's 2001 national championship team and on Amateur Athletic Union clubs. Wilson's portly build and unorthodox swing mechanics make many scouts ambivalent about his prospect status, but he continues to improve his efficiency both at the plate and behind it. He has above-average bat speed and slightly below-average power. Wilson has shortened his swing, enabling him to make more consistent contact and improve his ability to handle pitches on the inner half. He'll use the opposite field and his plate discipline and feel for the strike zone make him a tough out. Wilson also has a knack for collecting the clutch hit. He's not terribly nimble behind the plate, but his footwork and hands are adequate, he blocks balls well and shows an average arm. He threw out 43 percent of basestealers in 2006 after erasing 45 percent the year before. He was unable to catch for most of the final month of the season because of shoulder soreness and some scouts question his durability. He profiles as a part-time big leaguer, but could play his way into an everyday role on a second-division team.

| Year | Club (League) | Class | AVG | G | AB | R | H | 2B | 3B | HR | RBI | BB | SO | SB | OBP | SLG |
|------|---------------|-------|-----|---|----|---|---|----|----|----|-----|----|----|----|-----|-----|
| 2003 | Provo (Pio) | R | .284 | 57 | 236 | 36 | 67 | 12 | 0 | 6 | 62 | 18 | 31 | 0 | .329 | .411 |
| 2004 | Cedar Rapids (MWL) | A | .268 | 105 | 396 | 45 | 106 | 23 | 0 | 8 | 64 | 30 | 55 | 5 | .320 | .386 |
| 2005 | Rancho Cucamonga (Cal) | A | .290 | 115 | 466 | 66 | 135 | 32 | 1 | 14 | 77 | 30 | 61 | 2 | .333 | .453 |
| 2006 | Arkansas (TL) | AA | .286 | 103 | 374 | 45 | 107 | 26 | 0 | 9 | 53 | 33 | 47 | 1 | .350 | .428 |
| **MINOR LEAGUE TOTALS** | | | .282 | 380 | 1472 | 192 | 415 | 93 | 1 | 37 | 256 | 111 | 194 | 8 | .334 | .422 |

## RYAN MOUNT
2B

**Born:** Aug. 17, 1986. **B-T:** L-R. **Ht.:** 6-1. **Wt.:** 180. **Drafted:** HS—Chino Hills, Calif., 2005 (2nd round). **Signed by:** Tim Corcoran.

Mount made a late surge as a high school senior, going from a lightly recruited college prospect to a second-round pick who signed for $615,000. His approach at the plate has aided his transition to pro ball. He's patient, has good pitch recognition and uses the whole field. He makes hard contact and has a knack for putting the barrel on the ball. Mount could develop plus power as he gains strength in his upper body. He needs to cut down on his strikeouts and improve against lefthanders after batting .172 off them in 2006. Minor league

hitting instructor Ty Van Berkleo (now with the Athletics), who is lefthanded, spent hours tossing batting practice to him during instructional league, and Mount began to show confidence facing southpaws. He's a fringe-average runner. Mount has played most of his pro career at shortstop, but he lacks the actions and fluidity to remain there. His hands are adequate and he has a plus arm, but his range and footwork are concerns. He'll probably move to second base down the road, though he'll stay at shortstop this year in low Class A.

| Year | Club (League) | Class | AVG | G | AB | R | H | 2B | 3B | HR | RBI | BB | SO | SB | OBP | SLG |
|------|---------------|-------|-----|---|----|---|---|----|----|----|-----|----|----|----|-----|-----|
| 2005 | Angels (AZL) | R | .216 | 29 | 102 | 15 | 22 | 7 | 1 | 1 | 17 | 17 | 31 | 4 | .325 | .333 |
| 2006 | Orem (Pio) | R | .285 | 69 | 277 | 54 | 79 | 14 | 2 | 9 | 38 | 36 | 67 | 10 | .370 | .448 |
| **MINOR LEAGUE TOTALS** | | | .266 | 98 | 379 | 69 | 101 | 21 | 3 | 10 | 55 | 53 | 98 | 14 | .358 | .417 |

## 21 TREVOR BELL RHP

**Born:** Oct. 12, 1986. **B-T:** L-R. **Ht.:** 6-2. **Wt.:** 180. **Drafted:** HS—La Crescenta, Calif., 2005 (1st round supplemental). **Signed by:** Tim Corcoran.

Bell has one of the most intriguing backgrounds in the minors. The grandson of Bob Bell (aka Bozo the Clown), Bell has been around show business for most of his life and appeared in commercials for Hot Wheels, Kellogg's and Old Navy. His mother Barbara is a television casting director. Bell was recognized by Baseball America as the top 14-year-old in the nation in 2001. He was a two-way star as an amateur but when his fastball velocity climbed to the mid-90s during his senior year in high school, he made his money on the mound, signing for $925,000 as the 37th overall pick. His fastball velocity hasn't been the same as a pro. He pitched at 88-90 mph for most of 2006, bumping 92. After he analyzed video of himself as an amateur with Orem pitching coach Zeke Zimmerman, Bell improved the tempo of his delivery and found a little more velocity. He'll snap off a plus curveball will late bite, but he needs to improve the command and consistency of his secondary stuff. He also throws a slider and changeup. Bell made strides in his approach to pitching and gets ahead of hitters with his fastball. He led the Pioneer League in innings, and he profiles as a durable back-of-the-rotation starter or middle reliever. Bell should spend most of 2007 in low Class A.

| Year | Club (League) | Class | W | L | ERA | G | GS | CG | SV | IP | H | R | ER | HR | BB | SO | AVG |
|------|---------------|-------|---|---|-----|---|----|----|----|----|---|---|----|----|----|----|-----|
| 2005 | Angels (AZL) | R | 0 | 0 | 4.50 | 4 | 4 | 0 | 0 | 8 | 10 | 4 | 4 | 0 | 3 | 7 | .313 |
| 2006 | Orem (Pio) | R | 4 | 2 | 3.50 | 16 | 16 | 0 | 0 | 82 | 82 | 35 | 32 | 8 | 15 | 53 | .261 |
| **MINOR LEAGUE TOTALS** | | | 4 | 2 | 3.59 | 20 | 20 | 0 | 0 | 90 | 92 | 39 | 36 | 8 | 18 | 60 | .266 |

## 22 RAFAEL RODRIGUEZ RHP

**Born:** Sept. 24, 1984. **B-T:** R-R. **Ht.:** 6-1. **Wt.:** 175. **Signed:** Dominican Republic, 2001. **Signed by:** Leo Perez.

The Angels signed the live-armed Rodriguez for $780,000 in 2001, when he was just 16. He has battled elbow tenderness since then, and while he remained healthy in 2006, he has been slow to grasp the craft of pitching. He made three stellar starts in high Class A to start his season, then climbed to Double-A and never sustained success. His maximum-effort delivery prevents him from maintaining consistency with his stuff and command. His fastball sits between 90-94 mph with late life. One out of five of his mid-80s sliders will show plus hard, sharp break. He has rudimentary feel for his changeup. Rodriguez often overthrows, misses up in the zone and pitches behind in counts. He's vulnerable against lefthanders, one of several factors that point to a relief role in his future. The Angels would have had to place him on their 40-man roster in order to protect him from the Rule 5 draft, but changes in the new labor agreement gave them an additional year to see how he develops. He could open 2007 in Double-A or move to Triple-A with a successful spring.

| Year | Club (League) | Class | W | L | ERA | G | GS | CG | SV | IP | H | R | ER | HR | BB | SO | AVG |
|------|---------------|-------|---|---|-----|---|----|----|----|-----|-----|-----|-----|----|-----|-----|-----|
| 2002 | Angels (AZL) | R | 2 | 1 | 3.99 | 8 | 8 | 0 | 0 | 38 | 37 | 19 | 17 | 4 | 20 | 50 | .255 |
| | Provo (Pio) | R | 1 | 1 | 5.96 | 6 | 6 | 0 | 0 | 26 | 26 | 17 | 17 | 3 | 14 | 25 | .268 |
| 2003 | Cedar Rapids (MWL) | A | 10 | 11 | 4.31 | 26 | 26 | 1 | 0 | 144 | 129 | 85 | 69 | 7 | 59 | 100 | .236 |
| 2004 | Angels (AZL) | R | 0 | 2 | 6.46 | 4 | 4 | 0 | 0 | 15 | 18 | 12 | 11 | 1 | 5 | 13 | .295 |
| | Cedar Rapids (MWL) | A | 1 | 5 | 6.48 | 7 | 7 | 0 | 0 | 33 | 36 | 27 | 24 | 5 | 19 | 35 | .273 |
| 2005 | Cedar Rapids (MWL) | A | 5 | 2 | 2.78 | 13 | 13 | 0 | 0 | 74 | 61 | 24 | 23 | 5 | 27 | 74 | .220 |
| | Rancho Cucamonga (Cal) | A | 4 | 4 | 6.75 | 14 | 14 | 0 | 0 | 72 | 84 | 58 | 54 | 11 | 33 | 44 | .292 |
| 2006 | Rancho Cucamonga (Cal) | A | 3 | 0 | 0.53 | 3 | 3 | 0 | 0 | 17 | 15 | 1 | 1 | 0 | 2 | 20 | .234 |
| | Arkansas (TL) | AA | 5 | 10 | 6.63 | 24 | 24 | 0 | 0 | 133 | 175 | 111 | 98 | 28 | 55 | 83 | .321 |
| **MINOR LEAGUE TOTALS** | | | 31 | 36 | 5.11 | 105 | 105 | 1 | 0 | 553 | 581 | 354 | 314 | 64 | 234 | 444 | .269 |

## 23 NICK GREEN RHP

**Born:** Aug. 20, 1984. **B-T:** R-R. **Ht.:** 6-4. **Wt.:** 200. **Drafted:** Darton (Ga.) JC, 2004 (35th round). **Signed by:** Chris McAlpin.

Green was not even recruited by Abraham Baldwin Junior College in his hometown of

tiny Tifton, Ga., so he went to Darton Junior College in nearby Albany. He turned down $80,000 from the Astros as an 11th-rounder in 2003, and he wound up sliding to the 35th round a year later, when the Angels inked him for $1,500. He moved from the bullpen to the rotation in 2005 and has been a reliable, durable member of minor league rotations since. Green has a good feel for pitching and the best changeup in the system. His fastball velocity improved this year and sat between 88-92 mph. His arm works well and he uses a herky-jerky, deceptive delivery. Green's circle changeup has late, hard, screwball-like action with plus sink and fade. His 76-78 mph curveball is inconsistent, with occasional tight, 11-to-5 break. One scout graded it higher than Green's changeup after watching him strike out 11 in eight shutout innings in August. He mixes his pitches well, moves the ball around, pitches inside and gets ahead in counts. His willingness to pitch to contact is one of his assets. Ticketed for Double-A in 2007, Green profiles as a back-of-the-rotation starter.

| Year | Club (League) | Class | W | L | ERA | G | GS | CG | SV | IP | H | R | ER | HR | BB | SO | AVG |
|------|---------------|-------|---|---|-----|---|----|----|----|----|---|---|----|----|----|----|-----|
| 2004 | Provo (Pio) | R | 4 | 3 | 4.03 | 17 | 10 | 0 | 0 | 51 | 56 | 28 | 23 | 4 | 20 | 44 | .275 |
| 2005 | Cedar Rapids (MWL) | A | 3 | 3 | 3.58 | 26 | 8 | 1 | 2 | 101 | 95 | 47 | 40 | 11 | 14 | 74 | .249 |
| 2006 | Rancho Cucamonga (Cal) | A | 5 | 3 | 4.15 | 11 | 11 | 1 | 0 | 65 | 77 | 31 | 30 | 9 | 19 | 57 | .291 |
| | Arkansas (TL) | AA | 8 | 5 | 4.41 | 17 | 17 | 0 | 0 | 112 | 115 | 64 | 55 | 23 | 21 | 77 | .268 |
| **MINOR LEAGUE TOTALS** | | | 20 | 14 | 4.04 | 71 | 46 | 2 | 2 | 329 | 343 | 170 | 148 | 47 | 74 | 252 | .268 |

## 24 CHRIS RESOP RHP

**Born:** Nov. 4, 1982. **B-T:** R-R. **Ht.:** 6-3. **Wt.:** 200. **Drafted:** HS—Naples, Fla., 2001 (4th round). **Signed by:** Mike Tosar (Marlins).

The Angels acquired Resop from the Marlins in November in exchange for reliever Kevin Gregg. Resop spent much of last year shuttling between Florida and Triple-A Albuquerque, which partially explains his uneven showing in the majors. While he pounded the strike zone in the minors, Resop pitched too carefully on the big stage instead of trusting his 92-95 mph fastball and underutilized curve. Still, he was one of many relievers to get a crack at setting up for Marlins veteran closer Joe Borowski, and the experience should prove valuable. Armed with a big frame and a bulldog attitude, Resop has only been on the mound since July 2003, when he converted from the outfield at the urging of former Marlins farm director Marc DelPiano. Resop hit a combined .193 with one homer in 269 at-bats over his first three pro seasons. He'll head to spring training with a chance to win a role in the Los Angeles bullpen, though the competition will be stiffer than it would have been in Florida.

| Year | Club (League) | Class | W | L | ERA | G | GS | CG | SV | IP | H | R | ER | HR | BB | SO | AVG |
|------|---------------|-------|---|---|-----|---|----|----|----|----|---|---|----|----|----|----|-----|
| 2003 | Greensboro (SAL) | A | 0 | 1 | 4.97 | 11 | 0 | 0 | 0 | 13 | 11 | 7 | 7 | 1 | 5 | 15 | .224 |
| 2004 | Greensboro (SAL) | A | 3 | 1 | 1.94 | 41 | 0 | 0 | 13 | 42 | 26 | 11 | 9 | 1 | 7 | 68 | .173 |
| 2005 | Carolina (SL) | AA | 3 | 2 | 2.57 | 43 | 0 | 0 | 24 | 49 | 47 | 15 | 14 | 2 | 16 | 56 | .242 |
| | Florida (NL) | MLB | 2 | 0 | 8.47 | 15 | 0 | 0 | 0 | 17 | 22 | 16 | 16 | 1 | 9 | 15 | .324 |
| 2006 | Albuquerque (PCL) | AAA | 4 | 0 | 3.81 | 40 | 0 | 0 | 2 | 50 | 49 | 21 | 21 | 4 | 15 | 43 | .258 |
| | Florida (NL) | MLB | 1 | 2 | 3.38 | 22 | 0 | 0 | 0 | 21 | 26 | 9 | 8 | 1 | 16 | 10 | .310 |
| **MINOR LEAGUE TOTALS** | | | 10 | 4 | 3.00 | 135 | 0 | 0 | 39 | 153 | 133 | 54 | 51 | 8 | 43 | 182 | .228 |
| **MAJOR LEAGUE TOTALS** | | | 3 | 2 | 5.63 | 37 | 0 | 0 | 0 | 38 | 48 | 25 | 24 | 2 | 25 | 25 | .316 |

## 25 RICHARD ALDRIDGE RHP

**Born:** Sept. 10, 1983. **B-T:** R-R. **Ht.:** 6-2. **Wt.:** 210. **Drafted:** Middle Georgia JC, 2004 (17th round). **Signed by:** Chris McAlpin.

Aldridge was a Wayne County High (Jesup, Ga.) and Middle Georgia JC teammate of Barret Browning, who ranks No. 29 on this list. It was Browning, not Aldridge, whom scouts came to see when they were teenagers, but Aldridge steadily has built his own reputation as a bullpen prospect. He dominated low Class A hitters in 2006. His fastball sits at 92 mph and can run it up into the mid-90s, showing some sink and late life. His 78-79 mph slider has three-quarter tilt. It's a plus-plus pitch at times, albeit inconsistent. Aldridge doesn't repeat his delivery and has below-average command. He cuts his delivery off, losing extension and leaving his stuff up. Shoulder problems have hampered his development and 2006 was the first season he stayed healthy. He has a future as a middle reliever or setup man. He's headed back to high Class A after making five appearances there at the end of last season.

| Year | Club (League) | Class | W | L | ERA | G | GS | CG | SV | IP | H | R | ER | HR | BB | SO | AVG |
|------|---------------|-------|---|---|-----|---|----|----|----|----|---|---|----|----|----|----|-----|
| 2004 | Angels (AZL) | R | 0 | 3 | 6.25 | 13 | 5 | 0 | 1 | 40 | 41 | 30 | 28 | 2 | 28 | 43 | .258 |
| 2005 | Angels (AZL) | R | 0 | 0 | 1.00 | 7 | 0 | 0 | 0 | 9 | 6 | 1 | 1 | 0 | 7 | 19 | .194 |
| | Orem (Pio) | R | 0 | 0 | 0.00 | 2 | 0 | 0 | 0 | 4 | 1 | 0 | 0 | 0 | 2 | 4 | .083 |
| 2006 | Cedar Rapids (MWL) | A | 2 | 3 | 2.37 | 50 | 0 | 0 | 24 | 57 | 34 | 17 | 15 | 4 | 21 | 81 | .169 |
| | Rancho Cucamonga (Cal) | A | 0 | 0 | 9.00 | 5 | 0 | 0 | 1 | 4 | 5 | 4 | 4 | 0 | 6 | 6 | .333 |
| **MINOR LEAGUE TOTALS** | | | 2 | 6 | 3.78 | 77 | 5 | 0 | 26 | 114 | 87 | 52 | 48 | 6 | 64 | 153 | .208 |

## TOMMY MURPHY
**OF**

**Born:** Aug. 27, 1979. **B-T:** R-R. **Ht.:** 6-0. **Wt.:** 185. **Drafted:** Florida Atlantic, 2000 (3rd round). **Signed by:** Todd Claus.

Murphy made his major league debut on May 4, a banner day for recent graduates of the Angels system. Murphy had an RBI single, while Mike Napoli homered in his first big league at-bat (off Justin Verlander, no less), Casey Kotchman also took Verlander deep and Howie Kendrick delivered an RBI single of his own. Los Angeles moved Murphy from shortstop to the outfield in 2004, hoping to enhance his value as a utilityman, which is his future role. His swing has holes and his pitch recognition and plate discipline never have been his strong suit. Murphy might be the Angels' most athletic prospect, and his hand-eye coordination and quick hands enable him to compensate for his mechanical flaws. He has gap power and can sting balls into both alleys when he makes contact, which isn't often enough to allow him to play everyday. He has developed into an above-average defender with plus arm strength and speed. He and Reggie Willits will compete for a job as an extra outfielder in Los Angeles during spring training.

| Year | Club (League) | Class | AVG | G | AB | R | H | 2B | 3B | HR | RBI | BB | SO | SB | OBP | SLG |
|------|---------------|-------|-----|---|----|---|---|----|----|----|-----|----|----|----|-----|-----|
| 2000 | Boise (NWL) | A | .225 | 55 | 213 | 38 | 48 | 18 | 1 | 2 | 25 | 15 | 52 | 14 | .291 | .347 |
| 2001 | Cedar Rapids (MWL) | A | .204 | 74 | 280 | 32 | 57 | 15 | 3 | 4 | 31 | 16 | 94 | 7 | .259 | .321 |
|  | Rancho Cucamonga (Cal) | A | .190 | 50 | 200 | 16 | 38 | 8 | 0 | 0 | 11 | 5 | 69 | 7 | .214 | .230 |
| 2002 | Cedar Rapids (MWL) | A | .270 | 128 | 485 | 72 | 131 | 20 | 2 | 3 | 48 | 40 | 115 | 31 | .324 | .338 |
| 2003 | Rancho Cucamonga (Cal) | A | .267 | 132 | 565 | 74 | 151 | 25 | 6 | 11 | 43 | 31 | 138 | 24 | .313 | .391 |
| 2004 | Arkansas (TL) | AA | .260 | 129 | 477 | 77 | 124 | 24 | 6 | 7 | 45 | 36 | 113 | 27 | .310 | .379 |
| 2005 | Arkansas (TL) | AA | .288 | 135 | 500 | 85 | 144 | 24 | 11 | 17 | 76 | 43 | 97 | 26 | .346 | .482 |
| 2006 | Salt Lake (PCL) | AAA | .302 | 73 | 285 | 43 | 86 | 16 | 3 | 7 | 36 | 19 | 62 | 6 | .351 | .453 |
|  | Los Angeles (AL) | MLB | .229 | 48 | 70 | 12 | 16 | 4 | 1 | 1 | 6 | 5 | 21 | 4 | .276 | .357 |
| **MINOR LEAGUE TOTALS** | | | .259 | 776 | 3005 | 437 | 779 | 150 | 32 | 51 | 315 | 205 | 740 | 142 | .311 | .381 |
| **MAJOR LEAGUE TOTALS** | | | .229 | 48 | 70 | 12 | 16 | 4 | 1 | 1 | 6 | 5 | 21 | 4 | .276 | .357 |

## REGGIE WILLITS
**OF**

**Born:** May 30, 1981. **B-T:** B-R. **Ht.:** 5-11. **Wt.:** 185. **Drafted:** Oklahoma, 2003 (7th round). **Signed by:** Kevin Ham.

Outfield depth isn't a strength of the system, as the Angels have placed an emphasis on signing infielders and pitchers in recent years. Their player-development department deserves credit for molding Tommy Murphy and Willits into dependable reserve outfielders. Willits made his major league debut in 2006, singling and scoring in his first major league game against the Royals before driving in the winning run in the 10th inning. Willits was used sparingly in the majors, but he led Los Angeles' full-season minor leaguers with a .327 average during his stint in Triple-A. Willits has gap power and utilizes a short, quick swing from both sides of the plate. He has made strides in his plate discipline, bunting and bat control. Balls down and in give him trouble, especially when he's hitting righthanded. Willits is an above-average defensive center fielder with an average arm and plus speed. After signing free agent Gary Matthews Jr., the Angels are set in the outfield for the near future, meaning that Willits could make their club as a reserve or return to Triple-A.

| Year | Club (League) | Class | AVG | G | AB | R | H | 2B | 3B | HR | RBI | BB | SO | SB | OBP | SLG |
|------|---------------|-------|-----|---|----|---|---|----|----|----|-----|----|----|----|-----|-----|
| 2003 | Provo (Pio) | R | .300 | 59 | 230 | 53 | 69 | 14 | 4 | 4 | 27 | 37 | 52 | 14 | .410 | .448 |
| 2004 | Rancho Cucamonga (Cal) | A | .285 | 135 | 526 | 99 | 150 | 17 | 5 | 5 | 52 | 73 | 112 | 44 | .374 | .365 |
| 2005 | Arkansas (TL) | AA | .304 | 123 | 487 | 75 | 148 | 23 | 6 | 2 | 46 | 54 | 78 | 40 | .377 | .388 |
| 2006 | Salt Lake (PCL) | AAA | .327 | 97 | 352 | 85 | 115 | 18 | 4 | 3 | 39 | 77 | 50 | 31 | .448 | .426 |
|  | Los Angeles (AL) | MLB | .267 | 28 | 45 | 12 | 12 | 1 | 0 | 0 | 2 | 11 | 10 | 4 | .411 | .289 |
| **MINOR LEAGUE TOTALS** | | | .302 | 414 | 1595 | 312 | 482 | 72 | 19 | 14 | 164 | 241 | 292 | 129 | .397 | .397 |
| **MAJOR LEAGUE TOTALS** | | | .267 | 28 | 45 | 12 | 12 | 1 | 0 | 0 | 2 | 11 | 10 | 4 | .411 | .289 |

## BARRET BROWNING
**LHP**

**Born:** Dec. 28, 1984. **B-T:** L-L. **Ht.:** 6-1. **Wt.:** 170. **Drafted:** Florida State, 2006 (28th round). **Signed by:** Tom Kotchman.

Browning's stock was considerably higher in high school than it was in college. The Red Sox drafted him in the sixth round in 2002, after which he went in the 26th round to Cubs in 2003 following one year at Middle Georgia JC. He then transferred to Florida State, where he was a Rockies 38th-rounder in 2005 and an Angels 26th-rounder last June, when he signed for $1,000. When he arrived at Orem, pitching coach Zeke Zimmerman immediately cleaned up his delivery. Browning improved his tempo, attained better balance over the rubber and better direction to the plate. He varies his arm slot, working from three-quarters as well as low-three-quarters to provide deception, especially against lefthanders. He pitches between 86-92 mph with his fastball, which has armside run and comes out of his hand

easily. His slider and changeup have potential to be plus pitches, though both are inconsistent. Browning profiles as a reliever, either as a middle man or perhaps as a lefty specialist. He could move through the system quickly and should begin 2007 in low Class A.

| Year | Club (League) | Class | W | L | ERA | G | GS | CG | SV | IP | H | R | ER | HR | BB | SO | AVG |
|------|---------------|-------|---|---|-----|---|----|----|----|----|---|---|----|----|----|----|-----|
| 2006 | Orem (Pio) | R | 3 | 2 | 3.05 | 23 | 0 | 0 | 1 | 41 | 33 | 17 | 14 | 3 | 13 | 40 | .220 |
| **MINOR LEAGUE TOTALS** | | | 3 | 2 | 3.05 | 23 | 0 | 0 | 1 | 41 | 33 | 17 | 14 | 3 | 13 | 40 | .220 |

 ## MARK TRUMBO 1B

**Born:** Jan. 16, 1986. **B-T:** R-R. **Ht.:** 6-4. **Wt.:** 220. **Drafted:** HS—Villa Park, Calif., 2004 (18th round). **Signed by:** Tim Corcoran.

Trumbo was one of California's top two-way prep prospects in 2004, when he led Villa Park High (Orange, Calif.) to a final No. 11 national ranking. Most clubs were scared off by his exorbitant bonus demands, but the Angels signed him away from Southern California for an 18th-round-record $1.425 million. His swing was littered with holes as an amateur, and most of them remain two years into his pro career. Trumbo's best tool is plus-plus raw power, which hasn't consistently translated to games because of his inability to make consistent contact. He doesn't have much of a load and his hands are slow. His pitch recognition is adequate. His approach varies from at-bat to at-bat, and he struggles against lefthanders. He's a below-average defender with poor range and footwork to go with adequate hands. He ran his fastball into the mid-90s in high school but no longer show plus arm strength. He's a well-below-average runner, and lacks life in his body and actions. The Angels were pleased with Trumbo's showing in instructional league and hope he'll carry the momentum over into spring training. If he fails to do so, he could return to low Class A in 2007.

| Year | Club (League) | Class | AVG | G | AB | R | H | 2B | 3B | HR | RBI | BB | SO | SB | OBP | SLG |
|------|---------------|-------|-----|---|----|---|---|----|----|----|-----|----|----|----|-----|-----|
| 2005 | Orem (Pio) | R | .274 | 71 | 299 | 45 | 82 | 23 | 1 | 10 | 45 | 21 | 67 | 2 | .322 | .458 |
| 2006 | Cedar Rapids (MWL) | A | .220 | 118 | 428 | 43 | 94 | 19 | 0 | 13 | 59 | 44 | 99 | 5 | .293 | .355 |
| **MINOR LEAGUE TOTALS** | | | .242 | 189 | 727 | 88 | 176 | 42 | 1 | 23 | 104 | 65 | 166 | 7 | .304 | .398 |

 ## PHIL SEIBEL LHP

**Born:** Jan. 28, 1979. **B-T:** L-L. **Ht.:** 6-1. **Wt.:** 195. **Drafted:** Texas, 2000 (8th round). **Signed by:** Dennis Cardoza (Expos).

If Seibel is completely over his history of elbow problems, he could make the Angels bullpen after arriving in a December trade with the Red Sox for Brendan Donnelly. L.A. is Seibel's fourth organization, as he was drafted by the Expos in 2000 and sent to the Mets in a forgettable seven-player deal two years later. Claimed on waivers by Boston after the 2003 season, he made two relief appearances in the majors the following April but has pitched just 130 innings since. Seibel strained an elbow ligament while in college at Texas and required Tommy John surgery after the 2004 season, costing him all of 2005. He was lights out in his return last year, though a strained forearm aborted his chances for a September callup. Seibel's strong suits are his fastball command, his slider and his makeup. He easily locates his 86-88 mph fastball on both sides of the plate and commands his entire repertoire, which also includes a curveball and changeup. He's not overpowering, but he doesn't make mistakes and he gets outs. He limited lefties to a .147 average and righties to a .154 mark in 2006. The Red Sox kept Seibel's innings and pitch counts down last year as a precaution. He has recovered from the forearm strain, so he should be 100 percent for 2007.

| Year | Club (League) | Class | W | L | ERA | G | GS | CG | SV | IP | H | R | ER | HR | BB | SO | AVG |
|------|---------------|-------|---|---|-----|---|----|----|----|----|---|---|----|----|----|----|-----|
| 2001 | Jupiter (FSL) | A | 10 | 7 | 3.95 | 29 | 21 | 0 | 0 | 134 | 144 | 70 | 59 | 12 | 28 | 88 | .273 |
| 2002 | Binghamton (EL) | AA | 10 | 8 | 3.97 | 28 | 25 | 2 | 0 | 150 | 147 | 78 | 66 | 17 | 49 | 114 | .263 |
| 2003 | Norfolk (IL) | AAA | 2 | 3 | 6.03 | 11 | 5 | 0 | 0 | 34 | 38 | 25 | 23 | 5 | 17 | 25 | .281 |
| | Binghamton (EL) | AA | 5 | 5 | 3.59 | 17 | 17 | 0 | 0 | 83 | 79 | 48 | 33 | 6 | 32 | 71 | .253 |
| 2004 | Boston (AL) | MLB | 0 | 0 | 0.00 | 2 | 0 | 0 | 0 | 4 | 0 | 0 | 0 | 0 | 5 | 1 | .000 |
| | Pawtucket (IL) | AAA | 1 | 2 | 3.02 | 8 | 7 | 0 | 0 | 45 | 42 | 16 | 15 | 7 | 12 | 31 | .263 |
| | Red Sox (GCL) | R | 0 | 0 | 2.25 | 3 | 3 | 0 | 0 | 4 | 2 | 1 | 1 | 1 | 1 | 6 | .143 |
| | Portland (EL) | AA | 0 | 1 | 7.50 | 3 | 1 | 0 | 0 | 6 | 8 | 5 | 5 | 3 | 2 | 6 | .320 |
| 2005 | Did not play—injured | | | | | | | | | | | | | | | | |
| 2006 | Greenville (SAL) | A | 2 | 0 | 1.35 | 4 | 4 | 0 | 0 | 20 | 12 | 3 | 3 | 2 | 0 | 19 | .176 |
| | Portland (EL) | AA | 2 | 3 | 1.20 | 9 | 9 | 0 | 0 | 45 | 24 | 11 | 6 | 5 | 12 | 42 | .153 |
| | Pawtucket (IL) | AAA | 2 | 0 | 1.20 | 9 | 0 | 0 | 0 | 15 | 6 | 2 | 2 | 1 | 3 | 22 | .118 |
| **MINOR LEAGUE TOTALS** | | | 34 | 29 | 3.58 | 121 | 92 | 2 | 0 | 536 | 502 | 259 | 213 | 59 | 156 | 424 | .250 |
| **MAJOR LEAGUE TOTALS** | | | 0 | 0 | 0.00 | 2 | 0 | 0 | 0 | 3 | 0 | 0 | 0 | 0 | 5 | 1 | .000 |

# LOS ANGELES
# DODGERS

BY **ALAN MATTHEWS**

The Mets may have swept the Dodgers in the National League Division Series, but Los Angeles shouldn't be singing the blues. The previous year, the franchise suffered through its second-worst showing since moving from Brooklyn in 1958 and the faces on the roster were as random as those at a cabstand. Fans' groans grew louder than traffic on the 5 when owner Frank McCourt fired Paul DePodesta and named **Ned Colletti**—who had been an assistant general manager with the archrival Giants—the club's third GM in four years.

Yet most of Colletti's moves worked. He signed veterans, spun trades, promoted rookies and saw the Dodgers move from mediocrity to prosperity. Baseball America's Organization of the Year, Los Angeles has the foundation to contend for years to come.

The Dodgers had seven rookies on their postseason roster, all of whom helped them get there. Russell Martin seized the catching job and shined both offensively and defensively. Andre Ethier, acquired in an offseason Milton Bradley trade with the Athletics, carried the club for a stretch at midseason with clutch hitting and power few predicted. Matt Kemp scorched the ball at the outset of a brief big league stint. When James Loney wasn't leading the minors in hitting at Triple-A Las Vegas, he was filling in admirably for the injured Nomar Garciaparra and reasserted himself as a frontline prospect.

On the mound, Chad Billingsley and Jonathan Broxton assumed important roles slightly ahead of schedule and showed why they're projected as Los Angeles' No. 1 starter and closer, respectively, of the future. Enigmatic Hong-Chih Kuo resurfaced as the force the Dodgers thought they acquired when they signed him in 1999. Takashi Saito, a 36-year-old former Japanese big leaguer in his first year in the United States, took over as closer and amassed 24 saves.

In addition to reinforcements, the farm system also provided lots of trade fodder. Six players on our Dodgers Top 30 list a year ago were sent packing, enabling the club to acquire players such as Marlon Anderson, Danys Baez, Wilson Betemit and Julio Lugo.

The Dodgers graduated or traded nine of their top 17 prospects from a year ago, so the system naturally lost some depth. But it's far from barren. Andy LaRoche and Loney are close to taking over the club's corner-infield jobs, while 2006 first-round pick Clayton Kershaw and 2004 first-rounder Scott Elbert are two of the very best lefty pitching prospects in the game.

All four of those players were taken in the five drafts Logan White ran as scouting director. He was promoted to assistant GM for scouting in the offseason, with Tim Hallgren ascending from national crosschecker to replace White. DeJon Watson, formerly a Reds scouting director and most recently an Indians major league scout, takes over as farm director from Terry Collins, who left to manage Japan's Orix Buffaloes.

## TOP 30 PROSPECTS

| | |
|---|---|
| 1. Andy LaRoche, 3b | 16. Steven Johnson, rhp |
| 2. Clayton Kershaw, lhp | 17. Greg Miller, lhp |
| 3. Scott Elbert, lhp | 18. Brent Leach, lhp |
| 4. James Loney, 1b/of | 19. Cory Dunlap, 1b |
| 5. Etanislao Abreu, 2b | 20. Mark Alexander, rhp |
| 6. Ivan DeJesus Jr., ss | 21. Mike Megrew, lhp |
| 7. Jonathan Meloan, rhp | 22. Ramon Troncoso, rhp |
| 8. Blake DeWitt, 2b/3b | 23. Carlos Santana, of/3b/c |
| 9. Josh Bell, 3b | 24. Cody White, lhp |
| 10. Preston Mattingly, ss | 25. Kyle Orr, 1b |
| 11. Chin-Lung Hu, ss | 26. Xavier Paul, of |
| 12. Bryan Morris, rhp | 27. Casey Hoorelbeke, rhp |
| 13. Delwyn Young, of | 28. Miguel Sanfler, lhp |
| 14. Justin Orenduff, rhp | 29. Josh Wall, rhp |
| 15. Zach Hammes, rhp | 30. Wesley Wright, lhp |

# ORGANIZATION OVERVIEW

**General manager:** Ned Colletti. **Farm director:** DeJon Watson. **Scouting director:** Tim Hallgren.

## 2006 PERFORMANCE

| Class | Team | League | W | L | PCT | Finish* | Manager | Affiliated |
|-------|------|--------|---|---|-----|---------|---------|-----------|
| Majors | Los Angeles | National | 88 | 74 | .543 | 2nd (16) | Grady Little | — |
| Triple-A | Las Vegas 51s | Pacific Coast | 67 | 77 | .465 | 12th (16) | Jerry Royster | 2001 |
| Double-A | Jacksonville Suns | Southern | 86 | 54 | .614 | 1st (10) | John Shoemaker | 2002 |
| High A | #Vero Beach Dodgers | Florida State | 51 | 80 | .389 | 12th (12) | Luis Salazar | 1980 |
| Low A | †Columbus Catfish | South Atlantic | 72 | 68 | .514 | 7th (16) | Travis Barbary | 2002 |
| Rookie | Ogden Raptors | Pioneer | 37 | 39 | .487 | 5th (8) | Lance Parrish | 2003 |
| Rookie | GCL Dodgers | Gulf Coast | 32 | 22 | .593 | 4th (13) | Juan Bustabad | 2001 |

**OVERALL 2006 MINOR LEAGUE RECORD**  345 340 .504 14th (30)

*Finish in overall standings (No. of teams in league). +League champion. #Affiliate will be in Inland Empire (California) in 2007.
†Affiliate will be in Great Lakes (Midwest) in 2007.

## ORGANIZATION LEADERS

### BATTING
| | | |
|---|---|---|
| AVG | Loney, James, Las Vegas | .370 |
| R | Valdez, Wilson, Las Vegas | 94 |
| H | Valdez, Wilson, Las Vegas | 157 |
| 2B | Young, Delwyn, Las Vegas | 42 |
| 3B | May, Lucas, Columbus | 9 |
| HR | Pedroza, Sergio, Columbus/VB/Visalia | 24 |
| RBI | Young, Delwyn, Las Vegas | 98 |
| BB | Dunlap, Cory, Vero Beach/Las Vegas | 97 |
| SO | Paul, Xavier, Vero Beach | 133 |
| SB | Godwin, Adam, Columbus | 30 |
| | Rogowski, Ryan, Ogden | 30 |
| OBP | Dunlap, Cory, Vero Beach/Las Vegas | .433 |
| SLG | Pedroza, Sergio, Columbus/VB/Visalia | .548 |
| XBH | Mitchell, Russell, Columbus/Vero Beach | 61 |
| | Young, Delwyn, Las Vegas | 61 |

### PITCHING
| | | |
|---|---|---|
| W | Lundberg, Spike, Las Vegas/Jacksonville | 17 |
| L | Houlton, D.J., Las Vegas | 11 |
| | Stults, Eric, Las Vegas | 11 |
| ERA | Nunez, Jhonny, GCL Dodgers | 1.58 |
| G | Hoorelbeke, Casey, Jacksonville | 59 |
| SV | Alexander, Mark, Las Vegas/Jacksonville | 27 |
| IP | Lundberg, Spike, Las Vegas/Jacksonville | 187 |
| BB | Elbert, Scott, Vero Beach/Jacksonville | 85 |
| SO | Elbert, Scott, Vero Beach/Jacksonville | 173 |
| AVG | Nunez, Jhonny, GCL Dodgers | .177 |

## BEST TOOLS

| | |
|---|---|
| Best Hitter for Average | James Loney |
| Best Power Hitter | Andy LaRoche |
| Best Strike-Zone Discipline | Cory Dunlap |
| Fastest Baserunner | Trayvon Robinson |
| Best Athlete | Preston Mattingly |
| Best Fastball | Clayton Kershaw |
| Best Curveball | Scott Elbert |
| Best Slider | Jonathan Meloan |
| Best Changeup | Carlos Alvarez |
| Best Control | Clayton Kershaw |
| Best Defensive Catcher | Gabriel Gutierrez |
| Best Defensive Infielder | Ivan DeJesus Jr. |
| Best Infield Arm | Andy LaRoche |
| Best Defensive Outfielder | Jamie Hoffmann |
| Best Outfield Arm | Xavier Paul |

## PROJECTED 2010 LINEUP

| | |
|---|---|
| Catcher | Russell Martin |
| First Base | James Loney |
| Second Base | Etanislao Abreu |
| Third Base | Andy LaRoche |
| Shortstop | Rafael Furcal |
| Left Field | Andre Ethier |

| | |
|---|---|
| Center Field | Juan Pierre |
| Right Field | Matt Kemp |
| No. 1 Starter | Chad Billingsley |
| No. 2 Starter | Jason Schmidt |
| No. 3 Starter | Clayton Kershaw |
| No. 4 Starter | Scott Elbert |
| No. 5 Starter | Brad Penny |
| Closer | Jonathan Broxton |

## LAST YEAR'S TOP 20 PROSPECTS

| | |
|---|---|
| 1. Chad Billingsley, rhp | 11. James Loney, 1b |
| 2. Andy LaRoche, 3b | 12. Justin Orenduff, rhp |
| 3. Joel Guzman, ss/of | 13. Chuck Tiffany, lhp |
| 4. Russell Martin, c | 14. Hong-Chih Kuo, lhp |
| 5. Jonathan Broxton, rhp | 15. Delwyn Young, 2b/of |
| 6. Scott Elbert, lhp | 16. Julio Pimentel, rhp |
| 7. Blake DeWitt, 3b | 17. Blake Johnson, rhp |
| 8. Matt Kemp, of | 18. Greg Miller, lhp |
| 9. Etanislau Abreu, 2b | 19. Josh Wall, rhp |
| 10. Chin-Lung Hu, ss | 20. Juan Rivera, ss |

## TOP PROSPECTS OF THE DECADE

| Year | Player, Pos. | 2006 Org. |
|------|--------------|-----------|
| 1997 | Paul Konerko, 3b | White Sox |
| 1998 | Paul Konerko, 1b | White Sox |
| 1999 | Angel Pena, c | Tabasco (Mexican) |
| 2000 | Chin-Feng Chen, of | La New Bears (Taiwan) |
| 2001 | Ben Diggins, rhp | Windy City (Frontier) |
| 2002 | Ricardo Rodriguez, rhp | Cardinals |
| 2003 | James Loney, 1b | Dodgers |
| 2004 | Edwin Jackson, rhp | Devil Rays |
| 2005 | Joel Guzman, ss/of | Devil Rays |
| 2006 | Chad Billingsley, rhp | Dodgers |

## TOP DRAFT PICKS OF THE DECADE

| Year | Player, Pos. | 2006 Org. |
|------|--------------|-----------|
| 1997 | Glenn Davis, 1b | Out of baseball |
| 1998 | Bubba Crosby, of | Yankees |
| 1999 | Jason Repko, ss/of | Dodgers |
| 2000 | Ben Diggins, rhp | Windy City (Frontier) |
| 2001 | Brian Pilkington, rhp (2nd) | Out of baseball |
| 2002 | James Loney, 1b | Dodgers |
| 2003 | Chad Billingsley, rhp | Dodgers |
| 2004 | Scott Elbert, lhp | Dodgers |
| 2005 | *Luke Hochevar, rhp | Royals |
| 2006 | Clayton Kershaw, lhp | Dodgers |

*Did not sign.

## ALL-TIME LARGEST BONUSES

| | |
|---|---|
| Clayton Kershaw, 2006 | $2,300,000 |
| Joel Guzman, 2001 | $2,250,000 |
| Ben Diggins, 2000 | $2,200,000 |
| Hideo Nomo, 1995 | $2,000,000 |
| Scott Elbert, 2004 | $1,575,000 |

# MINOR LEAGUE DEPTH CHART

## Los Angeles Dodgers

**Impact: A.** Despite graduating four of last year's top eight prospects, LaRoche, Kershaw, Elbert, Loney and Abreu all possess impact potential and remain at the top of the system.

**Depth: C.** The Dodgers graduated or traded more than a third of the prospects from last year's Top 30, and while the system features a bevy of young arms at the lower levels, the talent falls off considerably following the top 10.

**Sleeper:** Francisco Lizarraga, ss. A 21-year-old switch-hitting Mexican shortstop, Lizarraga has intriguing tools on both sides of the game.

| LF | CF | RF |
|---|---|---|
| Preston Mattingly (10) | Jamie Hoffmann | Delwyn Young (13) |
| Anthony Raglani | Ryan Rogowski | Xavier Paul (26) |
| Bridger Hunt | Trayvon Robinson | |
| Scott Van Slyke | | |
| Andrew Locke | | |

| 3B | SS | 2B | 1B |
|---|---|---|---|
| Andy LaRoche (1) | Ivan DeJesus (6) | Etanislao Abreu (5) | James Loney (4) |
| Blake DeWitt (8) | Chin Lung-Hu (11) | Travis Denker | Cory Dunlap (19) |
| Josh Bell (9) | Francisco Lizarraga | Wilson Valdez | Kyle Orr (25) |
| Brian Mathews | Juan Rivera | | Jamie Ortiz |
| | | | David Sutherland |
| | | | Cole Bruce |

| C |
|---|
| Carlos Santana (23) |
| Kenley Jansen |
| Juan Apodaca |
| Gabriel Gutierrez |

| RHP | | LHP | |
|---|---|---|---|
| **Starters** | **Relievers** | **Starters** | **Relievers** |
| Bryan Morris (12) | Jonathan Meloan (7) | Clayton Kershaw (2) | Greg Miller (17) |
| Justin Orenduff (14) | Zach Hammes (15) | Scott Elbert (3) | Brent Leach (18) |
| Steven Johnson (16) | Mark Alexander (20) | Mike Megrew (21) | Cody White (24) |
| Josh Wall (29) | Ramon Troncoso (22) | Eric Stults | Miguel Sanfler (28) |
| Eric Hull | Casey Hoorelbeke (27) | Garrett White | Wesley Wright (30) |
| Javy Guerra | Chris Malone | Alberto Bastardo | Luis Gonzalez |
| Jesus Castillo | Brian Akin | | Carlos Alvarez |
| James McDonald | Kyle Wilson | | Tim Hamulack |
| Spike Lundberg | Mario Alvarez | | |
| Kyle Smit | Tommy Perez | | |
| Eric Thompson | B.J. LaMura | | |

# DRAFT ANALYSIS

## 2006     SIGNING BUDGET: $5.5 million

**Best Pro Debut:** LHP Clayton Kershaw (1), who went 2-0, 1.95 with a 54-5 K-BB ratio in 37 Gulf Coast League innings, and RHP Bryan Morris (1), who went 4-5, 5.13 with 79 strikeouts in 60 innings in the hitter-friendly Pioneer League, each rated as the No. 1 prospects in his circuit. Morris had Tommy John surgery in October, knocking him out for the entire 2007 season.

**Best Athlete:** SS Preston Mattingly (1) was an all-Indiana wide receiver and scored 20 points a game in basketball. All his tools are average or better, except his arm.

**Best Pure Hitter:** Mattingly, the son of former American League batting champion and MVP Don Mattingly, has great bloodlines, a quick bat and power potential. OF Bridger Hunt (9) hit .314 in low Class A.

**Best Raw Power:** 1B Kyle Orr (4) produces outstanding leverage with his 6-foot-5, 205-pound frame. Compared with Justin Morneau and Richie Sexson, Orr won a bronze medal with Team Canada at the World Junior Championship last summer before turning pro.

**Fastest Runner:** Much faster than his father was, Mattingly can cover 60 yards in 6.56 seconds.

**Best Defensive Player:** SS Justin Fuller (11) has the range and arm to make all the plays, but his bat is a question after he hit .230 in his pro debut.

**Best Fastball:** Both Kershaw and Morris pitched at 93-94 mph and hit 96 during the summer. Even before Morris got hurt, Kershaw would have rated a slight edge because he's a lefty and locates his heater better. He maintained his velocity in instructional league as well.

**Best Breaking Ball:** Morris had one of the best curveballs in the draft. Kershaw has a curve that shows plus break at times.

**Most Intriguing Background:** Mattingly is just one of several Dodgers draftees with baseball relatives. 2B Curt Bradley's (33) father Phil also was a big league all-star. Morris played for his father Ricky, an assistant at Motlow State (Tenn.) CC, while 2B Kody Kaiser (26) played for his uncle Sonny Golloway at Oklahoma, but Kaiser has since transferred to Oklahoma City JC. 3B Tanner Biagini's (48) late father Greg was a minor league manager for several years, while LHP Jake Debus' (39) uncle Jon was Los Angeles' bullpen coach. RHP Jordan Chambless (43) doubled as a defensive back and punt returner at Texas A&M before quitting football this summer. Of this group, only Morris and Mattingly signed.

**Closest To The Majors:** Kershaw. He was drafted out of high school, but he's a left-hander with three plus pitches, command, a durable frame and strong makeup.

**Best Late-Round Pick:** RHP Eric Thompson (23) is a 6-foot-7, 220-pounder who was headed to Southern Oregon on a basketball scholarship. His size gives him plenty of projection, and his fastball already sits at 89-91 mph. DH Matt Berezay (21) impressed the Dodgers with his bat by hitting .296/.415/.533 in the Pioneer League.

**The One Who Got Away:** RHP Alex White (14) has a first-round fastball, currently pitching at 90-94 mph with projections that he could reach 98. But his $1.4 million price tag scared off most clubs, and Los Angeles let him walk to North Carolina.

**Assessment:** Kershaw can make an argument for being the best lefthanded pitching prospect in baseball. The Dodgers debated offering Jeff Weaver arbitration last offseason, and their decision to do so paid off with the compensatory draft picks that became Morris and Mattingly.

## 2005     BUDGET: $2.2 million

The Dodgers' failure to sign RHP Luke Hochevar (1) was magnified when he went No. 1 overall in the 2006 draft. They salvaged depth with SS Ivan DeJesus Jr. (2), 3B Josh Bell (4) and RHPs John Meloan (5) and Steven Johnson (13). **GRADE: C**

## 2004     BUDGET: $5.6 million

Missouri high schools produced the top two picks, LHP Scott Elbert (1) and 2B/3B Blake DeWitt (1). RHP Justin Orenduff (1) was on the fast track before hurting his shoulder last year. **GRADE: B+**

## 2004     BUDGET: $3.4 million

It's rare to find three cornerstones in one draft, but Los Angeles may have done just that with this crop in RHP Chad Billingsley (1), OF Matt Kemp (6) and 3B Andy LaRoche (39). **GRADE: A**

*Draft analysis by Jim Callis. Numbers in parentheses indicate draft rounds. Budgets are bonuses in first 10 rounds.*

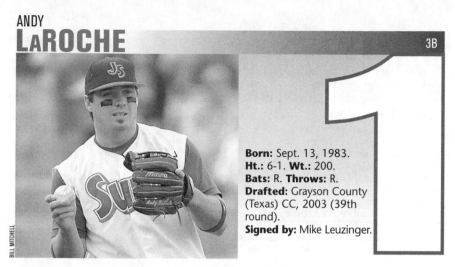

# ANDY
# LaROCHE

3B

**Born:** Sept. 13, 1983.
**Ht.:** 6-1. **Wt.:** 200.
**Bats:** R. **Throws:** R.
**Drafted:** Grayson County
(Texas) CC, 2003 (39th
round).
**Signed by:** Mike Leuzinger.

BILL MITCHELL

The son of former major league all-star Dave and the brother of Braves first baseman Adam, Andy could be the best big leaguer in the family. He graduated early from high school and attended Grayson County (Texas) CC in what would have been the spring of his senior year in 2002. The Padres took him in the 21st round that June as a draft and follow, but made little effort to sign him the following spring. By that point LaRoche had committed to Rice and several clubs viewed him as unsignable. The Dodgers took a 39th-round flier on him in the 2003 draft, and after he raked in the Cape Cod League that summer, they signed him for $1 million. LaRoche established himself as one of the top position players in the minors by slugging 30 homers in 2005, and he fortified that reputation with another strong campaign in 2006. He hit a career-high .315 with 19 homers (including one on the first pitch he saw in Triple-A) despite a torn labrum in his left shoulder that required surgery following the season. He also hurt his right shoulder, but played through both injuries.

Few players can cause a stir in batting practice like LaRoche can. He sometimes will take BP with a 36-ounce bat, which has helped him build remarkable strength in his hands and wrists. He has tremendous power and a ferocious approach, attacking pitches with a quick, leveraged swing. He can drive balls out to all parts of the park, but is at his best when he's hammering them from gap to gap. He lets the ball travel deep in the hitting zone. He's an intelligent hitter who made strides in 2006 with his plate discipline and willingness to work counts without sacrificing any power. For the first time as a pro, he drew more walks than strikeouts. Defensively, he has good hands and a solid-average arm. He's a reliable third baseman who committed just five errors in 54 games at Las Vegas.

LaRoche can fall into bad habits at the plate, at times losing balance, lengthening his swing and chasing pitches out of the zone when he tries to muscle up. He's geared to pull for power, and his average could suffer unless he tones down his swing. He has below-average range and speed. He always has had a big league mentality and his brashness rubs some the wrong way. The Dodgers are quick to praise him for his grit and determination, and they don't consider his makeup to be a detriment.

LaRoche profiles as an everyday third baseman and an occasional all-star with a .275-.285 average and 25-30 homer potential. He should be fully recovered by the start of spring training, where he'll compete with Wilson Betemit to start at third base in Los Angeles. If he doesn't win the job, LaRoche likely will play regularly in Triple-A instead of sitting on the big league bench to open the year.

| Year | Club (League) | Class | AVG | G | AB | R | H | 2B | 3B | HR | RBI | BB | SO | SB | OBP | SLG |
|------|---------------|-------|-----|---|-----|---|---|----|----|----|-----|----|----|----|-----|-----|
| 2003 | Ogden (Pio) | R | .211 | 6 | 19 | 1 | 4 | 1 | 0 | 0 | 5 | 1 | 4 | 0 | .238 | .263 |
| 2004 | Columbus (SAL) | A | .283 | 65 | 244 | 52 | 69 | 20 | 0 | 13 | 42 | 29 | 30 | 12 | .375 | .525 |
| | Vero Beach (FSL) | A | .237 | 62 | 219 | 26 | 52 | 13 | 0 | 10 | 34 | 17 | 42 | 2 | .295 | .434 |
| 2005 | Vero Beach (FSL) | A | .333 | 63 | 249 | 54 | 83 | 14 | 1 | 21 | 51 | 19 | 38 | 6 | .380 | .651 |
| | Jacksonville (SL) | AA | .273 | 64 | 227 | 41 | 62 | 12 | 0 | 9 | 43 | 32 | 54 | 2 | .367 | .445 |
| 2006 | Jacksonville (SL) | AA | .309 | 62 | 230 | 42 | 71 | 13 | 0 | 9 | 46 | 41 | 32 | 6 | .419 | .483 |
| | Las Vegas (PCL) | AAA | .322 | 55 | 202 | 35 | 65 | 14 | 1 | 10 | 35 | 25 | 32 | 3 | .400 | .550 |
| **MINOR LEAGUE TOTALS** | | | .292 | 377 | 1390 | 251 | 406 | 87 | 2 | 72 | 256 | 164 | 232 | 31 | .372 | .513 |

## 2 CLAYTON KERSHAW
LHP

**Born:** March 19, 1988. **B-T:** L-L. **Ht.:** 6-3. **Wt.:** 210. **Drafted:** HS—Dallas, 2006 (1st round). **Signed by:** Calvin Jones.

Kershaw established himself as the best high school prospect in the 2006 draft when he improved his stuff and dominated Texas high school competition last spring. When Andrew Miller fell to the Tigers at No. 6, Kershaw got to the Dodgers at No. 7. He signed for $2.3 million and ranked as the No. 1 prospect in the Gulf Coast League in his debut. Kershaw's stuff and body have plenty of projection, and his fastball is already well above-average. He paints both corners with 93-94 mph heat, topping out at 96. His curveball is a plus pitch with 71-77 mph velocity and 1-to-7 tilt. He has feel for a circle changeup that could become a third above-average pitch. He fills the strike zone with all three of his pitches. He has a durable frame and repeats his delivery. Laid-back and affable off the field, he's hard-nosed and tough-minded on it. Much more advanced than most young pitchers, Kershaw just needs to get more consistent with his pitches. His curve improved exponentially between his junior and senior seasons in high school, but it still gets loopy and hangs in the zone at times. Because of his impeccable fastball command, Kershaw should have no problem with older hitters, and he could begin 2007 at the club's new high Class A Inland Empire affiliate. He has top-of-the-rotation stuff, command and makeup.

| Year | Club (League) | Class | W | L | ERA | G | GS | CG | SV | IP | H | R | ER | HR | BB | SO | AVG |
|------|---------------|-------|---|---|-----|---|----|----|----|----|---|---|----|----|----|----|-----|
| 2006 | Dodgers (GCL) | R | 2 | 0 | 1.95 | 10 | 8 | 0 | 1 | 37 | 28 | 10 | 8 | 0 | 5 | 54 | .201 |
| **MINOR LEAGUE TOTALS** | | | 2 | 0 | 1.95 | 10 | 8 | 0 | 1 | 37 | 28 | 10 | 8 | 0 | 5 | 54 | .201 |

## 3 SCOTT ELBERT
LHP

**Born:** May 13, 1985. **B-T:** L-L. **Ht.:** 6-2. **Wt.:** 190. **Drafted:** HS—Seneca, Mo., 2004 (1st round). **Signed by:** Mitch Webster.

Elbert grew up less than 10 miles from where assistant GM Logan White went to grade school. He was an all-Missouri tailback as a high school junior, amassing 2,449 yards and 36 touchdowns before giving up football. The first prep lefty drafted in 2004, he signed for $1.575 million and reached Double-A last year at age 21. The fiercest competitor in the system, Elbert attacks both sides of the plate with his 90-92 mph fastball, which has late life and can reach 96. His two-plane curveball has hard, sharp break. He's merciless against lefthanders, who hit just .156 off him in 2006. He's athletic and durable. Elbert doesn't consistently repeat his delivery and overthrows, which leads to below-average command. He'll power through his curveball, which causes it to flatten out. He hasn't needed his circle changeup much, and it lags behind his other two offerings. Dodgers manager Grady Little could be tempted to add him to the big league bullpen in 2007, but Elbert has the stuff to develop into a workhorse No. 2 or 3 starter. He'll probably head back to Double-A to start the season.

| Year | Club (League) | Class | W | L | ERA | G | GS | CG | SV | IP | H | R | ER | HR | BB | SO | AVG |
|------|---------------|-------|---|---|-----|---|----|----|----|----|---|---|----|----|----|----|-----|
| 2004 | Ogden (Pio) | R | 2 | 3 | 5.26 | 12 | 12 | 0 | 0 | 50 | 47 | 33 | 29 | 5 | 30 | 45 | .270 |
| 2005 | Columbus (SAL) | A | 8 | 5 | 2.66 | 25 | 24 | 1 | 0 | 115 | 83 | 37 | 34 | 8 | 57 | 128 | .200 |
| 2006 | Vero Beach (FSL) | A | 5 | 5 | 2.37 | 17 | 15 | 0 | 0 | 84 | 57 | 27 | 22 | 4 | 41 | 97 | .193 |
| | Jacksonville (SL) | AA | 6 | 4 | 3.61 | 11 | 11 | 0 | 0 | 62 | 40 | 26 | 25 | 11 | 44 | 76 | .187 |
| **MINOR LEAGUE TOTALS** | | | 21 | 17 | 3.19 | 65 | 62 | 1 | 0 | 311 | 227 | 123 | 110 | 28 | 172 | 346 | .207 |

## 4 JAMES LONEY
1B/OF

**Born:** May 7, 1984. **B-T:** L-L. **Ht.:** 6-3. **Wt.:** 200. **Drafted:** HS—Missouri City, Texas, 2002 (1st round). **Signed by:** Chris Smith.

Loney was a two-way star on the Elkins High (Missouri City, Texas) team that won the 2002 national championship. When Nomar Gaciaparra began 2006 on the disabled list, Loney made his major league debut, singling off John Smoltz for his first hit. He also had a nine-RBI game at Colorado in September and went 3-for-4 in his lone postseason start. In between, he led the minors in hitting. Loney has an advanced feel for hitting and makes consistent hard contact. He has above-average bat speed and uses his hands well, allowing the barrel to remain in the hitting zone for an extended period. He uses all fields and exhibits plate discipline. He's a well above-average first baseman with supple hands and a plus arm, and he saw some time in the outfield in 2006. He's a hard worker with strong makeup. Loney's 12 home runs in 2006 were a career

high, and there's a wide range of opinion regarding his long-term power production. His swing path is fairly flat, and he could be more of a high-average doubles hitter in the mold of Mark Grace. He's a below-average runner. Los Angeles re-signed Garciaparra and he'll receive most of the playing time at first base. Loney should make the Dodgers as a backup and could see spot duty in right field in an effort to get his bat into the lineup.

| Year | Club (League) | Class | AVG | G | AB | R | H | 2B | 3B | HR | RBI | BB | SO | SB | OBP | SLG |
|------|---------------|-------|-----|---|-----|---|---|----|----|----|-----|----|----|----|-----|-----|
| 2002 | Great Falls (Pio) | R | .371 | 47 | 170 | 33 | 63 | 22 | 3 | 5 | 30 | 25 | 18 | 5 | .457 | .624 |
| | Vero Beach (FSL) | A | .299 | 17 | 67 | 6 | 20 | 6 | 0 | 0 | 5 | 6 | 10 | 0 | .356 | .388 |
| 2003 | Vero Beach (FSL) | A | .276 | 125 | 468 | 64 | 129 | 31 | 3 | 7 | 46 | 43 | 80 | 9 | .337 | .400 |
| 2004 | Jacksonville (SL) | AA | .238 | 104 | 395 | 39 | 94 | 19 | 2 | 4 | 35 | 42 | 75 | 5 | .314 | .327 |
| 2005 | Jacksonville (SL) | AA | .284 | 138 | 504 | 74 | 143 | 31 | 2 | 11 | 65 | 59 | 87 | 1 | .357 | .419 |
| 2006 | Las Vegas (PCL) | AAA | .380 | 98 | 366 | 64 | 139 | 33 | 2 | 8 | 67 | 32 | 34 | 9 | .426 | .546 |
| | Los Angeles (NL) | MLB | .284 | 48 | 102 | 20 | 29 | 6 | 5 | 4 | 18 | 8 | 10 | 1 | .342 | .559 |
| **MINOR LEAGUE TOTALS** | | | .298 | 529 | 1970 | 280 | 588 | 142 | 12 | 35 | 248 | 207 | 304 | 29 | .366 | .436 |
| **MAJOR LEAGUE TOTALS** | | | .284 | 48 | 102 | 20 | 29 | 6 | 5 | 4 | 18 | 8 | 10 | 1 | .342 | .559 |

## 5 ETANISLAO ABREU 2B

**Age:** Nov. 13, 1984. **B-T:** B-R. **Ht.:** 5-10. **Wt.:** 172. **Signed:** Dominican Republic, 2002. **Signed by:** Pablo Peguero.

Though often overshadowed in Los Angeles' deep system—he was accidentally left out of the team's 2006 media guide—Abreu quietly has established himself as one of its top position players. He won the 2005 high class A Florida State League batting title with a .327 average. Abreu is an aggressive, instinctual player with four plus tools. He has above-average bat speed and lashes line drives to all fields from both sides of the plate. He stays inside the ball well, has outstanding plate coverage, can turn around inside fastballs and maintains his balance through his swing. While he makes consistent contact, Abreu isn't selective and doesn't work deep counts. He could drive the ball better if he gets stronger, but projects to be more of a doubles hitter rather than a home run threat. A switch-hitter, he has more pop from the right side but uses the whole field better from the left. He's an above-average runner with plus range. He has soft hands and enough arm to handle shortstop. He could better utilize his speed on the basepaths. He's streaky and the Dodgers would like to see more consistency in his game. Abreu profiles as an everyday second baseman who can hit .280-.290 with 8-12 homers while playing quality defense. He should spend most of 2007 in Triple-A.

| Year | Club (League) | Class | AVG | G | AB | R | H | 2B | 3B | HR | RBI | BB | SO | SB | OBP | SLG |
|------|---------------|-------|-----|---|-----|---|---|----|----|----|-----|----|----|----|-----|-----|
| 2003 | Dodgers (GCL) | R | .294 | 45 | 163 | 30 | 48 | 7 | 5 | 0 | 20 | 11 | 24 | 9 | .358 | .399 |
| | Vero Beach (FSL) | A | .000 | 3 | 10 | 0 | 0 | 0 | 0 | 0 | 0 | 1 | 2 | 0 | .091 | .000 |
| 2004 | Columbus (SAL) | A | .301 | 104 | 359 | 50 | 108 | 21 | 8 | 8 | 54 | 8 | 59 | 16 | .326 | .471 |
| | Vero Beach (FSL) | A | .419 | 11 | 43 | 8 | 18 | 3 | 1 | 0 | 3 | 1 | 8 | 4 | .435 | .535 |
| 2005 | Vero Beach (FSL) | A | .327 | 96 | 394 | 54 | 129 | 23 | 7 | 4 | 43 | 15 | 56 | 14 | .356 | .452 |
| | Jacksonville (SL) | AA | .250 | 24 | 96 | 10 | 24 | 3 | 2 | 0 | 9 | 4 | 21 | 0 | .284 | .323 |
| 2006 | Jacksonville (SL) | AA | .287 | 118 | 457 | 66 | 131 | 24 | 3 | 6 | 55 | 33 | 69 | 8 | .343 | .392 |
| **MINOR LEAGUE TOTALS** | | | .301 | 401 | 1522 | 218 | 458 | 81 | 26 | 18 | 184 | 73 | 239 | 51 | .341 | .424 |

## 6 IVAN DeJESUS JR. SS

BILL MITCHELL

**Born:** May 1, 1987. **B-T:** R-R. **Ht.:** 5-11. **Wt.:** 182. **Drafted:** HS—Guaynabo, P.R., 2005 (2nd round). **Signed by:** Manuel Estrada.

DeJesus' father Ivan Sr. originally signed with Los Angeles and spent 15 years in the majors. A switch-hitter as an amateur, DeJesus batted solely righthanded last year. DeJesus has a rare blend of tools and instincts. His defense is ahead of his bat now, but he's patient, works counts and allows balls to travel deep in the hitting zone. He has good bat-head awareness and slaps the ball to all fields. DeJesus has pure shortstop actions with supple hands and plus range. He has an average arm with efficient exchanges. He's a slightly above-average runner. He lacks strength and DeJesus' power is well below-average. In 2006, he batted .228 away from hitter-friendly Golden Park in low Class A Columbus. As he grows into his wiry frame, DeJesus could improve his punch at the plate. He profiles as an everyday, defense-first big leaguer. He'll spend 2007 in high Class A.

| Year | Club (League) | Class | AVG | G | AB | R | H | 2B | 3B | HR | RBI | BB | SO | SB | OBP | SLG |
|------|---------------|-------|-----|---|-----|---|---|----|----|----|-----|----|----|----|-----|-----|
| 2005 | Dodgers (GCL) | R | .339 | 33 | 121 | 18 | 41 | 5 | 0 | 0 | 11 | 10 | 22 | 8 | .389 | .380 |
| | Ogden (Pio) | R | .208 | 20 | 72 | 4 | 15 | 1 | 0 | 0 | 3 | 6 | 18 | 3 | .296 | .222 |
| 2006 | Columbus (SAL) | A | .277 | 126 | 483 | 65 | 134 | 17 | 2 | 1 | 44 | 63 | 85 | 16 | .361 | .327 |
| **MINOR LEAGUE TOTALS** | | | .281 | 179 | 676 | 87 | 190 | 23 | 2 | 1 | 58 | 79 | 125 | 27 | .359 | .325 |

## 7 JONATHAN MELOAN — RHP

**Born:** July 11, 1984. **B-T:** R-R. **Ht.:** 6-3. **Wt.:** 225. **Drafted:** Arizona, 2005 (5th round). **Signed by:** Brian Stephenson.

Assistant GM Logan White first saw Meloan when he was a high school senior in 2002 and went up against Loney. Meloan's stuff wasn't overly impressive, but the fact he was pitching with a partially torn anterior cruciate ligament in his knee left an impression. Meloan signed for $155,000 after going 27-2 in his final two years at Arizona. He works primarily off a 92-94 mph fastball and mid-80s slider, which has been up to 88. He also has feel for a curveball and changeup, which are passable pitches. He has above-average fastball command and locates his secondary stuff well. Meloan has a ripped physique that lacks looseness. His max-effort delivery features some recoil, a huge red flag. Because of his mechanics and his heavy college workload, the Dodgers wisely limited his innings in 2006. He had elbow soreness during spring training, though an MRI in the off-season found nothing to cause alarm. After impressing scouts in the Arizona Fall League, Meloan could arrive quickly in Los Angeles as a setup man. His health and durability ultimately will determine his value. He'll likely open 2007 in Triple-A.

| Year | Club (League) | Class | W | L | ERA | G | GS | CG | SV | IP | H | R | ER | HR | BB | SO | AVG |
|------|---------------|-------|---|---|-----|---|----|----|----|----|----|---|----|----|----|----|-----|
| 2005 | Ogden (Pio) | R | 0 | 2 | 3.69 | 16 | 6 | 0 | 1 | 39 | 30 | 16 | 16 | 4 | 18 | 54 | .210 |
| 2006 | Columbus (SAL) | A | 1 | 1 | 1.54 | 12 | 0 | 0 | 1 | 23 | 9 | 5 | 4 | 2 | 7 | 41 | .118 |
| | Vero Beach (FSL) | A | 1 | 0 | 2.50 | 4 | 3 | 0 | 0 | 18 | 15 | 6 | 5 | 2 | 4 | 27 | .221 |
| | Jacksonville (SL) | AA | 1 | 0 | 1.69 | 5 | 0 | 0 | 0 | 11 | 3 | 2 | 2 | 1 | 5 | 23 | .086 |
| **MINOR LEAGUE TOTALS** | | | 3 | 3 | 2.67 | 37 | 9 | 0 | 2 | 91 | 57 | 29 | 27 | 9 | 34 | 145 | .177 |

## 8 BLAKE DeWITT — 2B/3B

**Born:** Aug. 20, 1985. **B-T:** L-R. **Ht.:** 5-11. **Wt.:** 195. **Drafted:** HS—Sikeston, Mo., 2004 (1st round). **Signed by:** Mitch Webster.

DeWitt's draft stock improved during his senior season and he was considered the best pure hitter in a lackluster 2004 high school draft class. He has been solid but not spectacular in three years in the minors. He moved from third base to second at high Class A Vero Beach last year, then back to the hot corner when promoted to Double-A. His tools aren't overwhelming, but DeWitt has good feel for the game. He has a knack for putting the barrel on the ball and he uses his hands well at the plate. His swing is short and fluid, and his bat stays in the hitting zone for a long time. He has a solid-average arm and quick release. DeWitt gets pull-happy and tends to drift during his swing, failing to keep his weight back. While he has enough bat speed to drive balls out of the park, he doesn't project to hit more than 12-18 homers annually in the big leagues. He's better suited for third base, so how much power he develops becomes vital to his value. He lacks the actions and range to stick in the middle infield and he's not a fluid fielder. He's a below-average runner. DeWitt's mature approach to hitting and excellent makeup should carry him to the majors. He should spend most of this year at Double-A.

| Year | Club (League) | Class | AVG | G | AB | R | H | 2B | 3B | HR | RBI | BB | SO | SB | OBP | SLG |
|------|---------------|-------|-----|---|----|---|---|----|----|----|-----|----|----|----|-----|-----|
| 2004 | Ogden (Pio) | R | .284 | 70 | 299 | 61 | 85 | 19 | 3 | 12 | 47 | 28 | 78 | 1 | .350 | .488 |
| 2005 | Columbus (SAL) | A | .283 | 120 | 481 | 61 | 136 | 31 | 3 | 11 | 65 | 34 | 79 | 0 | .333 | .428 |
| | Vero Beach (FSL) | A | .419 | 8 | 31 | 4 | 13 | 3 | 0 | 1 | 7 | 1 | 3 | 0 | .438 | .613 |
| 2006 | Vero Beach (FSL) | A | .268 | 106 | 425 | 61 | 114 | 18 | 1 | 18 | 61 | 45 | 79 | 8 | .339 | .442 |
| | Jacksonville (SL) | AA | .183 | 26 | 104 | 6 | 19 | 1 | 0 | 1 | 6 | 8 | 21 | 0 | .241 | .221 |
| **MINOR LEAGUE TOTALS** | | | .274 | 330 | 1340 | 193 | 367 | 72 | 7 | 43 | 186 | 116 | 260 | 9 | .334 | .434 |

## 9 JOSH BELL — 3B

**Born:** Nov. 13, 1986. **B-T:** B-R. **Ht.:** 6-1. **Wt.:** 205. **Drafted:** HS—Lantana, Fla., 2005 (4th round). **Signed by:** Manny Estrada.

Bell entered his senior season as one of the top position players in the high school draft class of 2005. But his approach and setup vacillated from at-bat to at-bat, he struggled mightily and slipped to the fourth round, where he signed for $212,000. He has hit .312 in two pro seasons and ranked among the Rookie-level Pioneer League's top power hitters in 2006. Bell's raw power ranks as at least a 70 on the 20-80 scouting scale. He has tremendous leverage in his quick, powerful stroke from both sides of the plate. His hands and footwork are adequate at third base, where he shows a plus arm. He has strong makeup. His approach and all-around game are unrefined. Like Andy LaRoche, Bell tends to swing from his heels, sacrificing his balance. He can beaten on the

inner half, especially when batting righthanded. His pitch recognition and plate discipline have a ways to go. He's doesn't have quick-twitch muscle movements, and he could improve his footwork defensively. Many of his 17 errors came on overthrows. He's a below-average runner. Bell profiles as an everyday third baseman with a .250-.260 average and 25-30 home runs annually. He'll probably begin 2007 in low Class A.

| Year | Club (League) | Class | AVG | G | AB | R | H | 2B | 3B | HR | RBI | BB | SO | SB | OBP | SLG |
|------|---------------|-------|-----|---|----|---|---|----|----|----|-----|----|----|----|-----|-----|
| 2005 | Dodgers (GCL) | R | .318 | 45 | 157 | 26 | 50 | 7 | 1 | 1 | 21 | 20 | 33 | 5 | .399 | .395 |
| 2006 | Ogden (Pio) | R | .308 | 64 | 250 | 45 | 77 | 17 | 3 | 12 | 53 | 23 | 72 | 4 | .367 | .544 |
| MINOR LEAGUE TOTALS | | | .312 | 109 | 407 | 71 | 127 | 24 | 4 | 13 | 74 | 43 | 105 | 9 | .380 | .486 |

## 10 PRESTON MATTINGLY                                         SS

**Born:** Aug. 28, 1987. **B-T:** R-R. **Ht.:** 6-3. **Wt.:** 205. **Drafted:** HS— Evansville, Ind., 2006 (1st round supplemental). **Signed by:** Marty Lamb.

Despite being a three-sport star and the son of former American League MVP and batting champ Don Mattingly, Preston somehow stayed off the radar of most area scouts in 2006. The Dodgers liked him all along, and made him a surprise supplemental first-round pick. After signing for $1 million, he acquitted himself well in the Gulf Coast League. An all-Indiana wide receiver in football and a 20-point-a-game scorer in basketball, Mattingly stands out for his athleticism, bat speed and raw power. Balls jump off his bat and he has power to all fields. He has a good feel for hitting and a sound approach. He's an above-average runner. He has good makeup. Mattingly is very raw. He needs to improve his pitch recognition, use the whole field and avoid chasing breaking balls. He lacks the actions and footwork to remain in the middle of the diamond, and he ultimately could wind up in left field. His throwing mechanics are poor and he has below-average arm strength. The Dodgers believe Mattingly will develop into a middle-of-the-order run producer. There are no immediate plans to change his position this year, which he'll probably spend in extended spring training and Rookie-level Ogden.

| Year | Club (League) | Class | AVG | G | AB | R | H | 2B | 3B | HR | RBI | BB | SO | SB | OBP | SLG |
|------|---------------|-------|-----|---|----|---|---|----|----|----|-----|----|----|----|-----|-----|
| 2006 | Dodgers (GCL) | R | .290 | 47 | 186 | 22 | 54 | 12 | 3 | 1 | 29 | 9 | 39 | 12 | .322 | .403 |
| MINOR LEAGUE TOTALS | | | .290 | 47 | 186 | 22 | 54 | 12 | 3 | 1 | 29 | 9 | 39 | 12 | .322 | .403 |

## 11 CHIN-LUNG HU                                              SS

**Born:** Feb. 2, 1984. **B-T:** R-R. **Ht.:** 5-9. **Wt.:** 150. **Signed:** Taiwan, 2003. **Signed by:** Pat Kelly/Vincent Liao.

The Dodgers have a history of success scouting the Pacific Rim and locked in on Hu as a teenager. Hu went 5-for-12 for Taiwan in the 2006 World Baseball Classic and was assigned to Double-A after two strong seasons in Class A. Hu's value lies in his glove, and he struggled to make consistent hard contact in 2006. He has a high front-leg kick to trigger his swing and tends to drift away from the plate. Fastballs in on his hands give him trouble, as he's geared to spray line drives up the middle and to the opposite field. He hits the top half of the ball well and has good pitch recognition. His 49 walks were almost twice as many as he had drawn in any previous season, and he made strides in his ability to command the strike zone. He has below-average power, though he can drive balls to both alleys when he gets his arms extended. He's a slightly above-average runner and has outstanding range and instincts at shortstop. He led Southern League shortstops with a .981 fielding percentage. Balls disappear in his glove and his hands are supple. He has a solid-average arm and makes clean, quick exchanges. He's quicker to his left than he is making plays to his backhand. Hu could develop into an everyday shortstop in the big leagues on a club that can supplement his lack of offense. He could repeat Double-A in 2007.

| Year | Club (League) | Class | AVG | G | AB | R | H | 2B | 3B | HR | RBI | BB | SO | SB | OBP | SLG |
|------|---------------|-------|-----|---|----|---|---|----|----|----|-----|----|----|----|-----|-----|
| 2003 | Ogden (Pio) | R | .305 | 53 | 220 | 34 | 67 | 9 | 5 | 3 | 23 | 14 | 33 | 5 | .343 | .432 |
| 2004 | Columbus (SAL) | A | .298 | 84 | 332 | 58 | 99 | 15 | 4 | 6 | 25 | 20 | 50 | 17 | .342 | .422 |
| | Vero Beach (FSL) | A | .307 | 20 | 75 | 12 | 23 | 4 | 1 | 0 | 10 | 5 | 6 | 3 | .350 | .387 |
| 2005 | Vero Beach (FSL) | A | .313 | 116 | 470 | 80 | 147 | 29 | 1 | 8 | 56 | 19 | 40 | 23 | .347 | .434 |
| 2006 | Jacksonville (SL) | AA | .254 | 125 | 488 | 71 | 124 | 20 | 2 | 5 | 34 | 49 | 63 | 11 | .326 | .334 |
| MINOR LEAGUE TOTALS | | | .290 | 398 | 1585 | 255 | 460 | 77 | 13 | 22 | 148 | 107 | 192 | 59 | .339 | .397 |

## 12 BRYAN MORRIS                                             RHP

**Born:** March 28, 1987. **B-T:** L-R. **Ht.:** 6-3. **Wt.:** 175. **Drafted:** Motlow State (Tenn.) CC, 2006 (1st round). **Signed by:** Marty Lamb.

After Tampa Bay drafted Morris in the third round in 2005 out of Tullahoma (Tenn.) High, the two sides agreed to a $1.4 million bonus that former Devil Rays ownership failed to fol-

low through on. Morris hedged on signing as well, mostly because his father Ricky wanted him to play at Motlow State (Tenn.) CC, where Ricky is an assistant coach. Morris dominated the juco circuit, went back into the draft, and signed for $1.325 million as the 26th overall choice in 2006. He's got huge stuff and a funky delivery. Following a fantastic debut in the Pioneer League, where he rated as the No. 1 prospect, Morris had Tommy John surgery and was expected to miss all of the 2007 season. The gangly righthander has a stiff front side and throws across his body. His arm is loose and quick, and he's a good athlete, but the torque created by his delivery might have led to his elbow injury. Erratic command was also a byproduct of his mechanics, but if his mid-90s fastball and hammer curveball come back, he has impact potential. Morris pitches at 93-94 mph and bumped 96 in Ogden. His downer breaking ball has excellent depth and grades as a plus pitch. He'll flash a rudimentary changeup and a fringy slider. If all goes well in rehabilitation, Morris might return to the mound in time for instructional league.

| Year | Club (League) | Class | W | L | ERA | G | GS | CG | SV | IP | H | R | ER | HR | BB | SO | AVG |
|------|---------------|-------|---|---|-----|---|----|----|----|----|---|---|----|----|----|----|-----|
| 2006 | Ogden (Pio) | R | 4 | 5 | 5.13 | 14 | 14 | 0 | 0 | 60 | 64 | 44 | 34 | 3 | 40 | 79 | .267 |
| **MINOR LEAGUE TOTALS** | | | 4 | 5 | 5.13 | 14 | 14 | 0 | 0 | 60 | 64 | 44 | 34 | 3 | 40 | 79 | .267 |

## 13 DELWYN YOUNG                                                  OF

**Born:** June 30, 1982. **B-T:** B-R. **Ht.:** 5-8. **Wt.:** 210. **Drafted:** Santa Barbara (Calif.) CC, 2002 (4th round). **Signed by:** James Merriweather.

The Braves failed to sign Young as a 19th-round draft-and-follow prior to the 2002 draft, and his stock soared after an impressive predraft workout at Dodger Stadium. He's quietly been one of the minors' most consistent offensive threats, climbing to Triple-A in 2006 and setting career highs in RBIs and doubles, marking his fourth consecutive season with at least 36 doubles. He led Dodgers minor leaguers in extra-base hits. Young's bat speed is among the best in the system. He's an aggressive hitter who looks to pull the ball early in the count and rarely gets cheated at the plate. He has the strength and bat control to pepper line drives to all parts of the park. He has solid-average power. His plate discipline and willingness to walk aren't pluses. His swing gets long, and has more holes from the right side, as he batted .198 against lefthanders in Triple-A last year. He's a below-average runner with below-average range and a plus arm suited for right field. His tools compare favorably to Matt Stairs', and Young will likely hit his way into a lineup as an everyday corner outfielder eventually. But he doesn't appear to be in the Dodgers' immediate outfield plans. Unless he's traded, he'll probably return to Triple-A in 2007.

| Year | Club (League) | Class | AVG | G | AB | R | H | 2B | 3B | HR | RBI | BB | SO | SB | OBP | SLG |
|------|---------------|-------|-----|---|----|---|---|----|----|----|-----|----|----|----|-----|-----|
| 2002 | Great Falls (Pio) | R | .300 | 59 | 240 | 42 | 72 | 18 | 1 | 10 | 41 | 27 | 60 | 4 | .380 | .508 |
| 2003 | South Georgia (SAL) | A | .323 | 119 | 443 | 67 | 143 | 38 | 7 | 15 | 73 | 36 | 87 | 5 | .381 | .542 |
| 2004 | Vero Beach (FSL) | A | .281 | 129 | 470 | 76 | 132 | 36 | 3 | 22 | 85 | 57 | 134 | 11 | .364 | .511 |
| 2005 | Jacksonville (SL) | AA | .296 | 95 | 371 | 52 | 110 | 25 | 1 | 16 | 62 | 27 | 86 | 1 | .346 | .499 |
|      | Las Vegas (PCL) | AAA | .325 | 36 | 160 | 23 | 52 | 12 | 0 | 4 | 14 | 8 | 35 | 0 | .361 | .475 |
| 2006 | Las Vegas (PCL) | AAA | .273 | 140 | 532 | 76 | 145 | 42 | 1 | 18 | 98 | 42 | 104 | 3 | .326 | .457 |
|      | Los Angeles (NL) | MLB | .000 | 8 | 5 | 0 | 0 | 0 | 0 | 0 | 0 | 0 | 1 | 0 | .000 | .000 |
| **MINOR LEAGUE TOTALS** | | | .295 | 578 | 2216 | 336 | 654 | 171 | 13 | 85 | 373 | 197 | 506 | 24 | .357 | .499 |
| **MAJOR LEAGUE TOTALS** | | | .000 | 8 | 5 | 0 | 0 | 0 | 0 | 0 | 0 | 0 | 1 | 0 | .000 | .000 |

## 14 JUSTIN ORENDUFF                                               RHP

**Born:** May 27, 1983. **B-T:** R-R. **Ht.:** 6-4. **Wt.:** 205. **Drafted:** Virginia Commonwealth, 2004 (1st round). **Signed by:** Clair Rierson.

Orenduff bolstered his draft stock in the summer of 2003 when he helped USA Baseball's college national team win a silver medal at the Pan American Games. He pitched alongside Cla Meredith (Padres) and Sean Marshall (Cubs) at Virginia Commonwealth after transferring from George Washington following his freshman year in 2002. Orenduff logged well over 300 innings in his college career, including summer ball, and has shown signs of wear since signing with the Dodgers for $1 million. He opened 2006 in Double-A before his balky shoulder forced him to shut it down in May. He had surgery in August. Orenduff operates with a heavy, 88-92 mph fastball and a hard, 81-83 mph slider. His slider rates as a plus for both its quality and its command. He uses it too often, but it was a big reason righthanders batted .164 against him last year, compared to .297 for lefthanders. He also features a fringy changeup. Orenduff could find himself in a middle relief or set-up role when he gets back on the mound. His ceiling is as a back-of-the-rotation starter. He's expected to return to the mound by spring training, but he might not be ready for a full-season assignment on Opening Day.

| Year | Club (League) | Class | W | L | ERA | G | GS | CG | SV | IP | H | R | ER | HR | BB | SO | AVG |
|---|---|---|---|---|---|---|---|---|---|---|---|---|---|---|---|---|---|
| 2004 | Ogden (Pio) | R | 2 | 3 | 4.74 | 13 | 10 | 0 | 0 | 44 | 46 | 26 | 23 | 4 | 25 | 57 | .272 |
| 2005 | Vero Beach (FSL) | A | 5 | 3 | 2.24 | 12 | 12 | 1 | 0 | 60 | 35 | 21 | 15 | 3 | 26 | 81 | .167 |
| | Jacksonville (SL) | AA | 5 | 2 | 4.07 | 14 | 13 | 0 | 0 | 66 | 59 | 33 | 30 | 6 | 24 | 65 | .241 |
| 2006 | Jacksonville (SL) | AA | 4 | 2 | 3.40 | 10 | 10 | 0 | 0 | 50 | 40 | 24 | 19 | 4 | 19 | 54 | .217 |
| **MINOR LEAGUE TOTALS** | | | 16 | 10 | 3.55 | 49 | 45 | 1 | 0 | 221 | 180 | 104 | 87 | 17 | 94 | 257 | .223 |

## 15 ZACH HAMMES                                                          RHP

**Born:** May 15, 1984. **B-T:** R-R. **Ht.:** 6-6. **Wt.:** 225. **Drafted:** HS—Iowa City, 2002 (2nd round). **Signed by:** Mitch Webster.

Following three straight years in low Class A with a combined ERA of 5.00, Hammes figured things out last year. He moved to the bullpen in 2005, and now that he pitches exclusively from the stretch, his delivery is simpler and more balanced than it was from the windup. He was added to the 40-man roster following the season. Hammes was clocked at 93 mph during his senior season in high school, but he was pitching around 88 before he cleaned up his delivery. He was up to 97 in Hawaii Winter Baseball, where he collected five saves as North Shore's closer. He sits at 92-94. His slider comes in at 81-84 with three-quarter tilt. It breaks out of his hand, but his 6-foot-6 frame and three-quarters arm slot give it enough angle and depth to grade as an above-average offering. His changeup is a legitimate third pitch that he uses effectively against lefthanders. Hammes' command is below average. He works deep counts and tends to miss up in the zone. He doesn't have exceptional feel for pitching. He should spend most of 2007 in Double-A.

| Year | Club (League) | Class | W | L | ERA | G | GS | CG | SV | IP | H | R | ER | HR | BB | SO | AVG |
|---|---|---|---|---|---|---|---|---|---|---|---|---|---|---|---|---|---|
| 2002 | Dodgers (GCL) | R | 2 | 2 | 3.27 | 10 | 8 | 0 | 0 | 33 | 26 | 14 | 12 | 0 | 15 | 27 | .217 |
| 2003 | South Georgia (SAL) | A | 7 | 11 | 5.54 | 25 | 24 | 0 | 0 | 117 | 138 | 91 | 72 | 11 | 65 | 75 | .295 |
| 2004 | Columbus (SAL) | A | 5 | 8 | 4.55 | 24 | 23 | 0 | 0 | 113 | 146 | 79 | 57 | 15 | 54 | 73 | .322 |
| 2005 | Columbus (SAL) | A | 3 | 4 | 4.81 | 22 | 8 | 0 | 1 | 64 | 69 | 43 | 34 | 7 | 52 | 46 | .273 |
| 2006 | Vero Beach (FSL) | A | 6 | 3 | 4.32 | 41 | 3 | 0 | 1 | 92 | 95 | 48 | 44 | 9 | 46 | 90 | .269 |
| | Las Vegas (PCL) | AAA | 0 | 0 | 5.63 | 2 | 1 | 0 | 0 | 8 | 7 | 5 | 5 | 1 | 5 | 8 | .241 |
| **MINOR LEAGUE TOTALS** | | | 23 | 28 | 4.73 | 124 | 67 | 0 | 2 | 426 | 481 | 280 | 224 | 43 | 237 | 319 | .287 |

## 16 STEVEN JOHNSON                                                       RHP

**Born:** Aug. 31, 1987. **B-T:** R-R. **Ht.:** 6-1. **Wt.:** 185. **Drafted:** HS—Kingsville, Md., 2005 (13th round). **Signed by:** Clair Rierson.

When the Dodgers needed a pitcher to fill in at Double-A in May, they called up Johnson from extended spring training. Though he was just 18, he handled himself with poise and maturity. After two scoreless relief appearances, he went back to extended spring training before reporting to Rookie-level Ogden. Johnson, whose father Dave pitched for the Pirates, Orioles and Tigers from 1987-93, led the Pioneer League with 86 strikeouts. He relies on feel and command and has a knack for setting up hitters. His delivery is clean and efficient. His fastball comes in at 90-91 mph, and he can add and subtract from it, as well as cut it. Johnson's slider and curveball last summer have potential to be above-average offerings, based more on his ability to spot them rather than their shape. His changeup is below-average. His frame doesn't lend considerable room for growth. He's a candidate to climb to high Class A in 2007. He has a ceiling as a back-of-the-rotation starter.

| Year | Club (League) | Class | W | L | ERA | G | GS | CG | SV | IP | H | R | ER | HR | BB | SO | AVG |
|---|---|---|---|---|---|---|---|---|---|---|---|---|---|---|---|---|---|
| 2005 | Dodgers (GCL) | R | 0 | 2 | 9.53 | 6 | 3 | 0 | 0 | 11 | 18 | 12 | 12 | 1 | 4 | 14 | .360 |
| 2006 | Jacksonville (SL) | AA | 0 | 0 | 0.00 | 2 | 0 | 0 | 0 | 5 | 2 | 0 | 0 | 0 | 2 | 3 | .133 |
| | Ogden (Pio) | R | 5 | 5 | 3.89 | 14 | 14 | 0 | 0 | 79 | 79 | 37 | 34 | 4 | 25 | 86 | .267 |
| **MINOR LEAGUE TOTALS** | | | 5 | 7 | 4.37 | 22 | 17 | 0 | 0 | 95 | 99 | 49 | 46 | 5 | 31 | 103 | .274 |

## 17 GREG MILLER                                                          LHP

**Born:** Nov. 3, 1984. **B-T:** L-L. **Ht.:** 6-5. **Wt.:** 195. **Drafted:** HS—Yorba Linda, Calif., 2002 (1st round supplemental). **Signed by:** Scott Groot.

Miller missed all of 2004 and the first half of 2005 with a shoulder injury that required two surgeries. He was used conservatively in 2006, opening the year in Double-A before spending most of it at Triple-A. He's not the same dominant pitcher and lacks consistency, but shows flashes of the velocity and stuff that made him the minors' best lefthanded pitching prospect before his injury. He doesn't repeat his arm slot, and seems to search for a release point that minimizes discomfort in his shoulder. As a result, his control suffers and he's erratic with all of his pitches. His fastball sits at 91-92 mph, touching 95 with nasty life and tail. His hard slider comes in between 80-86 mph with late, sharp break. He also throws a cutter, curveball and changeup, but worked with a two-pitch mix in his role as Vegas' setup man. He rarely worked more than two innings, and Miller's durability remains a concern.

The Dodgers could opt to return him to the rotation to test his stamina and give him more innings to work on his control. Miller's future lies in his health.

| Year | Club (League) | Class | W | L | ERA | G | GS | CG | SV | IP | H | R | ER | HR | BB | SO | AVG |
|------|---------------|-------|---|---|-----|---|----|----|----|----|----|---|----|----|----|----|-----|
| 2002 | Great Falls (Pio) | R | 3 | 2 | 2.37 | 11 | 7 | 0 | 0 | 38 | 27 | 14 | 10 | 1 | 13 | 37 | .199 |
| 2003 | Vero Beach (FSL) | A | 11 | 4 | 2.49 | 21 | 21 | 1 | 0 | 116 | 103 | 40 | 32 | 5 | 41 | 111 | .240 |
| | Jacksonville (SL) | AA | 1 | 1 | 1.01 | 4 | 4 | 0 | 0 | 27 | 15 | 5 | 3 | 1 | 7 | 40 | .156 |
| 2004 | Did not play—Injured | | | | | | | | | | | | | | | | |
| 2005 | Dodgers (GCL) | R | 0 | 0 | 2.25 | 4 | 3 | 0 | 0 | 12 | 7 | 5 | 3 | 0 | 4 | 14 | .159 |
| | Vero Beach (FSL) | A | 1 | 0 | 0.93 | 5 | 3 | 0 | 0 | 10 | 4 | 1 | 1 | 0 | 7 | 10 | .138 |
| | Jacksonville (SL) | AA | 0 | 0 | 2.77 | 12 | 0 | 0 | 2 | 13 | 14 | 6 | 4 | 1 | 15 | 17 | .275 |
| 2006 | Jacksonville (SL) | AA | 1 | 0 | 0.79 | 11 | 0 | 0 | 1 | 23 | 12 | 8 | 2 | 0 | 13 | 24 | .154 |
| | Las Vegas (PCL) | AAA | 3 | 0 | 4.38 | 33 | 0 | 0 | 0 | 37 | 33 | 19 | 18 | 1 | 33 | 32 | .243 |
| **MINOR LEAGUE TOTALS** | | | 20 | 7 | 2.39 | 101 | 38 | 1 | 3 | 275 | 215 | 98 | 73 | 9 | 133 | 285 | .215 |

## 18 BRENT LEACH
LHP

**Born:** Nov. 18, 1982. **B-T:** L-L. **Ht.:** 6-5. **Wt.:** 205. **Drafted:** Delta State (Miss.), 2005 (6th round). **Signed by:** Dennis Moeller.

Leach began his college career at Southern Mississippi, but he broke down and had Tommy John surgery in 2003. He transferred to nearby Delta State, where he was used primarily at the back of the bullpen. He suffers from hyperhidrosis, a condition that causes excessive sweating in the palms—which is decidedly inconvenient for a pitcher. His condition improved by having mild electrical shocks applied to his hands. He led the Pioneer League in ERA in 2005 and began 2006 in the low Class A rotation. Once he moved to high Class A, he went back to the bullpen, where he best profiles. Leach has a physical frame and two strong pitches in an 89-91 mph fastball that can touch 93 and a plus breaking ball at 78-81. He delivers his breaking ball from the same slot as his fastball and it has hard, late break. It's his greatest asset and is a legitimate strikeout pitch against lefties. He has some feel for a changeup. Leach has below-average command and his delivery isn't pretty. His arm slot is slightly lower than it was in college, which has aided his effectiveness against lefties. He also has an outstanding pickoff move and led the minors with 22 pickoffs last year. As a situational lefty or middle reliever, Leach could move quickly, and might begin 2007 in Double-A.

| Year | Club (League) | Class | W | L | ERA | G | GS | CG | SV | IP | H | R | ER | HR | BB | SO | AVG |
|------|---------------|-------|---|---|-----|---|----|----|----|----|----|---|----|----|----|----|-----|
| 2005 | Ogden (Pio) | R | 5 | 3 | 2.43 | 14 | 13 | 1 | 0 | 67 | 53 | 21 | 18 | 4 | 29 | 77 | .227 |
| 2006 | Columbus (SAL) | A | 4 | 2 | 3.27 | 10 | 10 | 0 | 0 | 52 | 41 | 22 | 19 | 2 | 31 | 67 | .230 |
| | Vero Beach (FSL) | A | 3 | 4 | 4.56 | 30 | 0 | 0 | 1 | 49 | 48 | 34 | 25 | 1 | 32 | 57 | .265 |
| **MINOR LEAGUE TOTALS** | | | 12 | 9 | 3.31 | 54 | 23 | 1 | 1 | 168 | 142 | 77 | 62 | 7 | 92 | 201 | .240 |

## 19 CORY DUNLAP
1B

**Born:** April 14, 1984. **B-T:** L-L. **Ht.:** 6-1. **Wt.:** 230. **Drafted:** Contra Costa (Calif.) CC, 2004 (3rd round). **Signed by:** Mark Sheehy.

While Dunlap continues to show an innate ability to hit, poor conditioning continues to hold him back. He ballooned to 300 pounds in high school in Alameda, Calif., where he played with Dontrelle Willis, but lost approximately 70 pounds and led all California junior college players with a .512 average in 2004. Former Dodgers farm director Terry Collins seemed to connect with Dunlap in his effort to promote better conditioning, but otherwise Dunlap hasn't shown enough drive to stay in shape. He came to camp well over his listed weight of 230 pounds last year and repeated high Class A. Dunlap has tremendous bat-head awareness and an advanced approach at the plate. He controls the strike zone, works counts and uses the entire field. He led the organization with a .435 on-base percentage. He shows plus raw power when he gets extended and finishes his swing. Dunlap can be beaten with fastballs in on his hands. He hit just .145 against lefties in 2006. He has adequate hands and instincts at first base. His range is well below-average, as is his speed. Dunlap will most likely spend most of 2007 at Double-A.

| Year | Club (League) | Class | AVG | G | AB | R | H | 2B | 3B | HR | RBI | BB | SO | SB | OBP | SLG |
|------|---------------|-------|-----|---|----|---|---|----|----|----|-----|----|----|----|-----|-----|
| 2004 | Ogden (Pio) | R | .351 | 71 | 245 | 57 | 86 | 18 | 1 | 7 | 53 | 68 | 40 | 0 | .492 | .518 |
| 2005 | Vero Beach (FSL) | A | .291 | 121 | 430 | 61 | 125 | 25 | 0 | 7 | 77 | 65 | 64 | 5 | .382 | .398 |
| 2006 | Vero Beach (FSL) | A | .261 | 89 | 284 | 43 | 74 | 15 | 0 | 14 | 47 | 88 | 69 | 0 | .435 | .461 |
| | Las Vegas (PCL) | AAA | .250 | 3 | 4 | 0 | 1 | 0 | 0 | 0 | 2 | 1 | 2 | 0 | .333 | .250 |
| **MINOR LEAGUE TOTALS** | | | .297 | 284 | 963 | 161 | 286 | 58 | 1 | 28 | 179 | 222 | 175 | 5 | .428 | .447 |

## 20 MARK ALEXANDER
RHP

**Born:** Dec. 6, 1980. **B-T:** R-R. **Ht.:** 5-11. **Wt.:** 200. **Drafted:** Missouri, 2004 (20th round). **Signed by:** Mitch Webster.

The Dodgers drafted a pair of first-rounders from the state of Missouri in 2004—Scott

Elbert and Blake DeWitt—and chose Alexander, a fifth-year senior from Mizzou, in the 20th round the same year. He blew out his elbow as a senior at Rockhurst (Mo.) High, had Tommy John surgery and pitched sparingly in college until his senior season. He was the organization's minor league pitcher of the year in 2006 and had a span of 23 appearances (26 innings) without allowing an earned run, a stretch that began in Double-A and continued in Triple-A. He works off a two-pitch mix and relies heavily on his 74-78 mph slider. It has short, sharp break, he has good feel for it and he'll throw it in any count and in any situation. He spots his 88-91 mph fastball to both corners, but it lacks significant life or movement. Alexander is meticulous in his preparation and takes detailed notes on opposing hitters. His stuff doesn't profile in the back of a big league bullpen, but he could break into the majors as a middle reliever. He will likely return to Triple-A to begin 2007.

| Year | Club (League) | Class | W | L | ERA | G | GS | CG | SV | IP | H | R | ER | HR | BB | SO | AVG |
|------|---------------|-------|---|---|-----|---|----|----|----|----|---|---|----|----|----|----|-----|
| 2004 | Ogden (Pio) | R | 4 | 1 | 2.65 | 25 | 0 | 0 | 9 | 34 | 30 | 10 | 10 | 4 | 8 | 37 | .227 |
| 2005 | Vero Beach (FSL) | A | 5 | 4 | 3.03 | 52 | 0 | 0 | 23 | 65 | 64 | 25 | 22 | 6 | 23 | 91 | .256 |
| 2006 | Jacksonville (SL) | AA | 3 | 2 | 0.96 | 40 | 0 | 0 | 26 | 47 | 26 | 8 | 5 | 2 | 13 | 72 | .158 |
| | Las Vegas (PCL) | AAA | 2 | 1 | 3.14 | 12 | 0 | 0 | 1 | 14 | 11 | 6 | 5 | 0 | 10 | 13 | .216 |
| **MINOR LEAGUE TOTALS** | | | 14 | 8 | 2.35 | 129 | 0 | 0 | 59 | 161 | 131 | 49 | 42 | 12 | 54 | 213 | .219 |

## 21 MIKE MEGREW LHP

**Born:** Jan. 29, 1984. **B-T:** L-L. **Ht.:** 6-6. **Wt.:** 210. **Drafted:** HS—Hope Valley, R.I., 2002 (5th round). **Signed by:** John Kosciak.

Greg Miller, Megrew and Eric Stults were three projectable lefthanders the Dodgers nabbed in the 2002 draft, and while only Stults has made it to the majors, all three remain prospects. Megrew's ascent was interrupted when recurring arm trouble eventually required Tommy John surgery following the 2004 season. The Marlins took a shot at Megrew in the 2005 major league Rule 5 draft based on his performance in instructional league that fall, then stashed him on the disabled list last March. But when his arm trouble persisted, they returned him to the Dodgers in April. Megrew made it back to the mound in June and eventually rejoined the Vero Beach rotation. His fastball typically sat between 87-89 mph, touching 91. He showed feel for two potentially plus secondary offerings in a circle changeup and a high-70s slider. His changeup has occasional plus sink and fade, and rivals lefty Carlos Alvarez' among the best in the system. Megrew's command has a long way to go, but his feel for pitching and control were assets before he had surgery, and he showed signs of both during instructional league. He was added to the 40-man roster after the season, and he will go to Double-A if he performs well during spring training in 2007.

| Year | Club (League) | Class | W | L | ERA | G | GS | CG | SV | IP | H | R | ER | HR | BB | SO | AVG |
|------|---------------|-------|---|---|-----|---|----|----|----|----|---|---|----|----|----|----|-----|
| 2002 | Dodgers (GCL) | R | 1 | 1 | 2.03 | 5 | 4 | 0 | 0 | 13 | 8 | 4 | 3 | 0 | 3 | 12 | .178 |
| 2003 | Ogden (Pio) | R | 5 | 3 | 3.40 | 14 | 14 | 0 | 0 | 77 | 64 | 40 | 29 | 6 | 24 | 99 | .222 |
| 2004 | Vero Beach (FSL) | A | 7 | 6 | 3.41 | 22 | 22 | 0 | 0 | 106 | 84 | 45 | 40 | 7 | 43 | 125 | .220 |
| 2005 | Dodgers (GCL) | R | 0 | 0 | 5.40 | 3 | 3 | 0 | 0 | 5 | 4 | 3 | 3 | 0 | 4 | 8 | .250 |
| | Vero Beach (FSL) | A | 0 | 2 | 20.25 | 2 | 2 | 0 | 0 | 4 | 9 | 9 | 9 | 1 | 2 | 2 | .429 |
| 2006 | Vero Beach (FSL) | A | 2 | 3 | 3.52 | 18 | 8 | 0 | 0 | 54 | 44 | 23 | 21 | 5 | 44 | 62 | .224 |
| **MINOR LEAGUE TOTALS** | | | 15 | 15 | 3.66 | 64 | 53 | 0 | 0 | 258 | 213 | 124 | 105 | 19 | 120 | 308 | .225 |

## 22 RAMON TRONCOSO RHP

**Born:** Feb. 16, 1983. **B-T:** R-R. **Ht.:** 6-2. **Wt.:** 187. **Signed:** Dominican Republic, 2002. **Signed by:** Pablo Peguero.

Dominican scout Pablo Peguero made a name for himself by signing Joel Guzman, and when he wound up in hot water for inking at least one Latin player before he was 16. Tony Abreu, lefty Miguel Sanfler and Troncoso were a few treats Peguero left L.A. before he was hired by the Giants. Troncoso spent three seasons in the Rookie-level Dominican Summer League before jumping to low Class A in 2005. He began 2006 at high Class A but was sent back to low A six weeks later and made good progress. He didn't allow an earned run in his final 13 innings of the season—six of which came in high Class A—and was lights-out during instructional league as well. He features a 91-95 mph fastball with sink and occasional bore. His secondary stuff is raw, though he added a changeup during instructional league that he showed feel for. He uses a change/splitter hybrid grip, and the pitch showed occasional plus action. His slider is hard and lacks depth. He has good control but below-average command. Troncoso's present package profiles in a middle-relief role, but he has good composure and if his secondary stuff comes around he could develop into a closer. He'll have a chance to climb to Double-A in 2007.

| Year | Club (League) | Class | W | L | ERA | G | GS | CG | SV | IP | H | R | ER | HR | BB | SO | AVG |
|------|---------------|-------|---|---|-----|---|----|----|----|----|---|---|----|----|----|----|-----|
| 2002 | Dodgers (DSL) | R | 2 | 4 | 2.27 | 11 | 7 | 0 | 0 | 40 | 47 | 23 | 10 | 0 | 14 | 29 | .287 |

| 2003 | Dodgers (DSL) | R | 2 | 2 | 2.47 | 11 | 7 | 0 | 0 | 47 | 39 | 23 | 13 | 1 | 13 | 38 | .228 |
|------|---------------|---|---|---|------|----|---|---|---|----|----|----|----|---|----|----|------|
| 2004 | Dodgers (DSL) | R | 2 | 0 | 0.00 | 9 | 0 | 0 | 3 | 12 | 9 | 0 | 0 | 0 | 3 | 8 | .220 |
| | Dodgers (DSL) | R | 0 | 3 | 5.73 | 8 | 0 | 0 | 2 | 22 | 27 | 17 | 14 | 0 | 9 | 21 | .293 |
| 2005 | Columbus (SAL) | A | 2 | 3 | 6.69 | 13 | 6 | 0 | 1 | 38 | 58 | 33 | 28 | 2 | 13 | 27 | .360 |
| | Ogden (PIO) | R | 6 | 2 | 3.68 | 29 | 0 | 0 | 13 | 37 | 40 | 19 | 15 | 0 | 12 | 30 | .278 |
| 2006 | Columbus (SAL) | A | 4 | 0 | 2.41 | 23 | 0 | 0 | 15 | 34 | 28 | 11 | 9 | 1 | 7 | 22 | .241 |
| | Vero Beach (FSL) | A | 1 | 3 | 6.75 | 18 | 0 | 0 | 0 | 29 | 43 | 27 | 22 | 1 | 14 | 31 | .347 |
| **MINOR LEAGUE TOTALS** | | | 19 | 17 | 3.87 | 122 | 20 | 0 | 34 | 258 | 291 | 153 | 111 | 5 | 85 | 206 | .287 |

## 23 CARLOS SANTANA

OF/3B/C

**Born:** April 8, 1986. **B-T:** B-R. **Ht.:** 5-11. **Wt.:** 170. **Signed:** Dominican Republic, 2004. **Signed by:** Andres Lopez.

Dodgers scouting chief Logan White encourages his scouts to target potential conversion candidates during evaluation, and Santana and third baseman Lucas May both spent time behind the plate during instructional league last fall. Santana showed passable catch-and-throws skills in his audition at catcher, and his bat also could make him an interesting prospect. Despite having just 78 minor league at-bats under his belt, he went to high Class A in May and hit safely in nine of his first 10 games and held his own all season. He then reported to Rookie-level Ogden, where he spent most of the summer manning right field to make room for Josh Bell at third base. He's athletic but his baseball acumen is limited. He uses his hands well at the plate and has above-average bat speed and good plate coverage. He maintains his balance better from the right side. His swing has some length. His lateral quickness, hands and instincts are pluses. He showed a solid-average arm behind the plate. He's a fringe-average runner. Santana could spend 2007 at Los Angeles' new low Class A Great Lakes affiliate.

| Year | Club (League) | Class | AVG | G | AB | R | H | 2B | 3B | HR | RBI | BB | SO | SB | OBP | SLG |
|------|---------------|-------|-----|---|----|---|---|----|----|----|-----|----|----|----|-----|-----|
| 2005 | Dodgers (GCL) | R | .295 | 32 | 78 | 14 | 23 | 4 | 1 | 1 | 14 | 16 | 8 | 0 | .412 | .410 |
| 2006 | Vero Beach (FSL) | A | .268 | 54 | 198 | 16 | 53 | 10 | 2 | 3 | 18 | 23 | 43 | 0 | .345 | .384 |
| | Ogden (Pio) | R | .303 | 37 | 132 | 31 | 40 | 5 | 1 | 7 | 27 | 30 | 19 | 4 | .423 | .515 |
| **MINOR LEAGUE TOTALS** | | | .284 | 123 | 408 | 61 | 116 | 19 | 4 | 11 | 59 | 69 | 70 | 4 | .385 | .431 |

## 24 CODY WHITE

LHP

**Born:** Feb. 27, 1985. **B-T:** L-L. **Ht.:** 6-3. **Wt.:** 185. **Drafted:** Texarkana (Texas) JC, D/F 2003 (12th round). **Signed by:** Mike Leuzinger.

At the outset of the season, it was uncertain whether White had much of a future in the organization. His flippant attitude toward his development was his most significant impediment, but he took his career more seriously in 2006 and turned a corner. He played on the same American Legion team in Texas as 2006 first-rounder Drew Stubbs. He was a talented hitter, and also played basketball in high school, indicators of his athletic ability. He was one of Ogden's most reliable relievers and followed the season up with an outstanding showing during instructional league. White has an aggressive approach and attacks both sides of the plate with a three-pitch mix. He works off an 88-92 mph fastball that has occasional plus sink. His curveball has good action down and away from lefthanders, and he has feel for a changeup, which fades from righties. Lefties hit .103 against him last year, and his calling could be out of the bullpen as a situational reliever. He will report to high Class A in 2007 to build on his success of last season.

| Year | Club (League) | Class | W | L | ERA | G | GS | CG | SV | IP | H | R | ER | HR | BB | SO | AVG |
|------|---------------|-------|---|---|-----|---|----|----|----|----|---|---|----|----|----|----|-----|
| 2004 | Dodgers (GCL) | R | 1 | 1 | 2.53 | 5 | 0 | 0 | 0 | 11 | 11 | 4 | 3 | 0 | 6 | 10 | .297 |
| 2005 | Ogden (Pio) | R | 1 | 3 | 6.92 | 17 | 6 | 0 | 0 | 40 | 59 | 35 | 31 | 2 | 27 | 36 | .351 |
| 2006 | Ogden (Pio) | R | 4 | 2 | 2.68 | 25 | 0 | 0 | 0 | 44 | 30 | 17 | 13 | 2 | 23 | 44 | .190 |
| **MINOR LEAGUE TOTALS** | | | 6 | 6 | 4.47 | 47 | 6 | 0 | 0 | 95 | 100 | 56 | 47 | 4 | 56 | 90 | .275 |

## 25 KYLE ORR

1B

**Born:** Sept. 9, 1988. **B-T:** L-R. **Ht.:** 6-5. **Wt.:** 205. **Drafted:** HS—Victoria, B.C., 2006 (4th round). **Signed by:** Hank Jones.

With a powerful lefthanded swing and a projectable 6-foot-5, 205-pound frame, Orr was considered the best draft-eligible player in Canada in 2006. He helped Canada's junior national team win a bronze medal in 2005 and 2006 in international competition, playing both ways as a hitter and pitcher. Orr originally sought a bonus near $500,000, sticking to his commitment to Kentucky as leverage, before finally settling on a $435,000 in October. His biggest tool is raw power and balls jump off his bat. His swing has looseness and life, but he's long-limbed and his swing also has length and lots of holes. His pitch recognition and plate discipline are unrefined. His power potential, athleticism and above-average arm strength profile in right field, but he has plenty of work to do on the nuances of defense.

First base might be his eventual destination. He's a below-average runner, though he's better under way. The Dodgers' player-development staff will have some work to do to mold Orr, but the raw material is there. He will open the season in extended spring training before reporting to a short-season team in June.

| Year | Club (League) | Class | AVG | G | AB | R | H | 2B | 3B | HR | RBI | BB | SO | SB | OBP | SLG |
|------|---------------|-------|-----|---|----|---|---|----|----|----|-----|----|----|----|-----|-----|
| 2006 | Did not play—Signed 2007 contract | | | | | | | | | | | | | | | |

## XAVIER PAUL
OF

**Born:** Feb. 25, 1985. **B-T:** L-R. **Ht.:** 6-0. **Wt.:** 200. **Drafted:** HS—Slidell, La., 2003 (4th round). **Signed by:** Clarence Johns.

Because of his size and commitment to Tulane, most teams passed on Paul during the draft, but area scout Clarence Johns (now with the Rockies) had a good rapport with Paul and his family and signed him for $270,000. He ranked among the system's top prospects following a strong debut but sustained success for the first time since then in his second season at high Class A. Paul is a plus runner with athleticism and bat speed. He's constantly tinkering with his approach at the plate and doesn't trust his hands. He can lash line drives to both alleys with average power, especially to the pull side. While his 133 strikeouts in 2006 were the most in the organization—and his career—he hit the ball with more authority. His front side often flies open, causing him to pull off the ball and making him vulnerable to pitches on the outer half. Paul has played all three outfield positions, but his best position is right. He made significant improvement last season defensively and has developed into an average defender with a plus, accurate arm. He needs to improve his technique playing balls hit in front of him. Paul must improve his overall consistency and ultimately could become a reliable outfielder with speed and pop. He'll climb to Double-A in 2007.

| Year | Club (League) | Class | AVG | G | AB | R | H | 2B | 3B | HR | RBI | BB | SO | SB | OBP | SLG |
|------|---------------|-------|------|-----|------|-----|-----|----|----|----|-----|-----|-----|----|------|------|
| 2003 | Ogden (Pio) | R | .307 | 69 | 264 | 60 | 81 | 15 | 6 | 7 | 47 | 34 | 58 | 11 | .384 | .489 |
| 2004 | Columbus (SAL) | A | .262 | 128 | 465 | 69 | 122 | 26 | 6 | 9 | 72 | 56 | 127 | 10 | .341 | .402 |
| 2005 | Vero Beach (FSL) | A | .247 | 85 | 288 | 42 | 71 | 15 | 3 | 7 | 41 | 32 | 81 | 1 | .328 | .392 |
| 2006 | Vero Beach (FSL) | A | .285 | 120 | 470 | 62 | 134 | 23 | 3 | 13 | 49 | 38 | 114 | 22 | .343 | .430 |
| **MINOR LEAGUE TOTALS** | | | .274 | 402 | 1487 | 233 | 408 | 79 | 18 | 36 | 209 | 160 | 380 | 44 | .347 | .424 |

## CASEY HOORELBEKE
RHP

**Born:** April 4, 1980. **B-T:** R-R. **Ht.:** 6-8. **Wt.:** 245. **Signed:** Lewis-Clark State (Idaho), NDFA 2003. **Signed by:** George Genovese.

Hoorelbeke is the son of Peter Rivera, the original lead singer, drummer and founder of the band Rare Earth. His brother Jesse is an outfielder in the Cubs system. Casey made a name for himself as a talented pitcher and basketball player at Coeur d' Alene (Idaho) High and transferred to Lewis-Clark State after pitching at North Idaho Junior College. After his first pro season in 2004, he moved to the bullpen where his low three-quarters arm slot and fringy three-pitch repertoire play best. He has a big, durable frame and an aggressive approach to pitching. He dominated at times in 2006 at Double-A before a viral infection slowed him in August, when he allowed 10 earned runs in seven appearances. His 88-90 mph sinker has average life and movement. His 10-to-4 slider is a fringe-average offering, as is his changeup. When he keeps the ball down in the zone he induces lots of ground balls. He has solid-average command and value as a middle reliever down the road. He was not placed on the 40-man roster and was Rule 5 eligible in 2006, but he wasn't taken in the draft and should spend most of 2007 in Triple-A.

| Year | Club (League) | Class | W | L | ERA | G | GS | CG | SV | IP | H | R | ER | HR | BB | SO | AVG |
|------|---------------|-------|---|---|------|-----|----|----|----|-----|-----|----|----|----|----|-----|------|
| 2004 | Columbus (SAL) | A | 0 | 1 | 2.57 | 3 | 3 | 0 | 0 | 14 | 13 | 7 | 4 | 1 | 2 | 8 | .271 |
| | Vero Beach (FSL) | A | 6 | 4 | 4.01 | 18 | 14 | 0 | 0 | 76 | 81 | 40 | 34 | 9 | 31 | 56 | .274 |
| 2005 | Vero Beach (FSL) | A | 9 | 3 | 2.40 | 42 | 1 | 0 | 4 | 83 | 74 | 25 | 22 | 0 | 35 | 58 | .253 |
| 2006 | Jacksonville (SL) | AA | 2 | 2 | 2.63 | 52 | 0 | 0 | 7 | 72 | 42 | 24 | 21 | 4 | 30 | 60 | .174 |
| **MINOR LEAGUE TOTALS** | | | 17 | 10 | 2.98 | 115 | 18 | 0 | 11 | 245 | 210 | 96 | 81 | 14 | 98 | 182 | .239 |

## MIGUEL SANFLER
LHP

**Born:** Oct. 5, 1984. **B-T:** L-L. **Ht.:** 5-11. **Wt.:** 165. **Signed:** Dominican Republic, 2002. **Signed by:** Pablo Peguero.

Sanfler began 2006 in low Class A and got off to an inauspicious start, which proved to be the beginning of a forgettable first full season. He allowed four earned runs on seven hits in his first appearance and things never got much better. He joined Ogden when its season opened in June and showed the stuff that makes him a prospect as a lefty reliever. With a compact, muscular frame reminiscent of a defensive back, Sanfler features outstanding arm strength and an aggressive approach. He can hit 97 mph, pitches at 92-93 and flashes a

power slider with hard tilt, as well as a promising splitter. His fastball has late life from a three-quarters arm slot. He's a thrower, but his arm works. He has little feel for pitching. His athleticism allows him to repeat his delivery and is a major reason the Dodgers believe he has a chance to become a valuable piece to add to their bullpen. He speaks little English and needs to improve his communication skills. He'll have another shot in low Class A this season.

| Year | Club (League) | Class | W | L | ERA | G | GS | CG | SV | IP | H | R | ER | HR | BB | SO | AVG |
|------|---------------|-------|---|---|-----|---|----|----|----|----|---|---|----|----|----|----|-----|
| 2004 | Dodgers (DSL) | R | 2 | 0 | 2.31 | 4 | 2 | 0 | 0 | 12 | 6 | 4 | 3 | 0 | 10 | 17 | .150 |
| 2005 | Dodgers (GCL) | R | 5 | 3 | 3.79 | 13 | 3 | 0 | 0 | 40 | 40 | 23 | 17 | 4 | 25 | 41 | .250 |
| 2006 | Columbus (SAL) | A | 1 | 4 | 9.14 | 15 | 0 | 0 | 1 | 22 | 25 | 26 | 22 | 1 | 21 | 16 | .294 |
| | Ogden (Pio) | R | 2 | 1 | 2.18 | 23 | 0 | 0 | 0 | 33 | 32 | 18 | 8 | 0 | 17 | 31 | .246 |
| **MINOR LEAGUE TOTALS** | | | 10 | 8 | 4.22 | 55 | 5 | 0 | 1 | 107 | 103 | 71 | 50 | 5 | 73 | 105 | .248 |

## 29 JOSH WALL                                                RHP

**Born:** Jan. 21, 1987. **B-T:** R-R. **Ht.:** 6-6. **Wt.:** 190. **Drafted:** HS—Walker, La., 2005 (2nd round). **Signed by:** Dennis Moeller.

Wall skyrocketed up the draft board in January 2005 when he flashed 95 mph heat at a Perfect Game showcase in Fort Myers, Fla. He joined Bryan Morris—a 2006 Dodgers draftee—as a second-team High School All-American with a 138-26 strikeout-walk ratio that spring, and signed with the Dodgers for $480,000. A half-brother of former Dodgers farmhand Lance Caraccioli, Wall may have been held back by his family's interest in his career in 2006. His father, who bird-dogs for Dodgers scout Dennis Moeller in Louisiana, spent most of the summer following his son around the Pioneer League and Josh at times lacked focus. Some scouts speculated that his dad's constant critiquing became counterproductive. His stuff backed up significantly and he pitched tentatively. His fastball was usually flat at 88 mph. His curveball, which showed promise and hard, downer action as an amateur, sat between 72-75 mph and lacked the depth it once showed. He gets around the ball, losing plane and command. If he cleans up his delivery and improves his mental approach, he has the frame and tools to develop into a middle-of-the-rotation starter. His performance in spring training will determine his assignment, but low Class A seems the likely destination.

| Year | Club (League) | Class | W | L | ERA | G | GS | CG | SV | IP | H | R | ER | HR | BB | SO | AVG |
|------|---------------|-------|---|---|-----|---|----|----|----|----|---|---|----|----|----|----|-----|
| 2005 | Dodgers (GCL) | R | 1 | 3 | 3.86 | 5 | 4 | 0 | 0 | 14 | 13 | 8 | 6 | 2 | 8 | 5 | .245 |
| 2006 | Ogden (Pio) | R | 3 | 5 | 5.86 | 14 | 14 | 0 | 0 | 66 | 80 | 56 | 43 | 5 | 33 | 41 | .305 |
| **MINOR LEAGUE TOTALS** | | | 4 | 8 | 5.51 | 19 | 18 | 0 | 0 | 80 | 93 | 64 | 49 | 7 | 41 | 46 | .295 |

## 30 WESLEY WRIGHT                                             LHP

**Born:** Jan. 28, 1985. **L-L. Ht.:** 5-11. **Wt.:** 160. **Drafted:** HS—Goshen, Ala., 2003 (7th round). **Signed by:** Clarence Johns.

Despite Wright's smallish frame and modest fastball velocity, former Dodgers area scout Clarence Johns (now with the Rockies) liked his aggressive attitude and feel for pitching and persuaded scouting director Logan White to take him in the seventh round in 2003. Wright passed up a scholarship from South Alabama and signed for $120,000. He had four stretches of at least 17 consecutive scoreless innings in 2006 between high A and Double-A. With a fastball described as "sneaky-fast" by minor league pitching coordinator Marty Reed, Wright has racked up impressive strikeout totals since signing, most of which come off his 88-91 mph heater that has late life. He has a slight wrist wrap in the back of his arm motion that doesn't hinder his control and gives his delivery some deception. Wright and Vero Beach pitching coach Glenn Dishman tweaked the grip on his spike curveball during his stint in Hawaii Winter Baseball, and the pitch has above-average break, with tight, 12-to-6 rotation. It's more consistent than his slider, which is little more than a chase pitch. He has rudimentary feel for his changeup. He can pitch to both sides of the plate and has average command. Wright climbed to Double-A as a 21-year-old late in 2006, and should spend most of 2007 there.

| Year | Club (League) | Class | W | L | ERA | G | GS | CG | SV | IP | H | R | ER | HR | BB | SO | AVG |
|------|---------------|-------|---|---|-----|---|----|----|----|----|---|---|----|----|----|----|-----|
| 2003 | Dodgers (GCL) | R | 3 | 1 | 3.58 | 14 | 5 | 0 | 0 | 38 | 37 | 15 | 15 | 1 | 19 | 26 | .270 |
| 2004 | Ogden (Pio) | R | 3 | 3 | 6.29 | 17 | 2 | 0 | 0 | 44 | 56 | 43 | 31 | 3 | 23 | 66 | .299 |
| 2005 | Columbus (SAL) | A | 1 | 5 | 1.93 | 30 | 0 | 0 | 1 | 61 | 38 | 21 | 13 | 2 | 33 | 68 | .178 |
| | Vero Beach (FSL) | A | 0 | 0 | 9.45 | 6 | 0 | 0 | 0 | 7 | 8 | 7 | 7 | 0 | 10 | 8 | .296 |
| 2006 | Vero Beach (FSL) | A | 3 | 3 | 1.49 | 26 | 0 | 0 | 0 | 42 | 29 | 11 | 7 | 0 | 23 | 51 | .197 |
| | Jacksonville (SL) | AA | 1 | 1 | 4.64 | 15 | 0 | 0 | 1 | 21 | 14 | 13 | 11 | 2 | 11 | 28 | .189 |
| **MINOR LEAGUE TOTALS** | | | 8 | 10 | 2.83 | 91 | 5 | 0 | 2 | 169 | 126 | 67 | 53 | 5 | 96 | 181 | .211 |

# MILWAUKEE
# BREWERS

BY **TOM HAUDRICOURT**

The Brewers were so upbeat about building around young infielders **Prince Fielder**, Bill Hall, J.J. Hardy and Rickie Weeks that they put them on the cover of their 2006 media guide. That promising foursome was supposed to help the club reach the next level after snapping a 12-year losing streak with an 81-81 record in 2005.

 Instead, Milwaukee took a step back and won just 75 games in a year where 84 would have meant a National League Central title. But that doesn't mean the club's optimism was misplaced. Instead, the 2006 Brewers succumbed to a series of damaging injuries as well as down years from some veterans.

The slope became slippery in May, when starting pitchers Ben Sheets and Tomo Ohka got hurt. Milwaukee tried a variety of minor leaguers in their place, including Ben Hendrickson and Dana Eveland, who flopped badly. The Brewers went 6-17 in those two spots in the rotation until Sheets and Ohka returned in the second half.

Then the infielders began to go down. Hardy was lost in mid-May with an ankle injury that later required surgery. Just when Weeks began to take off as a leadoff hitter, he hurt his wrist in late July and also needed an operation. Veteran third baseman Corey Koskie missed the entire second half with post-concussion syndrome.

The lone positive aspect of all the infield injuries was the emergence of Hall, who became the everyday shortstop when Hardy went out. Hall had a breakout season, leading Milwaukee with 35 homers and 85 RBIs and guaranteeing himself a regular job in

GEORGE GOJKOVICH

2007, possibly in the outfield.

The outfield picture became clouded when impending free agent Carlos Lee was traded in late July after turning down a $48 million contract extension, and Geoff Jenkins declined so precipitously that he was benched for a time in August. Corey Hart finally got a chance to play in the everyday lineup and performed well enough to put himself squarely in the club's plans.

A more surprising development was the emergence of Carlos Villanueva, who began the year in Double-A and found himself in the big league rotation for the final weeks. Showing poise and command not normally associated with a 22-year-old rookie, Villanueva gave the Brewers the confidence to trade Doug Davis (and Eveland) to the Diamondbacks in an offseason move that filled their catching void with Johnny Estrada.

Having advanced several solid everyday players to the majors in recent years, Milwaukee is developing some impressive arms to join them. Yovani Gallardo pitched himself into blue-chip prospect status in 2006, and Steve Hammond and Tim Dillard should be on the verge of the majors this season. Another wave loaded with dazzling potential is still a couple of years off.

With the division's best combination of young talent and payroll flexibility, the Brewers should contend in a weakened NL Central in 2007—if they can stay healthy.

## TOP 30 PROSPECTS

| | |
|---|---|
| 1. Yovani Gallardo, rhp | 16. Zach Jackson, lhp |
| 2. Ryan Braun, 3b | 17. Tony Gwynn Jr., of |
| 3. Will Inman, rhp | 18. Manny Parra, lhp |
| 4. Jeremy Jeffress, rhp | 19. Brent Brewer, ss |
| 5. Mark Rogers, rhp | 20. Chris Errecart, of/1b |
| 6. Lorenzo Cain, of | 21. Hernan Iribarren, 2b |
| 7. Steve Hammond, lhp | 22. Dennis Sarfate, rhp |
| 8. Cole Gillespie, of | 23. Joe Thatcher, lhp |
| 9. Alcides Escobar, ss | 24. Robert Hinton, rhp |
| 10. Mat Gamel, 3b | 25. R.J. Seidel, rhp |
| 11. Angel Salome, c | 26. Brendan Katin, of |
| 12. Charlie Fermaint, of | 27. Steve Garrison, lhp |
| 13. Darren Ford, of | 28. Stephen Chapman, of |
| 14. Yohannis Perez, ss | 29. Vinny Rottino, 3b/c/of |
| 15. Tim Dillard, rhp | 30. Rolando Pascual, rhp |

# ORGANIZATION OVERVIEW

**General manager:** Doug Melvin. **Farm director:** Reid Nichols. **Scouting director:** Jack Zduriencik.

## 2006 PERFORMANCE

| Class | Team | League | W | L | PCT | Finish* | Manager | Affiliated |
|---|---|---|---|---|---|---|---|---|
| Majors | Milwaukee | National | 75 | 87 | .463 | 13th (16) | Ned Yost | — |
| Triple-A | Nashville Sounds | Pacific Coast | 76 | 68 | .528 | 5th (16) | Frank Kremblas | 2005 |
| Double-A | Huntsville Stars | Southern | 67 | 71 | .486 | 6th (10) | Don Money | 1999 |
| High A | Brevard Co. Manatees | Florida State | 64 | 65 | .496 | 7th (12) | Ramon Aviles | 2005 |
| Low A | West Virginia Power | South Atlantic | 74 | 62 | .544 | 4th (16) | Mike Guerrero | 2005 |
| Rookie | Helena Brewers | Pioneer | 34 | 42 | .447 | 6th (8) | Eddie Sedar | 2003 |
| Rookie | AZL Brewers | Arizona | 21 | 35 | .375 | 8th (9) | Charlie Greene | 2001 |
| **OVERALL 2006 MINOR LEAGUE RECORD** | | | 336 | 343 | .495 | 18th (30) | | |

*Finish in overall standings (No. of teams in league). +League champion

## ORGANIZATION LEADERS

### BATTING
| | | |
|---|---|---|
| AVG | Lefave, Andrew, AZL Brewers | .353 |
| R | Ford, Darren, West Virginia | 103 |
| H | Cain, Lorenzo, West Virginia | 176 |
| 2B | Cain, Lorenzo, West Virginia | 37 |
| 3B | Chapman, Stephen, West Virginia/Helena | 8 |
| | Ezi, Travis, Brevard County/Huntsville | 8 |
| HR | Braun, Ryan, Brevard County/Huntsville | 27 |
| RBI | Braun, Ryan, Brevard County/Huntsville | 99 |
| BB | Nelson, Brad, Nashville/Huntsville | 81 |
| SO | Ford, Darren, West Virginia | 156 |
| SB | Ford, Darren, West Virginia | 76 |
| OBP | Gillespie, Cole, Helena | .464 |
| SLG | Gillespie, Cole, Helena | .548 |
| XBH | Braun, Ryan, Brevard County/Huntsville | 67 |

### PITCHING
| | | |
|---|---|---|
| W | Gallardo, Yovani, Brevard County/Huntsville | 11 |
| | Hammond, Steven, Brevard County/Huntsville | 11 |
| | Sarfate, Dennis, Nashville | 11 |
| | Villanueva, Carlos, Huntsville/Nashville | 11 |
| L | Hammond, Steven, Brevard County/Huntsville | 11 |
| | Thurman, Corey, Nashville/Huntsville | 11 |
| ERA | Gallardo, Yovani, Brevard County/Huntsville | 1.86 |
| G | Zumwalt, Alec, Huntsville/Nashville | 58 |
| SV | Zumwalt, Alec, Huntsville/Nashville | 20 |
| IP | Thurman, Corey, Nashville/Huntsville | 168 |
| BB | Sarfate, Dennis, Nashville | 80 |
| SO | Gallardo, Yovani, Brevard County/Huntsville | 188 |
| AVG | Gallardo, Yovani, Brevard County/Huntsville | .192 |

## BEST TOOLS

| | |
|---|---|
| Best Hitter for Average | Hernan Iribarren |
| Best Power Hitter | Ryan Braun |
| Best Strike-Zone Discipline | Cole Gillespie |
| Fastest Baserunner | Darren Ford |
| Best Athlete | Brent Brewer |
| Best Fastball | Jeremy Jeffress |
| Best Curveball | Yovani Gallardo |
| Best Slider | Robert Hinton |
| Best Changeup | R.J. Seidel |
| Best Control | Will Inman |
| Best Defensive Catcher | Lou Palmisano |
| Best Defensive Infielder | Alcides Escobar |
| Best Infield Arm | Ryan Braun |
| Best Defensive Outfielder | Tony Gwynn Jr. |
| Best Outfield Arm | Lorenzo Cain |

## PROJECTED 2010 LINEUP

| | |
|---|---|
| Catcher | Angel Salome |
| First Base | Prince Fielder |
| Second Base | Rickie Weeks |
| Third Base | Ryan Braun |
| Shortstop | J.J. Hardy |
| Left Field | Bill Hall |
| Center Field | Lorenzo Cain |
| Right Field | Corey Hart |
| No. 1 Starter | Ben Sheets |
| No. 2 Starter | Yovani Gallardo |
| No. 3 Starter | Dave Bush |
| No. 4 Starter | Will Inman |
| No. 5 Starter | Chris Capuano |
| Closer | Jeremy Jeffress |

## LAST YEAR'S TOP 20 PROSPECTS

| | |
|---|---|
| 1. Prince Fielder, 1b | 11. Will Inman, rhp |
| 2. Mark Rogers, rhp | 12. Charlie Fermaint, of |
| 3. Ryan Braun, 3b | 13. Manny Parra, lhp |
| 4. Yovani Gallardo, rhp | 14. Brad Nelson, of |
| 5. Corey Hart, of/3b | 15. Hernan Iribarren, 2b |
| 6. Alcides Escobar, ss | 16. Tim Dillard, rhp |
| 7. Dana Eveland, lhp | 17. Rolando Pascual, rhp |
| 8. Nelson Cruz, of | 18. Steve Hammond, lhp |
| 9. Jose Capellan, rhp | 19. Ben Hendrickson, rhp |
| 10. Zach Jackson, lhp | 20. Lou Palmisano, c |

## TOP PROSPECTS OF THE DECADE

| Year | Player, Pos. | 2006 Org. |
|---|---|---|
| 1997 | Todd Dunn, of | Out of baseball |
| 1998 | Valerio de los Santos, lhp | White Sox |
| 1999 | Ron Belliard, 2b | Cardinals |
| 2000 | Nick Neugebauer, rhp | Out of baseball |
| 2001 | Ben Sheets, rhp | Brewers |
| 2002 | Nick Neugebauer, rhp | Out of baseball |
| 2003 | Brad Nelson, 1b | Brewers |
| 2004 | Rickie Weeks, 2b | Brewers |
| 2005 | Rickie Weeks, 2b | Brewers |
| 2006 | Prince Fielder, 1b | Brewers |

## TOP DRAFT PICKS OF THE DECADE

| Year | Player, Pos. | 2006 Org. |
|---|---|---|
| 1997 | Kyle Peterson, rhp | Out of baseball |
| 1998 | J.M. Gold, rhp | Out of baseball |
| 1999 | Ben Sheets, rhp | Brewers |
| 2000 | Dave Krynzel, of | Brewers |
| 2001 | Mike Jones, rhp | Brewers |
| 2002 | Prince Fielder, 1b | Brewers |
| 2003 | Rickie Weeks, 2b | Brewers |
| 2004 | Mark Rogers, rhp | Brewers |
| 2005 | Ryan Braun, 3b | Brewers |
| 2006 | Jeremy Jeffress, rhp | Brewers |

## LARGEST BONUSES IN CLUB HISTORY

| | |
|---|---|
| Rickie Weeks, 2003 | $3,600,000 |
| Ben Sheets, 1999 | $2,450,000 |
| Ryan Braun, 2005 | $2,450,000 |
| Prince Fielder, 2002 | $2,400,000 |
| Mark Rogers, 2004 | $2,200,000 |

# MINOR LEAGUE DEPTH CHART

## Milwaukee Brewers

**Impact: A.** Impressive considering what the Brewers have graduated to Milwaukee, but Gallardo, Braun and others have potential to be regulars and more.
**Depth: B.** The talent doesn't run out in the Top 10, particularly in the outfield. Improved effort in Latin America may take a while to pay off.
**Sleeper:** Joe Thatcher, lhp. A late-blooming southpaw out of Indiana State, Thatcher dominated up to Double-A in 2006 and could help in the majors in '07.

*Numbers in parentheses indicate prospect rankings.*

| LF |
|---|
| Cole Gillespie (8) |
| Chris Errecart (20) |
| Drew Anderson |
| Michael Brantley |
| Kennard Bibbs |

| CF |
|---|
| Charlie Fermaint (12) |
| Darren Ford (13) |
| Tony Gwynn Jr. (17) |
| Steve Moss |
| Dave Krynzel |
| Mike Goetz |

| RF |
|---|
| Lorenzo Cain (6) |
| Brendan Katin (26) |
| Steve Chapman (28) |
| Freddy Parejo |

| 3B |
|---|
| Ryan Braun (2) |
| Matt Gamel (10) |
| Vinny Rottino (29) |
| Adam Heether |
| Carlos Hereaud |

| SS |
|---|
| Alcides Escobar (9) |
| Yohannis Perez (14) |
| Brent Brewer (19) |
| Chris Barnwell |
| Mike Bell |

| 2B |
|---|
| Hernan Iribarren (21) |
| Ryan Crew |
| Callix Crabbe |
| Ken Holmberg |

| 1B |
|---|
| Brad Nelson |
| Tony Festa |
| Ned Yost IV |
| John Alonso |

| C |
|---|
| Angel Salome (11) |
| Lou Palmisano |
| Carlos Corporan |
| Andy Bouchie |

| RHP | |
|---|---|
| **Starters** | **Relievers** |
| Yovani Gallardo (1) | Dennis Sarfate (22) |
| Will Inman (3) | Robert Hinton (24) |
| Jeremy Jeffress (4) | Steve Bray |
| Mark Rogers (5) | Alec Zumwalt |
| Tim Dillard (15) | Mike Meyers |
| R.J. Seidel (25) | Gerrit Simpson |
| Rolando Pascual (30) | Brett Evert |
| Kevin Roberts | Josh Alliston |
| Mike Jones | Ben Stanczyk |
| Wily Peralta | Patrick Ryan |
| Josh Wahpepah | Bo Hall |
| | Luis Pena |

| LHP | |
|---|---|
| **Starters** | **Relievers** |
| Steve Hammond (7) | Joe Thatcher (23) |
| Zach Jackson (16) | Mitch Stetter |
| Manny Parra (18) | Jeff Housman |
| Steve Garrison (27) | Jeremy Lewis |
| Derek Miller | Luis Ramirez |
| David Welch | |
| Brandon Parillo | |

## 2006 — SIGNING BUDGET: $3.4 million

**Best Pro Debut:** After helping Oregon State win the College World Series, OF Cole Gillespie (3) batted .344/.464/.548 with eight homers and 18 steals and led the Pioneer League in on-base percentage. Maybe he just likes wood bats, but OF/1B Chris Errecart (5) starred in the Cape Cod League last summer before slumping at California for most of the spring. He hit .316/.406/.518 with 13 homers and a Pioneer League-best 61 RBIs. OF Mike Goetz (25), the NCAA Division I batting champ, was old for the Arizona League but did top the circuit with 31 steals.

**Best Athlete:** SS Brent Brewer (2) would have played wide receiver at Florida State had he not turned pro. RHP Jeremy Jeffress (1) had his high school number retired—in basketball. RHP R.J. Seidel (16) was a three-sport star (football and basketball) at his Wisconsin high school.

**Best Pure Hitter:** Gillespie has solid tools across the board, but his bat is his best. He didn't display a lot of over-the-fence power in college, but the Brewers would be thrilled if he hit 20 homers a year.

**Best Raw Power:** Errecart. His 13 homers were five more than he hit as a college junior.

**Fastest Runner:** Brewer gets from the right side of the plate to first base in 4.2 seconds. OF Lee Haydel (19), whose rights the Brewers control after he attended Delgado (La.) CC, is even quicker, running a 6.39-second 60-yard dash.

**Best Defensive Player:** Milwaukee likes C Andy Boucie's (7) work behind the plate, which helped him make the Pioneer League all-star team. He also hit .265/.384/.417 with seven homers.

**Best Fastball:** Jeffress has effortless heat, reaching 95-97 mph in the late innings and touching at least 98 almost every time out this year. His fastball has been clocked as high as 102.

**Best Breaking Ball:** RHP Shane Hill (5), who helped Florida Christian earn a state title and a No. 5 national high school ranking this spring, has a plus curveball. With a 6-foot-4 frame, he projects to add velocity to his present 86-89 mph.

**Most Intriguing Background:** Brent is not related to Bernie. OF Chuckie Caufield's (39) sister LaNeishea played in the WNBA. Like Brewer, C Jesse D'Amico (21) turned down college football offers. He rushed for more than 1,600 yards as a senior. Draft-and-follow LHP Zach Braddock's grandfather Jim was a heavyweight boxing champion whose story was the basis for the film "Cinderella Man."

**Closest To The Majors:** Gillespie. He should be able to handle a promotion to high Class A to open his first full season.

Best Late-Round Pick: Seidel is a projectable 6-foot-6, 185-pounder with an 85-90 mph fastball and good athleticism. He signed for $415,000, the equivalent of third-round money.

**The One Who Got Away:** Scouts liked 1B Andrew Clark's (18) 91-92 mph fastball and his potential as a lefthander until he hurt his shoulder in 2005. He's still intriguing as a 6-foot-2, 205-pounder with power potential, and he could make an immediate impact at Mississippi.

**Assessment:** Milwaukee would have loved for a quality college pitcher to fall to them at No. 16, but it still was thrilled to add Jeffress' power arm to a stable that already includes Yovani Gallardo, Will Inman and Mark Rogers. Power-hitting outfielders are the Brewers' biggest need in the majors, and they found two interesting ones in Gillespie and Errecart.

## 2005 — BUDGET: $3.8 million

3B Ryan Braun (1) looks like the big bat the Brewers hoped they were getting. RHP Will Inman (3) has been unhittable, while 3B Mat Gamel (4) and LHP Steve Hammond (6) have been pleasant surprises.   **GRADE: A**

## 2004 — BUDGET: $4.3 million

Milwaukee found a frontline starter—but it's RHP Yovani Gallardo (2), and not RHP Mark Rogers (1), who has developed slowly since going fifth overall. C Angel Salome (5) and draft-and-follow OF Lorenzo Cain (17) could crack the big league lineup in time.   **GRADE: B+**

## 2003 — BUDGET: $6.1 million

2B Rickie Weeks (1) reached the majors quickly and may live up to his status as the No. 2 overall pick. OFs Tony Gwynn Jr. (2) and Charlie Fermaint (4) have some potential.   **GRADE: B**

*Draft analysis by Jim Callis. Numbers in parentheses indicate draft rounds. Budgets are bonuses in first 10 rounds.*

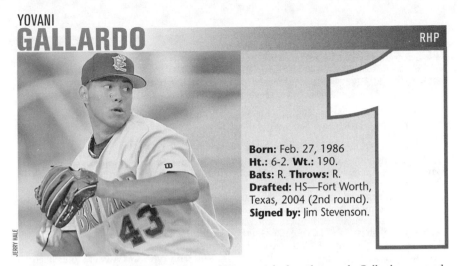

## YOVANI
# GALLARDO
RHP

**Born:** Feb. 27, 1986
**Ht.:** 6-2. **Wt.:** 190.
**Bats:** R. **Throws:** R.
**Drafted:** HS—Fort Worth, Texas, 2004 (2nd round).
**Signed by:** Jim Stevenson.

JERRY HALE

The Brewers thought they had something special when they made Gallardo a second-round pick and signed him for $725,000 in 2004, but he has exceeded expectations with his meteoric rise through the system. In 2006, he established himself as one of the game's elite pitching prospects. He began the season in the high Class A Florida State League and spent the second half dealing in the Double-A Southern League, ranking as the No. 2 prospect in both circuits behind Reds righthander Homer Bailey. Gallardo led the minor leagues in strikeouts (188), finished third in ERA (1.86) and strikeouts per nine innings (10.9) and pitched a scoreless inning for the World Team in the Futures Game. Gallardo has Mexican ancestry but grew up in Texas and signed out of Trimble Tech High in Fort Worth. He struck out 25 in an 11-inning game as a senior, and scouts weren't happy that his coach left him in for 148 pitches, but he has been healthy and durable in pro ball. With so many of their best pitching prospects breaking down or failing in the majors in recent years, Gallardo gives the Brewers something to get excited about.

Gallardo features a fastball that he consistently throws at 90-94 mph with armside run and sink, and he can reach back and get a little extra juice when he needs it. His sharp-breaking curveball is the best in the system, and his 85-89 mph slide became a plus pitch in 2006. His changeup has cutting action and continues to improve, and he'll throw it in any count. Beyond his impressive pure stuff, Gallardo shows savvy by adding and subtracting from his pitches and varying their looks to keep hitters off balance. He'll change arm slots at times to give hitters yet something else to think about and repeats his delivery easily, giving him strong command of his pitches. His poise on and off the field is something that can't be taught, especially considering his youth.

There's not much not to like about Gallardo. His frame might look a little soft, but he has a loose, easy delivery. Some observers think he can be too laid-back, but the Brewers say he's just quiet by nature and competes well without making a big show of it. Pitchers who use a drop-and-drive delivery like Gallardo does can elevate their pitches if they don't stay on top of them, but that's not an issue with him. He keeps the ball down in the zone and gave up just six homers in 155 innings last year.

After Gallardo moved up to Double-A Huntsville and had no problems making the adjustment, the Brewers began speculating about his arrival in the majors. He's likely to start 2007 with Triple-A Nashville, though it's not completely out of the question that he could make the big league rotation with a strong showing in spring training. Already ahead of schedule, he's young enough to allow more time to mature. Barring injury, it's going to be difficult to hold him back for long. Gallardo will challenge Ben Sheets for the designation as Milwaukee's No. 1 starter in the near future.

| Year | Club (League) | Class | W | L | ERA | G | GS | CG | SV | IP | H | R | ER | HR | BB | SO | AVG |
|------|---------------|-------|---|---|-----|---|----|----|----|----|---|---|----|----|----|----|-----|
| 2004 | Brewers (AZL) | R | 0 | 0 | 0.47 | 6 | 6 | 0 | 0 | 19 | 14 | 3 | 1 | 0 | 4 | 23 | .203 |
| | Beloit (MWL) | A | 0 | 1 | 12.27 | 2 | 2 | 0 | 0 | 7 | 12 | 10 | 10 | 2 | 4 | 8 | .400 |
| 2005 | West Virginia (SAL) | A | 8 | 3 | 2.74 | 26 | 18 | 0 | 1 | 121 | 100 | 46 | 37 | 5 | 51 | 110 | .230 |
| 2006 | Brevard County (FSL) | A | 6 | 3 | 2.09 | 13 | 13 | 0 | 0 | 78 | 54 | 24 | 18 | 4 | 23 | 103 | .196 |
| | Huntsville (SL) | AA | 5 | 2 | 1.63 | 13 | 13 | 0 | 0 | 77 | 50 | 18 | 14 | 2 | 28 | 85 | .187 |
| **MINOR LEAGUE TOTALS** | | | 19 | 9 | 2.38 | 60 | 52 | 0 | 1 | 303 | 230 | 101 | 80 | 13 | 110 | 329 | .214 |

## RYAN BRAUN

3B

**Born:** Nov. 17, 1983. **B-T:** R-R. **Ht.:** 6-2. **Wt.:** 200. **Drafted:** Miami, 2005 (1st round). **Signed by:** Larry Pardo.

Like Yovani Gallardo, Braun earned a trip to the Futures Game and a promotion to Double-A, where he stepped up his performance in the second half. The fifth overall pick in the 2005 draft, he rated as the top position prospect in the Florida State League. A rare five-tool corner infielder, Braun has tremendous bat speed and profiles as an impact hitter for average and power. He stays back on offspeed pitches and uses the entire field. His speed and arm strength are plus tools as well. He took yoga classes with Mike Lieberthal last offseason to improve his balance. After making 31 errors last season, Braun must improve his footwork at third base. Some scouts believe he'll eventually need to move to the outfield, but Milwaukee believes he'll be a sound defender at the hot corner. He doesn't have the most textbook swing, but it works for him. After hitting .326 in the Arizona Fall League, Braun definitely is ready for Triple-A. The Brewers expect him to complete their homegrown infield by 2008, though he could arrive by the all-star break.

| Year | Club (League) | Class | AVG | G | AB | R | H | 2B | 3B | HR | RBI | BB | SO | SB | OBP | SLG |
|---|---|---|---|---|---|---|---|---|---|---|---|---|---|---|---|---|
| 2005 | Helena (Pio) | R | .341 | 10 | 41 | 6 | 14 | 2 | 1 | 2 | 10 | 2 | 6 | 2 | .383 | .585 |
| | West Virginia (SAL) | A | .355 | 37 | 152 | 21 | 54 | 16 | 2 | 8 | 35 | 9 | 34 | 2 | .396 | .645 |
| 2006 | Brevard County (FSL) | A | .274 | 59 | 226 | 34 | 62 | 12 | 2 | 7 | 37 | 23 | 54 | 14 | .346 | .438 |
| | Huntsville (SL) | AA | .303 | 59 | 231 | 42 | 70 | 19 | 1 | 15 | 40 | 21 | 46 | 12 | .367 | .589 |
| **MINOR LEAGUE TOTALS** | | | .308 | 165 | 650 | 103 | 200 | 49 | 6 | 32 | 122 | 55 | 140 | 30 | .367 | .549 |

## WILL INMAN

RHP

**Born:** Feb. 6, 1987. **B-T:** R-R. **Ht.:** 6-0. **Wt.:** 200. **Drafted:** HS—Dry Fork, Va., 2005 (3rd round). **Signed by:** Grant Brittain.

After leading Tunstall High to back-to-back Virginia state titles and setting the state record for strikeouts, Inman spurned an Auburn commitment to sign for $500,000. He followed a strong pro debut in 2005 by posting the second-best ERA in the minors. Inman isn't overpowering, but he can consistently command his 89-92 mph fastball for strikes in any part of the zone. He stays ahead in the count and complements his fastball with a two-plane slurve that he's trying to develop into a more conventional curveball. He began using his changeup more last season. He is a fiery competitor. Inman missed a month last season with a sore shoulder, perhaps because he three too many breaking balls. He has eliminated much of the effort in his delivery and stayed on a straighter line to the plate, mechanical adjustments the Brewers hope will relieve stress on his arm. He's not projectable and needs to refine his secondary pitches. Any worries Milwaukee had about Inman's sore shoulder were quieted when he didn't allow an earned run in his first five outings after coming off the disabled list. He has the stuff and aggressiveness to move quickly, and he'll pitch at high Class A Brevard County as a 20-year-old.

| Year | Club (League) | Class | W | L | ERA | G | GS | CG | SV | IP | H | R | ER | HR | BB | SO | AVG |
|---|---|---|---|---|---|---|---|---|---|---|---|---|---|---|---|---|---|
| 2005 | Brewers (AZL) | R | 0 | 0 | 0.00 | 1 | 0 | 0 | 0 | 2 | 0 | 0 | 0 | 0 | 1 | 1 | .000 |
| | Helena (Pio) | R | 6 | 0 | 2.00 | 13 | 5 | 0 | 1 | 45 | 29 | 11 | 10 | 5 | 11 | 58 | .182 |
| 2006 | West Virginia (SAL) | A | 10 | 2 | 1.71 | 23 | 20 | 0 | 0 | 111 | 75 | 22 | 21 | 3 | 24 | 134 | .190 |
| **MINOR LEAGUE TOTALS** | | | 16 | 2 | 1.77 | 37 | 25 | 0 | 1 | 158 | 104 | 33 | 31 | 8 | 36 | 193 | .186 |

## JEREMY JEFFRESS

RHP

**Born:** Sept. 21, 1987. **B-T:** R-R. **Ht.:** 6-1. **Wt.:** 185. **Drafted:** HS—South Boston, Va., 2006 (1st round). **Signed by:** Tim McIlvaine.

Jeffress had more sheer velocity than any pitcher in the 2006 draft. The Brewers hoped for a quality college arm with the 16th overall pick, but changed gears and took Jeffress, who signed for $1.55 million. Despite control struggles in his pro debut, he rated as the top pitching prospect in the Rookie-level Arizona League. Jeffress regularly throws his fastball in the high 90s, hit 98 mph throughout 2006 and topped out at 102. He's an excellent athlete with smooth mechanics and utilizes his lower half well. He flashes a hard slider, but the pitch is a work in progress. He showed encouraging signs of progress with his offspeed stuff in instructional league. It's hard to succeed as a one-pitch pitcher, and Jeffress will have to refine his slider and changeup. His control is erratic and he wore down by the end of the summer. He's a project, but the long-term payoff could be huge, as scouts compare Jeffress to Dwight Gooden for his velocity, athleti-

cism and easy delivery. He should see low Class A at some point this season.

| Year | Club (League) | Class | W | L | ERA | G | GS | CG | SV | IP | H | R | ER | HR | BB | SO | AVG |
|------|---------------|-------|---|---|-----|---|----|----|----|----|---|---|----|----|----|----|-----|
| 2006 | Brewers (AZL) | R | 2 | 5 | 5.88 | 13 | 4 | 0 | 0 | 34 | 30 | 26 | 22 | 0 | 25 | 37 | .227 |
| **MINOR LEAGUE TOTALS** | | | 2 | 5 | 5.88 | 13 | 4 | 0 | 0 | 34 | 30 | 26 | 22 | 0 | 25 | 37 | .227 |

## 5 MARK ROGERS RHP

STEVE MOORE

**Born:** Jan. 30, 1986. **B-T:** R-R. **Ht.:** 6-2. **Wt.:** 205. **Drafted:** HS—Mount Ararat, Maine, 2004 (1st round). **Signed by:** Tony Blengino.

Two years after selecting Rogers with the fifth overall pick ahead of Jeremy Sowers and Homer Bailey, the Brewers still aren't quite sure what they have. Injuries and control issues have plagued Maine's first-ever high school first-rounder, yet he has averaged 11.0 strikeouts per nine innings as a pro. Rogers has two pitches that make him devastating when he commands them: a mid- to high-90s fastball and a 12-to-6 curveball. He's working on a changeup, and it can be effective because hitters have to watch out for his fastball and curve. A standout hockey and soccer player in high school, he has tremendous athleticism. The Brewers altered Rogers' mechanics because he threw across his body in high school. He still struggles at times to repeat his delivery, which leads to control and command difficulties. The inability to smooth out his mechanics led to shoulder problems in July, effectively ending his season. Rogers' shoulder continued to bother him during the offseason, and he was slated for arthroscopic surgery to pinpoint the cause. If he has surgery, he'll miss the start of the season. He remains a classic high-risk, high-reward player with the raw stuff to be a No. 1 starter or a closer.

| Year | Club (League) | Class | W | L | ERA | G | GS | CG | SV | IP | H | R | ER | HR | BB | SO | AVG |
|------|---------------|-------|---|---|-----|---|----|----|----|----|---|---|----|----|----|----|-----|
| 2004 | Brewers (AZL) | R | 0 | 3 | 4.73 | 9 | 6 | 0 | 0 | 27 | 30 | 21 | 14 | 0 | 14 | 35 | .294 |
| 2005 | West Virginia (SAL) | A | 2 | 9 | 5.11 | 25 | 20 | 0 | 1 | 99 | 87 | 65 | 56 | 11 | 70 | 109 | .238 |
| 2006 | Brevard County (FSL) | A | 1 | 2 | 5.07 | 16 | 16 | 0 | 0 | 71 | 68 | 46 | 40 | 6 | 53 | 96 | .253 |
| | Brewers (AZL) | R | 0 | 0 | 2.25 | 3 | 3 | 0 | 0 | 4 | 5 | 1 | 1 | 0 | 2 | 5 | .294 |
| **MINOR LEAGUE TOTALS** | | | 3 | 14 | 4.99 | 53 | 45 | 0 | 1 | 200 | 190 | 133 | 111 | 17 | 139 | 245 | .252 |

## 6 LORENZO CAIN OF

RICH ABEL

**Born:** April 13, 1986. **B-T:** R-R. **Ht.:** 6-2. **Wt.:** 170. **Drafted:** Tallahassee (Fla.) CC, D/F 2004 (17th round). **Signed by:** Doug Reynolds.

After signing as a draft-and-follow in 2005, Cain claimed Arizona League MVP honors in his pro debut. He followed up by leading the low Class A South Atlantic League in hits in 2006. As his wiry frame continues to fill out, Cain shows flashes of five-tool potential. He has a quick bat with projectable power potential, though his pop primarily comes to the gaps right now. He's a plus runner and a solid defensive outfielder with average arm strength. He shifted from center to right field last year. A bit of a free swinger, Cain is prone to strikeouts at times and still is learning the nuances of hitting. He tends to be pull-conscious and has worked with West Virginia hitting coach Mike Lum to use the whole field. Cain didn't play baseball until he was in high school and remains raw in all phases of the game. Once Cain develops physically and gains experience, the Brewers believe he could be something special. He'll move up to high Class A in 2007.

| Year | Club (League) | Class | AVG | G | AB | R | H | 2B | 3B | HR | RBI | BB | SO | SB | OBP | SLG |
|------|---------------|-------|-----|---|----|---|---|----|----|----|----|----|----|----|-----|-----|
| 2005 | Brewers (AZL) | R | .356 | 50 | 205 | 45 | 73 | 18 | 5 | 5 | 37 | 20 | 32 | 12 | .418 | .566 |
| | Helena (Pio) | R | .208 | 6 | 24 | 4 | 5 | 0 | 0 | 0 | 1 | 1 | 6 | 0 | .321 | .208 |
| 2006 | West Virginia (SAL) | A | .307 | 132 | 527 | 91 | 162 | 36 | 4 | 6 | 60 | 58 | 104 | 34 | .384 | .425 |
| **MINOR LEAGUE TOTALS** | | | .317 | 188 | 756 | 140 | 240 | 54 | 9 | 11 | 98 | 79 | 142 | 46 | .391 | .456 |

## 7 STEVE HAMMOND LHP

**Born:** April 30, 1982. **B-T:** R-L. **Ht.:** 6-2. **Wt.:** 205. **Drafted:** Long Beach State, 2005 (6th round). **Signed by:** Bruce Seid.

Hammond began his college career at Sacramento CC in 2001, but had bone spurs removed from his elbow and didn't pitch for Sac City again until 2004. He worked just 24 innings after transferring to Long Beach State in 2005, but he caught the eye of the Brewers, who signed him for $30,000 as a sixth-rounder. Put in the rotation to get innings, he has thrived as a starter, reaching Double-A in his first full season. Hammond's fastball sits at 88-92 mph and tops out at 94, and he has maintained his velocity while moving from reliever to starter. He spots his fastball well and complements it with an improving changeup. He throws strikes and pitches with poise.

Hammond's slider is average at best. Milwaukee wants him to continue starting, so he'll need three reliable pitches to continue to move through the system. He got a late start by signing at age 23, though concerns about his age were mitigated when he pitched well in Double-A. Hammond will continue to work out of the rotation this year in Triple-A and projects as a No. 4 starter. He also could be an asset in the bullpen, which would get him to the majors more quickly. He could make his big league debut late in 2007.

| Year | Club (League) | Class | W | L | ERA | G | GS | CG | SV | IP | H | R | ER | HR | BB | SO | AVG |
|---|---|---|---|---|---|---|---|---|---|---|---|---|---|---|---|---|---|
| 2005 | Helena (Pio) | R | 1 | 0 | 1.06 | 4 | 2 | 0 | 0 | 17 | 13 | 5 | 2 | 1 | 0 | 23 | .206 |
| | West Virginia (SAL) | A | 3 | 0 | 2.45 | 4 | 1 | 0 | 0 | 15 | 12 | 4 | 4 | 0 | 5 | 11 | .235 |
| | Brevard County (FSL) | A | 1 | 3 | 2.78 | 8 | 7 | 0 | 0 | 36 | 33 | 17 | 11 | 2 | 9 | 30 | .244 |
| 2006 | Brevard County (FSL) | A | 6 | 5 | 2.53 | 14 | 14 | 0 | 0 | 85 | 68 | 32 | 24 | 7 | 23 | 70 | .215 |
| | Huntsville (SL) | AA | 5 | 6 | 2.93 | 13 | 13 | 1 | 0 | 74 | 63 | 29 | 24 | 7 | 25 | 58 | .229 |
| MINOR LEAGUE TOTALS | | | 16 | 14 | 2.58 | 43 | 37 | 1 | 0 | 226 | 189 | 87 | 65 | 17 | 62 | 192 | .225 |

## 8 COLE GILLESPIE
OF

BILL MITCHELL

**Born:** June 20, 1984. **B-T:** R-R. **Ht.:** 6-1. **Wt.:** 205. **Drafted:** Oregon State, 2006 (3rd round). **Signed by:** Brandon Newell.

Undrafted as a sophomore-eligible in 2005, Gillespie won a College World Series championship and the Pacific-10 Conference player of the year award last spring. After signing for $417,500 as a third-round pick, he led the Rookie-level Pioneer League in on-base percentage. Gillespie is an advanced hitter with bat speed and tremendous balance at the plate. He exercises patience in working the count and makes adjustments easily. He should hit for average, and Milwaukee thinks he can produce 15-20 homers per year. He's a good athlete, with solid-average speed and outfield range as well as the instincts to steal bases. He also exhibits strong leadership skills. Gillespie missed time with shoulder problems during his college career, leaving the former pitching recruit with a below-average arm. He's limited to left field and doesn't quite fit the power profile for that position. The Brewers believe they got a steal with Gillespie as a third-rounder. His advanced hitting approach and strong makeup will allow him to skip a level and start his first full season in high Class A. His emergence and that of Lorenzo Cain bolsters the outfield depth the system had lacked.

| Year | Club (League) | Class | AVG | G | AB | R | H | 2B | 3B | HR | RBI | BB | SO | SB | OBP | SLG |
|---|---|---|---|---|---|---|---|---|---|---|---|---|---|---|---|---|---|
| 2006 | Helena (Pio) | R | .344 | 51 | 186 | 49 | 64 | 12 | 1 | 8 | 31 | 40 | 34 | 18 | .464 | .548 |
| MINOR LEAGUE TOTALS | | | .344 | 51 | 186 | 49 | 64 | 12 | 1 | 8 | 31 | 40 | 34 | 18 | .464 | .548 |

## 9 ALCIDES ESCOBAR
SS

STEVE MOORE

**Born:** Dec. 16, 1986. **B-T:** R-R. **Ht.:** 6-1. **Wt.:** 165. **Signed:** Venezuela, 2003. **Signed by:** Epy Guerrero.

The youngest regular in the Florida State League last season, Escobar broke his finger in mid-April. He missed three weeks and it continued to bother him after he returned. A rough year at the plate got worse in the final two months, when he hit .234 with just four extra-base hits. Escobar's defensive tools are far ahead of his bat at this point. He boats fluid actions, soft hands and a plus arm. As he continues to fill out and gain strength, he has a chance to grow into gap power. He makes contact with a slashing line-drive swing. He's an above-average runner with basestealing potential. Lean and wiry, Escobar lacks strength in his game, especially at the plate. He doesn't drive the ball and is overaggressive. His injury didn't help, but he didn't make many strides or adjustments after a promising 2005. Escobar was impressive in instructional league, and the Brewers were toying with the idea of promoting him to Double-A in 2007. Considering how much he struggled offensively last year, returning him to high Class A might make more sense. He'll have to hit if he's going to challenge J.J. Hardy for Milwaukee's shortstop job in the future.

| Year | Club (League) | Class | AVG | G | AB | R | H | 2B | 3B | HR | RBI | BB | SO | SB | OBP | SLG |
|---|---|---|---|---|---|---|---|---|---|---|---|---|---|---|---|---|---|
| 2004 | Helena (Pio) | R | .281 | 68 | 231 | 38 | 65 | 8 | 0 | 2 | 24 | 20 | 44 | 20 | .348 | .342 |
| 2005 | West Virginia (SAL) | A | .271 | 127 | 520 | 80 | 141 | 25 | 8 | 2 | 36 | 20 | 90 | 30 | .305 | .362 |
| 2006 | Brevard County (FSL) | A | .257 | 87 | 350 | 47 | 90 | 9 | 1 | 2 | 33 | 19 | 56 | 28 | .296 | .306 |
| MINOR LEAGUE TOTALS | | | .269 | 282 | 1101 | 165 | 296 | 42 | 9 | 6 | 93 | 59 | 190 | 78 | .311 | .340 |

RICH ABEL

## MAT GAMEL
3B

**Born:** July 26, 1985 **B-T:** L-R. **Ht.:** 6-0. **Wt.:** 205. **Drafted:** Chipola (Fla.) JC, 2005 (4th round). **Signed by:** Doug Reynolds.

Undrafted out of high school, Gamel spent a year Daytona Beach (Fla.) Community College before transferring to Chipola (Fla.) Junior College, where the Brewers spotted him while scouting teammate Darren Ford, a draft-and-follow. In his first full pro season, Gamel was named MVP of the South Atlantic League all-star game. He wowed the crowd by hitting 15 bombs in the second round of the home run derby, which he lost in the finals. Gamel can hit for average and power. He has a sound left-handed stroke, hits balls from gap to gap and can pull a pitch out of the park if a pitcher challenges him inside. A former pitcher, he has plus arm strength to go with decent speed and agility. His swing can get long at times, but Gamel doesn't strike out excessively. After making 52 errors in 157 pro games at third base, he must improve his footwork to reduce his wayward throws. With Ryan Braun ahead of him, he could move to the outfield in the future. There are no plans to shift Gamel off the hot corner this year. He'll make the jump to high Class A and could be big league-ready by the end of 2008.

| Year | Club (League) | Class | AVG | G | AB | R | H | 2B | 3B | HR | RBI | BB | SO | SB | OBP | SLG |
|------|---------------|-------|-----|---|----|---|---|----|----|----|-----|----|----|----|-----|-----|
| 2005 | West Virginia (SAL) | A | .174 | 8 | 23 | 2 | 4 | 0 | 0 | 1 | 1 | 5 | 9 | 0 | .321 | .304 |
| | Helena (Pio) | R | .327 | 50 | 199 | 34 | 65 | 15 | 2 | 5 | 37 | 12 | 49 | 7 | .375 | .497 |
| 2006 | West Virginia (SAL) | A | .288 | 129 | 493 | 65 | 142 | 28 | 5 | 17 | 88 | 52 | 81 | 9 | .359 | .469 |
| **MINOR LEAGUE TOTALS** | | | .295 | 187 | 715 | 101 | 211 | 43 | 7 | 23 | 126 | 69 | 139 | 16 | .362 | .471 |

## ANGEL SALOME
C

**Born:** June 8, 1986. **B-T:** R-R. **Ht.:** 5-7. **Wt.:** 190. **Drafted:** HS—New York, 2004 (5th round). **Signed by:** Tony Blengino.

Salome was born in the Dominican Republic and though his family moved between there and New York twice, they didn't settle permanently in New York until he was 12. He was leading the South Atlantic League in RBIs last season when he broke his ankle sliding into second in early August. He has compact strength in his short frame, prompting some to call him "Pocket Pudge." Salome has a 70 arm, helping him throw out 37 percent of basestealers despite needing overall work on his defensive mechanics. He drives the ball with a short, powerful stroke. Salome is a tireless, enthusiastic worker and made marked improvement defensively last year. He committed 15 errors and allowed 17 passed balls, however, and is still learning the basic catching fundamentals of shifting his weight, blocking balls and calling games. The Brewers have high hopes for their top catching prospect, who would fill an obvious hole in their lauded homegrown lineup. And while Salome is still at least a couple years away, the path is clear for him, as long as he continues to develop his defensive skills.

| Year | Club (League) | Class | AVG | G | AB | R | H | 2B | 3B | HR | RBI | BB | SO | SB | OBP | SLG |
|------|---------------|-------|-----|---|----|---|---|----|----|----|-----|----|----|----|-----|-----|
| 2004 | Brewers (AZL) | R | .235 | 20 | 81 | 7 | 19 | 7 | 0 | 0 | 8 | 4 | 14 | 2 | .271 | .321 |
| 2005 | West Virginia (SAL) | A | .254 | 29 | 118 | 15 | 30 | 7 | 1 | 4 | 21 | 8 | 17 | 1 | .302 | .432 |
| | Helena (Pio) | R | .415 | 37 | 159 | 34 | 66 | 17 | 0 | 8 | 50 | 15 | 16 | 6 | .469 | .673 |
| 2006 | West Virginia (SAL) | A | .292 | 105 | 418 | 63 | 122 | 31 | 2 | 10 | 85 | 39 | 63 | 7 | .349 | .447 |
| **MINOR LEAGUE TOTALS** | | | .305 | 191 | 776 | 119 | 237 | 62 | 3 | 22 | 164 | 66 | 110 | 16 | .359 | .478 |

## CHARLIE FERMAINT
OF

**Born:** Oct. 11, 1985. **B-T:** R-R. **Ht.:** 5-10. **Wt.:** 170. **Drafted:** HS—Dorado, P.R., 2003 (4th round). **Signed by:** Larry Pardo.

Fermaint has progressed steadily while being pushed aggressively, though he's been bothered by hamstring and shoulder issues during his ascent and was benched once in 2006 for not running a groundball out. One of the system's top athletes, he has quick hands and impressive bat speed, but hasn't tapped into his raw power potential. Fermaint is a plus runner who can cover 60 yards in 6.5 seconds as well as showing the makings of a plus center fielder defensively. His arm is solid-average. His instincts aren't helping him on his flyball reads and he was caught on 14 of 41 steal attempts. But club officials remind themselves that Fermaint played the entire season at age 20 in the Florida State League, a tough circuit for any hitter. He must learn to stay on offspeed pitches and stop pulling off. Overall, his strike-zone judgment has to improve, and he needs to find consistency at the plate and let his talent take over. He doesn't hit for power and is more valuable at the top of the order, so Fermaint must get on base and make things happen. The Brewers have something of a logjam in center field, with Gwynn at Triple-A, Steve Moss coming off a disappointing turn at Double-A and then Fermaint. All three are likely to repeat their 2006 levels, at least to start.

| Year | Club (League) | Class | AVG | G | AB | R | H | 2B | 3B | HR | RBI | BB | SO | SB | OBP | SLG |
|------|---------------|-------|-----|---|----|----|----|----|----|----|-----|----|----|----|-----|-----|
| 2003 | Brewers (AZL) | R | .300 | 25 | 100 | 16 | 30 | 3 | 3 | 1 | 9 | 3 | 19 | 6 | .327 | .420 |
| 2004 | Helena (Pio) | R | .229 | 58 | 218 | 30 | 50 | 14 | 2 | 5 | 39 | 19 | 83 | 8 | .300 | .381 |
| 2005 | Helena (Pio) | R | .364 | 31 | 129 | 46 | 47 | 9 | 2 | 12 | 32 | 15 | 28 | 11 | .419 | .744 |
| | West Virginia (SAL) | A | .248 | 27 | 113 | 18 | 28 | 7 | 0 | 5 | 17 | 8 | 39 | 4 | .301 | .442 |
| 2006 | Brevard County (FSL) | A | .276 | 110 | 424 | 67 | 117 | 20 | 4 | 7 | 33 | 42 | 119 | 27 | .349 | .392 |
| **MINOR LEAGUE TOTALS** | | | .276 | 251 | 984 | 177 | 272 | 53 | 11 | 30 | 130 | 87 | 288 | 56 | .340 | .444 |

## 13  DARREN FORD                                                     OF

**Born:** Oct. 1, 1985. **B-T:** R-R. **Ht.:** 6-1. **Wt.:** 195. **Drafted:** Chipola (Fla.) JC, D/F 2004 (18th round). **Signed by:** Tony Blengino.

One of the fastest players in the minor leagues, Ford reached the New Jersey state finals in the 100-meter dash in high school, and he led the South Atlantic League in swipes last year while ranking second in the minors. He uses top-of-the-scale speed to chase down balls in center, making him a prototype center fielder/leadoff hitter. A three-sport star in high school, he's still developing his approach to hitting. He remains undisciplined at the plate, striking out on pitches out of the zone and not drawing enough walks. Ford improved his pitch selection as the year progressed, and he showed flashes of the type of impact player he can be. The Brewers have stressed the importance of bunting and hitting the ball on the ground as often as possible, though Ford does have some sock in his bat. With a strong, solid body type, he's built for both speed and durability. He often beats out routine ground balls, flustering infielders into making poor throws. Ford can be brought along slowly, but needs to cut down on his strikeouts and make more contact to hit atop the order and take full advantage of his speed. He'll continue to develop in high Class A this season.

| Year | Club (League) | Class | AVG | G | AB | R | H | 2B | 3B | HR | RBI | BB | SO | SB | OBP | SLG |
|------|---------------|-------|-----|---|----|----|----|----|----|----|-----|----|----|----|-----|-----|
| 2005 | Helena (Pio) | R | .271 | 61 | 236 | 57 | 64 | 4 | 3 | 1 | 24 | 33 | 70 | 18 | .365 | .326 |
| 2006 | West Virginia (SAL) | A | .283 | 125 | 491 | 93 | 139 | 24 | 3 | 7 | 54 | 56 | 133 | 69 | .361 | .387 |
| **MINOR LEAGUE TOTALS** | | | .279 | 186 | 727 | 150 | 203 | 28 | 6 | 8 | 78 | 89 | 203 | 87 | .362 | .367 |

## 14  YOHANNIS PEREZ                                                  SS

**Born:** Oct. 11, 1982. **B-T:** R-R. **Ht.:** 6-0 **Wt.:** 192. **Signed:** Cuba, 2006. **Signed by:** Fernando Arango.

Perez was one of five Cuban defectors who worked out at the Diamondbacks' complex in the Dominican Republic last summer. Brewers international scouting director Fernando Arango is from Matanzas, Cuba, and Perez' hometown is in the same province. Arango spearheaded the charge to sign Perez for $450,000. Overjoyed at attaining his freedom, Perez broke down crying in his first visit to a U.S. grocery store and is driven to succeed. He has drawn comparisons to Rickie Weeks for his strong wrists and quick hands, and to Yuniesky Betancourt for his overall game. Perez, who hasn't played for two years after defecting, put on some weight during his downtime and should play lighter when he gets back in shape. Before the layoff, Perez was a plus runner, covering 60 yards in 6.4 seconds. He was timed at 6.6 in the tryout. In the field, he has shown good instincts to go with soft hands, a strong arm and outstanding range. The Brewers were unable to get Perez to instructional league in the fall because they had trouble unblocking him with the U.S. Treasury Department, a process all Cuban players must go through. The Brewers invited him to big league camp and envision him starting the 2007 season in Double-A.

| Year | Club (League) | Class | AVG | G | AB | R | H | 2B | 3B | HR | RBI | BB | SO | SB | OBP | SLG |
|------|---------------|-------|-----|---|----|---|---|----|----|----|-----|----|----|----|-----|-----|
| 2006 | Did Not Play—Signed 2007 Contract | | | | | | | | | | | | | | | |

## 15  TIM DILLARD                                                     RHP

**Born:** July 19, 1983. **B-T:** B-R. **Ht.:** 6-4. **Wt.:** 205. **Drafted:** Itawamba (Miss.) CC, D/F 2002 (34th round). **Signed by:** Doug Reynolds.

Dillard's father Steve was a second-rounder in 1972 and enjoyed parts of eight seasons as an infield reserve for three teams between 1975-82. Tim split his time between catching and pitching as an amateur, and the Brewers twice drafted him as a pitcher, in the 15th round in 2001 out of high school and again as a draft-and-follow in 2002. Dillard was the organization's pitcher of the year in 2005 after leading all full-season pitchers in innings, victories and ERA. Elevated to Double-A last year, he pitched163 innings, again tops in the system. With a big, strong frame, he's a bull on the mound yet pitches with command, staying ahead in the count and issuing few walks. Dillard's fastball sits at 88-92 mph for the most part with good sinking action, resulting in a better than 1.5 groundball-flyball ratio. Because he's around the plate a lot and doesn't possess a blazing fastball, he can be hittable. But Dillard doesn't give in. He is still working on making his slider a consistent pitch and needs

to continue developing his changeup. Dillard already has the savvy to succeed. He projects to the back half of the rotation, but that's OK with the Brewers because of his knack for eating innings.

| Year | Club (League) | Class | W | L | ERA | G | GS | CG | SV | IP | H | R | ER | HR | BB | SO | AVG |
|------|---------------|-------|---|---|-----|---|----|----|-----|-----|-----|-----|-----|-----|-----|-----|------|
| 2003 | Brewers (AZL) | R | 1 | 2 | 3.79 | 11 | 4 | 0 | 0 | 36 | 36 | 19 | 15 | 1 | 5 | 32 | .261 |
|  | Helena (Pio) | R | 0 | 0 | 0.00 | 3 | 0 | 0 | 0 | 5 | 5 | 0 | 0 | 0 | 2 | 6 | .250 |
| 2004 | Beloit (MWL) | A | 2 | 5 | 3.94 | 43 | 1 | 0 | 10 | 78 | 89 | 46 | 34 | 4 | 22 | 61 | .280 |
| 2005 | Brevard County (FSL) | A | 12 | 10 | 2.48 | 28 | 28 | 5 | 0 | 185 | 150 | 64 | 51 | 9 | 31 | 128 | .219 |
| 2006 | Huntsville (SL) | AA | 10 | 7 | 3.15 | 29 | 25 | 1 | 0 | 163 | 167 | 76 | 57 | 10 | 36 | 108 | .261 |
| **MINOR LEAGUE TOTALS** | | | 25 | 24 | 3.03 | 114 | 58 | 6 | 10 | 467 | 447 | 205 | 157 | 24 | 96 | 335 | .248 |

## 16  ZACH JACKSON                                                LHP

**Born:** May 13, 1983. **B-T:** L-L. **Ht.:** 6-5. **Wt.:** 220. **Drafted:** Texas A&M, 2004 (1st round supplemental). **Signed by:** Andy Beene (Blue Jays).

With Prince Fielder ready for the majors, the Brewers traded Lyle Overbay to the Blue Jays for Dave Bush, Gabe Gross and Jackson at the 2005 Winter Meetings. Milwaukee needed help when Ben Sheets and Tomo Ohka were sidelined at the same time last year, and Jackson was one of many rookies who got a chance to earn a permanent spot in the rotation. He showed an effective arsenal, but was inconsistent in seven big league starts. He was inconsistent in Triple-A as well and has never dominated in the upper levels, allowing more hits than innings over the course of his career. With an average 88-91 mph fastball, Jackson has to work his cutter inside on righthanders to be successful. His sweeping curve and average changeup aren't reliable pitches, leaving Jackson to get by with his hard stuff and funky delivery. Because his offspeed pitches were erratic, hitters can figure out his herky-jerky delivery and get better swings the second time through the lineup. Jackson works quickly but sometimes relies on his cutter too much and gives up too many hits. Until he develops more reliable offspeed pitches, it is difficult to project Jackson in the big league rotation. He may eventually slide into a relief role. The fact that he throws strikes and doesn't back down works in his favor.

| Year | Club (League) | Class | W | L | ERA | G | GS | CG | SV | IP | H | R | ER | HR | BB | SO | AVG |
|------|---------------|-------|---|---|-----|---|----|----|-----|-----|-----|-----|-----|-----|-----|-----|------|
| 2004 | Auburn (NYP) | A | 0 | 0 | 5.40 | 4 | 4 | 0 | 0 | 15 | 20 | 9 | 9 | 1 | 6 | 11 | .323 |
| 2005 | Dunedin (FSL) | A | 8 | 1 | 2.88 | 10 | 10 | 0 | 0 | 59 | 56 | 25 | 19 | 3 | 6 | 48 | .247 |
|  | New Hampshire (EL) | AA | 4 | 3 | 4.00 | 9 | 9 | 0 | 0 | 54 | 57 | 27 | 24 | 3 | 12 | 43 | .277 |
|  | Syracuse (IL) | AAA | 4 | 4 | 5.13 | 8 | 8 | 0 | 0 | 47 | 61 | 33 | 27 | 3 | 21 | 33 | .323 |
| 2006 | Milwaukee (NL) | MLB | 2 | 2 | 5.40 | 8 | 7 | 0 | 0 | 38 | 48 | 26 | 23 | 6 | 14 | 22 | .304 |
|  | Nashville (PCL) | AAA | 4 | 6 | 4.12 | 18 | 18 | 1 | 0 | 107 | 106 | 55 | 49 | 11 | 44 | 58 | .262 |
| **MINOR LEAGUE TOTALS** | | | 20 | 14 | 4.08 | 49 | 49 | 1 | 0 | 283 | 300 | 149 | 128 | 21 | 89 | 193 | .276 |
| **MAJOR LEAGUE TOTALS** | | | 2 | 2 | 5.40 | 8 | 7 | 0 | 0 | 38 | 48 | 26 | 23 | 6 | 14 | 22 | .304 |

## 17  TONY GWYNN JR.                                               OF

**Born:** Oct. 4, 1982. **B-T:** L-R. **Ht.:** 6-0. **Wt.:** 185. **Drafted:** San Diego State, 2003 (2nd round). **Signed by:** Bruce Seid.

Gwynn finally broke through to bat .300 in Triple-A last season, becoming the kind of pesky leadoff hitter the Brewers envisioned when they drafted him. No one has doubted his defensive prowess. An above-average runner but not an absolute burner, Gwynn can go get the ball in center field, covering territory gap to gap with excellent instincts. He has a decent arm, certainly enough to play in center. When he was drafted, he was not strong enough physically and pitchers would knock the bat out of his hands. But he has matured physically and understands the importance of hitting the ball on the ground. He offers little by way of extra-base power, though, which has been a knock dating back to San Diego State, where he was coached by his future Hall of Fame father, Tony Sr. Given his first taste of big league action early in the second half, Gwynn was effective off the Brewers' bench. But presented with the chance to play center field regularly for the Brewers as a September callup, he did not perform nearly as well at the plate, swinging at too many pitches early in the count and showing little plate discipline or pop. That audition left doubts about whether Gwynn will hit enough to be a regular in the majors or if he'll have to settle for reserve status. Milwaukee's crowded outfield could prompt a return to Triple-A for Gwynn.

| Year | Club (League) | Class | AVG | G | AB | R | H | 2B | 3B | HR | RBI | BB | SO | SB | OBP | SLG |
|------|---------------|-------|-----|---|-----|---|---|----|----|-----|-----|-----|-----|-----|------|------|
| 2003 | Beloit (MWL) | A | .280 | 61 | 236 | 35 | 66 | 8 | 0 | 1 | 33 | 32 | 31 | 14 | .364 | .326 |
| 2004 | Huntsville (SL) | AA | .243 | 138 | 534 | 74 | 130 | 20 | 5 | 2 | 37 | 53 | 95 | 34 | .318 | .311 |
| 2005 | Huntsville (SL) | AA | .271 | 133 | 509 | 83 | 138 | 21 | 5 | 1 | 41 | 76 | 75 | 34 | .370 | .338 |
| 2006 | Nashville (PCL) | AAA | .300 | 112 | 447 | 73 | 134 | 21 | 5 | 4 | 42 | 42 | 84 | 30 | .360 | .396 |
|  | Milwaukee (NL) | MLB | .260 | 32 | 77 | 5 | 20 | 2 | 1 | 0 | 4 | 2 | 15 | 3 | .275 | .312 |
| **MINOR LEAGUE TOTALS** | | | .271 | 444 | 1726 | 265 | 468 | 70 | 15 | 8 | 153 | 203 | 285 | 112 | .351 | .343 |
| **MAJOR LEAGUE TOTALS** | | | .260 | 32 | 77 | 5 | 20 | 2 | 1 | 0 | 4 | 2 | 15 | 3 | .275 | .312 |

## 18 MANNY PARRA
LHP

**Born:** Oct. 30, 1982. **B-T:** L-L. **Ht.:** 6-3. **Wt.:** 200. **Drafted:** American River (Calif.) JC, D/F 2001 (26th round). **Signed by:** Justin McCray.

Once considered one of the top pitching prospects in the organization, Parra has suffered ongoing shoulder problems that eventually led to surgery in 2005. He did a better job of staying on the mound last season but is now behind in his development, spending most of 2006 in high Class A after pitching in Double-A two years ago. When healthy, he has excellent stuff, beginning with a two-seam fastball at 88-92 mph. He works up in the zone with a four-seamer that tops out at 94-95 mph and has an average splitter and curveball. Parra is still working on controlling his changeup, which would make him a lot tougher to hit. The Brewers have worked with Parra on smoothing out his delivery and taking pressure off his shoulder. The rust showed last year, as Parra was more erratic with his control, but he still finished with more than a strikeout per inning and returned to Double-A by the end of the season. His control, once a strong suit, has regressed. Before his injuries, the Brewers figured Parra might make it to the majors at some point in 2006. That didn't happen, but he's still a lefty with a quality arm and will pitch in Triple-A this year at age 24.

| Year | Club (League) | Class | W | L | ERA | G | GS | CG | SV | IP | H | R | ER | HR | BB | SO | AVG |
|------|---------------|-------|---|---|-----|---|----|----|----|-----|-----|-----|-----|----|-----|-----|------|
| 2002 | Brewers (AZL) | R | 0 | 0 | 4.50 | 1 | 1 | 0 | 0 | 2 | 1 | 1 | 1 | 1 | 0 | 4 | .143 |
| | Ogden (Pio) | R | 3 | 1 | 3.21 | 11 | 10 | 0 | 0 | 48 | 59 | 30 | 17 | 3 | 10 | 51 | .298 |
| 2003 | Beloit (MWL) | A | 11 | 2 | 2.73 | 23 | 23 | 1 | 0 | 139 | 127 | 50 | 42 | 9 | 24 | 117 | .243 |
| 2004 | High Desert (Cal) | A | 5 | 2 | 3.48 | 13 | 12 | 1 | 0 | 67 | 76 | 41 | 26 | 3 | 19 | 64 | .290 |
| | Huntsville (SL) | AA | 0 | 1 | 3.00 | 3 | 3 | 0 | 0 | 6 | 5 | 3 | 2 | 0 | 0 | 10 | .217 |
| 2005 | Huntsville (SL) | AA | 5 | 6 | 3.96 | 16 | 16 | 0 | 0 | 91 | 111 | 47 | 40 | 4 | 21 | 86 | .295 |
| 2006 | Brevard County (FSL) | A | 1 | 3 | 2.96 | 15 | 14 | 0 | 0 | 55 | 47 | 29 | 18 | 4 | 32 | 61 | .235 |
| | Huntsville (SL) | AA | 3 | 0 | 2.87 | 6 | 6 | 0 | 0 | 31 | 26 | 13 | 10 | 0 | 8 | 29 | .232 |
| **MINOR LEAGUE TOTALS** | | | 28 | 15 | 3.20 | 88 | 85 | 2 | 0 | 439 | 452 | 214 | 156 | 24 | 114 | 422 | .266 |

## 19 BRENT BREWER
SS

**Born:** Dec. 19, 1987. **B-T:** R-R. **Ht.:** 6-2. **Wt.:** 190. **Drafted:** HS—Tyrone, Ga., 2006 (2nd round). **Signed by:** Doug Reynolds.

How could Milwaukee pass on a draft pick with this last name? It was athleticism that sealed the deal to draft the multisport star, who was to play wide receiver and shortstop at Florida State. One of the top wide-receiver recruits in the country, he turned pro and gave up football for $600,000. As might be expected from an athlete sought by Bobby Bowden, Brewer has a long list of physical attributes: speed, strength, a good arm and great range at shortstop. But he's a raw baseball player, as evidenced by his 24 errors in 45 games in the Arizona League. Still maturing physically, Brewer eventually may have to move off shortstop. Scouts believe he could be an outstanding center fielder. The Brewers just want him to play and gain experience after dividing his loyalties during high school between baseball and football. As he matures and gets stronger, the Brewers believe he'll develop power. Brewer tried too many batting stances but finally found a comfortable approach, then continued to make strides in instructional league. He must work hard on his strike-zone discipline, increase his on-base percentage and take advantage of his speed. The Brewers expect this will come from a gifted athlete who will play the entire 2007 season at 19, presumably in low Class A.

| Year | Club (League) | Class | AVG | G | AB | R | H | 2B | 3B | HR | RBI | BB | SO | SB | OBP | SLG |
|------|---------------|-------|-----|---|----|---|---|----|----|----|-----|----|----|----|-----|-----|
| 2006 | Brewers (AZL) | R | .264 | 45 | 182 | 25 | 48 | 3 | 6 | 3 | 22 | 16 | 53 | 10 | .328 | .396 |
| **MINOR LEAGUE TOTALS** | | | .264 | 45 | 182 | 25 | 48 | 3 | 6 | 3 | 22 | 16 | 53 | 10 | .328 | .396 |

## 20 CHRIS ERRECART
OF/1B

**Born:** Feb. 11, 1985. **B-T:** R-L. **Ht.:** 6-1. **Wt.:** 210. **Drafted:** California, 2006 (5th round). **Signed by:** Justin McCray.

Heading into last spring, nobody figured Errecart would last until the fifth round. But Errecart—who never hit .300 in college—had some draftitis as a junior, following his .303-6-22 performance in the 2005 Cape Cod League with a .268-8-30 effort with metal at California. Errecart's swing plays better with wood, though, and after signing for $166,000 he led the Pioneer League in RBIs and finished second in homers during his pro debut. Errecart reestablished himself as an offensive performer with plenty of pop, mainly to the pull side. He hit some legendary homers at Rookie-level Helena, flashing the raw power that the Brewers are lacking throughout their system. At times, he's jumpy at the plate and gets out front on offspeed pitches. He was overly pull-happy during the spring. He has average range and arm strength in the outfield but doesn't run well and probably projects as a first baseman down the road. Errecart played nearly half of his games at that position in his first

pro season but is a decent enough athlete to continue seeing time in the outfield as well. The Brewers' outfield situation is crowded at all levels, and Errecart will move faster—perhaps starting at high Class A—if he moves to first.

| Year | Club (League) | Class | AVG | G | AB | R | H | 2B | 3B | HR | RBI | BB | SO | SB | OBP | SLG |
|------|---------------|-------|-----|---|----|---|---|----|----|----|-----|----|----|----|-----|-----|
| 2006 | Helena (Pio) | R | .316 | 70 | 272 | 49 | 86 | 16 | 0 | 13 | 61 | 25 | 56 | 5 | .406 | .518 |
| **MINOR LEAGUE TOTALS** | | | .316 | 70 | 272 | 49 | 86 | 16 | 0 | 13 | 61 | 25 | 56 | 5 | .406 | .518 |

## HERNAN IRIBARREN                                                      2B

**Born:** June 29, 1984. **B-T:** L-R. **Ht.:** 6-1. **Wt.:** 170. **Signed:** Venezuela, 2002. **Signed by:** Epy Guerrero.

A .333 career hitter entering the year, Iribarren earned an asterisk next to his numbers last summer when he was caught using a corked bat, drawing suspensions from the Florida State League as well as the Brewers. He was better after the suspension than before, raking at a .344 clip the rest of the way, earning midseason and postseason all-star honors in the FSL. Iribarren has two above-average tools, but his plus speed doesn't play well—he lacks instincts and is a middling basestealer. Irribarren challenges for batting titles with a slashing hitting style that helps him take advantage of his quickness. He's displays the strike-zone discipline and patience to be a useful No. 2 hitter in the lineup despite a somewhat funky approach. His well below-average power makes the improvement of his basestealing ability a must. A solid defensive player in the past, Iribarren fought himself at times in the field last season and got into mental funks. He might have enough ability to make consistent contact and on-base skills to carry him to the big leagues. He is limited to second base, though, limiting his versatility as a role player. He will move up to Double-A in 2007, and likely continuing along the same career path as an above-average hitter.

| Year | Club (League) | Class | AVG | G | AB | R | H | 2B | 3B | HR | RBI | BB | SO | SB | OBP | SLG |
|------|---------------|-------|-----|---|----|---|---|----|----|----|-----|----|----|----|-----|-----|
| 2002 | Milwaukee (DSL) | R | .314 | 66 | 223 | 35 | 70 | 13 | 2 | 2 | 34 | 19 | 43 | 7 | .383 | .417 |
| 2003 | Milwaukee (DSL) | R | .344 | 64 | 227 | 43 | 78 | 12 | 7 | 2 | 27 | 24 | 36 | 17 | .403 | .485 |
| 2004 | Brewers (AZL) | R | .439 | 46 | 189 | 40 | 83 | 6 | 9 | 4 | 36 | 19 | 23 | 15 | .490 | .630 |
|  | Beloit (MWL) | A | .373 | 15 | 67 | 12 | 25 | 6 | 5 | 1 | 10 | 5 | 16 | 1 | .411 | .657 |
| 2005 | West Virginia (SAL) | A | .290 | 126 | 486 | 72 | 141 | 15 | 8 | 4 | 48 | 51 | 99 | 38 | .360 | .379 |
| 2006 | Brevard County (FSL) | A | .319 | 108 | 398 | 50 | 127 | 12 | 4 | 2 | 50 | 39 | 57 | 19 | .376 | .384 |
| **MINOR LEAGUE TOTALS** | | | .330 | 425 | 1590 | 252 | 524 | 64 | 35 | 15 | 205 | 157 | 274 | 97 | .391 | .442 |

## DENNIS SARFATE                                                       RHP

**Born:** April 9, 1981. **B-T:** R-R. **Ht.:** 6-4. **Wt.:** 220. **Drafted:** Chandler-Gilbert (Ariz.) CC, 2001 (9th round). **Signed by:** Brian Johnson.

Sarfate climbed the ladder as a starter, showing durability by averaging 25 starts and more than 130 innings in each of the three seasons after elbow surgery limited him in 2002. His inability to develop a reliable offspeed pitch to complement his 93-96 mph fastball and solid slider finally led him to the bullpen last year in Triple-A. Sarfate was excited about the shift, bought into it and prospered, with some impressive outings for the Brewers in September. He has a free-and-easy arm action and pitches up in the strike zone frequently, and isn't afraid to come inside on hitters and back them off the plate. Still erratic with his fastball command during stretches, Sarfate should benefit from the sharper focus of short relief. He never had much confidence in his changeup and doesn't have to worry about throwing it anymore, leaving his substandard curve, which has its moments, as his second pitch. Scouts thought for a long time that he profiled as a power reliever. Sarfate, who threw well both in the Arizona Fall League and the winter Mexican Pacific League, will compete for a bullpen role in the spring, and likely contribute at some point in 2007. His large physical frame is well equipped for multiple-inning appearances and durable enough to bounce back on consecutive nights.

| Year | Club (League) | Class | W | L | ERA | G | GS | CG | SV | IP | H | R | ER | HR | BB | SO | AVG |
|------|---------------|-------|---|---|-----|---|----|----|----|----|----|----|----|----|----|----|-----|
| 2001 | Ogden (Pio) | R | 1 | 2 | 4.63 | 9 | 4 | 0 | 1 | 23 | 20 | 13 | 12 | 4 | 10 | 32 | .230 |
| 2002 | Brewers (AZL) | R | 0 | 0 | 2.57 | 5 | 5 | 0 | 0 | 14 | 6 | 4 | 4 | 0 | 7 | 22 | .125 |
|  | Ogden (Pio) | R | 0 | 0 | 9.00 | 1 | 0 | 0 | 0 | 1 | 2 | 1 | 1 | 0 | 1 | 2 | .400 |
| 2003 | Beloit (MWL) | A | 12 | 2 | 2.84 | 26 | 26 | 0 | 0 | 140 | 114 | 50 | 44 | 11 | 66 | 140 | .227 |
| 2004 | Huntsville (SL) | AA | 7 | 12 | 4.05 | 28 | 25 | 0 | 0 | 129 | 128 | 71 | 58 | 12 | 78 | 113 | .278 |
| 2005 | Huntsville (SL) | AA | 9 | 9 | 3.88 | 24 | 24 | 1 | 0 | 130 | 120 | 65 | 56 | 13 | 59 | 110 | .245 |
|  | Nashville (PCL) | AAA | 0 | 1 | 2.25 | 2 | 1 | 0 | 0 | 12 | 6 | 3 | 3 | 1 | 4 | 10 | .150 |
| 2006 | Nashville (PCL) | AAA | 10 | 7 | 3.67 | 34 | 21 | 0 | 0 | 125 | 125 | 63 | 51 | 7 | 78 | 117 | .265 |
|  | Milwaukee (NL) | MLB | 0 | 0 | 4.32 | 8 | 0 | 0 | 0 | 8 | 9 | 4 | 4 | 0 | 4 | 11 | .265 |
| **MINOR LEAGUE TOTALS** | | | 39 | 33 | 3.59 | 129 | 106 | 1 | 1 | 574 | 521 | 270 | 229 | 48 | 303 | 546 | .248 |
| **MAJOR LEAGUE TOTALS** | | | 0 | 0 | 4.32 | 8 | 0 | 0 | 0 | 8 | 9 | 4 | 4 | 0 | 4 | 11 | .265 |

## JOE THATCHER

LHP

**Born:** Oct. 4, 1981. **B-T:** L-L. **Ht.:** 6-2. **Wt.:** 202. **Signed:** Frontier League (independent), 2005. **Signed by:** Brad Del Barba.

Thatcher went undrafted after his senior year at Indiana State, when he posted a 4-8, 5.60 mark before signing with independent River City in the Frontier League in 2004. He was closing games for River City and was noticed by scouts at the Frontier League all-star game before signing with the Brewers. He appears to have found his niche as a situational reliever, and despite getting there in roundabout way, he's moving quickly up the organizational ladder. He pitched at three different levels last season, finishing the year in Double-A while making huge strides. Thatcher operates with a cutting 88-91 mph fastball and sweeping slider from a low three-quarters slot. He throws strikes and provides a deceptive look with a funky cross-body delivery. He challenges hitters with his aggressive approach. He is the classic late bloomer who knows how to set up hitters and works ahead in the count with average stuff. He's working to improve his changeup to be more than just a lefty specialist. At 25, he's no kid, but he's so tough on lefthanders (who hit .145 against him in 55 regular-season at-bats), he could be knocking on the door in 2007. He dominated Hawaii Winter Baseball (0.73 ERA, .189 opponent average), further speeding his timetable.

| Year | Club (League) | Class | W | L | ERA | G | GS | CG | SV | IP | H | R | ER | HR | BB | SO | AVG |
|------|---------------|-------|---|---|-----|---|----|----|----|----|---|---|----|----|----|----|-----|
| 2004 | River City (FL) | IND | 2 | 3 | 2.98 | 29 | 0 | 0 | 5 | 42 | 38 | 15 | 14 | 3 | 15 | 55 | .239 |
| 2005 | River City (FL) | IND | 4 | 2 | 1.27 | 18 | 0 | 0 | 5 | 21 | 18 | 5 | 3 | 0 | 4 | 27 | .228 |
| | Helena (Pio) | R | 2 | 0 | 3.52 | 6 | 0 | 0 | 2 | 8 | 8 | 3 | 3 | 1 | 1 | 10 | .258 |
| | Brevard County (FSL) | A | 0 | 0 | 0.00 | 7 | 0 | 0 | 2 | 9 | 6 | 0 | 0 | 0 | 0 | 14 | .188 |
| 2006 | West Virginia (SAL) | A | 1 | 3 | 2.43 | 26 | 0 | 0 | 10 | 30 | 28 | 13 | 8 | 2 | 6 | 42 | .243 |
| | Brevard County (FSL) | A | 3 | 1 | 0.29 | 16 | 0 | 0 | 2 | 31 | 12 | 6 | 1 | 1 | 9 | 32 | .119 |
| | Huntsville (SL) | AA | 1 | 0 | 1.69 | 4 | 0 | 0 | 0 | 5 | 2 | 2 | 1 | 0 | 2 | 6 | .111 |
| **MINOR LEAGUE TOTALS** | | | 7 | 4 | 1.42 | 59 | 0 | 0 | 16 | 82 | 56 | 24 | 13 | 4 | 18 | 104 | .189 |

## ROBERT HINTON

RHP

**Born:** Aug. 13, 1984. **B-T:** R-R. **Ht.:** 6-2. **Wt.:** 190. **Drafted:** Manatee (Fla.) CC, D/F 2003 (40th round). **Signed by:** Charles Aliano/Fernando Arango.

Hinton was the Brewers' most significant draft-and-follow from 2003 and signed the next spring for $90,000. His father Rich pitched for five big league clubs over six journeyman big league seasons. Tabbed as a reliever for much of his career, Robert ended 2006 in the high Class A rotation. He opened eyes throughout the season by improving his fastball command. Hinton throws two fastballs—a four-seamer anywhere from 89-93 mph and an 87-90 mph two-seamer with sink. His hard slider, which sits in the mid-80s, grades out as a plus pitch, and at times has sharp, late break. He pitches inside aggressively with his fastball and slider to lefthanders and actually handled them better than righties last season. He needs to learn to spot his fastball better to all quadrants of the zone and to work the outside corner better, away from righthanders' power. He continued to work on fastball command and a changeup during a stellar stint in Hawaii Winter Baseball. Hinton may have a middle reliever's profile, but he's good in that role and is poised to jump to Double-A.

| Year | Club (League) | Class | W | L | ERA | G | GS | CG | SV | IP | H | R | ER | HR | BB | SO | AVG |
|------|---------------|-------|---|---|-----|---|----|----|----|----|---|---|----|----|----|----|-----|
| 2004 | Helena (Pio) | R | 4 | 4 | 5.15 | 15 | 5 | 0 | 1 | 51 | 55 | 31 | 29 | 5 | 17 | 50 | .278 |
| 2005 | West Virginia (SAL) | A | 3 | 4 | 2.53 | 46 | 0 | 0 | 14 | 75 | 54 | 24 | 21 | 7 | 27 | 77 | .199 |
| 2006 | Brevard County (FSL) | A | 5 | 4 | 3.31 | 36 | 6 | 0 | 2 | 90 | 88 | 40 | 33 | 6 | 26 | 95 | .255 |
| **MINOR LEAGUE TOTALS** | | | 12 | 12 | 3.47 | 97 | 11 | 0 | 17 | 215 | 197 | 95 | 83 | 18 | 70 | 222 | .242 |

## R.J. SEIDEL

RHP

**Born:** Sept. 3, 1987. **B-T:** R-R. **Ht.:** 6-6. **Wt.:** 185. **Drafted:** HS—LaCrosse, Wis., 2006 (16th round). **Signed By:** Harvey Kuenn Jr.

Seidel, whose father Dick pitched in the Yankees system in the early 1980s, ranked as the top prospect in Wisconsin for much of the spring. But he had a strong commitment to Arkansas and when he turned down predraft offers from at least two clubs, he slid to the 16th round. The Brewers evaluated him a bit more during the summer in American Legion ball, then signed him in early August for $415,000—just $2,500 less than third-round pick Cole Gillespie received. Seidel threw his fastball at 85-90 mph most of the spring, but he's so athletic and projectable that some scouts believe his heater eventually will reach the mid-90s. His curveball should become at least an average pitch, and he already has shown some mastery of a changeup. A three-sport star as a quarterback and basketball forward in high school, Seidel will jump up this list if he responds well to focusing on baseball. The Brewers usually move high school pitchers slowly, and he should begin his pro career in extended spring training before heading to Helena or the Arizona League in June.

| Year | Club (League) | Class | W | L | ERA | G | GS CG SV | IP | H | R | ER | HR | BB | SO | AVG |
|------|---------------|-------|---|---|-----|---|----------|----|---|---|----|----|----|----|-----|
| 2006 | Did not play—Signed 2007 contract | | | | | | | | | | | | | | |

## 26 BRENDAN KATIN                                          OF

**Born:** Jan. 28, 1983. **B-T:** R-R. **Ht.:** 6-1. **Wt.:** 235. **Drafted:** Miami, 2005 (23rd round). **Signed by:** Larry Pardo.

A low-round draft pick as a college senior who played most of the year at high Class A, Katin has a strong physique that gives him his one major calling card: raw power. Playing in a stadium in which the wind constantly is in the face of hitters, he managed to finish last season with 34 doubles and 13 homers before a promotion to Double-A. Katin was a college teammate of 2005 first-round pick Ryan Braun and has similar power and mental toughness. He takes an aggressive cut and his swing gets a bit long at times, making him strikeout-prone and especially susceptible to offspeed pitchers. Roving hitting instructor Jim Skaalen worked with Katin at toning down that swing and putting the ball in play more often. At 24, he can't afford to sacrifice any power as he faces the upper levels and must gain better control of the strike zone while doing so. Katin has decent speed for his size and a strong arm that allows him to play right field. With raw power that is missing for the most part in the organization, Katin only needs to continue working on keeping his stroke shorter and swinging at strikes. The Brewers have been impressed with his makeup and aggressive approach to the game. He will return to Double-A to start 2007.

| Year | Club (League) | Class | AVG | G | AB | R | H | 2B | 3B | HR | RBI | BB | SO | SB | OBP | SLG |
|------|---------------|-------|-----|---|----|---|---|----|----|----|-----|----|----|----|-----|-----|
| 2005 | Helena (Pio) | R | .386 | 33 | 114 | 30 | 44 | 6 | 0 | 8 | 26 | 17 | 25 | 3 | .471 | .649 |
| | West Virginia (SAL) | A | .202 | 23 | 84 | 7 | 17 | 1 | 0 | 1 | 5 | 8 | 29 | 0 | .287 | .250 |
| 2006 | Brevard County (FSL) | A | .289 | 116 | 450 | 64 | 130 | 34 | 3 | 13 | 75 | 34 | 112 | 4 | .349 | .464 |
| | Huntsville (SL) | AA | .224 | 15 | 58 | 11 | 13 | 2 | 0 | 4 | 8 | 1 | 11 | 0 | .250 | .466 |
| **MINOR LEAGUE TOTALS** | | | .289 | 187 | 706 | 112 | 204 | 43 | 3 | 26 | 114 | 60 | 177 | 7 | .355 | .469 |

## 27 STEVE GARRISON                                         LHP

**Born:** Sept. 12, 1986. **B-T:** L-L. **Ht.:** 6-1. **Wt.:** 185. **Drafted:** HS—Ewing, N.J., 2005 (10th round). **Signed by:** Tony Blengino.

As might be expected from a player who went to the elite Hun School of Princeton in New Jersey, Garrison is a smart, poised, sharp pitcher with an effervescent personality. He slipped to the 10th round in 2005 due to signability questions, because of his commitment to North Carolina. Nevertheless, Garrison signed for $160,000, a bonus commensurate with the middle of the fifth round. Garrison works with a four-pitch repertoire consisting of an 87-89 mph fastball, slider, curveball and changeup, which each rate average to a tick below average presently. The key is, he throws strikes and has an idea of how to attack hitters when he's on the mound. As he matures and gets stronger, he projects to pick up some velocity on his fastball, which has touched 91 from time to time, and slider, his best secondary pitch. He's athletic and has good arm speed. After spending time in extended spring training last year, Garrison pitched the remainder of the season at low Class A. He has a clean, effortless delivery and is a strike thrower who works ahead in the count, and mixes his offerings effectively. Because he doesn't overpower hitters, when Garrison does make a mistake, he can be susceptible to the long ball. The Brewers love the intangibles he brings to the mound, especially at a young age. Already on the fast track, he'll compete for a spot in the high Class A rotation this spring.

| Year | Club (League) | Class | W | L | ERA | G | GS | CG | SV | IP | H | R | ER | HR | BB | SO | AVG |
|------|---------------|-------|---|---|-----|---|----|----|----|----|---|---|----|----|----|----|-----|
| 2005 | Brewers (AZL) | R | 2 | 2 | 2.86 | 11 | 4 | 0 | 2 | 35 | 39 | 13 | 11 | 0 | 5 | 28 | .300 |
| 2006 | West Virginia (SAL) | A | 7 | 6 | 3.45 | 17 | 16 | 0 | 0 | 89 | 86 | 38 | 34 | 10 | 22 | 77 | .253 |
| **MINOR LEAGUE TOTALS** | | | 9 | 8 | 3.28 | 28 | 20 | 0 | 2 | 123 | 125 | 51 | 45 | 10 | 27 | 105 | .266 |

## 28 STEPHEN CHAPMAN                                        OF

**Born:** Oct. 12, 1985 **B-T:** L-L. **Ht.:** 6-0. **Wt.:** 180. **Drafted:** HS—Marianna, Fla., 2004 (6th round). **Signed by:** Doug Reynolds.

Chapman, who was selected to the roster for the inaugural Aflac All-American game in 2003, has scuffled at the plate since opting to sign for $159,000 with the Brewers instead of going to Auburn. On surface, you wouldn't think a player competing at the Rookie-level for a third consecutive year would be considered among a strong organization's top prospects. But, it became evident early that Chapman wasn't going to get regular at-bats in a loaded West Virginia outfield, the Brewers sent him back to Helena for a second season. As might be expected from an experienced player with added confidence, Chapman fared well offensively, and he's a solid defender in center field with an average arm that's good enough for him to fill in in right. He has some pop in his bat—31 of his 84 hits at Helena went for extra

bases—and he has plus speed that makes him a threat on the bases. He is a well-rounded player with solid tools across the board. He often struggles with his timing at the plate, however, and gets frustrated, becoming his own worst enemy and striking out in bunches. Chapman remains a work in progress and could be another in a series of late bloomers in their system. The Brewers will find out more about Chapman in 2007 when he's West Virginia's everyday center fielder.

| Year | Club (League) | Class | AVG | G | AB | R | H | 2B | 3B | HR | RBI | BB | SO | SB | OBP | SLG |
|------|---------------|-------|------|-----|-----|-----|-----|----|----|----|-----|----|-----|----|------|------|
| 2004 | Brewers (AZL) | R | .229 | 49 | 192 | 33 | 44 | 7 | 7 | 4 | 18 | 17 | 50 | 4 | .290 | .401 |
| 2005 | Helena (Pio) | R | .269 | 54 | 167 | 25 | 45 | 9 | 1 | 6 | 25 | 20 | 38 | 10 | .352 | .443 |
| 2006 | West Virginia (SAL) | A | .176 | 6 | 17 | 3 | 3 | 0 | 0 | 0 | 0 | 1 | 6 | 0 | .222 | .176 |
| | Helena (Pio) | R | .308 | 70 | 276 | 50 | 85 | 18 | 8 | 6 | 40 | 29 | 63 | 20 | .387 | .496 |
| **MINOR LEAGUE TOTALS** | | | .271 | 179 | 652 | 111 | 177 | 34 | 16 | 16 | 83 | 67 | 157 | 34 | .346 | .446 |

## 29 VINNY ROTTINO                                                   3B/C/OF

**Born:** April 7, 1980. **B-T:** R-R. **Ht.:** 6-1. **Wt.:** 200. **Signed:** NDFA/Wisconsin-La Crosse, 2003. **Signed by:** Brian Johnson.

Just over three years ago, Rottino went undrafted despite an all-American D-III career at Wisconsin-LaCrosse and had enrolled at University of Wisconsin's pharmaceutical school while playing in the Land O' Lakes baseball league. He worked out for several teams, before signing with the Brewers. He earned the organization's minor league player of the year in 2004 and parlayed his.303 career minor league average into a major league call-up in September. Rottino's calling card is his bat, though he's more of a gap hitter than a home run threat, which may preclude him from being an everyday player. His versatility, however, virtually assures big league time and he enhances his value in that department last year by being a passable catcher. A former college shortstop, he has seen time at third base, first base and the corner outfield slots. Rottino showed improvement behind the plate, with a strong arm and physique for the position. He threw out eight of 25 basestealers (32 percent) in Triple-A last season but just one of 16 (6 percent) in the Arizona Fall League. His best position is probably third base, where he handles himself well. With a short, smooth stroke and the ability to put the ball in play, he should make a decent utility player at the top level.

| Year | Club (League) | Class | AVG | G | AB | R | H | 2B | 3B | HR | RBI | BB | SO | SB | OBP | SLG |
|------|---------------|-------|------|-----|------|-----|-----|----|----|----|-----|-----|-----|----|------|------|
| 2003 | Helena (Pio) | R | .311 | 64 | 222 | 42 | 69 | 10 | 0 | 1 | 20 | 28 | 25 | 5 | .404 | .369 |
| 2004 | Beloit (MWL) | A | .304 | 140 | 529 | 78 | 161 | 25 | 9 | 17 | 124 | 40 | 71 | 5 | .352 | .482 |
| 2005 | Huntsville (SL) | AA | .296 | 120 | 469 | 63 | 139 | 20 | 6 | 6 | 52 | 40 | 68 | 2 | .351 | .403 |
| | Nashville (PCL) | AAA | .345 | 9 | 29 | 4 | 10 | 1 | 0 | 1 | 2 | 3 | 6 | 0 | .406 | .483 |
| 2006 | Nashville (PCL) | AAA | .314 | 117 | 398 | 55 | 125 | 25 | 2 | 7 | 42 | 40 | 74 | 12 | .379 | .440 |
| | Milwaukee (NL) | MLB | .214 | 9 | 14 | 1 | 3 | 1 | 0 | 0 | 1 | 1 | 2 | 1 | .267 | .286 |
| **MINOR LEAGUE TOTALS** | | | .306 | 450 | 1647 | 242 | 504 | 81 | 17 | 32 | 240 | 151 | 244 | 24 | .367 | .434 |
| **MAJOR LEAGUE TOTALS** | | | .214 | 9 | 14 | 1 | 3 | 1 | 0 | 0 | 1 | 1 | 2 | 1 | .267 | .286 |

## 30 ROLANDO PASCUAL                                                         RHP

**Born:** Feb. 8, 1989. **B-T:** B-R. **Ht.:** 6-6. **Wt.:** 218. **Signed:** Dominican Republic, 2005. **Signed by:** Fernando Arango.

The Brewers graded Pascual out as a second-round talent when they signed him for $710,000 out of the Dominican Republic in 2005. They believed he was advanced enough, despite his youth and lack of game experience, to skip past the Rookie-level Dominican Summer League and start his pro career in the Arizona League. Pascual proved to be not ready for that challenge. He had trouble throwing strikes to put it modestly, racking up 20 wild pitches to trail only the epically wild Jason Neighborgall among short-season pitchers. Taking into account the combination of the culture shock and Pascual's inexperience, the Brewers tried not to be alarmed. They knew their new approach of signing young Latin players and bringing them directly to the States would have its pitfalls. With a great pitcher's body, Pascual throws his fastball at 88-93 mph but is still working on commanding his curveball. His changeup also remains a work in progress. With a strong work ethic and willingness to listen to coaches, Pascual should eventually figure things out and be the pitcher the Brewers expect him to be. It certainlyl wasn't the best way to start his career, but not a sign of ultimate doom either. He has a loose, live arm and plenty of projection in his tall, rangy frame. He has plenty of time to develop as well, and won't turn 21 until the 2010 season. A Rookie-ball repeat is on tap for Pascual.

| Year | Club (League) | Class | W | L | ERA | G | GS | CG | SV | IP | H | R | ER | HR | BB | SO | AVG |
|------|---------------|-------|---|---|------|----|----|----|----|----|----|----|----|----|----|----|------|
| 2006 | Brewers (AZL) | R | 3 | 7 | 9.94 | 14 | 7 | 0 | 0 | 42 | 44 | 51 | 46 | 1 | 37 | 22 | .277 |
| **MINOR LEAGUE TOTALS** | | | 3 | 7 | 9.94 | 14 | 7 | 0 | 0 | 42 | 44 | 51 | 46 | 1 | 37 | 22 | .277 |

# MINNESOTA
# TWINS

BY **JOHN MANUEL**

The names change. The results, for the last five years, hardly have.

The Twins won their fourth American League Central title in the last five seasons under manager Ron Gardenhire, streaking past the Tigers in September after trailing by a dozen games at the all-star break. While they were doomed by uncharacteristically sloppy play in the Division Series and swept by the Athletics, 2006 was a success.

Minnesota rallied after it jettisoned some of the mistakes dotting its Opening Day roster and turned to internal candidates to get the team going. Jason Bartlett and Nick Punto replaced Juan Castro and Tony Batista on the left side of the infield, and while neither hit for much power, they provided much more offense and better defense.

On the mound, the Twins found middle-relief help in Pat Neshek after trading malcontent J.C. Romero for infield prospect Alexi Casilla during the offseason. When they gave up on Kyle Lohse, they turned loose **Francisco Liriano**, who was among baseball's most dominant pitchers before being sidelined late in the season by a strained elbow. Liriano complemented ace Johan Santana, Baseball America's Major League Player of the Year.

Postseason Tommy John surgery will sideline Liriano in 2007, and even Minnesota's abundant pitching depth may be hard-pressed to replace his brilliance. General manager Terry Ryan and his trusted, experienced staff do have options such as Boof Bonser, 2006 phenom Matt Garza, fellow righties J.D. Durbin and Kevin Slowey and

Minnesota native Glen Perkins.

The Twins have more questions when it comes to finding capable everyday players.

Catcher Joe Mauer won the AL batting title, while first baseman Justin Morneau became the first Twin since 1987 to hit 30 homers in a season (along with Torii Hunter). Add in right fielder Michael Cuddyer, a 1997 first-round pick who finally established himself as a regular and drove in 109 runs, and the Twins have a young, vibrant core for their lineup.

Hunter's one-year contract extension buys Minnesota another season there, but center field and third base remain problem positions for the long-term. The Twins focused on position players in a draft notable for its pitchers. However, in prep outfielders Chris Parmelee (first round, the fifth time in six years the Twins spent their top pick on a high school hitter) and Joe Benson (second), they may have found two more impact bats.

By then, their new ballpark should be ready. Scheduled for completion in 2010, the stadium took years of political wrangling before billionaire owner Carl Pohlad and the state could agree on a plan. The park secures the club's future in the Twin Cities.

Despite the increase in projected revenues with the new stadium, the Twins still have to plan ahead and rebuild from within. Few organizations do it better.

## TOP 30 PROSPECTS

| | |
|---|---|
| 1. Matt Garza, rhp | 16. Jay Rainville, rhp |
| 2. Glen Perkins, lhp | 17. David Winfree, 3b |
| 3. Kevin Slowey, rhp | 18. Brian Duensing, lhp |
| 4. Chris Parmelee, of/1b | 19. Trevor Plouffe, ss/3b |
| 5. Anthony Swarzak, rhp | 20. Kyle Waldrop, rhp |
| 6. Pat Neshek, rhp | 21. Eduardo Morlan, rhp |
| 7. Alexi Casilla, ss/2b | 22. Jose Mijares, lhp |
| 8. Joe Benson, of | 23. Whit Robbins, 3b |
| 9. Paul Kelly, ss | 24. Tyler Robertson, lhp |
| 10. J.D. Durbin, rhp | 25. Erik Lis, 1b |
| 11. Oswaldo Sosa, rhp | 26. Brandon Roberts, of |
| 12. Matt Moses, 3b | 27. Yohan Pino, rhp |
| 13. Denard Span, of | 28. Alex Burnett, rhp |
| 14. Jeff Manship, rhp | 29. David Shinskie, rhp |
| 15. Alexander Smit, lhp | 30. Alex Romero, of |

# ORGANIZATION OVERVIEW

**General manager:** Terry Ryan. **Farm director:** Jim Rantz. **Scouting director:** Mike Radcliff.

## 2006 PERFORMANCE

| Class | Team | League | W | L | PCT | Finish* | Manager | Affiliated |
|---|---|---|---|---|---|---|---|---|
| Majors | Minnesota | American | 96 | 66 | .593 | 2nd (14) | Ron Gardenhire | — |
| Triple-A | Rochester Red Wings | International | 79 | 64 | .552 | 3rd (14) | Stan Cliburn | 2003 |
| Double-A | New Britain Rock Cats | Eastern | 64 | 78 | .451 | 11th (12) | Riccardo Ingram | 1995 |
| High A | Fort Myers Miracle | Florida State | 80 | 60 | .571 | 1st (12) | Kevin Boles | 1993 |
| Low A | Beloit Snappers | Midwest | 74 | 62 | .536 | 6th (14) | Jeff Smith | 2005 |
| Rookie | Elizabethton Twins | Appalachian | 42 | 26 | .618 | 1st (10) | Ray Smith | 1974 |
| Rookie | GCL Twins | Gulf Coast | 26 | 27 | .491 | 7th (12) | Nelson Prada | 1989 |
| **OVERALL 2006 MINOR LEAGUE RECORD** | | | 365 | 319 | .534 | 6th (30) | | |

*Finish in overall standings (No. of teams in league). +League champion

## ORGANIZATION LEADERS

### BATTING
| | | |
|---|---|---|
| AVG | Lis, Erik, Beloit | .326 |
| R | Span, Denard, New Britain | 92 |
| H | Span, Denard, New Britain | 170 |
| 2B | Lis, Erik, Beloit | 37 |
| 3B | Oeltjen, Trent, New Britain | 10 |
| | Pickrel, Jeremy, Fort Myers | 10 |
| HR | Jones, Garrett, Rochester | 24 |
| RBI | Jones, Garrett, Rochester | 105 |
| BB | Deeds, Doug, New Britain | 70 |
| SO | Jones, Garrett, Rochester | 132 |
| SB | Casilla, Alexi, Fort Myers/New Britain | 50 |
| OBP | Lis, Erik, Beloit | .402 |
| SLG | Lis, Erik, Beloit | .547 |
| XBH | Jones, Garrett, Rochester | 61 |

### PITCHING
| | | |
|---|---|---|
| W | Pino, Yohan, Beloit | 14 |
| | Garza, Matt, FM/NB/Rochester | 14 |
| L | Simonitsch, Errol, New Britain | 15 |
| ERA | Slowey, Kevin, Fort Myers/New Britain | 1.90 |
| G | Shinskie, David, Beloit/New Britain | 59 |
| SV | Hernandez, Danny, Elizabethton | 18 |
| IP | Sosa, Oswaldo, Beloit/Fort Myers | 163 |
| BB | Harben, Adam, New Britain | 67 |
| SO | Slowey, Kevin, Fort Myers/New Britain | 158 |
| AVG | Garza, Matt, FM/NB/Rochester | .179 |

## BEST TOOLS

| | |
|---|---|
| Best Hitter for Average | Chris Parmelee |
| Best Power Hitter | Garrett Jones |
| Best Strike-Zone Discipline | Alexi Casilla |
| Fastest Baserunner | Brandon Roberts |
| Best Athlete | Joe Benson |
| Best Fastball | Matt Garza |
| Best Curveball | Jeff Manship |
| Best Slider | Danny Hernandez |
| Best Changeup | Brian Duensing |
| Best Control | Kevin Slowey |
| Best Defensive Catcher | Allan de San Miguel |
| Best Defensive Infielder | Alexi Casilla |
| Best Infield Arm | Paul Kelly |
| Best Defensive Outfielder | Denard Span |
| Best Outfield Arm | Eli Tintor |

## PROJECTED 2010 LINEUP

| | |
|---|---|
| Catcher | Joe Mauer |
| First Base | Justin Morneau |
| Second Base | Alexi Casilla |
| Third Base | Matt Moses |
| Shortstop | Jason Bartlett |
| Left Field | Chris Parmelee |
| Center Field | Torii Hunter |
| Right Field | Michael Cuddyer |
| Designated Hitter | Jason Kubel |
| No. 1 Starter | Johan Santana |
| No. 2 Starter | Francisco Liriano |
| No. 3 Starter | Matt Garza |
| No. 4 Starter | Glen Perkins |
| No. 5 Starter | Kevin Slowey |
| Closer | Joe Nathan |

## LAST YEAR'S TOP 20 PROSPECTS

1. Francisco Liriano, lhp
2. Jason Kubel, of
3. Matt Moses, 3b
4. Glen Perkins, lhp
5. Anthony Swarzak, rhp
6. Denard Span, of
7. Matt Garza, rhp
8. Jay Rainville, rhp
9. Trevor Plouffe, ss
10. Kyle Waldrop, rhp
11. Paul Kelly, ss
12. Adam Harben, rhp
13. Kevin Slowey, rhp
14. J.D. Durbin, rhp
15. Eduardo Morlan, rhp
16. Jose Mijares, lhp
17. David Winfree, 3b
18. Juan Portes, 2b/of
19. Drew Thompson, 2b/ss
20. Henry Sanchez, 1b

## TOP PROSPECTS OF THE DECADE

| Year | Player, Pos. | 2006 Org. |
|---|---|---|
| 1997 | Todd Walker, 2b | Padres |
| 1998 | Luis Rivas, ss | Devil Rays |
| 1999 | Michael Cuddyer, 3b | Twins |
| 2000 | Michael Cuddyer, 3b | Twins |
| 2001 | Adam Johnson, rhp | Athletics |
| 2002 | Joe Mauer, c | Twins |
| 2003 | Joe Mauer, c | Twins |
| 2004 | Joe Mauer, c | Twins |
| 2005 | Joe Mauer, c | Twins |
| 2006 | Francisco Liriano, lhp | Twins |

## TOP DRAFT PICKS OF THE DECADE

| Year | Player, Pos. | 2006 Org. |
|---|---|---|
| 1997 | Michael Cuddyer, ss | Twins |
| 1998 | Ryan Mills, lhp | Out of baseball |
| 1999 | B.J. Garbe, of | Marlins |
| 2000 | Adam Johnson, rhp | Athletics |
| 2001 | Joe Mauer, c | Twins |
| 2002 | Denard Span, of | Twins |
| 2003 | Matt Moses, 3b | Twins |
| 2004 | Trevor Plouffe, ss | Twins |
| 2005 | Matt Garza, rhp | Twins |
| 2006 | Chris Parmelee, of/1b | Twins |

## ALL-TIME LARGEST BONUSES

| | |
|---|---|
| Joe Mauer, 2001 | $5,150,000 |
| B.J. Garbe, 1999 | $2,750,000 |
| Adam Johnson, 2000 | $2,500,000 |
| Ryan Mills, 1998 | $2,000,000 |
| Michael Cuddyer, 1997 | $1,850,000 |

# MINOR LEAGUE DEPTH CHART

## Minnesota Twins

**Impact: C.** Give Matt Garza one more big league out, and the Twins don't have an obvious No. 1. No one has produced more impact bats of late in the Joe Mauer-Justin Morneau tandem, though.

**Depth: A.** Aside from catcher—due to Mauer's presence—and power bats, the Twins have a little bit of everything.

**Sleeper:** Nick Papasan, 2b. A smallish frame drove him down the draft, but Papasan was one of the better pure hitters available in 2006.

*Numbers in parentheses indicate prospect rankings.*

| LF | CF | RF |
|---|---|---|
| Alex Romero (30) | Joe Benson (8) | Chris Parmelee (4) |
| Garrett Guzman | Denard Span (13) | Trent Oeltjen |
| | Brandon Roberts (26) | Eli Tintor |
| | Danny Santiesteban | |
| | Edward Ovalle | |

| 3B | SS | 2B | 1B |
|---|---|---|---|
| Matt Moses (12) | Paul Kelly (9) | Alexi Casilla (7) | Erik Lis (25) |
| David Winfree (17) | Trevor Plouffe (19) | Drew Thompson | Hank Sanchez |
| Whit Robbins (23) | Steve Singleton | Nick Papasan | Garrett Jones |
| Danny Valencia | | Matt Tolbert | Doug Deeds |
| Garrett Olson | | Brian Dinkelman | Brock Peterson |
| Deibinson Romero | | Steven Tolleson | Jonathan Waltenbury |
| | | Juan Portes | |

| C |
|---|
| Allan de San Miguel |
| Wilson Ramos |
| Jeff Christy |

| RHP | | LHP | |
|---|---|---|---|
| **Starters** | **Relievers** | **Starters** | **Relievers** |
| Matt Garza (1) | Pat Neshek (6) | Glen Perkins (2) | Jose Mijares (22) |
| Kevin Slowey (3) | Eduardo Morlan (21) | Alexander Smit (15) | Ricky Barrett |
| Anthony Swarzak (5) | Alex Burnett (28) | Brian Duensing (18) | Jay Sawatski |
| J.D. Durbin (10) | David Shinskie (29) | Tyler Robertson (24) | |
| Oswaldo Sosa (11) | Zach Ward | Kyle Aselton | |
| Jeff Manship (14) | Tim Lahey | Errol Simonitsch | |
| Jay Rainville (16) | Danny Hernandez | Kyle Edlich | |
| Kyle Waldrop (20) | Danny Powers | Ryan Mullins | |
| Yohan Pino (27) | | | |
| Brian Kirwan | | | |
| Matt Fox | | | |
| Adam Hawes | | | |
| Ludovicus Van Mil | | | |

# DRAFT ANALYSIS

## 2006

SIGNING BUDGET: $3.2 million

**Best Pro Debut:** Most of the Twins' position-player signees performed well, starting with OF/1B Chris Parmelee (1). He batted .279/.369/.532 with eight homers in the Gulf Coast League, then held his own as an 18-year-old in low Class A. 3B Whit Robbins (4) headed straight to low Class A and hit .304/.421/.482. 3B Danny Valencia (19) was an Appalachian League all-star after batting .311/.365/.505 with eight homers.

**Best Athlete:** OF Joe Benson (2) could have played college football after rushing for 2,183 yards as a senior, including a 363-yard performance in the second round of the Illinois 6-A playoffs. He's a legitimate five-tool player with outstanding makeup. LHP Tyler Robertson (3) also had college-football potential as a quarterback.

**Best Pure Hitter:** Parmelee was one of the more advanced high school hitters in the draft. If Benson can tone down his aggressive approach, he has similar potential. SS Nick Papasan (24) also is a gifted hitter whose 5-foot-11 frame belies his strong hands and surprising pop.

**Best Raw Power:** Though they scouted Parmelee extensively before the draft, he surprised the Twins with the pop he showed during the summer. Hi

**Fastest Runner:** Benson can get from the right side of home plate to first base in 4.1 seconds, and he could get a step quicker after he loses his football stiffness. OF Mark Dolenc (15) is an above-average runner.

**Best Defensive Player:** C Jeff Christy's (6) work behind the plate earned him a late-season fill-in promotion to Double-A.

**Best Fastball:** Robertson is a 6-foot-5, 225-pound southpaw who already throws 90-91 mph and can reach 94. And his fastball ranks as his No. 2 pitch, behind his curveball.

**Best Breaking Ball:** Robertson's curveball is good, but RHP Jeff Manship's (14) is better. He's fully recovered from Tommy John surgery in 2004 and also has a solid-average fastball.

**Most Intriguing Backgroud:** OF Jared Mitchell (10) is an even more accomplished football player than Benson and Robertson, and he turned down the Twins to play wide receiver at Louisiana State. SS Derek McCallum (50) was a hockey defenseman who played with the U.S. national team. C Braxton Chisholm (29) decided to pursue a career in firefighting rather than baseball.

Robertson's father Jay is a former Indians scouting director who now scouts for the Rangers. Manship's brother Matt signed with the Athletics as a 29th-round pick. 2B Brian Dinkelman (8) was the NAIA player of the year after hitting .462 with 17 homers. He broke Randy Velarde's NAIA records for career hits (373) and assists (679) while also setting new standards for runs (303), doubles (96) and total bases (670).

**Closest to the Majors:** Manship, who would have been a third- or fourth-round pick if not for signability questions stemming from his sophomore-eligible status. He pitched well in a brief stint in high Class A.

**Best Late-Round Pick:** Manship and Papasan.

**The One Who Got Away:** The Twins would have considered Mitchell with their first-round pick if Parmelee hadn't been available. Though they offered Mitchell a significant bonus and he wanted to play baseball, the two sides couldn't reach a deal.

**Assessment:** After stocking up on pitching in recent drafts, the Twins bolstered their stock of hitters with Parmelee and Benson. Adding Mitchell would have been a coup.

## 2005      BUDGET: $5.2 million

Not even the Twins realized how talented RHP Matt Garza (1) was. RHP Kevin Slowey (2) could join him in the majors in the near future, and SS Paul Kelly (2) is off to a good start. 1B Henry Sanchez (1) hasn't gotten his big bat going yet, however.   **GRADE: B+**

## 2004      BUDGET: $7.5 million

A class that includes five first-rounders lost some of its luster last year but still offers depth. LHP Glen Perkins (1) has reached the majors, while SS Trevor Plouffe (1) and RHPs Kyle Waldrop (1) Anthony Swarzak (2) and Eduardo Morlan (3) could do the same. RHPs Matt Fox (1) and Jay Rainville (1) have had injury problems.   **GRADE: C+**

## 2003      BUDGET: $3.2 million

3B Matt Moses (1) and RHP Scott Baker (2) have leveled off significantly, so this grade drops from a B+ a year ago.   **GRADE: C**

*Draft analysis by Jim Callis. Numbers in parentheses indicate draft rounds. Budgets are bonuses in first 10 rounds.*

# MATT
# GARZA

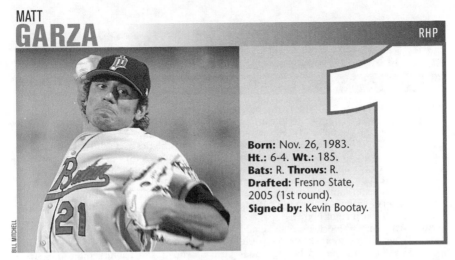

BILL MITCHELL

**Born:** Nov. 26, 1983.
**Ht.:** 6-4. **Wt.:** 185.
**Bats:** R. **Throws:** R.
**Drafted:** Fresno State,
2005 (1st round).
**Signed by:** Kevin Bootay.

Garza's rise has been even more meteoric than it looks. While he was a prospect in high school at Fresno's Washington Union High, where he also played quarterback, he didn't seriously consider signing when the Rockies drafted him in the 40th round in 2002. His son Matt Jr., born the day of the draft, was a big reason he went to college, and Matt and his girlfriend Serina Ortiz now have a daughter Sierra as well. Garza stayed home to attend Fresno State, a once-proud program in rebuilding mode. He was a part-time starter for his first two seasons, posting a 9.55 ERA as a freshman, before anchoring the Bulldogs rotation as a junior. He went 6-5, 3.07 and ranked second in the Western Athletic Conference with 120 strikeouts in 108 innings. The Twins took Garza 25th overall in 2005 and signed him for $1.35 million, and he paid immediate dividends. He finished his debut by excelling at low Class A Beloit. He was just getting warmed up for 2006, when he was the most dominant pitcher in the minors. Starting the year at high Class A Fort Myers and continuing to deal at Double-A New Britain and Triple-A Rochester, Garza was leading the minors in strikeouts when he was promoted to the big leagues in early August. He pitched 186 innings overall between the majors and minors and tired late, when the Twins left him off their postseason roster in favor of fellow rookie Glen Perkins.

Garza has evolved from a two-pitch power arm as a college freshman to a guy with a quality four-pitch repertoire. Yet he's still all about the fastball. While his heater usually sits at 90-94 mph, Garza showed the ability to dial it up to 97-98 at times in 2006, including late in games. It's his out pitch and has enough life that he trusts it in any count. He refined his delivery slightly, and his improved fastball command was another reason he dominated minor leaguers. Garza also throws a curveball, slider and changeup. Both the curve and the slider are above-average pitches at times, and he throws both with power, particularly his low-80s slider. His changeup grades out as solid-average and he spots it well against left-handers, who hit just two home runs against him all year. He has a smooth delivery that he repeats well, along with plenty of mound presence.

With his slender build, Garza appeared to wear down while facing his first full pro season and facing big league hitters. When he tired, his command suffered. Righthanders teed off on his fastball when he nibbled in the majors, tagging him for a 1.014 OPS, but Garza just needs to trust his stuff more and maintain his strength. His curveball and slider can get more consistent.

No one expected Garza to be this good this fast, not even the Twins. While his late-season fade means he probably has to earn a spot in the 2007 rotation, Francisco Liriano's injury and Brad Radke's retirement make Garza's inclusion a near certainty. Garza's ceiling is all that's in question, and calling him a No. 2 starter behind Johan Santana almost seems conservative.

| Year | Club (League) | Class | W | L | ERA | G | GS | CG | SV | IP | H | R | ER | HR | BB | SO | AVG |
|------|---------------|-------|---|---|-----|---|----|----|----|----|---|---|----|----|----|----|-----|
| 2005 | Elizabethton (Appy) | R | 1 | 1 | 3.66 | 4 | 4 | 0 | 0 | 20 | 14 | 10 | 8 | 3 | 6 | 25 | .200 |
| | Beloit (MWL) | A | 3 | 3 | 3.54 | 10 | 10 | 0 | 0 | 56 | 53 | 24 | 22 | 5 | 15 | 64 | .251 |
| 2006 | Fort Myers (FSL) | A | 5 | 1 | 1.42 | 8 | 8 | 0 | 0 | 44 | 27 | 13 | 7 | 3 | 11 | 53 | .169 |
| | New Britain (EL) | AA | 6 | 2 | 2.51 | 10 | 10 | 0 | 0 | 57 | 40 | 22 | 16 | 2 | 14 | 68 | .190 |
| | Rochester (IL) | AAA | 3 | 1 | 1.85 | 5 | 5 | 2 | 0 | 34 | 20 | 7 | 7 | 1 | 7 | 33 | .174 |
| | Minnesota (AL) | MLB | 3 | 6 | 5.76 | 10 | 9 | 0 | 0 | 50 | 62 | 33 | 32 | 6 | 23 | 38 | .301 |
| **MINOR LEAGUE TOTALS** | | | 18 | 8 | 2.56 | 37 | 37 | 2 | 0 | 211 | 154 | 76 | 60 | 14 | 53 | 243 | .201 |
| **MAJOR LEAGUE TOTALS** | | | 3 | 6 | 5.76 | 10 | 9 | 0 | 0 | 50 | 62 | 33 | 32 | 6 | 23 | 38 | .301 |

## ☑ **GLEN PERKINS** LHP

**Born:** March 2, 1983. **B-T:** L-L. **Ht.:** 5-11. **Wt.:** 200. **Drafted:** Minnesota, 2004 (1st round). **Signed by:** Mark Wilson.

A Minnesota native, Perkins starred for the hometown Golden Gophers for two years before the Twins took him 22nd overall in 2004. He finished the 2006 season with a September callup, pitching so well out of the bullpen that he beat out Matt Garza for a spot on the playoff roster. Perkins has above-average stuff and throws strikes. His fastball took a small jump in 2006, regularly sitting at 92-93 mph and touching 95. It has been his strikeout pitch for much of his career. His curveball is a put-away pitch, and he can add and subtract velocity from it. He long has shown a good feel for a solid-average changeup. While Perkins has matured, he still sometimes lets mistakes in the field get to him. He was more focused the higher up the ladder he pitched. Staying in top shape has been difficult for him, but he generally has succeeded. With Francisco Liriano shelved, Perkins is at the front of the line along with Garza to earn a spot in the big league rotation. At the least, the Twins believe Perkins can help them immediately as a reliever.

| Year | Club (League) | Class | W | L | ERA | G | GS | CG | SV | IP | H | R | ER | HR | BB | SO | AVG |
|------|---------------|-------|---|---|-----|---|----|----|----|----|---|---|----|----|----|----|-----|
| 2004 | Elizabethton (Appy) | R | 1 | 0 | 2.25 | 3 | 3 | 0 | 0 | 12 | 8 | 3 | 3 | 0 | 4 | 22 | .186 |
|  | Quad City (MWL) | A | 2 | 1 | 1.30 | 9 | 9 | 0 | 0 | 48 | 33 | 9 | 7 | 2 | 12 | 49 | .205 |
| 2005 | Fort Myers (FSL) | A | 3 | 2 | 2.13 | 10 | 9 | 2 | 0 | 55 | 41 | 14 | 13 | 2 | 13 | 66 | .205 |
|  | New Britain (EL) | AA | 4 | 4 | 4.90 | 14 | 14 | 0 | 0 | 79 | 80 | 45 | 43 | 4 | 35 | 67 | .263 |
| 2006 | New Britain (EL) | AA | 4 | 11 | 3.91 | 23 | 23 | 2 | 0 | 117 | 109 | 60 | 51 | 11 | 45 | 131 | .243 |
|  | Rochester (IL) | AAA | 0 | 1 | 2.08 | 1 | 1 | 0 | 0 | 4 | 6 | 1 | 1 | 0 | 5 | 3 | .333 |
|  | Minnesota (AL) | MLB | 0 | 0 | 1.59 | 4 | 0 | 0 | 0 | 6 | 3 | 1 | 1 | 0 | 0 | 6 | .150 |
| **MINOR LEAGUE TOTALS** | | | 14 | 19 | 3.36 | 60 | 59 | 4 | 0 | 316 | 277 | 132 | 118 | 19 | 114 | 338 | .236 |
| **MAJOR LEAGUE TOTALS** | | | 0 | 0 | 1.59 | 4 | 0 | 0 | 0 | 5 | 3 | 1 | 1 | 0 | 0 | 6 | .150 |

## ☑ **KEVIN SLOWEY** RHP

**Born:** May 4, 1984. **B-T:** R-R. **Ht.:** 6-3. **Wt.:** 190. **Drafted:** Winthrop, 2005 (2nd round). **Signed by:** Ricky Taylor.

Slowey finished 2006 with two pressure-packed starts: one in Cuba in the finale of the Americas Olympic qualifier against the host nation, the other with Triple-A Rochester in the International League playoffs. His bullpen blew a lead for him in the former—though Team USA rallied for the victory—and he won the latter. Slowey resembles Brad Radke for his fastball command, which some scouts rate an 8 on their 2-8 scale. He puts his 88-92 mph fastball wherever he wants, usually with good life. His delivery is so easy that it creates deception. In the high Class A Florida State League all-star game, Slowey threw nine straight fastballs to strike out the side, and only one drew a swing. His moxie makes his tools play up. He throws 90 percent fastballs with average velocity, and it's hard to see Slowey succeeding in the majors with that approach. He saw the benefits of pitching backward—throwing secondary pitches in fastball counts, and vice-versa—against Cuba, when he gave up only one run in five innings. His changeup is ahead of his slurvy breaking ball at this point, but both need more work. Slowey could use some Triple-A time, but he's also so polished, it would be no surprise if he won a roster spot in spring training. If he learns to use his secondary pitches effectively, his command could make him a frontline starter.

| Year | Club (League) | Class | W | L | ERA | G | GS | CG | SV | IP | H | R | ER | HR | BB | SO | AVG |
|------|---------------|-------|---|---|-----|---|----|----|----|----|---|---|----|----|----|----|-----|
| 2005 | Elizabethton (Appy) | R | 0 | 0 | 1.17 | 4 | 0 | 0 | 1 | 8 | 2 | 1 | 1 | 0 | 1 | 15 | .080 |
|  | Beloit (MWL) | A | 3 | 2 | 2.24 | 13 | 9 | 1 | 0 | 64 | 42 | 18 | 16 | 4 | 8 | 69 | .183 |
| 2006 | Fort Myers (FSL) | A | 4 | 2 | 1.01 | 14 | 14 | 0 | 0 | 89 | 52 | 19 | 10 | 2 | 9 | 99 | .164 |
|  | New Britain (EL) | AA | 4 | 3 | 3.19 | 9 | 9 | 1 | 0 | 59 | 50 | 23 | 21 | 6 | 13 | 52 | .223 |
| **MINOR LEAGUE TOTALS** | | | 11 | 7 | 1.96 | 40 | 32 | 2 | 1 | 221 | 146 | 61 | 48 | 13 | 30 | 235 | .183 |

## ☑ **CHRIS PARMELEE** OF/1B

**Born:** Feb. 24, 1988. **B-T:** L-L. **Ht.:** 6-1. **Wt.:** 200. **Drafted:** HS—Chino Hills, Calif., 2006 (1st round). **Signed by:** John Leavitt.

Parmelee cemented his place in the first round of the 2006 draft by adding game power to his patient, polished package. He hit 11 homers as a high school senior, then went deep in his first pro appearance after signing for $1.5 million as the 20th overall pick. He finished the season by holding his own in the low Class A Midwest League. With plate discipline, leverage and a short, repeatable stroke, Parmelee is the total package as a power hitter. He actually has shown the Twins more raw power than they

thought he had as an amateur, and he seems to swing better with wood than he did with metal. He has an above-average arm that fits in right field. A below-average runner, Parmelee will get bigger and slower as he gets older. His instincts, jumps and routes will have to compensate if he's to stay in the outfield. He's a solid defender at first base if he has to move there. Parmelee has the advanced bat to move quickly. He's similar to what the Twins thought they had in Jason Kubel before Kubel's knee injury, but with better power. Parmelee will start 2007 back in low Class A, but it would be an upset for him to spend the whole season there.

| Year | Club (League) | Class | AVG | G | AB | R | H | 2B | 3B | HR | RBI | BB | SO | SB | OBP | SLG |
|---|---|---|---|---|---|---|---|---|---|---|---|---|---|---|---|---|
| 2006 | Twins (GCL) | R | .279 | 45 | 154 | 29 | 43 | 7 | 4 | 8 | 32 | 23 | 47 | 3 | .369 | .532 |
|  | Beloit (MWL) | A | .227 | 11 | 22 | 2 | 5 | 1 | 0 | 0 | 2 | 5 | 9 | 0 | .370 | .273 |
| MINOR LEAGUE TOTALS |  |  | .273 | 56 | 176 | 31 | 48 | 8 | 4 | 8 | 34 | 28 | 56 | 3 | .369 | .500 |

## ⑤ ANTHONY SWARZAK
RHP

**Born:** Sept. 10, 1985. **B-T:** R-R. **Ht.:** 6-3. **Wt.:** 195. **Drafted:** HS—Fort Lauderdale, Fla., 2004 (2nd round). **Signed by:** Brad Weitzel.

He began 2006 in the same rotation as Matt Garza and Kevin Slowey, but Garza couldn't keep pace with his older teammates. Instead, he served as the rock of the Fort Myers rotation, making every start and leading the Florida State League in strikeouts. Swarzak has an ideal pitcher's body and has shown three solid-average to plus pitches at times. His fastball touched 94-95 mph in 2006, and his curveball is major league average already. It could be a plus pitch as he improves his consistency and command of it. Swarzak also shows a feel for his changeup and savvy beyond his years. Fastball velocity and command were issues for Swarzak, especially in the first half of the season. He pitched at 89-90 mph much of the year and had to learn to succeed without his best stuff. He'll need to pitch down in the zone more consistently without the FSL's big ballparks and heavy air to help him. Swarzak moves to Double-A, where he'll pitch the entire season at age 21. If his velocity bounces back to 2005 levels, he could speed up his accelerated timetable.

| Year | Club (League) | Class | W | L | ERA | G | GS | CG | SV | IP | H | R | ER | HR | BB | SO | AVG |
|---|---|---|---|---|---|---|---|---|---|---|---|---|---|---|---|---|---|
| 2004 | Twins (GCL) | R | 5 | 3 | 2.63 | 11 | 9 | 0 | 1 | 48 | 46 | 20 | 14 | 1 | 6 | 42 | .251 |
| 2005 | Beloit (MWL) | A | 9 | 5 | 4.04 | 18 | 18 | 0 | 0 | 91 | 81 | 48 | 41 | 7 | 32 | 101 | .238 |
|  | Fort Myers (FSL) | A | 3 | 4 | 3.66 | 10 | 10 | 0 | 0 | 59 | 72 | 25 | 24 | 3 | 11 | 55 | .300 |
| 2006 | Fort Myers (FSL) | A | 11 | 7 | 3.27 | 27 | 27 | 2 | 0 | 146 | 131 | 56 | 53 | 8 | 60 | 131 | .242 |
| MINOR LEAGUE TOTALS |  |  | 28 | 19 | 3.45 | 66 | 64 | 2 | 1 | 344 | 330 | 149 | 132 | 19 | 109 | 329 | .253 |

## ⑥ PAT NESHEK
RHP

**Born:** Sept. 4, 1980. **B-T:** B-R. **Ht.:** 6-3. **Wt.:** 205. **Drafted:** Butler, 2002 (6th round). **Signed by:** Billy Milos.

Neshek was voted top pitcher of the first Perfect Game World Wood Bat Association showcase back in 1998, and he had a stellar career at Butler, where he set records for strikeouts in a game (18), season (118) and career (280). He's an avid autograph collector, fully in evidence at his Website, patneshek.com. Neshek earned his way to the majors, posting a career 2.17 ERA over five minor league seasons. He has pinpoint command despite a unconventional sidearm delivery that creates tremendous deception. He annihilates righthanders (.140 average, 37 strikeouts in 86 big league at-bats) with his 86-91 mph sinking fastball and slurvy breaking ball. Lefthanders usually feast on sidearmers, and Neshek is susceptible as well. He gave up four home runs in 45 at-bats to major league lefties, who slugged .511 against him. He needs to focus on movement and command and use his changeup more to combat them. When he tries to overpower hitters, his stuff flattens out. Neshek is what he is. He already has demonstrated he can be an effective middle reliever, but that's also probably his ceiling.

| Year | Club (League) | Class | W | L | ERA | G | GS | CG | SV | IP | H | R | ER | HR | BB | SO | AVG |
|---|---|---|---|---|---|---|---|---|---|---|---|---|---|---|---|---|---|
| 2002 | Elizabethton (Appy) | R | 0 | 2 | 0.99 | 23 | 0 | 0 | 15 | 27 | 13 | 6 | 3 | 0 | 6 | 41 | .141 |
| 2003 | Quad City (MWL) | A | 3 | 2 | 0.52 | 28 | 0 | 0 | 14 | 34 | 20 | 3 | 2 | 0 | 11 | 53 | .165 |
|  | Fort Myers (FSL) | A | 4 | 1 | 2.15 | 20 | 0 | 0 | 2 | 29 | 22 | 8 | 7 | 2 | 6 | 29 | .202 |
|  | New Britain (EL) | AA | 1 | 1 | 5.87 | 5 | 1 | 0 | 1 | 8 | 7 | 5 | 5 | 2 | 3 | 5 | .233 |
| 2004 | New Britain (EL) | AA | 2 | 1 | 3.82 | 26 | 0 | 0 | 2 | 35 | 34 | 15 | 15 | 2 | 18 | 38 | .246 |
|  | Fort Myers (FSL) | A | 0 | 1 | 2.95 | 16 | 0 | 0 | 10 | 18 | 16 | 7 | 6 | 2 | 2 | 19 | .225 |
| 2005 | New Britain (EL) | AA | 6 | 4 | 2.19 | 55 | 0 | 0 | 24 | 82 | 69 | 25 | 20 | 9 | 21 | 95 | .225 |
| 2006 | Rochester (IL) | AAA | 6 | 2 | 1.95 | 33 | 0 | 0 | 14 | 60 | 41 | 13 | 13 | 7 | 14 | 87 | .189 |
|  | Minnesota (AL) | MLB | 4 | 2 | 2.19 | 32 | 0 | 0 | 0 | 37 | 23 | 9 | 9 | 6 | 6 | 53 | .176 |
| MINOR LEAGUE TOTALS |  |  | 22 | 14 | 2.17 | 206 | 1 | 0 | 82 | 295 | 222 | 82 | 71 | 24 | 81 | 367 | .205 |
| MAJOR LEAGUE TOTALS |  |  | 4 | 2 | 2.19 | 32 | 0 | 0 | 0 | 37 | 23 | 9 | 9 | 6 | 6 | 53 | .176 |

## 7 ALEXI CASILLA

SS/2B

**Born:** July 20, 1984. **B-T:** B-R. **Ht.:** 5-9. **Wt.:** 160. **Signed:** Dominican Republic, 2003. **Signed by:** Leo Perez (Angels).

The Twins were eager to get rid of J.C. Romero in a December 2005 trade with the Angels, and they were equally happy to get Casilla, whom they believed could be a solid utility player or second baseman. After making a poor first impression by failing to make the Double-A team out of spring training, he wowed the organization with a strong season, leading the system in stolen bases. Casilla is a top-of-the-lineup igniter who showed defensive ability at shortstop and second base. He's a well-above-average runner. His quick hands work well at the plate, where he's a spray hitter who makes excellent contact, and in the field. He also has more than enough arm for shortstop and turns the double play well at second. Slight and not exceptionally strong, Casilla has an utter lack of power that limits his ceiling. It will be hard for him to be an impact hitter if he doesn't draw more walks, get on base and steal a lot of bases. Big league second baseman Luis Castillo becomes a free agent after the 2007 season, and Casilla is poised to take over for him after spending a year in Triple-A. He may have played his way into the future shortstop discussion as well.

| Year | Club (League) | Class | AVG | G | AB | R | H | 2B | 3B | HR | RBI | BB | SO | SB | OBP | SLG |
|------|---------------|-------|-----|---|----|---|---|----|----|----|-----|----|----|----|-----|-----|
| 2003 | Anaheim (DSL) | R | .298 | 33 | 124 | 21 | 37 | 3 | 2 | 0 | 15 | 16 | 14 | 28 | .396 | .355 |
| 2004 | Cedar Rapids (MWL) | A | .310 | 9 | 29 | 6 | 9 | 2 | 1 | 0 | 1 | 5 | 4 | 1 | .412 | .448 |
| | AZL Angels (AZL) | R | .258 | 45 | 163 | 29 | 42 | 1 | 4 | 0 | 10 | 15 | 10 | 24 | .332 | .313 |
| | Provo (PIO) | R | .333 | 4 | 12 | 4 | 4 | 1 | 1 | 0 | 1 | 4 | 0 | 1 | .529 | .583 |
| 2005 | Arkansas (TEX) | AA | .211 | 7 | 19 | 4 | 4 | 0 | 0 | 0 | 4 | 2 | 3 | 1 | .286 | .211 |
| | Salt Lake (PCL) | AAA | .256 | 13 | 39 | 3 | 10 | 0 | 0 | 0 | 1 | 3 | 6 | 1 | .310 | .256 |
| | Cedar Rapids (MWL) | A | .325 | 78 | 308 | 62 | 100 | 11 | 3 | 3 | 17 | 29 | 31 | 47 | .392 | .409 |
| 2006 | Fort Myers (FSL) | A | .331 | 78 | 323 | 56 | 107 | 12 | 6 | 0 | 33 | 30 | 36 | 31 | .390 | .406 |
| | New Britain (EL) | AA | .294 | 45 | 170 | 28 | 50 | 10 | 1 | 1 | 13 | 18 | 20 | 19 | .375 | .382 |
| | Minnesota (AL) | MLB | .250 | 9 | 4 | 1 | 1 | 0 | 0 | 0 | 0 | 2 | 1 | 0 | .500 | .250 |
| **MINOR LEAGUE TOTALS** | | | .306 | 312 | 1187 | 213 | 363 | 40 | 18 | 4 | 95 | 122 | 124 | 153 | .379 | .380 |
| **MAJOR LEAGUE TOTALS** | | | .250 | 9 | 4 | 1 | 1 | 0 | 0 | 0 | 0 | 2 | 1 | 0 | .500 | .250 |

## 8 JOE BENSON

OF

**Born:** March 5, 1988. **B-T:** R-R. **Ht.:** 6-1. **Wt.:** 205. **Drafted:** HS—Joliet, Ill., 2006 (2nd round). **Signed by:** Billy Milos.

A high school catcher who also played some outfield, Benson is one of the organization's top athletes. He rushed for 2,183 yards as a senior and could have played college football if he hadn't signed for $575,000 as a second-round pick in June. He joined Chris Parmelee in jumping to low Class A late in the year, though he was gassed by season's end. Benson has first-round tools across the board and has the best power/speed combination of any Twins farmhand. He has above-average raw power and speed (4.1 seconds to first base from the right side), and with more experience he could be a center fielder. His average arm should play in either center or left field. Players with a football mentality like Benson's have to learn to grind their way through a baseball season, rather than going all-out all the time. His ability to make adjustments at the plate will determine whether his raw power becomes usable power. He's far less polished than Parmelee, but he also has a higher ceiling. Benson probably will need to rise one step at a time through the minor leagues, which means he'll return to low Class A in 2007.

| Year | Club (League) | Class | AVG | G | AB | R | H | 2B | 3B | HR | RBI | BB | SO | SB | OBP | SLG |
|------|---------------|-------|-----|---|----|---|---|----|----|----|-----|----|----|----|-----|-----|
| 2006 | Twins (GCL) | R | .260 | 52 | 196 | 30 | 51 | 11 | 5 | 5 | 28 | 21 | 41 | 9 | .335 | .444 |
| | Beloit (MWL) | A | .263 | 8 | 19 | 2 | 5 | 0 | 0 | 0 | 1 | 0 | 6 | 1 | .263 | .263 |
| **MINOR LEAGUE TOTALS** | | | .260 | 60 | 215 | 32 | 56 | 11 | 5 | 5 | 29 | 21 | 47 | 10 | .329 | .428 |

## 9 PAUL KELLY

SS

**Born:** Oct. 19, 1986. **B-T:** R-R. **Ht.:** 6-0. **Wt.:** 185. **Drafted:** HS—Flower Mound, Texas, 2005 (2nd round). **Signed by:** Marty Esposito.

Flower Mound (Texas) High righty Craig Italiano showed more velocity than any pitcher in the 2005 draft, and Kelly, his teammate, also threw 94-95 mph while doubling as a shortstop. His bat and defensive potential prompted the Twins to draft Kelly as a hitter in the second round— one pick after the Athletics chose Italiano—even though they selected prep shortstop Trevor Plouffe in the first round the year before. Kelly has passed Plouffe on the organization's shortstop depth chart. He knows the

strike zone and has power, leading some scouts to project him to hit 15 homers annually. He wows scouts with the organization's best infield arm and positions himself so well that he rarely has to rely on his arm strength to make plays. He's a quiet, confident leader. A torn meniscus in his left knee ended Kelly's season in late July, and he hadn't recovered sufficiently to make it through a full instructional league. A fringe-average runner before he got hurt, he'll have to prove his range is sufficient for shortstop once he returns. Offensively, his swing tends to be choppy and causes him to hit a lot of balls in the air, and some scouts doubt he's strong enough to translate those fly balls into home runs. The Twins believe in Kelly's bat, and some club officials think they may have a young Alan Trammell on their hands. A healthy Kelly could push Plouffe to third base in high Class A in 2007.

| Year | Club (League) | Class | AVG | G | AB | R | H | 2B | 3B | HR | RBI | BB | SO | SB | OBP | SLG |
|------|---------------|-------|-----|---|----|---|---|----|----|----|-----|----|----|----|-----|-----|
| 2005 | Twins (GCL) | R | .277 | 40 | 137 | 16 | 38 | 6 | 0 | 2 | 20 | 14 | 36 | 3 | .358 | .365 |
| | Beloit (MWL) | A | .313 | 5 | 16 | 2 | 5 | 2 | 0 | 1 | 4 | 2 | 3 | 0 | .368 | .625 |
| 2006 | Beloit (MWL) | A | .280 | 95 | 378 | 58 | 106 | 22 | 4 | 3 | 48 | 32 | 60 | 4 | .352 | .384 |
| **MINOR LEAGUE TOTALS** | | | .281 | 140 | 531 | 76 | 149 | 30 | 4 | 6 | 72 | 48 | 99 | 7 | .354 | .386 |

## 10 J.D. DURBIN

RHP

**Born:** Feb. 24, 1982. **B-T:** R-R. **Ht.:** 6-0. **Wt.:** 210. **Drafted:** HS—Scottsdale, Ariz., 2000 (2nd round). **Signed by:** Lee MacPhail IV.

Durbin dubbed himself "The Real Deal" early in his career, when he threw upper-90s gas and reached Minnesota at age 22. Then he was derailed by surgery to repair a partially torn labrum in 2004 and shoulder tendinitis in 2005. He was rolling in 2006 until missing the last two months with a nerve problem in his biceps, which didn't require surgery. Durbin still ranks among the Twins' hardest-throwing starters. His fastball sits at 92-94 mph and he still can reach back for more. His curveball, which managers rated the best in the Triple-A International League, is a power low-80s breaker that comes out of his hand looking like a fastball. He has improved his ability to throw his curve and changeup for strikes. He has matured into a gamer and takes his job more seriously. The missed time the last three years not only clouds Durbin's durability, but it also cost him development time he needed to hone his control. He was more pitch-efficient this season but still needs to improve in that regard. If he can't hold up, he may have to move to the bullpen. Just when he had turned the corner, Durbin had to combat one more obstacle with his biceps injury. He's out of options, so 2007 is likely his last chance with Minnesota. The Twins rotation has holes, and a healthy Durbin could step forward and seize a spot.

| Year | Club (League) | Class | W | L | ERA | G | GS | CG | SV | IP | H | R | ER | HR | BB | SO | AVG |
|------|---------------|-------|---|---|-----|---|----|----|----|----|----|----|----|----|----|----|-----|
| 2000 | Twins (GCL) | R | 0 | 0 | 0.00 | 2 | 0 | 0 | 0 | 2 | 2 | 0 | 0 | 0 | 0 | 4 | .222 |
| 2001 | Elizabethton (Appy) | R | 3 | 2 | 1.87 | 8 | 7 | 0 | 0 | 34 | 23 | 13 | 7 | 2 | 17 | 39 | .190 |
| 2002 | Quad City (MWL) | A | 13 | 4 | 3.19 | 27 | 27 | 0 | 0 | 161 | 144 | 66 | 57 | 14 | 51 | 163 | .239 |
| 2003 | Fort Myers (FSL) | A | 9 | 2 | 3.09 | 14 | 14 | 0 | 0 | 87 | 73 | 35 | 30 | 3 | 22 | 69 | .224 |
| | New Britain (EL) | AA | 6 | 3 | 3.14 | 14 | 14 | 2 | 0 | 95 | 102 | 39 | 33 | 10 | 29 | 70 | .278 |
| 2004 | New Britain (EL) | AA | 4 | 1 | 2.52 | 13 | 13 | 0 | 0 | 64 | 62 | 21 | 18 | 4 | 22 | 53 | .253 |
| | Rochester (IL) | AAA | 3 | 2 | 4.54 | 7 | 7 | 0 | 0 | 36 | 49 | 27 | 18 | 4 | 16 | 38 | .325 |
| | Minnesota (AL) | MLB | 0 | 1 | 7.36 | 4 | 1 | 0 | 0 | 7 | 12 | 6 | 6 | 0 | 6 | 6 | .387 |
| 2005 | Rochester (IL) | AAA | 5 | 5 | 4.33 | 22 | 19 | 0 | 0 | 104 | 97 | 52 | 50 | 8 | 51 | 90 | .251 |
| 2006 | Rochester (IL) | AAA | 4 | 3 | 2.33 | 16 | 16 | 0 | 0 | 89 | 67 | 27 | 23 | 3 | 50 | 81 | .209 |
| **MINOR LEAGUE TOTALS** | | | 47 | 22 | 3.16 | 123 | 117 | 2 | 0 | 672 | 619 | 280 | 236 | 48 | 258 | 607 | .245 |
| **MAJOR LEAGUE TOTALS** | | | 0 | 1 | 7.36 | 4 | 1 | 0 | 0 | 7 | 12 | 6 | 6 | 0 | 6 | 6 | .387 |

## 11 OSWALDO SOSA

RHP

**Born:** Sept. 19, 1985. **B-T:** R-R. **Ht.:** 6-4. **Wt.:** 225. **Signed:** Venezuela, 2002. **Signed by:** Jose Leon.

The Twins love Sosa's upside and consider him a success story for their pitching coaches and strength and conditioning staff. He has added two inches and nearly 40 pounds since signing and has added it the right way, in the right places. Sosa also has taken well to instruction, using drills to lengthen his stride and get proper extension in his delivery. Sosa's fastball has climbed from 86-88 mph when he signed to 89-93 now, touching 94. It has natural cutting action in on lefthanders, and he can throw a two-seamer at 90-92 with good sink. He throws downhill, and lefties were helpless against him—they had no home runs and just seven extra-base hits in 241 at-bats while hitting .191. He's able to work primarily off his fastball and throws a slider that lacks consistent depth but can be an average major league pitch. His curveball and changeup are serviceable but aren't out pitches yet. If he had more of a strikeout pitch, Sosa could profile as a No. 2 starter, but his current package looks

more like a durable, innings-eating workhorse who will rely on his defense. Sosa was tabbed as a potential rotation candidate at the Winter Meetings by manager Ron Gardenhire, but that seems unlikely given the depth of pitchers ahead of him in the system. Coming off a strong winter effort in his native Venezuela, he's likely headed to Double-A to start 2007.

| Year | Club (League) | Class | W | L | ERA | G | GS | CG | SV | IP | H | R | ER | HR | BB | SO | AVG |
|------|---------------|-------|---|---|-----|---|----|----|----|-----|-----|-----|-----|----|----|-----|------|
| 2003 | Tronconero 1 (VSL) | R | 1 | 2 | 3.02 | 11 | 10 | 0 | 0 | 54 | 44 | 24 | 18 | 0 | 18 | 40 | .221 |
| 2004 | Twins (GCL) | R | 1 | 2 | 2.20 | 8 | 5 | 0 | 0 | 29 | 27 | 13 | 7 | 0 | 4 | 30 | .239 |
| 2005 | Elizabethton (Appy) | R | 6 | 5 | 4.95 | 12 | 11 | 0 | 0 | 56 | 59 | 37 | 31 | 4 | 21 | 40 | .265 |
| 2006 | Beloit (MWL) | A | 9 | 7 | 2.75 | 20 | 20 | 1 | 0 | 118 | 102 | 44 | 36 | 1 | 36 | 95 | .233 |
| | Fort Myers (FSL) | A | 4 | 1 | 2.08 | 6 | 6 | 0 | 0 | 35 | 23 | 12 | 8 | 1 | 18 | 27 | .189 |
| **MINOR LEAGUE TOTALS** | | | 21 | 17 | 3.09 | 57 | 52 | 1 | 0 | 291 | 255 | 130 | 100 | 6 | 97 | 232 | .233 |

## 12 MATT MOSES                                      3B

**Born:** Feb. 20, 1985. **B-T:** L-R. **Ht.:** 6-0. **Wt.:** 215. **Drafted:** HS—Richmond, Va., 2003 (1st round). **Signed by:** John Wilson.

Moses, a 2003 first-round pick whose offensive ability once was compared with that of Hank Blalock, has followed Blalock's downward turn—only he's done it in the minors. He had been pushed aggressively, reaching Double-A by age 20, but the Twins slowed him down and had him repeat the level in 2006, and he didn't respond as well as expected. The Twins still see potential in his bat but have lowered the bar and now see Moses as more of a six-hole hitter and complementary player than a middle-of-the-lineup force. He has been a streak hitter who has above-average bat speed but goes into funks where he loses his plate discipline and gets pull happy. He doesn't control the strike zone well enough to hit for a high average and doesn't make enough contact for his above-average power potential to show itself. He is a below-average runner. Moses' defense also has not developed as hoped. He's inconsistent with his footwork and throws, and his fringy range doesn't help. He probably could handle left field defensively and may move there sooner than later because the Twins want to see how good his bat can be. The Twins drafted third baseman Brian Busher in the minor league phase of the Rule 5 draft in December, giving them a veteran option for Triple-A and likely pushing Moses back to Double-A.

| Year | Club (League) | Class | AVG | G | AB | R | H | 2B | 3B | HR | RBI | BB | SO | SB | OBP | SLG |
|------|---------------|-------|-----|---|----|---|---|----|----|----|-----|----|----|----|-----|-----|
| 2003 | Twins (GCL) | R | .385 | 18 | 65 | 6 | 25 | 5 | 1 | 0 | 11 | 5 | 9 | 0 | .417 | .492 |
| 2004 | Twins (GCL) | R | .250 | 1 | 4 | 0 | 1 | 0 | 0 | 0 | 1 | 0 | 0 | 0 | .250 | .250 |
| | Quad City (MWL) | A | .223 | 29 | 112 | 16 | 25 | 7 | 0 | 3 | 14 | 12 | 25 | 0 | .304 | .366 |
| 2005 | Fort Myers (FSL) | A | .306 | 73 | 265 | 37 | 81 | 16 | 1 | 7 | 42 | 28 | 59 | 13 | .376 | .453 |
| | New Britain (EL) | AA | .210 | 48 | 186 | 25 | 39 | 9 | 1 | 6 | 30 | 14 | 51 | 3 | .275 | .366 |
| 2006 | New Britain (EL) | AA | .249 | 125 | 474 | 47 | 118 | 16 | 2 | 15 | 72 | 35 | 113 | 2 | .303 | .386 |
| **MINOR LEAGUE TOTALS** | | | .261 | 294 | 1106 | 131 | 289 | 53 | 5 | 31 | 170 | 94 | 257 | 18 | .323 | .402 |

## 13 DENARD SPAN                                     OF

**Born:** Feb. 27, 1984. **B-T:** L-L. **Ht.:** 6-1. **Wt.:** 180. **Drafted:** HS—Tampa, 2002 (1st round). **Signed by:** Brad Weitzel.

The Twins have been patient with Span, and with Torii Hunter manning center field in Minnesota it was a luxury they could afford. Now Hunter has gotten expensive and has a contract that runs out after 2007, meaning Span is poised to replace him. That will only happen if Span makes a significant leap forward, for while he still has first-round tools and athleticism, he has not delivered first-round performance. Span remains among the fastest Twins, a 70 runner on the 20-80 scale, and he's a premium athlete. With a bit more polish, he should be a fine big league defender, though his arm is fringy. He lacks instincts and the savvy to take advantage of his speed on the basepaths, where he barely succeeded more than two-thirds of the time in 2006. Like Matt Moses, he's a streaky hitter who doesn't drive the ball consistently and is at times overpowered by hard stuff. He also tends to wear down over the course of long seasons and must get stronger. Span answered some concerns on that end—and in terms of his commitment, which has been questioned—by playing winter ball in Venezuela. Tools aren't Span's problem; putting those tools to use are. He has one more year to close the gap between prospect and polished pro, and he'll try to prove himself as a Triple-A leadoff hitter in 2007.

| Year | Club (League) | Class | AVG | G | AB | R | H | 2B | 3B | HR | RBI | BB | SO | SB | OBP | SLG |
|------|---------------|-------|-----|---|----|---|---|----|----|----|-----|----|----|----|-----|-----|
| 2003 | Elizabethton (Appy) | R | .271 | 50 | 207 | 34 | 56 | 5 | 1 | 1 | 18 | 23 | 34 | 14 | .355 | .319 |
| 2004 | Quad City (MWL) | A | .267 | 64 | 240 | 29 | 64 | 4 | 3 | 0 | 14 | 34 | 49 | 15 | .363 | .308 |
| 2005 | Fort Myers (FSL) | A | .339 | 49 | 186 | 38 | 63 | 3 | 3 | 1 | 19 | 22 | 25 | 13 | .410 | .403 |
| | New Britain (EL) | AA | .285 | 68 | 267 | 47 | 76 | 6 | 5 | 0 | 26 | 22 | 41 | 10 | .355 | .345 |
| 2006 | New Britain (EL) | AA | .285 | 134 | 536 | 80 | 153 | 16 | 6 | 2 | 45 | 40 | 78 | 24 | .340 | .349 |
| **MINOR LEAGUE TOTALS** | | | .287 | 365 | 1436 | 228 | 412 | 34 | 18 | 4 | 122 | 141 | 227 | 76 | .358 | .344 |

## JEFF MANSHIP
**RHP**

**Born:** Jan. 16, 1985. **B-T:** B-R. **Ht.:** 6-0. **Wt.:** 165. **Drafted:** Notre Dame, 2006 (14th round). **Signed by:** Billy Milos.

As a San Antonio prep star, Manship followed in the footsteps of his older brother Matt, who went to Stanford and was a 29th-round pick of the Athletics in 2006. Jeff was a member of USA Baseball's junior national team after his senior year in high school but threw too many of his signature curveballs in the event—he estimates he threw 130 pitches during a 15-strikeout effort against Curacao—and required Tommy John surgery that forced him to take a medical redshirt as a freshman at Notre Dame. He eased back into pitching in 2005, then proved himself as an ace again in 2006, going 9-2, 3.26 while leading the Big East Conference with 111 strikeouts in 94 innings. Manship signed as a redshirt sophomore for a $300,000 bonus. In an effort to finish his degree he attended classes at Notre Dame in the fall rather than going to instructional league. While Manship's curveball isn't quite as good as it used to be, it's still an above-average pitch and the Twins consider it the best in the system thanks to his command of it and its depth. Manship's 89-92 mph fastball can touch 93 and he throws plenty of strikes with it. He also uses a changeup and slider. While he's strong and well-built, Manship is undersized, and his durability and ability to keep his fastball down in the strike zone will be key in his first full season, which should start at high Class A.

| Year | Club (League) | Class | W | L | ERA | G | GS | CG | SV | IP | H | R | ER | HR | BB | SO | AVG |
|---|---|---|---|---|---|---|---|---|---|---|---|---|---|---|---|---|---|
| 2006 | Twins (GCL) | R | 0 | 0 | 0.00 | 2 | 0 | 0 | 0 | 6 | 3 | 0 | 0 | 0 | 1 | 10 | .150 |
| | Fort Myers (FSL) | A | 0 | 0 | 2.08 | 4 | 3 | 0 | 0 | 9 | 7 | 3 | 2 | 0 | 2 | 12 | .212 |
| **MINOR LEAGUE TOTALS** | | | 0 | 0 | 1.26 | 6 | 3 | 0 | 0 | 14 | 10 | 3 | 2 | 0 | 3 | 22 | .189 |

## ALEXANDER SMIT
**LHP**

**Born:** Oct. 2, 1985. **B-T:** L-L. **Ht.:** 6-4. **Wt.:** 205. **Signed:** Netherlands, 2002. **Signed by:** Howie Norsetter.

The Twins stopped fighting Smit in 2006, and he rewarded them with a breakthrough season. He still has yet to put all his stuff and deception and fearlessness together in a full, consistent season, but he did enough to earn a spot on the 40-man roster. Smit has put together strong second halves in the past two seasons and continues to rack up huge strikeout numbers at lower levels. The Twins allowed him to go back to his unconventional knuckle-curveball last year, an inconsistent pitch that can be a swing-and-miss offering at times. He pushes the pitch out with his thumb from the bottom, rather than producing spin from the top with his index or middle finger. Smit doesn't have a changeup, but he has plenty of feel for his fastball and spots it well, throwing it anywhere from the mid-80s to the low 90s, adding and subtracting as he goes. Since signing for $800,000 in 2002, Smit has lagged behind in figuring out how to be a professional, how to adopt a routine and how to stay in shape in the offseason. The Twins hope Smit will come to camp in better shape in 2007, avoid the poor spring training performances that have held him back and put together a strong season from start to finish for the first time, beginning in high Class A.

| Year | Club (League) | Class | W | L | ERA | G | GS | CG | SV | IP | H | R | ER | HR | BB | SO | AVG |
|---|---|---|---|---|---|---|---|---|---|---|---|---|---|---|---|---|---|
| 2003 | Twins (GCL) | R | 3 | 0 | 1.18 | 8 | 7 | 0 | 0 | 38 | 19 | 8 | 5 | 0 | 20 | 40 | .156 |
| 2004 | Elizabethton (Appy) | R | 1 | 1 | 2.54 | 6 | 5 | 0 | 0 | 28 | 25 | 9 | 8 | 0 | 10 | 43 | .248 |
| 2005 | Beloit (MWL) | A | 1 | 9 | 5.98 | 14 | 10 | 0 | 0 | 50 | 58 | 41 | 33 | 9 | 28 | 54 | .283 |
| | Elizabethton (Appy) | R | 6 | 1 | 1.97 | 21 | 0 | 0 | 3 | 46 | 25 | 12 | 10 | 3 | 12 | 86 | .157 |
| 2006 | Beloit (MWL) | A | 7 | 2 | 2.99 | 34 | 13 | 0 | 0 | 108 | 77 | 48 | 36 | 6 | 53 | 141 | .199 |
| **MINOR LEAGUE TOTALS** | | | 18 | 13 | 3.07 | 83 | 35 | 0 | 3 | 270 | 204 | 118 | 92 | 18 | 123 | 364 | .210 |

## JAY RAINVILLE
**RHP**

**Born:** Oct. 16, 1985. **B-T:** R-R. **Ht.:** 6-3. **Wt.:** 230. **Drafted:** HS—Pawtucket, R.I., 2004 (1st round supplemental). **Signed by:** Jay Weitzel.

Rainville ranked No. 8 on this list last year and was about to jump on the fast track when he felt pain in his throwing shoulder in spring training. Rainville had a compressed nerve and needed surgery, which he had in early April. His rehabilitation went well, however, and he was able to return to the mound in instructional league. Rainville's maturity showed through in his diligence in working his way back from surgery, and he was touching 90 mph by the end of instructs, where he got about 25 innings of needed work. His frame, work ethic, maturity and stuff have some members of the organization projecting Rainville as a future front-of-the-rotation starter. While he's regained his old velocity, the Twins also project him to gain more velocity in the future, possibly sitting in the low 90s and touching a bit higher. Rainville's curveball had potential to be a power, swing-and-miss 12-to-6 pitch before his injury, and the Twins saw glimpses of it in instructional league. He even throws

a changeup for strikes at times. The Twins are anxious to see what a healthy Rainville can do in 2007 and he'll begin by pitching in high Class A.

| Year | Club (League) | Class | W | L | ERA | G | GS | CG | SV | IP | H | R | ER | HR | BB | SO | AVG |
|------|---------------|-------|---|---|-----|---|----|----|----|----|---|---|----|----|----|----|-----|
| 2004 | Twins (GCL) | R | 3 | 2 | 1.84 | 8 | 7 | 0 | 0 | 34 | 39 | 19 | 7 | 1 | 3 | 38 | .273 |
| 2005 | Beloit (MWL) | A | 8 | 2 | 3.77 | 16 | 16 | 0 | 0 | 88 | 83 | 39 | 37 | 14 | 27 | 77 | .243 |
| | Fort Myers (FSL) | A | 4 | 3 | 2.67 | 9 | 9 | 1 | 0 | 54 | 54 | 22 | 16 | 7 | 6 | 35 | .256 |
| 2006 | Did not play—Injured | | | | | | | | | | | | | | | | |
| **MINOR LEAGUE TOTALS** | | | 15 | 7 | 3.06 | 33 | 32 | 1 | 0 | 177 | 176 | 80 | 60 | 22 | 36 | 150 | .253 |

## DAVID WINFREE                                              3B/1B

**Born:** Aug. 5, 1985. **B-T:** R-R. **Ht.:** 6-3. **Wt.:** 215. **Drafted:** HS—Virginia Beach, Va., 2003 (13th round). **Signed by:** John Wilson.

With a strong start and a full season, Winfree might have pushed his way into the top 10, but neither of those things happened. After getting off to an 8-for-25 start in high Class A, he went back home to Virginia Beach—with the club's permission—because he felt he needed to go away from the game for a bit and regain his confidence. The time away helped him, and after a brief spell in extended spring training he returned to the Miracle for the season's final two months. He tried to make up for lost time in the Arizona Fall League, working on taking more pitches and being more patient. The Twins want to be patient with Winfree because he has outstanding strength, good bat speed and above-average raw power. He also has shown a knack for picking up RBIs and adjusts well to situational hitting, but the fact that he went AWOL brings his commitment to baseball into question. Defensively, Winfree doesn't do anything pretty but maximizes his fringy range and arm by working hard and showing good footwork. He still may prove too big for third and saw action at first base last year, but if his bat plays he could develop into a middle-of-the-order threat at either corner infield spot. He's ticketed for Double-A, where he could repeat his role in the AFL and split time at third base and DH with Matt Moses.

| Year | Club (League) | Class | AVG | G | AB | R | H | 2B | 3B | HR | RBI | BB | SO | SB | OBP | SLG |
|------|---------------|-------|-----|---|----|---|---|----|----|----|-----|----|----|----|-----|-----|
| 2003 | Twins (GCL) | R | .129 | 23 | 70 | 4 | 9 | 1 | 2 | 0 | 3 | 2 | 16 | 0 | .164 | .200 |
| 2004 | Elizabethton (Appy) | R | .286 | 59 | 217 | 31 | 62 | 8 | 0 | 8 | 37 | 18 | 51 | 1 | .349 | .433 |
| 2005 | Beloit (MWL) | A | .294 | 135 | 562 | 80 | 165 | 31 | 5 | 16 | 101 | 22 | 93 | 3 | .329 | .452 |
| 2006 | Twins (GCL) | R | .200 | 4 | 15 | 2 | 3 | 1 | 0 | 0 | 1 | 1 | 4 | 0 | .250 | .267 |
| | Fort Myers (FSL) | A | .276 | 67 | 261 | 43 | 72 | 13 | 2 | 13 | 48 | 19 | 59 | 2 | .328 | .490 |
| **MINOR LEAGUE TOTALS** | | | .276 | 288 | 1125 | 160 | 311 | 54 | 9 | 37 | 190 | 62 | 223 | 6 | .322 | .439 |

## BRIAN DUENSING                                              LHP

**Born:** Feb. 22, 1983. **B-T:** L-L. **Ht.:** 5-11. **Wt.:** 195. **Drafted:** Nebraska, 2005 (3rd round). **Signed by:** Mark Wilson.

Duensing grew up in Omaha watching College World Series games, then pitched for the Cornhuskers in the CWS himself in 2005. He went 8-0 as a redshirt junior and pitched his way into high draft consideration, though he was surprised when the Twins took him as high as they did. He was a third-round pick even after an injury-interrupted career at Nebraska, which included 2004 Tommy John surgery. Duensing has stayed healthy as a pro with consistent stuff, and his feel for pitching keeps improving. His poor record obscured a year when his above-average control and average command helped him reach Double-A in his first full season. While he doesn't have a putaway pitch, all his offerings—both two- and four-seam fastballs that sit in the upper 80s, a curveball, slider and circle changeup—grade out as average or a tick above at times. He knows how to pitch backward, and his change-up and slider have been go-to pitches. Duensing will have to keep proving his durability and throw his breaking stuff with a bit more velocity to maintain separation between his fastballs and offspeed pitches. In a system fairly short on lefthanders, he'll be given every chance to succeed, and heads back to Double-A to open 2007.

| Year | Club (League) | Class | W | L | ERA | G | GS | CG | SV | IP | H | R | ER | HR | BB | SO | AVG |
|------|---------------|-------|---|---|-----|---|----|----|----|----|---|---|----|----|----|----|-----|
| 2005 | Elizabethton (Appy) | R | 4 | 3 | 2.32 | 12 | 9 | 0 | 0 | 50 | 49 | 19 | 13 | 4 | 16 | 55 | .249 |
| 2006 | Beloit (MWL) | A | 2 | 3 | 2.94 | 11 | 11 | 0 | 0 | 70 | 68 | 26 | 23 | 3 | 14 | 55 | .257 |
| | Fort Myers (FSL) | A | 2 | 5 | 4.24 | 7 | 7 | 0 | 0 | 40 | 47 | 25 | 19 | 4 | 8 | 33 | .296 |
| | New Britain (EL) | AA | 1 | 2 | 3.65 | 10 | 9 | 0 | 0 | 49 | 51 | 29 | 20 | 6 | 18 | 30 | .277 |
| **MINOR LEAGUE TOTALS** | | | 9 | 13 | 3.21 | 40 | 36 | 0 | 0 | 210 | 215 | 99 | 75 | 17 | 56 | 173 | .267 |

## TREVOR PLOUFFE                                              SS/3B

**Born:** June 15, 1986. **B-T:** R-R. **Ht.:** 6-2. **Wt.:** 175. **Drafted:** HS—Northridge, Calif., 2004 (1st round). **Signed by:** Bill Mele.

After two full seasons, the Twins remain unsure about Plouffe, who garnered attention on

the mound as well at shortstop as a high school All-American. Organization officials remain optimistic about his bat, more than his statistics suggest they should. He had an up-and-down season in high Class A but finished strong, hitting .299 with 13 of his 34 extra-base hits coming in his final 33 games. Plouffe also performed well in instructional league, and club officials don't think anything's wrong with his swing. Effort and competitiveness aren't the problem, and he's intense and works hard. He's fairly selective at the plate and was at his best when he was patient. Defensively, Plouffe has soft hands and an above-average arm. While his range isn't ideal, he's an average runner and he has retained his athleticism since high school, just not his performance. He's headed to Double-A for '07, but if his bat doesn't pick up soon he could get more work at second base and third base (where he played some in '06) in preparation for a future as a utility player.

| Year | Club (League) | Class | AVG | G | AB | R | H | 2B | 3B | HR | RBI | BB | SO | SB | OBP | SLG |
|------|--------------|-------|-----|---|-----|----|-----|----|----|----|-----|----|-----|----|------|------|
| 2004 | Elizabethton (Appy) | R | .283 | 60 | 237 | 29 | 67 | 7 | 2 | 4 | 28 | 19 | 34 | 2 | .340 | .380 |
| 2005 | Beloit (MWL) | A | .223 | 127 | 466 | 58 | 104 | 18 | 0 | 13 | 60 | 50 | 78 | 8 | .300 | .345 |
| 2006 | Fort Myers (FSL) | A | .246 | 125 | 455 | 60 | 112 | 26 | 4 | 4 | 45 | 58 | 93 | 8 | .333 | .347 |
| **MINOR LEAGUE TOTALS** | | | .244 | 312 | 1158 | 147 | 283 | 51 | 6 | 21 | 133 | 127 | 205 | 18 | .321 | .353 |

## 20 KYLE WALDROP RHP

**Born:** Oct. 27, 1985. **B-T:** R-R. **Ht.:** 6-4. **Wt.:** 200. **Drafted:** HS—Knoxville, Tenn., 2004 (1st round). **Signed by:** Tim O'Neil.

The Twins bucked the consensus in signing Waldrop as a first-round pick in 2004, after many teams thought he would go to Vanderbilt with lefthander David Price, who was considered the state of Tennessee's top prospect. While Price has blossomed at Vandy and is a top prospect for the '07 draft, Waldrop has made slow progress in pro ball but the Twins remain confident in his projection. While his fastball velocity has remained pedestrian—it's often at 86-89 mph and touches 90-91—it has plenty of sink and he has become a groundball machine (242-126 groundout-flyout ratio). Waldrop still has projection left and is still getting used to his growing body. He could wind up being 6-foot-6 and close to 230 pounds, and the Twins see him as an innings-eater. They love his makeup and hope he'll remain patient as his velocity improves and his body develops. Waldrop has a feel for his secondary stuff, and while his curveball, slider and changeup aren't plus pitches, they all play average because he commands them well. He needs to make slight adjustments to his arm action, which can get long in the back and provides little deception. Patience is the watchword for Waldrop, who will head back to high Class A to start 2007.

| Year | Club (League) | Class | W | L | ERA | G | GS | CG | SV | IP | H | R | ER | HR | BB | SO | AVG |
|------|--------------|-------|---|---|------|----|----|----|----|-----|-----|-----|-----|----|----|-----|------|
| 2004 | Twins (GCL) | R | 3 | 2 | 1.42 | 7 | 7 | 0 | 0 | 38 | 32 | 9 | 6 | 1 | 4 | 30 | .229 |
| | Elizabethton (Appy) | R | 2 | 0 | 3.24 | 4 | 4 | 0 | 0 | 25 | 21 | 10 | 9 | 1 | 3 | 25 | .221 |
| 2005 | Beloit (MWL) | A | 6 | 11 | 4.98 | 27 | 27 | 2 | 0 | 152 | 182 | 93 | 84 | 17 | 23 | 108 | .291 |
| 2006 | Beloit (MWL) | A | 6 | 3 | 3.85 | 18 | 18 | 1 | 0 | 110 | 110 | 54 | 47 | 8 | 17 | 62 | .259 |
| | Fort Myers (FSL) | A | 3 | 2 | 3.57 | 8 | 7 | 1 | 0 | 45 | 48 | 27 | 18 | 4 | 17 | 25 | .265 |
| **MINOR LEAGUE TOTALS** | | | 20 | 18 | 3.99 | 64 | 63 | 4 | 0 | 370 | 393 | 193 | 164 | 31 | 64 | 250 | .268 |

## 21 EDUARDO MORLAN RHP

**Born:** March 1, 1986. **B-T:** R-R. **Ht.:** 6-2. **Wt.:** 220. **Drafted:** HS—Miami, 2004 (3rd round). **Signed by:** Hector Otero.

The Twins still have high hopes for most of the pitchers from their deep 2004 draft, and Morlan may have the most arm strength of any of them. Born in Cuba, he arrived with his family in Miami when he was 12 during a relaxation in visa rules for Cubans in the late 1990s, though they had to make a detour through Spain. Morlan's fastball and hard breaking ball, usually described as a slider, can both be power pitches. His fastball has reached 97 mph and he throws his slider in the mid-80s, and at times he dominated. In the five starts when he pitched at least seven innings, he gave up just 17 hits and struck out 47. But Morlan is still learning to pitch and to have consistent stuff every time out. Most of the season, his average fastball velocity was right at 90, and he usually topped out at 92-93 mph. He's learning to take a little off his fastball and slider and not throw every pitch as hard as he can. His high-effort delivery and power repertoire profile him for the back of a bullpen, and if he makes the switch full-time in 2007, he could move quickly. He'll start at high Class A.

| Year | Club (League) | Class | W | L | ERA | G | GS | CG | SV | IP | H | R | ER | HR | BB | SO | AVG |
|------|--------------|-------|---|---|------|----|----|----|----|-----|-----|-----|-----|----|----|-----|------|
| 2004 | Twins (GCL) | R | 1 | 2 | 2.84 | 11 | 2 | 0 | 1 | 25 | 25 | 14 | 8 | 1 | 10 | 28 | .245 |
| 2005 | Elizabethton (Appy) | R | 2 | 0 | 0.82 | 4 | 4 | 0 | 0 | 22 | 6 | 2 | 2 | 0 | 6 | 30 | .085 |
| | Beloit (MWL) | A | 4 | 4 | 4.38 | 10 | 10 | 0 | 0 | 51 | 39 | 25 | 25 | 5 | 31 | 55 | .207 |
| 2006 | Beloit (MWL) | A | 5 | 5 | 2.29 | 28 | 18 | 1 | 2 | 106 | 78 | 31 | 27 | 6 | 38 | 125 | .202 |
| **MINOR LEAGUE TOTALS** | | | 12 | 11 | 2.72 | 53 | 34 | 1 | 3 | 205 | 148 | 72 | 62 | 12 | 85 | 238 | .198 |

**JOSE MIJARES**  LHP

**Born:** Oct. 29, 1984. **B-T:** L-L. **Ht.:** 6-0. **Wt.:** 230. **Signed:** Venezuela, 2002. **Signed by:** Jose Leon.

Mijares has the stuff to be a top prospect, but the off-field factors that help players have success have not aligned for him. A native of Caracas' shantytown slums, he has had a difficult life, using baseball as a positive outlet. Being a professional in all aspects has proven difficult. One organization coach estimated he quit four times during the 2006 season, and when the Twins tried to arrange for him to pitch in Venezuela's lower-level winter league, Mijares balked, changed his mind, then balked and quit again. He has trouble keeping weight off and has been described as a lefthanded Rich Garces, though he's not quite that big. He also has more stuff than Garces ever did, with three pitches that earn at least 70 grades (on the 20-80 scouting scale) from scouts in and out of the organization. Mijares' fastball reaches 95-96 mph as a starter and even a tick or two better in shorter stints. It's fairly straight, and might be his third-best pitch because when he elevates it, he gets in trouble. He throws both a slider and a curveball, and both are exceptional, with power, tilt and depth. He would stand a better chance of starting if he maintained his conditioning better. Mijares' best role seems to be as a lefty reliever because coming to the park with a chance to pitch every day seems to be the best motivation for him. He's expected to head to Double-A in 2007.

| Year | Club (League) | Class | W | L | ERA | G | GS | CG | SV | IP | H | R | ER | HR | BB | SO | AVG |
|------|---------------|-------|---|---|------|----|----|----|----|-----|-----|-----|----|----|-----|-----|------|
| 2002 | Twins (VSL) | R | 2 | 5 | 3.91 | 13 | 9 | 0 | 0 | 53 | 51 | 29 | 23 | 2 | 27 | 42 | .264 |
| 2003 | Twins (VSL) | R | 2 | 4 | 1.05 | 11 | 7 | 0 | 0 | 52 | 28 | 17 | 6 | 1 | 15 | 58 | .159 |
| 2004 | Twins (GCL) | R | 4 | 0 | 2.43 | 19 | 0 | 0 | 5 | 30 | 22 | 9 | 8 | 1 | 15 | 25 | .208 |
| 2005 | Beloit (MWL) | A | 6 | 3 | 4.31 | 20 | 6 | 0 | 2 | 54 | 43 | 28 | 26 | 6 | 40 | 78 | .219 |
|      | Fort Myers (FSL) | A | 0 | 0 | 1.50 | 5 | 1 | 0 | 0 | 12 | 5 | 4 | 2 | 1 | 5 | 17 | .116 |
| 2006 | Fort Myers (FSL) | A | 3 | 5 | 3.57 | 27 | 5 | 0 | 0 | 63 | 52 | 30 | 25 | 10 | 27 | 77 | .226 |
| **MINOR LEAGUE TOTALS** | | | 17 | 17 | 3.07 | 95 | 28 | 0 | 7 | 264 | 201 | 117 | 90 | 21 | 129 | 297 | .213 |

 **WHIT ROBBINS**  3B

**Born:** Sept. 25, 1984. **B-T:** L-R. **Ht.:** 6-0. **Wt.:** 205. **Drafted:** Georgia Tech, 2006 (4th round). **Signed by:** Ricky Taylor.

A product of suburban Atlanta's East Cobb summer teams, Robbins has a long track record for a player new to pro ball. He was a three-year starter at Georgia Tech and improved his draft stock significantly by shifting from first base to third when teammate Wes Hodges (who signed for $1 million with the Indians as a second-round pick) was limited by a leg injury. Robbins showed good hands and a strong arm, though he'll need work on his footwork and repetitions to become a good third baseman. He signed quickly with the Twins for $265,000 and hit the ground running, with 10 hits in his first 14 at-bats. Robbins has a sound lefthanded stroke and good bat speed to catch up with good fastballs. His season ended due to a balky back, which the Twins hope he took care of in the offseason with a combination of rest and rehabilitation. A healthy Robbins would quickly move into the team's wide-open third base mix, but Robbins will have to hit to stay ahead of fellow '06 draftees Garrett Olson and Danny Valencia, and to catch up to Matt Moses and David Winfree ahead of him. He's primed to be the third baseman in high Class A in 2007.

| Year | Club (League) | Class | AVG | G | AB | R | H | 2B | 3B | HR | RBI | BB | SO | SB | OBP | SLG |
|------|---------------|-------|------|----|-----|----|----|----|----|----|-----|----|----|----|------|------|
| 2006 | Beloit (MWL) | A | .304 | 32 | 112 | 12 | 34 | 9 | 1 | 3 | 26 | 22 | 17 | 1 | .421 | .482 |
| **MINOR LEAGUE TOTALS** | | | .304 | 32 | 112 | 12 | 34 | 9 | 1 | 3 | 26 | 22 | 17 | 1 | .421 | .482 |

 **TYLER ROBERTSON**  LHP

**Born:** Dec. 23, 1987. **B-T:** L-L. **Ht.:** 6-5. **Wt.:** 225. **Drafted:** HS—Fair Oaks, Calif., 2006 (3rd round). **Signed by:** Kevin Bootay.

Robertson attracted plenty of attention as a high schooler, both as a pitcher and a quarterback, but a commitment to Cal State Fullerton signaled his intention to focus on baseball. He eschewed the Titans for a $405,000 signing bonus and knew what he was getting into, as his father Jay scouts for the Rangers and has raised his son around the game. Robertson has soaked up instruction and knows his body and delivery well, which is a good thing because others have a hard time describing what he does. Scouts agree Robertson is unorthodox, and as Twins roving pitching coordinator Rick Knapp puts it, "He doesn't look lefthanded. Go take a picture of a big righthander and look at it in the mirror—that's what he looks like." After he begins his windup, Robertson's left arm, in the words of one scout, plunges straight down. He then brings the arm back up and goes to the plate. While he repeats the arm action and it creates deception, it's stiff, and the Twins hope to loosen him up to give his pitches a bit more life. His stuff is already solid average, with a 90-91 mph fastball that touches 94 and

a good curveball with depth. The Twins believe he's an important piece in increasing their depth of lefthanders and expect him to earn a spot in the low Class A rotation.

| Year | Club (League) | Class | W | L | ERA | G | GS | CG | SV | IP | H | R | ER | HR | BB | SO | AVG |
|------|---------------|-------|---|---|-----|---|----|----|----|----|---|---|----|----|----|----|-----|
| 2006 | Twins (GCL) | R | 4 | 2 | 4.25 | 11 | 10 | 0 | 0 | 49 | 54 | 23 | 23 | 2 | 15 | 54 | .280 |
| **MINOR LEAGUE TOTALS** | | | 4 | 2 | 4.25 | 11 | 10 | 0 | 0 | 49 | 54 | 23 | 23 | 2 | 15 | 54 | .280 |

## ERIK LIS                                                                1B

**Born:** March 8, 1984. **B-T:** L-L. **Ht.:** 6-1. **Wt.:** 220. **Drafted:** Evansville, 2005 (9th round). **Signed by:** Billy Milos.

Lis dominated the Midwest League in 2006, leading the league in batting, on-base and slugging percentage. He was just finding his power stroke, with four homers in six games, when he was hit by a pitch that broke the hamate bone in his right wrist and ended his season in mid-August. He has strength in his wrists and hands, repeats his swing and knows when to cheat to catch up to good fastballs. His innate feel for hitting helps him work counts to his advantage, and he's not afraid to use the whole field. His future home run power may just be average because he doesn't have great bat speed. His other tools are well below average, particularly in the case of his defense at first and his speed. Lis will end up as a 4-A player unless his home run power blossoms, but hitters like him are hard to find. He'll anchor the lineup at Fort Myers in his second full season.

| Year | Club (League) | Class | AVG | G | AB | R | H | 2B | 3B | HR | RBI | BB | SO | SB | OBP | SLG |
|------|---------------|-------|-----|---|----|---|---|----|----|----|-----|----|----|----|-----|-----|
| 2005 | Elizabethton (Appy) | R | .315 | 49 | 168 | 29 | 53 | 12 | 1 | 10 | 41 | 9 | 35 | 0 | .356 | .577 |
| 2006 | Beloit (MWL) | A | .326 | 105 | 411 | 69 | 134 | 37 | 3 | 16 | 70 | 51 | 83 | 4 | .402 | .547 |
| **MINOR LEAGUE TOTALS** | | | .323 | 154 | 579 | 98 | 187 | 49 | 4 | 26 | 111 | 60 | 118 | 4 | .389 | .556 |

## BRANDON ROBERTS                                                          OF

**Born:** Nov. 9, 1984. **B-T:** L-R. **Ht.:** 6-0. **Wt.:** 185. **Drafted:** Cal Poly, 2005 (7th round). **Signed by:** Mike Misuraca (Reds).

Roberts was traded just before the Florida State League all-star game, making that his first contest in a Fort Myers uniform. A 70 runner on the 20-80 scale, Roberts plays a good defensive center field with a fringy arm that plays well enough for the position. His biggest question will be how his bat plays. He batted .293 in 2006 but produced little power and doesn't project to hit for much more because of his swing. He hits the ball hard, but his swing is choppy and seems better suited for redirecting the ball rather than driving it. While it allows Roberts to take advantage of his speed by beating out infield hits now, that approach works less frequently against big league defenders. Roberts also needs to walk more to take greater advantage of his speed. He broke his left foot in the first workout of instructional league, so the Twins' look at him was shorter than they had hoped. They like what they've seen so far, though, and expect a healthy Roberts to jump to Double-A.

| Year | Club (League) | Class | AVG | G | AB | R | H | 2B | 3B | HR | RBI | BB | SO | SB | OBP | SLG |
|------|---------------|-------|-----|---|----|---|---|----|----|----|-----|----|----|----|-----|-----|
| 2005 | Billings (PIO) | R | .318 | 68 | 274 | 50 | 87 | 9 | 6 | 4 | 36 | 24 | 44 | 32 | .386 | .438 |
| 2006 | Fort Myers (FSL) | A | .316 | 71 | 285 | 40 | 90 | 12 | 1 | 3 | 34 | 20 | 43 | 27 | .370 | .396 |
|      | Sarasota (FSL) | A | .267 | 60 | 247 | 40 | 66 | 5 | 1 | 1 | 15 | 16 | 39 | 23 | .325 | .308 |
| **MINOR LEAGUE TOTALS** | | | .301 | 199 | 806 | 130 | 243 | 26 | 8 | 8 | 85 | 60 | 126 | 82 | .362 | .383 |

## YOHAN PINO                                                              RHP

**Born:** Dec. 26, 1983. **B-T:** R-R. **Ht.:** 6-3. **Wt.:** 171. **Signed:** Venezuela, 2004. **Signed by:** Jose Leon.

Some in the Twins system believe Pino could be the next Oswaldo Sosa, though he'll have a hard time coming in under the radar as Sosa did. Pino began the 2006 season in middle relief in low Class A but finished winning six of seven starts. Despite his inexperience, he also was pitching well in the Venezuelan League. Pino lacks physical maturity and is still filling out his 6-foot-3 frame, so his stuff is fringy or even a shade below. His fastball sits at 86-88 mph and has late run and sink. He throws two variations of both his curveball and slider, showing excellent feel for when to throw them harder and when to take something off. He can use either as a strikeout pitch. His best asset is his command of his overall repertoire, which is among the best in the organization. While Pino has shown he can start, he's also shown a resilient arm prized in relievers and has the same quality stuff even in back-to-back outings. With a good spring, Pino could jump to Double-A for 2007.

| Year | Club (League) | Class | W | L | ERA | G | GS | CG | SV | IP | H | R | ER | HR | BB | SO | AVG |
|------|---------------|-------|---|---|-----|---|----|----|----|----|---|---|----|----|----|----|-----|
| 2004 | Minnesota (DSL) | R | 10 | 1 | 0.53 | 13 | 12 | 3 | 0 | 86 | 49 | 12 | 5 | 0 | 5 | 81 | .161 |
| 2005 | Elizabethton (Appy) | R | 9 | 2 | 3.72 | 12 | 12 | 1 | 0 | 68 | 68 | 31 | 28 | 3 | 13 | 64 | .255 |
| 2006 | Beloit (MWL) | A | 14 | 2 | 1.91 | 42 | 7 | 0 | 3 | 94 | 69 | 25 | 20 | 4 | 20 | 99 | .198 |
| **MINOR LEAGUE TOTALS** | | | 33 | 5 | 1.93 | 67 | 31 | 4 | 3 | 247 | 186 | 68 | 53 | 7 | 38 | 244 | .202 |

## 28  ALEX BURNETT
RHP

**Born:** July 26, 1987. **B-T:** R-R. **Ht.:** 6-0. **Wt.:** 195. **Drafted:** HS—Huntington Beach, Calif., 2005 (12th round). **Signed by:** John Leavitt.

Burnett played his high school baseball in one of the nation's tougher leagues in Orange County, and led Ocean View High to three straight conference titles as well as a California section title. He has moved slowly as a pro, with two seasons in Rookie ball. He teamed with Brian Kirwan to give Rookie-level Elizabethton a powerful 1-2 punch in its rotation, and both are prospects. While Burnett isn't as physical as Kirwan, he's athletic, has good stuff and is poised to break out in 2007. His fastball sits at 92 mph and touches 94, and he has the athletic ability to repeat his delivery, maintain his stuff and keep his fastball down. He isn't afraid to elevate it, though, and then plays off it with a 72-76 mph downer curveball. His changeup is in the early stages of development. One club official, clearly excited by Burnett's package, said he has some Roy Oswalt in him, but others see him becoming a short reliever. He will head to low Class A to start 2007.

| Year | Club (League) | Class | W | L | ERA | G | GS | CG | SV | IP | H | R | ER | HR | BB | SO | AVG |
|------|---------------|-------|---|---|-----|---|----|----|----|----|----|----|----|----|----|----|-----|
| 2005 | Twins (GCL) | R | 4 | 2 | 4.10 | 13 | 8 | 0 | 0 | 48 | 50 | 25 | 22 | 6 | 14 | 33 | .267 |
| 2006 | Elizabethton (Appy) | R | 4 | 3 | 4.04 | 13 | 13 | 1 | 0 | 71 | 66 | 41 | 32 | 6 | 13 | 71 | .242 |
| **MINOR LEAGUE TOTALS** | | | 8 | 54.06 | | 26 | 21 | 1 | 0 | 120 | 116 | 66 | 54 | 12 | 27 | 104 | .252 |

## 29  DAVID SHINSKIE
RHP

**Born:** May 4, 1984. **B-T:** R-R. **Ht.:** 6-4. **Wt.:** 215. **Drafted:** HS—Kulpmont, Pa., 2003 (4th round). **Signed by:** Jay Weitzel.

Even for a player with athleticism, a plus arm, a pro body and good results, it's hard to make the Twins' 40-man roster. Such was the case for Shinskie, who didn't earn a 40-man spot and wasn't selected in the Rule 5 draft. Shinskie, a former high school quarterback, threw more strikes in low Class A than he had in previous seasons. He still blew six of 17 save opportunities because of his lack of feel for anything offspeed. He didn't respond to a promotion to Double-A, and the Twins realize that aptitude is not one of Shinskie's strengths. They hope being left off the 40-man gets a message through to a pitcher with a fastball that parks at 90-92 mph and tops out at 94-95. At times, Shinskie throws a plus hard slider in the mid-80s range, but he doesn't throw quality strikes with either pitch consistently enough to start. His future is in the bullpen, and he'll work in that role in high Class A in 2007.

| Year | Club (League) | Class | W | L | ERA | G | GS | CG | SV | IP | H | R | ER | HR | BB | SO | AVG |
|------|---------------|-------|---|---|-----|---|----|----|----|----|----|----|----|----|----|----|-----|
| 2003 | Twins (GCL) | R | 1 | 4 | 7.41 | 5 | 5 | 0 | 0 | 17 | 20 | 18 | 14 | 0 | 10 | 13 | .294 |
| 2004 | Elizabethton (Appy) | R | 7 | 3 | 4.19 | 11 | 11 | 0 | 0 | 54 | 59 | 31 | 25 | 6 | 17 | 28 | .289 |
| 2005 | Beloit (MWL) | A | 2 | 8 | 7.22 | 29 | 10 | 0 | 1 | 77 | 111 | 72 | 62 | 11 | 24 | 51 | .333 |
| 2006 | Beloit (MWL) | A | 6 | 7 | 2.13 | 48 | 0 | 0 | 11 | 76 | 76 | 25 | 18 | 3 | 15 | 61 | .260 |
| | New Britain (EL) | AA | 0 | 4 | 8.44 | 11 | 0 | 0 | 0 | 16 | 20 | 20 | 15 | 1 | 8 | 11 | .303 |
| **MINOR LEAGUE TOTALS** | | | 16 | 26 | 5.03 | 104 | 26 | 0 | 12 | 240 | 286 | 166 | 134 | 21 | 74 | 164 | .297 |

## 30  ALEX ROMERO
OF

**Born:** Sept. 9, 1983. **B-T:** B-R. **Ht.:** 6-0. **Wt.:** 190. **Signed:** Venezuela, 2000. **Signed by:** Rudy Hernandez.

Romero has the best tools among a trio of similar Twins minor league outfielders. Like Trent Oeltjen and Garrett Guzman, he has ability in all five tools and has had success at Double-A. None projects to have enough power to start at a corner spot for a championship big league team. Guzman, may have the best power of the group. Oeltjen, an Olympic silver medalist for Australia in 2004, is the most well-rounded but has the lowest ceiling. The Twins still like Romero's upside the best, though he's more of a tweener at this stage than a regular. He opened 2006 in Triple-A and couldn't build on the success he had in 2005, when he set career highs in homers and slugging percentage. Romero is tough to strike out and still runs well, and as a switch-hitter and competent defender in both corners, he has an excellent chance to be a fourth outfielder. Romero was regaining momentum in the Venezuelan League, and he could join Guzman and Oelten in the Rochester outfield in 2007.

| Year | Club (League) | Class | AVG | G | AB | R | H | 2B | 3B | HR | RBI | BB | SO | SB | OBP | SLG |
|------|---------------|-------|-----|---|----|----|----|----|----|----|-----|----|----|----|-----|-----|
| 2001 | San Joaquin (VSL) | R | .347 | 49 | 167 | 22 | 58 | 9 | 0 | 2 | 30 | 11 | 9 | 10 | .388 | .437 |
| 2002 | Twins (GCL) | R | .333 | 56 | 186 | 31 | 62 | 13 | 2 | 2 | 42 | 29 | 14 | 16 | .423 | .447 |
| 2003 | Quad City (MWL) | A | .296 | 120 | 423 | 50 | 125 | 16 | 3 | 4 | 40 | 43 | 43 | 11 | .359 | .376 |
| 2004 | Fort Myers (FSL) | A | .292 | 105 | 380 | 59 | 111 | 21 | 2 | 6 | 42 | 54 | 47 | 6 | .387 | .405 |
| 2005 | New Britain (EL) | AA | .301 | 139 | 509 | 65 | 153 | 31 | 2 | 15 | 77 | 36 | 69 | 12 | .354 | .458 |
| 2006 | New Britain (EL) | AA | .281 | 48 | 167 | 29 | 47 | 11 | 2 | 5 | 16 | 26 | 19 | 15 | .384 | .461 |
| | Rochester (IL) | AAA | .250 | 71 | 236 | 20 | 59 | 8 | 2 | 0 | 26 | 15 | 22 | 6 | .300 | .301 |
| **MINOR LEAGUE TOTALS** | | | .297 | 588 | 2068 | 276 | 615 | 109 | 13 | 34 | 273 | 214 | 223 | 76 | .367 | .412 |

# NEW YORK
# METS

BY **MATT MEYERS**

No team cruised to the postseason more easily then the Mets in 2006, who did so with a team built through a variety of ways. There were free agents (Carlos Beltran, Billy Wagner), homegrown talent (Jose Reyes, David Wright) and trade acquisitions (Carlos Delgado, Paul Lo Duca). A late-season injury to one of their biggest free-agent signings, Pedro Martinez, undermined New York in October. After winning 97 regular-season games the Mets fell to the Cardinals in a memorable seven-game Championship Series.

Though the season's finish was disappointing, New York should be in position to contend for several years. The Mets did their best to ensure that in August, when they locked up both Reyes and Wright beyond their arbitration years for a combined $88.25 million. Reyes is signed through 2010 with an option for 2011 and Wright through 2012 with a 2013 option. Combined with Carlos Beltran, who's signed through 2011 and has yet to turn 30, the Mets will continue to have one of the game's best position-player cores for years.

The Mets are still big spenders and can fill most major holes on the free-agent market. But their farm system has improved to the point where they have players at the upper levels ready to make an impact.

Mike Pelfrey and Philip Humber seem poised to help the rotation in 2007 and could be its anchors for years and Lastings Milledge (who missed qualifying for this list) and Carlos Gomez may factor into the outfield.

General manager **Omar Minaya** is always willing to trade prospects for big leaguers,

too. He parted with three good prospects (righthanders Gaby Hernandez and Yusmeiro Petit, plus first baseman Mike Jacobs) last season to get Delgado and Lo Duca in separate deals with the Marlins.

In recent years, the Mets have done a fine job of signing high-ceiling talent. Their drafts haven't been deep, in part because they've forfeited eight early picks in the last five years as free agent compensation, but since 2001 they've signed Aaron Heilman, Wright, Scott Kazmir, Milledge, Humber and Pelfrey before the second round.

A former Mets international scouting director, Minaya also has re-emphasized his club's efforts on the worldwide market since becoming GM in September 2004. New York invested a combined $2.1 million on Dominican outfielder Fernando Martinez and Venezuelan righthander Deolis Guerra in 2005, and both had outstanding debuts in full-season leagues at age 17. The Mets dipped into the international well again last summer to sign Dominican catcher Francisco Pena, the son of former all-star Tony Pena, for $750,000.

In just two years at the helm, Minaya has turned the Mets from a punchline into one of the teams best equipped for the next half-decade. He has big league talent, minor league talent and a budget as large as anyone in the NL. Like the Mets' offense in 2006, it's a lethal combination.

## TOP 30 PROSPECTS

1. Mike Pelfrey, rhp
2. Fernando Martinez, of
3. Carlos Gomez, of
4. Philip Humber, rhp
5. Deolis Guerra, rhp
6. Kevin Mulvey, rhp
7. Jon Niese, lhp
8. Mike Carp, 1b
9. Joe Smith, rhp
10. Alay Soler, rhp
11. Anderson Hernandez, ss/2b
12. Francisco Pena, c
13. Adam Bostick, lhp
14. Brett Harper, 1b
15. Emmanuel Garcia, ss
16. Jose Coronado, ss
17. Josh Stinson, rhp
18. Bobby Parnell, rhp
19. Dustin Martin, of
20. Eddie Camacho, lhp
21. Nick Evans, 1b
22. Tobi Stoner, rhp
23. Sean Henry, of
24. Todd Privett, lhp
25. Mike Devaney, rhp
26. John Holdzkom, rhp
27. Mike Nickeas, c
28. Eric Brown, rhp
29. Daniel Stegall, of
30. Corey Coles, of

# ORGANIZATION OVERVIEW

**General manager:** Omar Minaya. **Farm director:** Adam Wogan. **Scouting director:** Rudy Terrasas.

## 2006 PERFORMANCE

| Class | Team | League | W | L | PCT | Finish* | Manager | Affiliated |
|---|---|---|---|---|---|---|---|---|
| Majors | New York | National | 97 | 65 | .599 | 1st (16) | Willie Randolph | — |
| Triple-A | #Norfolk Tides | International | 57 | 84 | .404 | 13th (14) | Ken Oberkfell | 1969 |
| Double-A | Binghamton Mets | Eastern | 70 | 70 | .500 | 6th (12) | Juan Samuel | 1992 |
| High A | St. Lucie Mets | Florida State | 77 | 62 | .554 | +3rd (12) | Gary Carter | 1988 |
| Low A | †Hagerstown Suns | South Atlantic | 58 | 82 | .414 | 14th (16) | Frank Cacciatore | 2005 |
| Short-season | Brooklyn Cyclones | New York-Penn | 41 | 33 | .554 | 4th (14) | George Greer | 2001 |
| Rookie | Kingsport Mets | Appalachian | 34 | 33 | .507 | 6th (10) | Donovan Mitchell | 1980 |
| Rookie | GCL Mets | Gulf Coast | 23 | 30 | .434 | 9th (13) | Bobby Floyd | 2004 |
| **OVERALL 2006 MINOR LEAGUE RECORD** | | | 360 | 394 | .477 | 24th (30) | | |

*Finish in overall standings (No. of teams in league). +League champion. #Affiliate will be in New Orleans (Pacific Coast) in 2007. †Affiliate will be in Savannah (South Atlantic) in 2007.

## ORGANIZATION LEADERS

### BATTING
| | | |
|---|---|---|
| AVG | Coles, Corey, St. Lucie | .341 |
| R | Carp, Mike, St. Lucie | 77 |
| H | Coles, Corey, St. Lucie | 156 |
| 2B | Evans, Nick, Hagerstown | 33 |
| 3B | Gomez, Carlos, Binghamton | 8 |
| HR | Flores, Jesus, St. Lucie | 21 |
| RBI | Carp, Mike, St. Lucie | 98 |
| BB | Caligiuri, Jay, Binghamton | 59 |
| SO | Ragsdale, Corey, Binghamton | 182 |
| SB | Gomez, Carlos, Binghamton | 41 |
| OBP | Coles, Corey, St. Lucie | .407 |
| SLG | Abreu, Michel, St. Lucie/Binghamton | .546 |
| XBH | Abreu, Michel, St. Lucie/Binghamton | 54 |

### PITCHING
| | | |
|---|---|---|
| W | Devaney, Michael, St. Lucie/Binghamton | 12 |
| | MacLane, Evan, Binghamton/Norfolk/Tucson | 12 |
| L | Landing, Jeffrey, Hagerstown | 11 |
| | Niese, Jonathan, Hagerstown/St. Lucie | 11 |
| | Parnell, Robert, Hagerstown/St. Lucie | 11 |
| | Scobie, Jason, Norfolk/New Hampshire/Syracuse | 11 |
| ERA | Devaney, Michael, St. Lucie/Binghamton | 2.13 |
| G | Camacho, Eddie, Binghamton | 53 |
| SV | Muniz, Carlos, St. Lucie | 31 |
| IP | Pinango, Miguel, Binghamton | 160 |
| BB | Devaney, Michael, St. Lucie/Binghamton | 70 |
| SO | Niese, Jonathan, Hagerstown/St. Lucie | 142 |
| AVG | Devaney, Michael, St. Lucie/Binghamton | .196 |

## BEST TOOLS

| | |
|---|---|
| Best Hitter for Average | Fernando Martinez |
| Best Power Hitter | Fernando Martinez |
| Best Strike-Zone Discipline | Corey Coles |
| Fastest Baserunner | Carlos Gomez |
| Best Athlete | Carlos Gomez |
| Best Fastball | Mike Pelfrey |
| Best Curveball | Philip Humber |
| Best Slider | Joe Smith |
| Best Changeup | Deolis Guerra |
| Best Control | Willie Collazo |
| Best Defensive Catcher | Drew Butera |
| Best Defensive Infielder | Jose Coronado |
| Best Infield Arm | Corey Ragsdale |
| Best Defensive Outfielder | Carlos Gomez |
| Best Outfield Arm | Carlos Gomez |

## PROJECTED 2010 LINEUP

| | |
|---|---|
| Catcher | Francisco Pena |
| First Base | Carlos Delgado |
| Second Base | Anderson Hernandez |
| Third Base | David Wright |
| Shortstop | Jose Reyes |

| | |
|---|---|
| Left Field | Lastings Milledge |
| Center Field | Carlos Beltran |
| Right Field | Fernando Martinez |
| No. 1 Starter | Mike Pelfrey |
| No. 2 Starter | Philip Humber |
| No. 3 Starter | John Maine |
| No. 4 Starter | Deolis Guerra |
| No. 5 Starter | Kevin Mulvey |
| Closer | Billy Wagner |

## LAST YEAR'S TOP 20 PROSPECTS

| | |
|---|---|
| 1. Lastings Milledge, of | 11. Jose Coronado, ss |
| 2. Philip Humber, rhp | 12. Jesus Flores, c |
| 3. Carlos Gomez, of | 13. Jeff Keppinger, 2b |
| 4. Fernando Martinez, of | 14. Shawn Bowman, 3b |
| 5. Anderson Hernandez, ss/2b | 15. Bobby Parnell, rhp |
| 6. Brian Bannister, rhp | 16. Emmanuel Garcia, ss |
| 7. Alay Soler, rhp | 17. Mike Carp, 1b |
| 8. Deolis Guerra, rhp | 18. Hector Pellot, 2b |
| 9. Jon Niese, lhp | 19. Matt Durkin, rhp |
| 10. Brett Harper, 1b | 20. Aarom Baldiris, 2b |

## TOP PROSPECTS OF THE DECADE

| Year | Player, Pos. | 2006 Org. |
|---|---|---|
| 1997 | Jay Payton, of | Athletics |
| 1998 | Grant Roberts, rhp | Out of baseball |
| 1999 | Alex Escobar, of | Nationals |
| 2000 | Alex Escobar, of | Nationals |
| 2001 | Alex Escobar, of | Nationals |
| 2002 | Aaron Heilman, rhp | Mets |
| 2003 | Jose Reyes, ss | Mets |
| 2004 | Kazuo Matsui, ss | Rockies |
| 2005 | Lastings Milledge, of | Mets |
| 2006 | Lastings Milledge, of | Mets |

## TOP DRAFT PICKS OF THE DECADE

| Year | Player, Pos. | 2006 Org. |
|---|---|---|
| 1997 | Geoff Goetz, lhp | Nashua (Can-Am) |
| 1998 | Jason Tyner, of | Twins |
| 1999 | Neil Musser, lhp (2nd round) | Royals |
| 2000 | Billy Traber, lhp | Nationals |
| 2001 | Aaron Heilman, rhp | Mets |
| 2002 | Scott Kazmir, lhp | Devil Rays |
| 2003 | Lastings Milledge, of | Mets |
| 2004 | Philip Humber, rhp | Mets |
| 2005 | Mike Pelfrey, rhp | Mets |
| 2006 | Kevin Mulvey, rhp | Mets |

## ALL-TIME LARGEST BONUSES

| | |
|---|---|
| Mike Pelfrey, 2005 | $3,550,000 |
| Philip Humber, 2004 | $3,000,000 |
| Scott Kazmir, 2002 | $2,150,000 |
| Lastings Milledge, 2003 | $2,075,000 |
| Geoff Goetz, 1997 | $1,700,000 |

# MINOR LEAGUE DEPTH CHART

## New York Mets

**Impact: A.** Pelfrey and Humber give the Mets two righthanders on the verge of making an impact, while Martinez, Gomez and Guerra give them three players with enormous ceilings.

**Depth: C.** Years of forfeiting draft picks for free agents have caught up with them a bit. The drop-off after the top five is significant, and there is very little at the lower levels.

**Sleeper:** Josh Stinson, rhp. Slipped through the cracks to the 37th round, Stinson was so good in the GCL that he even got a late season promotion to low Class A.

*Numbers in parentheses indicate prospect rankings.*

| LF | CF | RF |
|---|---|---|
| Dustin Martin (19) | Fernando Martinez (2) | Daniel Stegall (29) |
| Corey Coles (30) | Carlos Gomez (3) | Ambiorix Concepcion |
| | Sean Henry (23) | Richard Pena |

| 3B | SS | 2B | 1B |
|---|---|---|---|
| Shawn Bowman | Jose Coronado (16) | Anderson Hernandez (11) | Mike Carp (8) |
| Chase Lambin | Emmanuel Garcia (15) | Hector Pellot | Brett Harper (14) |
| | Corey Ragsdale | | Nick Evans (21) |
| | Jose Castro | | Michel Abreu |
| | Luis Rivera | | Junior Contreras |

| C |
|---|
| Francisco Pena (12) |
| Mike Nickeas (27) |
| Drew Butera |
| Sean McCraw |

### RHP

| Starters | Relievers |
|---|---|
| Mike Pelfrey (1) | Joe Smith (9) |
| Philip Humber (4) | John Holdzkom (26) |
| Deolis Guerra (5) | Jeremy Mizell |
| Kevin Mulvey (6) | Steve Schmoll |
| Alay Soler (10) | Rafael Cova |
| Josh Stinson (17) | Jose De La Torre |
| Bobby Parnell (18) | |
| Tobi Stoner (22) | |
| Mike Devaney (25) | |
| Eric Brown (28) | |
| Jose Sanchez | |
| Stephen Holmes | |
| Matt Durkin | |
| Jorge Reyes | |

### LHP

| Starters | Relievers |
|---|---|
| Jon Niese (7) | Eddie Camacho (20) |
| Adam Bostick (13) | Mitch Wylie |
| Todd Privett (24) | Blake McGinley |

## 2006

**Best Pro Debut:** RHP Joe Smith (3) had a 0.45 ERA and 28-2 K-BB ratio in 20 New York-Penn League innings, earning a promotion to Double-A. RHP Tobi Stoner (16) went 6-2, 2.15 in the NY-P and allowed just five earned runs over his final eight starts.

**Best Athlete:** OF Daniel Stegall was a Miami quarterback recruit. He's raw as a hitter, but all of his other tools are above-average and he profiles as a classic right fielder.

**Best Pure Hitter:** OF Dustin Martin (26) won the Southland Conference batting title with a .389 average, then opened the Mets' eyes by hitting .315/.399/.454 in the NY-P and .269 in Hawaii Winter Baseball.

**Best Raw Power:** C Bradley Hubbert (32), a late-summer sign, runs well for a 6-foot-4, 210-pounder. Primarily an outfielder before transferring to Alcorn State in 2006, he showed enough behind the plate in instructional league for the Mets to believe he can stay there. OF Jeremy Barfield (9), now at San Jacinto (Texas) JC but under control to the Mets, has more power than Hubbert.

**Fastest Runner:** OF Will Bashelor (28) has 6.5-second speed in the 60-yard dash, making him slightly quicker than Stegall.

**Best Defensive Player:** SS/2B Ritchie Price (18) is a sound defender with quality instincts. He has a chance to reach the majors if he hits enough, a question after he batted .229 in his pro debut.

**Best Fastball:** RHP Kevin Mulvey (2), the Mets' top pick, throws 90-94 mph with little effort. He to--pped out at 96 during the summer. He has the best fastball based on a combination of velocity, life and command. For sheer ability to light up a radar gun, it's RHP John Holdzkom (4), who can hit 98 mph but doesn't always know where his heater is headed.

**Best Breaking Ball:** Most sidearmers lose velocity and have difficulty staying on top of a breaking pitch when they drop down, but not Smith. His fastball went from 85-87 mph to 88-91 (peaking at 94), and his slider was death on righthanders: They went just 7-for-67 (.104) with one extra-base hit (a double) against him in pro ball.

**Most Intriguing Background:** Barfield's father Jesse and C Stephen Puhl's (17) dad Terry are both former all-stars, and Barfield's brother Josh plays second base for the Padres. Holdzkom's brother Lincoln pitches in the Cubs system. Price's father Ritch coached him at Kansas. 1B Joel Wells (21)

declined the chance to turn pro to attend medical school at Tulane.

**Closest To The Majors:** Both Mulvey and Smith reached Double-A. Mulvey had more success there, but Smith will have an easier time reaching Shea Stadium as a reliever.

**Best Late-Round Pick:** RHP Josh Stinson (37) already works at 89-92 mph and touches 94, with a lot of projection remaining in his 6-foot-4, 190-pound frame. He also has the best curveball in New York's draft, though it's not as consistent as Smith's slider. He posted a 1.35 ERA in three low Class A starts at age 18.

**The One Who Got Away:** LHP/OF Justin Woodall (19) was one of the best athletes in the draft, a lefthander with a mid-90s fastball and an offensive threat with well-above-average power and speed. He's also a defensive back with NFL potential. While the Mets considered signing him to a two-sport deal, they decided the likelihood of losing him to football was too great. He's playing at Alabama.

**Assessment:** Rudy Terrassas didn't have a first-round pick in his first draft as Mets scouting director, but his first two choices advanced to Double-A. New York focused on pitching, with Stegall the only position player signed out of the first 11 rounds.

## 2005 BUDGET: $4.7 million

Good news: The Mets got the draft's consensus best pitching prospect, RHP Mike Pelfrey (1), at No. 9. Bad news: They failed to sign RHP Pedro Beato (17), who went 31st overall in 2006. **GRADE: B+**

## 2004 BUDGET: $5.3 million

RHP Philip Humber (1) has rebounded from Tommy John surgery and 1B Mike Carp (9) has a legitimate bat. RHP Gaby Hernandez (3) was used to get Paul LoDuca. **GRADE: C**

## 2003 BUDGET: $3.0 million

New York seemed to sour on OF Lastings Milledge (1) last year, but he still has huge potential. RHP Brian Bannister (7) was traded to the Royals for Ambiorix Burgos this offseason. **GRADE: B**

*Draft analysis by Jim Callis. Numbers in parentheses indicate draft rounds. Budgets are bonuses in first 10 rounds.*

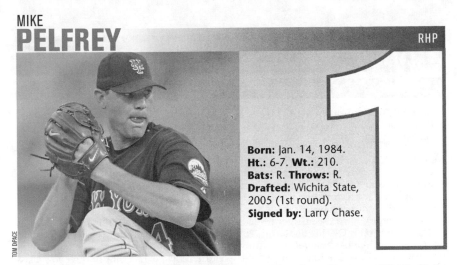

# MIKE
# PELFREY

RHP

**Born:** Jan. 14, 1984.
**Ht.:** 6-7. **Wt.:** 210.
**Bats:** R. **Throws:** R.
**Drafted:** Wichita State, 2005 (1st round).
**Signed by:** Larry Chase.

TOM DIPACE

After going 33-7 with a school-record 2.18 ERA in three seasons at Wichita State, Pelfrey was Baseball America's top-rated pitching prospect heading into the 2005 draft. The Diamondbacks considered him for the No. 1 overall pick, but he ultimately dropped to the Mets at No. 9 because of signability concerns. He didn't sign until January, when he received a club-record $3.55 million bonus as part of a $5.25 million big league contract. Pelfrey showed no ill effects from his layoff and needed just four starts at high Class A St. Lucie to earn a promotion to Double-A Binghamton. Pelfrey credits veteran catcher Mike DiFelice—whom the Mets sent to Binghamton solely to serve as mentor—with helping him gain confidence in his secondary stuff. He earned a major league callup when Pedro Martinez first went on the disabled list in July and won his first big league start before being sent to Triple-A Norfolk. If not for a sore back that limited him late in the season, Pelfrey would have been in the mix for a spot in the postseason bullpen. He might have gotten a playoff start, considering how beat up New York's starting pitchers were.

There are few pitchers in the minors whose fastball can rival Pelfrey's. His two-seamer sits at 92-95 mph with fierce sink and late life and rates as a 70 on the 20-80 scouting scale. He throws it effortlessly from a 6-foot-7 frame on a steep downhill plane with great extension and solid command. He also has a four-seamer for extra velocity higher in the zone. Though Pelfrey barely needed to use a changeup as an amateur, he already has a good feel for it and it's his No. 2 pitch. He fiddled with his grip in 2006 and improved his command of the pitch. He fields his position well and has a good pickoff move, though the Mets would like to see him get faster to the plate from the stretch.

A lack of a reliable breaking ball is the biggest thing holding Pelfrey back. He has thrown both a curveball and a slider but now favors the slider, which is better suited for his power arm. He throws it at 84-87 mph with some depth, and he can reduce the break on it to give it more of a cutter look against lefthanders. He has yet to learn how to command his slider consistently, and it probably always will be his third-best pitch. Though his mechanics are clean, he tends to over-rotate his lower half in his windup, which hurts his ability to locate his pitches.

Though he needs better command of his secondary stuff, there's little left for Pelfrey to prove in the minors. With Martinez out until at least the all-star break, Pelfrey will definitely be in the mix for the Opening Day rotation. He should be in the Mets rotation for years to come and has the potential to be a legitimate No. 1 starter.

| Year | Club (League) | Class | W | L | ERA | G | GS | CG | SV | IP | H | R | ER | HR | BB | SO | AVG |
|------|---------------|-------|---|---|-----|---|----|----|----|----|---|---|----|----|----|----|-----|
| 2006 | St. Lucie (FSL) | A | 2 | 1 | 1.64 | 4 | 4 | 0 | 0 | 22 | 17 | 5 | 4 | 1 | 2 | 26 | .224 |
| | Binghamton (EL) | AA | 4 | 2 | 2.71 | 12 | 12 | 0 | 0 | 66 | 60 | 23 | 20 | 2 | 26 | 77 | .244 |
| | New York (NL) | MLB | 2 | 1 | 5.48 | 4 | 4 | 0 | 0 | 21 | 25 | 14 | 13 | 1 | 12 | 13 | .305 |
| | Norfolk (IL) | AAA | 1 | 0 | 2.25 | 2 | 2 | 0 | 0 | 8 | 4 | 2 | 2 | 1 | 5 | 6 | .148 |
| **MINOR LEAGUE TOTALS** | | | 7 | 3 | 2.43 | 18 | 18 | 0 | 0 | 96 | 81 | 30 | 26 | 4 | 33 | 109 | .232 |
| **MAJOR LEAGUE TOTALS** | | | 2 | 1 | 5.48 | 4 | 4 | 0 | 0 | 21 | 25 | 14 | 13 | 1 | 12 | 13 | .305 |

## 2  FERNANDO MARTINEZ
OF

**Born:** Oct. 10, 1988. **B-T:** L-R. **Ht.:** 6-0. **Wt.:** 185. **Signed:** Dominican Republic, 2005. **Signed by:** Rafael Bournigal/Sandy Johnson/Eddy Toledo.

Martinez received the largest bonus of any international sign in 2005 ($1.4 million) and proved to be a good investment in his debut. Though he missed time with a bone bruise in his hand and a knee sprain, Martinez handled the low Class A South Atlantic League at age 17 and earned a promotion to high Class A. The youngest player in the Arizona Fall League, he recovered from a 1-for-18 start to hit .304 afterward. Martinez has an advanced approach well beyond his years. He has good pitch recognition, strike-zone awareness and power to all fields. He has slightly above-average speed, though he's better underway than down the line or as a basestealer. He has a strong outfield arm. Like many young hitters, Martinez tends to overswing when he gets in a funk but should outgrow that as he gets more reps against advanced pitching. He doesn't have a good first step and can take poor routes in center field, which likely means that he'll end up in right field. Martinez has the highest ceiling of any hitter in the system and will put himself into the discussion of the best prospects in baseball if he can build on his 2006 season. Even if he has to move from center field, his bat could make him an all-star. He should be back in high Class A to begin 2007.

| Year | Club (League) | Class | AVG | G | AB | R | H | 2B | 3B | HR | RBI | BB | SO | SB | OBP | SLG |
|------|---------------|-------|-----|---|----|---|---|----|----|----|-----|----|----|----|-----|-----|
| 2006 | GCL Mets (GCL) | R | .250 | 1 | 4 | 1 | 1 | 0 | 0 | 0 | 0 | 0 | 1 | 0 | .250 | .250 |
|  | St. Lucie (FSL) | A | .193 | 30 | 119 | 18 | 23 | 4 | 2 | 5 | 11 | 6 | 24 | 1 | .254 | .387 |
|  | Hagerstown (SAL) | A | .333 | 45 | 192 | 24 | 64 | 14 | 2 | 5 | 28 | 15 | 36 | 7 | .389 | .505 |
| **MINOR LEAGUE TOTALS** | | | .279 | 76 | 315 | 43 | 88 | 18 | 4 | 10 | 39 | 21 | 61 | 8 | .336 | .457 |

## 3  CARLOS GOMEZ
OF

**Born:** Dec. 4, 1985. **B-T:** R-R. **Ht.:** 6-2. **Wt.:** 175. **Signed:** Dominican Republic, 2002. **Signed by:** Eddy Toledo.

The Mets decided to let Gomez skip high Class A because they were so impressed with the way he responded to instruction and made adjustments during spring training. He started the season slow and spent some time in extended spring straining when a back injury sidelined him in May. Roving hitting instructor Lamar Johnson got him to relax the upper half in his swing, and Gomez batted .323 the rest of the way. Gomez' arm and speed both rate as a 70 on the 20-80 scouting scale. He's an above-average center fielder and he refined his basestealing technique to where he had 41 swipes in 50 attempts in 2006. His lightning-quick bat and natural swing path allow him to make consistent hard contact. His arm gives him yet another plus tool. Much of his game is still raw. Gomez is too aggressive at the plate and needs to improve his situational hitting. He has plus raw power that has yet to show up in game action. His flashy style has irked some his opponents, but the Mets don't see it as a problem and think it will diminish as he matures. With Carlos Beltran signed through 2011, Gomez' future with New York lies in right field. Ticketed for the Mets' new Triple-A New Orleans affiliate, he has a ceiling comparable with that of Fernando Martinez.

| Year | Club (League) | Class | AVG | G | AB | R | H | 2B | 3B | HR | RBI | BB | SO | SB | OBP | SLG |
|------|---------------|-------|-----|---|----|---|---|----|----|----|-----|----|----|----|-----|-----|
| 2003 | Mets (DSL) | R | .240 | 58 | 208 | 26 | 50 | 7 | 0 | 1 | 10 | 7 | 37 | 13 | .283 | .288 |
| 2004 | Kingsport (Appy) | R | .287 | 38 | 150 | 24 | 43 | 10 | 4 | 1 | 20 | 5 | 29 | 8 | .333 | .427 |
|  | Mets (GCL) | R | .268 | 19 | 71 | 10 | 19 | 7 | 0 | 0 | 11 | 2 | 9 | 9 | .303 | .366 |
| 2005 | Hagerstown (SAL) | A | .275 | 120 | 487 | 75 | 134 | 13 | 6 | 8 | 48 | 32 | 88 | 64 | .331 | .376 |
| 2006 | Binghamton (EL) | AA | .281 | 120 | 430 | 53 | 121 | 24 | 8 | 7 | 48 | 27 | 97 | 41 | .350 | .423 |
| **MINOR LEAGUE TOTALS** | | | .273 | 355 | 1346 | 188 | 367 | 61 | 18 | 17 | 137 | 73 | 260 | 135 | .329 | .383 |

## 4  PHILIP HUMBER
RHP

**Born:** Dec. 21, 1982. **B-T:** R-R. **Ht.:** 6-4. **Wt.:** 210. **Drafted:** Rice, 2004 (1st round). **Signed by:** Dave Lottsfeldt.

The winning pitcher in the championship game of the 2003 College World Series, Humber went third overall in the 2004 draft and signed the following January. His big league deal included a $3 million bonus and $4.2 million guarantee. Tommy John surgery in July 2005 cut his pro debut short, but he was on the field one year later and quickly returned to his previous form. Humber's curveball is one of the best in the minors. Thrown at 74-78 mph, it has tight rotation with a powerful downward action. His fastball sits at 90-94 mph. He also features a developing low-80s changeup with

late sink. He throws strikes with all three pitches. Humber has a tendency to overthrow, which tires him out and costs him his command. It also hurts his changeup, which loses its effectiveness when it climbs to 86-87 mph. As good as his curveball is, he could do a better job of throwing it for strikes because big league hitters will be less likely to chase it. Though his Arizona Fall League stint ended with a sore shoulder, an MRI revealed no damage and Humber is primed for his first full-season workload. Though his stuff is good enough to pitch in the big leagues, Humber will probably be better served with a full season in Triple-A to improve his endurance. He profiles as a No. 2 or 3 starter.

| Year | Club (League) | Class | W | L | ERA | G | GS | CG | SV | IP | H | R | ER | HR | BB | SO | AVG |
|------|---------------|-------|---|---|-----|---|----|----|----|----|---|---|----|----|----|----|-----|
| 2005 | St. Lucie (FSL) | A | 2 | 6 | 4.99 | 14 | 14 | 0 | 0 | 70 | 74 | 41 | 39 | 6 | 18 | 65 | .273 |
| | Binghamton (EL) | AA | 0 | 1 | 6.75 | 1 | 1 | 0 | 0 | 4 | 4 | 3 | 3 | 0 | 2 | 2 | .250 |
| 2006 | Mets (GCL) | R | 0 | 0 | 6.75 | 1 | 1 | 0 | 0 | 4 | 7 | 3 | 3 | 0 | 1 | 7 | .389 |
| | St. Lucie (FSL) | A | 3 | 1 | 2.37 | 7 | 7 | 0 | 0 | 38 | 24 | 12 | 10 | 4 | 9 | 36 | .178 |
| | Binghamton (EL) | AA | 2 | 2 | 2.88 | 6 | 6 | 0 | 0 | 34 | 25 | 12 | 11 | 4 | 10 | 36 | .195 |
| | New York (NL) | MLB | 0 | 0 | 0.00 | 2 | 0 | 0 | 0 | 2 | 0 | 0 | 0 | 0 | 1 | 2 | .000 |
| **MINOR LEAGUE TOTALS** | | | 7 | 10 | 3.94 | 29 | 29 | 0 | 0 | 151 | 134 | 71 | 66 | 14 | 40 | 146 | .236 |
| **MAJOR LEAGUE TOTALS** | | | 0 | 0 | 0.00 | 2 | 0 | 0 | 0 | 2 | 0 | 0 | 0 | 0 | 1 | 2 | .000 |

## 5 DEOLIS GUERRA                                           RHP

**Born:** April 17, 1989. **B-T:** R-R. **Ht.:** 6-5. **Wt.:** 200. **Signed:** Venezuela, 2005. **Signed by:** Rafael Bournigal.

After signing for $700,000 as the top prospect coming out of Venezuela in 2005, Guerra was challenged with an assignment to the South Atlantic League as the circuit's youngest player in 2006. He responded by shaking off a rocky start to go 6-5, 1.90 in the last three months and earn a late promotion to high Class A. Guerra stands out most with a feel for his changeup that's exceptional for a teenager. He maintains his normal arm action, setting up a fastball that sits at 88-90 mph and touches 92. His frame should allow for more velocity as he matures, making the gap between his changeup and fastball all the more difficult for hitters. Guerra's curveball is below average. He lacks confidence in his curve, and it has poor rotation and depth. The tilt and velocity on his breaking ball changes as he tries to figure it out, and it's possible it could morph into a slider. His delivery is repeatable but too slow and mechanical. With a little more velocity and an average curveball, Guerra would establish himself as an elite prospect. Time is certainly on his side, as he'll begin the season at age 17, making him a safe bet to be the youngest player in the Florida State League.

| Year | Club (League) | Class | W | L | ERA | G | GS | CG | SV | IP | H | R | ER | HR | BB | SO | AVG |
|------|---------------|-------|---|---|-----|---|----|----|----|----|---|---|----|----|----|----|-----|
| 2006 | Hagerstown (SAL) | A | 6 | 7 | 2.20 | 17 | 17 | 0 | 0 | 82 | 59 | 22 | 20 | 3 | 37 | 64 | .208 |
| | St. Lucie (FSL) | A | 1 | 1 | 6.14 | 2 | 2 | 0 | 0 | 7 | 9 | 6 | 5 | 1 | 6 | 5 | .290 |
| **MINOR LEAGUE TOTALS** | | | 7 | 8 | 2.53 | 19 | 19 | 0 | 0 | 89 | 68 | 28 | 25 | 4 | 43 | 69 | .217 |

## 6 KEVIN MULVEY                                            RHP

**Born:** May 26, 1985. **B-T:** R-R. **Ht.:** 6-1. **Wt.:** 175. **Drafted:** Villanova, 2006 (2nd round). **Signed by:** Scott Hunter.

Mulvey's mother was watching a Dwight Gooden start for the Mets when she went into labor with Kevin, so it was only fitting that the club made him its top pick in the 2006 draft. A second-rounder, he signed late for $585,000 but still reached Double-A. Mulvey came to pro ball with a feel for four pitches. His fastball sits at 90-93 mph and touches 96. He has good leverage in his delivery, which allows him to maintain his velocity and might give him more as he matures physically. His 82-84 mph slider has short, late break. He's effective at changing a batter's eye level with his mid-70s curveball. His changeup should at least provide a weapon against lefthanders. He throws from a high three-quarters arm slot with a fluid arm action and little effort. Though he can throw all four of his pitches for strikes, Mulvey's command within the zone needs work. His changeup is still a below-average pitch at this point, and he lacks a true putaway pitch. The Mets believe Mulvey has a chance to have four above-average pitches and could join their rotation in 2008. He may start his first full season in St. Lucie to avoid the cold April climate in Binghamton.

| Year | Club (League) | Class | W | L | ERA | G | GS | CG | SV | IP | H | R | ER | HR | BB | SO | AVG |
|------|---------------|-------|---|---|-----|---|----|----|----|----|---|---|----|----|----|----|-----|
| 2006 | Mets (GCL) | R | 0 | 0 | 0.00 | 1 | 1 | 0 | 0 | 2 | 1 | 0 | 0 | 0 | 0 | 1 | .143 |
| | Binghamton (EL) | AA | 0 | 1 | 1.35 | 3 | 3 | 1 | 0 | 13 | 10 | 4 | 2 | 1 | 5 | 10 | .217 |
| **MINOR LEAGUE TOTALS** | | | 0 | 1 | 1.17 | 4 | 4 | 1 | 0 | 15 | 11 | 4 | 2 | 1 | 5 | 11 | .208 |

## JON NIESE
LHP

STEVE MOORE

**Born:** Oct. 27, 1986. **B-T:** L-L. **Ht.:** 6-3. **Wt.:** 190. **Drafted:** HS—Defiance, Ohio, 2005 (7th round). **Signed by:** Erwin Bryant.

A product of the same Defiance (Ohio) High program that spawned Chad Billingsley, Niese was Ohio's first ever back-to-back state high school player of the year. He was deemed a tough sign coming out of high school, but a recruiting call from Hall of Fame catcher Gary Carter convinced Niese to sign for $175,000, the equivalent of early fifth-round money. Niese is at his best when he has command of his three-pitch mix. He has a lively fastball that sits at 87-90 mph. His big, looping 68-70 mph curveball is a strikeout pitch when it's on. He's willing to throw his 77-79 mph straight changeup to both lefthanders and righthanders. The Mets love his competitive fire. Though both his curveball and changeup have potential, Niese rarely has a feel for both of them on the same night. His curve could use more consistent rotation and he needs better command of both pitches. He can get overcompetitve and try to strike everyone out, which works against him. He'll have to get stronger after wearing down as his first full season progressed, resulting in some ugly late-season starts. Despite some inconsistency, Niese showed promise in 2006. He'll return to high Class A, where he made two late starts, and projects as a middle-of-the-rotation starter.

| Year | Club (League) | Class | W | L | ERA | G | GS | CG | SV | IP | H | R | ER | HR | BB | SO | AVG |
|---|---|---|---|---|---|---|---|---|---|---|---|---|---|---|---|---|---|
| 2005 | Mets (GCL) | R | 1 | 0 | 3.65 | 7 | 5 | 0 | 0 | 25 | 23 | 10 | 10 | 1 | 10 | 24 | .245 |
| 2006 | Hagerstown (SAL) | A | 11 | 9 | 3.93 | 25 | 25 | 1 | 0 | 124 | 121 | 67 | 54 | 7 | 62 | 132 | .256 |
| | St. Lucie (FSL) | A | 0 | 2 | 4.50 | 2 | 2 | 0 | 0 | 10 | 8 | 8 | 5 | 0 | 5 | 10 | .216 |
| **MINOR LEAGUE TOTALS** | | | 12 | 11 | 3.92 | 34 | 32 | 1 | 0 | 158 | 152 | 85 | 69 | 8 | 77 | 166 | .252 |

## MIKE CARP
1B

MARC S. LEVINE

**Born:** June 30, 1986. **B-T:** L-R. **Ht.:** 6-2. **Wt.:** 205. **Drafted:** HS—Lakewood, Calif., 2004 (9th round). **Signed by:** Steve Leavitt.

Carp hit 11 homers in his first 26 games at low Class A Hagertown in 2005 then fell into a deep slump before injuring his right wrist. He made adjustments, however, and rebounded to be named Mets minor league player of the year in 2006. After using more of the field and tightening his strike zone, he led both the system and the Florida State League in RBIs. Carp is an all-around hitter with good hand-eye coordination, pitch recognition and power. He makes consistent hard contact and can drive the ball from gap to gap. Though young for his leagues the last two years, he has shown an advanced approach at the plate. There are mixed reviews about Carp's defense. He's by no means a butcher, but he doesn't have quick feet and he has trouble receiving throws. He reaches for balls instead of letting them come to him, creating unnecessary errors. He's a below-average runner. Carp will need his bat to carry him, and it may do just that. The Mets will get a better read on his future after he spends 2007 in Double-A.

| Year | Club (League) | Class | AVG | G | AB | R | H | 2B | 3B | HR | RBI | BB | SO | SB | OBP | SLG |
|---|---|---|---|---|---|---|---|---|---|---|---|---|---|---|---|---|
| 2004 | Mets (GCL) | R | .267 | 57 | 191 | 30 | 51 | 12 | 0 | 4 | 26 | 22 | 51 | 2 | .358 | .393 |
| 2005 | Hagerstown (SAL) | A | .249 | 89 | 313 | 49 | 78 | 12 | 1 | 19 | 63 | 35 | 96 | 2 | .358 | .476 |
| 2006 | St. Lucie (FSL) | A | .287 | 137 | 491 | 69 | 141 | 27 | 1 | 17 | 88 | 51 | 107 | 2 | .379 | .450 |
| **MINOR LEAGUE TOTALS** | | | .271 | 283 | 995 | 148 | 270 | 51 | 2 | 40 | 177 | 108 | 254 | 6 | .368 | .447 |

## JOE SMITH
RHP

RICH ABEL

**Born:** March 22, 1984. **B-T:** R-R. **Ht.:** 6-2. **Wt.:** 205. **Drafted:** Wright State, 2006 (3rd round). **Signed by:** Erwin Bryant.

Smith had shoulder surgery as a senior in high school and couldn't make the Wright State roster as a freshman. After making the team as a walk-on in 2004, he dropped his arm angle from high three-quarters to sidearm a year later and his stuff improved appreciably. His 0.98 ERA would have led NCAA Division I last spring, but he fell five innings short of qualifying. A third-round pick, he signed for $410,000 and reached Double-A in August. Smith is unique because he throws much harder than typical sidearmers, and his 89-91 mph fastball has sinking, fading action. It tops out at 94. He stays on top of an 81-83 mph, two-plane slider that destroys righthanders. They hit just .104 against him in pro ball. The key to Smith reaching his ceiling is his changeup. He never needed it in college, but he does in pro ball to keep advanced lefthanders honest. They went 10-for-20 (.500) against him in his brief Double-A stint. If he can make his

changeup an average pitch, Smith should be an excellent setup man. Without it, he'd be just a righthanded specialist. Chad Bradford filled that role for the Mets in 2006, and his departure could allow Smith to make the team at some point in his first full season. He'll probably open in Triple-A.

| Year | Club (League) | Class | W | L | ERA | G | GS | CG | SV | IP | H | R | ER | HR | BB | SO | AVG |
|------|---------------|-------|---|---|-----|---|----|----|----|----|---|---|----|----|----|----|-----|
| 2006 | Brooklyn (NYP) | A | 0 | 1 | 0.45 | 17 | 0 | 0 | 9 | 20 | 10 | 3 | 1 | 0 | 3 | 28 | .141 |
| | Binghamton (EL) | AA | 0 | 2 | 5.68 | 10 | 0 | 0 | 0 | 13 | 12 | 8 | 8 | 1 | 11 | 12 | .267 |
| **MINOR LEAGUE TOTALS** | | | 0 | 3 | 2.48 | 27 | 0 | 0 | 9 | 33 | 22 | 11 | 9 | 1 | 14 | 40 | .190 |

## 10  ALAY SOLER                                     RHP

**Born:** Oct. 9, 1979. **B-T:** R-R. **Ht.:** 6-1. **Wt.:** 240. **Signed:** Cuba, 2004. **Signed by:** Rafael Bournigal.

After signing a $2.8 million major league contract in the fall of 2004, Soler missed all of 2005 because he couldn't secure a visa until October. He showed up to his first big league camp out of shape and had a poor spring training, though he bounced back to reach New York in May. He threw a two-hit shutout against the Diamondbacks, but struggled with his control shortly afterward and was demoted in early July. Soler has success when he attacks the strike zone with his low-90s fastball and above-average slider. The latter is his best pitch. He throws it at 80-81 mph with sharp, late break to righthanders and slows it down and backdoors it against lefties. Soler is his own worst enemy and gets in trouble when he tries to nibble and play around with his offspeed stuff in what looks like an attempt to emulate fellow Cuban Orlando Hernandez. He needs to dedicate himself much more to conditioning after making a bad first impression. After his midsummer demotion, he missed six weeks with a minor Achilles problem that isn't considered serious but wasn't helped by his excess weight. If Soler plays to his strengths, he has the chance to be a solid back-of-the-rotation starter or setup man. How much time he spends getting in shape likely will dictate his assignment in 2007, and when he could contribute in the majors.

| Year | Club (League) | Class | W | L | ERA | G | GS | CG | SV | IP | H | R | ER | HR | BB | SO | AVG |
|------|---------------|-------|---|---|-----|---|----|----|----|----|---|---|----|----|----|----|-----|
| 2005 | Mets (DSL) | R | 0 | 1 | 1.69 | 2 | 1 | 0 | 0 | 5 | 3 | 3 | 1 | 0 | 2 | 12 | .143 |
| 2006 | St. Lucie (FSL) | A | 2 | 0 | 0.60 | 6 | 6 | 0 | 0 | 30 | 13 | 2 | 2 | 0 | 9 | 33 | .129 |
| | Binghamton (EL) | AA | 1 | 0 | 2.75 | 3 | 3 | 0 | 0 | 20 | 16 | 6 | 6 | 0 | 3 | 22 | .222 |
| | New York (NL) | MLB | 2 | 3 | 6.00 | 8 | 8 | 1 | 0 | 45 | 50 | 33 | 30 | 7 | 21 | 23 | .275 |
| | Brooklyn (NYP) | A | 0 | 1 | 6.23 | 1 | 1 | 0 | 0 | 4 | 2 | 3 | 3 | 1 | 2 | 9 | .125 |
| | Norfolk (IL) | AAA | 1 | 1 | 6.30 | 2 | 2 | 0 | 0 | 10 | 13 | 7 | 7 | 0 | 4 | 12 | .317 |
| **MINOR LEAGUE TOTALS** | | | 4 | 3 | 2.47 | 14 | 13 | 0 | 0 | 69 | 47 | 21 | 19 | 1 | 20 | 88 | .187 |
| **MAJOR LEAGUE TOTALS** | | | 2 | 3 | 6.00 | 8 | 8 | 1 | 0 | 45 | 50 | 33 | 30 | 7 | 21 | 23 | .275 |

## 11  ANDERSON HERNANDEZ                                     SS/2B

**Born:** Oct. 30, 1982. **B-T:** B-R. **Ht.:** 5-9. **Wt.:** 170. **Signed:** Dominican Republic, 2001. **Signed by:** Ramon Pena (Tigers).

No Mets prospect took a bigger step forward in 2005, but few stalled as much as Hernandez in 2006. He opened the season as the Mets' second baseman, but he struggled with the bat and then was sidelined with a bulging disc. By the time he recovered, Jose Valentin had displaced him as the Mets' regular second baseman. Hernandez' strength is his defensive ability. He has soft hands, plus range and an above-average arm but sometimes gets lazy and doesn't charge balls aggressively enough. A natural righthanded hitter, Hernandez was adept from both sides of the plate in 2005 and hit .298 from the left side. That dropped to .232 in 2006 and he looked far better from his natural side. Hernandez gets too pull conscious and has excess movement in his stance. He needs to improve his plate discipline to reduce his strikeouts and take advantage of his above-average speed. After struggling in the big leagues and losing his job, he began to press to prove he belonged and it only made matters worse. The Mets still do not have a long-term solution at second base—Valentin is 37—so the opportunity is still there for Hernandez to establish himself, but it's looking more and more like he's destined for a utility role.

| Year | Club (League) | Class | AVG | G | AB | R | H | 2B | 3B | HR | RBI | BB | SO | SB | OBP | SLG |
|------|---------------|-------|-----|---|----|---|---|----|----|----|-----|----|----|----|-----|-----|
| 2001 | Tigers (GCL) | R | .264 | 55 | 216 | 37 | 57 | 5 | 11 | 0 | 18 | 13 | 38 | 34 | .303 | .389 |
| | Lakeland (FSL) | A | .190 | 7 | 21 | 2 | 4 | 0 | 1 | 0 | 1 | 0 | 8 | 0 | .190 | .286 |
| 2002 | Lakeland (FSL) | A | .259 | 123 | 410 | 52 | 106 | 13 | 7 | 2 | 42 | 33 | 102 | 16 | .310 | .339 |
| 2003 | Lakeland (FSL) | A | .229 | 106 | 380 | 47 | 87 | 11 | 4 | 2 | 28 | 27 | 69 | 15 | .278 | .295 |
| 2004 | Lakeland (FSL) | A | .295 | 32 | 122 | 20 | 36 | 4 | 3 | 0 | 11 | 6 | 26 | 7 | .326 | .377 |
| | Erie (EL) | AA | .274 | 101 | 394 | 65 | 108 | 19 | 3 | 5 | 29 | 26 | 89 | 17 | .326 | .376 |
| 2005 | Binghamton (EL) | AA | .326 | 66 | 273 | 46 | 89 | 14 | 1 | 7 | 24 | 14 | 58 | 11 | .360 | .462 |

| | | Class | AVG | G | AB | R | H | 2B | 3B | HR | RBI | BB | SO | SB | OBP | SLG |
|---|---|---|---|---|---|---|---|---|---|---|---|---|---|---|---|---|
| | Norfolk (IL) | AAA | .303 | 66 | 261 | 34 | 79 | 6 | 4 | 2 | 30 | 22 | 46 | 24 | .354 | .379 |
| | New York (NL) | MLB | .056 | 6 | 18 | 1 | 1 | 0 | 0 | 0 | 0 | 1 | 4 | 0 | .105 | .056 |
| 2006 | St. Lucie (FSL) | A | .111 | 2 | 9 | 0 | 1 | 0 | 0 | 0 | 0 | 0 | 1 | 0 | .111 | .111 |
| | Norfolk (IL) | AAA | .249 | 102 | 414 | 44 | 103 | 11 | 4 | 0 | 23 | 21 | 70 | 15 | .285 | .295 |
| | New York (NL) | MLB | .152 | 25 | 66 | 4 | 10 | 1 | 1 | 1 | 3 | 1 | 12 | 0 | .164 | .242 |
| **MINOR LEAGUE TOTALS** | | | .268 | 660 | 2500 | 347 | 670 | 83 | 38 | 18 | 206 | 162 | 507 | 139 | .312 | .353 |
| **MAJOR LEAGUE TOTALS** | | | .131 | 31 | 84 | 5 | 11 | 1 | 1 | 1 | 3 | 2 | 16 | 0 | .151 | .202 |

## 12 FRANCISCO PENA
C

**Born:** Oct. 12, 1989. **B-T:** R-R. **Ht.:** 6-2. **Wt.:** 210. **Signed:** Dominican Republic, 2006. **Signed by:** Ismael Cruz.

The son of former big league catcher Tony Pena and brother of Braves farmhand Tony Pena Jr., Francisco was at one time considered the top player on the international market in 2006, and rumors swirled that he could command as much as a $2 million bonus. He ended up getting $750,000, the seventh-largest bonus handed out to international players last summer. Pena stands out for his impressive catch-and-throw skills and he consistently posts 1.9-second pop times thanks to an above-average arm and quick release. He has an advanced offensive approach and is willing to go the other way, but his bat is still pretty raw and involves a lot of projection because his pitch recognition is rudimentary. There are some concerns that Pena's body is too thick and that he's not as athletic as his dad or brother. His biggest obstacle defensively is adjusting to the higher velocities he has to catch as a professional, but it's something that should come in time and isn't a serious concern. The Mets love Pena's cerebral nature and his bilingualism—products of having grown up around the game—which will serve him well as a catcher. He probably won't be ready for a full-season league, so Rookie-level Kingsport or short-season Brooklyn is his most likely destination.

| Year | Club (League) | Class | AVG | G | AB | R | H | 2B | 3B | HR | RBI | BB | SO | SB | OBP | SLG |
|---|---|---|---|---|---|---|---|---|---|---|---|---|---|---|---|---|
| 2006 | Did not play—Signed 2007 contract | | | | | | | | | | | | | | | |

## 13 ADAM BOSTICK
LHP

**Born:** March 17, 1983. **B-T:** L-L. **Ht.:** 6-1. **Wt.:** 220. **Drafted:** HS—Greensburg, Pa., 2001 (6th round). **Signed by:** Steve Mondile (Marlins).

Acquired from the Marlins along with Jason Vargas in the trade that sent relievers Henry Owens and Matt Lindstrom to Florida, Bostick missed the 2002 season following surgery to transpose a nerve in his elbow but came back strong and led the low Class A South Atlantic League in strikeouts in 2004. Bostick, who passed on a scholarship to play quarterback for NCAA Division II Slippery Rock (Pa.), has a sinking two-seam fastball with late life that sits from 88-91 mph. He complements it with a plus curveball with late bite that has a little more tilt then a typical 12-to-6 offering, and a four-seam fastball when he wants to work up in the zone. Bostick has a deceptive delivery that makes it hard for hitters to pick up his pitches. He's an excellent athlete who can make spectacular defensive plays, but he has difficulty repeating his mechanics. His right elbow and shoulder will often fly open early, which makes it hard for him to maintain his arm slot and causes him to spin off the mound. Bostick has worked on a changeup, but is still not comfortable with it and needs urging to throw it more. Even with a fringy changeup, his fastball-curve combo should be enough to make him a solid back-end starter. He'll head to Triple-A and could get a shot should an injury arise in the rotation.

| Year | Club (League) | Class | W | L | ERA | G | GS | CG | SV | IP | H | R | ER | HR | BB | SO | AVG |
|---|---|---|---|---|---|---|---|---|---|---|---|---|---|---|---|---|---|
| 2001 | Marlins (GCL) | R | 1 | 1 | 4.26 | 7 | 1 | 0 | 0 | 13 | 16 | 8 | 6 | 0 | 3 | 13 | .302 |
| 2002 | Did not play—Injured | | | | | | | | | | | | | | | | |
| 2003 | Greensboro (SAL) | A | 0 | 1 | 3.77 | 7 | 1 | 0 | 0 | 14 | 12 | 6 | 6 | 1 | 12 | 15 | .231 |
| | Jamestown (NYP) | A | 4 | 6 | 5.12 | 15 | 15 | 0 | 0 | 77 | 77 | 49 | 44 | 9 | 39 | 76 | .263 |
| 2004 | Greensboro (SAL) | A | 2 | 8 | 3.79 | 23 | 22 | 0 | 0 | 114 | 100 | 57 | 48 | 10 | 58 | 163 | .239 |
| 2005 | Jupiter (FSL) | A | 4 | 5 | 3.84 | 17 | 17 | 0 | 0 | 91 | 95 | 47 | 39 | 7 | 36 | 94 | .270 |
| | Carolina (SL) | AA | 4 | 3 | 4.67 | 9 | 9 | 0 | 0 | 44 | 42 | 26 | 23 | 3 | 25 | 39 | .250 |
| 2006 | Carolina (SL) | AA | 8 | 7 | 3.52 | 22 | 22 | 0 | 0 | 115 | 100 | 58 | 45 | 7 | 67 | 109 | .235 |
| | Albuquerque (PCL) | AAA | 1 | 2 | 4.67 | 5 | 5 | 0 | 0 | 27 | 39 | 20 | 14 | 4 | 13 | 30 | .339 |
| **MINOR LEAGUE TOTALS** | | | 24 | 33 | 4.08 | 105 | 92 | 0 | 0 | 496 | 481 | 271 | 225 | 41 | 253 | 539 | .256 |

## 14 BRETT HARPER
1B

**Born:** July 31, 1981. **B-T:** L-R. **Ht.:** 6-4. **Wt.:** 185. **Drafted:** Scottsdale (Ariz.) JC, D/F 2000 (45th round). **Signed by:** Kevin Frady.

The son of former Twins catcher Brian Harper showed his plus power in 2005 when he finished third in the minors in home runs with 36 after hitting just 22 over his first four pro seasons. He returned to Double-A in 2006 and was raking through 19 games before a shoulder injury knocked him out for the season. Unlike his father, who was known for his ability to put

the ball in play, Harper has an all-or-nothing approach. He's always looking for a fastball to drive and struggles with quality breaking pitches. He's a slow runner with below-average range at first base and doesn't look comfortable making even routine plays. His poor defense and lack of versatility limit his value as a reserve, but if he can continue to hit with tremendous power he should be able to find a job as a regular, even if it's not with the Mets. He'll be ready for spring training following shoulder surgery and will get a shot to prove himself in Triple-A.

| Year | Club (League) | Class | AVG | G | AB | R | H | 2B | 3B | HR | RBI | BB | SO | SB | OBP | SLG |
|------|---------------|-------|-----|---|----|---|---|----|----|----|-----|----|----|----|-----|-----|
| 2001 | Kingsport (Appy) | R | .336 | 38 | 146 | 24 | 49 | 9 | 1 | 0 | 19 | 8 | 30 | 3 | .386 | .411 |
| | Columbia (SAL) | A | .182 | 10 | 33 | 1 | 6 | 1 | 0 | 0 | 4 | 3 | 14 | 0 | .250 | .212 |
| 2002 | Brooklyn (NYP) | A | .279 | 53 | 183 | 21 | 51 | 6 | 0 | 1 | 20 | 14 | 37 | 2 | .333 | .328 |
| 2003 | St. Lucie (FSL) | A | .205 | 13 | 44 | 5 | 9 | 2 | 0 | 0 | 4 | 5 | 13 | 1 | .308 | .250 |
| | Capital City (SAL) | A | .329 | 23 | 79 | 5 | 26 | 6 | 0 | 1 | 9 | 4 | 20 | 1 | .376 | .443 |
| | Kingsport (Appy) | R | .429 | 11 | 35 | 6 | 15 | 8 | 0 | 2 | 10 | 3 | 9 | 0 | .500 | .829 |
| | Brooklyn (NYP) | A | .299 | 28 | 87 | 5 | 26 | 8 | 0 | 1 | 18 | 5 | 12 | 1 | .337 | .425 |
| 2004 | Mets (GCL) | R | .400 | 2 | 5 | 1 | 2 | 0 | 0 | 1 | 4 | 1 | 1 | 0 | .500 | 1.000 |
| | St. Lucie (FSL) | A | .350 | 60 | 220 | 32 | 77 | 18 | 1 | 9 | 55 | 35 | 53 | 1 | .440 | .564 |
| | Binghamton (EL) | AA | .247 | 45 | 174 | 24 | 43 | 12 | 0 | 7 | 26 | 14 | 60 | 0 | .309 | .437 |
| 2005 | St. Lucie (FSL) | A | .280 | 62 | 239 | 35 | 67 | 11 | 1 | 20 | 60 | 21 | 64 | 0 | .337 | .586 |
| | Binghamton (EL) | AA | .273 | 67 | 227 | 37 | 62 | 11 | 0 | 16 | 42 | 26 | 85 | 0 | .352 | .533 |
| 2006 | Binghamton (EL) | AA | .338 | 19 | 65 | 8 | 22 | 7 | 0 | 0 | 8 | 7 | 19 | 1 | .427 | .446 |
| **MINOR LEAGUE TOTALS** | | | .296 | 431 | 1537 | 204 | 455 | 99 | 3 | 58 | 279 | 146 | 417 | 10 | .363 | .478 |

## 15  EMMANUEL GARCIA                                                    SS

**Born:** March 4, 1986. **B-T:** L-R. **Ht.:** 6-2. **Wt.:** 180. **Signed:** NDFA/HS–Montreal, 2004. **Signed by:** Claude Pelletier.

A Montreal native born to an Italian father and Spanish mother who played professional tennis, Garcia went undrafted in 2004 when baseball had a shortage of visas for minor league players. Because of his relative lack of baseball experience, Garcia was sent to extended spring training and then Kingsport last year despite a promising debut in 2005. Garcia is a tick above average across the board—with the exception of his power—and one of the best all-around athletes in the system. He has a mature approach at the plate with excellent bat control that allows him to work deep counts and thrive at the top of the order. His speed and instincts make him a pest on the basepaths. Garcia responds well to instruction and has impressed the Mets with his steady improvement. There were questions about his ability to stay at shortstop, but he showed enough there in 2006 that he'll remain there for the time being, though his arm might not be good enough for him to be a regular there. He'll get his first crack at full-season ball as the regular shortstop at the Mets' new low Class A Savannah affiliate in 2007.

| Year | Club (League) | Class | AVG | G | AB | R | H | 2B | 3B | HR | RBI | BB | SO | SB | OBP | SLG |
|------|---------------|-------|-----|---|----|---|---|----|----|----|-----|----|----|----|-----|-----|
| 2005 | Mets (GCL) | R | .339 | 45 | 186 | 43 | 63 | 7 | 0 | 2 | 30 | 21 | 36 | 17 | .412 | .409 |
| | St. Lucie (FSL) | A | .222 | 2 | 9 | 1 | 2 | 1 | 0 | 0 | 0 | 0 | 2 | 0 | .222 | .333 |
| 2006 | Kingsport (Appy) | R | .291 | 51 | 206 | 35 | 60 | 5 | 2 | 3 | 25 | 27 | 41 | 19 | .373 | .379 |
| | Brooklyn (NYP) | A | .240 | 13 | 50 | 7 | 12 | 0 | 0 | 0 | 3 | 5 | 13 | 3 | .316 | .240 |
| **MINOR LEAGUE TOTALS** | | | .304 | 111 | 451 | 86 | 137 | 13 | 2 | 5 | 58 | 53 | 92 | 39 | .380 | .375 |

## 16  JOSE CORONADO                                                    SS

**Born:** April 13, 1986. **B-T:** B-R. **Ht.:** 6-1. **Wt.:** 175. **Signed:** Venezuela, 2003. **Signed by:** Gregorio Machado.

Coronado impressed the Mets so much in 2005 that he was promoted twice, and even saw some action in big league spring training games last year. The most advanced of a group of low-level shortstops, he was challenged with an assignment to high Class A, where he was overmatched offensively. Coronado's strength is his defense, so it's not a shock he struggled at the plate. He has hands that are quick and soft, excellent range and an above-average arm to go with a quick release. He can make the spectacular play at short, but needs to be more aggressive in charging slowly hit balls. A switch-hitter, Coronado lacks strength and needs to fill out so he can swing with more authority and increase his bat speed. He understands his offensive limitations and tries to play within them, using a slap-and-dash approach, but he still strikes out too often. He's an above-average runner, though not a burner. Coronado will likely repeat the level but needs to significantly improve his offensive game to ever profile as a regular.

| Year | Club (League) | Class | AVG | G | AB | R | H | 2B | 3B | HR | RBI | BB | SO | SB | OBP | SLG |
|------|---------------|-------|-----|---|----|---|---|----|----|----|-----|----|----|----|-----|-----|
| 2004 | Mets (VSL) | R | .248 | 33 | 121 | 19 | 30 | 6 | 0 | 3 | 17 | 20 | 23 | 0 | .354 | .372 |
| 2005 | Mets (GCL) | R | .404 | 11 | 47 | 9 | 19 | 1 | 1 | 0 | 4 | 1 | 9 | 1 | .429 | .468 |
| | Kingsport (Appy) | R | .266 | 39 | 139 | 24 | 37 | 5 | 1 | 1 | 8 | 22 | 27 | 6 | .382 | .338 |
| | Hagerstown (SAL) | A | .225 | 18 | 71 | 4 | 16 | 2 | 1 | 0 | 4 | 7 | 17 | 1 | .295 | .282 |
| 2006 | St. Lucie (FSL) | A | .226 | 138 | 544 | 61 | 123 | 20 | 4 | 0 | 37 | 41 | 119 | 4 | .283 | .278 |
| **MINOR LEAGUE TOTALS** | | | .244 | 239 | 922 | 117 | 225 | 34 | 7 | 4 | 70 | 91 | 195 | 12 | .317 | .309 |

## 17 JOSH STINSON
RHP

**Born:** March 14, 1988. **B-T:** R-R. **Ht.:** 6-4. **Wt.:** 190. **Drafted:** HS—Shreveport, La., 2006 (37th round). **Signed by:** Benny Latino.

Special assistant Benny Latino stayed on Stinson all year but knew there wasn't much buzz surrounding him, and the Mets patiently waited to grab him in the 37th round. Latino pulled the same act when he was with the Devil Rays, snagging big leaguers Joey Gathright (32nd) and Chad Gaudin (34th round) in the 2001 draft. Signed for $125,000, he pitched so well in the Rookie-level Gulf Coast League that he received a late-season promotion to low Class A. Stinson throws two- and four-seam fastballs that sit from 89-94 mph with a good downward plane. He works mostly off the two-seamer, which sits at 89-91 with heavy sink and was instrumental in his 2.00 ground-fly ratio in the GCL. Formerly a slurvy pitch, his breaking ball has developed into a hard 2-to-7 curve from 78-82 mph, and he spent much of the season working on his changeup. Stinson's mechanics lack consistency, and he has a tendency to fall off to the first-base side of the mound, which hinders his command. With an ideal frame and arm speed, Stinson offers projection and has the makeup to make the necessary adjustments. He'll spend 2007 in low Class A and has the makings of a middle-of-the-rotation starter.

| Year | Club (League) | Class | W | L | ERA | G | GS | CG | SV | IP | H | R | ER | HR | BB | SO | AVG |
|------|---------------|-------|---|---|-----|---|----|----|----|----|---|---|----|----|----|----|-----|
| 2006 | Mets (GCL) | R | 1 | 2 | 2.00 | 9 | 4 | 0 | 0 | 27 | 27 | 10 | 6 | 0 | 5 | 14 | .273 |
| | Hagerstown (SAL) | A | 0 | 1 | 1.35 | 3 | 3 | 0 | 0 | 13 | 11 | 2 | 2 | 0 | 4 | 5 | .239 |
| **MINOR LEAGUE TOTALS** | | | 1 | 3 | 1.79 | 12 | 7 | 0 | 0 | 40 | 38 | 12 | 8 | 0 | 9 | 19 | .262 |

## 18 BOBBY PARNELL
RHP

**Born:** Sept. 8, 1984. **B-T:** R-R. **Ht.:** 6-3. **Wt.:** 180. **Drafted:** Charleston Southern, 2005 (9th round). **Signed by:** Marlin McPhail.

Parnell burst onto the scene in 2005 when he led the short-season New York-Penn League in ERA in his pro debut, an impressive feat for someone who posted ERAs of 6.82 and 8.86 in his final two years at Charleston Southern. A strained oblique cost him much of spring training in 2006 and he never regained his 2005 form. Parnell has a lively sinker that tops out at 94 mph, but it's more effective at 91-92 because it has more movement when he takes a little off it. He complements it with a nasty 84-86 mph slider that is a swing-and-miss pitch. Because he struggles to throw the slider for strikes, it's more useful when he's ahead in the count and can get hitters to expand their zones. The Mets like his confidence and poise, but want him to throw his changeup more. Because he rarely uses the change, he doesn't throw it with conviction. Despite a poor 2006, he still has one of the stronger arms in the system and the Mets think he'll be fine with a full spring training. He'll probably spend 2007 in high Class A.

| Year | Club (League) | Class | W | L | ERA | G | GS | CG | SV | IP | H | R | ER | HR | BB | SO | AVG |
|------|---------------|-------|---|---|-----|---|----|----|----|----|---|---|----|----|----|----|-----|
| 2005 | Brooklyn (NYP) | A | 2 | 3 | 1.73 | 15 | 14 | 0 | 0 | 73 | 48 | 20 | 14 | 1 | 29 | 67 | .185 |
| 2006 | Hagerstown (SAL) | A | 5 | 10 | 4.04 | 18 | 18 | 1 | 0 | 94 | 84 | 50 | 42 | 7 | 40 | 84 | .239 |
| | St. Lucie (FSL) | A | 0 | 1 | 9.26 | 3 | 3 | 0 | 0 | 12 | 16 | 13 | 12 | 3 | 9 | 13 | .333 |
| **MINOR LEAGUE TOTALS** | | | 7 | 14 | 3.43 | 36 | 35 | 1 | 0 | 178 | 148 | 83 | 68 | 11 | 78 | 164 | .225 |

## 19 DUSTIN MARTIN
OF

**Born:** April 4, 1984. **B-T:** L-L. **Ht.:** 6-2. **Wt.:** 210. **Drafted:** Sam Houston State, 2006 (26th round). **Signed by:** Leroy Dreyer and Ray Corbett.

As a senior in college, Martin led the Southland Conference in hitting with a .389 average and was named all-conference for his efforts. Signed for a mere $1,000, he continued that hot hitting in his pro debut and finished in the top five in the New York-Penn League in hitting, on-base percentage, slugging and triples. He capped his fine debut by holding his own against more experienced pros in Hawaii Winter Baseball, hitting .269 in 78 at-bats (the league average was just .238). Though he lacks one standout tool, Martin's tools are average across the board. He is a smart hitter with a short, assertive stroke. Martin has more of a pull approach, but drives the ball up the middle and to right-center when he's locked in. He earned praise for making adjustments as the season progressed and staying very consistent with his performance and effort. His arm and speed are both a tick above average and he can handle all three outfield spots, though he spent most of the season in left. Martin doesn't appear to have the power to profile as a regular in an outfield corner, but could increase his stock by proving he can handle center. Either way, his approach and makeup could fit nicely as a reserve outfielder. As senior sign, he'll get a chance to move quickly if he continues to hit.

| Year | Club (League) | Class | AVG | G | AB | R | H | 2B | 3B | HR | RBI | BB | SO | SB | OBP | SLG |
|------|---------------|-------|-----|---|----|---|---|----|----|----|-----|----|----|----|-----|-----|
| 2006 | Brooklyn (NYP) | A | .315 | 72 | 251 | 22 | 79 | 15 | 7 | 2 | 35 | 28 | 50 | 7 | .399 | .454 |
| **MINOR LEAGUE TOTALS** | | | .315 | 72 | 251 | 22 | 79 | 15 | 7 | 2 | 35 | 28 | 50 | 7 | .399 | .454 |

## 20 EDDIE CAMACHO
LHP

**Born:** Sept. 17, 1982. **B-T:** L-L. **Ht.:** 6-1. **Wt.:** 180. **Signed:** NDFA/Cal State Northridge, 2004. **Signed by:** Steve Leavitt.

When the Mets were short a pitcher on their GCL club in 2004, they asked their area scouts for the names of the best pitcher they saw who went undrafted and signed Camacho on the recommendation of Steve Leavitt. Camacho signed for $500 and left his job at a canning plant to turn pro and has been solid ever since in a short relief role. His pitching style is reminiscent of former Mets closer John Franco in that he barely tops 90 mph with his fastball and succeeds on the strength of his changeup. Camacho actually throws two variations of the change, one that is straight that he spots for strikes and the other with sink that is a strikeout pitch against righthanders. His breaking ball lacks definition and is more of a slurvy pitch, though the Mets would like it to be more of a hard slider to give him a weapon against lefties. His current fast-ball-change repertoire is more effective against righties who hit .227 against him in 2006 while lefties hit .246. The Mets have pushed him the last two seasons and the Mets love that he has risen to the occasion both times. Considering his success at Double-A, he should be ticketed for Triple-A with a chance at a callup should an opening arise.

| Year | Club (League) | Class | W | L | ERA | G | GS | CG | SV | IP | H | R | ER | HR | BB | SO | AVG |
|---|---|---|---|---|---|---|---|---|---|---|---|---|---|---|---|---|---|
| 2004 | Mets (GCL) | R | 0 | 0 | 0.00 | 3 | 0 | 0 | 1 | 5 | 0 | 0 | 0 | 0 | 0 | 9 | .000 |
| | Brooklyn (NYP) | A | 3 | 1 | 0.69 | 18 | 0 | 0 | 1 | 39 | 19 | 4 | 3 | 1 | 11 | 38 | .140 |
| 2005 | St. Lucie (FSL) | A | 2 | 4 | 2.74 | 45 | 0 | 0 | 10 | 49 | 49 | 17 | 15 | 2 | 21 | 40 | .261 |
| 2006 | Binghamton (EL) | AA | 3 | 4 | 3.63 | 53 | 0 | 0 | 1 | 79 | 71 | 36 | 32 | 6 | 25 | 61 | .235 |
| **MINOR LEAGUE TOTALS** | | | 8 | 9 | 2.61 | 119 | 0 | 0 | 13 | 173 | 139 | 57 | 50 | 9 | 57 | 148 | .217 |

## 21 NICK EVANS
1B

**Born:** Jan. 30, 1986. **B-T:** R-R **Ht.:** 6-2. **Wt.:** 180. **Drafted:** HS—Phoenix, 2004 (5th round). **Signed by:** Dave Birecki.

A third baseman when he was drafted out of Phoenix' St. Mary's High, Evans was a minor bright spot on a Hagerstown club that was atrocious offensively (the Suns hit .238/.313/.348 collectively). He led the club in almost every counting statistic, but with the exception of a scorching June in which he hit .364/.430/.705, his performance was mediocre. Evans has some of the best raw power in the system and shows it off with his impressive batting practice displays. The ball jumps off his bat and he's at this best when he's driving balls up the middle, but often gets too pull happy in games. Since he was Hagerstown's only power threat for much of the season, teams pitched around him and he often expanded his strike zone. Because of his third-base background, he has the potential to be above average at first and has shown improvement there, though his 15 errors ranked second among South Atlantic League first basemen. The Mets have also been impressed with the way he has taken to their strength and agility programs. As a righthanded-hitting first baseman, his prospect status is tied up mostly in his power potential. His ability to translate his raw power into games with consistency is paramount. It will certainly be tested in the pitcher-friendly Florida State League in 2007.

| Year | Club (League) | Class | AVG | G | AB | R | H | 2B | 3B | HR | RBI | BB | SO | SB | OBP | SLG |
|---|---|---|---|---|---|---|---|---|---|---|---|---|---|---|---|---|
| 2004 | Mets (GCL) | R | .258 | 50 | 182 | 36 | 47 | 10 | 3 | 7 | 27 | 14 | 51 | 3 | .311 | .462 |
| 2005 | Kingsport (Appy) | R | .344 | 15 | 64 | 11 | 22 | 7 | 0 | 6 | 22 | 4 | 17 | 1 | .382 | .734 |
| | Brooklyn (NYP) | A | .252 | 57 | 226 | 30 | 57 | 11 | 3 | 6 | 33 | 17 | 34 | 0 | .302 | .407 |
| 2006 | Hagerstown (SAL) | A | .254 | 137 | 511 | 55 | 130 | 33 | 3 | 15 | 67 | 45 | 99 | 2 | .320 | .419 |
| **MINOR LEAGUE TOTALS** | | | .260 | 259 | 983 | 132 | 256 | 61 | 9 | 34 | 149 | 80 | 201 | 6 | .318 | .445 |

## 22 TOBI STONER
RHP

**Born:** December 3, 1984. **B-T:** B-R. **Ht.:** 6-2. **Wt.:** 192. **Drafted:** Davis & Elkins (W. Va.), 2006 (16th round). **Signed by:** Matt Wondolowski.

Scouting director Rudy Terraras asks each of his area scouts for their "gut-feel guy" leading up to the draft and scout Matt Wondolowski tabbed Stoner as his before the Mets took him in the 16th round. A two-way player at his Division II college, Stoner finished fourth in the New York-Penn League in ERA after signing for $1,000. He features an 89-92 mph fastball to go with a cutter, curveball and change. Stoner is receptive to coaching and picked up a changeup very quickly. He has confidence throwing the fastball to both sides of the plate and at times showed average command of all four pitches even mixing in a slider when ahead in the count. The key for Stoner will be streamlining his repertoire to improve his consistency. He's very athletic and fields his position well but will rush his delivery, which hinders his command. Stoner is a fierce competitor who is very hard on himself when things aren't going well. His performance at Brooklyn was a pleasant surprise and he'll get a taste of full-season ball in 2007, most likely in low Class A.

| Year | Club (League) | Class | W | L | ERA | G | GS | CG | SV | IP | H | R | ER | HR | BB | SO | AVG |
|------|---------------|-------|---|---|-----|---|----|----|----|----|---|---|----|----|----|----|-----|
| 2006 | Brooklyn (NYP) | A | 6 | 2 | 2.15 | 14 | 14 | 1 | 0 | 84 | 66 | 25 | 20 | 1 | 17 | 62 | .219 |
| **MINOR LEAGUE TOTALS** | | | 6 | 2 | 2.15 | 14 | 14 | 1 | 0 | 84 | 66 | 25 | 20 | 1 | 17 | 62 | .219 |

 ## SEAN HENRY

OF

**Born:** Aug. 18, 1985. **B-T:** R-R. **Ht.:** 5-10. **Wt.:** 154. **Drafted:** Diablo Valley (Calif.) CC, 2004 (20th round). **Signed by:** Chuck Hensley Jr.

Henry has one of the better amateur pedigrees of anyone in the Mets system and hit .481 for USA Baseball's 2003 junior national team that included Billy Butler (Royals) and Neil Walker (Pirates), among others. He has tantalized the Mets with his athleticism, but it took him almost three seasons to get out of rookie ball. Henry is an aggressive hitter with good bat speed and has impressive pop for someone of his size. He's a smart baserunner with above-average speed that plays well on the bases and in the field. The former shortstop moved to center field last year and showed excellent aptitude there. His clean routes made him look like a natural but he needs to make an adjustment with his footwork on throws, which differs from the infield. Henry also needs to stay within himself as a hitter because of his tendency to swing for the fences. The Mets were pleased with Henry's progress on both offense and defense in 2006 and he'll finally get his shot to open a season in a full-season league.

| Year | Club (League) | Class | AVG | G | AB | R | H | 2B | 3B | HR | RBI | BB | SO | SB | OBP | SLG |
|------|---------------|-------|-----|---|----|---|---|----|----|----|-----|----|----|----|-----|-----|
| 2004 | Mets (GCL) | R | .282 | 56 | 202 | 35 | 57 | 9 | 5 | 4 | 30 | 22 | 43 | 10 | .364 | .436 |
| 2005 | Kingsport (Appy) | R | .255 | 42 | 149 | 24 | 38 | 7 | 1 | 5 | 31 | 22 | 43 | 15 | .350 | .416 |
| 2006 | Kingsport (Appy) | R | .275 | 41 | 149 | 28 | 41 | 12 | 2 | 4 | 27 | 21 | 29 | 23 | .365 | .463 |
| | Hagerstown (SAL) | A | .254 | 21 | 71 | 7 | 18 | 5 | 0 | 3 | 14 | 3 | 16 | 7 | .280 | .451 |
| **MINOR LEAGUE TOTALS** | | | .270 | 160 | 571 | 94 | 154 | 33 | 8 | 16 | 102 | 68 | 131 | 55 | .351 | .440 |

 ## TODD PRIVETT

LHP

**Born:** April 22, 1986. **B-T:** L-L. **Ht.:** 6-0. **Wt.:** 185. **Drafted:** JC of Southern Idaho, 2006 (14th round). **Signed by:** Jim Reeves.

Privett was part of a talented JC of Southern Idaho staff that had a total of three pitchers drafted and also included his brother Zack. The first of that trio drafted, Privett signed for $37,500 as a 14th-rounder. He typically sits at 88-90 mph with his fastball, but was up to 92 mph during the college season where opponents batted just .168 against him. He's a finesse pitcher that works mostly off of a fastball-change combination from a three-quarters arm angle and pitches with little effort. He throws the fastball to both sides of the plate and isn't afraid to use his changeup, which has a little fade and sink, against both lefthanders and righthanders. Privett will also mix in a curveball at 72-73 mph with late bite when he's ahead in the count but he doesn't have the confidence to throw it for strikes. Privett struggled maintaining his velocity and appeared to wear down a little late in the season. In a system short on lefthanders, Privett is worth following and should begin 2007 in low Class A.

| Year | Club (League) | Class | W | L | ERA | G | GS | CG | SV | IP | H | R | ER | HR | BB | SO | AVG |
|------|---------------|-------|---|---|-----|---|----|----|----|----|---|---|----|----|----|----|-----|
| 2006 | Kingsport (Appy) | R | 1 | 2 | 4.03 | 5 | 5 | 0 | 0 | 22 | 24 | 12 | 10 | 1 | 4 | 22 | .264 |
| | Brooklyn (NYP) | A | 1 | 2 | 2.11 | 8 | 8 | 0 | 0 | 47 | 44 | 14 | 11 | 4 | 8 | 38 | .246 |
| **MINOR LEAGUE TOTALS** | | | 2 | 4 | 2.73 | 13 | 13 | 0 | 0 | 69 | 68 | 26 | 21 | 5 | 12 | 60 | .252 |

## MIKE DEVANEY

RHP

**Born:** July 31, 1982. **B-T:** R-R. **Ht.:** 6-4. **Wt.:** 220. **Drafted:** Concordia (Ore.), 2004 (23rd round). **Signed by:** Jim Reeves.

As a sophomore at NAIA Concordia University in Portland, Ore., Devaney threw a no-hitter in a start against Jeff Francis, now of the Rockies, and he has done nothing but win since signing with the Mets. Despite having fringe-average stuff, he has compiled a career record of 27-9, 2.77. He tied for the minor league lead in shutouts and complete games and led the organization in wins and ERA, ranked second in strikeouts and had a 32-inning scoreless streak in high Class A. Devaney's fastball tops out at 90 mph and he pitches at 88 with some arm-side run. He also mixes in a cutter, a changeup and a slow curveball with tight rotation at around 65 mph that hitters just can't seem to get good swings on. He has a funky arm action with a wrist curl in the back that prevents him from having pinpoint command, however, it's this deceptive motion that induces so many bad swings. With stuff that grades out as fringe average or below average across the board, Devaney hardly has a prospect's typical profile. But his continued success, particularly at Double-A, is an indication that he's doing something right. He'll be back there to begin 2007 and if his command improves and his success continues, he'll get more chances to keep proving himself.

| Year | Club (League) | Class | W | L | ERA | G | GS | CG | SV | IP | H | R | ER | HR | BB | SO | AVG |
|------|---------------|-------|---|---|-----|---|----|----|----|----|---|---|----|----|----|----|-----|
| 2004 | Brooklyn (NYP) | A | 5 | 0 | 1.95 | 14 | 14 | 0 | 0 | 69 | 58 | 19 | 15 | 1 | 29 | 56 | .248 |
| 2005 | Hagerstown (SAL) | A | 10 | 4 | 3.88 | 32 | 15 | 2 | 0 | 137 | 107 | 73 | 59 | 9 | 51 | 121 | .214 |
| 2006 | St. Lucie (FSL) | A | 8 | 3 | 1.62 | 16 | 16 | 2 | 0 | 95 | 63 | 26 | 17 | 4 | 35 | 86 | .188 |
| | Binghamton (EL) | AA | 4 | 2 | 3.06 | 11 | 10 | 2 | 0 | 53 | 39 | 19 | 18 | 5 | 35 | 43 | .211 |
| **MINOR LEAGUE TOTALS** | | | 27 | 9 | 2.77 | 73 | 55 | 6 | 0 | 354 | 267 | 137 | 109 | 19 | 150 | 306 | .213 |

## 26  JOHN HOLDZKOM                                                    RHP

**Born:** Oct. 19, 1987. **B-T:** R-R. **Ht.:** 6-7. **Wt.:** 225. **Drafted:** Salt Lake CC, 2006 (4th round). **Signed by:** Mike Baker.

The brother of Lincoln Holdzkom, a 2001 seventh-round pick of the Marlins who was taken by the Astros in the 2006 Rule 5 draft, John is a bit of an enigma. Despite an incredible arm, he fell to the Mariners in the 15th round of 2005 draft coming out of high school. He was academically ineligible for much of his senior season and pitched sparingly upon his return because of problems with his control and with his coach. A year of junior college in a wood-bat league helped his stock immensely and the Mets signed him for $210,000 as a fourth-rounder, though he certainly wasn't a consensus first-five-round pick. Holdzkom has a fastball that touches 98 mph and sits at 92-94 mph. He also features a hard slider in the high 80s that can be dominant. Because of his size, Holdzkom has a very hard time repeating his delivery. He has been working on a changeup in the bullpen but doesn't throw it in games as of yet. The Mets knew he was this raw when they drafted him but couldn't resist such a power arm. Though he profiles best as a reliever, the organization wants to use him as a starter and hope it helps the development of his change. He'll be back in extended spring training, with a likely assignment to Kingsport or Brooklyn come June.

| Year | Club (League) | Class | W | L | ERA | G | GS | CG | SV | IP | H | R | ER | HR | BB | SO | AVG |
|------|---------------|-------|---|---|-----|---|----|----|----|----|---|---|----|----|----|----|-----|
| 2006 | Mets (GCL) | R | 2 | 5 | 7.71 | 16 | 2 | 0 | 3 | 23 | 28 | 28 | 20 | 0 | 20 | 23 | .289 |
| **MINOR LEAGUE TOTALS** | | | 2 | 5 | 7.71 | 16 | 2 | 0 | 3 | 23 | 28 | 28 | 20 | 0 | 20 | 23 | .289 |

## 27  MIKE NICKEAS                                                      C

**Born:** Feb. 10, 1983. **B-T:** R-R. **Ht.:** 6-0. **Wt.:** 2005. **Drafted:** Georgia Tech, 2004 (5th round). **Signed by:** John Castleberry (Rangers).

When it became clear that they did not see Victor Diaz as part of their long-term plan, the Mets sent Diaz to Texas in exchange for Nickeas. Born in Canada, Nickeas' British father played for Vancouver in the North American Soccer League. Nickeas' spent most of his childhood in California though, and he played for the U.S. national team in both high school and college but fell to the fifth round of the 2004 draft when he slumped as a junior. After a strong debut the Rangers aggressively promoted him to Double-A for his first full season because they wanted him to work with their better pitching prospects, but he struggled terribly with the bat and has yet to recover offensively. Nickeas' strength is his defense, however, and he's a sound receiver with soft hands, good blocking instincts and a solid arm. As a hitter, Nickeas has good knowledge of the strike zone but doesn't make hard contact consistently. He's a bit stiff at the plate and it doesn't appear he'll hit enough to become a regular behind the plate. He missed time with a hamstring pull in 2006, and he's a below-average runner even when healthy. His defense and leadership should allow him to be a prototypical backup catcher and he'll likely spend some more time at Double-A in 2007. With Jesus Flores taken by the Nationals in the Rule 5 draft, Nickeas ranks as the best catcher in the system.

| Year | Club (League) | Class | AVG | G | AB | R | H | 2B | 3B | HR | RBI | BB | SO | SB | OBP | SLG |
|------|---------------|-------|-----|---|----|---|---|----|----|----|-----|----|----|----|-----|-----|
| 2004 | Spokane (NWL) | A | .288 | 62 | 233 | 42 | 67 | 18 | 0 | 10 | 55 | 33 | 53 | 2 | .384 | .494 |
| 2005 | AZL Rangers (AZL) | R | .286 | 6 | 21 | 2 | 6 | 1 | 0 | 1 | 6 | 3 | 4 | 0 | .400 | .476 |
| | Frisco (TL) | AA | .202 | 68 | 242 | 22 | 49 | 7 | 1 | 5 | 24 | 20 | 43 | 1 | .263 | .302 |
| 2006 | Frisco (TL) | AA | .248 | 39 | 113 | 15 | 28 | 7 | 0 | 2 | 15 | 21 | 22 | 1 | .382 | .363 |
| | Bakersfield (Cal) | A | .297 | 17 | 64 | 6 | 19 | 4 | 0 | 0 | 6 | 6 | 17 | 0 | .395 | .359 |
| | Binghamton (EL) | AA | .167 | 4 | 12 | 1 | 2 | 0 | 0 | 0 | 3 | 1 | 4 | 0 | .267 | .167 |
| **MINOR LEAGUE TOTALS** | | | .250 | 196 | 685 | 88 | 171 | 37 | 1 | 18 | 109 | 84 | 143 | 4 | .343 | .385 |

## 28  ERIC BROWN                                                        RHP

**Born:** Feb. 23, 1984. **B-T:** R-R. **Ht.:** 6-6. **Wt.:** 225. **Drafted:** Wingate (N.C.), 2005 (18th round). **Signed by:** Marlin McPhail.

The first Wingate player to be drafted in nine years, Brown had two seasons in one. He was sent to low Class A to begin 2006, but struggled terribly in a swingman role. He was demoted to Brooklyn and placed in the rotation where he flourished, ranking second in the New York-Penn League in ERA. Brown has tremendous size, though he's not a hard thrower and pitches at 86-90 mph with his fastball. It has late sink in the zone and he complements it with a slider and curveball. When he got to Brooklyn, the Mets had him move both his breaking pitch-

es further back in his hand and it increased their velocity and break. His slider sits at 80-83 mph with a two-plane break and is his second-best offering. He also has a changeup, though it's clearly his fourth pitch. He has above-average command, but he'll need more velocity to succeed at higher levels. Brown's size and easy arm action have the Mets optimistic he can increase his velocity, and club officials believe the five-day routine of being in a rotation suits Brown better than the bullpen. With a good spring, he could be bound for high Class A.

| Year | Club (League) | Class | W | L | ERA | G | GS | CG | SV | IP | H | R | ER | HR | BB | SO | AVG |
|------|---------------|-------|---|---|-----|---|----|----|----|----|---|---|----|----|----|----|-----|
| 2005 | Brooklyn (NYP) | A | 3 | 2 | 3.97 | 16 | 0 | 0 | 4 | 34 | 33 | 16 | 15 | 3 | 7 | 31 | .254 |
| 2006 | Hagerstown (SAL) | A | 3 | 2 | 5.29 | 20 | 6 | 1 | 0 | 63 | 74 | 42 | 37 | 5 | 24 | 51 | .288 |
| | Brooklyn (NYP) | A | 7 | 1 | 1.16 | 10 | 10 | 1 | 0 | 70 | 53 | 16 | 9 | 2 | 4 | 55 | .204 |
| **MINOR LEAGUE TOTALS** | | | 13 | 5 | 3.29 | 46 | 16 | 2 | 4 | 167 | 160 | 74 | 61 | 10 | 35 | 137 | .247 |

# DANIEL STEGALL
OF

**Born:** Sept. 24, 1987. **B-T:** L-R. **Ht.:** 6-3. **Wt.:** 180. **Drafted:** HS—Greenwood, Ark., 2006 (7th round). **Signed by:** Larry Chase.

Stegall was a two-way player at Greenwood (Ark.) High, where he also played quarterback on the football team. He had signed a letter of intent to play quarterback at Miami, but instead opted to sign with the Mets for a $145,000 bonus as a seventh-rounder. As a two-sport athlete from a small high school, Stegall is very raw but has as much upside as any position player the Mets have in the low minors. His best tool is his above-average raw power and the ball jumps off of his bat with excellent carry. He runs well for his size and has an above-average arm that allowed him to hit 91 mph off the mound in high school. Stegall struggled in the GCL with his pitch recognition and timing but the Mets were pleased with the way he made adjustments as the year went on and he ended on an 11-game hitting streak. He played center field this season, but his future is probably in right field. His reads and routes showed promise, but his throwing mechanics need work as he has a tendency to short-arm his throws. Stegall is the type of player that needs time and patience, but his raw package of tools offers promise. He likely will end up in Kingsport after opening 2007 in extended spring training.

| Year | Club (League) | Class | AVG | G | AB | R | H | 2B | 3B | HR | RBI | BB | SO | SB | OBP | SLG |
|------|---------------|-------|-----|---|----|---|---|----|----|----|-----|----|----|----|-----|-----|
| 2006 | Mets (GCL) | R | .214 | 40 | 145 | 18 | 31 | 5 | 1 | 0 | 18 | 23 | 42 | 5 | .324 | .262 |
| **MINOR LEAGUE TOTALS** | | | .214 | 40 | 145 | 18 | 31 | 5 | 1 | 0 | 18 | 23 | 42 | 5 | .324 | .262 |

# COREY COLES
OF

**Born:** Jan. 30, 1982. **B-T:** L-L. **Ht.:** 6-1. **Wt.:** 180. **Drafted:** Louisiana-Lafayette, 2003 (5th round). **Signed by:** Bob Rossi.

St. Lucie won the Florida State League title last season, and Coles was as big of a reason as anyone. A .292 hitter entering 2006, Coles led the FSL (and the Mets organization) with a .341 average. Coles' strength is his disciplined approach and his ability to make sound, consistent contact all over the field. He works counts and is tough to strike out but has well-below-average power as evidenced by his 31 extra-base hits. He makes quality reads and jumps in the outfield, which allows to him to play all three outfield positions. He has average speed and range and can steal a base here or there, though he doesn't walk enough or run well enough to profile as a leadoff hitter. Even though he pitched in all three of his seasons at Louisiana-Lafayette, his arm plays below average. Coles doesn't profile as a regular anywhere, but has a skill set that could make him an asset as a reserve. One scout compared him to Orlando Palmeiro who was also drafted out of college, lacks power and did not break into the big leagues until he was 26 years old. Coles will head to Double-A this year and try to prove that 2006 wasn't a fluke.

| Year | Club (League) | Class | AVG | G | AB | R | H | 2B | 3B | HR | RBI | BB | SO | SB | OBP | SLG |
|------|---------------|-------|-----|---|----|---|---|----|----|----|-----|----|----|----|-----|-----|
| 2003 | Brooklyn (NYP) | A | .167 | 15 | 36 | 5 | 6 | 0 | 1 | 0 | 3 | 3 | 4 | 3 | .231 | .222 |
| | Kingsport (Appy) | R | .333 | 27 | 96 | 19 | 32 | 5 | 1 | 0 | 6 | 8 | 17 | 6 | .396 | .406 |
| 2004 | Brooklyn (NYP) | A | .278 | 64 | 237 | 40 | 66 | 6 | 5 | 2 | 20 | 17 | 31 | 10 | .338 | .371 |
| 2005 | Hagerstown (SAL) | A | .307 | 69 | 264 | 27 | 81 | 16 | 0 | 4 | 33 | 12 | 40 | 11 | .342 | .413 |
| 2006 | St. Lucie (FSL) | A | .341 | 124 | 458 | 65 | 156 | 26 | 4 | 1 | 45 | 48 | 59 | 21 | .407 | .421 |
| **MINOR LEAGUE TOTALS** | | | .313 | 299 | 1091 | 156 | 341 | 53 | 11 | 7 | 107 | 88 | 151 | 51 | .370 | .401 |

# NEW YORK
# YANKEES

BY **JOHN MANUEL**

The Yankees farm system, which ranked among the worst in baseball in both 2004 and 2005, had reason to be proud during the 2006 stretch run.

In their first full seasons in New York, Chien-Ming Wang tied for the major league lead with 19 victories and Robinson Cano chased the American League batting crown with a .342 average. **Melky Cabrera**, who

stumbled badly in a brief 2005 callup, came through with a solid contribution while filling in for the injured Hideki Matsui. The Yankees also had enough lower-level prospects that they didn't have to part with any of their blue-chippers when they acquired outfielder Bob Abreu and righthander Cory Lidle from the Phillies in July. (New York's ability and willingness to absorb $23 million in contract obligations also was a major factor.)

But none of that seemed to matter in October. Lidle's sobering death in an airplane crash came on the heels of a first-round playoff loss to the Tigers. Alex Rodriguez, the game's highest-paid player, continued to run afoul of Yankees fans and capped an erratic season with a 1-for-14 postseason effort. Several media outlets called for the firing of Joe Torre, though owner George Steinbrenner chose to keep the manager after his 11th season.

General manager Brian Cashman clearly influenced that move and made most of the big decisions surrounding the Yankees this year as the 75-year-old Steinbrenner faded more into the background. Cashman has been GM during the club's nine-year run

atop the AL East. But New York hasn't won a World Series championship since 2000 despite spending nearly $1 billion on major league salaries.

The reasons for that failure can be debated, but having to start Jaret Wright against the Tigers in Game Four of the Division Series highlighted the Yankees' inability to develop pitching. The only postseason victory came from Wang—the lone starter they've developed and kept since Andy Pettitte.

In the near future, though, the Yankees should have plenty of homegrown options, both in the rotation and in the bullpen. Their last three drafts have brought in several significant arms, and Philip Hughes is arguably the best pitching prospect in the minors. He probably was ready to help New York in September, but the organization played it safe with its top prospect, who nearly doubled his career high for innings in a season.

The Yankees also replenished the bottom of their system, bringing in as much talent as any organization in 2006. New York spent roughly $7 million on the draft, landing three pitchers (Dellin Betances, Joba Chamberlain and Ian Kennedy) who jump into their top 10. The Yankees also spent heavily on a dozen international players, including $1.6 million for Venezuelan catcher Jesus Montero, widely regarded as having the most power among 2006 international signees.

## TOP 30 PROSPECTS

| | |
|---|---|
| 1. Philip Hughes, rhp | 16. Alan Horne, rhp |
| 2. Jose Tabata, of | 17. Angel Reyes, lhp |
| 3. Humberto Sanchez, rhp | 18. Austin Jackson, of |
| 4. Dellin Betances, rhp | 19. Chase Wright, lhp |
| 5. Joba Chamberlain, rhp | 20. George Kontos, rhp |
| 6. Ian Kennedy, rhp | 21. Jesus Montero, c |
| 7. Tyler Clippard, rhp | 22. Steven White, rhp |
| 8. J. Brent Cox, rhp | 23. T.J. Beam, rhp |
| 9. Kevin Whelan, rhp | 24. Zach McAllister, rhp |
| 10. Brett Gardner, of | 25. Colin Curtis, of |
| 11. Marcos Vechionacci, 3b | 26. Jeff Karstens, rhp |
| 12. Jeff Marquez, rhp | 27. Josue Calzado, of |
| 13. Eric Duncan, 1b/3b | 28. Bronson Sardinha, of |
| 14. Chris Garcia, rhp | 29. Tim Norton, rhp |
| 15. Mark Melancon, rhp | 30. Daniel McCutchen, rhp |

# ORGANIZATION OVERVIEW

**General Manager:** Brian Cashman. **Farm director:** Mark Newman. **Scouting director:** Damon Oppenheimer.

## 2006 PERFORMANCE

| Class | Team | League | W | L | PCT | Finish* | Manager | Affiliated |
|---|---|---|---|---|---|---|---|---|
| Majors | New York | American | 97 | 65 | .599 | 1st (14) | Joe Torre | — |
| Triple-A | #Columbus Clippers | International | 69 | 73 | .486 | 9th (14) | Dave Miley | 1979 |
| Double-A | Trenton Thunder | Eastern | 80 | 62 | .547 | 2nd (12) | Bill Masse | 2003 |
| High A | Tampa Yankees | Florida State | 75 | 62 | .547 | 4th (12) | Luis Sojo | 1994 |
| Low A | Charleston Riverdogs | South Atlantic | 78 | 62 | .557 | 3rd (16) | Bill Mosiello | 2005 |
| Short-season | Staten Island Yankees | New York-Penn | 45 | 29 | .608 | +1st (14) | Gaylen Pitts | 1999 |
| Rookie | GCL Yankees | Gulf Coast | 33 | 20 | .608 | 3rd (13) | Oscar Acosta | 1980 |
| **OVERALL 2006 MINOR LEAGUE RECORD** | | | 378 | 308 | .551 | 3rd (30) | | |

*Finish in overall standings (No. of teams in league). +League champion. #Affiliate will be in Scranton (International) in 2007.

## ORGANIZATION LEADERS

### BATTING
| | | |
|---|---|---|
| AVG | Pino, Wilmer, Staten Island | .326 |
| R | Gardner, Brett, Tampa/Trenton | 106 |
| H | Gardner, Brett, Tampa/Trenton | 152 |
| TB | Ruiz, Randy, Wichita/Trenton | 249 |
| 2B | Ehlers, Cody, Tampa | 38 |
| 3B | Gardner, Brett, Tampa/Trenton | 10 |
| HR | Ruiz, Randy, Wichita/Trenton | 26 |
| RBI | Ehlers, Cody, Tampa | 106 |
| BB | Gardner, Brett, Tampa/Trenton | 88 |
| SO | Jackson, Austin, Charleston | 151 |
| SB | Christian, Justin, Trenton | 76 |
| OBP | Gardner, Brett, Tampa/Trenton | .407 |
| SLG | Ruiz, Randy, Wichita/Trenton | .532 |
| XBH | Ruiz, Randy, Wichita/Trenton | 62 |

### PITCHING
| | | |
|---|---|---|
| W | Jones, Jason, Tampa/Trenton | 13 |
| L | De Paula, Jorge, Trenton/Columbus | 15 |
| ERA | Reyes, Angel, GCL Yankees/Staten Island | 1.40 |
| G | Casadiego, Gerardo, Tampa/Trenton | 58 |
| CG | White, Steven, Trenton/Columbus | 2 |
| | Wilson, Kris, Trenton/Columbus | 2 |
| SV | Pope, Justin, Columbus/Trenton | 23 |
| IP | White, Steven, Trenton/Columbus | 175 |
| BB | DeSalvo, Matt, Columbus/Trenton | 93 |
| SO | Clippard, Tyler, Trenton | 175 |
| AVG | Reyes, Angel, GCL Yankees/Staten Island | .171 |

## BEST TOOLS

| | |
|---|---|
| Best Hitter for Average | Jose Tabata |
| Best Power Hitter | Shelly Duncan |
| Best Strike-Zone Discipline | Brett Gardner |
| Fastest Baserunner | Brett Gardner |
| Best Athlete | Tim Battle |
| Best Fastball | Joba Chamberlain |
| Best Curveball | Philip Hughes |
| Best Slider | J. Brent Cox |
| Best Changeup | Tyler Clippard |
| Best Control | Philip Hughes |
| Best Defensive Catcher | Francisco Cervelli |
| Best Defensive Infielder | Ramiro Pena |
| Best Infield Arm | Marcos Vechionacci |
| Best Defensive Outfielder | Tim Battle |
| Best Outfield Arm | Seth Fortenberry |

## PROJECTED 2010 LINEUP

| | |
|---|---|
| Catcher | Jesus Montero |
| First Base | Eric Duncan |
| Second Base | Robinson Cano |
| Third Base | Alex Rodriguez |
| Shortstop | Derek Jeter |
| Left Field | Melky Cabrera |
| Center Field | Johnny Damon |
| Right Field | Jose Tabata |
| Designated Hitter | Bob Abreu |
| No. 1 Starter | Philip Hughes |
| No. 2 Starter | Chien-Ming Wang |
| No. 3 Starter | Humberto Sanchez |
| No. 4 Starter | Dellin Betances |
| No. 5 Starter | Joba Chamberlain |
| Closer | J. Brent Cox |

## LAST YEAR'S TOP 20 PROSPECTS

| | |
|---|---|
| 1. Philip Hughes, rhp | 11. J. Brent Cox, rhp |
| 2. Eric Duncan, 3b/1b | 12. Tim Battle, of |
| 3. Jose Tabata, of | 13. Brett Gardner, of |
| 4. C.J. Henry, ss | 14. Steven White, rhp |
| 5. Austin Jackson, of | 15. Melky Cabrera, of |
| 6. Eduardo Nunez, ss | 16. Matt DeSalvo, rhp |
| 7. Marcos Vechionacci, 3b | 17. Alan Horne, rhp |
| 8. Christian Garcia, rhp | 18. Sean Henn, lhp |
| 9. Jeff Marquez, rhp | 19. Kevin Howard, 2b/3b |
| 10. Tyler Clippard, rhp | 20. Matt Smith, lhp |

## TOP PROSPECTS OF THE DECADE

| Year | Player, Pos. | 2006 Org. |
|---|---|---|
| 1997 | Ruben Rivera, of | White Sox |
| 1998 | Eric Milton, lhp | Reds |
| 1999 | Nick Johnson, 1b | Nationals |
| 2000 | Nick Johnson, 1b | Nationals |
| 2001 | Nick Johnson, 1b | Nationals |
| 2002 | Drew Henson, 3b | Out of baseball |
| 2003 | Jose Contreras, rhp | White Sox |
| 2004 | Dioner Navarro, c | Devil Rays |
| 2005 | Eric Duncan, 3b | Yankees |
| 2006 | Philip Hughes, rhp | Yankees |

## TOP DRAFT PICKS OF THE DECADE

| Year | Player, Pos. | 2006 Org. |
|---|---|---|
| 1997 | *Tyrell Godwin, of | Nationals |
| 1998 | Andy Brown, of | Out of baseball |
| 1999 | David Walling, rhp | Out of baseball |
| 2000 | David Parrish, c | Pirates |
| 2001 | John-Ford Griffin, of | Blue Jays |
| 2002 | Brandon Weeden, rhp (2nd round) | Royals |
| 2003 | Eric Duncan, 3b | Yankees |
| 2004 | Philip Hughes, rhp | Yankees |
| 2005 | C.J. Henry, ss | Phillies |
| 2006 | Ian Kennedy, rhp | Yankees |

*Did not sign.

## ALL-TIME LARGEST BONUSES

| | |
|---|---|
| Hideki Irabu, 1997 | $8,500,000 |
| Jose Contreras, 2002 | $6,000,000 |
| Willy Mo Pena, 1999 | $2,440,000 |
| Ian Kennedy, 2006 | $2,250,000 |
| Drew Henson, 1998 | $2,000,000 |

# MINOR LEAGUE DEPTH CHART

## New York Yankees

**Impact: B.** Hughes and Tabata rank among the best in the minors at their positions, and Hughes might be the best pitcher in the minors.
**Depth: B.** The Yankees have enough righthanded pitching depth to absorb injuries to the likes of Chris Garcia and Mark Melancon.
**Sleeper:** Reegie Corona, 2b/ss. Middle infielder hit his way to being considered a prospect by the organization and fits the utility profile.

*Numbers in parentheses indicate prospect rankings.*

### LF
Austin Jackson (18)
Collin Curtis (25)
Justin Christian
Kevin Reese

### CF
Brett Gardner (10)
Tim Battle
Kevin Thompson
Carlos Martinez Urena

### RF
Jose Tabata (2)
Josue Calzado (27)
Bronson Sardinha (28)
Seth Fortenberry
Edwar Gonzalez
Arielky LaPay

### 3B
Marcos Vechionacci (11)
Mitch Hilligoss
Kevin Howard

### SS
Eduardo Nunez
Ramiro Pena
Andy Cannizaro
Jose Pirala

### 2B
Reegie Corona
Wilmer Pina
Mario Holmann

### 1B
Eric Duncan (13)
Shelley Duncan
Juan Miguel Miranda
Cody Ehlers
Ben Jones

### C
Jesus Montero (21)
Frank Cervelli
Joe Muich

### RHP

| Starters | Relievers |
| --- | --- |
| Philip Hughes (1) | J. Brent Cox (8) |
| Humberto Sanchez (3) | Mark Melancon (15) |
| Dellin Betances (4) | T.J. Beam (23) |
| Joba Chamberlain (5) | Tim Norton (29) |
| Ian Kennedy (6) | Daniel McCutchen (30) |
| Tyler Clippard (7) | Anthony Claggett |
| Jeff Marquez (12) | Grant Duff |
| Christian Garcia (14) | Francisco Butto |
| Alan Horne (16) | Eric Wordekemper |
| George Kontos (20) | Edwar Ramirez |
| Steven White (22) | |
| Zach McAllister (24) | |
| Jeff Karstens (26) | |
| Ivan Nova | |
| Darrell Rasner | |
| Brett Smith | |
| Erick Abreu | |
| Matt DeSalvo | |
| Jason Stephens | |

### LHP

| Starters | Relievers |
| --- | --- |
| Angel Reyes (17) | Garrett Patterson |
| Chase Wright (19) | Michael Dunn |
| Wilkins Arias | Sean Henn |
| Zack Kroenke | |
| Abel Gomez | |
| Edgar Soto | |

# DRAFT ANALYSIS

**Best Pro Debut:** Despite a 90-94 mph fastball and a hard slider, RHP George Kontos (5) went 3-10, 5.29 at Northwestern during the spring. The Yankees simplified his delivery, which improved his command, and he went 7-3, 2.64 with 82 strikeouts in 78 innings during the regular season before winning the clinching game of the short-season New York-Penn League playoffs. Counting the NY-P postseason, RHP Tim Norton (7) didn't allow an earned run in his final 30 innings. He throws a 90-93 mph fastball and a quality changeup.

**Best Athlete:** OF Seth Fortenberry (11), who just needs to make better contact to tap into his offensive potential. OF Colin Curtis (4) has average tools across the board.

**Best Pure Hitter:** 3B/SS Mitch Hilligoss (6) or Curtis. Hilligoss won the Big 10 Conference batting title (.404) in 2005 and finished second (.386) last spring.

**Best Raw Power:** The Yankees concentrated more on finding players who can hit now, and will worry about developing their power later. Curtis stands out the most with his average pop.

**Fastest Runner:** Fortenberry has plus speed. He has been clocked at 6.5 seconds in the 60 and 4.1 seconds from the left side of the plate to first base.

**Best Defensive Player:** New York envisions Curtis as a Mark Kotsay-type center fielder whose instincts allow him to play above his tools. Chris Kunda (19) was named the Pacific-10 Conference defensive player of the year while playing second base, then ably moved to shortstop as a pro.

**Best Fastball:** The Yankees gave above-slot seven-figure bonuses to RHPs Joba Chamberlain (1) and Dellin Betances (8), both of whom usually pitch at 92-94 mph and can reach back to get to 97. Betances may throw harder as he fills out his 6-foot-8, 210-pound frame and refines his mechanics.

**Best Breaking Ball:** Both Betances and RHP Mark Melancon (9) can throw a nasty curveball, with Melancon's more consistent. Melancon might have been a first-round pick had he not injured his elbow late in the spring, and he needed surgery in the fall.

**Most Intriguing Background:** At No. 41 overall, Chamberlain is the highest-selected Native American in draft history. RHP Casey Erickson's (10) uncle Roger once pitched for the Yankees. RHP David Robertson's (17) brother Connor plays in the Athletics system, as does C Brian Baisley's (24) brother Jeff. RHP Zach McAllister's (3) father Steve is a crosschecker with the Diamondbacks.

**Closest To The Majors:** RHP Ian Kennedy (1) doesn't have the big-time pure stuff of other pitchers in this draft class, but it's good enough when combined with his command and moxie.

**Best Late-Round Pick:** Though RHP Daniel McCutchen (13) drew a 50-game suspension for testing positive for performance-enhancing drugs, the Yankees were enthused by his sinker, which topped out at 95 mph, and his curveball.

**The One Who Got Away:** LHP Del Howell (18) took his 90-92 mph fastball to Alabama. LHP Eric Erickson (43), now at Miami, reminds some scouts of Jeremy Sowers.

**Assessment:** After years of playing the draft conservatively, the Yankees are flexing their financial muscle. They paid above-slot bonuses to Kennedy, Chamberlain, Curtis, Betances and Melancon, and this should be their best draft in a while.

## 2005      BUDGET: $3.7 million

Two premium athletes, SS C.J. Henry (1) and OF Austin Jackson (8), struggled with the bat in 2006, though Henry served a purpose as a piece in the Bob Abreu trade. RHP J. Brent Cox (2) could be the Yankees' closer of the future. **GRADE: C**

## 2004      BUDGET: $4.8 million

RHP Philip Hughes (1) has become one of the best pitching prospects in the minors and should arrive in New York any day now. RHP Jeff Marquez (1) is another talented arm, while OF Jon Poterson (1) has been a bust. **GRADE: B+**

## 2003      BUDGET: $3.8 million

1B/3B Eric Duncan (1) hasn't lived up to his hype and could become trade bait. RHP Tyler Clippard (9) has been a revelation, though not doing what it took to sign RHP Daniel Bard (20) was a mistake. **GRADE: C**

*Draft analysis by Jim Callis. Numbers in parentheses indicate draft rounds. Budgets are bonuses in first 10 rounds.*

PHILIP
# HUGHES

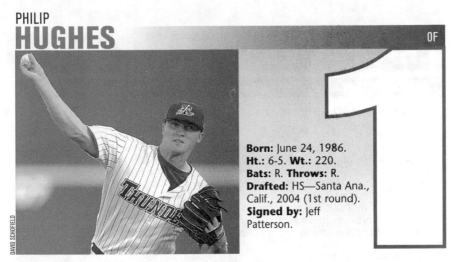

**Born:** June 24, 1986.
**Ht.:** 6-5. **Wt.:** 220.
**Bats:** R. **Throws:** R.
**Drafted:** HS—Santa Ana.,
Calif., 2004 (1st round).
**Signed by:** Jeff
Patterson.

DAVID SCHOFIELD

ughes entered 2006 as the top prospect in the Yankees system, and he handled that pressure better than many of his predecessors. The Yankees also have handled Hughes well. Due to injuries, he pitched just 91 innings in his first two years in pro ball. None of his physical problems had been major: A stubbed toe limited him to five innings in his 2004 pro debut, and he had two stints on the disabled list with shoulder tendinitis and a tired arm in 2005. So his workload wouldn't increase dramatically, New York limited him to 80 pitches or five innings for most of the second half of 2006. He turned in one of the minors' best seasons and finished with a kick that had Yankees fans calling for his promotion for the stretch run. Instead of tiring as he pushed past 100 innings for the first time, Hughes dominated, giving up just 10 hits and two runs in his last 30 innings, then striking out 13 in six innings against eventual champion Portland in the first game of the Double-A Eastern League playoffs.

Hughes has it all, with the combination of stuff, feel and command to profile as a No. 1 starter. In the words of one club official, "His stuff and his command keep getting better," and they were pretty good to begin with. Hughes sits at 91-95 mph with his four-seam fastball and touches 96. He can throw quality strikes with either his four-seamer or his upper-80s two-seamer. As he gains experience, his excellent control (his career K-BB ratio is 269-54) should evolve into above-average command. Hughes' greatest accomplishment as a pro has been to forsake his slider in favor of a knockout curveball, which is more of a strikeout pitch and produces less stress on his arm. It's a true power breaking ball that sits in the low 80s with 1-to-7 break. Club officials call it the best in the system because Hughes can throw it for quality strikes or bury it out of the zone, and because he uses the same arm slot and release point he uses for his fastball. While his slider is still a good pitch, he rarely throws it in games anymore.

The biggest concerns for Hughes entering the season were durability and his changeup. He answered the former question emphatically, but his changeup remains an unfinished project. While he made progress, he doesn't control his change as well as he does his fastball and curve. Because the curve is still relatively new to him, it sometimes morphs into more of a slurve, but that's happening less often.

The Yankees' biggest need is a homegrown ace to join Chien-Ming Wang at the front of their rotation, and Hughes is nearly ready to give them just that. Hughes hasn't pitched in Triple-A yet and probably will start 2007 there with the club's new Scranton/Wilkes-Barre affiliate, if only to get consistent work early in the season. No one would be shocked to see Hughes in the majors by June, just three years after being drafted.

| Year | Club (League) | Class | W | L | ERA | G | GS | CG | SV | IP | H | R | ER | HR | BB | SO | AVG |
|------|---------------|-------|---|---|------|----|----|----|----|-----|-----|----|----|----|----|-----|------|
| 2004 | Yankees (GCL) | R | 0 | 0 | 0.00 | 3 | 3 | 0 | 0 | 5 | 4 | 0 | 0 | 0 | 0 | 8 | .222 |
| 2005 | Charleston (SAL) | A | 7 | 1 | 1.97 | 12 | 12 | 1 | 0 | 69 | 46 | 19 | 15 | 1 | 16 | 72 | .192 |
| | Tampa (FSL) | A | 2 | 0 | 3.06 | 5 | 4 | 0 | 0 | 18 | 8 | 6 | 6 | 0 | 4 | 21 | .140 |
| 2006 | Tampa (FSL) | A | 2 | 3 | 1.80 | 5 | 5 | 0 | 0 | 30 | 19 | 7 | 6 | 0 | 2 | 30 | .178 |
| | Trenton (EL) | AA | 10 | 3 | 2.25 | 21 | 21 | 0 | 0 | 116 | 73 | 30 | 29 | 5 | 32 | 138 | .179 |
| **MINOR LEAGUE TOTALS** | | | 21 | 7 | 2.12 | 46 | 45 | 1 | 0 | 237 | 150 | 62 | 56 | 6 | 54 | 269 | .181 |

## JOSE TABATA
OF

**Born:** Aug. 12, 1988. **B-T:** R-R. **Ht.:** 5-11. **Wt.:** 160. **Signed:** Venezuela, 2005. **Signed by:** Ricardo Finol.

After signing for $550,000, Tabata raised expectations with an impressive debut in the Rookie-level Gulf Coast League in 2005. He was having a rousing encore at low Class A Charleston in 2006 before a thumb injury effectively ended his season in July. Some hitters just seem to be born with the innate ability to get the fat part of the bat to the ball quickly, consistently and with power. That's Tabata. He has the bat speed to catch up to good fastballs and drive any pitch to any part of the park. His other tools are at least average, as he has flashed plus speed and arm strength. His coaches praise his ability to compete and rise to the occasion. Because he makes such easy contact, Tabata doesn't walk much, though he improved as the season went on. Scouts have noticed that he tends to coast and turn his talent on and off. His lower half already has thickened somewhat, and some think he could lose significant athleticism and speed as he gets older, relegating him to left field instead of right. Tabata was healthy enough to return to the field in the Venezuelan League this winter, then had to leave early with wrist pain. A healthy Tabata should be poised for a breakout 2007 season. He has the talent to reach New York by the end of 2008.

| Year | Club (League) | Class | AVG | G | AB | R | H | 2B | 3B | HR | RBI | BB | SO | SB | OBP | SLG |
|------|---------------|-------|-----|---|----|----|----|----|----|----|-----|----|----|----|-----|-----|
| 2005 | Yankees (GCL) | R | .314 | 44 | 156 | 30 | 49 | 5 | 1 | 3 | 25 | 15 | 14 | 22 | .382 | .417 |
| 2006 | Charleston (SAL) | A | .298 | 86 | 319 | 50 | 95 | 22 | 1 | 5 | 51 | 30 | 66 | 15 | .377 | .420 |
| **MINOR LEAGUE TOTALS** | | | .303 | 130 | 475 | 80 | 144 | 27 | 2 | 8 | 76 | 45 | 80 | 37 | .379 | .419 |

## HUMBERTO SANCHEZ
RHP

**Born:** May 28, 1983. **B-T:** R-R. **Ht.:** 6-6. **Wt.:** 230. **Drafted:** Connors State (Okla.) JC, D/F 2001 (31st round). **Signed by:** Rob Guzik/Buddy Paine (Tigers).

The key player for the Yankees in their Gary Sheffield trade with the Tigers in November, Sanchez originally signed for $1 million as a draft-and-follow. Though he started the 2006 Futures Game for the World Team, Sanchez became expendable when Justin Verlander and Joel Zumaya passed him and the Tigers also drafted Andrew Miller. He's the young power arm New York lacked in Triple-A, where its rotation was loaded with finesse righties in 2006. Sanchez' fastball sits at 90-94 mph and he can dial it up to 97. His hard slider is a plus pitch at times, when it features so much downward break that it looks like a splitter. He'll also mix in a curveball and has an adequate changeup. Sanchez could use more consistency with his secondary pitches, mechanics and command, but his biggest need is to stay healthy. He hasn't done a good job of staying in shape, and while he reported to spring training last year in the best condition of his career, he still couldn't push his career high past 123 innings. Sanchez had oblique and groin injuries in 2005, then came down with a tender elbow and missed the last month of the 2006 season. He has a shot at making the Yankees rotation out of spring training, though his lack of durability lessens the likelihood of him throwing 160-180 big league innings. If he starts the season in Triple-A, he still should surface in New York before the year is out.

| Year | Club (League) | Class | W | L | ERA | G | GS | CG | SV | IP | H | R | ER | HR | BB | SO | AVG |
|------|---------------|-------|---|---|-----|---|----|----|----|----|---|---|----|----|----|----|-----|
| 2002 | Oneonta (NYP) | A | 2 | 2 | 3.62 | 9 | 9 | 0 | 0 | 32 | 29 | 18 | 13 | 1 | 21 | 26 | .244 |
| 2003 | West Michigan (MWL) | A | 7 | 7 | 4.42 | 23 | 23 | 0 | 0 | 116 | 107 | 71 | 57 | 3 | 78 | 96 | .249 |
| 2004 | Lakeland (FSL) | A | 7 | 11 | 5.21 | 19 | 19 | 3 | 0 | 105 | 103 | 67 | 61 | 9 | 51 | 115 | .263 |
| | Erie (EL) | AA | 1 | 0 | 2.13 | 2 | 2 | 0 | 0 | 13 | 10 | 5 | 3 | 1 | 6 | 15 | .213 |
| 2005 | Erie (EL) | AA | 3 | 5 | 5.57 | 15 | 11 | 0 | 0 | 65 | 72 | 42 | 40 | 10 | 27 | 65 | .283 |
| 2006 | Erie (EL) | AA | 5 | 3 | 1.76 | 11 | 11 | 0 | 0 | 72 | 47 | 17 | 14 | 2 | 27 | 86 | .190 |
| | Toledo (IL) | AAA | 5 | 3 | 3.86 | 9 | 9 | 0 | 0 | 51 | 50 | 23 | 22 | 2 | 20 | 43 | .260 |
| **MINOR LEAGUE TOTALS** | | | 30 | 31 | 4.16 | 88 | 84 | 3 | 0 | 454 | 418 | 243 | 210 | 28 | 230 | 446 | .249 |

## DELLIN BETANCES, RHP

**Born:** March 23, 1988. **B-T:** R-R. **Ht.:** 6-7. **Wt.:** 185. Drafted: HS—New York, 2006 (8th round). **Signed by:** Cesar Presbott/Brian Barber.

Betances was considered a probable first-round pick early in the 2006 draft cycle, but his slow start in the spring, high price tag and commitment to Vanderbilt scared off many clubs. The Yankees popped him in the eighth round and met his $1 million asking price, erasing the bonus record for that round—which they set a year earlier when they gave Austin Jackson $800,000. Betances' stuff is as good as anyone's in the system. His fastball sits at 93-94 mph and touched 98 in the club's fall mini-

camp. He uses a low-80s power curveball as an out pitch. His changeup has made significant strides in his short pro career and grades as a future plus pitch with sinking, diving action. He's athletic and intelligent, and adapted quickly to the mechanical adjustments New York asked him to make. While he's shown some feel for his changeup, Betances needs to throw it more to master it. At his size, he'll have to work to keep his mechanics in sync and maintain balance over the rubber. At times, he rushes his delivery, making it hard for his arm to keep up with his body and costing him command. The Yankees already consider Betances ahead of schedule. He should make his full-season debut in low Class A in 2007. A potential No. 1 starter, he could become a local product who stars for the Yankees.

| Year | Club (League) | Class | W | L | ERA | G | GS | CG | SV | IP | H | R | ER | HR | BB | SO | AVG |
|------|---------------|-------|---|---|-----|---|----|----|----|----|---|---|----|----|----|----|-----|
| 2006 | Yankees (GCL) | R | 0 | 1 | 1.16 | 7 | 7 | 0 | 0 | 23 | 14 | 5 | 3 | 1 | 7 | 27 | .173 |
| **MINOR LEAGUE TOTALS** | | | 0 | 1 | 1.16 | 7 | 7 | 0 | 0 | 23 | 14 | 5 | 3 | 1 | 7 | 27 | .173 |

## 5 JOBA CHAMBERLAIN                                    RHP

**Born:** Sept. 23, 1985. **B-T:** R-R. **Ht.:** 6-3. **Wt.:** 225. Drafted: Nebraska, 2006 (1st round supplemental). **Signed by:** Steve Lemke/Tim Kelly.

Chamberlain was hardly a pedigreed prospect as an amateur. He started pitching as a high school senior and went 3-6, 5.23 as a freshman for NCAA Division II Nebraska-Kearney. He transformed himself after transferring to Nebraska in Lincoln, having knee surgery, losing 25 pounds and blossoming into a dominant starter. When the Yankees drafted him 41st overall, he became the highest-drafted Native American ever. Chamberlain throws four pitches for strikes, and his fastball is his go-to pitch. It sat at 94-97 mph during the Hawaii Winter Baseball season, where he was named the top prospect in the league, and he throws it for quality strikes. His slider at times has depth and tilt and can be above-average, while his curveball and changeup are also solid. Projected to go in the first 10 picks, Chamberlain fell in the draft because of health questions. He missed time in the spring with triceps tendinitis, and his knee surgery and previous weight problems also scared off some clubs. He'll have to maintain his current body to maintain his stuff. Chamberlain has the best combination of power and polish among 2006 Yankees draftees and will move quickly if healthy. He'll start 2007 in high Class A and should move quickly.

| Year | Club (League) | Class | W | L | ERA | G | GS | CG | SV | IP | H | R | ER | HR | BB | SO | AVG |
|------|---------------|-------|---|---|-----|---|----|----|----|----|---|---|----|----|----|----|-----|
| 2006 | Did not play—Signed 2007 contract | | | | | | | | | | | | | | | | |

## 6 IAN KENNEDY                                        RHP

**Born:** Dec. 19, 1984. **B-T:** R-R. **Ht.:** 6-0. **Wt.:** 190. Drafted: Southern California, 2006 (1st round). **Signed by:** Bill Mele/Jeff Patterson.

A high school teammate of Rockies prospect Ian Stewart, Kennedy was a 14th-round pick of the Cardinals in 2003 but didn't sign. He succeeded Anthony Reyes as Southern California's ace but was much better as a sophomore (12-3, 2.54) than as a junior (5-7, 3.90). Nonetheless, the Yankees drafted him 21st overall and signed him for an above-slot $2.25 million bonus. Kennedy has excellent command, particularly for a young pitcher, thanks to his consistent delivery. His command helps his average stuff play up. He spots his fastball, which sits in the upper 80s and touches 92 mph when he's right, and throws a sinking changeup from the same arm slot and with similar arm speed. Even when he's not at his best, Kennedy keeps the ball down and doesn't give up many homers. He's savvy and intelligent and pitches with a plan. All of Kennedy's pitches took a step back during the spring, and his command wasn't enough to compensate. His changeup's regression and his loopy curveball kept him from putting away hitters with two strikes. His curve in particular needs help, as he tends to get around on it, costing it depth. He needs to stay tall in his delivery, lest his small stature work against him. The Yankees believe in pitching coordinator Nardi Contreras and consider Kennedy the perfect project for him. If Contreras can help him tighten his curve and regain confidence, Kennedy will hop on the fast track. He's likely headed for high Class A in 2007.

| Year | Club (League) | Class | W | L | ERA | G | GS | CG | SV | IP | H | R | ER | HR | BB | SO | AVG |
|------|-------------------|-------|---|---|------|---|----|----|----|----|---|---|----|----|----|----|------|
| 2006 | Staten Island (NYP) | A | 0 | 0 | 0.00 | 1 | 1 | 0 | 0 | 3 | 2 | 0 | 0 | 0 | 2 | 2 | .200 |
| **MINOR LEAGUE TOTALS** | | | 0 | 0 | 0.00 | 1 | 1 | 0 | 0 | 3 | 2 | 0 | 0 | 0 | 2 | 2 | .200 |

## 7 TYLER CLIPPARD RHP

DAVID SCHOFIELD

**Born:** Feb. 14, 1985. **B-T:** R-R. **Ht.:** 6-4. **Wt.:** 200. Drafted: HS—Trinity, Fla., 2003 (9th round). **Signed by:** Scott Pleis.

In his third full pro season, Clippard did what he has done every season—get better. He got off to a rough start at Double-A Trenton but recovered with a dominant second half that included the first no-hitter in the Thunder's 13-year franchise history. He led the Eastern League in strikeouts and ranked fifth in the entire minors. Clippard has figured out how put hitters away at every level without "wow" stuff. He frequently pitches backward because he can throw his curveball and changeup, both slightly above-average pitches, for quality strikes. His long arms and lanky body add deception to his delivery. Though he has filled out his frame to around 200 pounds, Clippard hasn't added fastball velocity. In fact, while he used to touch 94 mph, his fastball usually topped out around 92 in 2006 and sat at 88-90. When he misses, he misses up in the zone and is prone to giving up home runs. Clippard still could use polish to tweak his mechanics and improve his fastball. He won't be an ace, but he should be a solid option as a No. 4 starter in the near future. He'll continue to move up one step at a time, heading to Triple-A in 2007.

| Year | Club (League) | Class | W | L | ERA | G | GS | CG | SV | IP | H | R | ER | HR | BB | SO | AVG |
|------|---------------|-------|---|---|-----|---|----|----|----|-----|-----|-----|-----|----|-----|-----|------|
| 2003 | Yankees (GCL) | R | 3 | 3 | 2.89 | 11 | 5 | 0 | 0 | 44 | 33 | 16 | 14 | 3 | 5 | 56 | .212 |
| 2004 | Battle Creek (MWL) | A | 10 | 10 | 3.44 | 26 | 25 | 1 | 0 | 149 | 153 | 71 | 57 | 12 | 32 | 145 | .264 |
| 2005 | Charleston (SAL) | A | 0 | 1 | 7.50 | 1 | 1 | 0 | 0 | 6 | 9 | 5 | 5 | 1 | 0 | 10 | .333 |
| | Tampa (FSL) | A | 10 | 9 | 3.18 | 26 | 25 | 0 | 0 | 147 | 118 | 56 | 52 | 12 | 34 | 169 | .219 |
| | Columbus (IL) | AAA | 0 | 0 | 0.00 | 1 | 0 | 0 | 0 | 1 | 0 | 0 | 0 | 0 | 0 | 2 | .000 |
| 2006 | Trenton (EL) | AA | 12 | 10 | 3.35 | 28 | 28 | 1 | 0 | 166 | 118 | 72 | 62 | 14 | 55 | 175 | .200 |
| **MINOR LEAGUE TOTALS** | | | 35 | 33 | 3.33 | 93 | 84 | 2 | 0 | 513 | 431 | 220 | 190 | 42 | 126 | 557 | .227 |

## 8 J. BRENT COX RHP

KEVIN PATAKY

**Born:** May 13, 1984. **B-T:** R-R. **Ht.:** 6-3. **Wt.:** 205. Drafted: Texas, 2005 (2nd round). **Signed by:** Steve Boros.

The closer for Texas' 2005 College World Series championship team, Cox led NCAA Division I with 19 saves that spring. He spent his first full pro season at Double-A, helping Trenton overcome a 0-10 start by serving as a workhorse set-up man. He finished the year with Team USA in the Olympic qualifying tournament. Cox pounds the strike zone with pitches that hitters find nearly impossible to lift. His out pitch is a plus slider with depth that he can throw for strikes or bury to get strikeouts. His fastball sits at 88-91 mph and plays up because of its heavy sink and his ability to command it. His changeup made significant strides in 2006, helping him limit lefthanders to a .150 average. He's a fearless competitor who loves to pitch with the game on the line. Cox just doesn't have enough fastball to be a strikeout pitcher. He profiles better as a set-up man than as a closer, and that somewhat modest ceiling is the biggest knock on him. With a big spring, Cox could pitch his way onto the big league roster. If he doesn't, he'll head to Triple-A and continue preparing for a set-up role.

| Year | Club (League) | Class | W | L | ERA | G | GS | CG | SV | IP | H | R | ER | HR | BB | SO | AVG |
|------|---------------|-------|---|---|-----|---|----|----|----|-----|----|----|----|----|----|----|------|
| 2005 | Tampa (FSL) | A | 1 | 2 | 2.60 | 16 | 0 | 0 | 0 | 28 | 20 | 9 | 8 | 1 | 5 | 27 | .206 |
| 2006 | Trenton (EL) | AA | 6 | 2 | 1.75 | 41 | 0 | 0 | 3 | 77 | 54 | 21 | 15 | 2 | 24 | 60 | .196 |
| **MINOR LEAGUE TOTALS** | | | 7 | 4 | 1.98 | 57 | 0 | 0 | 3 | 105 | 74 | 30 | 23 | 3 | 29 | 87 | .199 |

## 9 KEVIN WHELAN RHP

RICH ABEL

**Born:** Jan. 8, 1984. **B-T:** R-R. **Ht.:** 6-0. **Wt.:** 200. Drafted: Texas A&M, 2005 (4th round). **Signed by:** Tim Grieve (Tigers).

Whelan arrived at Texas A&M as a catcher but his strong arm proved more valuable on the mound, and he's looked like a steal since Detroit took him in the fourth round in 2005, dominating three levels and earning 42 saves in 1 ½ seasons. He came to the Yankees in the Gary Sheffield trade in November. Whelan's out pitch is his splitter, clocked as high as 89 mph. He also has a strong four-seam fastball in the 92-94 mph range, as well as a two-seamer with plus sink. The residue of the throwing motion he used as a catcher adds deception. Whelan switched to pitching full-time only in 2005, and his inexperience remains evident. He sometimes loses his feel for the strike zone. Once he gains a better understanding of his delivery, he'll have an easier time repeating it. His slider, which could be a nice addition to his fastball-splitter combination, has remained

inconsistent. Whelan will start 2007 in Double-A, with an eye toward refining his pitches. Once everything clicks, he has the potential to sail through the system. He may get to New York at some point this season, and he should arrive in the majors to stay in 2008.

| Year | Club (League) | Class | W | L | ERA | G | GS | CG | SV | IP | H | R | ER | HR | BB | SO | AVG |
|------|---------------|-------|---|---|------|----|----|----|----|----|----|----|----|----|----|-----|------|
| 2005 | Oneonta (NYP) | A | 1 | 1 | 2.25 | 11 | 0 | 0 | 4 | 12 | 2 | 4 | 3 | 1 | 6 | 19 | .051 |
|  | West Michigan (MWL) | A | 0 | 0 | 0.73 | 14 | 0 | 0 | 11 | 12 | 4 | 1 | 1 | 0 | 2 | 22 | .098 |
| 2006 | Lakeland (FSL) | A | 4 | 1 | 2.67 | 51 | 0 | 0 | 27 | 54 | 33 | 20 | 16 | 1 | 29 | 69 | .178 |
| **MINOR LEAGUE TOTALS** |  |  | 5 | 2 | 2.30 | 76 | 0 | 0 | 42 | 78 | 39 | 25 | 20 | 2 | 37 | 110 | .147 |

## 10 BRETT GARDNER   OF

**Born:** Aug. 24, 1983. **B-T:** L-L. **Ht.:** 5-10. **Wt.:** 180. **Drafted:** College of Charleston, 2005 (3rd round). **Signed by:** Steve Swail.

A former walk-on, Gardner became the highest-drafted player in College of Charleston history as a senior in 2005. He reached Double-A and ranked ninth in the majors with 58 steals in his first full pro season. The organization's fastest runner, Gardner has earned 70 grades on the 20-80 scouting scale for his speed and consistently turns in 4.0-second times from the plate to first base. He's an adept basestealer who succeeded on 83 percent of his attempts in 2006, and he covers the gaps well in center field. Gardner endears himself to scouts with his all-out hustle, while his plate discipline ranks as the best in the system. He stays within himself at the plate and sprays line drives from gap to gap, using a short swing he repeats well. With no power to speak of, Gardner will have to keep proving that he can hold his own against better pitching as he moves up the ladder. He has the bat speed to turn on balls inside, but he frequently gets beat on the outer half and fails to adjust. His arm is below average and his routes are erratic, though he usually outruns his mistakes. With Johnny Damon signed for three more seasons, Gardner has time to prove he can drive the ball enough to become a regular. He's ticketed for Triple-A in 2007.

| Year | Club (League) | Class | AVG | G | AB | R | H | 2B | 3B | HR | RBI | BB | SO | SB | OBP | SLG |
|------|---------------|-------|-----|----|-----|----|----|----|----|----|-----|----|-----|----|------|------|
| 2005 | Staten Island (NYP) | A | .284 | 73 | 282 | 62 | 80 | 9 | 1 | 5 | 32 | 39 | 49 | 19 | .377 | .376 |
| 2006 | Tampa (FSL) | A | .323 | 63 | 232 | 46 | 75 | 12 | 5 | 0 | 22 | 43 | 51 | 30 | .433 | .418 |
| 2006 | Trenton (EL) | AA | .272 | 55 | 217 | 41 | 59 | 4 | 3 | 0 | 13 | 27 | 39 | 28 | .352 | .318 |
| **MINOR LEAGUE TOTALS** |  |  | .293 | 191 | 731 | 149 | 214 | 25 | 9 | 5 | 67 | 109 | 139 | 77 | .388 | .372 |

## 11 MARCOS VECHIONACCI   3B

**Born:** Aug. 7, 1986. **B-T:** B-R. **Ht.:** 6-2. **Wt.:** 170. **Signed:** Venezuela, 2002. **Signed by:** Ricardo Finol.

Vechionacci has a higher ceiling than almost any hitter in the system, and he's also a potentially premier defender on the left side of the infield. He has above-average raw power and a knack for centering the ball on the fat part of the bat. He's starting to use his pitch-recognition skills to select balls he can drive out of the park, and he could become a .279-.290 hitter with 30-homer power. A switch-hitter, he's slightly better from the left side but is sound from the right. While he probably could handle shortstop, Vechionacci has Gold Glove ability at third base, where his accurate, plus arm and soft hands suit him well. He's a solid-average runner. Vechionacci's emotional maturity, in terms of focus on a play-to-play and game-to-game basis, is beginning to catch up to his physical maturity. He still has some growing to do on both counts, though. He has been pushed, and his game collapsed when he opened 2006 in high Class A. He struggled offensively (specifically with pitch recognition) and defensively, and he lost confidence. One scout who saw Charleston still liked him better than Jose Tabata because of his body and future power potential. The Yankees hope this is Vechionacci's true breakout season, and if it is, he could finish it in Double-A.

| Year | Club (League) | Class | AVG | G | AB | R | H | 2B | 3B | HR | RBI | BB | SO | SB | OBP | SLG |
|------|---------------|-------|-----|-----|------|-----|-----|----|----|----|-----|-----|-----|----|------|------|
| 2003 | N.Y. Yankees 1 (DSL) | R | .300 | 62 | 200 | 28 | 60 | 10 | 4 | 2 | 30 | 37 | 22 | 4 | .410 | .420 |
| 2004 | Tampa (FSL) | A | .250 | 1 | 4 | 1 | 1 | 0 | 0 | 0 | 0 | 0 | 0 | 0 | .250 | .250 |
|  | Staten Island (NYP) | A | .292 | 19 | 72 | 13 | 21 | 5 | 0 | 0 | 8 | 11 | 13 | 0 | .393 | .361 |
|  | Yankees (GCL) | R | .336 | 36 | 131 | 24 | 44 | 9 | 1 | 4 | 22 | 12 | 19 | 5 | .392 | .511 |
| 2005 | Charleston (SAL) | A | .252 | 128 | 503 | 83 | 127 | 26 | 8 | 2 | 62 | 43 | 83 | 16 | .314 | .348 |
| 2006 | Tampa (FSL) | A | .178 | 36 | 135 | 15 | 24 | 3 | 1 | 1 | 15 | 11 | 29 | 1 | .242 | .237 |
|  | Charleston (SAL) | A | .255 | 98 | 368 | 56 | 94 | 15 | 6 | 7 | 44 | 55 | 52 | 7 | .357 | .386 |
| **MINOR LEAGUE TOTALS** |  |  | .263 | 380 | 1413 | 220 | 371 | 68 | 20 | 16 | 181 | 169 | 218 | 33 | .344 | .373 |

## 12  JEFF MARQUEZ                                                    RHP

**Born:** Aug. 10, 1984. **B-T:** L-R. **Ht.:** 6-2. **Wt.:** 175. Drafted: Sacramento CC, 2004 (1st round supplemental). **Signed by:** Jeff Patterson.

Marquez hasn't disappointed the Yankees since they took him with the 41st overall pick in 2004. His live arm produces fastballs that sit at 89-94 mph, and at times he's thrown even harder. His heater has natural sink, and he had a 2-1 ground/fly ratio in high Class A in 2006. His season was interrupted by a shoulder strain that landed him on the disabled list for all of July, but he returned to have his best month of the season in August and made up for lost time in Hawaii Winter Baseball. Though he had a 7.04 ERA, he ranked as HWB's No. 4 prospect. Marquez will go as far as his command and secondary stuff take him. He didn't throw enough strikes early in counts in 2006, making him more hittable than he should have been after he fell behind. He would have more swing-and-miss stuff if he stayed tall more in his delivery. While he has the ability to spin a curveball, both it and his changeup don't find the strike zone frequently enough. He throws his changeup too hard at times. Marquez has the raw stuff to start in the middle of a big league rotation, and his hard sinker would make him a valuable reliever if necessary. He should open this year in Double-A.

| Year | Club (League) | Class | W | L | ERA | G | GS | CG | SV | IP | H | R | ER | HR | BB | SO | AVG |
|------|---------------|-------|---|---|-----|---|----|----|----|----|---|---|----|----|----|----|-----|
| 2004 | Yankees (GCL) | R | 2 | 0 | 0.63 | 4 | 2 | 0 | 0 | 14 | 10 | 1 | 1 | 0 | 4 | 18 | .189 |
|      | Staten Island (NYP) | A | 2 | 4 | 3.02 | 11 | 11 | 0 | 0 | 51 | 51 | 26 | 17 | 2 | 20 | 36 | .267 |
| 2005 | Charleston (SAL) | A | 9 | 13 | 3.42 | 27 | 27 | 1 | 0 | 140 | 138 | 64 | 53 | 4 | 61 | 107 | .257 |
| 2006 | Yankees (GCL) | R | 0 | 1 | 3.18 | 2 | 2 | 0 | 0 | 6 | 7 | 2 | 2 | 1 | 1 | 8 | .304 |
|      | Tampa (FSL) | A | 7 | 5 | 3.61 | 18 | 17 | 0 | 0 | 92 | 102 | 56 | 37 | 4 | 29 | 82 | .279 |
| **MINOR LEAGUE TOTALS** | | | 20 | 23 | 3.27 | 62 | 59 | 1 | 0 | 303 | 308 | 149 | 110 | 11 | 115 | 251 | .264 |

## 13  ERIC DUNCAN                                                    1B/3B

**Born:** Dec. 7, 1984. **B-T:** L-R. **Ht.:** 6-3. **Wt.:** 195. Drafted: HS—West Orange, N.J., 2003 (1st round). **Signed by:** Cesar Presbott.

The Yankees have pushed Duncan aggressively ever since he responded positively in 2004 to a midseason promotion to high Class A. They thought Duncan had the right mix of power, patience and contact ability from the left side to be an ideal hitter for Yankee Stadium. However, the two years since he ranked No. 1 on this list haven't been good to Duncan. He struggled for most of 2005 at Double-A, yet he was promoted to Triple-A out of spring training in 2006 before he was ready. Back problems didn't help matters. Duncan gathered himself after a demotion to Double-A in June, but when the back injury—originally considered a lower-back strain, later diagnosed as a disc problem—cropped up again, he faltered and eventually ended his season in mid-August. He returned to play in the Arizona Fall League, though his performance was more modest. Duncan has the bat speed to turn on good fastballs, crushes balls on the inner half and isn't afraid to take a walk. His raw power ranks among the best in the system. However, back injuries tend to linger, and Duncan will have to work hard to remain in the lineup consistently. While he played some third base in 2006, he lacks the arm strength and agility to be effective there. He saw more action and is better suited for first base, where he has become adequate in a short time and should improve with experience. A healthy Duncan should be ready for a second stint at Triple-A in 2007, but it's becoming harder to see him as an eventual regular for the Yankees.

| Year | Club (League) | Class | AVG | G | AB | R | H | 2B | 3B | HR | RBI | BB | SO | SB | OBP | SLG |
|------|---------------|-------|-----|---|----|---|---|----|----|----|-----|----|----|----|-----|-----|
| 2003 | Yankees (GCL) | R | .278 | 47 | 180 | 24 | 50 | 12 | 2 | 2 | 28 | 18 | 33 | 0 | .348 | .400 |
|      | Staten Island (NYP) | A | .373 | 14 | 59 | 11 | 22 | 5 | 4 | 2 | 13 | 2 | 11 | 1 | .413 | .695 |
| 2004 | Battle Creek (MWL) | A | .260 | 78 | 288 | 52 | 75 | 23 | 2 | 12 | 57 | 38 | 84 | 7 | .351 | .479 |
|      | Tampa (FSL) | A | .254 | 51 | 173 | 23 | 44 | 20 | 2 | 4 | 26 | 31 | 47 | 0 | .366 | .462 |
| 2005 | Trenton (EL) | AA | .235 | 126 | 451 | 60 | 106 | 15 | 3 | 19 | 61 | 59 | 136 | 9 | .326 | .408 |
| 2006 | Columbus (IL) | AAA | .209 | 31 | 110 | 7 | 23 | 3 | 1 | 0 | 6 | 9 | 24 | 0 | .279 | .255 |
|      | Trenton (EL) | AA | .248 | 57 | 206 | 32 | 51 | 15 | 2 | 10 | 29 | 32 | 38 | 0 | .355 | .485 |
| **MINOR LEAGUE TOTALS** | | | .253 | 404 | 1467 | 209 | 371 | 93 | 16 | 49 | 220 | 189 | 373 | 17 | .343 | .438 |

## 14  CHRIS GARCIA                                                   RHP

**Born:** Aug. 24, 1985. **B-T:** R-R. **Ht.:** 6-4. **Wt.:** 175. Drafted: HS—Miami, 2004 (3rd round). **Signed by:** Dan Radison.

A high school catcher, Garcia shifted to the mound as a senior and emerged as a top pitching prospect. After missing a month in 2005 with an elbow strain, he was sidelined for much of 2006 by an oblique strain, but he looked strong when he returned. Yankees officials believe a healthy Garcia has almost as much upside as Hughes. While Hughes' curve has passed his as the organization's best, Garcia's is still a plus pitch, particularly when he throws it with purpose and power. His fastball is consistently in the low 90s, and as he refines his mechan-

ics and continues to gain experience, it could sit in the mid-90s. He's learning to work off his fastball more and rely on his curve less. Garcia has pitched just 197 innings in three years as a pro, and while his biggest needs are an improved changeup and experience, he's about to miss another year of development time. Garcia tried to make up for lost time in Hawaii Winter Baseball, but he injured his elbow. He had surgery to reinforce a torn ligament and isn't expected to pitch again until 2008.

| Year | Club (League) | Class | W | L | ERA | G | GS | CG | SV | IP | H | R | ER | HR | BB | SO | AVG |
|------|---------------|-------|---|---|------|----|----|----|----|-----|-----|-----|----|----|----|-----|------|
| 2004 | Yankees (GCL) | R | 3 | 4 | 2.84 | 13 | 6 | 0 | 0 | 38 | 26 | 13 | 12 | 1 | 17 | 47 | .188 |
| 2005 | Charleston (SAL) | A | 5 | 6 | 3.91 | 21 | 20 | 0 | 0 | 106 | 102 | 57 | 46 | 3 | 53 | 103 | .249 |
| 2006 | Yankees (GCL) | R | 0 | 1 | 9.53 | 5 | 3 | 0 | 0 | 11 | 15 | 13 | 12 | 1 | 4 | 15 | .313 |
| | Charleston (SAL) | A | 2 | 3 | 3.46 | 7 | 7 | 0 | 0 | 42 | 37 | 19 | 16 | 2 | 12 | 45 | .243 |
| **MINOR LEAGUE TOTALS** | | | 10 | 14 | 3.93 | 46 | 36 | 0 | 0 | 197 | 180 | 102 | 86 | 7 | 86 | 210 | .241 |

## 15 MARK MELANCON RHP

**Born:** March 28, 1985. **B-T:** R-R. **Ht.:** 6-2. **Wt.:** 210. **Drafted:** Arizona, 2006 (9th round). **Signed by:** Andy Stankiewicz.

Arizona's single-season (11) and career (18) saves leader, Melancon projected as a first-round pick until a strained elbow ligament ended his junior season in April. Satisfied by the results of an MRI exam, New York snapped him up in the ninth round and signed him for $600,000. He had to leave Hawaii Winter Baseball after just four appearances with what initially was characterized as a sore arm, but Melancon had Tommy John surgery in November and is expected to miss the 2007 season. At his best, Melancon has power stuff that fits the closer profile. His fastball ranges from 92-95 mph with late life. He attacks hitters high and low, with enough giddy-up on his heater to work up in and out of the strike zone, and a hammer 12-to-6 curveball. Coaches rave about Melancon's work ethic and positive contribution to team chemistry. Melancon's maximum-effort delivery put stress on his elbow, leading to his injury. However, the Yankees love his makeup and have no doubts that he'll attack his rehab and do everything he can to come back strong. The Yankees won't get to see if he can be their future closer until his first full season, in 2008.

| Year | Club (League) | Class | W | L | ERA | G | GS | CG | SV | IP | H | R | ER | HR | BB | SO | AVG |
|------|---------------|-------|---|---|------|---|----|----|----|----|---|---|----|----|----|----|------|
| 2006 | Staten Island (NYP) | A | 0 | 1 | 3.52 | 7 | 0 | 0 | 2 | 8 | 9 | 7 | 3 | 0 | 2 | 8 | .281 |
| **MINOR LEAGUE TOTALS** | | | 0 | 1 | 3.52 | 7 | 0 | 0 | 2 | 8 | 9 | 7 | 3 | 0 | 2 | 8 | .281 |

## 16 ALAN HORNE RHP

**Born:** Jan. 5, 1983. **B-T:** R-R. **Ht.:** 6-4. **Wt.:** 200. **Drafted:** Florida, 2005 (11th round). **Signed by:** Brian Barber.

Horne jumped straight to high Class A in his pro debut. While he needed a couple of months to adjust, the Yankees are encouraged by the progress of this highly-regarded arm. He was a 2001 first-round pick (Indians, 27th overall) out of Marianna High in Florida's panhandle, where he was a teammate of Angels catcher Jeff Mathis. While Mathis signed that year, Horne embarked on a college career that began at Mississippi, was interrupted by Tommy John surgery, detoured to Chipola (Fla.) JC and wound up at Florida. He helped pitch the Gators to the 2005 College World Series before signing for $400,000. At 6-foot-4 and 200 pounds, Horne has an ideal pitcher's frame. When he stays direct to the plate and doesn't over-rotate, he keeps his delivery shorter and more repeatable. Then he can throw strikes with two plus pitches, a 92-96 mph fastball and a curveball that at times has good depth. He worked on a changeup last year and made progress with the pitch. Horne is a high-risk, high-reward prospect. He'll head to Double-A hoping to build on his late-season momentum.

| Year | Club (League) | Class | W | L | ERA | G | GS | CG | SV | IP | H | R | ER | HR | BB | SO | AVG |
|------|---------------|-------|---|---|------|----|----|----|----|-----|-----|----|----|----|----|-----|------|
| 2006 | Tampa (FSL) | A | 6 | 9 | 4.84 | 28 | 26 | 0 | 0 | 123 | 105 | 72 | 66 | 10 | 61 | 122 | .230 |
| **MINOR LEAGUE TOTALS** | | | 6 | 9 | 4.84 | 28 | 26 | 0 | 0 | 123 | 105 | 72 | 66 | 10 | 61 | 122 | .230 |

## 17 ANGEL REYES LHP

**Born:** Jan. 8, 1987. **B-T:** L-L. **Ht.:** 5-11. **Wt.:** 170. **Signed:** Dominican Republic, 2003. **Signed by:** Victor Mata/Carlos Rios.

The Yankees have struggled to develop lefthanders since hitting the jackpot with 1990 draft-and-follow Andy Pettitte. Though senior vice president of baseball operations Mark Newman says the Yankees have the best pitching depth in his 15 years with the organization, they still have a distinct lack of lefthanders, particularly in the upper levels. Reyes, converted from an outfielder to a pitcher in 2004, has emerged as the lefty with the highest ceiling in the system. Though he's small, he has a quick arm and generates above-average velocity with his fastball, touching 93-94 mph at times. His curveball also has shown signs of

being a plus pitch, and he has shown glimpses of a changeup. Still raw, Reyes excited the Yankees with a three-start audition at short-season Staten Island shortly after he turned 19 last year, more than holding his own. The next stop will be full-season ball in low Class A, where he'll work on becoming more consistent.

| Year | Club (League) | Class | W | L | ERA | G | GS | CG | SV | IP | H | R | ER | HR | BB | SO | AVG |
|------|---------------|-------|---|---|-----|---|----|----|----|----|---|---|----|----|----|----|-----|
| 2004 | Yankees 2 (DSL) | R | 2 | 2 | 2.42 | 7 | 3 | 0 | 0 | 22 | 8 | 7 | 6 | 1 | 23 | 25 | .108 |
| 2005 | Yankees 2 (DSL) | R | 1 | 5 | 1.52 | 15 | 6 | 0 | 1 | 41 | 19 | 2 | 7 | 0 | 1 | 0 | .106 |
| 2006 | Yankees (GCL) | R | 3 | 2 | 1.35 | 11 | 5 | 0 | 3 | 47 | 25 | 10 | 7 | 1 | 14 | 45 | .156 |
|  | Staten Island (NYP) | A | 1 | 1 | 1.53 | 3 | 3 | 0 | 0 | 18 | 12 | 4 | 3 | 0 | 6 | 16 | .211 |
| **MINOR LEAGUE TOTALS** | | | 7 | 10 | 1.62 | 36 | 17 | 0 | 4 | 128 | 64 | 23 | 23 | 2 | 44 | 86 | .136 |

## 18  AUSTIN JACKSON                                                          OF

**Born:** Feb. 1, 1987. **B-T:** R-R. **Ht.:** 6-1. **Wt.:** 185. **Drafted:** HS—Denton, Texas, 2005 (8th round). **Signed by:** Mark Batchko.

Jackson has confused scouts as both an amateur and now as a pro. Recruited to play point guard at Georgia Tech, Jackson had scouts guessing whether he actually wanted to play pro baseball with some spotty efforts as a high school senior. However, he spurned the Yellow Jackets when the Yankees drafted him in 2005 and gave him $800,000, a record for a player selected in the eighth round. (New York broke the record last year with Dellin Betances' $1 million bonus.) After a solid debut in the Gulf Coast League, Jackson joined fellow phenoms Jose Tabata and C.J. Henry in low Class A. He was the only one to finish the season with Charleston, as Tabata got hurt and Henry went to the Phillies in the Bobby Abreu/Cory Lidle trade. Jackson learned what it takes to grind out a season, an important lesson because he didn't play like the premium athlete the Yankees thought they were getting. Premium athletes are quicker at making adjustments than Jackson is, and they run better. Jackson's 4.4-second times from the right side of the plate to first base were pedestrian, though he runs better underway. His fringy speed also limits his range in center field, where he'll have to improve his routes and instincts to become an average defender. Jackson has raw strength, stays inside the ball well and has patience, so he eventually could hit for above-average power. To do so, he'll have to dramatically improve his breaking-ball recognition and stop falling behind in the count so often. Unless Jackson can have his athletic ability play better on the field, he'll only go as far as his bat takes him as a left fielder. He's expected to move up to high Class A but could return to Charleston, at least to begin the year.

| Year | Club (League) | Class | AVG | G | AB | R | H | 2B | 3B | HR | RBI | BB | SO | SB | OBP | SLG |
|------|---------------|-------|-----|---|----|---|---|----|----|----|-----|----|----|----|-----|-----|
| 2005 | Yankees (GCL) | R | .304 | 40 | 148 | 32 | 45 | 11 | 2 | 0 | 14 | 18 | 26 | 11 | .374 | .405 |
| 2006 | Charleston (SAL) | A | .260 | 134 | 535 | 90 | 139 | 24 | 5 | 4 | 47 | 61 | 151 | 37 | .340 | .346 |
| **MINOR LEAGUE TOTALS** | | | .269 | 174 | 683 | 122 | 184 | 35 | 7 | 4 | 61 | 79 | 177 | 48 | .347 | .359 |

## 19  CHASE WRIGHT                                                           LHP

**Born:** Feb. 8, 1983. **B-T:** L-L. **Ht.:** 6-2. **Wt.:** 190. **Drafted:** HS—Iowa Park, Texas, 2001 (3rd round). **Signed by:** Mark Batchko.

A third-round pick back in 2001, Wright took a while to get going. His arm strength never has been a problem, but his lack of command was. He finally stuck as a starter in 2005 in low Class A and finally made significant progress last year, when he was the high Class A Florida State League's pitcher of the year. He began 2006 in the bullpen, joined the rotation in June and led the FSL in ERA. The Yankees consider him the most advanced lefty in the system. Wright's stuff is just solid—88-90 mph fastball, curveball, changeup—and could play better if he could use to learn the same arm slot for his curve as he does for his other pitches. He lowered his slot to get more movement and harnessed control of his heater in 2006, getting plenty of grounders and not allowing a homer in 343 at-bats by righthanders. Wright doesn't have a strikeout pitch and profiles best at the back of a rotation. Added to the 40-man roster, he will get his first taste of Double-A in his seventh pro season.

| Year | Club (League) | Class | W | L | ERA | G | GS | CG | SV | IP | H | R | ER | HR | BB | SO | AVG |
|------|---------------|-------|---|---|-----|---|----|----|----|----|---|---|----|----|----|----|-----|
| 2001 | Yankees (GCL) | R | 2 | 3 | 7.92 | 10 | 7 | 0 | 0 | 25 | 33 | 28 | 22 | 0 | 21 | 33 | .317 |
| 2002 | Yankees (GCL) | R | 2 | 3 | 3.43 | 10 | 7 | 0 | 0 | 42 | 32 | 19 | 16 | 0 | 39 | 23 | .218 |
| 2003 | Battle Creek (MWL) | A | 1 | 1 | 6.43 | 7 | 2 | 0 | 0 | 14 | 12 | 11 | 10 | 1 | 16 | 10 | .226 |
|  | Staten Island (NYP) | A | 3 | 5 | 3.56 | 14 | 14 | 1 | 0 | 81 | 82 | 42 | 32 | 2 | 30 | 68 | .269 |
| 2004 | Battle Creek (MWL) | A | 5 | 8 | 5.44 | 18 | 18 | 0 | 0 | 86 | 100 | 60 | 52 | 4 | 57 | 51 | .294 |
|  | Staten Island (NYP) | A | 0 | 1 | 9.00 | 1 | 1 | 0 | 0 | 3 | 5 | 5 | 3 | 0 | 3 | 3 | .333 |
| 2005 | Charleston (SAL) | A | 10 | 4 | 3.75 | 25 | 24 | 0 | 0 | 144 | 128 | 71 | 60 | 10 | 69 | 110 | .242 |
| 2006 | Tampa (FSL) | A | 12 | 3 | 1.88 | 37 | 14 | 1 | 0 | 120 | 95 | 32 | 25 | 1 | 43 | 100 | .218 |
| **MINOR LEAGUE TOTALS** | | | 35 | 28 | 3.85 | 122 | 87 | 2 | 0 | 515 | 487 | 268 | 220 | 18 | 278 | 398 | .253 |

## 20 GEORGE KONTOS RHP

**Born:** June 12, 1985. **B-T:** R-R. **Ht.:** 6-3. **Wt.:** 215. **Drafted:** Northwestern, 2006 (5th round).
**Signed by:** Steve Lemke.

Kontos was expected to be Northwestern's ace as a junior, with two years of experience and a solid 2005 summer in the Cape Cod League, where he ranked third in the league in strike-outs behind fellow 2006 Yankees draftee Tim Norton and Red Sox first-rounder Daniel Bard. Instead, Kontos went just 3-10, 5.29 last spring as his ability to throw strikes deserted him. The Yankees still drafted him in the fifth round based mostly off his good size and the stuff he showed in the Cape, and signed him for $158,000. He was impressive in his debut, winning seven straight starts and both playoff starts to help lead Staten Island to the short-season New York-Penn League title. Kontos has a fastball that sits at 90-92 mph and has touched 94. More important, he has shown a proclivity to challenge hitters with wood bats the he didn't show facing metal bats in college. The Yankees think there's more velocity in there, and they will let him keep his slider, which he can run into the mid-80s. Kontos has taken to a curveball taught to him by minor league pitching coordinator Nardi Contreras, and he has the potential for an average or better bender in the future. His changeup is too firm, and Kontos' track record is not one of sustained success. He'll head to Class A in 2007.

| Year | Club (League) | Class | W | L | ERA | G | GS | CG | SV | IP | H | R | ER | HR | BB | SO | AVG |
|---|---|---|---|---|---|---|---|---|---|---|---|---|---|---|---|---|---|
| 2006 | Staten Island (NYP) | A | 7 | 3 | 2.64 | 14 | 14 | 0 | 0 | 78 | 64 | 25 | 23 | 3 | 19 | 82 | .227 |
| **MINOR LEAGUE TOTALS** | | | 7 | 3 | 2.64 | 14 | 14 | 0 | 0 | 78 | 64 | 25 | 23 | 3 | 19 | 82 | .227 |

## 21 JESUS MONTERO C

**Born:** Nov. 28, 1989. **B-T:** R-R. **Ht.:** 6-3. **Wt.:** 220. **Signed:** Venezuela, 2006. **Signed by:** Carlos Rios/Ricardo Finol.

Montero was one of the more anticipated free agents on the 2006 international market when it opened in July, and New York moved quickly to land him for the second-highest bonus of the signing period. Then-international scouting director Lin Garrett raved about Montero's top-of-the-line power, as well as his makeup and work ethic. Despite the Yankees' impressive summer in Latin America, they fired Garrett after the summer. Scouts from other organizations agreed that Montero had more power—present and future—than any other international prospect available. However, Montero had his doubters, starting with his position. His physical, mature frame may yet outgrow the catcher's spot. One scout compared him to Travis Hafner physically, and it wasn't meant as a compliment. His maxed-out body also led to suspicions that Montero wasn't really 16. Club officials reiterated that there was no age issue, but in December they confirmed that his signing bonus, originally reported as $2 million, had been adjusted down to $1.6 million. Montero disappointed the Yankees at their fall minicamp with his hitting and his fielding. He has yet to play in an organized game and hitters with 80 power potential on the 20-80 scouting scale are hard to come by, so New York will give Montero time. He's likely to begin 2007 in extended spring training and make his pro debut in the Gulf Coast League in June.

| Year | Club (League) | Class | AVG | G | AB | R | H | 2B | 3B | HR | RBI | BB | SO | SB | OBP | SLG |
|---|---|---|---|---|---|---|---|---|---|---|---|---|---|---|---|---|
| 2006 | Did not play—Signed 2007 contract | | | | | | | | | | | | | | | |

## 22 STEVEN WHITE RHP

**Born:** June 15, 1981. **B-T:** R-R. **Ht.:** 6-5. **Wt.:** 205. **Drafted:** Baylor, 2003 (4th round).
**Signed by:** Steve Boros/Mark Newman.

No. 4 on this list two years ago, White is running out of time as the Yankees acquire more and more pitchers with similar or better stuff and more command. He's still a factor, though, as he's taken to minor league pitching coordinator Nardi Contreras' instruction and improved his curveball. At his best, White pounds the strike zone with a 90-93 mph four-seam fastball that he occasionally throws at 95, as well as his curveball and two versions of a changeup. One of his changes is straight, while the other has some sink. His whole package was more effective when he repeated Double-A last year, particularly against left-handers. In Triple-A, White got pounded when he elevated both his fastball and his changeups. He's worked hard to pick up a two-seam fastball and to improve his command. The Yankees are suddenly crowded with Triple-A righthanders, and White has little relief pitching in his past, so he could need time to adjust if asked to change roles. His ceiling is more likely at the back of the rotation, but he has more stuff than the likes of Jeff Karstens and Darrell Rasner. To pass them, White likely will have to master Triple-A in 2007.

| Year | Club (League) | Class | W | L | ERA | G | GS | CG | SV | IP | H | R | ER | HR | BB | SO | AVG |
|---|---|---|---|---|---|---|---|---|---|---|---|---|---|---|---|---|---|---|
| 2004 | Battle Creek (MWL) | A | 5 | 2 | 2.65 | 9 | 9 | 2 | 0 | 58 | 36 | 19 | 17 | 4 | 26 | 56 | .183 |

| | Club (League) | Class | W | L | ERA | G | GS | CG | SV | IP | H | R | ER | HR | BB | SO | AVG |
|---|---|---|---|---|---|---|---|---|---|---|---|---|---|---|---|---|---|
| | Tampa (FSL) | A | 6 | 2 | 2.56 | 12 | 12 | 1 | 0 | 60 | 51 | 26 | 17 | 4 | 19 | 44 | .232 |
| 2005 | Tampa (FSL) | A | 0 | 0 | 3.09 | 3 | 2 | 0 | 0 | 12 | 8 | 4 | 4 | 1 | 2 | 8 | .195 |
| | Trenton (EL) | AA | 2 | 7 | 6.44 | 11 | 11 | 0 | 0 | 50 | 61 | 41 | 36 | 9 | 26 | 54 | .296 |
| 2006 | Trenton (EL) | AA | 4 | 1 | 2.11 | 11 | 11 | 1 | 0 | 68 | 52 | 16 | 16 | 0 | 28 | 45 | .217 |
| | Columbus (IL) | AAA | 4 | 9 | 4.71 | 17 | 17 | 1 | 0 | 107 | 100 | 58 | 56 | 8 | 42 | 88 | .256 |
| **MINOR LEAGUE TOTALS** | | | 21 | 21 | 3.70 | 63 | 62 | 5 | 0 | 355 | 308 | 164 | 146 | 26 | 143 | 295 | .238 |

## T.J. BEAM
RHP

**Born:** Aug. 28, 1980. **B-T:** R-R. **Ht.:** 6-7. **Wt.:** 215. **Drafted:** Mississippi, 2003 (10th round). **Signed by:** D.J. Svihlik.

Beam did just what the Yankees hoped he would in 2006. He continued his adjustment from starter to reliever, dominated the minors and made his big league debut. Now, he has to take next step—having major league success and earning manager Joe Torre's trust in the late innings. Beam's stuff has improved the last two years, particularly his slider, which is now plus pitch at times. He stays tall in his delivery more consistently now and can hit 95 mph with his fastball, though it usually sits in the low 90s. Beam thrived in extended appearances in the minors, often pitching two or three innings per outing, and some Yankees officials worried that he had little experience throwing on back-to-back days prior to getting to the majors. Sure enough, he struggled in such appearances. When he's tired, his stuff flattens out and he's vulnerable to homers. Beam needs to get stronger. He'll have a chance to earn a big league bullpen spot in 2007 but will have to pitch a lot better in New York to stay there.

| Year | Club (League) | Class | W | L | ERA | G | GS | CG | SV | IP | H | R | ER | HR | BB | SO | AVG |
|---|---|---|---|---|---|---|---|---|---|---|---|---|---|---|---|---|---|---|
| 2003 | Staten Island (NYP) | A | 2 | 1 | 2.70 | 9 | 5 | 0 | 1 | 33 | 25 | 14 | 10 | 4 | 9 | 31 | .200 |
| | Battle Creek (MWL) | A | 2 | 1 | 5.82 | 5 | 5 | 0 | 0 | 22 | 27 | 16 | 14 | 3 | 8 | 19 | .300 |
| 2004 | Staten Island (NYP) | A | 2 | 4 | 2.57 | 12 | 12 | 1 | 0 | 67 | 61 | 28 | 19 | 4 | 14 | 69 | .251 |
| | Battle Creek (MWL) | A | 2 | 5 | 4.35 | 11 | 7 | 0 | 0 | 41 | 34 | 20 | 20 | 8 | 17 | 54 | .227 |
| 2005 | Tampa (FSL) | A | 1 | 1 | 3.12 | 12 | 0 | 0 | 1 | 17 | 14 | 7 | 6 | 2 | 7 | 27 | .215 |
| | Charleston (SAL) | A | 3 | 3 | 1.66 | 35 | 2 | 0 | 2 | 60 | 45 | 15 | 11 | 2 | 18 | 78 | .206 |
| 2006 | Trenton (EL) | AA | 4 | 0 | 0.86 | 18 | 0 | 0 | 3 | 42 | 26 | 5 | 4 | 1 | 12 | 34 | .182 |
| | Columbus (IL) | AAA | 2 | 0 | 1.71 | 19 | 0 | 0 | 1 | 32 | 16 | 6 | 6 | 1 | 13 | 37 | .151 |
| | New York (AL) | MLB | 2 | 0 | 8.50 | 20 | 0 | 0 | 0 | 18 | 26 | 17 | 17 | 5 | 6 | 12 | .338 |
| **MINOR LEAGUE TOTALS** | | | 18 | 15 | 2.58 | 121 | 31 | 1 | 8 | 314 | 248 | 111 | 90 | 25 | 98 | 349 | .218 |
| **MAJOR LEAGUE TOTALS** | | | 2 | 0 | 8.50 | 20 | 0 | 0 | 0 | 18 | 26 | 17 | 17 | 5 | 6 | 12 | .338 |

## ZACH McALLISTER
RHP

**Born:** Dec. 8, 1987. **B-T:** R-R. **Ht.:** 6-5. **Wt.:** 230. **Drafted:** HS—Chillicothe, Ill., 2006 (3rd round). **Signed by:** Steve Lemke.

The Yankees loaded up on college pitchers in the 2006 draft, but also grabbed a pair of physical high school arms who will need time to develop in Dellin Betances and McAllister. A third-round pick, McAllister was the top-rated prospect in Illinois last year (ahead of George Kontos) and signed for $368,000. His father Steve scouts for the Diamondbacks organization as a crosschecker. McAllister still is getting used to his body, as he has added six inches and more than 50 pounds to his frame in the last two years. Now he'll have to get used to essentially a new repertoire. In high school, he had a lower arm slot and used more of a sinker-slider approach, mixing in the rare changeup. With his body and arm strength, the Yankees believe he can be more of a power pitcher and have made some changes. They have raised McAllister's arm slot slightly, worked with him on a four-seam fastball and added a curveball, hoping he'll take to it and shelve his slider eventually. Used in a piggyback role in the Gulf Coast League with Betances, McAllister showed good arm strength, throwing in the low 90s. He also displayed an aggressiveness in the strike zone that New York likes to see. Because of the overhaul of his repertoire, McAllister may need longer to develop and could start this season in extended spring training.

| Year | Club (League) | Class | W | L | ERA | G | GS | CG | SV | IP | H | R | ER | HR | BB | SO | AVG |
|---|---|---|---|---|---|---|---|---|---|---|---|---|---|---|---|---|---|---|
| 2006 | Yankees (GCL) | R | 5 | 2 | 3.09 | 11 | 1 | 0 | 0 | 35 | 35 | 14 | 12 | 1 | 12 | 28 | .259 |
| **MINOR LEAGUE TOTALS** | | | 5 | 2 | 3.09 | 11 | 1 | 0 | 0 | 35 | 35 | 14 | 12 | 1 | 12 | 28 | .259 |

## COLIN CURTIS
OF

**Born:** Feb. 1, 1985. **B-T:** L-L. **Ht.:** 6-0. **Wt.:** 190. **Drafted:** Arizona State, 2006 (4th round). **Signed by:** Andy Stankiewicz.

A three-year starter at Arizona State, Curtis helped led the Sun Devils to the 2005 College World Series and won a New York-Penn League championship in his first taste of pro ball. Curtis was the Yankees' highest-drafted position player in 2006 and had a solid debut after signing for an above-slot $450,000 bonus. New York buys into his offensive ability, thanks to his short, quick swing, and offense may have to be his calling card. Area scouts in Arizona

considered him less athletic as a junior than he was as a freshman. All his tools play average, and his body leaves little room for projection. While he's a smart, aggressive baserunner and efficient basestealer, his speed is just average. He has some strength in his swing, which seems to work better with wood than with metal. Curtis played center field in Staten Island and his bat would fit best there. He'll have to maximize his average range, running smart routes and improving his instincts, to stay there. No one doubts his makeup, as Curtis was diagnosed with testicular cancer at age 15 and beat the disease. If the Yankees decide to keep Austin Jackson in low Class A, Curtis could get on the fast track and jump to high Class A.

| Year | Club (League) | Class | AVG | G | AB | R | H | 2B | 3B | HR | RBI | BB | SO | SB | OBP | SLG |
|---|---|---|---|---|---|---|---|---|---|---|---|---|---|---|---|---|
| 2006 | Yankees (GCL) | R | .500 | 3 | 8 | 3 | 4 | 2 | 0 | 1 | 4 | 1 | 0 | 1 | .600 | 1.125 |
| | Staten Island (NYP) | A | .302 | 44 | 159 | 25 | 48 | 9 | 2 | 1 | 18 | 12 | 19 | 4 | .362 | .403 |
| **MINOR LEAGUE TOTALS** | | | .311 | 47 | 167 | 28 | 52 | 11 | 2 | 2 | 22 | 13 | 19 | 5 | .374 | .437 |

## JEFF KARSTENS
RHP

**Born:** Sept. 24, 1982. **B-T:** R-R. **Ht.:** 6-3. **Wt.:** 175. **Drafted:** Texas Tech, 2003 (19th round). **Signed by:** Mark Batchko.

International League hitters had their way with Karstens in his first Triple-A stint, and he went 0-5, 7.01 in seven starts. Sent down to Double-A, Karstens turned his year around with the help of Trenton pitching coach Dave Eiland. He pitched aggressively and won all six of his decisions, earning a trip back to Triple-A, and the ride didn't stop until Karstens arrived in New York and nearly exhausted his rookie eligibility. He earned his first major league victory in his second start, pitched with moxie and earned the respect of manager Joe Torre. Karstens' stuff is fringe-average, particularly his fastball, which sat at 87 mph in the majors. However, he throws both a slider and curveball for strikes, and he can use his above-average changeup in any count. With Andy Pettitte and Kei Igawa added to the fold, Karstens will return to Triple-A to start the year and be near the front of the line for a promotion.

| Year | Club (League) | Class | W | L | ERA | G | GS | CG | SV | IP | H | R | ER | HR | BB | SO | AVG |
|---|---|---|---|---|---|---|---|---|---|---|---|---|---|---|---|---|---|
| 2003 | Staten Island (NYP) | A | 4 | 2 | 2.54 | 14 | 10 | 0 | 0 | 67 | 63 | 22 | 19 | 2 | 16 | 53 | .256 |
| 2004 | Tampa (FSL) | A | 6 | 9 | 4.02 | 24 | 24 | 1 | 0 | 139 | 151 | 70 | 62 | 11 | 31 | 116 | .284 |
| 2005 | Trenton (EL) | AA | 12 | 11 | 4.15 | 28 | 27 | 0 | 0 | 169 | 192 | 91 | 78 | 16 | 42 | 147 | .285 |
| 2006 | Trenton (EL) | AA | 6 | 0 | 2.31 | 11 | 11 | 0 | 0 | 74 | 54 | 20 | 19 | 4 | 14 | 67 | .198 |
| | Columbus (IL) | AAA | 5 | 5 | 4.28 | 14 | 14 | 1 | 0 | 74 | 80 | 42 | 35 | 9 | 30 | 48 | .275 |
| | New York (AL) | MLB | 2 | 1 | 3.80 | 8 | 6 | 0 | 0 | 43 | 40 | 20 | 18 | 6 | 11 | 16 | .242 |
| **MINOR LEAGUE TOTALS** | | | 33 | 27 | 3.67 | 91 | 86 | 2 | 0 | 523 | 540 | 245 | 213 | 42 | 133 | 431 | .268 |
| **MAJOR LEAGUE TOTALS** | | | 2 | 1 | 3.80 | 8 | 6 | 0 | 0 | 42 | 40 | 20 | 18 | 6 | 11 | 16 | .242 |

## JOSUE CALZADO
OF

**Born:** Nov. 6, 1985. **B-T:** R-R. **Ht.:** 6-2 **Wt.:** 190. **Signed:** Dominican Republic, 2003. **Signed by:** Carlos Rios/Victor Mata/Jose Luna.

Calzado, who signed for $110,000 in 2003, needed three years to get out of the Rookie-level Dominican Summer League. When he finally did, he was a different physical specimen from the 6-foot-1, 160-pounder they signed, having grown an inch and added 30 pounds. With five-tool potential, Calzado is still raw and a long way off from helping in New York, even after a successful cup of coffee in low Class A. Calzado has bat speed and raw power. He has plus speed but lacks the instincts and savvy to make the most of it on the bases and in center field. He often has to use his quickness to run down balls that he didn't read well off the bat. Calzado has a decent concept of the strike zone and an excellent work ethic. He's expected to return to Charleston, though New York's depth in outfielders and his lack of polish may dictate he opens in extended spring training before going to Staten Island.

| Year | Club (League) | Class | AVG | G | AB | R | H | 2B | 3B | HR | RBI | BB | SO | SB | OBP | SLG |
|---|---|---|---|---|---|---|---|---|---|---|---|---|---|---|---|---|
| 2003 | N.Y. Yankees 2 (DSL) | R | .223 | 57 | 184 | 23 | 41 | 5 | 1 | 1 | 14 | 11 | 43 | 9 | .350 | .277 |
| 2004 | N.Y. Yankees 1 (DSL) | R | .175 | 54 | 154 | 26 | 27 | 6 | 2 | 0 | 16 | 15 | 38 | 9 | .289 | .240 |
| 2005 | N.Y. Yankees 1 (DSL) | R | .291 | 60 | 182 | 28 | 53 | 9 | 3 | 2 | 31 | 26 | 41 | 18 | .399 | .407 |
| 2006 | Yankees (GCL) | R | .250 | 47 | 172 | 31 | 43 | 7 | 3 | 3 | 26 | 21 | 26 | 10 | .325 | .378 |
| | Charleston (SAL) | A | .375 | 12 | 40 | 4 | 15 | 3 | 0 | 0 | 6 | 2 | 8 | 2 | .419 | .450 |
| **MINOR LEAGUE TOTALS** | | | .245 | 230 | 732 | 112 | 179 | 30 | 9 | 6 | 93 | 95 | 156 | 48 | .347 | .335 |

## BRONSON SARDINHA
OF

**Born:** April 6, 1983. **B-T:** L-R. **Ht.:** 601. **Wt.:** 195. **Drafted:** HS—Honolulu, 2001 (1st round supplemental). **Signed by:** Gus Quattlebaum.

The Yankees have cooled on Sardinha over the years, citing his laid-back demeanor and inability to find a defensive home. But over the last two years, the former supplemental first-round pick made progress, and his natural hitting skills and athletic ability have him poised to contribute in the majors. Sardinha's bat has blossomed since his 2005 move to right field, where his arm strength plays average and he has solid range. His lefthanded swing remains

fluid and strong, he stays inside the ball well, and he has improved at letting his power come naturally as he concentrates on using the whole field. He played better after a promotion to Triple-A, thriving under Columbus manager Dave Miley. Sardinha, whose brothers Dane (Reds) and Duke (Rockies) were active minor leaguers in 2006, tied a career high with 16 homers, but his overall power potential falls shy of the ideal for a right fielder. And with Melky Cabrera ahead of him—not to mention Bob Abreu—it appears Sardinha would be a better fit in another organization.

| Year | Club (League) | Class | AVG | G | AB | R | H | 2B | 3B | HR | RBI | BB | SO | SB | OBP | SLG |
|------|---------------|-------|-----|---|----|---|---|----|----|----|-----|----|----|----|-----|-----|
| 2001 | Yankees (GCL) | R | .303 | 55 | 188 | 42 | 57 | 14 | 3 | 4 | 27 | 28 | 51 | 11 | .398 | .473 |
| 2002 | Greensboro (SAL) | A | .263 | 93 | 342 | 49 | 90 | 13 | 0 | 12 | 44 | 34 | 78 | 15 | .334 | .406 |
| | Staten Island (NYP) | A | .323 | 36 | 124 | 25 | 40 | 8 | 0 | 4 | 16 | 24 | 36 | 4 | .433 | .484 |
| 2003 | Tampa (FSL) | A | .193 | 59 | 212 | 23 | 41 | 8 | 2 | 1 | 17 | 24 | 57 | 8 | .279 | .264 |
| | Battle Creek (MWL) | A | .275 | 71 | 269 | 54 | 74 | 16 | 0 | 8 | 41 | 40 | 40 | 5 | .374 | .424 |
| 2004 | Tampa (FSL) | A | .315 | 63 | 248 | 37 | 78 | 12 | 2 | 2 | 33 | 29 | 39 | 9 | .389 | .403 |
| | Trenton (EL) | AA | .267 | 72 | 266 | 37 | 71 | 11 | 1 | 6 | 29 | 37 | 65 | 4 | .356 | .383 |
| 2005 | Trenton (EL) | AA | .258 | 133 | 503 | 63 | 130 | 30 | 2 | 12 | 68 | 55 | 115 | 11 | .338 | .398 |
| 2006 | Columbus (IL) | AAA | .286 | 52 | 185 | 27 | 53 | 10 | 5 | 6 | 27 | 23 | 36 | 3 | .365 | .492 |
| | Trenton (EL) | AA | .254 | 86 | 334 | 47 | 85 | 10 | 1 | 10 | 40 | 34 | 78 | 0 | .324 | .380 |
| **MINOR LEAGUE TOTALS** | | | .269 | 720 | 2671 | 404 | 719 | 132 | 16 | 65 | 342 | 328 | 595 | 70 | .352 | .404 |

## 29 TIM NORTON RHP

**Born:** May 23, 1983. **B-T:** R-R. **Ht.:** 6-5. **Wt.:** 230. **Drafted:** Connecticut, 2006 (7th round). **Signed by:** Matt Hyde.

Norton put up better numbers than George Kontos at Staten Island last summer, but Kontos rates as a slightly better prospect because he has more arm strength and is two years younger. A seventh-rounder who signed for $85,000, Norton operates at 90-93 mph with his four-seam fastball. He had a funky delivery when he first arrived in pro ball, but after a month, the Yankees were able to take some of the effort out of it. He threw consistent strikes with his fastball and didn't issue a walk in four of his final eight starts. He also gained better control his two-seamer, which he'll need to use more as he moves up. Norton's biggest problem is his lack of a breaking ball. His arm slot lends itself to a slider, and his isn't very good right now. He throws a nice changeup and a splitter, pitches that help him against left-handers. The total package makes Norton most likely to make an impact as a reliever, but the Yankees hope he can gain experience and develop a better breaking ball in a starting role in 2007, likely in low Class A.

| Year | Club (League) | Class | W | L | ERA | G | GS | CG | SV | IP | H | R | ER | HR | BB | SO | AVG |
|------|---------------|-------|---|---|-----|---|----|----|----|----|---|---|----|----|----|----|-----|
| 2006 | Staten Island (NYP) | A | 3 | 3 | 2.60 | 15 | 15 | 0 | 0 | 73 | 60 | 29 | 21 | 1 | 14 | 83 | .222 |
| **MINOR LEAGUE TOTALS** | | | 3 | 3 | 2.60 | 15 | 15 | 0 | 0 | 73 | 60 | 29 | 21 | 1 | 14 | 83 | .222 |

## 30 DANIEL McCUTCHEN RHP

**Born:** Sept. 26, 1982. **B-T:** R-R. **Ht.:** 6-2. **Wt.:** 195. **Drafted:** Oklahoma, 2006 (13th round). **Signed by:** Mark Batchko.

Most organizations wouldn't be as happy with a player who ran afoul of baseball's performance-enhancing drugs policy in his pro debut. But the Yankees love McCutchen's stuff and attitude, and they believe his contention that his positive test resulted from ephedra in a prescription drug he took during his career at Oklahoma. He became the Sooners' ace as a fifth-year senior in 2006, ranking third in NCAA Division I with 149 innings. In that respect, McCutchen's 50-game suspension didn't hurt too badly, because the time off was good for him. During his brief pro debut, he showed good control of four pitches. He works at 90-92 mph with both a two-seam fastball and a four-seamer, and he hits 94-95 at times with the latter. He also has a plus curveball he throws with power in the low 80s, as well as a change-up with late tail and sink. The Yankees want to smooth out his delivery, which had plenty of effort in his college days, and get all that energy going toward home plate. He had elbow problems at Grayson County (Texas) CC, and while he was healthy at Oklahoma, his college career lasted five years. At age 24, he has just 29 innings of pro experience. While McCutchen has a chance to start, he also could move quickly as a middle reliever—once his suspension is over. After he serves the final 23 games, he could open 2007 in high Class A.

| Year | Club (League) | Class | W | L | ERA | G | GS | CG | SV | IP | H | R | ER | HR | BB | SO | AVG |
|------|---------------|-------|---|---|-----|---|----|----|----|----|---|---|----|----|----|----|-----|
| 2006 | Staten Island (NYP) | A | 1 | 0 | 1.13 | 2 | 2 | 0 | 0 | 8 | 4 | 1 | 1 | 1 | 1 | 11 | .148 |
| | Charleston (SAL) | A | 1 | 0 | 2.14 | 7 | 0 | 0 | 1 | 21 | 13 | 5 | 5 | 2 | 5 | 18 | .186 |
| **MINOR LEAGUE TOTALS** | | | 2 | 0 | 1.86 | 9 | 2 | 0 | 1 | 29 | 17 | 6 | 6 | 3 | 6 | 29 | .175 |

# OAKLAND
# ATHLETICS

BY **JOHN MANUEL**

The Athletics haven't moved to their new home in Fremont, Calif., a bedroom community roughly 20 miles south of their current base in Oakland. The ink hasn't even dried on the blueprint for the club's plan to build a small, technology-driven ballpark, Cisco Field, by 2010 or 2011.

And yet the A's make significant changes every year, winning with different players and different styles. The biggest shift in the last year has been parting ways with manager Ken Macha—twice, in fact, rehiring him after letting his contract expire in 2005 but firing him after 2006.

In four seasons, Macha piloted a pair of American League West winners, never won fewer than 88 games and took the A's past the first round of the playoffs for the first time since 1990. But even as Oakland was sweeping the Twins in an AL Division Series—a prelude to getting swept by the Tigers in the AL Championship Series—it plainly wasn't Macha's team.

It also won't belong to Bob Geren, his replacement as manager. More than any general manager, **Billy Beane** has put his stamp on his franchise. Beane became GM after the 1997 season, and 1998 remains Oakland's only losing year with him in charge. While the winning has been constant, how the A's have won has changed substantially. The 2006 model was a defensive wonder, featuring six-time Gold Glove Award winner Eric Chavez, impenetrable second baseman Mark Ellis and three outfielders capable of playing center field. Oakland hit 175 home runs and had a .340 on-base percentage. By contrast,

LARRY GOREN

the first of Beane's teams to reach the postseason mashed 239 homers and had a .360 OBP. That 2000 club drew 100 more walks, had nearly 200 more strikeouts and played a very different style of baseball than the 2006 edition.

Oakland can't keep winning over the long haul without a productive farm system, and that's why the next few years will be crucial. The big league lineup had four homegrown regulars—Chavez, Bobby Crosby, Dan Johnson and Nick Swisher—and more appear to be on the way. The A's ability to draft and trade for position players remains impressive. Their top three prospects—outfielder Travis Buck, first baseman Daric Barton and catcher Kurt Suzuki—all have had success in Double-A, and all three could be big league starters by 2008.

The A's success has led to lower picks in the first round of the draft. They once drafted Mark Mulder and Barry Zito with top 10 choices in 1998 and 1999, but they haven't selected that high since. As a result, it has been harder to find quality arms. While Beane has remade the big league rotation, the farm system has little premium pitching to offer. To that end, the A's have gone for undervalued high school arms in the last two drafts, and have hopes for the likes of Jared Lansford, Craig Italiano, Vin Mazzaro and their top pick in 2006, second-rounder Trevor Cahill.

## TOP 30 PROSPECTS

| | |
|---|---|
| 1. Travis Buck, of | 16. Danny Putnam, of |
| 2. Daric Barton, 1b | 17. Myron Leslie, 3b/of |
| 3. Kurt Suzuki, c | 18. Vin Mazzaro, rhp |
| 4. Matt Sulentic, of | 19. Ryan Goleski, of |
| 5. Jermaine Mitchell, of | 20. Landon Powell, c |
| 6. Javier Herrera, of | 21. Jeff Baisley, 3b |
| 7. Jason Windsor, rhp | 22. Craig Italiano, rhp |
| 8. Marcus McBeth, rhp | 23. Anthony Recker, c |
| 9. Justin Sellers, ss | 24. Mike Mitchell, rhp |
| 10. Trevor Cahill, rhp | 25. Jason Ray, rhp |
| 11. Richie Robnett, of | 26. Ryan Webb, rhp |
| 12. Cliff Pennington, ss | 27. Ben Jukich, lhp |
| 13. Kevin Melillo, 2b | 28. Andrew Bailey, rhp |
| 14. Shane Komine, rhp | 29. Chad Lee, rhp |
| 15. Jared Lansford, rhp | 30. Larry Cobb, of |

# ORGANIZATION OVERVIEW

**General manager:** Billy Beane. **Farm director:** Keith Lieppman. **Scouting director:** Eric Kubota.

## 2006 PERFORMANCE

| Class | Team | League | W | L | PCT | Finish* | Manager | Affiliated |
|---|---|---|---|---|---|---|---|---|
| Majors | Oakland | American | 93 | 69 | .574 | 4th (14) | Ken Macha | — |
| Triple-A | Sacramento RiverCats | Pacific Coast | 78 | 66 | .542 | 4th (16) | Tony DeFrancesco | 2000 |
| Double-A | Midland RockHounds | Texas | 78 | 61 | .561 | 1st (8) | Von Hayes | 1999 |
| High A | Stockton Ports | California | 69 | 71 | .493 | 6th (10) | Todd Steverson | 2005 |
| Low A | Kane County Cougars | Midwest | 79 | 60 | .568 | 2nd (14) | Aaron Nieckula | 2003 |
| Short-season | Vancouver Canadians | Northwest | 39 | 37 | .513 | 4th (8) | Richard Magnante | 1979 |
| Rookie | AZL Athletics | Arizona | 24 | 31 | .436 | 6th (9) | Ruben Escalera | 1988 |
| **OVERALL 2006 MINOR LEAGUE RECORD** | | | 367 | 326 | .530 | 7th (30) | | |

*Finish in overall standings (No. of teams in league). +League champion

## ORGANIZATION LEADERS

### BATTING
| | | |
|---|---|---|
| AVG | Perez, Luis, Stockton | .333 |
| R | Clark, Doug, Sacramento | 108 |
| H | Clark, Doug, Sacramento | 155 |
| 2B | Buck, Travis, Stockton/Midland | 41 |
| 3B | Blasi, Nicholas, Kane County/Stockton | 8 |
| | Colamarino, Brant, Midland | 8 |
| | Petit, Gregorio, Stockton | 8 |
| HR | McClain, Scott, Sacramento | 28 |
| RBI | Baisley, Jeffrey, Kane County | 110 |
| BB | Stavisky, Brian, Sacramento/Midland | 80 |
| SO | Pineda, Jose, Kane County | 132 |
| SB | Clark, Doug, Sacramento | 25 |
| OBP | Stavisky, Brian, Sacramento/Midland | .406 |
| SLG | Baisley, Jeffrey, Kane County | .519 |
| XBH | McClain, Scott, Sacramento | 61 |

### PITCHING
| | | |
|---|---|---|
| W | Windsor, Jason, Midland/Sacramento | 17 |
| L | Ford, Ryan, Stockton | 12 |
| ERA | Piekarz, Joe, Kane County | 3.26 |
| G | McBeth, Marcus, Stockton/Sac./Midland | 65 |
| SV | McBeth, Marcus, Stockton/Sac./Midland | 34 |
| IP | Fritz, Benjamin, Midland/Sacramento | 168 |
| BB | Ray, Jason, Kane County/Stockton | 68 |
| SO | Windsor, Jason, Midland/Sacramento | 158 |
| AVG | Ray, Jason, Kane County/Stockton | .232 |

## BEST TOOLS

| | |
|---|---|
| Best Hitter for Average | Daric Barton |
| Best Power Hitter | Richie Robnett |
| Best Strike-Zone Discipline | Daric Barton |
| Fastest Baserunner | Jermaine Mitchell |
| Best Athlete | Javier Herrera |
| Best Fastball | Craig Italiano |
| Best Curveball | Ben Jukich |
| Best Slider | Santiago Casilla |
| Best Changeup | Marcus McBeth |
| Best Control | Scott Deal |
| Best Defensive Catcher | Kurt Suzuki |
| Best Defensive Infielder | Justin Sellers |
| Best Infield Arm | Cliff Pennington |
| Best Defensive Outfielder | Javier Herrera |
| Best Outfield Arm | Javier Herrera |

## PROJECTED 2010 LINEUP

| | |
|---|---|
| Catcher | Kurt Suzuki |
| First Base | Nick Swisher |
| Second Base | Mark Ellis |
| Third Base | Eric Chavez |
| Shortstop | Bobby Crosby |
| Left Field | Matt Sulentic |
| Center Field | Milton Bradley |
| Right Field | Travis Buck |
| Designated Hitter | Daric Barton |
| No. 1 Starter | Rich Harden |
| No. 2 Starter | Dan Haren |
| No. 3 Starter | Joe Blanton |
| No. 4 Starter | Kirk Saarloos |
| No. 5 Starter | Jason Windsor |
| Closer | Huston Street |

## LAST YEAR'S TOP 20 PROSPECTS

| | |
|---|---|
| 1. Daric Barton, 1b | 11. Kurt Suzuki, c |
| 2. Javier Herrera, of | 12. Jared Lansford, rhp |
| 3. Cliff Pennington, ss | 13. Richie Robnett, of |
| 4. Andre Ethier, of | 14. Danny Putnam, of |
| 5. Travis Buck, of | 15. Jason Windsor, rhp |
| 6. Kevin Melillo, 2b | 16. Gregorio Petit, inf |
| 7. Jairo Garcia, rhp | 17. Justin Sellers, ss |
| 8. Craig Italiano, rhp | 18. Jimmy Shull, rhp |
| 9. Shane Komine, rhp | 19. Dallas Braden, lhp |
| 10. Vince Mazzaro, rhp | 20. Landon Powell, c |

## TOP PROSPECTS OF THE DECADE

| Year | Player, Pos. | 2006 Org. |
|---|---|---|
| 1997 | Miguel Tejada, ss | Orioles |
| 1998 | Ben Grieve, of | Out of baseball |
| 1999 | Eric Chavez, 3b | Athletics |
| 2000 | Mark Mulder, lhp | Cardinals |
| 2001 | Jose Ortiz, 2b | Lancaster (Atlantic) |
| 2002 | Carlos Pena, 1b | Red Sox |
| 2003 | Rich Harden, rhp | Athletics |
| 2004 | Bobby Crosby, ss | Athletics |
| 2005 | Nick Swisher, of | Athletics |
| 2006 | Daric Barton, 1b | Athletics |

## TOP DRAFT PICKS OF THE DECADE

| Year | Player, Pos. | 2006 Org. |
|---|---|---|
| 1997 | Chris Enochs, rhp | Out of baseball |
| 1998 | Mark Mulder, lhp | Cardinals |
| 1999 | Barry Zito, lhp | Athletics |
| 2000 | Freddie Bynum, ss (2nd round) | Cubs |
| 2001 | Bobby Crosby, ss | Athletics |
| 2002 | Nick Swisher, of | Athletics |
| 2003 | Brad Sullivan, rhp | Athletics |
| 2004 | Landon Powell, c | Athletics |
| 2005 | Cliff Pennington, ss | Athletics |
| 2006 | Trevor Cahill, rhp (2nd round) | Athletics |

## LARGEST BONUSES IN CLUB HISTORY

| | |
|---|---|
| Mark Mulder, 1998 | $3,200,000 |
| Nick Swisher, 2002 | $1,780,000 |
| Barry Zito, 1999 | $1,625,000 |
| Cliff Pennington, 2005 | $1,475,000 |
| Joe Blanton, 2002 | $1,400,000 |

# MINOR LEAGUE DEPTH CHART

## Oakland Athletics

**Impact: D.** Every A's farmhand has some warts, from having to develop power to defensive shortcomings. No one here earns the "can't-miss" tag.

**Depth: C.** Oakland's talent among position players is fine, but the A's have tried to remedy their lack of power arms, spending serveral high draft picks on prep pitchers.

**Sleeper:** Myron Leslie, 3b/of. Having outgrown shortstop, Leslie is developing enough of a power bat to play any corner spot.

*Numbers in parentheses indicate prospect rankings.*

### LF
Travis Buck (1)
Matt Sulentic (4)
Danny Putnam (16)
Brian Stavisky
Jason Perry

### CF
Jermaine Mitchell (5)
Javi Herrera (6)
Larry Cobb (30)
Toddric Johnson
Eduardo Sierra
Shane Keough
Chad Boyd

### RF
Richie Robnett (11)
Myron Leslie (17)
Ryan Goleski (19)

### 3B
Jeff Baisley (21)

### SS
Justin Sellers (9)
Cliff Pennington (12)
Christian Vitters

### 2B
Kevin Melillo (13)
Donnie Murphy
Gregorio Petit
Mark Kiger

### 1B
Daric Barton (2)
Brant Colamarino
Vasili Spanos

### C
Kurt Suzuki (3)
Landon Powell (20)
Anthony Recker (23)
John Baker
Jeremy Brown
Raul Padron

### RHP

| Starters | Relievers |
| --- | --- |
| Jason Windsor (7) | Marcus McBeth (8) |
| Trevor Cahill (10) | Mike Mitchell (24) |
| Shane Komine (14) | Jason Ray (25) |
| Jared Lansford (15) | Santiago Casilla |
| Vin Mazzaro (18) | Connor Robertson |
| Craig Italiano (22) | Scott Moore |
| Ryan Webb (26) | Brad Zeigler |
| Andrew Bailey (28) | Earl Oakes |
| Chad Lee (29) | |
| Henry Alberto Rodriguez | |
| Scott Deal | |
| Brad Knox | |
| Mike Rogers | |
| Jason Fernandez | |
| Jimmy Shull | |

### LHP

| Starters | Relievers |
| --- | --- |
| Dan Meyer | Ben Jukich (27) |
| Dallas Braden | Jay Marshall |
| | Brad Kilby |
| | Brad Davis |

# DRAFT ANALYSIS

## 2006

**Best Pro Debut:** As an 18-year-old in the short-season Northwest League, OF Matt Sulentic (3) hit .354/.409/.479. OF Jermaine Mitchell (5) was older but just as impressive in the NWL, hitting .362/.460/.507 with 14 steals. RHP Scott Moore (23) had a 1.29 ERA, nine saves and a 30-5 K-BB ratio in 21 innings, mostly in the NWL.

**Best Athlete:** A two-way player in junior college, Mitchell has hitting ability, power potential, more speed than the A's realized and center-field skills. The Athletics drafted more well-rounded athletes than they usually do, also picking up OFs Angel Sierra (8) and Toddric Johnson (14).

**Best Pure Hitter:** Sulentic won the Dallas metroplex high school triple crown with a .654-20-59 performance. He's not physically imposing at 5-foot-10 and 170 pounds, but he's a gifted hitter with surprising pop and was able to bat .235 in low Class A in August. Early in his NWL career, an opposing team came out to watch him take batting practice after hearing the sound the ball made coming off his bat.

**Best Raw Power:** Mitchell's edge in size (6 feet, 200 pounds) gives him the edge in pop over Sulentic.

**Fastest Runner:** Mitchell or Sierra. Mitchell accelerates more quickly and has been timed as fast as 3.9 seconds from the left side of the plate to first base. Sierra would beat him in a 60-yard dash. He was part of a high school relay team that set a Puerto Rican record with a 42.78-second time in the 4x100 relay.

**Best Defensive Player:** OF Larry Cobb is an above-average center fielder who showed the ability to play at least an average second base in instructional league.

**Best Fastball:** RHP Chad Lee (4), barely a blip on the scouting radar before this year, pitches from 91-95 mph. RHP Andrew Bailey (6) had Tommy John surgery in 2005 and got back to 92-93 mph last spring, and he could rebound further in 2007.

**Best Breaking Ball:** LHP Ben Jukich (13) used his hard curveball to lead NAIA pitchers in strikeouts (144) and strikeouts per nine innings (13.7). He finished the summer in the Midwest League playoffs. RHP Trevor Cahill (2), Oakland's top pick, has a spike curveball with sharp downward break.

**Most Intriguing Background:** SS Christian Vitters' (10) younger brother Josh is one of the top high school hitters available in the 2007 draft. The A's picked the sons of farm director Keith Lieppman (1B Burke, 33) and former big leaguers Dave Cochrane (C Steve, 34) and Nelson Simmons (RHP Goldy, 40) as draft-and-follows. OF Lorenzo Macias' (28) brother Drew plays in the Padres system. RHP Matt Manship's (29) brother Jeff signed with the Twins as a 14th-round pick.

**Closest To The Majors:** The Athletics need lefthanded pitching, and they'll push Jukich because he's already 24.

**Best Late-Round Pick:** Jukich and Moore. Moore scared off some scouts with his 6-foot-2, 245-pound frame, but he has a low-90s fastball, an effective slider and the ability to throw strikes.

**The One Who Got Away:** Oakland took late-round fliers on potential five-tool OF Jon Pigott (31, now at Florida) and LHP Nick Hernandez (32, Tennessee), who has touched 90 mph.

**Assessment:** Despite lacking a first-round pick, the A's still hauled in an interesting mix of hitters and pitchers.

## 2005
BUDGET: $4.8 million

OF Travis Buck (1) has established himself as the system's best prospect. SS Cliff Pennington (1) regressed in 2006, but the Athletics still have hopes for him as well as RHP Jared Lansford (2) and SS Justin Sellers (6). Unsigned 1B Justin Smoak (16) could go No. 1 overall in 2008. **GRADE: C+**

## 2004
BUDGET: $6.3 million

RHP Huston Street (1) became a quality big league closer almost immediately. Oakland added plenty of depth in Cs Landon Powell (1) and Kurt Suzuki (2), OFs Richie Robnett (1) and Danny Putnam (1), RHP Jason Windsor (3), 2B Kevin Melillo (5) and 3B/OF Myron Leslie (8). **GRADE: A**

## 2003
BUDGET: $4.9 million

OF Andre Ethier (2) had a banner rookie season—after the A's had traded him for Milton Bradley. They may not get anything out of RHP Brad Sullivan (1) and 3B Brian Snyder (1), and dealt their other first-rounder, SS/2B Omar Quintanilla (1). **GRADE: B**

*Draft analysis by Jim Callis. Numbers in parentheses indicate draft rounds. Budgets are bonuses in first 10 rounds.*

# TRAVIS
# BUCK

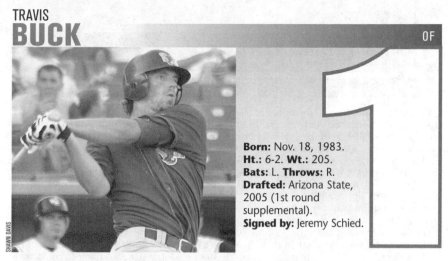

**Born:** Nov. 18, 1983.
**Ht.:** 6-2. **Wt.:** 205.
**Bats:** L. **Throws:** R.
**Drafted:** Arizona State, 2005 (1st round supplemental).
**Signed by:** Jeremy Schied.

SHAWN DAVIS

The 2006 season was more of the same for Buck, who has been an elite prospect since high school. He was part of a banner class of Washington state prep players in 2002 that included Red Sox lefthander Jon Lester, Pirates farmhand Brent Lillibridge and Giants prospect Travis Ishikawa, among others. Buck fell from top-round consideration in the 2002 draft after a modest senior season, going in the 23rd round to the Mariners, so he went to Arizona State. He had been an infielder but played outfield exclusively his first two seasons with the Sun Devils, then saw time at third base in 2005, when he helped the team reach the College World Series. Since signing with the Athletics as the 36th overall pick that year for $950,000, he has hit .328/.399/.511 with a staggering 53 doubles in 497 pro at-bats. He was leading the minors with 39 two-baggers in 2006 when he went down with an abdominal injury in July that ended his season. He returned briefly in the Arizona Fall League before being sidelined again, and his injury was finally diagnosed properly as a sports hernia.

While hitting comes naturally to Buck, he works hard at his craft, with an inner drive to be a great hitter. He has quick hands, strong wrists and outstanding pitch recognition. He has the bat speed to turn on good fastballs, yet trusts his hands enough to wait out breaking balls. The result is that he stays balanced, uses the whole field with a repeatable, low-maintenance swing and lashes line drives from foul line to foul line. As he gets stronger and learns to use his lower half better, many of his doubles should start going over the fence. Oakland conservatively projects Buck to produce Rusty Greer-like numbers with .300 batting averages and 15-20 homers annually. He covers the plate well and isn't afraid to take a walk. A solid athlete, Buck is a good baserunner who's improving as a basestealer.

Scouts long have projected home run pop for Buck. One scout projected his power as a 65 on the 20-80 scouting scale when he was in high school. Yet he hit just 19 homers in three years at Arizona State and has just 10 in 125 pro games. The A's believe Buck's power will emerge as he continues to fill out and gain experience. Their theory is that players such as Buck, Daric Barton and Kurt Suzuki—their top three prospects—develop more home run power because they hit the ball hard consistently and control the strike zone. Buck's defense is just OK. His speed plays better on the bases than in the outfield, and his fringy arm fits best in left field. He compensates for his lack of arm strength with good accuracy.

Buck should be fully recovered from his sports hernia and at full strength for spring training. It was his presence that made his former Sun Devils teammate, Andre Ethier, expendable in the Milton Bradley trade in December 2005. Buck is a bigger version of Ethier with similar tools but more projected power. While more minor league at-bats wouldn't hurt—he should start the year at Triple-A Sacramento—Buck should be big league-ready midway through the 2007 season.

| Year | Club (League) | Class | AVG | G | AB | R | H | 2B | 3B | HR | RBI | BB | SO | SB | OBP | SLG |
|------|---------------|-------|-----|---|----|---|---|----|----|----|-----|----|----|----|-----|-----|
| 2005 | Vancouver (NWL) | A | .361 | 9 | 36 | 7 | 13 | 1 | 0 | 2 | 9 | 5 | 8 | 1 | .439 | .556 |
|  | Kane County (MWL) | A | .341 | 32 | 123 | 17 | 42 | 13 | 0 | 1 | 22 | 19 | 19 | 3 | .427 | .472 |
| 2006 | Midland (TL) | AA | .302 | 50 | 212 | 32 | 64 | 22 | 1 | 4 | 22 | 22 | 39 | 9 | .376 | .472 |
|  | Stockton (Cal) | A | .349 | 34 | 126 | 24 | 44 | 17 | 3 | 3 | 26 | 14 | 18 | 2 | .400 | .603 |
| **MINOR LEAGUE TOTALS** | | | .328 | 125 | 497 | 80 | 163 | 53 | 4 | 10 | 79 | 60 | 84 | 15 | .399 | .511 |

## 2. DARIC BARTON 1B

STEVE MOORE

**Born:** Aug. 16, 1985. **B-T:** L-R. **Ht.:** 6-0. **Wt.:** 205. **Drafted:** HS—Huntington Beach, Calif., 2003 (1st round). **Signed by:** Dan Ontiveros (Cardinals).

Acquired from the Cardinals in the Mark Mulder trade in December 2004, Barton established himself as the A's top prospect and played in the Futures Game in 2005. In 2006, however, his progress halted when he broke his left elbow in a first-base collision with Tony Womack in Triple-A. Barton returned to the Rookie-level Arizona League briefly in August, then played full-time in the Dominican League. Oakland general manager Billy Beane called Barton the best hitter in the minors when he traded for him, and he remains the system's best pure hitter. He has a textbook swing, fluid and short with a bit of loft, hinting at future power. His exceptional plate discipline allowed him to control the strike zone at Triple-A as a 20-year-old, and he's advanced enough to know to use the whole field. Barton wasn't tearing up Triple-A before his injury. Even those who believe in Barton's power grade it as average at best, and if he doesn't develop that kind of pop he'll be a less-than-intimidating threat for a first baseman. To keep hitting for average and to make himself an average defender at first base, he'll have to work harder on staying in shape. His thickening lower half could leave him well-below-average as a runner. Frank Thomas' departure as a free agent could create an opportunity for Barton. He probably needs more minor league time, especially considering the former catcher still hasn't played the equivalent of a full season at first base. A big spring training could make it hard to keep his bat out of the Oakland lineup, however.

| Year | Club (League) | Class | AVG | G | AB | R | H | 2B | 3B | HR | RBI | BB | SO | SB | OBP | SLG |
|------|---------------|-------|-----|---|----|---|---|----|----|----|-----|----|----|----|-----|-----|
| 2003 | Johnson City (Appy) | R | .294 | 54 | 170 | 29 | 50 | 10 | 0 | 4 | 29 | 37 | 48 | 0 | .420 | .424 |
| 2004 | Peoria (MWL) | A | .313 | 90 | 313 | 63 | 98 | 23 | 0 | 13 | 77 | 69 | 44 | 4 | .445 | .511 |
| 2005 | Stockton (Cal) | A | .318 | 79 | 292 | 60 | 93 | 16 | 2 | 8 | 52 | 62 | 49 | 0 | .438 | .469 |
|      | Midland (TL) | AA | .316 | 56 | 212 | 38 | 67 | 20 | 1 | 5 | 37 | 35 | 30 | 1 | .410 | .491 |
| 2006 | Athletics (AZL) | R | .200 | 2 | 5 | 1 | 1 | 1 | 0 | 0 | 2 | 0 | 0 | 0 | .200 | .400 |
|      | Sacramento (PCL) | AAA | .259 | 43 | 147 | 25 | 38 | 6 | 4 | 2 | 22 | 32 | 26 | 1 | .389 | .395 |
| **MINOR LEAGUE TOTALS** | | | .305 | 324 | 1139 | 216 | 347 | 76 | 7 | 32 | 219 | 235 | 197 | 6 | .425 | .468 |

## 3. KURT SUZUKI C

STEVE MOORE

**Born:** Oct. 4, 1983. **B-T:** R-R. **Ht.:** 5-11. **Wt.:** 200. **Drafted:** Cal State Fullerton, 2004 (2nd round). **Signed by:** Randy Johnson.

Suzuki went from walk-on to hero at Cal State Fullerton, leading the Titans to the 2004 College World Series championship as the team's top hitter and emotional core. He built on his "Kurt Klutch" reputation in 2006 with USA Baseball's Olympic qualifying team, hitting .455 with a game-winning homer against Brazil. Team USA manager Davey Johnson called him the team's best player. Never satisfied, Suzuki keeps getting better. He repeats his short swing, geared to produce line drives, and has improved significantly in using the whole field. He draws plenty of walks and is tough to strike out. He's an athletic grinder who went from decent to above-average defensively through hard work and fundamentals, leading Double-A Texas League catchers in fielding percentage (.997) while ranking second in catching basestealers (47 percent). Suzuki doesn't project to hit for much power, though some scouts expect him to hit 10-15 homers a season because he controls the strike zone so well and hits the ball hard. Defense doesn't come naturally to him, but he has shown the ability to work at it with outstanding results. He's a below-average runner, though fine for a catcher. Suzuki's natural leadership ability and work ethic have drawn admiration from Jason Kendall during Suzuki's trips to big league camp. After a year in Triple-A, Suzuki should be ready to replace Kendall when his contract expires after the 2007 season.

| Year | Club (League) | Class | AVG | G | AB | R | H | 2B | 3B | HR | RBI | BB | SO | SB | OBP | SLG |
|------|---------------|-------|-----|---|----|---|---|----|----|----|-----|----|----|----|-----|-----|
| 2004 | Vancouver (NWL) | A | .297 | 46 | 175 | 27 | 52 | 10 | 3 | 3 | 31 | 18 | 26 | 0 | .394 | .440 |
| 2005 | Stockton (Cal) | A | .277 | 114 | 441 | 85 | 122 | 26 | 5 | 12 | 65 | 63 | 61 | 5 | .378 | .440 |
| 2006 | Midland (TL) | AA | .285 | 99 | 376 | 64 | 107 | 26 | 1 | 7 | 55 | 58 | 50 | 5 | .392 | .415 |
| **MINOR LEAGUE TOTALS** | | | .283 | 259 | 992 | 176 | 281 | 62 | 9 | 22 | 151 | 139 | 137 | 10 | .386 | .430 |

## 4 MATT SULENTIC OF

BILL MITCHELL

**Born:** Oct. 6, 1987. **B-T:** L-R. **Ht.:** 5-10. **Wt.:** 170. **Drafted:** HS—Hillcrest, Texas, 2006 (3rd round). **Signed by:** Blake Davis.

Sulentic won the high school triple crown in the Dallas Metroplex last spring, hitting .654-20-59. Area scout Blake Davis talked him up to Oakland's front office for four hours, and the A's took him in the third round and signed him for $395,000. After tearing up the short-season Northwest League, Sulentic finished his pro debut on fumes in the low Class A Midwest League. Few doubt he will hit, and he soon should rival Daric Barton and Travis Buck for the title of best hitter in the system. Sulentic has a pure lefthanded swing and an innate ability to get the barrel on the ball consistently. His strength and bat speed should produce above-average power. His toughness and makeup endeared him to the A's. Projecting a position for Sulentic, who played both middle-infield spots and all over the outfield in high school, already is a challenge. He took a stab at second base in instructional league before Oakland decided to leave him in left field for now. His arm is below-average. He's probably maxed out physically. Though he offers little projection, Sulentic is already very good and looks like a future No. 3 hitter. If he settles in as a left fielder, he could move quickly. He'll likely start 2007 back at low Class A Kane County.

| Year | Club (League) | Class | AVG | G | AB | R | H | 2B | 3B | HR | RBI | BB | SO | SB | OBP | SLG |
|------|---------------|-------|------|----|-----|----|----|----|----|----|-----|----|----|----|------|------|
| 2006 | Kane County (MWL) | A | .235 | 30 | 98 | 12 | 23 | 4 | 1 | 1 | 13 | 12 | 19 | 1 | .327 | .327 |
| | Vancouver (NWL) | A | .354 | 38 | 144 | 24 | 51 | 10 | 1 | 2 | 22 | 14 | 30 | 3 | .409 | .479 |
| **MINOR LEAGUE TOTALS** | | | .306 | 68 | 242 | 36 | 74 | 14 | 2 | 3 | 35 | 26 | 49 | 4 | .375 | .417 |

## 5 JERMAINE MITCHELL OF

BILL MITCHELL

**Born:** Nov. 2, 1984. **B-T:** L-L. **Ht.:** 6-0. **Wt.:** 200. **Drafted:** UNC Greensboro, 2006 (5th round). **Signed by:** Neil Avent.

Mitchell spent two years at Texarkana (Texas) Junior College before transferring to UNC Greensboro as a junior. A's area scout Neil Avent, a former UNCG assistant coach, stayed on Mitchell and the A's cross-checked him in the Southern Conference tournament. They popped Mitchell in the fifth round, signed him for $155,000 then watched him sizzle in his pro debut until he broke a bone in his right foot. Only injury slows Mitchell, who's the system's fastest runner with 70 speed on the 20-80 scouting scale. Unlike many speedsters, he's no slap hitter. He has powerful legs and a strong frame. He has the plate discipline to wait on his pitch and the swing plane to drive the ball to all fields. Mitchell's throwing arm is below-average but playable in center. He'll need experience and at-bats to adjust against better breaking balls, to translate his raw power into home runs and to hone his baserunning instincts. Mitchell could be a star if it all comes together, and his toolsy package makes him look like a fiffh-round steal. He should join Larry Cobb and Matt Sulentic in a dynamic Kane County outfield to start 2007.

| Year | Club (League) | Class | AVG | G | AB | R | H | 2B | 3B | HR | RBI | BB | SO | SB | OBP | SLG |
|------|---------------|-------|------|----|-----|----|----|----|----|----|-----|----|----|----|------|------|
| 2006 | Vancouver (NWL) | A | .362 | 37 | 138 | 23 | 50 | 7 | 2 | 3 | 23 | 22 | 27 | 14 | .460 | .507 |
| **MINOR LEAGUE TOTALS** | | | .362 | 37 | 138 | 23 | 50 | 7 | 2 | 3 | 23 | 22 | 27 | 14 | .460 | .507 |

## 6 JAVIER HERRERA OF

STEVE MOORE

**Born:** April 9, 1985. **B-T:** R-R. **Ht.:** 5-10. **Wt.:** 160. **Signed:** Venezuela, 2001. **Signed by:** Julio Franco.

Considered on the fast track after ranking as the Northwest League's top prospect in 2004, Herrera has hit significant speed bumps the last two seasons. He was suspended for violating baseball's performance-enhancing drug policy in 2005, then missed all of 2006 after injuring his elbow in spring training. He had Tommy John surgery and wasn't ready to return for instructional league. Herrera has more athletic ability than anyone in the system. He has above-average power and speed, a sound swing and center-field skills. He had the A's best outfield arm before his surgery and it should bounce back. He started drawing more walks in low Class A two years ago. Herrera has yet to play 100 games in a season and has played just five above low Class A. Many Tommy John surgery alumni—especially hitters—have returned quicker than Herrera, leading to suspicion that he didn't attack his rehabilitation as he should have. When he last played, he struck out 111 times in 372 at-bats in 2005 because he tends to overswing. Herrera may struggle in 2007 if his plan is to work his way back into shape. Even if he's a bit heavier and slower in his return, his power potential allows him to profile as a corner

outfielder. He'll head to high Class A Stockton as soon as he's healthy.

| Year | Club (League) | Class | AVG | G | AB | R | H | 2B | 3B | HR | RBI | BB | SO | SB | OBP | SLG |
|---|---|---|---|---|---|---|---|---|---|---|---|---|---|---|---|---|
| 2002 | Athletics (DSL) | R | .286 | 65 | 227 | 40 | 65 | 14 | 5 | 5 | 47 | 23 | 56 | 21 | .359 | .458 |
| 2003 | Athletics (AZL) | R | .230 | 17 | 61 | 12 | 14 | 3 | 1 | 2 | 13 | 7 | 19 | 3 | .329 | .410 |
| 2004 | Vancouver (NWL) | A | .331 | 65 | 263 | 50 | 87 | 15 | 4 | 12 | 47 | 24 | 59 | 23 | .392 | .555 |
| 2005 | Sacramento (PCL) | AAA | .417 | 5 | 12 | 5 | 5 | 1 | 0 | 1 | 3 | 1 | 1 | 1 | .533 | .750 |
| | Kane County (MWL) | A | .275 | 94 | 360 | 70 | 99 | 18 | 2 | 13 | 62 | 47 | 110 | 26 | .374 | .444 |
| 2006 | Did not play—Injured | | | | | | | | | | | | | | | |
| **MINOR LEAGUE TOTALS** | | | .293 | 246 | 923 | 177 | 270 | 51 | 12 | 33 | 172 | 102 | 245 | 74 | .375 | .481 |

## 7 JASON WINDSOR  RHP

BILL MITCHELL

**Born:** July 16, 1982. **B-T:** R-R. **Ht.:** 6-2. **Wt.:** 235. **Drafted:** Cal State Fullerton, 2004 (3rd round). **Signed by:** Randy Johnson.

Windsor was drafted three times between high school and junior college before leading Cal State Fullerton to back-to-back College World Series trips in 2003-04. He was the CWS outstanding player when the Titans won the national title in 2004. Windsor tied for the minor league victory lead and made his big league debut in 2006. His big heart and durable frame are key ingredients for Windsor, who often pitches off a mid-80s fastball that tops out at 90 mph. It plays up because of his plus changeup, which is the best among the system's starters and has good sink. He throws his curve and slider for strikes as well and isn't afraid to challenge hitters. Windsor must command his fastball better to have success if he's not going to throw harder. Major league hitters torched him during his brief stint with Oakland. Shane Komine has better stuff, but Windsor's bigger frame gives him the better chance at long-term success among the A's upper-level starters. The A's like Windsor's moxie, though scouts from other organizations consider him fringy. Another pitch—perhaps a cutter or splitter—could be the difference between Windsor becoming a back-of-the-rotation starter or a 4-A pitcher. He also could develop into a Justin Duchscherer-style set-up man.

| Year | Club (League) | Class | W | L | ERA | G | GS | CG | SV | IP | H | R | ER | HR | BB | SO | AVG |
|---|---|---|---|---|---|---|---|---|---|---|---|---|---|---|---|---|---|
| 2004 | Vancouver (NWL) | A | 0 | 0 | 0.00 | 4 | 0 | 0 | 1 | 5 | 4 | 0 | 0 | 0 | 0 | 5 | .211 |
| | Kane County (MWL) | A | 1 | 0 | 2.77 | 9 | 0 | 0 | 3 | 13 | 11 | 4 | 4 | 0 | 5 | 13 | .220 |
| 2005 | Stockton (Cal) | A | 2 | 2 | 3.58 | 10 | 10 | 0 | 0 | 55 | 52 | 28 | 22 | 5 | 8 | 64 | .244 |
| | Midland (TL) | AA | 3 | 6 | 5.72 | 11 | 11 | 0 | 0 | 57 | 69 | 40 | 36 | 5 | 23 | 39 | .303 |
| 2006 | Midland (TL) | AA | 4 | 1 | 2.97 | 6 | 6 | 0 | 0 | 33 | 27 | 12 | 11 | 2 | 10 | 35 | .227 |
| | Sacramento (PCL) | AAA | 13 | 1 | 3.81 | 20 | 20 | 1 | 0 | 118 | 128 | 53 | 50 | 7 | 32 | 123 | .272 |
| | Oakland (AL) | MLB | 0 | 1 | 6.59 | 4 | 3 | 0 | 0 | 14 | 21 | 12 | 10 | 2 | 5 | 6 | .375 |
| **MINOR LEAGUE TOTALS** | | | 23 | 10 | 3.93 | 60 | 47 | 1 | 4 | 281 | 291 | 137 | 123 | 19 | 78 | 279 | .265 |
| **MAJOR LEAGUE TOTALS** | | | 0 | 1 | 6.59 | 4 | 3 | 0 | 0 | 13 | 21 | 12 | 10 | 2 | 5 | 6 | .375 |

## 8 MARCUS McBETH  RHP

BILL MITCHELL

**Born:** Aug. 23, 1980. **B-T:** R-R. **Ht.:** 6-1. **Wt.:** 185. **Drafted:** South Carolina, 2001 (4th round). **Signed by:** Kelly Heath.

McBeth ranked seventh on this list in 2002—as a center fielder. A former kick returner on South Carolina's football team, he long has been one of the A's top athletes and always had well-above-average arm strength. After he hit .233 in three pro seasons, he moved to the mound in 2005 and ranked fifth in the minors in saves in 2006. Though he's relatively new to pitching, McBeth's athleticism has helped him made rapid strides. His changeup has become a plus pitch in short order and rates as the organization's best. He plays it off a 95-96 mph fastball that jumps out of his hand. His mid-80s slider has become an average pitch, even above-average at times. One A's official said McBeth's best attribute is his competitive fire. McBeth at times will miss up in the strike zone with his changeup and slider. He needs to locate his changeup better against left-handers. With more mound time, his ability to set hitters up should improve. McBeth will get the opportunity to join the Oakland bullpen in 2007. His power stuff would fit in well between set-up man Justin Duchscherer and closer Huston Street.

| Year | Club (League) | Class | AVG | G | AB | R | H | 2B | 3B | HR | RBI | BB | SO | SB | OBP | SLG |
|---|---|---|---|---|---|---|---|---|---|---|---|---|---|---|---|---|
| 2002 | Visalia (Cal) | A | .227 | 76 | 255 | 45 | 58 | 7 | 3 | 10 | 39 | 29 | 73 | 14 | .318 | .396 |
| | Athletics (AZL) | R | .333 | 4 | 9 | 5 | 3 | 0 | 0 | 0 | 0 | 3 | 0 | 3 | .500 | .333 |
| 2003 | Modesto (Cal) | A | .130 | 15 | 54 | 7 | 7 | 0 | 0 | 0 | 5 | 5 | 20 | 2 | .210 | .130 |
| | Kane County (MWL) | A | .256 | 68 | 234 | 30 | 60 | 9 | 3 | 4 | 26 | 28 | 57 | 8 | .349 | .372 |
| 2004 | Modesto (Cal) | A | .234 | 99 | 329 | 41 | 77 | 18 | 4 | 5 | 41 | 14 | 86 | 4 | .288 | .359 |
| **MINOR LEAGUE TOTALS** | | | .233 | 262 | 881 | 128 | 205 | 34 | 10 | 19 | 111 | 79 | 236 | 31 | .311 | .359 |

| Year | Club (League) | Class | W | L | ERA | G | GS | CG | SV | IP | H | R | ER | HR | BB | SO | AVG |
|------|---------------|-------|---|---|-----|---|----|----|----|----|---|---|----|----|----|----|-----|
| 2005 | Kane County (MWL) | A | 1 | 2 | 5.03 | 16 | 0 | 0 | 1 | 20 | 20 | 11 | 11 | 2 | 13 | 21 | .263 |
|  | Athletics (AZL) | R | 1 | 0 | 0.90 | 8 | 0 | 0 | 4 | 10 | 5 | 2 | 1 | 1 | 5 | 13 | .147 |
|  | Stockton (Cal) | A | 0 | 0 | 0.00 | 2 | 0 | 0 | 0 | 3 | 1 | 0 | 0 | 0 | 2 | 3 | .125 |
| 2006 | Stockton (Cal) | A | 0 | 0 | 0.00 | 8 | 0 | 0 | 7 | 9 | 1 | 0 | 0 | 0 | 2 | 14 | .037 |
|  | Sacramento (PCL) | AAA | 0 | 1 | 11.05 | 6 | 0 | 0 | 0 | 7 | 7 | 9 | 9 | 3 | 6 | 7 | .241 |
|  | Midland (TL) | AA | 3 | 2 | 2.48 | 45 | 0 | 0 | 25 | 54 | 43 | 16 | 15 | 4 | 20 | 65 | .213 |
| **MINOR LEAGUE TOTALS** | | | 5 | 5 | 3.16 | 85 | 0 | 0 | 37 | 103 | 77 | 38 | 36 | 10 | 48 | 123 | .205 |

## 9 JUSTIN SELLERS

SS

PAUL GIERHART

**Born:** Feb. 1, 1986. **B-T:** R-R. **Ht.:** 5-10. **Wt.:** 160. **Drafted:** HS—Huntington Beach, Calif., 2005 (6th round). **Signed by:** Randy Johnson.

The son of former big league righthander Jeff Sellers, Justin committed to play for Cal State Fullerton but signed for a relatively modest $150,000 bonus as a 2005 sixth-rounder. A Marina High (Huntington Beach, Calif.) teammate of Daric Barton in 2003, Sellers was the youngest Kane County player for much of 2006. Oakland has considered making him a switch-hitter but hasn't gone ahead with the experiment yet. Sellers has passed fellow 2005 draftee Cliff Pennington as the best defensive infielder in the system. He has a feel for defense, making difficult plays look easy thanks to soft hands, smooth footwork, surprising range and a solid-average, accurate arm. Offensively, he controls the strike zone and has the bat speed to sting balls from gap to gap. His above-average instincts play well defensively and on the bases, where he's a slightly above-average runner. Sellers had more fly outs than any A's farmhand in 2006. He hasn't adjusted his homer-oriented approach despite evidence that homers won't be a big part of his game. They definitely won't be if he doesn't respond to the organization's pleas that he hit the weight room and get stronger. Today's A's value defense more than most clubs. Sellers will need to show more professionalism to reach his ceiling as an everyday shortstop whose bats profiles for the bottom of a lineup. A stronger, more coachable Sellers will earn a spot in high Class A.

| Year | Club (League) | Class | AVG | G | AB | R | H | 2B | 3B | HR | RBI | BB | SO | SB | OBP | SLG |
|------|---------------|-------|-----|---|----|---|---|----|----|----|-----|----|----|----|-----|-----|
| 2005 | Vancouver (NWL) | A | .274 | 47 | 175 | 31 | 48 | 8 | 1 | 0 | 13 | 19 | 24 | 8 | .369 | .331 |
| 2006 | Kane County (MWL) | A | .241 | 119 | 411 | 75 | 99 | 21 | 2 | 5 | 46 | 58 | 65 | 17 | .346 | .338 |
| **MINOR LEAGUE TOTALS** | | | .251 | 166 | 586 | 106 | 147 | 29 | 3 | 5 | 59 | 77 | 89 | 25 | .353 | .336 |

## 10 TREVOR CAHILL

RHP

BILL MITCHELL

**Born:** March 1, 1988. **B-T:** R-R. **Ht.:** 6-3. **Wt.:** 195. **Drafted:** HS—Vista, Calif., 2006 (2nd round). **Signed by:** Craig Weissmann.

With just 19 innings under his belt entering his senior season in high school, Cahill was an unknown quantity leading up to the 2006 draft. His commitment to Dartmouth also complicated matters. He pitched his way into first-round consideration until strep throat resulted in a pair of poor outings in May. Oakland thought it would take a hitter with its top choice (second round), but changed gears when Cahill was available and signed him for $560,000. Cahill offers plenty of projection. At his best, his fastball sits at 92-94 mph and his spike curveball is a plus-plus pitch. His curve is a power breaker that could become a swing-and-miss big league pitch. A former high school shortstop, Cahill has the athletic ability to make quick adjustments and respond to coaching. It wasn't just strep throat that affected Cahill's stuff. His inexperience as a pitcher has led to an inability to hold his stuff, during starts and from outing to outing. The A's are confident Cahill will become more consistent with a professional approach to conditioning, training and preparation. He also needs to come up with a changeup. Cahill may be less refined than other young A's arms, but his combination of size, health, stuff and intelligence makes him the best bet among them. He may start 2007 in extended spring training and play in short-season Vancouver before making his full-season debut the following year.

| Year | Club (League) | Class | W | L | ERA | G | GS | CG | SV | IP | H | R | ER | HR | BB | SO | AVG |
|------|---------------|-------|---|---|-----|---|----|----|----|----|---|---|----|----|----|----|-----|
| 2006 | Athletics (AZL) | R | 0 | 0 | 3.00 | 4 | 4 | 0 | 0 | 9 | 2 | 4 | 3 | 0 | 7 | 11 | .071 |
| **MINOR LEAGUE TOTALS** | | | 0 | 0 | 3.00 | 4 | 4 | 0 | 0 | 9 | 2 | 4 | 3 | 0 | 7 | 11 | .071 |

## 11 RICHIE ROBNETT

OF

**Born:** Sept. 17, 1983. **B-T:** L-L. **Ht.:** 5-10. **Wt.:** 195. **Drafted:** Fresno State, 2004 (1st round). **Signed by:** Scott Kidd.

Scouts outside the A's organization frequently put Robnett at the top of their follow lists because his tools stand out in the system. Those tools got him picked in the first round in

2004 out of Fresno State and earned him a $1.325 million signing bonus. While he has athletic ability and still runs well, Robnett's best tool is his raw power. He's short but stocky and strong, quick to the ball and able to hit balls out of any ballpark. Harnessing his power remains a concern, though, because he lacks pitch recognition and strikes out too much. The rest of his tools don't play up to their grades because he's so raw, even after two full seasons. He has the speed to play center field and his slightly above-average arm would play in right, but he doesn't project as an above-average defender due to inconsistent routes and other fundamentals. A broken hamate bone in 2006 didn't help matters, and he struggled in a brief stint in the Mexican Pacific League. Robnett is headed to Double-A Midland, likely in center field, flanked by prospects Travis Buck, Myron Leslie and Danny Putnam.

| Year | Club (League) | Class | AVG | G | AB | R | H | 2B | 3B | HR | RBI | BB | SO | SB | OBP | SLG |
|---|---|---|---|---|---|---|---|---|---|---|---|---|---|---|---|---|
| 2004 | Vancouver (NWL) | A | .299 | 43 | 164 | 26 | 49 | 14 | 1 | 4 | 36 | 28 | 43 | 1 | .395 | .470 |
| 2005 | Stockton (Cal) | A | .243 | 115 | 457 | 77 | 111 | 30 | 0 | 20 | 74 | 56 | 151 | 8 | .324 | .440 |
| 2006 | Midland (TL) | AA | .357 | 5 | 14 | 5 | 5 | 1 | 0 | 1 | 2 | 4 | 4 | 0 | .474 | .643 |
| | Sacramento (PCL) | AAA | .091 | 5 | 11 | 0 | 1 | 1 | 0 | 0 | 0 | 0 | 3 | 0 | .091 | .182 |
| | Stockton (Cal) | A | .266 | 69 | 267 | 46 | 71 | 8 | 2 | 11 | 38 | 35 | 73 | 4 | .358 | .434 |
| **MINOR LEAGUE TOTALS** | | | .260 | 237 | 913 | 154 | 237 | 54 | 3 | 36 | 150 | 123 | 274 | 13 | .348 | .444 |

 ## CLIFF PENNINGTON                                                SS

**Born:** June 15, 1984. **B-T:** B-R. **Ht.:** 5-11. **Wt.:** 185. **Drafted:** Texas A&M, 2005 (1st round). **Signed by:** Blake Davis.

A third-team All-American and scouts' darling in college, Pennington seemed poised to break out in 2006. Instead, he had a lost season. After impressing the organization enough in his debut and first instructional league to earn an invitation to big league spring training, he struggled defensively in front of the big league staff. A's officials say the combination of a tweaked knee, lost confidence and jump to high Class A combined to bury Pennington, who got off to an 8-for-78 start in April. He battled leg problems and had hit safely in 14 of 15 games when he tore his left hamstring, effectively sidelining him for the rest of the season. He swung the bat well in instructional league in 2006 but wasn't moving as well as he had previously. A move to second base is possible for Pennington, who has soft hands, a quick transfer and strong arm. He could move to second in 2007 in a return trip to high Class A, teaming with Sellers in the middle infield, but the A's are waiting to see how Pennington looks in spring training before settling on his assignment.

| Year | Club (League) | Class | AVG | G | AB | R | H | 2B | 3B | HR | RBI | BB | SO | SB | OBP | SLG |
|---|---|---|---|---|---|---|---|---|---|---|---|---|---|---|---|---|
| 2005 | Kane County (MWL) | A | .276 | 69 | 290 | 49 | 80 | 15 | 0 | 3 | 29 | 39 | 47 | 25 | .364 | .359 |
| 2006 | Athletics (AZL) | R | .464 | 9 | 28 | 3 | 13 | 3 | 1 | 0 | 6 | 4 | 2 | 0 | .531 | .643 |
| | Stockton (Cal) | A | .203 | 46 | 177 | 36 | 36 | 7 | 0 | 2 | 21 | 24 | 35 | 7 | .302 | .277 |
| **MINOR LEAGUE TOTALS** | | | .261 | 124 | 495 | 88 | 129 | 25 | 1 | 5 | 56 | 67 | 84 | 32 | .352 | .345 |

 ## KEVIN MELILLO                                                2B

**Born:** May 14, 1982. **B-T:** L-R. **Ht.:** 6-0. **Wt.:** 190. **Drafted:** South Carolina, 2004 (5th round). **Signed by:** Michael Holmes.

Melillo broke out on his own with a huge 2005 season, smashing an organization-high 24 homers between three levels. In 2006 he focused on the other parts of his game, working diligently to become a better defender. He shocked many in the organization by leading the Texas League with a .990 fielding percentage while making just six errors in 134 games at second base. Always a confident player, Melillo translated that confidence to the defensive side after extensive work with Juan Navarette, the organization's infield rover. He still doesn't profile as an above-average defender at second due to his poor range, though. He turns double plays well enough with a strong arm, a tool that led the organization to give him time at third base in the Arizona Fall League. Melillo's power dipped significantly from his breakout 2005 season, and he's in danger of becoming a tweener. While he has power, he's not a masher, more Aaron Boone than Bret Boone. Without either Boone's defensive prowess, Melillo will have to combine his defensive chops of 2006 with his power of 2005 to supplant Mark Ellis as the A's future second baseman. He's ticketed for Triple-A in 2007.

| Year | Club (League) | Class | AVG | G | AB | R | H | 2B | 3B | HR | RBI | BB | SO | SB | OBP | SLG |
|---|---|---|---|---|---|---|---|---|---|---|---|---|---|---|---|---|
| 2004 | Vancouver (NWL) | A | .340 | 22 | 94 | 22 | 32 | 11 | 2 | 2 | 21 | 11 | 16 | 2 | .422 | .564 |
| 2005 | Kane County (MWL) | A | .286 | 78 | 280 | 47 | 80 | 18 | 3 | 8 | 36 | 53 | 40 | 10 | .399 | .457 |
| | Stockton (Cal) | A | .400 | 22 | 90 | 21 | 36 | 7 | 1 | 9 | 23 | 12 | 18 | 2 | .471 | .800 |
| | Midland (TL) | AA | .282 | 35 | 131 | 33 | 37 | 10 | 0 | 7 | 34 | 14 | 23 | 9 | .347 | .519 |
| 2006 | Midland (TL) | AA | .280 | 136 | 500 | 73 | 140 | 31 | 3 | 12 | 73 | 68 | 98 | 14 | .367 | .426 |
| **MINOR LEAGUE TOTALS** | | | .297 | 293 | 1095 | 196 | 325 | 77 | 9 | 38 | 187 | 158 | 195 | 37 | .386 | .488 |

## SHANE KOMINE                                                    RHP

**Born:** Oct. 18, 1980. **B-T:** R-R. **Ht.:** 5-9. **Wt.:** 180. **Drafted:** Nebraska, 2002 (9th round). **Signed by:** Jim Pransky.

A 5-foot-8, 135-pound high school pitcher, Komine grew into the pillar of Nebraska's baseball program, leading it from afterthought to back-to-back College World Series trips in 2001-02. The toll Komine paid in four seasons affected his professional career significantly. He had back and shoulder problems in college (the latter required surgery), and then had Tommy John surgery in 2004. Against all those odds, Komine reached the major leagues in 2006, and while he didn't pitch well, he handled himself well and took positives from the experience. Komine isn't the same pitcher as he was at Nebraska, and in fact, he's not the same pitcher from one start to the next, and that's the problem. At times, he throws a 91-94 mph fastball, and his curveball, slider and changeup all have their moments. His curve is his best secondary offering, and he throws all his pitches for strikes. His stuff fluctuated significantly last year, particularly his velocity on all his pitches. He's never been durable as a pro, surpassing 150 innings once. He loses velocity during games as well, making him better suited for the bullpen, but scouts question whether he can have his best stuff when pitching on back-to-back days. If the A's have decided to move him to a relief role, they haven't talked about it, and Komine appears ticketed for a return to the Triple-A rotation in 2007.

| Year | Club (League) | Class | W | L | ERA | G | GS | CG | SV | IP | H | R | ER | HR | BB | SO | AVG |
|------|---------------|-------|---|---|-----|---|----|----|----|----|---|---|----|----|----|----|-----|
| 2002 | Visalia (Cal) | A | 1 | 3 | 5.96 | 18 | 0 | 0 | 0 | 26 | 23 | 20 | 17 | 2 | 20 | 22 | .240 |
| 2003 | Kane County (MWL) | A | 6 | 0 | 1.82 | 8 | 8 | 1 | 0 | 54 | 45 | 12 | 11 | 1 | 9 | 50 | .223 |
| 2003 | Midland (TL) | AA | 4 | 6 | 3.75 | 19 | 18 | 1 | 0 | 103 | 108 | 51 | 43 | 6 | 30 | 75 | .271 |
| 2004 | Midland (TL) | AA | 4 | 5 | 4.77 | 17 | 17 | 0 | 0 | 94 | 103 | 56 | 50 | 10 | 28 | 65 | .281 |
| 2005 | Athletics (AZL) | R | 0 | 1 | 9.72 | 4 | 4 | 0 | 0 | 8 | 10 | 10 | 9 | 0 | 7 | 11 | .294 |
|  | Stockton (Cal) | A | 0 | 0 | 4.15 | 2 | 2 | 0 | 0 | 9 | 10 | 4 | 4 | 0 | 3 | 11 | .294 |
|  | Midland (TL) | AA | 2 | 1 | 3.16 | 5 | 5 | 0 | 0 | 31 | 27 | 12 | 11 | 5 | 7 | 33 | .235 |
| 2006 | Oakland (AL) | MLB | 0 | 0 | 5.00 | 2 | 2 | 0 | 0 | 9 | 10 | 5 | 5 | 3 | 8 | 1 | .270 |
|  | Sacramento (PCL) | AAA | 11 | 8 | 4.05 | 24 | 22 | 1 | 0 | 140 | 145 | 67 | 63 | 13 | 38 | 116 | .267 |
| **MINOR LEAGUE TOTALS** | | | 28 | 24 | 4.02 | 97 | 76 | 3 | 0 | 466 | 471 | 232 | 208 | 37 | 142 | 383 | .263 |
| **MAJOR LEAGUE TOTALS** | | | 0 | 0 | 5.00 | 2 | 2 | 0 | 0 | 9 | 10 | 5 | 5 | 3 | 8 | 1 | .270 |

## JARED LANSFORD                                                  RHP

**Born:** Oct. 22, 1986. **B-T:** R-R. **Ht.:** 6-2. **Wt.:** 190. **Drafted:** HS—Santa Clara, Calif., 2005 (2nd round). **Signed by:** Scott Kidd.

The son of former A's third baseman (and American League batting champion) Carney Lansford and brother of Cubs third baseman Josh, Jared had the most success of any of the prep pitchers the A's have drafted the last three years. A relative newcomer to pitching—he once was expected to join his brother as an infielder—Lansford proved a quick study, finishing his first pro season in high Class A. He was hit hard there, so the A's hope he'll make quick adjustments in 2007 in a return to Stockton. Lansford's success in 2006 hinged on his ability to keep the ball down. He works off a sinker that sits at 89-92 mph and touches 94, by far his best pitch. While he has effort in his delivery, it actually helps create deception. His slider is his second pitch, and it needs significant improvement in depth and tilt to be a swing-and-miss pitch at higher levels. His changeup is a distant third offering he doesn't trust, and he could use a split-finger fastball or cutter to give hitters a different look. The A's have hope his athletic ability will allow him to make adjustments and improve his stuff a tick, even though his frame doesn't offer classic projection.

| Year | Club (League) | Class | W | L | ERA | G | GS | CG | SV | IP | H | R | ER | HR | BB | SO | AVG |
|------|---------------|-------|---|---|-----|---|----|----|----|----|---|---|----|----|----|----|-----|
| 2005 | Athletics (AZL) | R | 0 | 1 | 1.27 | 7 | 6 | 0 | 0 | 21 | 16 | 4 | 3 | 0 | 5 | 20 | .216 |
| 2006 | Kane County (MWL) | A | 11 | 6 | 2.86 | 18 | 18 | 2 | 0 | 104 | 87 | 40 | 33 | 1 | 42 | 50 | .236 |
|  | Stockton (Cal) | A | 0 | 1 | 12.71 | 3 | 3 | 0 | 0 | 11 | 23 | 19 | 16 | 4 | 5 | 9 | .397 |
| **MINOR LEAGUE TOTALS** | | | 11 | 8 | 3.42 | 28 | 27 | 2 | 0 | 137 | 126 | 63 | 52 | 5 | 52 | 79 | .252 |

## DANNY PUTNAM                                                     OF

**Born:** Sept. 17, 1982. **B-T:** L-L. **Ht.:** 5-10. **Wt.:** 200. **Drafted:** Stanford, 2004 (1st round supplemental). **Signed by:** Scott Kidd.

A star at San Diego's Rancho Bernardo High and at Stanford (as well as with Team USA in 2003), Putnam's track record counters his short stature and lack of overwhelming tools. His 2006 season was essentially wasted due to a posterior cruciate ligament injury in his knee, however. A grinder, he played hurt before having surgery, then returned strong in Double-A, hitting .337 with seven homers in his final 104 at-bats. His strengths remain tied to his weaknesses. He's short, but that helps account for his compact stroke. He maximizes his offensive ability with an efficient approach. He swings with a purpose, works counts and

doesn't waste at-bats. Putnam is not a natural athlete, so he works hard to stay in shape and possesses plenty of strength in his hands and wrists. He's a below-average runner with just average arm strength, but he runs good routes and is an efficient defender, better suited for left but playable in right. A healthy Putnam would give the A's corner outfield depth to go with Travis Buck, Richie Robnett and Matt Sulentic, and with a strong spring, Putnam could earn his first shot at Triple-A.

| Year | Club (League) | Class | AVG | G | AB | R | H | 2B | 3B | HR | RBI | BB | SO | SB | OBP | SLG |
|------|---------------|-------|-----|---|----|---|---|----|----|----|-----|----|----|----|-----|-----|
| 2004 | Vancouver (NWL) | A | .289 | 11 | 38 | 10 | 11 | 2 | 0 | 2 | 3 | 14 | 8 | 1 | .481 | .500 |
| 2004 | Kane County (MWL) | A | .219 | 49 | 160 | 29 | 35 | 5 | 2 | 7 | 27 | 29 | 40 | 0 | .347 | .406 |
| 2005 | Stockton (Cal) | A | .307 | 131 | 514 | 97 | 158 | 37 | 3 | 15 | 100 | 66 | 92 | 1 | .388 | .479 |
| 2006 | Athletics (AZL) | R | .278 | 6 | 18 | 2 | 5 | 1 | 0 | 0 | 2 | 6 | 2 | 0 | .458 | .333 |
| | Midland (TL) | AA | .244 | 60 | 225 | 33 | 55 | 13 | 2 | 8 | 37 | 23 | 37 | 2 | .317 | .427 |
| | Stockton (Cal) | A | .375 | 10 | 40 | 7 | 15 | 2 | 0 | 1 | 9 | 6 | 8 | 0 | .457 | .500 |
| **MINOR LEAGUE TOTALS** | | | .280 | 267 | 995 | 178 | 279 | 60 | 7 | 33 | 178 | 144 | 187 | 4 | .374 | .454 |

## 17 MYRON LESLIE                                3B/OF

**Born:** May 2, 1982. **B-T:** B-R. **Ht.:** 6-2. **Wt.:** 220. **Drafted:** South Florida, 2004 (8th round). **Signed by:** Steve Barningham.

Leslie teamed with Jeff Baisley at South Florida for three seasons, playing shortstop while Baisley manned third. Leslie has made slow but steady progress as a pro, and some scouts believe he's about to break out. His overall ceiling resembles that of Bobby Bonilla, as a switch-hitter with power from both sides who doesn't look pretty but can play third base or a corner outfield spot. That's clearly a lofty comparison for Leslie, as Bonilla was in his second big league season at age 24. But Leslie could be an extra outfielder/first baseman who switch-hits with power but may not hit for enough average to be a regular. His long arms sometimes leave him tied up on balls on the inner half, but when he gets extended, the ball jumps off his bat to all fields. Scouts who didn't see him as an amateur have a hard time believing he played shortstop, and third base might be a stretch at his size, but he has the arm strength and perhaps enough athletic ability to stay on an outfield corner. His hands are good enough for third, but his feet leave him poorly positioned to throw at times. Leslie is ready to move to Double-A, likely moving to different positions to accommodate other prospects.

| Year | Club (League) | Class | AVG | G | AB | R | H | 2B | 3B | HR | RBI | BB | SO | SB | OBP | SLG |
|------|---------------|-------|-----|---|----|---|---|----|----|----|-----|----|----|----|-----|-----|
| 2004 | Vancouver (NWL) | A | .245 | 73 | 273 | 41 | 67 | 12 | 2 | 1 | 28 | 41 | 34 | 1 | .339 | .315 |
| 2005 | Kane County (MWL) | A | .275 | 131 | 472 | 77 | 130 | 32 | 2 | 15 | 68 | 78 | 89 | 2 | .377 | .447 |
| 2006 | Stockton (Cal) | A | .273 | 136 | 513 | 81 | 140 | 25 | 0 | 17 | 100 | 71 | 98 | 6 | .365 | .421 |
| **MINOR LEAGUE TOTALS** | | | .268 | 340 | 1258 | 199 | 337 | 69 | 4 | 33 | 196 | 190 | 221 | 9 | .364 | .408 |

## 18 VIN MAZZARO                                RHP

**Born:** Sept. 27, 1986. **B-T:** R-R. **Ht.:** 6-2. **Wt.:** 190. **Drafted:** HS—Rutherford, N.J., 2005 (3rd round). **Signed by:** Jeff Bittiger.

The third high school pitcher the A's picked in the 2005 draft, Mazzaro was ahead of Jared Lansford to open 2006, earning a spot on Kane County's Opening Day roster while Lansford was in extended spring training. But Mazzaro wrapped up his season in mid-August with an ERA north of 5.00 (he reached his innings limit), while Lansford earned a promotion. While Lansford is known as the sinkerballer, Mazzaro has natural sink as well, with similar upper-80s/low-90s velocity. His best secondary pitch is a changeup that was better in instructional league in 2005 than it was during his first regular season. His curveball has its moments, particularly when he throws it with power and confidence. As the season proved, though, Mazzaro didn't always do that, and the quality of his stuff fluctuated. Showing up on game day was enough against New Jersey high school players, but he learned that beating professionals requires better preparation, conditioning and mental toughness. The A's remain confident he'll learn his lessons and earn a spot in the high Class A rotation for 2007.

| Year | Club (League) | Class | W | L | ERA | G | GS | CG | SV | IP | H | R | ER | HR | BB | SO | AVG |
|------|---------------|-------|---|---|-----|---|----|----|----|----|---|---|----|----|----|----|-----|
| 2006 | Kane County (MWL) | A | 9 | 9 | 5.05 | 24 | 24 | 0 | 0 | 119 | 146 | 81 | 67 | 7 | 42 | 81 | .310 |
| **MINOR LEAGUE TOTALS** | | | 9 | 9 | 5.05 | 24 | 24 | 0 | 0 | 119 | 146 | 81 | 67 | 7 | 42 | 81 | .310 |

## 19 RYAN GOLESKI                                OF

**Born:** March 19, 1982. **B-T:** R-R. **Ht.:** 6-3. **Wt.:** 225. **Drafted:** Eastern Michigan, 2003 (24th round). **Signed by:** Bill Schudlich (Indians).

The A's picked up Goleski in the major league Rule 5 draft by sending cash to the Devil Rays for the No. 1 overall pick. They also added deceptive sidearmer Jay Marshall from the White Sox with their own choice, and Marshall could make the big league club as a situa-

tional lefthander. Oakland considered Goleski a candidate to get platoon at-bats as a corner outfielder before discovering he had aggravated a left wrist injury while taking batting practice two weeks after the season. He had surgery to repair ligament damage and wasn't expected to be ready for the start of spring training. Goleski was expected to go in the first three rounds in the 2003 draft, but his stock slipped after he broke his hand while breaking up a fight on Eastern Michigan's campus. The injury sapped his power and he fell to the Indians in the 24th round. A free swinger with plus raw power, Goleski hit 28 homers in low Class A in 2004. Poor pitch recognition and plate discipline doomed him in 2005, when he dropped to .212 with 17 homers. An extremely hard worker, he spent the offseason breaking down video of his swing and hours in the cage to make improvements in his approach. The biggest adjustment was finding much better balance at the plate. His patience and pitch recognition also improved significantly. An average runner, Goleski has above-average arm strength and takes good routes to balls in right field. To send Goleski and Marshall to the minors in 2007, Oakland first would have to slide them through waivers and then offer them back to their original clubs for half their $50,000 draft price.

| Year | Club (League) | Class | AVG | G | AB | R | H | 2B | 3B | HR | RBI | BB | SO | SB | OBP | SLG |
|------|---------------|-------|-----|---|----|---|---|----|----|----|-----|----|----|----|-----|-----|
| 2003 | Mahoning Valley (NYP) | A | .296 | 64 | 243 | 39 | 72 | 15 | 2 | 8 | 37 | 21 | 66 | 3 | .358 | .473 |
| 2004 | Lake County (SAL) | A | .295 | 130 | 505 | 83 | 149 | 22 | 5 | 28 | 104 | 55 | 100 | 6 | .370 | .525 |
| 2005 | Kinston (CL) | A | .212 | 122 | 458 | 59 | 97 | 27 | 0 | 17 | 67 | 39 | 134 | 6 | .276 | .382 |
| 2006 | Akron (EL) | AA | .296 | 87 | 324 | 48 | 96 | 24 | 0 | 17 | 63 | 36 | 87 | 4 | .370 | .528 |
| | Kinston (CL) | A | .331 | 38 | 121 | 28 | 40 | 7 | 0 | 10 | 43 | 25 | 30 | 2 | .441 | .636 |
| **MINOR LEAGUE TOTALS** | | | .275 | 441 | 1651 | 257 | 454 | 95 | 7 | 80 | 314 | 176 | 417 | 21 | .349 | .486 |

## 20 LANDON POWELL                                                                   C

**Born:** March 19, 1982. **B-T:** B-R. **Ht.:** 6-3. **Wt.:** 245. **Drafted:** South Carolina, 2004 (1st round). **Signed by:** Michael Holmes.

Powell has been on the radar since his sophomore year in high school. His high school and college track record are solid, but the same question that always has dogged him—what will his body look like as a pro?—continues to cloud his future. Powell has power from both sides of the plate, a cannon arm (a 70 on the 20-80 scouting scale) and hands as soft as butter. He's flexible, receives well and led California League catchers both with a .994 fielding percentage and by throwing out 52 percent of opposing basestealers. Playing every day in high Class A seemed to help Powell stay in shape, but he didn't handle the gap between the regular season (which he finished in Double-A) and the Arizona Fall League well. His weight ballooned again—one scout estimated Powell was as much as 40 pounds over his playing weight—and his well-below-average speed was exacerbated by a complete lack of agility. Several scouts said Powell struggled to get out of his crouch to field bunts. If he stays in shape, Powell could be an all-star. His track record argues against it. He'll head back to Double-A to open 2007.

| Year | Club (League) | Class | AVG | G | AB | R | H | 2B | 3B | HR | RBI | BB | SO | SB | OBP | SLG |
|------|---------------|-------|-----|---|----|---|---|----|----|----|-----|----|----|----|-----|-----|
| 2004 | Vancouver (NWL) | A | .237 | 38 | 135 | 24 | 32 | 6 | 1 | 3 | 19 | 26 | 22 | 0 | .362 | .363 |
| 2005 | Did not play—Injured | | | | | | | | | | | | | | | |
| 2006 | Midland (TL) | AA | .268 | 12 | 41 | 4 | 11 | 0 | 0 | 1 | 4 | 3 | 12 | 0 | .333 | .341 |
| | Stockton (Cal) | A | .264 | 90 | 326 | 44 | 86 | 12 | 0 | 15 | 47 | 43 | 77 | 0 | .350 | .439 |
| **MINOR LEAGUE TOTALS** | | | .257 | 140 | 502 | 72 | 129 | 18 | 1 | 19 | 70 | 72 | 111 | 0 | .352 | .410 |

## 21 JEFF BAISLEY                                                                    3B

**Born:** Dec. 19, 1982. **B-T:** R-R. **Ht.:** 6-3. **Wt.:** 210. **Drafted:** South Florida, 2005 (12th round). **Signed by:** Steve Barningham.

Weighed down by a stress fracture in his left foot as a junior in 2004, Baisley wasn't drafted and was just a 12th-rounder as a senior in 2005. He was the low Class A Midwest League's MVP as a 23-year-old while leading it in RBIs, runs and total bases. He wasn't promoted because the A's wanted Kane County to win and needed 2003 first-round pick Brian Snyder to get playing time in high Class A. Baisley will jump to Double-A in 2007 to see what he's made of. Scouts agree he's a sound defender at third base with good hands and footwork and an average arm. One of three brothers to play pro ball—older brother Brad was a second-round pick (Phillies) in 1998, while his twin Brian catches in the Yankees system—Baisley has good instincts and game savvy. His bat is the question. Scouts aren't sure he'll be able to catch up to power stuff in on his hands at higher levels, and some have him pegged as a minor league slugger. The A's will accelerate his timetable in 2007.

| Year | Club (League) | Class | AVG | G | AB | R | H | 2B | 3B | HR | RBI | BB | SO | SB | OBP | SLG |
|------|---------------|-------|-----|---|----|---|---|----|----|----|-----|----|----|----|-----|-----|
| 2005 | Vancouver (NWL) | A | .252 | 61 | 218 | 28 | 55 | 15 | 1 | 6 | 38 | 27 | 27 | 3 | .362 | .413 |
| 2006 | Kane County (MWL) | A | .298 | 124 | 466 | 86 | 139 | 35 | 1 | 22 | 110 | 62 | 86 | 6 | .382 | .519 |
| **MINOR LEAGUE TOTALS** | | | .284 | 185 | 684 | 114 | 194 | 50 | 2 | 28 | 148 | 89 | 113 | 9 | .375 | .485 |

## CRAIG ITALIANO

RHP

**Born:** July 22, 1986. **B-T:** R-R. **Ht.:** 6-3. **Wt.:** 195. **Drafted:** HS—Flower Mound, Texas, 2005 (2nd round). **Signed by:** Blake Davis.

A season ago, Italiano ranked ahead of his 2005 draft cohorts and was the top-ranked pitcher in the organization after Santiago Casilla—who was later found to be three years older than previously thought. He was a high school teammate of Twins infielder Paul Kelly at Flower Mound High and was committed to play at Texas Christian before the A's gave him a $725,500 signing bonus. He lasted just four starts in 2006, though, before his maximum-effort delivery and short arm action led to a labrum tear that required surgery. He has the system's best fastball when healthy, a power pitch that hit 98 mph in high school and has hit 96 repeatedly as a pro. His curveball also showed signs of being a plus, power breaking ball. Italiano was not ready to return to the mound by instructional league, and the A's won't know what his stuff looks like post-surgery until he takes the mound in spring training. He should return to low Class A once healthy.

| Year | Club (League) | Class | W | L | ERA | G | GS | CG | SV | IP | H | R | ER | HR | BB | SO | AVG |
|------|---------------|-------|---|---|-----|---|----|----|----|-----|----|----|----|----|----|----|-----|
| 2005 | Athletics (AZL) | R | 1 | 2 | 6.75 | 8 | 3 | 0 | 0 | 19 | 20 | 17 | 14 | 0 | 8 | 27 | .267 |
| 2006 | Kane County (MWL) | A | 0 | 1 | 3.50 | 4 | 4 | 0 | 0 | 18 | 18 | 12 | 7 | 1 | 9 | 23 | .261 |
| **MINOR LEAGUE TOTALS** | | | 1 | 3 | 5.15 | 12 | 7 | 0 | 0 | 37 | 38 | 29 | 21 | 1 | 17 | 50 | .264 |

## ANTHONY RECKER

C

**Born:** Aug. 29, 1983. **B-T:** R-R. **Ht.:** 6-3. **Wt.:** 230. **Drafted:** Alvernia (Pa.), 2005 (18th round). **Signed by:** Jeff Bittiger.

Recker was a star at Division II Alvernia (Pa.), becoming the first player drafted from the school since Wade Miller in 1998. Scouts consider Recker a favorite for his all-out approach and muscle-bound physique. He's perhaps the A's hardest worker and strongest player. Most important, he has tools. He has developed a lower set-up to his swing since college, improving his swing path. He's strong enough to drive the ball out of any park and has plus raw power, though he doesn't project to hit for a particularly high average. Defensively, Recker has an above-average arm and threw out 42 percent of basestealers in low Class A last season. His tools give him the profile for a backup catcher. Recker's biggest issue will be whether he can receive, block balls and handle pitching staffs up well enough to become a regular. Just three Midwest League catchers topped his 14 passed balls, and his 12 errors tied for the league's worst mark. He's headed to high Class A in 2007 to get more polish.

| Year | Club (League) | Class | AVG | G | AB | R | H | 2B | 3B | HR | RBI | BB | SO | SB | OBP | SLG |
|------|---------------|-------|-----|---|----|---|---|----|----|----|-----|----|----|----|-----|-----|
| 2005 | Vancouver (NWL) | A | .233 | 43 | 150 | 16 | 35 | 8 | 0 | 5 | 18 | 16 | 40 | 0 | .315 | .387 |
| 2006 | Kane County (MWL) | A | .287 | 109 | 407 | 52 | 117 | 24 | 3 | 14 | 57 | 42 | 115 | 5 | .358 | .464 |
| **MINOR LEAGUE TOTALS** | | | .273 | 152 | 557 | 68 | 152 | 32 | 3 | 19 | 75 | 58 | 155 | 5 | .346 | .443 |

## MIKE MITCHELL

RHP

**Born:** Oct. 27, 1981. **B-T:** R-R. **Ht.:** 6-2. **Wt.:** 185. **Drafted:** St. Charles (Mo.) CC, 2003 (35th round). **Signed by:** Jim Pransky.

Mitchell didn't sign when the Indians drafted him in 2002 (14th round), returned to school and hadn't made much of a splash with the Athletics since they signed him—until last season. He needed Tommy John surgery late in 2003, and 2006 was his first full, healthy season. He emerged as the closer at Stockton after Marcus McBeth's promotion, then earned his own promotions, first to Triple-A and then more reasonably to Double-A. He also did a nice job in the Arizona Fall League. Mitchell attacks hitters, starting with a fastball that sits in the low 90s with life down in the zone. His most trusted secondary pitch is a solid-average slider, which he also throws hard, at times in the mid-80s. He made progress with his changeup in the AFL, though it's still his third pitch. Mitchell doesn't have a great feel for pitching but generally throws strikes and challenges hitters. Mitchell will start 2007 in the minors—most likely in Double-A—but could earn a big league shot if he pitches like he did in 2006.

| Year | Club (League) | Class | W | L | ERA | G | GS | CG | SV | IP | H | R | ER | HR | BB | SO | AVG |
|------|---------------|-------|---|---|-----|---|----|----|----|-----|----|----|----|----|----|----|-----|
| 2004 | Athletics (AZL) | R | 1 | 0 | 1.35 | 7 | 0 | 0 | 1 | 13 | 14 | 4 | 2 | 0 | 1 | 7 | .275 |
| 2005 | Vancouver (NWL) | A | 0 | 0 | 0.00 | 7 | 0 | 0 | 5 | 9 | 4 | 1 | 0 | 0 | 4 | 6 | .118 |
| | Kane County (MWL) | A | 0 | 0 | 3.24 | 19 | 0 | 0 | 3 | 25 | 24 | 11 | 9 | 2 | 11 | 19 | .258 |
| 2006 | Stockton (Cal) | A | 1 | 1 | 2.85 | 33 | 0 | 0 | 18 | 41 | 37 | 14 | 13 | 0 | 14 | 41 | .240 |
| | Sacramento (PCL) | AAA | 0 | 0 | 4.50 | 5 | 0 | 0 | 0 | 6 | 5 | 3 | 3 | 1 | 1 | 3 | .227 |
| | Midland (TL) | AA | 2 | 1 | 3.60 | 14 | 0 | 0 | 0 | 20 | 24 | 11 | 8 | 1 | 11 | 15 | .316 |
| **MINOR LEAGUE TOTALS** | | | 4 | 2 | 2.75 | 85 | 0 | 0 | 27 | 115 | 108 | 44 | 35 | 4 | 42 | 91 | .251 |

## 25 JASON RAY
RHP

**Born:** July 14, 1984. **B-T:** R-R. **Ht.:** 5-11. **Wt.:** 195. **Drafted:** Azusa Pacific (Calif.), 2005 (8th round). **Signed by:** Randy Johnson.

The A's decided to give Ray a chance to start in his first full pro season, hoping they might have another Rich Harden on their hands—a short, hard-throwing starter. Instead, they found out Ray is not a starting pitcher. His stuff didn't hold through more than three innings, and the A's will concentrate on honing his work habits, repertoire and approach to that of a reliever. Ray has big stuff, and his high overhand delivery (a leftover of his days as a junior college outfielder) creates natural deception. He has one of the system's hardest fastballs, sitting at 92-94 mph and touching 95. Secondary stuff has been a problem for Ray—he was moved to the rotation to hone it—and in that regard, the move helped him because his curveball improved over the course of the season. He made more strides with it in instructional league. It's still inconsistent, however, and he also gets in trouble when he elevates his fastball, which happened a lot in high Class A. Ray likely will return to high Class A to start 2007, this time in the bullpen, and he could move quickly as long as he throws strikes.

| Year | Club (League) | Class | W | L | ERA | G | GS | CG | SV | IP | H | R | ER | HR | BB | SO | AVG |
|------|---------------|-------|---|---|-----|---|----|----|----|-----|-----|----|----|----|----|-----|------|
| 2005 | Vancouver (NWL) | A | 0 | 1 | 2.12 | 20 | 0 | 0 | 0 | 30 | 17 | 8 | 7 | 1 | 23 | 56 | .163 |
| 2006 | Kane County (MWL) | A | 6 | 1 | 3.02 | 13 | 13 | 2 | 0 | 66 | 48 | 29 | 22 | 1 | 35 | 68 | .201 |
| | Stockton (Cal) | A | 5 | 5 | 4.95 | 18 | 7 | 0 | 0 | 60 | 59 | 36 | 33 | 9 | 33 | 48 | .266 |
| **MINOR LEAGUE TOTALS** | | | 11 | 7 | 3.59 | 51 | 20 | 2 | 0 | 155 | 124 | 73 | 62 | 11 | 91 | 172 | .219 |

## 26 RYAN WEBB
RHP

**Born:** Feb. 5, 1986. **B-T:** R-R. **Ht.:** 6-6. **Wt.:** 190. **Drafted:** HS—Palm Harbor, Fla., 2004 (4th round). **Signed by:** Steve Barningham.

Despite two mediocre seasons, the A's consider Webb in the same group as the trio of high school pitchers they selected high in the 2005 draft and just a shade behind 2006 top pick Trevor Cahill. The A's are modifying their development program for high school pitchers like Webb and realize they have to handle them differently from the college pitchers they're used to drafting. Webb has adjustments to make as he fills out his generous 6-foot-6 frame. He's a sinker/slider pitcher who has good sinking life to his fastball. While his velocity and the quality of his stuff still fluctuates, at times both pitches are above-average, with his 89-91 mph fastball touching 93 and his slider showing occasional two-plane break. He made more progress with his changeup in 2006 than he had previously. He's much too hittable at this stage, though, for the A's to count on him as a big league starter. While he doesn't give up too many walks, Webb falls behind too often and gets torched in those situations. He'll go back to high Class A to see if he can miss more bats.

| Year | Club (League) | Class | W | L | ERA | G | GS | CG | SV | IP | H | R | ER | HR | BB | SO | AVG |
|------|---------------|-------|---|---|-----|---|----|----|----|-----|-----|-----|-----|----|----|-----|------|
| 2004 | Athletics (AZL) | R | 1 | 1 | 4.87 | 8 | 7 | 0 | 0 | 20 | 18 | 11 | 11 | 2 | 1 | 23 | .228 |
| 2005 | Kane County (MWL) | A | 5 | 11 | 4.76 | 24 | 23 | 0 | 0 | 129 | 139 | 82 | 68 | 16 | 41 | 84 | .280 |
| 2006 | Stockton (Cal) | A | 8 | 9 | 5.28 | 23 | 23 | 0 | 0 | 118 | 160 | 75 | 69 | 9 | 37 | 96 | .332 |
| **MINOR LEAGUE TOTALS** | | | 14 | 21 | 5.00 | 55 | 53 | 0 | 0 | 267 | 317 | 168 | 148 | 27 | 79 | 203 | .300 |

## 27 BEN JUKICH
LHP

**Born:** Oct. 17, 1982. **B-T:** L-L. **Ht.:** 6-4. **Wt.:** 190. **Drafted:** Dakota Wesleyan (S.D.), 2006 (13th round). **Signed by:** Kevin Mello.

Jukich's upside appears to be that of a lefthanded reliever, but with what he has accomplished already, perhaps expectations should be higher. Jukich graduated from a Minnesota high school in 2001 and flunked out of junior college the next year. He was close to joining the Army when one of his former teammates recommended him to Jeremy Jorgensen, the baseball coach at McCook (Neb.) Community College. Jukich made the most of his second chance, building up arm strength and staying eligible to pitch. He transferred after two seasons to Dakota Wesleyan in South Dakota, where he led the NAIA in strikeouts (144) and strikeouts per nine innings (13.7). The first player in school and Great Plains Athletic Conference history to be drafted, he signed for $20,000. Despite his inexperience, Jukich has a natural feel for pitching. He throws strikes with an active upper 80s fastball and a plus breaking ball. It's not a true 12-to-6 curve because of his lower arm angle, but it has depth and he can bury it or throw it for strikes. Jukich needs refinement with his changeup and is older than the typical draftee, but the A's intend to move him quickly. His success at Kane County likely means he's headed for high Class A to start 2007.

| Year | Club (League) | Class | W | L | ERA | G | GS | CG | SV | IP | H | R | ER | HR | BB | SO | AVG |
|------|---------------|-------|---|---|-----|---|----|----|----|-----|-----|----|----|----|----|-----|------|
| 2006 | Vancouver (NWL) | A | 0 | 0 | 3.24 | 3 | 1 | 0 | 2 | 8 | 9 | 3 | 3 | 0 | 5 | 10 | .273 |
| | Kane County (MWL) | A | 3 | 2 | 2.38 | 13 | 4 | 0 | 0 | 42 | 41 | 15 | 11 | 1 | 25 | 40 | .261 |
| **MINOR LEAGUE TOTALS** | | | 3 | 2 | 2.52 | 16 | 5 | 0 | 2 | 50 | 50 | 18 | 14 | 1 | 30 | 50 | .263 |

## 28 ANDREW BAILEY RHP

**Born:** May 31, 1984. **B-T:** R-R. **Ht.:** 6-3. **Wt.:** 220. **Drafted:** Wagner, 2006 (6th round). **Signed by:** Jeff Bittiger.

Bailey was another strong arm with an atypical background whom the A's added in the 2006. He's a raw Northeasterner who was having a fine college career, racking up impressive strikeout totals, when he had Tommy John surgery in May 2005. The A's were scouting him and might have drafted him in 2005 if they had been able to get him crosschecked prior to the surgery. Bailey returned to the mound in time to build momentum for the 2006 draft and recover his fastball velocity. Signed for $135,000, he has been able to overpower righthanders with his fastball so far. His heater has life, particularly with its arm-side run, and he isn't afraid to pitch inside with it. The pitch sits in the low 90s and touches 93 mph, and he uses it aggressively. His ERA would have ranked second in the Northwest League if he had enough innings to qualify. His curveball and changeup came and went in his pro debut, and maintaining consistency with those pitches—difficult to project because of his less-than-smooth delivery and mechanics—will be the key to whether he can remain in a rotation. Bailey will have a chance to earn a spot in the high Class A rotation out of spring training.

| Year | Club (League) | Class | W | L | ERA | G | GS | CG | SV | IP | H | R | ER | HR | BB | SO | AVG |
|---|---|---|---|---|---|---|---|---|---|---|---|---|---|---|---|---|---|
| 2006 | Vancouver (NWL) | A | 2 | 5 | 2.02 | 13 | 10 | 0 | 0 | 58 | 39 | 20 | 13 | 2 | 20 | 53 | .187 |
| **MINOR LEAGUE TOTALS** | | | 2 | 5 | 2.02 | 13 | 10 | 0 | 0 | 58 | 39 | 20 | 13 | 2 | 20 | 53 | .187 |

## 29 CHAD LEE RHP

**Born:** Dec. 20, 1985. **B-T:** R-R. **Ht.:** 6-4. **Wt.:** 200. **Drafted:** Barton County (Kan.) CC, 2006. **Signed by:** Jeremy Scheid.

After the Athletics spent years drafting polished college pitchers, followed by projectable high school arms, Lee stands out because he's neither. He was the sixth junior college player drafted in 2006, and he had drawn attention for the 2005 draft before he tore the anterior cruciate ligament in his left knee during a rundown drill in fall practice. He came back in April 2005 but didn't return to his top form until spring 2006, when he unleashed a 91-95 mph fastball and an 80-81 mph power curve. He shortened his arm action and threw more strikes with his improved health and mechanics. Lee felt forearm pain and was pitching out of the bullpen late in the spring, so that knocked him down the draft a bit, and the A's were happy to get him in the fourth round. He had less polish than they expected in terms of fundamentals such as holding runners, fielding his position and pitch selection, and he didn't touch 95 in his debut. He'll need time to learn the basics and could end up in the bullpen eventually, yet the A's were happy to get a potential power arm for a relative bargain price of $245,000. Lee will head to low Class A for his first full season.

| Year | Club (League) | Class | W | L | ERA | G | GS | CG | SV | IP | H | R | ER | HR | BB | SO | AVG |
|---|---|---|---|---|---|---|---|---|---|---|---|---|---|---|---|---|---|
| 2006 | Vancouver (NWL) | A | 3 | 2 | 4.29 | 12 | 10 | 0 | 0 | 50 | 50 | 28 | 24 | 5 | 15 | 31 | .254 |
| **MINOR LEAGUE TOTALS** | | | 3 | 2 | 4.29 | 12 | 10 | 0 | 0 | 50 | 50 | 28 | 24 | 5 | 15 | 31 | .254 |

## 30 LARRY COBB OF/2B

**Born:** July 10, 1985. **B-T:** R-R. **Ht.:** 5-9. **Wt.:** 175. **Drafted:** College of Charleston, 2006 (27th round). **Signed by:** Neil Avent.

David Eckstein has won two World Series championships as a starting shortstop, and teams still are trying to find their own models of the scrappy sparkplug. The A's candidate is Cobb, who won MVP honors both at Vancouver and in instructional league in his debut season. He's a bit bigger than Eckstein but earns the comparison because of his ability to grind quality efforts day after day, his one above-average tool (speed, though Cobb is faster than Eckstein) and his defensive versatility. Cobb was at Manatee (Fla.) Junior College before going to College of Charleston for a season, and the A's scouted him along with Jermaine Mitchell in the Southern Conference tournament. They correctly surmised he would sign even if he wasn't picked on the draft's first day and could be a true steal, especially if his experiment at second base takes. Cobb made adjustments with the glove, and the A's will give him reps there during spring training and in the regular season in low Class A. He's a quality defender in center field. Adding infield play to his repertoire would be key for Cobb, who also has the A's dreaming of Chone Figgins due to his versatility, size and speed.

| Year | Club (League) | Class | AVG | G | AB | R | H | 2B | 3B | HR | RBI | BB | SO | SB | OBP | SLG |
|---|---|---|---|---|---|---|---|---|---|---|---|---|---|---|---|---|
| 2006 | Sacramento (PCL) | AAA | .000 | 2 | 4 | 0 | 0 | 0 | 0 | 0 | 0 | 0 | 1 | 0 | .000 | .000 |
| | Vancouver (NWL) | A | .292 | 63 | 253 | 42 | 74 | 14 | 2 | 1 | 14 | 27 | 49 | 9 | .358 | .375 |
| **MINOR LEAGUE TOTALS** | | | .288 | 65 | 257 | 42 | 74 | 14 | 2 | 1 | 14 | 27 | 50 | 9 | .353 | .370 |

# PHILADELPHIA
# PHILLIES
## BY CHRIS KLINE

After dealing Bobby Abreu and Cory Lidle to the Yankees at the trade deadline, the Phillies appeared to be turning the page and starting to rebuild. But with Abreu gone, the clubhouse suddenly came together and homegrown talents **Ryan Howard**, Chase Utley, Jimmy Rollins and Cole Hamels led an improbable run at the wild card.

Though Philadelphia fell three games short of the Dodgers for the wild card, the Phillies served notice that they will be legitimate contenders in the National League East in 2007. Howard set a club record with 58 homers and won the league MVP award. Utley set a franchise record for second basemen with 32 homers and scored an NL-best 131 runs, four ahead of Rollins, who hit a career-high 25 homers. Hamels went 7-4, 2.60 over the final two months, which may be the first step in establishing himself as one of the game's top southpaws.

Furthermore, the Phillies re-energized the fan base in a city known to have more brotherly love for the NFL's Eagles or even the NHL's Flyers. Now the next task is to end a 13-year postseason drought.

To do that, Philadelphia will rely heavily on its homegrown core, which also includes Pat Burrell and Brett Myers. The farm system may make a couple of new contributions as well. Carlos Ruiz has flown under the radar during his eight-year pro career but could be Mike Lieberthal's successor at catcher. Outfielder Michael Bourn, lefthander J.A. Happ and righties Joe Bisenius and Zach Segovia probably will begin the season in the minors but are close to being ready if needed. The Phillies also had high hopes for

ED WOLFSTEIN

righthander Scott Mathieson—who floundered in his 2006 big league debut—but he'll miss most or all of 2007 after having Tommy John surgery.

Though the system has churned out Howard, Utley and Hamels in recent years, it has lacked depth. As a result, general manager Pat Gillick had assistant GM Mike Arbuckle get more involved in the draft. The club's scouting director from 1993-2001, Arbuckle oversaw drafts that included Scott Rolen, Adam Eaton, Rollins, Randy Wolf, Burrell, Ryan Madson, Myers, Utley and Howard.

In 2006 the Phillies kicked off their draft with a pair of intriguing picks who rank second and third on this prospect list. They gambled the 18th choice on mercurial righthander Kyle Drabek, who had one of the best arms but also one of the most questionable makeups available. In the supplemental first round they grabbed sweet-swinging shortstop Adrian Cardenas, Baseball America's High School Player of the Year.

Philadelphia's minor league affiliates combined for a .526 winning percentage, eighth-best in baseball, highlighted by low Class A Lakewood. The BlueClaws went 84-55 during the regular season and won the South Atlantic League playoffs behind a rotation led by the organization's top prospect, righthander Carlos Carrasco, and lefties Josh Outman and Matt Maloney.

## TOP 30 PROSPECTS

1. Carlos Carrasco, rhp
2. Kyle Drabek, rhp
3. Adrian Cardenas, ss
4. Edgar Garcia, rhp
5. Scott Mathieson, rhp
6. Josh Outman, lhp
7. Michael Bourn, of
8. J.A. Happ, lhp
9. Matt Maloney, lhp
10. Greg Golson, of
11. D'Arby Myers, of
12. Mike Costanzo, 3b
13. Carlos Ruiz, c
14. Zach Segovia, rhp
15. Kyle Kendrick, rhp
16. Joe Bisenius, rhp
17. Drew Carpenter, rhp
18. Brad Harman, ss
19. Lou Marson, c
20. C.J. Henry, ss
21. Welinson Baez, 3b
22. Dan Brauer, lhp
23. Pat Overholt, rhp
24. Jason Jaramillo, c
25. Jim Ed Warden, rhp
26. Jeremy Slayden, of
27. Jason Donald, ss
28. Heitor Correa, rhp
29. Alfredo Simon, rhp
30. Matt Smith, lhp

# ORGANIZATION OVERVIEW

**General manager:** Pat Gillick. **Farm director:** Steve Noworyta. **Scouting director:** Marti Wolever.

## 2006 PERFORMANCE

| Class | Team | League | W | L | PCT | Finish* | Manager | Affiliated |
|-------|------|--------|---|---|-----|---------|---------|-----------|
| Majors | Philadelphia | National | 85 | 77 | .525 | 4th (16) | Charlie Manuel | — |
| Triple-A | #Scranton/W-B Red Barons | International | 84 | 58 | .592 | 1st (14) | John Russell | 1989 |
| Double-A | Reading Phillies | Eastern | 71 | 69 | .507 | 5th (12) | P.J. Forbes | 1967 |
| High A | Clearwater Threshers | Florida State | 67 | 72 | .482 | 9th (12) | Greg Legg | 1985 |
| Low A | Lakewood BlueClaws | South Atlantic | 84 | 55 | .604 | +2nd (16) | Dave Huppert | 2001 |
| Short-season | †Batavia Muckdogs | New York-Penn | 35 | 38 | .479 | 10th (14) | Steve Roadcap | 1988 |
| Rookie | GCL Phillies | Gulf Coast | 18 | 31 | .367 | 12th (13) | Jim Morrison | 1999 |
| **OVERALL 2006 MINOR LEAGUE RECORD** | | | 359 | 323 | .526 | 8th (30) | | |

*Finish in overall standings (No. of teams in league). +League champion. #Affiliate will be in Ottawa (International) in 2007.
†Affiliate will be in Williamsport (New York-Penn) in 2007.

## ORGANIZATION LEADERS

### BATTING
| | | |
|---|---|---|
| AVG | Florence, Branden, Clearwater/Reading | .324 |
| R | Burgamy, Brian, Clearwater/Reading | 112 |
| H | Florence, Branden, Clearwater/Reading | 162 |
| 2B | Slayden, Jeremy, Lakewood | 44 |
| 3B | Bourn, Michael, Reading/Scranton/WB | 13 |
| HR | Burnham, Gary, Reading/Scranton/WB | 17 |
| RBI | Florence, Branden, Clearwater/Reading | 86 |
| BB | Burgamy, Brian, Clearwater/Reading | 95 |
| SO | Golson, Greg, Lakewood/Clearwater | 160 |
| SB | Bourn, Michael, Reading/Scranton/WB | 45 |
| OBP | Leon, Carlos, Reading/Scranton/WB | .394 |
| SLG | Slayden, Jeremy, Lakewood | .510 |
| XBH | Slayden, Jeremy, Lakewood | 57 |

### PITCHING
| | | |
|---|---|---|
| W | Segovia, Zach, Clearwater/Reading | 17 |
| L | Gonzalez, Gio, Reading | 12 |
| ERA | Maloney, Matt, Lakewood | 2.03 |
| G | Bisenius, Joseph, Clearwater/Reading | 52 |
| SV | Key, Chris, Clearwater/Reading | 21 |
| IP | Kendrick, Kyle, Lakewood/Clearwater | 182 |
| BB | Gonzalez, Gio, Reading | 84 |
| SO | Maloney, Matt, Lakewood | 180 |
| AVG | Carrasco, Carlos, Lakewood | .182 |

## BEST TOOLS

| | |
|---|---|
| Best Hitter for Average | Adrian Cardenas |
| Best Power Hitter | Mike Costanzo |
| Best Strike-Zone Discipline | Carlos Ruiz |
| Fastest Baserunner | Greg Golson |
| Best Athlete | Greg Golson |
| Best Fastball | Carlos Carrasco |
| Best Curveball | Kyle Drabek |
| Best Slider | Josh Outman |
| Best Changeup | J.A. Happ |
| Best Control | J.A. Happ |
| Best Defensive Catcher | Tim Gradoville |
| Best Defensive Infielder | Freddy Galvez |
| Best Infield Arm | Welinson Baez |
| Best Defensive Outfielder | Greg Golson |
| Best Outfield Arm | Greg Golson |

## PROJECTED 2010 LINEUP

| | |
|---|---|
| Catcher | Carlos Ruiz |
| First Base | Ryan Howard |
| Second Base | Chase Utley |
| Third Base | Mike Costanzo |
| Shortstop | Jimmy Rollins |
| Left Field | Pat Burrell |
| Center Field | Aaron Rowand |
| Right Field | Adrian Cardenas |

| | |
|---|---|
| No. 1 Starter | Cole Hamels |
| No. 2 Starter | Brett Myers |
| No. 3 Starter | Carlos Carrasco |
| No. 4 Starter | Kyle Drabek |
| No. 5 Starter | Freddy Garcia |
| Closer | Scott Mathieson |

## LAST YEAR'S TOP 20 PROSPECTS

1. Cole Hamels, lhp
2. Gio Gonzalez, lhp
3. Greg Golson, of
4. Michael Bourn, of
5. Scott Mathieson, rhp
6. Daniel Haigwood, lhp
7. Welinson Baez, 3b/ss
8. Mike Costanzo, 3b
9. Brad Harman, ss/2b
10. Jason Jaramillo, c
11. Tim Moss, 2b
12. Edgar Garcia, rhp
13. Chris Roberson, of
14. Shane Victorino, of
15. Eude Brito, lhp
16. Carlos Carrasco, rhp
17. Michael Durant, 1b
18. Carlos Ruiz, c
19. J.A. Happ, lhp
20. Jake Blalock, of

## TOP PROSPECTS OF THE DECADE

| Year | Player, Pos. | 2006 Org. |
|------|--------------|-----------|
| 1997 | Scott Rolen, 3b | Cardinals |
| 1998 | Ryan Brannan, rhp | Out of baseball |
| 1999 | Pat Burrell, 1b | Phillies |
| 2000 | Pat Burrell, 1b/of | Phillies |
| 2001 | Jimmy Rollins, ss | Phillies |
| 2002 | Marlon Byrd, of | Nationals |
| 2003 | Gavin Floyd, rhp | Phillies |
| 2004 | Cole Hamels, lhp | Phillies |
| 2005 | Ryan Howard, 1b | Phillies |
| 2006 | Cole Hamels, lhp | Phillies |

## TOP DRAFT PICKS OF THE DECADE

| Year | Player, Pos. | 2006 Org. |
|------|--------------|-----------|
| 1997 | *J.D. Drew, of | Dodgers |
| 1998 | Pat Burrell, 1b | Phillies |
| 1999 | Brett Myers, rhp | Phillies |
| 2000 | Chase Utley, 2b | Phillies |
| 2001 | Gavin Floyd, rhp | Phillies |
| 2002 | Cole Hamels, lhp | Phillies |
| 2003 | Tim Moss, 2b (3rd round) | Phillies |
| 2004 | Greg Golson, of | Phillies |
| 2005 | Mike Costanzo, 3b (2nd round) | Phillies |
| 2006 | Kyle Drabek, rhp | Phillies |

*Did not sign.

## LARGEST BONUSES IN CLUB HISTORY

| | |
|---|---|
| Gavin Floyd, 2001 | $4,200,000 |
| Pat Burrell, 1998 | $3,150,000 |
| Brett Myers, 1999 | $2,050,000 |
| Cole Hamels, 2002 | $2,000,000 |
| Chase Utley, 2000 | $1,780,000 |

# MINOR LEAGUE DEPTH CHART

## Philadelphia Phillies

**Impact: C.** The only impact the farm system will have in the short term are arms, but the top two arms are at least a year or two away. The 2006 draft brought in several potential impact position players.

**Depth: C.** The Phillies were so short on position talent at first base last year that they found former Phillie Gary Burnham playing in a semi-pro league and signed him. That sums up the depth overall of position players in the system, though it's not as thin as it used to be.

**Sleeper:** Michael Zagurski, lhp. Assistant GM Mike Arbuckle and the Phillies staff refer to Zagurski as "Mini-Me," as his body—thick through the middle like a barrel—resembles Arbuckle's. Zagurski's fastball was up to 92 mph and he has a plus slider out of the bullpen.

*Numbers in parentheses indicate prospect rankings.*

| LF | CF | RF |
|---|---|---|
| Jeremy Slayden (26) | Michael Bourn (7) | Dominic Brown |
| Chris Roberson | Greg Golson (10) | T.J. Warren |
| | D'Arby Myers (11) | |
| | Quintin Berry | |

| 3B | SS | 2B | 1B |
|---|---|---|---|
| Mike Costanzo (12) | Adrian Cardenas (3) | Tim Moss | Charlie Yarborough |
| Welinson Baez (21) | Brad Harman (18) | Avelino Asprilla | Michael Durant |
| | C.J. Henry (20) | | |
| | Jason Donald (27) | | |

**C**
Carlos Ruiz (13)
Lou Marson (19)
Jason Jaramillo (24)
Jesus Sanchez
Tim Gradoville

### RHP

| Starters | Relievers |
|---|---|
| Carlos Carrasco (1) | Joe Bisenius (16) |
| Kyle Drabek (2) | Pat Overholt (23) |
| Edgar Garcia (4) | Jim Ed Warden (25) |
| Scott Mathieson (5) | Brett Harker |
| Zach Segovia (14) | Nick Evangelista |
| Kyle Kendrick (15) | Sam Walls |
| Drew Carpenter (17) | Carlos Monasterios |
| Heitor Correa (28) | Yen-Feng Lin |
| Alfredo Simon (29) | |
| Ben Pfinsgraff | |
| Julio De La Cruz | |
| Justin Germano | |
| Michael Dubee | |
| Scott Mitchinson | |

### LHP

| Starters | Relievers |
|---|---|
| Josh Outman (6) | Matt Smith (30) |
| J.A. Happ (8) | Michael Zagurski |
| Matt Maloney (9) | Eude Brito |
| Dan Brauer (22) | Chris Key |

## 2006

**Best Pro Debut:** After winning BA's High School Player of the Year award, SS Adrian Cardenas (1) encored by hitting .318 with 13 steals to make the Rookie-level Gulf Coast League all-star team. OF D'Arby Myers (4) joined him on the squad after batting .313 with 11 swipes. RHP Ben Pfinsgraff (22), who competes very well with average stuff, had a 1.55 ERA and a 69-18 K-BB ratio in 64 innings.

**Best Athlete:** OF Dominic Brown (20) was recruited by Miami as a wide receiver, while OF Darin McDonald (12) could have played cornerback at Idaho State. Myers and OF T.J. Warren (8) are also quality athletes. RHP Kyle Drabek (1) could have gone in the second or third round as a shortstop.

**Best Pure Hitter:** Cardenas outperformed high school teammate Chris Marrero (a Nationals first-round pick) as a senior this spring. If he winds up at second base as many scouts suspect, Cardenas could develop along the lines of Chase Utley.

**Best Raw Power:** 1B Charlie Yarbrough (7), who stands 6-foot-6 and 250 pounds, or OF Gus Milner (14), who's a mere 6-foot-5 and 245.

**Fastest Runner:** The Phillies like to draft speed, and 2006 was no exception. OF Quintin Berry (5) has gone from the left side of home plate to first base in 3.9 seconds. Brown ran a 4.57-second 40-yard dash. 2B/SS Zach Penprase (13) tied for the NCAA Division I stolen-base crown with 56 in 63 attempts. Myers and Warren are also plus runners.

**Best Defensive Player:** Philadelphia sees Jason Donald (3) becoming a solid big league shortstop. He has a strong arm, and his hands and instincts help compensate for his ordinary range.

**Best Fastball:** Drabek had a rough debut with a 7.11 ERA in the GCL, but he has a 94-95 mph fastball that peaks at 97.

**Best Breaking Ball:** The Phillies thought Drabek's spike curveball was the best curve in the draft. It's a tremendous pitch, though he relies on it too much at times rather than pitching off his fastball.

**Most Intriguing Background:** Drabek's father Doug won a National League Cy Young Award. RHP Michael Dubee's (18) dad Rich is Philadelphia's pitching coach. McDonald's brothers Darnell and Donzell have gotten cups of coffee in the majors. OF Riley Cooper (15) is playing wide receiver at Florida, while RHP Will Savage played quarterback at the JC of the Canyons (Calif.).

**Closest To The Majors:** RHP Drew Carpenter (2) and LHP Dan Brauer (6) both are command specialists with solid stuff. Brauer has made a remarkably rapid recovery from labrum surgery that caused him to miss the entire 2005 season.

**Best Late-Round Pick:** Dubee and RHP Jarod Freeman (11) both have low-90s fastballs and promising curves. Dubee also has the feel for pitching to be expected from a pitching coach's son.

**The One Who Got Away:** Cooper has raw power to go with his 6.29-second speed in the 60-yard dash, but it was impossible to lure him away from football. Ultraprojectable Kyle Gibson (36) could blossom into a first-round pick after three years at Missouri.

**Assessment:** There are well-documented concerns about Drabek's makeup, but his talent made him an easy gamble to take with the No. 18 choice. The last time the Phillies got that much upside in that area of the first round, they shook off medical concerns and took Cole Hamels with the 17th pick in 2002, and that has worked out well.

## 2005    BUDGET: $1.8 million

3B Mike Costanzo (2) and LHPs Matt Maloney (3) and Josh Outman (10) all had solid first full seasons. The Phillies didn't have a first-rounder (though the Yankees took SS C.J. Henry with their pick and traded him to Philadelphia last year). **GRADE: C**

## 2004    BUDGET: $3.4 million

Spectacularly athletic OF Greg Golson (1) still is trying to figure out how to hit, so LHP J.A. Happ (3) may be the prize of this crop. RHP Andy Baldwin (5) was used in the Jamie Moyer trade last summer. **GRADE: C**

## 2003    BUDGET: $1.2 million

Philadelphia didn't pick until the third round, and Tim Moss (3) has stagnated. OF Michael Bourn (4) and RHP Kyle Kendrick (7) may contribute, but the best player selected was RHP Greg Reynolds (41), who became the No. 2 choice in 2006. **GRADE: D**

*Draft analysis by **Jim Callis**. Numbers in parentheses indicate draft rounds. Budgets are bonuses in first 10 rounds.*

# CARLOS
# CARRASCO

RHP

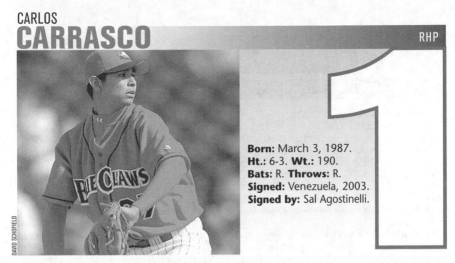

DAVID SCHOFIELD

**Born:** March 3, 1987.
**Ht.:** 6-3. **Wt.:** 190.
**Bats:** R. **Throws:** R.
**Signed:** Venezuela, 2003.
**Signed by:** Sal Agostinelli.

Signed for $300,000 out of Venezuela in 2003, Carrasco had a successful debut the following year in the Rookie-level Gulf Coast League. The Phillies take full blame for rushing him in 2005, pushing him to low Class A Lakewood at age 18 in a move that backfired when he posted a 7.04 ERA. He turned a corner in instructional league after the season, setting the stage for a return to Lakewood in 2006, when he blossomed into a legitimate frontline starter prospect. He ranked third in the system in wins and ERA and represented the organization in the Futures Game. He was a major part of Lakewood's South Atlantic League title run, though the Phillies were disappointed with the way Carrasco handled himself when he struggled. Since making strides in grasping English this season, Carrasco has taken to instruction more easily.

Carrasco has two plus pitches in his arsenal, starting with a consistent 90-92 mph fastball. His fastball has outstanding late life and finish, and he commands it to all four quadrants of the strike zone. He can dial it up to 93-94 when he needs to, and he could add more velocity as he matures physically. He complements his heater with one of the best changeups in the system. His changeup features excellent late fade and depth, and he'll throw it in any count. The biggest improvement Carrasco made in 2006 was with his curveball. He commanded his 71-77 mph curve better than he ever had, showing good tilt and late bite. He repeats his delivery and fields his position well. Though he didn't have an at-bat with the BlueClaws, Philadelphia raves about the pride Carrasco takes in the offensive side of the game. He's a good bunter and shows aptitude in understanding game situations from a hitter's perspective.

Carrasco has a simple, compact delivery, but he can rush it at times, leading to erratic command. He arguably commands his changeup better than any of his pitches, but slows down his arm action slightly when he throws it, tipping off hitters. While his curveball is his third-best pitch, he falls in love with it at times. He needs to improve its consistency and also throw it for strikes more often, because better hitters will be less likely to chase it off the plate. Carrasco needs to have a better overall rhythm on the mound. He'll speed up when things are going his way, and slow down to a snail's pace when he's scuffling.

The Phillies already tried to jump Carrasco once, and they won't make the same mistake again. Though he's shown much more maturity, there's really no reason to rush him. While other arms from Lakewood's championship staff might leap past him, Carrasco will start 2007 in high Class A Clearwater and won't see Double-A Reading before midseason, putting him on pace to arrive in Philadelphia at some point in 2009.

| Year | Club (League) | Class | W | L | ERA | G | GS | CG | SV | IP | H | R | ER | HR | BB | SO | AVG |
|------|---------------|-------|---|---|-----|---|----|----|----|----|---|---|----|----|----|----|-----|
| 2004 | Phillies (GCL) | R | 5 | 4 | 3.56 | 11 | 8 | 0 | 0 | 48 | 53 | 23 | 19 | 2 | 15 | 34 | .276 |
| 2005 | Lakewood (SAL) | A | 1 | 7 | 7.04 | 13 | 13 | 1 | 0 | 63 | 78 | 50 | 49 | 11 | 28 | 46 | .302 |
| | Batavia (NYP) | A | 0 | 3 | 13.50 | 4 | 4 | 0 | 0 | 15 | 29 | 25 | 23 | 8 | 5 | 12 | .392 |
| | Phillies (GCL) | R | 0 | 0 | 1.80 | 2 | 2 | 0 | 0 | 5 | 3 | 1 | 1 | 0 | 1 | 2 | .176 |
| 2006 | Lakewood (SAL) | A | 12 | 6 | 2.26 | 26 | 26 | 2 | 0 | 159 | 103 | 50 | 40 | 6 | 65 | 159 | .182 |
| **MINOR LEAGUE TOTALS** | | | 18 | 20 | 4.09 | 56 | 53 | 3 | 0 | 290 | 266 | 149 | 132 | 27 | 114 | 253 | .240 |

## 2 KYLE DRABEK

RHP

**Born:** Dec. 8, 1987. **B-T:** R-R. **Ht.:** 6-1. **Wt.:** 180. **Drafted:** HS—The Woodlands, 2006 (1st round). **Signed by:** Steve Cohen.

Many clubs thought Drabek had the best pure stuff in the 2006 draft, but huge makeup concerns scared teams away from the son of former Cy Young Award winner Doug Drabek. Kyle fell to the 18th pick, and the Phillies signed him for $1.55 million. He led The Woodlands (Texas) High to the national title during the spring, going 10-0, 1.18 on the mound and batting .479 with six homers as a short-stop. Drabek has better stuff than his father, starting with a 78-82 mph spike curveball with devastating late action. Scouts describe it as unhittable, and hitters also have to be wary of Drabek's mid-90s fastball that tops out at 97 mph. He made strides with his changeup's location during instructional league after he tinkered with his grip. Drabek generates lightning-fast arm speed through a compact, easily repeatable delivery. He's one of the best athletes in the system. Philadelphia wouldn't have had a chance to draft Drabek if not for a public-intoxication charge against him (later dropped) and a single-car accident in which he struck a tree. Clubs also were turned off by his temper, and he repeatedly lost his cool when things didn't go his way in pro ball. Also, Drabek doesn't get quite the extension from the windup as he does from the stretch. He tends to lean back on his heel too much, which costs him overall balance and command. His mid-80s slider and his changeup show promise, but they lag behind his curve and his fastball. Despite issues in Drabek's past, the Phillies could-n't pass him up a potential No. 1 starter in the draft. They believe he'll tone down his emotions as he grows up, and if he shows better maturity in spring training, he could open 2007 in low Class A.

| Year | Club (League) | Class | W | L | ERA | G | GS | CG | SV | IP | H | R | ER | HR | BB | SO | AVG |
|------|---------------|-------|---|---|-----|---|----|----|----|----|---|---|----|----|----|----|-----|
| 2006 | Phillies (GCL) | R | 1 | 3 | 7.71 | 6 | 6 | 0 | 0 | 23 | 33 | 24 | 20 | 2 | 11 | 14 | .333 |
| **MINOR LEAGUE TOTALS** | | | 1 | 3 | 7.71 | 6 | 6 | 0 | 0 | 23 | 33 | 24 | 20 | 2 | 11 | 14 | .333 |

## 3 ADRIAN CARDENAS

SS

**Born:** Oct. 10, 1987. **B-T:** L-R. **Ht.:** 5-11. **Wt.:** 185. **Drafted:** HS—Miami, 2006 (1st round supplemental). **Signed by:** Miguel Machado.

Cardenas entered last spring as the second-best player on his team—behind eventual Nationals first-rounder Chris Marrero—and as a projected fifth-round pick. By the end of the spring, he had led Miami's Monsignor Pace to a state title, set a school record with a .647 average and a Dade County mark with 18 homers and won Baseball America's High School Player of the Year award. After signing for $925,000 as the 37th overall pick, he made the Gulf Coast League all-star team. Cardenas has good strength and a short, compact swing from the left side. He has a knack for squaring up balls, making consistent hard contact and driving the ball to all fields. He profiles to hit 15-20 homers annually in the majors. He's presently a solid-average defender at shortstop, though most scouts believe he'll have to change positions down the road. He lacks first-step quickness and the range to play short, and his speed and arm strength are fringy. Cardenas probably will play second base alongside 2006 third-round pick Jason Donald in low Class A in 2007.

| Year | Club (League) | Class | AVG | G | AB | R | H | 2B | 3B | HR | RBI | BB | SO | SB | OBP | SLG |
|------|---------------|-------|-----|---|----|---|---|----|----|----|-----|----|----|----|-----|-----|
| 2006 | Phillies (GCL) | R | .318 | 41 | 154 | 22 | 49 | 5 | 4 | 2 | 21 | 17 | 28 | 13 | .384 | .442 |
| **MINOR LEAGUE TOTALS** | | | .318 | 41 | 154 | 22 | 49 | 5 | 4 | 2 | 21 | 17 | 28 | 13 | .384 | .442 |

## 4 EDGAR GARCIA

RHP

**Born:** Sept. 20, 1987. **B-T:** R-R. **Ht.:** 6-2. **Wt.:** 190. **Signed:** Dominican Republic, 2004. **Signed by:** Sal Agostinelli/Wil Tejada.

The Phillies followed Garcia as a 15-year-old in the Dominican in 2004 and signed him for $500,000 just before he planned to attend the Perfect Game/Baseball America World Wood Bat Championship. Garcia spent the bulk of his first full season in the United States in extended spring training, where he refined his delivery and worked on his secondary pitches. After rushing Carlos Carrasco, Philadelphia sent Garcia to short-season Batavia at age 18, and he had a successful summer. Garcia has excellent life on a 91-92 mph fastball that tops out at 95. He should

find more velocity as he grows into an already sturdy frame. He throws two variations of a curveball, a harder 81-83 mph version that more resembles a slider and a softer pitch with true 12-to-6 break. After working on the arm speed and command of his changeup, Garcia used it more in 2006 and showed flashes of making it a plus pitch. While Garcia's secondary pitches are improved, they still lack consistency. He tends to get around on his breaking pitches, resulting in erratic command. While his delivery is simple and repeatable, the arm speed on his changeup has to be practically flawless because he doesn't create a lot of deception. The Phillies compare Garcia to Carrasco for both his repertoire and his advanced feel for pitching. They'll continue to bring Garcia along slowly and can't wait to see what he does in his first taste of full-season ball at Lakewood.

| Year | Club (League) | Class | W | L | ERA | G | GS | CG | SV | IP | H | R | ER | HR | BB | SO | AVG |
|------|---------------|-------|---|---|-----|---|----|----|----|----|---|---|----|----|----|----|-----|
| 2005 | Phillies (GCL) | R | 4 | 4 | 3.56 | 10 | 10 | 0 | 0 | 56 | 63 | 26 | 22 | 4 | 13 | 42 | .284 |
| 2006 | Batavia (NYP) | A | 3 | 5 | 2.98 | 12 | 12 | 1 | 0 | 66 | 62 | 28 | 22 | 5 | 10 | 46 | .243 |
| **MINOR LEAGUE TOTALS** | | | 7 | 9 | 3.25 | 22 | 22 | 1 | 0 | 122 | 125 | 54 | 44 | 9 | 23 | 88 | .262 |

## 5 SCOTT MATHIESON RHP

STEVE MOORE

**Born:** Feb. 27, 1984. **B-T:** R-R. **Ht.:** 6-4. **Wt.:** 195. **Drafted:** HS—Aldergrove, B.C., 2002 (17th round). **Signed by:** Tim Kissner.

Mathieson has pitched all over the map in the last two years. He worked at the Futures Game, the World Cup and the Arizona Fall League in 2005, then pitched in the World Baseball Classic and jumped from Double-A to the majors in 2006. He was shut down in September with elbow problems that required Tommy John surgery. Mathieson lives off his low-90s fastball, which can climb as high as 97 mph. After working with a curveball for most of his first five seasons, he switched to a slider late in 2005 and worked on it exclusively in the AFL that fall. It quickly has become a plus pitch with good tilt and devastating late break. He maintains his arm speed on his changeup, which has good life down in the zone. Though the track record for Tommy John survivors is strong, Mathieson will miss most or all of the 2007 season. Just as quickly as his slider came on during the first half of 2006, he completely lost the feel for it when he was promoted to Philadelphia in mid-July. He started to regain command of the pitch after being reassigned to Triple-A Scranton/Wilkes-Barre. If all goes well, Mathieson will return to the mound during the summer at the Phillies' new short-season Williamsport affiliate. While he has the stuff to start, it gives him the potential to close games as well.

| Year | Club (League) | Class | W | L | ERA | G | GS | CG | SV | IP | H | R | ER | HR | BB | SO | AVG |
|------|---------------|-------|---|---|-----|---|----|----|----|----|---|---|----|----|----|----|-----|
| 2002 | Phillies (GCL) | R | 0 | 2 | 5.40 | 7 | 2 | 0 | 0 | 17 | 24 | 11 | 10 | 0 | 6 | 14 | .338 |
| 2003 | Phillies (GCL) | R | 2 | 7 | 5.52 | 11 | 11 | 0 | 0 | 59 | 59 | 42 | 36 | 5 | 13 | 51 | .247 |
| | Batavia (NYP) | A | 0 | 0 | 0.00 | 2 | 0 | 0 | 1 | 6 | 0 | 0 | 0 | 0 | 0 | 7 | .000 |
| 2004 | Lakewood (SAL) | A | 8 | 9 | 4.32 | 25 | 25 | 1 | 0 | 131 | 130 | 73 | 63 | 7 | 50 | 112 | .260 |
| 2005 | Clearwater (FSL) | A | 3 | 8 | 4.14 | 23 | 23 | 1 | 0 | 122 | 111 | 62 | 56 | 17 | 34 | 118 | .241 |
| 2006 | Reading (EL) | AA | 7 | 2 | 3.21 | 14 | 14 | 0 | 0 | 93 | 73 | 35 | 33 | 8 | 29 | 99 | .221 |
| | Scranton/W-B (IL) | AAA | 3 | 1 | 3.93 | 5 | 5 | 0 | 0 | 34 | 26 | 16 | 15 | 2 | 10 | 36 | .208 |
| | Philadelphia (NL) | MLB | 1 | 4 | 7.47 | 9 | 8 | 0 | 0 | 37 | 48 | 36 | 31 | 8 | 16 | 28 | .312 |
| **MINOR LEAGUE TOTALS** | | | 23 | 29 | 4.16 | 87 | 80 | 2 | 1 | 461 | 423 | 239 | 213 | 39 | 142 | 437 | .243 |
| **MAJOR LEAGUE TOTALS** | | | 1 | 4 | 7.47 | 9 | 8 | 0 | 0 | 37 | 48 | 36 | 31 | 8 | 16 | 28 | .312 |

## 6 JOSH OUTMAN LHP

DAVID SCHOFIELD

**Born:** Sept. 14, 1984. **B-T:** L-L. **Ht.:** 6-1. **Wt.:** 190. **Drafted:** Central Missouri State, 2005 (10th round). **Signed by:** Jerry Lafferty.

While at St. Louis Community College-Forest Park, Outman used a delivery developed by his father Fritz that scouts described as one of the strangest they'd ever seen. He extended his arm straight up, bent it down to nearly touch his opposite shoulder and then took a walking step rather than using a leg kick. After transferring to Central Missouri State, he reworked his mechanics while also starring as an outfielder/DH. Outman contributed to a South Atlantic League championship by winning 13 of his last 15 regular-season decisions in 2006. After making changes to his delivery, Outman has seen his fastball jump from 86-88 mph to 90-94. Lakewood pitching coach Steve Schrenk had him ditch his curveball in favor of a sharp slider that quickly became a plus pitch with excellent tilt and late life. His changeup grades as average. Outman has a good feel for his changeup, but wasn't consistent locat-

ing it in 2006. His arm speed slows down at times, which he can remedy by using the pitch more often. He puts away hitters easily when he gets ahead in the count but needs to do a better job of throwing strikes. Ticketed for high Class A, Outman could reach Double-A by the summer.

| Year | Club (League) | Class | W | L | ERA | G | GS | CG | SV | IP | H | R | ER | HR | BB | SO | AVG |
|------|---------------|-------|---|---|-----|---|----|----|----|----|---|---|----|----|----|----|-----|
| 2005 | Batavia (NYP) | A | 2 | 1 | 2.76 | 11 | 4 | 0 | 0 | 29 | 23 | 14 | 9 | 1 | 14 | 31 | .207 |
| 2006 | Lakewood (SAL) | A | 14 | 6 | 2.95 | 27 | 27 | 1 | 0 | 155 | 119 | 61 | 51 | 5 | 75 | 161 | .213 |
| **MINOR LEAGUE TOTALS** | | | 16 | 7 | 2.92 | 38 | 31 | 1 | 0 | 185 | 142 | 75 | 60 | 6 | 89 | 192 | .212 |

## 7 MICHAEL BOURN OF

**Born:** Dec. 27, 1982. **B-T:** L-R. **Ht.:** 5-11. **Wt.:** 180. **Drafted:** Houston, 2003 (4th round). **Signed by:** Dave Owen.

Though the Phillies have seen many of their prospects struggle after skipping a level, Bourn succeeded after skipping high Class A in 2005. He repeated Double-A in 2006, played half the year in Triple-A and finished it in Philadelphia. He has led the system in steals in each of his three full seasons. Bourn is the organization's best leadoff hitter and offers a package of line drives, plate discipline and speed. He bunts well and has game-changing quickness on the bases. Bourn is a plus defender in center field with outstanding range and a strong arm. He'll never hit for much power, though Bourn has worked on taking pitches to the opposite field. As a leadoff hitter he still needs to cut down on his strikeouts, be more patient and prove he can work deep counts consistently. If the Phillies trade Aaron Rowand, Bourn would be the best in-house candidate to replace him. Otherwise, he'll open 2007 at the club's new Triple-A Ottawa affiliate. He could become Philadelphia's version of Juan Pierre, with better plate discipline and a stronger arm.

| Year | Club (League) | Class | AVG | G | AB | R | H | 2B | 3B | HR | RBI | BB | SO | SB | OBP | SLG |
|------|---------------|-------|-----|---|----|---|---|----|----|----|-----|----|----|----|-----|-----|
| 2003 | Batavia (NYP) | A | .280 | 35 | 125 | 12 | 35 | 0 | 1 | 0 | 4 | 23 | 28 | 23 | .404 | .296 |
| 2004 | Lakewood (SAL) | A | .317 | 109 | 413 | 92 | 131 | 20 | 14 | 5 | 53 | 85 | 88 | 57 | .433 | .470 |
| 2005 | Reading (EL) | AA | .268 | 135 | 544 | 80 | 146 | 18 | 8 | 6 | 44 | 63 | 123 | 38 | .348 | .364 |
| 2006 | Reading (EL) | AA | .274 | 80 | 318 | 62 | 87 | 5 | 6 | 4 | 26 | 36 | 67 | 30 | .350 | .365 |
| | Scranton/W-B (IL) | AAA | .283 | 38 | 152 | 34 | 43 | 5 | 7 | 1 | 15 | 20 | 33 | 15 | .368 | .428 |
| | Philadelphia (NL) | MLB | .125 | 17 | 8 | 2 | 1 | 0 | 0 | 0 | 0 | 1 | 3 | 1 | .222 | .125 |
| **MINOR LEAGUE TOTALS** | | | .285 | 397 | 1552 | 280 | 442 | 48 | 36 | 16 | 142 | 227 | 339 | 163 | .379 | .393 |
| **MAJOR LEAGUE TOTALS** | | | .125 | 17 | 8 | 2 | 1 | 0 | 0 | 0 | 0 | 1 | 3 | 1 | .222 | .125 |

## 8 J.A. HAPP LHP

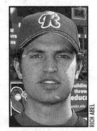

**Born:** Oct. 19, 1982. **B-T:** L-L. **Ht.:** 6-5. **Wt.:** 205. **Drafted:** Northwestern, 2004 (3rd round). **Signed by:** Bob Szymkowski.

The first Northwestern player ever to make the all-Big 10 Conference team three times, Happ has had no trouble adjusting to pro ball. He has posted a 2.49 ERA and reached Triple-A in just two and a half seasons. The Phillies worked with Happ to get him more upright in his delivery, which created more deception and velocity (up to 93 mph in the Arizona Fall League) on his fastball. He has always demonstrated an ability to locate the pitch wherever he wants. Even with the boost to his fastball, Happ's changeup remains his best pitch, featuring excellent depth and fade. After missing time with quadriceps and oblique injuries in 2005, Happ proved durable and tossed a career-high 175 innings (including the AFL) in 2006. He's one of the better athletes in the system. Happ's slider is too soft at times, turning into a loopy slurve. He made strides with its consistency in 2006, but it will improve more as he uses it more. Though he locates his fastball exceptionally well, he can rely on to it too much. Happ is the next starter in line for a promotion to Philadelphia and projects as a No. 3 or 4 starter. The offseason acquisitions of Adam Eaton and Freddy Garcia will buy him a full year of development time at Triple-A.

| Year | Club (League) | Class | W | L | ERA | G | GS | CG | SV | IP | H | R | ER | HR | BB | SO | AVG |
|------|---------------|-------|---|---|-----|---|----|----|----|----|---|---|----|----|----|----|-----|
| 2004 | Batavia (NYP) | A | 1 | 2 | 2.02 | 11 | 11 | 0 | 0 | 36 | 22 | 8 | 8 | 1 | 18 | 37 | .185 |
| 2005 | Lakewood (SAL) | A | 4 | 4 | 2.36 | 14 | 12 | 0 | 0 | 72 | 57 | 26 | 19 | 3 | 26 | 70 | .213 |
| | Reading (EL) | AA | 1 | 0 | 1.50 | 1 | 1 | 0 | 0 | 6 | 3 | 1 | 1 | 0 | 2 | 8 | .150 |
| | Clearwater (FSL) | A | 3 | 7 | 2.81 | 13 | 13 | 0 | 0 | 80 | 63 | 35 | 25 | 9 | 19 | 77 | .216 |
| 2006 | Reading (EL) | AA | 6 | 2 | 2.65 | 12 | 12 | 0 | 0 | 75 | 58 | 27 | 22 | 2 | 29 | 81 | .214 |
| | Scranton/W-B (IL) | AAA | 1 | 0 | 1.50 | 1 | 1 | 0 | 0 | 6 | 3 | 1 | 1 | 1 | 1 | 4 | .136 |
| **MINOR LEAGUE TOTALS** | | | 16 | 15 | 2.49 | 52 | 50 | 0 | 0 | 275 | 206 | 98 | 76 | 16 | 95 | 277 | .208 |

## MATT MALONEY                                                    LHP

**Born:** Jan. 16, 1984. **B-T:** L-L. **Ht.:** 6-4. **Wt.:** 220. **Drafted:** Mississippi, 2005 (3rd round). **Signed by:** Mike Stauffer.

Maloney was worn out from pitching Mississippi to the NCAA super regionals when he turned pro in 2005, so the Phillies didn't see him at his best until 2006. His best was very good, as he was named South Atlantic League pitcher of the year after leading the circuit in wins, innings and strikeouts while finishing second in ERA. Maloney attacks hitters by throwing four pitches for strikes. His stuff is average across the board but his advanced feel makes it play up, and he creates good deception with his easily repeatable delivery. His 86-88 mph sinker is his best pitch because of its late movement. His changeup isn't far behind and he'll throw it in any count. He also has an 11-to-5 curveball and a slider. Maloney's lack of velocity leaves him with little margin for error, and his secondary pitches need work to translate at the upper levels. His curveball has good downward spiral but can flatten out at times, and his slider needs to be tighter and harder if it's going to remain in his arsenal. On the high end, Maloney could be a No. 4 starter. Without better breaking stuff, he could be a middle reliever. Considering his savvy and that he'll be 23 in 2007, he could skip a level and head straight to Double-A.

| Year | Club (League) | Class | W | L | ERA | G | GS | CG | SV | IP | H | R | ER | HR | BB | SO | AVG |
|---|---|---|---|---|---|---|---|---|---|---|---|---|---|---|---|---|---|
| 2005 | Batavia (NYP) | A | 2 | 1 | 3.89 | 8 | 8 | 0 | 0 | 37 | 38 | 20 | 16 | 2 | 15 | 36 | .277 |
| 2006 | Lakewood (SAL) | A | 16 | 9 | 2.03 | 27 | 27 | 2 | 0 | 169 | 120 | 54 | 38 | 5 | 73 | 180 | .194 |
| **MINOR LEAGUE TOTALS** | | | 18 | 10 | 2.36 | 35 | 35 | 2 | 0 | 206 | 158 | 74 | 54 | 7 | 88 | 216 | .209 |

## GREG GOLSON                                                     OF

**Born:** Sept. 17, 1985. **B-T:** R-R. **Ht.:** 6-0. **Wt.:** 190. **Drafted:** HS—Austin, 2004 (1st round). **Signed by:** Steve Cohen.

The Phillies have been patient with Golson since signing him for $1.475 million as the 21st overall pick in 2004, and it may finally be starting to pay off. Though he repeated low Class A at the start of 2006 and hit just .220, he surged following a promotion to high Class A in late July. The best athlete in the 2004 draft, Golson possesses the best speed, center-field skills and outfield arm in the system. He consistently gets from the right side of the plate to first base in 4.0 seconds. He has above-average raw power to go along with those wheels. Area scouts who saw Golson as an amateur thought he'd have to make a lot of adjustments at the plate in pro ball, and he has struggled to do so. His pitch recognition and plate discipline are still very raw, and he's too pull-conscious. He has the speed to become an electrifying basestealer, but that hasn't happened. He was disappointed at returning to Lakewood, and his play reflected that. His upside is the highest among the system's position players, but he needs to start performing in what will be his fourth pro season.

| Year | Club (League) | Class | AVG | G | AB | R | H | 2B | 3B | HR | RBI | BB | SO | SB | OBP | SLG |
|---|---|---|---|---|---|---|---|---|---|---|---|---|---|---|---|---|
| 2004 | Phillies (GCL) | R | .295 | 47 | 183 | 34 | 54 | 8 | 5 | 1 | 22 | 10 | 54 | 12 | .345 | .410 |
| 2005 | Lakewood (SAL) | A | .264 | 89 | 375 | 51 | 99 | 19 | 8 | 4 | 27 | 26 | 106 | 25 | .322 | .389 |
| 2006 | Clearwater (FSL) | A | .264 | 40 | 159 | 31 | 42 | 11 | 2 | 6 | 17 | 11 | 53 | 7 | .324 | .472 |
| | Lakewood (SAL) | A | .220 | 93 | 387 | 56 | 85 | 15 | 4 | 7 | 31 | 19 | 107 | 23 | .258 | .333 |
| **MINOR LEAGUE TOTALS** | | | .254 | 269 | 1104 | 172 | 280 | 53 | 19 | 18 | 97 | 66 | 320 | 67 | .304 | .385 |

## D'ARBY MYERS                                                     OF

**Born:** Dec. 12, 1988. **B-T:** R-R. **Ht.:** 6-3. **Wt.:** 180. **Drafted:** HS—Los Angeles (4th round), 2006. **Signed by:** Tim Kissner.

Many clubs showed interest in Myers prior to the 2006 draft, and some teams originally had him slated as a second- or third-round pick, but his commitment to Southern California made it hard to get a read on his signability. The Phillies had the right info and popped him in the fourth round, signing him for $250,000. A plus runner, Myers also showed he could hit for average and power in his debut in the Gulf Coast League and carried that over into instructional league. Myers has a compact stroke that produces line drives to all fields, though he needs to recognize pitches better and work deeper counts. His route-running is suspect at times, but he has great closing speed. If he's going to remain a center fielder, he'll need to continue to work on getting better reads off the bat. Myers has all five tools, and some officials in the organization say his ceiling is higher than Golson's. He'll compete for a job in low Class A this spring.

| Year | Club (League) | Class | AVG | G | AB | R | H | 2B | 3B | HR | RBI | BB | SO | SB | OBP | SLG |
|------|---------------|-------|-----|---|----|---|---|----|----|----|-----|----|----|----|-----|-----|
| 2006 | Phillies (GCL) | R | .313 | 31 | 128 | 20 | 40 | 7 | 1 | 2 | 13 | 7 | 32 | 11 | .353 | .430 |
| **MINOR LEAGUE TOTALS** | | | .313 | 31 | 128 | 20 | 40 | 7 | 1 | 2 | 13 | 7 | 32 | 11 | .353 | .430 |

 ## MIKE COSTANZO                                                  3B

**Born:** Sept. 9, 1983. **B-T:** L-R. **Ht.:** 6-3. **Wt.:** 215. **Drafted:** Coastal Carolina, 2005 (2nd round). **Signed by:** Roy Tanner.

When he was born, Constanzo was brought home from the hospital in a Phillies jacket. After helping lead Coastal Carolina to prominence as a pitcher (8-1, 14 saves as a junior) and hitter in three seasons, he hasn't quite performed up to expectations with his hometown organization. Still, he ranked fifth in the high Class A Florida State League in RBIs in his first full season after playing in the New York-Penn League in his debut. His swing can get long, and at times he struggles mightily with offspeed pitches. Several scouts said he appeared to take at-bats off last summer. He worked hard on laying off pitches over the inner half—where he'd automatically go into pull mode—but he still has a ways to go. Virtually all of his power is to right and right-center and he rarely works to the opposite field. Defensively, Costanzo is arguably the best third baseman in the system. He has soft hands, a strong, accurate arm and good range, though he needs to work on his footwork to the right. Costanzo will get plenty of opportunities as the highest-drafted player in the system in 2005 and one of the top power prospects in the organization, but he needs to tighten up his approach and use the whole field more consistently. He'll likely play all of 2007 in Double-A.

| Year | Club (League) | Class | AVG | G | AB | R | H | 2B | 3B | HR | RBI | BB | SO | SB | OBP | SLG |
|------|---------------|-------|-----|---|----|---|---|----|----|----|-----|----|----|----|-----|-----|
| 2005 | Batavia (NYP) | A | .274 | 73 | 281 | 47 | 77 | 17 | 3 | 11 | 50 | 35 | 89 | 0 | .356 | .473 |
| 2006 | Clearwater (FSL) | A | .258 | 135 | 504 | 72 | 130 | 33 | 1 | 14 | 81 | 74 | 133 | 3 | .364 | .411 |
| **MINOR LEAGUE TOTALS** | | | .264 | 208 | 785 | 119 | 207 | 50 | 4 | 25 | 131 | 109 | 222 | 3 | .361 | .433 |

 ## CARLOS RUIZ                                                    C

**Born:** Jan. 22, 1979. **B-T:** R-R. **Ht.:** 5-10. **Wt.:** 180. **Signed:** Panama, 1998. **Signed by:** Sal Agostinelli.

It's been a slow, steady development road for Ruiz since international scouting director Sal Agostinelli signed him for the bargain basement price of $8,000 in 1998. Ruiz impressed scouts with his defense in the Arizona Fall League in 2004, but it's been his development as a hitter that has the Phillies envisioning Ruiz carrying the bulk of the catching load in the big leagues this season. Ruiz, who played for his native Panama in the World Baseball Classic, has a line-drive stroke that produces natural loft and surprising power. Defensively he remains adequate, with an above-average arm, solid mechanics in his transfer, good blocking ability and a strong lower half. He threw out 35 percent of basestealers in Triple-A but just 21 percent in his big league stint. Barring a move on the free agent market, Ruiz is the frontrunner to be the everyday catcher in Philadelphia in 2007, sharing duty with another minor league veteran, Chris Coste.

| Year | Club (League) | Class | AVG | G | AB | R | H | 2B | 3B | HR | RBI | BB | SO | SB | OBP | SLG |
|------|---------------|-------|-----|---|----|---|---|----|----|----|-----|----|----|----|-----|-----|
| 1999 | Phillies (DSL) | R | .305 | 60 | 226 | 39 | 69 | 15 | 5 | 4 | 35 | 9 | 11 | 3 | .351 | .469 |
| 2000 | Phillies (GCL) | R | .277 | 38 | 130 | 11 | 36 | 7 | 1 | 1 | 22 | 9 | 9 | 3 | .329 | .369 |
| 2001 | Lakewood (SAL) | A | .261 | 73 | 249 | 21 | 65 | 14 | 3 | 4 | 32 | 10 | 27 | 5 | .290 | .390 |
| 2002 | Clearwater (FSL) | A | .213 | 92 | 342 | 35 | 73 | 18 | 3 | 5 | 32 | 18 | 30 | 3 | .264 | .327 |
| 2003 | Clearwater (FSL) | A | .315 | 15 | 54 | 5 | 17 | 0 | 0 | 2 | 9 | 2 | 5 | 2 | .339 | .426 |
|  | Reading (EL) | AA | .266 | 52 | 169 | 22 | 45 | 6 | 0 | 2 | 16 | 12 | 15 | 1 | .321 | .337 |
| 2004 | Reading (EL) | AA | .284 | 101 | 349 | 45 | 99 | 15 | 2 | 17 | 50 | 22 | 37 | 8 | .338 | .484 |
| 2005 | Scranton/W-B (IL) | AAA | .300 | 100 | 347 | 50 | 104 | 25 | 9 | 4 | 40 | 30 | 48 | 4 | .354 | .458 |
| 2006 | Scranton/W-B (IL) | AAA | .307 | 100 | 368 | 56 | 113 | 25 | 0 | 16 | 69 | 42 | 56 | 4 | .389 | .505 |
|  | Philadelphia (NL) | MLB | .261 | 27 | 69 | 5 | 18 | 1 | 1 | 3 | 10 | 5 | 8 | 0 | .316 | .435 |
| **MINOR LEAGUE TOTALS** | | | .278 | 631 | 2234 | 284 | 621 | 125 | 23 | 55 | 305 | 154 | 238 | 33 | .333 | .428 |
| **MAJOR LEAGUE TOTALS** | | | .261 | 27 | 69 | 5 | 18 | 1 | 1 | 3 | 10 | 5 | 8 | 0 | .316 | .435 |

## ZACH SEGOVIA                                                   RHP

**Born:** April 11, 1983. **B-T:** R-R. **Ht.:** 6-2. **Wt.:** 220. **Drafted:** HS—Forney, Texas, 2002 (2nd round). **Signed by:** Dave Owen.

A classic late bloomer, Segovia is one of the best development stories in the system. After signing for $712,500 as a second-round pick out of high school, Segovia made his debut in the Gulf Coast League and had Tommy John surgery the following season. It took him nearly two years to fully recover, and he easily put up his best numbers last season—finishing it in the Arizona Fall League after winning two games for Team USA in the Olympic Qualifying tournament in Cuba. Segovia's velocity hasn't returned to

its pre-surgery form, as his fastball now sits at 88-92 mph, topping out at 93. Without the velocity, Segovia compensated by becoming a more complete pitcher. He can now sink his heater much better, and he'll cut it or run it in to either side of the plate when he needs to. His slider and changeup are at least average offerings. Segovia's best asset is his fastball command, and his secondary stuff needs to improve. He gets around on his slider, which leaves the pitch hanging in the upper quadrant of the zone. While durability is no longer a concern, Segovia must maintain a strict training regimen to keep his weight in check. The Phillies will give Segovia a long look for a rotation spot in 2007, but he likely opens the year in the Triple-A rotation.

| Year | Club (League) | Class | W | L | ERA | G | GS | CG | SV | IP | H | R | ER | HR | BB | SO | AVG |
|---|---|---|---|---|---|---|---|---|---|---|---|---|---|---|---|---|---|
| 2002 | Phillies (GCL) | R | 3 | 2 | 2.10 | 8 | 8 | 0 | 0 | 34 | 21 | 11 | 8 | 0 | 3 | 30 | .174 |
| 2003 | Phillies (GCL) | R | 0 | 1 | 4.00 | 5 | 4 | 0 | 0 | 9 | 8 | 5 | 4 | 0 | 0 | 6 | .235 |
|  | Lakewood (SAL) | A | 1 | 5 | 3.99 | 11 | 10 | 0 | 0 | 50 | 63 | 25 | 22 | 2 | 14 | 27 | .307 |
| 2004 | Did not play—Injured |  |  |  |  |  |  |  |  |  |  |  |  |  |  |  |  |
| 2005 | Clearwater (FSL) | A | 4 | 14 | 5.54 | 27 | 27 | 0 | 0 | 145 | 168 | 98 | 89 | 18 | 48 | 83 | .291 |
| 2006 | Clearwater (FSL) | A | 5 | 1 | 2.19 | 7 | 7 | 0 | 0 | 49 | 39 | 14 | 12 | 2 | 12 | 41 | .222 |
|  | Reading (EL) | AA | 11 | 5 | 3.11 | 17 | 16 | 3 | 0 | 107 | 90 | 45 | 37 | 8 | 24 | 75 | .226 |
| **MINOR LEAGUE TOTALS** |  |  | 24 | 28 | 3.93 | 75 | 72 | 3 | 0 | 394 | 389 | 198 | 172 | 30 | 101 | 262 | .257 |

## 15 KYLE KENDRICK                                                    RHP

**Born:** Aug. 26, 1984. **B-T:** R-R. **Ht.:** 6-3. **Wt.:** 185. **Drafted:** HS—Mount Vernon, Wash., 2003 (7th round). **Signed by:** Tim Kissner.

One of the better athletes in the system, Kendrick was lured away from a football scholarship at Washington State when the Phillies signed him for $135,000 in 2003. After two years of scuffling through the system, Kendrick emerged in 2006 and finished among the organization leaders in ERA and led all farmhands with 176 innings. The biggest difference has been his 82-84 mph slider, which served as his primary out pitch after being promoted to high Class A. Kendrick commands his fastball well, sitting at 91-94 mph with good movement, and his changeup also improved last season to become at least an average pitch. Though his slider became his go-to pitch, he can still get around on it at times when he rushes his delivery. Kendrick is one of the most durable pitchers in the system and he should begin the season in the Double-A rotation.

| Year | Club (League) | Class | W | L | ERA | G | GS | CG | SV | IP | H | R | ER | HR | BB | SO | AVG |
|---|---|---|---|---|---|---|---|---|---|---|---|---|---|---|---|---|---|
| 2003 | Phillies (GCL) | R | 0 | 4 | 5.46 | 9 | 5 | 0 | 0 | 31 | 40 | 24 | 19 | 3 | 12 | 26 | .305 |
| 2004 | Lakewood (SAL) | A | 3 | 8 | 6.08 | 15 | 15 | 0 | 0 | 67 | 85 | 56 | 45 | 9 | 33 | 36 | .318 |
|  | Batavia (NYP) | A | 2 | 8 | 5.48 | 13 | 12 | 0 | 0 | 71 | 94 | 52 | 43 | 6 | 18 | 53 | .330 |
| 2005 | Clearwater (FSL) | A | 0 | 1 | 0.00 | 1 | 1 | 0 | 0 | 4 | 5 | 1 | 0 | 0 | 2 | 1 | .333 |
|  | Lakewood (SAL) | A | 0 | 3 | 9.13 | 5 | 5 | 0 | 0 | 23 | 38 | 24 | 23 | 2 | 10 | 11 | .369 |
|  | Batavia (NYP) | A | 5 | 4 | 3.74 | 14 | 14 | 1 | 0 | 91 | 94 | 49 | 38 | 7 | 22 | 70 | .262 |
| 2006 | Lakewood (SAL) | A | 3 | 2 | 2.15 | 7 | 7 | 0 | 0 | 46 | 34 | 14 | 11 | 0 | 15 | 54 | .199 |
|  | Clearwater (FSL) | A | 9 | 7 | 3.53 | 21 | 20 | 2 | 0 | 130 | 117 | 59 | 51 | 15 | 37 | 79 | .241 |
| **MINOR LEAGUE TOTALS** |  |  | 22 | 37 | 4.47 | 85 | 79 | 3 | 0 | 463 | 507 | 279 | 230 | 42 | 149 | 330 | .279 |

## 16 JOE BISENIUS                                                     RHP

**Born:** Sept. 18, 1982. **B-T:** R-R. **Ht.:** 6-5. **Wt.:** 210. **Drafted:** Oklahoma City, 2004 (12th round). **Signed by:** Paul Scott.

Bisenius played a major role on Oklahoma City College's NAIA record 70-win season in 2004, and despite having the highest ERA on the team (3.19), he went 12-0 for the Stars. Bisenius came into his own in 2006 after struggling at low Class A the previous year, jumping up to Double-A where he held opposing hitters to a .182 average. Bisenius pounds the zone with his 91-94 fastball, attacking both sides of the plate. Scouts differ on what to call his breaking ball—Bisenius calls it a slider, but scouts refer to it as a hard curveball. Regardless, it emerged as a plus pitch in 2006, with good depth and devastating late movement. He can sometimes get around on his breaking ball, leaving it up in the zone. After competing in Venezuela's winter league for Magallanes, Bisenius will get a long look in big league camp this spring, and should battle for a bullpen spot in Philly. He has better pure stuff than Rule 5 selection Jim Ed Warden, but the difference in arm angle might be enough to prompt the Phillies to keep both.

| Year | Club (League) | Class | W | L | ERA | G | GS | CG | SV | IP | H | R | ER | HR | BB | SO | AVG |
|---|---|---|---|---|---|---|---|---|---|---|---|---|---|---|---|---|---|
| 2004 | Batavia (NYP) | A | 0 | 1 | 1.43 | 11 | 11 | 0 | 0 | 50 | 39 | 12 | 8 | 5 | 14 | 38 | .219 |
| 2005 | Lakewood (SAL) | A | 6 | 4 | 5.88 | 40 | 4 | 1 | 4 | 64 | 66 | 45 | 42 | 5 | 37 | 56 | .264 |
| 2006 | Clearwater (FSL) | A | 4 | 1 | 1.93 | 35 | 0 | 0 | 2 | 61 | 48 | 17 | 13 | 4 | 22 | 62 | .216 |
|  | Reading (EL) | AA | 4 | 2 | 3.09 | 16 | 0 | 0 | 5 | 23 | 14 | 9 | 8 | 2 | 8 | 33 | .182 |
| **MINOR LEAGUE TOTALS** |  |  | 14 | 8 | 3.22 | 102 | 15 | 1 | 11 | 199 | 167 | 83 | 71 | 16 | 81 | 189 | .230 |

## 17 DREW CARPENTER                                                    RHP

**Born:** May 18, 1985. **B-T:** R-R. **Ht.:** 6-3. **Wt.:** 230. **Drafted:** Long Beach State, 2006 (2nd round). **Signed by:** Tim Kissner.

Carpenter was slated to go to Oklahoma when he transferred from Sacramento City College, but a coaching change with the Sooners (and the staff's willingness to let him out of his national letter of intent) prompted him to choose Long Beach State instead. His talent and the work of pitching coach Troy Buckley—who mentored four first- or second-round picks between 2004-2005—helped push Carpenter into the second round in 2006. Carpenter features a low-90s fastball with good movement and commands it to all parts of the zone. He rounds out his repertoire with an average-to-plus slider and changeup. While Carpenter repeats his delivery well, his arm can drag behind slightly with his offspeed pitches, and tends to leave them up in the zone as a result. That is especially true of his changeup, which now grades out as below average but should be an average pitch down the road. He'll begin the season in high Class A.

| Year | Club (League) | Class | W | L | ERA | G | GS | CG | SV | IP | H | R | ER | HR | BB | SO | AVG |
|------|---------------|-------|---|---|-----|---|----|----|----|----|----|---|----|----|----|----|-----|
| 2006 | Phillies (GCL) | R | 0 | 0 | 0.00 | 2 | 1 | 0 | 0 | 3 | 2 | 0 | 0 | 0 | 0 | 4 | .200 |
|      | Batavia (NYP) | A | 0 | 0 | 0.77 | 3 | 3 | 0 | 0 | 12 | 10 | 1 | 1 | 0 | 5 | 12 | .250 |
| **MINOR LEAGUE TOTALS** | | | 0 | 0 | 0.61 | 5 | 4 | 0 | 0 | 15 | 12 | 1 | 1 | 0 | 5 | 16 | .240 |

## 18 BRAD HARMAN                                                         SS

**Born:** Nov. 19, 1985. **B-T:** R-R. **Ht.:** 6-1. **Wt.:** 180. **Signed:** Australia, 2003. **Signed by:** Kevin Hooker.

The Phillies have a strong presence in Australia, and Harman is arguably the best player they've signed out of the lower Pacific Rim. Signed for $50,000, Harman started 2006 on a high note, playing in the World Baseball Classic, but it became his toughest season after his mother passed away. Things snowballed on him and he never got on track. But Harman still shows good tools. He has slightly above-average speed and some loft power with the aptitude and work ethic to improve. The Phillies believe he can stay at shortstop because of his soft hands, slightly above-average range and arm strength. His arm doesn't jump out, but it's strong and his throws are always on the money. He still needs to improve his first-step quickness at times to maximize his effectiveness defensively, and he needs to bounce back from a disappointing season at the plate. Because of what he went through personally at his age in 2006, the organization is being patient with Harman. If he has a good spring, Harman could jump into an everyday role in Double-A.

| Year | Club (League) | Class | AVG | G | AB | R | H | 2B | 3B | HR | RBI | BB | SO | SB | OBP | SLG |
|------|---------------|-------|-----|---|----|---|---|----|----|----|-----|----|----|----|-----|-----|
| 2004 | Clearwater (FSL) | A | — | 1 | 0 | 1 | 0 | 0 | 0 | 0 | 0 | 1 | 0 | 0 | 1.000 | — |
|      | Phillies (GCL) | R | .230 | 51 | 183 | 23 | 42 | 10 | 0 | 2 | 19 | 11 | 41 | 2 | .281 | .317 |
| 2005 | Lakewood (SAL) | A | .303 | 105 | 419 | 63 | 127 | 23 | 1 | 11 | 58 | 45 | 89 | 5 | .380 | .442 |
| 2006 | Clearwater (FSL) | A | .241 | 119 | 423 | 59 | 102 | 19 | 1 | 2 | 25 | 48 | 102 | 6 | .322 | .305 |
| **MINOR LEAGUE TOTALS** | | | .264 | 276 | 1025 | 146 | 271 | 52 | 2 | 15 | 102 | 105 | 232 | 13 | .339 | .363 |

## 19 LOU MARSON                                                          C

**Born:** July 26, 1986. **B-T:** R-R. **Ht.:** 6-1. **Wt.:** 195. **Drafted:** HS—Scottsdale, Ariz., 2004 (4th round). **Signed by:** Therron Brockish.

A two-sport star in high school, Marson broke his collarbone just three games into his senior year and saw his dream of playing quarterback in college diminish significantly. With football behind him and despite three unexceptional years in the organization offensively, the Phillies feel Marson is headed in the right direction as one of the best catchers in the system. Marson handled the best pitching staff in the organization by far at Lakewood, and his receiving skills, game-calling and blocking abilities all blossomed in 2006. Marson hasn't concentrated on his approach as a hitter nearly as much as he's tried to become better defensively, and he'll need to balance out his game as he moves forward. His swing can become very long at times, and breaking balls give him fits. Marson is slated to move to high Class A, but Double-A isn't being ruled out simply because of how much he's grown defensively.

| Year | Club (League) | Class | AVG | G | AB | R | H | 2B | 3B | HR | RBI | BB | SO | SB | OBP | SLG |
|------|---------------|-------|-----|---|----|---|---|----|----|----|-----|----|----|----|-----|-----|
| 2004 | Phillies (GCL) | R | .257 | 38 | 113 | 18 | 29 | 3 | 0 | 4 | 8 | 13 | 18 | 4 | .333 | .389 |
| 2005 | Batavia (NYP) | A | .245 | 60 | 220 | 25 | 54 | 11 | 3 | 5 | 25 | 27 | 52 | 0 | .329 | .391 |
| 2006 | Lakewood (SAL) | A | .243 | 104 | 350 | 44 | 85 | 16 | 5 | 4 | 39 | 49 | 82 | 4 | .343 | .351 |
| **MINOR LEAGUE TOTALS** | | | .246 | 202 | 683 | 87 | 168 | 30 | 8 | 13 | 72 | 89 | 152 | 8 | .337 | .370 |

## 20 C.J. HENRY SS

**Born:** May 31, 1986. **B-T:** R-R. **Ht.:** 6-3. **Wt.:** 205. **Drafted:** HS—Putnam City, Okla., 2005 (1st round). **Signed by:** Mark Batchko (Yankees).

Henry ranked No. 4 on the Yankees list last year before the club packaged him with lefthander Matt Smith, catcher Jesus Sanchez and righthander Carlos Monasterios in exchange for Bobby Abreu and Cory Lidle. New York swayed Henry away from a future in basketball—which his parents both played at Kansas—with $1.75 million as the 17th overall pick in 2005, but the offensive results haven't shown up. Henry's best tools are his strength, bat speed and athleticism. He has well-above-average power, but his swing can get long and mechanical at times and he strikes out in bunches as a result. Some scouts think he's better suited for third base or a corner outfield spot down the road, as his arm rates as fringe-average and his body continues to fill out. There is still a lot of projection left with Henry, but the track record isn't there, particularly in translating his above-average raw power. Henry worked out at third base during instructional league and likely faces the position change when he returns to high Class A this year.

| Year | Club (League) | Class | AVG | G | AB | R | H | 2B | 3B | HR | RBI | BB | SO | SB | OBP | SLG |
|------|---------------|-------|-----|---|-----|---|---|----|----|----|-----|----|----|----|-----|-----|
| 2005 | Yankees (GCL) | R | .249 | 48 | 181 | 32 | 45 | 9 | 3 | 3 | 17 | 17 | 39 | 17 | .333 | .381 |
| 2006 | Charleston (SAL) | A | .240 | 77 | 275 | 35 | 66 | 19 | 3 | 2 | 33 | 32 | 86 | 14 | .330 | .353 |
| | Lakewood (SAL) | A | .253 | 25 | 91 | 13 | 23 | 3 | 4 | 1 | 16 | 7 | 25 | 1 | .313 | .407 |
| **MINOR LEAGUE TOTALS** | | | .245 | 150 | 547 | 80 | 134 | 31 | 10 | 6 | 66 | 56 | 150 | 32 | .328 | .371 |

## 21 WELINSON BAEZ 3B

**Born:** July 7, 1984. **B-T:** R-R. **Ht.:** 6-3. **Wt.:** 190. **Signed:** Dominican Republic, 2002. **Signed by:** Wil Tejeda.

Baez has incredible physical ability, but other than 170 at-bats in short-season ball two years ago, the Phillies haven't seen much out of their $250,000 investment out of the Dominican in 2002. Phillies officials rave about how Baez plays during instructional league and spring training, but the production hasn't been there when it counts. Baez drips tools, with his power and arm strength rating as his best assets. Baez has a 70 arm on the 20-80 scouting scale, and the potential for huge raw pop. He has good hands for third base and has shown above-average range. Baez went through his toughest year in 2006—his first full season—as he failed to recognize breaking balls and his plate discipline was abysmal. The Phillies want to see more aggressiveness out of Baez, who often fell behind in counts in low Class A and struggled against quality breaking pitches, leading to him topping the South Atlantic League in strikeouts. Baez should return to low Class A to build on the confidence he once again built up during instructional league.

| Year | Club (League) | Class | AVG | G | AB | R | H | 2B | 3B | HR | RBI | BB | SO | SB | OBP | SLG |
|------|---------------|-------|-----|---|-----|---|---|----|----|----|-----|----|----|----|-----|-----|
| 2003 | Phillies (GCL) | R | .246 | 41 | 142 | 20 | 35 | 6 | 1 | 3 | 17 | 12 | 37 | 3 | .319 | .366 |
| 2004 | Phillies (GCL) | R | .234 | 51 | 171 | 24 | 40 | 7 | 2 | 4 | 18 | 21 | 62 | 3 | .320 | .368 |
| 2005 | Phillies (GCL) | R | .267 | 15 | 45 | 6 | 12 | 4 | 1 | 2 | 6 | 8 | 14 | 1 | .400 | .533 |
| | Batavia (NYP) | A | .324 | 45 | 170 | 34 | 55 | 14 | 1 | 6 | 37 | 22 | 45 | 2 | .408 | .524 |
| 2006 | Lakewood (SAL) | A | .232 | 122 | 427 | 48 | 99 | 34 | 3 | 6 | 51 | 41 | 158 | 5 | .305 | .368 |
| **MINOR LEAGUE TOTALS** | | | .252 | 274 | 955 | 132 | 241 | 65 | 8 | 21 | 129 | 104 | 316 | 14 | .333 | .403 |

## 22 DAN BRAUER LHP

**Born:** Oct. 14, 1983. **B-T:** L-L. **Ht.:** 6-0. **Wt.:** 210. **Drafted:** Northwestern, 2006 (6th round). **Signed by:** Bob Szymkowski.

After tying for the Cape Cod League in wins and ranking second in strikeouts in 2004, Brauer was set to be an early-round pick in 2005. But he started having shoulder problems at the end of that summer and needed surgery to repair a torn labrum. It didn't take long for Brauer to make a strong recovery, however, as he was the Big Ten Conference pitcher of the year and he threw a no-hitter against Michigan State. Brauer might be the poster child for successful labrum surgery survivors, as his velocity jumped from 86-90 mph as an amateur to 92-93 mph in his pro debut after he signed as a sixth-rounder for $150,000. He commands his curveball well, and the pitch grades out as solid average. He creates excellent deception from the left side, and can locate all his pitches to either side of the plate. Brauer will need to further develop his changeup if he is going to stay in the rotation. The Phillies will move Brauer quickly and he will start 2007 in high Class A.

| Year | Club (League) | Class | W | L | ERA | G | GS | CG | SV | IP | H | R | ER | HR | BB | SO | AVG |
|------|---------------|-------|---|---|-----|---|----|----|----|----|---|---|----|----|----|----|-----|
| 2006 | Batavia (NYP) | A | 3 | 4 | 1.96 | 11 | 10 | 0 | 0 | 55 | 39 | 14 | 12 | 1 | 18 | 65 | .206 |
| | Lakewood (SAL) | A | 0 | 1 | 4.50 | 3 | 2 | 0 | 0 | 8 | 10 | 9 | 4 | 1 | 5 | 10 | .303 |
| **MINOR LEAGUE TOTALS** | | | 3 | 5 | 2.29 | 14 | 12 | 0 | 0 | 63 | 49 | 23 | 16 | 2 | 23 | 75 | .221 |

## PAT OVERHOLT

RHP

**Born:** Feb. 8, 1984. **B-T:** R-R. **Ht.:** 6-0. **Wt.:** 190. **Drafted:** Santa Clara, 2005 (22nd round). **Signed by:** Joey Davis.

Overholt always had arm strength, serving as the starting shortstop for three seasons in high school. One of the best athletes in the system, Overholt was also a standout basketball player and golfer at Brighton High in Salt Lake City. However, after a standout freshman season at Santa Clara, where he saved 10 games, he struggled and went just 2-7, 5.09 while trying to become a starter. Primarily used as a reliever after signing as a 22nd-round pick, Overholt blossomed in 2006. He commands his 90-96 mph fastball to both sides of the plate, and his 84-85 mph slider emerged as his out pitch. His slider is a plus pitch, featuring good tilt and deadly late break. Overholt also started implementing a changeup into his repertoire last season, but it's still a work in progress. The Phillies tried to extend Overholt's outings in 2006, pitching him in two- or three-inning stints, and if his changeup shows development, they haven't ruled out a rotation spot in the future. He's a flyball pitcher and homer-prone, giving up one longball every eight innings, but has power reliever stuff. Overholt will return to high Class A to start 2007, but could move quickly once his role is defined.

| Year | Club (League) | Class | W | L | ERA | G | GS | CG | SV | IP | H | R | ER | HR | BB | SO | AVG |
|---|---|---|---|---|---|---|---|---|---|---|---|---|---|---|---|---|---|
| 2005 | Batavia (NYP) | A | 2 | 3 | 2.65 | 21 | 0 | 0 | 5 | 34 | 28 | 12 | 10 | 1 | 13 | 51 | .224 |
| 2006 | Lakewood (SAL) | A | 3 | 3 | 3.15 | 29 | 0 | 0 | 2 | 46 | 37 | 17 | 16 | 4 | 26 | 52 | .223 |
| | Clearwater (FSL) | A | 5 | 3 | 4.10 | 15 | 0 | 0 | 0 | 26 | 20 | 17 | 12 | 5 | 10 | 41 | .196 |
| **MINOR LEAGUE TOTALS** | | | 10 | 9 | 3.23 | 65 | 0 | 0 | 7 | 106 | 85 | 46 | 38 | 10 | 49 | 144 | .216 |

## JASON JARAMILLO

C

**Born:** Oct. 9, 1982. **B-T:** B-R. **Ht.:** 6-0. **Wt.:** 200. **Drafted:** Oklahoma State, 2004 (2nd round). **Signed by:** Paul Scott.

The Phillies have been on Jaramillo since 2001, when they selected him in the 42nd round out of high school. Three years later, they signed him in the second round for $585,000 out of Oklahoma State. Jaramillo broke a bone in his right hand in Double-A last May, costing him three weeks. He never really got on track after that, but finished with a strong showing offensively in the Arizona Fall League, where he hit .379 with a pair of homers in 66 at-bats. Jaramillo started switch-hitting in high school, and he's equally adept from either side of the plate. He has a line-drive stroke that produces gap power, and he'll probably never hit for much pop in the majors. While Jaramillo was rated the best defensive catcher in the South Atlantic League in 2005, scouts were less impressed during his AFL stint, criticizing his game-calling ability as well as his receiving skills. Jaramillo has the best arm in the system behind the plate, and should play in Triple-A this year.

| Year | Club (League) | Class | AVG | G | AB | R | H | 2B | 3B | HR | RBI | BB | SO | SB | OBP | SLG |
|---|---|---|---|---|---|---|---|---|---|---|---|---|---|---|---|---|
| 2004 | Phillies (GCL) | R | .667 | 1 | 3 | 1 | 2 | 0 | 0 | 0 | 1 | 0 | 0 | 0 | .667 | .667 |
| | Batavia (NYP) | A | .223 | 31 | 112 | 11 | 25 | 5 | 0 | 1 | 14 | 12 | 27 | 0 | .299 | .295 |
| 2005 | Lakewood (SAL) | A | .304 | 119 | 448 | 46 | 136 | 28 | 4 | 8 | 63 | 44 | 72 | 2 | .368 | .438 |
| 2006 | Reading (EL) | AA | .248 | 93 | 322 | 35 | 80 | 25 | 1 | 6 | 39 | 32 | 55 | 0 | .320 | .388 |
| | Scranton/W-B (IL) | AAA | .167 | 2 | 6 | 0 | 1 | 0 | 0 | 0 | 1 | 0 | 1 | 0 | .143 | .167 |
| **MINOR LEAGUE TOTALS** | | | .274 | 246 | 891 | 93 | 244 | 58 | 5 | 15 | 118 | 88 | 155 | 2 | .341 | .401 |

## JIM ED WARDEN

RHP

**Born:** May 7, 1979. **B-T:** R-R. **Ht.:** 6-7. **Wt.:** 195. **Drafted:** Tennessee Tech, 2001 (6th round). **Signed by:** Phil Rossi (Indians).

Warden was the first NCAA Division I scholarship athlete out of Middle Tennessee Christian School, a disctinction he earned after he walked on at Tennessee Tech. While he had some success there and showed power stuff, he also set the single-season record of 16 wild pitches for the Golden Eagles. Things didn't go well during much of Warden's pro career either until the Indians switched his arm slot to a low three-quarters angle in 2005. The Phillies took a chance on Warden in the Rule 5 draft, selecting him in the second round of the major league phase. With the new release point, he took off, hitting 90-93 mph consistently with his fastball that tops out at 95. His slider has become a plus pitch, but his changeup was the biggest reason for his success last season in Double-A. Warden is new to the two big changes in his career, both in his arm angle and the bullpen role, and his confidence needs to be stoked. He also needs to be more consistent with his release point, as he'll still come over the top from time to time. He'll need better command if he's going to stick on the Phillies' 25-man roster all season.

| Year | Club (League) | Class | W | L | ERA | G | GS | CG | SV | IP | H | R | ER | HR | BB | SO | AVG |
|---|---|---|---|---|---|---|---|---|---|---|---|---|---|---|---|---|---|
| 2001 | Burlington (Appy) | R | 4 | 5 | 4.27 | 12 | 12 | 0 | 0 | 53 | 56 | 32 | 25 | 6 | 13 | 52 | .265 |
| 2002 | Kinston (CL) | A | 2 | 4 | 6.61 | 7 | 7 | 0 | 0 | 33 | 38 | 27 | 24 | 3 | 30 | 29 | .290 |
| 2003 | Kinston (CL) | A | 0 | 4 | 7.52 | 7 | 7 | 1 | 0 | 26 | 32 | 23 | 22 | 4 | 25 | 21 | .302 |
| | Lake County (SAL) | A | 4 | 3 | 2.86 | 14 | 13 | 0 | 0 | 69 | 49 | 30 | 22 | 5 | 44 | 61 | .197 |
| | Akron (EL) | AA | 0 | 1 | 9.00 | 1 | 1 | 0 | 0 | 4 | 6 | 4 | 4 | 0 | 5 | 1 | .400 |
| 2004 | Lake County (SAL) | A | 5 | 1 | 3.00 | 41 | 1 | 0 | 13 | 54 | 43 | 22 | 18 | 6 | 27 | 63 | .213 |
| | Akron (EL) | AA | 0 | 1 | 9.53 | 4 | 0 | 0 | 0 | 6 | 7 | 7 | 6 | 1 | 7 | 5 | .292 |
| 2005 | Kinston (CL) | A | 3 | 5 | 3.72 | 46 | 0 | 0 | 4 | 68 | 68 | 38 | 28 | 8 | 32 | 72 | .266 |
| 2006 | Akron (EL) | AA | 5 | 2 | 2.90 | 55 | 0 | 0 | 11 | 59 | 35 | 25 | 19 | 3 | 29 | 47 | .172 |
| **MINOR LEAGUE TOTALS** | | | 23 | 26 | 4.07 | 187 | 41 | 1 | 28 | 371 | 334 | 208 | 168 | 36 | 212 | 351 | .239 |

## JEREMY SLAYDEN                                                             OF

**Born:** July 28, 1982. **B-T:** L-R. **Ht.:** 6-0. **Wt.:** 185. **Drafted:** Georgia Tech, 2005 (8th round). **Signed by:** Chip Lawrence.

Slayden was considered a first-round talent in 2004, but injuries plagued him over his last two years at Georgia Tech—most notably a torn rotator cuff in his throwing shoulder. A 20th-round pick of the Padres out of high school and an 18th-round pick by the Athletics in 2004, Slayden ultimately signed for $95,000 as an eighth-rounder with the Phillies a year later. Slayden hit 40 homers during his college career, and he's continued to show power and a solid approach to hitting as a pro. He shortened his stroke in 2006 to make better contact, and used the whole field much better than he ever had. He also commanded the zone and his pitch recognition improved significantly as a result. Because of the shoulder surgery, Slayden is limited to left field defensively, and his arm strength will never be anything more than average. He's never been overly athletic and is a below-average runner. Slayden needs to remain consistent and keep his strikeout totals down. Already 24, he'll jump to Double-A in 2007.

| Year | Club (League) | Class | AVG | G | AB | R | H | 2B | 3B | HR | RBI | BB | SO | SB | OBP | SLG |
|---|---|---|---|---|---|---|---|---|---|---|---|---|---|---|---|---|
| 2005 | Batavia (NYP) | A | .268 | 54 | 194 | 35 | 52 | 11 | 0 | 9 | 36 | 28 | 45 | 1 | .373 | .464 |
| 2006 | Lakewood (SAL) | A | .310 | 107 | 400 | 65 | 124 | 44 | 3 | 10 | 81 | 41 | 89 | 5 | .381 | .510 |
| **MINOR LEAGUE TOTALS** | | | .296 | 161 | 594 | 100 | 176 | 55 | 3 | 19 | 117 | 69 | 134 | 6 | .378 | .495 |

## JASON DONALD                                                             SS

**Born:** Sept. 8, 1984. **B-T:** R-R. **Ht.:** 6-1. **Wt.:** 200. **Drafted:** Arizona, 2006 (3rd round). **Signed by:** Theron Brockish.

Donald turned down big money out of high school to attend Arizona. Donald helped the Wildcats to the College World Series in 2004, then hit .272 in the Cape Cod League in 2005 before eventually signing for $400,000 as a third-round pick last June. Scouts love his gamer mentality and overall makeup, but Donald has one true above-average tool—his plus throwing arm. Donald has a compact, line-drive stroke that produces gap power. The Phillies grade him as a 55 runner on the 20-80 scouting scale, and though he lacks range defensively, his instincts and hands allow him to make up for it. For as compact as Donald's swing is, he goes through mechanical breakdowns at times, and it tends to become long and slow as a result. His arm strength grades higher than Brad Harman's at shortstop, though Harman is the better overall defender. Donald will start his first full season in low Class A.

| Year | Club (League) | Class | AVG | G | AB | R | H | 2B | 3B | HR | RBI | BB | SO | SB | OBP | SLG |
|---|---|---|---|---|---|---|---|---|---|---|---|---|---|---|---|---|
| 2006 | Batavia (NYP) | A | .263 | 63 | 213 | 33 | 56 | 14 | 2 | 1 | 24 | 23 | 42 | 12 | .347 | .362 |
| **MINOR LEAGUE TOTALS** | | | .263 | 63 | 213 | 33 | 56 | 14 | 2 | 1 | 24 | 23 | 42 | 12 | .347 | .362 |

## HEITOR CORREA                                                             RHP

**Born:** Aug. 25, 1989. **B-T:** R-R. **Ht.:** 6-2. **Wt.:** 180. **Signed:** Brazil, 2006. **Signed by:** Sal Agostinelli.

One of four players the Phillies signed out of Brazil for a total of $200,000 in 2006, Correa has the highest ceiling of the group. Some club officials already compare his stuff to Carlos Carrasco's, and they rave about Correa's maturity level and aptitude. He throws three pitches for strikes, working with a 90-94 mph fastball, a curveball with above-average potential and a changeup that shows flashes of being a plus offering. Though he has promising secondary pitches, Correa is reluctant to use them and is content to change speeds with his fastball and vary his location. He's very raw and still learning how to attack hitters in different situations, but his upside is exceptional. He'll battle for a job in the low Class A rotation, but with his age and experience level, Williamsport is a more likely destination.

| Year | Club (League) | Class | W | L | ERA | G | GS | CG | SV | IP | H | R | ER | HR | BB | SO | AVG |
|------|---------------|-------|---|---|-----|---|----|----|----|----|---|---|----|----|----|----|-----|
| 2006 | Phillies (GCL) | R | 0 | 3 | 7.83 | 8 | 4 | 0 | 0 | 23 | 35 | 21 | 20 | 1 | 7 | 14 | .365 |
| **MINOR LEAGUE TOTALS** | | | 0 | 3 | 7.83 | 8 | 4 | 0 | 0 | 23 | 35 | 21 | 20 | 1 | 7 | 14 | .365 |

## 29 ALFREDO SIMON RHP

**Born:** May 8, 1981. **B-T:** R-R. **Ht.:** 6-4. **Wt.:** 230. **Signed:** Dominican Republic, 1999. **Signed by:** Sal Agostinelli.

The Phillies got Simon back in the system after pulling off a Rule 5 draft day trade with the Orioles, dealing the 19th pick in the draft (catcher Adam Donachie from the Royals) and cash for the righthander. Philadelphia was developing Simon nicely for nearly five seasons before dealing him to San Francisco in July 2004 for Felix Rodriguez. As a Giant, Simon struggled in the rotation and moved to the bullpen in 2005. The Rangers signed Simon as a six-year minor league free agent prior to the Rule 5 draft, but he never pitched for them. Simon has a big body and power stuff. He touched 97 several times for in the Dominican Winter League, and several scouts compared him to Freddy Garcia. The problem is that Simon doesn't have Garcia-like secondary pitches. His slider, curveball and changeup are all fringe-average and he doesn't command the zone well with any of them. Simon struggled terribly in the bullpen at Triple-A Fresno last season, and there were reports he had elbow tenderness in the Dominican. The Phillies would like to try him back in the rotation, but they won't if they have to keep him on their 25-man roster all season.

| Year | Club (League) | Class | W | L | ERA | G | GS | CG | SV | IP | H | R | ER | HR | BB | SO | AVG |
|------|---------------|-------|---|---|-----|---|----|----|----|----|---|---|----|----|----|----|-----|
| 2000 | Phillies (DSL) | R | 0 | 0 | 1.46 | 4 | 4 | 0 | 0 | 12 | 6 | 3 | 2 | 0 | 9 | 10 | .136 |
| 2001 | Phillies (GCL) | R | 2 | 2 | 2.91 | 10 | 8 | 0 | 0 | 43 | 35 | 23 | 14 | 2 | 23 | 40 | .220 |
| 2002 | Batavia (NYP) | A | 9 | 2 | 3.59 | 15 | 14 | 0 | 0 | 90 | 79 | 44 | 36 | 5 | 46 | 77 | .237 |
| 2003 | Lakewood (SAL) | A | 5 | 0 | 3.79 | 14 | 7 | 0 | 2 | 71 | 59 | 32 | 30 | 4 | 25 | 66 | .224 |
| 2004 | Clearwater (FSL) | A | 7 | 9 | 3.27 | 22 | 21 | 4 | 0 | 135 | 121 | 58 | 49 | 13 | 38 | 107 | .242 |
|  | San Jose (Cal) | A | 1 | 2 | 5.68 | 6 | 6 | 0 | 0 | 32 | 44 | 24 | 20 | 7 | 12 | 21 | .352 |
| 2005 | Norwich (EL) | AA | 3 | 8 | 5.03 | 43 | 9 | 0 | 19 | 91 | 104 | 54 | 51 | 6 | 24 | 60 | .293 |
| 2006 | Fresno (PCL) | AAA | 0 | 6 | 6.75 | 10 | 10 | 0 | 0 | 52 | 76 | 41 | 39 | 8 | 19 | 35 | .349 |
|  | San Jose (Cal) | A | 2 | 4 | 6.44 | 18 | 7 | 0 | 0 | 36 | 43 | 28 | 26 | 7 | 14 | 35 | .299 |
| **MINOR LEAGUE TOTALS** | | | 29 | 33 | 4.27 | 142 | 86 | 4 | 21 | 563 | 567 | 307 | 267 | 52 | 210 | 451 | .265 |

## 30 MATT SMITH LHP

**Born:** June 15, 1979. **B-T:** L-L. **Ht.:** 6-5. **Wt.:** 225. **Drafted:** Oklahoma State, 2000 (4th round). **Signed by:** Mark Batchko (Yankees).

No stranger to the big game atmosphere, Smith was Oklahoma State's No. 1 starter as a sophomore on the school's last team to go to Omaha. He also pitched in the same rotation as Mark Prior for Team USA in 1999, but injuries plagued him throughout his pro career and he never panned out as a starter. The Yankees moved Smith to the bullpen in 2002, where he steadily climbed through the system working with a fastball/slider mix. Smith gets good late life on his 90-93 mph fastball, and his sweeping slider with 1-to-7 break can be a plus pitch at times. The slider is Smith's best pitch, and gives him a chance to start the year in the Philadelphia bullpen. A middle or situational reliever who could help the big league club immediately, Smith's ceiling is limited to a solid-average lefty setup man with not much upside beyond that.

| Year | Club (League) | Class | W | L | ERA | G | GS | CG | SV | IP | H | R | ER | HR | BB | SO | AVG |
|------|---------------|-------|---|---|-----|---|----|----|----|----|---|---|----|----|----|----|-----|
| 2000 | Staten Island (NYP) | A | 5 | 4 | 2.38 | 14 | 14 | 0 | 0 | 76 | 74 | 32 | 20 | 1 | 20 | 59 | .261 |
| 2001 | Greensboro (SAL) | A | 5 | 3 | 2.59 | 16 | 16 | 1 | 0 | 97 | 69 | 37 | 28 | 1 | 32 | 116 | .197 |
|  | Tampa (FSL) | A | 6 | 2 | 2.24 | 11 | 11 | 0 | 0 | 68 | 54 | 21 | 17 | 2 | 22 | 71 | .215 |
| 2002 | Norwich (EL) | AA | 3 | 8 | 5.44 | 17 | 17 | 0 | 0 | 89 | 112 | 63 | 54 | 8 | 37 | 70 | .305 |
|  | Tampa (FSL) | A | 0 | 4 | 6.59 | 8 | 6 | 0 | 0 | 27 | 37 | 23 | 20 | 1 | 17 | 20 | .330 |
| 2003 | Tampa (FSL) | A | 2 | 3 | 2.23 | 6 | 6 | 0 | 0 | 32 | 20 | 11 | 8 | 0 | 12 | 25 | .175 |
|  | Trenton (EL) | AA | 2 | 3 | 4.26 | 9 | 9 | 0 | 0 | 51 | 57 | 29 | 24 | 6 | 24 | 36 | .291 |
| 2004 | Trenton (EL) | AA | 4 | 4 | 4.96 | 14 | 11 | 0 | 0 | 62 | 67 | 34 | 34 | 5 | 31 | 56 | .285 |
| 2005 | Trenton (EL) | AA | 3 | 4 | 2.80 | 22 | 4 | 0 | 2 | 55 | 46 | 24 | 17 | 2 | 23 | 59 | .230 |
|  | Columbus (IL) | AAA | 2 | 0 | 2.60 | 25 | 0 | 0 | 1 | 28 | 24 | 9 | 8 | 3 | 13 | 33 | .226 |
| 2006 | New York (AL) | MLB | 0 | 0 | 0.00 | 12 | 0 | 0 | 0 | 12 | 4 | 0 | 0 | 0 | 8 | 9 | .105 |
|  | Columbus (IL) | AAA | 0 | 1 | 2.08 | 24 | 0 | 0 | 0 | 26 | 27 | 9 | 6 | 3 | 8 | 22 | .267 |
|  | Scranton/W-B (IL) | AAA | 0 | 0 | 2.00 | 9 | 0 | 0 | 4 | 9 | 5 | 2 | 2 | 1 | 6 | 6 | .161 |
|  | Clearwater (FSL) | A | 0 | 0 | 0.00 | 2 | 0 | 0 | 0 | 2 | 0 | 0 | 0 | 0 | 0 | 6 | .000 |
|  | Philadelphia (NL) | MLB | 0 | 1 | 2.08 | 14 | 0 | 0 | 0 | 9 | 3 | 2 | 2 | 0 | 4 | 12 | .111 |
| **MINOR LEAGUE TOTALS** | | | 32 | 36 | 3.44 | 177 | 94 | 1 | 7 | 622 | 592 | 294 | 238 | 33 | 245 | 579 | .252 |
| **MAJOR LEAGUE TOTALS** | | | 0 | 1 | 0.87 | 26 | 0 | 0 | 0 | 20 | 7 | 2 | 2 | 0 | 12 | 21 | .108 |

# PITTSBURGH
# PIRATES

BY **JOHN PERROTTO**

For years the Pirates have said the key to building a winning team is scouting and player development. Yet seemingly each winter, they would add fading veterans to provide quick fixes.

After going 67-95 in 2005, Pittsburgh traded for Sean Casey and signed Jeromy Burnitz and Joe Randa. That plan backfired badly, as the three combined to hit just 23 home runs and drive in 106 runs en route to another 67-95 season in 2006.

Those failures finally spurred the Pirates to do more than just pay lip service to the idea of building from within. Following a 30-60 record before the all-star break, they got younger in the second half by benching Burnitz and Randa and dealing Casey to the Tigers. Pittsburgh went 37-35, its first winning record after the break since 1992, which also happens to be the last season it finished on the positive side of .500.

For a change, the Pirates entered the off-season legitimately feeling they had a nucleus of young players who could help the franchise end its string of 14 consecutive losing seasons. That's just two shy of the major legue record set by the 1933-48 Phillies.

The biggest reason for optimism is that Pittsburgh finished the season with four starting pitchers 24 or younger in Zach Duke, **Tom Gorzelanny**, Paul Maholm and Ian Snell. The Pirates also had a 28-year-old closer in Mike Gonzalez, who converted all 24 of his save opportunities in his first full season on the job, and a 23-year-old heir apparent in Matt Capps, who set a franchise rookie record by pitching in 89 games.

Ronny Paulino was called up from Triple-A

in mid-April and seized the starting catching job by hitting .310. By the end of the season, Pittsburgh's entire starting lineup consisted of players 28 or younger, including Jason Bay, who has one National League rookie of the year award and two all-star berths in three years with the Bucs, and National League batting champion Freddy Sanchez.

After infusing so much youth into their big league roster, however, the Pirates now have a thin farm system with few premium prospects. Most of their younger players were drafted during Mickey White's three-year run as scouting director from 1999-2001, which included taking Snell in the 26th round in 2000 and Duke in the 20th round in 2001.

One of general manager Dave Littlefield's first moves after taking over midway through the 2001 season was to fire White and replace him with Ed Creech. Creech's last three first-round picks—outfielder Andrew McCutchen (2005), catcher Neil Walker (2004) and righthander Brad Lincoln (2006)—are Pittsburgh's best prospects, but his drafts haven't been as deep as White's.

It's hard to pin all the blame on Creech, though. Pirates ownership went through a period where it overruled the scouting department's desire to draft high-ceiling prospects in favor of college players. While Pittsburgh currently has a young team, the number of potential contributors coming up behind them is minimal.

## TOP 30 PROSPECTS

| | |
|---|---|
| 1. Andrew McCutchen, of | 16. Pat Bresnehan, rhp |
| 2. Neil Walker, c | 17. Dave Davidson, lhp |
| 3. Brad Lincoln, rhp | 18. James Boone, of |
| 4. Brent Lillibridge, ss | 19. Josh Shortslef, lhp |
| 5. Yoslan Herrera, rhp | 20. Joe Bauserman, rhp |
| 6. Josh Sharpless, rhp | 21. Shelby Ford, 2b |
| 7. Steven Pearce, 1b | 22. Brandon Holden, rhp |
| 8. Brian Bixler, ss | 23. Steve Lerud, c |
| 9. Brad Corley, of | 24. Jesse Chavez, rhp |
| 10. Todd Redmond, rhp | 25. Franquelis Osoria, rhp |
| 11. Mike Felix, lhp | 26. Brian Rogers, rhp |
| 12. John Van Benschoten, rhp | 27. Rajai Davis, of |
| 13. Bryan Bullington, rhp | 28. Jim Negrych, 2b |
| 14. Wardell Starling, rhp | 29. Jared Hughes, rhp |
| 15. Jonah Bayliss, rhp | 30. Romulo Sanchez, rhp |

# ORGANIZATION OVERVIEW

**General manager:** David Littlefield. **Farm director:** Brian Graham. **Scouting director:** Ed Creech.

## 2006 PERFORMANCE

| Class | Team | League | W | L | PCT | Finish* | Manager | Affiliated |
|---|---|---|---|---|---|---|---|---|
| Majors | Pittsburgh | National | 67 | 95 | .414 | 15 (16) | Jim Tracy | — |
| Triple-A | Indianapolis Indians | International | 76 | 66 | .535 | 4th (14) | Trent Jewett | 2005 |
| Double-A | Altoona Curve | Eastern | 75 | 64 | .540 | 3rd (12) | Tim Leiper | 1999 |
| High A | Lynchburg Hillcats | Carolina | 63 | 75 | .457 | 7th (8) | Gary Green | 1995 |
| Low A | Hickory Crawdads | South Atlantic | 67 | 70 | .489 | 10th (16) | Jeff Branson | 1999 |
| Short-season | #Williamsport Crosscutters | New York-Penn | 28 | 47 | .373 | 13th (14) | Tom Prince | 1999 |
| Rookie | GCL Pirates | Gulf Coast | 27 | 26 | .509 | 6th (13) | Turner Ward | 1967 |
| **OVERALL 2006 MINOR LEAGUE RECORD** | | | 336 | 348 | .491 | 19th (30) | | |

*Finish in overall standings (No. of teams in league). +League champion. #Affiliate will be in State College (New York-Penn) in 2007.

## ORGANIZATION LEADERS

**BATTING**

| | | |
|---|---|---|
| AVG | Keel, Jared, GCL Pirates/Williamsport | .313 |
| R | Lillibridge, Brent, Hickory/Lynchburg | 106 |
| H | Bixler, Brian, Lynchburg/Altoona | 164 |
| 2B | Pearce, Steven, Hickory/Lynchburg | 40 |
| 3B | Buttler, Vic, Altoona/Indianapolis | 15 |
| HR | Pearce, Steven, Hickory/Lynchburg | 26 |
| RBI | Corley, Brad, Hickory | 100 |
| BB | Lillibridge, Brent, Hickory/Lynchburg | 87 |
| SO | Lerud, Steve, Hickory | 160 |
| SB | Morgan, Nyjer, Lynchburg/Altoona | 72 |
| OBP | Lillibridge, Brent, Hickory/Lynchburg | .419 |
| SLG | Pearce, Steven, Hickory/Lynchburg | .523 |
| XBH | Pearce, Steven, Hickory/Lynchburg | 68 |

**PITCHING**

| | | |
|---|---|---|
| W | Jacobsen, Landon, Indianapolis/Altoona | 14 |
| L | Four players tied at | 11 |
| ERA | Bresnahan, Pat, Williamsport | 2.25 |
| G | Knight, Brandon, Altoona | 58 |
| | Nitkowski, C.J., Indianapolis | 58 |
| SV | Knight, Brandon, Altoona | 32 |
| IP | Starling, Wardell, Lynchburg/Altoona | 179 |
| BB | Connolly, Michael, Indianapolis/Altoona | 62 |
| SO | Redmond, Todd, Hickory | 148 |
| AVG | Bresnahan, Pat, Williamsport | .201 |

## BEST TOOLS

| | |
|---|---|
| Best Hitter for Average | Andrew McCutchen |
| Best Power Hitter | Neil Walker |
| Best Strike-Zone Discipline | Brent Lillibridge |
| Fastest Baserunner | Rajai Davis |
| Best Athlete | Andrew McCutchen |
| Best Fastball | Brad Lincoln |
| Best Curveball | Brad Lincoln |
| Best Slider | Josh Sharpless |
| Best Changeup | Todd Redmond |
| Best Control | Josh Shortslef |
| Best Defensive Catcher | Matt Clarkson |
| Best Defensive Infielder | Brent Lillibridge |
| Best Infield Arm | Javier Guzman |
| Best Defensive Outfielder | Andrew McCutchen |
| Best Outfield Arm | Austin McClune |

## PROJECTED 2010 LINEUP

| | |
|---|---|
| Catcher | Ronny Paulino |
| First Base | Steven Pearce |
| Second Base | Freddy Sanchez |
| Third Base | Neil Walker |
| Shortstop | Brent Lillibridge |
| Left Field | Jason Bay |
| Center Field | Andrew McCutchen |
| Right Field | Xavier Nady |
| No. 1 Starter | Brad Lincoln |
| No. 2 Starter | Ian Snell |
| No. 3 Starter | Zach Duke |
| No. 4 Starter | Tom Gorzelanny |
| No. 5 Starter | Paul Maholm |
| Closer | Matt Capps |

## LAST YEAR'S TOP 20 PROSPECTS

1. Neil Walker, c
2. Andrew McCutchen, of
3. Tom Gorzelanny, lhp
4. Paul Maholm, lhp
5. Jose Bautista, 3b
6. Nate McLouth, of
7. Bryan Bullington, rhp
8. John Van Benschoten, rhp
9. Chris Duffy, of
10. Matt Capps, rhp
11. Rajai Davis, of
12. Craig Stansberry, 2b
13. Ronny Paulino, c
14. James Boone, of
15. Brad Corley, of
16. Mike Johnston, lhp
17. Josh Sharpless, rhp
18. Joe Bauserman, rhp
19. Todd Redmond, rhp
20. Adam Boeve, of

## TOP PROSPECTS OF THE DECADE

| Year | Player, Pos. | 2006 Org. |
|---|---|---|
| 1997 | Kris Benson, rhp | Orioles |
| 1998 | Kris Benson, rhp | Orioles |
| 1999 | Chad Hermansen, of | Sioux Falls (Am. Assoc.) |
| 2000 | Chad Hermansen, of | Sioux Falls (Am. Assoc.) |
| 2001 | J.R. House, c | Astros |
| 2002 | J.R. House, c | Astros |
| 2003 | John Van Benschoten, rhp | Pirates |
| 2004 | John Van Benschoten, rhp | Pirates |
| 2005 | Zack Duke, lhp | Pirates |
| 2006 | Andrew McCutchen, cf | Pirates |

## TOP DRAFT PICKS OF THE DECADE

| Year | Player, Pos. | 2006 Org. |
|---|---|---|
| 1997 | J.J. Davis, of | Out of baseball |
| 1998 | Clint Johnson, lhp/of | Out of baseball |
| 1999 | Bobby Bradley, rhp | Out of baseball |
| 2000 | Sean Burnett, lhp | Pirates |
| 2001 | John Van Benschoten, rhp/of | Pirates |
| 2002 | Bryan Bullington, rhp | Pirates |
| 2003 | Paul Maholm, lhp | Pirates |
| 2004 | Neil Walker, c | Pirates |
| 2005 | Andrew McCutchen, of | Pirates |
| 2006 | Brad Lincoln, rhp | Pirates |

## ALL-TIME LARGEST BONUSES

| | |
|---|---|
| Bryan Bullington, 2002 | $4,000,000 |
| Brad Lincoln, 2006 | $2,750,000 |
| John Van Benschoten, 2001 | $2,400,000 |
| Bobby Bradley, 1999 | $2,225,000 |
| Paul Maholm, 2003 | $2,200,000 |

# MINOR LEAGUE DEPTH CHART

## Pittsburgh Pirates

**Impact: B.** McCutchen and Lincoln cover for some of the organization's missteps, but the prospect list suffers from players who face either significant injury questons or limited ceilings.

**Depth: D.** Losing six players—including Tom Gorzelanny, Paul Maholm and Matt Capps—from last year's list doesn't help, but draft misses have been more damaging and leave the Pirates with few prospects who will be able to step in this season.

**Sleeper:** Victor Igsema, of. Old for the Gulf Coast League, the Pirates will be patient with Igsema because he has huge raw power.

*Numbers in parentheses indicate prospect rankings.*

| LF | CF | RF |
|---|---|---|
| Jason Delaney | Andrew McCutchen (1) | Brad Corley (9) |
| Justin Byler | James Boone (18) | Victor Igsema |
| Tom Hagan | Rajai Davis (27) | Adam Boeve |
| | Nyjer Morgan | |

| 3B | SS | 2B | 1B |
|---|---|---|---|
| Eddie Prasch | Brent Lillibridge (4) | Shelby Ford (21) | Steven Pearce (7) |
| Jared Keel | Brian Bixler (8) | Jim Negrych (28) | Kent Sakamoto |
| | Javier Guzman | Craig Stansberry | Daniel Rios |
| | Jose Luis de los Santos | Cameron Blair | |
| | Angel Gonzalez | | |

| C |
|---|
| Neil Walker (2) |
| Steve Lerud (23) |
| Mike McCuistion |

### RHP

| Starters | Relievers |
|---|---|
| Brad Lincoln (3) | Josh Sharpless (6) |
| Yuslan Herrera (5) | Jonah Bayliss (15) |
| Todd Redmond (10) | Jesse Chavez (24) |
| John Van Benschoten (12) | Franquelis Osoria (25) |
| Bryan Bullington (13) | Brian Rogers (26) |
| Wardell Starling (14) | Romulo Sanchez (30) |
| Pat Bresnehan (16) | Justin Vaclavik |
| Joe Bauserman (20) | Jason Quarles |
| Brandon Holden (22) | Eric Ridener |
| Jared Hughes (29) | Chris Hernandez |
| Clayton Hamilton | Jonathan Albaladejo |
| Brad Clapp | Chad Blackwell |
| Matt Peterson | |

### LHP

| Starters | Relievers |
|---|---|
| Mike Felix (11) | Dave Davidson (17) |
| Josh Shortslef (19) | Juan Perez |
| Shane Youman | |

# DRAFT ANALYSIS

## 2006 — SIGNING BUDGET: $4.9 million

**Best Pro Debut:** The Pirates put RHP Pat Bresnehan's (5) delivery more in line with the plate, resulting in improved command. He had a 2.25 ERA in his debut, which concluded with 34 consecutive scoreless innings. He sat at 92 mph and showed better feel for his secondary pitches.

**Best Athlete:** OF Austin McClune (7) was a star defensive back in high school. His best tools are his speed and arm strength, and he started to translate his raw power into game action during instructional league. RHP Brad Lincoln (1) and LHP Mike Felix (2) were two-way stars in college but too talented on the mound to pursue hitting in pro ball. 1B Tom Hagan (39) punted at Virginia.

**Best Pure Hitter:** 2B Shelby Ford (3) has a solid stroke from both sides of the plate and hit .278/.345/.452 with most of his action coming in low Class A. He'll be better once he adds some strength to his 6-foot-3, 190-pound frame.

**Best Raw Power:** Probably Lincoln, who was one of the most dangerous power hitters in the Cape Cod League in 2005, though he won't get many at-bats in the future because he'll be pitching. Pittsburgh mainly drafted line-drive hitters who produce more for average than for pop. 2B Jim Negrych (6) has the most present power—more average than plus—with Ford in line to pass him if he fills out.

**Fastest Runner:** OF James Barksdale (15) has plus-plus speed and led NCAA Division II with 59 steals in 69 attempts. McClune is nearly as fast.

**Best Defensive Player:** Alex Presley (8) is an instinctive center fielder. McClune has the tools to surpass him once he gains more experience.

**Best Fastball:** Lincoln sits at 92-93 mph and touches 97 with good life on his four-seam fastball. He also can get groundballs with his darting 88-91 mph two-seamer. Bresnehan and RHP Steve MacFarland (9) both can reach 94 mph.

**Best Breaking Ball:** Lincoln's hard curveball is just as impressive as his fastball, and he can throw it for strikes or entice hitters to chase it out of the zone. Felix and RHP Brandon Holden (13) have above-average curves.

**Most Intriguing Background:** Unsigned SS Brandon Wilkerson's (47) father Curtis played in the majors.

**Closest To The Majors:** Though a strained oblique muscle slowed Lincoln in his debut, he still should speed toward PNC Park. He could arrive by late 2007.

**Best Late-Round Pick:** Holden would have gone in the second or third round had he not come down with triceps tendinitis during the spring. He showed an 88-93 mph fastball and a hammer curveball when healthy. Pittsburgh signed him away from Florida for $155,000 in late August.

**The One Who Got Away:** The Pirates really liked 3B Lonnie Chisenhall's (11) left-handed bat. There were teams that would have taken him as early as the supplemental first round if he were considered signable, and Pittsburgh couldn't deter him from attending South Carolina.

**Assessment:** After focusing more on bats in the previous two drafts, the Pirates went for college pitchers. They got one of the best with Lincoln at No. 4 overall, and Felix, RHP Jared Hughes (4) and Bresnehan could join him on the fast track.

## 2005 — BUDGET: $3.7 million

OF Andrew McCutchen (1) has a higher ceiling than anyone the Pirates have drafted in years. SS Brent Lillibridge (4) joins him among the system's small number of truly quality prospects, while 1B Steven Pearce (8) got attention by hitting 26 homers in his first full season. **GRADE: B+**

## 2004 — BUDGET: $4.1 million

C Neil Walker (1), a local product, is the real deal, and SS Brian Bixler (2) started to hit in 2006. But this crop drops off quickly after that. **GRADE: C+**

## 2003 — BUDGET: $4.4 million

Pittsburgh found not one but two lefty starters in Paul Maholm (1) and Tom Gorzelanny (2). RHP Josh Sharpless (24), another local product, could provide bullpen help. **GRADE: B**

*Draft analysis by Jim Callis. Numbers in parentheses indicate draft rounds. Budgets are bonuses in first 10 rounds.*

# ANDREW
# McCUTCHEN

RHP

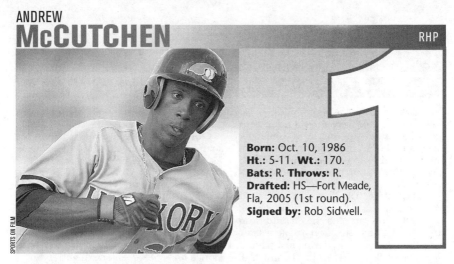

SPORTS ON FILM

**Born:** Oct. 10, 1986
**Ht.:** 5-11. **Wt.:** 170.
**Bats:** R. **Throws:** R.
**Drafted:** HS—Fort Meade, Fla, 2005 (1st round).
**Signed by:** Rob Sidwell.

A first-team All-American and Florida's high school player of the year in 2005, McCutchen hit .709 with 11 homers as a senior at Fort Meade High, located in the heart of phosphate mining country in Central Florida. He spent time singing in the choir at the church where his father is a youth minister, writing poetry and drawing when he wasn't leading the state in hitting. McCutchen also was a potential big-time football recruit as a wide receiver until suffering a serious right knee injury in his sophomore season and undergoing reconstructive surgery. He comes from a very athletic background, as his father was a running back at Division II power Carson-Newman (Tenn.) and his mother was a Florida junior college volleyball standout. The 11th overall pick in the 2005 draft, McCutchen signed for $1.9 million and immediately jumped on the fast track to the major leagues. Baseball America rated him the No. 1 prospect in the Rookie-level Gulf Coast League in 2005 and in the low Class A South Atlantic League in 2006. He skipped a level and jumped to Altoona last August, and he had no trouble performing in Double-A as a 19-year-old.

McCutchen already has shown the ability to hit for average with his quick wrists and simple swing, and he's also developing over-the-fence power as his body begins to fill out. He already drives the ball to all fields, and scouts project him as a .300 hitter with 20-25 homers per season in the major leagues. He especially wears out lefthanders, batting .318/.469/.549 with eight home runs in 154 at-bats against them in 2006. McCutchen has tremendous speed, which he uses to cover plenty of ground in center field. He's a potential Gold Glover. His arm is his only tool that isn't a plus, but it's average and he hits the cutoff man and throws to the right base. He also wins high marks for his attitude, maturity and passion for the game.

While McCutchen has a better concept of the strike zone than most hitters his age, his plate discipline slipped in his first full season and will need some refinement. Though he has succeeded on 40 of 50 (80 percent) steal attempts in pro ball, he has the speed to be much more dangerous on the basepaths. He says his primary goal for 2007 is to improve his basestealing knowledge. Once he does, there's no reason he couldn't contend for stolen base titles once he reaches the majors.

McCutchen has advanced faster than the Pirates ever could have hoped when they drafted him. He'll likely open 2007 back in Double-A, putting him in position to spend September in the majors if he continues to progress. He has leadoff skills but he has hit primarily out of the No. 3 slot in pro ball. With his power continuing to develop, Pittsburgh envisions him as a middle-of-the-order hitter.

| Year | Club (League) | Class | AVG | G | AB | R | H | 2B | 3B | HR | RBI | BB | SO | SB | OBP | SLG |
|------|---------------|-------|------|-----|-----|-----|-----|-----|-----|-----|-----|-----|-----|-----|------|------|
| 2005 | Pirates (GCL) | R | .297 | 45 | 158 | 36 | 47 | 9 | 3 | 2 | 30 | 29 | 24 | 13 | .411 | .430 |
| | Williamsport (NY-P) | A | .346 | 13 | 52 | 12 | 18 | 3 | 1 | 0 | 5 | 8 | 6 | 4 | .443 | .442 |
| 2006 | Hickory (SAL) | A | .291 | 114 | 453 | 77 | 132 | 20 | 4 | 14 | 62 | 42 | 91 | 22 | .356 | .446 |
| | Altoona (EL) | AA | .308 | 20 | 78 | 12 | 24 | 4 | 0 | 3 | 12 | 8 | 20 | 1 | .379 | .474 |
| **MINOR LEAGUE TOTALS** | | | .298 | 192 | 741 | 137 | 221 | 36 | 8 | 19 | 109 | 87 | 141 | 40 | .377 | .445 |

## 2 NEIL WALKER C

STEVE MOORE

**Born:** Sept. 10, 1985. **B-T:** B-R. **Ht.:** 6-3. **Wt.:** 211. **Drafted:** HS—Gibsonia, Pa., 2004 (1st round). **Signed by:** Jon Mercurio.

After starring at Pine-Richland High, Walker became the first Pittsburgh-area player ever selected in the first round by the Pirates. He hurt his left wrist swinging a bat in the Arizona Fall League after the 2005 season and had surgery that November. He missed the first six weeks of 2006 and had limited power all season, though he did make it to Pittsburgh for the Futures Game. Walker is a rarity, a switch-hitting catcher with the potential to hit 30 home runs a season. He has plus power from the left side, though it was muted as he recovered from his wrist surgery. He also makes good contact at the plate. He's a good athlete with average speed. His arm is strong and he has a quick release. Because he doesn't walk much, pitchers at higher levels could exploit Walker's lack of patience. He threw out just 29 percent of basestealers in 2006 because his sloppy footwork costs him accuracy. His receiving also needs refinement, though he's doing better at shifting for balls. The Pirates might get more long-term production out of him by shifting him to another position, and he has the athleticism to handle third base or the outfield. Ronny Paulino's presence might also dictate a move for Walker, but he'll start 2007 as a catcher in Double-A.

| Year | Club (League) | Class | AVG | G | AB | R | H | 2B | 3B | HR | RBI | BB | SO | SB | OBP | SLG |
|------|---------------|-------|-----|---|----|---|---|----|----|----|-----|----|----|----|-----|-----|
| 2004 | Pirates (GCL) | R | .271 | 52 | 192 | 28 | 52 | 12 | 3 | 4 | 20 | 10 | 33 | 3 | .313 | .427 |
| | Williamsport (NY-P) | A | .313 | 8 | 32 | 2 | 10 | 3 | 0 | 0 | 7 | 2 | 1 | 1 | .343 | .406 |
| 2005 | Hickory (SAL) | A | .301 | 120 | 485 | 78 | 146 | 33 | 2 | 12 | 68 | 20 | 71 | 7 | .332 | .452 |
| | Lynchburg (Car) | A | .262 | 9 | 42 | 4 | 11 | 2 | 1 | 0 | 12 | 0 | 12 | 0 | .244 | .357 |
| 2006 | Lynchburg (Car) | A | .284 | 72 | 264 | 32 | 75 | 22 | 1 | 3 | 35 | 19 | 41 | 3 | .345 | .409 |
| | Altoona (EL) | AA | .161 | 10 | 31 | 5 | 5 | 0 | 0 | 2 | 3 | 1 | 4 | 0 | .188 | .355 |
| **MINOR LEAGUE TOTALS** | | | .286 | 271 | 1046 | 149 | 299 | 72 | 7 | 21 | 145 | 52 | 162 | 14 | .324 | .428 |

## 3 BRAD LINCOLN RHP

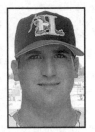

**Born:** May 25, 1985 **B-T:** L-R. **Ht.:** 6-0. **Wt.:** 200. **Drafted:** Houston, 2006 (1st round). **Signed by:** Everett Russell.

Lincoln was the Conference USA player of the year in 2006, when he went 12-2, 1.69 and hit .295 with 14 homers as a first baseman/DH. He went fourth overall in the draft and signed for $2.75 million, but he was limited in his pro debut and instructional league by a strained right oblique. Lincoln's fastball sits at 92-93 mph and touches 97, breaking bats with its boring action. He also has a two-seam, 88-91 mph version that induces grounders. His hard curveball may be a better pitch than his fastball, but he commands them both well. Though he's just 6 feet tall, he does a good job of throwing downhill. As a hitter, he has more raw power than almost any Pirates farmhand. His biggest need is to gain more consistency with his changeup, which should come as he uses it more often in pro ball. It should become an average pitch. His velocity was down in his pro debut, but that was likely just the combination of fatigue after pulling double duty in college and his oblique injury. The Pirates usually downplay their draft picks, but they believe Lincoln could be a No. 1 starter. He likely will begin 2007 at high Class A Lynchburg with an eye on making his major league debut no later than 2008.

| Year | Club (League) | Class | W | L | ERA | G | GS | CG | SV | IP | H | R | ER | HR | BB | SO | AVG |
|------|---------------|-------|---|---|-----|---|----|----|----|----|---|---|----|----|----|----|-----|
| 2006 | Pirates (GCL) | R | 0 | 0 | 0.00 | 2 | 2 | 0 | 0 | 8 | 6 | 1 | 0 | 0 | 1 | 9 | .222 |
| | Hickory (SAL) | A | 1 | 2 | 6.75 | 4 | 4 | 0 | 0 | 16 | 25 | 15 | 12 | 2 | 6 | 10 | .368 |
| **MINOR LEAGUE TOTALS** | | | 1 | 2 | 4.56 | 6 | 6 | 0 | 0 | 24 | 31 | 16 | 12 | 2 | 7 | 19 | .326 |

## 4 BRENT LILLIBRIDGE SS

RICH ABEL

**Born:** Sept, 18, 1983. **B-T:** R-R. **Ht.:** 5-11. **Wt.:** 182. **Drafted:** Washington, 2005 (4th round). **Signed by:** Greg Hopkins.

Lillibridge was a three-time all-Pac-10 Conference selection at Washington, as a center fielder in his freshman season then as a shortstop the next two years. After a so-so pro debut, he had an outstanding first full season, leading the system in hitting (.319), runs (106), walks (87) and on-base percentage (.419) while adding 53 steals in 64 tries. Lillibridge hits for average, has solid gap power and showed improved plate discipline in 2006. He has above-average speed and very good instincs on the bases Defensively, he has outstanding range, especially to his right, and a solid arm. He projects as a possible leadoff hitter, but to fill that role Lillibridge will need to

shorten his swing and cut down on his strikeouts. Though he can make acrobatic plays at shortstop, he sometimes tries to pull off impossible ones, leading to 47 errors in 169 pro games. He'll return to Double-A after participating in the Eastern League playoffs at the end of 2006. Though Pirates incumbent Jack Wilson has three years and $19.6 million remaining on his contract, Lillibridge could enter the picture by September.

| Year | Club (League) | Class | AVG | G | AB | R | H | 2B | 3B | HR | RBI | BB | SO | SB | OBP | SLG |
|------|---------------|-------|-----|---|----|---|---|----|----|----|-----|----|----|----|-----|-----|
| 2005 | Williamsport (NY-P) | A | .243 | 42 | 169 | 19 | 41 | 12 | 4 | 4 | 18 | 14 | 35 | 10 | .305 | .432 |
| 2006 | Hickory (SAL) | A | .299 | 74 | 274 | 59 | 82 | 18 | 5 | 11 | 43 | 51 | 61 | 29 | .414 | .522 |
| | Lynchburg (Car) | A | .313 | 54 | 201 | 47 | 63 | 10 | 3 | 2 | 28 | 36 | 43 | 24 | .426 | .423 |
| **MINOR LEAGUE TOTALS** | | | .289 | 170 | 644 | 125 | 186 | 40 | 12 | 17 | 89 | 101 | 139 | 63 | .391 | .467 |

## 5 YOSLAN HERRERA

RHP

**Born:** April 28, 1981. **B-T:** R-R. **Ht.:** 6-2. **Wt.:** 200. **Signed:** Cuba, 2006. **Signed by:** Rene Gayo/Louie Eljaua.

Herrera defected from Cuba after being left off the Olympic roster in 2004 because of injury. He impressed Pittsburgh general manager Dave Littlefield during a workout last August in the Dominican Republic, and signed a three-year, $1.92 million major league contract (including a $750,000 bonus) in December. Loathe to participate in the international market in recent years because of soaring costs, the Pirates hadn't signed a Cuban since the 1950s. Herrera has a good feel for pitching with an above-average curveball and a splitter that drops off the table. He has good mound presence and was a disciple of Jose Contreras when both pitched for Pinar del Rio in Cuba. His fastball has fringy velocity, sitting at 88 mph and touching 92, though some scouts project Herrera to work in the low 90s once he gets established in the United States. He'll have to adapt to a new culture, a challenge that has undone several Cuban defectors in the past. Herrera will have a chance to compete for a job in Pittsburgh's rotation this spring, though he may need some minor league seasoning after not pitching competitively for nearly three years. He projects as a possible No. 3 starter.

| Year | Club (League) | Class | W | L | ERA | G | GS | CG | SV | IP | H | R | ER | HR | BB | SO | AVG |
|------|---------------|-------|---|---|-----|---|----|----|----|----|---|---|----|----|----|----|-----|
| 2006 | Did not play—Signed 2007 contract | | | | | | | | | | | | | | | | |

## 6 JOSH SHARPLESS

RHP

**Born:** Jan. 26, 1981. **B-T:** R-R. **Ht.:** 6-5. **Wt.:** 235. **Drafted:** Allegheny (Pa.), 2003 (24th round). **Signed by:** Jon Mercurio.

Sharpless was lightly recruited by colleges out of high school in suburban Pittsburgh, and he pitched just 19 innings as a senior after getting mononucleosis. He spent four years at Division III Allegheny (Pa.) before signing for $1,500 as a 24th-rounder. He returned home twice in 2006, first for the Futures Game in July and then when the Pirates called him up in August. Sharpless put up video-game numbers in the minors (2.20 ERA, 12.5 strikeouts per nine innings) and succeeded in the majors because hitters have such a difficult time picking up his pitches. He throws straight over the top, and his outstanding slider breaks so big and so late that batters have almost no time to react. His 92 mph fastball occasionally hits 95 and looks faster because of his long wingspan. He has struggled with his control at times, most notably after his big league callup. However, Sharpless began throwing more strikes after Pirates pitching coach Jim Colborn made a mechanical adjustment late in 2006. He's not athletic and doesn't field his position well. Sharpless has a good chance of winning a middle-relief job in Pittsburgh during spring training. If can find the strike zone consistently, he has the ability to eventually become a set-up man and perhaps even a closer.

| Year | Club (League) | Class | W | L | ERA | G | GS | CG | SV | IP | H | R | ER | HR | BB | SO | AVG |
|------|---------------|-------|---|---|-----|---|----|----|----|----|---|---|----|----|----|----|-----|
| 2003 | Williamsport (NY-P) | A | 1 | 1 | 2.59 | 22 | 0 | 0 | 5 | 31 | 19 | 9 | 9 | 2 | 17 | 45 | .173 |
| 2004 | Hickory (SAL) | A | 6 | 2 | 3.03 | 44 | 0 | 0 | 4 | 74 | 42 | 28 | 25 | 4 | 55 | 109 | .158 |
| 2005 | Lynchburg (Car) | A | 3 | 0 | 0.00 | 17 | 0 | 0 | 5 | 27 | 7 | 1 | 0 | 0 | 11 | 46 | .081 |
| | Altoona (EL) | AA | 1 | 0 | 2.89 | 7 | 0 | 0 | 0 | 9 | 6 | 3 | 3 | 0 | 3 | 13 | .171 |
| 2006 | Altoona (EL) | AA | 2 | 0 | 0.86 | 14 | 0 | 0 | 8 | 21 | 8 | 2 | 2 | 0 | 9 | 30 | .114 |
| | Indianapolis (IL) | AAA | 1 | 1 | 2.45 | 23 | 0 | 0 | 1 | 33 | 32 | 11 | 9 | 1 | 15 | 30 | .250 |
| | Pittsburgh (NL) | MLB | 0 | 0 | 1.50 | 14 | 0 | 0 | 0 | 12 | 7 | 2 | 2 | 0 | 11 | 7 | .175 |
| **MINOR LEAGUE TOTALS** | | | 14 | 4 | 2.20 | 127 | 0 | 0 | 23 | 196 | 114 | 54 | 48 | 7 | 110 | 273 | .164 |
| **MAJOR LEAGUE TOTALS** | | | 0 | 0 | 1.50 | 14 | 0 | 0 | 0 | 12 | 7 | 2 | 2 | 0 | 11 | 7 | .175 |

## 7  STEVEN PEARCE
1B

**Born:** April 13, 1983. **B-T:** R-R. **Ht.:** 5-11. **Wt.:** 198. **Drafted:** South Carolina, 2005 (8th round). **Signed by:** Jack Powell.

Pearce turned down the Red Sox as a 10th-round pick after hitting .346 with 21 homers for South Carolina's 2004 College World Series team, then batted .358 with 21 homers as a senior and went in the eighth round in 2005. He has continued to slug his way through the lower minors, leading the short-season New York-Penn League with 26 doubles in his pro debut and hitting 26 homers in his first full season. Pearce generates his power with bat speed and an aggressive approach. Though he looks to punish pitchers, he's also willing to take a walk. Pearce is solid defensively at first base, with decent range and soft hands. Pitchers can fool Pearce with offspeed stuff and he has particular trouble staying back against changeups. At 5-foot-11, he presents a small target for a first baseman. He's a below-average runner but will take an extra base on occasion. Like most of Pittsburgh's best prospects, Pearce will open 2007 in Double-A. That will be a good test after he has been old for his previous levels. The Pirates lack power on their major league club, so an opportunity awaits when he's ready.

| Year | Club (League) | Class | AVG | G | AB | R | H | 2B | 3B | HR | RBI | BB | SO | SB | OBP | SLG |
|------|---------------|-------|-----|---|----|---|---|----|----|----|-----|----|----|----|-----|-----|
| 2005 | Williamsport (NY-P) | A | .301 | 72 | 272 | 48 | 82 | 26 | 0 | 7 | 52 | 35 | 43 | 2 | .381 | .474 |
| 2006 | Hickory (SAL) | A | .288 | 41 | 160 | 35 | 46 | 13 | 1 | 12 | 38 | 15 | 32 | 1 | .363 | .606 |
| | Lynchburg (Car) | A | .265 | 90 | 328 | 48 | 87 | 27 | 1 | 14 | 60 | 34 | 65 | 7 | .348 | .482 |
| **MINOR LEAGUE TOTALS** | | | .283 | 203 | 760 | 131 | 215 | 66 | 2 | 33 | 150 | 84 | 140 | 10 | .363 | .505 |

## 8  BRIAN BIXLER
SS

**Born:** Oct. 22, 1982. **B-T:** R-R. **Ht.:** 6-1. **Wt.:** 190. **Drafted:** Eastern Michigan, 2004 (2nd round). **Signed by:** Duane Gustavson.

Bixler was the Mid-American Conference player of the year in 2004, setting Eastern Michigan records for hitting (.453) and runs (74) and league marks for hits (110) and hitting streak (32 games). After a lackluster first 1½ pro seasons, he made the high Class A Carolina League all-star team and reached Double-A in 2006, batting better than .300 at both stops. The most improved player in the system in 2006, Bixler tightened his strike zone, which allowed him to be more productive at the plate. He has gotten stronger over the last two years, giving him decent gap power. With above-average speed, he's a threat to steal bases and beat out infield hits. Bixler strikes out too much, particularly for a top-of-the-order hitter. He can improve the frequency and the success rate (71 percent) with which he steals bases. His arm and range are average at best, so he faces an eventual move to second base. Coupled with Pittsburgh's lack of middle-infield prospects in the upper levels, a good spring performance could push Bixler to Triple-A Indianapolis to start 2007. With shortstop Jack Wilson signed through 2009 in Pittsburgh, it would be easier for Bixler to push underachieving Jose Castillo off second base.

| Year | Club (League) | Class | AVG | G | AB | R | H | 2B | 3B | HR | RBI | BB | SO | SB | OBP | SLG |
|------|---------------|-------|-----|---|----|---|---|----|----|----|-----|----|----|----|-----|-----|
| 2004 | Williamsport (NY-P) | A | .276 | 59 | 228 | 40 | 63 | 7 | 4 | 0 | 21 | 15 | 51 | 14 | .321 | .342 |
| 2005 | Hickory (SAL) | A | .281 | 126 | 502 | 74 | 141 | 23 | 2 | 9 | 50 | 38 | 134 | 21 | .343 | .388 |
| 2006 | Lynchburg (Car) | A | .303 | 73 | 267 | 46 | 81 | 16 | 2 | 5 | 33 | 35 | 58 | 18 | .402 | .434 |
| | Altoona (EL) | AA | .301 | 60 | 226 | 36 | 68 | 13 | 1 | 3 | 19 | 16 | 57 | 6 | .363 | .407 |
| **MINOR LEAGUE TOTALS** | | | .289 | 318 | 1223 | 196 | 353 | 59 | 9 | 17 | 123 | 104 | 300 | 59 | .356 | .393 |

## 9  BRAD CORLEY
OF

**Born:** Dec. 28, 1983. **B-T:** R-R. **Ht.:** 6-2. **Wt.:** 198. **Drafted:** Mississippi State, 2005 (2nd round). **Signed by:** Everett Russell.

Corley set himself up as a possible first-round pick by hitting .380 with 19 homers as a Mississippi State sophomore, but he hit just five homers as a junior after breaking a thumb while trying out for Team USA the previous summer. He led both the system and the South Atlantic League with 100 RBIs in 2006, his first full pro season. Corley has good tools, including plus power and a strong arm. He struggled early in his pro debut, leading to talk the Pirates had overdrafted him in the second round, but he shortened his swing and began to hit better. Primarily a right fielder, he has enough speed to get by in center if needed. The knock on Corley in college was that he lacked plate discipline, and his 109-18 K-BB ratio as an older player in the SAL shows that he hasn't made much progress. Pitchers continually get him to chase high fastballs and

breaking balls in the dirt. His tools are intriguing, especially in an organization lacking power-hitting prospects, but Corley will have to make more consistent contact to become a big league regular. He'll move up to high Class A to start 2007.

| Year | Club (League) | Class | AVG | G | AB | R | H | 2B | 3B | HR | RBI | BB | SO | SB | OBP | SLG |
|------|---------------|-------|-----|---|----|---|---|----|----|----|-----|----|----|----|-----|-----|
| 2005 | Williamsport (NY-P) | A | .279 | 68 | 265 | 29 | 74 | 10 | 6 | 4 | 35 | 16 | 56 | 3 | .331 | .408 |
| 2006 | Hickory (SAL) | A | .281 | 134 | 534 | 87 | 150 | 32 | 2 | 16 | 100 | 18 | 109 | 9 | .323 | .438 |
| **MINOR LEAGUE TOTALS** | | | .280 | 202 | 799 | 116 | 224 | 42 | 8 | 20 | 135 | 34 | 165 | 12 | .326 | .428 |

## TODD REDMOND
RHP

**Born:** May 17, 1985. **B-T:** R-R. **Ht.:** 6-3. **Wt.:** 210. **Drafted:** St. Petersburg (Fla.) JC, 2004 (39th round). **Signed by:** Rob Sidwell.

Redmond led St. Petersburg (Fla.) to a runner-up finish at the Junior College World Series championship in 2005, then signed with the Pirates as a draft-and-follow. He finished second in the New York-Penn League in ERA during his pro debut, and continued to impress in 2006, ranking fourth in the South Atlantic League in wins and ERA. Redmond has exceptional command of his low-90s fastball and gets a lot of swings and misses with it, particularly up in the strike zone. He complements his fastball with an outstanding changeup and a solid curveball. He's very efficient with his pitches, which should allow him to work deeper into games as he gets older, and wins high marks for his competitiveness. He lacks a dominant pitch, and Redmond's stuff may not play as well against more experienced hitters. He gives up a lot of fly balls, which could be a problem if he stops missing bats. Redmond likely will start 2007 in high Class A and should make a midseason move to Double-A. If he continues to prove himself, he could fit into the majors as a No. 3 or 4 starter.

| Year | Club (League) | Class | W | L | ERA | G | GS | CG | SV | IP | H | R | ER | HR | BB | SO | AVG |
|------|---------------|-------|---|---|-----|---|----|----|----|----|---|---|----|----|----|----|-----|
| 2005 | Williamsport (NY-P) | A | 1 | 2 | 1.98 | 15 | 14 | 0 | 0 | 73 | 62 | 22 | 16 | 2 | 21 | 63 | .232 |
| 2006 | Hickory (SAL) | A | 13 | 6 | 2.75 | 27 | 27 | 0 | 0 | 160 | 137 | 64 | 49 | 13 | 33 | 148 | .227 |
| **MINOR LEAGUE TOTALS** | | | 14 | 8 | 2.51 | 42 | 41 | 0 | 0 | 233 | 199 | 86 | 65 | 15 | 54 | 211 | .228 |

## MIKE FELIX
LHP

**Born:** Aug. 13, 1985. **B-T:** L-L. **Ht.:** 5-11. **Wt.:** 190. **Drafted:** Troy, 2006 (2nd round). **Signed by:** Darren Mazeroski.

After barely playing as a sophomore at Auburn, Felix transferred to Troy at the urging of high school teammate Jared Keel. Felix starred as a two-way player for the Trojans in 2006, and the Pirates jumped on him in the second round of the draft and signed him for $725,000. Pittsburgh also landed Keel in the 31st round and sent them both to short-season Williamsport. Felix has a big-breaking curveball that is tough on lefthanders, though they batted .379 against him in his pro debut. At times, his fastball will reach as high as 93 mph. He's a good athlete, drawing comparisons to Mike Hampton for his hitting and fielding ability. Except for the curveball, the rest of Felix's arsenal is nondescript. His fastball usually sits around 88 mph and his changeup is below-average. He's inconsistent with his control and command, regressing after making progess at Troy during the spring. Felix will open his first full season as a starter in low Class A. If he can't improve his command and his changeup, his ceiling will be limited to being a setup man. With his curveball alone, he should be able to become at least a lefty specialist.

| Year | Club (League) | Class | W | L | ERA | G | GS | CG | SV | IP | H | R | ER | HR | BB | SO | AVG |
|------|---------------|-------|---|---|-----|---|----|----|----|----|---|---|----|----|----|----|-----|
| 2006 | Williamsport (NY-P) | A | 1 | 6 | 3.56 | 13 | 13 | 0 | 0 | 48 | 41 | 24 | 19 | 3 | 33 | 49 | .236 |
| **MINOR LEAGUE TOTALS** | | | 1 | 6 | 3.56 | 13 | 13 | 0 | 0 | 48 | 41 | 24 | 19 | 3 | 33 | 49 | .236 |

## JOHN VAN BENSCHOTEN
RHP

**Born:** April 14, 1980. **B-T:** R-R. **Ht.:** 6-4. **Wt.:** 215. **Drafted:** Kent State, 2001 (1st round). **Signed by:** Duane Gustavson.

The Pirates bucked conventional draft wisdom by taking Van Benschoten as a pitcher in 2001, after he hit a Division I-leading 31 home runs and stole 23 bases in his junior season at Kent State. He showed great promise early in his pro career and was ranked as the Pirates' top prospect going into the 2003 and 2004 season, but he has been beset by injuries the past two years, having two arthroscopic surgeries on his right shoulder and one on his left. After sitting out all of 2005, Van Benschoten made five minor league starts at the end of the 2006 season, and the Pirates were pleased that his fastball velocity was close to its previous 91-94 mph. He also has a plus curveball and a slider that can be an out pitch when he throws it for strikes. He's athletic, capable of helping himself at the plate and in the field. Van Benschoten's biggest

problem isn't only that he hasn't been able to stay healthy, but also that he hasn't been able to gain the experience necessary for someone who pitched only as a reliever in college. He also hasn't been able to develop a feel for his changeup. He still has the talent to be a No. 2 starter but needs to get on the mound consistently. He'll likely begin the season in Triple-A.

| Year | Club (League) | Class | W | L | ERA | G | GS | CG | SV | IP | H | R | ER | HR | BB | SO | AVG |
|---|---|---|---|---|---|---|---|---|---|---|---|---|---|---|---|---|---|
| 2001 | Williamsport (NY-P) | A | 0 | 2 | 3.51 | 9 | 9 | 0 | 0 | 26 | 23 | 11 | 10 | 0 | 10 | 19 | .247 |
| 2002 | Hickory (SAL) | A | 11 | 4 | 2.80 | 27 | 27 | 0 | 0 | 148 | 119 | 57 | 46 | 6 | 62 | 145 | .219 |
| 2003 | Lynchburg (Car) | A | 6 | 0 | 2.22 | 9 | 9 | 0 | 0 | 49 | 33 | 14 | 12 | 1 | 18 | 49 | .192 |
| | Altoona (EL) | AA | 7 | 6 | 3.69 | 17 | 17 | 1 | 0 | 90 | 95 | 46 | 37 | 5 | 34 | 78 | .268 |
| 2004 | Nashville (PCL) | AAA | 4 | 11 | 4.72 | 23 | 23 | 0 | 0 | 132 | 135 | 75 | 69 | 16 | 49 | 101 | .264 |
| | Pittsburgh (NL) | MLB | 1 | 3 | 6.91 | 6 | 5 | 0 | 0 | 29 | 33 | 27 | 22 | 3 | 19 | 18 | .300 |
| 2005 | Did not play—Injured | | | | | | | | | | | | | | | | |
| 2006 | Pirates (GCL) | R | 0 | 1 | 4.50 | 1 | 1 | 0 | 0 | 6 | 1 | 3 | 3 | 1 | 2 | 4 | .053 |
| | Altoona (EL) | AA | 1 | 0 | 3.60 | 1 | 1 | 0 | 0 | 5 | 3 | 2 | 2 | 0 | 3 | 3 | .176 |
| | Indianapolis (IL) | AAA | 1 | 1 | 5.40 | 3 | 3 | 0 | 0 | 12 | 10 | 7 | 7 | 2 | 7 | 13 | .233 |
| **MINOR LEAGUE TOTALS** | | | 30 | 25 | 3.58 | 90 | 90 | 1 | 0 | 467 | 419 | 215 | 186 | 31 | 185 | 412 | .239 |
| **MAJOR LEAGUE TOTALS** | | | 1 | 3 | 6.91 | 6 | 5 | 0 | 0 | 28 | 33 | 27 | 22 | 3 | 19 | 18 | .300 |

## BRYAN BULLINGTON RHP

**Born:** Sept. 30, 1980. **B-T:** R-R. **Ht.:** 6-5. **Wt.:** 220. **Drafted:** Ball State, 2002 (1st round). **Signed by:** Duane Gustavson.

Bullington has been under the microscope since the Pirates used the first overall pick to take him rather than B.J. Upton in the 2002 draft. They signed him for a club-record signing bonus of $4 million. After four seasons in the organization, he has pitched in just one major league game, though he's 34-17, 3.33 in 69 minor league games. However, he missed all of last season after shoulder surgery in October 2005. Bullington's fastball was clocked as high as 95 mph at Ball State, but he has never touched that in pro ball. His heater now sits at 88-91, far from overpowering, though he has good command of it. He rediscovered his slider in Triple-A in 2005 and it became a strikeout pitch for him. His curveball and changeup are also serviceable pitches. While he's getting older and his chance of becoming a star has likely passed, he could still develop into a decent starter if healthy. He'll go back to Triple-A to start the 2007 season.

| Year | Club (League) | Class | W | L | ERA | G | GS | CG | SV | IP | H | R | ER | HR | BB | SO | AVG |
|---|---|---|---|---|---|---|---|---|---|---|---|---|---|---|---|---|---|
| 2003 | Hickory (SAL) | A | 5 | 1 | 1.39 | 8 | 7 | 0 | 0 | 45 | 25 | 10 | 7 | 3 | 11 | 46 | .155 |
| | Lynchburg (Car) | A | 8 | 4 | 3.05 | 17 | 17 | 2 | 0 | 97 | 101 | 39 | 33 | 5 | 27 | 67 | .270 |
| 2004 | Altoona (EL) | AA | 12 | 7 | 4.10 | 26 | 26 | 0 | 0 | 145 | 160 | 77 | 66 | 18 | 47 | 100 | .289 |
| 2005 | Indianapolis (IL) | AAA | 9 | 5 | 3.38 | 18 | 18 | 1 | 0 | 109 | 104 | 48 | 41 | 11 | 26 | 82 | .251 |
| | Pittsburgh (NL) | MLB | 0 | 0 | 13.50 | 1 | 0 | 0 | 0 | 1 | 1 | 2 | 2 | 0 | 1 | 1 | .250 |
| 2006 | Did not play—Injured | | | | | | | | | | | | | | | | |
| **MINOR LEAGUE TOTALS** | | | 34 | 17 | 3.33 | 69 | 68 | 3 | 0 | 397 | 390 | 174 | 147 | 37 | 111 | 295 | .259 |
| **MAJOR LEAGUE TOTALS** | | | 0 | 0 | 13.85 | 1 | 0 | 0 | 0 | 1 | 1 | 2 | 2 | 0 | 1 | 1 | .250 |

## WARDELL STARLING RHP

**Born:** March 14, 1983. **B-T:** R-R. **Ht.:** 6-4. **Wt.:** 205. **Drafted:** Odessa (Texas) JC, D/F 2002 (4th round). **Signed by:** Tom Barnard.

Starling was a highly regarded high school player in the Houston area, and he and James Loney led Elkins High (Missouri City, Texas) to a Texas state title and national championship in 2002. Starling opted to attend Odessa (Texas) Junior College, then signed with the Pirates as a draft-and-follow just before the 2003 draft. Consistency had been Starling's biggest problem since coming into pro ball, but he made gains in that department last season. He pitched well in his second try at high Class A, then continued to get hitters out at Double-A. His fastball velocity was erratic earlier in his career but stayed consistently at 91-93 mph in 2006. He also improved his changeup. Starling's curveball continues to be inconsistent and occasionally gets loopy. The downside to what was otherwise a breakout season was that his strikeout rate dropped and he tended to tire after five innings. He's likely to go back to Double-A to start the season. If he continues to show improvement, he'll be in line for a promotion to Triple-A, putting him on the cusp of the major leagues, where he projects as a middle-of-the-rotation starter.

| Year | Club (League) | Class | W | L | ERA | G | GS | CG | SV | IP | H | R | ER | HR | BB | SO | AVG |
|---|---|---|---|---|---|---|---|---|---|---|---|---|---|---|---|---|---|
| 2003 | Pirates (GCL) | R | 4 | 1 | 3.94 | 11 | 11 | 0 | 0 | 48 | 47 | 23 | 21 | 5 | 13 | 52 | .247 |
| 2004 | Hickory (SAL) | A | 11 | 8 | 4.11 | 26 | 26 | 1 | 0 | 140 | 132 | 84 | 64 | 10 | 51 | 114 | .253 |
| 2005 | Lynchburg (Car) | A | 10 | 10 | 5.22 | 28 | 28 | 1 | 0 | 153 | 168 | 98 | 89 | 18 | 55 | 102 | .279 |
| 2006 | Lynchburg (Car) | A | 4 | 4 | 3.18 | 13 | 13 | 0 | 0 | 74 | 53 | 35 | 26 | 3 | 17 | 45 | .202 |
| | Altoona (EL) | AA | 6 | 5 | 2.80 | 15 | 15 | 1 | 0 | 87 | 81 | 36 | 27 | 6 | 27 | 42 | .249 |
| **MINOR LEAGUE TOTALS** | | | 35 | 28 | 4.07 | 93 | 93 | 4 | 0 | 502 | 481 | 276 | 227 | 42 | 163 | 355 | .253 |

## JONAH BAYLISS                                                    RHP

**Born:** Aug. 13, 1980. **B-T:** R-R. **Ht.:** 6-2. **Wt.:** 200. **Drafted:** Trinity (Conn.), 2002 (7th round). **Signed by:** Steve Connelly (Royals).

The Pirates were happy just to shed themselves of Mark Redman's $4.5 million salary when they traded him to Kansas City in 2005. They got two minor league relievers in return, and it turns out they got a useful piece in Bayliss, who finished fourth in the Triple-A International League in saves last season. His career took a major step forward in 2005 when the Royals converted him from starter to reliever. Bullpen work fits the former high school hockey star's mentality better and allows him to more often use his best pitch, a fastball that picked up a few ticks in 2006 to 94-95 mph with good movement. Bayliss, befitting a former starter, still has a slider, split-finger fastball and changeup in his arsenal. While the slider became more reliable last season, he needs to throw it for strikes more often. The other pitches are now pretty much just for show. Bayliss enjoys the challenge of closing and will handle that role again if he's sent back to Triple-A to begin this season. However, he'll have a good shot to earn a spot on the major league roster in spring training and work in middle relief.

| Year | Club (League) | Class | W | L | ERA | G | GS | CG | SV | IP | H | R | ER | HR | BB | SO | AVG |
|------|---------------|-------|---|---|-----|---|----|----|----|----|---|---|----|----|----|----|-----|
| 2002 | Spokane (NWL) | A | 4 | 8 | 5.35 | 15 | 15 | 0 | 0 | 71 | 70 | 46 | 42 | 9 | 29 | 38 | .264 |
| 2003 | Burlington (MWL) | A | 7 | 12 | 3.86 | 26 | 26 | 2 | 0 | 140 | 129 | 78 | 60 | 11 | 69 | 133 | .242 |
| 2004 | Wilmington (Car) | A | 6 | 6 | 4.93 | 24 | 24 | 0 | 0 | 111 | 119 | 70 | 61 | 11 | 44 | 79 | .287 |
| 2005 | Kansas City (AL) | MLB | 0 | 0 | 4.63 | 11 | 0 | 0 | 0 | 12 | 7 | 6 | 6 | 2 | 4 | 10 | .167 |
| | Wichita (TL) | AA | 1 | 2 | 2.84 | 30 | 0 | 0 | 8 | 57 | 43 | 19 | 18 | 5 | 26 | 63 | .208 |
| 2006 | Indianapolis (IL) | AAA | 3 | 3 | 2.17 | 46 | 0 | 0 | 23 | 58 | 37 | 15 | 14 | 4 | 28 | 67 | .181 |
| | Pittsburgh (NL) | MLB | 1 | 1 | 4.30 | 11 | 0 | 0 | 0 | 15 | 13 | 7 | 7 | 1 | 11 | 15 | .241 |
| **MINOR LEAGUE TOTALS** | | | 21 | 31 | 4.02 | 141 | 65 | 2 | 31 | 437 | 398 | 228 | 195 | 40 | 196 | 380 | .245 |
| **MAJOR LEAGUE TOTALS** | | | 1 | 1 | 4.44 | 22 | 0 | 0 | 0 | 26 | 20 | 13 | 13 | 3 | 15 | 25 | .208 |

## PAT BRESNEHAN                                                    RHP

**Born:** April 23, 1985. **B-T:** R-R. **Ht.:** 6-1. **Wt.:** 195. **Drafted:** Arizona State, 2006 (5th round). **Signed by:** Ted Williams.

Bresnehan led the state with 109 strikeouts in 49 innings during his sophomore season of high school in 2001 in Dover, Mass. He went to school in Connecticut for a year, then he struck out 21 in a one-hitter during the first start of his senior year back in Massachusetts. Because of his commitment to Arizona State, however, he lasted until the 23rd round of the 2003 draft, and he didn't sign with the Royals. He had an up-and-down career with the Sun Devils, going 10-9, 5.01 in 193 innings over three seasons before Pittsburgh signed him for $202,500. He got on a roll in pro ball, finishing the summer with 34 straight scoreless innings. Bresnehan's fastball consistently hits 91 mph and tops out at 94, and it looks even faster because of its exceptional movement. He also has a hard slider to go along with a curveball and a changeup. He had control problems throughout his college career, but Williamsport pitching coach Bruce Tanner suggested some mechanical adjustments which seemed to help. Bresnehan has a maximum-effort delivery and tends to throw across his body, which raises long-term injury concerns. But he was a pleasant surprise in his first pro season, and will begin 2007 in low Class A. His arsenal suggests his future could be in the bullpen—and his stuff held up better in that role in college—but mastering the changeup would make him a viable starter.

| Year | Club (League) | Class | W | L | ERA | G | GS | CG | SV | IP | H | R | ER | HR | BB | SO | AVG |
|------|---------------|-------|---|---|-----|---|----|----|----|----|---|---|----|----|----|----|-----|
| 2006 | Williamsport (NY-P) | A | 4 | 5 | 2.25 | 15 | 10 | 0 | 0 | 68 | 50 | 21 | 17 | 3 | 17 | 59 | .201 |
| **MINOR LEAGUE TOTALS** | | | 4 | 5 | 2.25 | 15 | 10 | 0 | 0 | 68 | 50 | 21 | 17 | 3 | 17 | 59 | .201 |

## DAVE DAVIDSON                                                    LHP

**Born:** April 23, 1984. **B-T:** L-L. **Ht.:** 6-1. **Wt.:** 188. **Drafted:** HS—Thorold, Ont., 2002 (10th round). **Signed by:** Charlie Sullivan.

The Pirates saw plenty of upside in Davidson when they drafted him out of Canada, but he didn't have much opportunity to show his ability until last year. He signed too late to play professionally in 2002, then was limited in his first three seasons because of a variety of injuries. The Pirates decided to move him to the bullpen last season because of his durability problems, and he had a 2.01 ERA and 96 strikeouts in a combined 76 innings at three levels. Davidson's fastball rarely tops 90 mph, but he has an outstanding curveball that eats up hitters from both sides of the plate. He struggled in the past to command his pitches, illustrated by his 50 walks in 62 innings in his first three seasons. But having the chance to pitch more consistently helped him cut that rate to 3.9 per nine innings in 2006. He lacks experi-

ence with a changeup, though he won't need it in the bullpen. He has a good chance to begin the 2007 season in Triple-A and be knocking on the door of the major leagues by midseason.

| Year | Club (League) | Class | W | L | ERA | G | GS | CG | SV | IP | H | R | ER | HR | BB | SO | AVG |
|------|---------------|-------|---|---|-----|---|----|----|----|----|---|---|----|----|----|----|-----|
| 2003 | Pirates (GCL) | R | 0 | 2 | 12.91 | 7 | 0 | 0 | 0 | 8 | 10 | 12 | 11 | 0 | 7 | 8 | .357 |
| 2004 | Pirates (GCL) | R | 1 | 0 | 3.44 | 7 | 1 | 0 | 0 | 18 | 16 | 11 | 7 | 0 | 14 | 24 | .235 |
| 2005 | Hickory (SAL) | A | 1 | 2 | 9.78 | 10 | 2 | 0 | 0 | 19 | 16 | 22 | 21 | 4 | 21 | 23 | .225 |
| | Williamsport (NY-P) | A | 1 | 1 | 3.18 | 5 | 4 | 0 | 0 | 17 | 14 | 7 | 6 | 0 | 8 | 23 | .226 |
| 2006 | Hickory (SAL) | A | 2 | 1 | 1.93 | 27 | 0 | 0 | 0 | 56 | 39 | 18 | 12 | 2 | 21 | 72 | .195 |
| | Lynchburg (Car) | A | 0 | 0 | 2.16 | 5 | 0 | 0 | 0 | 8 | 6 | 2 | 2 | 0 | 2 | 11 | .194 |
| | Altoona (EL) | AA | 1 | 1 | 2.31 | 10 | 1 | 0 | 0 | 12 | 8 | 4 | 3 | 0 | 10 | 13 | .186 |
| **MINOR LEAGUE TOTALS** | | | 6 | 7 | 4.03 | 71 | 8 | 0 | 0 | 138 | 109 | 76 | 62 | 6 | 83 | 174 | .217 |

## 18 JAMES BOONE                                                             OF

**Born:** March 16, 1983. **B-T:** B-R. **Ht.:** 6-2. **Wt.:** 191. **Drafted:** Missouri, 2005 (3rd round). **Signed by:** Jim Rough.

The Pirates thought they drafted a potential star when they took Boone in 2005, but he hasn't seen the field much in his two seasons because of injuries. A cousin of former American League batting champion Carney Lansford, Boone had a pinched nerve in his final season at Missouri, and it affected him during his first year in pro ball as well when he spent time on the disabled list at Williamsport. A broken foot kept him on the DL at low Class A Hickory until May 24 in 2005, and he played just 28 games before shoulder problems sidelined him for the rest of the year. Boone has a multitude of tools, as he's a switch-hitter with the potential to hit for average and power. He's also an above-average center fielder with good range and a decent arm. He has good speed, though it hasn't translated into many stolen bases yet. Boone will go back to low Class A after his aborted 2006 season. While his future is intriguing and his work ethic is outstanding, he's at an age where he'll need to start moving up the organizational ladder quickly to have a chance to be a major league regular.

| Year | Club (League) | Class | AVG | G | AB | R | H | 2B | 3B | HR | RBI | BB | SO | SB | OBP | SLG |
|------|---------------|-------|-----|---|----|---|---|----|----|----|-----|----|----|----|-----|-----|
| 2005 | Williamsport (NY-P) | A | .291 | 68 | 278 | 44 | 81 | 12 | 4 | 8 | 42 | 16 | 85 | 8 | .343 | .450 |
| 2006 | Hickory (SAL) | A | .192 | 28 | 99 | 11 | 19 | 3 | 0 | 0 | 3 | 13 | 30 | 3 | .302 | .222 |
| **MINOR LEAGUE TOTALS** | | | .265 | 96 | 377 | 55 | 100 | 15 | 4 | 8 | 45 | 29 | 115 | 11 | .332 | .390 |

## 19 JOSH SHORTSLEF                                                          LHP

**Born:** Feb. 1, 1982. **B-T:** R-L. **Ht.:** 6-4. **Wt.:** 242. **Drafted:** HS—Sterling, N.Y., 2000 (6th round). **Signed by:** Charlie Sullivan.

Shortslef has made slow progress through the Pirates system since being drafted in 2000, leading the New York-Penn League with 10 wins in 2002 but also being beset by a series of arm injuries. He showed enough at Double-A in 2006—despite being sidelined for 10 weeks by a strained forearm—to be placed on the 40-man roster at the end of the season and sent to the Arizona Fall League. Shortslef's fastball reaches 93 mph and usually sits at 89-91. He also has a big-breaking curveball that's particularly effective against lefthanders, who hit just .188 against him last season. His changeup still needs work. Shortslef was a good athlete in high school, averaging 21 points a game as a power forward in basketball during his senior year, but he has gotten heavier in recent years, leading to concern about his conditioning. He needs more time at Double-A to start the season but could move quickly to Triple-A if he pitches well early in the season. The Pirates still think he can be a major league starter, but his ability to get lefthanders out could mean a move to the bullpen.

| Year | Club (League) | Class | W | L | ERA | G | GS | CG | SV | IP | H | R | ER | HR | BB | SO | AVG |
|------|---------------|-------|---|---|-----|---|----|----|----|----|---|---|----|----|----|----|-----|
| 2000 | Pirates (GCL) | R | 3 | 2 | 3.73 | 11 | 3 | 0 | 0 | 31 | 26 | 15 | 13 | 1 | 11 | 19 | .224 |
| 2001 | Pirates (GCL) | R | 2 | 3 | 3.63 | 10 | 4 | 1 | 0 | 35 | 39 | 23 | 14 | 1 | 9 | 14 | .293 |
| 2002 | Williamsport (NY-P) | A | 10 | 4 | 3.33 | 14 | 13 | 0 | 0 | 76 | 84 | 36 | 28 | 2 | 18 | 37 | .284 |
| 2003 | Hickory (SAL) | A | 0 | 5 | 7.50 | 5 | 5 | 0 | 0 | 18 | 21 | 15 | 15 | 0 | 6 | 14 | .296 |
| 2004 | Hickory (SAL) | A | 11 | 5 | 4.42 | 30 | 18 | 0 | 0 | 124 | 134 | 65 | 61 | 11 | 38 | 92 | .278 |
| 2005 | Lynchburg (Car) | A | 10 | 5 | 4.58 | 22 | 22 | 1 | 0 | 120 | 132 | 69 | 61 | 8 | 44 | 84 | .284 |
| 2006 | Altoona (EL) | AA | 6 | 2 | 4.45 | 12 | 12 | 0 | 0 | 61 | 62 | 33 | 30 | 4 | 13 | 50 | .262 |
| | Pirates (GCL) | R | 1 | 1 | 3.78 | 3 | 2 | 0 | 0 | 17 | 15 | 9 | 7 | 1 | 3 | 12 | .246 |
| **MINOR LEAGUE TOTALS** | | | 43 | 27 | 4.28 | 107 | 79 | 2 | 0 | 481 | 513 | 265 | 229 | 28 | 142 | 322 | .276 |

## 20 JOE BAUSERMAN                                                           RHP

**Born:** Oct. 4, 1985. **B-T:** R-R. **Ht.:** 6-2. **Wt.:** 238. **Drafted:** HS—Tallahassee, Fla, 2004 (4th round). **Signed by:** Rob Sidwell.

Bauserman was a high school standout in both baseball and football. His father moved the family from Winchester, Va., to Tallahassee, Fla., after his son's sophomore year in order to increase his exposure and chances of getting a scholarship. It worked, as Bauserman

signed to play quarterback at Ohio State, but he wound up choosing baseball when the Pirates gave him a $300,000 signing bonus as their fourth-round pick in 2004. He missed the final month of last season with shoulder tendinitis, but the condition wasn't considered serious and he has a solid build. Bauserman's fastball was clocked as high as 96 mph in high school, but has usually been at 90-92 in pro ball. He has outstanding secondary pitches and has continually tightened his curveball since becoming a pro. He also throws a good changeup that has the potential to become an above-average pitch. He needs to pitch off his fastball more because his curve and change are so good that he tends to rely too much on them at times. Bauserman is making steady progress and will begin 2007 in high Class A. He projects as a solid mid-rotation starter in the major leagues.

| Year | Club (League) | Class | W | L | ERA | G | GS | CG | SV | IP | H | R | ER | HR | BB | SO | AVG |
|------|---------------|-------|---|---|-----|---|----|----|----|----|---|---|----|----|----|----|-----|
| 2004 | Pirates (GCL) | R | 2 | 2 | 2.79 | 9 | 8 | 0 | 0 | 39 | 26 | 13 | 12 | 4 | 10 | 35 | .187 |
| 2005 | Williamsport (NY-P) | A | 6 | 2 | 2.84 | 14 | 14 | 0 | 0 | 70 | 64 | 30 | 22 | 3 | 26 | 45 | .253 |
| 2006 | Hickory (SAL) | A | 6 | 8 | 4.01 | 21 | 21 | 0 | 0 | 110 | 117 | 66 | 49 | 11 | 38 | 63 | .267 |
| **MINOR LEAGUE TOTALS** | | | 14 | 12 | 3.42 | 44 | 43 | 0 | 0 | 218 | 207 | 109 | 83 | 18 | 74 | 143 | .249 |

## 21 SHELBY FORD 2B

**Born:** Dec. 15, 1984. **B-T:** B-R. **Ht.:** 6-3. **Wt.:** 190. **Drafted:** Oklahoma State, 2006 (3rd round). **Signed by:** Mike Leuzinger.

Ford was a three-time all-state selection as a high school player in Fort Worth and decided to stay home to play at Texas Christian. He transferred to Oklahoma State following his sophomore season, however, and played one year with the Cowboys before being drafted in the third round. Signed for $450,000, he spent just seven games at Williamsport after signing before he was promoted to low Class A. He has good power potential for a middle infielder. He hit 35 home runs in three college seasons, including 16 as a freshman, then slugged .452 in his pro debut. More experienced pro pitchers were able to get Ford to chase pitches, though plate discipline wasn't an issue in college. Ford converted to second base as a junior at Oklahoma State after playing third base at Texas Christian and shortstop in high school, and the Pirates plan to keep him there. He has his share of rough edges at second, particularly with footwork and turning the double play, but he has a plus arm. Ford has decent speed but isn't a burner. Ford will begin this season in high Class A, and if he continues to improve defensively and cut down on his strikeouts, he could move quickly through the system.

| Year | Club (League) | Class | AVG | G | AB | R | H | 2B | 3B | HR | RBI | BB | SO | SB | OBP | SLG |
|------|---------------|-------|-----|---|----|---|---|----|----|----|-----|----|----|----|-----|-----|
| 2006 | Williamsport (NY-P) | A | .400 | 7 | 25 | 3 | 10 | 3 | 0 | 0 | 2 | 3 | 3 | 1 | .483 | .520 |
| | Hickory (SAL) | A | .265 | 55 | 223 | 43 | 59 | 16 | 3 | 6 | 27 | 14 | 51 | 4 | .329 | .444 |
| **MINOR LEAGUE TOTALS** | | | .278 | 62 | 248 | 46 | 69 | 19 | 3 | 6 | 29 | 17 | 54 | 5 | .345 | .452 |

## 22 BRANDON HOLDEN RHP

**Born:** Jan. 1, 1988. **B-T:** R-R **Ht:** 6-4, **Wt.:** 185. **Drafted:** HS—Parkland, Fla., 2006 (13th round). **Signed by:** Everett Russell.

Holden was considered a potential high draft pick last year, with some projecting him to go as early as the second round, before triceps tendinitis ended his senior high school season early. He pitched just 28 innings, though he went 5-0, 0.99 with 45 strikeouts and led Florida's Douglas High to a national ranking when he was healthy. The Pirates took a flyer on Holden in the 13th round and wound up signing him for $155,000 in mid August. Because of his late signing and injury questions, he didn't play last summer. Holden's fastball is firm and sits at 88-93 mph, though he'll need to command it better. His out pitch is a big-breaking curveball that overwhelmed high school hitters. Like many young pitchers, he needs to work on his changeup. Because of his arm problems in 2006, there's a natural cause for concern that Holden is an injury risk, though the Pirates are convinced he's healthy. He showed a loose, quick arm in high school, though his mechanics will need to be cleaned up a bit. The Pirates will take it slowly with Holden after last spring, and he likely will remain in extended spring training and make his pro debut in June in the Gulf Coast League.

| Year | Club (League) | Class | W | L | ERA | G | GS | CG | SV | IP | H | R | ER | HR | BB | SO | AVG |
|------|---------------|-------|---|---|-----|---|----|----|----|----|---|---|----|----|----|----|-----|
| 2006 | Did not play—Signed 2007 contract | | | | | | | | | | | | | | | | |

## 23 STEVE LERUD C

**Born:** Oct. 13, 1984. **B-T:** L-R. **Ht.:** 6-1. **Wt.:** 210. **Drafted:** HS—Reno, Nev., 2003 (3rd round). **Signed by:** Jaron Madison.

Lerud's 60 home runs at Galena High in Reno broke the Nevada career record that had been held by longtime big leaguer Matt Williams. Interestingly, Lerud's parents once shared

a duplex with Williams' parents in Carson City, Nev., after they were first married. Lerud has outstanding power potential from the left side, a rarity for a catcher, but he has yet to match his high school home run proficiency because of inconsistency and injuries. He had a broken foot that delayed the start of his career and a broken arm that ruined his 2005 season. He has loft in his batting stroke that will enable him to hit 20-25 home runs a year if he cuts down on his strikeouts. Lerud has struck out in more than a quarter of his plate appearances in the minors. While he sometimes chases bad pitches, he also goes through spells when he's hesitant to swing and gets himself behind in the count. Lerud had 35 passed balls last season and needs to improve his footwork behind the plate, though he's a willing worker. He lacks experience because of his injuries, and he has a fringe-average arm. He's a below-average runner. Lerud will move up to high Class A this season. His age and power potential make him a candidate for a position switch if his defense doesn't improve.

| Year | Club (League) | Class | AVG | G | AB | R | H | 2B | 3B | HR | RBI | BB | SO | SB | OBP | SLG |
|------|---------------|-------|-----|---|----|---|---|----|----|----|-----|----|----|----|-----|-----|
| 2004 | Pirates (GCL) | R | .246 | 48 | 175 | 22 | 43 | 12 | 1 | 5 | 20 | 11 | 38 | 0 | .297 | .411 |
| | Williamsport (NY-P) | A | .241 | 8 | 29 | 2 | 7 | 0 | 0 | 0 | 2 | 4 | 6 | 0 | .353 | .241 |
| 2005 | Hickory (SAL) | A | .088 | 25 | 80 | 6 | 7 | 2 | 2 | 2 | 13 | 4 | 27 | 0 | .149 | .238 |
| | Pirates (GCL) | R | .267 | 18 | 60 | 13 | 16 | 3 | 1 | 2 | 15 | 7 | 13 | 0 | .351 | .450 |
| | Williamsport (NY-P) | A | .125 | 10 | 32 | 3 | 4 | 0 | 0 | 1 | 2 | 2 | 14 | 0 | .176 | .219 |
| 2006 | Hickory (SAL) | A | .239 | 117 | 393 | 45 | 94 | 28 | 0 | 12 | 57 | 40 | 146 | 4 | .330 | .402 |
| **MINOR LEAGUE TOTALS** | | | .222 | 226 | 769 | 91 | 171 | 45 | 4 | 22 | 109 | 68 | 244 | 4 | .301 | .377 |

 ## JESSE CHAVEZ — RHP

**Born:** Aug. 21, 1983. **B-T:** R-R. **Ht.:** 6-1. **Wt.:** 160. **Drafted:** Riverside (Calif.) CC, D/F 2002 (42nd round). **Signed by:** Steve Flores (Rangers).

Chavez was the Cubs' 39th-round pick in 2001 out of high school in Fontana, Calif. He went to nearby Riverside Community College but didn't sign with the Cubs. He went in the 42nd round to the Rangers in 2002 and they signed him just before the 2003 draft. The Pirates acquired Chavez in a deadline deal last year for Kip Wells, and he showed them enough that he was sent to the Arizona Fall League. Chavez' fastball reaches 95 mph, but he has trouble consistently throwing it for strikes. He also has trouble commanding his best pitch, a big-breaking curveball that's tough on righthanders. Lefties have more success against Chavez, and he needs to either add cutting action to his fastball or sharpen his changeup in order to combat that tendency. He's slightly built, and concerns about his durability caused the Rangers to move him to the bullpen in 2005. While Chavez has struggled at times while making the conversion, he has a good enough arm and competitiveness to pitch in middle relief in the major leagues after more seasoning in Triple-A this year.

| Year | Club (League) | Class | W | L | ERA | G | GS | CG | SV | IP | H | R | ER | HR | BB | SO | AVG |
|------|---------------|-------|---|---|-----|---|----|----|----|----|---|---|----|----|----|----|-----|
| 2003 | Spokane (NWL) | A | 2 | 2 | 4.55 | 17 | 8 | 0 | 1 | 55 | 63 | 30 | 28 | 5 | 31 | 48 | .286 |
| 2004 | Clinton (MWL) | A | 6 | 10 | 4.68 | 27 | 22 | 0 | 0 | 123 | 148 | 75 | 64 | 8 | 35 | 96 | .306 |
| 2005 | Bakersfield (Cal) | A | 0 | 0 | 2.22 | 11 | 0 | 0 | 2 | 24 | 16 | 6 | 6 | 2 | 9 | 31 | .182 |
| | Frisco (TL) | AA | 4 | 3 | 5.68 | 31 | 0 | 0 | 1 | 57 | 71 | 43 | 36 | 10 | 25 | 27 | .316 |
| 2006 | Frisco (TL) | AA | 2 | 5 | 4.42 | 38 | 0 | 0 | 4 | 59 | 54 | 33 | 29 | 5 | 28 | 70 | .245 |
| | Oklahoma (PCL) | AAA | 0 | 0 | 4.50 | 1 | 0 | 0 | 0 | 2 | 3 | 1 | 1 | 0 | 0 | 3 | .333 |
| | Indianapolis (IL) | AAA | 2 | 1 | 4.24 | 12 | 0 | 0 | 0 | 17 | 18 | 9 | 8 | 0 | 9 | 15 | .273 |
| **MINOR LEAGUE TOTALS** | | | 16 | 21 | 4.58 | 137 | 30 | 0 | 8 | 338 | 373 | 197 | 172 | 30 | 137 | 290 | .285 |

## FRANQUELIS OSORIA — RHP

**Born:** Sept, 12, 1981. **B-T:** R-R. **Ht:** 5-11. **Wt:** 200. **Signed:** Dominican Republic, 1999. **Signed by:** Pablo Peguero/Ramon Perez (Dodgers).

The Pirates claimed Osoria off waivers in December after the Dodgers dropped him from their 40-man roster to clear space for free-agent acquisitions. Pirates manager Jim Tracy is familiar with Osoria from his time as Los Angeles' skipper in 2005, when the Dominican Republic native made his major league debut. His best pitch is a sinking fastball that usually parks at 88-92 mph. He throws it from a low-three-quarter arm slot, sometimes dropping down to almost sidearm, and the pitch produces one ground ball after another when it is working. Osoria has six digits on his right hand, which also helps him put sinking action on the ball. The sinker is his only plus pitch, so he has trouble against lefthanders. He has a frisbee slider that has a side-to-side break, and his changeup is strictly for show. Osoria has trouble throwing either pitch for strikes consistently. He's one of a sizable group of righthanded relievers with limited or no major league experience who will compete for a job in the Pirates bullpen in spring training. If he makes the club, he'll work in the middle innings and as a specialist against righthanders.

| Year | Club (League) | Class | W | L | ERA | G | GS | CG | SV | IP | H | R | ER | HR | BB | SO | AVG |
|---|---|---|---|---|---|---|---|---|---|---|---|---|---|---|---|---|---|
| 2000 | Dodgers (DSL) | R | 3 | 4 | 2.52 | 13 | 12 | 0 | 0 | 64 | 58 | 33 | 18 | 1 | 23 | 46 | .230 |
| 2001 | Dodgers (DSL) | R | 4 | 4 | 3.16 | 15 | 11 | 0 | 0 | 77 | 69 | 38 | 27 | 5 | 16 | 67 | .237 |
| 2002 | Vero Beach (FSL) | A | 0 | 1 | 2.45 | 3 | 0 | 0 | 0 | 7 | 4 | 2 | 2 | 0 | 2 | 10 | .154 |
|  | So. Georgia (SAL) | A | 2 | 2 | 3.32 | 21 | 1 | 0 | 1 | 43 | 40 | 22 | 16 | 1 | 13 | 30 | .226 |
| 2003 | Vero Beach (FSL) | A | 3 | 6 | 3.00 | 33 | 3 | 0 | 6 | 75 | 69 | 34 | 25 | 4 | 19 | 53 | .244 |
| 2004 | Las Vegas (PCL) | AAA | 0 | 0 | 6.48 | 4 | 0 | 0 | 0 | 8 | 13 | 6 | 6 | 0 | 1 | 3 | .342 |
|  | Jacksonville (SL) | AA | 8 | 5 | 3.67 | 51 | 0 | 0 | 5 | 81 | 71 | 36 | 33 | 2 | 18 | 73 | .229 |
| 2005 | Las Vegas (PCL) | AAA | 6 | 4 | 2.62 | 40 | 0 | 0 | 9 | 55 | 63 | 18 | 16 | 3 | 13 | 35 | .299 |
|  | Los Angeles (NL) | MLB | 0 | 2 | 3.94 | 24 | 0 | 0 | 0 | 30 | 28 | 14 | 13 | 3 | 8 | 15 | .259 |
| 2006 | Los Angeles (NL) | MLB | 0 | 2 | 7.13 | 12 | 0 | 0 | 0 | 18 | 27 | 14 | 14 | 4 | 9 | 13 | .360 |
|  | Las Vegas (PCL) | AAA | 2 | 2 | 4.35 | 44 | 0 | 0 | 2 | 52 | 81 | 31 | 25 | 2 | 21 | 28 | .362 |
| **MINOR LEAGUE TOTALS** | | | 28 | 28 | 3.27 | 224 | 27 | 0 | 23 | 463 | 468 | 220 | 168 | 18 | 126 | 345 | .258 |
| **MAJOR LEAGUE TOTALS** | | | 0 | 4 | 5.13 | 36 | 0 | 0 | 0 | 47 | 55 | 28 | 27 | 7 | 17 | 28 | .301 |

## 26 BRIAN ROGERS

RHP

**Born:** July 17, 1982. **B-T:** R-R. **Ht.:** 6-4. **Wt.:** 195. **Drafted:** Georgia Southern, 2003 (11th round). **Signed by:** Gary York (Tigers).

Rogers had quite an eventful final two months of the 2006 season, getting dealt from the Tigers to the Pirates for Sean Casey at the trading deadline, then making his major league debut on Sept. 1. The Tigers moved Rogers from the rotation to the bullpen at the start of 2005 season, and he has since posted a fine 2.09 ERA in 97 minor league relief appearances. Rogers isn't overpowering, and his sinking fastball rarely touches 90 mph. However, he spots it well and complements it with a slider that's particularly tough on righthanders. He also makes up for his lack of pure stuff by not walking batters. His arsenal does leave him with little margin for error, so it remains to be seen if he can get veteran hitters out on a consistent basis. He also has a tendency to give up a lot of fly balls. Rogers will likely begin the season in Triple-A, but expect to see him back in the major leagues at some point in 2007. He has enough pitching savvy to carve out a career as a middle reliever in the big leagues.

| Year | Club (League) | Class | W | L | ERA | G | GS | CG | SV | IP | H | R | ER | HR | BB | SO | AVG |
|---|---|---|---|---|---|---|---|---|---|---|---|---|---|---|---|---|---|
| 2003 | Oneonta (NY-P) | A | 3 | 2 | 3.34 | 12 | 12 | 0 | 0 | 57 | 49 | 23 | 21 | 2 | 18 | 66 | .232 |
| 2004 | West Michigan (MWL) | A | 6 | 8 | 4.55 | 25 | 25 | 0 | 0 | 142 | 163 | 76 | 72 | 9 | 44 | 120 | .293 |
| 2005 | Lakeland (FSL) | A | 4 | 1 | 2.06 | 52 | 1 | 0 | 2 | 66 | 50 | 16 | 15 | 2 | 21 | 65 | .212 |
| 2006 | Erie (EL) | AA | 3 | 2 | 2.39 | 37 | 0 | 0 | 1 | 64 | 49 | 19 | 17 | 7 | 14 | 69 | .210 |
|  | Altoona (EL) | AA | 0 | 0 | 0.00 | 2 | 0 | 0 | 1 | 4 | 2 | 0 | 0 | 0 | 2 | 5 | .167 |
|  | Indianapolis (IL) | AAA | 1 | 1 | 1.08 | 7 | 0 | 0 | 1 | 8 | 2 | 1 | 1 | 1 | 1 | 8 | .077 |
|  | Pittsburgh (NL) | MLB | 0 | 0 | 8.31 | 10 | 0 | 0 | 0 | 9 | 11 | 8 | 8 | 2 | 2 | 7 | .324 |
| **MINOR LEAGUE TOTALS** | | | 17 | 14 | 3.33 | 135 | 38 | 0 | 5 | 341 | 315 | 135 | 126 | 21 | 100 | 333 | .247 |
| **MAJOR LEAGUE TOTALS** | | | 0 | 0 | 8.31 | 10 | 0 | 0 | 0 | 8 | 11 | 8 | 8 | 2 | 2 | 7 | .324 |

## 27 RAJAI DAVIS

OF

**Born:** Oct. 19, 1980. **B-T:** R-R. **Ht.:** 5-11. **Wt.:** 197. **Drafted:** Connecticut-Avery Point JC, 2001 (38th round). **Signed by:** Charlie Sullivan.

Baseball was a sidelight for Davis in high school in New London, Conn., as his true love seemed to be playing point guard in basketball. But he continued playing baseball at a branch campus of the University of Connecticut, and the Pirates took a shot at him late in the 2001 draft. He worked his way through the farm system until landing in the major leagues last August. Davis' calling card is his great speed, which has allowed him to steal 224 bases in six minor league seasons. It also enables to cover plenty of ground in center field and to make up for mistakes when he takes bad routes. Davis led the Gulf Coast League with a .384 average in 2002, then hit better than .300 at both Class A stops. His average and plate discipline have suffered against more experienced pitchers since reaching Double-A. Davis spent the final six weeks of last season with the Pirates and didn't start a game, an indication the organization views him as a reserve outfielder long-term.

| Year | Club (League) | Class | AVG | G | AB | R | H | 2B | 3B | HR | RBI | BB | SO | SB | OBP | SLG |
|---|---|---|---|---|---|---|---|---|---|---|---|---|---|---|---|---|
| 2001 | Williamsport (NY-P) | A | .083 | 6 | 12 | 1 | 1 | 0 | 0 | 0 | 0 | 2 | 4 | 0 | .214 | .083 |
|  | Pirates (GCL) | R | .262 | 26 | 84 | 19 | 22 | 1 | 0 | 0 | 4 | 13 | 26 | 11 | .364 | .274 |
| 2002 | Pirates (GCL) | R | .384 | 58 | 224 | 38 | 86 | 16 | 5 | 4 | 35 | 20 | 25 | 24 | .436 | .554 |
|  | Williamsport (NY-P) | A | .000 | 1 | 4 | 0 | 0 | 0 | 0 | 0 | 0 | 0 | 1 | 0 | .000 | .000 |
|  | Hickory (SAL) | A | .429 | 6 | 14 | 4 | 6 | 0 | 0 | 0 | 3 | 6 | 2 | 2 | .619 | .429 |
| 2003 | Hickory (SAL) | A | .305 | 125 | 478 | 84 | 146 | 21 | 7 | 6 | 54 | 55 | 65 | 40 | .383 | .416 |
| 2004 | Lynchburg (Car) | A | .314 | 127 | 509 | 91 | 160 | 27 | 7 | 5 | 38 | 59 | 60 | 57 | .388 | .424 |
| 2005 | Altoona (EL) | AA | .281 | 123 | 499 | 82 | 140 | 22 | 5 | 4 | 34 | 43 | 76 | 45 | .351 | .369 |
| 2006 | Indianapolis (IL) | AAA | .283 | 100 | 385 | 53 | 109 | 17 | 1 | 2 | 21 | 27 | 59 | 45 | .335 | .348 |
|  | Pittsburgh (NL) | MLB | .143 | 20 | 14 | 1 | 2 | 1 | 0 | 0 | 0 | 0 | 3 | 1 | .250 | .214 |
| **MINOR LEAGUE TOTALS** | | | .303 | 572 | 2209 | 372 | 670 | 104 | 25 | 21 | 189 | 225 | 318 | 224 | .374 | .402 |
| **MAJOR LEAGUE TOTALS** | | | .143 | 20 | 14 | 1 | 2 | 1 | 0 | 0 | 0 | 0 | 3 | 1 | .250 | .214 |

## 28 JIM NEGRYCH 2B

**Born:** March 2, 1985. **B-T:** L-R. **Ht.:** 5-10. **Wt.:** 180. **Drafted:** Pittsburgh, 2006 (6th round). **Signed by:** Jon Mercurio.

Ed Creech has made a concerted effort to draft more local players since taking over as scouting director in 2002. The Pirates made Negrych, an All-American who hit .396 with 11 homers, the first player drafted by the club out of the University of Pittsburgh since Ken Macha in 1972. Signed for $150,000, he went down in August with a torn ligament in his left thumb, requiring surgery. Negrych's best tool is clearly his bat, and he has the ability to hit for a high average with solid power while also showing good plate discipline. He's not a naturally gifted athlete, and his defense at second base is below-average, especially his footwork in turning the double play. He's also a below-average runner. His work ethic is legendary, however, and he spent countless hours in the batting cage and weight room at Pitt. Negrych may begin the season on the disabled list, but he'll go to low Class A when he's ready. How the injury affects his hitting will be a major question because his bat will determine if he gets to the major leagues.

| Year | Club (League) | Class | AVG | G | AB | R | H | 2B | 3B | HR | RBI | BB | SO | SB | OBP | SLG |
|------|---------------|-------|-----|---|-----|---|----|----|----|----|-----|----|----|----|------|------|
| 2006 | Williamsport (NY-P) | A | .267 | 42 | 146 | 12 | 39 | 7 | 2 | 2 | 17 | 13 | 19 | 1 | .327 | .384 |
| **MINOR LEAGUE TOTALS** | | | .267 | 42 | 146 | 12 | 39 | 7 | 2 | 2 | 17 | 13 | 19 | 1 | .327 | .384 |

## 29 JARED HUGHES RHP

**Born:** July 4, 1985. **B-T:** R-R. **Ht.:** 6-7. **Wt.:** 220. **Drafted:** Long Beach State, 2006 (4th round). **Signed by:** Brad Cameron.

Hughes was one of the top high school pitchers in the nation after his junior year in Laguna Beach, Calif., but his stock dropped after a subpar senior year as he struggled with a back injury and questions about his makeup. He decided to play college ball at Santa Clara after the Devil Rays drafted him in the 16th round in 2003, and he transferred to Long Beach State after one season. He signed last June for $305,000 as a fourth-round pick. Hughes' fastball was clocked at high as 97 mph in high school, but he doesn't throw that hard anymore, working more at 90-92, albeit with better sink. The fastball gets on hitters quickly, though, because of the deception his 6-foot-7 frame creates in his delivery. Hughes' slider is an above-average pitch and he's able to change speeds on it, but he has trouble commanding his changeup. The knock on Hughes has long been that he lacks competitiveness, and he has never dominated hitters as his stuff suggests he should. He often nibbled in his first pro season rather than attacking hitters and had an uneven debut. Hughes will go back to low Class A to begin the 2007 season. At this point he projects as a pitcher at the back end of a rotation.

| Year | Club (League) | Class | W | L | ERA | G | GS | CG | SV | IP | H | R | ER | HR | BB | SO | AVG |
|------|---------------|-------|---|---|------|----|----|----|----|----|----|----|----|----|----|----|------|
| 2006 | Williamsport (NY-P) | A | 1 | 2 | 2.74 | 5 | 5 | 0 | 0 | 23 | 14 | 7 | 7 | 2 | 7 | 11 | .179 |
| 2006 | Hickory (SAL) | A | 5 | 4 | 5.77 | 10 | 10 | 0 | 0 | 48 | 46 | 38 | 31 | 6 | 31 | 25 | .250 |
| **MINOR LEAGUE TOTALS** | | | 6 | 6 | 4.79 | 15 | 15 | 0 | 0 | 71 | 60 | 45 | 38 | 8 | 38 | 36 | .229 |

## 30 ROMULO SANCHEZ RHP

**Born:** April 28, 1984. **B-T:** R-R. **Ht.:** 6-5. **Wt.:** 242. **Signed:** Venezuela, 2002. **Signed by:** Camilo Pascual/Doug Carpenter (Dodgers).

Latin American scouting coordinator Rene Gayo has tried to increase the Pirates presence in Latin America since being hired in 2004. His first move was to sign Sanchez, who had been released by the Dodgers. He missed the final two months of the 2006 season with shoulder tendinitis and has battled similar nagging injuries throughout his career. Sanchez' calling card is a 96 mph fastball that he can throw past most hitters, especially working out of the bullpen. Sanchez needs to command his fastball better, and he lacks a quality secondary pitch, which is why the Pirates converted him from starter to reliever last season. His slider became much sharper after the conversion. He'll likely start this season in Double-A and will move quickly if he improves his control.

| Year | Club (League) | Class | W | L | ERA | G | GS | CG | SV | IP | H | R | ER | HR | BB | SO | AVG |
|------|---------------|-------|---|---|------|----|----|----|----|-----|-----|-----|-----|----|----|-----|------|
| 2002 | Dodgers East (DSL) | R | 1 | 4 | 4.44 | 15 | 0 | 0 | 1 | 24 | 24 | 16 | 12 | 4 | 10 | 22 | .242 |
| 2003 | Dodgers East (DSL) | R | 2 | 3 | 4.46 | 9 | 9 | 0 | 0 | 38 | 40 | 25 | 19 | 1 | 10 | 21 | .255 |
| 2004 | Pirates (VSL) | R | 4 | 2 | 1.03 | 21 | 2 | 1 | 6 | 44 | 33 | 9 | 5 | 0 | 7 | 49 | .202 |
| 2005 | Pirates (GCL) | R | 1 | 0 | 1.80 | 2 | 1 | 0 | 0 | 10 | 7 | 2 | 2 | 1 | 4 | 7 | .206 |
| | Altoona (EL) | AA | 1 | 0 | 3.60 | 2 | 2 | 0 | 0 | 10 | 11 | 4 | 4 | 2 | 4 | 5 | .282 |
| | Hickory (SAL) | A | 3 | 3 | 4.70 | 10 | 10 | 0 | 0 | 54 | 59 | 34 | 28 | 5 | 19 | 24 | .292 |
| 2006 | Hickory (SAL) | A | 0 | 3 | 7.08 | 21 | 3 | 0 | 4 | 41 | 51 | 36 | 32 | 4 | 18 | 28 | .302 |
| | Lynchburg (Car) | A | 0 | 0 | 1.04 | 8 | 0 | 0 | 1 | 9 | 7 | 1 | 1 | 0 | 4 | 6 | .212 |
| | Altoona (EL) | AA | 0 | 0 | 5.00 | 8 | 0 | 0 | 0 | 9 | 8 | 5 | 5 | 1 | 8 | 5 | .242 |
| **MINOR LEAGUE TOTALS** | | | 12 | 15 | 4.08 | 96 | 27 | 1 | 12 | 238 | 240 | 132 | 108 | 18 | 84 | 167 | .258 |

# ST. LOUIS
# CARDINALS

BY **DERRICK GOOLD**

LARRY GOREN

Several weeks after ownership shook up the player-development department, the Cardinals rode a sampling of players gathered and groomed by their system to a World Series title.

Seeking to bridge talent procurement with talent development, the Cardinals added farm director to scouting director Jeff Luhnow's responsibilities in September. Three years into his career with St. Louis, Luhnow has run two drafts and has overseen the establishment of baseball academies in the Dominican Republic and Venezuela. Luhnow said his joint responsibilities should eliminate what he called a natural tension between scouting and development.

The move irritated some in the front office, because farm director Bruce Manno was reassigned as a major league scout and because Lunhow comes from a business background. The move came the same day the team extended general manager Walt Jocketty's contract through 2008, prompting manager Tony La Russa to say, "Nothing wrong with our development. Just have to get the talent."

Though many of the players on the franchise's 10th World Series championship team were acquired via free agency and trades, the system did make some significant contributions. Most notable, of course, is Albert Pujols, who went from 13th-round pick in 1999 to superstar seemingly overnight. **Chris Duncan** (supplemental first round, 1999) cranked 22 homers during the regular season to help St. Louis sneak into the playoffs. Yadier Molina (fourth round,

2000) surprisingly led the team in hits during the postseason.

On the mound, Anthony Reyes (15th round, 2003) pitched eight strong innings to win Game One of the World Series. Adam Wainwright (who came from Atlanta in the J.D. Drew trade) got the final outs in the National League Championship Series and World Series after taking over for injured closer Jason Isringhausen. St. Louis might not have successfully negotiated the first two rounds of the playoffs without the bullpen work of Tyler Johnson (34th round, 2000) and Josh Kinney (signed out of the independent Frontier League in 2001).

Those are real contributions from a system that has lacked depth in recent years. It remains thin at the upper levels, as evidenced by Triple-A Memphis' 58-86 record and 15th-place finish in the 16-team Pacific Coast League. The bulk of St. Louis' best prospects was concentrated in Class A, the result of an infusion of talent from the last two drafts, when it owned a total of 11 picks in the first two rounds. Eight of the players on the Cardinals top 10 list were drafted in either 2005 or 2006. No. 1-ranked outfielder Colby Rasmus was St. Louis' top pick in 2005, when the club also nabbed righthander Mark McCormick in the supplemental first round, outfielder Daryl Jones in the third, catcher Bryan Anderson in the fourth and lefty Jaime Garcia in the 22nd.

## TOP 30 PROSPECTS

| | |
|---|---|
| 1. Colby Rasmus, of | 16. Cody Haerther, of |
| 2. Jaime Garcia, lhp | 17. Tyler Greene, ss |
| 3. Chris Perez, rhp | 18. Tyler Herron, rhp |
| 4. Blake Hawksworth, rhp | 19. Tyler Johnson, lhp |
| 5. Jon Jay, of | 20. Nick Stavinoha, of |
| 6. Bryan Anderson, c | 21. Trey Hearne, rhp |
| 7. Adam Ottavino, rhp | 22. Tommy Pham, ss |
| 8. Mark McCormick, rhp | 23. Brad Furnish, lhp |
| 9. Josh Kinney, rhp | 24. Mark Worrell, rhp |
| 10. Darryl Jones, of | 25. Dennis Dove, rhp |
| 11. Mitchell Boggs, rhp | 26. Mike Sillman, rhp |
| 12. Brendan Ryan, ss | 27. Jon Edwards, of |
| 13. Mark Hamilton, 1b | 28. Shane Robinson, of |
| 14. Chris Lambert, rhp | 29. Skip Schumaker, of |
| 15. Chris Narveson, lhp | 30. Amaury Cazana-Marti, of |

# ORGANIZATION OVERVIEW

**General manager:** Walt Jocketty. **Farm and scouting director:** Jeff Luhnow.

## 2006 PERFORMANCE

| Class | Team | League | W | L | PCT | Finish* | Manager | Affiliated |
|---|---|---|---|---|---|---|---|---|
| Majors | St. Louis | National | 83 | 78 | .516 | 5th (16) | Tony La Russa | — |
| Triple-A | Memphis Redbirds | Pacific Coast | 58 | 86 | .403 | 15th (16) | Danny Sheaffer | 1998 |
| Double-A | Springfield Cardinals | Texas | 66 | 72 | .478 | 6th (8) | Chris Maloney | 2005 |
| High A | Palm Beach Cardinals | Florida State | 75 | 60 | .556 | 2nd (12) | Ron Warner | 2003 |
| Low A | Swing of the Quad Cities | Midwest | 76 | 61 | .555 | 3rd (14) | Keith Mitchell | 2005 |
| Short-season | #State College Spikes | New York-Penn | 39 | 36 | .420 | 8th (14) | Mark DeJohn | 2006 |
| Rookie | Johnson City Cardinals | Appalachian | 34 | 34 | .500 | 7th (10) | Dan Radison | 1974 |
| **OVERALL 2006 MINOR LEAGUE RECORD** | | | 348 | 349 | .499 | 15th (30) | | |

*Finish in overall standings (No. of teams in league). +League champion. #Affiliate will be in Batavia (New York-Penn) in 2007.

## ORGANIZATION LEADERS

### BATTING
| | | |
|---|---|---|
| AVG | Garcia, Isaias, Johnson City | .339 |
| R | Greene, Tyler, Palm Beach/Quad Cities | 80 |
| H | Roth, Randy, Quad Cities/Palm Beach | 149 |
| 2B | Roth, Randy, Quad Cities/Palm Beach | 35 |
| 3B | Rasmus, Colby, Quad Cities/Palm Beach | 8 |
| HR | Evans, Terry, Palm Beach/Spring./Arkansas | 22 |
| RBI | Rasmus, Colby, Quad Cities/Palm Beach | 85 |
| BB | Washington, Rico, Springfield/Memphis | 77 |
| SO | Greene, Tyler, Palm Beach/Quad Cities | 155 |
| SB | Greene, Tyler, Palm Beach/Quad Cities | 33 |
| OBP | Garcia, Isaias, Johnson City | .395 |
| SLG | Garcia, Isaias, Johnson City | .510 |
| | Shorey, Mark, Johnson City | .510 |
| XBH | Roth, Randy, Quad Cities/Palm Beach | 57 |

### PITCHING
| | | |
|---|---|---|
| W | Meacham, Cory, Quad Cities/Palm Beach | 13 |
| L | Tankersley, Dennis, Memphis | 15 |
| ERA | Hearne, Trey, Quad Cities | 2.25 |
| G | Cavazos, Andy, Springfield/Memphis | 67 |
| SV | Sillman, Mike, Palm Beach | 35 |
| IP | Webb, John, Memphis | 200 |
| BB | Parisi, Mike, Springfield | 68 |
| SO | Garcia, Jaime, Quad Cities/Palm Beach | 131 |
| AVG | King, Blake, Johnson City | 167 |

## BEST TOOLS

| | |
|---|---|
| Best Hitter for Average | Colby Rasmus |
| Best Power Hitter | Mark Hamilton |
| Best Strike-Zone Discipline | Jon Jay |
| Fastest Baserunner | Daryl Jones |
| Best Athlete | Daryl Jones |
| Best Fastball | Mark McCormick |
| Best Curveball | Jaime Garcia |
| Best Slider | Chris Perez |
| Best Changeup | Blake Hawksworth |
| Best Control | Jaime Garcia |
| Best Defensive Catcher | Matt Pagnozzi |
| Best Defensive Infielder | Brendan Ryan |
| Best Infield Arm | Tyler Greene |
| Best Defensive Outfielder | Skip Schumaker |
| Best Outfield Arm | Jon Edwards |

## PROJECTED 2010 LINEUP

| | |
|---|---|
| Catcher | Yadier Molina |
| First Base | Albert Pujols |
| Second Base | Adam Kennedy |
| Third Base | Scott Rolen |
| Shortstop | David Eckstein |
| Left Field | Jon Jay |
| Center Field | Colby Rasmus |

| | |
|---|---|
| Right Field | Chris Duncan |
| No. 1 Starter | Chris Carpenter |
| No. 2 Starter | Adam Wainwright |
| No. 3 Starter | Anthony Reyes |
| No. 4 Starter | Jaime Garcia |
| No. 5 Starter | Blake Hawksworth |
| Closer | Chris Perez |

## LAST YEAR'S TOP 20 PROSPECTS

| | |
|---|---|
| 1. Anthony Reyes, rhp | 11. Daryl Jones, of |
| 2. Colby Rasmus, of | 12. Tyler Herron, rhp |
| 3. Tyler Greene, ss | 13. Brendan Ryan, ss |
| 4. Chris Lambert, rhp | 14. Tyler Johnson, lhp |
| 5. Mark McCormick, rhp | 15. Chris Duncan, 1b/of |
| 6. Adam Wainwright, rhp | 16. Juan Mateo, rhp |
| 7. Travis Hanson, 3b | 17. Juan Lucena, ss |
| 8. Cody Haerther, of | 18. Nick Stavinoha, of |
| 9. Nick Webber, rhp | 19. Skip Schumaker, of |
| 10. Stuart Pomeranz, rhp | 20. Rick Ankiel, of |

## TOP PROSPECTS OF THE DECADE

| Year | Player, Pos. | 2006 Org. |
|---|---|---|
| 1997 | Matt Morris, rhp | Giants |
| 1998 | Rick Ankiel, lhp | Cardinals |
| 1999 | J.D. Drew, of | Dodgers |
| 2000 | Rick Ankiel, lhp | Cardinals |
| 2001 | Bud Smith, lhp | Long Beach (Golden) |
| 2002 | Jimmy Journell, rhp | Bridgeport (Atlantic) |
| 2003 | Dan Haren, rhp | Athletics |
| 2004 | Blake Hawksworth, rhp | Cardinals |
| 2005 | Anthony Reyes, rhp | Cardinals |
| 2006 | Anthony Reyes, rhp | Cardinals |

## TOP DRAFT PICKS OF THE DECADE

| Year | Player, Pos. | 2006 Org. |
|---|---|---|
| 1997 | Adam Kennedy, ss | Angels |
| 1998 | J.D. Drew, of | Dodgers |
| 1999 | Chance Caple, rhp | Out of baseball |
| 2000 | Shaun Boyd, of | Cardinals |
| 2001 | Justin Pope, rhp | Yankees |
| 2002 | Calvin Hayes, ss (3rd round) | Cardinals |
| 2003 | Daric Barton, c | Athletics |
| 2004 | Chris Lambert, rhp | Cardinals |
| 2005 | Colby Rasmus, of | Cardinals |
| 2006 | Adam Ottavino, rhp | Cardinals |

## ALL-TIME LARGEST BONUSES

| | |
|---|---|
| J.D. Drew, 1998 | $3,000,000 |
| Rick Ankiel, 1997 | $2,500,000 |
| Chad Hutchinson, 1998 | $2,300,000 |
| Shaun Boyd, 2000 | $1,750,000 |
| Braden Looper, 1996 | $1,675,000 |

# MINOR LEAGUE DEPTH CHART

## St. Louis Cardinals

**Impact: D.** Colby Rasmus has significant upside, but most of the rest of the system is dominated by college products with modest hopes or players with track records of injuries or limited success.

**Depth: C.** The Cardinals do have more to work with than they used to, with solid early returns on their 2006 draft class.

**Sleeper:** Randy Roth, 1b/of. Older prospects can still be prospects if they have tools, and Roth (power, arm) made a strong case with his debut.

*Numbers in parentheses indicate prospect rankings.*

### LF
Jon Jay (5)
Cody Haerther (16)
Amaury Cazana-Marti (30)
Nathan Southard

### CF
Colby Rasmus (1)
Darryl Jones (10)
Shane Robinson (28)
Skip Schumaker (29)
James Rapoport
Reid Gorecki

### RF
Nick Stavinoha (20)
Jon Edwards (27)
Joe Mather

### 3B
Tyler Greene (17)
Travis Hanson

### SS
Brendan Ryan (12)
Tommy Pham (22)

### 2B
Juan Lucena
Isa Garcia
Jose Martinez
Jarrett Hoffpauir
Casey Rowlett

### 1B
Mark Hamilton (13)
Randy Roth
Mike Ferris
A.J. Van Slyke

### C
Bryan Anderson (6)
Brandon Yarbrough

### RHP

| Starters | Relievers |
|---|---|
| Blake Hawksworth (4) | Chris Perez (3) |
| Adam Ottavino (7) | Josh Kinney (9) |
| Mark McCormick (8) | Mark Worrell (24) |
| Mitchell Boggs (11) | Dennis Dove (25) |
| Chris Lambert (14) | Mike Sillman (26) |
| Tyler Herron (18) | Blake King |
| Trey Hearne (21) | Andy Cavazos |
| Stuart Pomeranz | Kenny Maiques |
| Mike Parisi | Cory Doyne |
| Gary Daley Jr. | Matthew Trent |
| Nick Webber | |
| Eddie Degerman | |
| P.J. Walters | |
| Elvis Hernandez | |
| Cory Meacham | |

### LHP

| Starters | Relievers |
|---|---|
| Jaime Garcia (2) | Tyler Johnson (19) |
| Chris Narveson (15) | Troy Cate |
| Brad Furnish (23) | Kevin Ool |
| Eric Haberer | Zachary Zuercher |
| Tyler Norrick | |
| Adam Daniels | |

# DRAFT ANALYSIS

## 2006

**Best Pro Debut:** The Cardinals had a number of impressive first-year performances, none moreso than former Miami teammates OF John Jay (2) and RHP Chris Perez (1) in low Class A. Jay hit .342/.416/.462, while Perez had 12 saves, a 1.84 ERA and 32 strikeouts in 29 innings. St. Louis had several league leaders, with 1B Mark Hamilton (2) and OF Mark Shorey (31) winning home run titles with eight in the New York-Penn League and 13 in the Rookie-level Appalachian League, respectively. 2B Isa Garcia (34) won the Appy batting title at .339 and OF Jim Rapoport (34) led the league in steals with 24.

**Best Athlete:** SS Tommy Pham (16) has offensive potential, plus speed and was clocked at 90-92 mph when he pitched in high school. Jay has solid if not spectacular tools across the board.

**Best Pure Hitter:** St. Louis' hitting instructors say Jay has the talent to win a big league batting title someday.

**Best Raw Power:** Hamilton first caught the Cardinals' attention by driving balls to the train tracks at Minute Maid Park during a February tournament. He shared the NY-P home run crown despite spending just a month in the league. Shorey also owns plenty of pop, and St. Louis is toying with the idea of making him a catcher.

**Fastest Runner:** Rapoport's speed rates a 7 on the 2-8 scouting scale. That puts him ahead of OF Shane Robinson (5), the first Florida State player to steal 100 bases.

**Best Defensive Player:** C David Carpenter (12) has standout catch-and-throw skills, starting with a well above-average arm. Jay, Robinson, Nathan Southard (17) and Rapoport are all legitimate center fielders.

**Best Fastball:** Perez has a 92-95 mph heater that's electric when he locates it down in the zone. RHP Adam Ottavino (1), who didn't allow an earned run in his first four pro starts, can maintain his 90-95 mph velocity throughout a game.

**Best Breaking Ball:** Perez' slider is a put-away pitch that eats up righthanders. RHP Gary Daley (3) struggles with his command, but his curveball can be a plus offering.

**Most Intriguing Background:** The Cardinals tried to sign OF Amaury Marti (18), a Cuban defector, as a free agent during the spring but had to wait until they could draft him. C Scott Thomas' (38) father Lee (farm director) and RHP Kyle Mura's

(42) dad Steve (pitcher) were members of the 1982 Cardinals. Thomas was also an all-star outfielder and a Phillies general manager. Hamilton's grandfather Ralph played in the NBA in 1949. LHP Brian Schroeder's (33) father Jay was the third overall pick in the June 1979 baseball draft and played quarterback in the NFL.

**Closest To The Majors:** Jay and Perez. Because he's a reliever, Perez could move past Jay once he improves his command.

**Best Late-Round Pick:** Pham, who signed for third-round money at $325,000. Among players who signed for slot money, it's RHP Luke Gregerson (28). He has good control and a potential plus slider, helping him strike out 46 batters in 32 pro innings.

**The One Who Got Away:** Sophomore-eligible C Mitch Canham (41) helped Oregon State win the College World Series and had a productive summer in the Cape Cod League. He'll probably go in the second or third round in 2007.

**Assessment:** After using a more balanced approach in 2005, the Cardinals loaded up on college players with good statistical track records. They did the same thing with little to show for it in 2004, but the earlier returns on this crop are much better.

## 2005 — BUDGET: $5.6 million

The Cardinals mixed college and high school talent and hit the jackpot with OF Colby Rasmus (1) and super-sleeper LHP Jaime Garcia (22), now their top two prospects. **GRADE: A**

## 2004 — BUDGET: $3.2 million

St. Louis focused on college talent, a myopic approach that undermined its efforts. RHP Chris Lambert (1) is the best of this group, and his stuff has regressed. **GRADE: F**

## 2003 — BUDGET: $2.8 million

The Cards gave up 1B Daric Barton (1) in the Mark Mulder trade. But they found a possible frontline starter in RHP Anthony Reyes (15), and drafted three more in Ian Kennedy (14), Brett Sinkbeil (38) and Max Scherzer (43)—all first-round picks in 2006. **GRADE: B+**

*Draft analysis by Jim Callis. Numbers in parentheses indicate draft rounds. Budgets are bonuses in first 10 rounds.*

## COLBY
# RASMUS

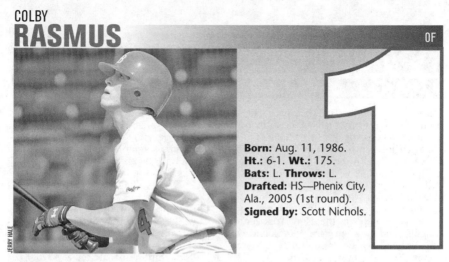

**Born:** Aug. 11, 1986.
**Ht.:** 6-1. **Wt.:** 175.
**Bats:** L. **Throws:** L.
**Drafted:** HS—Phenix City, Ala., 2005 (1st round).
**Signed by:** Scott Nichols.

S eeing snow for the third time in his life wasn't the rarest event Rasmus weathered at the start of his first full season in pro baseball. The player with the best blend of tools, upside and instincts in the system opened the year in a bona fide slump. Through his first seven games with low Class A Quad Cities, Rasmus was 2-for-28. But he quickly snapped the cold spell, muscled his way into a promotion and affirmed his reputation as the highest-watt position prospect the Cardinals have had since Albert Pujols. Rasmus has been an elite player for his age group since winning a U.S. championship at the 1999 Little League World Series. His father Tony was an Angels 10th-round pick in January 1986, and coached Russell County High (Seale, Ala.) and Colby, brother Cory (a Braves supplemental first-rounder in 2006) and Kaser Kiker (the Rangers' first-round pick in June) to the national high school title in 2005. After switching from pitching to hitting in high school, Rasmus broke Bo Jackson's Alabama state single-season record with 24 homers. St. Louis drafted Rasmus 28th overall in 2005 and signed him for $1 million. After shaking off his early slump, Rasmus earned a promotion to high Class A Palm Beach and led Cardinals farmhands with 85 RBIs.

Rasmus has a balanced, disciplined approach and a loose swing—all signs of burgeoning power potential in his wiry strong frame. Even with quick hands and a penchant for pulling the ball, he has become adept at hitting to all fields. With his speed and instincts on the basepaths, he should be at least a 20-20 threat once he gets to the majors. One of the most athletic players in the system, he's a quality defender. He gets good jumps and covers enough ground to play center field, and his arm is strong enough for right. He was clocked at 91 mph off the mound in high school.

At both stops this past season, Rasmus got off to slow starts. The Cardinals weren't alarmed, but they'd like to see him make quicker adjustments. He sometimes hurries his throws, costing him accuracy. He still has plenty of room to grow into his body, and certainly more strength will be required for him to reach his power potential. Coaches have tried to impress upon him the importance of developing and adhering to a pregame routine.

The two-year contract Jim Edmonds signed in November was a bridge, connecting the end of his era to the beginning of another. Rasmus should continue the tradition of center field being the franchise's most stable position, as Willie McGee, Ray Lankford and Edmonds have patrolled the middle garden in St. Louis for most of the last 25 years. Rasmus should continue to move steadily through the system, reaching Double-A Springfield at some point in 2007.

| Year | Club (League) | Class | AVG | G | AB | R | H | 2B | 3B | HR | RBI | BB | SO | SB | OBP | SLG |
|---|---|---|---|---|---|---|---|---|---|---|---|---|---|---|---|---|
| 2005 | Johnson City (Appy) | R | .296 | 62 | 216 | 47 | 64 | 16 | 5 | 7 | 27 | 21 | 73 | 13 | .362 | .514 |
| 2006 | Palm Beach (FSL) | A | .254 | 53 | 193 | 22 | 49 | 4 | 5 | 5 | 35 | 27 | 35 | 11 | .351 | .404 |
| | Quad Cities (MWL) | A | .310 | 78 | 303 | 49 | 94 | 22 | 3 | 11 | 50 | 29 | 55 | 17 | .373 | .512 |
| **MINOR LEAGUE TOTALS** | | | .291 | 193 | 712 | 118 | 207 | 42 | 13 | 23 | 112 | 77 | 163 | 41 | .364 | .483 |

## ② JAIME GARCIA  LHP

**Born:** June 2, 1981. **B-T:** L-L. **Ht.:** 6-1. **Wt.:** 200. **Drafted:** HS—Mission, Texas, 2005 (22nd round). **Signed by:** Joe Almaraz.

First noticed as a two-way player on the Mexican junior national team, Garcia fell to the Orioles in the 30th round in 2004, mostly because of confusion about his eligibility for the draft. He didn't sign and hurt his prospect stock by falling out of shape. Joe Almaraz, the area scout who covered him for the Orioles in 2004, joined the Cardinals for 2005 and talked St. Louis into drafting Garcia. He made his pro debut in 2006, reaching high Class A and representing St. Louis at the Futures Game. Garcia fools hitters with a wicked downward-breaking curveball he lands for strikes. His fastball features natural sinking life and consistently reaches the low 90s and tops out at 94. He operates with a clean, easy arm action and repeats his delivery, allowing him to fill the zone with strikes. He shows an advanced touch with his changeup. While he throws strikes, Garcia still is refining his command and learning how to set hitters up. He tends to fall in love with his curveball and needs to do a better job of varying his pitch sequences. He's a fiery competitor who has to keep his emotions in check. Garcia is on the fast track. He should move up to Double-A this year, and he could crack the big league rotation by 2008.

| Year | Club (League) | Class | W | L | ERA | G | GS | CG | SV | IP | H | R | ER | HR | BB | SO | AVG |
|------|---------------|-------|---|---|------|----|----|----|----|----|----|----|----|----|----|-----|------|
| 2006 | Quad Cities (MWL) | A | 5 | 4 | 2.90 | 13 | 13 | 1 | 0 | 78 | 67 | 28 | 25 | 1 | 18 | 80 | .229 |
|      | Palm Beach (FSL) | A | 5 | 4 | 3.84 | 12 | 12 | 0 | 0 | 77 | 84 | 33 | 33 | 3 | 16 | 51 | .282 |
| **MINOR LEAGUE TOTALS** | | | 10 | 8 | 3.37 | 25 | 25 | 1 | 0 | 155 | 151 | 61 | 58 | 4 | 34 | 131 | .256 |

## ③ CHRIS PEREZ  RHP

**Born:** July 1, 1985. **B-T:** R-R. **Ht.:** 6-4. **Wt.:** 225. **Drafted:** Miami, 2006 (1st round supplemental). **Signed by:** Steve Turco.

After brief dalliance as a starter, Perez spent his final two years in college as Miami's closer and had 12 saves to go with a 1.88 ERA last spring. The Cardinals took him 42nd overall in June and signed him for $800,000, earmarking him for a click climb through the system by send him to low Class A to close for a playoff-bound team. Perez has one of the best fastballs in the organization, throwing it consistently at 92-95 mph. His best pitch, however, is a devilish 83-87 mph slider that overmatches righthanders. They hit just .159 against him last summer. Perez' biggest challenge is harnessing his stuff. He walks too many batters, especially lefthanders, against whom his slider is less effective. He gets good life on his fastball when he locates it down in the zone, but he can't do that consistently yet. With his stuff and experience, Perez should rush through the system. St. Louis will continue to bring him along as a closer and believes he eventually can inherit that role in the majors. He'll open 2007 in high Class A.

| Year | Club (League) | Class | W | L | ERA | G | GS | CG | SV | IP | H | R | ER | HR | BB | SO | AVG |
|------|---------------|-------|---|---|------|----|----|----|----|----|----|----|----|----|----|-----|------|
| 2006 | Quad Cities (MWL) | A | 2 | 0 | 1.84 | 25 | 0 | 0 | 12 | 29 | 20 | 9 | 6 | 0 | 19 | 32 | .198 |
| **MINOR LEAGUE TOTALS** | | | 2 | 0 | 1.84 | 25 | 0 | 0 | 12 | 29 | 20 | 9 | 6 | 0 | 19 | 32 | .198 |

## ④ BLAKE HAWKSWORTH  RHP

**Born:** March 1, 1983. **B-T:** R-R. **Ht.:** 6-3. **Wt.:** 195. **Drafted:** Bellevue (Wash.) CC, D/F 2001 (28th round). **Signed by:** Dane Walker.

After signing for $1.475 million as a draft-and-follow in 2002, Hawksworth ranked as the Cardinals' top prospect heading into 2004 before serious injuries knocked him off track. He totaled just 25 innings in 2004-05 because of bone spurs in his right ankle and a partially torn labrum. He returned to work 163 innings last year after totaling 188 in his first four pro seasons. Hawksworth's velocity has returned to the low 90s. He also regained the touch on his changeup, which has graded as one of the best in the system for years. He uses both a curveball and a slider, with the curve the more consistent of his breaking pitches. He retained his control and savvy after his convalescence, and he finished the season strong. Before he got hurt, Hawksworth had the potential to be a frontline starter. To get there, he needs to develop a stronger breaking ball that he can rely on. He had occasional issues with fastball command in the past, and they cropped up again after his promotion to Double-A. His durability is still somewhat a question, though everything went well last year. Hawksworth went a long way to make up for lost time in 2006. Now he'll join the Triple-A Memphis rotation and be just one step from the majors.

| Year | Club (League) | Class | W | L | ERA | G | GS | CG | SV | IP | H | R | ER | HR | BB | SO | AVG |
|---|---|---|---|---|---|---|---|---|---|---|---|---|---|---|---|---|---|
| 2002 | Johnson City (Appy) | R | 2 | 4 | 3.14 | 13 | 12 | 0 | 0 | 66 | 58 | 31 | 23 | 8 | 18 | 61 | .232 |
| | New Jersey (NYP) | A | 1 | 0 | 0.00 | 2 | 2 | 0 | 0 | 10 | 6 | 0 | 0 | 0 | 2 | 8 | .171 |
| 2003 | Peoria (MWL) | A | 5 | 1 | 2.30 | 10 | 10 | 0 | 0 | 55 | 37 | 16 | 14 | 0 | 12 | 57 | .187 |
| | Palm Beach (FSL) | A | 1 | 3 | 3.94 | 6 | 6 | 0 | 0 | 32 | 28 | 14 | 14 | 2 | 11 | 32 | .235 |
| 2004 | Palm Beach (FSL) | A | 1 | 0 | 5.91 | 2 | 2 | 0 | 0 | 11 | 10 | 7 | 7 | 2 | 3 | 11 | .250 |
| 2005 | New Jersey (NYP) | A | 0 | 3 | 7.98 | 7 | 6 | 0 | 0 | 15 | 18 | 18 | 13 | 0 | 10 | 12 | .321 |
| 2006 | Palm Beach (FSL) | A | 7 | 2 | 2.47 | 14 | 14 | 0 | 0 | 84 | 75 | 23 | 23 | 0 | 19 | 55 | .247 |
| | Springfield (TL) | AA | 4 | 2 | 3.39 | 13 | 13 | 0 | 0 | 80 | 72 | 34 | 30 | 8 | 31 | 66 | .248 |
| **MINOR LEAGUE TOTALS** | | | 21 | 15 | 3.18 | 67 | 65 | 0 | 0 | 351 | 304 | 143 | 124 | 20 | 106 | 302 | .235 |

## 5 JON JAY OF

PAUL GIERHART

**Born:** March 15, 1985. **B-T:** L-L. **Ht.:** 6-0. **Wt.:** 200. **Drafted:** Miami, 2006 (2nd round). **Signed by:** Steve Turco.

Jay consistently produced as a collegian for both Miami and Team USA, but many teams saw him as a tweener who didn't profile as a regular. As a result, the Cardinals were able to land him in the second round of the 2006 draft and sign him for $480,000. He had a spectacular pro debut, batting .342 in low Class A. Jay has an unorthodox approach but he consistently shows the ability to hit pitches in all parts of the zone. His game is built around hitting line drives and making the most of his solid-average speed. Some Cardinals coaches already are predicting that he'll win a major league batting title. While he doesn't have a standout tool, he's pretty solid across the board. He's a capable center fielder with an accurate arm. He pumps his hands and uses a wide stance at the plate, quirky habits that scared off some scouts but haven't hurt him yet. He does have some length to his swing. He doesn't hit for much power, so he'll have to stay in center field to profile as a regular. It's possible he'll leapfrog Colby Rasmus and beat him to the majors. They also could wind up playing alongside each other in the Springfield outfield this season.

| Year | Club (League) | Class | AVG | G | AB | R | H | 2B | 3B | HR | RBI | BB | SO | SB | OBP | SLG |
|---|---|---|---|---|---|---|---|---|---|---|---|---|---|---|---|---|
| 2006 | Quad Cities (MWL) | A | .342 | 60 | 234 | 42 | 80 | 13 | 3 | 3 | 45 | 28 | 27 | 9 | .416 | .462 |
| **MINOR LEAGUE TOTALS** | | | .342 | 60 | 234 | 42 | 80 | 13 | 3 | 3 | 45 | 28 | 27 | 9 | .416 | .462 |

## 6 BRYAN ANDERSON C

PAUL GIERHART

**Born:** Dec. 16, 1986. **B-T:** L-R. **Ht.:** 6-1. **Wt.:** 200. **Drafted:** HS—Simi Valley, Calif., 2005 (4th round). **Signed by:** Jay North.

Anderson had a disappointing performance as a high school senior in 2005, but he has done nothing but produce since signing as a fourth-round pick that June. He parlayed a strong pro debut into an invitation to big league camp last spring; he was the youngest player in attendance at age 19. Anderson is a rare commodity, a lefty-hitting catcher with the potential to produce for average and gap power. He controls the strike zone very well for someone his age. He draws raves for his leadership skills and is a good receiver. He has an average, accurate arm and threw out 36 percent of basestealers last year. While he polices the run game effectively, Anderson's throwing mechanics aren't smooth and it's uncertain whether his success throwing out runners will carry over to the upper levels. He's also working on improving his blocking skills. He's a below-average runner. Ticketed for high Class A in 2007, Anderson will present the Cardinals with an interesting dilemma if he continues to hit. Yadier Molina is one of the better defensive catchers in the majors, but his offensive potential is far less than Anderson's.

| Year | Club (League) | Class | AVG | G | AB | R | H | 2B | 3B | HR | RBI | BB | SO | SB | OBP | SLG |
|---|---|---|---|---|---|---|---|---|---|---|---|---|---|---|---|---|
| 2005 | Johnson City (Appy) | R | .331 | 51 | 154 | 28 | 51 | 8 | 1 | 6 | 36 | 15 | 29 | 6 | .383 | .513 |
| 2006 | Quad Cities (MWL) | A | .302 | 109 | 381 | 50 | 115 | 29 | 3 | 3 | 51 | 42 | 66 | 2 | .377 | .417 |
| **MINOR LEAGUE TOTALS** | | | .310 | 160 | 535 | 78 | 166 | 37 | 4 | 9 | 87 | 57 | 95 | 8 | .379 | .445 |

## 7 ADAM OTTAVINO RHP

MIKE JANES

**Born:** Nov. 22, 1985. **B-T:** R-R. **Ht.:** 6-5. **Wt.:** 215. **Drafted:** Northeastern, 2006 (1st round). **Signed by:** Kobe Perez.

Ottavino caught scouts' attention with several notable performances during the spring. He held his own against the Red Sox in an exhibition game, no-hit Georgia Tech for six innings and later completed a 14-strikeout no-hitter against James Madison. He broke the Northeastern single-season strikeout record in each of the last two years before going 30th overall in the 2006 draft and signing for $950,000. He didn't allow an earned run in his first four pro starts. He can maintain mid-90s veloc-

ity on a four-seam fastball throughout a game, but Ottavino downshifted to a low-90s two-seamer at the Cardinals' request and excelled. He can get strikeouts with his slider and also mixes in a changeup and slurvy curveball. Ottavino tends to tilt back in his delivery, causing him to get under his pitches and leave them in the strike zone. He's still figuring out how to harness his stuff on a consistent basis. His changeup will need to improve if he's going to remain in the rotation. Ottavino will continue to start for now, moving up to high Class A. But his fastball/slider combination could make him a dynamic reliever.

| Year | Club (League) | Class | W | L | ERA | G | GS | CG | SV | IP | H | R | ER | HR | BB | SO | AVG |
|------|---------------|-------|---|---|-----|---|----|----|----|----|----|----|----|----|----|----|-----|
| 2006 | State College (NYP) | A | 2 | 2 | 3.14 | 6 | 6 | 0 | 0 | 29 | 23 | 12 | 10 | 1 | 13 | 26 | .211 |
| | Quad Cities (MWL) | A | 2 | 3 | 3.44 | 8 | 8 | 0 | 0 | 37 | 28 | 21 | 14 | 3 | 19 | 38 | .211 |
| **MINOR LEAGUE TOTALS** | | | 4 | 5 | 3.31 | 14 | 14 | 0 | 0 | 65 | 51 | 33 | 24 | 4 | 32 | 64 | .211 |

## 8 MARK MCCORMICK                                       RHP

**Born:** Oct. 15, 1983. **B-T:** R-R. **Ht.:** 6-2. **Wt.:** 195. **Drafted:** Baylor, 2005 (1st round supplemental). **Signed by:** Joe Almaraz.

McCormick has been a top prospect since high school. In his first full pro season, he earned a promotion after 11 starts in low Class A, but pitched just four more innings because of shoulder inflammation. McCormick consistently brings power stuff to the mound. He was blowing mid- to upper-90s fastballs as a prep phenom and continues to throw in that range as a starter when he's mechanically sound. His hard curveball is one of the best breaking pitches in the system. Despite his electric stuff, McCormick never has consistently dominated opponents. He walks too many hitters and runs up high pitch counts. He's still trying to find a comfortable grip for a changeup. McCormick should be 100 percent for spring training after resting in the offseason. The Cardinals will use him as a starter in high Class A this year, but he long has been considered a possible closer candidate. In that role, he could flourish with just two pitches.

| Year | Club (League) | Class | W | L | ERA | G | GS | CG | SV | IP | H | R | ER | HR | BB | SO | AVG |
|------|---------------|-------|---|---|-----|---|----|----|----|----|----|----|----|----|----|----|-----|
| 2005 | New Jersey (NYP) | A | 0 | 0 | 0.00 | 2 | 2 | 0 | 0 | 6 | 1 | 0 | 0 | 0 | 3 | 10 | .053 |
| | Quad Cities (MWL) | A | 1 | 2 | 5.48 | 9 | 9 | 0 | 0 | 43 | 41 | 27 | 26 | 4 | 28 | 45 | .253 |
| 2006 | Quad Cities (MWL) | A | 2 | 4 | 3.78 | 11 | 11 | 0 | 0 | 52 | 38 | 25 | 22 | 3 | 38 | 63 | .207 |
| | Palm Beach (FSL) | A | 0 | 0 | 11.25 | 2 | 2 | 0 | 0 | 4 | 5 | 5 | 5 | 0 | 3 | 5 | .294 |
| **MINOR LEAGUE TOTALS** | | | 3 | 6 | 4.54 | 24 | 24 | 0 | 0 | 105 | 85 | 57 | 53 | 7 | 72 | 123 | .223 |

## 9 JOSH KINNEY                                          RHP

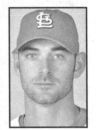

**Born:** March 31, 1979. **B-T:** R-R. **Ht.:** 6-1. **Wt.:** 195. **Signed:** Frontier League (independent), 2001. **Signed by:** Scott Melvin.

Kinney had accepted a job as a fly-fishing tour guide, packed his car and was driving away from baseball when the Cardinals signed him off an independent Frontier League team in suburban St. Louis. Five years later, he got six key outs in the National League Division Series, 10 more in the NL Championship Series and three more in the World Series. He didn't allow any runs in the postseason. Pitching coach Dave Duncan lauds Kinney's fearless approach and his ability to generate strikeouts and grounders. He works with an 89-90 mph sinker and a sweeping slider. He throws strikes and keeps the ball down in the zone. But he is what he is: a short reliever who's not overpowering and has little margin for error. He'll continue to succeed as long as he locates his pitches well, and he'll be in trouble if he can't. The Cardinals are counting on him to be a key cog in their bullpen again this year, capable of getting a clutch whiff or groundout when needed.

| Year | Club (League) | Class | W | L | ERA | G | GS | CG | SV | IP | H | R | ER | HR | BB | SO | AVG |
|------|---------------|-------|---|---|-----|---|----|----|----|----|----|----|----|----|----|----|-----|
| 2001 | New Jersey (NYP) | A | 2 | 0 | 0.00 | 3 | 0 | 0 | 0 | 6 | 2 | 0 | 0 | 0 | 0 | 5 | .111 |
| | River City (FL) | IND | 1 | 0 | 1.71 | 3 | 3 | 0 | 0 | 21 | 18 | 7 | 4 | 1 | 7 | 18 | .237 |
| | Peoria (MWL) | A | 1 | 4 | 4.39 | 27 | 0 | 0 | 0 | 41 | 47 | 24 | 20 | 1 | 15 | 35 | .287 |
| 2002 | Potomac (CAR) | A | 1 | 3 | 2.29 | 44 | 0 | 0 | 7 | 55 | 52 | 21 | 14 | 2 | 23 | 42 | .248 |
| 2003 | Palm Beach (FSL) | A | 3 | 0 | 1.52 | 31 | 0 | 0 | 3 | 41 | 38 | 7 | 7 | 0 | 10 | 35 | .245 |
| | Tennessee (SL) | AA | 2 | 1 | 0.68 | 29 | 0 | 0 | 2 | 40 | 19 | 4 | 3 | 2 | 12 | 48 | .142 |
| 2004 | Palm Beach (FSL) | A | 0 | 1 | 4.32 | 7 | 0 | 0 | 0 | 8 | 8 | 6 | 4 | 1 | 6 | 12 | .216 |
| | Tennessee (SL) | AA | 3 | 8 | 5.50 | 50 | 0 | 0 | 4 | 56 | 67 | 40 | 34 | 6 | 34 | 48 | .288 |
| 2005 | Memphis (PCL) | AAA | 1 | 2 | 7.36 | 26 | 0 | 0 | 0 | 26 | 40 | 21 | 21 | 4 | 19 | 25 | .354 |
| | Springfield (TL) | AA | 5 | 2 | 1.29 | 32 | 0 | 0 | 11 | 42 | 28 | 9 | 6 | 2 | 12 | 42 | .185 |
| 2006 | Memphis (PCL) | AAA | 2 | 2 | 1.52 | 51 | 0 | 0 | 3 | 71 | 46 | 16 | 12 | 2 | 29 | 76 | .186 |
| | St. Louis (NL) | MLB | 0 | 0 | 3.24 | 21 | 0 | 0 | 0 | 25 | 17 | 9 | 9 | 3 | 8 | 22 | .189 |
| **MINOR LEAGUE TOTALS** | | | 20 | 23 | 2.83 | 300 | 0 | 0 | 30 | 385 | 347 | 148 | 121 | 20 | 160 | 368 | .237 |
| **MAJOR LEAGUE TOTALS** | | | 0 | 0 | 3.24 | 21 | 0 | 0 | 0 | 25 | 17 | 9 | 9 | 3 | 8 | 22 | .189 |

## 10  DARRYL JONES                                    OF

**Born:** June 25, 1987. **B-T:** L-L. **Ht.:** 5-11. **Wt.:** 180. **Drafted:** HS—Spring Texas, 2005 (3rd round). **Signed by:** Joe Almaraz.

Jones caught 20 touchdown passes in his final two seasons of high school football, and he was coveted by NCAA Division I-A programs as a wide receiver because of his speed and agility. He opted instead for a baseball scholarship to Rice, and the Cardinals wooed him into pro ball with a $450,000 bonus. He spent most of his first two seasons at Rookie-level Johnson City, making good progress from 2005 to 2006. Jones is the fastest player and best athlete in the system, drawing comparisons to a young Kenny Lofton. Focusing on baseball for the first time in his life, he has started to hit to all fields and develop power in his stroke. He can cover a lot of ground in center field. He's still raw in most phases of the game. Jones still can get pull-happy and overaggressive at the plate, and needs to realize his main goal should be getting on base. His instincts on the bases and in the outfield need improvement. His arm is a tick below-average. Jones missed time last year with hamstring problems, and St. Louis is eager to see what he can do over a full season when he's healthy. He should spend all or most of 2006 in low Class A.

| Year | Club (League) | Class | AVG | G | AB | R | H | 2B | 3B | HR | RBI | BB | SO | SB | OBP | SLG |
|---|---|---|---|---|---|---|---|---|---|---|---|---|---|---|---|---|
| 2005 | Johnson City (Appy) | R | .209 | 61 | 182 | 36 | 38 | 6 | 1 | 2 | 10 | 15 | 41 | 10 | .311 | .286 |
| 2006 | Johnson City (Appy) | R | .265 | 20 | 68 | 15 | 18 | 3 | 1 | 3 | 13 | 8 | 8 | 3 | .367 | .471 |
|  | Quad Cities (MWL) | A | .235 | 26 | 81 | 15 | 19 | 5 | 1 | 1 | 7 | 6 | 23 | 2 | .308 | .358 |
| **MINOR LEAGUE TOTALS** | | | .227 | 107 | 331 | 66 | 75 | 14 | 3 | 6 | 30 | 29 | 72 | 15 | .322 | .341 |

## 11  MITCHELL BOGGS                                  RHP

**Born:** Feb. 15, 1984. **B-T:** R-R. **Ht.:** 6-3. **Wt.:** 195. **Drafted:** Georgia, 2005 (5th round). **Signed by:** Roger Smith.

Coming out of high school as a dual-sport star, Boggs committed to play baseball at Georgia, then had regrets and transferred to Tennessee-Chattanooga (which doesn't have a baseball team) to play football in the fall of his sophomore year. After playing in three games as a quarterback (he rushed three times for nine yards), he returned to Georgia as a sophomore to focus again on baseball. He finished his college career with a 5.62 ERA, but his raw ability attracted scouts. He began to establish himself as one of the organization's better young arms last summer. He ranked second in the Florida State League in strikeouts and took a perfect game into the ninth inning of a game in June, finishing with a one-hit shutout. His fastball runs consistently in the low 90s, though it can touch 94-95 mph. He mixes in an average slider with sharp break and a workable changeup. It's the hard, boring sink on his fastball that further adds to his reputation within the organization. He'll head to Double-A in 2007, and while he'll remain in a starting role for now he may eventually require a move to the bullpen to reach the big leagues.

| Year | Club (League) | Class | W | L | ERA | G | GS | CG | SV | IP | H | R | ER | HR | BB | SO | AVG |
|---|---|---|---|---|---|---|---|---|---|---|---|---|---|---|---|---|---|
| 2005 | New Jersey (NYP) | A | 4 | 4 | 3.89 | 15 | 14 | 0 | 0 | 72 | 77 | 38 | 31 | 5 | 24 | 61 | .271 |
| 2006 | Palm Beach (FSL) | A | 10 | 6 | 3.41 | 27 | 27 | 1 | 0 | 145 | 153 | 69 | 55 | 7 | 51 | 126 | .271 |
| **MINOR LEAGUE TOTALS** | | | 14 | 10 | 3.57 | 42 | 41 | 1 | 0 | 217 | 230 | 107 | 86 | 12 | 75 | 187 | .271 |

## 12  BRENDAN RYAN                                     SS

**Born:** March 26, 1982. **B-T:** R-R. **Ht.:** 6-2. **Wt.:** 195. **Drafted:** Lewis-Clark State (Idaho), 2003 (7th round). **Signed by:** Dane Walker.

Ryan missed more than four months of the season because of ligament injuries to his ring finger and wrist on his left hand, after missing time with hamstring injuries in 2005. He had a barnstorm rehab through four levels of the organization that also gave him his first look at Triple-A. Just two years removed from being considered the club's top position prospect, he saved what was almost a lost season by leading the Arizona Fall League in hits. An athletic player with solid tools, Ryan was smoothing out his rough edges as a fielder and a hitter before his injury, showing a better approach at the plate. He has good speed but his quickness plays better in the field than on the bases, where his steals have dwindled from 30 in 2004. He has an average arm. Ryan can be unsettled at the plate, and his unbridled play in the field leads to unnecessary errors. He led AFL shortstops with eight. He has matured on and off the field but needs to remain focused to continue his improvement. Injuries have cost him significant time in consecutive seasons. The Cardinals have a need for an infielder to emerge from the minors ready to play in the middle of the diamond. Ryan is headed back to Triple-A and hopes to emerge in that role by September, but if he doesn't hit better he could end up as a utility player.

| Year | Club (League) | Class | AVG | G | AB | R | H | 2B | 3B | HR | RBI | BB | SO | SB | OBP | SLG |
|---|---|---|---|---|---|---|---|---|---|---|---|---|---|---|---|---|
| 2003 | New Jersey (NYP) | A | .311 | 53 | 193 | 20 | 60 | 14 | 4 | 0 | 13 | 14 | 25 | 11 | .363 | .425 |
| 2004 | Peoria (MWL) | A | .322 | 105 | 426 | 72 | 137 | 21 | 4 | 2 | 59 | 24 | 42 | 30 | .356 | .404 |
| 2005 | Palm Beach (FSL) | A | .303 | 49 | 188 | 29 | 57 | 17 | 0 | 1 | 16 | 15 | 20 | 8 | .355 | .410 |
|  | Springfield (TL) | AA | .273 | 43 | 154 | 28 | 42 | 8 | 1 | 2 | 9 | 15 | 19 | 6 | .343 | .377 |
| 2006 | Palm Beach (FSL) | A | .429 | 3 | 14 | 2 | 6 | 1 | 0 | 0 | 1 | 0 | 2 | 1 | .429 | .500 |
|  | Springfield (TL) | AA | .302 | 10 | 43 | 6 | 13 | 1 | 0 | 0 | 3 | 3 | 6 | 1 | .348 | .326 |
|  | Memphis (PCL) | AAA | .154 | 7 | 26 | 4 | 4 | 0 | 0 | 1 | 6 | 1 | 3 | 1 | .185 | .269 |
|  | State College (NYP) | A | .235 | 8 | 34 | 5 | 8 | 0 | 0 | 0 | 3 | 3 | 4 | 1 | .282 | .235 |
| **MINOR LEAGUE TOTALS** |  |  | .303 | 278 | 1078 | 166 | 327 | 62 | 9 | 6 | 110 | 75 | 121 | 59 | .349 | .394 |

## 13   MARK HAMILTON                                                    1B

**Born:** July 29, 1984. **B-T:** L-L. **Ht.:** 6-3. **Wt.:** 220. **Drafted:** Tulane, 2006 (2nd round supplemental). **Signed by:** Scott Nichols.

Hamilton swatted 20 home runs last spring for Tulane and finished second in Conference USA with a .461 on-base percentage. He got the Cardinals' attention when he hit balls to the train tracks in left field at Minute Maid Park in Houston during a February tournament. He signed quickly for $465,000, then tied for the New York-Penn League home run title with eight (despite leaving State College after just 30 games). Hamilton has been a known commodity to scouts since his junior year of high school, but despite his power production at Tulane, some scouts have never warmed up to him, questioning how his power would translate as a pro and where he'd play on defense. Hamilton has a seasoned approach to go with his muscular frame and powerful lefthanded swing. He's willing to work deep into a count to find a pitch to drive, and he has tremendous power, though he could add more by using his whole body when he swings. He can drive anything on the inner half, but his swing has holes. His other tools don't measure up. He has settled in at first base, but even in college moved around the field to keep his bat in the lineup. He's a marginal defender at first and needs work there. His arm and speed are below-average. A lack of a position won't hold him out of high Class A this year, though he may find himself pigeonholed as a future DH—a problem for a National League club.

| Year | Club (League) | Class | AVG | G | AB | R | H | 2B | 3B | HR | RBI | BB | SO | SB | OBP | SLG |
|---|---|---|---|---|---|---|---|---|---|---|---|---|---|---|---|---|
| 2006 | Quad Cities (MWL) | A | .254 | 38 | 142 | 16 | 36 | 8 | 0 | 3 | 25 | 10 | 32 | 0 | .307 | .373 |
|  | State College (NYP) | A | .264 | 30 | 106 | 18 | 28 | 3 | 1 | 8 | 24 | 13 | 24 | 1 | .347 | .538 |
| **MINOR LEAGUE TOTALS** |  |  | .258 | 68 | 248 | 34 | 64 | 11 | 1 | 11 | 49 | 23 | 56 | 1 | .325 | .444 |

## 14   CHRIS LAMBERT                                                    RHP

**Born:** March 3, 1983. **B-T:** R-R. **Ht.:** 6-1. **Wt.:** 205. **Drafted:** Boston College, 2004 (1st round). **Signed by:** Joe Rigoli.

Since getting his career off to a promising start, Lambert hasn't adjusted to the upper levels and has struggled to maintain the stuff he showed in college. He has 41 Double-A starts on his resume and an ERA that hasn't yet dipped below 5.00, and as he was getting on a bit of a roll last year he missed time in August with a pulled muscle in his right biceps. Consistency has been the biggest obstacle in his advancement. Lambert was still somewhat raw after three years at Boston College, but he still has the attributes that led to him being a first-round pick: a big, sturdy frame, a low-90s fastball, an improving curveball and a big league changeup. He also throws a slider now, and in fact sometimes relies on it too much instead of working off his fastball. He has made progress with his delivery, reducing his effort, but still needs work on his command and the consistency of all his pitches. He has never shown dominant stuff as a pro. Lambert would have been a tough call for the 40-man roster if the new labor agreement hadn't changed the rules, so he needs to use his extra year to prove something to the Cardinals. They'd like him to win a job in the Triple-A rotation in spring training.

| Year | Club (League) | Class | W | L | ERA | G | GS | CG | SV | IP | H | R | ER | HR | BB | SO | AVG |
|---|---|---|---|---|---|---|---|---|---|---|---|---|---|---|---|---|---|
| 2004 | Peoria (MWL) | A | 1 | 1 | 2.58 | 9 | 9 | 0 | 0 | 38 | 31 | 15 | 11 | 2 | 24 | 46 | .218 |
| 2005 | Palm Beach (FSL) | A | 7 | 1 | 2.63 | 10 | 10 | 0 | 0 | 55 | 53 | 20 | 16 | 4 | 15 | 46 | .255 |
|  | Springfield (TL) | AA | 3 | 8 | 6.35 | 18 | 18 | 0 | 0 | 85 | 97 | 69 | 60 | 10 | 48 | 69 | .291 |
| 2006 | Memphis (PCL) | AAA | 0 | 1 | 6.75 | 1 | 1 | 0 | 0 | 4 | 5 | 3 | 3 | 0 | 0 | 2 | .357 |
|  | Springfield (TL) | AA | 10 | 9 | 5.30 | 23 | 23 | 0 | 0 | 121 | 126 | 84 | 71 | 20 | 63 | 113 | .268 |
| **MINOR LEAGUE TOTALS** |  |  | 21 | 20 | 4.79 | 61 | 61 | 0 | 0 | 303 | 312 | 191 | 161 | 36 | 150 | 276 | .267 |

## 15   CHRIS NARVESON                                                   LHP

**Born:** Dec. 20, 1981. **B-T:** L-L. **Ht.:** 6-3. **Wt.:** 205. **Drafted:** HS—Asheville, N.C., 2000 (2nd round). **Signed by:** Randy Benson.

In the time between being lauded as one of the organization's golden prospects and mak-

ing his major league debut with the Cardinals, Narveson was traded twice, had shoulder surgery, was plucked off waivers and finally landed back in St. Louis. He was riding the fast track before being dealt to the Rockies in the Larry Walker deal in 2004. Narveson was shipped to the Red Sox in 2005, and he returned to the Cardinals in 2005 via waivers. He spent most of last season on the shelf, recovering from offseason labrum surgery. It was the second major operation of his career. Tommy John surgery knocked him off track in 2001-2002. Narveson made encouraging progress upon his return last season, allowing two or fewer runs in eight of his final 10 Triple-A starts, earning a look in St. Louis in September. He operates with a fringe-average 87-89 mph fastball, though it's not quite as firm as it was prior to the shoulder troubles. His fastball sometimes starts out in the mid-80s before reaching as high as the low 90s in later innings. He also has a sharp cutter, a curveball and a solid changeup with fading action. His curve is too slow and hangs at times. He isn't overpowering and lacks a plus pitch, but he throws strikes and has reliable secondary offerings that he mixes well. He will vie for a job in St. Louis in spring training, be it in the revamped rotation or in an apprentice season as a reliever.

| Year | Club (League) | Class | W | L | ERA | G | GS | CG | SV | IP | H | R | ER | HR | BB | SO | AVG |
|---|---|---|---|---|---|---|---|---|---|---|---|---|---|---|---|---|---|
| 2000 | Johnson City (Appy) | R | 2 | 4 | 3.27 | 12 | 12 | 0 | 0 | 55 | 57 | 33 | 20 | 7 | 25 | 63 | .263 |
| 2001 | Peoria (MWL) | A | 3 | 3 | 1.98 | 8 | 8 | 0 | 0 | 50 | 32 | 14 | 11 | 3 | 11 | 53 | .185 |
| | Potomac (CL) | A | 4 | 3 | 2.57 | 11 | 11 | 1 | 0 | 67 | 52 | 22 | 19 | 4 | 13 | 53 | .212 |
| 2002 | Johnson City (Appy) | R | 0 | 2 | 4.91 | 6 | 6 | 0 | 0 | 18 | 23 | 12 | 10 | 2 | 6 | 16 | .307 |
| | Peoria (MWL) | A | 2 | 1 | 4.46 | 9 | 9 | 0 | 0 | 42 | 49 | 24 | 21 | 5 | 8 | 36 | .283 |
| 2003 | Palm Beach (FSL) | A | 7 | 7 | 2.86 | 15 | 14 | 1 | 0 | 91 | 83 | 34 | 29 | 4 | 19 | 65 | .242 |
| | Tennessee (SL) | AA | 4 | 3 | 3.00 | 10 | 10 | 0 | 0 | 57 | 56 | 21 | 19 | 6 | 26 | 34 | .262 |
| 2004 | Tennessee (SL) | AA | 5 | 10 | 4.16 | 23 | 23 | 0 | 0 | 128 | 114 | 64 | 59 | 11 | 51 | 121 | .244 |
| | Tulsa (TL) | AA | 0 | 3 | 3.15 | 4 | 4 | 0 | 0 | 20 | 16 | 14 | 7 | 1 | 13 | 14 | .235 |
| 2005 | Pawtucket (IL) | AAA | 4 | 5 | 4.77 | 21 | 20 | 0 | 0 | 111 | 109 | 62 | 59 | 15 | 46 | 66 | .262 |
| | Memphis (PCL) | AAA | 0 | 1 | 12.15 | 2 | 2 | 0 | 0 | 7 | 11 | 9 | 9 | 2 | 7 | 8 | .379 |
| 2006 | Palm Beach (FSL) | A | 0 | 0 | 2.12 | 3 | 3 | 0 | 0 | 17 | 9 | 4 | 4 | 2 | 1 | 13 | .150 |
| | Memphis (PCL) | AAA | 8 | 5 | 2.81 | 15 | 15 | 0 | 0 | 80 | 70 | 26 | 25 | 9 | 33 | 58 | .238 |
| | St. Louis (NL) | MLB | 0 | 0 | 4.82 | 5 | 1 | 0 | 0 | 9 | 6 | 5 | 5 | 1 | 5 | 12 | .176 |
| **MINOR LEAGUE TOTALS** | | | 39 | 47 | 3.54 | 139 | 137 | 2 | 0 | 743 | 681 | 339 | 292 | 71 | 259 | 600 | .245 |
| **MAJOR LEAGUE TOTALS** | | | 0 | 0 | 4.82 | 5 | 1 | 0 | 0 | 9 | 6 | 5 | 5 | 1 | 5 | 12 | .176 |

## 16 CODY HAERTHER                                                      OF

**Born:** July 14, 1983. **B-T:** L-R. **Ht.:** 6-0. **Wt.:** 190. **Drafted:** HS—Chatsworth, Calif., 2002 (6th round). **Signed by:** Steve Gossett.

Haerther started his career with three consecutive .300-plus seasons, but fell short last year after slumping to a .222 clip in the first half. He reclaimed his reputation as one of the best hitting prospects in the organization by hitting .322 after the all-star break His younger brother Casey was drafted by the Padres in 2006, but didn't sign and is likely to start as a freshman at UCLA. Until the last two drafts infused the system with outfield talent, Haerther was the top prospect at the position, and by far the best hitter. He has sharp strength to his swing, with an ear-catching pop when he connects (41 extra-base hits last year) and a fluid stroke to go with his keen approach. He has yet to strike out 60 times in a season, and in 2006 he drew a career-high 37 walks. A former third baseman, he has adapted well to the outfield and plays a capable left field. He will be rewarded with an invitation to big league camp this spring, and a strong spring training performance will put him in Triple-A and on the verge of the big leagues, though he's unlikely to be considered for a major league role until 2008.

| Year | Club (League) | Class | AVG | G | AB | R | H | 2B | 3B | HR | RBI | BB | SO | SB | OBP | SLG |
|---|---|---|---|---|---|---|---|---|---|---|---|---|---|---|---|---|
| 2003 | Johnson City (Appy) | R | .332 | 63 | 226 | 31 | 75 | 12 | 6 | 3 | 39 | 22 | 30 | 2 | .390 | .478 |
| 2004 | Peoria (MWL) | A | .316 | 86 | 326 | 48 | 103 | 20 | 2 | 5 | 45 | 32 | 59 | 7 | .383 | .436 |
| 2005 | Palm Beach (FSL) | A | .318 | 47 | 173 | 29 | 55 | 8 | 7 | 8 | 30 | 17 | 31 | 8 | .380 | .584 |
| | Springfield (TL) | AA | .298 | 65 | 208 | 30 | 62 | 10 | 1 | 10 | 37 | 9 | 44 | 0 | .333 | .500 |
| 2006 | Springfield (TL) | AA | .277 | 120 | 412 | 56 | 114 | 27 | 3 | 11 | 52 | 37 | 59 | 3 | .336 | .437 |
| **MINOR LEAGUE TOTALS** | | | .304 | 381 | 1345 | 194 | 409 | 77 | 19 | 37 | 203 | 117 | 223 | 20 | .362 | .472 |

## 17 TYLER GREENE                                                       SS

**Born:** Aug. 17, 1983. **B-T:** R-R. **Ht.:** 6-2. **Wt.:** 185. **Drafted:** Georgia Tech, 2005 (1st round). **Signed by:** Roger Smith.

Greene capped his uneven college career by batting .372 as a junior at Georgia Tech in 2005, yet questions still surrounded his bat and future profile in the scouting community. After a solid pro debut, he seemed primed to take off, but stumbled in his return to Palm Beach last year. Greene was erratic in the field and wasn't producing at the plate when he was demoted to low Class A. He turned 23 at the end of the season, so the organization is anxious to see some returns on his $1.1 million bonus. One of the organization's top athletes, he

may be its swiftest basestealer, with a sprinter's legs and a pickpocket's timing. He made adjustments at the plate after his demotion and learned to use the middle of the field and stop chasing pitches. He showed power potential at Quad Cities, but scouts wonder if he'll be able to handle better pitching. He has the strongest infield arm in the system, though he committed 23 errors in 71 games before his demotion because of poor footwork. Some scouts project him as a third baseman, where he thrived while playing for USA Baseball's college national team in 2003. Greene will give Palm Beach another try to open the season.

| Year | Club (League) | Class | AVG | G | AB | R | H | 2B | 3B | HR | RBI | BB | SO | SB | OBP | SLG |
|------|---------------|-------|-----|---|-----|-----|-----|----|----|----|-----|----|-----|----|------|------|
| 2005 | New Jersey (NYP) | A | .261 | 35 | 138 | 28 | 36 | 12 | 0 | 1 | 18 | 15 | 37 | 13 | .352 | .370 |
| | Palm Beach (FSL) | A | .271 | 20 | 85 | 17 | 23 | 4 | 0 | 2 | 5 | 5 | 28 | 6 | .326 | .388 |
| 2006 | Palm Beach (FSL) | A | .224 | 71 | 268 | 38 | 60 | 10 | 1 | 5 | 19 | 29 | 90 | 22 | .308 | .325 |
| | Quad Cities (MWL) | A | .287 | 59 | 223 | 42 | 64 | 8 | 3 | 15 | 47 | 20 | 65 | 11 | .375 | .552 |
| **MINOR LEAGUE TOTALS** | | | .256 | 185 | 714 | 125 | 183 | 34 | 4 | 23 | 89 | 69 | 220 | 52 | .340 | .412 |

## 18  TYLER HERRON                                                    RHP

**Born:** Aug. 5, 1986. **B-T:** R-R. **Ht.:** 6-3. **Wt.:** 190. **Drafted:** HS—Wellington, Fla., 2005 (1st round supplemental). **Signed by:** Steve Turco.

The Cardinals are taking their second stab at a pitcher from Florida's Wellington High, though when they took Justin Pope in the first round in 2001, it was after Pope had spent three seasons at Central Florida. Herron is moving slowly, as he bombed in his pro debut in the Appy League over 50 innings. His return trip began in similar fashion until he picked up his first pro win in late July, a prelude to going 4-1, 2.67 in five August starts. Better command of his low-90s sinker helped Herron get going, as he was able to locate the pitch to minimize hard contact. He also began mixing in his changeup up to 20 times a game with success. The Cardinals believe his curveball can become a plus pitch. Herron impressed Johnson City manager Dan Radison with his maturity, taking sloppy defensive play behind him in stride.

| Year | Club (League) | Class | W | L | ERA | G | GS | CG | SV | IP | H | R | ER | HR | BB | SO | AVG |
|------|---------------|-------|---|---|-----|---|----|----|----|-----|-----|----|----|----|----|-----|------|
| 2005 | Johnson City (Appy) | R | 0 | 3 | 5.62 | 13 | 13 | 0 | 0 | 50 | 47 | 35 | 31 | 11 | 27 | 49 | .245 |
| 2006 | Johnson City (Appy) | R | 5 | 6 | 4.13 | 13 | 13 | 1 | 0 | 70 | 69 | 41 | 32 | 6 | 22 | 54 | .259 |
| | State College (NYP) | A | 0 | 1 | 3.00 | 1 | 1 | 1 | 0 | 6 | 7 | 2 | 2 | 1 | 1 | 3 | .318 |
| **MINOR LEAGUE TOTALS** | | | 5 | 10 | 4.67 | 27 | 27 | 2 | 0 | 125 | 123 | 78 | 65 | 18 | 50 | 106 | .256 |

## 19  TYLER JOHNSON                                                   LHP

**Born:** June 7, 1981. **B-T:** B-L. **Ht.:** 6-2. **Wt.:** 180. **Drafted:** Moorpark (Calif.) JC, D/F 2000 (34th round). **Signed by:** Chuck Fick.

Johnson was in spring training with the A's in 2005 as a major league Rule 5 pick, but he failed to make the team and was returned to the Cardinals. A year later, he emerged as a critical piece in the team's postseason run. Of the eight outs he got in the National League Division Series, six were strikeouts. He finished with 12 strikeouts in 7⅓ playoff innings. After he baffled the Padres with his breaking ball, some hitters called it one of the best in the majors. The hard, late-biting pitch has been called both a slider and a curveball, and it has a natural loopy break to it. The pitch is hard to pick up and harder to hit by lefties, who hit .221 against him. He throws an average fastball that peaks in the high 80s. Johnson, sporting the clubhouse's most colorful tattoos, was labeled as loopy as his breaking ball before he returned to the Cardinals from the A's with his laid-back vibe still intact, but tempered by focus. The organization has learned how to handle his personality and believes his attitude keeps him from dwelling on bad outing. He had his bouts with wildness and was erratic late in the season, even against lefties. St. Louis has Randy Flores and Ricardo Rincon with more experience in the same role, but neither has as good a pitch as Johnson's, so he will continue to share the specialist job and may branch out to a less lefty-specific role.

| Year | Club (League) | Class | W | L | ERA | G | GS | CG | SV | IP | H | R | ER | HR | BB | SO | AVG |
|------|---------------|-------|---|---|-----|---|----|----|----|-----|-----|-----|-----|----|-----|-----|------|
| 2001 | Johnson City (Appy) | R | 1 | 1 | 2.66 | 9 | 9 | 0 | 0 | 41 | 26 | 17 | 12 | 1 | 21 | 58 | .181 |
| | Peoria (MWL) | A | 0 | 1 | 3.95 | 3 | 3 | 0 | 0 | 14 | 14 | 9 | 6 | 1 | 10 | 15 | .255 |
| 2002 | Peoria (MWL) | A | 15 | 3 | 2.00 | 22 | 18 | 0 | 0 | 121 | 96 | 35 | 27 | 7 | 42 | 132 | .218 |
| 2003 | Palm Beach (FSL) | A | 5 | 5 | 3.08 | 22 | 10 | 0 | 0 | 79 | 79 | 29 | 27 | 2 | 38 | 81 | .262 |
| | Tennessee (SL) | AA | 1 | 0 | 1.65 | 20 | 0 | 0 | 0 | 27 | 16 | 7 | 5 | 1 | 15 | 39 | .168 |
| 2004 | Tennessee (SL) | AA | 2 | 2 | 4.79 | 53 | 0 | 0 | 4 | 56 | 48 | 32 | 30 | 4 | 37 | 77 | .221 |
| 2005 | Memphis (PCL) | AAA | 2 | 1 | 4.27 | 57 | 0 | 0 | 7 | 59 | 51 | 31 | 28 | 6 | 26 | 77 | .232 |
| | St. Louis (NL) | MLB | 0 | 0 | 0.00 | 5 | 0 | 0 | 0 | 3 | 3 | 0 | 0 | 0 | 3 | 4 | .300 |
| 2006 | Memphis (PCL) | AAA | 0 | 0 | 8.64 | 8 | 0 | 0 | 0 | 8 | 12 | 8 | 8 | 1 | 4 | 8 | .316 |
| | St. Louis (NL) | MLB | 2 | 4 | 4.95 | 56 | 0 | 0 | 0 | 36 | 33 | 21 | 20 | 5 | 23 | 37 | .244 |
| **MINOR LEAGUE TOTALS** | | | 26 | 13 | 3.17 | 194 | 40 | 0 | 11 | 406 | 342 | 168 | 143 | 23 | 193 | 487 | .226 |
| **MAJOR LEAGUE TOTALS** | | | 2 | 4 | 4.62 | 61 | 0 | 0 | 0 | 39 | 36 | 21 | 20 | 5 | 26 | 41 | .248 |

## 20 NICK STAVINOHA OF

**Born:** May 3, 1982. **B-T:** R-R. **Ht.:** 6-2. **Wt.:** 225. **Drafted:** Louisiana State, 2005 (7th round). **Signed by:** Steve Gossett.

Stavinoha has proven to be a bargain since the Cardinals signed him as a fifth-year senior for $15,000 in 2005. He's come a long way from his freshman year at Houston, where he was a linebacker recruit and long snapper on the football team, before opting to attend San Jacinto (Texas) Junior College to pursue his baseball career. He ultimately ended up at Louisiana State for his final two years of eligibility. He jumped to Double-A in his first full season, though he missed time with an ankle injury and then with inflammation in his right elbow. His .218 average in 78 at-bats in the Arizona Fall League was really his first hiccup as a hitter. He has a sound approach at the plate and above-average power. A former catcher in junior college, Stavinoha played both corner outfield slots last year, spending the majority of his time in right field. He has the arm to play there but is a slightly below-average runner. Regardless of which corner he plays on, Stavinoha will go where his bat takes him. He'll advance to Triple-A this season and try to show he can hit against top-level pitching.

| Year | Club (League) | Class | AVG | G | AB | R | H | 2B | 3B | HR | RBI | BB | SO | SB | OBP | SLG |
|------|---------------|-------|-----|---|----|---|---|----|----|----|-----|----|----|----|-----|-----|
| 2005 | Quad Cities (MWL) | A | .344 | 65 | 250 | 54 | 86 | 9 | 2 | 14 | 53 | 23 | 25 | 4 | .398 | .564 |
| 2006 | Springfield (TL) | AA | .297 | 111 | 417 | 55 | 124 | 26 | 3 | 12 | 73 | 28 | 81 | 2 | .340 | .460 |
| **MINOR LEAGUE TOTALS** | | | .315 | 176 | 667 | 109 | 210 | 35 | 5 | 26 | 126 | 51 | 106 | 6 | .362 | .499 |

## 21 TREY HEARNE RHP

**Born:** Aug. 19, 1983. **B-T:** R-R. **Ht.:** 6-1. **Wt.:** 190. **Drafted:** Texas A&M-Corpus Christi, 2005 (28th round). **Signed by:** Joe Almaraz.

A darling of the Cardinals results-oriented evaluation, Hearne doesn't have a fastball that lights up radar guns or a breaking pitch that buckles knees. He has unblinking control and uncanny performance, though, and he continues to have success. An academic all-American at Texas A&M-Corpus Christi, he established the school's season record with 116 strikeouts in 2005. He's the seven-year-old program's winningest pitcher, and his 16-5 mark as a pro is a testament to his savvy. He bounced between the rotation and the bullpen in low Class A last year. At one point he retired 21 consecutive batters as a reliever before returning to the rotation. He works with a sneaky-fast fastball that explodes out of his smooth delivery and has late movement. At his best, he tops out at 88-89 mph, but his pitches are difficult to square. He uses his changeup as a chase pitch and can throw his curveball while behind in the count. Control is his best asset, and he keeps the ball down and works both sides of the zone. Hearn understands his abilities and is ready to prove himself at a higher level. He profiles as a middle reliever but could keep surprising people.

| Year | Club (League) | Class | W | L | ERA | G | GS | CG | SV | IP | H | R | ER | HR | BB | SO | AVG |
|------|---------------|-------|---|---|-----|---|----|----|----|----|---|---|----|----|----|----|-----|
| 2005 | New Jersey (NYP) | A | 4 | 2 | 2.56 | 24 | 1 | 0 | 0 | 39 | 25 | 15 | 11 | 2 | 12 | 42 | .181 |
| 2006 | Quad Cities (MWL) | A | 12 | 3 | 2.25 | 31 | 17 | 0 | 0 | 128 | 102 | 42 | 32 | 10 | 34 | 106 | .216 |
| **MINOR LEAGUE TOTALS** | | | 16 | 5 | 2.32 | 55 | 18 | 0 | 0 | 167 | 127 | 57 | 43 | 12 | 46 | 148 | .208 |

## 22 TOMMY PHAM SS

**Born:** March 8, 1988. **B-T:** R-R. **Ht.:** 6-1. **Wt.:** 175. **Drafted:** HS—Las Vegas, 2006 (16th round). **Signed by:** Manny Guerra.

Pham was the consensus pick as the best draft-eligible high school player in Nevada in 2006. Though he pitched fewer than 10 innings in high school, Pham attracted attention on the mound in short stints on the showcase circuit by showing a 90-92 mph fastball and surprising feel for a slider. Scouts and college coaches were split on which position suited him best, but Pham was clear that he wanted to hit. The Cardinals hinted at taking him in the third round, but Pham's agent (since fired) priced him out of the first five rounds. The Cardinals took a flier on him in the 16th round and signed him for $325,000, the same bonus they gave to third-rounder Gary Daley. Pham has the tools to stay at shortstop in pro ball with a plus arm and good footwork. His indifference to improving defensively turned off some area scouts, but his bat should allow him to profile for second base or third if he needs to move. Offensively, he has good bat speed and the ball jumps off his bat. He's an above-average runner who can cover 60 yards in 6.7 seconds. He had four hits in his first game but didn't make many adjustments in his debut and struggled with sprained fingers on his right hand. He still has a higher ceiling than many of the more polished college hitters in the Cardinals system and should anchor the infield at Quad Cities this year.

| Year | Club (League) | Class | AVG | G | AB | R | H | 2B | 3B | HR | RBI | BB | SO | SB | OBP | SLG |
|------|---------------|-------|-----|---|----|---|---|----|----|----|-----|----|----|----|-----|-----|
| 2006 | Johnson City (Appy) | R | .231 | 54 | 182 | 26 | 42 | 8 | 3 | 1 | 19 | 26 | 42 | 12 | .340 | .324 |
| **MINOR LEAGUE TOTALS** | | | .231 | 54 | 182 | 26 | 42 | 8 | 3 | 1 | 19 | 26 | 42 | 12 | .340 | .324 |

## 23 BRAD FURNISH
LHP

**Born:** Jan. 19, 1985. **B-T:** B-L. **Ht.:** 6-1. **Wt.:** 185. **Drafted:** Texas Christian, 2006 (2nd round). **Signed by:** Joe Almaraz.

Furnish began his college career at Nebraska, then transferred to Texas Christian and helped the Horned Frogs to a pair of regional appearances. A polished lefthander, Furnish has shown flashes of dominance as an amateur despite average stuff. He had a seven-inning no-hitter with 13 strikeouts against Texas-Pan American in February 2006 and pitched his way into second round. His fastball sat in the 88-92 mph range in college, and he liked to work up and out of the strike zone with it after setting hitters up with his overhand curveball, a solid average offering. Furnish gets good extension in his delivery and has good control of both pitches, which helps them both play up. His approach makes Furnish a flyball pitcher and leaves him susceptible to home runs when he isn't precise. His velocity was down a tick after signing, natural after throwing 100 innings at TCU (with four of his 20 appearances coming in relief) and another 75 for State College. A fresh Furnish could skip a level and start his first full season at Palm Beach. He profiles as a back-of-the-rotation southpaw.

| Year | Club (League) | Class | W | L | ERA | G | GS | CG | SV | IP | H | R | ER | HR | BB | SO | AVG |
|------|---------------|-------|---|---|-----|---|----|----|----|----|----|----|----|----|----|----|-----|
| 2006 | State College (NYP) | A | 3 | 6 | 3.94 | 15 | 15 | 0 | 0 | 75 | 65 | 36 | 33 | 5 | 19 | 68 | .234 |
| **MINOR LEAGUE TOTALS** | | | 3 | 6 | 3.94 | 15 | 15 | 0 | 0 | 75 | 65 | 36 | 33 | 5 | 19 | 68 | .234 |

## 24 MARK WORRELL
RHP

**Born:** March 8, 1983. **B-T:** R-R. **Ht.:** 6-1. **Wt.:** 190. **Drafted:** Florida International, 2004 (12th round). **Signed by:** Steve Turco.

Worrell recorded a minors-best 35 saves in 2005, and he followed that performance up with a Texas League-leading 27 saves last season. It's his quirky, unique delivery, however, that continues to attract all the attention. "It's unorthodox," Worrell has said of his self-taught mechanics. "But it works to my advantage." He never throws from a windup. His front shoulder stays closed to the hitter until his right arm forces it open. He throws from a variety of arm angles and uses a different fastball for righthanders than he does for lefties. Both cruise in the low 90s, offset by a wily slider. He also has a changeup with down and in action to lefties. He held righthanded hitters to a .198 average and struck out more than a third of the righties he faced. Lefties had more success, hitting six home runs while recording a .263 average. Worrell doesn't have overpowering stuff but has perfect makeup for relief and a resilient arm. He will close again in Triple-A this season, and his deception could help present him with an opportunity in the major league bullpen, which is ever dependent on situational matchups under Tony La Russa and Dave Duncan.

| Year | Club (League) | Class | W | L | ERA | G | GS | CG | SV | IP | H | R | ER | HR | BB | SO | AVG |
|------|---------------|-------|---|---|-----|---|----|----|----|----|----|----|----|----|----|----|-----|
| 2004 | Johnson City (Appy) | R | 1 | 0 | 1.21 | 17 | 0 | 0 | 6 | 22 | 12 | 3 | 3 | 1 | 7 | 35 | .152 |
| | Peoria (MWL) | A | 0 | 2 | 4.30 | 12 | 0 | 0 | 6 | 15 | 9 | 10 | 7 | 2 | 6 | 20 | .170 |
| 2005 | Palm Beach (FSL) | A | 2 | 3 | 2.25 | 53 | 0 | 0 | 35 | 56 | 38 | 20 | 14 | 6 | 19 | 53 | .191 |
| 2006 | Springfield (TL) | AA | 3 | 7 | 4.52 | 57 | 0 | 0 | 27 | 62 | 52 | 34 | 31 | 10 | 20 | 75 | .226 |
| **MINOR LEAGUE TOTALS** | | | 6 | 12 | 3.20 | 139 | 0 | 0 | 74 | 155 | 111 | 67 | 55 | 19 | 52 | 183 | .198 |

## 25 DENNIS DOVE
RHP

**Born:** Aug. 31, 1981. **B-T:** R-R. **Ht.:** 6-4. **Wt.:** 205. **Drafted:** Georgia Southern, 2003 (5th round). **Signed by:** Roger Smith.

Dove needed some kind of jump-start to his career after making 42 starts, none above Class A, in two and a half seasons. He shifted to the bullpen last year and advanced to Double-A in the second half. With one plus pitch, he finally began to blossom in relief. Dove has long sported one of the best fastballs in the organization, a lively hopper he can run up to 96-97 mph at times. He consistently is able to pump 92-94 mph heat with a funky, max-effort delivery that gives him some deception. He hadn't learned to harness his stuff as a starter, and poor control plagued him. He works almost exclusively with fastballs, mixing in an occasional slider that doesn't feature the same type of power you'd expect from a pitcher with his arm strength. He also largely scrapped the changeup he tried as a starter. He was more aggressive in relief, and his control showed marked improvement. He built upon his breakthrough season with a promising stint in the Arizona Fall League, going 1-0, 1.93 over nine innings. The Cardinals added him to the 40-man roster after the season, and he'll get a chance to garner attention in major league spring training while also auditioning for the Triple-A bullpen.

| Year | Club (League) | Class | W | L | ERA | G | GS | CG | SV | IP | H | R | ER | HR | BB | SO | AVG |
|---|---|---|---|---|---|---|---|---|---|---|---|---|---|---|---|---|---|
| 2003 | New Jersey (NYP) | A | 1 | 3 | 3.51 | 7 | 7 | 0 | 0 | 26 | 29 | 15 | 10 | 1 | 15 | 15 | .284 |
| 2004 | Peoria (MWL) | A | 0 | 1 | 4.97 | 3 | 3 | 0 | 0 | 13 | 11 | 8 | 7 | 1 | 10 | 4 | .234 |
| | New Jersey (NYP) | A | 0 | 5 | 8.06 | 6 | 6 | 0 | 0 | 22 | 31 | 20 | 20 | 3 | 13 | 24 | .344 |
| 2005 | Quad Cities (MWL) | A | 7 | 5 | 3.88 | 18 | 18 | 2 | 0 | 102 | 93 | 47 | 44 | 6 | 30 | 72 | .242 |
| | Palm Beach (FSL) | A | 2 | 4 | 4.85 | 8 | 8 | 0 | 0 | 43 | 48 | 24 | 23 | 1 | 15 | 23 | .286 |
| 2006 | Palm Beach (FSL) | A | 3 | 3 | 2.81 | 41 | 0 | 0 | 4 | 51 | 38 | 20 | 16 | 3 | 13 | 56 | .212 |
| | Springfield (TL) | AA | 0 | 3 | 8.79 | 13 | 0 | 0 | 0 | 14 | 18 | 16 | 14 | 6 | 8 | 15 | .295 |
| **MINOR LEAGUE TOTALS** | | | 13 | 24 | 4.45 | 96 | 42 | 2 | 4 | 271 | 268 | 150 | 134 | 21 | 104 | 209 | .260 |

## MIKE SILLMAN
RHP

**Born:** Dec. 3, 1981. **B-T:** R-R. **Ht.:** 6-1. **Wt.:** 190. **Drafted:** Nebraska, 2004 (21st round). **Signed by:** Mike Roberts.

Inheriting the role that Mark Worrell used as a launching pad to the organization's pitcher of the year award in 2005, Sillman found similar success as Palm Beach's closer and his 35 saves were second in the minors. Sillman attacks hitters from a sidearm, almost submarine delivery that's funky and deceptive to hitters. He dropped his arm slot prior to his junior year at Nebraska at the urging of his coaches. He surrendered just two home runs in 2006 and can be death to righthanded hitters, who managed a meager .142 average against him last year. He hides the ball well and his fastball ranges from 89-91 mph with late life down in the zone. When he throws his slider, it's usually too late for hitters to pick up, and it features hard, darting action down and in on lefties. He can spin it for strikes or use it as a swing-and-miss chase pitch, running out of the zone or in the dirt. Sandwiched by Worrell above and Chris Perez below, Sillman will close in Double-A this season.

| Year | Club (League) | Class | W | L | ERA | G | GS | CG | SV | IP | H | R | ER | HR | BB | SO | AVG |
|---|---|---|---|---|---|---|---|---|---|---|---|---|---|---|---|---|---|
| 2004 | Johnson City (Appy) | R | 1 | 1 | 2.00 | 6 | 0 | 0 | 1 | 9 | 5 | 2 | 2 | 1 | 2 | 13 | .156 |
| | New Jersey (NYP) | A | 0 | 0 | 1.35 | 16 | 0 | 0 | 2 | 20 | 12 | 3 | 3 | 1 | 8 | 28 | .167 |
| 2005 | Quad Cities (MWL) | A | 8 | 2 | 2.74 | 56 | 0 | 0 | 22 | 66 | 39 | 23 | 20 | 3 | 49 | 77 | .171 |
| 2006 | Palm Beach (FSL) | A | 4 | 3 | 1.10 | 57 | 0 | 0 | 35 | 57 | 34 | 10 | 7 | 2 | 20 | 86 | .167 |
| **MINOR LEAGUE TOTALS** | | | 13 | 6 | 1.89 | 135 | 0 | 0 | 60 | 152 | 90 | 38 | 32 | 7 | 79 | 204 | .168 |

## JON EDWARDS
OF

**Born:** Jan. 8, 1988. **B-T:** R-R. **Ht.:** 6-5. **Wt.:** 230. **Drafted:** HS—Keller, Texas, 2006 (14th round). **Signed by:** Joe Almaraz.

Because he was ineligible for half his senior season in high school, Edwards dropped to the 14th round in June and signed for $100,000. He already looks like a steal after ranking among the Top 10 Prospects in the Appalachian League despite being hampered by a sore wrist and hamstring. At a hulking 6-foot-5, 230 pounds he presents plus raw power, both pulling the ball and to straightaway center, and is cast in the mold of a prototypical right fielder. He has plus arm strength but below-average range. He moves well for his size but struggled on balls hit right at him. Edwards has a long swing, but it's not unwieldy, and he has better pitch recognition than most young hitters. He struck out 33 times to 20 walks in 154 at-bats, showing good discipline. He should step into the middle of the Quad Cities lineup as a 19-year-old this summer.

| Year | Club (League) | Class | AVG | G | AB | R | H | 2B | 3B | HR | RBI | BB | SO | SB | OBP | SLG |
|---|---|---|---|---|---|---|---|---|---|---|---|---|---|---|---|---|
| 2006 | Johnson City (Appy) | R | .266 | 48 | 154 | 23 | 41 | 16 | 1 | 4 | 27 | 20 | 33 | 0 | .360 | .461 |
| **MINOR LEAGUE TOTALS** | | | .266 | 48 | 154 | 23 | 41 | 16 | 1 | 4 | 27 | 20 | 33 | 0 | .360 | .461 |

## SHANE ROBINSON
OF

**Born:** Oct. 30, 1984. **B-T:** R-R. **Ht.:** 5-9. **Wt.:** 165. **Drafted:** Florida State, 2006 (5th round). **Signed by:** Scott Melvin.

Evaluations of Robinson entering the draft varied. Some scouts saw him as a valuable, on-base pest with an ability to play center field, while others had little interest, seeing him as a righthanded-hitting version of former Athletics minor leaguer Steve Stanley, without Stanley's speed. As a sophomore at Florida State in 2005, Robinson had a school-record 40-game hitting streak and became the only college player that year with 100 hits and 40 stolen bases, finishing with 122 hits, a .427 average and .532 on-base percentage. He was less productive as a junior (his OPS dropped nearly 200 points), fell to the fifth round and signed for $175,000. He had three hits in his pro debut in low Class A. Robinson is a slap hitter who tries to push the ball around the diamond. His lack of physical strength leaves him with below-average bat speed and well-below-average power. He has good plate discipline and works counts well. He handles the bat well and bunts effectively. He's a solid-average runner, with good instincts on the bases and in center field, where he's an average defender with fringy range. His arm is below-average but accurate. His slight frame lends little room

for projection, and his best profile is as a second-hole hitter and center fielder. He'll have to prove he can hit power pitching at higher levels, starting in 2007 at Palm Beach.

| Year | Club (League) | Class | AVG | G | AB | R | H | 2B | 3B | HR | RBI | BB | SO | SB | OBP | SLG |
|---|---|---|---|---|---|---|---|---|---|---|---|---|---|---|---|---|
| 2006 | Quad Cities (MWL) | A | .282 | 63 | 252 | 41 | 71 | 9 | 2 | 0 | 21 | 20 | 20 | 13 | .346 | .333 |
| **MINOR LEAGUE TOTALS** | | | .282 | 63 | 252 | 41 | 71 | 9 | 2 | 0 | 21 | 20 | 20 | 13 | .346 | .333 |

## SKIP SCHUMAKER OF

**Born:** Feb. 3, 1980. **B-T:** L-R. **Ht.:** 5-10. **Wt.:** 175. **Drafted:** UC Santa Barbara, 2001 (5th round). **Signed by:** Steve Gossett.

One of the lone bright spots in a sour season at Triple-A Memphis was Schumaker overcoming the club's struggles and hitting a team-best .306/.348/.382. Then he really broke out after leaving the Redbirds early to compete in the Olympic qualifying tournament with Team USA. He was the leadoff hitter and center fielder and hit .405 in the tournament and scored 15 runs. USA Baseball CEO Paul Seiler called him the MVP of the club that beat Cuba, won the tournament and qualified the U.S. for the 2008 Games. The swift fielder was on the Cardinals' Opening Day roster and for most of the first month of the regular season, he had the only home run by a Cardinals starting left fielder. Center fielder Jim Edmonds took a shine to Schumaker in 2005 and continued promoting him during spring training last year. He was stellar, making some of the spring's most dynamic defensive plays. He has the defensive ability to play all three outfield positions well, and has enough arm for those spots too. Few players in the entire organization get better jumps and have the closing speed that Schumaker has. He has found a way to channel his line-drive approach into a .300 average, though he could make better use of his running ability on the bases. He has minimal power, so he has to get on base. He is slated to join the major league club as an extra outfielder in 2007 and will become the first glove off the bench late in games, and that's his long-term role as well.

| Year | Club (League) | Class | AVG | G | AB | R | H | 2B | 3B | HR | RBI | BB | SO | SB | OBP | SLG |
|---|---|---|---|---|---|---|---|---|---|---|---|---|---|---|---|---|
| 2001 | New Jersey (NYP) | A | .253 | 49 | 162 | 22 | 41 | 10 | 1 | 0 | 14 | 29 | 33 | 11 | .368 | .327 |
| 2002 | Potomac (CAR) | A | .287 | 136 | 551 | 71 | 158 | 22 | 4 | 2 | 44 | 45 | 84 | 26 | .342 | .352 |
| 2003 | Tennessee (SL) | AA | .251 | 91 | 342 | 43 | 86 | 20 | 3 | 2 | 22 | 37 | 54 | 6 | .330 | .345 |
| 2004 | Tennessee (SL) | AA | .316 | 138 | 516 | 78 | 163 | 29 | 6 | 4 | 43 | 60 | 61 | 19 | .389 | .419 |
| 2005 | Memphis (PCL) | AAA | .287 | 115 | 443 | 66 | 127 | 24 | 3 | 7 | 34 | 29 | 54 | 14 | .330 | .402 |
| | St. Louis (NL) | MLB | .250 | 27 | 24 | 9 | 6 | 1 | 0 | 0 | 1 | 2 | 2 | 1 | .308 | .292 |
| 2006 | Memphis (PCL) | AAA | .306 | 95 | 369 | 47 | 113 | 13 | 3 | 3 | 27 | 23 | 48 | 11 | .348 | .382 |
| | St. Louis (NL) | MLB | .185 | 28 | 54 | 3 | 10 | 1 | 0 | 1 | 2 | 5 | 6 | 2 | .254 | .259 |
| **MINOR LEAGUE TOTALS** | | | .289 | 624 | 2383 | 327 | 688 | 118 | 20 | 18 | 184 | 223 | 334 | 87 | .351 | .378 |
| **MAJOR LEAGUE TOTALS** | | | .205 | 55 | 78 | 12 | 16 | 2 | 0 | 1 | 3 | 7 | 8 | 3 | .271 | .269 |

## AMAURY CAZANA-MARTI OF

**Born:** Sept. 2, 1974. **B-T:** R-R. **Ht.:** 6-1. **Wt.:** 212. **Drafted:** Miami (no school), 2006 (18th round). **Signed by:** Koby Perez.

The day the Cardinals took the Cuban defector in the 18th round, they believed he was 27. Around the time he jumped to Double-A his age leapt, too—up to 32 by the time he was assigned to the Arizona Fall League. At either age, Marti has to move fast to keep the Cardinals interested. His teammates at Palm Beach nicknamed him "God" for his muscular Rickey Henderson-like physique. Marti first came to the Cardinals' attention during spring training, when they thought he was a pitcher. After some research, they found out he was an outfielder signed to an independent league contract (he played in the Can-Am League in 2005), and thus eligible for the draft. Marti displayed his raw power early, launching what some say is the longest home run hit at Palm Beach's home park. He regularly hit light-tower shots during batting practice, but his susceptibility to breaking balls didn't allow his power to fully manifest in games. He has plus bat speed, with an over-aggressive approach at times. He often expands the strike zone early in the count. He hit lefties at a .455 clip with an .848 slugging percentage in Double-A. Defensively, he is athletic enough to play anywhere in the outfield, and he has average arm strength. He doesn't take great routes to the ball. Though he's a good runner under way, his speed doesn't translate to stealing bases and he gets down the line slow because of his big swing. No matter his age, if he doesn't hit, he won't have any value. He'll try to earn a spot in the Memphis outfield in spring training.

| Year | Club (League) | Class | AVG | G | AB | R | H | 2B | 3B | HR | RBI | BB | SO | SB | OBP | SLG |
|---|---|---|---|---|---|---|---|---|---|---|---|---|---|---|---|---|
| 2006 | Palm Beach (FSL) | A | .282 | 20 | 85 | 17 | 24 | 6 | 0 | 4 | 16 | 9 | 26 | 3 | .351 | .494 |
| | Springfield (TL) | AA | .227 | 40 | 132 | 17 | 30 | 4 | 0 | 6 | 13 | 13 | 41 | 1 | .315 | .394 |
| **MINOR LEAGUE TOTALS** | | | .249 | 60 | 217 | 34 | 54 | 10 | 0 | 10 | 29 | 22 | 67 | 4 | .329 | .433 |

# SAN DIEGO
# PADRES

BY **MATT EDDY**

The Padres repeated as National League West champions and had their third consecutive winning season in 2006, both firsts in franchise history. Neither would have happened if not for some astute trades on the part of general manager Kevin Towers.

His biggest deal came in January, when he acquired **Adrian Gonzalez**, Chris Young and minor league outfielder Terrmel Sledge from the Rangers for Adam Eaton, Akinori Otsuka and catching prospect Billy Killian. Gonzalez, the No. 1 overall pick in the 2000 draft, topped San Diego with a .304 average and 24 homers, while Young won 11 games with a team-best 3.46 ERA and NL-best .206 opponents' average.

Two other trades strengthened areas of weakness. After coming over from the Mets in November for Xavier Nady, Mike Cameron won a Gold Glove in center field and led the Padres with 83 RBIs. In May, the Red Sox wanted Doug Mirabelli back and parted with Josh Bard, who hit .338 as a part-timer, and Cla Meredith, whose 1.07 ERA was the lowest among NL pitchers with at least 50 innings.

One of the reasons San Diego was active on the trade market is that its farm system lacks depth in the upper levels. Since-traded Josh Barfield hit .280 with 13 homers and played a steady second base as a rookie in 2006, while Clay Hensley (originally signed by the Giants and traded for Matt Herges in 2003) won 11 games. But weak drafts in 2003 and 2004—typified by spending the No. 1 overall choice in the latter draft on Matt Bush—undermined the Padres' prospect pipeline.

Eight of the club's top 10 prospects have

ANDREW WOOLLEY

come from the last two drafts, highlighting the efforts of vice president of scouting and player development Grady Fuson and scouting director Bill Gayton to supplement the system. San Diego aggressively landed two premium draft-and-follows last spring in righthanders Drew Miller and Aaron Breit.

International scouting director Randy Smith's work also has been magnified as the Padres search for their first homegrown Latin American star. Their best hope is Dominican outfielder Yefri Carvajal, signed in 2005 after the Padres lost out in the Fernando Martinez bidding to the Mets.

Led by the organization's top prospect, outfielder Cedric Hunter, the Arizona League Padres won the league championship and were one of three San Diego affiliates to qualify for the postseason. Padres farm clubs combined for a .513 winning percentage, their best mark since 2002. After 10 years in Mobile, San Diego will shift its Double-A affiliate to San Antonio in 2007.

The Padres ended an even longer association when they allowed manager Bruce Bochy to take the same job with the Giants after the season. The skipper of four of the five division winners in franchise history, Bochy had been at San Diego's helm since 1995, a run surpassed only by Atlanta's Bobby Cox among active managers. The Padres hired Angels pitching coach Bud Black to replace Bochy.

## TOP 30 PROSPECTS

| | |
|---|---|
| 1. Cedric Hunter, of | 16. Wade LeBlanc, lhp |
| 2. Cesar Carrillo, rhp | 17. Kevin Cameron, rhp |
| 3. Matt Antonelli, 3b | 18. Paul McAnulty, 1b/3b |
| 4. Kevin Kouzmanoff, 3b | 19. Matt Bush, ss |
| 5. Will Venable, of | 20. Luis Cruz, 2b/ss |
| 6. Chase Headley, 3b | 21. Felix Carrasco, 3b |
| 7. Chad Huffman, of | 22. Andrew Brown, rhp |
| 8. Nick Hundley, c | 23. Sean Thompson, lhp |
| 9. Jared Wells, rhp | 24. Matt Buschmann, rhp |
| 10. Cesar Ramos, lhp | 25. Mike Ekstrom, rhp |
| 11. Aaron Breit, rhp | 26. Colt Morton, c |
| 12. Drew Miller, rhp | 27. Pablo Menchaca, rhp |
| 13. Yefri Carvajal, of | 28. Simon Castro, rhp |
| 14. Kyler Burke, of | 29. Kyle Blanks, 1b |
| 15. David Freese, 3b | 30. John Hussey, rhp |

**General manager:** Kevin Towers. **Farm director:** Grady Fuson. **Scouting director:** Bill Gayton.

## 2006 PERFORMANCE

| Class | Team | League | W | L | PCT | Finish* | Manager | Affiliated |
|---|---|---|---|---|---|---|---|---|
| Majors | San Diego | National | 88 | 74 | .543 | 3rd (16) | Bruce Bochy | — |
| Triple-A | Portland Beavers | Pacific Coast | 68 | 76 | .472 | 11th (16) | Craig Colbert | 2001 |
| Double-A | #Mobile BayBears | Southern | 62 | 76 | .449 | 7th (10) | Gary Jones | 1997 |
| High A | Lake Elsinore Storm | California | 74 | 66 | .529 | 3rd (10) | Rick Renteria | 2001 |
| Low A | Fort Wayne Wizards | Midwest | 71 | 66 | .518 | 8th (14) | Randy Ready | 1999 |
| Short-season | Eugene Emeralds | Northwest | 43 | 33 | .566 | 3rd (8) | Doug Dascenzo | 2001 |
| Rookie | AZL Padres | Arizona | 36 | 19 | .655 | +1st (9) | Carlos Lezcano | 2004 |
| **OVERALL 2006 MINOR LEAGUE RECORD** | | | 354 | 336 | .513 | 12th (30) | | |

*Finish in overall standings (No. of teams in league). +League champion. #Affiliate will be in San Antonio (Texas) in 2007.

## ORGANIZATION LEADERS

### BATTING
| | | |
|---|---|---|
| AVG | Durango, Luis, AZL Padres | .378 |
| R | Kazmar, Sean, Lake Elsinore | 98 |
| H | Venable, Will, Fort Wayne | 160 |
| 2B | Cruz, Luis, Mobile | 39 |
| 2B | Venable, William, Fort Wayne | 39 |
| 3B | Baxter, Michael, Fort Wayne | 7 |
| HR | Knott, Jon, Portland | 32 |
| RBI | Knott, Jon, Portland | 113 |
| BB | Cust, Jack, Portland | 143 |
| SO | Adams, Skip, Lake Elsinore | 137 |
| SB | Ramirez, Yordany, Lake Elsinore | 23 |
| OBP | Durango, Luis, AZL Padres | .470 |
| SLG | Sledge, Terrmel, Portland | .583 |
| XBH | Knott, Jon, Portland | 70 |

### PITCHING
| | | |
|---|---|---|
| W | Geer, Joshua, Fort Wayne/Lake Elsinore | 13 |
| L | Hayhurst, Dirk, L.E./Mobile/Portland | 14 |
| ERA | Dunn, Brooks, Eugene | 2.41 |
| G | Jamison, Neil, Fort Wayne/Lake Elsinore | 74 |
| SV | Jamison, Neil, Fort Wayne/Lake Elsinore | 37 |
| IP | Ekstrom, Michael, Lake Elsinore/Mobile | 167 |
| BB | Oyervidez, Jose, Mobile | 75 |
| SO | Thompson, Sean, Mobile | 134 |
| AVG | Dunn, Brooks, Eugene | .232 |

## BEST TOOLS

| | |
|---|---|
| Best Hitter for Average | Cedric Hunter |
| Best Power Hitter | Kevin Kouzmanoff |
| Best Strike-Zone Discipline | Matt Antonelli |
| Fastest Baserunner | Luis Durango |
| Best Athlete | Matt Antonelli |
| Best Fastball | Drew Miller |
| Best Curveball | Sean Thompson |
| Best Slider | Jared Wells |
| Best Changeup | Wade LeBlanc |
| Best Control | Mike Ekstrom |
| Best Defensive Catcher | Luke Carlin |
| Best Defensive Infielder | Luis Cruz |
| Best Infield Arm | Matt Bush |
| Best Defensive Outfielder | Yordany Ramirez |
| Best Outfield Arm | Yordany Ramirez |

## PROJECTED 2010 LINEUP

| | |
|---|---|
| Catcher | Nick Hundley |
| First Base | Adrian Gonzalez |
| Second Base | Matt Antonelli |
| Third Base | Kevin Kouzmanoff |
| Shortstop | Khalil Greene |
| Left Field | Will Venable |
| Center Field | Cedric Hunter |

| | |
|---|---|
| Right Field | Mike Cameron |
| No. 1 Starter | Jake Peavy |
| No. 2 Starter | Chris Young |
| No. 3 Starter | Cesar Carrillo |
| No. 4 Starter | Clay Hensley |
| No. 5 Starter | Cesar Ramos |
| Closer | Scott Linebrink |

## LAST YEAR'S TOP 20 PROSPECTS

1. Cesar Carrillo, rhp
2. George Kottaras, c
3. Josh Barfield, 2b
4. Ben Johnson, of
5. Chase Headley, 3b
6. Clay Hensley, rhp
7. Jared Wells, rhp
8. Paul McAnulty, of/1b
9. Nick Hundley, c
10. Freddy Guzman, of
11. Cesar Ramos, lhp
12. Sean Thompson, lhp
13. Matt Bush, ss
14. Ben Krosschell, rhp
15. Kyle Blanks, 1b
16. Joel Santo, rhp
17. Ernesto Frieri, rhp
18. Josh Geer, rhp
19. Yefri Carvajal, of
20. Kenny Baugh, rhp

## TOP PROSPECTS OF THE DECADE

| Year | Player, Pos. | 2006 Org. |
|---|---|---|
| 1997 | Derrek Lee, 1b | Cubs |
| 1998 | Matt Clement, rhp | Red Sox |
| 1999 | Matt Clement, rhp | Red Sox |
| 2000 | Sean Burroughs, 3b | Devil Rays |
| 2001 | Sean Burroughs, 3b | Devil Rays |
| 2002 | Sean Burroughs, 3b | Devil Rays |
| 2003 | Xavier Nady, of | Pirates |
| 2004 | Josh Barfield, 2b | Padres |
| 2005 | Josh Barfield, 2b | Padres |
| 2006 | Cesar Carrillo, rhp | Padres |

## TOP DRAFT PICKS OF THE DECADE

| Year | Player, Pos. | 2006 Org. |
|---|---|---|
| 1997 | Kevin Nicholson, ss | Somerset (Atlantic) |
| 1998 | Sean Burroughs, 3b | Devil Rays |
| 1999 | Vince Faison, of | Yankees |
| 2000 | Mark Phillips, lhp | Out of baseball |
| 2001 | Jake Gautreau, 3b | Indians |
| 2002 | Khalil Greene, ss | Padres |
| 2003 | Tim Stauffer, rhp | Padres |
| 2004 | Matt Bush, ss | Padres |
| 2005 | Cesar Carrillo, rhp | Padres |
| 2006 | Matt Antonelli, 3b | Padres |

## LARGEST BONUSES IN CLUB HISTORY

| | |
|---|---|
| Matt Bush, 2004 | $3,150,000 |
| Mark Phillips, 2000 | $2,200,000 |
| Sean Burroughs, 1998 | $2,100,000 |
| Jake Gautreau, 2001 | $1,875,000 |
| Matt Antonelli, 2006 | $1,575,000 |

# MINOR LEAGUE DEPTH CHART

## San Diego Padres

**Impact: D.** All the system's top prospects come with considerable question marks, from Carrillo's health, to Antonelli's and Hunter's power, to Kouzmanoff's ability to hold down third base.

**Depth: D.** More than half the system's prospects have been acquired in the past two years—by draft, signing or trade—leaving the Padres noticeably thin at the upper levels.

**Sleeper:** Simon Castro, rhp. Though he did not pitch in the States, Castro has one of the biggest arms in the system and could move quickly if he can adjust to pro ball.

*Numbers in parentheses indicate prospect rankings.*

| LF | CF | RF |
|---|---|---|
| Willl Venable (5) | Cedric Hunter (1) | Yefri Carvajal (13) |
| Chad Huffman (7) | Luis Durango | Kyler Burke (14) |
| Jon Knott | Javis Diaz | Nick Crosta |
| Vince Sinisi | Drew Macias | Yordany Ramirez |

| 3B | SS | 2B | 1B |
|---|---|---|---|
| Kevin Kouzmanoff (4) | Matt Bush (19) | Matt Antonelli (3) | Paul McAnulty (18) |
| Chase Headley (6) | Jesus Lopez | Luis Cruz (20) | Kyle Blanks (29) |
| David Freese (15) | Juan Ciriaco | Sean Kazmar | Craig Cooper |
| Felix Carrasco (21) | | | Daryl Jones |
| Rayner Contreras | | | |

| C |
|---|
| Nick Hundley (8) |
| Colt Morton (26) |
| Luke Carlin |

| RHP | | LHP | |
|---|---|---|---|
| **Starters** | **Relievers** | **Starters** | **Relievers** |
| Cesar Carrillo (2) | Jared Wells (9) | Cesar Ramos (10) | Sean Thompson (23) |
| Aaron Breit (11) | Kevin Cameron (17) | Wade LeBlanc (16) | Royce Ring |
| Drew Miller (12) | Andrew Brown (22) | Nate Culp | Ryan Ketchner |
| Matt Buschmann (24) | John Madden | Brooks Dunn | Orlando Lara |
| Mike Ekstrom (25) | Neil Jamison | | Pascual Juan |
| Pablo Menchaca (27) | Tyler Mead | | |
| Simon Castro (28) | Leo Rosales | | |
| John Hussey (30) | Manny Ayala | | |
| Rolando Valdez | Jose Oyervidez | | |
| Rob Garramone | Jonathan Ellis | | |
| John Hudgins | Ernesto Frieri | | |
| Richie Daigle | Josh Geer | | |

# DRAFT ANALYSIS

## 2006　SIGNING BUDGET: $4.7 million

**Best Pro Debut:** OF Cedric Hunter (3) won Rookie-level Arizona League MVP honors after batting .371/.467/.484 with 17 steals and league highs in runs (46) and hits (79). 3B David Freese (9) spent most of the summer in low Class A and batted .317/.395/.569 with 13 homers and 70 RBIs. OF Chad Huffman (2) hit .335 with nine homers and a Northwest League-best .439 on-base percentage. 1B Craig Cooper (7) joined Huffman on the NWL all-star team by batting .320/.418/.485.

**Best Athlete:** In 2002-03, 3B Matt Antonelli (1) was the Massachusetts high school player of the year in football and hockey and the runner-up in baseball. Huffman was a backup quarterback at Texas Christian. OF Kyler Burke (1) was a prep linebacker who won a high school slam-dunk contest.

**Best Pure Hitter:** Hunter and Huffman spray line drives to all fields while doing a masterful job of controlling the strike zone. Freese is another advanced hitter, though he sacrifices some contact by using more of a power approach.

**Best Raw Power:** Freese. Huffman has some interesting power potential if he can learn to lift more balls in the air.

**Fastest Runner:** 2B Ray Stokes (16) is a plus-plus runner who stole a Cal State East Bay-record 29 bases in 31 attempts last spring. He's still learning on the bases after making the jump from NCAA Division III to pro ball, and swiped just three bases in five tries in his debut. OF Michael Epping (13) and Antonelli have above-average speed.

**Best Defensive Player:** Antonelli has the tools but needs some more polish at third base. The Padres may move him to second base, where his power would be a better fit. For now, Cooper is the slickest fielder as an agile first baseman with outstanding hands.

**Best Fastball:** The Padres signed mostly finesse pitchers out of the draft, though draft-and-follows Drew Miller (92-96 mph) and Aaron Breit (91-94) have good velocity. Among the 2006 draftees, RHP Matt Buschmann (15) has the best fastball at 89-93 mph.

**Best Breaking Ball:** Buschmann's 84-85 mph slider. The best secondary pitch in San Diego's draft is LHP Wade LeBlanc's (2) changeup.

**Most Intriguing Background:** Huffman's brothers Scott and Royce also played football and baseball in college, and Royce played in Triple-A for the Astros in 2006. 3B Luke Stewart's (43) father Jeff is a Padres area scout. 3B Bryce Lefebvre's (45) dad Jim was the 1965 National League Rookie of the Year and managed three big league clubs. 1B Casey Haerther's (34) brother Cody is one of the Cardinals' better outfield prospects.

**Closest To The Majors:** The Padres will push Freese because he signed as a 23-year-old fifth-year senior, and his bat will help him move quickly as well. He'll take more time if San Diego continues to try him behind the plate.

**Best Late-Round Pick:** Buschmann.

**The One Who Got Away:** San Diego still controls the rights to RHP Matt Latos (11), who has touched 100 mph and is now at Broward (Fla.) CC. But it lost out on slick-fielding SS Grant Green (14), who headed to Southern California when he didn't get a seven-figure bonus.

**Assessment:** Hunter, who exceeded initial expectations, and Antonelli are two of the Padres' best prospects already. They added position-player depth with Burke, Huffman and Freese, and they needed it.

## 2005　BUDGET: $3.0 million

After successive poor drafts, the Padres desperately needed to restock their system, and they did with RHP Cesar Carrillo (1), LHP Cesar Ramos (1), 3B Chase Headley (2), C Nick Hundley (2), OF Max Venable (7) and draft-and-follow RHPs Aaron Breit (12) and Drew Miller (37) .　**GRADE: B**

## 2004　BUDGET: $4.5 million

Upper management decided Stephen Drew was too expensive, and San Diego compounded that mistake by taking SS Matt Bush (1) No. 1 overall. He ranks 19th on our Padres Top 30 list, and that still makes him the best prospect from this crop. **GRADE: F**

## 2003　BUDGET: $2.8 million

After taking him fourth overall, San Diego learned that RHP Tim Stauffer (1) had a previously undiagnosed shoulder injury. He hasn't been the same since, and no one else has stepped forward.　**GRADE: F**

*Draft analysis by Jim Callis. Numbers in parentheses indicate draft rounds. Budgets are bonuses in first 10 rounds.*

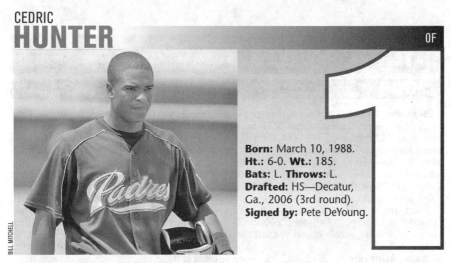

# CEDRIC
# HUNTER

**Born:** March 10, 1988.
**Ht.:** 6-0. **Wt.:** 185.
**Bats:** L. **Throws:** L.
**Drafted:** HS—Decatur, Ga., 2006 (3rd round).
**Signed by:** Pete DeYoung.

BILL MITCHELL

Hunter has stood out as a hitter everywhere he has played. He held up under the scrutiny of the showcase circuit, thrived against top competition in the East Cobb summer league program in suburban Atlanta and went 1-for-2 in the 2005 Aflac High School All-America Classic. It was no surprise, then, when Hunter hit .580 with 12 homers in 69 at-bats and added 20 steals as a senior at Martin Luther King Jr. High (Lithonia, Ga.) last spring to earn All-America honors. The Padres made him a third round pick last June and signed him for $415,000. While Hunter wasn't as hyped as other high school hitters in his draft class, San Diego was happy to add his polished offensive approach and workmanlike demeanor to the organization. And he delivered right out of the gate, reaching base in his first 49 pro games in the Rookie-level Arizona League, including a 23-game hitting streak. Hunter won AZL MVP honors by leading the complex league in runs, hits and total bases (103) while finishing second to teammate Luis Durango in on-base percentage.

Hunter's bat is clearly his best tool. He has excellent hand-eye coordination and impressive balance. He commands the strike zone like a much more experienced hitter—he walked nearly twice as often as he struck out in his pro debut—and laces line drives to all fields with a slashing swing. Hunter showed the ability to let the ball get deep before committing to a pitch and he was rarely fooled by AZL pitchers. A high leg kick serves as his trigger, but he gets his foot down in time and loads his hands well in the process. Hunter's plus instincts help bolster his average speed and range in center field. Because of his impressive first-step quickness, he has a knack for stealing bases. His overall game often gets compared with that of Jacque Jones.

While he possesses plenty of raw bat speed, Hunter didn't hit for much power in his first taste of pro ball. He makes enough hard contact, though, to become a 15-20 homer hitter down the road. A slight loop in his swing would be of more concern if he didn't square the ball up so consistently. Despite spending time on the mound as a sophomore and hitting 87 mph, Hunter has below-average arm strength. He was limited by a tender elbow in his debut, which often forced him to DH.

Hunter has the natural hitting instincts and quiet confidence to suggest he'll continue to hit for high averages as he moves up. While his swing and approach don't portend raw power, he has a lean, athletic frame that could add strength as he fills out. If Hunter can stay in center field, that will be a bonus. At this stage, none of his non-hitting tools projects as a plus, but he's intelligent and has tremendous desire to improve. He should be ready for a full-season assignment in 2007, in all likelihood to low Class A Fort Wayne.

| Year | Club (League) | Class | AVG | G | AB | R | H | 2B | 3B | HR | RBI | BB | SO | SB | OBP | SLG |
|------|---------------|-------|-----|---|----|---|---|----|----|----|-----|----|----|----|-----|-----|
| 2006 | Padres (AZL) | R | .371 | 52 | 213 | 46 | 79 | 13 | 4 | 1 | 44 | 40 | 22 | 17 | .467 | .484 |
| | Eugene (NWL) | A | .267 | 5 | 15 | 0 | 4 | 0 | 0 | 0 | 0 | 1 | 3 | 0 | .313 | .267 |
| **MINOR LEAGUE TOTALS** | | | .364 | 57 | 228 | 46 | 83 | 13 | 4 | 1 | 44 | 41 | 25 | 17 | .458 | .469 |

## 2 CESAR CARRILLO
RHP

**Born:** April 29, 1984. **B-T:** R-R. **Ht.:** 6-3. **Wt.:** 175. **Drafted:** Miami, 2005 (1st round). **Signed by:** Joe Bochy.

Carrillo's strong commitment to Miami and a bout with biceps tendinitis dropped him into the 33rd round of the 2002 draft. After sitting out 2003 in a dispute between the university and the NCAA over his ACT score, he won the first 24 decisions of his college career, two shy of the NCAA Division I record. The 18th overall pick in 2005 and the recipient of a $1.55 million bonus, he made just 10 starts last season before straining an elbow ligament in June. Carrillo possesses an above-average 90-94 mph fastball that can reach 96 and features late life and natural sink. His curveball has tight downward break, with the potential to become a plus pitch. Using a three-quarters delivery, he pitches in on righthanders as well as anyone in the system, but doesn't command his fastball to the other side of the plate with the same aplomb. His delivery is a little herky-jerky but the deception it provides makes it tough for hitters to pick the ball up. He's a tough competitor. Though Carrillo didn't need surgery, his elbow didn't heal in time for him to attend instructional league or the Arizona Fall League. Because he didn't need it in college, his changeup still is developing. The Padres hope that Carrillo will be 100 percent after an offseason of rest. If he is, he'll open the season at Triple-A Portland with a chance for a big league callup later in the year. If he isn't, he could be headed for surgery.

| Year | Club (League) | Class | W | L | ERA | G | GS | CG | SV | IP | H | R | ER | HR | BB | SO | AVG |
|------|---------------|-------|---|---|-----|---|----|----|----|----|---|---|----|----|----|----|-----|
| 2005 | Mobile (SL) | AA | 4 | 0 | 3.23 | 5 | 5 | 0 | 0 | 31 | 23 | 11 | 11 | 2 | 7 | 35 | .204 |
| | Lake Elsinore (Cal) | A | 1 | 2 | 7.01 | 7 | 7 | 0 | 0 | 26 | 30 | 21 | 20 | 3 | 9 | 29 | .280 |
| 2006 | Mobile (SL) | AA | 1 | 3 | 3.02 | 9 | 9 | 0 | 0 | 51 | 45 | 23 | 17 | 5 | 15 | 43 | .239 |
| | Portland (PCL) | AAA | 0 | 0 | 6.75 | 1 | 1 | 0 | 0 | 3 | 2 | 2 | 2 | 0 | 3 | 1 | .222 |
| **MINOR LEAGUE TOTALS** | | | 6 | 5 | 4.10 | 22 | 22 | 0 | 0 | 110 | 100 | 57 | 50 | 10 | 34 | 108 | .240 |

## 3 MATT ANTONELLI
3B

**Born:** April 8, 1985. **B-T:** R-R. **Ht.:** 6-1. **Wt.:** 190. **Drafted:** Wake Forest, 2006 (1st round). **Signed by:** Ash Lawson.

As a high school senior, Antonelli was the Massachusetts state player of the year in football and hockey—and the runner-up in baseball. He improved his game in each of his three seasons at Wake Forest and turned in two strong summers in the Cape Cod League. The Padres made him the 17th overall pick last June and signed him for $1.575 million. Antonelli has excellent pitch recognition skills and makes consistent contact. His swing is compact, though his bat speed is only average. He hits the ball hard to all fields because he stays back well on offspeed pitches. A rare athlete for a third baseman, Antonelli has above-average quickness and speed, with soft hands and a solid arm at the hot corner. The big question with Antonelli is his power. He hit just three homers in two summers using wood bats on the Cape and didn't go deep in his debut. As a result, he worked to improve the load of his swing in instructional league. Because his two-strike approach is so good, he works a lot of deep counts, and some observers think he can get too passive. For such a good athlete, at times he looks like he's exerting maximum effort. He has the tools to play just about anywhere on the diamond and might settle in at second base—where he auditioned in instructional league—or in center field if he doesn't develop the power of a prototypical third baseman. He'll probably jump to high Class A Lake Elsinore for his first full season.

| Year | Club (League) | Class | AVG | G | AB | R | H | 2B | 3B | HR | RBI | BB | SO | SB | OBP | SLG |
|------|---------------|-------|-----|---|----|---|---|----|----|----|----|----|----|----|----|-----|
| 2006 | Fort Wayne (MWL) | A | .125 | 5 | 16 | 3 | 2 | 1 | 1 | 0 | 0 | 2 | 6 | 0 | .222 | .313 |
| | Eugene (NWL) | A | .286 | 55 | 189 | 38 | 54 | 12 | 1 | 0 | 22 | 46 | 31 | 9 | .426 | .360 |
| **MINOR LEAGUE TOTALS** | | | .273 | 60 | 205 | 41 | 56 | 13 | 2 | 0 | 22 | 48 | 37 | 9 | .412 | .356 |

## 4 KEVIN KOUZMANOFF
3B

**Born:** July 25, 1981. **B-T:** R-R. **Ht.:** 6-1. **Wt.:** 200. **Drafted:** Nevada, 2003 (6th round). **Signed by:** Don Lyle (Indians).

Kouzmanoff earned the nickname "The Crushin' Russian" (though he's actually of Macedonian decent) after homering in each of his first two games in the majors, including a grand slam on the first big league pitch he ever saw. An unheralded prospect when he signed as a sixth-rounder in 2003, he led the minors in slugging (.656) last year while finishing second in hitting (.379) and fourth in on-base percentage (.437). Because the Indians also had Andy Marte at third base, they felt com-

fortable including him with righthander Andrew Brown in a November trade for Josh Barfield. Kouzmanoff has a compact, line-drive stroke that produces power to all fields. He's not a tremendous athlete, but he maximizes his physical skills with all-out play on the bases and in the field. He shows a strong arm and makes the routine plays at third base. Some scouts question Kouzmanoff's ability to stay at the hot corner, but the Padres believe he can. He's a below-average runner. Injuries have dogged him the last two years, as he missed two months with a back injury in 2005 and lost time to back and hamstring strains in 2006. After hitting .332/.395/.556 in the minors, Kouzmanoff has nothing left to prove there. He would have faced another year in Triple-A had Cleveland held onto him, but he's the front-runner to start at third base for San Diego.

| Year | Club (League) | Class | AVG | G | AB | R | H | 2B | 3B | HR | RBI | BB | SO | SB | OBP | SLG |
|------|---------------|-------|-----|---|----|---|---|----|----|----|-----|----|----|----|-----|-----|
| 2003 | Mahoning Valley (NYP) | A | .272 | 54 | 206 | 31 | 56 | 8 | 1 | 8 | 33 | 21 | 36 | 2 | .342 | .437 |
| 2004 | Akron (EL) | AA | .208 | 7 | 24 | 3 | 5 | 1 | 1 | 1 | 6 | 2 | 5 | 0 | .259 | .458 |
| | Lake County (SAL) | A | .330 | 123 | 473 | 74 | 156 | 35 | 5 | 16 | 87 | 44 | 75 | 5 | .394 | .526 |
| 2005 | Mahoning Valley (NYP) | A | .143 | 3 | 7 | 0 | 1 | 0 | 0 | 0 | 0 | 1 | 2 | 0 | .250 | .143 |
| | Kinston (Car) | A | .339 | 68 | 254 | 47 | 86 | 20 | 4 | 12 | 58 | 24 | 51 | 3 | .401 | .591 |
| 2006 | Akron (EL) | AA | .389 | 67 | 244 | 46 | 95 | 19 | 1 | 15 | 55 | 23 | 34 | 2 | .449 | .660 |
| | Buffalo (IL) | AAA | .353 | 27 | 102 | 22 | 36 | 9 | 0 | 7 | 20 | 10 | 12 | 2 | .409 | .647 |
| | Cleveland (AL) | MLB | .214 | 16 | 56 | 4 | 12 | 2 | 0 | 3 | 11 | 5 | 12 | 0 | .279 | .411 |
| **MINOR LEAGUE TOTALS** | | | .332 | 349 | 1310 | 223 | 435 | 92 | 12 | 59 | 259 | 125 | 215 | 14 | .395 | .556 |
| **MAJOR LEAGUE TOTALS** | | | .214 | 16 | 56 | 4 | 12 | 2 | 0 | 3 | 11 | 5 | 12 | 0 | .279 | .411 |

## 5 WILL VENABLE
OF

**Born:** Oct. 29, 1982. **B-T:** L-L. **Ht.:** 6-2. **Wt.:** 205. **Drafted:** Princeton, 2005 (7th round). **Signed by:** Jim Bretz.

Venable focused on basketball through high school and college, and was an all-Ivy League selection in both hoops and baseball as a senior at Princeton. Because he's the son of former big leaguer Max Venable, Will had more exposure to baseball than most two-sport stars. In 2006, his first full season, he led the low Class A Midwest League in runs while ranking second in hitting and third in on-base percentage—with Max watching as Fort Wayne's hitting coach. The Padres love Venable's makeup and have been pleasantly surprised by his aptitude for baseball. His pure lefthanded stroke and bat speed produce plenty of line drives, and more homers should come as he learns to get back-spin on the ball. He has drawn comparisons to Garrett Anderson (including early-career questions about power) and Dave Justice (more for his athletic frame). Venable's strike-zone judgment is sound. He has average speed and refined baserunning instincts for such an inexperienced player. Venable doesn't throw well and has below-average range, limiting him to left field. While 2006 was a success, at 23 Venable was older than most of his competition. He'll move to high Class A this year with a chance for a promotion to San Diego's new Double-A San Antonio affiliate at midseason. He projects as a decent regular or good fourth outfielder.

| Year | Club (League) | Class | AVG | G | AB | R | H | 2B | 3B | HR | RBI | BB | SO | SB | OBP | SLG |
|------|---------------|-------|-----|---|----|---|---|----|----|----|-----|----|----|----|-----|-----|
| 2005 | Padres (AZL) | R | .322 | 15 | 59 | 13 | 19 | 4 | 2 | 1 | 12 | 2 | 9 | 4 | .385 | .508 |
| | Eugene (NWL) | A | .216 | 42 | 139 | 17 | 30 | 5 | 2 | 2 | 14 | 14 | 38 | 2 | .295 | .324 |
| 2006 | Fort Wayne (MWL) | A | .314 | 124 | 472 | 86 | 148 | 34 | 5 | 11 | 91 | 55 | 81 | 18 | .389 | .477 |
| **MINOR LEAGUE TOTALS** | | | .294 | 181 | 670 | 116 | 197 | 43 | 9 | 14 | 117 | 71 | 128 | 24 | .369 | .448 |

## 6 CHASE HEADLEY
3B

**Born:** May 9, 1984. **B-T:** B-R. **Ht.:** 6-2. **Wt.:** 195. **Drafted:** Tennessee, 2005 (2nd round). **Signed by:** Billy Merkel.

Headley spent his freshman year at Pacific before transferring to Tennessee, where he missed significant time as a sophomore with hamstring trouble. After a strong summer in the Cape Cod League. he finished second in NCAA Division I with 63 walks and got drafted in the second round in 2005. He earned all-star recognition in the high Class A California League last season. Headley stands out most with his outstanding pitch recognition, allowing him to hit for average and get on base. He's a switch-hitter who has hit significantly better from the left side in pro ball. Defensively, he has a plus arm and clean hands. A high school valedictorian and academic all-American in college, he's intelligent and has strong makeup. In the context of the hitter-friendly Cal League, Headley's 12 homers and .434 slugging percentage were unimpressive. The Padres think he can learn to pull the ball with more authority and develop average power. At times he opens up early on throws, resulting in low tosses to first base. He's a

below-average runner with heavy feet. Though he has no outstanding tool, Headley projects as a potential regular because of his on-base skills and instincts. Destined for Double-A this year, he could push Kevin Kouzmanoff from third base to left field when he's ready.

| Year | Club (League) | Class | AVG | G | AB | R | H | 2B | 3B | HR | RBI | BB | SO | SB | OBP | SLG |
|------|---------------|-------|-----|---|-----|-----|-----|----|----|----|-----|-----|-----|----|------|------|
| 2005 | Eugene (NWL) | A | .268 | 57 | 220 | 29 | 59 | 14 | 3 | 6 | 33 | 34 | 48 | 1 | .375 | .441 |
| | Fort Wayne (MWL) | A | .200 | 4 | 15 | 2 | 3 | 0 | 0 | 0 | 1 | 1 | 4 | 0 | .250 | .200 |
| 2006 | Lake Elsinore (Cal) | A | .291 | 129 | 484 | 79 | 141 | 33 | 0 | 12 | 73 | 74 | 96 | 4 | .389 | .434 |
| **MINOR LEAGUE TOTALS** | | | .282 | 190 | 719 | 110 | 203 | 47 | 3 | 18 | 107 | 109 | 148 | 5 | .382 | .431 |

## 7 CHAD HUFFMAN                                      OF

**Born:** April 29, 1985. **B-T:** R-R. **Ht.:** 6-1. **Wt.:** 205. **Drafted:** Texas Christian, 2006 (2nd round). **Signed by:** Tim Holt.

Like his two older brothers, Huffman played both college baseball and football. And like Royce Huffman, a first baseman the Padres signed as minor league free agent in the offseason, Chad was a quarterback and infielder at Texas Christian. He broke Royce's school record for hits as a freshman in 2004, and the Padres signed Chad for $660,000 after making him their second-round pick last June. Scouts always have liked Huffman's bat, and he delivered in his pro debut, leading the Northwest League in on-base percentage while finishing second in hitting and slugging. He's a strong athlete with above-average power and a good hand path that should allow him to hit for average. He shows great plate coverage and tremendous balance throughout his swing, with the ball carrying very well off his bat. He thrives on competition, takes instruction well and always works to improve. Huffman has a tendency to get a little wide at the plate, becoming back-leg oriented and showing a little loop in his swing. A second baseman in college, he didn't have the range or footwork to profile as a pro infielder. His speed is average at best, and his range and arm are just playable in left field. Because he's advanced at the plate, Huffman could go straight to high Class A, and could challenge for a big league job in late 2008.

| Year | Club (League) | Class | AVG | G | AB | R | H | 2B | 3B | HR | RBI | BB | SO | SB | OBP | SLG |
|------|---------------|-------|-----|---|-----|-----|-----|----|----|----|-----|-----|-----|----|------|------|
| 2006 | Fort Wayne (MWL) | A | .214 | 5 | 14 | 2 | 3 | 0 | 1 | 0 | 0 | 2 | 2 | 0 | .313 | .357 |
| | Eugene (NWL) | A | .343 | 54 | 198 | 41 | 68 | 17 | 1 | 9 | 40 | 25 | 34 | 2 | .439 | .576 |
| **MINOR LEAGUE TOTALS** | | | .335 | 59 | 212 | 43 | 71 | 17 | 2 | 9 | 40 | 27 | 36 | 2 | .431 | .561 |

## 8 NICK HUNDLEY                                      C

**Born:** Sept. 8, 1983. **B-T:** R-R. **Ht.:** 6-1. **Wt.:** 210. **Drafted:** Arizona, 2005 (2nd round). **Signed by:** Dave Lottsfeldt.

A fifth-round pick by the Marlins out of high school, Hundley went three rounds earlier in 2005 after establishing himself as one of college baseball's best all-around catchers. His father Tim is the defensive coordinator for Texas-El Paso's football team. After a slow start in low Class A last year, Nick hit .410 with seven homers in June to earn a promotion. Hundley has sound strike-zone discipline and uses the entire field. He has some strength and power, and should hit enough to profile as an everyday catcher. He has a chance to be the total package as a receiver, with good hands and a strong, accurate arm. He consistently gets the ball to second base in an above-average 1.9 seconds. Hundley frequently tries to make the exchange from mitt to hand too quickly, resulting in throws without care because his legs aren't underneath him. Nevertheless, he threw out 36 percent of basestealers in 2006. His receiving and blocking skills are inconsistent and would benefit if he added flexibility. He's a below-average runner but good for a catcher. The Padres want to keep him and Colt Morton on different teams so they each can catch full time, so Hundley could return to high Class A to open 2007.

| Year | Club (League) | Class | AVG | G | AB | R | H | 2B | 3B | HR | RBI | BB | SO | SB | OBP | SLG |
|------|---------------|-------|-----|---|-----|----|-----|----|----|----|-----|----|-----|----|------|------|
| 2005 | Eugene (NWL) | A | .250 | 43 | 148 | 30 | 37 | 7 | 1 | 7 | 22 | 33 | 35 | 1 | .391 | .453 |
| | Fort Wayne (MWL) | A | .222 | 10 | 36 | 2 | 8 | 2 | 0 | 0 | 5 | 4 | 9 | 0 | .310 | .278 |
| 2006 | Fort Wayne (MWL) | A | .274 | 57 | 215 | 29 | 59 | 19 | 0 | 8 | 44 | 25 | 45 | 1 | .355 | .474 |
| | Lake Elsinore (Cal) | A | .278 | 47 | 176 | 18 | 49 | 13 | 0 | 3 | 23 | 20 | 44 | 1 | .357 | .403 |
| **MINOR LEAGUE TOTALS** | | | .266 | 157 | 575 | 79 | 153 | 41 | 1 | 18 | 94 | 82 | 133 | 3 | .363 | .435 |

## 9 JARED WELLS
RHP

**Born:** Oct. 31, 1981. **B-T:** R-R. **Ht.:** 6-4. **Wt.:** 200. **Drafted:** San Jacinto (Texas) JC, D/F 2002 (31st round). **Signed by:** Jay Darnell.

STEVE MOORE

After struggling with consistency early in his career, Wells led the California League with a 3.44 ERA and was the top starter on the U.S. World Cup team in 2005. In each of the last two seasons, he has pitched well early but had problems adjusting after a midseason promotion. Wells generates 90-92 mph fastballs and touches 94 from a sturdy pitcher's frame. When he's going well, he features good sink on his two-seam fastball and nice depth on a hard slider that grades as average. He's starting to recognize the value of throwing a changeup. Wells struggled to locate his fastball, leaving it up in the zone too often. His slider will flatten out and isn't a true strikeout pitch, and his changeup is still below average. His stubbornness was a barrier to him learning the pitch sequences he needs to succeed in Triple-A. Though athletic, Wells tends to rush his delivery. He has the stuff to pitch at the back of a big league rotation, but without a consistent changeup, he profiles better as a reliever. The Padres believe his Triple-A struggles will benefit him in the long run, and they sent him to the Arizona Fall League to work on commanding his fastball. He'll be back in Portland to start 2007.

| Year | Club (League) | Class | W | L | ERA | G | GS | CG | SV | IP | H | R | ER | HR | BB | SO | AVG |
|------|---------------|-------|---|---|-----|---|----|----|----|----|----|----|----|----|----|----|-----|
| 2003 | Eugene (NWL) | A | 4 | 6 | 2.75 | 14 | 14 | 0 | 0 | 79 | 77 | 34 | 24 | 6 | 32 | 53 | .256 |
| 2004 | Fort Wayne (MWL) | A | 4 | 6 | 4.09 | 14 | 14 | 1 | 0 | 81 | 91 | 42 | 37 | 6 | 19 | 72 | .283 |
| | Lake Elsinore (Cal) | A | 4 | 6 | 4.52 | 13 | 12 | 0 | 0 | 72 | 81 | 44 | 36 | 5 | 30 | 38 | .290 |
| 2005 | Lake Elsinore (Cal) | A | 11 | 3 | 3.44 | 19 | 19 | 2 | 0 | 120 | 116 | 51 | 46 | 6 | 26 | 80 | .257 |
| | Mobile (SL) | AA | 2 | 5 | 4.40 | 7 | 7 | 0 | 0 | 43 | 51 | 25 | 21 | 3 | 16 | 22 | .307 |
| 2006 | Mobile (SL) | AA | 4 | 3 | 2.64 | 12 | 12 | 1 | 0 | 61 | 53 | 20 | 18 | 4 | 27 | 49 | .235 |
| | Portland (PCL) | AAA | 2 | 9 | 7.27 | 15 | 15 | 0 | 0 | 73 | 87 | 66 | 59 | 8 | 46 | 55 | .296 |
| **MINOR LEAGUE TOTALS** | | | 31 | 38 | 4.10 | 94 | 93 | 4 | 0 | 529 | 556 | 282 | 241 | 38 | 196 | 369 | .273 |

## 10 CESAR RAMOS
LHP

**Born:** June 22, 1984. **B-T:** L-L. **Ht.:** 6-2. **Wt.:** 190. **Drafted:** Long Beach State, 2005 (1st round supplemental). **Signed by:** Brendan Hause.

BILL MITCHELL

Ramos turned down the Devil Rays as a sixth-round pick out of high school and became the winningest lefthander in Long Beach State history. Ramos had a 5.01 ERA in his debut but rebounded to post the second-best ERA in the California League in 2006. Ramos has four pitches, a compact delivery and great confidence on the mound. His best offering is probably his slider, which he uses to attack righthanders. He does a nice job of locating his lively 86-90 mph four-seam fastball. He began going to his changeup more often last season, especially to keep righties off balance, and his arm speed on the pitch improved dramatically. Ramos lacks the secondary stuff to consistently put away batters. He can sometimes rush his delivery and get off line to the plate, resulting in pitches left up and over the plate. His curveball is below average and not much more than a show pitch. He has to get stronger after wearing down at the end of his first full pro season. Ramos has the makeup and the feel to be a No. 4 or 5 starter in the big leagues, though he has to hit his spots and change speeds to succeed. He'll pitch in Double-A this season.

| Year | Club (League) | Class | W | L | ERA | G | GS | CG | SV | IP | H | R | ER | HR | BB | SO | AVG |
|------|---------------|-------|---|---|-----|---|----|----|----|----|----|----|----|----|----|----|-----|
| 2005 | Eugene (NWL) | A | 0 | 1 | 6.53 | 6 | 4 | 0 | 0 | 21 | 27 | 21 | 15 | 3 | 7 | 13 | .303 |
| | Fort Wayne (MWL) | A | 3 | 2 | 4.19 | 7 | 7 | 1 | 0 | 39 | 42 | 19 | 18 | 0 | 7 | 32 | .282 |
| 2006 | Lake Elsinore (Cal) | A | 7 | 8 | 3.70 | 26 | 24 | 0 | 0 | 141 | 161 | 72 | 58 | 9 | 44 | 70 | .292 |
| **MINOR LEAGUE TOTALS** | | | 10 | 11 | 4.09 | 39 | 35 | 1 | 0 | 200 | 230 | 112 | 91 | 12 | 58 | 115 | .291 |

## 11 AARON BREIT
RHP

**Born:** April 19, 1986. **B-T:** R-R. **Ht.:** 6-3. **Wt.:** 180. **Drafted:** Garden City (Kan.) CC, D/F 2005 (12th round). **Signed by:** Lane Decker.

The Padres drafted Breit twice—in both 2004 and 2005—and finally signed him as a draft-and-follow for $150,000 in spring 2006. They first made him a 46th-round pick out of Thomas More Prep High in Hays, Kan., then took him again the following year in the 12th round, ultimately signing him away from a Kansas commitment. Breit set the Garden City (Kan.) Community College record with 108 strikeouts in 2006. Breit throws a lively fastball on good downward plane, usually pitching at 91-94 mph. His hard, true curveball features good bite and has a chance to develop into a plus pitch. Breit also shows good touch with his changeup and has a good feel for the strike zone overall. He gets high marks for his maturity and clean mechanics. Breit uses a slider at times, but it's more of a show pitch. Like

a lot of young pitchers, he occasionally overthrows his curveball and changeup. He struggles at times to repeat his delivery, lunging toward the plate and getting off line, costing him command. Because of the crispness of his stuff, his pitcher's build and knack for pitching, Breit projects as a No. 3 or 4 starter in the big leagues. He'll start 2007 in low Class A, with an outside chance to open in high Class A.

| Year | Club (League) | Class | W | L | ERA | G | GS | CG | SV | IP | H | R | ER | HR | BB | SO | AVG |
|------|---------------|-------|---|---|-----|---|----|----|----|----|----|----|----|----|----|----|-----|
| 2006 | Eugene (NWL) | A | 2 | 3 | 3.08 | 18 | 12 | 0 | 0 | 64 | 60 | 31 | 22 | 2 | 22 | 69 | .250 |
| **MINOR LEAGUE TOTALS** | | | 2 | 3 | 3.08 | 18 | 12 | 0 | 0 | 64 | 60 | 31 | 22 | 2 | 22 | 69 | .250 |

## 12 DREW MILLER
RHP

**Born:** Feb. 24, 1986. **B-T:** R-R. **Ht.:** 6-4. **Wt.:** 190. **Drafted:** Seminole State (Okla.) JC, D/F 2005 (37th round). **Signed by:** Lane Decker.

Decker, the same scout who signed since-traded catcher George Kottaras as a draft-and-follow in 2003, also signed Miller and Aaron Breit as draft-and-follows last spring. Miller posted dominant strikeout totals in junior college but struggled to a 4.29 ERA in his sophomore year at Seminole State (Okla.) Junior College. The Padres gave him early fourth-round money ($300,000) to sign. Miller offers athleticism and one of the best arms in the system. He generates easy low-90s velocity, topping out at 96 mph. He's just starting to scratch the surface of his ability, though, and he could develop more velocity as he matures. Miller's secondary stuff is inconsistent. He struggles to throw his slider and curveball for strikes because he lacks confidence in either pitch, so the Padres tried to get him to focus on perfecting just one of his breaking balls. His changeup is a work in progress, and he often showed more command of the pitch than his slider. Miller sometimes rushes his delivery and needs to develop a more compact motion, as he tends to stay upright. Miller profiles as a No. 3 or 4 starter in the big leagues, but he's a long way off. The potential is there for four pitches, but Miller will need time to harness his potential. He'll probably begin this season in low Class A.

| Year | Club (League) | Class | W | L | ERA | G | GS | CG | SV | IP | H | R | ER | HR | BB | SO | AVG |
|------|---------------|-------|---|---|-----|---|----|----|----|----|----|----|----|----|----|----|-----|
| 2006 | Padres (AZL) | R | 3 | 0 | 3.47 | 7 | 4 | 0 | 0 | 23 | 19 | 15 | 9 | 1 | 10 | 14 | .218 |
| | Eugene (NWL) | A | 2 | 1 | 3.62 | 9 | 8 | 0 | 0 | 37 | 39 | 24 | 15 | 0 | 20 | 23 | .267 |
| **MINOR LEAGUE TOTALS** | | | 5 | 1 | 3.56 | 16 | 12 | 0 | 0 | 61 | 58 | 39 | 24 | 1 | 30 | 37 | .249 |

## 13 YEFRI CARVAJAL
OF

**Born:** Jan. 22, 1989. **B-T:** R-R. **Ht.:** 5-11. **Wt.:** 190. **Signed:** Dominican Republic, 2005. **Signed by:** Felix Francisco.

Signed for $350,000 in 2005 when the club lost out on Dominican outfield prospect Fernando Martinez to the Mets, Carvajal debuted in the Arizona League last season but missed time with shin splints and a hamate bone injury. His hitting seemed to suffer as a result, because his hitting and power tools are among the best in the system, thanks to the type of bat speed that can't be taught. He makes consistent, loud contact while being very aggressive at the plate. Thus the Padres stressed pitch recognition in instructional league and worked to close his stance for better balance. While he's extremely raw, the Padres are excited by Carvajal's potential because they believe his bat is special, but also because he loves to play and takes instruction well. He draws comparisons with Kirby Puckett and Gary Matthews Sr. from Padres officials for his bat and body type, which is strong and stocky. Even at age 17, Carvajal is mature physically and will always have to make conditioning a priority. His other tools are average and he's rapidly improving in the outfield, to the point where his range and solid-average arm might eventually play in right field. He would have to have a great spring to make a full-season team in 2007, but could see short-season Eugene by season's end.

| Year | Club (League) | Class | AVG | G | AB | R | H | 2B | 3B | HR | RBI | BB | SO | SB | OBP | SLG |
|------|---------------|-------|-----|---|----|---|---|----|----|----|----|----|----|----|----|-----|
| 2006 | Padres (AZL) | R | .253 | 19 | 75 | 14 | 19 | 3 | 0 | 2 | 9 | 3 | 16 | 2 | .288 | .373 |
| **MINOR LEAGUE TOTALS** | | | .253 | 19 | 75 | 14 | 19 | 3 | 0 | 2 | 9 | 3 | 16 | 2 | .288 | .373 |

## 14 KYLER BURKE
OF

**Born:** April 20, 1988. **B-T:** L-L. **Ht.:** 6-3. **Wt.:** 205. **Drafted:** HS—Ooltewah, Tenn., 2006 (1st round supplemental). **Signed by:** Ash Lawson.

The first Tennessee high school player to hit 20 home runs since 1998, Burke also pitched and played linebacker for the Ooltewah High football team. Burke is a natural athlete, but his prep performance may have been aided by substandard competition in southeast Tennessee and a short right-field fence at his home field. The Padres keyed in on Burke's all-around potential and sound batting eye, and took him with the 35th overall pick in June, then signed him for $950,000. As a pro, he showcased a clean swing, but tended to drift with his body into pitches and get out on his front foot. He also had a tough time making con-

tact when Arizona League pitchers began feeding him a steady diet of breaking balls and changeups. In fact, after hitting safely in 11 of his first 13 games, Burke batted just .168 afterward, which included a 4-for-47 slump. Because it was his first taste of failure, he lost confidence and assertiveness. But the Padres think highly of Burke's potential to hit for average and power, and believe it's just a matter of finding rhythm and timing at the plate. His range and speed are average at best, but plus arm strength—he hit 91 mph off the mound in high school—will allow him to handle right field. Burke will have every chance to make the low Class A Fort Wayne roster.

| Year | Club (League) | Class | AVG | G | AB | R | H | 2B | 3B | HR | RBI | BB | SO | SB | OBP | SLG |
|------|---------------|-------|-----|---|----|---|---|----|----|----|-----|----|----|----|-----|-----|
| 2006 | Padres (AZL) | R | .209 | 45 | 163 | 24 | 34 | 3 | 4 | 1 | 15 | 26 | 56 | 1 | .313 | .294 |
| **MINOR LEAGUE TOTALS** | | | .209 | 45 | 163 | 24 | 34 | 3 | 4 | 1 | 15 | 26 | 56 | 1 | .313 | .294 |

## 15 DAVID FREESE 3B

**Born:** April 28, 1983. **B-T:** R-R. **Ht.:** 6-2. **Wt.:** 220. **Drafted:** South Alabama, 2006 (9th round). **Signed by:** Bob Filotei.

Freese and Blue Jays top prospect Adam Lind starred on the infield corners for South Alabama in 2003 and 2004. A fifth-year senior last year, Freese could have signed as a free agent before the draft, but the Jaguars qualified for NCAA playoffs and shrunk his window to one day. The Sun Belt conference player of the year opted to take his chances in the draft and wound up with $6,000 as a ninth-round pick. Freese quickly established himself as one of the top value picks when he demolished the Northwest League and slugged 13 home runs on his way to playing at low Class A in his first half-season. Naturally, it is Freese's big-time bat that will be his ticket to the big leagues, as his strength, bat speed and strike-zone judgment are all above average. In his short low Class A stint, he showed the ability to stay inside the ball and drive it the other way with authority. The Padres would like Freese to stand more upright at the plate to generate more lift to his pull side, and he needs to prove he can hit major league caliber breaking balls. Accounts of his defense vary, as area scouts regarded Freese as a first baseman coming out of college, but Padres officials saw the potential to become at least an average defender at third base. His infield actions, range and arm rate average at best, but his technique needs refinement. He did some catching in instructional league and flashed a few 1.9 seconds pop times, but at 24 a move to catcher probably isn't in the offing. It would surprise no one if he flourishes in high Class A and moves rapidly to Double-A this season.

| Year | Club (League) | Class | AVG | G | AB | R | H | 2B | 3B | HR | RBI | BB | SO | SB | OBP | SLG |
|------|---------------|-------|-----|---|----|---|---|----|----|----|-----|----|----|----|-----|-----|
| 2006 | Fort Wayne (MWL) | A | .299 | 53 | 204 | 27 | 61 | 13 | 3 | 8 | 44 | 21 | 44 | 1 | .374 | .510 |
| | Eugene (NWL) | A | .379 | 18 | 58 | 19 | 22 | 8 | 0 | 5 | 26 | 7 | 12 | 0 | .465 | .776 |
| **MINOR LEAGUE TOTALS** | | | .317 | 71 | 262 | 46 | 83 | 21 | 3 | 13 | 70 | 28 | 56 | 1 | .395 | .569 |

## 16 WADE LeBLANC LHP

**Born:** Aug. 7, 1984. **B-T:** L-L. **Ht.:** 6-3. **Wt.:** 190. **Drafted:** Alabama, 2006 (2nd round). **Signed by:** Bob Filotei.

LeBlanc was bound for hometown McNeese State when he blossomed as a senior at Barbe High in Lake Charles, La., earning first-team All-America honors. McNeese coach Todd Butler left for a job with Alabama, though, and LeBlanc followed. He was BA's Freshman of the Year in 2004, going 8-4, 2.08, and while he missed much of his sophomore season, he led the Tide to super-regionals as a junior. The Padres made LeBlanc, a classic college lefty with command and feel for pitching, their second-round pick last June and signed him for $590,000. He's proven durable, and his smooth, repeatable delivery allows him to throw three pitches for strikes. His best offerings are his curveball and plus changeup. He possesses two versions of the latter: a get-me-over pitch and a strikeout changeup that one Padres official said appears to stop in midair. His curve has average spin and break, but he lands it for strikes. LeBlanc has average command of a deceptive 84-88 mph fastball, which peaks at 90, but he can get in trouble with the pitch because it's straight at lower speeds and hard to command when thrown harder. To combat this, LeBlanc is experimenting with a two-seam fastball, a cutter and a slider. The Padres would like him to stick with just his three pitches and instead improve his pitch location and sequencing. LeBlanc is poised and highly competitive and projects as a back of the rotation starter in the big leagues. He'll probably follow Ramos' path by getting an extended look in high Class A this season.

| Year | Club (League) | Class | W | L | ERA | G | GS | CG | SV | IP | H | R | ER | HR | BB | SO | AVG |
|------|---------------|-------|---|---|-----|---|----|----|----|----|----|---|----|----|----|----|-----|
| 2006 | Eugene (NWL) | A | 1 | 0 | 4.29 | 7 | 3 | 0 | 0 | 21 | 19 | 10 | 10 | 0 | 6 | 20 | .250 |
| | Fort Wayne (MWL) | A | 4 | 1 | 2.20 | 7 | 7 | 0 | 0 | 33 | 31 | 8 | 8 | 1 | 10 | 27 | .250 |
| **MINOR LEAGUE TOTALS** | | | 5 | 1 | 3.02 | 14 | 10 | 0 | 0 | 54 | 50 | 18 | 18 | 1 | 16 | 47 | .250 |

## 17 KEVIN CAMERON RHP

**Born:** Dec. 15, 1979. **B-T:** R-R. **Ht.:** 6-1. **Wt.:** 192. **Drafted:** Georgia Tech, 2001 (13th round). **Signed by:** Ricky Taylor (Twins).

Though he posted a 8.59 ERA as a Twins farmhand in the Arizona Fall League, opposing scouts were excited by Cameron's live cutter/slider mix, and the Padres took him in the major league Rule 5 draft. The Twins converted Cameron to relief after drafting him in 2001 and he began generating easy 97-mph velocity. He missed the entire 2002 season with a labrum tear in right shoulder. Tendinitis in the same shoulder caused him to miss about a month in both 2003 and 2005. Cameron has generated about twice as many groundouts as flyouts at both Double-A and Triple-A with his moving cut fastball, which he can dial up to 92 mph. His four-seam fastball can still reach 97 on occasion. Cameron's hard 86-88 mph slider is a strike-out pitch and has similar lateral movement as his cutter but more depth. In fact, everything Cameron throws moves, in part because his arm wasn't set properly after he broke it as a child. He still struggles to hold runners and nine of 12 basestealers were successful in 2005 and 2006. As a Rule 5 pick, he'll have to remain on San Diego's major league roster or else he has to clear waivers and then be offered back to Minnesota for half his $50,000 draft price.

| Year | Club (League) | Class | W | L | ERA | G | GS | CG | SV | IP | H | R | ER | HR | BB | SO | AVG |
|---|---|---|---|---|---|---|---|---|---|---|---|---|---|---|---|---|---|
| 2001 | Elizabethton (Appy) | R | 1 | 1 | 1.57 | 22 | 0 | 0 | 13 | 23 | 16 | 4 | 4 | 0 | 5 | 30 | .186 |
| 2002 | Did not play—Injured | | | | | | | | | | | | | | | | |
| 2003 | Quad City (MWL) | A | 1 | 5 | 3.92 | 39 | 0 | 0 | 2 | 62 | 57 | 30 | 27 | 2 | 33 | 58 | .238 |
| 2004 | Fort Myers (FSL) | A | 2 | 3 | 3.13 | 22 | 0 | 0 | 1 | 32 | 23 | 13 | 11 | 1 | 13 | 22 | .195 |
| | New Britain (EL) | AA | 1 | 3 | 2.33 | 26 | 0 | 0 | 3 | 46 | 47 | 20 | 12 | 1 | 21 | 47 | .253 |
| 2005 | New Britain (EL) | AA | 6 | 2 | 2.72 | 43 | 0 | 0 | 6 | 79 | 76 | 38 | 24 | 8 | 27 | 60 | .244 |
| 2006 | Rochester (IL) | AAA | 6 | 4 | 2.98 | 40 | 0 | 0 | 9 | 66 | 53 | 25 | 22 | 2 | 26 | 65 | .216 |
| **MINOR LEAGUE TOTALS** | | | 17 | 18 | 2.92 | 192 | 0 | 0 | 34 | 309 | 272 | 130 | 100 | 14 | 125 | 282 | .229 |

## 18 PAUL McANULTY 1B/3B

**Born:** Feb. 24, 1981. **B-T:** L-R. **Ht.:** 5-10. **Wt.:** 220. **Drafted:** Long Beach State, 2002 (12th round). **Signed by:** Jason McLeod.

McAnulty continued his assault on minor league pitching in 2006, finishing fifth in the Pacific Coast League in both hits and doubles. One thing was different, though: McAnulty shifted from first base, his natural position, to third base. The move was precipitated by the Padres giving up on Vinny Castilla and Mark Bellhorn as everyday third-base options. The conversion proved to be a slow process, though, as McAnulty showed limited agility and an erratic arm at the hot corner. He played just six games in the outfield last season and is on the short side to make an ideal first baseman. A pure hitter, McAnulty boasts one of the best strokes—short and direct—in the system. He combines that with strength and a tremendous batting eye to profile as a major league hitter. He's a below-average runner. McAnulty got more reps at third base in instructional league and could break camp with the big league team if the Padres need a bat off the bench. He was initially scheduled to play third base in Hawaii Winter Baseball, but those plans were altered when his knee required offseason surgery. McAnulty can hit, knows he can hit and might have a career along the lines of former Padre Mark Sweeney as a pinch-hitter and occasional first baseman and outfielder.

| Year | Club (League) | Class | AVG | G | AB | R | H | 2B | 3B | HR | RBI | BB | SO | SB | OBP | SLG |
|---|---|---|---|---|---|---|---|---|---|---|---|---|---|---|---|---|
| 2002 | Idaho Falls (Pio) | R | .379 | 67 | 235 | 56 | 89 | 29 | 0 | 8 | 51 | 49 | 43 | 7 | .488 | .604 |
| 2003 | Fort Wayne (MWL) | A | .273 | 133 | 455 | 48 | 124 | 27 | 0 | 7 | 73 | 67 | 82 | 5 | .370 | .378 |
| 2004 | Lake Elsinore (Cal) | A | .297 | 133 | 495 | 98 | 147 | 36 | 3 | 23 | 87 | 88 | 106 | 3 | .404 | .521 |
| 2005 | Mobile (SL) | AA | .282 | 79 | 298 | 39 | 84 | 17 | 2 | 10 | 42 | 34 | 66 | 5 | .364 | .453 |
| | Portland (PCL) | AAA | .344 | 38 | 151 | 27 | 52 | 15 | 0 | 6 | 27 | 16 | 29 | 0 | .405 | .563 |
| | San Diego (NL) | MLB | .208 | 22 | 24 | 4 | 5 | 0 | 0 | 0 | 0 | 3 | 7 | 1 | .321 | .208 |
| 2006 | Portland (PCL) | AAA | .310 | 125 | 478 | 76 | 148 | 34 | 5 | 19 | 79 | 62 | 79 | 1 | .388 | .521 |
| | San Diego (NL) | MLB | .231 | 16 | 13 | 3 | 3 | 1 | 0 | 1 | 3 | 2 | 4 | 0 | .333 | .538 |
| **MINOR LEAGUE TOTALS** | | | .305 | 575 | 2112 | 344 | 644 | 158 | 10 | 73 | 359 | 316 | 405 | 21 | .398 | .493 |
| **MAJOR LEAGUE TOTALS** | | | .216 | 38 | 37 | 7 | 8 | 1 | 0 | 1 | 3 | 5 | 11 | 1 | .326 | .324 |

## 19 MATT BUSH SS

**Born:** Feb. 8, 1986. **B-T:** R-R. **Ht.:** 5-11. **Wt.:** 170. **Drafted:** HS—El Cajon, Calif., 2004 (1st round). **Signed by:** Tim McWilliam.

You know the story by now: The Padres opted for Bush, the local high school two-way standout, with the No. 1 overall pick in the 2004 draft instead of going with more dynamic—but also more expensive—college stars Stephen Drew, Jeff Niemann or Jered Weaver. They settled for Bush just three days before the draft because he agreed to a $3.15 million bonus. He's now three years into his pro career, but hasn't played above low Class A because of injuries and poor hitting. He broke his ankle during spring training last year and was hampered by

hamstring injuries twice during the season and again during instructional league. Bush continues to show the outstanding arm that helped make him a consensus first-round talent, but his range, hands and foot speed are just slightly above average. He showed outstanding lateral movement as an amateur, but now needs to clean up his defensive footwork. Bush is a .221 hitter in 624 minor league at-bats and his hitting tools remain unrefined. Good health would help, but his swing path and strike-zone judgment need to be addressed. The Padres would like for him gain strength. At this stage, Bush projects as a utility infielder, but he won't reach even that modest ceiling if he doesn't rededicate himself to the game. He should finally get a taste of high Class A this season, but without rapid improvement, the Padres might be tempted to convert Bush's arm strength—he hit 95 mph in high school—to the mound.

| Year | Club (League) | Class | AVG | G | AB | R | H | 2B | 3B | HR | RBI | BB | SO | SB | OBP | SLG |
|------|---------------|-------|-----|---|----|---|---|----|----|----|-----|----|----|----|-----|-----|
| 2004 | Padres (AZL) | R | .181 | 21 | 72 | 12 | 13 | 2 | 1 | 0 | 10 | 11 | 17 | 4 | .302 | .236 |
| | Eugene (NWL) | A | .222 | 8 | 27 | 1 | 6 | 2 | 0 | 0 | 3 | 2 | 9 | 0 | .276 | .296 |
| 2005 | Fort Wayne (MWL) | A | .221 | 126 | 453 | 56 | 100 | 13 | 3 | 2 | 32 | 33 | 76 | 8 | .279 | .276 |
| 2006 | Padres (AZL) | R | .000 | 1 | 1 | 0 | 0 | 0 | 0 | 0 | 1 | 3 | 0 | 0 | .750 | .000 |
| | Fort Wayne (MWL) | A | .268 | 21 | 71 | 8 | 19 | 3 | 0 | 0 | 7 | 6 | 13 | 2 | .333 | .310 |
| **MINOR LEAGUE TOTALS** | | | .221 | 177 | 624 | 78 | 138 | 20 | 4 | 2 | 53 | 55 | 115 | 14 | .291 | .276 |

## 20 LUIS CRUZ                                                                2B/SS

**Born:** Feb. 10, 1984. **B-T:** R-R. **Ht.:** 6-1. **Wt.:** 180. **Signed:** Mexico, 2000. **Signed by:** Ray Poitevint/Lee Sigman (Red Sox).

It has taken Cruz six minor league seasons, two organizations and two seasons in Double-A to find even the modest level of offensive success he attained last year. Acquired from the Red Sox in a December 2002 trade for Cesar Crespo, Cruz finished third in the Double-A Southern League in doubles and fourth in extra-base hits (50), and was selected to play in both the SL all-star game and the Futures Game. The Padres noticed a distinct improvement in his work habits when he returned from the Mexican Pacific League in the 2005 offseason. Cruz is the system's top defensive infielder with the hands, range, quick feet and arm strength to play anywhere on the infield. Most of his minor league career has been spent at shortstop, but that changed last season when he spent a lot of time playing second and third base in deference to Juan Ciriaco. Cruz makes it look very easy defensively, though he did commit 29 errors because of erratic throwing. Cruz has surprising pop but remains a streaky hitter because his plate discipline needs a lot of refinement. He can catch up with any fastball, but struggles against quality breaking balls. He's an average runner. If Cruz continues to hit, he projects at worst as a utility infielder at the major league level. He's ready for Triple-A.

| Year | Club (League) | Class | AVG | G | AB | R | H | 2B | 3B | HR | RBI | BB | SO | SB | OBP | SLG |
|------|---------------|-------|-----|---|----|---|---|----|----|----|-----|----|----|----|-----|-----|
| 2001 | Red Sox (GCL) | R | .259 | 53 | 197 | 18 | 51 | 9 | 0 | 3 | 18 | 7 | 17 | 1 | .285 | .350 |
| 2002 | Red Sox (GCL) | R | .292 | 21 | 72 | 10 | 21 | 4 | 0 | 0 | 9 | 3 | 6 | 2 | .329 | .347 |
| | Augusta (SAL) | A | .188 | 58 | 202 | 16 | 38 | 7 | 1 | 3 | 15 | 9 | 30 | 0 | .221 | .277 |
| 2003 | Fort Wayne (MWL) | A | .231 | 129 | 481 | 55 | 111 | 24 | 1 | 8 | 53 | 30 | 55 | 2 | .279 | .335 |
| 2004 | Lake Elsinore (Cal) | A | .277 | 124 | 512 | 75 | 142 | 35 | 3 | 8 | 72 | 24 | 56 | 3 | .310 | .404 |
| 2005 | Mobile (SL) | AA | .159 | 44 | 151 | 14 | 24 | 2 | 1 | 3 | 6 | 9 | 31 | 0 | .215 | .245 |
| 2006 | Mobile (SL) | AA | .261 | 130 | 499 | 65 | 130 | 35 | 3 | 12 | 65 | 29 | 62 | 8 | .301 | .415 |
| **MINOR LEAGUE TOTALS** | | | .245 | 559 | 2114 | 253 | 517 | 116 | 9 | 37 | 238 | 111 | 257 | 16 | .284 | .360 |

## 21 FELIX CARRASCO                                                              3B

**Born:** Feb. 14, 1987. **B-T:** B-R. **Ht.:** 6-1. **Wt.:** 220. **Signed:** Dominican Republic, 2006. **Signed by:** Randy Smith/Felix Francisco.

Carrasco joined the organization in March and made a louder pro debut than outfielder Yefri Carvajal, his Arizona League teammate. And like Carvajal, Carrasco is a high-energy, physically mature player, for whom hitting is the name of the game. A switch-hitter, Carrasco has top-of-the-scale power potential from the left side, but is more of a line-drive hitter from the right. Observers wonder how much average Carrasco will hit for because he drops his hands low in the zone, making it difficult for him to recover and leading to an uppercut in his swing. He could also tighten his strike-zone discipline. Athletic and agile for his size, he has a chance to be a solid-average defender at third base. His 23 errors in 46 games were caused more by carelessness and being worn down than by fundamental deficiencies. Carrasco has well above-average arm strength for the position and his infield range and actions are average. He'll also need to pay attention to physical conditioning, as he already weighs in at a burly 220 pounds. Carrasco is an average runner but doesn't get out of the box quickly because of a big swing. He's likely headed to low Class A for his full-season debut.

| Year | Club (League) | Class | AVG | G | AB | R | H | 2B | 3B | HR | RBI | BB | SO | SB | OBP | SLG |
|------|---------------|-------|-----|---|----|---|---|----|----|----|-----|----|----|----|-----|-----|
| 2006 | Padres (AZL) | R | .273 | 46 | 172 | 32 | 47 | 12 | 1 | 4 | 37 | 17 | 48 | 2 | .347 | .424 |
| **MINOR LEAGUE TOTALS** | | | .273 | 46 | 172 | 32 | 47 | 12 | 1 | 4 | 37 | 17 | 48 | 2 | .347 | .424 |

## ANDREW BROWN

RHP

**Born:** Feb. 17, 1981. **B-T:** R-R. **Ht.:** 6-6. **Wt.:** 230. **Drafted:** HS—Jacksonville, Fla., 1999 (6th round). **Signed by:** Marco Paddy (Braves).

Brown joined the Padres along with Kevin Kouzmanoff in the November trade that sent Josh Barfield to the Indians. While Brown has a history of elbow issues, including Tommy John surgery in 2000, the mental side of the game has been a bigger factor in slowing his climb to the majors. The Indians questioned his mental toughness in 2004, but he showed more aggressiveness after moving to the bullpen the following season. Brown has power stuff, with a fastball that sits in the mid-90s and a wipeout slider. When the Indians scouted him in 2004, Brown was sitting at 95-96 mph, topping out at 98—a velocity he never approached with the Indians. Mechanical issues are partly to blame, as Brown is often long, slow and unbalanced in his delivery. That doesn't bode well for controlling runners or his command, which took a major hit last year. Brown could still be valuable coming out of the pen if he irons out the kinks in his delivery, but it will have to be this season because he's out of options.

| Year | Club (League) | Class | W | L | ERA | G | GS | CG | SV | IP | H | R | ER | HR | BB | SO | AVG |
|------|---------------|-------|---|---|-----|---|----|----|----|----|---|---|----|----|----|----|-----|
| 1999 | Braves (GCL) | R | 1 | 1 | 2.34 | 11 | 11 | 0 | 0 | 42 | 40 | 15 | 11 | 4 | 16 | 57 | .247 |
| 2000 | Did not play—Injured | | | | | | | | | | | | | | | | |
| 2001 | Jamestown (NYP) | A | 3 | 4 | 3.92 | 14 | 12 | 0 | 0 | 64 | 50 | 29 | 28 | 5 | 31 | 59 | .215 |
| 2002 | Vero Beach (FSL) | A | 10 | 10 | 4.11 | 25 | 24 | 1 | 0 | 127 | 97 | 63 | 58 | 13 | 62 | 129 | .215 |
| 2003 | Jacksonville (SL) | AA | 0 | 0 | 0.00 | 1 | 1 | 0 | 0 | 1 | 0 | 0 | 0 | 0 | 0 | 1 | .000 |
| 2004 | Jacksonville (SL) | AA | 1 | 3 | 4.02 | 8 | 8 | 0 | 0 | 40 | 36 | 23 | 18 | 5 | 14 | 58 | .235 |
| | Buffalo (IL) | AAA | 1 | 0 | 0.00 | 1 | 1 | 0 | 0 | 5 | 4 | 0 | 0 | 0 | 3 | 4 | .222 |
| | Akron (EL) | AA | 3 | 6 | 4.66 | 17 | 17 | 0 | 0 | 77 | 66 | 44 | 40 | 7 | 36 | 67 | .234 |
| 2005 | Buffalo (IL) | AAA | 4 | 2 | 3.36 | 49 | 0 | 0 | 4 | 70 | 52 | 28 | 26 | 7 | 19 | 81 | .204 |
| 2006 | Buffalo (IL) | AAA | 5 | 4 | 2.60 | 39 | 0 | 0 | 5 | 62 | 52 | 21 | 18 | 5 | 36 | 53 | .228 |
| | Cleveland (AL) | MLB | 0 | 0 | 3.60 | 9 | 0 | 0 | 0 | 10 | 6 | 4 | 4 | 0 | 8 | 7 | .171 |
| **MINOR LEAGUE TOTALS** | | | 28 | 30 | 3.66 | 165 | 74 | 1 | 9 | 489 | 397 | 223 | 199 | 46 | 217 | 509 | .222 |
| **MAJOR LEAGUE TOTALS** | | | 0 | 0 | 3.60 | 9 | 0 | 0 | 0 | 10 | 6 | 4 | 4 | 0 | 8 | 7 | .171 |

 ## SEAN THOMPSON

LHP

**Born:** Oct. 13, 1982. **B-T:** L-L. **Ht.:** 5-11. **Wt.:** 170. **Drafted:** HS—Denver, 2002 (5th round). **Signed by:** Darryl Milne.

Thompson spent two years in short-season ball before tackling low Class A. He began 2005 in high Class A and quickly jumped to Double-A early in the season, but got hit hard. His maturation continued with a repeat of the level last year. This time he finished fourth in the Southern League in strikeouts, but also fourth in most home runs allowed. The organization attributes Thompson's success to improved command of his 85-88 mph fastball, especially in the second half of the season. Getting ahead in the count allowed him to work his two best offerings—a very good changeup and occasionally very good curveball—into sequences that worked for him. Both pitches are among the best in the system. Thompson's high strikeouts total is a testament to the effectiveness of his secondary stuff because his fastball is below average. Like many lefthanders, Thompson fields his position well and controls the running game with one of the system's best pickoff moves. He needs to gain more focus and better control his emotions on the mound. Thompson is bound for Triple-A, and has a chance to become at best a back-end major league starter or a left-on-left reliever, at worst.

| Year | Club (League) | Class | W | L | ERA | G | GS | CG | SV | IP | H | R | ER | HR | BB | SO | AVG |
|------|---------------|-------|---|---|-----|---|----|----|----|----|---|---|----|----|----|----|-----|
| 2002 | Idaho Falls (Pio) | R | 4 | 3 | 3.83 | 13 | 11 | 0 | 0 | 56 | 51 | 34 | 24 | 4 | 38 | 69 | .249 |
| 2003 | Eugene (NWL) | A | 7 | 1 | 2.48 | 15 | 15 | 0 | 0 | 80 | 58 | 28 | 22 | 5 | 39 | 97 | .204 |
| 2004 | Fort Wayne (MWL) | A | 9 | 6 | 3.10 | 27 | 27 | 0 | 0 | 148 | 124 | 60 | 51 | 15 | 57 | 157 | .239 |
| 2005 | Lake Elsinore (Cal) | A | 4 | 1 | 2.16 | 6 | 6 | 0 | 0 | 33 | 26 | 15 | 8 | 4 | 13 | 45 | .210 |
| | Mobile (SL) | AA | 4 | 5 | 4.67 | 20 | 20 | 0 | 0 | 114 | 127 | 67 | 59 | 10 | 55 | 94 | .294 |
| 2006 | Mobile (SL) | AA | 6 | 10 | 3.86 | 27 | 27 | 2 | 0 | 154 | 148 | 79 | 66 | 18 | 46 | 134 | .255 |
| **MINOR LEAGUE TOTALS** | | | 34 | 26 | 3.54 | 108 | 106 | 2 | 0 | 585 | 534 | 283 | 230 | 56 | 248 | 596 | .249 |

 ## MATT BUSCHMANN

RHP

**Born:** Feb. 13, 1984. **B-T:** R-R. **Ht.:** 6-3. **Wt.:** 195. **Drafted:** Vanderbilt, 2006 (15th round). **Signed by:** Ash Lawson.

Buschmann stepped into Vanderbilt's rotation and thrived as its Friday starter when David Price (the possible No. 1 overall pick in the 2007 draft) hit a slump last spring. The Padres were pleased that Buschmann made it to high Class A in his pro debut, especially considering he was a senior sign for $2,000. He tops out at 92 mph and pitches at 86-90 with a lively fastball he delivers from a three-quarter arm slot, generating good sink and bore. Buschmann gets in trouble when he gets under his pitches and has a habit of flying open. He throws an 84-85 mph slider that can be a plus offering on occasion. Buschmann gets good side-to-side break on the

pitch, but is working on adding tilt to the pitch to locate it down on the zone. He commands the inside portion of the strike zone against righthanders but needs to improve his ability to throw strikes down and away. His changeup is an average offering. Buschmann has the makings of a future No. 4 or 5 starter with the ability to pitch to contact and generate groundball outs. He'll likely begin 2007 back in high Class A, where he finished strong in the postseason.

| Year | Club (League) | Class | W | L | ERA | G | GS | CG | SV | IP | H | R | ER | HR | BB | SO | AVG |
|---|---|---|---|---|---|---|---|---|---|---|---|---|---|---|---|---|---|
| 2006 | Eugene (NWL) | A | 3 | 4 | 3.12 | 15 | 10 | 0 | 0 | 61 | 54 | 26 | 21 | 5 | 11 | 63 | .242 |
| | Lake Elsinore (Cal) | A | 1 | 0 | 3.55 | 2 | 2 | 0 | 0 | 13 | 9 | 5 | 5 | 0 | 4 | 5 | .205 |
| MINOR LEAGUE TOTALS | | | 4 | 4 | 3.19 | 17 | 12 | 0 | 0 | 73 | 63 | 31 | 26 | 5 | 15 | 68 | .236 |

## 25  MIKE EKSTROM                                                    RHP

**Born:** Aug. 30, 1983. **B-T:** R-R. **Ht.:** 6-0. **Wt.:** 185. **Drafted:** Point Loma Nazarene (Calif.), 2004 (12th round). **Signed by:** Tim McWilliam.

Ekstrom spent two years at Oregon State before transferring to Point Loma Nazarene in San Diego, where he was named Golden State Athletic Conference player of the year as a senior. Command of three pitches served Ekstrom well as he put Class A behind him in a season and a half, making 28 starts for Fort Wayne in 2005 and 14 for Lake Elsinore in 2005. He made his Double-A debut last June, where his strikeout and hit rates slipped. He was durable, though, and earned organizational pitcher of the year honors. Because he doesn't have exceptional velocity and because he's a 6-foot righthander, Ekstrom will have to earn his promotions. But for what he lacks in raw stuff, he makes up for with composure, presence and for having a real plan on the mound. Ekstrom attacks the strike zone with an 88-92 mph sinking fastball, a hard slider and a changeup. As it is with all pitchers who rely on control, Ekstrom's success hinges on his ability to change speeds, hit his spots and induce soft contact.

| Year | Club (League) | Class | W | L | ERA | G | GS | CG | SV | IP | H | R | ER | HR | BB | SO | AVG |
|---|---|---|---|---|---|---|---|---|---|---|---|---|---|---|---|---|---|
| 2004 | Eugene (NWL) | A | 3 | 1 | 3.69 | 12 | 7 | 0 | 0 | 39 | 38 | 18 | 16 | 1 | 10 | 42 | .250 |
| | Fort Wayne (MWL) | A | 0 | 2 | 8.16 | 3 | 3 | 0 | 0 | 14 | 21 | 15 | 13 | 1 | 3 | 10 | .368 |
| 2005 | Fort Wayne (MWL) | A | 13 | 6 | 3.70 | 28 | 28 | 1 | 0 | 168 | 167 | 76 | 69 | 11 | 36 | 112 | .257 |
| 2006 | Lake Elsinore (Cal) | A | 7 | 4 | 2.30 | 14 | 14 | 1 | 0 | 82 | 76 | 32 | 21 | 2 | 21 | 68 | .251 |
| | Mobile (SL) | AA | 3 | 7 | 3.84 | 14 | 14 | 3 | 0 | 84 | 87 | 46 | 36 | 2 | 19 | 49 | .261 |
| MINOR LEAGUE TOTALS | | | 26 | 20 | 3.60 | 71 | 66 | 5 | 0 | 388 | 389 | 187 | 155 | 17 | 89 | 281 | .260 |

## 26  COLT MORTON                                                       C

**Born:** April 10, 1982. **B-T:** R-R. **Ht.:** 6-5. **Wt.:** 230. **Drafted:** North Carolina State, 2003 (3rd round). **Signed by:** Mike Rikard.

Morton shortened his swing and showed the lowest strikeout rate of his career in his repeat of high Class A. He made it to Double-A for the first time in July, despite being a 2003 third-round pick out of college. Morton was willing to adjust his all-or-nothing swing mechanics last season in high Class A, closing his stance and minimizing extraneous movement. His raw power is unparalleled in the system, but he'll likely always hit for a low average. Morton is a natural leader behind the plate and pitchers like throwing to him. He moves exceptionally for someone who stands 6-feet-5 due to impressive flexibility, and blocks and receives the ball well. Morton's throwing, while always strong, was improved last season, but he still had to work to synchronize his footwork and exchange to increase the accuracy of his throws. Morton missed time in 2006 with a groin injury and the Padres sent him to the Arizona Fall League to make up for lost time. He projects as a backup catcher in the Mark Parent mold.

| Year | Club (League) | Class | AVG | G | AB | R | H | 2B | 3B | HR | RBI | BB | SO | SB | OBP | SLG |
|---|---|---|---|---|---|---|---|---|---|---|---|---|---|---|---|---|
| 2003 | Eugene (NWL) | A | .278 | 25 | 97 | 14 | 27 | 6 | 0 | 7 | 20 | 10 | 29 | 0 | .346 | .557 |
| | Fort Wayne (MWL) | A | .171 | 22 | 76 | 5 | 13 | 4 | 0 | 2 | 7 | 5 | 28 | 0 | .222 | .303 |
| 2004 | Fort Wayne (MWL) | A | .150 | 36 | 127 | 10 | 19 | 5 | 1 | 4 | 11 | 16 | 45 | 0 | .260 | .299 |
| | Eugene (NWL) | A | .239 | 66 | 243 | 43 | 58 | 13 | 0 | 17 | 45 | 33 | 75 | 2 | .340 | .502 |
| | Mobile (SL) | AA | .333 | 1 | 3 | 1 | 1 | 0 | 0 | 1 | 1 | 1 | 0 | 0 | .500 | 1.333 |
| 2005 | Fort Wayne (MWL) | A | .261 | 63 | 222 | 27 | 58 | 15 | 0 | 10 | 46 | 35 | 57 | 0 | .362 | .464 |
| | Lake Elsinore (Cal) | A | .323 | 26 | 96 | 19 | 31 | 4 | 0 | 9 | 19 | 14 | 30 | 0 | .407 | .646 |
| 2006 | Mobile (SL) | AA | .266 | 41 | 139 | 15 | 37 | 10 | 0 | 6 | 21 | 11 | 44 | 0 | .329 | .468 |
| | Lake Elsinore (Cal) | A | .227 | 53 | 176 | 30 | 40 | 15 | 0 | 5 | 22 | 36 | 44 | 0 | .374 | .398 |
| MINOR LEAGUE TOTALS | | | .241 | 333 | 1179 | 164 | 284 | 72 | 1 | 61 | 192 | 161 | 352 | 2 | .340 | .459 |

## 27  PABLO MENCHACA                                                  RHP

**Born:** Nov. 28, 1987. **B-T:** R-R. **Ht.:** 6-4. **Wt.:** 225. **Signed:** Mexico, 2005. **Signed by:** Randy Smith/Robert Rowley.

Menchaca notched the win in the Arizona League championship game and finished ninth in the league in ERA. Strong and durable, Menchaca resembles a young Freddy Garcia, with his quick, efficient arm action and a heavy sinking fastball that sits at 88-90 mph and peaks

at 93. The pitch explodes on hitters and he should get into the low 90s with consistency as he matures. Menchaca's secondary offerings aren't nearly so advanced. He shows some feel for a changeup, but his breaking ball needs a lot of work. His low three-quarters curveball sometimes sweeps or bites, and he's also working on developing a slider. The organization thinks with refinement he'll be able to develop one or the other as his go-to breaking ball. He tends to rush his delivery and needs to stay back. Menchaca shows a feel for pitching and is a future starter who will eat innings and get ground balls, but he's a long way from the majors.

| Year | Club (League) | Class | W | L | ERA | G | GS | CG | SV | IP | H | R | ER | HR | BB | SO | AVG |
|------|---------------|-------|---|---|------|----|---|----|----|----|----|----|----|----|----|----|------|
| 2006 | Padres (AZL) | R | 3 | 1 | 3.35 | 13 | 7 | 0 | 0 | 51 | 52 | 23 | 19 | 0 | 9 | 39 | .265 |
| | Eugene (NWL) | A | 0 | 0 | 3.00 | 1 | 0 | 0 | 0 | 3 | 3 | 1 | 1 | 0 | 1 | 2 | .273 |
| MINOR LEAGUE TOTALS | | | 3 | 1 | 3.33 | 14 | 7 | 0 | 0 | 54 | 55 | 24 | 20 | 0 | 10 | 41 | .266 |

## 28 SIMON CASTRO RHP

**Born:** April 9, 1988. **B-T:** R-R. **Ht.:** 6-5. **Wt.:** 203. **Signed:** Dominican Republic, 2006. **Signed by:** Randy Smith/Felix Francisco.

Despite a shaky showing in instructional league and not yet pitching in the U.S., Castro has one of the highest ceilings among pitchers in the organization. After trading pitchers Evan Meek, Jose Ceda, Joel Santo and Cesar Rojas last summer—and after losing Joakim Soria in the major league Rule 5 draft—Castro is one of the best raw power arms remaining in the system. He already possesses a plus fastball with life at 93-96 mph. Castro gets good extension on his fastball and the pitch shows good armside sink and run. He has an outstanding pitcher's body—short torso, long arms and legs—and shows good arm action. Castro pitches from a high three-quarters delivery and sometimes drops his elbow, guiding the ball to the plate, but this is common in young pitchers and easily correctable. He has the makings of a changeup, but tends to get under and around his slider. Both pitches need a lot of work. Castro has excellent makeup and has a chance to develop into a frontline starting pitcher.

| Year | Club (League) | Class | W | L | ERA | G | GS | CG | SV | IP | H | R | ER | HR | BB | SO | AVG |
|------|---------------|-------|---|---|------|----|----|----|----|----|----|----|----|----|----|----|------|
| 2006 | Padres (DSL) | R | 1 | 3 | 4.63 | 12 | 12 | 0 | 0 | 47 | 40 | 33 | 24 | 2 | 21 | 58 | .219 |
| MINOR LEAGUE TOTALS | | | 1 | 3 | 4.63 | 12 | 12 | 0 | 0 | 47 | 40 | 33 | 24 | 2 | 21 | 58 | .219 |

## 29 KYLE BLANKS 1B

**Born:** Sept. 11, 1986. **B-T:** R-R. **Ht.:** 6-6. **Wt.:** 270. **Drafted:** Yavapai (Ariz.) JC, D/F 2004, (42nd round). **Signed by:** Jake Wilson.

Blanks led the wood-bat Arizona Community College Athletic Conference in batting (.440), doubles (25) and RBIs (47) in 2004, after which the Padres signed him for $260,000 before he could enter the 2005 draft. Blanks is a good defender at first base with soft feet and mobility for someone listed at 6-foot-6 and 270 pounds, though he was up near 300 pounds by the end of the season. His arm is solid-average. Blanks has tremendous strength and raw power from the right side, but can be pitched to because he loses his sense of timing at the plate and gives away too many at-bats. Blanks is susceptible to the high fastball. The Padres would like Blanks to play closer to his listed weight of 270 pounds, but he got off track last season when a major leg infection sidelined him after mid-July. Blanks needs a big power year in high Class A to re-establish himself as a prospect.

| Year | Club (League) | Class | AVG | G | AB | R | H | 2B | 3B | HR | RBI | BB | SO | SB | OBP | SLG |
|------|---------------|-------|------|-----|-----|----|-----|----|----|----|-----|----|-----|----|------|------|
| 2005 | Padres (AZL) | R | .299 | 48 | 164 | 33 | 49 | 10 | 1 | 7 | 30 | 25 | 49 | 3 | .420 | .500 |
| 2006 | Fort Wayne (MWL) | A | .292 | 86 | 308 | 41 | 90 | 20 | 0 | 10 | 52 | 36 | 79 | 2 | .382 | .455 |
| MINOR LEAGUE TOTALS | | | .294 | 134 | 472 | 74 | 139 | 30 | 1 | 17 | 82 | 61 | 128 | 5 | .395 | .470 |

## 30 JOHN HUSSEY RHP

**Born:** Nov. 22, 1986. **B-T:** R-R. **Ht.:** 6-3. **Wt.:** 172. **Signed:** Australia, 2004. **Signed by:** Trevor Schumm.

Hussey, signed out of Australia, repeated the Arizona League in 2006 and finished with fifth-best ERA in the league. Not yet physically mature, Hussey has a good frame with room to fill out. He has the potential to develop three average to slightly above-average offerings. He pitches at 88-90 mph with excellent arm action, and he touched 93 this summer. Hussey has a chance to develop an outstanding curveball, but for now it's an average offering, much like his changeup, and he experimented with a cut fastball last season. Hussey's delivery is smooth, though like most teenage pitchers he struggles to stay on line to the plate. With continued improvement, Hussey could become a middle- or back-of-the-rotation starter.

| Year | Club (League) | Class | W | L | ERA | G | GS | CG | SV | IP | H | R | ER | HR | BB | SO | AVG |
|------|---------------|-------|---|---|------|----|---|----|----|----|----|----|----|----|----|----|------|
| 2005 | Padres (AZL) | R | 1 | 3 | 6.44 | 9 | 9 | 0 | 0 | 36 | 38 | 30 | 26 | 2 | 13 | 31 | .275 |
| 2006 | Padres (AZL) | R | 3 | 1 | 2.44 | 13 | 7 | 0 | 0 | 44 | 39 | 16 | 12 | 1 | 16 | 32 | .253 |
| MINOR LEAGUE TOTALS | | | 4 | 4 | 4.24 | 22 | 16 | 0 | 0 | 81 | 77 | 46 | 38 | 3 | 29 | 63 | .264 |

# SAN FRANCISCO
# GIANTS

BY **ANDY BAGGARLY**

A day after the Giants finished with a sub-.500 record for the second consecutive year, general manager Brian Sabean admitted the organization had to change its decade-long plan of surrounding **Barry Bonds** with older, short-term veterans.

Then San Francisco went out and committed $64 million to six free agents, none younger then 31, before re-signing the 42-year-old Bonds to a one-year, $16 million contract.

Nevertheless, the Giants have begun a shift in philosophy, even if it won't be apparent at AT&T Park in 2007.

In August, they paid $2.1 million to sign 16-year-old Dominican third baseman Angel Villalona. That broke the franchise record for a bonus given to an amateur, besting the $2.025 million given to first-round righthander Tim Lincecum two months earlier. The signings were an about-face for a club that had intentionally sacrificed draft picks and diverted bonus money to the major league payroll in previous years.

While Bonds is back and taking aim at Hank Aaron's all-time home run record, owner Peter Magowan stated that if the slugger returned, he would be a complement and no longer a centerpiece. The new nucleus of the Giants is their young pitching staff.

With Jason Schmidt departing for the Dodgers as a free agent, Matt Cain becomes the staff ace at age 22. Under-recognized amid baseball's hailstorm of spectacular rookies in 2006, he won a team-high 13 games and showed marked improvement in the second half. San Francisco also expects big things from Lincecum, who's on the cusp of making an impact in his first full pro season. Noah Lowry, and Jonathan Sanchez, give the Giants a solid pair of lefty starters.

San Francisco hired manager Bruce Bochy away from the Padres partly because of his track record working with young pitchers and his judicious use of the bullpen. He replaces 71-year-old Felipe Alou, a man held in high esteem but not the right leader for a club that Sabean pledges to make younger.

After years of foregoing premium draft choices, there's little talent at the upper levels of the system, and Triple-A Fresno and Double-A Connecticut finished a combined 35 games under .500.

Scouting director Dick Tidrow has a knack for unearthing talented arms in the draft, but in 2006 he found several promising position players. Players like outfielder Mike McBryde, middle infielder Brian Bocock and catcher Adam Witter teamed with shortstop Emmanuel Burriss to help Salem-Keizer win the short-season Northwest League title.

Those hitters won't arrive in time to help the Giants in 2007 and they won't shake the skepticism about whether homegrown players will be given fair chances to sink or swim. Kevin Frandsen, their second baseman of the future, might apprentice in a utility role. No other position prospect is ready to contribute, with the possible exception of Fred Lewis, who could make the club as a fourth outfielder.

## TOP 30 PROSPECTS

| | |
|---|---|
| 1. Tim Lincecum, rhp | 16. Marcus Sanders, ss |
| 2. Jonathan Sanchez, lhp | 17. Dan Griffin, rhp |
| 3. Angel Villalona, 3b | 18. Merkin Valdez, rhp |
| 4. Emmanuel Burriss, ss | 19. Brian Anderson, rhp |
| 5. Brian Wilson, rhp | 20. Joey Martinez, rhp |
| 6. Kevin Frandsen, 2b | 21. Sharlon Schoop, ss |
| 7. Fred Lewis, of | 22. Thomas Neal, of |
| 8. Nate Schierholtz, of | 23. Justin Hedrick, rhp |
| 9. Eddy Martinez-Esteve, of | 24. Erick Threets, lhp |
| 10. Billy Sadler, rhp | 25. Ben Copeland, of |
| 11. Travis Ishikawa, 1b | 26. Brian Bocock, 2b/ss |
| 12. Mike McBryde, of | 27. David Quinowski, lhp |
| 13. Clayton Tanner, lhp | 28. Dan Ortmeier, of |
| 14. Osiris Matos, rhp | 29. Jose Valdez, rhp |
| 15. Nick Pereira, rhp | 30. Brian Horwitz, of/1b |

# ORGANIZATION OVERVIEW

**General manager:** Brian Sabean. **Farm director:** Jack Hiatt. **Scouting director:** Matt Nerland.

## 2006 PERFORMANCE

| Class | Team | League | W | L | PCT | Finish* | Manager | Affiliated |
|---|---|---|---|---|---|---|---|---|
| Majors | San Francisco | National | 76 | 85 | .472 | 10th | Felipe Alou | — |
| Triple-A | Fresno Grizzlies | Pacific Coast | 61 | 83 | .424 | 14th (16) | Shane Turner | 1998 |
| Double-A | Connecticut Defenders | Eastern | 64 | 77 | .454 | 10th (12) | Dave Machemer | 2003 |
| High A | San Jose Giants | California | 82 | 58 | .586 | 1st (10) | Lenn Sakata | 1988 |
| Low A | Augusta GreenJackets | South Atlantic | 92 | 47 | .662 | 1st (16) | Roberto Kelly | 2005 |
| Short-season | Salem-Keizer Volcanoes | Northwest | 55 | 21 | .724 | +1st (8) | Steve Decker | 1997 |
| Rookie | AZL Giants | Arizona | 33 | 22 | .600 | 4th (9) | Bert Hunter | 2000 |
| **OVERALL 2006 MINOR LEAGUE RECORD** | | | 387 | 308 | .557 | 1st (30) | | |

*Finish in overall standings (No. of teams in league). +League champion

## ORGANIZATION LEADERS

### BATTING
| | | |
|---|---|---|
| *AVG | Janeway, Rich, AZL Giants | .324 |
| R | Three players tied at | 90 |
| H | Minicozzi, Mark, San Jose | 160 |
| 2B | Bowker, John, Fresno/San Jose | 32 |
| 3B | Velez, Eugenio, Augusta | 20 |
| HR | Three players tied at | 16 |
| RBI | Minicozzi, Mark, San Jose | 93 |
| BB | Copeland, Benjamin, Augusta | 73 |
| SO | Maroul, David, Augusta | 123 |
| SB | Richardson, Antoan, Augusta | 66 |
| OBP | Burriss, Emmanuel, Salem-Keizer | .384 |
| SLG | Witter, Adam, Salem-Keizer | .585 |
| XBH | Velez, Eugenio, Augusta | 63 |

### PITCHING
| | | |
|---|---|---|
| W | Martinez, Joseph, Augusta | 15 |
| L | Floyd, Jesse, Connecticut | 14 |
| ERA | Cowart, Adam, Salem-Keizer | 1.08 |
| G | Hedrick, Justin, San Jose | 64 |
| SV | Anderson, Brian, San Jose | 37 |
| IP | Begg, Chris, Connecticut | 175 |
| BB | Garcia, James, San Jose/Fresno/Connecticut | 72 |
| SO | Misch, Patrick, Connecticut/Fresno | 136 |
| | Pereira, Nick, San Jose/Fresno | 136 |
| AVG | Cowart, Adam, Salem-Keizer | .178 |

## BEST TOOLS

| | |
|---|---|
| Best Hitter for Average | Eddy Martinez-Esteve |
| Best Power Hitter | Angel Villalona |
| Best Strike-Zone Discipline | Brian Horwitz |
| Fastest Baserunner | Mike McBryde |
| Best Athlete | Fred Lewis |
| Best Fastball | Tim Lincecum |
| Best Curveball | Tim Lincecum |
| Best Slider | Brian Wilson |
| Best Changeup | Jonathan Sanchez |
| Best Control | Adam Cowart |
| Best Defensive Catcher | Justin Knoedler |
| Best Defensive Infielder | Emmanuel Burriss |
| Best Infield Arm | Brian Bocock |
| Best Defensive Outfielder | Clay Timpner |
| Best Outfield Arm | Mike McBryde |

## PROJECTED 2010 LINEUP

| | |
|---|---|
| Catcher | Eliezer Alfonzo |
| First Base | Travis Ishikawa |
| Second Base | Kevin Frandsen |
| Third Base | Angel Villalona |
| Shortstop | Emmanuel Burriss |
| Left Field | Eddy Martinez-Esteve |
| Center Field | Fred Lewis |
| Right Field | Nate Schierholtz |
| No. 1 Starter | Matt Cain |
| No. 2 Starter | Tim Lincecum |
| No. 3 Starter | Jonathan Sanchez |
| No. 5 Starter | Matt Morris |
| Closer | Brian Wilson |

## LAST YEAR'S TOP 20 PROSPECTS

1. Matt Cain, rhp
2. Marcus Sanders, ss/2b
3. Eddy Martinez-Esteve, of
4. Travis Ishikawa, 1b
5. Merkin Valdez, rhp
6. Jonathan Sanchez, lhp
7. Nate Schierholtz, of
8. Fred Lewis, of
9. Kevin Frandsen, 2b/ss
10. Craig Whitaker, rhp
11. Dan Ortmeier, of
12. Brian Wilson, rhp
13. Jeremy Accardo, rhp
14. Clay Timpner, of
15. Pablo Sandoval, 3b
16. Dan Griffin, rhp
17. Scott Munter, rhp
18. Jack Taschner, lhp
19. Waldis Joaquin, rhp
20. Jon Coutlangus, lhp

## TOP PROSPECTS OF THE DECADE

| Year | Player, Pos. | 2006 Org. |
|---|---|---|
| 1997 | Joe Fontenot, rhp | Out of baseball |
| 1998 | Jason Grilli, rhp | Tigers |
| 1999 | Jason Grilli, rhp | Tigers |
| 2000 | Kurt Ainsworth, rhp | Dodgers |
| 2001 | Jerome Williams, rhp | Athletics |
| 2002 | Jerome Williams, rhp | Athletics |
| 2003 | Jesse Foppert, rhp | Mariners |
| 2004 | Merkin Valdez, rhp | Giants |
| 2005 | Matt Cain, rhp | Giants |
| 2006 | Matt Cain, rhp | Giants |

## TOP DRAFT PICKS OF THE DECADE

| Year | Player, Pos. | 2006 Org. |
|---|---|---|
| 1997 | Jason Grilli, rhp | Tigers |
| 1998 | Tony Torcato, of | White Sox |
| 1999 | Kurt Ainsworth, rhp | Dodgers |
| 2000 | Boof Bonser, rhp | Twins |
| 2001 | Brad Hennessey, rhp | Giants |
| 2002 | Matt Cain, rhp | Giants |
| 2003 | David Aardsma, rhp | Cubs |
| 2004 | Eddy Martinez-Esteve, of | Giants |
| 2005 | Ben Copeland, of | Giants |
| 2006 | Tim Lincecum, rhp | Giants |

## LARGEST BONUSES IN CLUB HISTORY

| | |
|---|---|
| Angel Villalona, 2006 | $2,100,000 |
| Tim Lincecum, 2006 | $2,025,000 |
| Jason Grilli, 1997 | $1,875,000 |
| David Aardsma, 2003 | $1,425,000 |
| Brad Hennessey, 2001 | $1,380,000 |

# MINOR LEAGUE DEPTH CHART

## San Francisco Giants

**Impact: B.** Tim Lincecum and Angel Villalona couldn't be more different—college pitcher close to majors and 16-year-old Dominican infielder—but they received two of the largest bonuses in Giants' history.

**Depth: D.** The organization's upper levels are filled with at best role players, at worst roster filler, particularly among hitters. Developing middle relievers remains the Giants' strongsuit.

**Sleeper:** Ben Copeland, of. The Giants' first position player drafted in 2005, Copeland remains raw for a college player but has offensive upside—rare in the organization.

*Numbers in parentheses indicate prospect rankings.*

| LF |
|---|
| Eddy Martinez-Esteve (9) |
| Brian Horwitz (30) |
| Robert Felmy |
| John Bowker |
| Michael Mooney |
| Carlos Sosa |

| CF |
|---|
| Fred Lewis (7) |
| Mike McBryde (12) |
| Ben Copeland (25) |
| Clay Timpner |
| Antoan Richardson |

| RF |
|---|
| Nate Schierholtz (8) |
| Thomas Neal (22) |
| Dan Ortmeier (28) |

| 3B |
|---|
| Angel Villalona (3) |
| David Maroul |
| Ryan Rohlinger |
| Brian Buscher |

| SS |
|---|
| Emmanuel Burriss (4) |
| Sharlon Schoop (21) |
| Brian Bocock (26) |

| 2B |
|---|
| Kevin Frandsen (6) |
| Marcus Sanders (16) |
| Mark Minicozzi |
| Eugenio Velez |
| Derin McMains |

| 1B |
|---|
| Travis Ishikawa (11) |
| Pablo Sandoval |
| William Thompson |
| Brett Pill |
| Matthew Weston |

| C |
|---|
| Adam Witter |
| Justin Knoedler |
| Todd Jennings |
| Matthew Klimas |
| Henry Gutierrez |

| RHP | |
|---|---|
| **Starters** | **Relievers** |
| Tim Lincecum (1) | Brian Wilson (5) |
| Nick Pereira (15) | Billy Sadler (10) |
| Dan Griffin (17) | Osiris Matos (14) |
| Merkin Valdez (18) | Brian Anderson (19) |
| Joey Martinez (20) | Justin Hedrick (23) |
| Jose Valdez (29) | David Newton |
| Adam Cowart | Wayne Foltin |
| Craig Whitaker | Kelvin Pichardo |
| Kelyn Acosta | Sergio Romo |
| Waldis Joaquin | Dave McKae |
| Henry Sosa | Orlando Yntema |
| Matt Palmer | |
| Manny Cabeza | |
| Chris Begg | |

| LHP | |
|---|---|
| **Starters** | **Relievers** |
| Jonathan Sanchez (2) | Erick Threets (24) |
| Clayton Tanner (13) | David Quinowski (27) |
| Ben Snyder | Jack Taschner |
| Pat Misch | Paul Oseguera |
| | Alex Hinshaw |

## 2006     SIGNING BUDGET: $4.3 million

**Best Pro Debut:** RHP Adam Cowart (35) didn't allow an earned run in his first four starts and earned short-season Northwest League pitcher-of-the-year honors by leading the circuit in wins (10-1), ERA (1.08) and K-BB ratio (55-8 in 83 innings). RHP Tim Lincecum (1) was just as unhittable as he had been in college, reaching high Class A while posting a 1.71 ERA. SS Emmanuel Burriss (1) made the NWL all-star team after hitting .307 with a league-high 35 steals.

**Best Athlete:** OF Mike McBryde, who missed almost the entire spring with a torn hamstring, is the fastest of the three pure speedsters the Giants signed out of the draft. He also has some strength in his 6-foot-2, 190-pound frame and threw in the low 90s as a closer at Florida Atlantic.

**Best Pure Hitter:** San Francisco focused more on all-around players than pure bats, so there's no obvious choice. Burriss hit .307, but he's more of a slap hitter who relies on his speed. 3B Matt Downs (36) might have the most hitting ability in this crop.

**Best Raw Power:** OF Bobby Felmy (22). C Adam Witter, signed as a fifth-year senior free agent before the draft, led NWL champion Salem-Keizer with 16 homers, while Felmy ranked second with eight.

**Fastest Runner:** Burriss, who can run a 6.3-second 60-yard dash, was considered the fastest early-round prospect in the draft, but Giants officials swear McBryde is quicker. OF Tyler Graham (19) also has 8 speed on the 2-8 scouting scale.

**Best Defensive Player:** Salem-Keizer won the NWL title thanks in large part to a stellar defense with standouts all over the field: Burriss, McBryde, Graham, Felmy, 3B Ryan Rohlinger (6), 2B/SS Brian Bocock (9), 2B Brad Boyer (13) and 1B Brett Pill (7). Rohlinger is an outstanding third baseman who's capable of playing shortstop. The best of the outfielders is McBryde, who showed a well-above-average arm in center field.

**Best Fastball:** Lincecum maintained 91-96 mph velocity and topped out at 98 throughout the season. His fastball also has good life, and it may not be his best pitch.

**Best Breaking Ball:** One veteran scout said he'd never seen a pitcher get as many called strikeouts with a curveball in college as Lincecum did, and he led NCAA Division I in strikeouts (199) and whiffs per nine innings (14.3). He had the best 1-2 combo of pitches in the draft.

**Most Intriguing Background:** LHP Ben Snyder's (4) brother Brad was an Indians first-round pick in 2003. OF Dusty Harvard (28) was recruited by the Colorado State and Wyoming football programs, and also played basketball and ran track in high school. He was the first high school player drafted out of Wyoming since the Rangers took Tony Piazza in the 33rd round in 1999.

**Closest To The Majors:** Lincecum could have helped the Giants in September if they needed him. San Francisco hasn't been afraid to push players who show they can handle it, so look for him in AT&T Park in early 2007.

**Best Late-Round Pick:** The Giants have hopes for several of their later choices. Boyer and Felmy are the best prospects from a tools standpoint, Graham can fly and Cowart and Downs had strong debuts.

**The One Who Got Away:** San Francisco liked Harvard's raw athleticism but he wound up at Oklahoma State.

**Assessment:** Getting Lincecum at No. 10 was a steal, and he'll pay almost immediate dividends. The Giants also were pleasantly surprised to get Burriss at No. 33 in a draft light on middle infielders.

## 2005     BUDGET: $502,000

At least they saved money. The Giants didn't have picks in the first three rounds, and the best prospect they landed, RHP Dan Griffin (5) ranks 17th in the top 30. **GRADE: F**

## 2004     BUDGET: $1.5 million

OF Eddy Martinez-Esteve (2) and 2B Kevin Frandsen (12) are two of the system's better position players, and LHP Jonathan Sanchez (27) was a steal. **GRADE: C+**

## 2003     BUDGET: $4.4 million

Both first-rounders, RHPs David Aardsma (since traded) and Craig Whitaker, have been disappointments. But RHP Brian Wilson (24), who had Tommy John surgery two months before the draft, could be the Giants' closer of the future and OF Nate Schierholtz (3) has his moments at the plate. **GRADE: C+**

*Draft analysis by Jim Callis. Numbers in parentheses indicate draft rounds. Budgets are bonuses in first 10 rounds.*

# TIM
# LINCECUM

RHP

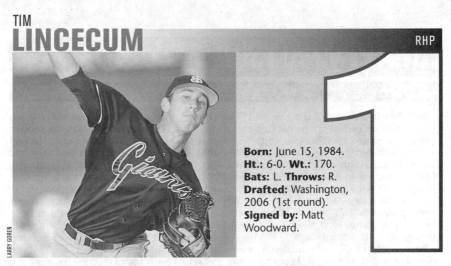

**Born:** June 15, 1984.
**Ht.:** 6-0. **Wt.:** 170.
**Bats:** L. **Throws:** R.
**Drafted:** Washington, 2006 (1st round).
**Signed by:** Matt Woodward.

LARRY GOREN

**W**hen Lincecum was available with the 10th overall pick in the 2006 draft, the Giants felt like they had just won the lottery. A month earlier, they figured there was no chance Lincecum would last beyond the third or fourth pick. But while his size and unorthodox delivery scared off some organizations, San Francisco saw him as a once-in-a-decade talent who was ready to dominate major league hitters straight out of college. Lincecum was draft-eligible the year before as a 21-year-old sophomore, but his seven-figure bonus demands dropped him to the 42nd round and the Indians. Cleveland made a run at him after he led the Cape Cod League with a 0.69 ERA but wouldn't meet his price. Lincecum returned to the Huskies, won his second straight Pacific-10 Conference pitcher of the year award and led NCAA Division I in strikeouts (199) and strikeouts per nine innings (14.3). He also added the Golden Spikes Award a week before signing for $2.025 million, a club record for a drafted player. After a couple of tuneups with short-season Salem Keizer, Lincecum dominated at high Class A San Jose and struck out 10 over seven innings to win his lone playoff start.

Lincecum throws a 91-96 mph fastball that tops out at 98. If that weren't enough, he also has a true hammer curveball that breaks early and keeps on breaking. Giants scouts believe he might have the best curve of any drafted player since Kerry Wood. He added a change-up during his Cape stint, and at times it's a swing-and-miss pitch that bottoms out at the plate. During the spring, he also unveiled a hard slider that he can throw for strikes. Lincecum's combination of stuff and deception makes him close to unhittable. He gains maximum leverage, belying his short stature, by over-rotating his body, using a high leg kick and then seemingly catapulting the ball with a lightning-quick over-the-top delivery. He almost leaps off the mound and his stride is so long that he appears to deliver the ball directly on top of hitters. He's incredibly strong for a pitcher his size, and some old-timers say he reminds them of Bob Feller or a righthanded Sandy Koufax because of his delivery and flexibility. That's no coincidence, because Lincecum's father watched Koufax pitch and taught his son to copy the Hall of Famer's mechanics.

Lincecum's delivery requires incredible focus because he takes his eye off the target during his Kevin Brown-style turn. It also requires Cirque du Soleil-style athleticism and coordination to keep him on center to the plate. He can suffer through bouts with his command because of all the moving parts in his delivery. Lincecum logged 342 innings in his three seasons at Washington, frequently exceeding 120 pitches per start. While he claims to have never felt soreness in his arm, some scouts believe he's a breakdown waiting to happen. San Francisco doesn't share those fears, believing he generates his power through leverage and not by overtaxing his arm.

He could be the devastating closer the Giants have lacked since Robb Nen injured his shoulder in 2002, but they say Lincecum will be a starter until he proves he can't handle the role. If he dominates, San Francisco will have a hard time keeping him off the Opening Day roster. He's more likely headed for Double-A until the club has a vacancy in the rotation.

| Year | Club (League) | Class | W | L | ERA | G | GS | CG | SV | IP | H | R | ER | HR | BB | SO | AVG |
|------|---------------|-------|---|---|-----|---|----|----|----|----|---|---|----|----|----|----|-----|
| 2006 | Salem-Keizer (NWL) | A | 0 | 0 | 0.00 | 2 | 2 | 0 | 0 | 4 | 1 | 0 | 0 | 0 | 0 | 10 | .071 |
|      | San Jose (Cal) | A | 2 | 0 | 1.95 | 6 | 6 | 0 | 0 | 28 | 13 | 7 | 6 | 3 | 12 | 48 | .135 |
| **MINOR LEAGUE TOTALS** | | | 2 | 0 | 1.71 | 8 | 8 | 0 | 0 | 32 | 14 | 7 | 6 | 3 | 12 | 58 | .127 |

## 2 JONATHAN SANCHEZ LHP

**Born:** Nov. 19, 1982. **B-T:** L-L. **Ht.:** 6-2. **Wt.:** 165. **Drafted:** Ohio Dominican, 2004 (27th round). **Signed by:** Sean O'Connor.

Sanchez profiles as a quality starter, but the Giants' bullpen need was so acute that they moved him to short relief after three dominating Double-A starts last year. He was in the big leagues a few weeks later. He finished the year in the San Francisco rotation, though he was much more effective coming out of the bullpen. Sanchez's low-90s fastball is sneaky-fast and can hit 95 mph on occasion. He partners it with a plus changeup that has fooled hitters at every level. The Giants aren't sure if Sanchez is ready to shoulder a full-season workload. He never has thrown more than 126 innings in a season and he has trouble maintaining his velocity when he's used on consecutive days. He also throws a slider but hasn't mastered it, in part because it's hard to stay on top of it with his low three-quarters delivery. Because he worked just 95 innings in 2006, the Giants had no reservations about letting Sanchez play winter ball in his native Puerto Rico. With a solid spring, he'll crack their rotation as a fifth starter.

| Year | Club (League) | Class | W | L | ERA | G | GS | CG | SV | IP | H | R | ER | HR | BB | SO | AVG |
|------|---------------|-------|---|---|-----|---|----|----|----|----|---|---|----|----|----|----|-----|
| 2004 | AZL Giants (AZL) | R | 5 | 0 | 2.77 | 9 | 3 | 0 | 1 | 26 | 22 | 9 | 8 | 0 | 9 | 27 | .229 |
| | Salem-Keizer (NWL) | A | 2 | 1 | 4.84 | 6 | 6 | 0 | 0 | 22 | 16 | 13 | 12 | 3 | 19 | 34 | .203 |
| 2005 | Augusta (SAL) | A | 5 | 7 | 4.08 | 25 | 25 | 0 | 0 | 126 | 122 | 59 | 57 | 8 | 39 | 166 | .254 |
| 2006 | Connecticut (EL) | AA | 2 | 1 | 1.15 | 13 | 3 | 0 | 2 | 31 | 14 | 7 | 4 | 0 | 9 | 46 | .137 |
| | Fresno (PCL) | AAA | 2 | 2 | 3.80 | 6 | 6 | 0 | 0 | 24 | 13 | 10 | 10 | 1 | 13 | 28 | .163 |
| | San Francisco (NL) | MLB | 3 | 1 | 4.95 | 27 | 4 | 0 | 0 | 40 | 39 | 26 | 22 | 2 | 23 | 33 | .250 |
| **MINOR LEAGUE TOTALS** | | | 16 | 11 | 3.58 | 59 | 43 | 0 | 3 | 229 | 187 | 98 | 91 | 12 | 89 | 301 | .223 |
| **MAJOR LEAGUE TOTALS** | | | 3 | 1 | 4.95 | 27 | 4 | 0 | 0 | 40 | 39 | 26 | 22 | 2 | 23 | 33 | .250 |

## 3 ANGEL VILLALONA 3B

BILL MITCHELL

**Born:** Aug. 13, 1990. **B-T:** R-R. **Ht.:** 6-2. **Wt.:** 210. **Signed:** Dominican Republic, 2006. **Signed by:** Rick Ragazzo/Pablo Peguero.

San Francisco doesn't often compete for top Latin American talent, but its didn't flinch at offering Villalona a club-record $2.1 million bonus. International scouting director Rick Ragazzo first noticed Villalona taking batting practice as a 13-year-old and maintained a close relationship with the family. Villalona developed such a comfort level with the Giants that he reportedly turned down larger offers from other clubs. Agent Scott Boras accused the Giants of circumventing him, but they insist they acted in good faith and Major League Baseball approved the contract. Though Villalona would be a high school sophomore in the United States, he already looks like a man. He combines size and power with athleticism. The ball makes a special sound off his bat and he has 40-plus home run potential. He doesn't need to make square contact to hit the ball a long way. He has good hands and instincts, and his plus arm allows him to make plays on balls hit down the line. Villalona has yet to face pro pitching, and the Giants must resist the temptation to move him too quickly. They're trying to be patient, bringing him to instructional league to introduce him to coaches and to American baseball culture. He'll be a below-average runner once he fills out. Villalona projects as an elite power-hitting prospect, but his arrival is probably at least four years away. It's possible Villalona could start his pro career with low Class Augusta as a 16-year-old, but he'll probably start the season in extended spring training before heading to the Rookie-level Arizona League.

| Year | Club (League) | Class | AVG | G | AB | R | H | 2B | 3B | HR | RBI | BB | SO | SB | OBP | SLG |
|------|---------------|-------|-----|---|----|----|----|----|----|----|-----|----|----|----|-----|-----|
| 2006 | Did Not Play—Signed 2007 Contract | | | | | | | | | | | | | | | |

## 4 EMMANUEL BURRISS SS

RICH ABEL

**Born:** Jan. 17, 1985. **B-T:** B-R. **Ht.:** 6-0. **Wt.:** 170. **Drafted:** Kent State, 2006 (1st round supplement). **Signed by:** Sean O'Connor.

Burriss established himself as a top prospect for the 2006 draft by stealing a Cape Cod League-high 37 bases in 44 games the previous summer. He led the Mid-American Conference with 42 steals last spring, then paced the short-season Northwest League with 35 after signing for $1 million as a supplemental first-round pick. A leadoff hitter in the mold of Luis Castillo, Burriss plays the game with poise and polish. He makes excellent contact and is a threat to reach base on anything in play. One club official wasn't shy about comparing his playmaking abilities to Willie Mays, while

another called him Jose Reyes with less power. He has top-of-the-line speed, outstanding range, soft hands and very good instincts. Burriss' arm grades a tick below average, leading to some doubts that he'll stick at shortstop, but his footwork is so good that he seldom fails to make plays. He has very little pop, and pitchers at higher levels may be able to over-power him. A switch-hitter, he's working on a more consistent approach from the left side. Omar Vizquel will be 40 in 2007, and the Giants will need a new shortstop in the near future. That figures to be Burriss, who may skip a level and begin at high Class A in 2007. That would allow fellow 2006 draftee Brian Bocock to play every day at shortstop in low Class A.

| Year | Club (League) | Class | AVG | G | AB | R | H | 2B | 3B | HR | RBI | BB | SO | SB | OBP | SLG |
|------|---------------|-------|-----|---|----|---|---|----|----|----|-----|----|----|----|-----|-----|
| 2006 | Salem-Keizer (NWL) | A | .307 | 65 | 254 | 50 | 78 | 8 | 2 | 1 | 27 | 27 | 22 | 35 | .384 | .366 |
| **MINOR LEAGUE TOTALS** | | | .307 | 65 | 254 | 50 | 78 | 8 | 2 | 1 | 27 | 27 | 22 | 35 | .384 | .366 |

## 5 BRIAN WILSON                                              RHP

**Born:** March 16, 1982. **B-T:** R-R. **Ht.:** 6-1. **Wt.:** 205. **Drafted:** Louisiana State, 2003 (24th round). **Signed by:** Tom Korenek.

The Giants drafted Wilson in the 24th round in 2003, knowing he wouldn't be able to pitch for a year because he had to recover from Tommy John surgery. Four years earlier, San Francisco had taken anoth-er Tommy John survivor out of Louisiana State, Kurt Ainsworth. Wilson's first pro season was a disaster, and he admitted he sometimes skated through his rehab work before rededicating himself and dominating the last two years. Wilson's biting 90-mph slider is the best in the system and is reminiscent of Robb Nen's signature pitch. He throws in the mid- to upper 90s with his fastball and hit 98 mph in the big leagues. Quietly intense and armed with a huge water ser-pent tattooed on his left arm, Wilson has the look of a closer. Fastball command was an issue for Wilson in San Francisco, and it may be partially explained by an oblique strain that kept him from getting into a consistent rhythm. He feeds off adrenaline, which can work against him when he overthrows or tries for a strikeout. He hasn't learned to handle poor outings yet. The Giants prefer an established presence in the ninth inning, so Wilson may have to settle for a setup role this year. If he succeeds there, he could close for San Francisco in 2008.

| Year | Club (League) | Class | W | L | ERA | G | GS | CG | SV | IP | H | R | ER | HR | BB | SO | AVG |
|------|---------------|-------|---|---|-----|---|----|----|----|----|---|---|----|----|----|----|-----|
| 2004 | Hagerstown (SAL) | A | 2 | 5 | 5.34 | 23 | 3 | 0 | 3 | 57 | 63 | 37 | 34 | 7 | 22 | 41 | .269 |
| 2005 | Augusta (SAL) | A | 5 | 1 | 0.82 | 26 | 0 | 0 | 13 | 33 | 23 | 7 | 3 | 0 | 7 | 30 | .190 |
| | Norwich (EL) | AA | 0 | 0 | 0.57 | 15 | 0 | 0 | 8 | 16 | 6 | 1 | 1 | 0 | 5 | 22 | .115 |
| | Fresno (PCL) | AAA | 1 | 1 | 3.97 | 9 | 0 | 0 | 0 | 11 | 8 | 7 | 5 | 0 | 8 | 13 | .190 |
| 2006 | San Jose (Cal) | A | 0 | 0 | 9.00 | 1 | 0 | 0 | 0 | 1 | 1 | 1 | 1 | 0 | 1 | 1 | .200 |
| | Fresno (PCL) | AAA | 1 | 3 | 2.89 | 24 | 0 | 0 | 7 | 28 | 20 | 9 | 9 | 2 | 14 | 30 | .202 |
| | San Francisco (NL) | MLB | 2 | 3 | 5.40 | 31 | 0 | 0 | 1 | 30 | 32 | 19 | 18 | 1 | 21 | 23 | .281 |
| **MINOR LEAGUE TOTALS** | | | 9 | 10 | 3.26 | 98 | 3 | 0 | 31 | 146 | 121 | 62 | 53 | 9 | 57 | 137 | .219 |
| **MAJOR LEAGUE TOTALS** | | | 2 | 3 | 5.40 | 31 | 0 | 0 | 1 | 30 | 32 | 19 | 18 | 1 | 21 | 23 | .281 |

## 6 KEVIN FRANDSEN                                            2B

**Born:** May 24, 1982. **B-T:** R-R. **Ht.:** 6-0. **Wt.:** 175. **Drafted:** San Jose State, 2004 (12th round). **Signed by:** Matt Nerland.

Frandsen was one of the Giants' most heartwarming stories in 2006. He dedicated himself to making the big leagues to honor his brother D.J., who lost a lifelong battle with cancer in 2004. After he got there, pitch-ing coach Dave Righetti, who was D.J.'s favorite player, quietly insisted that Kevin take his uniform No. 19, which he had worn the number since 1981. Frandsen has marvelous bat control and profiles as a solid No. 2 hitter in the mold of Robby Thompson. He puts the ball in play consistently, uses the whole field and has occasional gap power. His baseball IQ is off the charts and he has plus makeup and maturity. Even when temperatures hit 112 degrees at Triple-A Fresno, he pestered the coaches for extra infield practice. Frandsen knows he must improve his on-base percentage and limit himself to pitches he can drive—a difficult task because he can put almost any pitch into play. He focused on working counts in the Arizona Fall League and had success. While he also played shortstop and third base in Triple-A, his range and arm are merely adequate and limit him to second base. The Giants would like him to polish his bunting skills. By hitting .388 in the Arizona Fall League, Frandsen improved his chances of opening 2007 as San Francisco's second baseman. But the Giants subse-quently re-signed Ray Durham, so Frandsen will apprentice in a utility role.

| Year | Club (League) | Class | AVG | G | AB | R | H | 2B | 3B | HR | RBI | BB | SO | SB | OBP | SLG |
|------|---------------|-------|-----|---|----|---|---|----|----|----|-----|----|----|----|-----|-----|
| 2004 | Salem-Keizer (NWL) | A | .296 | 25 | 98 | 22 | 29 | 5 | 0 | 3 | 14 | 9 | 9 | 0 | .369 | .439 |
| 2005 | San Jose (Cal) | A | .351 | 75 | 291 | 57 | 102 | 22 | 3 | 2 | 40 | 26 | 22 | 13 | .429 | .467 |
|  | Norwich (EL) | AA | .287 | 33 | 129 | 22 | 37 | 8 | 0 | 2 | 20 | 4 | 14 | 7 | .336 | .395 |
|  | Fresno (PCL) | AAA | .351 | 20 | 94 | 18 | 33 | 10 | 1 | 2 | 16 | 2 | 5 | 1 | .378 | .543 |
| 2006 | Fresno (PCL) | AAA | .304 | 71 | 293 | 46 | 89 | 25 | 3 | 3 | 30 | 12 | 30 | 7 | .358 | .440 |
|  | San Jose (Cal) | A | .429 | 2 | 7 | 1 | 3 | 0 | 0 | 0 | 1 | 0 | 0 | 0 | .556 | .429 |
|  | San Francisco (NL) | MLB | .215 | 41 | 93 | 12 | 20 | 4 | 0 | 2 | 7 | 3 | 14 | 0 | .284 | .323 |
| **MINOR LEAGUE TOTALS** | | | .307 | 73 | 300 | 47 | 92 | 25 | 3 | 3 | 31 | 12 | 30 | 7 | .364 | .440 |
| **MAJOR LEAGUE TOTALS** | | | .215 | 41 | 93 | 12 | 20 | 4 | 0 | 2 | 7 | 3 | 14 | 0 | .284 | .323 |

## 7 FRED LEWIS OF

**Born:** Dec. 9, 1980. **B-T:** L-R. **Ht.:** 6-2. **Wt.:** 190. **Drafted:** Southern, 2002 (2nd round). **Signed by:** Tom Korenek.

Lewis was a wide receiver at Mississippi Gulf Coast Junior College and wasn't serious about baseball until he transferred to Southern. His lack of baseball experience showed early in his career, as he needed to repeat levels and struggled with slow starts. But when he arrived as a major league callup in September, Lewis went 3-for-3 as a pinch-hitter and wowed the coaches with his athleticism. The best all-around athlete in the system, Lewis does things on the basepaths the Giants haven't seen from a position prospect since Darren Lewis (no relation). He has the raw skills (bat speed, strength, speed) to hit .300 with 20-25 homers and 30-40 steals annually. He does a good job of recognizing pitches and taking walks. At 26, Lewis is still more about potential than production. He strikes out too much, though he would benefit from swinging at more early count strikes. He doesn't use his speed as well as he could on the bases or in the outfield. He takes poor routes to balls, prompting his move from center field to left last summer. Lewis is ready for a major league role as a spare outfielder, but the Giants want him to play every day to see if he can finally figure things out. There's a good chance he'll return to Triple-A.

| Year | Club (League) | Class | AVG | G | AB | R | H | 2B | 3B | HR | RBI | BB | SO | SB | OBP | SLG |
|------|---------------|-------|-----|---|----|---|---|----|----|----|-----|----|----|----|-----|-----|
| 2002 | Salem-Keizer (NWL) | A | .322 | 58 | 239 | 43 | 77 | 9 | 3 | 1 | 23 | 26 | 58 | 9 | .396 | .397 |
| 2003 | Hagerstown (SAL) | A | .250 | 114 | 420 | 61 | 105 | 17 | 8 | 1 | 27 | 68 | 112 | 30 | .361 | .336 |
| 2004 | San Jose (Cal) | A | .301 | 115 | 439 | 88 | 132 | 20 | 11 | 8 | 57 | 84 | 109 | 33 | .424 | .451 |
|  | Fresno (PCL) | AAA | .304 | 6 | 23 | 3 | 7 | 1 | 0 | 1 | 2 | 5 | 5 | 1 | .429 | .478 |
| 2005 | Norwich (EL) | AA | .273 | 137 | 512 | 79 | 140 | 28 | 7 | 7 | 47 | 69 | 124 | 30 | .361 | .396 |
| 2006 | Fresno (PCL) | AAA | .276 | 120 | 439 | 85 | 121 | 20 | 11 | 12 | 56 | 68 | 105 | 18 | .375 | .453 |
|  | San Francisco (NL) | MLB | .455 | 13 | 11 | 5 | 5 | 1 | 0 | 0 | 2 | 0 | 3 | 0 | .455 | .545 |
| **MINOR LEAGUE TOTALS** | | | .276 | 120 | 439 | 85 | 121 | 20 | 11 | 12 | 56 | 68 | 105 | 18 | .375 | .453 |
| **MAJOR LEAGUE TOTALS** | | | .455 | 13 | 11 | 5 | 5 | 1 | 0 | 0 | 2 | 0 | 3 | 0 | .455 | .545 |

## 8 NATE SCHIERHOLTZ OF

**Born:** Feb. 15, 1984. **B-T:** L-R. **Ht.:** 6-2. **Wt.:** 215. **Drafted:** Chabot (Calif.) JC, 2003 (2nd round). **Signed by:** Matt Nerland.

A surprise second-round pick in 2003, Schierholtz looked like he might fall into the trap of becoming a power hitter without a position. But he converted from third base to right field in late 2004 and has worked hard on his defense. He struggled at the plate in Double-A in 2006, and it took a Connecticut-record 25-game hitting streak in August to rescue his season. Schierholtz has a bodybuilder's physique and tremendous power. He was a sight to behold in spring training, when his mammoth shots cleared a 100-foot netting and peppered a neighboring apartment complex. He runs well for his size, looks to take the extra base and always hustles. He has a strong outfield arm. He has a clean lefthanded swing, but there's some length to it and Schierholtz struggles with plate discipline. He cut down on his strikeouts last season, but he still doesn't walk nearly enough. A promotion to the Triple-A Pacific Coast League, which favors hitters, should help Schierholtz' confidence. If he shows more consistency at the plate, he could compete for a big league starting job in 2008.

| Year | Club (League) | Class | AVG | G | AB | R | H | 2B | 3B | HR | RBI | BB | SO | SB | OBP | SLG |
|------|---------------|-------|-----|---|----|---|---|----|----|----|-----|----|----|----|-----|-----|
| 2003 | Giants (AZL) | R | .400 | 11 | 45 | 5 | 18 | 0 | 2 | 0 | 5 | 3 | 8 | 4 | .449 | .489 |
|  | Salem-Keizer (NWL) | A | .306 | 35 | 124 | 23 | 38 | 6 | 2 | 3 | 29 | 12 | 15 | 0 | .382 | .460 |
| 2004 | Hagerstown (SAL) | A | .296 | 58 | 233 | 41 | 69 | 22 | 0 | 15 | 53 | 18 | 52 | 1 | .353 | .584 |
|  | San Jose (Cal) | A | .295 | 62 | 258 | 39 | 76 | 18 | 9 | 3 | 31 | 15 | 41 | 3 | .338 | .469 |
| 2005 | San Jose (Cal) | A | .319 | 128 | 502 | 83 | 160 | 37 | 8 | 15 | 86 | 32 | 132 | 5 | .363 | .514 |
| 2006 | Connecticut (EL) | AA | .270 | 125 | 470 | 55 | 127 | 25 | 7 | 14 | 54 | 27 | 81 | 8 | .325 | .443 |
| **MINOR LEAGUE TOTALS** | | | .299 | 419 | 1632 | 246 | 488 | 108 | 28 | 50 | 258 | 107 | 329 | 21 | .351 | .491 |

## 9  EDDY MARTINEZ-ESTEVE                                            OF

**Born:** July 14, 1983. **B-T:** R-R. **Ht.:** 6-2. **Wt.:** 215. **Drafted:** Florida State, 2004 (2nd round). **Signed by:** Paul Turco Jr.

STEVE MOORE

Drafted with San Francisco's first pick (second round) in 2004, Martinez-Esteve hasn't been able to stay healthy. He was nagged by injuries during his college career, and he has undergone elective surgeries on his right shoulder and foot as a pro. He made it through just 27 games last season before hyperextending his left shoulder and had surgery to repair a torn labrum in June. Martinez-Esteve is the best pure hitter in the system, with the ability to hit for average and power. Coaches noted that his maturity improved last year and he reported to instructional league having lost almost 20 pounds. Martinez-Esteve might finally be getting the message that he can't DH in the National League. He's putting more effort into improving his defensive skills, though his range, arm and instincts all rate below average in left field. First base remains an option, but only if he's up for the challenge. Martinez-Esteve should be fine for spring training, when he'll make his first appearance in big league camp. Following his lost season, he'll probably return to Double-A, but he could be in the mix for a starting job with the Giants in 2008.

| Year | Club (League) | Class | AVG | G | AB | R | H | 2B | 3B | HR | RBI | BB | SO | SB | OBP | SLG |
|------|---------------|-------|------|-----|-----|----|-----|----|----|----|-----|----|----|----|------|------|
| 2004 | Giants (AZL) | R | .357 | 4 | 14 | 2 | 5 | 2 | 0 | 0 | 4 | 0 | 2 | 2 | .375 | .500 |
|      | Salem-Keizer (NWL) | A | .286 | 10 | 35 | 5 | 10 | 4 | 0 | 0 | 2 | 6 | 7 | 0 | .405 | .400 |
|      | Hagerstown (SAL) | A | .217 | 13 | 46 | 4 | 10 | 1 | 1 | 1 | 11 | 8 | 8 | 1 | .339 | .348 |
|      | San Jose (Cal) | A | .420 | 17 | 69 | 11 | 29 | 7 | 2 | 0 | 14 | 4 | 9 | 0 | .446 | .580 |
| 2005 | San Jose (Cal) | A | .313 | 132 | 479 | 89 | 150 | 44 | 3 | 17 | 94 | 89 | 82 | 4 | .427 | .524 |
| 2006 | Connecticut (EL) | AA | .272 | 27 | 92 | 8 | 25 | 10 | 0 | 2 | 11 | 9 | 14 | 0 | .324 | .446 |
| **MINOR LEAGUE TOTALS** | | | .272 | 27 | 92 | 8 | 25 | 10 | 0 | 2 | 11 | 9 | 14 | 0 | .324 | .446 |

## 10  BILLY SADLER                                                   RHP

**Born:** Sept. 21, 1981. **B-T:** R-R. **Ht.:** 6-0. **Wt.:** 190. **Drafted:** Louisiana State, 2003 (6th round). **Signed by:** Tom Korenek.

The Giants dodged a bullet when they didn't lose Sadler in the major league Rule 5 draft after the 2005 season. They knew he had a big arm, but he had control problems and is quite a bit shorter than his listed height. Sadler earned a September callup and a roster spot in 2006 by saving 21 games with a 2.43 ERA in the minors. A teammate of Brian Wilson at Louisiana State, Sadler also had Tommy John surgery in college, though his came at Pensacola (Fla.) JC. Sadler throws a two-seam fastball that sits in the low 90s and can touch 96 mph. It has good, tailing action and locks up righthanders. His curveball also gives them fits, and his changeup has become more consistent during the last two seasons. Sadler still has issues with his control and command. He needs to do a better job of locating his fastball and of getting ahead in the count to set up hitters for his curveball. His mound presence was a concern early in his career but isn't any longer. He continued to dominate in the Arizona Fall League and appears destined for a role in the San Francisco bullpen. If Wilson doesn't claim the Giants' closer job in the future, it could fall to Sadler.

| Year | Club (League) | Class | W | L | ERA | G | GS | CG | SV | IP | H | R | ER | HR | BB | SO | AVG |
|------|---------------|-------|----|----|------|-----|----|----|----|-----|-----|----|----|----|-----|-----|------|
| 2003 | Hagerstown (SAL) | A | 0 | 0 | 4.80 | 12 | 0 | 0 | 1 | 15 | 15 | 8 | 8 | 4 | 13 | 10 | .263 |
| 2004 | San Jose (Cal) | A | 2 | 2 | 2.38 | 30 | 3 | 0 | 0 | 57 | 29 | 17 | 15 | 1 | 40 | 66 | .149 |
|      | Norwich (EL) | AA | 0 | 3 | 3.86 | 17 | 0 | 0 | 0 | 30 | 22 | 16 | 13 | 3 | 18 | 24 | .195 |
| 2005 | Norwich (EL) | AA | 6 | 5 | 3.31 | 47 | 0 | 0 | 5 | 84 | 64 | 34 | 31 | 4 | 33 | 81 | .208 |
| 2006 | Connecticut (EL) | AA | 4 | 3 | 2.56 | 44 | 0 | 0 | 20 | 46 | 23 | 14 | 13 | 1 | 29 | 67 | .146 |
|      | Fresno (PCL) | AAA | 2 | 0 | 1.80 | 7 | 0 | 0 | 1 | 10 | 5 | 2 | 2 | 1 | 2 | 12 | .156 |
|      | San Francisco (NL) | MLB | 0 | 0 | 6.75 | 5 | 0 | 0 | 0 | 4 | 5 | 3 | 3 | 2 | 2 | 6 | .294 |
| **MINOR LEAGUE TOTALS** | | | 14 | 13 | 3.05 | 157 | 3 | 0 | 27 | 242 | 158 | 91 | 82 | 14 | 135 | 260 | .183 |
| **MAJOR LEAGUE TOTALS** | | | 0 | 0 | 6.75 | 5 | 0 | 0 | 0 | 4 | 5 | 3 | 3 | 2 | 2 | 6 | .294 |

## 11  TRAVIS ISHIKAWA                                                1B

**Born:** Sept. 24, 1983. **B-T:** L-L. **Ht.:** 6-3. **Wt.:** 210. **Drafted:** HS—Federal Way, Wash., 2002 (21st round). **Signed by:** Matt Woodward.

Ishikawa made his major league debut in April and didn't look overmatched at the plate, and he also impressed the coaching staff with his smooth fielding at first base. But he was optioned to Double-A when Lance Niekro returned from the bereavement list and fared so poorly that the Giants didn't bring him back in September. The club signed him to a $955,000 bonus in 2002 to steer him away from Oregon State and expected his line-drive

swing to translate into more home runs as he matured physically. Ishikawa has filled out and he has tremendous lower-body strength, but his development with the bat has been erratic and his best tool remains his glove. He regressed a bit with his strike zone discipline, taking too many strikes early in the count and failing to hone his two-strike approach. A move to the hitter-friendly Pacific Coast League should help Ishikawa regain confidence this season.

| Year | Club (League) | Class | AVG | G | AB | R | H | 2B | 3B | HR | RBI | BB | SO | SB | OBP | SLG |
|------|---------------|-------|-----|---|----|---|---|----|----|----|-----|----|----|----|-----|-----|
| 2002 | Giants (AZL) | R | .279 | 19 | 68 | 10 | 19 | 4 | 2 | 1 | 10 | 7 | 20 | 7 | .364 | .441 |
| | Salem-Keizer (NWL) | A | .307 | 23 | 88 | 14 | 27 | 2 | 1 | 1 | 17 | 5 | 22 | 1 | .347 | .386 |
| 2003 | Hagerstown (SAL) | A | .206 | 57 | 194 | 20 | 40 | 5 | 0 | 3 | 22 | 33 | 69 | 3 | .329 | .278 |
| | Salem-Keizer (NWL) | A | .254 | 66 | 248 | 53 | 63 | 17 | 4 | 3 | 31 | 44 | 77 | 0 | .376 | .391 |
| 2004 | Hagerstown (SAL) | A | .256 | 97 | 355 | 59 | 91 | 19 | 2 | 15 | 54 | 45 | 110 | 10 | .357 | .448 |
| | San Jose (Cal) | A | .232 | 16 | 56 | 10 | 13 | 7 | 0 | 1 | 10 | 10 | 16 | 0 | .353 | .411 |
| 2005 | San Jose (Cal) | A | .282 | 127 | 432 | 87 | 122 | 28 | 7 | 22 | 79 | 70 | 129 | 1 | .387 | .532 |
| 2006 | Connecticut (EL) | AA | .232 | 86 | 298 | 33 | 69 | 13 | 4 | 10 | 42 | 35 | 88 | 0 | .316 | .403 |
| | San Francisco (NL) | MLB | .292 | 12 | 24 | 1 | 7 | 3 | 1 | 0 | 4 | 1 | 6 | 0 | .320 | .500 |
| **MINOR LEAGUE TOTALS** | | | .255 | 491 | 1739 | 286 | 444 | 95 | 20 | 56 | 265 | 249 | 531 | 22 | .357 | .430 |
| **MAJOR LEAGUE TOTALS** | | | .292 | 12 | 24 | 1 | 7 | 3 | 1 | 0 | 4 | 1 | 6 | 0 | .320 | .500 |

## 12 MIKE McBRYDE OF

**Born:** March 22, 1985. **B-T:** R-R. **Ht.:** 6-2. **Wt.:** 190. **Drafted:** Florida Atlantic, 2006 (5th round). **Signed by:** Steve Arnieri.

McBryde missed all but three games in his junior season at Florida Atlantic because of a strained hamstring, but the Giants had heavily scouted him in 2005. They were delighted to snap him up in the fifth round last June and sign him for $180,000. He previously had turned down the Red Sox as a 38th-rounder out of high school. A center fielder and closer for the Owls, he hit .370 in both his freshman and sophomore seasons. He also threw in the low 90s with a plus curveball, but the Giants kept him in the outfield. He showed off his arm strength by recording eight assists in his first three weeks for Salem-Keizer. The Giants say McBryde is already an above-average major league center fielder defensively, and most consider him the fastest player in an organization with several top sprinters. The organization knows it will have to work hard to make McBryde a legitimate hitter, but he surprised people by staying afloat in the Northwest League in spite of his injury layoff. While not a power-hitting prospect, McBryde is a threat to take extra bases because of his wheels. He'll move up the ladder quickly if he's not overmatched at the plate, and could be pushed as high as high Class A to start the season.

| Year | Club (League) | Class | AVG | G | AB | R | H | 2B | 3B | HR | RBI | BB | SO | SB | OBP | SLG |
|------|---------------|-------|-----|---|----|---|---|----|----|----|-----|----|----|----|-----|-----|
| 2006 | Salem-Keizer (NWL) | A | .276 | 71 | 225 | 38 | 62 | 9 | 5 | 3 | 34 | 22 | 59 | 16 | .344 | .400 |
| **MINOR LEAGUE TOTALS** | | | .276 | 71 | 225 | 38 | 62 | 9 | 5 | 3 | 34 | 22 | 59 | 16 | .344 | .400 |

## 13 CLAYTON TANNER LHP

**Born:** Dec. 5, 1987. **B-T:** R-L. **Ht.:** 6-1. **Wt.:** 180. **Drafted:** HS—Concord, Calif., 2006 (3rd round). **Signed by:** Keith Snider.

Several high school lefthanders were on the Giants' board in the third round of the 2006 draft, but Tanner was a known commodity and based on their scouting reports the organization believed he had a deep inner drive to match his ability. Tanner grew up a Giants fan, another fact that helped the organization persuade him to sign for $425,000 rather than fulfill his commitment to Pepperdine. Outside of Jonathan Sanchez, Tanner has the highest ceiling of any lefty starter prospect in the system. He throws a plus fastball with late life that tops out at 91 mph, though the Giants believe he'll add velocity as he matures. He worked out at AT&T Park all winter as part of a conditioning program. He competed well against older players in the Northwest League, showing the ability to mix his fastball, curve and slider. He's working on a changeup, which will be essential as he advances. Tanner is probably headed for low Class A, though the Giants had him skip the Arizona League in his debut year and it wouldn't be a shock to see him competing in high Class A before long.

| Year | Club (League) | Class | W | L | ERA | G | GS | CG | SV | IP | H | R | ER | HR | BB | SO | AVG |
|------|---------------|-------|---|---|-----|---|----|----|----|----|---|---|----|----|----|----|-----|
| 2006 | Salem-Keizer (NWL) | A | 2 | 2 | 3.46 | 13 | 0 | 0 | 1 | 26 | 17 | 11 | 10 | 1 | 8 | 25 | .183 |
| **MINOR LEAGUE TOTALS** | | | 2 | 2 | 3.46 | 13 | 0 | 0 | 1 | 26 | 17 | 11 | 10 | 1 | 8 | 25 | .183 |

## 14 OSIRIS MATOS RHP

**Born:** Nov. 6, 1984. **B-T:** R-R. **Ht.:** 6-1. **Wt.:** 180. **Signed:** Dominican Republic, 2002. **Signed by:** Rick Ragazzo.

Matos is named for the Egyptian god of the underworld, and he was almost that intimidating in the low Class A South Atlantic League, striking out 81 while walking just 12 in 61

innings. Matos was used as a starter until last season, but he had some arm fatigue and the Giants figured his fearlessness would allow him to blossom in relief. They were right. He doesn't pitch around hitters, relying on his mid-90s fastball and a quick, hard slider that breaks straight down. He can hit 97 mph, but his strength is his ability to work the ladder, throwing a low fastball with good sink and a letter-high ball with rise and carry. The Giants are tutoring him on another offspeed pitch to combat lefties. In spite of his success out of the bullpen, it's too early to pigeonhole Matos as a reliever. His development mirrors that of Russ Ortiz, who went on to a successful career as a starter. Matos finished the season in Double-A, a sign he's on the fast track. He'll probably return to Connecticut to start the season and is a good bet to make his major league debut this year.

| Year | Club (League) | Class | W | L | ERA | G | GS | CG | SV | IP | H | R | ER | HR | BB | SO | AVG |
|------|---------------|-------|---|---|-----|---|----|----|----|-----|-----|-----|-----|----|----|-----|------|
| 2002 | Giants (AZL) | R | 4 | 2 | 4.65 | 13 | 13 | 0 | 0 | 62 | 63 | 35 | 32 | 3 | 22 | 51 | .266 |
| 2003 | Giants (AZL) | R | 2 | 2 | 4.67 | 9 | 6 | 0 | 0 | 35 | 35 | 21 | 18 | 1 | 10 | 28 | .261 |
| 2004 | Giants (AZL) | R | 2 | 0 | 2.44 | 11 | 8 | 0 | 1 | 48 | 43 | 23 | 13 | 1 | 20 | 47 | .230 |
| 2005 | Augusta (SAL) | A | 8 | 8 | 4.99 | 29 | 22 | 0 | 0 | 135 | 162 | 83 | 75 | 12 | 31 | 79 | .297 |
| 2006 | Augusta (SAL) | A | 7 | 3 | 1.76 | 44 | 0 | 0 | 13 | 61 | 42 | 13 | 12 | 3 | 12 | 81 | .193 |
| | Connecticut (EL) | AA | 0 | 0 | 3.72 | 6 | 0 | 0 | 2 | 10 | 11 | 4 | 4 | 0 | 2 | 5 | .282 |
| **MINOR LEAGUE TOTALS** | | | 23 | 15 | 3.95 | 112 | 49 | 0 | 16 | 351 | 356 | 179 | 154 | 20 | 97 | 291 | .262 |

## 15  NICK PEREIRA                                                    RHP

**Born:** Sept. 22, 1982. **B-T:** R-R. **Ht.:** 6-1. **Wt.:** 190. **Drafted:** San Francisco, 2005 (10th round). **Signed by:** Matt Nerland.

Like former Giants prospect Jesse Foppert, Pereira is a University of San Francisco product who jumped onto the radar screen with a strong showing in the college summer Valley League. While he hasn't dominated the minor leagues as Foppert did, Pereira is progressing almost as quickly. The Giants aren't afraid to push college pitchers who match smarts with stuff, and Pereira jumped from high Class A to Triple-A with plenty of the summer to spare. He represented the Giants in the Futures Game but didn't pitch. Pereira reminds some in the organization of Brad Hennessey, a command pitcher with an even temperament who competes well. He struggled at times in Triple-A but impressed coaches with the way he bounced back and made adjustments. He pitches with a fastball at 88-90 mph and can hit 93, but the key is the good sink and run he generates. He's still learning fastball command, but it helps that he can throw his changeup and curveball for strikes and isn't afraid to go to his offspeed stuff when behind in the count. Pereira fields his position well and runs the bases better than many of his position teammates. He's expected to return to Triple-A to open the season and should provide valuable depth to the big league club.

| Year | Club (League) | Class | W | L | ERA | G | GS | CG | SV | IP | H | R | ER | HR | BB | SO | AVG |
|------|---------------|-------|---|---|-----|---|----|----|----|-----|-----|-----|-----|----|----|-----|------|
| 2005 | Salem-Keizer (NWL) | A | 5 | 3 | 3.04 | 14 | 9 | 0 | 0 | 50 | 54 | 21 | 17 | 0 | 14 | 41 | .277 |
| 2006 | San Jose (Cal) | A | 7 | 1 | 2.06 | 13 | 13 | 0 | 0 | 79 | 65 | 21 | 18 | 1 | 16 | 76 | .222 |
| | Fresno (PCL) | AAA | 4 | 3 | 5.92 | 15 | 15 | 0 | 0 | 79 | 87 | 55 | 52 | 10 | 48 | 60 | .281 |
| **MINOR LEAGUE TOTALS** | | | 16 | 7 | 3.76 | 42 | 37 | 0 | 0 | 208 | 206 | 97 | 87 | 11 | 78 | 177 | .258 |

## 16  MARCUS SANDERS                                                   SS

**Born:** Aug. 25, 1985. **B-T:** R-R. **Ht.:** 6-0. **Wt.:** 160. **Drafted:** South Florida CC, D/F 2003 (17th round). **Signed by:** Paul Turco, Jr.

The Giants had high hopes for Sanders after surgery on his right shoulder following the 2005 season. The surgery reversed a procedure he had in high school to tighten his shoulder capsule after he dislocated it in a football game. But Sanders struggled with his arm more than ever last year, leaving his prospect status in serious doubt. Once considered a plus defensive shortstop with some of the best hands in the system, Sanders had to play DH just to get at-bats. For the first time, his shoulder also affected him at the plate and he lost both his ability to make contact and any pop he had in his bat. Sanders was healthy enough to play in instructional league, but he couldn't move to second base because it was too taxing for him to throw across his body. The Giants were planning to seek more medical opinions on Sanders this winter. If he can get past his shoulder issues, he remains a terrific athlete with plus speed, above-average baseball smarts and surprising power. The Giants are hoping he will be ready when full-season affiliates begin play. If so, he'll probably return to high Class A.

| Year | Club (League) | Class | AVG | G | AB | R | H | 2B | 3B | HR | RBI | BB | SO | SB | OBP | SLG |
|------|---------------|-------|-----|---|----|---|---|----|----|----|-----|----|----|----|-----|-----|
| 2004 | Giants (AZL) | R | .292 | 55 | 209 | 54 | 61 | 12 | 4 | 3 | 21 | 35 | 45 | 28 | .415 | .431 |
| 2005 | Augusta (SAL) | A | .300 | 111 | 420 | 86 | 126 | 19 | 4 | 5 | 40 | 69 | 90 | 57 | .407 | .400 |
| 2006 | San Jose (Cal) | A | .213 | 54 | 211 | 39 | 45 | 9 | 1 | 0 | 17 | 25 | 43 | 24 | .302 | .265 |
| | Giants (AZL) | R | .121 | 10 | 33 | 7 | 4 | 1 | 0 | 0 | 3 | 7 | 11 | 4 | .275 | .152 |
| **MINOR LEAGUE TOTALS** | | | .270 | 230 | 873 | 186 | 236 | 41 | 9 | 8 | 81 | 136 | 189 | 113 | .379 | .365 |

## DAN GRIFFIN                                                          RHP

**Born:** Sept. 29, 1984. **B-T:** R-R. **Ht.:** 6-7. **Wt.:** 231. **Drafted:** Niagara, 2005 (5th round). **Signed by:** Sean O'Connor.

Griffin opened the season as one of the most promising arms in the South Atlantic League, and Augusta had one of the most effective pitching staffs in all of minor league base-ball. But Griffin turned out to be the exception. He struggled to command his hard fastball and had trouble repeating his delivery in 16 starts before he was diagnosed with rotator cuff tendinitis and a scapular stress reaction in his upper back. Griffin responded to rehab and the Giants were confident he would be 100 percent in the spring. A hulking presence on the mound, Griffin throws a slider and a sweeping curveball to complement a fastball that sits at 91-94 mph and tops out a bit higher. He throws from a high three-quarters arm slot, and when he dips down it's not by design. He's unsure of himself at times and is more of a thrower right now, but he has shown coaches signs that he's learning how to pitch. Griffin probably needs to develop a changeup to remain a starter, but once he becomes a consistent strike-thrower he'll move quickly. Expect him to start in high Class A this season.

| Year | Club (League) | Class | W | L | ERA | G | GS | CG | SV | IP | H | R | ER | HR | BB | SO | AVG |
|------|---------------|-------|---|---|-----|---|----|----|----|-----|-----|----|----|----|----|-----|------|
| 2005 | Giants (AZL) | R | 0 | 0 | 0.75 | 4 | 4 | 0 | 0 | 12 | 9 | 2 | 1 | 0 | 6 | 20 | .214 |
|      | Salem-Keizer (NWL) | A | 3 | 2 | 2.39 | 8 | 8 | 0 | 0 | 38 | 33 | 11 | 10 | 1 | 12 | 49 | .241 |
| 2006 | Augusta (SAL) | A | 5 | 5 | 4.46 | 16 | 16 | 1 | 0 | 73 | 78 | 44 | 36 | 7 | 33 | 78 | .266 |
| **MINOR LEAGUE TOTALS** | | | 8 | 7 | 3.46 | 28 | 28 | 1 | 0 | 122 | 120 | 57 | 47 | 8 | 51 | 147 | .254 |

 ## MERKIN VALDEZ                                                      RHP

**Born:** Nov. 10, 1981. **B-T:** R-R. **Ht.:** 6-3. **Wt.:** 220. **Signed:** Dominican Republic, 1999. **Signed by:** Felix Francisco (Braves).

The Giants have been excited about Valdez' arm ever since he arrived in the December 2002 trade that sent Russ Ortiz to the Braves, but a lack of consistency has kept him from breaking through. Valdez appeared to be on the doorstep in spring training, when he blew away hitters with a 99-mph fastball and super-tight slider, but the former top prospect was dropped from the closer role to middle relief in Triple-A and had trouble repeating his deliv-ery or throwing strikes. When it became clear Valdez wasn't ready to help the Giants in the bullpen, he was moved to the rotation in August in the hopes he could iron out his issues by working in three- and four-inning stints. The plan appeared to be working, but Valdez grabbed his arm in the third inning of a start Aug. 27 and had Tommy John surgery a month later. On the day he was injured, Giants officials said Valdez was throwing with the best combination of command and velocity that they had seen in two years. He won't be able to get back on the mound until winter ball at the earliest.

| Year | Club (League) | Class | W | L | ERA | G | GS | CG | SV | IP | H | R | ER | HR | BB | SO | AVG |
|------|---------------|-------|---|---|-----|---|----|----|----|-----|-----|-----|-----|----|-----|-----|------|
| 2000 | Braves (DSL) | R | 1 | 5 | 1.57 | 14 | 7 | 0 | 0 | 57 | 52 | 27 | 10 | 2 | 14 | 32 | .234 |
| 2001 | Braves (DSL) | R | 6 | 7 | 2.93 | 15 | 14 | 1 | 0 | 92 | 93 | 41 | 30 | 0 | 18 | 48 | .258 |
| 2002 | Braves (GCL) | R | 7 | 3 | 1.98 | 12 | 8 | 1 | 0 | 68 | 47 | 18 | 15 | 0 | 12 | 76 | .193 |
| 2003 | Hagerstown (SAL) | A | 9 | 5 | 2.25 | 26 | 26 | 2 | 0 | 156 | 119 | 42 | 39 | 11 | 49 | 166 | .213 |
| 2004 | Fresno (PCL) | AAA | 0 | 0 | 7.20 | 1 | 1 | 0 | 0 | 5 | 6 | 4 | 4 | 0 | 4 | 5 | .316 |
|      | San Jose (Cal) | A | 3 | 1 | 2.52 | 7 | 7 | 0 | 0 | 36 | 30 | 12 | 10 | 4 | 5 | 44 | .219 |
|      | San Francisco (NL) | MLB | 0 | 0 | 27.00 | 2 | 0 | 0 | 0 | 2 | 4 | 5 | 5 | 1 | 3 | 2 | .444 |
|      | Norwich (EL) | AA | 1 | 4 | 4.32 | 10 | 7 | 0 | 1 | 42 | 35 | 21 | 20 | 3 | 15 | 31 | .229 |
| 2005 | Norwich (EL) | AA | 5 | 6 | 3.53 | 24 | 19 | 1 | 0 | 107 | 99 | 48 | 42 | 7 | 45 | 96 | .252 |
| 2006 | Fresno (PCL) | AAA | 0 | 4 | 5.80 | 46 | 3 | 0 | 5 | 50 | 52 | 42 | 32 | 6 | 39 | 48 | .268 |
| **MINOR LEAGUE TOTALS** | | | 32 | 35 | 2.97 | 155 | 92 | 5 | 6 | 613 | 533 | 255 | 202 | 33 | 201 | 546 | .234 |
| **MAJOR LEAGUE TOTALS** | | | 0 | 0 | 27.00 | 2 | 0 | 0 | 0 | 1 | 4 | 5 | 5 | 1 | 3 | 2 | .444 |

 ## BRIAN ANDERSON                                                     RHP

**Born:** May 25, 1983. **B-T:** R-R. **Ht.:** 6-3. **Wt.:** 210. **Drafted:** Long Beach State, 2005 (14th round). **Signed by:** Ray Krawczyk.

Anderson was the set-up man for Padres prospect Neil Jamison at Long Beach State, but there's no doubt be can handle the pressure that comes with pitching the ninth inning. The southern California native set a high Class A California League record and led the minor leagues with 37 saves last year. He's 56-for-59 in save chances in his pro career, and he saw a little more action under San Jose manager Lenn Sakata in Hawaii Winter Baseball. Sakata probably won't see Anderson again this year. A control artist, he throws an 86-88 mph fast-ball than hits 90 on occasion and cuts back across the plate, similar to that of Paul Quantrill. Anderson also commands a slider and seldom pitches from behind in the count. Giants coaches like his size and his ability to bounce back—an attribute he doesn't abuse because he often needs so few pitches to record three outs. Anderson had a career highlight when

he appeared as the closer for the Cal League all-star team. His set-up man? None other than Jamison. Anderson will move up to Double-A this season and has a chance to contribute at the big league level in September.

| Year | Club (League) | Class | W | L | ERA | G | GS | CG | SV | IP | H | R | ER | HR | BB | SO | AVG |
|------|---------------|-------|---|---|-----|---|----|----|----|----|---|---|----|----|----|----|-----|
| 2005 | Salem-Keizer (NWL) | A | 3 | 1 | 1.95 | 27 | 0 | 0 | 19 | 28 | 16 | 6 | 6 | 2 | 3 | 42 | .162 |
| 2006 | San Jose (Cal) | A | 1 | 1 | 1.86 | 54 | 0 | 0 | 37 | 68 | 44 | 14 | 14 | 5 | 17 | 85 | .183 |
| MINOR LEAGUE TOTALS | | | 4 | 2 | 1.89 | 81 | 0 | 0 | 56 | 95 | 60 | 20 | 20 | 7 | 20 | 127 | .176 |

## 20 JOEY MARTINEZ                                                                  RHP

**Born:** Feb. 26, 1983. **B-T:** L-R. **Ht.:** 6-2. **Wt.:** 175. **Drafted:** Boston College, 2005 (12th round). **Signed by:** Glenn Tufts.

Few pitchers in the Giants system have a baseball IQ to match that of Martinez, who was a 15-game winner and the ace of a strong Augusta staff in 2006. Martinez led his Boston College staff in innings and threw four straight complete games before the Giants drafted him, so it's not surprising that he was tired by the time he made his pro debut with Salem-Keizer in 2005. He was competing against younger players in low Class A, but the Giants believe his changes speeds well enough to succeed at higher levels. Martinez competes with a two-seam fastball that sits at 84-88 mph and touches 90, along with a changeup and curveball that he throws for reliable strikes. But his real strength is his ability to add and subtract from his fastball to keep hitters off balance. Like most pitchers on the Augusta staff, Martinez compiled an impressive strikeout-walk ratio. His 11 hit batters showed he's not afraid to pitch inside despite having less than a huge fastball. The Giants compare Martinez to Ryan Vogelsong, whom they used to fetch Jason Schmidt in a 2001 deadline deal with the Pirates. If Martinez isn't used as a trade chip, he's ticketed for high Class A this season.

| Year | Club (League) | Class | W | L | ERA | G | GS | CG | SV | IP | H | R | ER | HR | BB | SO | AVG |
|------|---------------|-------|---|---|-----|---|----|----|----|----|---|---|----|----|----|----|-----|
| 2005 | Salem-Keizer (NWL) | A | 4 | 3 | 4.30 | 15 | 13 | 0 | 0 | 69 | 69 | 33 | 33 | 9 | 15 | 59 | .264 |
| 2006 | Augusta (SAL) | A | 15 | 5 | 3.01 | 27 | 27 | 1 | 0 | 168 | 156 | 66 | 56 | 9 | 26 | 135 | .246 |
| MINOR LEAGUE TOTALS | | | 19 | 8 | 3.38 | 42 | 40 | 1 | 0 | 237 | 225 | 99 | 89 | 18 | 41 | 194 | .251 |

## 21 SHARLON SCHOOP                                                                   SS

**Born:** April 15, 1987. **B-T:** R-R. **Ht.:** 6-2. **Wt.:** 180. **Signed:** Curacao, 2004. **Signed by:** Rick Ragazzo.

Not long ago, the Giants considered Schoop the second-best defensive infielder in the organization, behind only Omar Vizquel. But after taking several impressive college shortstops in the 2006 draft, the Giants have no reason to rush the Curacao native up the ladder. They even moved him to second base during instructional league because of arm fatigue. Schoop repeated the Arizona League as a 19-year-old, and while the Giants expected improvement at the plate, they didn't expect him to hit .421 over his first 17 games, including hitting for the cycle in a game. Schoop finished with a .310 average and continued to show advanced plate discipline. He drew 26 walks against 15 strikeouts and his .437 on-base percentage ranked fifth in the league. Still just a teenager, the Giants project he'll hit for power as he continues to mature. The Giants like his hands and lateral quickness, but were puzzled when he started making inaccurate throws across the diamond. Wherever he reports in 2007—likely Salem-Keizer after another stint in extended spring training—Schoop will be missing his best pal. The Giants traded countryman Shairon Martis to the Nationals for Mike Stanton last summer.

| Year | Club (League) | Class | AVG | G | AB | R | H | 2B | 3B | HR | RBI | BB | SO | SB | OBP | SLG |
|------|---------------|-------|-----|---|----|---|---|----|----|----|-----|----|----|----|-----|-----|
| 2004 | Giants (DSL) | R | .251 | 59 | 199 | 40 | 50 | 11 | 3 | 0 | 24 | 27 | 22 | 8 | .353 | .337 |
| 2005 | Giants (AZL) | R | .254 | 48 | 169 | 29 | 43 | 4 | 0 | 1 | 19 | 14 | 18 | 10 | .328 | .296 |
| 2006 | Giants (AZL) | R | .310 | 38 | 126 | 29 | 39 | 7 | 1 | 1 | 21 | 26 | 15 | 8 | .437 | .405 |
|      | Salem-Keizer (NWL) | A | .286 | 4 | 7 | 1 | 2 | 0 | 0 | 0 | 1 | 2 | 0 | 0 | .500 | .286 |
| MINOR LEAGUE TOTALS | | | .267 | 149 | 501 | 99 | 134 | 22 | 4 | 2 | 65 | 69 | 55 | 26 | .370 | .339 |

## 22 THOMAS NEAL                                                                     OF

**Born:** Aug. 17, 1987. **B-T:** R-R. **Ht.:** 6-1. **Wt.:** 205. **Drafted:** Riverside (Calif.) CC, D/F 2005 (36th round). **Signed by:** Lee Carballo.

The Giants offered Neal $7,000 to sign out of high school in Southern California in 2005, but he went to nearby Riverside Community College instead and boosted his stock with a huge season (.637 slugging and .504 on-base percentage). San Francisco signed him as a draft-and-follow for $220,000. Neal has what the Giants describe as light-tower power and a righthanded swing that has excellent balance. He battled against older competition in his pro debut with Salem-Keizer and didn't get to show his true ability because he dislocated his shoulder on a dive and struggled the rest of the season. Neal is far from a dead-pull hitter.

He has power to right-center and has a knack for squaring up strikes, but tends to get over-anxious at the plate. He played third base in high school but profiles as a corner outfielder. His range and speed are below average, but he has an above-average arm, which means he'll probably continue to start in right field as he moves through the system. Expect Neal to graduate to low Class A in 2007, along with a host of interesting position players.

| Year | Club (League) | Class | AVG | G | AB | R | H | 2B | 3B | HR | RBI | BB | SO | SB | OBP | SLG |
|------|---------------|-------|-----|---|-----|----|----|----|----|----|-----|----|----|----|------|------|
| 2006 | Salem-Keizer (NWL) | A | .250 | 50 | 176 | 26 | 44 | 6 | 2 | 4 | 20 | 7 | 44 | 1 | .289 | .375 |
| **MINOR LEAGUE TOTALS** | | | .250 | 50 | 176 | 26 | 44 | 6 | 2 | 4 | 20 | 7 | 44 | 1 | .289 | .375 |

 ## JUSTIN HEDRICK                                                                   RHP

**Born:** June 8, 1982. **B-T:** R-R. **Ht.:** 6-3. **Wt.:** 225. **Drafted:** Northeastern, 2004 (6th round). **Signed by:** Glenn Tufts.

Hedrick was invited to major league spring training camp last year but didn't perform well. The Giants felt he lacked focus, so he wasn't assigned when full-season affiliates began the season. After a few weeks, Hedrick reported to high Class A and it didn't take long for him to turn things around. A rare four-pitch reliever, he pitches off a fastball that sits at 88-90 mph but gets on hitters quicker because of his size and long arms. He has a breaking ball he throws wide like a slurve or tight like a true slider. His other weapon is a splitter that is usually in the dirt but is a good strikeout pitch when he gets ahead. If he throws strikes and keeps his fastball on a downward plane, Hedrick should continue to progress in a relief role. But because he has such a wide assortment of pitches, the Giants haven't ruled out starting him down the road. Hedrick is a good bet to continue up the line with his closer, Brian Anderson, in Double-A this season.

| Year | Club (League) | Class | W | L | ERA | G | GS | CG | SV | IP | H | R | ER | HR | BB | SO | AVG |
|------|---------------|-------|---|---|------|-----|----|----|----|-----|-----|----|----|----|----|-----|------|
| 2004 | Giants (AZL) | R | 0 | 0 | 10.13 | 2 | 0 | 0 | 0 | 3 | 6 | 3 | 3 | 0 | 1 | 4 | .462 |
| | Salem-Keizer (NWL) | A | 1 | 2 | 3.27 | 11 | 4 | 0 | 0 | 33 | 22 | 14 | 12 | 3 | 17 | 44 | .196 |
| 2005 | San Jose (Cal) | A | 3 | 4 | 3.55 | 51 | 0 | 0 | 12 | 58 | 42 | 24 | 23 | 7 | 23 | 75 | .195 |
| 2006 | San Jose (Cal) | A | 6 | 4 | 2.00 | 56 | 0 | 0 | 6 | 86 | 53 | 19 | 19 | 3 | 30 | 110 | .182 |
| **MINOR LEAGUE TOTALS** | | | 10 | 10 | 2.86 | 120 | 4 | 0 | 18 | 180 | 123 | 60 | 57 | 13 | 71 | 233 | .195 |

 ## ERICK THREETS                                                                   LHP

**Born:** Nov. 4, 1981. **B-T:** L-L. **Ht.:** 6-5. **Wt.:** 240. **Drafted:** Modesto (Calif.) JC, 2000 (7th round). **Signed by:** Matt Nerland.

It seems the whole organization is rooting for Threets, a one-time Nuke LaLoosh story who was on the verge of making his major league debut last September. After years of erratic command and injury problems mixed with incendiary stuff—including a fastball that legend holds once hit 104 mph—Threets began throwing strikes in Triple-A. He had a 2.87 ERA in 49 games, kept his fastballs from sailing to the screen and got over a changeup and little cut slider with consistency. The Giants were giddy with his progress. Then he sustained a severe tear in his lat muscle on his throwing side on Aug. 27—the same day Merkin Valdez tore an elbow ligament. While his velocity wasn't in the triple digits, Threets was consistently in the upper 90s last year and was gunned at 97 mph on the day of his injury. He spent the winter rehabbing his side and was expected to be healthy when he reports to spring training. He could be a candidate for the Opening Day roster, but more likely the Giants will want him to repeat Triple-A.

| Year | Club (League) | Class | W | L | ERA | G | GS | CG | SV | IP | H | R | ER | HR | BB | SO | AVG |
|------|---------------|-------|---|----|------|-----|----|----|----|-----|-----|-----|-----|----|-----|-----|------|
| 2001 | San Jose (Cal) | A | 0 | 10 | 4.25 | 14 | 14 | 0 | 0 | 59 | 49 | 34 | 28 | 2 | 40 | 60 | .224 |
| | Hagerstown (SAL) | A | 2 | 0 | 0.75 | 12 | 0 | 0 | 1 | 24 | 13 | 3 | 2 | 1 | 9 | 32 | .155 |
| 2002 | San Jose (Cal) | A | 0 | 1 | 6.67 | 26 | 0 | 0 | 0 | 28 | 23 | 24 | 21 | 2 | 28 | 43 | .225 |
| 2003 | Norwich (EL) | AA | 0 | 0 | 15.88 | 11 | 0 | 0 | 0 | 11 | 15 | 20 | 20 | 1 | 21 | 16 | .306 |
| | Hagerstown (SAL) | A | 2 | 3 | 3.26 | 22 | 0 | 0 | 0 | 50 | 26 | 20 | 18 | 2 | 42 | 47 | .159 |
| 2004 | Did not play—Injured | | | | | | | | | | | | | | | | |
| 2005 | Norwich (EL) | AA | 1 | 2 | 5.06 | 30 | 0 | 0 | 2 | 43 | 43 | 28 | 24 | 2 | 31 | 35 | .259 |
| 2006 | Fresno (PCL) | AAA | 2 | 1 | 2.87 | 49 | 0 | 0 | 0 | 63 | 51 | 26 | 20 | 4 | 44 | 51 | .223 |
| **MINOR LEAGUE TOTALS** | | | 7 | 17 | 4.31 | 164 | 14 | 0 | 3 | 278 | 220 | 155 | 133 | 14 | 215 | 284 | .217 |

 ## BEN COPELAND                                                                   OF

**Born:** Dec. 17, 1983. **B-T:** L-L. **Ht.:** 6-1. **Wt.:** 195. **Drafted:** Pittsburgh, 2005 (4th round). **Signed by:** Sean O'Connor.

The Giants' top draft choice in 2005 (though not until the fourth round because of draft picks lost as free-agent compensation), Copeland played a full season in low Class A and his performance was in line with expectations. He makes consistent, squared-up contact, which is no surprise for a player who won a Big East Conference batting title, destroyed several Pitt

single-season offensive records and was a third-team All-America selection in 2005. He's considered a good athlete and a total package, but none of his tools stands out. He has quick hands and can turn on good fastballs, but he might need to get a little stronger to emerge as a No. 2 hitter in the big leagues. The Giants would also like Copeland to eliminate some of his many fly outs, which aren't a good match for his baserunning skills and instincts. He plays a good, instinctive center field with a playable throwing arm and good range thanks to his above-average speed. Copeland should have little trouble adjusting to high Class A this season.

| Year | Club (League) | Class | AVG | G | AB | R | H | 2B | 3B | HR | RBI | BB | SO | SB | OBP | SLG |
|------|---------------|-------|-----|---|----|---|---|----|----|----|-----|----|----|----|-----|-----|
| 2005 | Giants (AZL) | R | .333 | 18 | 60 | 16 | 20 | 4 | 2 | 1 | 14 | 5 | 14 | 2 | .388 | .517 |
| | Salem-Keizer (NWL) | A | .306 | 29 | 121 | 25 | 37 | 5 | 4 | 4 | 23 | 11 | 25 | 2 | .364 | .512 |
| 2006 | Augusta (SAL) | A | .281 | 135 | 527 | 90 | 148 | 29 | 12 | 5 | 71 | 73 | 90 | 30 | .368 | .410 |
| **MINOR LEAGUE TOTALS** | | | .290 | 182 | 708 | 131 | 205 | 38 | 18 | 10 | 108 | 89 | 129 | 34 | .369 | .436 |

## 26  BRIAN BOCOCK                                                2B/SS

**Born:** March 9, 1985. **B-T:** R-R. **Ht.:** 5-11. **Wt.:** 185. **Drafted:** Stetson, 2006 (9th round). **Signed by:** Glenn Tufts.

The Giants suddenly have a stockpile of burners in the middle infield, and Bocock might be the best pure playmaker among them. His defensive skills stood out even as he played alongside 33rd overall pick Emmanuel Burris at Salem-Keizer. Signed for $72,500 as a ninth-rounder, Bocock has excellent range, above-average hands and a strong arm that allows him to make plays deep in the hole. His skill set and quiet intensity remind some of former Giants infielder Mike Benjamin, and he had a good showing in instructional league. The Giants expect to take the slow road as Bocock learns to recognize offspeed pitches and develop a consistent approach. He struggled at the plate in his pro debut, over-rotating his shoulder and rolling over a lot of outside pitches. But as one coach said, "If we can make him a .260 hitter, he'll make a lot of money." He has sneaky gap power, but the Giants would be satisfied if he could make more consistent contact, drive balls up the middle and learn to drop a few bunt singles after he heads to a full-season affiliate. He'll probably begin the season in low Class A.

| Year | Club (League) | Class | AVG | G | AB | R | H | 2B | 3B | HR | RBI | BB | SO | SB | OBP | SLG |
|------|---------------|-------|-----|---|----|---|---|----|----|----|-----|----|----|----|-----|-----|
| 2006 | Salem-Keizer (NWL) | A | .223 | 39 | 103 | 12 | 23 | 6 | 0 | 0 | 7 | 12 | 29 | 6 | .305 | .282 |
| | Augusta (SAL) | A | .000 | 2 | 1 | 1 | 0 | 0 | 0 | 0 | 1 | 0 | 0 | 0 | .000 | .000 |
| **MINOR LEAGUE TOTALS** | | | .221 | 41 | 104 | 13 | 23 | 6 | 0 | 0 | 8 | 12 | 29 | 6 | .300 | .279 |

## 27  DAVID QUINOWSKI                                                LHP

**Born:** April 23, 1986. **B-T:** L-L. **Ht.:** 5-10. **Wt.:** 170. **Drafted:** Riverside (Calif.) CC, D/F 2004 (46th round). **Signed by:** Lee Carballo.

The Giants might have a scout running the concession stand at the Riverside Community College baseball field. Quinowski is one of several players the organization has snapped up from the program, including lefthander Ben Nieto and outfielder Thomas Neal. Like Neal, Quinowski signed as a draft-and-follow and struggled with his command in his pro debut, walking a batter an inning at Salem-Keizer in 2005. But when he arrived at low Class A last year, the Giants worked with him to shorten up a slow delivery and move from a high leg kick to a slide step. The unintended result was a deceptive motion that allows Quinowski to overpower hitters despite a fastball in the mid- to upper 80s. Even the better righthanders in the South Atlantic League had a hard time getting good swings on him. Quinowski also throws a plus changeup and continued to work on his breaking stuff in an assignment to Hawaii Winter Baseball, where he performed well. The Giants are also fond of another lefty reliever they picked up in the 2006 draft, Paul Oseguera, which could make Quinowski expendable in a trade. He's expected to begin in high Class A in 2007.

| Year | Club (League) | Class | W | L | ERA | G | GS | CG | SV | IP | H | R | ER | HR | BB | SO | AVG |
|------|---------------|-------|---|---|-----|---|----|----|----|----|---|---|----|----|----|----|-----|
| 2005 | Salem-Keizer (NWL) | A | 2 | 1 | 3.21 | 19 | 0 | 0 | 0 | 14 | 12 | 7 | 5 | 1 | 14 | 19 | .235 |
| 2006 | Augusta (SAL) | A | 4 | 2 | 1.43 | 44 | 0 | 0 | 4 | 75 | 36 | 14 | 12 | 1 | 24 | 76 | .145 |
| **MINOR LEAGUE TOTALS** | | | 6 | 3 | 1.71 | 63 | 0 | 0 | 4 | 89 | 48 | 21 | 17 | 2 | 38 | 95 | .160 |

## 28  DAN ORTMEIER                                                OF

**Born:** May 11, 1981. **B-T:** B-L. **Ht.:** 6-4. **Wt.:** 214. **Drafted:** Texas-Arlington, 2002 (3rd round). **Signed by:** Todd Thomas.

A perennial member of Giants prospect lists, Ortmeier retains his prospect status because his tools are undeniable. He's switch-hitter with a line-drive swing from both sides of the plate, above-average defense in right or center field, a plus arm and surprising speed for a

player his size. Ortmeier made a contribution at the big league level last season, hitting a game-tying pinch-hit single off the Dodgers' Danys Baez in the ninth inning of a game the Giants won 6-5. But he sat for a long stretch before the Giants returned him to Triple-A, and a poor showing there found him back in Double-A with bruised confidence. His lefthanded hitting mechanics were a mess, and pitchers noticed they could take advantage of his long, open stride and his tendency to rotate off pitches. As a result, he saw a lot of fastballs up and breaking balls away. While Ortmeier had a more consistent swing from the right side, he'll need to reestablish himself as a lefty hitter to move back into the Giants' plans. He competes well, always hustles and is one of the most likeable players in the system. He'll probably look for a fresh start in Triple-A this season.

| Year | Club (League) | Class | AVG | G | AB | R | H | 2B | 3B | HR | RBI | BB | SO | SB | OBP | SLG |
|------|---------------|-------|-----|---|----|---|---|----|----|----|-----|----|----|----|-----|-----|
| 2002 | Salem-Keizer (NWL) | A | .292 | 49 | 195 | 32 | 57 | 9 | 1 | 5 | 31 | 18 | 37 | 3 | .352 | .426 |
| 2003 | San Jose (Cal) | A | .304 | 115 | 408 | 62 | 124 | 32 | 6 | 8 | 56 | 39 | 89 | 13 | .378 | .471 |
| 2004 | Norwich (EL) | AA | .252 | 106 | 377 | 55 | 95 | 23 | 6 | 10 | 48 | 47 | 110 | 18 | .352 | .424 |
| 2005 | Norwich (EL) | AA | .274 | 135 | 503 | 85 | 138 | 23 | 6 | 20 | 79 | 48 | 115 | 35 | .360 | .463 |
|  | San Francisco (NL) | MLB | .136 | 15 | 22 | 1 | 3 | 0 | 0 | 0 | 1 | 3 | 5 | 1 | .269 | .136 |
| 2006 | Fresno (PCL) | AAA | .244 | 68 | 262 | 37 | 64 | 14 | 3 | 6 | 33 | 16 | 40 | 8 | .293 | .389 |
|  | San Francisco (NL) | MLB | .250 | 9 | 12 | 0 | 3 | 1 | 0 | 0 | 2 | 0 | 4 | 0 | .250 | .333 |
|  | Connecticut (EL) | AA | .251 | 47 | 167 | 17 | 42 | 9 | 1 | 2 | 11 | 17 | 38 | 7 | .328 | .353 |
| **MINOR LEAGUE TOTALS** | | | .247 | 115 | 429 | 54 | 106 | 23 | 4 | 8 | 44 | 33 | 78 | 15 | .307 | .375 |
| **MAJOR LEAGUE TOTALS** | | | .250 | 9 | 12 | 0 | 3 | 1 | 0 | 0 | 2 | 0 | 4 | 0 | .250 | .333 |

## 29 JOSE VALDEZ

RHP

**Born:** Aug. 1, 1988. **B-T:** R-R. **Ht.:** 6-7. **Wt.:** 190. **Drafted:** Dominican Republic, 2005. **Signed by:** Rick Ragazzo.

The Giants might restrict Valdez from drinking milk. He was listed at 6-foot-5 when he signed, but club officials say he had grown another inch or two by the time instructional league rolled around last fall. With Valdez' youth and size, the Giants have modest plans for him at present: to find a consistent delivery and repeat it. He had trouble repeating his arm slot during the Arizona League season, and his velocity was all over the board. When he's on his fastball is a plus-plus pitch in the mid-90s with good run and sink. Valdez made steady progress throwing competitive pitches, and he's starting to command a curveball. The Giants see him as a starter, and to that end, they hope to teach him a changeup. But that's probably down the road a bit. For now they want him to focus on the catcher's mitt with what he has. Valdez could be a standout in the Arizona League in 2007, and if he develops quickly could earn a ticket to Salem-Keizer.

| Year | Club (League) | Class | W | L | ERA | G | GS | CG | SV | IP | H | R | ER | HR | BB | SO | AVG |
|------|---------------|-------|---|---|-----|---|----|----|----|----|---|---|----|----|----|----|-----|
| 2005 | Giants (DSL) | R | 2 | 1 | 3.12 | 10 | 9 | 0 | 0 | 35 | 36 | 15 | 12 | 1 | 12 | 35 | .275 |
| 2006 | Giants (AZL) | R | 1 | 3 | 7.38 | 12 | 8 | 0 | 0 | 39 | 48 | 36 | 32 | 3 | 25 | 40 | .304 |
| **MINOR LEAGUE TOTALS** | | | 3 | 4 | 5.38 | 22 | 17 | 0 | 0 | 74 | 84 | 51 | 44 | 4 | 37 | 75 | .291 |

## 30 BRIAN HORWITZ

OF/1B

**Born:** Nov. 7, 1982. **B-T:** R-R. **Ht.:** 6-1. **Wt.:** 180. **Signed:** California, NDFA 2004. **Signed by:** Matt Nerland.

Horwitz was batting .324 when the Giants promoted him from high Class A to Double-A in June, spoiling any chance for him to win his third batting title in three pro seasons. But he wasn't complaining, and some in the organization believed that he should have been challenged that way to start the season after hitting .347 in short-season ball in 2004 and .349 in low Class A in 2005. Like many nondrafted free agents, Horwitz must continuarlly prove himself and he continues to do so, hitting at every level with his inside-out swing. He uses every inch between the chalk lines, keeps a consistent approach and has excelled with runners on base. He runs well enough to keep his bat moving up the system, and while he's not a polished left fielder, his arm grades a bit above average. Every manager who has had Horwitz on his team raves about him. He would project a little better if he could play another position. He played some first base last year, but he doesn't have the power to fit the profile there. He got a brief look at Triple-A in 2006 but might have to earn his way back there.

| Year | Club (League) | Class | AVG | G | AB | R | H | 2B | 3B | HR | RBI | BB | SO | SB | OBP | SLG |
|------|---------------|-------|-----|---|----|---|---|----|----|----|-----|----|----|----|-----|-----|
| 2004 | Salem-Keizer (NWL) | A | .347 | 71 | 268 | 41 | 93 | 24 | 1 | 2 | 44 | 21 | 34 | 3 | .407 | .466 |
| 2005 | Augusta (SAL) | A | .349 | 123 | 470 | 77 | 164 | 38 | 4 | 2 | 88 | 50 | 39 | 6 | .415 | .460 |
| 2006 | San Jose (Cal) | A | .324 | 56 | 207 | 26 | 67 | 11 | 2 | 2 | 31 | 30 | 23 | 0 | .414 | .425 |
|  | Fresno (PCL) | AAA | .125 | 5 | 16 | 1 | 2 | 1 | 0 | 0 | 1 | 2 | 2 | 0 | .222 | .188 |
|  | Connecticut (EL) | AA | .286 | 78 | 269 | 23 | 77 | 9 | 1 | 2 | 29 | 31 | 35 | 3 | .365 | .349 |
| **MINOR LEAGUE TOTALS** | | | .297 | 139 | 492 | 50 | 146 | 21 | 3 | 4 | 61 | 63 | 60 | 3 | .381 | .376 |

# SEATTLE
# MARINERS

BY **JIM CALLIS**

Bill Bavasi helped lay the foundation for a 2002 World Series championship as Angels general manager from 1994-99, but he has struggled in three years as Mariners general manager. Bavasi's Seattle clubs have averaged 70 wins per season, a steep drop from the 98 victories the M's averaged in four years under his predecessor, Pat Gillick.

 Seattle has gone from 63 wins to 69 to 78 under Bavasi, but that incremental progress hasn't been enough to get out of last place. The Mariners were a tease in 2006. They were 41-39 and just two games back in the American League West on June 30, when they traded one of their top infield prospects, Asdrubal Cabrera, to the Indians for platoon DH Eduardo Perez. By July 26, Seattle had dropped into last place, yet Bavasi dealt another of his best prospects, outfielder Shin-Soo Choo, in a deal to get the other half of Cleveland's DH platoon, Ben Broussard.

With dreams of contending again in the offseason, Bavasi continued to make more short-sighted deals. He dispatched live-armed Rafael Soriano to the Braves for Horacio Ramirez, then trumped that by picking up Jose Vidro from the Nationals for Chris Snelling and Emiliano Fruto.

The highlight of Bavasi's tenure has been the major league ascendancy of homegrown prospects Yuniesky Betancourt, Felix Hernandez, Jose Lopez and **J.J. Putz**. But all of them except for Betancourt were signed by the previous front-office regime, as was their latest phenom, outfielder Adam Jones. Bavasi has tried to put his stamp on the club by signing big-ticket free agents Adrian

Beltre ($64 million), Richie Sexson ($50 million) and Jarrod Washburn ($37.5 million), but they haven't lived up to their contracts or changed Seattle's fortunes.

Because the Mariners' major league record has been so poor, free-agent compensation rules have protected their recent first-round picks after they forfeited four of them and failed to sign a fifth from 2000-04. Seattle took catcher Jeff Clement with the No. 3 choice in 2005 and righthander Brandon Morrow at No. 5 in 2006, selections it hopes will help reverse a series of poor drafts that have undermined the farm system. Most of the Mariners' recent top prospects have been the results of their efforts on the international scouting market.

More losing won't be tolerated. The day after he announced that Bavasi and manager Mike Hargrove would return in 2007, M's chairman and CEO Howard Lincoln said he expected a dramatic turnaround. That will be difficult, considering Seattle finished next to last in the AL in scoring and won't bring back two of the top starters (Jamie Moyer and free agent Gil Meche) on its pitching staff.

"I don't want to leave any doubt in anybody's mind," Lincoln said. "Mike Hargrove and Bill Bavasi are on my hot seat, and I expect that they are going to work even harder than they're already working to produce the results the fans and, I think, the ownership group expects."

## TOP 30 PROSPECTS

1. Adam Jones, of
2. Jeff Clement, c
3. Brandon Morrow
4. Tony Butler, lhp
5. Ryan Feierabend, lhp
6. Wladimir Balentien, of
7. Mark Lowe, rhp
8. Chris Tillman, rhp
9. Yung-Chi Chen, 2b
10. Eric O'Flaherty, lhp
11. Carlos Triunfel, ss
12. Justin Thomas, lhp
13. Jon Huber, rhp
14. Michael Wilson, of
15. Rob Johnson, c
16. Bryan LaHair, 1b
17. Matt Tuiasosopo, 3b/ss
18. Stephen Kahn, rhp
19. Anthony Varvaro, rhp
20. Luis Valbuena, 2b
21. Jose de la Cruz, rhp
22. Travis Blackley, lhp
23. Robert Rohrbaugh, lhp
24. Michael Saunders, of
25. Greg Halman, of
26. Alex Liddi, 3b
27. Carlos Peguero, of
28. Cesar Jimenez, lhp
29. Oswaldo Navarro, ss
30. Michael Garciaparra, 2b

# ORGANIZATION OVERVIEW

**General manager:** Bill Bavasi. **Farm director:** Benny Looper. **Scouting director:** Bob Fontaine.

## 2006 PERFORMANCE

| Class | Team | League | W | L | PCT | Finish* | Manager | Affiliated |
|---|---|---|---|---|---|---|---|---|
| Majors | Seattle | American | 78 | 84 | .481 | 10th (14) | Mike Hargrove | — |
| Triple-A | Tacoma Rainiers | Pacific Coast | 74 | 70 | .514 | 7th (16) | Dave Brundage | 1995 |
| Double-A | #San Antonio Missions | Texas | 60 | 78 | .435 | 7th (8) | Daren Brown | 2001 |
| High A | †Inland Empire 66ers | California | 72 | 68 | .514 | +5th (10) | Gary Thurman | 2001 |
| Low A | Wisconsin Timber Rattlers | Midwest | 54 | 86 | .386 | 13th (14) | Jim Horner | 1993 |
| Short-season | Everett AquaSox | Northwest | 31 | 45 | .408 | 6th (8) | Dave Myers | 1995 |
| Rookie | AZL Mariners | Arizona | 25 | 30 | .455 | 5th (9) | Dana Williams | 2001 |
| **OVERALL 2006 MINOR LEAGUE RECORD** | | | 316 | 377 | .456 | 27th (30) | | |

*Finish in overall standings (No. of teams in league). +League champion. #Affiliate will be in West Tenn (Southern) in 2007. †Affiliate will be in High Desert (California) in 2007.

## ORGANIZATION LEADERS

### BATTING
| | | |
|---|---|---|
| AVG | Chen, Yung Chi, I. Empire/AZL/San Antonio | .324 |
| R | Johnson, Brent, Inland Empire | 82 |
| H | LaHair, Bryan, San Antonio/Tacoma | 145 |
| 2B | Hubbard, Thomas, I. Empire/San Antonio | 32 |
| 3B | Boucher, Sebastien, San Antonio | 9 |
| | Womack, Josh, Inland Empire | 9 |
| HR | Wilson, Michael, Inland Empire/San Antonio | 23 |
| RBI | Wilson, Michael, Inland Empire/San Antonio | 95 |
| BB | Boucher, Sebastien, San Antonio | 73 |
| SO | Wilson, Michael, Inland Empire/San Antonio | 156 |
| SB | Boucher, Sebastien, San Antonio | 27 |
| | Sabatella, Bryan, Wisconsin/Everett | 27 |
| OBP | White, Joseph, Everett | .424 |
| SLG | Peguero, Carlos, AZL Mariners/Everett | .520 |
| XBH | Wilson, Michael, Inland Empire/San Antonio | 56 |

### PITCHING
| | | |
|---|---|---|
| W | Thomas, Justin, Wisconsin/Inland Empire | 14 |
| L | Fagan, Paul, Wisconsin | 14 |
| ERA | Salinas, Doug, AZL Mariners | 2.84 |
| G | Woerman, Joseph, Wisconsin/Inland Empire | 61 |
| SV | Huber, Jon, San Antonio/Tacoma | 23 |
| IP | Thomas, Justin, Wisconsin/Inland Empire | 166 |
| BB | Bello, Cibney, Inland Empire | 82 |
| SO | Cruceta, Francisco, Tacoma | 185 |
| AVG | Salinas, Doug, AZL Mariners | .219 |

## BEST TOOLS

| | |
|---|---|
| Best Hitter for Average | Yung-Chi Chen |
| Best Power Hitter | Jeff Clement |
| Best Strike-Zone Discipline | Brent Johnson |
| Fastest Baserunner | Sebastien Boucher |
| Best Athlete | Adam Jones |
| Best Fastball | Brandon Morrow |
| Best Curveball | Tony Butler |
| Best Slider | Mark Lowe |
| Best Changeup | Ryan Feierabend |
| Best Control | Ryan Feierabend |
| Best Defensive Catcher | Rob Johnson |
| Best Defensive Infielder | Oswaldo Navarro |
| Best Infield Arm | Carlos Triunfel |
| Best Defensive Outfielder | Adam Jones |
| Best Outfield Arm | Adam Jones |

## PROJECTED 2010 LINEUP

| | |
|---|---|
| Catcher | Kenji Johjima |
| First Base | Richie Sexson |
| Second Base | Jose Lopez |
| Third Base | Adrian Beltre |
| Shortstop | Yuniesky Betancourt |
| Left Field | Wladimir Balentien |
| Center Field | Ichiro Suzuki |
| Right Field | Adam Jones |
| Designated Hitter | Jeff Clement |
| No. 1 Starter | Felix Hernandez |
| No. 2 Starter | Brandon Morrow |
| No. 3 Starter | Tony Butler |
| No. 4 Starter | Ryan Feierabend |
| No. 5 Starter | Chris Tillman |
| Closer | J.J. Putz |

## LAST YEAR'S TOP 20 PROSPECTS

1. Jeff Clement, c
2. Adam Jones, of/ss
3. Kenji Johjima, c
4. Chris Snelling, of
5. Matt Tuiasosopo, ss
6. Asdrubal Cabrera, ss
7. Shin-Soo Choo, of
8. Emiliano Fruto, rhp
9. Clint Nageotte, rhp
10. Rob Johnson, c
11. Wladimir Balentien, of
12. Michael Saunders, of
13. Yorman Bazardo, rhp
14. Luis Valbuena, 2b
15. Stephen Kahn, rhp
16. Ryan Feierabend, lhp
17. Cesar Jimenez, lhp
18. Bobby Livingston, lhp
19. Sebastien Boucher, of
20. T.J. Bohn, of

## TOP PROSPECTS OF THE DECADE

| Year | Player, Pos. | 2006 Org. |
|---|---|---|
| 1997 | Jose Cruz Jr., of | Dodgers |
| 1998 | Ryan Anderson, lhp | Out of baseball |
| 1999 | Ryan Anderson, lhp | Out of baseball |
| 2000 | Ryan Anderson, lhp | Out of baseball |
| 2001 | Ryan Anderson, lhp | Out of baseball |
| 2002 | Ryan Anderson, lhp | Out of baseball |
| 2003 | Rafael Soriano, rhp | Mariners |
| 2004 | Felix Hernandez, rhp | Mariners |
| 2005 | Felix Hernandez, rhp | Mariners |
| 2006 | Jeff Clement, c | Mariners |

## TOP DRAFT PICKS OF THE DECADE

| Year | Player, Pos. | 2006 Org. |
|---|---|---|
| 1997 | Ryan Anderson, lhp | Out of baseball |
| 1998 | Matt Thornton, lhp | White Sox |
| 1999 | Ryan Christianson, c | Devil Rays |
| 2000 | Sam Hays, lhp (4th round) | Out of baseball |
| 2001 | Michael Garciaparra, ss | Mariners |
| 2002 | *John Mayberry Jr., of | Rangers |
| 2003 | Adam Jones, ss/rhp | Mariners |
| 2004 | Matt Tuiasosopo, ss | Mariners |
| 2005 | Jeff Clement, c | Mariners |
| 2006 | Brandon Morrow, rhp | Mariners |

*Did not sign.

## ALL-TIME LARGEST BONUSES

| | |
|---|---|
| Ichiro Suzuki, 2000 | $5,000,000 |
| Jeff Clement, 2005 | $3,400,000 |
| Brandon Morrow, 2006 | $2,450,000 |
| Matt Tuiasosopo, 2004 | $2,290,000 |
| Ryan Anderson, 1997 | $2,175,000 |

## Seattle Mariners

**Impact: C.** The Mariners have some impact talent, led by Adam Jones. Hard-throwing Brandon Morrow and powerful catcher Jeff Clement have big tools but erratic track records of performance.

**Depth: D.** A slew of poor drafts, long covered up by an even bigger slew of international signings, has caught up to the organization, leaving it dangerously thin at the upper levels. A pair of 2006 trades that gave up three players for a pair of Indians DHs didn't help.

**Sleeper:** Graham Godfrey, rhp. Though the sophomore-eligible draftee has not yet thrown a pro pitch, his fastball-curveball combo could enable him to shoot into next year's top 10.

*Numbers in parentheses indicate prospect rankings.*

| LF | CF | RF |
|---|---|---|
| Michael Wilson (14) | Adam Jones (1) | Wladimir Balentien (6) |
| Casey Craig | Greg Halman (25) | Michael Saunders (24) |
| Jon Nelson | Kuo-Hui Lo | Carlos Peguero (27) |
| | Sebastien Boucher | Kalian Sams |
| | Brent Johnson | Josh Womack |
| | Welington Dotel | |

| 3B | SS | 2B | 1B |
|---|---|---|---|
| Matt Tuiasosopo (17) | Carlos Triunfel (11) | Yung-Chi Chen (9) | Bryan LaHair (16) |
| Alex Liddi (26) | Oswaldo Navarro (29) | Luis Valbuena (20) | Gerardo Avila |
| | Mario Martinez | Michael Garciaparra (30) | |
| | | Chris Minaker | |

| C |
|---|
| Jeff Clement (2) |
| Rob Johnson (15) |
| Adam Moore |

| RHP | | LHP | |
|---|---|---|---|
| **Starters** | **Relievers** | **Starters** | **Relievers** |
| Brandon Morrow (3) | Mark Lowe (7) | Tony Butler (4) | Eric O'Flaherty (10) |
| Chris Tillman (8) | Jon Huber (13) | Ryan Feierabend (5) | Cesar Jimenez (28) |
| Anthony Varvaro (19) | Stephen Kahn (18) | Justin Thomas (12) | Ryan Rowland-Smith |
| Andrew Baldwin | Jose de la Cruz (21) | Travis Blackley (22) | |
| Doug Fister | Kam Mickolio | Robert Rohrbaugh (23) | |
| Ricky Orta | Austin Dirkx | Bobby Livingston | |
| Doug Salinas | Andrew Barb | Steve Uhlmansiek | |
| Juan Carlos Ramirez | Joe Woerman | Jose Escalona | |
| Victor Duarte | Travis Chick | | |
| | Yorman Bazardo | | |

# DRAFT ANALYSIS

## 2006
SIGNING BUDGET: $4.4 million

**Best Pro Debut:** Though he was an 18-year-old from the non-hotbed of Wisconsin, LHP Tony Butler (3) pitched as well in the Northwest League as he did in Rookie ball, going a combined 3-2, 2.72 with 77 strikeouts in 56 innings. RHP Austin Dirkx (16) had a 1.64 ERA, five saves and 49 strikeouts in 38 innings—including five whiffs in a two-inning Triple-A stint.

**Best Athlete:** OF Gavin Dickey (12) was a backup quarterback at Florida. He's still raw with the bat, but he has arm strength and uses his speed well on the bases and in the outfield.

**Best Pure Hitter:** SS Chris Minaker (10) improved in each of his four years at Stanford, setting career highs across the board as a senior last spring. He continued to hit in pro ball, batting .315 with four homers in 40 games in low Class A.

**Best Raw Power:** The Mariners knew that C Adam Moore (6), who missed all of 2005 with a knee injury, had power. They've also been pleased with the improvement he has shown throwing and receiving since turning pro, and they believe he can stay behind the plate.

**Fastest Runner:** Dickey has plus speed and stole 16 bases in 18 attempts in pro ball.

**Best Defensive Player:** Seattle didn't sign any premium defenders. Dickey still needs work on his routes and instincts, but he has the potential become an above-average center fielder.

**Best Fastball:** The Mariners needed power arms and they tried to load up on them. RHP Brandon Morrow (1) pitches in the mid-90s and has topped out at 99 mph. Butler worked at 86-87 mph for much of the spring before suddenly soaring to 93-95 mph, and he stayed there in pro ball. RHPs Justin Souza (9) and Aaron Solomon (11) have touched 96, while RHPs Chris Tillman (2) and Ricky Orta (4) can get to 94.

**Best Breaking Ball:** Tillman and Butler have a chance to develop outstanding breaking pitches. Tillman has more power to his slider, while Butler's curveball is tough on righthanders because it breaks down and in on them.

**Most Intriguing Background:** Minaker not only graduated from Stanford, but he completed a master's degree in sociology in his four years there. OF Stan Posluszny's (34) brother Paul is a Penn State football star who won the Bednarik (nation's top defend-er) and Butkus (nation's top linebacker) awards in 2005. Unsigned RHP Bryan Earley's (44) father Bill pitched briefly in the big leagues. LHP Greg Moviel's (26) brother Paul pitches in the White Sox system.

**Closest To The Majors:** Morrow, who has a mid-80s slider to go with his heat, projects as a future closer and may not need much more than a full season in the minors before he's ready for Seattle.

**Best Late-Round Pick:** Dirkx' sinker and slider move so much that hitters have trouble making hard contact against him. RHP Kam Mickolio (18) can get inconsistent with his delivery, but he's 6-foot-9 and has flashed a 92-93 mph fastball.

**The One Who Got Away:** 3B Jared Baehl (14) was a two-way and football star in high school. His power potential is his best feature, and he'll show it off at Evansville.

**Assessment:** The Mariners addressed the lack of pitching in their system by signing arms with their first five and eight of their first 10 selections. Butler looks like one of the steals of the draft to this point.

## 2005
BUDGET: $4.1 million

For the first time since 1999, the Mariners had a true first-round choice. They selected power-hitting C Jeff Clement (1) and LHP Justin Thomas (4) with their top two picks, and so far they haven't regretted either decision. **GRADE: B**

## 2004
BUDGET: $3.2 million

Without picks in the first two rounds, Seattle gave 3B/SS Matt Tuiasosopo (3) $2.29 million to buy him away from football, and he hasn't lived up to his bonus yet. RHP Mark Lowe (5) had a breakthrough 2006, but it ended with major elbow surgery. **GRADE: C**

## 2003
BUDGET: $2.8 million

Some teams would have made OF Adam Jones (1) a pitcher, but he has become the system's best prospect as an everyday player. LHPs Ryan Feierabend (3) and Erik O'Flaherty (6) went from high school to the majors in three years. **GRADE: B**

*Draft analysis by Jim Callis. Numbers in parentheses indicate draft rounds. Budgets are bonuses in first 10 rounds.*

# ADAM JONES

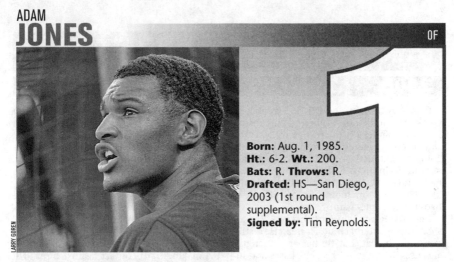

**Born:** Aug. 1, 1985.
**Ht.:** 6-2. **Wt.:** 200.
**Bats:** R. **Throws:** R.
**Drafted:** HS—San Diego, 2003 (1st round supplemental).
**Signed by:** Tim Reynolds.

W hen Seattle took Jones with the 37th overall pick in 2003, it put an end to a dismal string of top draft choices that began with Ryan Anderson in 1997. Many teams preferred Jones as a pitcher after seeing him top out at 96 mph in high school, but he wanted to play every day and the Mariners granted his wish after signing him for $925,000. Jones has improved steadily as he has climbed the minor league ladder, and he has quickened his pace the last two seasons, opening 2005 at high Class A Inland Empire and reaching Seattle in mid-2006. Changing positions didn't slow him down. Jones spent his three years in pro ball at shortstop, but Yuniesky Betancourt seized that spot with the Mariners thanks to his defensive wizardry. Jones played two games in the outfield at the end of the 2005 season and worked on his center-field skills in the Arizona Fall League. In his first full year at the position, managers rated Jones the best defensive outfielder in the Triple-A Pacific Coast League.

Jones has drawn Mike Cameron comparisons since changing positions. He's an excellent athlete who has gotten both stronger and quicker since turning pro. He has increased his power output each year and still has room to add another 20 pounds to his frame. He's an above-average runner, a long strider who's more effective taking an extra base rather than stealing one. The Mariners believe he can become a consistent 20-20 man like Cameron, and that might be a conservative estimate of Jones' power. He also has the tools to emulate Cameron and become a Gold Glove outfielder. Jones tracks balls very well, covers plenty of ground and has one of the strongest center-field arms in the game. He recorded five assists in 26 major league games. If needed Jones also could return to shortstop and become at least a solid-average defender there. He has shown a strong work ethic and the ability to adapt to tougher competition throughout his pro career.

Jones can be too aggressive for his own good. Plate discipline never has been his strong suit, and the biggest difference between him and Cameron is that Cameron walks more. Jones swings and misses enough that he may not hit for a high average and will pile up some strikeouts, though he's still young enough to make further adjustments. Breaking balls still give him trouble on occasion. Defensively, he can improve his routes, especially on balls hit over his heads. He made some errors early in 2006 due to too many needless throws.

One of the youngest and best players from his 2003 draft class, Jones has the ability to become a much-needed building block for the Mariners. He could use a little more time to polish his game, so he probably will open 2007 at Triple-A Tacoma. When he returns to Seattle, he could face another position switch. The Mariners plan on playing Ichiro in center field, so Jones could move to right, where he has played briefly in the minors.

| Year | Club (League) | Class | AVG | G | AB | R | H | 2B | 3B | HR | RBI | BB | SO | SB | OBP | SLG |
|------|---------------|-------|-----|---|-----|---|---|----|----|----|-----|----|----|----|-----|-----|
| 2003 | Mariners (AZL) | R | .284 | 28 | 109 | 18 | 31 | 5 | 1 | 0 | 8 | 5 | 19 | 5 | .368 | .349 |
| | Everett (NWL) | A | .462 | 3 | 13 | 2 | 6 | 1 | 0 | 0 | 4 | 1 | 3 | 0 | .467 | .538 |
| 2004 | Wisconsin (MWL) | A | .267 | 130 | 510 | 76 | 136 | 23 | 7 | 11 | 72 | 33 | 124 | 8 | .314 | .404 |
| 2005 | Inland Empire (Cal) | A | .295 | 68 | 271 | 43 | 80 | 20 | 5 | 8 | 46 | 29 | 64 | 4 | .374 | .494 |
| | San Antonio (TL) | AA | .298 | 63 | 228 | 33 | 68 | 10 | 3 | 7 | 20 | 22 | 48 | 9 | .365 | .461 |
| 2006 | Tacoma (PCL) | AAA | .287 | 96 | 380 | 69 | 109 | 19 | 4 | 16 | 62 | 28 | 78 | 13 | .345 | .484 |
| | Seattle (AL) | MLB | .216 | 32 | 74 | 6 | 16 | 4 | 0 | 1 | 8 | 2 | 22 | 3 | .237 | .311 |
| **MINOR LEAGUE TOTALS** | | | .285 | 388 | 1511 | 241 | 430 | 78 | 20 | 42 | 212 | 118 | 336 | 39 | .346 | .446 |
| **MAJOR LEAGUE TOTALS** | | | .216 | 32 | 74 | 6 | 16 | 4 | 0 | 1 | 8 | 2 | 22 | 3 | .237 | .311 |

## 2 JEFF CLEMENT  C

**Born:** Aug. 21, 1983. **B-T:** L-R. **Ht.:** 6-2. **Wt.:** 215. **Drafted:** Southern California, 2005 (1st round). **Signed by:** Greg Whitworth.

The third overall pick in the 2005 draft, Clement signed for a Mariners draft-record $3.4 million. His first full pro season was interrupted for seven weeks when he needed May operations to repair a torn meniscus in his left knee and remove a bone chip from his left elbow. When he returned, Seattle promoted him to Triple-A, where he predictably struggled. Power is Clement's calling card. He broke Drew Henson's national prep mark with 75 career homers, then hit 46 more in three years at Southern California, eight shy of Mark McGwire's school record. Clement shortened his swing in 2005 and should hit for a solid average as well. He has worked hard to improve as a catcher, and Seattle believes he'll become an average defender. Scouts from outside the organization have less faith in Clement's athletic and catching ability, and he definitely needs to get better behind the plate. He has an average arm but doesn't always get his feet set, costing him strength and accuracy. He threw out just 26 percent of basestealers in 2006. He's a below-average runner. Clement concluded his year by hitting .189 in Hawaii Winter Baseball, but the Mariners expect him to rebound in 2007. They want to get his bat into their big league lineup as soon as possible, though he may have to break in as a DH with Kenji Johjima at catcher and Richie Sexson at first base. For now, Clement will stay behind the plate and open the season in Triple-A.

| Year | Club (League) | Class | AVG | G | AB | R | H | 2B | 3B | HR | RBI | BB | SO | SB | OBP | SLG |
|------|---------------|-------|-----|---|----|---|---|----|----|----|-----|----|----|----|-----|-----|
| 2005 | Wisconsin (MWL) | A | .319 | 30 | 113 | 17 | 36 | 5 | 0 | 6 | 20 | 12 | 25 | 1 | .386 | .522 |
| 2006 | San Antonio (TL) | AA | .288 | 15 | 59 | 7 | 17 | 6 | 1 | 2 | 10 | 7 | 8 | 0 | .386 | .525 |
| | Tacoma (PCL) | AAA | .257 | 67 | 245 | 23 | 63 | 10 | 0 | 4 | 32 | 16 | 53 | 0 | .321 | .347 |
| **MINOR LEAGUE TOTALS** | | | .278 | 112 | 417 | 47 | 116 | 21 | 1 | 12 | 62 | 35 | 86 | 1 | .348 | .420 |

## 3 BRANDON MORROW  RHP

**Born:** July 26, 1984. **B-T:** R-R. **Ht.:** 6-3. **Wt.:** 190. **Drafted:** California, 2006 (1st round). **Signed by:** Stacey Pettis.

Morrow posted a 7.57 ERA over his first two seasons at California before emerging as a prime prospect in the Cape Cod League in 2005. He became the highest draft pick in school history, going fifth overall last June and signing for $2.45 million. A diabetic, he wears an insulin pump when not on the mound and monitors his blood sugar during games. His condition shouldn't limit him in baseball. Morrow is a true power pitcher. He has a mid-90s fastball that has reached 99 mph, and he maintains his velocity into the late innings. He backs up his heat with a mid-80s slider and a hard splitter. While some teams projected Morrow as a closer, the Mariners will try to make him a starter. To stay in the rotation, Morrow will need to improve his command and feel for pitching. He'll also have to refine his barely-used changeup, and while he works on that pitch Seattle will limit how many splitters he throws. Soreness in his forearm limited him to 16 innings in his pro debut. Morrow returned to the mound in September and was lights out in a three-inning stint in high Class A. He may return to that level with the M's new High Desert affiliate or open 2007 in Double-A West Tenn. If his command and changeup improve quickly, he could reach the majors in 2008.

| Year | Club (League) | Class | W | L | ERA | G | GS | CG | SV | IP | H | R | ER | HR | BB | SO | AVG |
|------|---------------|-------|---|---|-----|---|----|----|----|----|---|---|----|----|----|----|-----|
| 2006 | Mariners (AZL) | R | 0 | 2 | 2.77 | 7 | 4 | 0 | 0 | 13 | 10 | 4 | 4 | 0 | 9 | 13 | .227 |
| | Inland Empire (Cal) | A | 0 | 0 | 0.00 | 1 | 1 | 0 | 0 | 3 | 0 | 0 | 0 | 0 | 0 | 4 | .000 |
| **MINOR LEAGUE TOTALS** | | | 0 | 2 | 2.25 | 8 | 5 | 0 | 0 | 16 | 10 | 4 | 4 | 0 | 9 | 17 | .189 |

## 4 TONY BUTLER  LHP

**Born:** Nov. 18, 1987. **B-T:** L-L. **Ht.:** 6-7. **Wt.:** 205. **Drafted:** HS—Oak Creek, Wis., 2006 (3rd round). **Signed by:** Joe Bohringer.

Butler spent much of the spring pitching at 86-87 mph, and the consensus was that his projection wasn't enough to warrant buying him away from an Arkansas scholarship. But area scout Joe Bohringer and Midwest supervisor Ken Madeja stayed on Butler, who suddenly jumped to 94-95 right before the draft. Seattle stole him with a third-round pick and signed him for $445,000. Butler maintained his newfound velocity in his debut, working at 89-92 mph and touching 95. His fastball has late life and he uses his 6-foot-7 frame to leverage it down in the strike zone. He also can buck-

le knees with his 76-80 mph curveball, which already ranks as the best in the system. He has feel for a changeup with late fade and deception. Mature and intelligent, he showed no fear while blowing away hitters at two levels. While Butler has made some adjustments to his mechanics, becoming more fluid and reducing the stress on his shoulder, he still can improve the timing with his leg drive. His changeup and control need more consistency, as he walked 34 batters in 56 pro innings. Butler will open his first pro season in his native Wisconsin, and if he pitches like he did last summer he won't stay long in low Class A. He has a ceiling as a No. 2 starter.

| Year | Club (League) | Class | W | L | ERA | G | GS | CG | SV | IP | H | R | ER | HR | BB | SO | AVG |
|------|---------------|-------|---|---|-----|---|----|----|----|----|---|---|----|----|----|----|-----|
| 2006 | Mariners (AZL) | R | 2 | 0 | 2.57 | 5 | 3 | 0 | 0 | 14 | 5 | 4 | 4 | 0 | 9 | 25 | .116 |
| | Everett (NWL) | A | 1 | 2 | 2.76 | 9 | 9 | 0 | 0 | 42 | 23 | 16 | 13 | 2 | 25 | 52 | .160 |
| **MINOR LEAGUE TOTALS** | | | 3 | 2 | 2.72 | 14 | 12 | 0 | 0 | 56 | 28 | 20 | 17 | 2 | 34 | 77 | .150 |

## 5 RYAN FEIERABEND                                         LHP

**Born:** Aug. 22, 1985. **B-T:** L-L. **Ht.:** 6-3. **Wt.:** 190. **Drafted:** HS—Grafton, Ohio, 2003 (3rd round). **Signed by:** Ken Madeja.

The youngest regular starting pitcher in the high Class A California and Double-A Texas leagues the last two seasons, Feierabend also became the youngest rookie pitcher in the majors when Seattle called him up in September. With Felix Hernandez, Feierabend and Adam Jones, the Mariners had three of the four youngest players in the big leagues in 2006. Feierabend has the best command in the system. His best pitch is his circle changeup, which he sets up with an 88-92 mph fastball that he can sink or cut. He's athletic and still has some projection remaining in his lanky frame. His pickoff move is as good as any in the game, as he has led each of his full-season leagues in basestealers caught and has permitted just three swipes in 33 attempts over the last two years. Feierabend has made strides with his breaking pitch but still seeks a truly reliable third pitch. He throws both a slider and a curveball, with the slider rating a slight edge. His delivery can get inconsistent, as he sometimes lands awkwardly on the side of his front foot. His maturity, intelligence and work ethic have allowed Feierabend to move quickly. While he'll probably spend most of 2007 in Triple-A, the Mariners trust he'll respond well if needed in the majors. He's not overpowering but should become a solid No. 4 starter.

| Year | Club (League) | Class | W | L | ERA | G | GS | CG | SV | IP | H | R | ER | HR | BB | SO | AVG |
|------|---------------|-------|---|---|-----|---|----|----|----|----|---|---|----|----|----|----|-----|
| 2003 | Mariners (AZL) | R | 2 | 3 | 2.61 | 6 | 5 | 0 | 1 | 21 | 23 | 11 | 6 | 0 | 6 | 12 | .288 |
| 2004 | Wisconsin (MWL) | A | 9 | 7 | 3.63 | 26 | 26 | 1 | 0 | 161 | 158 | 78 | 65 | 17 | 44 | 106 | .263 |
| 2005 | Inland Empire (Cal) | A | 8 | 7 | 3.88 | 29 | 29 | 0 | 0 | 151 | 186 | 80 | 65 | 16 | 51 | 122 | .310 |
| 2006 | San Antonio (TL) | AA | 9 | 12 | 4.28 | 28 | 28 | 0 | 0 | 154 | 156 | 87 | 73 | 16 | 55 | 127 | .267 |
| | Seattle (AL) | MLB | 0 | 1 | 3.71 | 4 | 2 | 0 | 0 | 17 | 15 | 7 | 7 | 3 | 7 | 11 | .231 |
| **MINOR LEAGUE TOTALS** | | | 28 | 29 | 3.87 | 89 | 88 | 1 | 1 | 486 | 523 | 256 | 209 | 49 | 156 | 367 | .280 |
| **MAJOR LEAGUE TOTALS** | | | 0 | 1 | 3.71 | 4 | 2 | 0 | 0 | 17 | 15 | 7 | 7 | 3 | 7 | 11 | .231 |

## 6 WLADIMIR BALENTIEN                                      OF

**Born:** July 2, 1984. **B-T:** R-R. **Ht.:** 6-2. **Wt.:** 190. **Signed:** Curacao, 2000. **Signed by:** Karel Williams.

Balentien arrived in the United States by hitting a Rookie-level Arizona League-record 16 homers in 2004, and he has been crushing homers and striking out in bunches ever since. A member of the 2004 Dutch Olympic team, he won San Antonio's MVP award and the Texas League home run derby in 2006. He also smacked two doubles in the Futures Game. Few players in the game can match Balentien's raw power. Though his approach remains simplistic, he made progress in 2006 with his plate discipline (more than doubling his career high in walks) and using the opposite field. Far from a one-dimensional slugger, he has average speed and a plus arm that managers rated the best among TL outfielders. A right fielder who can play some center, he led the league with 17 outfield assists. Balentien's all-out, all-the-time approach limits his ability to make contact and hit for average. He'll chase any pitch he can reach, and he swings so hard that he'll pull his head off the ball. His stroke is long, he can be helpless against breaking stuff and he doesn't adjust when he falls behind in the count. He can get out of control in the field as well, topping TL outfielders with 11 errors. Balentien's power is undeniable, but how usable it will be in the majors remains in question. The Mariners love his ceiling and will hope he can find a more balanced approach this year in Triple-A.

| Year | Club (League) | Class | AVG | G | AB | R | H | 2B | 3B | HR | RBI | BB | SO | SB | OBP | SLG |
|------|---------------|-------|-----|---|----|----|----|----|----|----|-----|----|----|----|------|------|
| 2001 | Aguirre (VSL) | R | .206 | 53 | 131 | 27 | 27 | 2 | 1 | 0 | 9 | 25 | 48 | 7 | .333 | .237 |
| 2002 | Aguirre (VSL) | R | .279 | 59 | 197 | 41 | 55 | 13 | 4 | 10 | 39 | 34 | 52 | 6 | .390 | .538 |
| 2003 | Mariners (AZL) | R | .283 | 50 | 187 | 42 | 53 | 12 | 5 | 16 | 52 | 22 | 55 | 4 | .363 | .658 |
| 2004 | Wisconsin (MWL) | A | .277 | 76 | 260 | 39 | 72 | 12 | 3 | 15 | 46 | 12 | 77 | 10 | .315 | .519 |
|  | Inland Empire (Cal) | A | .289 | 10 | 38 | 5 | 11 | 1 | 0 | 2 | 5 | 4 | 10 | 1 | .357 | .474 |
| 2005 | Inland Empire (Cal) | A | .291 | 123 | 492 | 76 | 143 | 38 | 8 | 25 | 93 | 33 | 160 | 9 | .338 | .553 |
| 2006 | San Antonio (TL) | AA | .230 | 121 | 444 | 76 | 102 | 23 | 1 | 22 | 82 | 70 | 140 | 14 | .337 | .435 |
| **MINOR LEAGUE TOTALS** | | | .265 | 492 | 1749 | 306 | 463 | 101 | 22 | 90 | 326 | 200 | 542 | 51 | .344 | .502 |

## 7  MARK LOWE

RHP

STEVE MOORE

**Born:** June 7, 1983. **B-T:** R-R. **Ht.:** 6-3. **Wt.:** 190. **Drafted:** Texas-Arlington, 2004 (5th round). **Signed by:** Mark Lummus.

Lowe's first full pro season was rough, as he posted a 5.47 ERA as a starter in low Class A in 2005. Moved to the bullpen in 2006, he was named Seattle's minor league pitcher of the year after needing just three months to go from high Class A to the majors. Lowe always projected as a reliever and his stuff jumped when he switched roles. His fastball went from 89-93 mph to a consistent 94-96 with quality life. His hard slider has late, quick break and chews up righthanders. He also has a change-up for lefties, and all three of his pitches are plus-plus at times. Lowe did a better job of throwing strikes when he didn't have to worry about doing anything more than cutting loose in short stints. Lowe missed three weeks in May with a shoulder impingement and was shut down in August with what was believed to be elbow tendinitis. Doctors planned to clean up his elbow with arthroscopy but found that he had no cartilage in the joint and had to perform a more drastic microfracture operation. Lowe's outlook is uncertain. If the surgery doesn't regenerate enough cartilage, he'd have to try to pitch with bone rubbing on bone. If he regains his health and stuff, he'll be a future closer. There's no exact timetable for his return, though the Mariners hope he can get back on the mound in May.

| Year | Club (League) | Class | W | L | ERA | G | GS | CG | SV | IP | H | R | ER | HR | BB | SO | AVG |
|------|---------------|-------|---|---|-----|---|----|----|----|----|---|---|----|----|----|----|-----|
| 2004 | Everett (NWL) | A | 1 | 2 | 4.93 | 18 | 3 | 0 | 7 | 38 | 42 | 22 | 21 | 4 | 14 | 38 | .276 |
| 2005 | Wisconsin (MWL) | A | 6 | 6 | 5.47 | 22 | 22 | 0 | 0 | 104 | 107 | 72 | 63 | 12 | 49 | 72 | .264 |
| 2006 | Inland Empire (Cal) | A | 1 | 0 | 1.84 | 13 | 2 | 0 | 2 | 29 | 14 | 10 | 6 | 0 | 11 | 46 | .132 |
|  | San Antonio (TL) | AA | 0 | 2 | 2.16 | 11 | 0 | 0 | 4 | 17 | 14 | 4 | 4 | 1 | 3 | 14 | .233 |
|  | Seattle (AL) | MLB | 1 | 0 | 1.93 | 15 | 0 | 0 | 0 | 19 | 12 | 4 | 4 | 1 | 9 | 20 | .190 |
| **MINOR LEAGUE TOTALS** | | | 8 | 10 | 4.50 | 64 | 27 | 0 | 13 | 188 | 177 | 108 | 94 | 17 | 77 | 170 | .244 |
| **MAJOR LEAGUE TOTALS** | | | 1 | 0 | 1.93 | 15 | 0 | 0 | 0 | 18 | 12 | 4 | 4 | 1 | 9 | 20 | .190 |

## 8  CHRIS TILLMAN

RHP

BILL MITCHELL

**Born:** April 15, 1988. **B-T:** R-R. **Ht.:** 6-5. **Wt.:** 195. **Drafted:** HS—Fountain Valley, Calif., 2006 (2nd round). **Signed by:** Tim Reynolds.

It's no coincidence that three of the Mariners' top four starting pitching prospects came from the 2006 draft. They targeted their biggest weakness by choosing Brandon Morrow, Tillman and Tony Butler with their first three picks. Tillman projected as an early first-rounder entering 2006, but an inconsistent senior season dropped him to the second round, where he signed for $680,000. Tillman owns two plus pitches in his lively 91-94 mph fastball and his slider. He generates velocity with little effort, as he has a loose arm and clean delivery, and he can add more once he fills out his lean 6-foot-5 frame. He showed some aptitude for throwing a changeup during instructional league. Tillman's velocity dipped in the spring when he fell in love with his splitter, and he'll need to recognize that his changeup is more vital to him as a starter than his split. He's not as mature as fellow high school draftee Butler, and some scouts questioned his mental toughness when Tillman struggled to live up to expectations as a senior. Tillman will team with Butler at the front of Seattle's low Class A rotation in 2007. If they and Morrow develop as hoped, the Mariners will have landed three first-round talents at the top of their 2006 draft.

| Year | Club (League) | Class | W | L | ERA | G | GS | CG | SV | IP | H | R | ER | HR | BB | SO | AVG |
|------|---------------|-------|---|---|-----|---|----|----|----|----|---|---|----|----|----|----|-----|
| 2006 | Mariners (AZL) | R | 2 | 0 | 0.82 | 5 | 0 | 0 | 1 | 11 | 9 | 4 | 1 | 0 | 5 | 16 | .214 |
|  | Everett (NWL) | A | 1 | 3 | 7.78 | 5 | 5 | 0 | 0 | 20 | 25 | 17 | 17 | 4 | 15 | 29 | .325 |
| **MINOR LEAGUE TOTALS** | | | 3 | 3 | 5.28 | 10 | 5 | 0 | 1 | 31 | 34 | 21 | 18 | 4 | 20 | 45 | .286 |

## ⑨ YUNG-CHI CHEN
2B

**Born:** July 13, 1983. **B-T:** R-R. **Ht.:** 5-11. **Wt.:** 170. **Signed:** Taiwan, 2004. **Signed by:** Jamey Storvick.

A mainstay on Taiwanese national teams, Chen was the youngest member of his 2004 Olympic team and earned all-tournament honors at the 2005 World Cup and 2006 Intercontinental Cup. He led Taiwan with one homer and five RBIs at the inaugural World Baseball Classic. Chen also played in the Futures Game in 2006, when he batted a career-high .324. Chen has an innate feel for putting the barrel of the bat on the ball. He easily makes contact, uses the entire field and employs a buggy-whip swing to generate surprising gap power for his size. He has the ability to make adjustments from at-bat to at-bat, not just game to game. He has average speed and good baserunning instincts. He's reliable at second base, committing just eight errors in 100 games in 2006, including none in 35 Double-A contests. At best, Chen is an adequate defender. His range and arm are just ordinary and he's not aggressive on ground balls. His double-play pivot also needs improvement. Though he easily hits for average, the rest of his offensive game (power, on-base skills, speed) is just fair. Chen has proven himself at every level so far, stalled only by a partially dislocated shoulder that cost him three weeks in late 2006. He should reach Triple-A at some point in 2007, though he's blocked by all-star Jose Lopez in Seattle.

| Year | Club (League) | Class | AVG | G | AB | R | H | 2B | 3B | HR | RBI | BB | SO | SB | OBP | SLG |
|------|---------------|-------|-----|---|----|---|---|----|----|----|-----|----|----|----|-----|-----|
| 2004 | Everett (NWL) | A | .300 | 49 | 200 | 37 | 60 | 13 | 1 | 3 | 34 | 16 | 36 | 25 | .353 | .420 |
| 2005 | Wisconsin (MWL) | A | .292 | 121 | 503 | 77 | 147 | 27 | 7 | 7 | 80 | 37 | 76 | 15 | .339 | .416 |
| 2006 | Mariners (AZL) | R | .273 | 3 | 11 | 1 | 3 | 1 | 1 | 0 | 2 | 1 | 0 | 0 | .385 | .545 |
|  | San Antonio (TL) | AA | .295 | 40 | 149 | 22 | 44 | 9 | 2 | 3 | 22 | 18 | 23 | 5 | .365 | .443 |
|  | Inland Empire (Cal) | A | .342 | 67 | 278 | 49 | 95 | 17 | 3 | 5 | 48 | 22 | 40 | 21 | .388 | .478 |
| **MINOR LEAGUE TOTALS** | | | .306 | 280 | 1141 | 186 | 349 | 67 | 14 | 18 | 186 | 94 | 175 | 66 | .357 | .436 |

## ⑩ ERIC O'FLAHERTY
LHP

**Born:** Feb. 2, 1985. **B-T:** L-L. **Ht.:** 6-2. **Wt.:** 195. **Drafted:** HS—Walla Walla, Wash., 2003 (6th round). **Signed by:** Phil Geisler.

If O'Flaherty had followed through on his commitment to Oregon State, he could have been part of a College World Series championship in 2006. He has no regrets, however, as he jumped from high Class A to the majors during the year. When he's fresh, O'Flaherty throws a 90-94 mph fastball that darts all over the place and an 85-86 mph slider. He also can mix in an 87-89 mph cutter and a changeup to combat righthanders. His deceptive delivery makes it tough to pick up his pitches, and he has the moxie to pitch in late-inning situations. O'Flaherty needs to get stronger after wearing down by the time he joined the Mariners in August. He had less arm speed in the majors, dropping his fastball velocity to 87-90 mph and costing his slider some bite. While he has enough pitches to start, he struggled physically in that role and missed much of 2004 with back problems. He still needs to fine-tune his control and command. If Jake Woods moves into the rotation, O'Flaherty could stick as the second lefty in Seattle's bullpen. Getting some more Triple-A seasoning wouldn't be bad for him either.

| Year | Club (League) | Class | W | L | ERA | G | GS | CG | SV | IP | H | R | ER | HR | BB | SO | AVG |
|------|---------------|-------|---|---|-----|---|----|----|----|----|---|---|----|----|----|----|-----|
| 2003 | Mariners (AZL) | R | 3 | 0 | 1.95 | 13 | 1 | 0 | 0 | 28 | 17 | 10 | 6 | 1 | 7 | 20 | .173 |
|  | Everett (NWL) | A | 1 | 0 | 3.38 | 3 | 1 | 0 | 0 | 11 | 8 | 5 | 4 | 1 | 3 | 7 | .235 |
| 2004 | Wisconsin (MWL) | A | 3 | 3 | 6.12 | 12 | 10 | 0 | 0 | 57 | 83 | 43 | 39 | 3 | 23 | 38 | .344 |
| 2005 | Wisconsin (MWL) | A | 4 | 4 | 3.75 | 45 | 0 | 0 | 13 | 70 | 73 | 35 | 29 | 2 | 30 | 51 | .268 |
| 2006 | Inland Empire (Cal) | A | 0 | 1 | 3.45 | 16 | 0 | 0 | 1 | 29 | 31 | 11 | 11 | 1 | 6 | 33 | .292 |
|  | San Antonio (TL) | AA | 2 | 2 | 1.14 | 25 | 0 | 0 | 7 | 39 | 45 | 10 | 5 | 0 | 15 | 36 | .300 |
|  | Tacoma (PCL) | AAA | 1 | 0 | 0.00 | 2 | 0 | 0 | 0 | 4 | 3 | 0 | 0 | 0 | 1 | 4 | .214 |
|  | Seattle (AL) | MLB | 0 | 0 | 4.09 | 15 | 0 | 0 | 0 | 11 | 18 | 9 | 5 | 2 | 6 | 6 | .360 |
| **MINOR LEAGUE TOTALS** | | | 14 | 10 | 3.57 | 116 | 12 | 0 | 21 | 237 | 260 | 114 | 94 | 8 | 85 | 189 | .284 |
| **MAJOR LEAGUE TOTALS** | | | 0 | 0 | 4.09 | 15 | 0 | 0 | 0 | 11 | 18 | 9 | 5 | 2 | 6 | 6 | .360 |

## ⑪ CARLOS TRIUNFEL
SS

**Born:** Feb. 27, 1990. **B-T:** R-R. **Ht.:** 6-2. **Wt.:** 180. **Signed:** Dominican Republic, 2006. **Signed by:** Patrick Guerrero/Franklin Tavares/Bob Engle.

Long a major player on the international stage, the Mariners shelled out $1.9 million last summer to sign a pair of Latin American middle infielders. Triunfel, a Dominican, received $1.3 million, while Mario Martinez, a Venezuelan, got $600,000. Other clubs offered Triunfel more money, but he felt most comfortable signing with Seattle. A potential five-tool

shortstop, he looked so good on offense and defense in instructional league that the Mariners will consider allowing him to start his pro career in low Class A—at age 17. Triunfel has the ability to hit for average and power. He has natural strength and already drives balls with backspin that will allow them to carry out of the park once he matures physically. He has an advanced approach and hung in well against more advanced pitchers in instructional league. Triunfel is an above-average runner with good hands and a strong, accurate arm. Seattle can't wait to see what he will do in 2007.

| Year | Club (League) | Class | AVG | G | AB | R | H | 2B | 3B | HR | RBI | BB | SO | SB | OBP | SLG |
|------|---------------|-------|-----|---|----|---|---|----|----|----|-----|----|----|----|-----|-----|
| 2006 | Did not play—Signed 2007 contract | | | | | | | | | | | | | | | |

## JUSTIN THOMAS
LHP

**Born:** Jan. 18, 1984. **B-T:** L-L. **Ht.:** 6-3. **Wt.:** 220. **Drafted:** Youngstown State, 2005 (4th round). **Signed by:** Ken Madeja.

After Tony Butler, Thomas has the best stuff among the lefthanders in the system. He gets good life on an 88-92 mph fastball, backs it up with a solid slider and mixes in a changeup. All three pitches rate as plus at times, though not on a consistent basis. They all move, with his fastball cutting and sinking, his slider breaking laterally and his changeup fading down and away. Thomas also can throw all three of them for strikes, and he has the durable frame to absorb a lot of innings. He gets extra credit for his makeup and was at his best while Inland Empire was winning the California League championship. Thomas struck out 17 and didn't allow a run in 13 innings over two postseason starts. Though he had no problems while reaching high Class A in his first full season, he still has work to do. His command isn't as impressive as his control, he needs to do a better job of staying on top of his slider and his changeup needs to become more reliable. If he can improve in all of those areas, he could become a No. 3 starter. Thomas will open 2007 in Double-A.

| Year | Club (League) | Class | W | L | ERA | G | GS | CG | SV | IP | H | R | ER | HR | BB | SO | AVG |
|------|---------------|-------|---|---|-----|---|----|----|----|-----|-----|-----|-----|----|----|-----|-----|
| 2005 | Everett (NWL) | A | 3 | 3 | 3.81 | 18 | 6 | 0 | 0 | 59 | 63 | 31 | 25 | 2 | 20 | 48 | .272 |
| 2006 | Wisconsin (MWL) | A | 5 | 5 | 3.10 | 11 | 11 | 0 | 0 | 61 | 69 | 29 | 21 | 4 | 17 | 51 | .286 |
| | Inland Empire (Cal) | A | 9 | 4 | 4.10 | 17 | 17 | 1 | 0 | 105 | 108 | 58 | 48 | 10 | 45 | 111 | .269 |
| **MINOR LEAGUE TOTALS** | | | 17 | 12 | 3.75 | 46 | 34 | 1 | 0 | 225 | 240 | 118 | 94 | 16 | 82 | 210 | .275 |

## JON HUBER
RHP

**Born:** July 7, 1981. **B-T:** R-R. **Ht.:** 6-2. **Wt.:** 195. **Drafted:** HS—Fort Myers, Fla., 2000 (5th round). **Signed by:** Joe Bochy (Padres).

Looking for a pinch-hitter for the 2004 stretch drive, the Padres dispatched Huber to the Mariners in exchange for Dave Hansen. Huber scuffled along as a starter until the Mariners moved him to the bullpen last year, rejuvenating his career. He saved 23 games between Double-A and Triple-A and saved his best pitching for the majors, where he posted a 1.08 ERA in 16 appearances. Huber used four pitches as a starter but focused mainly on his fastball and slider as a reliever. Both improved as he worked in shorter stints, with his fastball ranging from 91-95 mph and his slider getting quicker and tighter. Huber also threw more strikes in his new role. He still has a curveball and changeup he can use to keep hitters off balance. He can rely too much on his slider at times, but he already has found a formula that works in the majors. Barring a disastrous spring training, Huber will have a job in Seattle's bullpen.

| Year | Club (League) | Class | W | L | ERA | G | GS | CG | SV | IP | H | R | ER | HR | BB | SO | AVG |
|------|---------------|-------|---|---|-----|---|----|----|----|-----|-----|-----|-----|----|----|-----|-----|
| 2000 | AZL Padres (AZL) | R | 1 | 4 | 6.60 | 14 | 10 | 0 | 0 | 45 | 54 | 49 | 33 | 1 | 32 | 39 | .293 |
| 2001 | Idaho Falls (PIO) | R | 5 | 9 | 6.04 | 15 | 15 | 0 | 0 | 73 | 77 | 61 | 49 | 7 | 48 | 75 | .274 |
| 2002 | Ft. Wayne (MWL) | A | 8 | 12 | 5.12 | 28 | 26 | 2 | 0 | 146 | 168 | 99 | 83 | 7 | 59 | 86 | .292 |
| 2003 | Ft. Wayne (MWL) | A | 1 | 1 | 3.76 | 7 | 7 | 0 | 0 | 38 | 31 | 18 | 16 | 2 | 11 | 34 | .226 |
| | Lake Elsinore (Cal) | A | 3 | 5 | 5.18 | 12 | 11 | 0 | 0 | 57 | 69 | 41 | 33 | 2 | 31 | 43 | .300 |
| 2004 | Lake Elsinore (Cal) | A | 8 | 6 | 3.70 | 20 | 20 | 0 | 0 | 107 | 107 | 53 | 44 | 9 | 44 | 100 | .262 |
| | Inland Empire (Cal) | A | 4 | 1 | 6.12 | 7 | 5 | 0 | 0 | 32 | 42 | 24 | 22 | 4 | 14 | 38 | .302 |
| 2005 | San Antonio (TL) | AA | 7 | 8 | 4.74 | 26 | 26 | 1 | 0 | 148 | 159 | 87 | 78 | 11 | 49 | 110 | .276 |
| 2006 | San Antonio (TL) | AA | 0 | 3 | 4.88 | 21 | 0 | 0 | 11 | 24 | 30 | 13 | 13 | 0 | 4 | 19 | .316 |
| | Tacoma (PCL) | AAA | 3 | 1 | 2.61 | 29 | 0 | 0 | 12 | 41 | 46 | 14 | 12 | 3 | 10 | 38 | .280 |
| | Seattle (AL) | MLB | 2 | 1 | 1.08 | 16 | 0 | 0 | 0 | 17 | 10 | 3 | 2 | 0 | 6 | 11 | .172 |
| **MINOR LEAGUE TOTALS** | | | 40 | 50 | 4.84 | 179 | 120 | 3 | 23 | 712 | 783 | 459 | 383 | 46 | 302 | 584 | .280 |
| **MAJOR LEAGUE TOTALS** | | | 2 | 1 | 1.08 | 16 | 0 | 0 | 0 | 16 | 10 | 3 | 2 | 0 | 6 | 11 | .172 |

## MICHAEL WILSON
OF

**Born:** June 29, 1983. **B-T:** R-R. **Ht.:** 6-2. **Wt.:** 215. **Drafted:** HS—Tulsa, 2001 (2nd round). **Signed by:** Mark Lummus.

Wilson was headed to Oklahoma to play linebacker until Seattle took him in the second round and signed him for $900,000. Wilson developed at a painstakingly slow rate in his first

three pro seasons, failing to get to full-season ball and struggling with switch-hitting and nagging groin and hamstring injuries. Once he gave up hitting lefthanded in 2005, he began to make progress. He has reached Double-A and hit 40 homers over the last two years while showing better instincts at the plate, on the bases and in the field. He now drives the ball to all fields rather than being a dead-pull hitter. He has shed some of his football bulk without losing strength, and his swing is now much looser than it had been. He runs well once he gets going and has gotten much better in left field, where he's now adequate. His arm has improved from awful to playable, a credit to his diligent work, and he threw out 17 baserunners last year. While he has made significant strides, Wilson still has a ways to go. He has an abrupt hitch in his swing and still chases sliders, though he now will handle some breaking balls he used to miss by two feet. He continues to draw walks but his strikeout rate spiked in 2006, even moreso after he reached Double-A. His routes in the outfield could still use some more improvement. Wilson has to close the holes in the game, but he has legitimate power and has a ceiling as an everyday left fielder. He'll probably open this year back in Double-A.

| Year | Club (League) | Class | AVG | G | AB | R | H | 2B | 3B | HR | RBI | BB | SO | SB | OBP | SLG |
|------|---------------|-------|-----|---|----|---|---|----|----|----|-----|----|----|----|-----|-----|
| 2002 | Mariners (AZL) | R | .238 | 41 | 143 | 28 | 34 | 5 | 0 | 4 | 19 | 18 | 52 | 4 | .357 | .357 |
| 2003 | Mariners (AZL) | R | .311 | 48 | 177 | 33 | 55 | 9 | 3 | 3 | 25 | 20 | 46 | 6 | .391 | .446 |
| 2004 | Everett (NWL) | A | .259 | 66 | 239 | 45 | 62 | 15 | 0 | 9 | 51 | 25 | 61 | 10 | .357 | .435 |
| 2005 | Wisconsin (MWL) | A | .266 | 127 | 463 | 93 | 123 | 29 | 3 | 19 | 84 | 57 | 107 | 10 | .360 | .464 |
| 2006 | San Antonio (TL) | AA | .245 | 67 | 249 | 32 | 61 | 12 | 1 | 12 | 43 | 28 | 85 | 1 | .336 | .446 |
| | Inland Empire (Cal) | A | .315 | 52 | 200 | 38 | 63 | 15 | 3 | 9 | 38 | 22 | 59 | 4 | .389 | .555 |
| **MINOR LEAGUE TOTALS** | | | .271 | 401 | 1471 | 269 | 398 | 85 | 10 | 56 | 260 | 170 | 410 | 35 | .363 | .456 |

## 15 ROB JOHNSON    C

**Born:** July 22, 1983. **B-T:** R-R. **Ht.:** 6-1. **Wt.:** 200. **Drafted:** Houston, 2004 (4th round). **Signed by:** Kyle Van Hook.

In 2005, his first full pro season, Johnson rated as the best defensive catcher in the low Class A Midwest League, reached high Class A and finished by playing for Team USA in the World Cup. With Kenji Johjima signed through 2008, the Mariners have no glaring need for a catcher. Yet they promoted Johnson all the way to Triple-A and compounded that decision by having him share time with Guillermo Quiroz and eventually Jeff Clement. As a result, Johnson caught just 74 games at a level at which he wasn't ready for offensively. His plate discipline eroded and his swing looked long. He has good raw power but has hit just 16 homers in 221 pro games. To produce more pop, he needs to add some loft to his swing, maintain his strength better over the course of a season and do a better job of waiting for pitches he can punish. Johnson is more athletic and runs better than most catchers. Throw in his arm strength, which enabled him to throw out 45 percent of basestealers in 2006, and he should be able to at least fill in at both infield and outfield corners. Though Johnson is the best defensive catcher in the system, his receiving can leave a lot to be desired. Despite his lack of playing time, he tied for the Pacific Coast League lead with 11 passed balls. Seattle plans on sending him back to Triple-A. With Johjima and Clement ahead of him on the depth chart, Johnson's best shot at having a role with Seattle is as a catcher/utilityman.

| Year | Club (League) | Class | AVG | G | AB | R | H | 2B | 3B | HR | RBI | BB | SO | SB | OBP | SLG |
|------|---------------|-------|-----|---|----|---|---|----|----|----|-----|----|----|----|-----|-----|
| 2004 | Everett (NWL) | A | .234 | 20 | 77 | 17 | 18 | 3 | 1 | 1 | 7 | 4 | 10 | 6 | .286 | .338 |
| | Mariners (AZL) | R | .222 | 8 | 27 | 4 | 6 | 1 | 0 | 0 | 1 | 3 | 7 | 1 | .323 | .259 |
| 2005 | Wisconsin (MWL) | A | .272 | 77 | 305 | 41 | 83 | 19 | 1 | 9 | 51 | 20 | 31 | 10 | .319 | .430 |
| | Inland Empire (Cal) | A | .314 | 19 | 70 | 15 | 22 | 3 | 0 | 2 | 12 | 10 | 14 | 2 | .381 | .443 |
| 2006 | Tacoma (PCL) | AAA | .231 | 97 | 337 | 28 | 78 | 9 | 4 | 4 | 33 | 13 | 74 | 14 | .261 | .318 |
| **MINOR LEAGUE TOTALS** | | | .254 | 221 | 816 | 105 | 207 | 35 | 6 | 16 | 104 | 50 | 136 | 33 | .299 | .370 |

## 16 BRYAN LAHAIR    1B

**Born:** Nov. 5, 1982. **B-T:** L-R. **Ht.:** 6-5. **Wt.:** 215. **Drafted:** St. Petersburg (Fla.) JC, D/F 2002 (39th round). **Signed by:** Mark Leavitt.

LaHair followed up his breakout 2005 performance by proving it was no fluke, earning Seattle's minor league player of the year award. He has become a regular for Team USA, playing in its last three tournaments: the World Cup and Olympic regional qualifier in 2005, and the Olympic qualifier in 2006. LaHair's resurgence began when he started getting his front foot down quicker, improving his timing at the plate. LaHair offers Sean Casey-like production as a first baseman and may have even more power, as he as started to drive the ball more regularly during game action and not just in batting practice. He uses the entire field and has good plate coverage. Originally drafted as a corner outfielder/third baseman, LaHair isn't very athletic and is limited to first base. He has below-average speed and defensive skills. While he has become an organization favorite, his lack of versatility presents a problem. Richie Sexson has two years and $28 million remaining on his contract, closing

off any opportunity at first base. LaHair has hit just .218 and .209 versus lefthanders over the last two seasons, so he may not be more than a platoon player. He'll probably open the season back in Triple-A but should get his first shot at the majors at some point in 2007.

| Year | Club (League) | Class | AVG | G | AB | R | H | 2B | 3B | HR | RBI | BB | SO | SB | OBP | SLG |
|------|---------------|-------|-----|---|----|---|---|----|----|----|-----|----|----|----|-----|-----|
| 2003 | Everett (NWL) | A | .244 | 57 | 201 | 26 | 49 | 14 | 0 | 2 | 20 | 11 | 40 | 4 | .286 | .343 |
| 2004 | Everett (NWL) | A | .440 | 7 | 25 | 5 | 11 | 6 | 0 | 1 | 7 | 1 | 3 | 0 | .464 | .800 |
| | Wisconsin (MWL) | A | .279 | 67 | 262 | 30 | 73 | 24 | 0 | 5 | 28 | 16 | 66 | 0 | .323 | .427 |
| 2005 | Inland Empire (Cal) | A | .310 | 126 | 509 | 81 | 158 | 28 | 2 | 22 | 113 | 51 | 125 | 0 | .373 | .503 |
| 2006 | San Antonio (TL) | AA | .293 | 60 | 222 | 22 | 65 | 12 | 0 | 6 | 30 | 24 | 52 | 0 | .371 | .428 |
| | Tacoma (PCL) | AAA | .327 | 54 | 202 | 36 | 66 | 10 | 0 | 10 | 44 | 23 | 49 | 3 | .393 | .525 |
| **MINOR LEAGUE TOTALS** | | | .297 | 371 | 1421 | 200 | 422 | 94 | 2 | 46 | 242 | 126 | 335 | 7 | .356 | .463 |

## 17 MATT TUIASOSOPO                                               3B/SS

**Born:** May 10, 1986. **B-T:** R-R. **Ht.:** 6-2. **Wt.:** 210. **Drafted:** HS—Woodinville, Wash., 2004 (3rd round). **Signed by:** Phil Geisler.

Tuiasosopo's father Manu and brother Marques both have played in the NFL, and Tuiasosopo was on a football path when he accepted a scholarship to play quarterback at Washington. Then the Mariners stepped in, taking him with their top pick in the 2004 draft and signing him for a third-round-record $2.29 million bonus. Tuiasosopo has mostly struggled as a pro. His athleticism and strength are still evident, and it's easy to see his potential, but he hasn't produced much at the plate. He uses an inside-out swing and takes most balls the other way, short-circuiting his power. He hasn't made effective adjustments or adopted a consistent approach. His stroke is long and he has a high leg kick that throws his timing off. His pitch recognition still needs work and he tends to dive into balls, leaving him vulnerable on the inner half. When his bat started to get going in the hitter-friendly California League last year, the Mariners promoted him to Double-A at age 20 and he was overmatched. He has good speed for his size and runs well underway. In his first two years in pro ball, Tuiasosopo played shortstop, where his actions and quickness were short. He moved to third base last June, and has the soft hands, arm strength and agility to be an asset there. The Mariners hope Tuiasosopo will start a Michael Wilson-like turnaround this year in Double-A.

| Year | Club (League) | Class | AVG | G | AB | R | H | 2B | 3B | HR | RBI | BB | SO | SB | OBP | SLG |
|------|---------------|-------|-----|---|----|---|---|----|----|----|-----|----|----|----|-----|-----|
| 2004 | Mariners (AZL) | R | .412 | 20 | 68 | 18 | 28 | 5 | 2 | 4 | 12 | 13 | 14 | 1 | .528 | .721 |
| | Everett (NWL) | A | .248 | 29 | 101 | 18 | 25 | 6 | 1 | 2 | 14 | 10 | 36 | 4 | .336 | .386 |
| 2005 | Wisconsin (MWL) | A | .276 | 107 | 409 | 72 | 113 | 21 | 3 | 6 | 45 | 44 | 96 | 8 | .359 | .386 |
| 2006 | San Antonio (TL) | AA | .185 | 62 | 216 | 16 | 40 | 4 | 0 | 1 | 10 | 20 | 64 | 2 | .259 | .218 |
| | Inland Empire (Cal) | A | .306 | 59 | 232 | 31 | 71 | 14 | 0 | 1 | 34 | 14 | 58 | 5 | .359 | .379 |
| **MINOR LEAGUE TOTALS** | | | .270 | 277 | 1026 | 155 | 277 | 50 | 6 | 14 | 115 | 101 | 268 | 20 | .349 | .371 |

## 18 STEPHEN KAHN                                                      RHP

**Born:** Dec. 14, 1983. **B-T:** L-R. **Ht.:** 6-3. **Wt.:** 215. **Drafted:** Loyola Marymount, 2005 (5th round). **Signed by:** Greg Whitworth.

Kahn had first-round aspirations in the 2005 draft, but he lost his fastball command and went just 5-6, 5.60 as a junior, and he fell to the Mariners in the fifth round. Seattle decided he would fit best into the bullpen and moved him there in pro ball. He had little trouble in the lower minors, blowing away hitters with a 94-97 mph fastball. But when he got to Double-A last summer, his lack of command quickly caught up to him. There's a lot of effort and a head jerk in his delivery, and he doesn't help matters by trying to throw harder when he gets into trouble. Kahn has good depth on his 12-to-6 curveball, but it's a loose, loopy pitch and he has trouble controlling it as well. He has a decent changeup but seems more interested in lighting up radar guns. Despite his big fastball, Kahn may never have the second pitch, command or mentality to be trusted as more than a setup man. He'll give Double-A another try in 2007.

| Year | Club (League) | Class | W | L | ERA | G | GS | CG | SV | IP | H | R | ER | HR | BB | SO | AVG |
|------|---------------|-------|---|---|-----|---|----|----|----|----|---|---|----|----|----|----|-----|
| 2005 | Mariners (AZL) | R | 0 | 0 | 0.00 | 1 | 0 | 0 | 0 | 1 | 1 | 0 | 0 | 0 | 1 | 1 | .333 |
| | Everett (NWL) | A | 3 | 0 | 3.93 | 17 | 0 | 0 | 12 | 18 | 14 | 9 | 8 | 1 | 14 | 22 | .209 |
| 2006 | Inland Empire (Cal) | A | 2 | 0 | 1.95 | 20 | 0 | 0 | 8 | 28 | 16 | 7 | 6 | 1 | 15 | 35 | .167 |
| | San Antonio (TL) | AA | 1 | 3 | 6.23 | 31 | 0 | 0 | 0 | 39 | 50 | 30 | 27 | 3 | 31 | 33 | .316 |
| **MINOR LEAGUE TOTALS** | | | 6 | 3 | 4.29 | 69 | 0 | 0 | 20 | 86 | 81 | 46 | 41 | 5 | 61 | 91 | .250 |

## 19 ANTHONY VARVARO                                                  RHP

**Born:** Oct. 31, 1984. **B-T:** R-R. **Ht.:** 6-0. **Wt.:** 180. **Drafted:** St. John's, 2005 (12th round). **Signed by:** David May.

Varvaro averaged more strikeouts per nine innings (12.1, ranking sixth in NCAA Division I) than St. John's teammate Craig Hansen (11.9), now with the Red Sox, in 2005. However,

Varvaro blew out his elbow that May, and the Mariners took a flier on him in the 12th round. Prior to the injury, he had a 92-94 mph fastball, a hard curveball and a chance to go as high as the supplemental first round. Since signing him for $500,000, Varvaro has pitched just 11 innings in the Arizona League. That was long enough for him to show that his stuff should bounce back, as he showed good arm speed and pitched at 90-91 mph. There was also tightness to his curve. Varvaro should be at full strength this year, though the Mariners could have him open the year in extended spring training rather than pitching in the cold April climate of the Midwest League. Varvaro needs work on developing a better changeup and reducing the effort in his delivery. He has the upside of a No. 3 starter.

| Year | Club (League) | Class | W | L | ERA | G | GS | CG | SV | IP | H | R | ER | HR | BB | SO | AVG |
|------|---------------|-------|---|---|-----|---|----|----|----|----|---|---|----|----|----|----|-----|
| 2006 | Mariners (AZL) | R | 0 | 2 | 1.64 | 5 | 3 | 0 | 0 | 11 | 7 | 3 | 2 | 0 | 5 | 15 | .184 |
| **MINOR LEAGUE TOTALS** | | | 0 | 2 | 1.64 | 5 | 3 | 0 | 0 | 11 | 7 | 3 | 2 | 0 | 5 | 15 | .184 |

## LUIS VALBUENA
2B

**Born:** Nov. 30, 1985. **B-T:** L-R. **Ht.:** 5-10. **Wt.:** 175. **Signed:** Venezuela, 2002. **Signed by:** Emilio Carrasquel.

Valbuena hit just .224 in April in his first shot at full-season ball, but hit .305 in the Midwest League the rest of the way, then finished the season in high Class A as a 20-year-old. He has a very good approach at the plate, handles the bat well and draws walks. He also has some pull-side power, which will be more evident as he gets stronger. Valbuena has slightly below-average speed coming out of the box and is an average runner underway. He doesn't have a lot of range at second base, but he makes the routine play. He encouraged the Mariners with some defensive improvements in 2006, as he looked lighter on his feet and slicker on his double-play pivot. Valbuena is comparable to Yung-Chi Chen; Chen has more power and runs better, while Valbuena is a better defender. He'll open 2007 in high Class A.

| Year | Club (League) | Class | AVG | G | AB | R | H | 2B | 3B | HR | RBI | BB | SO | SB | OBP | SLG |
|------|---------------|-------|-----|---|----|----|----|----|----|----|-----|----|----|----|-----|-----|
| 2003 | Aguirre (VSL) | R | .228 | 50 | 167 | 26 | 38 | 11 | 4 | 1 | 22 | 20 | 25 | 3 | .323 | .359 |
| 2004 | Aguirre (VSL) | R | .361 | 61 | 216 | 44 | 78 | 24 | 6 | 2 | 34 | 27 | 15 | 11 | .444 | .556 |
| 2005 | Tacoma (PCL) | AAA | .000 | 3 | 4 | 0 | 0 | 0 | 0 | 0 | 0 | 1 | 2 | 0 | .200 | .000 |
| | Everett (NWL) | A | .261 | 74 | 287 | 47 | 75 | 10 | 3 | 12 | 51 | 31 | 37 | 14 | .333 | .443 |
| 2006 | Inland Empire (Cal) | A | .252 | 43 | 163 | 18 | 41 | 10 | 1 | 2 | 10 | 14 | 26 | 1 | .315 | .362 |
| | Wisconsin (MWL) | A | .286 | 89 | 325 | 45 | 93 | 16 | 6 | 3 | 38 | 44 | 44 | 21 | .371 | .400 |
| **MINOR LEAGUE TOTALS** | | | .280 | 320 | 1162 | 180 | 325 | 71 | 20 | 20 | 155 | 137 | 149 | 50 | .360 | .427 |

## JOSE DE LA CRUZ
RHP

**Born:** Sept. 23, 1983. **B-T:** R-R. **Ht.:** 6-7. **Wt.:** 245. **Signed:** Dominican Republic, 2002. **Signed by:** Junior Ramirez (Devil Rays).

The Mariners traded righthander Marcos Carvajal to the Devil Rays for de la Cruz four months after acquiring Carvajal. In his first year in the system, de la Cruz was named Inland Empire's pitcher of the year and saved the final game of the California League playoffs. There's no deception involved with de la Cruz. He's a 6-foot-7, 245-pound hulk who tries to throw his heavy 91-95 mph sinker by hitters. His second pitch is a slider that can be a plus pitch at times and can flatten out at others. His delivery has some effort to it, but it works for him. De la Cruz managed to significantly improve his control last season, but his command still needs some work. He has a closer's mindset and has the stuff to pitch in the late innings. Still a couple of years away from the majors, he'll move up to Double-A in 2007.

| Year | Club (League) | Class | W | L | ERA | G | GS | CG | SV | IP | H | R | ER | HR | BB | SO | AVG |
|------|---------------|-------|---|---|-----|---|----|----|----|----|----|----|----|----|----|----|-----|
| 2003 | Princeton (APP) | R | 0 | 2 | 1.33 | 15 | 1 | 0 | 1 | 27 | 25 | 8 | 4 | 1 | 9 | 15 | .248 |
| 2004 | Hudson Valley (NYP) | A | 2 | 0 | 1.10 | 17 | 0 | 0 | 7 | 41 | 28 | 8 | 5 | 0 | 11 | 42 | .185 |
| 2005 | SW Michigan (MWL) | A | 3 | 6 | 3.94 | 50 | 0 | 0 | 19 | 62 | 51 | 33 | 27 | 2 | 35 | 60 | .224 |
| 2006 | Inland Empire (Cal) | A | 2 | 4 | 2.97 | 50 | 0 | 0 | 21 | 61 | 50 | 26 | 20 | 4 | 19 | 52 | .220 |
| **MINOR LEAGUE TOTALS** | | | 7 | 12 | 2.65 | 132 | 1 | 0 | 48 | 190 | 154 | 75 | 56 | 7 | 74 | 169 | .218 |

## TRAVIS BLACKLEY
LHP

**Born:** Nov. 4, 1982. **B-T:** L-L. **Ht.:** 6-3. **Wt.:** 200. **Signed:** Australia, 2000. **Signed by:** Jim Colborn.

Blackley was the system's best lefty prospect when he reached Seattle in July 2004, but then things started to unravel for him. He changed his approach and tried to pitch away from contact, falling behind in counts and then getting crushed when he came back over the plate. After returning to Triple-A, he went on the disabled list with shoulder tendinitis, and during the offseason doctors found two small tears in his labrum. Blackley had shoulder surgery in February 2005 and missed that season, but he was able to make 27 starts last year. His stuff is starting to get back to where it was. Blackley's best pitch is still his change-up, and he still throws it with the same arm speed as his fastball. He worked mostly at 84-

89 mph with his fastball in 2006, down from 87-92 in the past. His fastball's command and movement always trumped its velocity anyway. His 74-76 mph curveball features some bite and depth, but not on a consistent basis. The Mariners were most pleased that Blackley regained his aggressive nature and confidence and hope his stuff can get a tick better as he puts the surgery further behind him. The back of Seattle's rotation is unsettled, so Blackley could fit into that mix, though he could use some time in Triple-A first.

| Year | Club (League) | Class | W | L | ERA | G | GS | CG | SV | IP | H | R | ER | HR | BB | SO | AVG |
|------|---------------|-------|---|---|-----|---|----|----|----|----|---|---|----|----|----|----|-----|
| 2001 | Everett (NWL) | A | 6 | 1 | 3.32 | 14 | 14 | 0 | 0 | 79 | 60 | 34 | 29 | 7 | 29 | 90 | .211 |
| 2002 | San Bernardino (Cal) | A | 5 | 9 | 3.49 | 21 | 20 | 1 | 0 | 121 | 102 | 52 | 47 | 11 | 44 | 152 | .227 |
| 2003 | San Antonio (TL) | AA | 17 | 3 | 2.61 | 27 | 27 | 0 | 0 | 162 | 125 | 55 | 47 | 11 | 62 | 144 | .215 |
| 2004 | Seattle (AL) | MLB | 1 | 3 | 10.04 | 6 | 6 | 0 | 0 | 26 | 35 | 31 | 29 | 9 | 22 | 16 | .321 |
|      | Tacoma (PCL) | AAA | 8 | 6 | 3.83 | 19 | 18 | 2 | 0 | 110 | 100 | 49 | 47 | 14 | 47 | 80 | .251 |
| 2006 | San Antonio (TL) | AA | 8 | 11 | 4.06 | 25 | 25 | 0 | 0 | 144 | 139 | 77 | 65 | 18 | 45 | 100 | .255 |
|      | Tacoma (PCL) | AAA | 1 | 1 | 4.09 | 2 | 2 | 0 | 0 | 11 | 10 | 5 | 5 | 2 | 5 | 5 | .233 |
| **MINOR LEAGUE TOTALS** | | | 45 | 31 | 3.44 | 108 | 106 | 3 | 0 | 628 | 536 | 272 | 240 | 63 | 232 | 571 | .233 |
| **MAJOR LEAGUE TOTALS** | | | 1 | 3 | 10.04 | 6 | 6 | 0 | 0 | 26 | 35 | 31 | 29 | 9 | 22 | 16 | .321 |

## 23 ROBERT ROHRBAUGH — LHP

**Born:** Dec. 28, 1983. **B-T:** R-L. **Ht.:** 6-2. **Wt.:** 195. **Drafted:** Clemson, 2005 (7th round). **Signed by:** Craig Bell.

Rohrbaugh's best attribute may be his mound presence, which enabled him to succeed in Double-A during his first full pro season. He repeats his simple delivery extremely well, which allows him to throw all three of his pitches for strikes. His fastball arrives at just 86-90 mph, but hitters don't get good swings against it. His fastball has some cutter action on it, and he throws on a good downward plane from a high three-quarters angle. Rohrbaugh throws a three-quarters breaking ball, somewhere between a curveball and slider, that draws mixed reviews from scouts. It doesn't fool lefthanders, who had much more success (batting .305) against him than righties (.229) did last year. His average changeup features some fade and sink. Rohrbaugh projects as a back-of-the-rotation starter and has proven himself at a top college program and up through Double-A, and he should reach Triple-A some time in 2007.

| Year | Club (League) | Class | W | L | ERA | G | GS | CG | SV | IP | H | R | ER | HR | BB | SO | AVG |
|------|---------------|-------|---|---|-----|---|----|----|----|----|---|---|----|----|----|----|-----|
| 2005 | Everett (NWL) | A | 5 | 2 | 3.84 | 14 | 12 | 0 | 0 | 68 | 68 | 33 | 29 | 7 | 18 | 71 | .262 |
| 2006 | Inland Empire (Cal) | A | 7 | 1 | 1.46 | 10 | 9 | 1 | 0 | 55 | 43 | 11 | 9 | 2 | 8 | 47 | .214 |
|      | San Antonio (TL) | AA | 5 | 5 | 3.78 | 14 | 14 | 0 | 0 | 86 | 87 | 37 | 36 | 9 | 27 | 64 | .268 |
| **MINOR LEAGUE TOTALS** | | | 17 | 8 | 3.19 | 38 | 35 | 1 | 0 | 209 | 198 | 81 | 74 | 18 | 53 | 182 | .252 |

## 24 MICHAEL SAUNDERS — OF

**Born:** Nov. 19, 1986. **B-T:** L-R. **Ht.:** 6-4. **Wt.:** 205. **Drafted:** Tallahassee (Fla.) CC, D/F 2004 (11th round). **Signed by:** Phil Geisler.

When the Mariners drafted Saunders out of a British Columbia high school in 2004, baseball faced a visa shortage that would have made it impossible to start his pro career. So he attended Tallahassee (Fla.) CC for a year before signing as a draft-and-follow for $237,500. He showed promise in his pro debut but had difficulty solving low Class A pitching in his first full season in 2006. While Saunders has raw tools and a fluid stroke, he was unprepared mentally or physically for playing on an everyday basis. He did make some adjustments, batting .298 from July until mid-August, when he left to play for Canada at an Olympic qualifying tournament in Cuba, where he hit a team-best .448. A multisport athlete growing up, Saunders showed NHL potential in hockey and also starred in basketball, lacrosse and soccer. He also showed an 88-91 mph fastball as a pitcher. His best tool is his raw power, created by natural loft in his swing, but he'll have to make more consistent contact in order to tap into it. He has solid speed but could slow down as he fills out, making a move from center to right field likely in his future. Seattle may have him repeat low Class A, which would give Wisconsin a very toolsy outfield of Saunders, Greg Halman and Carlos Peguero.

| Year | Club (League) | Class | AVG | G | AB | R | H | 2B | 3B | HR | RBI | BB | SO | SB | OBP | SLG |
|------|---------------|-------|-----|---|----|---|---|----|----|----|----|----|----|----|-----|-----|
| 2005 | Everett (NWL) | A | .270 | 56 | 196 | 24 | 53 | 13 | 3 | 7 | 39 | 27 | 74 | 2 | .361 | .474 |
| 2006 | Wisconsin (MWL) | A | .240 | 104 | 359 | 48 | 86 | 10 | 8 | 4 | 39 | 48 | 103 | 22 | .329 | .345 |
| **MINOR LEAGUE TOTALS** | | | .250 | 160 | 555 | 72 | 139 | 23 | 11 | 11 | 78 | 75 | 177 | 24 | .340 | .391 |

## 25 GREG HALMAN — OF

**Born:** Aug. 26, 1987. **B-T:** R-R. **Ht.:** 6-4. **Wt.:** 190. **Signed:** Netherlands, 2004. **Signed by:** Peter Van Dalen.

Halman signed after winning the MVP award in the Dutch league as a 17-year-old. The popular comparison among Mariners officials is Andre Dawson, because Halman is long-limbed, high-waisted athlete. He has a projectable frame and present strength, and Seattle

envisions him hitting for power and average once he matures physically, gains more experience and tightens his strike zone. He needs to improve his approach, because he's a dead-pull hitter who chases pitches. Halman is a long-strider who runs well for his size, especially once he gets going. Halman may be able to stay in center field, and if he can't he has more than enough arm and bat projection to play in right. The biggest negative about his 2006 season was that it lasted just a month because he broke his right hand in an on-field brawl. Though he's still young and raw, Seattle will promote him to low Class A this year as a 19-year-old.

| Year | Club (League) | Class | AVG | G | AB | R | H | 2B | 3B | HR | RBI | BB | SO | SB | OBP | SLG |
|------|---------------|-------|-----|---|----|---|---|----|----|----|-----|----|----|----|-----|-----|
| 2005 | Mariners (AZL) | R | .258 | 26 | 89 | 17 | 23 | 2 | 3 | 3 | 11 | 10 | 19 | 1 | .350 | .449 |
| 2006 | Everett (NWL) | A | .259 | 28 | 116 | 19 | 30 | 6 | 4 | 5 | 15 | 3 | 32 | 10 | .295 | .509 |
| MINOR LEAGUE TOTALS | | | .259 | 54 | 205 | 36 | 53 | 8 | 7 | 8 | 26 | 13 | 51 | 11 | .320 | .483 |

## 26 ALEX LIDDI                                                     3B

**Born:** Aug. 14, 1988. **B-T:** R-R. **Ht.:** 6-4. **Wt.:** 176. **Signed:** Italy, 2005. **Signed by:** Wayne Norton/Mario Mazzotti.

Liddi is one of two Italian-born players in professional baseball; Cubs minor league righthander Alessandro Maestri is the other. They were two of the four prospects signed out of Major League Baseball International's inaugural European Baseball Academy, held at the Italian national Olympic training center in Tirrenia in 2005. Seattle signed him for $55,000. He made his pro debut in 2006 and finished fifth in the Arizona League batting race as a 17-year-old. It's easy to dream about Liddi's projected power, as he has a good swing and lots of room to add strength to his skinny 6-foot-4, 176-pound frame. He shows an aptitude for driving the ball to right-center and should learn to turn on pitches in time. As with most of Seattle's young international players, he still has a lot to learn about plate discipline. It's possible he could outgrow the hot corner if he fills out, but he has a plus arm (he touched 88 mph off the mound as an amateur), soft hands and the agility to make plays. He moves well for his size but probably will slow down to a below-average runner once he physically matures. Besides his tools, the Mariners also rave about Liddi's love for the game and work ethic. He'll be one of the youngest players in the Midwest League this year.

| Year | Club (League) | Class | AVG | G | AB | R | H | 2B | 3B | HR | RBI | BB | SO | SB | OBP | SLG |
|------|---------------|-------|-----|---|----|---|---|----|----|----|-----|----|----|----|-----|-----|
| 2006 | Mariners (AZL) | R | .313 | 47 | 182 | 31 | 57 | 13 | 6 | 3 | 25 | 12 | 48 | 9 | .355 | .500 |
| | Wisconsin (MWL) | A | .184 | 11 | 38 | 4 | 7 | 1 | 0 | 0 | 2 | 1 | 8 | 0 | .200 | .211 |
| MINOR LEAGUE TOTALS | | | .291 | 58 | 220 | 35 | 64 | 14 | 6 | 3 | 27 | 13 | 56 | 9 | .329 | .450 |

## 27 CARLOS PEGUERO                                                 OF

**Born:** Feb. 22, 1987. **B-T:** L-L. **Ht.:** 6-5. **Wt.:** 220. **Signed:** Dominican Republic, 2005. **Signed by:** Patrick Guerrero/Bob Engle.

Three Mariners farmhands shared the Arizona League home run title last summer: first baseman/outfielder Gerardo Avila, outfielder Welington Dotel and Peguero. Peguero, who also led the league in slugging percentage, tied them even though he moved up to Everett for the final month. He has plenty of strength in his 6-foot-5, 220-pound frame, but he's more than just a masher. He uses the whole field and shows some aptitude for hitting for average as well as power. One club official compared his swing to Fred McGriff's. Peguero is a good athlete and he has above-average speed, though he'll slow down as he gets older and fills out. He has a plus arm as well and should be able to stick in right field. Still raw overall, Peguero's control of the strike zone is rudimentary, and he struggled against better quality pitching in the Northwest League. He also needs to hone his baserunning and defensive instincts. Peguero will be a regular in low Class A this year at age 20.

| Year | Club (League) | Class | AVG | G | AB | R | H | 2B | 3B | HR | RBI | BB | SO | SB | OBP | SLG |
|------|---------------|-------|-----|---|----|---|---|----|----|----|-----|----|----|----|-----|-----|
| 2005 | Seattle (DSL) | R | .251 | 59 | 179 | 31 | 45 | 8 | 4 | 6 | 30 | 22 | 66 | 1 | .337 | .441 |
| 2006 | Mariners (AZL) | R | .313 | 34 | 134 | 27 | 42 | 10 | 7 | 7 | 30 | 13 | 49 | 3 | .380 | .649 |
| | Everett (NWL) | A | .204 | 25 | 93 | 7 | 19 | 4 | 1 | 2 | 9 | 2 | 34 | 0 | .221 | .333 |
| MINOR LEAGUE TOTALS | | | .261 | 118 | 406 | 65 | 106 | 22 | 12 | 15 | 69 | 37 | 149 | 4 | .327 | .485 |

## 28 CESAR JIMENEZ                                                  LHP

**Born:** Nov. 12, 1984. **B-T:** L-L. **Ht.:** 5-11. **Wt.:** 180. **Signed:** Venezuela, 2001. **Signed by:** Emilio Carrasquel.

After spending the previous two seasons working mainly out of the bullpen, Jimenez operated out of the rotation for most of 2006 and hit his stride last summer, allowing only one earned run in 43 innings over six Triple-A starts. He wore down afterward, as he had as a starter in the past. He spent three weeks on the Tacoma disabled list in August with a sore elbow and got hammered when he made his big league debut in September. Jimenez likely will wind up as a reliever because he holds up better and shows better stuff in that role.

Hovever, he could open 2007 back in the Triple-A rotation His best pitch is his changeup, making him effective against righthanders. His fastball has some cut action and sits at 88-89 mph and touches 92 when he operates out of the bullpen—2-3 mph quicker than when he starts. He also does a better job of throwing strikes and keeping the ball down in relief.

| Year | Club (League) | Class | W | L | ERA | G | GS | CG | SV | IP | H | R | ER | HR | BB | SO | AVG |
|------|---------------|-------|---|---|-----|---|----|----|----|----|---|---|----|----|----|----|-----|
| 2001 | Aguirre (VSL) | R | 7 | 1 | 0.83 | 11 | 11 | 2 | 0 | 65 | 37 | 6 | 6 | 0 | 12 | 67 | .167 |
| 2002 | Mariners (AZL) | R | 0 | 0 | 3.38 | 1 | 0 | 0 | 0 | 3 | 3 | 2 | 1 | 0 | 0 | 3 | .300 |
| | Everett (NWL) | A | 2 | 1 | 2.70 | 8 | 0 | 0 | 1 | 20 | 12 | 7 | 6 | 2 | 5 | 25 | .174 |
| 2003 | Wisconsin (MWL) | A | 8 | 11 | 2.94 | 28 | 20 | 0 | 0 | 126 | 134 | 61 | 41 | 7 | 46 | 76 | .273 |
| 2004 | Inland Empire (Cal) | A | 6 | 7 | 2.29 | 43 | 2 | 0 | 6 | 86 | 80 | 28 | 22 | 3 | 19 | 81 | .241 |
| 2005 | Tacoma (PCL) | AAA | 0 | 0 | 9.39 | 4 | 0 | 0 | 0 | 8 | 9 | 8 | 8 | 5 | 1 | 9 | .290 |
| | San Antonio (TL) | AA | 3 | 5 | 2.62 | 45 | 1 | 0 | 4 | 69 | 64 | 21 | 20 | 3 | 24 | 54 | .250 |
| 2006 | San Antonio (TL) | AA | 0 | 2 | 2.76 | 3 | 3 | 0 | 0 | 16 | 10 | 5 | 5 | 0 | 5 | 10 | .179 |
| | Tacoma (PCL) | AAA | 5 | 10 | 4.36 | 24 | 19 | 1 | 3 | 107 | 107 | 54 | 52 | 8 | 55 | 66 | .266 |
| | Seattle (AL) | MLB | 0 | 0 | 14.73 | 4 | 1 | 0 | 0 | 7 | 13 | 12 | 12 | 4 | 4 | 3 | .382 |
| **MINOR LEAGUE TOTALS** | | | 31 | 37 | 2.90 | 167 | 56 | 3 | 14 | 500 | 456 | 192 | 161 | 28 | 167 | 391 | .244 |
| **MAJOR LEAGUE TOTALS** | | | 0 | 0 | 14.73 | 4 | 1 | 0 | 0 | 7 | 13 | 12 | 12 | 4 | 4 | 3 | .382 |

## 29 OSWALDO NAVARRO SS

**Born:** Oct. 2, 1984. **B-T:** B-R. **Ht.:** 6-0. **Wt.:** 155. **Signed:** Venezuela, 2001. **Signed by:** Emilio Carrasquel.

Managers rated Navarro the top defensive shortstop in the Texas League last year, and he has been the best defensive infielder on our Mariners tools list for three years running. Navarro still has to prove he can hit enough to earn a big league role. Defensively, he could play in the majors right now. He has above-average hands, actions and instincts at shortstop, and scouts grade his arm and range from solid to plus. Nothing stands out about his offensive game, and his strikeout rate spiked in the upper minors last year. He doesn't hit for much average or power, and his average speed doesn't lend itself to basestealing. His plate discipline improved last season but still took a hit when he was pushed to Triple-A. His ceiling is as a defensive-minded utilityman. He'll spend most of 2007 in Triple-A.

| Year | Club (League) | Class | AVG | G | AB | R | H | 2B | 3B | HR | RBI | BB | SO | SB | OBP | SLG |
|------|---------------|-------|-----|---|----|---|---|----|----|----|-----|----|----|----|-----|-----|
| 2002 | Aguirre (VSL) | R | .261 | 37 | 119 | 13 | 31 | 4 | 1 | 0 | 9 | 12 | 21 | 3 | .338 | .311 |
| 2003 | Everett (NWL) | A | .258 | 61 | 233 | 42 | 60 | 12 | 1 | 0 | 23 | 10 | 39 | 16 | .302 | .318 |
| 2004 | Wisconsin (MWL) | A | .211 | 40 | 109 | 13 | 23 | 4 | 0 | 0 | 7 | 11 | 19 | 4 | .295 | .248 |
| | Everett (NWL) | A | .273 | 68 | 267 | 38 | 73 | 27 | 1 | 1 | 30 | 21 | 59 | 17 | .331 | .393 |
| 2005 | Wisconsin (MWL) | A | .269 | 120 | 450 | 57 | 121 | 29 | 0 | 9 | 69 | 39 | 60 | 11 | .329 | .393 |
| 2006 | San Antonio (TL) | AA | .267 | 79 | 266 | 27 | 71 | 13 | 1 | 1 | 24 | 39 | 57 | 7 | .371 | .335 |
| | Tacoma (PCL) | AAA | .246 | 55 | 183 | 15 | 45 | 9 | 0 | 2 | 21 | 19 | 33 | 1 | .314 | .328 |
| | Seattle (AL) | MLB | .667 | 4 | 3 | 0 | 2 | 0 | 0 | 0 | 0 | 0 | 1 | 0 | .667 | .667 |
| **MINOR LEAGUE TOTALS** | | | .261 | 460 | 1627 | 205 | 424 | 98 | 4 | 13 | 183 | 151 | 288 | 59 | .329 | .350 |
| **MAJOR LEAGUE TOTALS** | | | .667 | 4 | 3 | 0 | 2 | 0 | 0 | 0 | 0 | 0 | 1 | 0 | .667 | .667 |

## 30 MICHAEL GARCIAPARRA RHP

**Born:** April 2, 1982. **B-T:** R-R. **Ht.:** 6-1. **Wt.:** 175. **Drafted:** HS—La Habra Heights, Calif., 2001 (1st round supplemental). **Signed by:** Derek Venezuela.

Nomar Garciaparra's younger brother did little to justify his $2 million signing bonus in his first four years of pro ball, repeatedly missing time with nagging injuries and hitting just .257. He decided to change his outlook in 2006, focusing on enjoying the game and not worrying about his pedigree or performance. That worked, as he reached Triple-A and hit .342 in the Arizona Fall League. Now, Garciaparra is hitting the ball where it's pitched and using the opposite field more than ever before. He doesn't have a lot of pop, but he can sting the ball into the gaps on occasion. He does a good job with pitch recognition and draws some walks. He has average speed. Signed as a shortstop, Garciaparra moved to second base, where his range and arm profile better, full-time in 2005. His reliable hands are his best defensive trait. He's one of the hardest workers in the system, and the Mariners admire his perserverance. He may never get the chance to be a regular in Seattle, but he could carve out a utility role.

| Year | Club (League) | Class | AVG | G | AB | R | H | 2B | 3B | HR | RBI | BB | SO | SB | OBP | SLG |
|------|---------------|-------|-----|---|----|---|---|----|----|----|-----|----|----|----|-----|-----|
| 2002 | Mariners (AZL) | R | .275 | 46 | 160 | 27 | 44 | 8 | 5 | 0 | 20 | 20 | 42 | 13 | .383 | .388 |
| | Everett (NWL) | A | .161 | 9 | 31 | 3 | 5 | 2 | 0 | 0 | 3 | 4 | 15 | 0 | .257 | .226 |
| 2003 | Wisconsin (MWL) | A | .243 | 122 | 440 | 55 | 107 | 12 | 1 | 2 | 38 | 38 | 80 | 14 | .314 | .289 |
| 2004 | Mariners (AZL) | R | .273 | 3 | 11 | 4 | 3 | 0 | 1 | 0 | 4 | 2 | 5 | 0 | .429 | .455 |
| | Inland Empire (Cal) | A | .226 | 70 | 234 | 48 | 53 | 12 | 3 | 1 | 26 | 31 | 44 | 5 | .333 | .316 |
| 2005 | Inland Empire (Cal) | A | .298 | 84 | 336 | 60 | 100 | 15 | 3 | 6 | 33 | 35 | 64 | 10 | .387 | .414 |
| 2006 | Mariners (AZL) | R | .313 | 4 | 16 | 3 | 5 | 3 | 0 | 1 | 2 | 1 | 0 | 1 | .353 | .688 |
| | San Antonio (TL) | AA | .305 | 28 | 105 | 13 | 32 | 3 | 1 | 1 | 16 | 8 | 21 | 1 | .375 | .381 |
| | Tacoma (PCL) | AAA | .316 | 42 | 136 | 26 | 43 | 5 | 0 | 1 | 10 | 22 | 26 | 3 | .422 | .375 |
| **MINOR LEAGUE TOTALS** | | | .267 | 408 | 1469 | 239 | 392 | 60 | 14 | 12 | 152 | 161 | 297 | 47 | .357 | .351 |

# TAMPA BAY
# DEVIL RAYS

BY **BILL BALLEW**

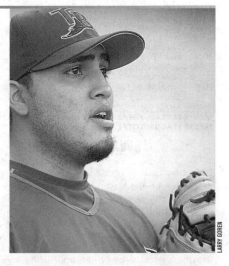

The Devil Rays had to keep telling themselves that it's always darkest before the dawn. Otherwise, the team's revamped ownership and front office never would have kept its sanity in 2006.

Tampa Bay entered the season trying to change the tone of a franchise that has struggled on most fronts since it started play in 1998.

Despite the best of intentions, trouble reared its head, with many of the problems occurring at Triple-A Durham. Delmon Young, the 2005 Minor League Player of the Year, received a 50-game suspension for tossing his bat and striking an umpire in April. Elijah Dukes was sent home twice after altercations with teammates, the coaching staff and an umpire. Bulls manager John Tamargo was suspended for 10 games by the International League for a run-in with an umpire in May, while B.J. Upton was charged with driving while impaired in June.

Dukes, Upton and Young are three of the most talented young players in baseball, and they all were critical of the organization in interviews with USA Today in July. Upton and Young concluded the campaign in the majors. Dukes, who didn't play after July 26, contemplated giving up the game. The Rays fired Tamargo and the rest of his Durham staff after the season ended.

All the turmoil in Durham overshadowed the Devil Rays' efforts in building what has become the strongest system in baseball. Young remains among the game's elite prospects and has been joined by Evan Longoria and Reid Brignac, who should take over the left side of Tampa Bay's infield in short order. The Rays finally are having some success developing pitching, with Jacob McGee, Wade Davis, Matt Walker and Jeremy Hellickson showing off quality arms in the lower minors.

Tampa Bay had good depth to begin with and added to it in trades, adding players such as J.P. Howell, **Dioner Navarro** and Ben Zobrist to their big league club and prospects such as Joel Guzman, Sergio Pedroza and Mitch Talbot to their system.

First-year scouting director R.J. Harrison nabbed Longoria with the third overall pick in the draft and also added talents such as righthander Josh Butler (second round), catcher Nevin Ashley (sixth) and outfielder Desmond Jennings (10th). Given the problems with several high-profile prospects, Harrison pushed his staff to find players with strong character and makeup to match their physical promise. The Rays also are trying to make a more concerted effort to find talent in Latin America.

Tampa Bay won one minor league championship (Double-A Montgomery in the Southern League) and narrowly missed another (high Class A Visalia lost in the California League finals), and hopes that core of players eventually will enjoy similar success at the big league level. For a team that has yet to break the 70-win plateau in the majors, anything positive must be considered a step in the right direction.

## TOP 30 PROSPECTS

| | |
|---|---|
| 1. Delmon Young, of | 16. Shawn Riggans, c |
| 2. Evan Longoria, 3b | 17. Andrew Sonnanstine, rhp |
| 3. Reid Brignac, ss | 18. John Jaso, c |
| 4. Jeff Niemann, rhp | 19. Jeff Ridgway, lhp |
| 5. Jacob McGee, lhp | 20. Elliot Johnson, 2b |
| 6. Elijah Dukes, of | 21. James Houser, lhp |
| 7. Akinori Iwamura, 3b | 22. Wes Bankston, 1b/3b |
| 8. Wade Davis, rhp | 23. Chris Mason, rhp |
| 9. Matt Walker, rhp | 24. Jonathan Barratt, lhp |
| 10. Jeremy Hellickson, rhp | 25. Josh Butler, rhp |
| 11. Joel Guzman, of/1b/3b | 26. Wade Townsend, rhp |
| 12. Jason Hammel, rhp | 27. Sergio Pedroza, of |
| 13. Mitch Talbot, rhp | 28. Chris Nowak, 1b |
| 14. Juan Salas, rhp | 29. Shaun Cumberland, of |
| 15. Fernando Perez, of | 30. Desmond Jennings, of |

# ORGANIZATION OVERVIEW

**General manager:** Andrew Friedman. **Farm director:** Mitch Lukevics. **Scouting director:** R.J. Harrison.

## 2006 PERFORMANCE

| Class | Team | League | W | L | PCT | Finish* | Manager | Affiliated |
|---|---|---|---|---|---|---|---|---|
| Majors | Tampa Bay | American | 61 | 101 | .377 | 14th (14) | Joe Maddon | — |
| Triple-A | Durham Bulls | International | 64 | 78 | .451 | 11th (14) | John Tamargo | 1998 |
| Double-A | Montgomery Biscuits | Southern | 77 | 62 | .554 | +3rd (10) | Charlie Montoyo | 2004 |
| High A | #Visalia Oaks | California | 75 | 65 | .536 | 2nd (10) | Joe Szekely | 2005 |
| Low A | †Southwest Michigan Devil Rays | Midwest | 62 | 77 | .446 | 12th (14) | Skeeter Barnes | 2005 |
| Short-season | Hudson Valley Renegades | New York-Penn | 31 | 43 | .419 | 12th (14) | Matt Quatraro | 1996 |
| Rookie | Princeton Devil Rays | Appalachian | 28 | 36 | .438 | 9th (10) | Jamie Nelson | 1997 |
| **OVERALL 2006 MINOR LEAGUE RECORD** | | | 337 | 361 | .483 | 22nd (30) | | |

*Finish in overall standings (No. of teams in league). +League champion. #Affiliate will be in Vero Beach (Florida State) in 2007.
†Affiliate will be in Columbus (South Atlantic) in 2007.

## ORGANIZATION LEADERS

### BATTING
| | | |
|---|---|---|
| AVG | Ashley, Nevin, Princeton | .333 |
| R | Perez, Fernando, Visalia | 137 |
| H | Perez, Fernando, Visalia | 182 |
| TB | Brignac, Reid, Visalia/Montgomery | 281 |
| 2B | Nowak, Chris, Visalia | 45 |
| 3B | Johnson, Elliot, Montgomery | 10 |
| HR | Witt, Kevin, Durham | 36 |
| RBI | Nowak, Chris, Visalia | 103 |
| BB | Perez, Fernando, Visalia | 88 |
| SO | Perez, Fernando, Visalia | 149 |
| SB | Upton, B.J., Durham | 46 |
| OBP | Ashley, Nevin, Princeton | .440 |
| SLG | Witt, Kevin, Durham | .577 |
| XBH | Witt, Kevin, Durham | 66 |

### PITCHING
| | | |
|---|---|---|
| W | Sonnanstine, Andrew, Montgomery | 15 |
| L | Peguero, Tony, Montgomery | 13 |
| ERA | Hellickson, Jeremy, Hudson Valley | 2.43 |
| G | Rodriguez, Jose, Montgomery/Durham | 61 |
| CG | Sonnanstine, Andrew, Montgomery | 4 |
| SV | Dupas, Greg, Southwest Michigan | 25 |
| IP | Sonnanstine, Andrew, Montgomery | 186 |
| BB | Mann, Brandon, Visalia | 66 |
| SO | McGee, Jacob, Southwest Michigan | 171 |
| AVG | Hellickson, Jeremy, Hudson Valley | .193 |

## BEST TOOLS

| | |
|---|---|
| Best Hitter for Average | Delmon Young |
| Best Power Hitter | Evan Longoria |
| Best Strike-Zone Discipline | Chris Nowak |
| Fastest Baserunner | Fernando Perez |
| Best Athlete | Elijah Dukes |
| Best Fastball | Juan Salas |
| Best Curveball | Matt Walker |
| Best Slider | Jeff Niemann |
| Best Changeup | Mitch Talbot |
| Best Control | Andy Sonnanstine |
| Best Defensive Catcher | Shawn Riggans |
| Best Defensive Infielder | Patrick Cottrell |
| Best Infield Arm | Neil Walton |
| Best Defensive Outfielder | Fernando Perez |
| Best Outfield Arm | Delmon Young |

## PROJECTED 2010 LINEUP

| | |
|---|---|
| Catcher | Dioner Navarro |
| First Base | Joel Guzman |
| Second Base | Jorge Cantu |
| Third Base | Evan Longoria |
| Shortstop | Reid Brignac |
| Left Field | Carl Crawford |
| Center Field | Rocco Baldelli |

| | |
|---|---|
| Right Field | Delmon Young |
| Designated Hitter | B.J. Upton |
| No. 1 Starter | Scott Kazmir |
| No. 2 Starter | Jeff Niemann |
| No. 3 Starter | Jake McGee |
| No. 4 Starter | Wade Davis |
| No. 5 Starter | Matt Walker |
| Closer | Juan Salas |

## LAST YEAR'S TOP 20 PROSPECTS

1. Delmon Young, of
2. Jeff Niemann, rhp
3. Jason Hammel, rhp
4. Reid Brignac, ss
5. Elijah Dukes, of
6. Wade Davis, rhp
7. Wes Bankston, 1b
8. Chad Orvella, rhp
9. Matt Walker, rhp
10. Chris Mason, rhp
11. Shawn Riggans, c
12. Jamie Shields, rhp
13. Fernando Perez, of
14. Wade Townsend, rhp
15. John Jaso, c/dh
16. Jacob McGee, lhp
17. Shaun Cumberland, of
18. Elliot Johnson, 2b
19. Jeremy Hellickson, rhp
20. Andy Sonnanstine, rhp

## TOP PROSPECTS OF THE DECADE

| Year | Player, Pos. | 2006 Org. |
|---|---|---|
| 1997 | Matt White, rhp | Out of baseball |
| 1998 | Matt White, rhp | Out of baseball |
| 1999 | Matt White, rhp | Out of baseball |
| 2000 | Josh Hamilton, of | Devil Rays |
| 2001 | Josh Hamilton, of | Devil Rays |
| 2002 | Josh Hamilton, of | Devil Rays |
| 2003 | Rocco Baldelli, of | Devil Rays |
| 2004 | B.J. Upton, ss | Devil Rays |
| 2005 | Delmon Young, of | Devil Rays |
| 2006 | Delmon Young, of | Devil Rays |

## TOP DRAFT PICKS OF THE DECADE

| Year | Player, Pos. | 2006 Org. |
|---|---|---|
| 1997 | Paul Wilder, of | Out of baseball |
| 1998 | Josh Pressley, 1b (4) | Marlins |
| 1999 | Josh Hamilton, of | Devil Rays |
| 2000 | Rocco Baldelli, of | Devil Rays |
| 2001 | Dewon Brazelton, rhp | Padres |
| 2002 | B.J. Upton, ss | Devil Rays |
| 2003 | Delmon Young, of | Devil Rays |
| 2004 | Jeff Niemann, rhp. | Devil Rays |
| 2005 | Wade Townsend, rhp | Devil Rays |
| 2006 | Evan Longoria, 3b | Devil Rays |

## ALL-TIME LARGEST BONUSES

| | |
|---|---|
| Matt White, 1996 | $10,200,000 |
| Rolando Arrojo, 1997 | $7,000,000 |
| B.J. Upton, 2002 | $4,600,000 |
| Dewon Brazelton, 2001 | $4,200,000 |
| Josh Hamilton, 1999 | $3,960,000 |

# MINOR LEAGUE DEPTH CHART

## Tampa Bay Devil Rays

**Impact: A.** Through astute drafting the Rays have stockpiled three of the games best prospects at their positions in right fielder Young, shortstop Brignac and third baseman Longoria.

**Depth: A.** Power righthanders make the difference. Niemann, Davis, Walker, Hellickson and Talbot give Rays a stable of arms to nearly match their impressive bats.

**Sleeper:** Elliott Johnson, 2b. Huge year contributed to Double-A Montgomery's Southern League title, and with a vacancy at second in Tampa Bay, Johnson might not be far off.

*Numbers in parentheses indicate prospect rankings.*

### LF
Sergio Pedroza (27)
Francisco Leandro
Ryan Royster
Andy Lopez

### CF
Fernando Perez (15)
Desmond Jennings (30)
John Matulia

### RF
Delmon Young (1)
Elijah Dukes (6)
Shaun Cumberland (29)

### 3B
Evan Longoria (2)
Akinori Iwamura (7)
Patrick Cottrell
Gabby Martinez
Mike McCormick

### SS
Reid Brignac (3)
Shawn O'Malley
Neil Walton

### 2B
Elliott Johnson (20)
Josh Asanovich

### 1B
Joel Guzman (11)
Wes Bankston (22)
Chris Nowak (28)
Henry Wrigley

### C
Shawn Riggans (16)
John Jaso (18)
Nevin Ashley
Christian Lopez
Craig Albernaz

### RHP

| Starters | Relievers |
| --- | --- |
| Jeff Niemann (4) | Juan Salas (14) |
| Wade Davis (8) | Chris Mason (23) |
| Matt Walker (9) | Brian Stokes |
| Jeremy Hellickson (10) | Greg Dupas |
| Jason Hammel (12) | Heath Rollins |
| Mitch Talbot (13) | Richard de los Santos |
| Andy Sonnanstine (17) | Shinji Mori |
| Josh Butler (25) | |
| Wade Townsend (26) | |
| Josh Butler | |
| Alex Cobb | |
| Woods Fines | |
| Evan Meek | |
| Ryan Reid | |
| Derek Feldkamp | |
| Tyree Hayes | |
| Chris Andujar | |
| Greg Reinhard | |

### LHP

| Starters | Relievers |
| --- | --- |
| Jacob McGee (5) | Jeff Ridgway (19) |
| James Houser (21) | Jon Switzer |
| Jonathan Barratt (24) | |
| Chuck Tiffany | |
| Mike Wlodarczyk | |
| Chris Seddon | |

# DRAFT ANALYSIS

## 2006 — SIGNING BUDGET: $5.0 million

**Best Pro Debut:** 3B Evan Longoria (1) was the consensus best hitter in the draft and lived up to that billing, batting .315/.360/.597 while reaching Double-A. OF Desmond Jennings (10) hit .277 and led the Rookie-level Appalachian League with 48 runs and 32 steals. C Nevin Ashley (6) topped the Appy in OBP (.440) and made the league all-star team.

**Best Athlete:** Jennings originally signed with Alabama's football team before becoming a junior college all-America wide receiver at Itawamba (Miss.) CC, leading the nation with 6.75 catches per game in 2005. SS Shawn O'Malley's (5) speed made him a dual threat as a wide receiver and defensive back for his high school football team. RHP Heath Rollins (11) played outfield at Winthrop and ran a 6.5-second 60-yard dash.

**Best Pure Hitter:** In a draft lacking in position players, Longoria was considered the one sure bet to hit .300. He has a smooth swing, quick hands and plenty of bat speed.

**Best Raw Power:** The Devil Rays projected Longoria as a 20-25 homer threat, but they may have to revise that total upward after he bashed 18 homers in his first pro summer. OF Quinn Stewart, signed before the draft as a fifth-year senior free agent, finished second in the NCAA Division I home run race with 23 during the spring, then hit six more in pro ball.

**Fastest Runner:** Jennings can run the 40 in 4.45 seconds, giving him top-of-the-line speed on baseball's scouting scale. O'Malley is nearly as quick.

**Best Defensive Player:** O'Malley covers a lot of ground at shortstop and has reliable hands, topping Appy League shortstops with a .963 fielding percentage.

**Best Fastball:** RHP Josh Butler (2) pitches from 91-95 with his fastball when he's fresh. The Devil Rays shut him down for two months with a mild case of biceps tendinitis, but he returned at the end of the summer.

**Best Breaking Ball:** RHP Alex Cobb (4) throws a true 12-to-6 curveball. RHP Ryan Reid (7) throws his power slider at 84-85 mph and buries it under the hands of lefties.

**Most Intriguing Background:** Unsigned OF Leon Johnson (29), a former Arizona state 100-meter champion who recently returned from a two-year Mormon mission to Siberia, is the brother of Elliot Johnson, one of the Rays' best infield prospects. RHP Tyree Hayes' (8) father Charlie and unsigned OF Candy Maldonado's (46) dad Candy each won World Series rings at the end of lengthy big league careers. 3B Jimmy Mayer's (30) father Bob is an Indians area scout.

**Closest To The Majors:** Longoria could open 2007 in Triple-A and may claim Tampa Bay's third-base job before the end of his first full season.

**Best Late-Round Pick:** Jennings. LHP Ryan Owen (16) has ordinary stuff, but competes hard and throws strikes from a variety of arm angles.

**The One Who Got Away:** The Rays hoped RHP Nick Fuller (3) would sign, but he took his power repertoire to South Carolina.

**Assessment:** In 2005, Rays brass insisted on since-injured Wade Townsend in the first round and ruined an agreement with third-rounder Bryan Morris, who went in 2006's first round to the Dodgers. Tampa Bay's new regime didn't interfere with R.J. Harrison's first draft as scouting director, and he added another elite hitting prospect to the game's most talented farm system.

## 2005 — BUDGET: $3.4 million

The old front-office regime insisted on RHP Wade Townsend (1), only to see him blow out his elbow three months later, and messed up a deal with RHP Bryan Morris (3), who became a first-round pick last year. On the positive side, RHP Jeremy Hellickson (4) was the New York-Penn League's top prospect in 2006. **GRADE: C**

## 2004 — BUDGET: $6.3 million

RHP Jeff Niemann (1) finally got healthy in the second half last year and showed why he went fourth overall. SS Reid Brignac (2), RHPs Wade Davis (3) and Matt Walker (10) and LHP Jacob McGee (5) could all be studs. **GRADE: A**

## 2003 — BUDGET: $5.7 million

OF Delmon Young's (1) performance has justified his No. 1 overall selection. RHP Chad Orvella (13) has helped the big league bullpen. Unsigned LHP Andrew Miller (3) was the consensus top prospect in the 2006 draft. **GRADE: B+**

*Draft analysis by Jim Callis. Numbers in parentheses indicate draft rounds. Budgets are bonuses in first 10 rounds.*

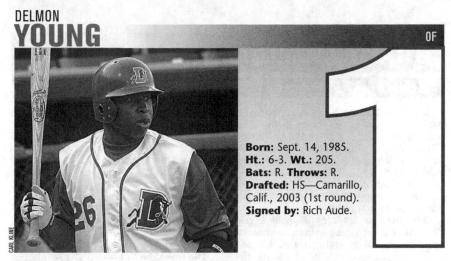

CARL KLINE

**Born:** Sept. 14, 1985.
**Ht.:** 6-3. **Wt.:** 205.
**Bats:** R. **Throws:** R.
**Drafted:** HS—Camarillo, Calif., 2003 (1st round).
**Signed by:** Rich Aude.

The first overall pick in the 2003 draft and BA's 2005 Minor League Player of the Year, Young made national headlines in late April. He threw his bat after being called out on strikes and it hit a replacement umpire, earning Young a 50-game suspension, the longest in the history of the Triple-A International League. After returning, he kept hitting but also created more controversy in late July, when he criticized the Devil Rays for not having promoted him. Young, who voiced similar displeasure at the end of the 2005 season, proved ready for the majors when he finally got the call in late August. After Freddy Garcia delivered a message by hitting the rookie in his first major league at-bat, Young became the first player to stroke eight hits in his first three games since Hall of Famer Willie McCovey in 1959. His older brother Dmitri had a difficult year as well, checking into a rehabilitation center for depression and alcohol abuse, getting released by the Tigers in September and drawing a year's probation for assaulting a former girlfriend.

Young has been well ahead of the curve in terms of polish since he signed. That continued to be the case during his big league debut, as he showed solid fundamentals with an aggressive approach in all phases of the game. Young possesses a smooth and consistent righthanded swing that produces line drives and the occasional cannon shot. He has an excellent approach, trying to drive every pitch back up the middle, which allows him to use the entire field and drive the ball consistently from gap to gap. He has the potential to contend for batting titles with at least 25-30 homers per season. His baseball instincts also are obvious on the basepaths as well as in the outfield. Young has above-average speed and arm strength, along with plus accuracy on his throws from right field.

Young comes across as aloof and standoffish, which only added fuel to the fire regarding his character after his incidents in 2006. The Rays believe added maturity will smooth some the rough spots. Several observers noted Young's progress once he reached the big leagues, pointing to his lack of retaliation after Garcia drilled him. On the field, his plate discipline is lacking, particularly against veteran pitchers who know how to set up an overaggressive hitter. While he has above-average power potential, he hit just 14 homers in 570 Triple-A at-bats. Learning to get himself into better hitter's counts will make him more of a home run threat. He's still young, so he has plenty of time to develop.

The Devil Rays held Young out of a game in the season's final week so he'd retain his rookie eligibility for 2007, when he should be a leading candidate for American League rookie of the year. By waiting so long to promote him, Tampa Bay's front office got its wish by ensuring that he won't be arbitration-eligible until after the 2009 season. He still reached the majors before he turned 21. As long as he stops being his own worst enemy, he should become a star.

| Year | Club (League) | Class | AVG | G | AB | R | H | 2B | 3B | HR | RBI | BB | SO | SB | OBP | SLG |
|------|---------------|-------|-----|---|-----|---|---|----|----|----|-----|----|----|----|-----|-----|
| 2004 | Charleston, S.C. (SAL) | A | .320 | 131 | 513 | 95 | 164 | 26 | 5 | 25 | 115 | 53 | 120 | 21 | .386 | .536 |
| 2005 | Montgomery (SL) | AA | .336 | 84 | 330 | 59 | 111 | 13 | 4 | 20 | 71 | 25 | 66 | 25 | .386 | .582 |
| 2005 | Durham (IL) | AAA | .285 | 52 | 228 | 33 | 65 | 13 | 3 | 6 | 28 | 4 | 33 | 7 | .303 | .447 |
| 2006 | Durham (IL) | AAA | .316 | 86 | 342 | 50 | 108 | 22 | 4 | 8 | 59 | 15 | 65 | 22 | .341 | .474 |
| 2006 | Tampa Bay (AL) | MLB | .317 | 30 | 126 | 16 | 40 | 9 | 1 | 3 | 10 | 1 | 24 | 2 | .336 | .476 |
| **MINOR LEAGUE TOTALS** | | | .317 | 353 | 1413 | 237 | 448 | 74 | 16 | 59 | 273 | 97 | 284 | 75 | .363 | .517 |
| **MAJOR LEAGUE TOTALS** | | | .317 | 30 | 126 | 16 | 40 | 9 | 1 | 3 | 10 | 1 | 24 | 2 | .336 | .476 |

## 2 EVAN LONGORIA 3B

ED WOLFSTEIN

**Born:** Oct. 7, 1985. **B-T:** R-R. **Ht.:** 6-2. **Wt.:** 213. **Drafted:** Long Beach State, 2006 (1st round). **Signed by:** Fred Repke.

The Devil Rays planned on taking a pitcher with the third overall pick in the June draft, but changed their plans when Longoria unexpectedly fell to them. The 2005 Cape Cod League MVP signed for $3 million on draft day after batting .353/.468/.602 as a junior at Long Beach State. Known for his bat, he hit even more than expected in his pro debut, whacking 21 homers (counting the playoffs) and reaching Double-A Montgomery. Longoria had no problem adjusting to wood bats in pro ball. His quick hands generate plenty of bat speed, allowing him to hit for average and power. He projects as a .300 hitter with 30 or more homers annually. He played some shortstop in college and shows soft hands and a solid arm at third base. His competitiveness and makeup are considered major pluses. Longoria has no glaring shortcomings. He just needs to be more consistent in all phases of his game, something that should come easily with experience. His worst tool is his speed but even that is average. Easily the most advanced hitter in the 2006 draft, Longoria may reach Tampa Bay sooner than initially expected. He could push for a big league job in mid-2007 and has the talent to become an all-star at third base.

| Year | Club (League) | Class | AVG | G | AB | R | H | 2B | 3B | HR | RBI | BB | SO | SB | OBP | SLG |
|------|---------------|-------|-----|---|-----|----|----|----|----|----|-----|----|----|----|------|------|
| 2006 | Montgomery (SL) | AA | .267 | 26 | 105 | 14 | 28 | 5 | 0 | 6 | 19 | 1 | 20 | 2 | .266 | .486 |
| | Visalia (Cal) | A | .327 | 28 | 110 | 22 | 36 | 8 | 0 | 8 | 28 | 13 | 19 | 1 | .402 | .618 |
| | Hudson Valley (NYP) | A | .424 | 8 | 33 | 5 | 14 | 1 | 1 | 4 | 11 | 5 | 5 | 1 | .487 | .879 |
| **MINOR LEAGUE TOTALS** | | | .315 | 62 | 248 | 41 | 78 | 14 | 1 | 18 | 58 | 19 | 44 | 4 | .360 | .597 |

## 3 REID BRIGNAC SS

LARRY GOREN

**Born:** Jan. 16, 1986. **B-T:** L-R. **Ht.:** 6-3. **Wt.:** 200. **Drafted:** HS—St. Amant, La., 2004 (2nd round). **Signed by:** Benny Latino.

Brignac grew two inches and added 15 pounds of muscle last offseason, and his increased strength and stamina resulted in one of the biggest breakout performances in the minors. He was named MVP and rated as the No. 1 prospect in the high Class A California League, hit well after a promotion to Double-A and won the Rays' minor league player of the year award. Brignac has strong hands and good bat speed. He stays through the ball at the plate and drive pitches to all fields, and also has natural loft in his swing. He should be good for 25-plus homers on an annual basis. There were concerns that he might outgrow shortstop, but he eased them in 2006 and continued to show plus arm strength. His makeup is exceptional. After committing 70 errors over the last two seasons, Brignac needs more consistency with his defense, particularly his throwing. While he has solid-average speed and quickness, he has yet to parlay that into his baserunning. At the plate, he needs to reduce his strikeouts and improve his knowledge of what pitchers are trying to do to get him out. Brignac has the talent and the intangibles to be Tampa Bay's starting shortstop within the next two years. He's likely to return to Double-A to start the season with a promotion to Triple-A Durham at midseason a possibility.

| Year | Club (League) | Class | AVG | G | AB | R | H | 2B | 3B | HR | RBI | BB | SO | SB | OBP | SLG |
|------|---------------|-------|-----|---|-----|----|-----|----|----|----|-----|----|-----|----|------|------|
| 2004 | Princeton (Appy) | R | .361 | 25 | 97 | 16 | 35 | 4 | 2 | 1 | 25 | 9 | 10 | 2 | .413 | .474 |
| | Charleston, S.C. (SAL) | A | .500 | 3 | 14 | 3 | 7 | 1 | 0 | 0 | 5 | 1 | 2 | 0 | .533 | .571 |
| 2005 | SW Michigan (MWL) | A | .264 | 127 | 512 | 77 | 135 | 29 | 2 | 15 | 61 | 40 | 131 | 5 | .319 | .416 |
| 2006 | Montgomery (SL) | AA | .300 | 28 | 110 | 18 | 33 | 6 | 2 | 3 | 16 | 7 | 31 | 3 | .355 | .473 |
| | Visalia (Cal) | A | .326 | 100 | 411 | 82 | 134 | 26 | 3 | 21 | 83 | 35 | 82 | 12 | .382 | .557 |
| **MINOR LEAGUE TOTALS** | | | .301 | 283 | 1144 | 196 | 344 | 66 | 9 | 40 | 190 | 92 | 256 | 22 | .356 | .479 |

## 4 JEFF NIEMANN RHP

**Born:** Feb. 28, 1983. **B-T:** R-R. **Ht.:** 6-9. **Wt.:** 281. **Drafted:** Rice, 2004 (1st round). **Signed by:** Jonathan Bonifay.

Niemann might have gone No. 1 overall in 2004 if he hadn't been recovering from arthroscopic elbow surgery and battling a groin strain, and he has fought physical problems since signing a $5.2 million big league contract. He pitched just 31 innings in his 2005 pro debut because of shoulder tenderness and more groin problems, and spent the first half of 2006 in extended spring training after surgery to shave the joint between his collarbone and shoulder. Niemann is a monster on the mound with a 92-96 mph fastball and an intimidating presence. He mixes the heater with a low-80s slider and does a good job of working both sides of the plate with both offerings. His curveball and change-

up showed improvement in 2006, and they give hitters a different look. All five pitchers drafted in the first round out of Rice this decade have needed surgery, and health is the biggest concern with Niemann. Physical setbacks have limited him to 108 pro innings, yet he dominated at times in Double-A and isn't far from being big league-ready. His top priority on the mound is to command the strike zone better with all of his pitches. Niemann has all the stuff and intangibles to be a top-of-the-rotation pitcher. The Rays want him to spend at least part of 2007 in Triple-A, though an impressive spring could accelerate his timetable.

| Year | Club (League) | Class | W | L | ERA | G | GS | CG | SV | IP | H | R | ER | HR | BB | SO | AVG |
|------|---------------|-------|---|---|-----|---|----|----|----|-----|----|----|----|----|----|-----|------|
| 2005 | Visalia (Cal) | A | 0 | 1 | 3.98 | 5 | 5 | 0 | 0 | 20 | 12 | 10 | 9 | 3 | 10 | 28 | .167 |
| | Montgomery (SL) | AA | 0 | 1 | 4.35 | 6 | 3 | 0 | 0 | 10 | 7 | 7 | 5 | 0 | 5 | 14 | .184 |
| 2006 | Montgomery (SL) | AA | 5 | 5 | 2.68 | 14 | 14 | 0 | 0 | 77 | 56 | 24 | 23 | 6 | 29 | 84 | .202 |
| **MINOR LEAGUE TOTALS** | | | 5 | 7 | 3.08 | 25 | 22 | 0 | 0 | 108 | 75 | 41 | 37 | 9 | 44 | 126 | .194 |

## 5 JACOB McGEE                                    LHP

PAUL GIERHART

**Born:** Aug. 6, 1986. **B-T:** L-L. **Ht.:** 6-3. **Wt.:** 190. **Drafted:** HS—Sparks, Nev., 2004 (5th round). **Signed by:** Fred Repke.

McGee's 2006 breakout was nearly as impressive as Reid Brignac's. In his first taste of full-season ball, he was the most impressive member of a talented low Class A Southwest Michigan staff that also included Wade Davis and Matt Walker. Managers rated McGee's fastball as the best in the Midwest League, and he led both the MWL and Rays farmhands in strikeouts. McGee has an advanced feel for pitching, particularly for a left-hander who spent most of 2006 as a teenager. He has added velocity to his fastball, now popping 90-94 mph consistently and touching 96 with above-average life. His curveball and changeup have a chance to become plus offerings. His curve has good tilt and movement, while his changeup has depth and fade. He shows good poise on the mound. McGee tends to battle with the command of his fastball when he tries to reach peak velocity, and he has yet to fully harness his lively stuff. He has worked hard to stay on top of his three-quarters delivery in order to keep his pitches down in the strike zone. He also needs to refine his secondary pitches. McGee is developing as hoped as he continues to mature physically. He'll spend the 2007 at high Class A Vero Beach and could blossom into a No. 2 starter.

| Year | Club (League) | Class | W | L | ERA | G | GS | CG | SV | IP | H | R | ER | HR | BB | SO | AVG |
|------|---------------|-------|---|---|-----|---|----|----|----|-----|-----|-----|-----|----|-----|-----|------|
| 2004 | Princeton (Appy) | R | 4 | 1 | 3.97 | 12 | 12 | 0 | 0 | 57 | 49 | 30 | 25 | 5 | 25 | 53 | .244 |
| 2005 | Hudson Valley (NYP) | A | 5 | 4 | 3.64 | 15 | 14 | 0 | 0 | 77 | 64 | 32 | 31 | 4 | 23 | 89 | .226 |
| 2006 | Southwest Michigan (MWL) | A | 7 | 9 | 2.96 | 26 | 26 | 0 | 0 | 134 | 103 | 54 | 44 | 7 | 65 | 171 | .211 |
| **MINOR LEAGUE TOTALS** | | | 16 | 14 | 3.37 | 53 | 52 | 0 | 0 | 267 | 216 | 116 | 100 | 16 | 113 | 313 | .222 |

## 6 ELIJAH DUKES                                    OF

SPORTS ON FILM

**Born:** June 26, 1984. **B-T:** B-R. **Ht.:** 6-2. **Wt.:** 240. **Drafted:** HS—Tampa, Fla., 2002 (3rd round). **Signed by:** Kevin Elfering.

Already the owner of a dubious track record of on- and off-field behavior, Dukes continued to self-destruct once the season began, getting sent home on two occasions after run-ins with his manager, teammates and an umpire. He finished the season on a 30-game suspension but returned to the field in the Arizona Fall League. A phenomenal athlete who was a top college football prospect as a linebacker, Dukes has made progress honing his skills and improving his overall knowledge of the game. He's one of the strongest players in baseball and also has the ability to control the strike zone. He combines his above-average speed and an aggressive approach to shine on the basepaths and in the outfield. He is strong arm adds to his right-field profile. Dukes' ceiling is limited only by his outbursts, a major shortcoming that dates back to high school. Though parts of his game are still somewhat rough around the edges, he can make up for small deficiencies with sheer talent. His biggest problem at the plate comes when he tries too hard to hit for power. Dukes is at a crossroads. A change of scenery may be in order, and Tampa Bay is loaded with outfielders, precipitating Dukes getting some work at first base in the AFL. If he can stay focused and control himself, he could develop into an impact player.

| Year | Club (League) | Class | AVG | G | AB | R | H | 2B | 3B | HR | RBI | BB | SO | SB | OBP | SLG |
|------|---------------|-------|-----|---|----|---|---|----|----|----|-----|----|----|----|-----|------|
| 2003 | Charleston, S.C. (SAL) | A | .245 | 117 | 383 | 51 | 94 | 17 | 4 | 7 | 53 | 45 | 130 | 33 | .338 | .366 |
| 2004 | Charleston, S.C. (SAL) | A | .288 | 43 | 163 | 26 | 47 | 12 | 2 | 2 | 15 | 18 | 47 | 14 | .368 | .423 |
| | Bakersfield (Cal) | A | .332 | 58 | 211 | 44 | 70 | 16 | 2 | 8 | 34 | 26 | 50 | 16 | .416 | .540 |
| 2005 | Montgomery (SL) | AA | .287 | 120 | 446 | 73 | 128 | 21 | 5 | 18 | 73 | 45 | 83 | 19 | .355 | .478 |
| 2006 | Durham (IL) | AAA | .293 | 80 | 283 | 58 | 83 | 15 | 5 | 10 | 50 | 44 | 47 | 9 | .401 | .488 |
| **MINOR LEAGUE TOTALS** | | | .284 | 418 | 1486 | 252 | 422 | 81 | 18 | 45 | 225 | 178 | 357 | 91 | .370 | .454 |

## 7 AKINORI IWAMURA
3B

LARRY GOREN

**Born:** Feb. 9, 1979. **B-T:** L-R. **Ht.:** 5-11. **Wt.:** 176. **Signed:** Japan, 2006. **Signed by:** Carlos Alfonso.

The Devil Rays won the bidding for Iwamura by posting $4.55 million. The club then signed him to a three-year contract worth $7.7 million. A five-time all-star in Japan, Iwamura kicked off his 2006 by batting .389 to help Japan win the World Baseball Classic. Though he's a free swinger, he was a career .300 hitter in Japan and scouts believe his batting average and on-base percentage will remain solid in the U.S. He averaged 35 homers over the past three seasons, though Japanese ballparks are more conducive to longballs and he's projected as more of a gap hitter here. He's a slightly above-average runner. Iwamura won six Japanese Gold Gloves as a third baseman, showing good agility and a strong arm. With third basemen B.J. Upton and Evan Longoria close to being ready for the majors, Tampa Bay may move Iwamura to second base. The Rays also think he could handle center field if needed. He's brimming with confidence, which should help him make the transition.

| Year | Club (League) | Class | AVG | G | AB | R | H | 2B | 3B | HR | RBI | BB | SO | SB | OBP | SLG |
|------|---------------|-------|-----|---|-----|----|------|-----|----|-----|-----|-----|-----|----|------|------|
| 1998 | Yakult (CL) | JAP | .000 | 1 | 3 | 0 | 0 | 0 | 0 | 0 | 0 | 0 | 2 | 0 | .000 | .000 |
| 1999 | Yakult (CL) | JAP | .294 | 83 | 252 | 28 | 74 | 11 | 4 | 11 | 35 | 18 | 46 | 7 | .341 | .500 |
| 2000 | Yakult (CL) | JAP | .278 | 130 | 436 | 67 | 121 | 13 | 9 | 18 | 66 | 39 | 103 | 13 | .342 | .472 |
| 2001 | Yakult (CL) | JAP | .287 | 136 | 520 | 79 | 149 | 24 | 4 | 18 | 81 | 32 | 111 | 15 | .329 | .452 |
| 2002 | Yakult (CL) | JAP | .320 | 140 | 510 | 67 | 163 | 35 | 2 | 23 | 71 | 58 | 114 | 5 | .390 | .531 |
| 2003 | Yakult (CL) | JAP | .263 | 60 | 232 | 43 | 61 | 6 | 2 | 12 | 35 | 22 | 55 | 5 | .328 | .461 |
| 2004 | Yakult (CL) | JAP | .300 | 138 | 533 | 99 | 160 | 19 | 0 | 44 | 103 | 70 | 173 | 8 | .383 | .583 |
| 2005 | Yakult (CL) | JAP | .319 | 144 | 548 | 83 | 175 | 31 | 4 | 30 | 102 | 63 | 146 | 6 | .388 | .555 |
| 2006 | Yakult (CL) | JAP | .311 | 145 | 546 | 84 | 170 | 27 | 2 | 32 | 77 | 70 | 128 | 8 | .389 | .544 |
| **JAPANESE TOTALS** | | | .300 | 977 | 3580 | 550 | 1073 | 166 | 27 | 188 | 570 | 372 | 878 | 67 | .366 | .519 |

## 8 WADE DAVIS
RHP

PAUL GIERHART

**Born:** Sept. 7, 1985. **B-T:** R-R. **Ht.:** 6-5. **Wt.:** 220. **Drafted:** HS—Lake Wales, Fla., 2004 (3rd round). **Signed by:** Kevin Elfering.

Davis did not begin pitching until his sophomore season in high school and turned down a scholarship to Florida in exchange for a $475,000 signing bonus. He led the short-season New York-Penn League in strikeouts in 2005 and ranked second in the Midwest League behind Jacob McGee in 2006. He slumped for two months at midseason before finishing strong in August, throwing a seven-inning no-hitter (and taking a 1-0 loss) in his final start. Davis throws his 92-95 mph fastball on an excellent downhill plane and has touched 98 mph. Both his 11-to-5 curveball and his slider are tight breaking balls with sharp movement, and he also has an effective changeup. He's a tough competitor and a good all-around athlete who fields his position as well as any pitcher in the system. Improved command of all his pitches within the strike zone and more confidence in his changeup would help Davis take the next step. While his fastball has above-average velocity, it tends to flatten out. All these issues are related to his inability to repeat his delivery on a straight line to the plate. While he can be inconsistent, Davis has the potential to have three plus pitches. The Rays project him in the middle of a major league rotation and will send him to high Class A in 2007.

| Year | Club (League) | Class | W | L | ERA | G | GS | CG | SV | IP | H | R | ER | HR | BB | SO | AVG |
|------|---------------|-------|---|---|-----|---|----|----|----|----|---|---|----|----|----|----|-----|
| 2004 | Princeton (Appy) | R | 3 | 5 | 6.09 | 13 | 13 | 0 | 0 | 58 | 71 | 46 | 39 | 8 | 19 | 38 | .301 |
| 2005 | Hudson Valley (NYP) | A | 7 | 4 | 2.72 | 15 | 15 | 0 | 0 | 86 | 75 | 35 | 26 | 5 | 23 | 97 | .234 |
| 2006 | Southwest Michigan (MWL) | A | 7 | 12 | 3.02 | 27 | 27 | 1 | 0 | 146 | 124 | 61 | 49 | 5 | 64 | 165 | .234 |
| **MINOR LEAGUE TOTALS** | | | 17 | 21 | 3.54 | 55 | 55 | 1 | 0 | 290 | 270 | 142 | 114 | 18 | 106 | 300 | .248 |

## 9 MATT WALKER
RHP

**Born:** Aug. 16, 1986. **B-T:** R-R. **Ht.:** 6-3. **Wt.:** 193. **Drafted:** HS—Baton Rouge, 2004 (10th round). **Signed by:** Benny Latino.

As they do with most of their high school pitching prospects, the Devil Rays kept Walker in extended spring training to begin his first full pro season. Once he got to low Class A, he gave up two earned runs or less in 13 of his 15 starts. A highly regarded prep quarterback, he signed for second-round money ($600,000) as a 10th-round pick in 2004. Walker's overhand 12-to-6 curveball rated as the best breaking ball in the MWL and is the best in the Rays system. His fastball has increased in velocity

since he signed and also features heavy sink. He sits at 92-94 mph and touches 96 with the ability to maintain his velocity throughout games. His changeup can become a plus pitch with good depth and fade. Scouts love the consistency and ease of his arm action, which creates impressive deception. Walker is working on refining his control and command. He tries to overpower hitters on occasion instead of using his secondary pitches. He also needs to improve his mechanics in order to repeat his delivery more consistently. Scouts are mixed on whether Walker will be a solid mid-rotation or a power reliever, but the Rays will continue to develop him in the rotation for now. He'll move up to high Class A in 2007.

| Year | Club (League) | Class | W | L | ERA | G | GS | CG | SV | IP | H | R | ER | HR | BB | SO | AVG |
|---|---|---|---|---|---|---|---|---|---|---|---|---|---|---|---|---|---|
| 2005 | Princeton (Appy) | R | 2 | 3 | 5.31 | 13 | 12 | 0 | 1 | 58 | 63 | 39 | 34 | 2 | 22 | 71 | .274 |
| | Hudson Valley (NYP) | A | 0 | 0 | 10.80 | 1 | 1 | 0 | 0 | 3 | 5 | 4 | 4 | 0 | 4 | 5 | .357 |
| 2006 | Southwest Michigan (MWL) | A | 5 | 5 | 3.18 | 15 | 15 | 0 | 0 | 82 | 66 | 34 | 29 | 5 | 41 | 68 | .223 |
| **MINOR LEAGUE TOTALS** | | | 7 | 8 | 4.22 | 29 | 28 | 0 | 1 | 143 | 134 | 77 | 67 | 7 | 67 | 144 | .248 |

## 10 JEREMY HELLICKSON                                    RHP

MIKE JANES

**Born:** April 8, 1987. **B-T:** R-R. **Ht.:** 6-1. **Wt.:** 185. **Drafted:** HS—Des Moines, 2005 (4th round). **Signed by:** Tom Couston.

Hellickson, who had committed to Louisiana State, turned pro for $500,000. He started 2006 in extended spring training to work with pitching coach Dick Bosman on his delivery and location. When Hellickson got on the mound, he led the New York-Penn league in strikeouts, never allowed more than three runs in a start and rated as the loop's top prospect. Hellickson has learned to work off his low-90s fastball and commands the pitch with impressive accuracy. He works effortlessly with smooth mechanics and a clean arm action. His sharp curveball has the promise to be a plus pitch with true downer bite, and his changeup showed improvement in 2006. His competitiveness is also a plus. Hellickson needs to upgrade the command of his curveball and fine-tune his changeup. With his deliberate delivery, he could be easy prey for basestealers at higher levels. The Rays want Hellickson, despite his considerable polish, to establish a strong foundation at every level and expect to keep him in low Class A for the entire 2007 season.He could be poised for a breakout like Jacob McGee had in the Midwest League.

| Year | Club (League) | Class | W | L | ERA | G | GS | CG | SV | IP | H | R | ER | HR | BB | SO | AVG |
|---|---|---|---|---|---|---|---|---|---|---|---|---|---|---|---|---|---|
| 2005 | Princeton (Appy) | R | 0 | 0 | 6.00 | 4 | 0 | 0 | 0 | 6 | 6 | 4 | 4 | 1 | 1 | 11 | .240 |
| 2006 | Hudson Valley (NYP) | A | 4 | 3 | 2.43 | 15 | 14 | 0 | 0 | 78 | 55 | 24 | 21 | 3 | 16 | 96 | .193 |
| **MINOR LEAGUE TOTALS** | | | 4 | 3 | 2.69 | 19 | 14 | 0 | 0 | 84 | 61 | 28 | 25 | 4 | 17 | 107 | .197 |

## 11 JOEL GUZMAN                                    OF/1B/3B

**Born:** Nov. 24, 1984. **B-T:** R-R. **Ht.:** 6-5. **Wt.:** 250. **Signed:** Dominican Republic, 2001. **Signed by:** Pablo Peguero (Dodgers).

The Dodgers signed Guzman for a Dominican-record $2.25 million in 2001, and he rated as their top prospect after 2004. He leveled off for the next two seasons before Los Angeles traded him and outfield prospect Sergio Pedroza to the Rays for Julio Lugo at the trade deadline. Primarily a shortstop before 2006, Guzman split time between the outfield, first and third base in Triple-A. Few minor leaguers can match his raw power. His hands work well and stay inside of the ball, and he's particularly adept at hitting low pitches a long way. He remains very athletic and agile despite his increased size. His arm strength is above average and more than enough for right field. Guzman has hit just 31 homers over the last two seasons. His best chance at playing time with Tampa Bay is at first base, and he'll have to unleash his power to stick there. He struggles with inside pitches and never has been very selective. He seemed to grow frustrated at the lack of big league opportunity with the Dodgers. The Rays will use spring training to determine where he fits best in 2007.

| Year | Club (League) | Class | AVG | G | AB | R | H | 2B | 3B | HR | RBI | BB | SO | SB | OBP | SLG |
|---|---|---|---|---|---|---|---|---|---|---|---|---|---|---|---|---|
| 2002 | GCL Dodgers (GCL) | R | .212 | 10 | 33 | 4 | 7 | 2 | 0 | 0 | 2 | 5 | 8 | 1 | .316 | .273 |
| | Great Falls (Pio) | R | .252 | 43 | 151 | 19 | 38 | 8 | 2 | 3 | 27 | 18 | 54 | 5 | .331 | .391 |
| 2003 | South Georgia (SAL) | A | .235 | 58 | 217 | 33 | 51 | 13 | 0 | 8 | 29 | 9 | 62 | 4 | .263 | .406 |
| | Vero Beach (FSL) | A | .246 | 62 | 240 | 30 | 59 | 13 | 1 | 5 | 24 | 11 | 60 | 0 | .279 | .371 |
| 2004 | Vero Beach (FSL) | A | .307 | 87 | 329 | 52 | 101 | 22 | 8 | 14 | 51 | 21 | 78 | 8 | .349 | .550 |
| | Jacksonville (SL) | AA | .280 | 46 | 182 | 25 | 51 | 11 | 3 | 9 | 35 | 13 | 44 | 1 | .325 | .522 |
| 2005 | Jacksonville (SL) | AA | .287 | 122 | 442 | 63 | 127 | 31 | 2 | 16 | 75 | 42 | 128 | 7 | .351 | .475 |
| 2006 | Los Angeles (NL) | MLB | .211 | 8 | 19 | 2 | 4 | 0 | 0 | 0 | 3 | 3 | 2 | 0 | .348 | .211 |
| | Durham (IL) | AAA | .193 | 25 | 88 | 7 | 17 | 5 | 0 | 4 | 9 | 4 | 23 | 0 | .228 | .386 |
| | Las Vegas (PCL) | AAA | .297 | 85 | 317 | 44 | 94 | 16 | 2 | 11 | 55 | 26 | 72 | 9 | .353 | .464 |
| **MINOR LEAGUE TOTALS** | | | .273 | 538 | 1999 | 277 | 545 | 121 | 18 | 70 | 307 | 149 | 529 | 35 | .324 | .456 |
| **MAJOR LEAGUE TOTALS** | | | .211 | 8 | 19 | 2 | 4 | 0 | 0 | 0 | 3 | 3 | 2 | 0 | .348 | .211 |

## 12  JASON HAMMEL                                                      RHP

**Born:** Sept. 2, 1982. **B-T:** R-R. **Ht.:** 6-6. **Wt.:** 200. **Drafted:** Treasure Valley (Ore.) CC, 2002 (10th round). **Signed by:** Paul Kirsch.

After reaching double digits in victories in both 2004 and 2005, Hammel had a better season than his statistics suggest last year, his first full season at the Triple-A level. He had a seven-start stretch in May and June where he went winless despite posting a 3.64 ERA, part of an overall 11-start victory drought. He did bounce back to pitch his best ball of the year in August, setting a Durham Triple-A franchise record with a 13-strikeout game just before his promotion to Tampa Bay. Hammel can locate his pitches to both sides of the plate and has learned to work off his low-90s fastball. His hard-breaking curveball is also a plus pitch, residing in the upper 70s, yet tends to be inconsistent. His changeup showed significant improvement in 2006 and he also did a better job of using his height to work on a downward plane. Hammel's difficulties arise when he leaves his pitches up in the strike zone. There were some concerns about how hard he was hit in his initial taste of the big leagues, but the Rays believe that was simply the result of relying too heavily on his fastball. He'll get the opportunity to win a job in Tampa Bay's rotation in spring training and profiles as a No. 3 or No. 4 starter.

| Year | Club (League) | Class | W | L | ERA | G | GS | CG | SV | IP | H | R | ER | HR | BB | SO | AVG |
|------|---------------|-------|---|---|-----|---|----|----|----|----|---|---|----|----|----|----|-----|
| 2002 | Princeton (Appy) | R | 0 | 0 | 0.00 | 2 | 0 | 0 | 1 | 5 | 7 | 0 | 0 | 0 | 0 | 5 | .318 |
| | Hudson Valley (NYP) | A | 1 | 5 | 5.23 | 13 | 10 | 0 | 1 | 52 | 71 | 41 | 30 | 0 | 14 | 38 | .314 |
| 2003 | Charleston, S.C. (SAL) | A | 6 | 2 | 3.40 | 14 | 12 | 1 | 0 | 77 | 70 | 32 | 29 | 2 | 27 | 50 | .246 |
| 2004 | Charleston, S.C. (SAL) | A | 4 | 7 | 3.23 | 18 | 18 | 0 | 0 | 95 | 94 | 54 | 34 | 7 | 27 | 88 | .257 |
| | Bakersfield (Cal) | A | 6 | 2 | 1.89 | 11 | 11 | 0 | 0 | 71 | 52 | 18 | 15 | 4 | 20 | 65 | .211 |
| 2005 | Montgomery (SL) | AA | 8 | 2 | 2.66 | 12 | 12 | 3 | 0 | 81 | 70 | 26 | 24 | 5 | 19 | 76 | .235 |
| | Durham (IL) | AAA | 3 | 2 | 4.12 | 10 | 10 | 0 | 0 | 55 | 57 | 31 | 25 | 8 | 27 | 48 | .264 |
| 2006 | Durham (IL) | AAA | 5 | 9 | 4.23 | 24 | 24 | 1 | 0 | 128 | 133 | 71 | 60 | 11 | 36 | 117 | .270 |
| | Tampa Bay (AL) | MLB | 0 | 6 | 7.77 | 9 | 9 | 0 | 0 | 44 | 61 | 38 | 38 | 7 | 21 | 32 | .333 |
| **MINOR LEAGUE TOTALS** | | | 33 | 29 | 3.47 | 104 | 97 | 5 | 2 | 563 | 554 | 273 | 217 | 37 | 170 | 487 | .257 |
| **MAJOR LEAGUE TOTALS** | | | 0 | 6 | 7.77 | 9 | 9 | 0 | 0 | 44 | 61 | 38 | 38 | 7 | 21 | 32 | .333 |

## 13  MITCH TALBOT                                                      RHP

**Born:** Oct. 17, 1983. **B-T:** R-R. **Ht.:** 6-2. **Wt.:** 199. **Drafted:** HS—Cedar City, Utah, 2002 (2nd round). **Signed by:** Doug Deutsch (Astros).

The Rays couldn't be happier with the package they received from Houston for Aubrey Huff at the All-Star break. While Ben Zobrist emerged as the starting shortstop in Tampa and should be at least a solid utilityman in the future, Talbot has an even better ceiling. He was dominant after changing organizations and at his best in the Double-A Southern League playoffs, tossing two complete-game shutouts while fanning 24 batters and walking just two in 18 innings. It took him a while, but Talbot finally grew into the velocity the Astros expected when they drafted him in the second-round in 2002. He pitched consistently at 90-93 mph last year, and the command of his secondary pitches improved. His changeup always has been effective, and he made strides picking up a third pitch, which is a cross between a cutter and a slider. He didn't have much luck trying to develop a consistent curveball or slider while in the Houston system. Talbot has a clean delivery and plenty of athleticism. Talbot could challenge for a spot in Tampa Bay's rotation by the end of 2007.

| Year | Club (League) | Class | W | L | ERA | G | GS | CG | SV | IP | H | R | ER | HR | BB | SO | AVG |
|------|---------------|-------|---|---|-----|---|----|----|----|----|---|---|----|----|----|----|-----|
| 2003 | Martinsville (Appy) | R | 4 | 4 | 2.83 | 12 | 12 | 0 | 0 | 54 | 45 | 26 | 17 | 1 | 11 | 46 | .224 |
| 2004 | Lexington (SAL) | A | 10 | 10 | 3.83 | 27 | 27 | 1 | 0 | 153 | 145 | 78 | 65 | 16 | 49 | 115 | .252 |
| 2005 | Salem (CL) | A | 8 | 11 | 4.34 | 27 | 27 | 1 | 0 | 151 | 169 | 90 | 73 | 15 | 46 | 100 | .280 |
| 2006 | Corpus Christi (TL) | AA | 6 | 4 | 3.39 | 18 | 17 | 0 | 1 | 90 | 94 | 49 | 34 | 4 | 29 | 96 | .269 |
| | Montgomery (SL) | AA | 4 | 3 | 1.90 | 10 | 10 | 0 | 0 | 66 | 51 | 16 | 14 | 2 | 18 | 59 | .214 |
| **MINOR LEAGUE TOTALS** | | | 32 | 32 | 3.55 | 94 | 93 | 2 | 1 | 515 | 504 | 259 | 203 | 38 | 153 | 416 | .256 |

## 14  JUAN SALAS                                                        RHP

**Born:** Nov. 7, 1978. **B-T:** R-R. **Ht.:** 6-2. **Wt.:** 210. **Signed:** Dominican Republic, 1998. **Signed by:** Rudy Santin.

Salas was as close to perfect as any reliever could be during the first three months of the 2006 season. The righthander didn't allow an earned run in 48⅓ innings to start the year. When the streak ended on July 14, Salas recovered to record the last two outs of a combined no-hitter with Jason Hammel in his next outing. Salas has been a full-time pitcher for little more than two years, having signed for $600,000 as a third baseman and hitting .264/.296/.361 in his first six seasons in pro ball. He has had a much easier time preventing hits than he did collecting them, as hit .128 opponent average ranked second among minor league relievers in 2006. Salas has a mid-90s fastball with a natural cutting action that evokes

comparisons to Mariano Rivera's out pitch. It moves so much that one scout called it "the best 95 mph slider I've ever seen." He succeeds mostly by overpowering hitters with his fastball, though he also has an actual mid-80s slider. A solid athlete with a long, loose arm action, Salas has low mileage on his arm and has made rapid strides in harnessing his control. His command needs improvement, as does his ability to repeat his delivery. But he could make the Tampa Bay bullpen in 2007 and emerge as the team's closer in the near future.

| Year | Club (League) | Class | W | L | ERA | G | GS | CG | SV | IP | H | R | ER | HR | BB | SO | AVG |
|------|---------------|-------|---|---|-----|---|----|----|----|----|---|---|----|----|----|----|-----|
| 2004 | Princeton (Appy) | R | 1 | 0 | 4.82 | 8 | 0 | 0 | 0 | 9 | 10 | 7 | 5 | 2 | 6 | 6 | .263 |
| 2005 | Visalia (Cal) | A | 2 | 1 | 3.52 | 25 | 0 | 0 | 1 | 38 | 30 | 19 | 15 | 6 | 18 | 47 | .216 |
| 2005 | Montgomery (SL) | AA | 1 | 0 | 3.68 | 15 | 0 | 0 | 0 | 22 | 25 | 12 | 9 | 2 | 12 | 18 | .281 |
| 2006 | Montgomery (SL) | AA | 3 | 0 | 0.00 | 23 | 0 | 0 | 14 | 35 | 13 | 4 | 0 | 0 | 14 | 52 | .110 |
|  | Durham (IL) | AAA | 1 | 1 | 1.57 | 27 | 0 | 0 | 3 | 29 | 15 | 5 | 5 | 3 | 11 | 33 | .149 |
|  | Tampa Bay (AL) | MLB | 0 | 0 | 5.40 | 8 | 0 | 0 | 0 | 10 | 13 | 7 | 6 | 1 | 3 | 8 | .295 |
| **MINOR LEAGUE TOTALS** | | | 8 | 2 | 2.30 | 98 | 0 | 0 | 18 | 133 | 93 | 47 | 34 | 13 | 61 | 156 | .192 |
| **MAJOR LEAGUE TOTALS** | | | 0 | 0 | 5.40 | 8 | 0 | 0 | 0 | 10 | 13 | 7 | 6 | 1 | 3 | 8 | .295 |

##  FERNANDO PEREZ
OF

**Born:** April 23, 1983. **B-T:** B-R. **Ht.:** 6-1. **Wt.:** 195. **Drafted:** Columbia, 2004 (7th round). **Signed by:** Brad Matthews.

Perez continued to make progress toward becoming a quality leadoff man and center fielder. The highest-drafted player ever out of Columbia, Perez hit .339 over the final two months, led the minors in runs scored and earned the managers' vote as the best defensive outfielder in the California League. He combines athleticism and intelligence to get the most out of his ability. A natural righthanded hitter, Perez began to switch-hit in 2006. With top-of-the-line speed, he focuses on hitting the ball on the ground, believing if it bounces twice he'll beat it out for an infield hit. Though he hit .303 from the left side, he needs to do a better job of making contact against righthanders. Perez has more to learn about basestealing as well, as he was caught 16 times in 49 attempts, too often for a player with his speed. He also can improve at taking the proper angles on fly balls instead of relying on his speed to recover from mistakes. His arm is average. Perez isn't as one-dimensional as former Devil Rays speedster Joey Gathright, whom they traded to the Royals in 2006. He'll move up to Double-A this year, and Tampa Bay continues to have high hopes for him.

| Year | Club (League) | Class | AVG | G | AB | R | H | 2B | 3B | HR | RBI | BB | SO | SB | OBP | SLG |
|------|---------------|-------|-----|---|----|---|---|----|----|----|-----|----|----|----|-----|-----|
| 2004 | Hudson Valley (NYP) | A | .232 | 69 | 267 | 46 | 62 | 8 | 5 | 2 | 20 | 30 | 70 | 24 | .314 | .322 |
| 2005 | SW Michigan (MWL) | A | .289 | 134 | 522 | 93 | 151 | 17 | 13 | 6 | 48 | 58 | 80 | 57 | .361 | .406 |
| 2006 | Visalia (Cal) | A | .307 | 133 | 547 | 123 | 168 | 19 | 9 | 4 | 56 | 78 | 134 | 33 | .398 | .397 |
| **MINOR LEAGUE TOTALS** | | | .285 | 336 | 1336 | 262 | 381 | 44 | 27 | 12 | 124 | 166 | 284 | 114 | .367 | .385 |

## SHAWN RIGGANS
C

**Born:** July 25, 1980. **B-T:** R-R. **Ht.:** 6-2. **Wt.:** 197. **Drafted:** Indian River (Fla.) CC, 2000 (24th round). **Signed by:** Kevin Elfering.

Injuries plagued Riggans early in his career, beginning with Tommy John surgery in 2001, further elbow problems in 2004 and a sprained ankle early in 2005. He has stayed healthy since. He has solid power and would be a good run producer in the lower half of a major league lineup. He showed more consistency with the bat in 2006 by lessening his tendency to pull most pitches. He still gets too aggressive at times, however. Like most catchers, he doesn't run well, but he does show excellent bounce behind the plate. Managers rated him the International League's best defensive catcher. Though he threw out just 25 percent of basestealers last year, Riggans' arm strength is a tick above average, and he possesses a quick release with solid accuracy on his throws. His game-calling continues to improve, and scouts and managers love his hard-nosed approach. His window of opportunity closed somewhat when the Devil Rays traded for Dioner Navarro in mid-2006. But Riggans can be at least a solid backup, and given the chance he could be an effective regular.

| Year | Club (League) | Class | AVG | G | AB | R | H | 2B | 3B | HR | RBI | BB | SO | SB | OBP | SLG |
|------|---------------|-------|-----|---|----|---|---|----|----|----|-----|----|----|----|-----|-----|
| 2001 | Princeton (Appy) | R | .345 | 15 | 58 | 15 | 20 | 4 | 0 | 8 | 17 | 9 | 18 | 1 | .433 | .828 |
| 2002 | Hudson Valley (NYP) | A | .263 | 73 | 266 | 34 | 70 | 13 | 0 | 9 | 48 | 32 | 72 | 2 | .343 | .414 |
| 2003 | Charleston, S.C. (SAL) | A | .280 | 68 | 232 | 33 | 65 | 17 | 0 | 3 | 34 | 19 | 35 | 3 | .340 | .392 |
|  | Orlando (SL) | AA | .274 | 22 | 62 | 7 | 17 | 6 | 0 | 1 | 11 | 4 | 14 | 0 | .319 | .419 |
| 2004 | Bakersfield (Cal) | A | .346 | 34 | 127 | 20 | 44 | 11 | 0 | 5 | 22 | 15 | 23 | 0 | .417 | .551 |
|  | Montgomery (SL) | AA | .222 | 10 | 36 | 3 | 8 | 1 | 0 | 2 | 7 | 2 | 14 | 0 | .282 | .417 |
| 2005 | Montgomery (SL) | AA | .310 | 89 | 313 | 40 | 97 | 21 | 0 | 8 | 53 | 26 | 69 | 1 | .365 | .454 |
| 2006 | Durham (IL) | AAA | .293 | 115 | 417 | 43 | 122 | 26 | 2 | 11 | 54 | 27 | 88 | 2 | .341 | .444 |
|  | Tampa Bay (AL) | MLB | .172 | 10 | 29 | 3 | 5 | 1 | 0 | 0 | 1 | 4 | 7 | 0 | .273 | .207 |
| **MINOR LEAGUE TOTALS** | | | .293 | 426 | 1511 | 195 | 443 | 99 | 2 | 47 | 246 | 134 | 333 | 9 | .354 | .455 |
| **MAJOR LEAGUE TOTALS** | | | .172 | 10 | 29 | 3 | 5 | 1 | 0 | 0 | 1 | 4 | 7 | 0 | .273 | .207 |

## 17 ANDREW SONNANSTINE                                                    RHP

**Born:** March 18, 1983. **B-T:** R-R. **Ht.:** 6-3. **Wt.:** 185. **Drafted:** Kent State, 2004 (13th round). **Signed by:** James Bonnici.

The Rays' 2006 minor league pitcher of the year, Sonnanstine finished first in the minors in shutouts (four) and second in innings. He won nine straight decisions at midseason, allowing just nine earned runs during that stretch, and added two more victories in the Southern League playoffs. His lone plus pitch is a changeup that Tampa Bay righty Jamie Shields taught him. Sonnanstine mixes the changeup well with his upper-80s fastball and sneaky slurve, and few pitches in the minors throw more quality strikes. He has more career starts (63) than walks (62), and managers rated his control the best in the Southern League last summer. Athletic and competitive, Sonnanstine is a durable workhorse who must continue to prove himself at every level. He has enough stuff and the guile to pitch in the lower half of a big league rotation. He'll spend most of 2007 in Triple-A.

| Year | Club (League) | Class | W | L | ERA | G | GS | CG | SV | IP | H | R | ER | HR | BB | SO | AVG |
|------|---------------|-------|---|---|-----|---|----|----|----|----|---|---|----|----|----|----|-----|
| 2004 | Hudson Valley (NYP) | A | 3 | 1 | 1.00 | 9 | 2 | 0 | 1 | 27 | 18 | 4 | 3 | 0 | 3 | 24 | .176 |
| | Charleston, S.C. (SAL) | A | 2 | 0 | 0.59 | 8 | 5 | 0 | 0 | 31 | 18 | 5 | 2 | 0 | 7 | 42 | .167 |
| 2005 | SW Michigan (MWL) | A | 10 | 4 | 2.55 | 18 | 18 | 1 | 0 | 117 | 103 | 42 | 33 | 10 | 11 | 103 | .232 |
| | Visalia (Cal) | A | 4 | 1 | 3.80 | 10 | 10 | 0 | 0 | 64 | 71 | 29 | 27 | 5 | 7 | 75 | .277 |
| 2006 | Montgomery (SL) | AA | 15 | 8 | 2.67 | 28 | 28 | 4 | 0 | 186 | 151 | 63 | 55 | 15 | 34 | 153 | .224 |
| **MINOR LEAGUE TOTALS** | | | 34 | 14 | 2.55 | 73 | 63 | 5 | 1 | 424 | 361 | 143 | 120 | 30 | 62 | 397 | .228 |

## 18 JOHN JASO                                                              C

**Born:** Sept. 19, 1983. **B-T:** L-R. **Ht.:** 6-2. **Wt.:** 205. **Drafted:** Southwestern (Calif.) JC, 2003 (12th round). **Signed by:** Craig Weissmann.

Jaso has the bat and overall ability to becoming a starting big league catcher, but he'll have to prove he can stay healthy first. Rotator-cuff problems and subsequent arthroscopic surgery limited him to 92 games in 2005, with most of those coming as a DH. He didn't go behind the plate in 2006 until mid-June, and even then he didn't catch in consecutive games. The Devil Rays are being cautious with Jaso because of his upside. He makes solid contact, drives the ball to all fields and could hit 20-plus homers annually. When healthy, he has above-average arm strength with good accuracy, but he threw out just 21 percent of basestealers while at less than 100 percent last year. He has excellent mobility and agility and is adept at blocking balls in the dirt, though his game-calling remains undeveloped due in part to playing time lost to injuries. Tampa Bay hopes he can put in a healthy season in Double-A this year.

| Year | Club (League) | Class | AVG | G | AB | R | H | 2B | 3B | HR | RBI | BB | SO | SB | OBP | SLG |
|------|---------------|-------|-----|---|----|---|---|----|----|----|-----|----|----|----|-----|-----|
| 2003 | Hudson Valley (NYP) | A | .227 | 47 | 154 | 20 | 35 | 7 | 0 | 2 | 20 | 25 | 26 | 2 | .344 | .312 |
| 2004 | Hudson Valley (NYP) | A | .302 | 57 | 199 | 34 | 60 | 17 | 2 | 2 | 35 | 22 | 32 | 1 | .378 | .437 |
| 2005 | SW Michigan (MWL) | A | .307 | 92 | 332 | 61 | 102 | 25 | 1 | 14 | 50 | 42 | 53 | 3 | .383 | .515 |
| 2006 | Visalia (Cal) | A | .309 | 95 | 366 | 58 | 113 | 22 | 0 | 10 | 55 | 31 | 48 | 1 | .362 | .451 |
| **MINOR LEAGUE TOTALS** | | | .295 | 291 | 1051 | 173 | 310 | 71 | 3 | 28 | 160 | 120 | 159 | 7 | .369 | .448 |

## 19 JEFF RIDGWAY                                                          LHP

**Born:** Aug. 17, 1980. **B-T:** R-L. **Ht.:** 6-3. **Wt.:** 189. **Drafted:** HS—Port Angeles, Wash., 1999 (14th round). **Signed by:** Paul Kirsch.

Ridgway missed all of the 2002 season with Tommy John surgery and half of the 2004 slate with an inflamed left shoulder. He found his rhythm during the second half of 2005 and was impressive last summer. He allowed earned runs in just 13 of 50 relief appearances and, more important, showed his arm is fully recovered. He threw more free and easy in 2006 than he had the year before, and had confidence in his arm for the first time in years. Ridgway pitches mostly with his 90-93 mph fastball and hard slurve, though he'll mix in a changeup on occasion. He does a nice job of working on both sides of the plate and keeping his pitches down in the strike zone. A hard worker and one of the feel-good stories in the organization, Ridgway is fearless on the mound. He should battle for a bullpen job with the Rays this spring and will earn one if he can show more consistency with his stuff.

| Year | Club (League) | Class | W | L | ERA | G | GS | CG | SV | IP | H | R | ER | HR | BB | SO | AVG |
|------|---------------|-------|---|---|-----|---|----|----|----|----|---|---|----|----|----|----|-----|
| 2000 | Princeton (Appy) | R | 3 | 4 | 2.47 | 12 | 12 | 0 | 0 | 55 | 47 | 24 | 15 | 2 | 30 | 60 | .230 |
| 2001 | Charleston, S.C. (SAL) | A | 7 | 8 | 4.07 | 22 | 22 | 0 | 0 | 104 | 110 | 55 | 47 | 4 | 42 | 71 | .273 |
| 2002 | Did not play—Injured | | | | | | | | | | | | | | | | |
| 2003 | Charleston, S.C. (SAL) | A | 5 | 8 | 4.17 | 24 | 19 | 0 | 0 | 99 | 102 | 63 | 46 | 2 | 41 | 74 | .268 |
| 2004 | Bakersfield (Cal) | A | 2 | 3 | 2.31 | 15 | 1 | 0 | 1 | 35 | 32 | 17 | 9 | 0 | 19 | 27 | .241 |
| 2005 | Visalia (Cal) | A | 3 | 4 | 5.20 | 24 | 0 | 0 | 0 | 45 | 43 | 31 | 26 | 2 | 36 | 56 | .257 |
| 2006 | Montgomery (SL) | AA | 1 | 0 | 2.33 | 16 | 0 | 0 | 2 | 19 | 10 | 5 | 5 | 1 | 7 | 29 | .152 |
| | Durham (IL) | AAA | 1 | 4 | 3.03 | 34 | 0 | 0 | 0 | 39 | 35 | 15 | 13 | 3 | 13 | 38 | .238 |
| **MINOR LEAGUE TOTALS** | | | 22 | 31 | 3.66 | 147 | 54 | 0 | 3 | 396 | 379 | 210 | 161 | 14 | 188 | 355 | .253 |

## ELLIOT JOHNSON 2B

**Born:** March 9, 1984. **B-T:** B-R. **Ht.:** 6-0. **Wt.:** 185. **Signed:** NDFA/HS—Thatcher, Ariz., 2002. **Signed by:** Craig Weissmann.

Johnson, whose brother Leon has been drafted three times by the Devil Rays and is now at Brigham Young, played his high school ball in a small mining town in eastern Arizona that isn't on any of the scouting trails. He would have headed to Eastern Arizona JC had Rays scout Craig Weissmann hadn't headed to an all-star game while on a trip to sign 2002 second-round pick Jason Pridie. Weissmann spotted Johnson and signed him as a nondrafted free agent. Since then, Johnson has made steady progress. Plus speed has long been his best tool, but he also has developed solid power from both sides of the plate in the last two years. He was just one of six minor leaguers to reach double digits in doubles, triples and homers in 2006. He came just the second player in pro baseball history to hit three homers in the first three innings of a game, joining Carl Reynolds of the 1930 White Sox when he accomplished the feat in 2004. Johnson is still somewhat raw at the plate and on the bases. His swing gets long when he tires, which results in high strikeout totals that he'll need to reduce in order to become a true leadoff man. He also could stand to draw more walks. After stealing 43 bases in each of the previous two seasons, he dropped to just 20 and was caught 18 times in 2006, illustrating the need for improving his reads and jumps. Johnson's range at second base is above average, and he has made steady improvement with his ability to turn the double play. His defensive consistency also has gotten better, and he made just 13 errors in 2006—down from 30 the year before. Johnson should make the jump to Triple-A in 2007 and could make his big league debut at some point during the year. His combination of speed and pop should enable him to stick in the majors, but his consistency will determine whether he becomes a starter or a utilityman.

| Year | Club (League) | Class | AVG | G | AB | R | H | 2B | 3B | HR | RBI | BB | SO | SB | OBP | SLG |
|------|---------------|-------|-----|---|----|---|---|----|----|----|-----|----|----|----|-----|-----|
| 2002 | Princeton (Appy) | R | .263 | 42 | 152 | 21 | 40 | 10 | 1 | 1 | 13 | 18 | 48 | 14 | .345 | .362 |
| 2003 | Charleston, S.C. (SAL) | A | .212 | 54 | 151 | 22 | 32 | 4 | 0 | 0 | 15 | 38 | 32 | 8 | .370 | .238 |
| 2004 | Charleston, S.C. (SAL) | A | .262 | 126 | 503 | 92 | 132 | 22 | 7 | 6 | 41 | 54 | 91 | 43 | .339 | .370 |
| 2005 | Visalia (Cal) | A | .273 | 56 | 227 | 42 | 62 | 10 | 3 | 8 | 33 | 24 | 49 | 28 | .350 | .449 |
| | Montgomery (SL) | AA | .261 | 63 | 264 | 31 | 69 | 9 | 6 | 3 | 21 | 13 | 68 | 15 | .305 | .375 |
| 2006 | Montgomery (SL) | AA | .281 | 122 | 494 | 69 | 139 | 21 | 10 | 15 | 50 | 39 | 122 | 20 | .335 | .455 |
| **MINOR LEAGUE TOTALS** | | | .265 | 463 | 1791 | 277 | 474 | 76 | 27 | 33 | 173 | 186 | 410 | 128 | .338 | .393 |

## JAMES HOUSER LHP

**Born:** Dec. 15, 1984. **B-T:** L-L. **Ht.:** 6-4. **Wt.:** 185. **Drafted:** HS—Sarasota, Fla., 2003 (2nd round). **Signed by:** Kevin Elfering.

Houser could be close to re-establishing himself as one of the premier prospects in the organization. Lean and wiry when he signed with the Rays as a second-rounder in 2003, Houser dealt with health and durability concerns after pitching just 33 innings in 2004 and missing most of July 2005 with shoulder problems that didn't require surgery. Last year, Houser made every start and tossed a career-high 151 innings at high Class A Visalia. He didn't lose after May 12 and added two more victories in the California League playoffs. Houser has added strength in the past two years. His fastball, once a low-90s offering, now lives at 87-90 mph but features impressive late movement that generates swings-and-misses. He runs his cutter in on the hands of righthanders and away from lefties, and he also throws a sweeping curveball and a straight changeup. The most impressive aspects of Houser's game are his mound presence and his ability to mix all of his pitches. Houser has an easy delivery but struggles on occasion with his release point. He's ready for Double-A.

| Year | Club (League) | Class | W | L | ERA | G | GS | CG | SV | IP | H | R | ER | HR | BB | SO | AVG |
|------|---------------|-------|---|---|-----|---|----|----|----|-----|---|---|----|----|----|----|-----|
| 2003 | Princeton (Appy) | R | 0 | 4 | 3.73 | 10 | 10 | 0 | 0 | 41 | 43 | 23 | 17 | 1 | 13 | 44 | .262 |
| 2004 | Charleston, S.C. (SAL) | A | 3 | 1 | 2.20 | 7 | 7 | 0 | 0 | 33 | 27 | 9 | 8 | 1 | 13 | 27 | .239 |
| 2005 | SW Michigan (MWL) | A | 8 | 8 | 3.76 | 22 | 22 | 0 | 0 | 115 | 100 | 50 | 48 | 12 | 31 | 109 | .239 |
| 2006 | Visalia (Cal) | A | 12 | 4 | 4.41 | 28 | 27 | 0 | 0 | 151 | 140 | 80 | 74 | 20 | 46 | 137 | .246 |
| **MINOR LEAGUE TOTALS** | | | 23 | 17 | 3.89 | 67 | 66 | 0 | 0 | 340 | 310 | 162 | 147 | 34 | 103 | 317 | .245 |

## WES BANKSTON 1B/3B

**Born:** Nov. 23, 1983. **B-T:** R-R. **Ht.:** 6-4. **Wt.:** 200. **Drafted:** HS—Plano, Texas, 2002 (4th round). **Signed by:** Milt Hill.

The first half of the 2006 season was a lost cause for Bankston. He missed all of May with a strained oblique and struggled in all phases of the game when the Rays attempted to fill an organizational need by moving him from first base to third. He returned to first exclusively after his mid-July promotion to Triple-A and once again displayed a keen eye and solid stroke at the plate. Bankston has above-average raw power but has not parlayed that

asset into big home run numbers the last two years. He's a below-average runner and doesn't move as well as a 23-year-old should, which led to his problems at third base. He's only adequate at first base, where he's going to have to start hitting homers if he hopes to play regularly in the big leagues. Maintaining better overall conditioning would be a step in the right direction. Bankston will spend at least another half-season in Triple-A before getting serious consideration from the Devil Rays, who have no obvious first baseman of the future.

| Year | Club (League) | Class | AVG | G | AB | R | H | 2B | 3B | HR | RBI | BB | SO | SB | OBP | SLG |
|------|---------------|-------|-----|---|----|---|---|----|----|----|-----|----|----|----|-----|-----|
| 2002 | Princeton (Appy) | R | .301 | 62 | 246 | 48 | 74 | 10 | 1 | 18 | 57 | 18 | 46 | 2 | .346 | .569 |
|  | Hudson Valley (NYP) | A | .303 | 8 | 33 | 2 | 10 | 1 | 0 | 0 | 1 | 0 | 6 | 1 | .294 | .333 |
| 2003 | Charleston, S.C. (SAL) | A | .256 | 103 | 375 | 46 | 96 | 18 | 1 | 12 | 60 | 53 | 94 | 2 | .346 | .405 |
| 2004 | Charleston, S.C. (SAL) | A | .289 | 127 | 470 | 82 | 136 | 30 | 3 | 23 | 101 | 73 | 104 | 9 | .390 | .513 |
| 2005 | Visalia (Cal) | A | .387 | 17 | 62 | 15 | 24 | 4 | 1 | 3 | 23 | 15 | 17 | 0 | .513 | .629 |
|  | Montgomery (SL) | AA | .292 | 82 | 301 | 42 | 88 | 17 | 2 | 12 | 47 | 30 | 64 | 3 | .362 | .482 |
| 2006 | Durham (IL) | AAA | .297 | 52 | 195 | 22 | 58 | 13 | 0 | 5 | 29 | 10 | 40 | 0 | .333 | .441 |
|  | Montgomery (SL) | AA | .263 | 45 | 167 | 20 | 44 | 7 | 1 | 4 | 19 | 12 | 37 | 4 | .322 | .389 |
| **MINOR LEAGUE TOTALS** |  |  | .287 | 496 | 1849 | 277 | 530 | 100 | 9 | 77 | 337 | 211 | 408 | 21 | .362 | .475 |

## 23 CHRIS MASON
RHP

**Born:** July 1, 1984. **B-T:** R-R. **Ht.:** 6-0. **Wt.:** 185. **Drafted:** UNC Greensboro, 2005 (2nd round). **Signed by:** Brad Matthews.

Mason starred as a two-way player for UNC Greensboro in 2005 before signing as a second-rounder and having a strong debut when the Devil Rays eased him into pro ball as a reliever. Back in the rotation for his first full pro season, Mason continued to show flashes of potential while experiencing his share of adversity. Mason appeared to run out of gas late in the year, posting a 7.34 ERA over the final two months. The velocity and movement on his normally live low-90s fastball was down for most of the second half; he mustered an eight-inning one-hitter in his final start. At his best, Mason mixes his plus fastball with a hard slurve. He worked a decent changeup, which needs more consistent depth, into his repertoire last season. He has a bulldog demeanor and is so competitive that he's sometimes too stubborn for his own good. Mason throws strikes with ease but still is working on consistently locating his pitches where he wants in the zone. It's possible that he'll end up as a reliever, but Tampa Bay will keep trying to develop him as a starter this year in Double-A.

| Year | Club (League) | Class | W | L | ERA | G | GS | CG | SV | IP | H | R | ER | HR | BB | SO | AVG |
|------|---------------|-------|---|---|-----|---|----|----|----|----|---|---|----|----|----|----|-----|
| 2005 | Hudson Valley (NYP) | A | 1 | 1 | 2.40 | 9 | 0 | 0 | 2 | 15 | 11 | 4 | 4 | 0 | 8 | 14 | .220 |
| 2005 | SW Michigan (MWL) | A | 1 | 0 | 1.45 | 10 | 0 | 0 | 0 | 19 | 17 | 8 | 3 | 0 | 5 | 16 | .246 |
| 2006 | Visalia (Cal) | A | 12 | 10 | 5.02 | 28 | 27 | 0 | 0 | 152 | 177 | 96 | 85 | 17 | 44 | 111 | .289 |
| **MINOR LEAGUE TOTALS** |  |  | 14 | 11 | 4.45 | 47 | 27 | 0 | 2 | 186 | 205 | 108 | 92 | 17 | 57 | 141 | .280 |

## 24 JONATHAN BARRATT
LHP

**Born:** March 19, 1985. **B-T:** R-L. **Ht.:** 5-9. **Wt.:** 165. **Drafted:** HS—Springfield, Mo., 2004 (5th round). **Signed by:** Rickey Drexler.

The Rays realize they made a mistake with Barratt in 2005. After his impressive pro debut at short-season Hudson Valley in 2004, he moved from the rotation to the bullpen and jumped to high Class A. Battling his control and confidence, he wound up posting a 6.59 ERA in 36 outings. Tampa Bay thought the lefty's small frame would respond better to a relief role, but corrected its error and sent Barratt back to the California League as a starter in 2006. If he hadn't finished four outs short of qualifying for the ERA title after skipping his final start to rest a groin injury, his 2.93 mark would have led the league by 0.75. Though he's just 5-foot-9 and 165 pounds, Barratt throws with little effort and has an exceptionally quick arm that delivers low-90s fastballs. His hard curve is one of the best lefty breaking balls in the system, and he throws his offspeed pitches from a variety of arm angles. The Rays also like his toughness and resiliency and saw his confidence return with every start he made last year. Barratt needs to become more consistent with his changeup while moving up to Double-A in 2007. The scrappy southpaw will remain a starter for the foreseeable future.

| Year | Club (League) | Class | W | L | ERA | G | GS | CG | SV | IP | H | R | ER | HR | BB | SO | AVG |
|------|---------------|-------|---|---|-----|---|----|----|----|----|---|---|----|----|----|----|-----|
| 2004 | Hudson Valley (NYP) | A | 2 | 3 | 2.74 | 10 | 10 | 1 | 0 | 43 | 38 | 21 | 13 | 2 | 11 | 50 | .233 |
| 2005 | Visalia (Cal) | A | 2 | 6 | 6.59 | 36 | 5 | 0 | 1 | 71 | 85 | 59 | 52 | 9 | 52 | 79 | .293 |
| 2006 | Visalia (Cal) | A | 9 | 6 | 2.93 | 21 | 20 | 1 | 0 | 111 | 93 | 43 | 36 | 8 | 37 | 100 | .229 |
| **MINOR LEAGUE TOTALS** |  |  | 13 | 15 | 4.05 | 67 | 35 | 2 | 1 | 224 | 216 | 123 | 101 | 19 | 100 | 229 | .251 |

## 25 JOSH BUTLER
RHP

**Born:** Dec. 11, 1984. **B-T:** R-R. **Ht.:** 6-5. **Wt.:** 200. **Drafted:** San Diego, 2006 (2nd round). **Signed by:** Dan Drake.

The 47th overall pick in the 2006 draft, Butler signed with Tampa Bay for $725,000 after

an up-and-down college season at San Diego. He didn't allow a run in his first 27 innings but tired late in the spring and wound up pitching just 13 innings in his pro debut. The Devil Rays shut him down for two months after he came down with a mild case of biceps tendinitis. When he's 100 percent, Butler possesses a 91-95 mph fastball with above-average life. He also has two plus breaking balls, a tight 12-to-6 overhand curveball and a sweeping slider. His changeup also shows promise with decent fade and depth. Tampa Bay is working on refining Butler's mechanics to help him drive more with his lower body in order to take stress off his arm and shoulder. At 6-foot-5, he gets out of kilter with his mechanics on occasion, but the Rays believe the entire package should come together nicely once his body fully matures. While they'll continue to be careful with him, Butler has the arm to move quickly through the minors. He'll open 2007 season in high Class A.

| Year | Club (League) | Class | W | L | ERA | G | GS | CG | SV | IP | H | R | ER | HR | BB | SO | AVG |
|------|---------------|-------|---|---|-----|---|----|----|----|----|---|---|----|----|----|----|-----|
| 2006 | Hudson Valley (NYP) | A | 0 | 3 | 5.40 | 5 | 2 | 0 | 0 | 13 | 13 | 9 | 8 | 0 | 7 | 12 | .265 |
| **MINOR LEAGUE TOTALS** | | | 0 | 3 | 5.40 | 5 | 2 | 0 | 0 | 13 | 13 | 9 | 8 | 0 | 7 | 12 | .265 |

## 26 WADE TOWNSEND                                             RHP

**Born:** Feb. 22, 1983. **B-T:** R-R. **Ht.:** 6-4. **Wt.:** 230. **Drafted:** Dripping Springs, Texas, 2005 (1st round). **Signed by:** Jonathan Bonifay.

Townsend went eighth overall in both the 2004 and 2005 drafts, though neither the Orioles nor the Devil Rays would have drafted him that high had the scouting departments gotten their way. He was part of one of the most successful college rotations ever at Rice from 2002-2004. Townsend, Philip Humber and Jeff Niemann won the 2003 College World Series together and all three went in the first eight picks of the 2004 draft. The Orioles low-balled Townsend in 2003, and he got angry and returned to Rice to complete his degree. Townsend hadn't pitched for nearly a year when he worked out for clubs in April and May in 2005, and he appealed to Tampa Bay's former upper-management team because he had no bargaining power. Townsend signed for $1.5 million—$700,000 below MLB's slot projection—and little has gone right for him since. He strained his neck in his first pro outing, went winless in 12 outings and then blew out his elbow in the Arizona Fall League. Tommy John surgery sidelined him for the entire 2006 slate. When he was starring at Rice, Townsend had a low-90s fastball and a devastating spike curveball, and he'd also flash an above-average changeup. In his pro debut, he pitched at 85-88 and didn't have the usual bite on his curve. Some scouts believe his future will be in the bullpen, in part because he has an intense competitive drive and wouldn't have to try to pace himself. At this point, the Rays just want to get Townsend back on the mound early in 2007 and see what they have.

| Year | Club (League) | Class | W | L | ERA | G | GS | CG | SV | IP | H | R | ER | HR | BB | SO | AVG |
|------|---------------|-------|---|---|-----|---|----|----|----|----|---|---|----|----|----|----|-----|
| 2005 | Hudson Valley (NYP) | A | 0 | 4 | 5.49 | 12 | 10 | 0 | 0 | 39 | 44 | 28 | 24 | 4 | 24 | 33 | .275 |
| 2006 | Did not play—Injured | | | | | | | | | | | | | | | | |
| **MINOR LEAGUE TOTALS** | | | 0 | 4 | 5.49 | 12 | 10 | 0 | 0 | 39 | 44 | 28 | 24 | 4 | 24 | 33 | .275 |

## 27 SERGIO PEDROZA                                             OF

**Born:** Feb. 23, 1984. **B-T:** L-R. **Ht.:** 6-1. **Wt.:** 180. **Drafted:** Cal State Fullerton, 2005 (3rd round). **Signed by:** Tim Kelly (Dodgers).

Pedroza has put up impressive numbers as a pro. He hit 16 homers in a half-season after signing with the Dodgers as a 2005 third-round pick, then smacked 28 homers, drew 101 walks and led the low Class A South Atlantic League with a .437 on-base percentage and .562 slugging percentage. While Pedroza did reach high Class A, he did most of his damage in SAL, where he was older than most of his competition at 22. But the Rays thought enough of his offensive potential to get him included in the July trade that sent Julio Lugo to the Dodgers. Pedroza has some juice in his bat and is capable of driving the ball out of the park to all fields. He's a free swinger who strikes out a lot yet still manages to draw a ton of walks. Without question, Pedroza's live bat will have to carry him at higher levels. He's a below-average runner who was caught eight times in 10 steals attempts last year, and he's no more than an adequate defender on the outfield corners. Besides his bat, his arm is his best tool. He'll open this season in Double-A, which will be a fairer test of his talents.

| Year | Club (League) | Class | AVG | G | AB | R | H | 2B | 3B | HR | RBI | BB | SO | SB | OBP | SLG |
|------|---------------|-------|-----|---|----|---|---|----|----|----|-----|----|----|----|-----|-----|
| 2005 | Ogden (Pio) | R | .500 | 12 | 46 | 13 | 23 | 1 | 0 | 4 | 18 | 6 | 8 | 4 | .574 | .783 |
| | Columbus (SAL) | A | .207 | 49 | 179 | 31 | 37 | 11 | 1 | 12 | 30 | 16 | 58 | 0 | .294 | .480 |
| 2006 | Vero Beach (FSL) | A | .154 | 13 | 39 | 7 | 6 | 2 | 0 | 3 | 9 | 8 | 18 | 0 | .292 | .436 |
| | Columbus (SAL) | A | .281 | 89 | 317 | 61 | 89 | 24 | 1 | 21 | 75 | 73 | 91 | 2 | .437 | .562 |
| | Visalia (Cal) | A | .313 | 29 | 99 | 23 | 31 | 9 | 1 | 4 | 9 | 20 | 26 | 0 | .447 | .545 |
| **MINOR LEAGUE TOTALS** | | | .274 | 192 | 680 | 135 | 186 | 47 | 3 | 44 | 141 | 123 | 201 | 6 | .404 | .546 |

## 28 CHRIS NOWAK 1B

**Born:** Feb. 21, 1983. **B-T:** R-R. **Ht.:** 6-5. **Wt.:** 225. **Drafted:** South Carolina-Spartanburg, 2004 (19th round). **Signed by:** Hank King.

At 23, Nowak was a little old to be considered a top prospect in the California League last year, but he made the most of the situation. Sent to high Class A in part because Kevin Witt and Wes Bankston were ahead of him on the organization depth chart, Nowak led the Cal League in doubles and RBIs. His compact stroke allows him to hit for average and for gap power to all fields. He controls the strike zone well, making him dangerous in RBI situations. Nowak also runs well for a first baseman and stole 17 bases in 23 tries in 2006. He offers a big target at first base and has experience at third base. The Rays also credit Nowak with taking a leadership role at Visalia following Reid Brignac's promotion to Double-A. He'll need to hit for more home run power at higher levels, but his stock is on the rise. He'll move to Double-A and could emerge as the system's top first-base prospect in 2007.

| Year | Club (League) | Class | AVG | G | AB | R | H | 2B | 3B | HR | RBI | BB | SO | SB | OBP | SLG |
|------|---------------|-------|-----|---|----|---|---|----|----|----|-----|----|----|----|-----|-----|
| 2004 | Hudson Valley (NYP) | A | .279 | 62 | 219 | 26 | 61 | 18 | 3 | 1 | 32 | 16 | 35 | 1 | .347 | .402 |
| 2005 | SW Michigan (MWL) | A | .304 | 105 | 368 | 55 | 112 | 28 | 1 | 7 | 65 | 56 | 58 | 2 | .398 | .443 |
| 2006 | Visalia (Cal) | A | .308 | 130 | 494 | 93 | 152 | 45 | 3 | 11 | 103 | 69 | 83 | 17 | .397 | .478 |
| **MINOR LEAGUE TOTALS** | | | .301 | 297 | 1081 | 174 | 325 | 91 | 7 | 19 | 200 | 141 | 176 | 20 | .387 | .451 |

## 29 SHAUN CUMBERLAND OF

**Born:** Aug. 1, 1984. **B-T:** L-R. **Ht.:** 6-2. **Wt.:** 185. **Drafted:** HS—Milton, Fla., 2003 (10th round). **Signed by:** Skip Bundy.

The Rays continue to believe that Cumberland is on the verge of breaking out and becoming a blue-chip outfield prospect. After putting together a strong second half in low Class A the previous year, he ranked fourth in the organization in RBIs despite hitting .258 in 2006. Cumberland has all the tools to achieve Tampa Bay's projections. He shows budding power from the left side as well as above-average speed and an arm strong enough to man right field at higher levels. He's a good defender capable of handling any of the three outfield spots. He's also an aggressive and smart baserunner who succeeded on 29 of his 38 steal attempts and hit into just four double plays last year. The problem for Cumberland is that he gives away too many at-bats by chasing too many pitches. The Rays believe he can be a .300 hitter once he channels his competitiveness in the right direction. He'll try to make the necessary adjustments this season in Double-A.

| Year | Club (League) | Class | AVG | G | AB | R | H | 2B | 3B | HR | RBI | BB | SO | SB | OBP | SLG |
|------|---------------|-------|-----|---|----|---|---|----|----|----|-----|----|----|----|-----|-----|
| 2003 | Princeton (Appy) | R | .252 | 62 | 218 | 28 | 55 | 11 | 5 | 1 | 32 | 19 | 41 | 12 | .314 | .362 |
| 2004 | Hudson Valley (NYP) | A | .329 | 50 | 164 | 25 | 54 | 7 | 4 | 1 | 11 | 11 | 23 | 9 | .375 | .439 |
| 2005 | SW Michigan (MWL) | A | .268 | 119 | 436 | 62 | 117 | 22 | 3 | 13 | 69 | 37 | 100 | 23 | .326 | .422 |
| 2006 | Visalia (Cal) | A | .258 | 126 | 520 | 86 | 134 | 18 | 3 | 16 | 98 | 42 | 133 | 29 | .319 | .396 |
| **MINOR LEAGUE TOTALS** | | | .269 | 357 | 1338 | 201 | 360 | 58 | 15 | 31 | 210 | 109 | 297 | 73 | .327 | .404 |

## 30 DESMOND JENNINGS OF

**Born:** Oct. 30, 1986. **B-T:** R-R. **Ht.:** 6-2. **Wt.:** 180. **Drafted:** Itawamba (Miss.) CC, 2006 (10th round). **Signed by:** Rickey Drexler.

Jennings, whose $150,000 bonus was the highest in the 10th round of the 2006 draft, also had a bright future in football. A three-sport star (baseball, basketball, football) in high school, he signed to play football at Alabama before winding up at Itawamba (Miss.) CC. As a freshman at Itawamba in the fall of 2005, he earned juco all-America honors by topping all juco players with 6.75 catches per game. Last spring, he led the baseball team to the regional playoff finals. In his pro debut, Jennings used his 80 speed on the 20-80 scouting scale to pace the Appalachian League in runs and steals. He displays incredible athletic ability in all phases of the game. He has considerable range, plus instincts and a lightning-quick first step in center field. Right now, he steals bases on speed alone and will become even more of a threat on the bases once he gets comfortable reading pitchers and taking larger leads. He has a good idea at the plate with solid bat speed and decent power that should continue to increase. His worst tool may be his arm, which rates as average. His biggest weakness is his routes on fly balls, though his quickness makes up for most of his mistakes. He has the package to be a top-of-the-lineup hitter with power. He'll advance to Tampa Bay's new low Class A Columbus affiliate in 2007.

| Year | Club (League) | Class | AVG | G | AB | R | H | 2B | 3B | HR | RBI | BB | SO | SB | OBP | SLG |
|------|---------------|-------|-----|---|----|---|---|----|----|----|-----|----|----|----|-----|-----|
| 2006 | Princeton (Appy) | R | .277 | 56 | 213 | 48 | 59 | 10 | 1 | 4 | 20 | 22 | 39 | 32 | .360 | .390 |
| **MINOR LEAGUE TOTALS** | | | .277 | 56 | 213 | 48 | 59 | 10 | 1 | 4 | 20 | 22 | 39 | 32 | .360 | .390 |

# TEXAS
# RANGERS

BY **AARON FITT**

In his first year as Rangers general manager, **Jon Daniels** proved he wasn't afraid to take risks. He also wasn't willing to compromise his vision for the future of the franchise. That vision began to materialize in 2006, just perhaps not as quickly as Texas hoped.

With a potent offense, the Rangers hung around in the American League West race until the middle of the summer. They finished 80-82, good enough for third place. Afterward, Daniels fired manager Buck Showalter and replaced him with former Oakland bench coach Ron Washington.

As usual, Texas was undone by its lack of pitching. Kevin Millwood, who signed a five-year, $60 million free agent contract before the 2006 season, gave the Rangers a reliable workhorse at the front of their staff for the first time in years. Fellow Daniels acquisitions Vicente Padilla and Robinson Tejeda were solid for 47 starts between them, but the rest of the rotation was riddled with question marks.

Adam Eaton, acquired from San Diego to be the No. 2 starter in a deal for Chris Young and Adrian Gonzalez, was a major disappointment with a finger injury and departed for the Phillies as a free agent in November. Edinson Volquez, No. 1 on this list a year ago, couldn't adjust to the majors, and Kameron Loe couldn't make the transition from reliever to starter.

The two biggest deals Daniels made in his first year do not look good thus far. Prior to the season, he shipped free-agent-to-be Alfonso Soriano to the Nationals for Brad Wilkerson, Terrmel Sledge and minor league righthander Armando Galarraga. Soriano became the fourth member of the 40-40 club while Wilkerson and Galarraga were busts.

Just before the July trade deadline, Daniels picked up another pending free agent, Carlos Lee, and outfield prospect Nelson Cruz from the Brewers for Francisco Cordero, Kevin Mench, Laynce Nix and minor league righty Julian Cordero. Lee couldn't put Texas over the top and signed with the Astros in November. Cruz could become the Rangers' everyday right fielder in 2007.

Despite his willingness to make moves, Daniels refused to mortgage Texas' pitching future, holding on to John Danks, Eric Hurley, Volquez and Thomas Diamond. They continued their steady development under first-year farm director Scott Servais, though all four struggled at different times in 2006.

It wasn't a great year for Texas' farm system, as several of its most heralded prospects leveled off and the six U.S. affiliates combined for the worst winning percentage (.423) in baseball. But a number of the Rangers' 2006 draftees made impressive pro debuts, including lefty Kasey Kiker (first round), shortstop Marcus Lemon (fourth) and first baseman Chris Davis (fifth). Led by international scouting director A.J. Preller, Texas brought in another impressive haul in Latin America, highlighted by 16-year-old hurlers Wilmer Font and Geuris Grullon and 17-year-old third baseman/catcher Emmanuel Solis.

## TOP 30 PROSPECTS

1. John Danks, lhp
2. Eric Hurley, rhp
3. Edinson Volquez, rhp
4. Thomas Diamond, rhp
5. John Mayberry Jr., of
6. Joaquin Arias, ss
7. Kasey Kiker, lhp
8. Nick Masset, rhp
9. Jason Botts, of/dh
10. Josh Rupe, rhp
11. Chris Davis, of/1b
12. Marcus Lemon, ss
13. Taylor Teagarden, c
14. Omar Poveda, rhp
15. Armando Galarraga, rhp
16. Chad Tracy, c
17. Ben Harrison, of
18. Johnny Whittleman, 3b
19. Fabio Castillo, rhp
20. Francisco Cruceta, rhp
21. Wes Littleton, rhp
22. Daniel Haigwood, lhp
23. Freddy Guzman, of
24. Michael Schlact, rhp
25. Anthony Webster, of
26. Jesse Ingram, rhp
27. Doug Mathis, rhp
28. Danny Ray Herrera, lhp
29. Jose Vallejo, 2b
30. Jacob Rasner, rhp

# ORGANIZATION OVERVIEW

**General manager:** Jon Daniels. **Farm director:** John Lombardo. **Scouting director:** Ron Hopkins.

## 2006 PERFORMANCE

| Class | Team | League | W | L | PCT | Finish* | Manager | Affiliated |
|---|---|---|---|---|---|---|---|---|
| Majors | Texas | American | 80 | 82 | .494 | 9th (14) | Buck Showalter | — |
| Triple-A | Oklahoma RedHawks | Pacific Coast | 74 | 70 | .503 | 8th (16) | Tim Ireland | 1983 |
| Double-A | Frisco RoughRiders | Texas | 72 | 68 | .514 | 5th (8) | Darryl Kennedy | 2003 |
| High A | Bakersfield Blaze | California | 58 | 82 | .414 | 10th (10) | Arnie Beyeler | 2005 |
| Low A | Clinton LumberKings | Midwest | 45 | 94 | .324 | 14th (14) | Carlos Subero | 2003 |
| SS A | Spokane Indians | Northwest | 26 | 50 | .342 | 8th (8) | Mike Micucci | 2003 |
| Rookie | AZL Rangers | Arizona | 19 | 37 | .339 | 9th (9) | Bob Skube | 2003 |
| **OVERALL 2006 MINOR LEAGUE RECORD** | | | 294 | 401 | .423 | 30th (30) | | |

*Finish in overall standings (No. of teams in league). +League champion

## ORGANIZATION LEADERS

### BATTING

| | | |
|---|---|---|
| *AVG | Frostad, Emerson, Bakersfield | .320 |
| R | Harrison, Ben, Bakersfield/Frisco | 89 |
| H | Harrison, Ben, Bakersfield/Frisco | 164 |
| TB | Harrison, Ben, Bakersfield/Frisco | 287 |
| 2B | Mahar, Kevin, Frisco | 38 |
| 2B | Murphy, Steve, AZL Rangers/Bakersfield | 38 |
| 3B | Hulett, Tug, Bakersfield/Frisco | 11 |
| HR | Gold, Nate, Frisco | 34 |
| RBI | Gold, Nate, Frisco | 107 |
| RBI | Harrison, Ben, Bakersfield/Frisco | 107 |
| BB | Hulett, Tug, Bakersfield/Frisco | 92 |
| SO | Gac, Ian, Bakersfield/Clinton | 179 |
| SB | Guzman, Freddy, Portland/Oklahoma | 31 |
| *OBP | Hulett, Tug, Bakersfield/Frisco | .411 |
| *SLG | Gold, Nate, Frisco | .564 |
| XBH | Gold, Nate, Frisco | 67 |

### PITCHING #Minimum 75 innings

| | | |
|---|---|---|
| W | Diamond, Thomas, Frisco | 12 |
| W | Kometani, Kea, Bakersfield/Frisco | 12 |
| L | Rasner, Jacob, Clinton | 16 |
| #ERA | Volquez, Edinson, Oklahoma | 3.21 |
| G | Ramirez, Erasmo, Oklahoma | 54 |
| CG | Dickey, R.A., Oklahoma | 3 |
| SV | Corey, Bryan, Frisco/Oklahoma/Pawtucket | 15 |
| IP | Mathis, Doug, Bakersfield/Frisco | 161 |
| BB | Diamond, Thomas, Frisco | 78 |
| SO | Danks, John, Frisco/Oklahoma | 154 |
| AVG | Volquez, Edinson, Oklahoma | .203 |

## BEST TOOLS

| | |
|---|---|
| Best Hitter for Average | Joaquin Arias |
| Best Power Hitter | John Mayberry Jr. |
| Best Strike-Zone Discipline | Tug Hulett |
| Fastest Baserunner | Freddy Guzman |
| Best Athlete | John Mayberry Jr. |
| Best Fastball | Eric Hurley |
| Best Curveball | John Danks |
| Best Slider | Josh Rupe |
| Best Changeup | Edinson Volquez |
| Best Control | Danny Ray Herrera |
| Best Defensive Catcher | Taylor Teagarden |
| Best Defensive Infielder | Joaquin Arias |
| Best Infield Arm | Joaquin Arias |
| Best Defensive Outfielder | Freddy Guzman |
| Best Outfield Arm | John Mayberry Jr. |

## PROJECTED 2010 LINEUP

| | |
|---|---|
| Catcher | Gerald Laird |
| First Base | Mark Teixeira |
| Second Base | Ian Kinsler |
| Third Base | Hank Blalock |
| Shortstop | Michael Young |
| Left Field | John Mayberry Jr. |
| Center Field | Brad Wilkerson |
| Right Field | Nelson Cruz |
| Designated Hitter | Jason Botts |
| No. 1 Starter | John Danks |
| No. 2 Starter | Eric Hurley |
| No. 3 Starter | Kevin Millwood |
| No. 4 Starter | Vicente Padilla |
| No. 5 Starter | Thomas Diamond |
| Closer | Edinson Volquez |

## LAST YEAR'S TOP 20 PROSPECTS

1. Edison Volquez, rhp
2. John Danks, lhp
3. Thomas Diamond, rhp
4. Joaquin Arias, ss
5. Eric Hurley, rhp
6. Ian Kinsler, 2b
7. Armando Galarraga, rhp
8. Jason Botts, of
9. Taylor Teagarden, c
10. John Mayberry Jr., of
11. Johnny Whittleman, 3b
12. Josh Rupe, rhp
13. Michael Schlact, rhp
14. C.J. Wilson, lhp
15. Scott Feldman, rhp
16. Fabio Castro, lhp
17. Travis Metcalf, 3b
18. Vince Sinisi, of
19. John Hudgins, rhp
20. Jose Vallejo, 2b

## TOP PROSPECTS OF THE DECADE

| Year | Player, Pos. | 2006 Org. |
|---|---|---|
| 1997 | Danny Kolb, rhp | Brewers |
| 1998 | Ruben Mateo, of | Out of baseball |
| 1999 | Ruben Mateo, of | Out of baseball |
| 2000 | Ruben Mateo, of | Out of baseball |
| 2001 | Carlos Pena, 1b | Red Sox |
| 2002 | Hank Blalock, 3b | Rangers |
| 2003 | Mark Teixeira, 3b | Rangers |
| 2004 | Adrian Gonzalez, 1b | Padres |
| 2005 | Thomas Diamond, rhp. | Rangers |
| 2006 | Edison Volquez, rhp | Rangers |

## TOP DRAFT PICKS OF THE DECADE

| Year | Player, Pos. | 2006 Org. |
|---|---|---|
| 1997 | Jason Romano, 3b | Devil Rays |
| 1998 | Carlos Pena, 1b | Red Sox |
| 1999 | Colby Lewis, rhp | Tigers |
| 2000 | Scott Heard, c | Out of baseball |
| 2001 | Mark Teixeira, 3b | Rangers |
| 2002 | Drew Meyer, ss | Rangers |
| 2003 | John Danks, lhp | Rangers |
| 2004 | Thomas Diamond, rhp. | Rangers |
| 2005 | John Mayberry Jr., of | Rangers |
| 2006 | Kasey Kiker, lhp | Rangers |

## LARGEST BONUSES IN CLUB HISTORY

| | |
|---|---|
| Mark Teixeira, 2001 | $4,500,000 |
| John Danks, 2003 | $2,100,000 |
| Vincent Sinisi, 2003 | $2,070,000 |
| Thomas Diamond, 2004 | $2,025,000 |
| Drew Meyer, 2002 | $1,875,000 |

# MINOR LEAGUE DEPTH CHART

## Texas Rangers

**Impact: D.** The Rangers have some solid pitching prospects, but they lack any single elite prospect with superstar potential. John Mayberry is the only position player with real all-star potential.

**Depth: C.** Texas' strength is its pitching depth, but a number of its top arms have not developed as planned and have wound up in the bullpen. The system is devoid of impact bats at the higher levels.

**Sleeper:** Jose Vallejo, 2b. Though his numbers were not impressive, Vallejo made progress from the left side of the plate in just his first full year as a switch-hitter—also his first full professional season. His instincts and tools stand out in the system.

*Numbers in parentheses indicate prospect rankings.*

| LF | CF | RF |
|---|---|---|
| Jason Botts (9) | Freddy Guzman (23) | John Mayberry (5) |
| Anthony Webster (25) | Craig Gentry | Ben Harrison (17) |
| Kevin Mahar | Cody Podraza | Steve Murphy |
| K.C. Herren | Brandon Boggs | Tim Rodriguez |
| Jake Blalock | R.J. Anderson | |
| Grant Gerrard | | |

| 3B | SS | 2B | 1B |
|---|---|---|---|
| Johnny Whittleman (18) | Joaquin Arias (6) | Jose Vallejo (29) | Chris Davis (11) |
| Travis Metcalf | Marcus Lemon (12) | Tug Hulett | Nate Gold |
| Emmanuel Solis | Drew Meyer | Aarom Baldiris | Ian Gac |
| Steven Marquardt | Enrique Cruz | German Duran | Freddie Thon |
| Johan Yan | | | Jim Fasano |

| C |
|---|
| Taylor Teagarden (13) |
| Chad Tracy (16) |
| Cristian Santana |
| Emerson Frostad |
| Manuel Pina |
| Billy Killian |

### RHP

| Starters | Relievers |
|---|---|
| Eric Hurley (2) | Nick Masset (8) |
| Edinson Volquez (3) | Josh Rupe (10) |
| Thomas Diamond (4) | Wes Littleton (21) |
| Omar Poveda (14) | Jesse Ingram (26) |
| Armando Galarraga (15) | Omar Beltre |
| Fabio Castillo (19) | Alexi Ogando |
| Francisco Cruceta (20) | Luis Mendoza |
| Michael Schlact (24) | John Lujan |
| Doug Mathis (27) | Brennan Garr |
| Jacob Rasner (30) | Jose Marte |
| Kea Kometani | Nate Fogle |
| Jacob Brigham | |
| Kyle Rogers | |
| Edwin Vera | |
| John Bannister | |

### LHP

| Starters | Relievers |
|---|---|
| John Danks (1) | Danny Ray Herrera (28) |
| Kasey Kiker (7) | Jesse Carlson |
| Daniel Haigwood (22) | |
| Zach Phillips | |
| Geuris Grullon | |
| A.J. Murray | |
| Broc Coffman | |
| Michael Kirkman | |

## 2006

**Best Pro Debut:** Little LHP Danny Ray Herrera (45) used his unhittable changeup with screwball action to go 4-3, 1.45 with a 72-12 K-BB ratio in 62 innings and reach high Class A. C Chad Tracy (3) and OF/1B Chris Davis (5) made the Northwest League all-star team. Tracy hit .262 with 11 homers, while Davis batted .277 with 15 blasts.

**Best Athlete:** OF Craig Gentry (10) is still raw, in part because he had Tommy John surgery and an infected knee while at Arkansas. But he's a graceful center fielder with well above-average speed and raw power. OF Grant Gerrard (7) is a 6-foot-4, 215-pounder with average to slightly above-average tools.

**Best Pure Hitter:** Tracy has a good approach and innate ability to center balls well on the bat. His power in his debut came as a bit of a surprise.

**Best Raw Power:** Navarro (Texas) JC coach Skip Johnson compared Davis to another of his former stars, Brad Hawpe, and Davis has more pop in his bat than Hawpe does. Davis also showed power on the mound in junior college, pitching at 90-92 mph when his back wasn't bothering him.

**Fastest Runner:** Gentry, who swiped 20 bases in 26 attempts as a pro.

**Best Defensive Player:** SS Marcus Lemon (4), who signed for $1 million, and Gentry are solid defenders up the middle. Lemon's hands and instincts enhance his average range. Some scouts questioned his bat, but he got off to a good start by hitting .310 in Rookie ball.

**Best Fastball:** LHP Kasey Kiker (1) is just 5-foot-11, but his quick arm and easy delivery allow him to unleash 90-93 mph heat and top out at 97. RHP Brennan Garr (9), a converted third baseman, can hit 95 mph. RHP Jake Brigham's (6) stock dropped when he struggled with his delivery this spring, but his fastball has touched 94.

**Best Breaking Ball:** Kiker's curveball. His changeup could give him a third plus pitch.

**Most Intriguing Background:** Listed at 5-foot-7 and 145 pounds-which may be generous-Herrera may be the smallest pitcher ever drafted. Tracy's father Jim man-ages the Pirates and played in the majors. Lemon's dad was a three-time all-star and now runs Chet Lemon's Juice, one of the nation's best AAU baseball programs. Unsigned OF Clint Stubbs' (49) brother Drew went eighth overall to the Reds in the 2006 draft.

**Closest To The Majors:** Herrera, because his changeup and location are exceptional. LHP Glenn Swanson, a draft-and-follow from 2005, also could move quickly in a lefthanded relief role.

**Best Late-Round Pick:** Herrera.

**The One Who Got Away:** RHP Brandt Walker (21) is wiry strong and features a nice three-pitch mix. He could contribute quickly at Stanford. The Rangers hoped to keep LHP Lance McClain's (24) rights by having him stay at national champion Walters State (Tenn.) CC, but he transferred to Tennessee.

**Assessment:** The Rangers hoped to get a quality lefthander with the 12th overall pick, and they accomplished that mission with Kiker. Tracy, Lemon and Davis all have some upside.

## 2005     BUDGET: $3.9 million

OF John Mayberry Jr. (1) started to blossom late in 2006. C Taylor Teagarden (3) spent the season recovering from Tommy John surgery. **GRADE: C**

## 2004     BUDGET: $5.0 million

RHPs Thomas Diamond (1) and Eric Hurley (1) are on the verge of giving the Rangers some much-needed pitching help. OF Ben Harrison (7) is one of their top power prospects. **GRADE: B**

## 2003     BUDGET: $5.5 million

LHP John Danks (1) is the system's top prospect, while 2B Ian Kinsler (17) has blown away expectations. Texas rues not signing RHP Brad Lincoln (29), who became the fourth overall pick in 2006. **GRADE: B**

*Draft analysis by Jim Callis. Numbers in parentheses indicate draft rounds. Budgets are bonuses in first 10 rounds.*

# JOHN
# DANKS

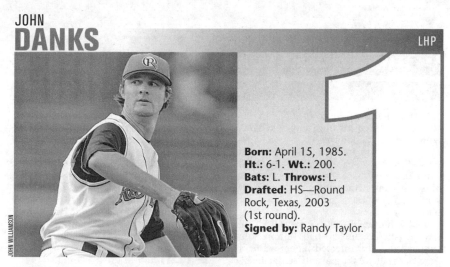

JOHN WILLIAMSON

**Born:** April 15, 1985.
**Ht.:** 6-1. **Wt.:** 200.
**Bats:** L. **Throws:** L.
**Drafted:** HS—Round
Rock, Texas, 2003
(1st round).
**Signed by:** Randy Taylor.

Throughout his career, Danks has been one of the youngest pitchers in his league and has started off each new stop by struggling against older competition. But every year, he makes adjustments, masters the level and advances to the next challenge. After he stumbled to a 7.15 ERA in April at Double-A Frisco, he went 4-0, 2.70 in his next eight starts to earn a promotion. He posted a 5.90 ERA in his first eight starts at Triple-A Oklahoma, then rallied to turn in a 2.32 ERA in his final six. Because he's lefthanded and has a deeper and more consistent repertoire, he has passed the other members of the DVD trio (Edinson Volquez, Thomas Diamond) to become the top pitching prospect in the system. The ninth overall pick in the 2003 draft, Danks comes from an athletic family. His father John played basketball at Texas, younger brother Jordan is a sophomore outfielder for the Longhorns and a possible first-rounder in the 2008 draft, and younger sister Emily is a standout high school volleyball player.

Danks offers a rare package for a 21-year-old lefthander, with a polished three-pitch mix and a track record of success up through Triple-A. His tight 1-to-7 curveball rated as his best pitch coming out of high school, but since then his tumbling changeup has also become a plus offering. His changeup is now more reliable than his curveball. He also has a four-seam fastball that sits at 90-92 mph and tops out at 94. Danks added a two-seam version in 2006 to help him widen the strike zone. He has a clean arm action from a high-three-quarters slot and does a good job repeating his easy delivery. Danks has started to fill out his durable, athletic frame, and he could add a little more velocity. His baseball IQ is outstanding, and he has a better feel for pitching than most hurlers his age. He does a good job of holding runners, as nine of 21 basestealers (43 percent) were caught on his watch in 2006.

At this point, it's just a matter of fine-tuning for Danks. He still needs to command his fastball better, because while he can throw it for strikes at any time, he gets punished sometimes when he leaves it up in the zone. His fastball is firm but not overpowering, so he needs to get ahead with it early in the count. Danks' command of his curveball comes and goes, though his changeup often bails him out. He'll need a more consistent curve in order to reach his ceiling as a No. 2 starter.

There was some sentiment that Danks could have started 2006 in the big leagues, but the Rangers were determined not to rush him and will continue to be patient. He'll have a chance to force his way into the big league rotation during spring training, but the more likely scenario is a return to Triple-A and a midseason debut in the majors. Once he settles in, Danks should pitch at or near the front of the Texas rotation for years to come.

| Year | Club (League) | Class | W | L | ERA | G | GS | CG | SV | IP | H | R | ER | HR | BB | SO | AVG |
|------|---------------|-------|---|---|-----|---|----|----|----|----|---|---|----|----|----|----|-----|
| 2003 | Rangers (AZL) | R | 1 | 0 | 0.69 | 5 | 3 | 0 | 0 | 13 | 6 | 3 | 1 | 0 | 4 | 22 | .136 |
| | Spokane (NWL) | A | 0 | 2 | 8.53 | 5 | 5 | 0 | 0 | 13 | 12 | 12 | 12 | 0 | 7 | 13 | .267 |
| 2004 | Clinton (MWL) | A | 3 | 2 | 2.17 | 14 | 8 | 0 | 0 | 50 | 38 | 17 | 12 | 4 | 14 | 64 | .210 |
| | Stockton (Cal) | A | 1 | 4 | 5.24 | 13 | 13 | 0 | 0 | 55 | 62 | 38 | 32 | 5 | 26 | 48 | .297 |
| 2005 | Bakersfield (Cal) | A | 3 | 3 | 2.50 | 10 | 10 | 0 | 0 | 58 | 50 | 18 | 16 | 5 | 16 | 53 | .228 |
| | Frisco (TL) | AA | 4 | 10 | 5.49 | 18 | 17 | 0 | 0 | 98 | 117 | 66 | 60 | 12 | 34 | 85 | .297 |
| 2006 | Frisco (TL) | AA | 5 | 4 | 4.15 | 13 | 13 | 0 | 0 | 69 | 74 | 38 | 32 | 11 | 22 | 82 | .273 |
| | Oklahoma (PCL) | AAA | 4 | 5 | 4.33 | 14 | 13 | 0 | 0 | 71 | 67 | 43 | 34 | 11 | 34 | 72 | .248 |
| **MINOR LEAGUE TOTALS** | | | 21 | 30 | 4.20 | 92 | 82 | 0 | 0 | 426 | 426 | 235 | 199 | 48 | 157 | 439 | .261 |

## ERIC HURLEY
RHP

STEVE MOORE

**Born:** Sept. 17, 1985. **B-T:** R-R. **Ht.:** 6-4. **Wt.:** 195. **Drafted:** HS—Jacksonville, 2004 (1st round). **Signed by:** Guy DeMutis.

Hurley survived the hitter-happy high Class A California League in the first half of the season, though he went 0-2, 9.45 in three July starts after returning from the Futures Game. Nonetheless, the Rangers promoted him to the Double-A Texas League, where he snapped out of his midseason funk and finished strong. Hurley is a true power pitcher with a pair of plus pitches and a chance for a third. He gets stronger as the game progresses, so if opponents don't get to him early in the game when his fastball is sitting around 90 mph, they soon have to contend with 93-96 mph heat, even in the late innings. He has developed enough confidence in his above-average slider to throw it in any count, an improvement from 2005. He's driven to reach the big leagues and receptive to instruction. Hurley's changeup remains underutilized and below-average, though he does have a good feel for it. Hurley could be a top-end starter if his changeup develops. He'll likely begin 2007 back in Double-A, though he could see the majors by the end of the season.

| Year | Club (League) | Class | W | L | ERA | G | GS | CG | SV | IP | H | R | ER | HR | BB | SO | AVG |
|------|---------------|-------|---|---|-----|---|----|----|----|-----|-----|-----|-----|-----|-----|-----|-----|
| 2004 | Rangers (AZL) | R | 0 | 1 | 2.35 | 6 | 2 | 0 | 0 | 15 | 20 | 8 | 4 | 1 | 4 | 15 | .317 |
| | Spokane (NWL) | A | 0 | 2 | 5.40 | 8 | 6 | 0 | 0 | 28 | 31 | 18 | 17 | 6 | 6 | 21 | .295 |
| 2005 | Clinton (MWL) | A | 12 | 6 | 3.77 | 28 | 28 | 0 | 0 | 155 | 135 | 72 | 65 | 11 | 59 | 152 | .234 |
| 2006 | Bakersfield (Cal) | A | 5 | 6 | 4.11 | 18 | 18 | 1 | 0 | 101 | 92 | 60 | 46 | 12 | 32 | 106 | .239 |
| | Frisco (TL) | AA | 3 | 1 | 1.95 | 6 | 6 | 0 | 0 | 37 | 21 | 9 | 8 | 4 | 11 | 31 | .168 |
| **MINOR LEAGUE TOTALS** | | | 20 | 16 | 3.74 | 66 | 60 | 1 | 0 | 337 | 299 | 167 | 140 | 34 | 112 | 325 | .238 |

## EDINSON VOLQUEZ
RHP

**Born:** July 3, 1983. **B-T:** R-R. **Ht.:** 6-1. **Wt.:** 200. **Signed:** Dominican Republic, 2001. **Signed by:** Rodolfo Rosario.

Volquez ranked as the Rangers' top prospect a year ago, but questions emerged about his ability to make adjustments after his disastrous big league stint in 2006. His career 9.20 ERA is the highest in baseball's modern era for a pitcher with at least 10 career starts. Volquez still has the electric stuff that fueled sky-high expectations a year ago, with a plus fastball that sits in the mid-90s and a plus changeup in the mid-70s. He always has been lauded for his makeup and work ethic, and he held his own in Triple-A prior to his big league callup. His curveball is erratic at best, as Volquez struggles to stay on top of it and can't throw it for strikes. He needs to do a better job of getting ahead in the count and commanding his fastball. The Rangers want him to stay on the rubber longer to give his arm a chance to catch up, allowing him to get more downhill plane on his pitches. If he can refine his curve and command, Volquez can earn a rotation spot in the spring and eventually emerge as a frontline starter. If he can't, he soon could find himself in the bullpen.

| Year | Club (League) | Class | W | L | ERA | G | GS | CG | SV | IP | H | R | ER | HR | BB | SO | AVG |
|------|---------------|-------|---|---|-----|---|----|----|----|-----|-----|-----|-----|-----|-----|-----|-----|
| 2002 | Texas (DSL) | R | 1 | 2 | 2.68 | 14 | 8 | 0 | 0 | 47 | 45 | 19 | 14 | 1 | 14 | 58 | .254 |
| 2003 | Rangers (AZL) | R | 2 | 1 | 4.00 | 10 | 4 | 0 | 1 | 27 | 24 | 14 | 12 | 1 | 11 | 28 | .245 |
| 2004 | Clinton (MWL) | A | 4 | 4 | 4.21 | 21 | 15 | 0 | 3 | 88 | 82 | 49 | 41 | 8 | 27 | 74 | .246 |
| | Stockton (Cal) | A | 4 | 1 | 2.95 | 8 | 8 | 0 | 0 | 40 | 31 | 16 | 13 | 6 | 14 | 34 | .221 |
| 2005 | Bakersfield (Cal) | A | 5 | 4 | 4.19 | 11 | 11 | 1 | 0 | 67 | 64 | 34 | 31 | 9 | 12 | 77 | .252 |
| | Rangers (AZL) | R | 0 | 0 | 0.00 | 1 | 1 | 0 | 0 | 2 | 2 | 0 | 0 | 0 | 0 | 2 | .222 |
| | Frisco (TL) | AA | 1 | 5 | 4.14 | 10 | 10 | 1 | 0 | 59 | 58 | 29 | 27 | 6 | 17 | 49 | .258 |
| | Texas (AL) | MLB | 0 | 4 | 14.21 | 6 | 3 | 0 | 0 | 13 | 25 | 22 | 20 | 3 | 10 | 11 | .403 |
| 2006 | Oklahoma (PCL) | AAA | 6 | 6 | 3.21 | 21 | 21 | 0 | 0 | 121 | 86 | 51 | 43 | 9 | 72 | 130 | .203 |
| | Texas (AL) | MLB | 1 | 6 | 7.29 | 8 | 8 | 0 | 0 | 33 | 52 | 28 | 27 | 7 | 17 | 15 | .359 |
| **MINOR LEAGUE TOTALS** | | | 23 | 23 | 3.63 | 96 | 78 | 2 | 4 | 449 | 392 | 212 | 181 | 40 | 167 | 452 | .236 |
| **MAJOR LEAGUE TOTALS** | | | 1 | 10 | 9.20 | 14 | 11 | 0 | 0 | 46 | 77 | 50 | 47 | 10 | 27 | 26 | .372 |

## THOMAS DIAMOND
RHP

STEVE MOORE

**Born:** April 6, 1983. **B-T:** R-R. **Ht.:** 6-3. **Wt.:** 245. **Drafted:** New Orleans, 2004 (1st round). **Signed by:** Randy Taylor.

In his second tour of duty at Double-A, Diamond struggled with his control at times, causing his walk totals and pitch counts to climb. As a result, he failed to last six innings in any of his final nine starts and pitched past six innings just once. But he still led the Texas League in strikeouts and lowered his Double-A ERA by 1.11 from 2005. A big, barrel-chested pitcher, Diamond can pitch up in the zone with a high-riding 91-94 mph fastball that touches 95-96 when he needs it. His plus

changeup gives him an effective weapon against lefthanders, and he has found success with his 82-83 mph slider now that he has mostly abandoned his overhand curveball. Diamond began throwing his slider with more conviction late in the season, but he still needs to develop it into a consistent out pitch. He also needs to throw more strikes so he can avoid the long at-bats that plagued him in 2006. Diamond still could become a mid-rotation workhorse if his slider emerges. Otherwise he could be ticketed for a late-inning role down the road. He'll open 2007 in Triple-A barring unforeseen developments in spring training.

| Year | Club (League) | Class | W | L | ERA | G | GS | CG | SV | IP | H | R | ER | HR | BB | SO | AVG |
|---|---|---|---|---|---|---|---|---|---|---|---|---|---|---|---|---|---|
| 2004 | Spokane (NWL) | A | 0 | 2 | 2.35 | 5 | 3 | 0 | 1 | 15 | 13 | 5 | 4 | 0 | 5 | 26 | .220 |
|  | Clinton (MWL) | A | 1 | 0 | 2.05 | 7 | 7 | 0 | 0 | 31 | 18 | 8 | 7 | 1 | 8 | 42 | .175 |
| 2005 | Bakersfield (Cal) | A | 8 | 0 | 1.99 | 14 | 14 | 1 | 0 | 81 | 53 | 20 | 18 | 3 | 31 | 101 | .191 |
|  | Frisco (TL) | AA | 5 | 4 | 5.35 | 14 | 14 | 0 | 0 | 69 | 66 | 44 | 41 | 8 | 38 | 68 | .249 |
| 2006 | Frisco (TL) | AA | 12 | 5 | 4.24 | 27 | 27 | 1 | 0 | 129 | 104 | 65 | 61 | 14 | 78 | 145 | .219 |
| MINOR LEAGUE TOTALS |  |  | 26 | 11 | 3.62 | 67 | 65 | 2 | 1 | 326 | 254 | 142 | 131 | 26 | 160 | 382 | .215 |

## 5 JOHN MAYBERRY JR. OF

STEVE MOORE

**Born:** Dec. 21, 1983. **B-T:** R-R. **Ht.:** 6-6. **Wt.:** 230. **Drafted:** Stanford, 2005 (1st round). **Signed by:** Tim Fortugno.

The son of a former all-star and somewhat of a surprise pick at No. 19 overall in the 2005 draft, Mayberry pulled a hamstring in spring training and struggled in the first half of his first full season. After changing his batting practice routine and working to shorten his swing, he improved against inside fastballs and hit .304 with 11 homers in the final two months. He kept it going in Hawaii Winter Baseball, leading all hitters with a .545 slugging percentage. Long and athletic, Mayberry's raw tools are exceptional, and he's starting to tap into his mammoth raw power, though the Rangers want him to improve his overall hitting with the belief his power will come later. Mayberry has good speed, a plus arm and is getting more comfortable in right field. The Rangers knew Mayberry would be a long-term project when they drafted him, and despite his progress he still needs to improve his timing and patience at the plate, as well as his ability to pull the ball. More of a first baseman in college, he's working on his jumps and throwing accuracy in the outfield. Mayberry's exceptional tools could make him a superstar if he figures everything out. He'll likely advance one level a year, making high Class A Bakersfield his next step.

| Year | Club (League) | Class | AVG | G | AB | R | H | 2B | 3B | HR | RBI | BB | SO | SB | OBP | SLG |
|---|---|---|---|---|---|---|---|---|---|---|---|---|---|---|---|---|
| 2005 | Spokane (NWL) | A | .253 | 71 | 265 | 51 | 67 | 16 | 0 | 11 | 26 | 26 | 71 | 7 | .341 | .438 |
| 2006 | Clinton (MWL) | A | .268 | 126 | 459 | 77 | 123 | 26 | 4 | 21 | 77 | 59 | 117 | 9 | .358 | .479 |
| MINOR LEAGUE TOTALS |  |  | .262 | 197 | 724 | 128 | 190 | 42 | 4 | 32 | 103 | 85 | 188 | 16 | .352 | .464 |

## 6 JOAQUIN ARIAS SS

**Born:** Sept. 21, 1984. **B-T:** R-R. **Ht.:** 6-2. **Wt.:** 165. **Signed:** Dominican Republic, 2001. **Signed by:** Victor Mata/Carlos Rios/Freddy Tiburcio (Yankees).

The player to be named in the 2004 Alex Rodriguez trade with the Yankees, Arias failed to hit .300 for the first time in the Rangers system in 2006. He got off to his customary slow start, and though he rebounded his performance might have been hindered by a twisted ankle that he played through for a month. Arias always has stood out for his athleticism. His plus range and plus-plus arm allow him to make sensational plays at shortstop, and he's starting to become a more consistent defender as well. Arias has quick hands and consistently puts the bat on the ball. Though Arias flashes power in batting practice, he has yet to translate it into game action. He has an aggressive approach at the plate and the Rangers would like him to improve his selectivity. He still needs to add strength and improve his durability. For all his plus-plus speed, he has succeeded in just 68 percent of his pro steal attempts. Arias will repeat a level for the first time in his career in 2007, as the Rangers will be patient while he fills out his frame and refines his game.

| Year | Club (League) | Class | AVG | G | AB | R | H | 2B | 3B | HR | RBI | BB | SO | SB | OBP | SLG |
|---|---|---|---|---|---|---|---|---|---|---|---|---|---|---|---|---|
| 2002 | GCL Yankees (GCL) | R | .300 | 57 | 203 | 29 | 61 | 7 | 6 | 0 | 21 | 12 | 16 | 2 | .338 | .394 |
| 2003 | Battle Creek (MWL) | A | .266 | 130 | 481 | 60 | 128 | 12 | 8 | 3 | 48 | 26 | 44 | 12 | .306 | .343 |
| 2004 | Stockton (Cal) | A | .300 | 123 | 500 | 77 | 150 | 20 | 8 | 4 | 62 | 31 | 53 | 30 | .344 | .396 |
| 2005 | Frisco (TL) | AA | .315 | 120 | 499 | 65 | 157 | 23 | 8 | 5 | 56 | 17 | 46 | 20 | .335 | .423 |
| 2006 | Oklahoma (PCL) | AAA | .268 | 124 | 493 | 56 | 132 | 14 | 10 | 4 | 49 | 19 | 64 | 26 | .296 | .361 |
|  | Texas (AL) | MLB | .545 | 6 | 11 | 4 | 6 | 1 | 0 | 0 | 1 | 1 | 0 | 0 | .583 | .636 |
| MINOR LEAGUE TOTALS |  |  | .289 | 554 | 2176 | 287 | 628 | 76 | 40 | 16 | 236 | 105 | 223 | 90 | .322 | .382 |
| MAJOR LEAGUE TOTALS |  |  | .545 | 6 | 11 | 4 | 6 | 1 | 0 | 0 | 1 | 1 | 0 | 0 | .583 | .636 |

## KASEY KIKER
LHP

**Born:** Nov. 19, 1987. **B-T:** L-L. **Ht.:** 5-11. **Wt.:** 170. **Drafted:** HS—Seale, Ala., 2006 (1st round). **Signed by:** Jeff Wood.

Kiker had a lengthy track record as the ace at Russell County High, winning a national title in 2005 and striking out 143 in 70 innings as a senior. Texas drafted him 12th overall and signed him for $1.6 million. His heavy prep workload mandated a strict pitch count in his pro debut, but he held his own against older competition in the short-season Northwest League. Kiker has a quick arm and a strong lower half, helping him rev his lively fastball as high as 97 mph and keep it at 90-93. His changeup is his second-best pitch, though his 12-to-6 curveball also has tight rotation and hard break. He could have three average to plus pitches in time. He has a clean arm action from a high three-quarters slot. He struggled to command all of his pitches at times this summer, though he was better down the stretch. He also needs to work on holding runners and fielding his position after mostly neglecting those aspects and focusing on fastball command in his debut. Kiker earns comparisons to Randy Wolf but throws harder. His slight frame lacks projection, but he already has quality stuff and could wind up in the middle of a big league rotation. He should be able to handle a promotion to low Class A Clinton in 2007.

| Year | Club (League) | Class | W | L | ERA | G | GS | CG | SV | IP | H | R | ER | HR | BB | SO | AVG |
|------|---------------|-------|---|---|-----|---|----|----|----|----|---|---|----|----|----|----|-----|
| 2006 | Spokane (NWL) | A | 0 | 7 | 4.13 | 16 | 15 | 0 | 0 | 52 | 44 | 34 | 24 | 5 | 35 | 51 | .232 |
| **MINOR LEAGUE TOTALS** | | | 0 | 7 | 4.13 | 16 | 15 | 0 | 0 | 52 | 44 | 34 | 24 | 5 | 35 | 51 | .232 |

## NICK MASSET
RHP

**Born:** May 17, 1982. **B-T:** R-R. **Ht.:** 6-4. **Wt.:** 190. **Drafted:** St. Petersburg (Fla.) CC, D/F 2000 (8th round). **Signed by:** Ray Jackson.

Masset has possessed tantalizing stuff ever since his high school days, when Tommy John surgery as a senior hurt his draft stock. Signed as a draft-and-follow for $225,000, he appeared on the verge of big things after his breakout 2004 season, but got crushed in 2005 and was inconsistent in 2006. He finished the season in the majors before dominating as a closer in the Mexican Pacific League. Masset throws his fastball at 89-95 mph as a starter but ran it up to 97-98 in bullpen in Texas and Mexico. His hard 85-86 mph curveball with sharp downward bite rates as a plus pitch. His changeup and cutter/slider are at least average and help him against lefthanders. Erratic command spoiled Masset's 2005 season and still makes him more hittable than he should be. Despite his impressive array of four pitches, he has yet to locate them well enough to be a reliable starter. He showed plenty of moxie to bounce back from 2005 but must prove he can sustain success. Masset may have pitched his way into a big league bullpen role with his strong winter.

| Year | Club (League) | Class | W | L | ERA | G | GS | CG | SV | IP | H | R | ER | HR | BB | SO | AVG |
|------|---------------|-------|---|---|-----|---|----|----|----|----|----|----|----|----|----|----|-----|
| 2001 | GCL Rangers (GCL) | R | 0 | 6 | 4.35 | 15 | 14 | 0 | 0 | 31 | 34 | 21 | 15 | 2 | 7 | 32 | .281 |
| 2002 | Savannah (SAL) | A | 5 | 8 | 4.56 | 33 | 16 | 0 | 0 | 120 | 129 | 75 | 61 | 11 | 47 | 93 | .276 |
| 2003 | Clinton (MWL) | A | 7 | 7 | 4.08 | 30 | 20 | 0 | 2 | 124 | 144 | 75 | 56 | 7 | 43 | 63 | .292 |
| 2004 | Stockton (Cal) | A | 6 | 5 | 3.51 | 16 | 11 | 0 | 0 | 77 | 71 | 38 | 30 | 6 | 19 | 43 | .242 |
| | Frisco (TL) | AA | 1 | 0 | 1.80 | 2 | 1 | 0 | 0 | 10 | 8 | 2 | 2 | 0 | 4 | 8 | .267 |
| 2005 | Frisco (TL) | AA | 7 | 12 | 6.18 | 29 | 27 | 1 | 0 | 157 | 197 | 124 | 108 | 19 | 61 | 105 | .313 |
| 2006 | Frisco (TL) | AA | 2 | 2 | 2.06 | 8 | 8 | 0 | 0 | 48 | 38 | 16 | 11 | 0 | 20 | 40 | .213 |
| | Oklahoma (PCL) | AAA | 4 | 5 | 4.81 | 24 | 7 | 1 | 3 | 67 | 79 | 48 | 36 | 4 | 28 | 65 | .293 |
| | Texas (AL) | MLB | 0 | 0 | 4.15 | 8 | 0 | 0 | 0 | 9 | 9 | 4 | 4 | 0 | 2 | 4 | .300 |
| **MINOR LEAGUE TOTALS** | | | 32 | 45 | 4.52 | 157 | 104 | 2 | 5 | 635 | 700 | 399 | 319 | 49 | 229 | 449 | .282 |
| **MAJOR LEAGUE TOTALS** | | | 0 | 0 | 4.15 | 8 | 0 | 0 | 0 | 8 | 9 | 4 | 4 | 0 | 2 | 4 | .300 |

## JASON BOTTS
OF/DH

**Born:** July 26, 1980. **B-T:** B-R. **Ht.:** 6-5. **Wt.:** 250. **Drafted:** Glendale (Calif.) JC, D/F 1999 (46th round). **Signed by:** Tim Fortugno.

The Rangers summoned Botts to the majors in May when DH Phil Nevin was struggling, and Botts showed flashes of promise in his sporadic playing time. He continued to hit when he was returned to Triple-A before breaking his hamate bone and missing three weeks in August. Botts has huge power from both sides of the plate, and he has shown the ability to hit for average as well. He commands the strike zone and takes plenty of walks. He runs well for a 6-foot-5, 250-pounder, especially once he gets going. Despite his sincere efforts to improve his defense, Botts remains a below-average defender in left field and at first base, so he will likely be primarily a DH. His willingness to

work deep counts results in more than his share of strikeouts. There's still some question about his long swing and how well it will work against quality pitching in the big leagues. Botts should earn a spot on the Rangers' Opening Day roster, either as the everyday DH or a power bat off the bench. He's 26 years old and has nothing left to prove in the minors.

| Year | Club (League) | Class | AVG | G | AB | R | H | 2B | 3B | HR | RBI | BB | SO | SB | OBP | SLG |
|---|---|---|---|---|---|---|---|---|---|---|---|---|---|---|---|---|
| 2000 | GCL Rangers (GCL) | R | .319 | 48 | 163 | 36 | 52 | 12 | 0 | 6 | 34 | 26 | 29 | 4 | .440 | .503 |
| 2001 | Savannah (SAL) | A | .309 | 114 | 392 | 63 | 121 | 24 | 2 | 9 | 50 | 53 | 88 | 13 | .416 | .449 |
| | Charlotte (FSL) | A | .167 | 4 | 12 | 1 | 2 | 1 | 0 | 0 | 0 | 4 | 4 | 0 | .375 | .250 |
| 2002 | Charlotte (FSL) | A | .254 | 116 | 401 | 67 | 102 | 22 | 5 | 9 | 54 | 75 | 99 | 7 | .387 | .401 |
| 2003 | Stockton (Cal) | A | .314 | 76 | 283 | 58 | 89 | 14 | 2 | 9 | 61 | 45 | 59 | 12 | .409 | .473 |
| | Frisco (TL) | AA | .263 | 55 | 194 | 26 | 51 | 11 | 1 | 4 | 27 | 21 | 45 | 6 | .341 | .392 |
| 2004 | Frisco (TL) | AA | .293 | 133 | 481 | 85 | 141 | 25 | 3 | 24 | 92 | 77 | 126 | 7 | .399 | .507 |
| 2005 | Oklahoma (PCL) | AAA | .286 | 133 | 510 | 93 | 146 | 31 | 7 | 25 | 102 | 67 | 152 | 2 | .375 | .522 |
| | Texas (AL) | MLB | .296 | 10 | 27 | 4 | 8 | 0 | 0 | 0 | 3 | 3 | 13 | 0 | .367 | .296 |
| 2006 | Texas (AL) | MLB | .220 | 20 | 50 | 8 | 11 | 4 | 0 | 1 | 6 | 8 | 18 | 0 | .317 | .360 |
| | Rangers (AZL) | R | .250 | 3 | 12 | 1 | 3 | 2 | 0 | 0 | 1 | 2 | 1 | 0 | .357 | .417 |
| | Frisco (TL) | AA | .125 | 5 | 16 | 3 | 2 | 0 | 0 | 0 | 2 | 3 | 3 | 0 | .250 | .125 |
| | Oklahoma (PCL) | AAA | .309 | 63 | 220 | 43 | 68 | 19 | 1 | 13 | 39 | 31 | 61 | 6 | .398 | .582 |
| **MINOR LEAGUE TOTALS** | | | .289 | 750 | 2684 | 476 | 777 | 161 | 21 | 99 | 462 | 404 | 667 | 57 | .394 | .476 |
| **MAJOR LEAGUE TOTALS** | | | .247 | 30 | 77 | 12 | 19 | 4 | 0 | 1 | 9 | 11 | 31 | 0 | .333 | .338 |

## 10 JOSH RUPE — RHP

**Born:** Aug. 18, 1982. **B-T:** R-R. **Ht.:** 6-2. **Wt.:** 210. **Drafted:** Louisburg (N.C.) JC, 2002 (3rd round). **Signed by:** John Tumminia (White Sox).

Part of the July 2003 Carl Everett trade with the White Sox, Rupe entered spring training with a legitimate chance to win a big league rotation spot but came down with elbow tendinitis. He didn't get going until June and the Rangers decided to use him out of the Double-A bullpen to get him back to the majors more quickly. He reached Texas in late July and proved to be an effective reliever. Rupe has a starter's repertoire, with four average or better pitches he can throw for strikes. His 91-94 mph fastball has plenty of late sink and his plus slider is an out pitch. He also throws a solid 12-to-6 curveball and a changeup. Despite his stuff, Rupe hasn't stuck as a starter because he hasn't been able to stay healthy in that role. His mechanics are still inconsistent, though he has settled into a three-quarters arm slot. Barring injury, Rupe will be on Texas' Opening Day roster, likely as a set-up man, though the Rangers haven't given up on the idea that he can help their rotation.

| Year | Club (League) | Class | W | L | ERA | G | GS | CG | SV | IP | H | R | ER | HR | BB | SO | AVG |
|---|---|---|---|---|---|---|---|---|---|---|---|---|---|---|---|---|---|
| 2002 | Bristol (Appy) | R | 3 | 3 | 5.26 | 17 | 2 | 0 | 0 | 38 | 38 | 23 | 22 | 4 | 22 | 40 | .260 |
| 2003 | Kannapolis (SAL) | A | 5 | 5 | 3.02 | 26 | 7 | 2 | 6 | 66 | 50 | 27 | 22 | 0 | 36 | 69 | .212 |
| | Clinton (MWL) | A | 4 | 1 | 3.90 | 6 | 5 | 0 | 0 | 28 | 29 | 14 | 12 | 1 | 7 | 23 | .266 |
| 2004 | Spokane (NWL) | A | 2 | 0 | 1.50 | 4 | 3 | 0 | 0 | 18 | 14 | 3 | 3 | 1 | 3 | 19 | .209 |
| | Stockton (Cal) | A | 2 | 0 | 0.98 | 4 | 3 | 0 | 0 | 18 | 12 | 4 | 2 | 0 | 4 | 14 | .182 |
| | Frisco (TL) | AA | 2 | 2 | 4.38 | 7 | 6 | 0 | 0 | 37 | 41 | 23 | 18 | 5 | 16 | 16 | .281 |
| 2005 | Frisco (TL) | AA | 4 | 3 | 3.74 | 11 | 10 | 0 | 0 | 65 | 64 | 29 | 27 | 7 | 26 | 55 | .261 |
| | Oklahoma (PCL) | AAA | 6 | 7 | 6.25 | 17 | 17 | 0 | 0 | 94 | 116 | 75 | 65 | 12 | 38 | 62 | .306 |
| | Texas (AL) | MLB | 1 | 0 | 2.79 | 4 | 1 | 0 | 0 | 10 | 7 | 4 | 3 | 0 | 4 | 6 | .219 |
| 2006 | Frisco (TL) | AA | 0 | 0 | 10.50 | 6 | 0 | 0 | 0 | 6 | 7 | 7 | 7 | 2 | 4 | 3 | .280 |
| | Oklahoma (PCL) | AAA | 1 | 1 | 3.38 | 12 | 0 | 0 | 2 | 13 | 13 | 6 | 5 | 0 | 6 | 4 | .271 |
| | Texas (AL) | MLB | 0 | 1 | 3.41 | 16 | 0 | 0 | 0 | 29 | 33 | 11 | 11 | 2 | 9 | 14 | .287 |
| **MINOR LEAGUE TOTALS** | | | 29 | 22 | 4.31 | 110 | 53 | 2 | 8 | 382 | 384 | 211 | 183 | 32 | 162 | 305 | .262 |
| **MAJOR LEAGUE TOTALS** | | | 1 | 1 | 3.26 | 20 | 1 | 0 | 0 | 38 | 40 | 15 | 14 | 2 | 13 | 20 | .272 |

## 11 CHRIS DAVIS — OF/1B

**Born:** March 17, 1986. **B-T:** L-R. **Ht.:** 6-3. **Wt.:** 210. **Drafted:** Navarro (Texas) JC, 2006 (5th round). **Signed by:** Randy Taylor.

A two-way star in high school, Davis began his college career at Texas but transferred to Navarro (Texas) JC before his freshman season began. He still pitched last spring, hitting 90-92 mph, but back problems limited his time on the mound. He hit 17 homers and Navarro coach Skip Johnson compared him to another of his former standouts, Brad Hawpe. Drafted in the fifth round—30 rounds earlier than the Angels selected him in 2005—Davis signed for $172,500 and earned Northwest League all-star honors in his debut. Davis' best tool is his above-average power from the left side. A streaky hitter, he's downright scary when he's locked in, as evidenced by two games against Vancouver when he hit four consecutive home runs and just missed a fifth, backing the right fielder up against the wall. Davis could be exploited on the outer half when he was mostly a pull hitter early in the summer, but he adjusted as the year progressed and began hitting with some authority to the opposite field. His swing has

some length to it, but he has impressive bat speed and leverage. He'll have to tighten his strike zone at higher levels. Davis played mostly outfield but is more comfortable at first base, where he's an adequate defender with a strong arm. He's a below-average runner. Davis should start 2007 in low Class A and has enough power to profile as an everyday first baseman.

| Year | Club (League) | Class | AVG | G | AB | R | H | 2B | 3B | HR | RBI | BB | SO | SB | OBP | SLG |
|------|---------------|-------|-----|---|----|---|---|----|----|----|-----|----|----|----|-----|-----|
| 2006 | Spokane (NWL) | A | .277 | 69 | 253 | 38 | 70 | 18 | 1 | 15 | 42 | 23 | 65 | 2 | .343 | .534 |
| **MINOR LEAGUE TOTALS** | | | .277 | 69 | 253 | 38 | 70 | 18 | 1 | 15 | 42 | 23 | 65 | 2 | .343 | .534 |

## 12 MARCUS LEMON SS

**Born:** June 3, 1988. **B-T:** L-R. **Ht.:** 5-11. **Wt.:** 173. **Drafted:** HS—Eustis, Fla., 2006 (4th round). **Signed by:** Guy DeMutis.

The son of former major league all-star Chet Lemon has baseball instincts to match his bloodlines. Though he had an accomplished amateur career that included standout performances for his father's Amateur Athletic Union club (Chet Lemon's Juice), Lemon's college commitment to Texas scared off many teams in the draft. The Rangers took a shot on him and signed him for $1 million, the highest bonus in 2006's fourth round. Lemon showed off his baseball savvy and solid all-around tools in his pro debut in the Rookie-level Arizona League. He has an advanced offensive approach for his age, plus a short stroke with snap in his hands. He can turn around quality fastballs to the pull side, though his power is more to the gaps than over the fence. Lemon has slightly above-average speed and baserunning smarts. Defensively, he has sure hands to go with an average arm and range, though he needs to work on his consistency. Lemon lacks a standout tool and isn't a sure thing to stick at shortstop, but the Rangers will leave him there as long as possible. He should have little trouble handling the jump to low Class A in 2007.

| Year | Club (League) | Class | AVG | G | AB | R | H | 2B | 3B | HR | RBI | BB | SO | SB | OBP | SLG |
|------|---------------|-------|-----|---|----|---|---|----|----|----|-----|----|----|----|-----|-----|
| 2006 | AZL Rangers (AZL) | R | .310 | 24 | 84 | 16 | 26 | 4 | 2 | 0 | 9 | 16 | 10 | 11 | .420 | .405 |
| **MINOR LEAGUE TOTALS** | | | .310 | 24 | 84 | 16 | 26 | 4 | 2 | 0 | 9 | 16 | 10 | 11 | .420 | .405 |

## 13 TAYLOR TEAGARDEN C

**Born:** Dec. 21, 1983. **B-T:** B-R. **Ht.:** 6-1. **Wt.:** 200. **Drafted:** Texas, 2005 (3rd round). **Signed by:** Randy Taylor.

Teagarden followed up a whirlwind 2005 with a quiet 2006. After helping lead Texas to the College World Series championship, signing for a $725,000 bonus and swatting seven homers in his pro debut, he capped his 2005 by having Tommy John surgery. He missed almost all of 2006 while rehabbing his elbow and a disc problem in his back, getting just 20 at-bats as a DH in Rookie ball. His back was completely healed and he swung the bat fairly well in instructional league, and he even caught the Rangers' final instructional league game, throwing out a baserunner. At full strength, Teagarden is an exceptional defensive catcher, with soft hands, quick feet and a strong, accurate throwing arm. His defense figures to carry him, as he still needs to refine his offensive approach and shore up some holes in his swing. Teagarden does have decent pop in his bat, and his overall package gives him a shot to be an everyday big league catcher. He should be fully healthy by spring training and could start 2007 in high Class A to make up for lost time.

| Year | Club (League) | Class | AVG | G | AB | R | H | 2B | 3B | HR | RBI | BB | SO | SB | OBP | SLG |
|------|---------------|-------|-----|---|----|---|---|----|----|----|-----|----|----|----|-----|-----|
| 2005 | Spokane (NWL) | A | .281 | 31 | 96 | 23 | 27 | 5 | 4 | 7 | 16 | 23 | 32 | 1 | .426 | .635 |
| 2006 | AZL Rangers (AZL) | R | .050 | 7 | 20 | 4 | 1 | 0 | 0 | 0 | 1 | 9 | 7 | 1 | .345 | .050 |
| **MINOR LEAGUE TOTALS** | | | .241 | 38 | 116 | 27 | 28 | 5 | 4 | 7 | 17 | 32 | 39 | 2 | .411 | .534 |

## 14 OMAR POVEDA RHP

**Born:** Sept. 28, 1987. **B-T:** R-R. **Ht.:** 6-4. **Wt.:** 200. **Signed:** Venezuela, 2004. **Signed by:** Andres Espinosa/Manny Batista.

The Rangers believe Poveda's peripheral numbers in his first full professional season in the United States paint a more accurate picture of his performance than his ugly win-loss record. He spent the entire season as an 18-year-old in low Class A and posted a 133-37 K-BB ratio, a reflection of his advanced feel for pitching. He even held his own in an emergency spot start at Double-A Frisco in July, allowing just one earned run in five innings, though he walked five. Tall and rangy with a loose arm and easy delivery, Poveda remains a projection guy, but his savvy and businesslike mound presence are positive indicators for his future. He has begun to fill out his frame and increased his fastball velocity from the mid-80s to the low 90s, typically sitting at 88-92 mph. He easily could add more velocity as he gets stronger. His best pitch is a plus changeup that is effective against both lefthanders and righthanders, and he does a good job mixing locations and keeping hitters off balance. His slurvy break-

ing ball lags behind his changeup and needs to be tightened up. Poveda figures to start 2007 in high Class A and he could become a mid-rotation big league starter.

| Year | Club (League) | Class | W | L | ERA | G | GS | CG | SV | IP | H | R | ER | HR | BB | SO | AVG |
|------|---------------|-------|---|---|-----|---|----|----|----|----|---|---|----|----|----|----|-----|
| 2005 | AZL Rangers (AZL) | R | 2 | 6 | 5.71 | 14 | 9 | 0 | 0 | 52 | 64 | 38 | 33 | 1 | 12 | 56 | .305 |
| 2006 | Frisco (TL) | AA | 0 | 1 | 1.80 | 1 | 1 | 0 | 0 | 5 | 4 | 2 | 1 | 0 | 5 | 1 | .222 |
| | Clinton (MWL) | A | 4 | 13 | 4.88 | 26 | 26 | 0 | 0 | 149 | 167 | 92 | 81 | 12 | 37 | 133 | .286 |
| **MINOR LEAGUE TOTALS** | | | 6 | 20 | 5.02 | 41 | 36 | 0 | 0 | 206 | 235 | 132 | 115 | 13 | 54 | 190 | .290 |

## 15  ARMANDO GALARRAGA                                            RHP

**Born:** Jan. 15, 1982. **B-T:** R-R. **Ht.:** 6-4. **Wt.:** 170. **Signed:** Venezuela, 2000. **Signed by:** Fred Ferreira (Expos).

Acquired along with Brad Wilkerson and Terrmel Sledge in the December 2005 Alfonso Soriano trade, Galarraga was coming off a season in which he pitched 156 innings—46 more than his previous career high. A survivor of Tommy John surgery in 2002, he added another 50 innings in the Venezuelan Winter League, and the Rangers believe the heavy workload caught up with him in 2006. He struggled out of the gate in Double-A Frisco before Texas shut him down for nearly two months with shoulder fatigue. When Galarraga returned to action later in the summer, he once again showed a lively low-90s sinker that touches 94 and a plus slider that ranks as one of the best in the system. He also has shown some feel for a changeup, which he'll need to develop in order to stick as a starter. Otherwise, he has the power stuff and aggressive approach to succeed as a reliever. Galarraga could return to Double-A to start 2007 but should move quickly if he's fully healthy.

| Year | Club (League) | Class | W | L | ERA | G | GS | CG | SV | IP | H | R | ER | HR | BB | SO | AVG |
|------|---------------|-------|---|---|-----|---|----|----|----|----|---|---|----|----|----|----|-----|
| 1999 | San Joaquin (VSL) | R | 1 | 2 | 4.98 | 21 | 3 | 0 | 2 | 43 | 49 | 37 | 24 | 4 | 28 | 31 | .283 |
| 2000 | Cagua (VSL) | R | 1 | 5 | 5.24 | 14 | 9 | 0 | 1 | 46 | 49 | 35 | 27 | 0 | 22 | 47 | .266 |
| 2001 | GCL Expos (GCL) | R | 1 | 3 | 3.12 | 14 | 1 | 0 | 2 | 35 | 37 | 21 | 12 | 2 | 15 | 24 | .274 |
| 2002 | GCL Expos (GCL) | R | 0 | 0 | 2.45 | 2 | 2 | 0 | 0 | 4 | 1 | 1 | 1 | 1 | 0 | 1 | .083 |
| 2003 | GCL Expos (GCL) | R | 1 | 1 | 1.80 | 5 | 5 | 0 | 0 | 15 | 13 | 5 | 3 | 0 | 5 | 7 | .241 |
| 2004 | Savannah (SAL) | A | 5 | 5 | 4.65 | 23 | 19 | 2 | 0 | 110 | 104 | 64 | 57 | 14 | 31 | 94 | .248 |
| 2005 | Potomac (CL) | A | 3 | 4 | 2.48 | 14 | 14 | 0 | 0 | 80 | 69 | 30 | 22 | 7 | 23 | 79 | .228 |
| | Harrisburg (EL) | AA | 3 | 4 | 5.19 | 13 | 13 | 1 | 0 | 76 | 80 | 47 | 44 | 10 | 21 | 58 | .275 |
| 2006 | Frisco (TL) | AA | 1 | 6 | 5.49 | 9 | 9 | 0 | 0 | 41 | 56 | 34 | 25 | 5 | 13 | 38 | .327 |
| | AZL Rangers (AZL) | R | 0 | 2 | 3.31 | 6 | 6 | 0 | 0 | 16 | 18 | 8 | 6 | 0 | 6 | 16 | .290 |
| | Spokane (NWL) | A | 0 | 1 | 4.50 | 1 | 1 | 0 | 0 | 4 | 4 | 2 | 2 | 1 | 0 | 3 | .250 |
| | Bakersfield (Cal) | A | 0 | 1 | 6.23 | 2 | 2 | 0 | 0 | 9 | 9 | 9 | 6 | 2 | 7 | 7 | .176 |
| **MINOR LEAGUE TOTALS** | | | 16 | 34 | 4.30 | 124 | 84 | 3 | 5 | 480 | 486 | 293 | 229 | 46 | 171 | 405 | .262 |

## 16  CHAD TRACY                                                     C

**Born:** July 4, 1985. **B-T:** R-R. **Ht.:** 6-3. **Wt.:** 200. **Drafted:** Pepperdine, 2006 (3rd round). **Signed by:** Todd Guggiana.

A year after smacking 12 home runs for Pepperdine and winning West Coast Conference player-of-the-year honors in 2005, Tracy slumped as a junior, finishing with just six homers in 254 at-bats. He nearly doubled that output in his pro debut after signing for $427,500 as a third-round pick. Tracy, whose father Jim manages the Pirates, has slightly above-average power and could get stronger if he can add about 15 pounds to his frame. Most of his home run pop comes to left field, but he can drive the ball to the right-center gap when pitchers work him away. It will take plenty of hard work to improve his catch-and-throw skills enough to make him passable defensively, but Tracy is receptive to instruction. When he arrived at short-season Spokane, Tracy was putting his body in bad position to catch the ball, struggling to block balls in the dirt and throwing across his body without putting any weight on his back foot. He made some progress correcting the flaws, but he threw out just 23 percent of basestealers and seemed to wear out by the end of the summer. Even if Tracy has to move, he could hit enough for first base. For now, he'll remain a full-time catcher as he heads to low Class A.

| Year | Club (League) | Class | AVG | G | AB | R | H | 2B | 3B | HR | RBI | BB | SO | SB | OBP | SLG |
|------|---------------|-------|-----|---|----|---|---|----|----|----|-----|----|----|----|-----|-----|
| 2006 | Spokane (NWL) | A | .262 | 66 | 252 | 41 | 66 | 14 | 1 | 11 | 35 | 23 | 46 | 4 | .339 | .456 |
| **MINOR LEAGUE TOTALS** | | | .262 | 66 | 252 | 41 | 66 | 14 | 1 | 11 | 35 | 23 | 46 | 4 | .339 | .456 |

## 17  BEN HARRISON                                                   OF

**Born:** Sept. 18, 1981. **B-T:** R-R. **Ht.:** 6-4. **Wt.:** 203. **Drafted:** Florida, 2004 (7th round). **Signed by:** Guy DeMutis.

A high school teammate of Khalil Greene at Key West High, Harrison has always had good tools, and he finished his four-year college career with 40 homers and 192 RBIs—both good for second all-time in Florida history. His problem as a pro has been staying on the field. Hamstring and vision problems limited him in 2005, and he went down 12 games after a pro-

motion to high Class A with a broken hand. Harrison stayed healthy throughout the 2006 regular season, easily setting career highs with 26 homers and 101 RBIs, but he separated a shoulder trying to make a play in the outfield in the Venezuelan Winter League. He had surgery and should be 100 percent for spring training. An outstanding fastball hitter who can also punish hanging breaking balls, Harrison stands out most for his above-average power. He struggles against quality breaking balls, but his pitch recognition and plate discipline are improving. He plays the game hard and emerged as a clubhouse leader in Bakersfield. Defensively, Harrison has a strong enough arm for right field, but his fringy speed and range probably ticket him for left. He has a chance to be a fourth outfielder in the majors, and maybe even a regular corner outfielder. He should start the year in Triple-A.

| Year | Club (League) | Class | AVG | G | AB | R | H | 2B | 3B | HR | RBI | BB | SO | SB | OBP | SLG |
|------|---------------|-------|-----|---|----|---|---|----|----|----|-----|----|----|----|-----|-----|
| 2004 | Spokane (NWL) | A | .271 | 55 | 214 | 41 | 58 | 11 | 0 | 11 | 33 | 22 | 64 | 2 | .358 | .477 |
| 2005 | Clinton (MWL) | A | .250 | 83 | 308 | 56 | 77 | 14 | 2 | 6 | 37 | 31 | 72 | 13 | .323 | .367 |
| | Bakersfield (Cal) | A | .318 | 12 | 44 | 4 | 14 | 2 | 0 | 1 | 7 | 3 | 13 | 2 | .367 | .432 |
| 2006 | Frisco (TL) | AA | .282 | 42 | 163 | 27 | 46 | 8 | 1 | 8 | 27 | 10 | 32 | 6 | .341 | .491 |
| | Bakersfield (Cal) | A | .293 | 87 | 331 | 52 | 97 | 19 | 1 | 18 | 74 | 49 | 85 | 9 | .397 | .520 |
| **MINOR LEAGUE TOTALS** | | | .275 | 279 | 1060 | 180 | 292 | 54 | 4 | 44 | 178 | 115 | 266 | 32 | .358 | .458 |

## 18 JOHNNY WHITTLEMAN                                                                 3B

**Born:** Feb. 11, 1987. **B-T:** L-R. **Ht.:** 6-2. **Wt.:** 195. **Drafted:** HS—Kingwood, Texas, 2005 (2nd round). **Signed by:** Randy Taylor.

The Rangers thought the 19-year-old Whittleman was ready for low Class A in his first full pro season, but he struggled for much of the year against more advanced pitching. He did get hot midway through 2006, and all nine of his home runs came in a span of just over a month between late June and late July. Whittleman showed mental toughness in the face of adversity, not surprising given his track record as a star football quarterback and leader of a Texas 5-A championship baseball team in high school. Whittleman flashed plus raw power in batting practice and in Hawaii Winter Baseball, but his best tool is his pure hitting ability. He has plenty of bat speed and can smoke line drives from foul pole to foul pole. Though he had a rough year, he actually controlled the strike zone very well. Whittleman's lower half is a little stiff, with a small hitch that throws off his timing at the plate, and it remains to be seen if his power will be usable enough for him to stay at third base. He also has to prove he can stick there defensively. Whittleman had 34 errors and an .891 fielding percentage in 2006, though he has the arm strength and instincts to become an average third baseman. Whittleman could return to low Class A to start 2007, with a promotion likely once he has some success.

| Year | Club (League) | Class | AVG | G | AB | R | H | 2B | 3B | HR | RBI | BB | SO | SB | OBP | SLG |
|------|---------------|-------|-----|---|----|---|---|----|----|----|-----|----|----|----|-----|-----|
| 2005 | Rangers (AZL) | R | .279 | 51 | 190 | 31 | 53 | 12 | 8 | 0 | 35 | 35 | 42 | 11 | .393 | .426 |
| 2006 | Clinton (MWL) | A | .227 | 130 | 466 | 56 | 106 | 21 | 3 | 9 | 43 | 60 | 97 | 7 | .313 | .343 |
| **MINOR LEAGUE TOTALS** | | | .242 | 181 | 656 | 87 | 159 | 33 | 11 | 9 | 78 | 95 | 139 | 18 | .337 | .367 |

## 19 FABIO CASTILLO                                                                    RHP

**Born:** Feb. 19, 1989. **B-T:** R-R. **Ht.:** 6-3. **Wt.:** 220. **Signed:** Dominican Republic, 2005. **Signed by:** Danilo Troncoso/Don Welke/Manny Bautista.

The Rangers signed Castillo and catcher Cristian Santana as the jewels of a banner haul from the Dominican Republic in 2005. Texas gave Castillo a taste of the United States with one start in the Arizona League last June, and he struck out four in three shutout innings. The Rangers then sent him to the Rookie-level Dominican Summer League, where he showed flashes of brilliance, striking out 14 in one outing. When he returned to Arizona for instructional league, he carried himself as a leader among the Rangers' young Latin contingent. With a big, physical frame reminiscent of Juan Guzman, Castillo might have the highest ceiling of any pitcher in the system. He already pitches in the 94-97 mph range with his fastball, and he has shown a power curveball with tight downward action and feel for a changeup. Castillo is raw and needs experience, but he displays good aptitude and maturity for his age. He should spend 2007 with the AZL Rangers and might not be far from exploding onto the prospect landscape.

| Year | Club (League) | Class | W | L | ERA | G | GS | CG | SV | IP | H | R | ER | HR | BB | SO | AVG |
|------|---------------|-------|---|---|-----|---|----|----|----|----|---|---|----|----|----|----|-----|
| 2006 | AZL Rangers (AZL) | R | 0 | 0 | 0.00 | 1 | 1 | 0 | 0 | 3 | 1 | 0 | 0 | 0 | 2 | 4 | .100 |
| | DSL Rangers (DSL) | R | 1 | 4 | 3.46 | 7 | 6 | 0 | 0 | 26 | 21 | 13 | 10 | 0 | 12 | 37 | .216 |
| **MINOR LEAGUE TOTALS** | | | 1 | 4 | 3.10 | 8 | 7 | 0 | 0 | 29 | 22 | 13 | 10 | 0 | 14 | 41 | .206 |

## 20 FRANCISCO CRUCETA                                                                 RHP

**Born:** July 4, 1981. **B-T:** R-R. **Ht.:** 6-2. **Wt.:** 215. **Signed:** Dominican Republic, 1999. **Signed by:** Pablo Peguero (Dodgers).

The Mariners appeared to have found a steal when they claimed Cruceta off waivers from the Indians in August 2005, as he led the Triple-A Pacific Coast League in wins and strikeouts

last year. But Seattle placed him on waivers after 2006, and the Rangers eagerly snatched him up. Cruceta has swing-and-miss stuff with a sinking 89-92 mph fastball that tops out at 94, a splitter that can be above-average at times and a decent slider. His major flaw continues to be his command. He doesn't throw strikes consistently and finished second in the PCL in walks. He works high in the zone too often, and he topped the league in homers allowed. Cruceta needs to do a better job pitching with his fastball to get ahead in the count, and he needs to become less predictable in his pitch selection. The Rangers aren't sure if Cruceta fits best as a starter or reliever, but he'll likely get a shot to make the Opening Day roster as a swingman.

| Year | Club (League) | Class | W | L | ERA | G | GS | CG | SV | IP | H | R | ER | HR | BB | SO | AVG |
|------|---------------|-------|---|---|-----|---|----|----|----|----|---|---|----|----|----|----|-----|
| 1999 | Dodgers (DSL) | R | 3 | 2 | 7.56 | 14 | 1 | 0 | 0 | 25 | 33 | 34 | 21 | 4 | 15 | 21 | .308 |
| 2000 | Dodgers (DSL) | R | 4 | 2 | 3.31 | 21 | 6 | 0 | 3 | 49 | 33 | 29 | 18 | 1 | 36 | 49 | .180 |
| 2001 | Dodgers (DSL) | R | 0 | 4 | 1.50 | 11 | 9 | 0 | 0 | 48 | 35 | 24 | 8 | 1 | 24 | 47 | .200 |
| 2002 | South Georgia (SAL) | A | 8 | 5 | 2.80 | 20 | 20 | 3 | 0 | 113 | 98 | 42 | 35 | 7 | 34 | 111 | .231 |
| | Kinston (CL) | A | 2 | 0 | 2.50 | 7 | 7 | 0 | 0 | 40 | 31 | 13 | 11 | 2 | 25 | 37 | .217 |
| 2003 | Akron (EL) | AA | 13 | 9 | 3.09 | 27 | 25 | 6 | 0 | 163 | 141 | 70 | 56 | 7 | 66 | 134 | .232 |
| 2004 | Akron (EL) | AA | 4 | 8 | 5.28 | 15 | 15 | 1 | 0 | 89 | 89 | 58 | 52 | 11 | 33 | 45 | .261 |
| | Buffalo (IL) | AAA | 6 | 5 | 3.25 | 14 | 14 | 1 | 0 | 83 | 78 | 35 | 30 | 6 | 36 | 62 | .259 |
| | Cleveland (AL) | MLB | 0 | 1 | 9.39 | 2 | 2 | 0 | 0 | 8 | 10 | 9 | 8 | 1 | 4 | 9 | .303 |
| 2005 | Buffalo (IL) | AAA | 6 | 4 | 5.19 | 30 | 13 | 1 | 0 | 102 | 123 | 65 | 59 | 16 | 32 | 92 | .297 |
| | Tacoma (PCL) | AAA | 1 | 1 | 5.00 | 2 | 2 | 0 | 0 | 9 | 11 | 6 | 5 | 3 | 3 | 10 | .297 |
| 2006 | Tacoma (PCL) | AAA | 13 | 9 | 4.38 | 28 | 28 | 1 | 0 | 160 | 150 | 81 | 78 | 25 | 76 | 185 | .247 |
| | Seattle (AL) | MLB | 0 | 0 | 10.80 | 4 | 1 | 0 | 0 | 7 | 10 | 8 | 8 | 2 | 6 | 2 | .370 |
| **MINOR LEAGUE TOTALS** | | | 60 | 49 | 3.81 | 189 | 140 | 13 | 3 | 881 | 822 | 457 | 373 | 83 | 380 | 793 | .246 |
| **MAJOR LEAGUE TOTALS** | | | 0 | 1 | 10.05 | 6 | 3 | 0 | 0 | 14 | 20 | 17 | 16 | 3 | 10 | 11 | .333 |

## 21  WES LITTLETON                                          RHP

**Born:** Sept. 2, 1982. **B-T:** R-R. **Ht.:** 6-2. **Wt.:** 210. **Drafted:** Cal State Fullerton, 2003 (4th round). **Signed by:** Steve Flores.

Littleton moved to the bullpen in 2005, when his velocity was down early. He was at his best in the Arizona Fall League after the season, but took the entire winter off afterward. He entered spring training out of shape and topping out in the mid-80s with his fastball. But once again, Littleton got stronger as the year progressed and he emerged as one of the Rangers' most reliable setup men. He was pitching at 87-92 mph and topping out at 94 by midseason. Littleton dropped his arm slot even lower than a sidearm angle late in 2005, giving him good deception and sink on his fastball. He also uses a changeup that has proven surprisingly effective against lefthanders, and a sweeping Frisbee slider that he can throw to both sides of the plate. Littleton's herky-jerky delivery also makes his pitches tough to pick up, but he doesn't always repeat it, and the possibility exists that major leaguers will adjust to his funky motion and start to hit him. For now, at least, he figures to be a key part of the Texas bullpen in 2007.

| Year | Club (League) | Class | W | L | ERA | G | GS | CG | SV | IP | H | R | ER | HR | BB | SO | AVG |
|------|---------------|-------|---|---|-----|---|----|----|----|----|---|---|----|----|----|----|-----|
| 2003 | Spokane (NWL) | A | 6 | 0 | 1.56 | 12 | 8 | 0 | 0 | 52 | 36 | 9 | 9 | 2 | 8 | 47 | .198 |
| 2004 | Stockton (Cal) | A | 8 | 10 | 4.15 | 30 | 23 | 0 | 0 | 141 | 139 | 76 | 65 | 7 | 56 | 72 | .273 |
| 2005 | Frisco (TL) | AA | 2 | 3 | 3.97 | 48 | 0 | 0 | 3 | 82 | 93 | 37 | 36 | 9 | 24 | 71 | .293 |
| 2006 | Frisco (TL) | AA | 3 | 0 | 0.66 | 17 | 0 | 0 | 3 | 27 | 13 | 3 | 2 | 1 | 7 | 25 | .137 |
| | Oklahoma (PCL) | AAA | 4 | 1 | 2.16 | 13 | 0 | 0 | 2 | 17 | 14 | 4 | 4 | 3 | 5 | 15 | .233 |
| | Texas (AL) | MLB | 2 | 1 | 1.73 | 33 | 0 | 0 | 1 | 36 | 23 | 7 | 7 | 2 | 13 | 17 | .189 |
| **MINOR LEAGUE TOTALS** | | | 23 | 14 | 3.28 | 120 | 31 | 0 | 8 | 319 | 295 | 129 | 116 | 22 | 100 | 230 | .254 |
| **MAJOR LEAGUE TOTALS** | | | 2 | 1 | 1.73 | 33 | 0 | 0 | 1 | 36 | 23 | 7 | 7 | 2 | 13 | 17 | .189 |

## 22  DANIEL HAIGWOOD                                        LHP

**Born:** Nov. 19, 1983. **B-T:** B-L. **Ht.:** 6-2. **Wt.:** 200. **Drafted:** HS—Pleasant Plains, Ark., 2002, (16th round). **Signed by:** Alex Slattery (White Sox).

After compiling a 43-1 career record in high school and a 32-11 mark over his first four pro seasons, Haigwood suffered through a losing season in 2006, which he spent in two new organizations. He began the year in the Phillies system, having been acquired from the White Sox in the 2005 Jim Thome trade, and was dealt to Texas in June for lefthander Fabio Castro. An intelligent lefty with a four-pitch mix, Haigwood has an innate ability to pitch his way out of jams, but he needs to do a better job avoiding jams in the first place. His best pitch is a plus changeup that's effective against righthanders, and his sharp curveball gives him an out pitch against lefties. Haigwood also has a workable slider and a fringe-average high-80s fastball that he needs to learn to trust. With less than overpowering stuff, his strength has always been his feel for pitching, but his high walk total in 2006 was indicative of his occasional command problems. Headed for Triple-A this year, he profiles as a back-of-the-rotation starter.

| Year | Club (League) | Class | W | L | ERA | G | GS | CG | SV | IP | H | R | ER | HR | BB | SO | AVG |
|------|---------------|-------|---|---|-----|---|----|----|----|----|---|---|----|----|----|----|-----|
| 2002 | White Sox (AZL) | R | 8 | 4 | 2.28 | 14 | 14 | 0 | 0 | 75 | 69 | 31 | 19 | 2 | 26 | 74 | .244 |

| | | | | | | | | | | | | | | | | |
|---|---|---|---|---|---|---|---|---|---|---|---|---|---|---|---|---|
| 2003 | Did not play—Injured | | | | | | | | | | | | | | | |
| 2004 | Kannapolis (SAL) | A | 10 | 4 | 4.76 | 21 | 21 | 0 | 0 | 113 | 97 | 63 | 60 | 10 | 56 | 99 | .246 |
| 2005 | Winston-Salem (CL) | A | 8 | 2 | 3.77 | 15 | 15 | 0 | 0 | 76 | 79 | 39 | 32 | 8 | 33 | 84 | .265 |
| | Birmingham (SL) | AA | 6 | 1 | 1.74 | 11 | 11 | 0 | 0 | 67 | 39 | 14 | 13 | 0 | 31 | 76 | .170 |
| 2006 | Reading (EL) | AA | 2 | 5 | 3.54 | 15 | 15 | 0 | 0 | 84 | 72 | 36 | 33 | 7 | 42 | 85 | .231 |
| | Frisco (TL) | AA | 1 | 2 | 3.63 | 12 | 12 | 1 | 0 | 62 | 66 | 29 | 25 | 4 | 44 | 57 | .280 |
| **MINOR LEAGUE TOTALS** | | | 35 | 18 | 3.43 | 88 | 88 | 1 | 0 | 478 | 422 | 212 | 182 | 31 | 232 | 475 | .241 |

## 23 FREDDY GUZMAN
OF

**Born:** Jan. 20, 1981. **B-T:** B-R. **Ht.:** 5-10. **Wt.:** 165. **Signed:** Dominican Republic, 2000. **Signed by:** Bill Clark/Modesto Ulloa (Padres).

Two years after he was on the verge of winning the Padres' starting center-field job, Guzman was traded to the Rangers with righthander Cesar Rojas last May for John Hudgins and Vince Sinisi. After missing all of 2005 while recovering from Tommy John surgery, Guzman won the Pacific Coast League stolen-base title with 42 after doing the same in 2004 with 48. He led the minors with 90 swipes in 2003 and has succeeded on 82 percent of his attempts as a pro. Guzman always has had well-above-average speed and good basestealing instincts, and he has improved his plate discipline and his bunting. His bat remains a question, however. He's not physical and never will hit for power, but if he continues to put the ball in play he could be a serviceable offensive player. Guzman is an outstanding defensive center fielder who gets excellent jumps and has the range to track down balls in both gaps. His arm remains below average, as it was before he blew out his elbow. Guzman profiles best as a fourth outfielder.

| Year | Club (League) | Class | AVG | G | AB | R | H | 2B | 3B | HR | RBI | BB | SO | SB | OBP | SLG |
|---|---|---|---|---|---|---|---|---|---|---|---|---|---|---|---|---|
| 2000 | San Diego (DSL) | R | .210 | 49 | 167 | 38 | 35 | 6 | 1 | 1 | 10 | 46 | 38 | 24 | .386 | .275 |
| 2001 | Idaho Falls (Pio) | R | .348 | 12 | 46 | 11 | 16 | 4 | 1 | 0 | 5 | 2 | 10 | 5 | .388 | .478 |
| 2002 | Lake Elsinore (Cal) | A | .259 | 21 | 81 | 13 | 21 | 3 | 0 | 1 | 6 | 8 | 12 | 14 | .326 | .333 |
| | Ft. Wayne (MWL) | A | .279 | 47 | 190 | 35 | 53 | 7 | 5 | 0 | 18 | 18 | 37 | 39 | .341 | .368 |
| | Eugene (NWL) | A | .225 | 21 | 80 | 14 | 18 | 2 | 1 | 0 | 8 | 7 | 15 | 16 | .293 | .275 |
| 2003 | Lake Elsinore (Cal) | A | .285 | 70 | 281 | 64 | 80 | 12 | 3 | 2 | 22 | 40 | 60 | 49 | .375 | .370 |
| | Mobile (SL) | AA | .271 | 46 | 177 | 30 | 48 | 5 | 2 | 1 | 11 | 26 | 34 | 38 | .368 | .339 |
| | Portland (PCL) | AAA | .300 | 2 | 10 | 1 | 3 | 0 | 0 | 0 | 0 | 0 | 1 | 3 | .300 | .300 |
| 2004 | Mobile (SL) | AA | .283 | 35 | 138 | 21 | 39 | 5 | 2 | 1 | 7 | 16 | 28 | 17 | .359 | .370 |
| | Portland (PCL) | AAA | .292 | 66 | 264 | 48 | 77 | 12 | 4 | 1 | 19 | 30 | 46 | 48 | .365 | .379 |
| | San Diego (NL) | MLB | .211 | 20 | 76 | 8 | 16 | 3 | 0 | 0 | 5 | 3 | 13 | 5 | .250 | .250 |
| 2005 | Did not play—Injured | | | | | | | | | | | | | | | |
| 2006 | Texas (AL) | MLB | .286 | 9 | 7 | 1 | 2 | 0 | 0 | 0 | 0 | 1 | 1 | 0 | .444 | .286 |
| | Oklahoma (PCL) | AAA | .282 | 69 | 252 | 45 | 71 | 9 | 2 | 1 | 14 | 36 | 36 | 31 | .375 | .345 |
| | Portland (PCL) | AAA | .274 | 30 | 124 | 15 | 34 | 7 | 2 | 2 | 14 | 14 | 19 | 11 | .348 | .411 |
| **MINOR LEAGUE TOTALS** | | | .273 | 468 | 1810 | 335 | 495 | 72 | 23 | 10 | 134 | 243 | 336 | 295 | .362 | .355 |
| **MAJOR LEAGUE TOTALS** | | | .217 | 29 | 83 | 9 | 18 | 3 | 0 | 0 | 5 | 4 | 14 | 5 | .270 | .253 |

## 24 MICHAEL SCHLACT
RHP

**Born:** Dec. 9, 1985. **B-T:** R-R. **Ht.:** 6-8. **Wt.:** 205. **Drafted:** HS—Marietta, Ga., 2004 (3rd round). **Signed by:** John Castleberry.

Following a breakout 2005 season in low Class A, Schlact took his lumps in 2006, as might be expected from a 20-year-old in the California League. A groundball pitcher, he wasn't helped by Bakersfield's porous infield defense. Schlact, who actually grew another inch in the past year, generates plenty of downhill leverage and gets good sink on his 90-92 mph fastball. Though his changeup continues to be a reliable offering and he made progress with his low-80s slider, Schlact ran into too many deep counts because he lacks a swing-and-miss pitch. Schlact always has been skinny, dating back to his prep career at Wheeler High, the same school that produced recent first-round picks Josh Burrus and Jeremy Hermida. Though he has added some weight since he was drafted, Schlact remains thin. Still, he didn't wear down in 2006, showing life on his fastball late in the season. The Rangers believe Schlact has the strong makeup to learn from his tough season and move forward in 2007, possibly in Double-A.

| Year | Club (League) | Class | W | L | ERA | G | GS | CG | SV | IP | H | R | ER | HR | BB | SO | AVG |
|---|---|---|---|---|---|---|---|---|---|---|---|---|---|---|---|---|---|
| 2004 | AZL Rangers (AZL) | R | 1 | 1 | 3.52 | 10 | 5 | 0 | 0 | 31 | 32 | 18 | 12 | 0 | 9 | 22 | .264 |
| 2005 | Clinton (MWL) | A | 10 | 7 | 4.17 | 28 | 28 | 0 | 0 | 168 | 184 | 85 | 78 | 10 | 37 | 90 | .280 |
| 2006 | Bakersfield (Cal) | A | 4 | 13 | 5.99 | 26 | 26 | 0 | 0 | 138 | 179 | 112 | 92 | 15 | 61 | 81 | .317 |
| **MINOR LEAGUE TOTALS** | | | 15 | 21 | 4.86 | 64 | 59 | 0 | 0 | 337 | 395 | 215 | 182 | 25 | 107 | 193 | .295 |

## 25 ANTHONY WEBSTER
OF

**Born:** April 10, 1983. **B-T:** L-R. **Ht.:** 6-0. **Wt.:** 197. **Drafted:** HS—Parsons, Tenn., 2001 (15th round). **Signed by:** Larry Grefer (White Sox).

A Tennessee high school football star at tailback, Webster has never been able to fully translate his considerable athleticism into results on the diamond. Acquired from the White

Sox in the July 2003 Carl Everett trade, he put up another solid but unspectacular year in 2006, playing his way out of Double-A and holding his own in Triple-A. Webster has an unorthodox offensive approach, with an excessive weight transfer from front to back, but he remedied that somewhat last year by going into more of a crouch, which allowed him to drive the ball better. With a tools package similar to that of Jacque Jones, Webster has become a better player as he has bought into stealing bases and mixing in some bunts so he can take advantage of his speed. His bat, raw power and defense are all average tools, but he has yet to hit for enough power to stick as a corner outfielder. Webster's weakest tool is his below-average arm and he's more of a left fielder despite spending much of 2006 in right. With another good season in Triple-A, Webster could force his way into the Rangers' outfield picture, most likely as a versatile fourth outfielder.

| Year | Club (League) | Class | AVG | G | AB | R | H | 2B | 3B | HR | RBI | BB | SO | SB | OBP | SLG |
|------|---------------|-------|-----|---|----|---|---|----|----|----|-----|----|----|----|-----|-----|
| 2001 | AZL White Sox (AZL) | R | .307 | 55 | 225 | 38 | 69 | 9 | 7 | 0 | 30 | 9 | 33 | 18 | .332 | .409 |
| 2002 | Bristol (Appy) | R | .352 | 61 | 244 | 58 | 86 | 7 | 3 | 1 | 30 | 38 | 38 | 16 | .448 | .418 |
| 2003 | Kannapolis (SAL) | A | .289 | 94 | 363 | 68 | 105 | 18 | 1 | 2 | 33 | 31 | 58 | 20 | .353 | .361 |
| | Clinton (MWL) | A | .270 | 18 | 74 | 11 | 20 | 7 | 0 | 1 | 9 | 0 | 8 | 4 | .286 | .405 |
| 2004 | Stockton (Cal) | A | .287 | 99 | 380 | 66 | 109 | 20 | 7 | 8 | 44 | 39 | 69 | 20 | .363 | .439 |
| 2005 | Bakersfield (Cal) | A | .301 | 122 | 498 | 93 | 150 | 36 | 11 | 11 | 73 | 31 | 55 | 25 | .346 | .484 |
| 2006 | Frisco (TL) | AA | .310 | 59 | 216 | 37 | 67 | 10 | 4 | 5 | 19 | 18 | 25 | 3 | .364 | .463 |
| | Oklahoma (PCL) | AAA | .269 | 69 | 242 | 30 | 65 | 15 | 2 | 3 | 19 | 13 | 36 | 16 | .317 | .384 |
| **MINOR LEAGUE TOTALS** | | | .299 | 577 | 2242 | 401 | 671 | 122 | 35 | 31 | 257 | 179 | 322 | 122 | .358 | .426 |

## 26  JESSE INGRAM                                                        RHP

**Born:** April 27, 1982. **B-T:** R-R. **Ht.:** 6-1. **Wt.:** 200. **Drafted:** California, 2004 (36th round). **Signed by:** Tim Fortugno.

Ingram dominated in his 2004 pro debut after setting California's single-season save record with 10 that spring. He pitched just eight innings in 2005 before he was shut down with soreness in his rotator cuff, and no one in the organization expected his breakout last year. Ingram's stuff isn't as overwhelming as his strikeout numbers, but his command is impeccable. He thrives on spotting his 90-92 mph fastball on the outside corner against righthanders, and he's not afraid to drop in a back-door slider against lefties in any count. Ingram dabbles with a changeup, but he's really a two-pitch guy. He handled a number of bullpen roles with aplomb in 2006, sometimes closing multiple days in a row, sometimes pitching four innings in a single outing. Ingram's ceiling is not particularly high, as his fastball velocity is nothing special and his slider can be slurvy at times, but his savvy makes up for his stuff. He should return to Double-A in 2007 and might not be far from a role in the big leagues.

| Year | Club (League) | Class | W | L | ERA | G | GS | CG | SV | IP | H | R | ER | HR | BB | SO | AVG |
|------|---------------|-------|---|---|-----|---|----|----|----|----|---|---|----|----|----|----|-----|
| 2004 | Spokane (NWL) | A | 4 | 1 | 1.42 | 22 | 0 | 0 | 4 | 32 | 19 | 7 | 5 | 1 | 16 | 45 | .167 |
| | Clinton (MWL) | A | 0 | 0 | 0.00 | 1 | 0 | 0 | 1 | 2 | 0 | 0 | 0 | 0 | 0 | 0 | .000 |
| 2005 | Bakersfield (Cal) | A | 0 | 2 | 21.00 | 8 | 0 | 0 | 2 | 6 | 15 | 15 | 14 | 1 | 11 | 8 | .517 |
| 2006 | Bakersfield (Cal) | A | 6 | 0 | 2.43 | 27 | 0 | 0 | 9 | 59 | 34 | 20 | 16 | 3 | 22 | 95 | .163 |
| | Frisco (TL) | AA | 3 | 2 | 5.21 | 15 | 0 | 0 | 4 | 19 | 20 | 13 | 11 | 2 | 5 | 22 | .274 |
| **MINOR LEAGUE TOTALS** | | | 13 | 5 | 3.52 | 73 | 0 | 0 | 20 | 118 | 88 | 55 | 46 | 7 | 54 | 170 | .205 |

## 27  DOUG MATHIS                                                        RHP

**Born:** June 7, 1983. **B-T:** R-R. **Ht.:** 6-3. **Wt.:** 220. **Drafted:** Missouri, 2005 (13th round). **Signed by:** Mike Grouse.

Though Mathis had a strong pro debut in 2005, the Rangers wanted him to make some adjustments for his first full season. They told him to focus on getting a more consistent balance point through his delivery so his arm could catch up, and to work on throwing more quality strikes at the bottom of the zone. He struggled with the adjustments at first, posting an 8.61 ERA in April. But he trusted the organization and stayed on the program, and the results followed. Mathis came out of college with a three-pitch mix but took it upon himself to add a curveball. That pitch gives him a fourth average offering, joining a sinker that tops out at 92 mph, a solid changeup and a slider that serves as his out pitch. Mathis commands his entire repertoire well, and he has learned to trust his fastball instead of leaning heavily on his slider like he did in college. Now the trick will be to build on the lessons of the past year and show he can be effective for an entire season. Mathis figures to open 2007 in Double-A, with a chance to be a No. 4 starter in Texas by 2008 or 2009.

| Year | Club (League) | Class | W | L | ERA | G | GS | CG | SV | IP | H | R | ER | HR | BB | SO | AVG |
|------|---------------|-------|---|---|-----|---|----|----|----|----|---|---|----|----|----|----|-----|
| 2005 | Spokane (NWL) | A | 4 | 7 | 2.68 | 17 | 16 | 0 | 0 | 84 | 78 | 33 | 25 | 2 | 17 | 78 | .243 |
| 2006 | Bakersfield (Cal) | A | 10 | 7 | 4.18 | 26 | 25 | 2 | 0 | 151 | 160 | 76 | 70 | 14 | 47 | 109 | .275 |
| | Frisco (TL) | AA | 0 | 0 | 3.60 | 2 | 2 | 0 | 0 | 10 | 14 | 5 | 4 | 0 | 5 | 10 | .326 |
| **MINOR LEAGUE TOTALS** | | | 14 | 14 | 3.64 | 45 | 43 | 2 | 0 | 245 | 252 | 114 | 99 | 16 | 69 | 197 | .266 |

## 28 DANNY RAY HERRERA
LHP

**Born:** Oct. 21, 1984. **B-T:** L-L. **Ht.:** 5-7. **Wt.:** 145. **Drafted:** New Mexico, 2006 (45th round). **Signed by:** Rick Schroeder.

When the Rangers were planning their draft, one of their scouts called in and announced over the speakerphone that Herrera can get Albert Pujols out right now, and the room erupted with laughter. No one was laughing after Herrera's tour de force debut, during which he silenced the bats of the offense-oriented California League. Herrera was already accustomed to thriving in harsh conditions, as he posted a 10-0, 2.24 record during his All-America senior season at New Mexico despite pitching in the high altitude of one of college baseball's best hitter's parks. Generously listed at 5-foot-7 and 145 pounds, Herrera may be the smallest pitcher ever drafted. He's also unique because he thrives with an 80-82 mph fastball that tops out at 84. Herrera can locate his fastball wherever he wants to, setting up batters for his changeup. It's a tumbler with true screwball action and arrives at 55-60 mph, making his fastball look an awful lot harder than it is. He also throws a sharp, late-breaking slider, and he mixes all of his pitches extremely well to keep hitters off balance. Nobody knows for sure whether Herrera will continue to have success at higher levels or if hitters will figure out his gimmick pitch and render him ineffective, but he'll likely get a chance to prove himself in Double-A this year.

| Year | Club (League) | Class | W | L | ERA | G | GS | CG | SV | IP | H | R | ER | HR | BB | SO | AVG |
|------|---------------|-------|---|---|-----|---|----|----|----|-----|----|----|----|----|----|----|-----|
| 2006 | AZL Rangers (AZL) | R | 0 | 1 | 2.08 | 3 | 0 | 0 | 2 | 9 | 5 | 2 | 2 | 0 | 0 | 11 | .172 |
| | Bakersfield (Cal) | A | 4 | 2 | 1.35 | 14 | 5 | 0 | 1 | 53 | 39 | 16 | 8 | 0 | 12 | 61 | .201 |
| **MINOR LEAGUE TOTALS** | | | 4 | 3 | 1.45 | 17 | 5 | 0 | 3 | 62 | 44 | 18 | 10 | 0 | 12 | 72 | .197 |

## 29 JOSE VALLEJO
2B

**Born:** Sept. 11, 1986. **B-T:** B-R. **Ht.:** 6-0. **Wt.:** 175. **Signed:** Dominican Republic, 2004. **Signed by:** Rodolfo Rosario/Manny Batista.

Vallejo persevered through the deaths of his father (killed by a drunk driver in a car accident) and his mother (cancer), and the Rangers firmly believe he'll have no problem overcoming something as relatively trivial as a tough 2006 season at the plate. He didn't learn to switch-hit until the previous year, when Rangers special assistant Terry Shumpert suggested it. Vallejo is making progress from the left side, as evidenced by his .240 batting average against righthanders last year, compared to his .220 mark against lefties. With above-average speed and improving bunting skills, he has a good idea how to play small ball, and he also has strength in his swing and could develop some gap power. Vallejo is a very slick defender at second base, with plenty of range, sure hands, good footwork around the bag and a strong arm for the position. He just lacks polish as a defender, but he's got a longer way to go as an offensive player. It remains to be seen if Vallejo will hit enough to reach the majors, but he owns the tools to do so and may just need time and at-bats. The Rangers could push him to high Class A in 2007, though a return to low Class A seems more likely.

| Year | Club (League) | Class | AVG | G | AB | R | H | 2B | 3B | HR | RBI | BB | SO | SB | OBP | SLG |
|------|---------------|-------|-----|---|----|----|-----|----|----|----|-----|----|-----|----|-----|-----|
| 2004 | Texas (DSL) | R | .212 | 52 | 170 | 23 | 36 | 4 | 1 | 1 | 19 | 16 | 52 | 9 | .302 | .265 |
| 2005 | AZL Rangers (AZL) | R | .291 | 52 | 203 | 28 | 59 | 7 | 2 | 1 | 15 | 19 | 49 | 18 | .364 | .360 |
| 2006 | Clinton (MWL) | A | .234 | 127 | 496 | 62 | 116 | 11 | 4 | 2 | 29 | 32 | 104 | 24 | .289 | .284 |
| **MINOR LEAGUE TOTALS** | | | .243 | 231 | 869 | 113 | 211 | 22 | 7 | 4 | 63 | 67 | 205 | 51 | .310 | .298 |

## 30 JACOB RASNER
RHP

**Born:** Dec. 4, 1986. **B-T:** R-R. **Ht.:** 6-4. **Wt.:** 195. **Drafted:** HS—Reno, Nev., 2005 (7th round). **Signed by:** Tim Fortugno.

Rasner was set to follow in the footsteps of his cousin, Yankees righthander Darrell Rasner, by pitching for Nevada until Texas signed him as a seventh-round pick out of high school in 2005. His pro debut was rocky, but he showed progress in his first full season as a 19-year-old in low Class A despite finishing second in the minors in losses. The Rangers like his intensity, toughness and arm. With a big, durable frame, Rasner pitches from a downhill plane and gets good sink and armside run on his promising fastball, which sits at 90-92 mph and tops out at 94. He flashes a decent slider and began utilizing a changeup in the second half of the season, but both offerings are underdeveloped. Rasner remains raw in all facets, but Texas believes his coordination and delivery will smooth out over time. He has started to fill out his lanky frame, and he profiles as a workhorse starter as he continues to get stronger. He could earn a spot in the high Class A rotation in 2007, but he also might benefit from more time in low Class A.

| Year | Club (League) | Class | W | L | ERA | G | GS | CG | SV | IP | H | R | ER | HR | BB | SO | AVG |
|------|---------------|-------|---|----|------|----|----|----|----|-----|-----|-----|-----|----|----|-----|------|
| 2005 | AZL Rangers (AZL) | R | 1 | 5 | 8.37 | 14 | 10 | 0 | 0 | 47 | 79 | 57 | 44 | 6 | 15 | 31 | .374 |
| 2006 | Clinton (MWL) | A | 6 | 16 | 5.41 | 27 | 27 | 1 | 0 | 145 | 154 | 102 | 87 | 14 | 52 | 117 | .274 |
| **MINOR LEAGUE TOTALS** | | | 7 | 21 | 6.14 | 41 | 37 | 1 | 0 | 192 | 233 | 159 | 131 | 20 | 67 | 148 | .301 |

# TORONTO
# BLUE JAYS

BY **MATT EDDY**

The Blue Jays have come a long way from their last-place 2004 season, and they managed to finish higher than third place for the first time since they won back-to-back World Series in 1993. To take the next step—making the playoffs—Toronto once again will have to rely on an increased payroll rather than major contributions from its farm system.

Toronto had baseball's sixth-lowest payroll at $46 million in 2005, but jumped to 16th overall at $72 million by Opening Day 2006. With little impact talent in their farm system, the Blue Jays signed free agents A.J. Burnett and B.J. Ryan and traded for Troy Glaus and Lyle Overbay.

Ownership again signed off on a payroll increase, and Ricciardi likely will have as much as $95 million at his disposal for 2007. He acted quickly in signing DH Frank Thomas, then spent $126 million to lock up Vernon Wells with a seven-year deal. Finding a shortstop was Toronto's top offseason priority, though the best it could do was sign 37-year-old Royce Clayton. The club's hole at that position is all the more glaring considering the Blue Jays used first-round picks on college shortstops Russ Adams and Hill in Ricciardi's first two drafts.

In their five drafts under Ricciardi, the Blue Jays have focused almost solely on college players, with more of an emphasis on track records of statistical success than on potential high ceilings. Adam Lind, who hit .367 in his September debut, may be the first impact bat drafted since Ricciardi's arrival, but there are few behind him in the system with the exception of 2006 first-round pick

Travis Snider. The system is stocked primarily with control pitchers, with most of the electric arms (led by 2006 rookie right-handers **Brandon League**, Dustin McGowan and Francisco Rosario) signed on former GM Gord Ash's watch.

Snider, a high school outfielder, snapped Toronto's five-year streak of taking a college player with their top pick. He won MVP honors in the Rookie-level Appalachian League, as did Lind in the Double-A Eastern League. Because the Blue Jays gave up their second- and third-round picks to sign Burnett and Ryan, they invested $725,000 in 16-year-old Venezuelan third baseman Balbino Fuenmayor. They also gave six-figure bonuses to four late-round choices: right-handers Chase Lirette (16th), Kyle Ginley (17th) and Graham Godfrey (34th), plus second baseman Jonathan del Campo (20th).

On the field, the Blue Jays' aggregate minor league winning percentage slipped under .500 for the first time since 2002. Three teams advanced to the playoffs, with Dunedin advancing the furthest, losing to St. Lucie in the high Class A Florida State League finals. Toronto announced at season's end that it won't operate an Appy League team in 2007, ending a four-year stint at Pulaski. If the Jays don't add an affiliate in the Rookie-level Gulf Coast League, they would be the only organization with just five North American affiliates.

## TOP 30 PROSPECTS

1. Adam Lind, of
2. Travis Snider, of
3. Ricky Romero, lhp
4. Ryan Patterson, of
5. Curtis Thigpen, c
6. Francisco Rosario, rhp
7. Brandon Magee, rhp
8. Jesse Litsch, rhp
9. David Purcey, lhp
10. Balbino Fuenmayor, 3b
11. Eric Fowler, lhp
12. Josh Banks, rhp
13. Chi-Hung Cheng, lhp
14. Ryan Klosterman, ss
15. Kyle Yates, rhp
16. Sergio Santos, ss
17. Anthony Hatch, inf
18. Graham Godfrey, rhp
19. Kyle Ginley, rhp
20. Davis Romero, lhp
21. Paul Phillips, rhp
22. Brian Pettway, of
23. Yohermyn Chavez, of
24. Ismael Ramirez, rhp
25. Ty Taubenheim, rhp
26. Ryan Roberts, 2b
27. Chip Cannon, 1b
28. Robinzon Diaz, c
29. Chase Lirette, rhp
30. Brian Jeroloman, c

# ORGANIZATION OVERVIEW

**General manager:** J.P. Ricciardi. **Farm director:** Dick Scott. **Scouting director:** Jon Lalonde.

## 2006 PERFORMANCE

| Class | Team | League | W | L | PCT | Finish* | Manager | Affiliated |
|---|---|---|---|---|---|---|---|---|
| Majors | Toronto | American | 87 | 75 | .537 | 7th (14) | John Gibbons | — |
| Triple-A | Syracuse SkyChiefs | International | 64 | 79 | .448 | 12th (14) | Mike Basso | 1978 |
| Double-A | New Hampshire Fisher Cats | Eastern | 68 | 73 | .482 | 7th (12) | Doug Davis | 2003 |
| High A | Dunedin Blue Jays | Florida State | 68 | 69 | .496 | 8th (12) | Omar Malave | 1987 |
| Low A | Lansing Lugnuts | Midwest | 72 | 65 | .526 | 7th (14) | Ken Joyce | 2005 |
| Short-season | Auburn Doubledays | New York-Penn | 42 | 32 | .568 | 3rd (14) | Dennis Holmberg | 2001 |
| Rookie | #Pulaski Blue Jays | Appalachian | 35 | 33 | .515 | 3rd (10) | Dave Pano | 2003 |
| **OVERALL 2006 MINOR LEAGUE RECORD** | | | 349 | 351 | .499 | 16th (30) | | |

*Finish in overall standings (No. of teams in league). #Blue Jays won't operate in Appalachian League in 2007.

## ORGANIZATION LEADERS

### BATTING
| | | |
|---|---|---|
| AVG | Lind, Adam, New Hampshire/Syracuse | .330 |
| R | Cannon, Chip, New Hampshire | 94 |
| H | Patterson, Ryan, Dunedin/New Hampshire | 161 |
| 2B | Patterson, Ryan, Dunedin/New Hampshire | 42 |
| 3B | Lydon, Wayne, Syracuse | 12 |
| HR | Cannon, Chip, New Hampshire | 34 |
| RBI | Patterson, Ryan, Dunedin/New Hampshire | 93 |
| BB | Majewski, Dustin, Dunedin/New Hamp. | 100 |
| SO | Cannon, Chip, New Hampshire | 176 |
| SB | Klosterman, Ryan, Dunedin/New Hampshire | 27 |
| OBP | Emanuele, Chris, Pulaski/Auburn | .412 |
| | Snider, Travis, Pulaski | .412 |
| SLG | Snider, Travis, Pulaski | .567 |
| XBH | Patterson, Ryan, Dunedin/New Hampshire | 70 |

### PITCHING
| | | |
|---|---|---|
| W | MacDonald, Michael, New Hampshire | 13 |
| | Trias, Orlando, Dunedin | 13 |
| L | Isenberg, Kurt, New Hampshire/Dunedin | 12 |
| | Purcey, David, Syracuse/New Hampshire | 12 |
| ERA | Ramirez, Ismael, New Hampshire/Syracuse | 2.42 |
| G | Thorpe, Tracy, New Hampshire | 60 |
| SV | Tavarez, Milton, Dunedin | 21 |
| IP | MacDonald, Michael, New Hampshire | 171 |
| BB | Purcey, David, Syracuse/New Hampshire | 82 |
| SO | Cheng, Chi-Hung, Lansing | 154 |
| AVG | Carnline, William, Lansing/Dunedin | .220 |

## TOP PROSPECTS OF THE DECADE

| Year | Player, Pos. | 2006 Org. |
|---|---|---|
| 1997 | Roy Halladay, rhp | Blue Jays |
| 1998 | Roy Halladay, rhp | Blue Jays |
| 1999 | Roy Halladay, rhp | Blue Jays |
| 2000 | Vernon Wells, of | Blue Jays |
| 2001 | Vernon Wells, of | Blue Jays |
| 2002 | Josh Phelps, c | Tigers |
| 2003 | Dustin McGowan, rhp | Blue Jays |
| 2004 | Alexis Rios, of | Blue Jays |
| 2005 | Brandon League, rhp | Blue Jays |
| 2006 | Dustin McGowan, rhp | Blue Jays |

## TOP DRAFT PICKS OF THE DECADE

| Year | Player, Pos. | 2006 Org. |
|---|---|---|
| 1997 | Vernon Wells, of | Blue Jays |
| 1998 | Felipe Lopez, ss | Nationals |
| 1999 | Alexis Rios, of | Blue Jays |
| 2000 | Miguel Negron, of | Cubs |
| 2001 | Gabe Gross, of | Brewers |
| 2002 | Russ Adams, ss | Blue Jays |
| 2003 | Aaron Hill, ss | Blue Jays |
| 2004 | David Purcey, lhp | Blue Jays |
| 2005 | Ricky Romero, lhp | Blue Jays |

| | | |
|---|---|---|
| 2006 | Travis Snider, of | Blue Jays |

## BEST TOOLS

| | |
|---|---|
| Best Hitter for Average | Adam Lind |
| Best Power Hitter | Travis Snider |
| Best Strike-Zone Discipline | Curtis Thigpen |
| Fastest Baserunner | Adam Calderone |
| Best Athlete | Yuber Rodriguez |
| Best Fastball | Francisco Rosario |
| Best Curveball | Chi-Hung Cheng |
| Best Slider | Brandon Magee |
| Best Changeup | Ricky Romero |
| Best Control | Josh Banks |
| Best Defensive Catcher | Brian Jeroloman |
| Best Defensive Infielder | Jonathan Diaz |
| Best Infield Arm | Sergio Santos |
| Best Defensive Outfielder | Chris Emanuele |
| Best Outfield Arm | Brian Pettway |

## PROJECTED 2010 LINEUP

| | |
|---|---|
| Catcher | Curtis Thigpen |
| First Base | Lyle Overbay |
| Second Base | Russ Adams |
| Third Base | Troy Glaus |
| Shortstop | Aaron Hill |
| Left Field | Travis Snider |
| Center Field | Vernon Wells |
| Right Field | Alex Rios |
| Designated Hitter | Adam Lind |
| No. 1 Starter | Roy Halladay |
| No. 2 Starter | A.J. Burnett |
| No. 3 Starter | Ricky Romero |
| No. 4 Starter | Dustin McGowan |
| No. 5 Starter | Gustavo Chacin |
| Closer | B.J. Ryan |

## LAST YEAR'S TOP 20 PROSPECTS

1. Dustin McGowan, rhp
2. Ricky Romero, lhp
3. David Purcey, lhp
4. Adam Lind, of
5. Josh Banks, rhp
6. Casey Janssen, rhp
7. Brandon League, rhp
8. Francisco Rosario, rhp
9. Curtis Thigpen, c
10. Vince Perkins, rhp
11. Shaun Marcum, rhp
12. Guillermo Quiroz, c
13. Ryan Patterson, of
14. Chi-Hung Cheng, lhp
15. Kyle Yates, rhp
16. Chip Cannon, 1b
17. Rob Cosby, 3b
18. Ismael Ramirez, rhp
19. Brian Pettway, of
20. Robinzon Diaz, c

## ALL-TIME LARGEST BONUSES

| | |
|---|---|
| Ricky Romero, 2005 | $2,400,000 |
| Felipe Lopez, 1998 | $2,000,000 |
| Gabe Gross, 2001 | $1,865,000 |
| Russ Adams, 2002 | $1,785,000 |
| Travis Snider, 2006 | $1,700,000 |

# MINOR LEAGUE DEPTH CHART

## Toronto Blue Jays

**Impact: C.** The Jays have two of the better-hitting outfielders in the minors in Lind and Snider—as well as Romero, the first pitcher taken in the 2005 draft—but no other frontline prospects.

**Depth: D.** Toronto's lack of up-the-middle prospects was apparent by Toronto's playing John McDonald 100 times in middle infield during 2007. On the other hand, players like Lind, Patterson, Thigpen, Rosario and Klosterman are nearly big league ready.

**Sleeper:** Graham Godfrey, rhp. Though the sophomore-eligible draftee has not yet thrown a pro pitch, his fastball-curveball combo could enable him to shoot into next year's top 10.

*Numbers in parentheses indicate prospect rankings.*

| LF | CF | RF |
|---|---|---|
| Adam Lind (1) | Chris Emanuele | Travis Snider (2) |
| Brian Pettway (22) | Dustin Majewski | Ryan Patterson (4) |
| Rob Cosby | Yuber Rodriguez | Yohermyn Chavez (23) |
| Jacob Butler | | Shawn Scobee |
| Jonathan Baksh | | |

| 3B | SS | 2B | 1B |
|---|---|---|---|
| Balbino Fuenmayor (10) | Ryan Klosterman (14) | Ryan Roberts (26) | Chip Cannon (27) |
| Anthony Hatch (17) | Sergio Santos (16) | Sean Shoffit | Luke Hopkins |
| John Hattig | Jonathan Diaz | Scott Campbell | Joey Metropoulos |
| Raul Barron | Jesus Gonzalez | Wes Stone | |

| C |
|---|
| Curtis Thigpen (5) |
| Robinzon Diaz (28) |
| Brian Jeroloman (30) |
| Josh Bell |
| Jonathan Jaspe |

### RHP

| Starters | Relievers |
|---|---|
| Francisco Rosario (6) | Kyle Yates (15) |
| Brandon Magee (7) | Paul Phillips (21) |
| Jesse Litsch (8) | Ismael Ramirez (24) |
| Josh Banks (12) | Chase Lirette (29) |
| Graham Godfrey (18) | Po-Hsuan Keng |
| Kyle Ginley (19) | Ryan Houston |
| Ty Taubenheim (25) | Tracy Thorpe |
| Orlando Trias | Billy Carnline |
| Jamie Vermilyea | Connor Falkenbach |
| Mike MacDonald | Lee Gronkiewicz |
| Shane Benson | Danny Hill |
| | Jordan De Jong |
| | Kristian Bell |

### LHP

| Starters | Relievers |
|---|---|
| Ricky Romero (3) | Chi-Hung Cheng (13) |
| David Purcey (9) | Davis Romero (20) |
| Eric Fowler (11) | Edgar Estanga |

# DRAFT ANALYSIS

## 2006
SIGNING BUDGET: $2.5 million

**Best Pro Debut:** OF Travis Snider (1) was the MVP and No. 1 prospect in the Appalachian League, batting .325/.412/.567 and leading the league in slugging. RHP Pat McGuigan's (27) ability to locate his slider allowed him to record nine saves with a 1.65 ERA and a 32-5 K-BB ratio in 27 innings.

**Best Athlete:** OF Adam Calderone (23) and Chris Emanuele (26) are similar, late-rounders with plus speed, line-drive bats and good defensive skills.

**Best Pure Hitter:** The Blue Jays were one of several teams that considered Snider the best high school hitter in the draft. He has no obvious weakness at the plate, as he hangs in well against lefthanders and stays back on breaking balls.

**Best Raw Power:** Snider has the size (6 feet, 220 pounds), strength and bat speed to launch tape-measure home runs on a consistent basis.

**Fastest Runner:** Toronto didn't sign any blazers. Calderone and Emanuele are above-average runners.

**Best Defensive Player:** C Brian Jeroloman (6) slumped at Florida last spring, which is why the Jays were able to draft him as low as they did. He did continue to play quality defense, however, and threw out 42 percent of basestealers in his pro debut. SS Jonathan Diaz (12) is this crop's best middle infielder. Both need to show more with the bat, as Jeroloman hit .241 in his debut and Diaz batted .200.

**Best Fastball:** RHP Brandon Magee (4), a senior sign, not only throws 90-94 mph, but he gets a lot of life on his fastball and uses his 6-foot-5 frame to throw on an extreme downward plane. RHP Graham Godfrey (34) can match Magee's velocity.

**Best Breaking Ball:** Magee's 81-84 mph slider is often a plus pitch. Midwest area scouts are kicking themselves for not doing a better job of gauging his signability in 2005. Godfrey has the best curveball.

**Most Intriguing Background:** 2B Scott Campbell (10), who played at Gonzaga, is the first New Zealander ever drafted. SS Jonathan Fernandez' (48) father Tony was a five-time all-star, four-time Gold Glover and one of the greatest players in franchise history. SS Cole (9) and 2B Justin Figueroa (42) could have given the Jays an all-twin double-play combination, but neither signed. They're the sons of former big leaguer Bien Figueroa, who manages high Class A Frederick in the Orioles

system. Nondrafted free agent RHP Drew Taylor's father Ron pitched for 11 years in the majors and is Toronto's team doctor.

**Closest To The Majors:** The Blue Jays will push Magee because he's already 23, and he'll be able to handle it. Snider should be one of the first high school bats from the '06 draft class to reach the big leagues.

**Best Late-Round Pick:** Godfrey dropped because of questionable signability as a draft-eligible sophomore but turned pro for $200,000. RHPs Chase Lirette (16) and Kyle Ginley (17) also received six-figure bonuses in later rounds. Lirette's splitter can be nasty.

**The One Who Got Away:** SS Cole Figueroa (9) was headed to St. Petersburg (Fla.) Junior College, which would have allowed the Jays to control his rights, but they lost him when he changed course and went to Florida.

**Assessment:** For the first time under general manager J.P. Ricciardi, the Blue Jays spent their first-rounder on a high school player. They tried to compensate for lacking second- and third-round picks by spending later in the draft on Godfrey, Lirette, Ginley and 2B Jonathan del Campo (20).

## 2005
BUDGET: $3.6 million

The Jays need a shortstop but passed up Troy Tulowitzki to take LHP Ricky Romero (1). OF Ryan Patterson (4) continues to prove scouts underestimated him. **GRADE: C**

## 2004
BUDGET: $4.6 million

The best draft of J.P. Ricciardi's reign landed the system's top prospect, OF Adam Lind (3); LHP Casey Janssen (6), who raced to the majors; and three other prospects in LHP David Purcey (1), C Curtis Thigpen (2) and draft-and-follow RHP Jesse Litsch (24). LHP Zach Jackson (1) was included in a deal for Lyle Overbay. **GRADE: B**

## 2003
BUDGET: $3.6 million

2B/SS Aaron Hill (1) and RHP Shaun Marcum (3) reached the majors quickly. Since-traded RHP Tom Mastny (11) closed games for the Indians at one point last year. **GRADE: C+**

*Draft analysis by Jim Callis. Numbers in parentheses indicate draft rounds. Budgets are bonuses in first 10 rounds.*

# LIND

OF

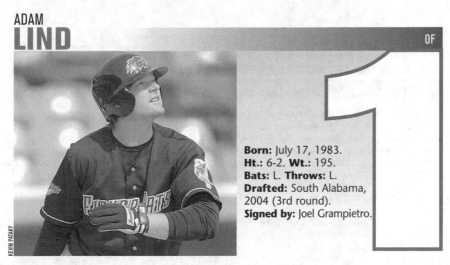

**Born:** July 17, 1983.
**Ht.:** 6-2. **Wt.:** 195.
**Bats:** L. **Throws:** L.
**Drafted:** South Alabama,
2004 (3rd round).
**Signed by:** Joel Grampietro.

KEVIN PATAKY

L ind was an eighth-round pick by the Twins out of an Indiana high school in 2002 but opted to attend South Alabama. He showed a fluid stroke and promising raw power in college, but only hinted at the hitter he would become. He hit a more-than-respectable .269 with wood bats in the Cape Cod League in the summer of 2003, then won the Sun Belt Conference batting title with a .392 average as a draft-eligible sophomore in 2004. After the Blue Jays took him in the third round, he signed for $445,000. He had no problem adapting to pro ball, leading the short-season New York-Penn League in doubles (23) and ranking second in extra-base hits (30) and RBIs (50). In his first full season, Lind jumped to high Class A and topped the Florida State League in doubles (42) and extra-base hits (58). He began to develop more over-the-fence power in 2006, when he won the Double-A Eastern League MVP award despite being promoted in late July. The Jays have named him his team's MVP in each of his three pro seasons, and only Carlos Delgado and Luis Lopez have won the award three times as well. Lind had one of the best seasons in the minors—batting a cumulative .330/.394/.556—and was just as dangerous during his September callup. In the final game of the season, he pushed Toronto into sole possession of second place in the American League East with a ninth-inning, two-run shot to dead-center off a 98 mph fastball from Kyle Farnsworth at Yankee Stadium.

Lind's classic lefthanded swing projects more power because his bat stays in the zone longer than that of most hitters. His hands are quiet and he's adept at staying inside the ball. Lind has exceptional balance at the plate and hits for power from line to line. His spread and slight crouch help him stay back on breaking balls. Every time he has moved up to a new level in pro ball, he initially has tried to go up the middle and to the opposite field. His first major league home run went to left-center. Once comfortable, though, he began to pull the ball with more authority. Lind doesn't seem to let anything bother him and is comfortable hitting behind in the count.

A first baseman in college, Lind isn't a great athlete and never has been much of a defender. He has come a long way with the glove in left field, working in batting practice by taking live rounds off the bat to improve from well below average to adequate. His arm is also below average but playable. Some scouts believe he'll eventually wind up at first base or DH. Lind is slow coming out of the batter's box, though he has average speed once he gets underway. His strike-zone judgment is certainly acceptable, but he could stand to draw a few more walks.

With Frank Catalanotto's departure for Texas as a free agent, Lind and Reed Johnson are frontrunners for Toronto's left-field job. But with Frank Thomas on board, DH is no longer an option for Lind. Either way, he should be one of the AL's top-hitting rookies. He figures to be batting in the middle of the Jays lineup by no later than 2008.

| Year | Club (League) | Class | AVG | G | AB | R | H | 2B | 3B | HR | RBI | BB | SO | SB | OBP | SLG |
|------|---------------|-------|-----|---|----|---|---|----|----|----|-----|----|----|----|-----|-----|
| 2004 | Auburn (NY-P) | A | .312 | 70 | 266 | 43 | 83 | 23 | 0 | 7 | 50 | 24 | 36 | 1 | .371 | .477 |
| 2005 | Dunedin (FSL) | A | .313 | 126 | 495 | 80 | 155 | 42 | 4 | 12 | 84 | 49 | 77 | 2 | .375 | .487 |
| 2006 | New Hampshire (EL) | AA | .310 | 91 | 348 | 43 | 108 | 24 | 0 | 19 | 71 | 25 | 87 | 2 | .357 | .543 |
|  | Syracuse (IL) | AAA | .394 | 34 | 109 | 20 | 43 | 7 | 0 | 5 | 18 | 23 | 18 | 1 | .496 | .596 |
|  | Toronto (AL) | MLB | .367 | 18 | 60 | 8 | 22 | 8 | 0 | 2 | 8 | 5 | 12 | 0 | .415 | .600 |
| **MINOR LEAGUE TOTALS** | | | .319 | 321 | 1218 | 186 | 389 | 96 | 4 | 43 | 223 | 121 | 218 | 6 | .382 | .511 |
| **MAJOR LEAGUE TOTALS** | | | .367 | 18 | 60 | 8 | 22 | 8 | 0 | 2 | 8 | 5 | 12 | 0 | .415 | .600 |

## 2 TRAVIS SNIDER OF

**Born:** Feb. 2, 1988. **B-T:** L-L. **Ht.:** 6-0. **Wt.:** 220. **Drafted:** HS—Everett, Wash., 2006 (1st round). **Signed by:** Brandon Mozley.

One of the top high school bats available in the 2006 draft, Snider led Jackson High (Mill Creek, Wash.) to a No. 2 national ranking. After signing for $1.7 million as the 14th overall pick, he won MVP honors and rated as the No. 1 prospect in the Rookie-level Appalachian League. He was leading the league in home runs when wrist tendinitis shelved him for the final week of the season. Snider is physically mature with a muscular frame that served him well as a high school running back until he broke his leg as a junior. Hitting and hitting for power are Snider's best tools, as his powerful swing generates above-average bat speed and tremendous raw power. He displays advanced hitting instincts, stays back on breaking balls and hangs in against lefties. His mental and competitive makeup is off the charts. The only knock on Snider leading up to the draft was his thick frame, especially his heavy lower half, and concerns about how it would project down the line. He worked hard on his conditioning and is more athletic than he appears. With work, he can be an average right fielder with a solid-average arm. He's a below-average runner but hustles. Snider will head to low Class A Lansing to begin 2007. He has the tools and desire to become an impact corner outfielder in the majors, and his bat should allow him to move more quickly than most high schoolers.

| Year | Club (League) | Class | AVG | G | AB | R | H | 2B | 3B | HR | RBI | BB | SO | SB | OBP | SLG |
|------|---------------|-------|-----|---|----|---|---|----|----|----|-----|----|----|----|-----|-----|
| 2006 | Pulaski (Appy) | R | .325 | 54 | 194 | 36 | 63 | 12 | 1 | 11 | 41 | 30 | 47 | 6 | .412 | .567 |
| **MINOR LEAGUE TOTALS** | | | .325 | 54 | 194 | 36 | 63 | 12 | 1 | 11 | 41 | 30 | 47 | 6 | .412 | .567 |

## 3 RICKY ROMERO LHP

**Born:** Nov. 6, 1984. **B-T:** R-L. **Ht.:** 6-1. **Wt.:** 200. **Drafted:** Cal State Fullerton, 2005 (1st round). **Signed by:** Demerius Pittman.

The first pitcher selected in the 2005 draft, Romero went sixth overall and signed for a club-record $2.4 million. He teamed with Jason Windsor (now with the Athletics) to lead Cal State Fullerton to the 2004 national title as a sophomore, and was a second-team All-American as a junior. Romero missed the first month of the 2006 season with mild elbow stiffness, though it's not a concern. Romero's best pitch is a plus changeup, which bottoms out and is highly effective against righthanders. He pitches at 91 mph with his fastball and can go get 93 when he needs it. He features above-average life on his fastball, including good arm-side movement with his two-seamer. His curveball is average if inconsistent. Romero struggled upon his promotion to Double-A New Hampshire when he couldn't locate his curve. He developed some bad habits at high Class A Dunedin, where he could put hitters away using just his fastball and changeup. Everything seemed to click, though, once he adjusted his delivery to improve his direction to the plate. His fastball and curveball command improved, and he threw on a better downhill plane. Romero advanced to Double-A in his first full season and finished strong, going 2-3, 2.75 in the final month. He'll likely return there to begin 2007 but should reach Triple-A Syracuse at some point during the season. He's on schedule to join the Toronto rotation no later than 2008.

| Year | Club (League) | Class | W | L | ERA | G | GS | CG | SV | IP | H | R | ER | HR | BB | SO | AVG |
|------|---------------|-------|---|---|-----|---|----|----|----|----|---|---|----|----|----|----|-----|
| 2005 | Auburn (NY-P) | A | 0 | 0 | 0.00 | 1 | 1 | 0 | 0 | 2 | 2 | 0 | 0 | 0 | 1 | 2 | .250 |
|  | Dunedin (FSL) | A | 1 | 0 | 3.82 | 8 | 8 | 0 | 0 | 31 | 36 | 13 | 13 | 2 | 7 | 22 | .283 |
| 2006 | Dunedin (FSL) | A | 2 | 1 | 2.47 | 10 | 10 | 1 | 0 | 58 | 48 | 17 | 16 | 5 | 14 | 61 | .224 |
|  | New Hampshire (EL) | AA | 2 | 7 | 5.08 | 12 | 12 | 0 | 0 | 67 | 65 | 43 | 38 | 7 | 26 | 41 | .256 |
| **MINOR LEAGUE TOTALS** | | | 5 | 8 | 3.81 | 31 | 31 | 1 | 0 | 158 | 151 | 73 | 67 | 14 | 48 | 126 | .250 |

## 4 RYAN PATTERSON OF

**Born:** May 2, 1983. **B-T:** R-R. **Ht.:** 5-11. **Wt.:** 210. **Drafted:** Louisiana State, 2005 (4th round). **Signed by:** Matt Briggs.

Patterson had a successful career at Louisiana State but wasn't drafted as a junior in 2004, nor was he signed as a free agent after winning the Cape Cod League batting title with a .327 mark that summer. He tore up the New York-Penn League in his pro debut in 2005, leading the league in extra-base hits (40), RBIs (65) and slugging percentage (.595). Proving that was no fluke, he led the Florida State League in slugging percentage in his first full season before a promotion to Double-A. Strong and compact, Patterson is a hitting machine. He ranked second in the Jays system in homers and

RBIs and finished among the minor league leaders in extra-base hits (65) and total bases (266). Though he doesn't employ a classic swing, he's short and direct to the ball. Because he sinks into his load, he has a flatter swing plane than the typical power hitter, enabling him to get backspin on the ball. He shows the instincts to make adjustments during an at-bat. He has average speed and is a good baserunner. Patterson likes to jump on the first pitch he can handle, though he's not a free swinger. The Blue Jays believe his plate discipline will catch up with his level of competition. Patterson can play center field in a pinch, but his range and arm fit best in left. Toronto pushed Patterson to Double-A in his first full season, and he responded after a rough start. He'll likely begin 2007 back with New Hampshire, and he could see Triple-A and maybe the majors later in the year.

| Year | Club (League) | Class | AVG | G | AB | R | H | 2B | 3B | HR | RBI | BB | SO | SB | OBP | SLG |
|------|---------------|-------|-----|---|----|---|---|----|----|----|-----|----|----|----|-----|-----|
| 2005 | Auburn (NY-P) | A | .339 | 71 | 274 | 52 | 93 | 23 | 4 | 13 | 65 | 21 | 53 | 5 | .386 | .595 |
| 2006 | Dunedin (FSL) | A | .288 | 84 | 354 | 65 | 102 | 25 | 0 | 19 | 69 | 20 | 61 | 2 | .327 | .520 |
| | New Hampshire (EL) | AA | .257 | 49 | 187 | 19 | 48 | 14 | 1 | 6 | 20 | 13 | 50 | 2 | .310 | .439 |
| **MINOR LEAGUE TOTALS** | | | .298 | 204 | 815 | 136 | 243 | 62 | 5 | 38 | 154 | 54 | 164 | 9 | .344 | .526 |

## 5 CURTIS THIGPEN                                         C

**Born:** April 19, 1983. **B-T:** R-R. **Ht.:** 5-10. **Wt.:** 185. **Drafted:** Texas, 2004 (2nd round). **Signed by:** Andy Beene.

Thigpen was a member of three College World Series teams at Texas from 2002-04. The Blue Jays drafted him as a catcher, even though he got little time behind the plate as a teammate of defensive standout Taylor Teagarden. More advanced as a catcher than Toronto thought, Thigpen reached Double-A in his first full season, and managers rated him the Eastern League's top defensive catcher in 2006. Thigpen commands the strike zone and excels at making contact, spraying the ball all over the field. His power is gap-to-gap, and he generates good backspin and carry on the ball. Behind the plate, Thigpen is extremely mobile and athletic for a catcher. He's a solid-average defender with good hands and slightly above-average receiving and blocking skills. His makeup is impeccable and he has the agility to handle the corner infield or outfield positions. Thigpen has average arm strength and a quick release, but his mechanics are inconsistent. He threw out just 24 percent of basestealers in 2006, including one of 14 in Triple-A. New Hampshire manager Doug Davis focused his attention last season on getting Thigpen's feet in sync with his release. An early-season staph infection cut into Thigpen's development time behind the plate. Toronto views Thigpen as its catcher of the future. His bat was probably ready for Triple-A this season, but the organization left him at Double-A to get extra time with Davis. Ticketed for Triple-A in 2007, he could make his major league debut in the second half.

| Year | Club (League) | Class | AVG | G | AB | R | H | 2B | 3B | HR | RBI | BB | SO | SB | OBP | SLG |
|------|---------------|-------|-----|---|----|---|---|----|----|----|-----|----|----|----|-----|-----|
| 2004 | Auburn (NY-P) | A | .301 | 45 | 166 | 34 | 50 | 11 | 2 | 7 | 29 | 23 | 32 | 1 | .390 | .518 |
| 2005 | Lansing (MWL) | A | .287 | 79 | 293 | 41 | 84 | 18 | 2 | 5 | 35 | 54 | 34 | 5 | .397 | .413 |
| | New Hampshire (EL) | AA | .284 | 39 | 141 | 18 | 40 | 8 | 0 | 4 | 15 | 9 | 19 | 0 | .340 | .426 |
| 2006 | New Hampshire (EL) | AA | .259 | 87 | 309 | 49 | 80 | 25 | 5 | 5 | 36 | 52 | 61 | 5 | .370 | .421 |
| | Syracuse (IL) | AAA | .264 | 13 | 53 | 3 | 14 | 3 | 0 | 1 | 9 | 2 | 9 | 0 | .304 | .377 |
| **MINOR LEAGUE TOTALS** | | | .279 | 263 | 962 | 145 | 268 | 65 | 9 | 22 | 124 | 140 | 155 | 11 | .374 | .433 |

## 6 FRANCISCO ROSARIO                                     RHP

**Born:** Sept. 28, 1980. **B-T:** R-R. **Ht.:** 6-1. **Wt.:** 215. **Signed:** Dominican Republic, 1999. **Signed by:** Tony Arias.

Rosario has been a member of the organization for eight seasons and a fixture on this list since his breakout 2002 season, after which he zoomed to No. 4. He tore a ligament in his elbow in the Arizona Fall League that fall, requiring Tommy John surgery that cost him all of 2003 and much of 2004. He has bounced between starting and relieving the last two seasons, and didn't pitch again after experiencing lower back pain in early August. Rosario employs true power stuff: a mid-90s fastball peaking at 98 mph with life, an 85-88 mph slider and a hard split-grip changeup. He located his fastball in the second half in Triple-A, working more aggressively on the inside part of the plate. After pitching tentatively in 2005, he seemed to clear that hurdle both physically and mentally. Despite his experience, Rosario still isn't a finished product. He can't reach his potential as a mid-rotation starter without learning to command his slider. He would benefit from greater focus on the mound. While in the majors, he sometimes overthrew and tried to muscle his way out of jams, which resulted in more hittable pitches. Rosario is out of options, so he'll have to be exposed to waivers if he can't crack Toronto's roster out of spring train-

ing. Unless he makes strides with his slider command, he'll probably have to make the club as a middle reliever.

| Year | Club (League) | Class | W | L | ERA | G | GS | CG | SV | IP | H | R | ER | HR | BB | SO | AVG |
|------|---------------|-------|---|---|-----|---|----|----|----|-----|-----|-----|-----|----|-----|-----|-----|
| 1999 | Blue Jays (DSL) | R | 1 | 0 | 3.06 | 18 | 0 | 0 | 3 | 32 | 26 | 16 | 11 | 0 | 11 | 38 | .208 |
| 2000 | Blue Jays (DSL) | R | 2 | 0 | 1.21 | 26 | 0 | 0 | 16 | 37 | 21 | 5 | 5 | 0 | 7 | 51 | .160 |
| 2001 | Medicine Hat (Pio) | R | 3 | 7 | 5.59 | 16 | 15 | 0 | 0 | 76 | 79 | 61 | 47 | 8 | 38 | 55 | .271 |
| 2002 | Charleston, W.Va. (SAL) | A | 6 | 1 | 2.57 | 13 | 13 | 1 | 0 | 67 | 50 | 22 | 19 | 5 | 14 | 78 | .206 |
|  | Dunedin (FSL) | A | 3 | 3 | 1.29 | 13 | 12 | 0 | 0 | 63 | 33 | 10 | 9 | 3 | 25 | 65 | .151 |
| 2003 | Did not play—Injured |  |  |  |  |  |  |  |  |  |  |  |  |  |  |  |  |
| 2004 | Dunedin (FSL) | A | 1 | 1 | 4.67 | 6 | 6 | 0 | 0 | 17 | 16 | 12 | 9 | 2 | 11 | 16 | .239 |
|  | New Hampshire (EL) | AA | 2 | 4 | 4.31 | 12 | 12 | 0 | 0 | 48 | 48 | 25 | 23 | 6 | 16 | 45 | .271 |
| 2005 | Syracuse (IL) | AAA | 2 | 7 | 3.95 | 30 | 18 | 0 | 2 | 116 | 111 | 59 | 51 | 16 | 42 | 80 | .258 |
| 2006 | Toronto (AL) | MLB | 1 | 2 | 6.65 | 17 | 1 | 0 | 0 | 23 | 24 | 17 | 17 | 4 | 16 | 21 | .264 |
|  | Syracuse (IL) | AAA | 0 | 3 | 2.79 | 14 | 8 | 0 | 1 | 42 | 29 | 14 | 13 | 2 | 13 | 50 | .196 |
| **MINOR LEAGUE TOTALS** |  |  | 20 | 26 | 3.38 | 148 | 84 | 1 | 22 | 499 | 413 | 224 | 187 | 42 | 177 | 478 | .226 |
| **MAJOR LEAGUE TOTALS** |  |  | 1 | 2 | 6.65 | 17 | 1 | 0 | 0 | 23 | 24 | 17 | 17 | 4 | 16 | 21 | .264 |

## 7  BRANDON MAGEE — RHP

**Born:** July 26, 1983. **B-T:** R-R. **Ht.:** 6-5. **Wt.:** 205. **Drafted:** Bradley, 2006 (4th round). **Signed by:** Aaron Jerslid.

Magee began his college career as Bradley's closer but blossomed into a starter and finished with 260 strikeouts, one shy of the school record. He would have gone between the eighth and 12th round as a junior in 2005 had his signability not been cloudy. He became one of the top senior signs in 2006, turning pro for $155,000 in the fourth round. Added strength allowed the tall, lean Magee to increase and hold his fastball velocity in the low 90s as a senior. He gets well above-average sink on his two-seamer, can dial it up to 94 when needed and delivers it on a steep downward plane from a high three-quarters delivery. He posted a strong 2.1 ground/fly ratio in his debut. Magee's plus slider was his bread-and-butter pitch in college and is the best in the system. Magee's slider was so good that he used it too much in college, and the Jays tried to get him to de-emphasize it somewhat and mix in more changeups. He also showed a tendency to keep his back foot locked to the rubber after delivering a pitch, and made a slight mechanical adjustment to correct it. There's some effort in his delivery, and some scouts believe he's better suited to be a reliever. The Jays believe Magee's ceiling, as a No. 3 starter, rivals that of any pitcher they've drafted in the past five years. Because he's already 23, he likely will be challenged with an Opening Day assignment to high Class A.

| Year | Club (League) | Class | W | L | ERA | G | GS | CG | SV | IP | H | R | ER | HR | BB | SO | AVG |
|------|---------------|-------|---|---|-----|---|----|----|----|----|----|----|----|----|----|----|-----|
| 2006 | Auburn (NY-P) | A | 3 | 1 | 3.10 | 11 | 11 | 0 | 0 | 52 | 51 | 23 | 18 | 1 | 19 | 40 | .254 |
| **MINOR LEAGUE TOTALS** |  |  | 3 | 1 | 3.10 | 11 | 11 | 0 | 0 | 52 | 51 | 23 | 18 | 1 | 19 | 40 | .254 |

## 8  JESSE LITSCH — RHP

**Born:** March 9, 1985. **B-T:** R-R. **Ht.:** 6-1. **Wt.:** 205. **Drafted:** South Florida CC, D/F 2004 (24th round). **Signed by:** Tony Arias.

The Rockies failed to sign Litsch as a 37th-rounder out of high school in 2003, and the Jays had to wait an additional year to land him as a draft-and-follow after taking him in the 24th round in 2004. He moved to high Class A to start his first full season after spending much of his pro debut dominating the Appy League, and he earned a promotion to Double-A by July. The aggressive Litsch is unafraid of contact. He has no knockout pitch, but he commands an 88-92 mph four-seam fastball with enough natural cutting action to put hitters away. He also throws a two-seamer, curveball, slider and changeup. He's able to throw his curveball for strikes and get hitters to chase it out of the zone. The Blue Jays can't say enough about his makeup. Litsch struggled in his first exposure to Double-A because he relied too much on his cutter, which hitters recognized. His slider was also less effective because it was too similar to his cutter. Toronto would like to see Litsch incorporate more curveballs and changeups into his mix. Litsch recovered to give up just two runs in his final three Double-A starts and is a safe bet to begin back at New Hampshire in 2007. He profiles as a back-of-the-rotation starter.

| Year | Club (League) | Class | W | L | ERA | G | GS | CG | SV | IP | H | R | ER | HR | BB | SO | AVG |
|------|---------------|-------|----|----|------|----|----|----|----|-----|-----|-----|----|----|----|-----|------|
| 2005 | Pulaski (Appy) | R | 5 | 1 | 2.74 | 11 | 11 | 0 | 0 | 66 | 51 | 22 | 20 | 6 | 10 | 67 | .212 |
|  | Auburn (NY-P) | A | 0 | 1 | 3.60 | 4 | 3 | 0 | 0 | 10 | 11 | 9 | 4 | 0 | 6 | 7 | .268 |
| 2006 | New Hampshire (EL) | AA | 3 | 4 | 5.06 | 12 | 12 | 1 | 0 | 69 | 85 | 44 | 39 | 6 | 13 | 54 | .309 |
|  | Dunedin (FSL) | A | 6 | 6 | 3.53 | 16 | 15 | 2 | 0 | 89 | 94 | 39 | 35 | 5 | 8 | 81 | .267 |
| **MINOR LEAGUE TOTALS** |  |  | 14 | 12 | 3.76 | 43 | 41 | 3 | 0 | 234 | 241 | 114 | 98 | 17 | 37 | 209 | .265 |

# DAVID PURCEY
LHP

RICH ABEL

**Born:** April 22, 1982. **B-T:** L-L. **Ht.:** 6-5. **Wt.:** 235. **Drafted:** Oklahoma, 2004 (1st round). **Signed by:** Ty Nichols.

Following a strong spring training, Purcey opened 2006 in Triple-A. He pitched well in April, but shaky command got the best of him in May and he was sent down to Double-A in June. He never got untracked at New Hampshire, so it was mostly a lost season. Few lefthanders can match the raw stuff Purcey possesses. His fastball and biting curveball are plus offerings when he commands them. He likes to dial up his four-seam fastball to 93-95 mph, but achieves more sinking and boring action when he throws his two-seamer at 90-92 mph. He works on a good downhill plane and has made some progress with a slider. Because of his large build and inconsistent release point, Purcey continues to battle his mechanics and to find command elusive. He frequently runs up high pitch counts and backs off once batters string together a few hits. He has made just modest strides with his changeup, which remains a below-average pitch. Purcey's first trip to Triple-A was a false start, and the Blue Jays acknowledge they may have pushed him too fast. Because he's inefficient with his pitches but durable, he might be better suited to relief. Toronto remains optimistic that he's taking a bit longer to harness his power stuff, which they feel is good enough to dominate with even slightly below-average command.

| Year | Club (League) | Class | W | L | ERA | G | GS | CG | SV | IP | H | R | ER | HR | BB | SO | AVG |
|---|---|---|---|---|---|---|---|---|---|---|---|---|---|---|---|---|---|
| 2004 | Auburn (NY-P) | A | 1 | 0 | 1.50 | 3 | 2 | 0 | 0 | 12 | 6 | 2 | 2 | 0 | 1 | 13 | .158 |
| 2005 | Dunedin (FSL) | A | 5 | 4 | 3.63 | 21 | 21 | 0 | 0 | 94 | 80 | 51 | 38 | 8 | 56 | 116 | .229 |
| | New Hampshire (EL) | AA | 4 | 3 | 2.93 | 8 | 8 | 1 | 0 | 43 | 32 | 17 | 14 | 2 | 25 | 45 | .205 |
| 2006 | Syracuse (IL) | AAA | 2 | 7 | 5.40 | 12 | 12 | 1 | 0 | 52 | 49 | 41 | 31 | 7 | 38 | 45 | .249 |
| | New Hampshire (EL) | AA | 4 | 5 | 5.60 | 16 | 16 | 0 | 0 | 88 | 101 | 59 | 55 | 9 | 44 | 81 | .287 |
| **MINOR LEAGUE TOTALS** | | | 16 | 19 | 4.35 | 60 | 59 | 2 | 0 | 289 | 268 | 170 | 140 | 26 | 164 | 300 | .245 |

# BALBINO FUENMAYOR
3B

JERRY HALE

**Born:** Nov. 26, 1989. **B-T:** R-R. **Ht.:** 6-2. **Wt.:** 195. **Signed:** Venezuela, 2006. **Signed by:** Rafael Moncada.

Following an impressive workout at Rogers Centre in front of general manager J.P. Ricciardi, Fuenmayor signed with the Blue Jays for $750,000. Toronto last invested heavily in a Venezuelan talent when they signed catcher Guillermo Quiroz for $1.2 million in 1998. Quiroz once ranked among the club's best prospects but was derailed by injuries and was claimed off waivers by the Mariners last April. Fuenmayor is athletic and has a chance to grow into power as he fills out. He has a lot of polish for a youngster, and his hitting ability is more advanced than his pop at this stage. He has a compact stroke with solid bat speed and the ability to drive the ball to the opposite field. At third base, he shows easy arm strength to go with good hands, footwork and range. As with many teenagers, Fuenmayor isn't very refined defensively. While his arm is strong, he'll have to improve his throwing accuracy. Questions about his power potential will remain unanswered until he shows what he can do in pro ball. Because the Blue Jays won't operate an Appy League club in 2007, it's unclear where Fuenmayor will be assigned at the conclusion of extended spring training.

| Year | Club (League) | Class | AVG | G | AB | R | H | 2B | 3B | HR | RBI | BB | SO | SB | OBP | SLG |
|---|---|---|---|---|---|---|---|---|---|---|---|---|---|---|---|---|
| 2006 | Did not play—Signed 2007 contract | | | | | | | | | | | | | | | |

# ERIC FOWLER
LHP

**Born:** March 18, 1983. **B-T:** L-L. **Ht.:** 6-3. **Wt.:** 220. **Drafted:** Mississippi, 2005 (5th round). **Signed by:** Matt Briggs.

Fowler was the fifth of five Ole Miss players to go in the top five rounds of the 2005 draft, a group that includes Blue Jays outfielder Brian Pettway. Fowler had no trouble in his debut and didn't miss a beat when he skipped a level and went to high Class A last season, finishing 10th in the Florida State League with a 3.74 ERA. Fowler is a three-pitch lefthander who has made strides with his fastball command. While he won't blow anybody away with his 88-91 mph velocity, he locates his fastball to both sides of the plate and gets groundballs with its plus sink. Fastball command is key for Fowler, who needs it to set up his sharp curveball, his out pitch. He has a fluid, repeatable delivery. To combat righthanders at higher levels, he'll need to continue improving his average changeup. As far as Fowler came with his fastball command this season, he'll need to take it a step further by throwing more strikes early in the count. He's ready for Double-A and profiles as either a back-end starter or a middle reliever.

| Year | Club (League) | Class | W | L | ERA | G | GS | CG | SV | IP | H | R | ER | HR | BB | SO | AVG |
|------|---------------|-------|---|---|-----|---|----|----|----|----|---|---|----|----|----|----|-----|
| 2005 | Auburn (NY-P) | A | 4 | 2 | 3.02 | 15 | 10 | 0 | 0 | 57 | 42 | 24 | 19 | 1 | 29 | 55 | .202 |
| 2006 | Dunedin (FSL) | A | 8 | 11 | 3.74 | 28 | 27 | 1 | 0 | 149 | 164 | 82 | 62 | 10 | 36 | 116 | .274 |
| **MINOR LEAGUE TOTALS** | | | 12 | 13 | 3.54 | 43 | 37 | 1 | 0 | 206 | 206 | 106 | 81 | 11 | 65 | 171 | .256 |

 ## JOSH BANKS

RHP

**Born:** July 18, 1982. **B-T:** R-R. **Ht.:** 6-3. **Wt.:** 215. **Drafted:** Florida International, 2003 (2nd round). **Signed by:** Tony Arias.

Banks entered 2006 as one of the system's top pitching prospects after finishing among the innings and strikeout leaders in the Eastern League, and he did the same in the Triple-A International League last season. But his status has taken a hit. While Banks is durable and has fine control, he hasn't fooled upper-level hitters. Banks has a 5.05 ERA in Double-A and Triple-A, and his 35 homers allowed last year were by far the most of any Triple-A pitcher. His 90-91 mph fastball has below-average movement and often catches too much of the plate. He would benefit from pitching more out of the zone, expanding it when he gets ahead. His best pitch is his plus splitter, but his curveball, slider and changeup are all below average. Banks is an intense competitor who's working to enhance the movement on his fastball, either by cutting it or sinking it. The Blue Jays once hoped he could become a No. 3 starter, but at this point he looks more like a back-end starter or a middle reliever.

| Year | Club (League) | Class | W | L | ERA | G | GS | CG | SV | IP | H | R | ER | HR | BB | SO | AVG |
|------|---------------|-------|---|---|-----|---|----|----|----|----|---|---|----|----|----|----|-----|
| 2003 | Auburn (NY-P) | A | 7 | 2 | 2.43 | 15 | 15 | 0 | 0 | 67 | 58 | 21 | 18 | 1 | 10 | 81 | .233 |
| 2004 | Dunedin (FSL) | A | 7 | 1 | 1.80 | 11 | 11 | 0 | 0 | 60 | 49 | 17 | 12 | 4 | 8 | 60 | .225 |
| | New Hampshire (EL) | AA | 6 | 6 | 5.03 | 18 | 17 | 1 | 0 | 91 | 89 | 54 | 51 | 15 | 28 | 76 | .256 |
| 2005 | New Hampshire (EL) | AA | 8 | 12 | 3.83 | 27 | 27 | 2 | 0 | 162 | 159 | 76 | 69 | 18 | 11 | 145 | .256 |
| 2006 | Syracuse (IL) | AAA | 10 | 11 | 5.17 | 29 | 29 | 0 | 0 | 171 | 184 | 108 | 98 | 35 | 28 | 126 | .267 |
| **MINOR LEAGUE TOTALS** | | | 38 | 32 | 4.05 | 100 | 99 | 3 | 0 | 551 | 539 | 276 | 248 | 73 | 85 | 488 | .253 |

 ## CHI-HUNG CHENG

LHP

**Born:** June 20, 1985. **B-T:** L-L. **Ht.:** 6-1. **Wt.:** 200. **Signed:** Taiwan, 2003. **Signed by:** J.P. Ricciardi.

Cheng has pitched three seasons in the U.S. without advancing past low Class A since signing for $400,000 following the 2003 World Cup. The Blue Jays wanted him to iron out his command issues before tackling high Class A, so he repeated the Midwest League and again finished among the league leaders in ERA, strikeouts and walks. Cheng achieved better balance and fastball command in part by separating his hands over the rubber, rather than over his head, though he still didn't throw strikes consistently. MWL observers said they were more impressed with him in 2005 than in 2006. Not a hard thrower, Cheng occasionally hits 90 mph but pitches at 84-87 with above-average life. His curveball is his best pitch, though he relies on it too much at times and scouts question whether his approach will work at higher levels. His changeup has the potential to become a plus pitch. Cheng has learned English and adapted to U.S. life quickly. His heavy amateur workload concerned some teams, but he showed no physical problems until he needed to have a slight tear in his labrum repaired in October. The Jays characterize the surgery as minor and believe he'll be throwing again by spring training. Cheng will try to develop a better fastball and changeup to go with his curve this year in high Class A. If he can't, he's likely destined for a relief role.

| Year | Club (League) | Class | W | L | ERA | G | GS | CG | SV | IP | H | R | ER | HR | BB | SO | AVG |
|------|---------------|-------|---|---|-----|---|----|----|----|----|---|---|----|----|----|----|-----|
| 2004 | Pulaski (Appy) | R | 3 | 1 | 2.82 | 14 | 14 | 0 | 0 | 61 | 47 | 27 | 19 | 4 | 35 | 74 | .219 |
| | Auburn (NY-P) | A | 0 | 0 | 4.50 | 1 | 0 | 0 | 0 | 2 | 1 | 1 | 1 | 1 | 0 | 3 | .143 |
| 2005 | Lansing (MWL) | A | 7 | 6 | 3.15 | 26 | 25 | 0 | 0 | 137 | 109 | 61 | 48 | 8 | 72 | 142 | .215 |
| 2006 | Lansing (MWL) | A | 11 | 5 | 2.70 | 28 | 28 | 0 | 0 | 143 | 129 | 57 | 43 | 5 | 68 | 154 | .244 |
| **MINOR LEAGUE TOTALS** | | | 21 | 12 | 2.91 | 69 | 67 | 0 | 0 | 343 | 286 | 146 | 111 | 18 | 175 | 373 | .228 |

## RYAN KLOSTERMAN

SS

**Born:** May 28, 1982. **B-T:** R-R. **Ht.:** 5-11. **Wt.:** 185. **Drafted:** Vanderbilt, 2004 (5th round). **Signed by:** Matt Briggs.

Regarded as the top defensive shortstop in the Cape Cod League in 2003, Klosterman went in the fifth round of the draft the following year. His heady play and polished approach served him well in his pro debut, then he slumped in 2005 before rebounding with surprising pop in high Class A last season. None of Klosterman's tools stands out, but he can make the routine play at shortstop, hit a few home runs and steal a few bases. He's short to the ball and exhibits surprising pull power for his size, though he could stand to make better contact. An average but smart runner, Klosterman is fast out of the box and succeeded on 26 of 29 steal attempts in 2006. His range and arm are merely adequate at shortstop, though he compensates with strong footwork and a quick transfer. He turns the dou-

ble play well, but he needs to improve his reads on balls off the bat and his ability to gauge the speed of baserunners. Klosterman began playing some second base in Double-A to prepare him for a potential big league role as a utilityman. He also saw time at third base in the Arizona Fall League, where he broke the knuckle on his right middle finger. He should be 100 percent by spring training. Klosterman did little with the bat following a midseason promotion to New Hampshire, so he'll return there in 2007.

| Year | Club (League) | Class | AVG | G | AB | R | H | 2B | 3B | HR | RBI | BB | SO | SB | OBP | SLG |
|------|---------------|-------|-----|---|----|---|---|----|----|----|-----|----|----|----|-----|-----|
| 2004 | Auburn (NY-P) | A | .275 | 66 | 269 | 50 | 74 | 13 | 4 | 5 | 32 | 22 | 55 | 16 | .343 | .409 |
| 2005 | Lansing (MWL) | A | .241 | 129 | 452 | 85 | 109 | 26 | 4 | 13 | 69 | 62 | 99 | 30 | .343 | .403 |
| 2006 | Dunedin (FSL) | A | .287 | 85 | 321 | 55 | 92 | 27 | 3 | 12 | 64 | 24 | 78 | 19 | .350 | .502 |
| | New Hampshire (EL) | AA | .248 | 43 | 137 | 22 | 34 | 5 | 0 | 4 | 16 | 17 | 37 | 7 | .358 | .372 |
| MINOR LEAGUE TOTALS | | | .262 | 323 | 1179 | 212 | 309 | 71 | 11 | 34 | 181 | 125 | 269 | 72 | .347 | .427 |

## 15  KYLE YATES                                                    RHP

**Born:** Jan. 8, 1983. **B-T:** R-R. **Ht.:** 5-11. **Wt.:** 190. **Drafted:** Texas, 2004 (13th round). **Signed by:** Andy Beene.

Accustomed to pitching in obscurity in the same University of Texas bullpen as Huston Street and J. Brent Cox, Yates broke out by going 11-6, 3.22 as a starter in his first full pro season in 2005. While he struggled in his first crack at Double-A this season, he got back on track during a brief demotion to high Class A and regrouped when he returned to New Hampshire. Yates' plus secondary offerings are ahead of his fringy fastball, which sits at 87-88 mph and sometimes creeps into the low 90s when he works in relief. He has tight spin on a hard curveball that can buckle the knees of lefties and righties alike. He trusts his changeup and the action he generates on the pitch makes it a key weapon against lefties. His stuff plays up out of the bullpen, where he moved in late July. Yates led the Arizona Fall League in strikeouts and could be a darkhorse candidate for the major league bullpen in 2007 if he polishes his command.

| Year | Club (League) | Class | W | L | ERA | G | GS | CG | SV | IP | H | R | ER | HR | BB | SO | AVG |
|------|---------------|-------|---|---|-----|---|----|----|----|----|---|---|----|----|----|----|-----|
| 2004 | Auburn (NY-P) | A | 0 | 1 | 6.75 | 9 | 0 | 0 | 0 | 9 | 9 | 7 | 7 | 0 | 5 | 11 | .243 |
| 2005 | Lansing (MWL) | A | 4 | 3 | 4.43 | 14 | 14 | 1 | 0 | 81 | 82 | 41 | 40 | 6 | 19 | 81 | .265 |
| | Dunedin (FSL) | A | 7 | 3 | 1.91 | 14 | 14 | 0 | 0 | 75 | 69 | 30 | 16 | 4 | 19 | 67 | .242 |
| 2006 | Dunedin (FSL) | A | 2 | 0 | 0.64 | 4 | 2 | 0 | 0 | 14 | 8 | 1 | 1 | 0 | 0 | 13 | .163 |
| | New Hampshire (EL) | AA | 6 | 9 | 3.75 | 28 | 18 | 1 | 1 | 127 | 118 | 60 | 53 | 10 | 38 | 102 | .246 |
| MINOR LEAGUE TOTALS | | | 19 | 16 | 3.43 | 69 | 48 | 2 | 1 | 307 | 286 | 139 | 117 | 20 | 81 | 274 | .247 |

## 16  SERGIO SANTOS                                                  SS

**Born:** July 4, 1983. **B-T:** R-R. **Ht.:** 6-3. **Wt.:** 225. **Drafted:** HS—Hacienda Heights, Calif., 2002 (1st round). **Signed by:** Mark Baca (Diamondbacks).

Not much went right for Santos in his first year in the organization after coming over in the trade that sent Miguel Batista and Orlando Hudson to Arizona for Troy Glaus. Renowned as an amateur for his power, Santos has struggled to do much of anything with the bat in two seasons in Triple-A, though he did have a 20-game hitting streak in 2006 and flashed as much raw power as any Syracuse batter. Quality breaking balls fool Santos—he batted just .194 against righthanders—and his swing gets out of whack when he tries too hard to make things happen. He needs to do a better job of identifying hittable pitches and of getting his legs underneath him on his swing. His plus-plus arm strength and accuracy were evident, however, and he has the best infield arm in the system. Though he makes most routine plays, Santos' average wheels limit his range at shortstop, a problem compounded by Syracuse's rough-hewn artificial turf. He might profile better at second or third base, but his future hinges on his ability to hit at this point. Santos will try to get going again at Triple-A this year.

| Year | Club (League) | Class | AVG | G | AB | R | H | 2B | 3B | HR | RBI | BB | SO | SB | OBP | SLG |
|------|---------------|-------|-----|---|----|---|---|----|----|----|-----|----|----|----|-----|-----|
| 2002 | Missoula (Pio) | R | .272 | 54 | 202 | 38 | 55 | 19 | 2 | 9 | 37 | 29 | 49 | 6 | .367 | .520 |
| 2003 | Lancaster (Cal) | A | .287 | 93 | 341 | 55 | 98 | 13 | 2 | 8 | 49 | 41 | 64 | 5 | .368 | .408 |
| | El Paso (TL) | AA | .255 | 37 | 137 | 13 | 35 | 7 | 1 | 2 | 16 | 8 | 25 | 0 | .293 | .365 |
| 2004 | El Paso (TL) | AA | .282 | 89 | 347 | 53 | 98 | 19 | 5 | 11 | 52 | 24 | 89 | 3 | .332 | .461 |
| 2005 | Tucson (PCL) | AAA | .239 | 132 | 490 | 55 | 117 | 21 | 3 | 12 | 68 | 34 | 108 | 2 | .288 | .367 |
| 2006 | Syracuse (IL) | AAA | .214 | 128 | 481 | 48 | 103 | 24 | 1 | 5 | 38 | 24 | 96 | 1 | .254 | .299 |
| MINOR LEAGUE TOTALS | | | .253 | 533 | 1998 | 262 | 506 | 103 | 14 | 47 | 260 | 160 | 431 | 17 | .311 | .389 |

## 17  ANTHONY HATCH                                                 INF

**Born:** Aug. 30, 1983. **B-T:** L-R. **Ht.:** 6-4. **Wt.:** 185. **Drafted:** Nicholls State, 2005 (13th round). **Signed by:** Matt Briggs.

Hatch has provided good value for a 13th-round pick, hitting for average and power in the Midwest League, where scouts and league managers viewed him as a sleeper prospect.

He has surprised the Blue Jays with his bat speed and the leverage in his fluid lefty stroke. He also has one of the best batting eyes in the system. Drafted as a third baseman, Hatch also played shortstop and second base last year. His range, arm and speed all rate as average, though he lacks the actions to profile as a regular shortstop. Toronto hoped to get him more time at second base, but injuries to both wrists shelved Hatch in late July and he missed instructional league for the second straight year. At 6-foot-4, angular and wiry strong, he might not be agile enough for second base, either. But whatever his future position, Hatch has more than enough bat to become a contributing backup or possibly more. He'll get more exposure to second base in high Class A this year.

| Year | Club (League) | Class | AVG | G | AB | R | H | 2B | 3B | HR | RBI | BB | SO | SB | OBP | SLG |
|------|---------------|-------|-----|---|----|----|----|----|----|----|-----|----|----|----|-----|-----|
| 2005 | Pulaski (Appy) | R | .273 | 41 | 128 | 16 | 35 | 11 | 2 | 5 | 26 | 9 | 30 | 0 | .331 | .508 |
| 2006 | Dunedin (FSL) | A | .500 | 3 | 8 | 3 | 4 | 2 | 0 | 0 | 2 | 2 | 0 | 0 | .600 | .750 |
| | Lansing (MWL) | A | .314 | 70 | 239 | 46 | 75 | 23 | 3 | 9 | 37 | 35 | 37 | 5 | .406 | .548 |
| **MINOR LEAGUE TOTALS** | | | .304 | 114 | 375 | 65 | 114 | 36 | 5 | 14 | 65 | 46 | 67 | 5 | .386 | .539 |

## 18  GRAHAM GODFREY                                                 RHP

**Born:** Aug. 9, 1984. **B-T:** R-R. **Ht.:** 6-3. **Wt.:** 195. **Drafted:** College of Charleston, 2006 (34th round). **Signed by:** Marc Tramuta.

To compensate for losing their 2006 second- and third-round picks for signing free agents A.J. Burnett and B.J. Ryan, the Blue Jays added talent by handing out six-figure bonuses to four players drafted after the 15th round. The most promising of the group is Godfrey, a draft-eligible sophomore who signed for $200,000 as a 34th-rounder. Godfrey was a junior college all-American in 2005 at Wallace State (Ala.) Community College, where he fashioned a 41-inning scoreless streak and went 8-1, 0.99 as a freshman. After transferring to the College of Charleston, he helped the Cougars win the first NCAA regional tournament in the mid-major program's history. Godfrey signed after Toronto followed him during the summer in the Cape Cod League. He already throws 90-94 mph with projection still remaining in his 6-foot-3, 195-pound frame. His curveball is a solid No. 2 pitch and ranks as the best bender among the Jays' 2006 draftees. Control, command and an improved changeup will be his points of emphasis when he makes his pro debut this year, most likely in low Class A.

| Year | Club (League) | Class | W | L | ERA | G | GS | CG | SV | IP | H | R | ER | HR | BB | SO | AVG |
|------|---------------|-------|---|---|-----|---|----|----|----|----|---|---|----|----|----|----|-----|
| 2006 | Did not play—Signed 2007 contract | | | | | | | | | | | | | | | | |

## 19  KYLE GINLEY                                                   RHP

**Born:** Sept. 1, 1986. **B-T:** R-R. **Ht.:** 6-2. **Wt.:** 225. **Drafted:** St. Petersburg (Fla.) JC, 2006 (17th round). **Signed by:** Joel Grampietro.

Another of Toronto's late-round investments in the 2006 draft, Ginley turned down a Florida Southern commitment for a $155,000 bonus. He possesses a true swing-and-miss fastball, and he lasted 17 rounds only because of questions about his signability. He throws downhill effectively, getting above-average sink on his 91-93 mph fastball. He has the potential to add velocity as he matures, as he's the youngest pitcher on this list. Though Ginley is around the plate, he'll need to sharpen his secondary offerings, a slider and changeup, both fringy pitches at this stage. The slider shows more promise. Ginley should be able to handle a jump to a full-season league to begin 2007. His ultimate role may be in the bullpen, but he'll remain a starter for now to hone his breaking ball.

| Year | Club (League) | Class | W | L | ERA | G | GS | CG | SV | IP | H | R | ER | HR | BB | SO | AVG |
|------|---------------|-------|---|---|------|---|----|----|----|----|----|----|----|----|----|----|------|
| 2006 | Pulaski (Appy) | R | 1 | 1 | 4.73 | 8 | 1 | 0 | 0 | 27 | 22 | 14 | 14 | 3 | 11 | 42 | .222 |
| | Auburn (NY-P) | A | 1 | 0 | 0.00 | 2 | 1 | 0 | 0 | 10 | 5 | 0 | 0 | 0 | 5 | 6 | .147 |
| **MINOR LEAGUE TOTALS** | | | 2 | 1 | 3.44 | 10 | 2 | 0 | 0 | 37 | 27 | 14 | 14 | 3 | 16 | 48 | .203 |

## 20  DAVIS ROMERO                                                  LHP

**Born:** March 30, 1983. **B-T:** L-L. **Ht.:** 5-10. **Wt.:** 170. **Signed:** Panama, 1999. **Signed by:** Giovany Miranda/Tony Arias.

Romero continued to overachieve in 2006, pitching in the Futures Game and making short work of Double-A and Triple-A on his way to Toronto. He also represented Panama in the World Baseball Classic, surrendering three unearned runs in his one-third of an inning. Though his listed height of 5-foot-10 is probably generous, Romero throws deceptively hard, consistently reaching 88-90 mph with his fringe-average fastball and usually pitching a tick below that. He hides the ball well and his three-quarters delivery and sweeping curveball are assets in left-on-left matchups. With four pitches, he has the stuff to attack righthanders, too. He keeps them honest with a slider he can get in on their hands and finishes them off

with a fading changeup. Romero is a strike-thrower and while he started exclusively in Double-A, his stuff translates better to a relief role. He's a prime contender for a spot in Toronto's 2007 bullpen.

| Year | Club (League) | Class | W | L | ERA | G | GS | CG | SV | IP | H | R | ER | HR | BB | SO | AVG |
|------|---------------|-------|---|---|-----|---|----|----|----|----|---|---|----|----|----|----|-----|
| 2000 | Blue Jays (DSL) | R | 1 | 0 | 2.65 | 13 | 2 | 0 | 4 | 34 | 15 | 10 | 10 | 1 | 10 | 45 | .129 |
| 2001 | Blue Jays (DSL) | R | 4 | 3 | 2.47 | 10 | 9 | 0 | 0 | 51 | 35 | 19 | 14 | 1 | 12 | 85 | .187 |
| 2002 | Medicine Hat (Pio) | R | 3 | 2 | 5.19 | 27 | 4 | 0 | 2 | 50 | 49 | 38 | 29 | 7 | 18 | 76 | .249 |
| 2003 | Auburn (NY-P) | A | 4 | 1 | 2.38 | 30 | 0 | 0 | 2 | 42 | 31 | 13 | 11 | 1 | 8 | 53 | .199 |
| 2004 | Charleston, W.Va. (SAL) | A | 5 | 4 | 2.53 | 32 | 14 | 0 | 1 | 103 | 77 | 36 | 29 | 6 | 30 | 108 | .209 |
| 2005 | Dunedin (FSL) | A | 9 | 6 | 3.47 | 34 | 18 | 0 | 1 | 125 | 133 | 60 | 48 | 10 | 34 | 136 | .273 |
| 2006 | New Hampshire (EL) | AA | 6 | 5 | 2.93 | 12 | 12 | 1 | 0 | 74 | 57 | 27 | 24 | 3 | 19 | 70 | .213 |
| | Syracuse (IL) | AAA | 4 | 4 | 3.83 | 18 | 3 | 0 | 1 | 45 | 46 | 25 | 19 | 3 | 7 | 36 | .264 |
| | Toronto (AL) | MLB | 1 | 0 | 3.86 | 7 | 0 | 0 | 0 | 16 | 19 | 7 | 7 | 1 | 6 | 10 | .297 |
| **MINOR LEAGUE TOTALS** | | | 36 | 25 | 3.16 | 176 | 62 | 1 | 11 | 523 | 443 | 228 | 184 | 32 | 138 | 609 | .227 |
| **MAJOR LEAGUE TOTALS** | | | 1 | 0 | 3.86 | 7 | 0 | 0 | 0 | 16 | 19 | 7 | 7 | 1 | 6 | 10 | .297 |

 ## 21  PAUL PHILLIPS
RHP

**Born:** Jan. 26, 1984. **B-T:** R-R. **Ht.:** 6-2. **Wt.:** 225. **Drafted:** Oakland, 2005 (9th round). **Signed by:** Kevin Briand.

Phillips has some of the best raw arm strength in the system, but his command comes and goes. At times he showed first- or second-round potential as an amateur, but labrum surgery forced him to miss part of 2003 and all of 2004 and scared many clubs off. Phillips pitches at 92-93 mph and tops out at 96 with his fastball. He shows better control at lower velocities and can fall in love with his radar-gun readings. When it's on, his mid-80s slider is a plus pitch, but his command of his slider is even more tenuous than that of his fastball. Phillips looks like an elite relief prospect if both pitches are working, but he struggled mightily when the Blue Jays pushed him to Double-A. He doesn't have much of a changeup, so lefthanders could give him trouble at higher levels. Phillips in an intense competitor and has a strong frame, though he tends to drag his shoulder in his delivery. He'll probably open 2007 in high Class A next season, and if he stops trying to make a perfect pitch every time and his command falls into place, he could move fast.

| Year | Club (League) | Class | W | L | ERA | G | GS | CG | SV | IP | H | R | ER | HR | BB | SO | AVG |
|------|---------------|-------|---|---|-----|---|----|----|----|----|---|---|----|----|----|----|-----|
| 2005 | Auburn (NY-P) | A | 2 | 1 | 2.29 | 26 | 0 | 0 | 13 | 39 | 31 | 14 | 10 | 2 | 13 | 41 | .214 |
| 2006 | New Hampshire (EL) | AA | 0 | 0 | 7.71 | 3 | 0 | 0 | 0 | 2 | 2 | 3 | 2 | 0 | 3 | 5 | .222 |
| | Dunedin (FSL) | A | 1 | 3 | 6.97 | 15 | 0 | 0 | 0 | 21 | 27 | 17 | 16 | 1 | 7 | 21 | .314 |
| | Lansing (MWL) | A | 5 | 3 | 2.01 | 31 | 0 | 0 | 14 | 40 | 36 | 12 | 9 | 2 | 13 | 37 | .231 |
| **MINOR LEAGUE TOTALS** | | | 8 | 7 | 3.24 | 75 | 0 | 0 | 27 | 103 | 96 | 46 | 37 | 5 | 36 | 104 | .242 |

 ## 22  BRIAN PETTWAY
OF

**Born:** July 29, 1983. **B-T:** R-R. **Ht.:** 6-1. **Wt.:** 225. **Drafted:** Mississippi, 2005 (3rd round). **Signed by:** Matt Briggs.

Pettway hasn't come close as a pro to living up to his billing as a top Southeastern Conference slugger. He has struck out 211 times in 181 pro games, and adversity has yet to result in motivating him to improve his pitch-recognition skills and two-strike approach. Sharpening both would enable Pettway to use his raw power, the equal of any Jays farmhand's, in game situations. He finished fifth in the Midwest League in extra-base hits in 2006, but he also was quite old for low Class A. Pettway played at a lower level because he lacked the advanced wood-bat experience as an amateur. Pettway is a hard worker who was equally hard on himself when he struggled. He has a strong throwing arm from his days as a two-way player in college, but his below-average range probably limits him to left field and he's not a factor on the bases. His bat will have to carry him and he needs to kick into gear at high Class A this year.

| Year | Club (League) | Class | AVG | G | AB | R | H | 2B | 3B | HR | RBI | BB | SO | SB | OBP | SLG |
|------|---------------|-------|-----|---|-----|---|---|----|----|----|-----|----|----|----|-----|-----|
| 2005 | Auburn (NY-P) | A | .225 | 56 | 200 | 19 | 45 | 10 | 2 | 6 | 25 | 16 | 66 | 0 | .288 | .385 |
| 2006 | Lansing (MWL) | A | .246 | 125 | 452 | 58 | 111 | 31 | 6 | 16 | 54 | 39 | 145 | 1 | .320 | .447 |
| **MINOR LEAGUE TOTALS** | | | .239 | 181 | 652 | 77 | 156 | 41 | 8 | 22 | 79 | 55 | 211 | 1 | .310 | .428 |

 ## 23  YOHERMYN CHAVEZ
OF

**Born:** Jan. 26, 1989. **B-T:** R-R. **Ht.:** 6-3. **Wt.:** 200. **Signed:** Venezuela, 2005. **Signed by:** Tony Arias.

The most promising of Toronto's international signees in 2005, Chavez made enough improvement with his swing and approach in extended spring training to warrant a roster spot with Rookie-level Pulaski at age 17. While he seemed a little timid at first, he more than held his own, though a sore wrist at midseason cut into his playing time and likely hampered

his power output. He showed much more present ability and aptitude than Dominican third baseman Lee Soto, who also signed with Toronto in 2005. While Chavez already has good size for his age, he likely will fill out more and add the ability to drive the ball to the opposite field. Like a lot of young batters, he's prone to chasing pitches out of the strike zone because he doesn't go the plate with a plan. His defensive game also has room for growth. Without the speed or instincts for center field, Chavez is a corner outfielder with an arm that presently rates as fringe-average. He has adapted well to a new culture. Chavez will go as far as his bat takes him, and he'll likely play at short-season Auburn in 2007.

| Year | Club (League) | Class | AVG | G | AB | R | H | 2B | 3B | HR | RBI | BB | SO | SB | OBP | SLG |
|------|---------------|-------|-----|---|----|---|---|----|----|----|-----|----|----|----|-----|-----|
| 2006 | Pulaski (Appy) | R | .276 | 36 | 105 | 19 | 29 | 9 | 0 | 0 | 18 | 9 | 23 | 1 | .371 | .362 |
| **MINOR LEAGUE TOTALS** | | | .276 | 36 | 105 | 19 | 29 | 9 | 0 | 0 | 18 | 9 | 23 | 1 | .371 | .362 |

## 24  ISMAEL RAMIREZ                                    RHP

**Born:** March 3, 1981. **B-T:** R-R. **Ht.:** 6-2. **Wt.:** 205. **Signed:** Venezuela, 1998. **Signed by:** Emilio Carrasquel.

Ramirez has toiled for eight years in the organization and started to garner attention the past three seasons. The Florida State League's 2004 pitcher of the year, Ramirez has posted consecutive solid seasons in Double-A. His solid-average fastball sits at 90-92 mph and has reached 94, but he has trouble locating it down in the zone because he struggles to get over his front side in his delivery. He also has trouble repeating his mechanics, as he frequently flies open, affecting his command. His sharp slider is his best pitch and his below-average changeup will need more refinement for him to succeed against lefthanders. Soreness in his triceps delayed Ramirez' promotion to Triple-A. He'll probably open 2007 in the Syracuse rotation, though his long-term future is likely as a swingman or middle reliever.

| Year | Club (League) | Class | W | L | ERA | G | GS | CG | SV | IP | H | R | ER | HR | BB | SO | AVG |
|------|---------------|-------|---|---|-----|---|----|----|----|----|---|---|----|----|----|----|-----|
| 1999 | Blue Jays (VSL) | R | 1 | 0 | 4.20 | 3 | 3 | 0 | 0 | 15 | 16 | 10 | 7 | 0 | 1 | 8 | .281 |
| 2000 | Blue Jays (VSL) | R | 2 | 0 | 3.15 | 4 | 4 | 0 | 0 | 20 | 20 | 7 | 7 | 4 | 2 | 13 | .253 |
| | Blue Jays (DSL) | R | 3 | 1 | 3.72 | 11 | 7 | 0 | 2 | 46 | 51 | 24 | 19 | 1 | 6 | 26 | .276 |
| 2001 | Medicine Hat (Pio) | R | 5 | 6 | 5.35 | 14 | 14 | 0 | 0 | 74 | 77 | 48 | 44 | 12 | 21 | 35 | .267 |
| 2002 | Charleston, W.Va. (SAL) | A | 0 | 1 | 4.86 | 6 | 1 | 0 | 0 | 17 | 20 | 10 | 9 | 2 | 7 | 14 | .290 |
| | Auburn (NY-P) | A | 0 | 2 | 7.15 | 3 | 3 | 0 | 0 | 11 | 17 | 10 | 9 | 2 | 2 | 7 | .354 |
| | Medicine Hat (Pio) | R | 4 | 2 | 2.98 | 11 | 10 | 0 | 0 | 54 | 51 | 23 | 18 | 4 | 14 | 51 | .249 |
| 2003 | Charleston, W.Va. (SAL) | A | 6 | 5 | 3.02 | 24 | 22 | 1 | 0 | 119 | 110 | 51 | 40 | 6 | 31 | 70 | .243 |
| 2004 | Dunedin (FSL) | A | 15 | 6 | 2.72 | 28 | 27 | 0 | 0 | 165 | 151 | 57 | 50 | 5 | 25 | 131 | .245 |
| 2005 | New Hampshire (EL) | AA | 8 | 13 | 4.12 | 27 | 27 | 0 | 0 | 151 | 155 | 75 | 69 | 19 | 32 | 125 | .267 |
| 2006 | New Hampshire (EL) | AA | 7 | 5 | 2.08 | 20 | 19 | 0 | 0 | 108 | 85 | 31 | 25 | 10 | 32 | 75 | .218 |
| | Syracuse (IL) | AAA | 2 | 0 | 4.50 | 3 | 3 | 0 | 0 | 18 | 16 | 9 | 9 | 3 | 3 | 8 | .242 |
| **MINOR LEAGUE TOTALS** | | | 53 | 41 | 3.45 | 154 | 140 | 1 | 2 | 799 | 769 | 355 | 306 | 68 | 176 | 563 | .253 |

## 25  TY TAUBENHEIM                                    RHP

**Born:** Nov. 17, 1982. **B-T:** R-R. **Ht.:** 6-6. **Wt.:** 250. **Drafted:** Edmonds (Wash.) CC, 2003 (19th round). **Signed by:** Brandon Newell (Brewers).

Taubenheim made one of the more remarkable jumps in the organization last season after being acquired in the trade that sent David Bush, Gabe Gross and Zach Jackson to the Brewers for Lyle Overbay. Taubenheim ended 2005 in Double-A and found himself starting for the Blue Jays in late May because of injuries to A.J. Burnett and Gustavo Chacin. Despite his large frame, Taubenehim is a control pitcher without an above-average offering. He's fearless and often shows plus command. He spots his fastball on the corners and is usually clocked at 89-91 mph with above-average sink. He complements it with an average slider he throws in any count and a fringe-average changeup. He also has a curveball he seldom uses. Taubenheim exceeded expectations with a solid spring training and had modest success as a big league starter, but profiles as a back-of-the-rotation guy. He tended to rely too heavily on scouting reports instead of pitching to his strengths in the big leagues. Taubenheim was placed on the disabled list in July with a staph infection in his left ankle, but he'll be fully recovered in time for spring training. He'll likely begin the season in Triple-A and be on call if an opening in the big league rotation arises.

| Year | Club (League) | Class | W | L | ERA | G | GS | CG | SV | IP | H | R | ER | HR | BB | SO | AVG |
|------|---------------|-------|---|---|-----|---|----|----|----|----|---|---|----|----|----|----|-----|
| 2003 | Helena (Pio) | R | 6 | 1 | 2.15 | 14 | 0 | 0 | 1 | 50 | 47 | 13 | 12 | 3 | 3 | 44 | .251 |
| 2004 | Beloit (MWL) | A | 5 | 3 | 3.61 | 47 | 0 | 0 | 12 | 92 | 81 | 41 | 37 | 10 | 17 | 106 | .227 |
| 2005 | Brevard County (FSL) | A | 10 | 2 | 2.63 | 16 | 16 | 2 | 0 | 106 | 86 | 34 | 31 | 7 | 26 | 75 | .224 |
| | Huntsville (SL) | AA | 2 | 6 | 4.36 | 11 | 11 | 0 | 0 | 64 | 64 | 36 | 31 | 7 | 24 | 44 | .269 |
| 2006 | Toronto (AL) | MLB | 1 | 5 | 4.89 | 12 | 7 | 0 | 0 | 35 | 40 | 22 | 19 | 5 | 18 | 26 | .282 |
| | Syracuse (IL) | AAA | 2 | 4 | 2.85 | 18 | 14 | 0 | 0 | 76 | 75 | 25 | 24 | 9 | 18 | 48 | .261 |
| **MINOR LEAGUE TOTALS** | | | 25 | 16 | 3.13 | 106 | 41 | 2 | 13 | 388 | 353 | 149 | 135 | 36 | 88 | 317 | .243 |
| **MAJOR LEAGUE TOTALS** | | | 1 | 5 | 4.89 | 12 | 7 | 0 | 0 | 35 | 40 | 22 | 19 | 5 | 18 | 26 | .282 |

## 26 RYAN ROBERTS 2B

**Born:** Sept. 19, 1980. **B-T:** R-R. **Ht.:** 5-11. **Wt.:** 190. **Drafted:** Texas-Arlington, 2003 (18th round). **Signed by:** Andy Beene.

Roberts was the Southland Conference player of the year and nearly won the league triple crown as a senior in 2003, yet lasted until the 18th round. He completed his climb to the majors last August by homering off the late Cory Lidle. Roberts has more power than his frame suggests, with the ability to drive the ball from right-center field to the left-field line. While his swing stays on a level plane for a long time, it can get big, diminishing his ability to hit for average. Drafted as a third baseman, he moved to second base in instructional league in 2003 and has made steady progress ever since. His range, hands and arm are average, and he turns the double play well. He's a below-average runner and brings very little on the bases. Roberts is a hard-nosed, high-energy player who may be able to carve out a utility role in the majors.

| Year | Club (League) | Class | AVG | G | AB | R | H | 2B | 3B | HR | RBI | BB | SO | SB | OBP | SLG |
|------|---------------|-------|-----|---|----|----|---|----|----|----|-----|----|----|----|-----|-----|
| 2003 | Auburn (NY-P) | A | .278 | 66 | 248 | 52 | 69 | 10 | 3 | 8 | 36 | 35 | 63 | 7 | .374 | .440 |
| 2004 | Charleston, W.Va. (SAL) | A | .283 | 64 | 226 | 38 | 64 | 9 | 0 | 13 | 39 | 55 | 50 | 0 | .440 | .496 |
| | Dunedin (FSL) | A | .239 | 59 | 205 | 29 | 49 | 1 | 1 | 7 | 25 | 36 | 51 | 0 | .350 | .356 |
| 2005 | Dunedin (FSL) | A | .287 | 42 | 164 | 33 | 47 | 9 | 0 | 9 | 35 | 24 | 27 | 6 | .380 | .506 |
| | New Hampshire (EL) | AA | .272 | 92 | 338 | 54 | 92 | 19 | 3 | 15 | 44 | 55 | 94 | 5 | .379 | .479 |
| 2006 | Toronto (AL) | MLB | .077 | 9 | 13 | 1 | 1 | 0 | 0 | 1 | 1 | 1 | 4 | 0 | .143 | .308 |
| | Syracuse (IL) | AAA | .273 | 98 | 362 | 44 | 99 | 28 | 1 | 10 | 49 | 30 | 86 | 5 | .330 | .439 |
| **MINOR LEAGUE TOTALS** | | | .272 | 421 | 1543 | 250 | 420 | 76 | 8 | 62 | 228 | 235 | 371 | 23 | .373 | .452 |
| **MAJOR LEAGUE TOTALS** | | | .077 | 9 | 13 | 1 | 1 | 0 | 0 | 1 | 1 | 1 | 4 | 0 | .143 | .308 |

## 27 CHIP CANNON 1B

**Born:** Nov. 30, 1981. **B-T:** L-R. **Ht.:** 6-5. **Wt.:** 225. **Drafted:** The Citadel, 2004 (8th round). **Signed by:** Marc Tramuta.

Area scout Marc Tramuta was such a big Cannon booster that he pushed to draft him in 2004's second round, though the Jays were able to wait until the eighth and sign him for $25,000 as a college senior. Cannon has justified Tramuta's faith by slugging 32 homers at three stops in 2005 to rank fifth in the minors, then topping the Eastern League with 27 last year. He continued to mash in the offseason, earning MVP honors in the Arizona Fall League by leading the league in homers (11), RBIs (29) and slugging (.714). For all his power—and he has few rivals in the system—he needs to develop a more consistent approach, especially with two strikes. He has the discipline to draw walks, but struck out 158 times in 135 games last season. He made improvements against lefthanders, hitting .265 with nine homers in 136 at-bats, after they fanned him 25 times in 48 Double-A at-bats in 2005. Because Cannon was born with two club feet and had three operations on each as a child, he has trouble starting and stopping on the bases and in the field. His range suffers as a result, though he has an above-average arm. Because he hit just .248, the Blue Jays may send Cannon back to New Hampshire to begin 2007, though his AFL performance may help him get to Triple-A.

| Year | Club (League) | Class | AVG | G | AB | R | H | 2B | 3B | HR | RBI | BB | SO | SB | OBP | SLG |
|------|---------------|-------|-----|---|----|----|---|----|----|----|-----|----|----|----|-----|-----|
| 2004 | Auburn (NY-P) | A | .271 | 62 | 210 | 33 | 57 | 15 | 1 | 10 | 41 | 22 | 55 | 0 | .338 | .495 |
| 2005 | Lansing (MWL) | A | .268 | 46 | 168 | 22 | 45 | 9 | 2 | 11 | 36 | 20 | 47 | 0 | .351 | .542 |
| | Dunedin (FSL) | A | .384 | 29 | 112 | 28 | 43 | 4 | 2 | 14 | 39 | 16 | 32 | 0 | .465 | .830 |
| | New Hampshire (EL) | AA | .247 | 47 | 170 | 15 | 42 | 13 | 1 | 7 | 23 | 10 | 58 | 2 | .293 | .459 |
| 2006 | New Hampshire (EL) | AA | .248 | 135 | 475 | 78 | 118 | 25 | 1 | 27 | 69 | 51 | 158 | 0 | .335 | .476 |
| **MINOR LEAGUE TOTALS** | | | .269 | 319 | 1135 | 176 | 305 | 66 | 7 | 69 | 208 | 119 | 350 | 2 | .345 | .522 |

## 28 ROBINZON DIAZ C

**Born:** Sept. 19, 1983. **B-T:** R-R. **Ht.:** 5-11. **Wt.:** 210. **Signed:** Dominican Republic, 2000. **Signed by:** Hilario Soriano.

Diaz has been remarkably consistent. Starting in 2003, when he won the Appalachian League batting title, he has earned all-star recognition and ranked among the top contact hitters in each of his leagues. He repeated high Class A in 2006 because the Jays wanted him to improve his game-calling and had Curtis Thigpen in Double-A. Diaz is a classic bad-ball hitter who puts the ball in play in nearly every at-bat, resulting in low strikeout and walk totals. With a flat plane to his swing and an inside-out approach, he doesn't hit many homers. He runs well for a catcher and threw out 31 percent of basestealers in 2006 with a strong, accurate arm. His blocking and receiving skills are average. He doesn't project as a regular but he could eventually become Thigpen's backup in Toronto. Diaz will move up to Double-A this year.

| Year | Club (League) | Class | AVG | G | AB | R | H | 2B | 3B | HR | RBI | BB | SO | SB | OBP | SLG |
|------|---------------|-------|-----|---|-----|----|-----|-----|-----|-----|-----|-----|-----|-----|------|------|
| 2001 | Blue Jays (DSL) | R | .312 | 65 | 253 | 49 | 79 | 17 | 2 | 2 | 45 | 20 | 19 | 4 | .374 | .419 |
| 2002 | Dunedin (FSL) | A | .120 | 10 | 25 | 3 | 3 | 0 | 0 | 0 | 1 | 1 | 4 | 0 | .148 | .120 |
|  | Medicine Hat (Pio) | R | .297 | 58 | 192 | 29 | 57 | 9 | 0 | 0 | 20 | 13 | 19 | 7 | .345 | .344 |
| 2003 | Pulaski (Appy) | R | .374 | 48 | 182 | 33 | 68 | 20 | 2 | 1 | 44 | 10 | 14 | 1 | .407 | .522 |
| 2004 | Charleston, W.Va. (SAL) | A | .287 | 105 | 407 | 62 | 117 | 20 | 2 | 2 | 42 | 27 | 31 | 10 | .341 | .361 |
| 2005 | Dunedin (FSL) | A | .294 | 100 | 388 | 47 | 114 | 17 | 6 | 1 | 65 | 15 | 28 | 5 | .325 | .376 |
| 2006 | Dunedin (FSL) | A | .306 | 104 | 418 | 59 | 128 | 21 | 1 | 3 | 44 | 20 | 37 | 8 | .341 | .383 |
| **MINOR LEAGUE TOTALS** | | | .303 | 490 | 1865 | 282 | 566 | 104 | 13 | 9 | 261 | 106 | 152 | 35 | .347 | .388 |

## 29 CHASE LIRETTE                                                   RHP

**Born:** June 9, 1985. **B-T:** R-R. **Ht.:** 6-3. **Wt.:** 210. **Drafted:** South Florida, 2006 (16th round). **Signed by:** Joel Grampietro.

Despite strong performances in the Cape Cod League in 2005 and at South Florida last spring, Lirette lasted 16 rounds in the 2006 draft. After signing for $135,000, Lirette's first task was to make mechanical adjustments. He worked to not stay so tall in his delivery and to become more flexible in his upper body. Once he got accustomed to the changes, he pitched better toward the end of his pro debut. Lirette gets good downhill plane on an 89-91 mph fastball and shows a real feel for the strike zone. He gained confidence in his slider and changeup as the season wore on, but both pitches need improvement. A fast worker on the mound, Lirette has begun to get a feel for adapting to what batters are trying to do against him. Mostly a reliever in college, he likely will wind up in the bullpen but may pitch out of the rotation in low Class A this season to get innings.

| Year | Club (League) | Class | W | L | ERA | G | GS | CG | SV | IP | H | R | ER | HR | BB | SO | AVG |
|------|---------------|-------|---|---|-----|---|----|----|----|----|---|---|----|----|----|----|-----|
| 2006 | Auburn (NY-P) | A | 4 | 1 | 2.23 | 10 | 6 | 0 | 1 | 40 | 32 | 11 | 10 | 1 | 7 | 37 | .219 |
| **MINOR LEAGUE TOTALS** | | | 4 | 1 | 2.23 | 10 | 6 | 0 | 1 | 40 | 32 | 11 | 10 | 1 | 7 | 37 | .219 |

## 30 BRIAN JEROLOMAN                                                   C

**Born:** May 10, 1985. **B-T:** L-R. **Ht.:** 6-0. **Wt.:** 195. **Drafted:** Florida, 2006 (6th round). **Signed by:** Joel Grampietro.

On the strength of his defensive tools, Jeroloman entered 2006 as the top catching prospect in college baseball. Though not much was expected from him with the bat, he hit just .242 as a junior and was just the eighth college catcher drafted in June. His brother Chuck is an infielder in the Red Sox system. Brian, who signed for $165,000, came as advertised. He receives high marks for his sure hands, sound footwork and above-average blocking and receiving skills. His arm strength is above-average and he features a quick, accurate release, which he used to throw out 42 percent of basestealers. Jeroloman is agile behind the plate and has advanced game-calling skills. At the plate, Jeroloman still showed traces of a metal-bat swing, and he had trouble keeping his hands inside the ball and getting the barrel on the ball. He has below-average power and speed. While his hitting needs work, Jeroloman's lefty bat, willingness to take walks and impeccable defensive tools make for an intriguing package. He may open 2007 in low Class A in an attempt to build his confidence at the plate.

| Year | Club (League) | Class | AVG | G | AB | R | H | 2B | 3B | HR | RBI | BB | SO | SB | OBP | SLG |
|------|---------------|-------|-----|---|-----|----|----|-----|-----|-----|-----|-----|-----|-----|------|------|
| 2006 | Auburn (NY-P) | A | .241 | 45 | 141 | 27 | 34 | 10 | 1 | 0 | 21 | 26 | 38 | 0 | .363 | .326 |
| **MINOR LEAGUE TOTALS** | | | .241 | 45 | 141 | 27 | 34 | 10 | 1 | 0 | 21 | 26 | 38 | 0 | .363 | .326 |

# WASHINGTON
# NATIONALS

BY **AARON FITT**

The Nationals finally found some stability in their second season in Washington, as a new ownership group led by developer Ted Lerner took over the reins of the franchise from Major League Baseball in late July. Former Braves executive Stan Kasten became team president, and general manager Jim Bowden and his staff were given the security of knowing their jobs were no longer in limbo.

Bowden's major offseason acquisition, Alfonso Soriano, became the fourth member of the 40-40 club. Soriano's big season and **Ryan Zimmerman's** 110-RBI rookie year didn't pay off in the standings, however. The Nationals finished in last place in the National League East at 71-91, 10 games worse than in 2005. Washington let manager Frank Robinson go after the season, replacing him with Mets third-base coach Manny Acta.

But the Nationals are about the future, not the present. With a new ballpark set to open in 2008, they spent 2006 trying to build a long-term foundation by acquiring as many young players as they could through trades, the draft and the international market.

Though he didn't trade Soriano, who left as a free agent after the season, Bowden did make some slick trades during the summer. He acquired big leaguers Austin Kearns and Felipe Lopez from the Reds and pitching prospects Luis Atilano (Braves), Matt Chico and Garrett Mock (Diamondbacks), Shairon Martis (Giants) and Jhonny Nunez (Dodgers) without giving up anyone in Washington's long-term plans. In December, Bowden unloaded declining veteran Jose Vidro and

his $12 million in salary obligations to the Mariners for outfielder Chris Snelling and righthander Emiliano Fruto.

For the first time in five years, the Nationals could spend freely in the draft, and they had two first-round picks and two second-rounders. Though they didn't sign second-round righty Sean Black, the Nationals spent $5.3 million on the draft, the 10th-highest amount in baseball. They also signed 16-year-old Dominican shortstop Esmailyn Gonzalez for $1.4 million. They trumpeted that bonus in their official press release, making a statement that they will be major players in Latin America for years to come.

The end result of all the moves is that Washington has vastly improved the depth in its farm system, though it will take some time for the talent to progress to the upper levels. The Nationals hope to build their club with homegrown talent, much like the Braves did under Kasten.

To that end, the Nationals hired Diamondbacks scouting director Mike Rizzo as assistant GM and vice president of baseball operations. Washington added 10 scouts, including former Devil Rays GM Chuck LaMar, in November to augment a scouting staff that had been ravaged during MLB's ownership. Even with a skeleton staff, scouting director Dana Brown has proven resourceful with help from scouts like Tony Arango, who signed the first three prospects on this list.

## TOP 30 PROSPECTS

1. Collin Balester, rhp
2. Chris Marrero, of
3. Colton Willems, rhp
4. Kory Casto, 3b/of
5. Esmailyn Gonzalez, ss
6. Zech Zinicola, rhp
7. Glenn Gibson, lhp
8. Matt Chico, lhp
9. Stephen King, ss
10. Ian Desmond, ss
11. Jesus Flores, c
12. Garrett Mock, rhp
13. Emiliano Fruto, rhp
14. Jhonny Nunez, rhp
15. Shairon Martis, rhp
16. Larry Broadway, 1b
17. Stephen Englund, of
18. Justin Maxwell, of
19. Adam Carr, rhp
20. John Lannan, lhp
21. Craig Stammen, rhp
22. Marco Estrada, rhp
23. Brian Peacock, c
24. Clint Everts, rhp
25. Shawn Hill, rhp
26. Devin Ivany, c
27. Frank Diaz, of
28. Cory Van Allen, lhp
29. Levale Speigner, rhp
30. Mike Hinckley, lhp

# ORGANIZATION OVERVIEW

**General manager:** Jim Bowden. **Farm director:** Andy Dunn. **Scouting director:** Dana Brown.

## 2006 PERFORMANCE

| Class | Team | League | W | L | PCT | Finish* | Manager | Affiliated |
|---|---|---|---|---|---|---|---|---|
| Majors | Washington | National | 71 | 91 | .438 | 14th (16) | Frank Robinson | — |
| Triple-A | #New Orleans Zephyrs | Pacific Coast | 72 | 71 | .503 | 9th (16) | Tim Foli | 2005 |
| Double-A | Harrisburg Senators | Eastern | 67 | 75 | .472 | 9th (12) | John Stearns | 1991 |
| High A | Potomac Nationals | Carolina | 64 | 76 | .457 | 6th (8) | Randy Knorr | 2005 |
| Low A | †Savannah Sand Gnats | South Atlantic | 56 | 83 | .403 | 15th (16) | Bobby Williams | 2003 |
| Short-season | Vermont Expos | New York-Penn | 23 | 52 | .307 | 14th (14) | Jose Alguacil | 1994 |
| Rookie | GCL Nationals | Gulf Coast | 23 | 31 | .426 | 10th (13) | Bob Henley | 1998 |
| **OVERALL 2006 MINOR LEAGUE RECORD** | | | 305 | 388 | .440 | 28th (30) | | |

*Finish in overall standings (No. of teams in league). +League champion. #Affiliate will be in Columbus (International) in 2007.
†Affiliate will be in Hagerstown (South Atlantic) in 2007.

## ORGANIZATION LEADERS

### BATTING
| | | |
|---|---|---|
| AVG | Broadway, Larry, New Orleans | .288 |
| R | Casto, Kory, Harrisburg | 89 |
| H | Casto, Kory, Harrisburg | 142 |
| TB | Casto, Kory, Harrisburg | 243 |
| 2B | Powell, Brandon, Potomac | 34 |
| 3B | Godwin, Tyrell, New Orleans | 7 |
| 3B | Pahuta, Tim, Savannah | 7 |
| HR | Casto, Kory, Harrisburg | 21 |
| HR | Whitesell, Josh, Harrisburg | 21 |
| RBI | Casto, Kory, Harrisburg | 89 |
| BB | Casto, Kory, Harrisburg | 90 |
| SO | Whitesell, Josh, Harrisburg | 139 |
| SB | Dorta, Melvin, Harrisburg/New Orleans | 36 |
| OBP | Casto, Kory, Harrisburg | .392 |
| SLG | Casto, Kory, Harrisburg | .479 |
| XBH | Casto, Kory, Harrisburg | 53 |

### PITCHING
| | | |
|---|---|---|
| W | Bouknight, Kip, Harrisburg/New Orleans | 9 |
| W | Good, Andrew, New Orleans | 9 |
| L | Trahan, David, Savannah/Potomac | 13 |
| ERA | Perez, Beltran, Harrisburg | 3.11 |
| G | Gryboski, Kevin, New Orleans | 52 |
| CG | Bouknight, Kip, Harrisburg/New Orleans | 2 |
| SV | Corcoran, Roy, Harrisburg/New Orleans | 27 |
| IP | Bouknight, Kip, Harrisburg/New Orleans | 158 |
| BB | Echols, Justin, New Orleans/Harrisburg | 81 |
| SO | Martinez, Anastacio, Harrisburg/New Orleans | 126 |
| AVG | Martinez, Anastacio, Harrisburg/New Orleans | .249 |

## BEST TOOLS

| | |
|---|---|
| Best Hitter for Average | Chris Marrero |
| Best Power Hitter | Chris Marrero |
| Best Strike-Zone Discipline | Kory Casto |
| Fastest Baserunner | Justin Maxwell |
| Best Athlete | Justin Maxwell |
| Best Fastball | Colton Willems |
| Best Curveball | Glenn Gibson |
| Best Slider | Zech Zinicola |
| Best Changeup | Emiliano Fruto |
| Best Control | Glenn Gibson |
| Best Defensive Catcher | Devin Ivany |
| Best Defensive Infielder | Esmailyn Gonzalez |
| Best Infield Arm | Ian Desmond |
| Best Defensive Outfielder | Frank Diaz |
| Best Outfield Arm | Ryan DeLaughter |

## PROJECTED 2010 LINEUP

| | |
|---|---|
| Catcher | Brian Schneider |
| First Base | Nick Johnson |
| Second Base | Felipe Lopez |
| Third Base | Ryan Zimmerman |
| Shortstop | Esmailyn Gonzalez |

| | |
|---|---|
| Left Field | Kory Casto |
| Center Field | Austin Kearns |
| Right Field | Chris Marrero |
| No. 1 Starter | Collin Balester |
| No. 2 Starter | Colton Willems |
| No. 3 Starter | John Patterson |
| No. 4 Starter | Glenn Gibson |
| No. 5 Starter | Matt Chico |
| Closer | Chad Cordero |

## LAST YEARS TOP 20 PROSPECTS

1. Ryan Zimmerman, 3b
2. Collin Balester, rhp
3. Clint Everts, rhp
4. Ian Desmond, ss
5. Armando Galarraga, rhp
6. Kory Casto, 3b
7. Mike Hinckley, lhp
8. Bill Bray, lhp
9. Larry Broadway, 1b
10. Daryl Thompson, rhp
11. Jason Bergmann, rhp
12. Frank Diaz, of
13. Justin Maxwell, of
14. Travis Hughes, rhp
15. Josh Whitesell, 1b
16. Darrell Rasner, rhp
17. Shawn Hill, rhp
18. Brandon Watson, of
19. Brendan Harris, 2b/3b
20. Devin Ivany, c

## TOP PROSPECTS OF THE DECADE

| Year | Player, Pos. | 2006 Org. |
|---|---|---|
| 1997 | Vladimir Guerrero, of | Angels |
| 1998 | Brad Fullmer, 1b | Out of baseball |
| 1999 | Michael Barrett, 3b/c | Cubs |
| 2000 | Tony Armas, rhp | Nationals |
| 2001 | Donnie Bridges, rhp | Alexandria (United) |
| 2002 | Brandon Phillips, ss | Reds |
| 2003 | Clint Everts, rhp | Nationals |
| 2004 | Clint Everts, rhp | Nationals |
| 2005 | Mike Hinckley, lhp | Nationals |
| 2006 | Ryan Zimmerman, 3b | Nationals |

## TOP DRAFT PICKS OF THE DECADE

| Year | Player, Pos. | 2006 Org. |
|---|---|---|
| 1997 | Donnie Bridges, rhp | Alexandria (United) |
| 1998 | Josh McKinley, ss | Out of baseball |
| 1999 | Josh Girdley, lhp | Out of baseball |
| 2000 | Justin Wayne, rhp | Out of baseball |
| 2001 | Josh Karp, rhp | Nationals |
| 2002 | Clint Everts, rhp | Nationals |
| 2003 | Chad Cordero, rhp | Nationals |
| 2004 | Bill Bray, lhp | Reds |
| 2005 | Ryan Zimmerman, 3b | Nationals |
| 2006 | Chris Marrero, of | Nationals |

## LARGEST BONUSES IN CLUB HISTORY

| | |
|---|---|
| Ryan Zimmerman | $2,975,000 |
| Justin Wayne, 2000 | $2,950,000 |
| Josh Karp, 2001 | $2,650,000 |
| Clint Everts, 2002 | $2,500,000 |
| Grady Sizemore, 2000 | $2,000,000 |

# MINOR LEAGUE DEPTH CHART

## Washington Nationals

**Impact: D.** Collin Balester is a nice prospect, but he's one of the weaker No. 1 prospects in baseball. Chris Marrero, Colton Willems, Esmailyn Gonzalez and Stephen King, among others, have a chance to become high-impact prospects, but all are far away.

**Depth: F.** Thanks to trades and the draft, the Nationals have built plenty of pitching and outfield depth. But Kory Casto is their only accomplished player above A-ball.

**Sleeper:** Brian Peacock, c. Peacock was hitting for average and power before shoulder soreness and appendicitis derailed him. With plenty of raw power and even some speed, Peacock is an athletic, energetic young catcher who could be in for a big year.

*Numbers in parentheses indicate prospect rankings.*

| LF | CF | RF |
|---|---|---|
| Chris Marrero (2) | Stephen Englund (17) | Ryan DeLaughter |
| Kory Casto (4) | Justin Maxwell (18) | Edgardo Baez |
| Mike Daniel | Frank Diaz (27) | |
| Dee Brown | Rogearvin Bernadina | |
| Marvin Lowrance | Francisco Plasencia | |

| 3B | SS | 2B | 1B |
|---|---|---|---|
| Leonard Davis | Esmailyn Gonzalez (5) | Melvin Dorta | Larry Broadway (16) |
| | Stephen King (9) | Michael Martinez | Josh Whitesell |
| | Ian Desmond (10) | Ofilio Castro | |
| | Josh Wilson | | |
| | Seth Bynum | | |
| | Jean Alvarez | | |

| C |
|---|
| Jesus Flores (11) |
| Brian Peacock (23) |
| Devin Ivany (26) |
| Sean Rooney |
| Luke Montz |
| Erick San Pedro |

| RHP | | LHP | |
|---|---|---|---|
| **Starters** | **Relievers** | **Starters** | **Relievers** |
| Collin Balester (1) | Zech Zinicola (6) | Glenn Gibson (7) | Juan De Los Santos |
| Colton Willems (3) | Emiliano Fruto (13) | Matt Chico (8) | Coby Mavroulis |
| Garrett Mock (12) | Adam Carr (19) | John Lannan (20) | Gerald Plexico |
| Jhonny Nunez (14) | Levale Speigner (29) | Cory Van Allen (28) | |
| Shairon Martis (15) | Jermaine Van Buren | Mike Hinckley (30) | |
| Craig Stammen (21) | Brett Campbell | Justin Jones | |
| Marco Estrada (22) | Alexis Morales | Jack Spradlin | |
| Clint Everts (24) | Devin Perrin | Jon Felfoldi | |
| Shawn Hill (25) | Danny Rueckel | Yunior Novoa | |
| Luis Atilano | Cole Kimball | Wuillys Bravo | |
| Hassan Pena | Andre Enriquez | | |
| Joel Hanrahan | | | |
| Chris Lugo | | | |
| T.J. Nall | | | |
| Carlos Martinez | | | |

# DRAFT ANALYSIS

**Best Pro Debut:** RHP Zech Zinicola (6) didn't join the organization until June, but he did enough in three months to earn the Nationals' minor league pitcher of the year award. He went 4-1, 1.65 with 12 saves and 31 strikeouts in 33 innings while advancing to Double-A.

**Best Athlete:** Stephen Englund (2) made an easy transition from prep shortstop to pro center fielder. His tools are ahead of his baseball skills for now—he batted .183 in his debut—but he can put on a show with his batting-practice power and throwing arm. Stephen King (3) is a possible five-tool shortstop.

**Best Pure Hitter:** OF Chris Marrero (1) batted .309 as a pro before coming down with viral meningitis in August. He has more pure hitting ability than King, an offensive shortstop.

**Best Raw Power:** Though Marrero didn't homer in his pro debut, his power rates as a 7 on the 2-8 scouting scale. The leverage in his swing gives him pop to all fields.

**Fastest Runner:** OF Chris French (21) can run 60 yards in 6.4 seconds, Oddly, he tried just three steal attempts in pro ball.

**Best Defensive Player:** King in the infield, Englund in the outfield and Sean Rooney (8) behind the plate.

**Best Fastball:** RHP Colton Willems (1) had one of the best high school heaters in the draft, working at 92-95 mph and topping out at 97. As a bonus, he locates his fastball well within the strike zone. Zinicola threw 92-93 mph every time out in pro ball, peaking at 95.

**Best Breaking Ball:** LHP Glenn Gibson's (4) curveball. Zinicola has the best slider, and he throws it at 82-85 mph.

**Most Intriguing Background:** C Josh Rodriguez' (47) father Eddie and OF Kyle Page's (48) dad Mitchell served on Washington's big league coaching staff in 2006. Mitchell Page also played in the majors, as did the fathers of Gibson (Paul) and OF Khris Davis (29, Rodney). RHP Hassan Pena (13) is a Cuban defector who can run his fastball up to 93 mph. RHP Cory Anderson (43) was a starting quarterback at the U.S. Coast Guard Academy, while OF D'Vontrey Richardson (35) is a backup passer at Florida State. RHP Javier Martinez' (42) brother Joe pitches in the Giants system. Davis, Richardson, Martinez, Rodriguez and Page failed to sign.

**Closest To The Majors:** Zinicola may push for a job in the Washington bullpen as early as 2007.

**Best Late-Round Pick:** RHP Adam Carr (18) was a slugging first baseman at Oklahoma State and pitched only in fall practice. But in that limited exposure on the mound, area scout Ryan Fox saw him touch 94 mph with his fastball and 85 with his slider. Carr had a 2.81 ERA and 27 strikeouts in 26 pro innings. He also hit .302 with three homers in 63 at-bats.

**The One Who Got Away:** RHP Sean Black (2) is the highest pick in the 2006 draft to turn down pro ball, opting instead for Seton Hall. A converted shortstop who's still developing on the mound, he'll show a plus fastball and curve when he's on. The Nationals took several gambles on tough signs and couldn't land RHP Sam Brown (7, now at North Carolina State), 3B Dustin Dickerson (15, Baylor) and RHP Sam Dyson (19, South Carolina).

**Assessment:** Free of Major League Baseball ownership for the first time since 2002, the franchise didn't have to take any shortcuts in the draft. The Nationals took two legitimate first-rounders in Marrero and Willems and went over slot recommendations to sign King, Gibson and Pena.

## 2005          BUDGET: $4.0 million

3B Ryan Zimmerman (1) drove in 110 runs as a big league rookie last year and makes the draft himself. The Nationals didn't have second- or third-round picks.          **GRADE: A**

## 2004          BUDGET: $3.7 million

RHP Collin Balester (4) is the system's best prospect, and SS Ian Desmond (3) is a slick fielder. LHP Bill Bray (1) was a key part of a trade last summer that netted Austin Kearns and Felipe Lopez.          **GRADE: C**

## 2003          BUDGET: $3.1 million

RHP Chad Cordero (1) was considered a bit of a reach, but he already has notched 91 saves in the majors. 3B/OF Kory Casto (3) is the Nats' top hitting prospect in the upper levels.          **GRADE: B+**

*Draft analysis by **Jim Callis**. Numbers in parentheses indicate draft rounds. Budgets are bonuses in first 10 rounds.*

# COLLIN
# BALESTER

RHP

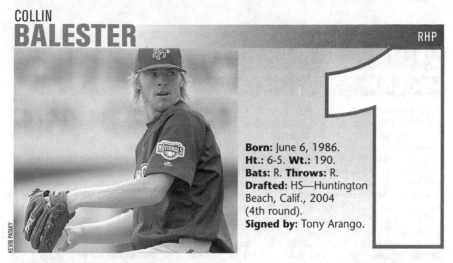

**Born:** June 6, 1986.
**Ht.:** 6-5. **Wt.:** 190.
**Bats:** R. **Throws:** R.
**Drafted:** HS—Huntington Beach, Calif., 2004 (4th round).
**Signed by:** Tony Arango.

KEVIN PATAKY

Going into his freshman year at Huntington Beach (Calif.) High, Balester spent much more time surfing than pitching. He admits that he knew about major league baseball but had no idea farm systems existed until his junior year of high school. His father Tom, who has spent 25 years shaving surfboards, worried about Balester falling in with the hard-partying surfer crowd, so he made him focus on baseball. It turned out the younger Balester had quite a knack for pitching, but he lacked the grades for college and signed for $290,000 as a fourth-round pick in 2004. He developed faster than the Nationals anticipated over his first two pro seasons, pushing his way to high Class A Potomac as a 19-year-old to start 2006. Early in the year, Washington wanted him to work on staying taller in his delivery to maximize leverage in his lanky frame, and he struggled with the adjustment, going 1-3, 6.91 over his first nine starts. His fastball velocity dropped to 88-90 mph and his command was very erratic. When Balester decided to return to his drop-and-drive roots, his stuff and control came back. He rebounded to earn three late-season starts at Double-A Harrisburg.

When Balester is on, he has two above-average pitches and a chance for a third. Once he went back to pushing off the rubber with his back foot, he regained the life and velocity on his 91-94 fastball and had much more success busting hitters inside and breaking bats. With a durable frame and an electric arm, he holds his velocity deep into games and still projects to add a little more zip to his fastball as he fills out. Balester's out pitch is a power 76-78 mph curveball with sharp downward bite. His command of his curve came on in the second half of 2006, when he had success throwing it for strikes or as a chase pitch. He has good feel for his 80-84 mph changeup, which the Nationals forced him to begin throwing late in 2005. The changeup is becoming an effective weapon against lefthanders, thanks to its good fade. Balester doesn't rack up huge strikeout totals, but that's in part because he tries to be efficient and keep his pitch counts down.

Balester still needs to learn to trust his changeup and develop a better feel for how much to put on or take off the pitch. It shows signs of being at least an average offering, and he'll need it to become more consistent in order to succeed as a starter in the big leagues. Though he tries to pitch to contact, he's still been too hittable because his location remains a work in progress. He has come a long way with the command of his fastball, but isn't as far along with his curve. While Balester has a gregarious, easygoing personality, he can get too emotional on the mound and lets his frustration with umpires get the better of him. Early in 2006, he struggled not just with mechanics but also with expectations, and he needs to be careful not to try to do too much.

At 20, Balester will be one of the youngest pitchers to open 2007 in Double-A. The Nationals have plenty of uncertainty in their starting rotation, and it's possible Balester could see the big leagues late in the year, but another full season in the minors would be good for his development. He has the stuff and the moxie to be Washington's No. 1 starter in a few years.

| Year | Club (League) | Class | W | L | ERA | G | GS | CG | SV | IP | H | R | ER | HR | BB | SO | AVG |
|------|---------------|-------|---|---|-----|---|----|----|----|----|----|----|----|----|----|----|-----|
| 2004 | Expos (GCL) | R | 1 | 2 | 2.19 | 5 | 4 | 0 | 0 | 25 | 20 | 8 | 6 | 0 | 5 | 21 | .215 |
| 2005 | Savannah (SAL) | A | 8 | 6 | 3.67 | 24 | 23 | 1 | 0 | 125 | 105 | 62 | 51 | 11 | 42 | 95 | .222 |
| 2006 | Potomac (CL) | A | 4 | 5 | 5.20 | 23 | 22 | 0 | 0 | 118 | 126 | 71 | 68 | 12 | 53 | 87 | .280 |
| | Harrisburg (EL) | AA | 1 | 0 | 1.83 | 3 | 3 | 0 | 0 | 20 | 15 | 5 | 4 | 0 | 6 | 10 | .231 |
| **MINOR LEAGUE TOTALS** | | | 14 | 13 | 4.05 | 55 | 52 | 1 | 0 | 287 | 266 | 146 | 129 | 23 | 106 | 213 | .246 |

## CHRIS MARRERO
OF

**Born:** July 2, 1988. **B-T:** R-R. **Ht.:** 6-3. **Wt.:** 210. **Drafted:** HS—Opa Locka, Fla., 2006 (1st round). **Signed by:** Tony Arango.

Marrero was the nation's top prep position player entering 2006, but he slumped during the spring. But after joking around with Nationals GM Jim Bowden at a workout in RFK Stadium, he crushed one mammoth homer after another, and onlooking Ryan Zimmerman couldn't believe Marrero was a high schooler. After he went 15th overall and signed for $1.625 million, Marrero had a solid pro debut until it was cut shot by viral meningitis in early August. Marrero's best tool is his plus-plus raw power from foul pole to foul pole. He has decent plate discipline and pitch recognition, and he gets his hands ready early in his smooth, quiet swing. With a big, athletic frame and fringe-average speed, he played a solid left field after spending his high school career at third base. He has an above-average arm. Marrero re-injured his hamstring last spring and developed bad habits to compensate, stepping in the bucket and pulling off pitches on the outer half. He seemed to correct the problem last summer, but he still needs to show he can make consistent hard contact. Marrero should be ready to push for an everyday job at Washington's new low Class A Hagerstown affiliate in 2007. He could be the Nationals' cleanup hitter of the future.

| Year | Club (League) | Class | AVG | G | AB | R | H | 2B | 3B | HR | RBI | BB | SO | SB | OBP | SLG |
|------|---------------|-------|-----|---|----|---|---|----|----|----|-----|----|----|----|-----|-----|
| 2006 | Nationals (GCL) | R | .309 | 22 | 81 | 10 | 25 | 9 | 0 | 0 | 16 | 8 | 19 | 0 | .374 | .420 |
| **MINOR LEAGUE TOTALS** | | | .309 | 22 | 81 | 10 | 25 | 9 | 0 | 0 | 16 | 8 | 19 | 0 | .374 | .420 |

## COLTON WILLEMS
RHP

**Born:** July 30, 1988. **B-T:** R-R. **Ht.:** 6-3. **Wt.:** 175. **Drafted:** HS—Fort Pierce, Fla, 2006 (1st round). **Signed by:** Tony Arango.

Willems surfaced as an elite arm in the summer of 2005, garnering most-valuable-pitcher honors at the Cape Cod Classic in July. He shut it down after the Aflac All-American game, and as a result had the freshest arm in Florida's deep high school pitching crop last spring. He went 22nd overall in June and signed for $1.425 million. Willems has a lightning-quick arm and a clean, easy delivery from a high three-quarters slot. His velocity spiked in the spring, when he came out pitching at 92 mph and bumped 97 in a relief outing, and he pitched at 91-93 as a starter last summer. With a tall, projectable frame, he gets good downward angle on his pitches. He secured his first-round status after his high school pitching coach, former major leaguer David West, taught him a mid-80s slider to replace his curveball. Though Willems locates his fastball well on both sides of the plate, he needs to command his slider better in order to make it a plus pitch. His changeup could become average, but it's in the very early stages of its development. The Nationals shut down Willems with mild elbow soreness in August, though they say they were just being extra cautious and it's not a long-term concern. Willems has the stuff to become a No. 1 starter, but he'll need time and patience to reach his ceiling. He could start 2007 in low Class A.

| Year | Club (League) | Class | W | L | ERA | G | GS | CG | SV | IP | H | R | ER | HR | BB | SO | AVG |
|------|---------------|-------|---|---|-----|---|----|----|----|----|---|---|----|----|----|----|-----|
| 2006 | Nationals (GCL) | R | 0 | 1 | 3.38 | 5 | 5 | 0 | 0 | 16 | 23 | 8 | 6 | 1 | 3 | 8 | .338 |
| **MINOR LEAGUE TOTALS** | | | 0 | 1 | 3.38 | 5 | 5 | 0 | 0 | 16 | 23 | 8 | 6 | 1 | 3 | 8 | .338 |

## KORY CASTO
3B/OF

**Born:** Dec. 8, 1981. **B-T:** L-R. **Ht.:** 6-1. **Wt.:** 200. **Drafted:** Portland, 2003 (3rd round). **Signed by:** Doug McMillan.

An outfielder in college, Casto moved to third base in 2004 and gradually became a very solid defender there. But when Ryan Zimmerman seized the Nationals' hot-corner job, they decided to move Casto back to the outfield after the 2006 all-star break. He had another solid year with the bat and continued to hit in the Arizona Fall League, despite missing three weeks for his wedding and honeymoon. A mature, disciplined hitter, Casto rarely chases pitches out of the zone and excels at working counts. He has average power and can use the whole field, and he's not afraid to jump on hanging breaking balls or high fastballs early in the count. He had no problem getting reacquainted with the outfield, where his arm is slightly above-average and his range is fringy. Casto has always been a streaky hitter because he'll fall into the trap of making too many adjustments at times. He's an extremely hard worker, but sometimes his drive to succeed gets the better of him. With the departure of Alfonso Soriano via free agency, Casto should have a chance to earn Washington's

left-field job. He should be a solid everyday player capable of hitting 20 homers per year.

| Year | Club (League) | Class | AVG | G | AB | R | H | 2B | 3B | HR | RBI | BB | SO | SB | OBP | SLG |
|------|---------------|-------|-----|---|-----|----|-----|----|----|----|-----|----|----|----|------|------|
| 2003 | Vermont (NYP) | A | .239 | 71 | 259 | 26 | 62 | 14 | 2 | 4 | 28 | 30 | 47 | 1 | .322 | .355 |
| 2004 | Savannah (SAL) | A | .286 | 124 | 483 | 67 | 138 | 35 | 4 | 16 | 88 | 31 | 70 | 1 | .337 | .474 |
| 2005 | Potomac (CL) | A | .290 | 135 | 500 | 86 | 145 | 36 | 4 | 22 | 90 | 84 | 98 | 6 | .394 | .510 |
| 2006 | Harrisburg (EL) | AA | .272 | 140 | 489 | 84 | 133 | 24 | 6 | 20 | 80 | 81 | 104 | 6 | .379 | .468 |
| **MINOR LEAGUE TOTALS** | | | .276 | 470 | 1731 | 263 | 478 | 109 | 16 | 62 | 286 | 226 | 319 | 14 | .364 | .465 |

## ⑤ ESMAILYN GONZALEZ ~ SS

**Born:** Sept. 21, 1989. **B-T:** B-R. **Ht.:** 5-11. **Wt.:** 175. **Signed:** Dominican Republic, 2006. **Signed by:** Jose Rijo.

Nationals special assistant Jose Rijo first discovered Gonzalez when the shortstop was 14, and he played at Rijo's Dominican baseball academy for a year. Their close relationship—and a $1.4 million signing bonus—helped Washington beat out four teams for his services last summer. He impressed in Dominican instructional league during the fall. A switch-hitter, Gonzalez has a short stroke with a good swing path, and he knows the strike zone very well for his age. Though he's just a fringe-average runner, he has good range and a solid-average arm at shortstop, where his actions are quick and easy and his hands are special. He has amazing instincts and is exceptionally skilled. During warmups he'll occasionally perform tricks like flipping the ball to first base behind his back. A high-energy player whose enthusiasm for the game is contagious, he goes by the nickname "Smiley." Like most 17-year-olds, Gonzalez needs to add strength, and a conditioning program will help. He has a mature offensive approach for his age, but he still needs plenty of polish. Despite good bat speed, he has below-average power. Gonzalez will come to the United States for spring training and likely will make his pro debut in the Rookie-level Gulf Coast League, though he has a shot to go to low Class A.

| Year | Club (League) | Class | AVG | G | AB | R | H | 2B | 3B | HR | RBI | BB | SO | SB | OBP | SLG |
|------|---------------|-------|-----|---|-----|---|---|----|----|----|-----|----|----|----|------|------|
| 2006 | Did not play—Signed 2007 contract | | | | | | | | | | | | | | | |

## ⑥ ZECH ZINICOLA ~ RHP

**Born:** March 2, 1985. **B-T:** R-R. **Ht.:** 6-1. **Wt.:** 220. **Drafted:** Arizona State, 2006 (6th round). **Signed by:** Mitch Sokol.

A free spirit who lived in a mobile home while he attended Arizona State, Zinicola settled in as the Sun Devils' closer his junior season after playing both ways his first two years. He signed for $147,500 as a sixth-rounder in June, then was named Nationals minor league pitcher of the year after dominating at three levels and finishing at Double-A. Zinicola has a power repertoire perfect for the back of the bullpen. He runs his plus fastball up to 95 mph routinely, and he complements it with an above-average 82-85 mph slider with tight bite. In college he threw an average changeup with splitter action, but he rarely used the pitch during his pro debut. Zinicola has a bulldog mentality, a physical frame and a clean, repeatable delivery. He needs to fine-tune his command, which lapsed late in the season as a heavy workload took its toll. Scouts questioned Zinicola's maturity at times in college, but it wasn't an issue in pro ball. Similar to former top Washington first-rounders Chad Cordero and Bill Bray, Zinicola is on the fast track. He could be a set-up man in the big leagues as soon as 2007, and he could be in line to replace Cordero as the closer in the future.

| Year | Club (League) | Class | W | L | ERA | G | GS | CG | SV | IP | H | R | ER | HR | BB | SO | AVG |
|------|---------------|-------|---|---|------|----|----|----|----|----|----|---|----|----|----|----|------|
| 2006 | Vermont (NYP) | A | 0 | 0 | 0.00 | 8 | 0 | 0 | 4 | 9 | 6 | 0 | 0 | 0 | 1 | 10 | .182 |
| | Potomac (CL) | A | 3 | 0 | 1.98 | 9 | 0 | 0 | 3 | 14 | 11 | 3 | 3 | 0 | 3 | 13 | .229 |
| | Harrisburg (EL) | AA | 1 | 1 | 2.70 | 10 | 0 | 0 | 5 | 10 | 11 | 6 | 3 | 0 | 11 | 8 | .256 |
| **MINOR LEAGUE TOTALS** | | | 4 | 1 | 1.65 | 27 | 0 | 0 | 12 | 33 | 28 | 9 | 6 | 0 | 15 | 31 | .226 |

## ⑦ GLENN GIBSON ~ LHP

**Born:** Sept. 21, 1987. **B-T:** L-L **Ht.:** 6-4. **Wt.:** 195. **Drafted:** HS—Center Moriches, N.Y., 2006 (4th round). **Signed by:** Guy Mader.

The son of former big league lefthander Paul Gibson, Glenn turned down a commitment to Central Florida for an above-slot $350,000 bonus in the fourth round. He signed late in the summer so he had a limited pro debut, but he did show off his polish with three scoreless outings at short-season Vermont. It's evident that Gibson learned a lot from his father, because he really knows how to pitch. His best offering is an above-average 76-77 mph curveball with good downward bite that was a revelation this spring after his dad moved his arm slot from three-quarters to high three-quarters. He has

always trusted his changeup, which already rates as an average pitch and could get better. Gibson projects to add velocity to his 86-88 mph fastball as he fills out his lanky frame, and he already ratchets it up to 91 on occasion. His delivery is clean and easy. Despite hiring a personal trainer and adding 15 pounds as a high school senior, Gibson remains skinny and needs to get stronger. He commands his fastball well but needs to add velocity to pitch toward the front of a big league rotation. Because he's so advanced, Gibson will push for a rotation spot in low Class A as a 19-year-old. He could become a No. 3 starter if he develops physically.

| Year | Club (League) | Class | W | L | ERA | G | GS | CG | SV | IP | H | R | ER | HR | BB | SO | AVG |
|------|---------------|-------|---|---|-----|---|----|----|----|----|---|---|----|----|----|----|-----|
| 2006 | Vermont (NYP) | A | 0 | 0 | 0.00 | 3 | 3 | 0 | 0 | 6 | 2 | 0 | 0 | 0 | 0 | 7 | .100 |
| **MINOR LEAGUE TOTALS** | | | 0 | 0 | 0.00 | 3 | 3 | 0 | 0 | 6 | 2 | 0 | 0 | 0 | 0 | 7 | .100 |

## 8 MATT CHICO
LHP

**Born:** June 10, 1983. **B-T:** L-L. **Ht.:** 5-11. **Wt.:** 200. **Drafted:** Palomar (Calif.) JC, 2003 (3rd round). **Signed by:** Mark Baca (Diamondbacks).

After turning down $700,000 as a Red Sox second-round pick out of high school, Chico flunked out of Southern California and a junior college, landing in a San Diego semipro league when the Diamondbacks drafted him in 2003. He showed flashes of promise in his first three seasons in the Arizona system before coming over to the Nationals along with Garrett Mock in an August deal for Livan Hernandez. With a build reminiscent of Mike Hampton's and a tenacious mindset to match, Chico has a deceptive delivery and keeps hitters off balance with a four-pitch mix. He spots his fastball to all four quadrants of the strike zone, relying heavily on an 88-91 mph two-seamer and mixing in a four-seamer that he can run up to 93-94. He adds and subtracts from his average curveball and throws his average changeup for strikes any time he wants. Chico isn't a softtosser, but he's also far from overpowering. He gets into trouble when he tries to blow hitters away, though he has done a better job of setting them up since getting rocked in Double-A at the beginning of 2005. Chico could be a No. 4 starter in the big leagues as soon as 2007 for the pitching-starved Nationals. He'll probably open the year at Washington's new Triple-A Columbus affiliate unless he's lights out in spring training.

| Year | Club (League) | Class | W | L | ERA | G | GS | CG | SV | IP | H | R | ER | HR | BB | SO | AVG |
|------|---------------|-------|---|---|-----|---|----|----|----|-----|-----|-----|-----|----|-----|-----|-----|
| 2003 | Yakima (NWL) | A | 7 | 4 | 3.53 | 17 | 13 | 0 | 0 | 71 | 75 | 28 | 28 | 4 | 25 | 71 | .274 |
| 2004 | South Bend (MWL) | A | 8 | 5 | 2.57 | 14 | 14 | 2 | 0 | 88 | 59 | 26 | 25 | 9 | 27 | 89 | .190 |
|  | El Paso (TL) | AA | 3 | 7 | 5.78 | 14 | 12 | 0 | 0 | 62 | 82 | 53 | 40 | 7 | 36 | 59 | .323 |
| 2005 | Tennessee (SL) | AA | 1 | 7 | 5.98 | 10 | 10 | 0 | 0 | 53 | 75 | 44 | 35 | 8 | 15 | 35 | .341 |
|  | Lancaster (Cal) | A | 7 | 2 | 3.76 | 18 | 18 | 0 | 0 | 110 | 101 | 50 | 46 | 13 | 39 | 102 | .243 |
| 2006 | Lancaster (Cal) | A | 3 | 4 | 3.75 | 10 | 10 | 0 | 0 | 50 | 48 | 25 | 21 | 5 | 11 | 49 | .239 |
|  | Tennessee (SL) | AA | 7 | 2 | 2.22 | 13 | 13 | 0 | 0 | 81 | 62 | 22 | 20 | 6 | 21 | 63 | .211 |
|  | Harrisburg (EL) | AA | 2 | 0 | 3.27 | 4 | 4 | 0 | 0 | 22 | 28 | 9 | 8 | 3 | 8 | 13 | .318 |
| **MINOR LEAGUE TOTALS** | | | 38 | 31 | 3.74 | 100 | 94 | 2 | 0 | 537 | 530 | 257 | 223 | 55 | 182 | 481 | .258 |

## 9 STEPHEN KING
SS

**Born:** Oct. 27, 1987. **B-T:** R-R. **Ht.:** 6-3. **Wt.:** 193. **Drafted:** HS—Winter Park, Fla., 2006 (3rd round). **Signed by:** Tony Arango.

A preseason high school All-American, King had a mediocre senior season thanks in large part to nagging leg injuries. The Nationals saw enough physical ability to take him in the second round, and they bought him out of a commitment to Louisiana State with a $750,000 bonus. He signed too late to make his pro debut. King has a tantalizing five-tool package that earns comparisons to Bobby Crosby and J.J. Hardy, and he has a chance to be a similar offensive-minded shortstop. With a strong, wiry frame and good bat speed, he projects to have at least average power, and he has a good enough feel for the zone to become an above-average hitter. Defensively, he has good actions up the middle, sure hands and plus arm strength. He's a solid-average runner. King will have to make adjustments in his swing to improve his load and trigger. Good fastballs tend to tie him up. Some scouts are concerned he could outgrow shortstop, and he's not in the same defensive class as Esmailyn Gonzalez or Ian Desmond. King may compete with Gonzalez for the starting shortstop job in low Class A, but he's more likely to spend 2007 at short-season Vermont. If he eventually moves off shortstop, King has enough bat and arm to play third base or the outfield.

| Year | Club (League) | Class | W | L | ERA | G | GS | CG | SV | IP | H | R | ER | HR | BB | SO | AVG |
|------|---------------|-------|---|---|-----|---|----|----|----|----|---|---|----|----|----|----|-----|
| 2006 | Did not play—Signed 2007 contract | | | | | | | | | | | | | | | | |

## IAN DESMOND · SS

**Born:** Sept. 20, 1985. **B-T:** R-R. **Ht.:** 6-2. **Wt.:** 185. **Drafted:** HS—Sarasota, Fla., 2004 (3rd round). **Signed by:** Russ Bove.

Though Desmond entered 2006 with a .244 career batting average, the Nationals saw enough in his confident approach to believe he could handle a promotion to Double-A. He got off to a slow start after getting few at-bats in big league camp, and he never recovered. Washington realized it rushed him and demoted him to high Class A in May, when he also missed two weeks with a back injury. Desmond still makes plenty of errors, but he has the tools to be an above-average defender at shortstop with plus-plus arm strength, plus range and soft hands. He started to make some offensive adjustments after his demotion, driving the ball the opposite way and learning to stay back on offspeed pitches. He has above-average speed. His best attributes might be his work ethic and leadership. The Nationals want Desmond to let the ball travel a little farther before he swings, so they opened his stance to improve his vision. He has gotten bigger but still doesn't hit for much power. He needs to focus more on getting on base. In the field, he needs to concentrate more on making the routine plays and do a better job anticipating ground balls. He's no longer the clear choice as Washington's shortstop of the future with Esmailyn Gonzalez and Stephen King now in the system, but Desmond is just 21 and still has a chance to be an everyday player. He'll need a lot of at-bats to improve offensively. He'll give Double-A another try in 2007.

| Year | Club (League) | Class | AVG | G | AB | R | H | 2B | 3B | HR | RBI | BB | SO | SB | OBP | SLG |
|------|---------------|-------|-----|---|-----|----|-----|----|----|----|-----|----|-----|----|------|------|
| 2004 | Expos (GCL) | R | .227 | 55 | 216 | 28 | 49 | 11 | 0 | 1 | 27 | 10 | 40 | 13 | .272 | .292 |
| | Vermont (NYP) | A | .250 | 4 | 12 | 2 | 3 | 0 | 0 | 1 | 1 | 0 | 2 | 0 | .308 | .500 |
| 2005 | Savannah (SAL) | A | .247 | 73 | 296 | 37 | 73 | 10 | 2 | 4 | 23 | 13 | 60 | 20 | .291 | .334 |
| | Potomac (CL) | A | .256 | 55 | 219 | 37 | 56 | 13 | 3 | 3 | 15 | 21 | 53 | 13 | .325 | .384 |
| 2006 | Harrisburg (EL) | AA | .182 | 37 | 121 | 8 | 22 | 4 | 1 | 0 | 3 | 5 | 35 | 4 | .214 | .231 |
| | Potomac (CL) | A | .244 | 92 | 365 | 50 | 89 | 20 | 2 | 9 | 45 | 29 | 79 | 14 | .313 | .384 |
| **MINOR LEAGUE TOTALS** | | | .238 | 316 | 1229 | 162 | 292 | 58 | 8 | 18 | 114 | 78 | 269 | 64 | .293 | .342 |

## JESUS FLORES · C

**Born:** Oct. 26, 1984. **B-T:** R-R. **Ht.:** 6-1. **Wt.:** 180. **Signed:** Venezuela, 2002. **Signed by:** Gregorio Machado (Mets).

After floundering in a 2005 season marred by a broken thumb, Flores rebounded to show why the Mets were so high on him after his breakout 2004. He tied for the high Class A Florida State League lead in home runs while finishing fourth in extra-base hits and slugging. The Nationals grabbed him in December in the major league Rule 5 draft. Flores is the rare power-hitting catcher who is also an asset defensively. He has a pull approach, so most of his power is to left field, though he will drive some balls to center. His arm is above-average and it plays up because of his quick release. With pop times consistently in the 1.85-1.95-second range, Flores can control the running game, and he threw out 39 percent of basestealers last season. He has an athletic frame and good lateral range that helps him block balls in the dirt. Because of his pull approach, Flores sometimes opens up his front side too early, which makes him susceptible to sliders away, and he needs better plate discipline. In the past he has been hard on himself when he was not hitting and let it affect his defense, but he has gotten better at channeling his emotions. He can get lazy behind the plate and is a slow runner. Catchers with his blend of power and defense are tough to find, but he's not ready to jump from Class A to the majors. If the Nationals can't work out a trade with the Mets, they can't send him to the minors without putting him through waivers and then offering him back to New York for half his $50,000 draft price. A year on Washington's big league bench would hurt his development.

| Year | Club (League) | Class | AVG | G | AB | R | H | 2B | 3B | HR | RBI | BB | SO | SB | OBP | SLG |
|------|---------------|-------|-----|---|-----|----|-----|----|----|----|-----|----|-----|----|------|------|
| 2002 | Mets (VSL) | R | .203 | 40 | 123 | 10 | 25 | 8 | 0 | 1 | 8 | 10 | 29 | 2 | .305 | .293 |
| | Mets (DSL) | R | .292 | 19 | 65 | 19 | 19 | 3 | 1 | 3 | 10 | 11 | 14 | 8 | .403 | .508 |
| 2003 | Mets (VSL) | R | .255 | 52 | 165 | 25 | 42 | 16 | 0 | 4 | 32 | 21 | 24 | 2 | .383 | .424 |
| 2004 | Mets (GCL) | R | .319 | 45 | 141 | 16 | 45 | 12 | 3 | 4 | 25 | 8 | 26 | 1 | .368 | .532 |
| | Brooklyn (NYP) | A | .333 | 3 | 6 | 1 | 2 | 0 | 0 | 1 | 3 | 0 | 1 | 0 | .333 | .833 |
| 2005 | Hagerstown (SAL) | A | .216 | 82 | 319 | 34 | 69 | 18 | 0 | 7 | 42 | 12 | 90 | 2 | .250 | .339 |
| 2006 | St. Lucie (FSL) | A | .266 | 120 | 429 | 66 | 114 | 32 | 0 | 21 | 70 | 28 | 127 | 2 | .335 | .487 |
| **MINOR LEAGUE TOTALS** | | | .253 | 361 | 1248 | 171 | 316 | 89 | 4 | 41 | 190 | 90 | 311 | 17 | .326 | .429 |

## GARRETT MOCK · RHP

**Born:** April 25, 1983. **B-T:** R-R. **Ht.:** 6-4. **Wt.:** 215. **Drafted:** Houston, 2004 (3rd round). **Signed by:** Trip Couch (Diamondbacks).

In his first full season in 2005, Mock led the high Class A California League in wins and

strikeouts despite pitching in Lancaster, one of baseball's best hitter havens. He came to big league camp the following spring and nearly earned a job on Arizona's Opening Day roster before heading to Double-A. He struggled all season with a slight tear under the meniscus in his left knee, and he was shelled after coming to the Nationals along with Matt Chico in an August trade for Livan Hernandez. A big, strong Texan with a fierce competitive streak, Mock did not let on that he was hurt, but it was obvious something was wrong when his fastball sat at 89-90 mph and topped out at 92. In years past he pitched at 92 and topped out at 95 with a heavy, boring fastball. When he's right, Mock's hard, short-breaking slider is an out pitch, and his changeup and overhand curveball are at least average. He got into bad mechanical habits because he couldn't extend on his landing leg, so he was searching for a comfortable arm slot. He had surgery to repair his knee and should be healthy by spring training, and the Nationals hope he will trust his stuff when he's back to 100 percent. He should push for a job in Triple-A in 2007, and he could be a middle-of-the-rotation workhorse by 2008.

| Year | Club (League) | Class | W | L | ERA | G | GS | CG | SV | IP | H | R | ER | HR | BB | SO | AVG |
|------|---------------|-------|---|---|-----|---|----|----|----|----|---|---|----|----|----|----|-----|
| 2004 | Yakima (NWL) | A | 2 | 0 | 1.54 | 5 | 5 | 0 | 0 | 23 | 18 | 8 | 4 | 1 | 4 | 14 | .228 |
| | South Bend (MWL) | A | 3 | 2 | 3.00 | 8 | 8 | 1 | 0 | 54 | 49 | 21 | 18 | 2 | 12 | 37 | .251 |
| 2005 | Lancaster (Cal) | A | 14 | 7 | 4.18 | 28 | 28 | 0 | 0 | 174 | 202 | 95 | 81 | 19 | 33 | 160 | .284 |
| 2006 | Tennessee (SL) | AA | 4 | 8 | 4.95 | 23 | 23 | 0 | 0 | 131 | 144 | 81 | 72 | 14 | 50 | 117 | .280 |
| | Harrisburg (EL) | AA | 0 | 4 | 10.26 | 4 | 4 | 0 | 0 | 17 | 29 | 21 | 19 | 2 | 5 | 9 | .387 |
| **MINOR LEAGUE TOTALS** | | | 23 | 21 | 4.37 | 68 | 68 | 1 | 0 | 399 | 442 | 226 | 194 | 38 | 104 | 337 | .281 |

## 13 EMILIANO FRUTO RHP

**Born:** June 6, 1984. **B-T:** R-R. **Ht.:** 6-3. **Wt.:** 235. **Signed:** Colombia, 2000. **Signed by:** Curtis Wallace (Mariners).

Though Fruto made his big league debut in 2006, he remained an enigma. No Mariners farmhand had as many different quality pitches, yet his ceiling probably is no more than a setup man. While he has progressed from the days when Seattle's minor league managers didn't want to use him with games on the line, the M's parted with him and outfielder Chris Snelling in a December trade for Jose Vidro. Fruto's best offering is a changeup that at times has screwball action and grades as a plus-plus pitch. He throws it with the same arm speed he uses for his lively 92-96 mph fastball. He also has one of the best curveballs in the system and a slider that has its moments. That's more than enough stuff to start, but Fruto lacks the control and focus to handle that role. He's still searching for command and a consistent plan. He'll fall in love with his offspeed stuff and not trust his fastball, and he'll throw his slider more than his curve, which is his superior breaking pitch. Though he's athletic for a 6-foot-3, 235-pounder, he doesn't do a good job of repeating his delivery and arm action. Fruto took a huge step forward in 2005, only to show up overweight in spring training. Washington hopes he learned his lesson and will be more reliable in 2007, when he'll get a chance to further establish himself in the majors.

| Year | Club (League) | Class | W | L | ERA | G | GS | CG | SV | IP | H | R | ER | HR | BB | SO | AVG |
|------|---------------|-------|---|---|-----|---|----|----|----|----|---|---|----|----|----|----|-----|
| 2001 | Mariners (AZL) | R | 5 | 3 | 5.84 | 12 | 12 | 0 | 0 | 62 | 73 | 45 | 40 | 3 | 22 | 51 | .291 |
| 2002 | Wisconsin (MWL) | A | 6 | 6 | 3.55 | 33 | 13 | 0 | 1 | 112 | 101 | 57 | 44 | 6 | 55 | 99 | .239 |
| 2003 | Tacoma (PCL) | AAA | 1 | 0 | 0.00 | 1 | 0 | 0 | 0 | 4 | 1 | 0 | 0 | 0 | 2 | 2 | .083 |
| | Inland Empire (Cal) | A | 7 | 8 | 3.78 | 42 | 4 | 0 | 7 | 79 | 80 | 43 | 33 | 5 | 38 | 83 | .267 |
| 2004 | San Antonio (TL) | AA | 3 | 3 | 5.66 | 43 | 1 | 0 | 1 | 68 | 77 | 47 | 43 | 6 | 37 | 56 | .277 |
| 2005 | San Antonio (TL) | AA | 2 | 3 | 2.57 | 40 | 0 | 0 | 12 | 67 | 56 | 22 | 19 | 6 | 22 | 63 | .231 |
| | Tacoma (PCL) | AAA | 1 | 2 | 13.09 | 9 | 0 | 0 | 0 | 11 | 11 | 17 | 16 | 1 | 11 | 12 | .268 |
| 2006 | Tacoma (PCL) | AAA | 1 | 3 | 3.18 | 28 | 0 | 0 | 10 | 45 | 33 | 23 | 16 | 1 | 21 | 55 | .204 |
| | Seattle (AL) | MLB | 2 | 2 | 5.50 | 23 | 0 | 0 | 1 | 36 | 34 | 24 | 22 | 4 | 24 | 34 | .246 |
| **MINOR LEAGUE TOTALS** | | | 26 | 28 | 4.25 | 208 | 30 | 0 | 31 | 447 | 432 | 254 | 211 | 28 | 208 | 421 | .253 |
| **MAJOR LEAGUE TOTALS** | | | 2 | 2 | 5.50 | 23 | 0 | 0 | 1 | 36 | 34 | 24 | 22 | 4 | 24 | 34 | .246 |

## 14 JHONNY NUNEZ RHP

**Born:** Nov. 26, 1985. **B-T:** R-R. **Ht.:** 6-3. **Wt.:** 185. **Signed:** Dominican Republic, 2003. **Signed by:** Andres Lopez (Dodgers).

In his domestic debut in the Dodgers system last summer, Nunez led the Gulf Coast League in wins and innings and finished second in strikeouts and ERA. He got better as the season went on, culminating in six shutout innings against the Red Sox in the first game of the GCL championship series. Nunez caught the attention of GCL Nationals manager Bobby Henley, who pushed for his acquisition in the Marlon Anderson trade. Nunez is a long way from the big leagues, but he has a live arm and a pair of potential plus pitches. He works at 89-92 mph with his fastball, touching 94, and he could add velocity as he fills out his wiry frame. He also throws a slider that can be hard with late snap, but it gets slurvy and the Nationals want him to add power to it. Nunez has a smooth arm action, but he needs to

repeat his delivery more consistently. Sometimes he overthrows, missing up in the zone. Nunez also needs to develop a changeup to stick as a starter. He showed quality stuff and moxie in dominating the GCL, giving him a chance to be a No. 2 or 3 starter if it all comes together. He'll get a crack at the low Class A South Atlantic League in 2007.

| Year | Club (League) | Class | W | L | ERA | G | GS | CG | SV | IP | H | R | ER | HR | BB | SO | AVG |
|---|---|---|---|---|---|---|---|---|---|---|---|---|---|---|---|---|---|
| 2004 | Dodgers (DSL) | R | 2 | 1 | 1.73 | 7 | 7 | 0 | 0 | 36 | 30 | 8 | 7 | 1 | 6 | 23 | .229 |
|  | Dodgers (DSL) | R | 2 | 0 | 4.60 | 4 | 3 | 0 | 0 | 16 | 17 | 9 | 8 | 0 | 4 | 12 | .262 |
| 2005 | Dodgers (DSL) | R | 4 | 3 | 1.92 | 15 | 8 | 1 | 0 | 52 | 29 | 13 | 11 | 0 | 13 | 40 | .153 |
| 2006 | Dodgers (GCL) | R | 6 | 0 | 1.58 | 10 | 7 | 0 | 0 | 57 | 35 | 12 | 10 | 0 | 19 | 56 | .177 |
| MINOR LEAGUE TOTALS |  |  | 14 | 4 | 2.02 | 36 | 25 | 1 | 0 | 161 | 111 | 42 | 36 | 1 | 42 | 131 | .190 |

## 15 SHAIRON MARTIS                                                                      RHP

**Born:** March 30, 1987. **B-T:** R-R. **Ht.:** 6-1. **Wt.:** 175. **Signed:** Curacao, 2004. **Signed by:** Philip Elhage (Giants).

Martis made a name for himself in the World Baseball Classic last March by throwing a no-hitter for the Netherlands against a Panama team that included Carlos Lee, Olmedo Saenz and Ruben Rivera. The 10-0 win was shortened to seven innings by the tournament's mercy rule, allowing Martis to complete the game in 65 pitches—the limit allowed by WBC rules. Martis then held his own in the low Class A South Atlantic League, and the Nationals acquired him from the Giants for reliever Mike Stanton in July. With a loose arm and an advanced feel for pitching for his age, Martis looked good in a late-season stint in high Class A. He pitches in the low 90s with a solid-average fastball, touching 94, and he could add velocity as he matures. His changeup became his best pitch over the last year, an above-average pitch with fade and deception. Martis needs to improve his inconsistent breaking ball, which tends to get slurvy. Given time, he has the solid repertoire and mound presence to be a No. 3 starter in the big leagues. He'll start back at high Class A in 2007.

| Year | Club (League) | Class | W | L | ERA | G | GS | CG | SV | IP | H | R | ER | HR | BB | SO | AVG |
|---|---|---|---|---|---|---|---|---|---|---|---|---|---|---|---|---|---|
| 2004 | Giants (DSL) | R | 4 | 3 | 1.79 | 14 | 12 | 0 | 0 | 70 | 55 | 15 | 14 | 2 | 17 | 63 | .221 |
| 2005 | Giants (AZL) | R | 2 | 1 | 1.85 | 11 | 5 | 0 | 1 | 34 | 28 | 10 | 7 | 1 | 9 | 50 | .226 |
| 2006 | Augusta (SAL) | A | 6 | 4 | 3.64 | 15 | 15 | 0 | 0 | 77 | 76 | 39 | 31 | 3 | 21 | 66 | .257 |
|  | Savannah (SAL) | A | 1 | 1 | 3.80 | 4 | 4 | 0 | 0 | 21 | 23 | 9 | 9 | 2 | 4 | 14 | .284 |
|  | Potomac (CL) | A | 0 | 2 | 3.00 | 2 | 2 | 0 | 0 | 12 | 9 | 5 | 4 | 0 | 3 | 7 | .209 |
|  | Harrisburg (EL) | AA | 0 | 1 | 12.60 | 1 | 1 | 0 | 0 | 5 | 8 | 7 | 7 | 4 | 3 | 1 | .348 |
| MINOR LEAGUE TOTALS |  |  | 13 | 12 | 2.95 | 47 | 39 | 0 | 1 | 219 | 199 | 85 | 72 | 12 | 57 | 201 | .244 |

## 16 LARRY BROADWAY                                                                     1B

**Born:** Dec. 17, 1980. **B-T:** L-L. **Ht.:** 6-4. **Wt.:** 230. **Drafted:** Duke, 2002 (3rd round). **Signed by:** Dana Brown.

Broadway was the top hitting prospect in the Nationals system entering the 2005 season, when a knee injury derailed him. He rebounded with a solid 2006 campaign in his first extended taste of Triple-A, leading Nationals farmhands with a .288 average, and he would have been in line for a big league promotion when Nick Johnson got hurt if he hadn't dislocated his shoulder diving for a ground ball in late August. He did not need surgery and planned to spend all winter strengthening the joint for spring training. Broadway's best tool is his above-average power. He can drive the ball to all fields, and he's always had a solid offensive approach and drawn plenty of walks. Broadway is a reliable defender at first base, with sure hands and a plus arm, but he has lost a step since his knee injury—and he was a below-average runner to begin with. The Nationals have talked with Broadway a lot about his physical condition, and they expect him to enter spring training ready to play first base in the big leagues in case Johnson is not fully recovered from his broken femur. He doesn't look like a future star, but he still has a chance to be a solid everyday player. That chance may have to come with another organization, however.

| Year | Club (League) | Class | AVG | G | AB | R | H | 2B | 3B | HR | RBI | BB | SO | SB | OBP | SLG |
|---|---|---|---|---|---|---|---|---|---|---|---|---|---|---|---|---|
| 2002 | Expos (GCL) | R | .250 | 4 | 8 | 1 | 2 | 0 | 0 | 0 | 0 | 4 | 4 | 0 | .500 | .250 |
|  | Vermont (NYP) | A | .315 | 35 | 127 | 13 | 40 | 3 | 0 | 4 | 23 | 13 | 33 | 0 | .379 | .433 |
| 2003 | Savannah (SAL) | A | .307 | 83 | 290 | 56 | 89 | 25 | 4 | 14 | 51 | 44 | 70 | 3 | .400 | .566 |
|  | Brevard County (FSL) | A | .224 | 25 | 76 | 8 | 17 | 7 | 1 | 1 | 7 | 18 | 20 | 0 | .367 | .382 |
|  | Harrisburg (EL) | AA | .321 | 21 | 78 | 13 | 25 | 3 | 0 | 5 | 18 | 7 | 15 | 0 | .371 | .551 |
| 2004 | Harrisburg (EL) | AA | .270 | 131 | 477 | 70 | 129 | 20 | 0 | 22 | 72 | 68 | 103 | 2 | .362 | .451 |
| 2005 | New Orleans (PCL) | AAA | .193 | 18 | 57 | 4 | 11 | 3 | 0 | 0 | 5 | 7 | 17 | 2 | .281 | .246 |
|  | Nationals (GCL) | R | .429 | 8 | 28 | 3 | 12 | 5 | 0 | 1 | 4 | 7 | 3 | 0 | .543 | .714 |
|  | Harrisburg (EL) | AA | .269 | 52 | 186 | 29 | 50 | 14 | 0 | 12 | 24 | 17 | 37 | 0 | .329 | .538 |
| 2006 | New Orleans (PCL) | AAA | .288 | 123 | 444 | 60 | 128 | 25 | 2 | 15 | 78 | 45 | 116 | 5 | .353 | .455 |
| MINOR LEAGUE TOTALS |  |  | .284 | 500 | 1771 | 257 | 503 | 105 | 7 | 74 | 282 | 230 | 418 | 12 | .366 | .477 |

## 17 STEPHEN ENGLUND OF

**Born:** June 6, 1988. **B-T:** R-R. **Ht.:** 6-3. **Wt.:** 190. **Drafted:** HS—Bellevue, Wash., 2006 (2nd round). **Signed by:** Doug McMillan.

Englund looks the part of a big-time prospect, so scouts expected big things from the third-team BA Preseason All-American in his senior year at Bellevue (Wash.) High. His bat was inconsistent, but the Nationals saw enough five-tool potential to draft him in the second round and give him a $515,000 bonus, buying him out of a commitment to Washington State. A shortstop in high school, Englund moved to the outfield after signing. A slightly above-average runner, he has a chance to stay in center field, but some scouts compare him to Jay Buhner and project him in right. Like Buhner, Englund has a plus arm and plus raw power, and he is capable of hitting long home runs in batting practice thanks to his excellent bat speed and a swing with good leverage. But as his rough debut in the Gulf Coast League suggests, he is raw in all facets of the game. He's adjusting to playing every day and using a wood bat, and he's working on shortening his swing and improving his two-strike approach. He also needs to mature, as his drama-filled high school career included being kicked off the team once and reinstated. Englund's exciting package of tools gives him a chance to be a star, but it's going to take a while. He should open at Vermont in 2007.

| Year | Club (League) | Class | AVG | G | AB | R | H | 2B | 3B | HR | RBI | BB | SO | SB | OBP | SLG |
|------|---------------|-------|-----|---|----|---|---|----|----|----|-----|----|----|----|-----|-----|
| 2006 | Nationals (GCL) | R | .183 | 35 | 115 | 16 | 21 | 3 | 0 | 1 | 12 | 17 | 41 | 5 | .307 | .235 |
| **MINOR LEAGUE TOTALS** | | | .183 | 35 | 115 | 16 | 21 | 3 | 0 | 1 | 12 | 17 | 41 | 5 | .307 | .235 |

## 18 JUSTIN MAXWELL OF

**Born:** Nov. 6, 1983. **B-T:** R-R. **Ht.:** R-R. **Wt.:** 225. **Drafted:** Maryland, 2005 (4th round). **Signed by:** Alex Smith.

Considered a potential first-round pick as a junior in 2004, Maxwell battled freak injuries his final two seasons at Maryland. He signed late with the Nationals for a $390,000 bonus in 2005, and he was held back in extended spring training to start 2006 in order to find his rhythm. Maxwell hit a three-run homer in his pro debut in low Class A in late April before heading to the disabled list two weeks later after breaking his toe. He returned to the field a month later but played most of the second half at Vermont, where he flashed the power-speed mix that has tantalized scouts for years. Maxwell is a true five-tool talent with above-average speed that translates well on the basepaths and in the outfield. A long strider, Maxwell has excellent range and a solid-average arm in center field. He shows plus raw power in batting practice but has yet to harness it. Maxwell's swing tends to get long and he has trouble with pitches on the outer half. He has a solid approach at the plate, but he needs an uninterrupted string of at-bats so he can polish his offensive game. Maxwell should return to low Class A to open 2007, but at age 23 he needs to get moving, so the Nationals figure to push him once he gets his feet wet.

| Year | Club (League) | Class | AVG | G | AB | R | H | 2B | 3B | HR | RBI | BB | SO | SB | OBP | SLG |
|------|---------------|-------|-----|---|----|---|---|----|----|----|-----|----|----|----|-----|-----|
| 2006 | Savannah (SAL) | A | .172 | 17 | 58 | 8 | 10 | 2 | 2 | 1 | 7 | 8 | 23 | 1 | .294 | .328 |
| | Vermont (NYP) | A | .269 | 74 | 271 | 36 | 73 | 11 | 3 | 4 | 33 | 27 | 61 | 20 | .346 | .376 |
| **MINOR LEAGUE TOTALS** | | | .252 | 91 | 329 | 44 | 83 | 13 | 5 | 5 | 40 | 35 | 84 | 21 | .337 | .368 |

## 19 ADAM CARR RHP

**Born:** April 1, 1984. **B-T:** R-R. **Ht.:** 6-1. **Wt.:** 185. **Drafted:** Oklahoma State, 2006 (18th round). **Signed by:** Ryan Fox.

Carr led the Big 12 Conference with 22 home runs as a first baseman at Oklahoma State in 2005, when Nationals area scout Ryan Fox happened to be on hand for two of his five career pitching appearances. Fox saw Carr throw one inning in fall practice that year as well, and he was impressed enough to push the Nationals to draft him as a pitcher even though he didn't pitch at all as a senior in 2006. Signed for $1,000 as an 18th-rounder, Carr was disappointed he wasn't drafted as a hitter, so the Nationals let him DH on days he wasn't pitching, and he batted a combined .302 with three homers in 63 at-bats between two levels. He was even better off the mound, and better still in Hawaii Winter Baseball, going 1-0, 1.64 with a pair of saves in 11 innings. Carr has a surprisingly clean delivery given his inexperience as a pitcher. He has an electric, fresh arm and a lively fastball that touches 95 mph. Carr also throws a low-80s slider that can be an above-average pitch, and he's dabbling with a changeup that could give him a third average offering. His biggest weakness is simply his lack of experience and polish, but he's got a good feel for pitching and a strong, durable frame. He should start 2007 with a full-season Class A club and could be a power arm at the back of a big league bullpen sooner rather than later.

| Year | Club (League) | Class | W | L | ERA | G | GS | CG | SV | IP | H | R | ER | HR | BB | SO | AVG |
|------|---------------|-------|---|---|-----|---|----|----|----|----|---|---|----|----|----|----|-----|
| 2006 | Nationals (GCL) | R | 1 | 0 | 3.06 | 10 | 0 | 0 | 1 | 18 | 13 | 6 | 6 | 1 | 7 | 19 | .200 |
| | Savannah (SAL) | A | 0 | 0 | 2.25 | 6 | 0 | 0 | 0 | 8 | 8 | 2 | 2 | 0 | 4 | 8 | .267 |
| **MINOR LEAGUE TOTALS** | | | 1 | 0 | 2.81 | 16 | 0 | 0 | 1 | 26 | 21 | 8 | 8 | 1 | 11 | 27 | .221 |

## JOHN LANNAN
LHP

**Born:** Sept. 27, 1984. **B-T:** L-L. **Ht.:** 6-5. **Wt.:** 200. **Drafted:** Siena, 2005 (11th round). **Signed by:** Dana Brown.

A native of Long Beach, N.Y., Lannan is a classic late-blooming Northern pitcher. He dominated as a starter his junior year at Siena, going 10-2, 2.29 with 83 strikeouts in 83 innings, but he fell to the 11th round of the 2005 draft because his fastball topped out at 88 mph. He added strength to his wiry frame in the offseason, and his velocity increased as a result. Lannan pitched at 89-91 mph for low Class A Savannah in 2006, touching 93. He also improved his mid-70s curveball, which was rather loopy in 2005 but showed good break and depth in 2006. Lannan's best pitch is a plus changeup in the low 80s that he commands to both sides of the plate. After posting a 1.61 ERA in April, he struggled with his command in the middle of the season before regrouping over the final two months, and he'll have to learn to avoid the big inning. He needs to sharpen his curveball and add strength, but projectable lefthanders capable of throwing three average or better pitches are hard to find. Lannan has a chance to be a No. 3 or 4 starter in the big leagues, and he'll open 2007 at high Class A.

| Year | Club (League) | Class | W | L | ERA | G | GS | CG | SV | IP | H | R | ER | HR | BB | SO | AVG |
|------|---------------|-------|---|---|-----|---|----|----|----|----|---|---|----|----|----|----|-----|
| 2005 | Vermont (NYP) | A | 3 | 5 | 5.26 | 14 | 11 | 0 | 0 | 63 | 74 | 46 | 37 | 5 | 31 | 41 | .287 |
| 2006 | Savannah (SAL) | A | 6 | 8 | 4.76 | 27 | 25 | 1 | 0 | 138 | 149 | 83 | 73 | 11 | 54 | 114 | .275 |
| **MINOR LEAGUE TOTALS** | | | 9 | 13 | 4.92 | 41 | 36 | 1 | 0 | 201 | 223 | 129 | 110 | 16 | 85 | 155 | .279 |

## CRAIG STAMMEN
RHP

**Born:** March 9, 1984. **B-T:** R-R. **Ht.:** 6-3. **Wt.:** 200. **Drafted:** Dayton, 2005 (12th round). **Signed by:** Ben Jones.

Stammen finished his three-year college career as the all-time strikeout leader at Dayton, where he recorded nine saves as a closer his sophomore year and nine complete games as a starter his junior year. He suffered from poor run support during his first full pro season in 2006, when he started 0-6 in low Class A before going 3-0 in June. Stammen has a similar repertoire to teammate Marco Estrada, but he's got a more physical build. Stammen's best offering is a plus curveball with sharp 12-to-6 action that he can throw for strikes or as a chase pitch. His fringe-average fastball sits at 89-91 mph, touches 92 and has late life. He mixes in a two-seam fastball, but his four-seamer is better. He's still trying to harness the command of his high-70s changeup, but he throws it with good arm speed and it can be average at times. He throws across his body, causing his walk totals to climb, but his arm action is quick and easy. Stammen figures to start 2007 at high Class A and profiles as a No. 4 starter.

| Year | Club (League) | Class | W | L | ERA | G | GS | CG | SV | IP | H | R | ER | HR | BB | SO | AVG |
|------|---------------|-------|---|---|-----|---|----|----|----|----|---|---|----|----|----|----|-----|
| 2005 | Vermont (NYP) | A | 4 | 5 | 4.06 | 13 | 7 | 0 | 0 | 51 | 62 | 36 | 23 | 2 | 12 | 32 | .297 |
| 2006 | Savannah (SAL) | A | 6 | 9 | 3.58 | 21 | 21 | 0 | 0 | 113 | 110 | 55 | 45 | 10 | 29 | 93 | .251 |
| | Potomac (CL) | A | 0 | 2 | 5.76 | 7 | 6 | 0 | 0 | 30 | 34 | 20 | 19 | 5 | 7 | 16 | .288 |
| **MINOR LEAGUE TOTALS** | | | 10 | 16 | 4.04 | 41 | 34 | 0 | 0 | 194 | 206 | 111 | 87 | 17 | 48 | 141 | .269 |

## MARCO ESTRADA
RHP

**Born:** July 5, 1983. **B-T:** R-R. **Ht.:** 6-0. **Wt.:** 180. **Drafted:** Long Beach State, 2005 (6th round). **Signed by:** Brian Hunter/Brian Parker.

Estrada and his mother moved from Mexico to California in 1989. He pitched at Glendale (Calif.) Community College in 2002 and '03 before sitting out a year while taking the two courses he needed to transfer to Long Beach State, where he jumped right into the weekend rotation. The Nationals had high hopes for Estrada in his first full pro season, but he broke his collarbone just before spring training while roller-blading, causing him to miss the first two and a half months. It took him a while to get going in low Class A, but he came on strong in Hawaii Winter Baseball, where he was the No. 10 prospect. Estrada's best pitch is an above-average curveball that he uses to put hitters away, and he has good feel for a changeup. His fastball is underwhelming, sitting at 88-90 mph and occasionally bumping 92 when he needs it. He needs to cut down on his walks. With a slight build, Estrada will never dominate, but he could be a No. 4 starter in the majors. He could move fast in 2007, starting at high Class A.

| Year | Club (League) | Class | W | L | ERA | G | GS | CG | SV | IP | H | R | ER | HR | BB | SO | AVG |
|------|---------------|-------|---|---|-----|---|----|----|----|----|---|---|----|----|----|----|-----|
| 2006 | Nationals (GCL) | R | 2 | 0 | 1.52 | 5 | 4 | 0 | 0 | 24 | 14 | 4 | 4 | 1 | 6 | 27 | .165 |
| | Savannah (SAL) | A | 1 | 4 | 5.59 | 8 | 8 | 0 | 0 | 37 | 44 | 23 | 23 | 6 | 14 | 29 | .301 |
| **MINOR LEAGUE TOTALS** | | | 3 | 4 | 4.01 | 13 | 12 | 0 | 0 | 61 | 58 | 27 | 27 | 7 | 20 | 56 | .251 |

## BRIAN PEACOCK                                                         C

**Born:** August 26, 1984. **B-T:** R-R. **Ht.:** 6-1. **Wt.:** 185. **Drafted:** Manatee (Fla.) CC, D/F 2004 (39th round). **Signed by:** Tony Arango/Russ Bove.

Peacock turned down a chance to transfer to Auburn when he signed with the Nationals as a draft-and-follow before the 2005 draft. After a trying pro debut in the Gulf Coast League, Peacock spent the winter before the 2006 season working with former big league catcher Randy Knorr, who helped the hyper Peacock learn to play under control and shorten his swing. He also improved his glovework and footwork behind the plate. He hit .288 with seven homers over the first two months last season at low Class A before shoulder soreness limited his effectiveness. An appendectomy in August ended his season. Peacock is an excellent athlete with solid-average speed, slightly above-average raw power, plus arm strength and a quick release when healthy. He needs to refine his offensive approach because he tries to pull everything and strikes out too much. He has the tools to be an average defensive catcher, but he needs to improve his hands and receiving skills. Peacock is a natural leader with an impeccable work ethic, giving him a chance to be an everyday catcher down the road. He could head back to low Class A to start 2007, but he'll get a chance to earn a job at high Class A.

| Year | Club (League) | Class | AVG | G | AB | R | H | 2B | 3B | HR | RBI | BB | SO | SB | OBP | SLG |
|------|---------------|-------|-----|---|----|---|---|----|----|----|-----|----|----|----|-----|-----|
| 2005 | Nationals (GCL) | R | .219 | 42 | 160 | 18 | 35 | 6 | 3 | 0 | 12 | 17 | 49 | 1 | .296 | .294 |
| 2006 | Savannah (SAL) | A | .232 | 88 | 314 | 46 | 73 | 15 | 2 | 12 | 42 | 24 | 102 | 1 | .300 | .408 |
| **MINOR LEAGUE TOTALS** | | | .228 | 130 | 474 | 64 | 108 | 21 | 5 | 12 | 54 | 41 | 151 | 2 | .299 | .369 |

## CLINT EVERTS                                                        RHP

**Born:** Aug. 10, 1984. **B-T:** B-R. **Ht.:** 6-2. **Wt.:** 170. **Drafted:** HS—Houston, 2002 (1st round). **Signed by:** Ray Corbett.

A two-way star in high school who signed for a $2.5 million bonus after being drafed fifth overall in 2002, Everts was the top prospect in the system in 2003 and 2004 before having Tommy John surgery in September 2004. He returned earlier than expected in 2005, taking the mound in late June, and it now looks like he returned too early. Everts is still trying to regain the low-90s fastball he showed prior to his injury. He worked mostly in the mid-80s in a rough 2006 season in high Class A. His changeup and curveball, which have previously rated as plus-plus offerings, still have good movement, but he struggled to command the curveball as well as he once did. Everts fell into a number of bad habits right before his surgery when he was favoring his arm. He spent 2006 almost having to relearn his rhythm and hip loads, and he had trouble finding a consistent release point. The Nationals planned to send Everts to the same long-toss program in Southern California this winter that Joel Zumaya once attended, with the hope he can regain some arm strength. If that plan works, he still has the terrific secondary stuff to be a frontline starter. But first, he'll have to conquer high Class A in 2007.

| Year | Club (League) | Class | W | L | ERA | G | GS | CG | SV | IP | H | R | ER | HR | BB | SO | AVG |
|------|---------------|-------|---|---|-----|---|----|----|----|----|---|---|----|----|----|----|-----|
| 2003 | Vermont (NYP) | A | 2 | 4 | 4.17 | 10 | 10 | 0 | 0 | 54 | 49 | 26 | 25 | 4 | 35 | 50 | .247 |
| | Savannah (SAL) | A | 0 | 3 | 3.46 | 5 | 5 | 0 | 0 | 26 | 23 | 13 | 10 | 1 | 10 | 21 | .230 |
| 2004 | Savannah (SAL) | A | 7 | 3 | 2.49 | 17 | 17 | 1 | 0 | 90 | 67 | 29 | 25 | 3 | 21 | 103 | .208 |
| | Brevard County (FSL) | A | 2 | 2 | 2.25 | 4 | 4 | 0 | 0 | 20 | 16 | 5 | 5 | 2 | 10 | 19 | .239 |
| 2005 | Nationals (GCL) | R | 0 | 1 | 3.38 | 7 | 7 | 0 | 0 | 16 | 18 | 9 | 6 | 0 | 8 | 15 | .269 |
| | Vermont (NYP) | A | 0 | 1 | 3.79 | 8 | 1 | 0 | 0 | 19 | 21 | 12 | 8 | 0 | 12 | 21 | .266 |
| 2006 | Potomac (CL) | A | 5 | 10 | 6.00 | 20 | 19 | 0 | 0 | 90 | 96 | 69 | 60 | 11 | 53 | 92 | .264 |
| **MINOR LEAGUE TOTALS** | | | 16 | 23 | 3.98 | 63 | 62 | 1 | 0 | 296 | 269 | 151 | 131 | 21 | 137 | 300 | .241 |

## SHAWN HILL                                                           RHP

**Born:** April 28,1981. **B-T:** R-R. **Ht.:** 6-2. **Wt.:** 185. **Drafted:** HS—Georgetown, Ont., 2000 (6th round). **Signed by:** Alex Agostino.

Hill appeared on the verge of cementing a rotation spot in Washington in 2004, when he also went 1-0, 1.64 in 11 innings for Canada in the Olympics. But Tommy John surgery ended his season prematurely, and he missed all of 2005 while rehabbing. Hill returned to the mound in 2006 and got off to a terrific start in Double-A, going 2-1, 1.86 with 22 strikeouts and just three walks in 29 innings in April. He pitched well in the big leagues before experiencing tightness in his surgically repaired elbow in June and missing nearly all of the second half. Hill relies on an 88-92 mph sinker that he spots to both sides of the plate. He also has good command of a solid curveball and adequate changeup. With an athletic frame, Hill fields his position well, and he is a fearless competitor. The Nationals hope he'll be ready to withstand the rigors of a full season in 2007, with his surgery more than two years behind him. Assuming he's healthy—not necessarily the safest assumption—he should earn a spot in a wide-open big league rotation out of spring training, and he profiles as a solid back-of-the-rotation starter.

| Year | Club (League) | Class | W | L | ERA | G | GS | CG | SV | IP | H | R | ER | HR | BB | SO | AVG |
|------|---------------|-------|---|---|-----|---|----|----|----|----|---|---|----|----|----|----|-----|
| 2000 | Expos (GCL) | R | 1 | 3 | 4.81 | 7 | 7 | 0 | 0 | 24 | 25 | 17 | 13 | 0 | 10 | 20 | .250 |
| 2001 | Vermont (NYP) | A | 2 | 2 | 2.27 | 7 | 7 | 0 | 0 | 36 | 22 | 12 | 9 | 0 | 8 | 23 | .172 |
| 2002 | Clinton (MWL) | A | 12 | 7 | 3.44 | 25 | 25 | 0 | 0 | 147 | 149 | 75 | 56 | 7 | 35 | 99 | .261 |
| 2003 | Brevard County (FSL) | A | 9 | 4 | 2.56 | 22 | 21 | 2 | 0 | 127 | 118 | 47 | 36 | 3 | 26 | 66 | .248 |
| | Harrisburg (EL) | AA | 3 | 1 | 3.54 | 4 | 4 | 0 | 0 | 20 | 23 | 12 | 8 | 0 | 11 | 12 | .280 |
| 2004 | Montreal (NL) | MLB | 1 | 2 | 16.00 | 3 | 3 | 0 | 0 | 9 | 17 | 16 | 16 | 1 | 7 | 10 | .415 |
| | Harrisburg (EL) | AA | 5 | 7 | 3.39 | 17 | 17 | 2 | 0 | 88 | 90 | 39 | 33 | 4 | 20 | 53 | .274 |
| 2005 | Did not play—Injured | | | | | | | | | | | | | | | | |
| 2006 | New Orleans (PCL) | AAA | 0 | 0 | 3.60 | 1 | 1 | 0 | 0 | 5 | 6 | 2 | 2 | 0 | 2 | 2 | .286 |
| | Washington (NL) | MLB | 1 | 3 | 4.66 | 6 | 6 | 0 | 0 | 37 | 43 | 20 | 19 | 2 | 12 | 16 | .297 |
| | Harrisburg (EL) | AA | 3 | 3 | 2.68 | 10 | 10 | 0 | 0 | 50 | 46 | 20 | 15 | 2 | 5 | 32 | .237 |
| MINOR LEAGUE TOTALS | | | 35 | 27 | 3.12 | 93 | 92 | 4 | 0 | 497 | 479 | 224 | 172 | 16 | 117 | 307 | .252 |
| MAJOR LEAGUE TOTALS | | | 2 | 5 | 6.90 | 9 | 9 | 0 | 0 | 45 | 60 | 36 | 35 | 3 | 19 | 26 | .323 |

## DEVIN IVANY                                               C

**Born:** July 27, 1982. **B-T:** R-R. **Ht.:** 6-2. **Wt.:** 185. **Drafted:** South Florida, 2004 (6th round). **Signed by:** Russ Bove.

One of the hardest-working players in the system, Ivany put himself on the prospect map through sheer force of will in 2005, when he reinvented his swing on his own during the off-season. He struggled out of the gate at high Class A in 2006, hitting just .229 in April before turning things around to finish the season at .262 for the second year in a row. He also showed some pop in Hawaii Winter Baseball, slugging .536 in 56 at-bats. Ivany's strength is his defense behind the plate. He's major league-ready as a defender. He has soft hands, quick feet and a solid-average arm, and he earns plaudits from his pitching staff for his ability to call a game and command the field. He's a good athlete who runs well for a catcher, even stealing the occasional base. At the plate, he's a line-drive, gap-to-gap hitter with occasional pull power, but he needs to work on his load and get his hands into position quicker. He has below-average raw power and doesn't figure to ever hit better than .270. Ivany looks like a future backup catcher, but his makeup gives him an outside chance to be a regular. He'll go to Double-A in 2007.

| Year | Club (League) | Class | AVG | G | AB | R | H | 2B | 3B | HR | RBI | BB | SO | SB | OBP | SLG |
|------|---------------|-------|-----|---|----|---|---|----|----|----|-----|----|----|----|-----|-----|
| 2004 | Vermont (NYP) | A | .125 | 12 | 48 | 4 | 6 | 0 | 0 | 0 | 1 | 1 | 5 | 1 | .143 | .125 |
| | Savannah (SAL) | A | .170 | 32 | 106 | 7 | 18 | 4 | 0 | 0 | 4 | 8 | 21 | 2 | .239 | .208 |
| 2005 | Savannah (SAL) | A | .262 | 113 | 409 | 52 | 107 | 27 | 1 | 13 | 54 | 25 | 65 | 7 | .315 | .428 |
| 2006 | Potomac (CL) | A | .262 | 115 | 446 | 62 | 117 | 19 | 3 | 6 | 55 | 25 | 64 | 12 | .311 | .359 |
| MINOR LEAGUE TOTALS | | | .246 | 272 | 1009 | 125 | 248 | 50 | 4 | 19 | 114 | 59 | 155 | 22 | .297 | .360 |

## FRANK DIAZ                                               OF

**Born:** Oct. 6, 1983. **B-T:** R-R. **Ht.:** 6-2. **Wt.:** 180. **Signed:** Venezuela, 2000. **Signed by:** Carlos Acosta.

A converted pitcher, Diaz had a breakout year in 2005, his fourth season as an outfielder, when he represented the Nationals in the Futures Game. He built on that success in April of 2006, when he batted .356 in Double-A, but he slumped badly in May before rebounding in June and wearing down late in the season. That's Diaz—a streaky hitter with average or better tools across the board. One of the best defensive outfielders in the system, he gets good jumps in center field and covers plenty of ground, and he has a strong, accurate arm. He has fringe-average power and solid-average speed. Diaz still has work to do at the plate, where he sometimes gets tied up because of a late trigger. He needs to trust that he can get started early without becoming a lunger. He also needs to work on his pitch recognition and plate discipline, as he has a tendency to chase fastballs up and out of the zone. At this point, Diaz looks like a fourth outfielder in the majors thanks to his defense. He should advance to Triple-A in 2007.

| Year | Club (League) | Class | AVG | G | AB | R | H | 2B | 3B | HR | RBI | BB | SO | SB | OBP | SLG |
|------|---------------|-------|-----|---|----|---|---|----|----|----|-----|----|----|----|-----|-----|
| 2001 | Expos (GCL) | R | .219 | 38 | 128 | 10 | 28 | 5 | 1 | 0 | 8 | 12 | 27 | 10 | .297 | .273 |
| 2002 | Expos (GCL) | R | .277 | 51 | 173 | 33 | 48 | 8 | 2 | 5 | 24 | 19 | 28 | 8 | .370 | .434 |
| | Brevard County (FSL) | A | .226 | 10 | 31 | 3 | 7 | 2 | 0 | 0 | 1 | 6 | 4 | 3 | .351 | .290 |
| 2003 | Savannah (SAL) | A | .270 | 122 | 440 | 63 | 119 | 28 | 4 | 7 | 49 | 15 | 73 | 19 | .298 | .400 |
| 2004 | Brevard County (FSL) | A | .242 | 114 | 413 | 46 | 100 | 17 | 8 | 8 | 57 | 31 | 76 | 16 | .303 | .380 |
| 2005 | Potomac (CL) | A | .312 | 134 | 554 | 85 | 173 | 45 | 5 | 16 | 74 | 20 | 67 | 14 | .342 | .498 |
| 2006 | Harrisburg (EL) | AA | .259 | 107 | 402 | 44 | 104 | 17 | 1 | 9 | 50 | 19 | 59 | 5 | .296 | .373 |
| MINOR LEAGUE TOTALS | | | .270 | 576 | 2141 | 284 | 579 | 122 | 21 | 45 | 263 | 122 | 334 | 75 | .317 | .410 |

## CORY VAN ALLEN                                           LHP

**Born:** Dec. 24, 1984. **B-T:** L-L. **Ht.:** 6-3. **Wt.:** 180. **Drafted:** Baylor, 2006 (5th round). **Signed by:** Bob Laurie.

The third-highest unsigned pick from the 2003 draft, Van Allen fell to the fifth round in 2006 after failing to develop his secondary pitches or command as scouts hoped in three

years at Baylor. With an ideal pitcher's frame, experience at a big-time college program and tantalizing stuff, the Nationals considered Van Allen a steal in the fifth round and signed him for $170,000. He attacks hitters with a changeup that can be above-average at times, though he doesn't always locate it where he wants. Van Allen also has good fastball velocity for a left-hander, pitching at 89-91 mph and touching 93, but the pitch lacks life. He threw a slider and a curveball in college, but his three-quarters arm slot is better suited for the slider, which is still developing. The Nationals want Van Allen to sharpen the slider and learn to command it more consistently. He has the build, stuff and control to be a No. 4 starter in the big leagues, but he's got work to do to reach that ceiling. He should begin 2007 in low Class A.

| Year | Club (League) | Class | W | L | ERA | G | GS | CG | SV | IP | H | R | ER | HR | BB | SO | AVG |
|---|---|---|---|---|---|---|---|---|---|---|---|---|---|---|---|---|---|
| 2006 | Vermont (NYP) | A | 1 | 4 | 4.06 | 13 | 9 | 0 | 0 | 58 | 53 | 29 | 26 | 5 | 16 | 41 | .248 |
| **MINOR LEAGUE TOTALS** | | | 1 | 4 | 4.06 | 13 | 9 | 0 | 0 | 58 | 53 | 29 | 26 | 5 | 16 | 41 | .248 |

## 29 LEVALE SPEIGNER RHP

**Born:** Sept. 24, 1980. **B-T:** R-R. **Ht.:** 5-11. **Wt.:** 175. **Drafted:** Auburn, 2003 (14th round). **Signed by:** Mark Quimuyog (Twins).

A good athlete who played shortstop and pitched for Thomasville (Ga.) High, Speigner worked mostly as a starter his first three years at Auburn, but he allowed 18 home runs as a junior and the Tigers moved him to the bullpen for his 2003 senior year. He flourished in the role, going 10-0, 2.42, and the Twins drafted him in the 14th round. Speigner continued to work out of the bullpen in his first two pro seasons before moving back to the rotation at Double-A New Britain in 2005. He had his best pro season as a closer in 2006, and the Nationals took him with the first pick of the second round of the major league Rule 5 draft. Speigner attacks hitters with a two-pitch mix—an 89-94 mph fastball with good life, and a hard curveball that can be an above-average pitch at times. He has never posted big strikeout numbers, and he needs to improve against lefthanders, but he has the stuff to be a useful reliever in the majors for Washington in 2007. If he doesn't stick on the big league roster, he'll have to clear waivers and be offered back to Minnesota for half of his $50,000 draft price.

| Year | Club (League) | Class | W | L | ERA | G | GS | CG | SV | IP | H | R | ER | HR | BB | SO | AVG |
|---|---|---|---|---|---|---|---|---|---|---|---|---|---|---|---|---|---|
| 2003 | Elizabethton (Appy) | R | 5 | 2 | 3.94 | 22 | 0 | 0 | 4 | 30 | 31 | 13 | 13 | 1 | 4 | 35 | .265 |
| 2004 | Quad City (MWL) | A | 2 | 2 | 2.84 | 22 | 0 | 0 | 9 | 32 | 27 | 14 | 10 | 1 | 15 | 29 | .216 |
| | Fort Myers (FSL) | A | 4 | 3 | 1.10 | 22 | 1 | 0 | 2 | 73 | 46 | 15 | 9 | 3 | 14 | 49 | .250 |
| 2005 | Rochester (IL) | AAA | 0 | 1 | 7.36 | 2 | 1 | 0 | 0 | 7 | 14 | 7 | 6 | 0 | 1 | 5 | .412 |
| | New Britain (EL) | AA | 6 | 10 | 4.13 | 23 | 23 | 2 | 0 | 144 | 149 | 75 | 66 | 14 | 28 | 94 | .268 |
| 2006 | New Britain (EL) | AA | 3 | 2 | 3.26 | 40 | 0 | 0 | 13 | 58 | 61 | 27 | 21 | 5 | 14 | 37 | .266 |
| | Rochester (IL) | AAA | 1 | 1 | 4.97 | 9 | 0 | 0 | 1 | 13 | 16 | 7 | 7 | 1 | 5 | 8 | .296 |
| **MINOR LEAGUE TOTALS** | | | 21 | 21 | 3.33 | 140 | 25 | 2 | 29 | 356 | 344 | 158 | 132 | 25 | 81 | 257 | .265 |

## 30 MIKE HINCKLEY LHP

**Born:** Oct. 5, 1982. **B-T:** R-L. **Ht.:** 6-3. **Wt.:** 170. **Drafted:** HS—Moore, Okla., 2001 (3rd round). **Signed by:** Darrell Brown.

Hinckley looked to be on the fast track in 2004, when he posted a 2.87 ERA in 94 innings in Double-A and finished the season as Washington's No. 1 prospect. He went to big league spring training in 2005 with a chance to earn a spot in the Opening Day rotation, but he began overthrowing and his arm action got longer, creating strain on his shoulder that caused him to miss the first month of the season. He pitched with a sore shoulder in 2005, and had posterior capsule relief surgery after the season. Hinckley returned to high Class A in 2006, where he struggled to regain his stuff and his command. At times he showed flashes of what he once was, but for most of the year his fastball sat in the mid- to upper 80s, not approaching the low 90s he pitched at two years ago. When he was at his best, Hinckley had excellent command of a three-pitch mix, but he had trouble commanding his changeup in 2006, and his curveball did not have the bite it once did. This season will be critical for Hinckley. He needs to return to Double-A and show that his stuff has come all the way back. The Nationals aren't giving up on a lefthander with Hinckley's pedigree yet, but time is running out.

| Year | Club (League) | Class | W | L | ERA | G | GS | CG | SV | IP | H | R | ER | HR | BB | SO | AVG |
|---|---|---|---|---|---|---|---|---|---|---|---|---|---|---|---|---|---|
| 2001 | Expos (GCL) | R | 2 | 2 | 5.24 | 8 | 5 | 0 | 0 | 34 | 46 | 23 | 20 | 1 | 12 | 28 | .329 |
| 2002 | Vermont (NYP) | A | 6 | 2 | 1.37 | 16 | 16 | 0 | 0 | 92 | 60 | 19 | 14 | 4 | 30 | 66 | .188 |
| 2003 | Savannah (SAL) | A | 9 | 5 | 3.64 | 23 | 23 | 2 | 0 | 121 | 124 | 54 | 49 | 4 | 41 | 111 | .271 |
| | Brevard County (FSL) | A | 4 | 0 | 0.72 | 4 | 4 | 1 | 0 | 25 | 14 | 2 | 2 | 1 | 1 | 23 | .159 |
| 2004 | Brevard County (FSL) | A | 6 | 2 | 2.61 | 10 | 10 | 0 | 0 | 62 | 47 | 23 | 18 | 6 | 18 | 51 | .211 |
| | Harrisburg (EL) | AA | 5 | 2 | 2.87 | 16 | 16 | 0 | 0 | 94 | 83 | 34 | 30 | 5 | 23 | 80 | .250 |
| 2005 | Potomac (CL) | A | 3 | 9 | 4.93 | 22 | 21 | 1 | 0 | 128 | 151 | 90 | 70 | 10 | 51 | 80 | .293 |
| 2006 | Potomac (CL) | A | 6 | 8 | 5.52 | 28 | 28 | 0 | 0 | 148 | 178 | 102 | 91 | 18 | 63 | 79 | .303 |
| **MINOR LEAGUE TOTALS** | | | 41 | 30 | 3.76 | 127 | 123 | 4 | 0 | 704 | 703 | 347 | 294 | 49 | 239 | 518 | .264 |

# APPENDIX

By the end of the summer, 29 of the 30 first-round picks had agreed to terms. The lone exception was Max Scherzer, who went 11th overall to the Diamondbacks. He remained in negotiations as this book went to print but was expected to sign before spring training. Another player of note who had not signed but was expected to was Japanese lefthander Kei Igawa. He had agreed to terms with the Yankees but had not signed at our transaction deadline.

We present their scouting reports below. Had they signed in time to be included in the book, Scherzer would have ranked No. 6 on our Diamondbacks prospects list (between Miguel Montero and Micah Owings), while Igawa would have ranked No. 9.

## MAX SCHERZER                                                                            RHP
**Born:** July 27, 1984. **B-T:** R-R. **Ht.:** 6-2. **Wt.:** 210. **Drafted:** Missouri, 2006 (1st round).

Scherzer entered last year rated as the top righthander available in the 2006 draft, but he slipped a few notches during the spring. He missed an early-season start after slamming a door on the middle finger of his pitching hand, and five more at midseason with biceps tendinitis. He helped Missouri reach the NCAA super regionals and went 7-3, 2.25 with 78 strikeouts in 80 innings, good but not great numbers for a college pitcher of his caliber. After coming back from the tendinitis, Scherzer only flashed the mid- to upper-90s velocity he showed throughout 2005 with Missouri and with Team USA during the summer. He pitched more at 91-92 mph, often peaking at 95. While he had one of the best pure arms in the draft, he doesn't consistently have a second plus pitch. His slider is inconsistent, though when it's at its best it will hit 87-88 mph. The Diamondbacks believe it will become a reliable out pitch in time. Scherzer has added a wide-grip changeup and a two-seam fastball in the last year, and he's still refining his secondary pitches. While he has toned down his delivery in college, he still throws with some effort. More than most of the top pitching prospects in the 2006 draft, he may be better suited to be a closer than a frontline starter. The highest-drafted player in the history of the Missouri program, Scherzer marks the third straight first-round pick who has had protracted negotiations with the Diamondbacks, following fellow Scott Boras client Stephen Drew (2004) and Justin Upton (2005). Neither side has commented much on the talks, and it's unclear how far apart they are. Scherzer went 11th overall on merit, not because of signability. Several clubs had concerns about his shoulder, though Arizona scouting director Mike Rizzo wasn't worried about Scherzer's health and was delighted to grab him. Rizzo left during the summer to become an assistant general manager and vice president of baseball operations with the Nationals, leaving the Diamondbacks' negotiations in the hands of GM Josh Byrnes.

## KEI IGAWA                                                                               LHP
**Born:** July 13, 1979. **B-T:** L-L. **Ht.:** 6-0. **Wt.:** 192. **Signed:** Japan, 2006.

After losing out to the Red Sox for the rights to Daisuke Matsuzaka, the Yankees won the posting of Igawa with a bid of $26,000,194. He agreed in December to a five-year big league contract worth $20 million. He put up power-pitcher numbers in Japan without power-pitcher stuff, winning a Central League MVP award in 2003 and leading the circuit in strikeouts three times in the last five seasons. The "194" at the end of New York's bid was a nod to his CL-best strikeout total in 2006. Former big leaguer manager Bobby Valentine, now the skipper of Japan's Chiba Lotte Marines, said Igawa was better four years ago but still called him a capable lefthander for a big league rotation. One international scout who saw Igawa in 2006 said he profiled at the back of the rotation and didn't have stuff to rival the last lefty starter to come out of Japan with any fanfare, Kazuo Ishii. Igawa's fastball sat at 86-91 mph last year, though he can reach back and hit 93. His strikeout pitch is a hard breaking ball in the upper 70s, alternately described as a curveball or slurve. He also throws a changeup that at times is an average pitch. Scouts say his best attributes are his fearlessness and willingness to challenge hitters. He'll pitch inside with his fastball and isn't afraid to use something off-speed in a fastball count. He's better suited to adjusting to the American style of play than Ishii was, even though he doesn't have Ishii's stuff. Igawa will pitch at the back of the Yankees rotation in 2007 and gives them another lefty to complement Randy Johnson and Andy Pettitte.

# SCOUTING DICTIONARY

**-a·bil·i·ty** *suffix* : applied to an action, implying competence or skill in a certain area of the game, i.e., pitchability, hittability, catchability; term often considered not very useful on scouting reports because it lacks detail and explanation. "Jason Repko and Albert Pujols both have hittability—but what kind of hittability are you talking about? It can mean many things." *(Logan White)*

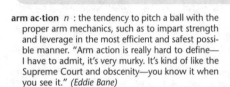

**al·u·mi·num-bat swing** *n* : a batting stroke, particularly in high school or college, which is either too long or can't protect the inside part of the plate, hurting its ability to translate to pro ball. "Joe Borchard in Stanford had an aluminum-bat swing. He extended too far and had a spot inside where you could pitch him." *(Mickey White)*

**arm ac·tion** *n* : the tendency to pitch a ball with the proper arm mechanics, such as to impart strength and leverage in the most efficient and safest possible manner. "Arm action is really hard to define—I have to admit, it's very murky. It's kind of like the Supreme Court and obscenity—you know it when you see it." *(Eddie Bane)*

**Bar·ney Rub·ble** *n* : **1** : short and stocky, as in the Flintstones character **2** : slightly dopey-looking. "Matt Stairs is kind of a Barney Rubble. Not too many guys make it with that kind of body." *(Anonymous)*

**base-clog·ger** *n* : a runner whose lack of speed and/or baserunning skill routinely keeps him from advancing from first to third on a single or scoring from first on a double. "Jim Thome can really hit, but he's definitely a base-clogger." *(Deric Ladnier)*

**bat·boy** *adj* : unimpressively scrawny and skinny. "When you see a guy with a batboy body they look like they should be carrying the ballbag, not actually playing. But middle infielders with batboy bodies usually can get playably stronger with weight training." *(Doug Carpenter)*

**be·hind** *prep* : positioned with one's fingers on the backside of the ball, rather than under, over or off to the side of it, thus imparting greater force and accuracy. "An outfielder always wants to stay behind the ball. If you're an infielder, say a second baseman, it's not as important because you can make up for it with good footwork and a quick release." *(Jack Zduriencik)*

**big eat·er** *n* : a hitter who will hit for outright power rather than slash balls down the line or into gaps; often applied to separate different types of corner infielders. "Paul Konerko was a big eater in high school in Scottsdale—you knew he was gonna hit for real power. Todd Helton was a good hitter, but not necessarily a big eater." *(Eddie Bane)*

**blood·lines** *n* : pedigree; being related to another accomplished baseball player or athlete, usually a parent. "A lot of people love it if a kid has good bloodlines, but the first question should be whether the guy can play. Genetics don't always play out."*(Mickey White)*

**boat race** *n* : a blowout, often leaving scouts unable to properly gauge the ability of the winning side's starting pitcher; derives from America's Cup competitions won by five or more miles. "I hate boat races, like games in Oklahoma that get called after five innings, because you don't really get a good look at the guy you came to see." *(Eddie Bane)*

**bor·ing** *adj* : driving down into the lower part of the strike zone, as in a drill; to move with heavy sink and lateral movement. "Carlos Zambrano's sinker has incredible boring action, particularly down and in to righthanders." *(Mike Arbuckle)*—**bore** *v* **syn** heavy

**bow-and-ar·row** *adj* : applied to a pitching motion, one where the pitcher pulls the ball out the glove directly behind his ear rather than in the proper circle, i.e. Keith Foulke. "Bow-and-arrow guys create deception, because the ball is hidden and then—surprise! Here it is." *(Doug Carpenter)*

**Bugs Bun·ny change·up** *n* : an offspeed pitch that moves so slowly and leaves the hitter so far out in front that he could swing and miss three times before it reaches the plate (as in Bugs Bunny's, "One, two, three strikes you're out!" pitch that confounded the Gas House Gorillas). "Trevor Hoffman has a Bugs Bunny changeup. It's so funny. It's comical." (Dan Jennings)

**can·kles** *n* : *pl* : a pairing of ankles and calves that show no distinguishing musculature features, as if they were one body part. "Guys with cankles are usually horrendous middle infielders—their first step is usually slow, so they're destined to be corner infielders." *(Dan Jennings)*

**car·ry** *n* : extra distance an outfielder's throw travels, seemingly longer than otherwise expected. "Some players, their good carry means their

throws stay in the air longer. It's a good thing. If you have too much arc, it's tough to have good carry." *(Jack Zduriencik)*

**cak·ey** *adj* : of a body type that is particularly soft and spongy, as in a pound cake. "Guys who are cakey are not quite doughy, but they're getting there." *(Dan Jennings)*

**cast** *v* : to lead with one's elbow while delivering a breaking ball, leaving the hand too far behind the arm and decreasing the potential to impart power spin. "Jason Johnson didn't get out in front of his breaking ball last night—he slowed his arm and casted his curveballs." *(Mike Arbuckle)*

**cei·ling** *n* : the maximum level of skill to which a player or prospect can conceivably develop at his peak; **syn** upside. "Delmon Young's physical tools allow him to have the ceiling of a frontline all-star caliber player for years." *(Mike Arbuckle)*

**cheat** *v* : primarily regarding a hitter's approach to fastballs, to stride and swing too early in anticipation of a fastball, and in so doing leaving one unable to adjust to anything offspeed. "You see hitters cheating when they don't have the bat speed to catch up to good fastballs—otherwise they'll be tardy and kill someone in the opposing dugout." *(Doug Carpenter)*

**chick·en-wing·er** *n* : a pitcher who leads with his elbow with limited extension, shortening his delivery into a more awkward and less fluid motion; generally applied to lefthanded pitchers without strong fastballs. "We scout away from chicken-wingers— you don't see many of them today. Billy Wagner is one. John Tudor was a classic chicken-winger." *(Mike Arbuckle)*

**close the gap** *v* : to cut off hits to the outfield that might otherwise reach the left- or right-center field walls. "Devon White could really close the gap, because he had the speed, first-step quickness and angle management." *(Jack Zduriencik)*

**come·back** *adj* : as in a pitch, moving from a few inches inside over the plate at the final moment. "Greg Maddux has a comeback fastball—lefthanded hitters flinch at it because it starts right at them but it breaks back over the plate." *(Deric Ladnier)*

**com·mand** *n or v* **1** : the ability to throw pitches at the intended spots within the strike zone **2** : to exhibit command. "Control is the ability to throw strikes—command is the ability to throw quality strikes." *(Curt Schilling)*

**com·pact** *adj* : applied to either a swing or pitching motion, efficient and with no wasted movement. "Compact doesn't necessarily mean quick, but it looks quick because there are shorter paths to what the player is doing." *(Logan White)*

**cush·ion** *v* : to field a ball in such a relaxed way that it settles easily into the glove ready to be smoothly transferred to the throwing hand. "When a guy cushions the ball, he's fielding it lovingly—it implies a confidence with what he's doing. An ease." *(Deacon Jones)*

**cut off ex·ten·sion** *v* : to deliver a pitch without the elbow too close to the body, impeding the proper exertion of force and follow-through. "We also call that having alligator arms—put your arm at your side and try to throw, you'll see. When you cut off extension you don't have your arm in the right place to deliver the ball." *(Doug Carpenter)*

**cut·ter** *n* : a fastball that, because the fingers are held slightly off to the side, breaks hard inside to lefties when thrown from a righthander or vice versa; a pitch that has the speed of a fastball but not quite the break of a slider. **syn** *cut fastball.* "Mariano Rivera has the best cutter out there—he throws it to lefties and boom, it's right in on their hands." *(Jack Zduriencik)*

**D·F·E** *abbr v or n* : **1** : draft, follow and evaluate **2** : a player selected as a draft-and-follow or recommended for that path; **syn** DNF (draft and follow).

**dart-throw·er** *n* : a pitcher who excessively aims the ball, implying some hesitancy or timidity. "Vern Ruhle used to be a dart-thrower for me, but then he got a little more confidence and let it go." *(Deacon Jones)*

**down·hill** *adj* : applied to a pitcher, throwing the ball from the highest release point possible, thereby applying a steeper angle to the pitch and giving the impression of extra downward movement; does not necessarily imply an over-the-top delivery. "Throwing downhill makes it harder to hit the baseball—Roy Oswalt does it really well for a smaller guy, and Curt Schilling's another example." *(Jack Zduriencik)*

**draft-and-fol·low** *n* : a player who, after being selected in the amateur draft, elects to attend junior college, thereby allowing his drafting club to continue to evaluate and perhaps sign him until a week before the following draft; practice eliminated by new draft rules as of 2007. "I liked Andy Pettitte out of high school but thought he'd be better off spending a year filling out in junior college, so I put him down as a draft-and-follow." *(Dan Jennings)*

**draft·i·tis** *n* : an affliction whereby a draft-eligible player withers under scouts' scrutiny and fails to display the skills he once did. "Ryan Howard had draftitis at Southwest Missouri, but the joke was on me. I allowed myself not to see him because we'd heard he was so bad." *(Mickey White)*

**drop-and-drive** *n* : the tendency for a pitcher to plant his lead leg and flex at the knee such that his body gets very low to the ground while delivering the ball; connotes power pitcher such as Tom Seaver, though is used less positively today

because drop-and-drive pitchers often have difficulty staying on top of the ball. "Roy Oswalt is an example of a drop-and-drive pitcher, but there aren't that many today. It's more stay tall and fall." *(Mike Arbuckle)*

**Eck·stein** *n* : **1** : a player, often undersized, who has seemingly little physical ability but exhibits enough desire and hustle to remain a prospect **2** : a player who after reaching the major leagues is a surprisingly difficult out. "Placido Polanco is an Eckstein—a pain in the ass player who keeps coming at you, a get-dirty type guy. Chone Figgins is, too." *(Deacon Jones)*

 **fall-down range** *n* : such limited lateral mobility that the only way to reach a ground ball would be to fall on top of it; usually used for corner infielders. "Frank Thomas at first base has fall-down range. So did Mo Vaughn." *(Mike Arbuckle)*

**fence shy** *adj* : applied to an outfielder or corner infielder, having a tendency to give up on fly or foul balls at the wall for fear of a collision; cautious. "Aaron Rowand will always sacrifice his body to make a catch. Other guys are more fence shy and are afraid of getting hurt." *(Jack Zduriencik)*

**five o'·clock hit·ter** *n* : a hitter who shows tremendous power but only in batting practice, unable to carry it over against game-speed pitching. "Russell Branyan was a notorious five o'clock hitter, but he has turned the corner." *(Mike Arbuckle)*

**five-tool play·er** *n* : a position player who exhibits all five of the primary physical skills required of them, i.e., hitting for average and power, running, fielding and throwing. "Derrek Lee in his good years was a five-tool player. That sounds strange for a first baseman, but he can actually do everything." *(Logan White)*

**frame** *v* : as in a catcher, to receive pitches just on or off the strike zone in such a manner as to convince the umpire that the pitch was a strike; to smoothly bring such pitches over the plate. "All good major league catchers frame the ball—it's a must. Mike Piazza has a below-average arm, but he frames pitches well so he helps his pitchers that way." *(Doug Mapson)*

**frin·gy** *adj* : on the borderline of being useful in the major leagues; slightly worse than playable. "You find a lot of guys who have two above-average pitches, but their changeup is fringy." *(Mike Arbuckle)*

**gap-to-gap** *adj* : having the tendency to hit doubles and triples to left-center and right-center fields, rather than shooting balls down the lines; implies limited power as much as good speed. "Craig Biggio had some power in his prime, but he was more of a gap-to-gap hitter—and a good one." *(Mike Arbuckle)*

**good/bad face** *n* : **1** : having an either strong or weak chin **2** : having a face that implies athleticism or a hard-nosed attitude toward sports; primarily used by older rather than younger scouts. "You sometimes have to fight to get some scouts past a guy with a bad face. I thought it was crazy, but there's something to it. You see almost no one in the big leagues with a bad face." *(Eddie Bane)*

**gid·dy-up** *n* : the tendency for a fastball to appear as if it explodes or rises as it crosses the plate, an illusion often caused by a smooth delivery that hides how fast the pitch will be. "Joel Zumaya had a good fastball in high school, but it didn't have the incredible giddy-up that it has now." *(Al Avila)* **syn** late life

**hap·py feet** *n pl* : the tendency for a hitter moving his feet in the batter's box as if to start toward first base while making contact, often too early to remain in proper batting position. "Ichiro is one of the few hitters who has the hand-eye coordination to get away with having happy feet." *(Deric Ladnier)*

**heavy** *adj* : **1** : as in a pitch, having hard downward action that will often rattle the bat in a hitter's hands **2** : accentuated forceful movement, perhaps laterally. "You love to see guys with heavy action on their pitches, because when they get to the plate they overbear on hitters." *(Doug Carpenter)*

**heavy-legged** *adj* : running with a laboring stride and effort; has less to do with weight or musculature of legs than the lack of grace or efficiency a runner exhibits. "It's really hard to find a catcher who isn't heavy-legged. That's one of the things that make Jason Kendall and Joe Mauer special." *(Doug Mapson)*

**hitch** *n* : a hitting trigger in which the batter drops his hands up or down rather than back, keeping him from starting his swing properly. "Matt Williams had a huge hitch coming out of UNLV, but had the hand-eye coordination and strength to make it work for him." *(Doug Mapson)*

**in·stincts** *n pl* : the trait in some players to immediately determine what will happen on the field, as if knowing in advance; usually applied in judging whether a fly ball will drop or be caught, anticipating pitch sequences or in defensive positioning. "A player with good instincts will already be moving toward a ground ball because of the pitch or the bat angle. Mark Kotsay is a guy who doesn't have one tool that stands out but his instincts make the whole package." *(Al Avila)*

**KP** *abbrev* : can't play; opposite of CP (can play). "When we put down KP for an amateur, that won't even be an organizational player—even Triple-A or Double-A. He's probably just a college player. No interest." *(Logan White)*

**kill zone** *n* : the area of the strike zone in which a hitter or pitcher enjoys particular success. "Dave Winfield's kill zone was away from him because his

arms were so long. You wanted to try to bust him in, like Derek Jeter." *(Mickey White)* **syn** *wheelhouse* (for hitters)

**life** *n* : movement of a pitch, but only within the strike zone. "Life can be run, cut, ride, sink—it's that little extra surge of movement." *(Al Avila)*

**lift** *n* : the tendency to swing in such a manner as to give batted balls consistent loft and therefore distance. "Robin Ventura was one of the best college hitters I ever saw—you knew that when he learned to add some loft, he would really hit some home runs." *(Jack Zduriencik)*

**load** *n* : a hesitation in a windup in which the pitcher stays back before he starts his full delivery, often helping him keep consistent mechanics and release point. "Jered Weaver has great load—he stays back really long over the rubber. A lot of kids rush, especially out of the stretch." *(Eddie Bane)*

**long** *adj* : applied to a swing, implies that the barrel of the bat takes an extended arc to the ball; opposite of *short* or *compact*. "If you have a long swing it's tough to make work, unless you have the pure leverage and strength of a Richie Sexson or Mark McGwire." *(Doug Mapson)*

**loo·py** *adj* : lacking the proper bite and sharpness, as in a breaking ball, implying a soft, predictable arc. "It's very hard to have a plus loopy curveball. Guys make money hitting loopy into the upper deck." *(Doug Carpenter)* **syn** *flippy*

**lose your ath·lete** *v* : to suffer a decline in quickness and agility while physically maturing, as opposed to outright laziness. "It's always disappointing when a great high school shortstop loses his athlete and has to wind up at first base." *(Logan White)*

**Mad·dux** n a relatively short righthanded pitcher who, without an above-average fastball, might still succeed primarily with control and intelligence. "A lot of mistakes are made when they think someone's a Maddux. He's a pretty rare animal." *(Logan White)*

**make·up** n **1** : competitive maturity **2** : the ability to withstand adversity and distraction; focus. "We never had to worry about Scott Rolen becoming as good as he could be. His makeup was off the charts." *(Mike Arbuckle)*

**mar·lin** *n* : a tale about a prospect that is hard to believe; fish story. "Art Stewart's one of my favorite people in the world, but he'll always say, 'Right after you left, the kid hit two homers, one of them 600 feet!' You just sit back and smile and go, 'marlin'." *(Eddie Bane)*

**max-effort** *adj* : exhibiting grunts and other signs of exertion, oftentimes more than would be seemingly necessary; laboring. "Max-effort guys, it

seems like nothing is easy about the game. Kevin Appier was max-effort — he threw everything he had into every pitch." *(Eddie Bane)*

**mus·cle** *v* : **1** : to impart a forced effort in either pitching or swinging **2** : to use extra exertion. "Everyone will occasionally muscle the ball, but young guys don't realize that it's better to be free and easy. Their mechanics go out the window when they muscle it." *(Doug Carpenter)*

**NP** *abbrev* : non-prospect; won't reach the major leagues. "You want to use NP and other shorthand like that because people look over our shoulders in the stands, friends and parents, and you don't want to crush a kid." *(Doug Carpenter)* **syn** *KP*

**pa·ra·chute** *v* : **1** : to float toward a target, as in an outfield throw without enough oomph behind it **2** : to fall out of the strike zone, as in a changeup. "Bernie Williams' throws tended to parachute, but because of his instincts and accuracy his arm was playable." *(Doug Mapson)*

**pie-throw·er** *n* : a pitcher who, while throwing a pitch, holds his palm too far under the ball rather than having his fingers on top of it, as if throwing a pie. "If you're a pie-thrower, you tend to end up in the zone a lot with your pitches flattening out. And you'll very well have a short career — it puts tremendous stress on the elbow and shoulder." *(Mike Arbuckle)*

**ping hit·ter** *n* : a weak hitter who doesn't swing the bat or connect with any force or resulting power; term precedes aluminum bats, so does not necessarily imply *aluminum-bat swing*. "We're not looking for ping hitters. We want guys who drive the ball with authority." *(Doug Mapson)*

**pitch re·cog·ni·tion** *n* : **1** a hitter's ability to identify the type and location of pitches almost immediately out of the pitcher's hand **2** : the act of adding the situation (man on third, one out, etc.) to the decision to swing. "You can tell that Albert Pujols has great pitch recognition because he has a balanced stride with his weight back, and he swings easy. He knows when a pitch isn't a strike and won't be fooled." *(Doug Carpenter)*

**plate dis·ci·pline** *n* : the ability to not swing at pitches out of the strike zone, or pitches that are less hittable than those that might follow; **syn** strike-zone judgment. "Kevin Youkilis sees the ball immediately out of the pitcher's hand—hitters with great discipline see and identify pitches very early." *(Mickey White)*

**play·able** *adj* : perhaps below average but adequate enough to survive in the major leagues. "David Eckstein doesn't have a strong arm at shortstop, but it's playable because of his quickness and instincts." *(Doug Mapson)*

**plus** *adj* : above average, usually compared to average major leaguer. "Derek Jeter had plus arm strength in high school—it was body control that

he needed work on because he was growing into his frame." *(Mickey White)*

**plus-plus** *adj* : far above average; outstanding. "Rafael Furcal has a plus-plus arm—he's so fluid and has such great finish. The ball leaves his hand real easy and explodes at the end." *(Logan White)*; **syn** double-plus

**plow·horse** *n* : a player who grinds out solid performances after most would have expected them to let up. "Darin Erstad is a real plowhorse—he's like a farmer who works in the field all day long." *(Deric Ladnier)*

**pop** *v* : to select a player in the draft, often somewhat unexpectedly. "It's hard to believe now, but when I popped Manny Ramirez in the first round in 1991, people were really surprised." *(Mickey White)*

**pole-to-pole** adj : the ability to hit with power throughout all 90 degrees of fair territory; whereas gap-to-gap implies the ability to hit doubles and triples to the middle of the park, pole-to-pole connotes dominance to all fields. "Ryan Howard has legitimate pole-to-pole power. He can hit them out anywhere." *(Mike Arbuckle)*

**pop time** *n* : the time (in seconds), on a stolen-base attempt, between a pitch hitting the catcher's glove and when his throw hits the middle-infielder's glove. "The typical pop time for major leaguers is two seconds flat, but Yadier Molina has an impressive pop time of about 1.85." *(Mike Arbuckle)*

**pop·eye** *v or n* : **1** : to elicit suspicion that a player is taking steroids or other illegal performance-enhancing substances **2** : a player suspected of using such substances. "I gotta tell you, it's not really hard to look at a player and see that he's popeyeing you." *(Anonymous)*

**pull off** *v* : to turn one's shoulder toward third base (for a righthanded hitter) while batting, creating a hitting position that is too open and inside-oriented to reach an outside pitch. "Manny Ramirez and Derek Jeter never pull off the ball—they keep their head down and their hands back. That's why they have so much power to right-center field." *(Deacon Jones)*

**quick·ness** *n* : **1** : the ability of a defensive player to take an immediate first step toward a ground or fly ball **2** : the speed with which a basestealer can reach top speed toward the next base. "If you have first-step quickness, you're going to get to balls faster than someone who is just really fast." *(Al Avila)*

**re·coil** *v or n* : **1** : to pull one's pitching arm back toward the body after delivering the ball, often

violently **2** : the movement imparted while recoiling. "When pitchers recoil they think they're getting more velocity, but they're really not. Guys who recoil are usually max-effort guys—they're not that smooth." *(Eddie Bane)* **syn** *bounceback*

**run** *n* : the act of a pitch moving laterally, usually from righthanders inside on righty hitters. "A cutter is the opposite of a runner because it moves inside to lefthanders. A righthanded runner breaks righthanded bats, because it runs in hitters' hands while they try to shorten their swing." *(Dan Jennings)*

**sign·a·bil·i·ty** *n* : the perceived chance that a draft pick will turn professional rather than enter or continue college. "Most area scouts worry too much about signability—they eliminate a guy because they assume he won't sign, when that's really the scouting director's job to worry about." *(Mickey White)*

**slash·er** *n* : a player who does not apply lift to the ball, instead surviving on hard ground balls and line drives; a player without power but with the speed and bat control to survive. "Willie McGee back in the day was a slasher. Kenny Lofton, too—he'll shorten his swing and hit the ball the other way and run." *(Logan White)* **syn** *slapper*

**slot** *n, v or adj* : **1** : the angle the pitching arm makes to the ground or body while delivering the ball **2** : to pay a draft pick a bonus that is comparable with what players picked around him received; implying such a bonus. "I think you change a pitcher's slot only as a last measure—you're messing with muscle memory, and sometimes they can't go back to the old slot afterward." *(Logan White)*

**slurve** *n* : a pitch that because of its speed and break acts halfway between a slider and a curveball. "Jeff Weaver changes speeds so much on his breaking ball it can come off as a slurve—there's a 74-76-mph one that's more like a curve and a 78-82-mph one that's more like a slider." *(Deacon Jones)* **slurvy** *adj*

**snap dra·gon** *n* : a particularly nasty curveball with a perfect snap of the wrist. "I took one look at that snap dragon and my knees buckled as much as the hitter's." *(Dan Jennings)* **syn** *yakker, yellow hammer*

**solid-average** *adj* : average, but with greater consistency than merely average would imply. "Dan Uggla has a solid-average arm at second base. It's more reliable than a guy who's just average. It's more trustworthy." *(Doug Carpenter)*

**special player** *n* : an amateur prospect who, because he is represented by Scott Boras and deemed by the agent to have particular promise, will probably cost a lot of money and time to get under contract. "Jered Weaver was a special player and was worth it. You don't stay away from those guys in the draft, but it's a consideration." *(Eddie Bane)* **syn** icon player

**spin off** *v* : to pitch with such force and lateral momentum as to land on the side of one's foot and move violently toward first or third base, out of proper fielding position. "Bob Gibson spun off a ton, and most left-handers spin off a bit." *(Eddie Bane)*

**stab·ber** *n* : a pitcher who stops his motion soon after removing the ball from his glove and sticks his arm toward the ground away from his body; **syn** plunger or sweeper. "Very few stabbers have much success—it breaks the rhythm of their arm moving in a circle. Rick Sutcliffe was a little bit of one." *(Dan Jennings)* **stab** *v*

**stay tall and fall** *v* : as in a pitcher, to remain primarily upright during his windup and let gravity take his body toward the plate rather than pushing off more strenuously lower to the ground. "A vast majority of pitchers today stay tall and fall. It's an easier delivery." *(Mike Arbuckle)*

**throw ac·ross bo·dy** *v* : to pitch in a manner where the arm must twist slightly to redirect the ball toward the plate, passing over the chest rather than being open and unimpeded; caused by, in the case of a righthander, the lead foot landing about three inches too far to the right, leaving the arm having to compensate for the pitch to travel toward the target. "We like guys to be closed a little bit, but when you throw across your body, you're asking for arm trouble. Joe Kennedy is probably the most severe guy in the big leagues right now." *(Eddie Bane)*

**tight·ly wound** *adj* : **1** : having a cut and strong physique with almost no apparent fat; can imply inflexibility **2** : having an uptight mental approach to the game; opposite of *loose*. "Baseball players who have played other sports can enter pro ball tightly wound, but they get looser the more they focus on the game." *(Jack Zduriencik)*

**tilt** *n* : movement of a pitch, primarily a slider, which takes place late at the plate as it falls off the hitting plane. "Randy Johnson had just about the best tilt I'd ever seen. Francisco Liriano's is pretty impressive, too." *(Dan Jennings)*

**tool** *n* : a physical skill used on the baseball field, usually confined to position players as hitting for average, hitting for power, running, fielding and throwing. "When you're scouting an amateur player, you want to see at least two above-average tools—because then you know the guy has a shot of being a major league regular." *(Logan White)*

**tool shed** *n* : **1** : a five-tool player **2** : a player who exhibits not only the five traditional tools but others such as quickness and agility. "When you think about everything he could do, Bo Jackson was a tool shed. I felt honored to watch him play." *(Jack Zduriencik)*

**trans·fer** *n* : the fielder's act of taking the ball out of his glove and getting it in throwing position; applies to both infielders and outfielders. "Bill Mazeroski and Derek Jeter both had excellent transfers—both smooth without any wasted time at all." *(Jack Zduriencik)*

**trig·ger** *n* : a hitter's timing mechanism, in which he brings his hands back before moving forward in a hitting motion, that initiates the swing. "It's impossible to get the bat going through the zone if you don't have the proper trigger. You're going to be late on the ball." *(Doug Mapson)*

**12-to-6** *adj* : Traveling from the equivalent of the 12 on a standard clock face down to the 6, as in an over-the-top curveball; also 1-to-7, etc; **syn** nose-to-toes. "Bert Blyleven's curve was a perfect 12-to-6 — it moved from the catcher's head right down to the plate." *(Mickey White)*

**us·a·bil·i·ty** *n* : The capability of a prospect's tool to actually be of use in game competition. "I've seen plenty of young pitchers with great fastballs but no usability, because they can't control it." *(Dan Jennings)*

**wet-news·pa·per** *adj* : Hitting with no authority, as if with a roll of damp newsprint. "When you see a wet-newspaper hitter, balls he hits have no sound. It's just a thud and it doesn't go anywhere." *(Deric Ladnier)*

**yel·low ham·mer** *n* : An exceptionally good curveball. "When you see a kid in high school who can throw an 85-mph yellow hammer, one that starts at the shoulders and ends at the knees, you're pretty excited." *(Deric Ladnier)*

# SIGNING BONUSES
## 2006 DRAFT

TOP 100 PICKS

### FIRST ROUND

| No. Team. Player, Pos. | Bonus |
|---|---|
| 1. Royals. Luke Hochevar, rhp | $3,500,000 |
| 2. Rockies. Greg Reynolds, rhp | $3,250,000 |
| 3. Devil Rays. Evan Longoria, 3b | $3,000,000 |
| 4. Pirates. Brad Lincoln, rhp | $2,750,000 |
| 5. Mariners. Brandon Morrow, rhp | $2,450,000 |
| 6. Tigers. Andrew Miller, lhp | $3,550,000 |
| 7. Dodgers. Clayton Kershaw, lhp | $2,300,000 |
| 8. Reds. Drew Stubbs, of | $2,000,000 |
| 9. Orioles. Bill Rowell, 3b | $2,100,000 |
| 10. Giants. Tim Lincecum, rhp | $2,025,000 |
| 11. Diamondbacks. Max Scherzer, rhp | Unsigned |
| 12. Rangers. Kasey Kiker, lhp | $1,600,000 |
| 13. Cubs. Tyler Colvin, of | $1,475,000 |
| 14. Blue Jays. Travis Snider, of | $1,700,000 |
| 15. Nationals. Chris Marrero, of | $1,625,000 |
| 16. Brewers. Jeremy Jeffress, rhp | $1,550,000 |
| 17. Padres. Matt Antonelli, 3b | $1,575,000 |
| 18. Phillies. Kyle Drabek, rhp/ss | $1,550,000 |
| 19. Marlins. Brett Sinkbeil, rhp | $1,525,000 |
| 20. Twins. Chris Parmelee, of/1b | $1,500,000 |
| 21. Yankees. Ian Kennedy, rhp | $2,250,000 |
| 22. Nationals. Colton Willems, rhp | $1,425,000 |
| 23. Astros. Max Sapp, c | $1,400,000 |
| 24. Braves. Cody Johnson, 1b | $1,375,000 |
| 25. Angels. Hank Conger, c | $1,350,000 |
| 26. Dodgers. Bryan Morris, rhp | $1,325,000 |
| 27. Red Sox. Jason Place, of | $1,300,000 |
| 28. Red Sox. Daniel Bard, rhp | $1,550,000 |
| 29. White Sox. Kyle McCulloch, rhp | $1,050,000 |
| 30. Cardinals. Adam Ottavino, rhp | $950,000 |

### SUPPLEMENTAL FIRST ROUND

| No. Team. Player, Pos. | Bonus |
|---|---|
| 31. Dodgers. Preston Mattingly, ss | $1,000,000 |
| 32. Orioles. Pedro Beato, rhp | $1,000,000 |
| 33. Giants. Emmanuel Burriss, ss | $1,000,000 |
| 34. Diamondbacks. Brooks Brown, rhp | $900,000 |
| 35. Padres. Kyler Burke, of | $950,000 |
| 36. Marlins. Chris Coghlan, 3b | $950,000 |
| 37. Phillies. Adrian Cardenas, ss | $925,000 |
| 38. Braves. Cory Rasmus, rhp | $900,000 |
| 39. Indians. David Huff, lhp | $900,000 |
| 40. Red Sox. Kris Johnson, lhp | $850,000 |
| 41. Yankees. Joba Chamberlain, rhp | $1,100,000 |
| 42. Cardinals. Chris Perez, rhp | $800,000 |
| 43. Braves. Steve Evarts, lhp | $800,000 |
| 44. Red Sox. Caleb Clay, rhp | $775,000 |

### SECOND ROUND

| No. Team. Player, Pos. | Bonus |
|---|---|
| 45. Royals. Jason Taylor, of | $762,500 |
| 46. Rockies. David Christensen, of | $750,000 |
| 47. Devil Rays. Josh Butler, rhp | $725,000 |
| 48. Pirates. Mike Felix, lhp | $725,000 |
| 49. Mariners. Chris Tillman, rhp | $680,000 |
| 50. Tigers. Ronnie Bourquin, 3b | $690,000 |

| No. Team. Player, Pos. | Bonus |
|---|---|
| 51. Braves. Jeff Locke, lhp | $675,000 |
| 52. Reds. Sean Watson, rhp | $670,000 |
| 53. Padres. Chad Huffman, of | $660,000 |
| 54. Cardinals. Brad Furnish, lhp | $600,000 |
| 55. Diamondbacks. Brett Anderson, lhp | $950,000 |
| 56. Indians. Steven Wright, rhp | $630,000 |
| 57. Indians. Josh Rodriguez, ss | $625,000 |
| 58. Orioles. Ryan Adams, 2b | $675,000 |
| 59. Nationals. Sean Black, rhp | Did Not Sign |
| 60. Brewers. Brent Brewer, ss | $600,000 |
| 61. Padres. Wade LeBlanc, lhp | $590,000 |
| 62. Mets. Kevin Mulvey, rhp | $585,000 |
| 63. Marlins. Tom Hickman, of | $575,000 |
| 64. Twins. Joe Benson, of | $575,000 |
| 65. Phillies. Drew Carpenter, rhp | $570,000 |
| 66. Athletics. Trevor Cahill, rhp | $560,000 |
| 67. Astros. Sergio Perez, rhp | $550,000 |
| 68. Braves. Dustin Evans, rhp | $530,000 |
| 69. Indians. Wes Hodges, 3b | $1,000,000 |
| 70. Nationals. Stephen Englund, of | $515,000 |
| 71. Red Sox. Justin Masterson, rhp | $510,000 |
| 72. Braves. Chase Fontaine, ss | $500,000 |
| 73. White Sox. Matt Long, rhp | $330,000 |
| 74. Cardinals. Jon Jay, of | $480,000 |

### SUPPLEMENTAL SECOND ROUND

| No. Team. Player, Pos. | Bonus |
|---|---|
| 75. Indians. Matt McBride, c | $445,000 |
| 76. Cardinals. Mark Hamilton, 1b | $465,000 |

### THIRD ROUND

| No. Team. Player, Pos. | Bonus |
|---|---|
| 77. Royals. Blake Wood, rhp | $460,000 |
| 78. Rockies. Keith Weiser, lhp | $455,000 |
| 79. Devil Rays. Nick Fuller, rhp | Did Not Sign |
| 80. Pirates. Shelby Ford, 2b | $450,000 |
| 81. Mariners. Tony Butler, lhp | $445,000 |
| 82. Tigers. Brennan Boesch, of | $445,000 |
| 83. Red Sox. Aaron Bates, 1b | $440,000 |
| 84. Reds. Chris Valaika, ss | $437,500 |
| 85. Orioles. Zach Britton, lhp | $435,000 |
| 86. Diamondbacks. Dallas Buck, rhp | $250,000 |
| 87. Diamondbacks. Cyle Hankerd, of | $430,000 |
| 88. Rangers. Chad Tracy, c | $427,500 |
| 89. Giants. Clayton Tanner, lhp | $425,000 |
| 90. Marlins. Torre Langley, c | $422,500 |
| 91. Nationals. Stephen King, ss | $750,000 |
| 92. Brewers. Cole Gillespie, of | $417,500 |
| 93. Padres. Cedric Hunter, of | $415,000 |
| 94. Mets. Joe Smith, rhp | $410,000 |
| 95. Marlins. Scott Cousins, of | $407,500 |
| 96. Twins. Tyler Robertson, lhp | $405,000 |
| 97. Phillies. Jason Donald, ss | $400,000 |
| 98. Athletics. Matt Sulentic, of | $395,000 |
| 99. Astros. Nick Moresi, of | $390,000 |
| 100. Braves. Chad Rodgers, lhp | $385,000 |

# SIGNING BONUSES
## 2005 DRAFT

### FIRST ROUND

| No. Team. Player, Pos. | Bonus |
|---|---|
| 1. Diamondbacks. Justin Upton, ss | $6,100,000 |
| 2. Royals. Alex Gordon, 3b | 4,000,000 |
| 3. Mariners. Jeff Clement, c | 3,400,000 |
| 4. Nationals. Ryan Zimmerman, 3b | 2,975,000 |
| 5. Brewers. Ryan Braun, 3b | 2,450,000 |
| 6. Blue Jays. Ricky Romero, lhp | 2,400,000 |
| 7. Rockies. Troy Tulowitzki, ss | 2,300,000 |
| 8. Devil Rays. Wade Townsend, rhp | 1,500,000 |
| 9. Mets. Mike Pelfrey, rhp | 3,550,000 |
| 10. Tigers. Cameron Maybin, of | 2,650,000 |
| 11. Pirates. Andrew McCutchen, of | 1,900,000 |
| 12. Reds. Jay Bruce, of | 1,800,000 |
| 13. Orioles. Brandon Snyder, c | 1,700,000 |
| 14. Indians. Trevor Crowe, of | 1,695,000 |
| 15. White Sox. Lance Broadway, rhp | 1,570,000 |
| 16. Marlins. Chris Volstad, rhp | 1,600,000 |
| 17. Yankees. C.J. Henry, ss | 1,575,000 |
| 18. Padres. Cesar Carrillo, rhp | 1,550,000 |
| 19. Rangers. John Mayberry, of | 1,525,000 |
| 20. Cubs. Mark Pawelek, lhp | 1,750,000 |
| 21. Athletics. Cliff Pennington, ss | 1,475,000 |
| 22. Marlins. Aaron Thompson, lhp | 1,225,000 |
| 23. Red Sox. Jacoby Ellsbury, of | 1,400,000 |
| 24. Astros. Brian Bogusevic, lhp | 1,375,000 |
| 25. Twins. Matt Garza, rhp | 1,350,000 |
| 26. Red Sox. Craig Hansen, rhp | 1,325,000 |
| 27. Braves. Joey Devine, rhp | 1,300,000 |
| 28. Cardinals. Colby Rasmus, of | 1,000,000 |
| 29. Marlins. Jacob Marceaux, rhp | 1,000,000 |
| 30. Cardinals. Tyler Greene, ss | 1,100,000 |

### SUPPLEMENTAL FIRST ROUND

| No. Team. Player, Pos. | Bonus |
|---|---|
| 31. Diamondbacks. Matt Torra, rhp | $1,025,000 |
| 32. Rockies. Chaz Roe, rhp | 1,025,000 |
| 33. Indians. John Drennen, of | 1,000,000 |
| 34. Marlins. Ryan Tucker, rhp | 975,000 |
| 35. Padres. Cesar Ramos, lhp | 950,000 |
| 36. Athletics. Travis Buck, of | 950,000 |
| 37. Angels. Trevor Bell, rhp | 925,000 |
| 38. Astros. Eli Iorg, of | 900,000 |
| 39. Twins. Henry Sanchez, 1b | 900,000 |
| 40. Dodgers. Luke Hochevar, rhp | Unsigned |
| 41. Braves. Beau Jones, lhp | $825,000 |
| 42. Red Sox. Clay Buchholz, rhp | 800,000 |
| 43. Cardinals. Mark McCormick, rhp | 800,000 |
| 44. Marlins. Sean West, lhp | 775,000 |
| 45. Red Sox. Jed Lowrie, 2b | 762,500 |
| 46. Cardinals. Tyler Herron, rhp | 675,000 |
| 47. Red Sox. Michael Bowden, rhp | 730,000 |
| 48. Orioles. Garrett Olson, lhp | 650,000 |

### SECOND ROUND

| No. Team. Player, Pos. | Bonus |
|---|---|
| 49. Diamondbacks. Matt Green, rhp | $500,000 |
| 50. Royals. Jeff Bianchi, ss | 690,000 |

| No. Team. Player, Pos. | Bonus |
|---|---|
| 51. Dodgers. Ivan De Jesus, ss | $675,000 |
| 52. Rockies. Daniel Carte, of | 670,000 |
| 53. Athletics. Craig Italiano, rhp | 725,500 |
| 54. Twins. Paul Kelly, ss | 650,000 |
| 55. Rockies. Zach Simons, rhp | 635,000 |
| 56 Devil Rays. Chris Mason, rhp | 630,000 |
| 57. Red Sox. Jon Egan, c | 625,000 |
| 58. Angels. Ryan Mount, ss | 615,000 |
| 59. Pirates. Brad Corley, of | 605,000 |
| 60. Reds. Travis Wood, lhp | 600,000 |
| 61. Orioles. Nolan Reimold, of | 590,000 |
| 62. Indians. Stephen Head, 1b | 605,000 |
| 63. Yankees. J. Brent Cox, rhp | 550,000 |
| 64. Marlins. Kris Harvey, of | 575,000 |
| 65. Phillies. Mike Costanzo, 3b | 570,000 |
| 66. Padres. Chase Headley, 3b | 560,000 |
| 67. Rangers. Johnny Whittleman, 3b | 650,000 |
| 68. Cubs. Donald Veal, lhp | 530,000 |
| 69. Athletics. Jared Lansford, rhp | 525,000 |
| 70. Cardinals. Josh Wilson, rhp | 515,000 |
| 71. Angels. P.J. Phillips, ss | 505,000 |
| 72. Astros. Ralph Henriquez, c | 485,000 |
| 73. Twins. Kevin Slowey, rhp | 490,000 |
| 74. Dodgers. Josh Wall, rhp | 480,000 |
| 75. Braves. Yunel Escobar, ss | 475,000 |
| 76. Padres. Nick Hundley, c | 465,000 |
| 77. Braves. Jeff Lyman, rhp | 460,000 |
| 78. Cardinals. Nick Webber, rhp | 425,000 |

### SUPPLEMENTAL SECOND ROUND

| No. Team. Player, Pos. | Bonus |
|---|---|
| 79. Marlins. Brett Hayes, c | $450,000 |
| 80. Twins. Drew Thompson, ss | 475,000 |

### THIRD ROUND

| No. Team. Player, Pos. | Bonus |
|---|---|
| 81. D'backs. Jason Neighborgall, rhp | $500,000 |
| 82. Royals. Chris Nicoll, rhp | 445,000 |
| 83. D'backs. Micah Owings, rhp | 440,000 |
| 84. Twins. Brian Duensing, lhp | 400,000 |
| 85. Brewers. Will Inman, rhp | 500,000 |
| 86. Blue Jays. Brian Pettway, of | 440,000 |
| 87. Rockies. Kyle Hancock, rhp Contract voided | |
| 88. Devil Rays. Bryan Morris, rhp | Unsigned |
| 89. Astros. Tommy Manzella, ss | $289,000 |
| 90. Tigers. Chris Robinson, c | 422,000 |
| 91. Pirates. James Boone, of | 420,000 |
| 92. Reds. Zach Ward, rhp | 420,000 |
| 93. Orioles. Brandon Erbe, rhp | 415,000 |
| 94. Indians. Nick Weglarz, 1b | 435,000 |
| 95. White Sox. Ricky Brooks, rhp | 300,000 |
| 96. Marlins. Matt Goyen, lhp | 340,000 |
| 97. Phillies. Matt Maloney, lhp | 400,000 |
| 98. Padres. Josh Geer, rhp | 395,000 |
| 99. Rangers. Taylor Teagarden, c | 725,000 |
| 100. Cubs. Mark Holliman, rhp | 385,000 |

# TOP 20 PROSPECTS
## FROM EVERY MINOR LEAGUE

As a complement to our organizational prospect rankings, Baseball America also ranks prospects in every minor league after each season. Like the organizational lists, they place more weight on potential than present performance and should not be regarded as minor league all-star teams.

The league lists do differ from the organizational lists, which are taken more from a scouting perspective. The league lists are based on conversations with league managers as well as scouts. They are not strictly polls, though we do try to talk with every manager. Some players on these lists, such as Stephen Drew and Matt Kemp, were not eligible for our organization prospect lists because they are no longer rookie-eligible. Such players are indicated with an asterisk (*). Players who have been traded from the organizations they are listed with are indicated with a pound sign (#).

Remember that managers and scouts tend to look at players differently. Managers give more weight to what a player does on the field, while scouts look at what a player might eventually do. We think both perspectives are useful, so we give you both even though they don't always match up with each other.

For a player to qualify for a league prospect list, he much have spent at least one-third of the season in a league. Position players must have one plate appearance per league game. Pitchers must pitch ⅓ inning per league game. Relievers must make at least 20 appearances in a full-season league or 10 appearances in a short-season league.

### INTERNATIONAL LEAGUE
1. Delmon Young, of, Durham (Devil Rays)
2. *Lastings Milledge, of, Norfolk (Mets)
3. *Jeremy Sowers, lhp, Buffalo (Indians)
4. *Tom Gorzelanny, lhp, Indianapolis (Pirates)
5. Ryan Sweeney, of, Charlotte (White Sox)
6. Josh Fields, 3b, Charlotte (White Sox)
7. *Hayden Penn, rhp, Ottawa (Orioles)
8. *Andy Marte, 3b, Buffalo (Indians)
9. #Humberto Sanchez, rhp, Toledo (Tigers)
10. *Jamie Shields, rhp, Durham (Devil Rays)
11. Elijah Dukes, of, Durham (Devil Rays)
12. Scott Thorman, 1b/of, Richmond (Braves)
13. *Brandon League, rhp, Syracuse (Blue Jays)
14. Jason Hammel, rhp, Durham (Devil Rays)
15. Dustin McGowan, rhp, Syracuse (Blue Jays)
16. Pat Neshek, rhp, Rochester (Twins)
17. Michael Bourn, of, Scranton/Wilkes-Barre (Phillies)
18. Dustin Pedroia, ss/2b, Pawtucket (Red Sox)
19. Charlie Haeger, rhp, Charlotte (White Sox)
20. *Chris Denorfia, of, Louisville (Reds)

### PACIFIC COAST LEAGUE
1. *Stephen Drew, ss, Tucson (Diamondbacks)
2. *Jered Weaver, rhp, Salt Lake (Angels)
3. *Howie Kendrick, 2b, Salt Lake (Angels)
4. *Chad Billingsley, rhp, Las Vegas (Dodgers)
5. Andy LaRoche, 3b, Las Vegas (Dodgers)
6. *Matt Kemp, of, Las Vegas (Dodgers)
7. Chris Young, of, Tucson (Diamondbacks)
8. Adam Jones, of, Tacoma (Mariners)
9. #Jason Hirsh, rhp, Round Rock (Astros)
10. *Carlos Quentin, of, Tucson (Diamondbacks)
11. Felix Pie, of, Iowa (Cubs)
12. James Loney, 1b, Las Vegas (Dodgers)
13. *Anthony Reyes, rhp, Memphis (Cardinals)
14. John Danks, lhp, Oklahoma (Rangers)
15. Erick Aybar, ss, Salt Lake (Angels)
16. *Rich Hill, lhp, Iowa (Cubs)
17. Miguel Montero, c, Tucson (Diamondbacks)
18. Chris Iannetta, c, Colorado Springs (Rockies)
19. Edinson Volquez, rhp, Oklahoma (Rangers)
20. #Joel Guzman, 3b/of, Las Vegas (Dodgers)

### EASTERN LEAGUE
1. Philip Hughes, rhp, Trenton (Yankees)
2. Matt Garza, rhp, New Britain (Twins)
3. Mike Pelfrey, rhp, Binghamton (Mets)
4. Adam Miller, rhp, Akron (Indians)
5. Adam Loewen, lhp, Bowie (Orioles)
6. Adam Lind, of, New Hampshire (Blue Jays)
7. Jacoby Ellsbury, of, Portland (Red Sox)
8. Carlos Gomez, of, Binghamton (Mets)
9. #Humberto Sanchez, rhp, Erie (Tigers)
10. Tyler Clippard, rhp, Trenton (Yankees)
11. Jonathan Sanchez, lhp, Connecticut (Giants)
12. Trevor Crowe, of, Akron (Indians)
13. #Kevin Kouzmanoff, 3b, Akron (Indians)
14. Kory Casto, 3b/of, Harrisburg (Nationals)
15. Alexi Casilla, ss, New Britain (Twins)
16. Scott Mathieson, rhp, Reading (Phillies)
17. Jair Jurrjens, rhp, Erie (Tigers)
18. #Gio Gonzalez, lhp, Reading (Phillies)
19. Radhames Liz, rhp, Bowie (Orioles)
20. Garrett Olson, lhp, Bowie (Orioles)

### SOUTHERN LEAGUE
1. Homer Bailey, rhp, Chattanooga (Reds)
2. Yovani Gallardo, rhp, Huntsville (Brewers)
3. Scott Elbert, lhp, Jacksonville (Dodgers)
4. *Matt Kemp, of, Jacksonville (Dodgers)
5. Andy LaRoche, 3b, Jacksonville (Dodgers)
6. Ryan Braun, 3b, Huntsville (Brewers)
7. Joey Votto, 1b, Chattanooga (Reds)
8. Jeff Niemann, rhp, Montgomery (Devil Rays)
9. Anibal Sanchez, rhp, Carolina (Marlins)
10. Jarrod Saltalamacchia, c, Mississippi (Braves)
11. Miguel Montero, c, Tennessee (Diamondbacks)
12. Sean Gallagher, rhp, West Tenn (Cubs)

13. #Tyler Lumsden, lhp, Birmingham (White Sox)
14. #George Kottaras, c, Mobile (Padres)
15. Alberto Gonzalez, ss, Tennessee (Diamondbacks)
16. Mitch Talbot, rhp, Montgomery (Devil Rays)
17. Eric Patterson, 2b, West Tenn (Cubs)
18. Juan Salas, rhp, Montgomery (Devil Rays)
19. Andy Sonnastine, rhp, Montgomery (Devil Rays)
20. Lance Broadway, rhp, Birmingham (White Sox)

## TEXAS LEAGUE

1. Alex Gordon, 3b, Wichita (Royals)
2. Brandon Wood, ss, Arkansas (Angels)
3. Troy Tulowitzki, ss, Tulsa (Rockies)
4. Billy Butler, of, Wichita (Royals)
5. Travis Buck, of, Midland (Athletics)
6. Ubaldo Jimenez, rhp, Tulsa (Rockies)
7. John Danks, lhp, Frisco (Rangers)
8. Hunter Pence, of, Corpus Christi (Astros)
9. Juan Gutierrez, rhp, Corpus Christi (Astros)
10. Ian Stewart, 3b, Tulsa (Rockies)
11. Chris Iannetta, c, Tulsa (Rockies)
12. Mitch Talbot, rhp, Corpus Christi (Astros)
13. Joe Koshansky, 1b, Tulsa (Rockies)
14. Kurt Suzuki, c, Midland (Athletics)
15. Matt Albers, rhp, Corpus Christi (Astros)
16. Chris Lubanski, of, Wichita (Royals)
17. Juan Morillo, rhp, Tulsa (Rockies)
18. Marcus McBeth, rhp, Midland (Athletics)
19. Terry Evans, of, Springfield/Arkansas (Cardinals/Angels)
20. Wladimir Balentien, of, San Antonio (Mariners)

## CALIFORNIA LEAGUE

1. Reid Brignac, ss, Visalia (Devil Rays)
2. Carlos Gonzalez, of, Lancaster (Diamondbacks)
3. Franklin Morales, lhp, Modesto (Rockies)
4. Nick Adenhart, rhp, Rancho Cucamonga (Angels)
5. Eric Hurley, rhp, Bakersfield (Rangers)
6. Travis Buck, of, Stockton (Athletics)
7. Jose Arredondo, rhp, Rancho Cucamonga (Angels)
8. Greg Reynolds, rhp, Modesto (Rockies)
9. Greg Smith, lhp, Lancaster (Diamondbacks)
10. Jonathan Herrera, ss, Modesto (Rockies)
11. Emilio Bonifacio, 2b, Lancaster (Diamondbacks)
12. Sean Rodriguez, ss, Rancho Cucamonga (Angels)
13. Mark Reynolds, if, Lancaster (Diamondbacks)
14. Ben Harrison, of, Bakersfield (Rangers)
15. Landon Powell, c, Stockton (Athletics)
16. Yung Chi Chen, 2b, Inland Empire (Mariners)
17. Fernando Perez, of, Visalia (Devil Rays)
18. Samuel Deduno, rhp, Modesto (Rockies)
19. Cesar Ramos, lhp, Lake Elsinore (Rockies)
20. Chase Headley, 3b, Lake Elsinore (Padres)

## CAROLINA LEAGUE

1. Chuck Lofgren, lhp, Kinston (Indians)
2. Jacoby Ellsbury, of, Wilmington (Red Sox)
3. Troy Patton, lhp, Salem (Astros)
4. Trevor Crowe, of, Kinston (Indians)
5. Jimmy Barthmaier, rhp, Salem (Astros)
6. Nolan Reimold, of, Frederick (Orioles)
7. Matt Harrison, lhp, Myrtle Beach (Braves)
8. Neil Walker, c, Lynchburg (Pirates)
9. Radhames Liz, rhp, Frederick (Orioles)
10. Scott Lewis, lhp, Kinston (Indians)
11. Brandon Jones, of, Myrtle Beach (Braves)
12. Collin Balester, rhp, Potomac (Nationals)
13. Van Pope, 3b, Myrtle Beach (Braves)
14. Felipe Paulino, rhp, Salem (Astros)

15. Garrett Olson, lhp, Frederick (Orioles)
16. Brian Barton, of, Kinston (Indians)
17. Brett Lillibridge, ss, Lynchburg (Pirates)
18. Chad Reineke, rhp, Salem (Astros)
19. Brian Bixler, ss, Lynchburg (Pirates)
20. Jed Lowrie, ss, Wilmington (Red Sox)

## FLORIDA STATE LEAGUE

1. Homer Bailey, rhp, Sarasota (Reds)
2. Yovanni Gallardo, rhp, Brevard County (Brewers)
3. Scott Elbert, lhp, Vero Beach (Dodgers)
4. Ryan Braun, 3b, Brevard County (Brewers)
5. Donald Veal, lhp, Daytona (Cubs)
6. Colby Rasmus, of, Palm Beach (Cardinals)
7. Mark Rogers, rhp, Brevard County (Brewers)
8. Mike Carp, 1b, St. Lucie (Mets)
9. Blake DeWitt, 2b/3b, Vero Beach (Dodgers)
10. Kevin Slowey, rhp, Fort Myers (Twins)
11. Sean Gallagher, rhp, Daytona (Cubs)
12. #Terry Evans, of, Palm Beach (Cardinals)
13. Gaby Hernandez, rhp, Jupiter (Marlins)
14. Johnny Cueto, rhp, Sarasota (Reds)
15. Jaime Garcia, lhp, Palm Beach (Cardinals)
16. Jair Jurrjens, rhp, Lakeland (Tigers)
17. Jose Mijares, lhp, Fort Myers (Twins)
18. Alexi Casilla, ss/2b, Fort Myers (Twins)
19. Ryan Patterson, of, Dunedin (Blue Jays)
20. Greg Golson, of, Clearwater (Phillies)

## MIDWEST LEAGUE

1. Jay Bruce, of, Dayton (Reds)
2. Cameron Maybin, of, West Michigan (Tigers)
3. Justin Upton, of, South Bend (Diamondbacks)
4. Colby Rasmus, of, Quad Cities (Cardinals)
5. Nick Adenhart, rhp, Cedar Rapids (Angels)
6. Jacob McGee, lhp, Southwest Michigan (Devil Rays)
7. Jaime Garcia, lhp, Quad Cities (Cardinals)
8. Wade Davis, rhp, Southwest Michigan (Devil Rays)
9. Donald Veal, lhp, Peoria (Cubs)
10. Matt Walker, rhp, Southwest Michigan (Devil Rays)
11. Stephen Marek, rhp, Cedar Rapids (Angels)
12. Johnny Cueto, rhp, Dayton (Reds)
13. Bryan Anderson, c, Quad Cities (Cardinals)
14. Oswaldo Sosa, rhp, Beloit (Twins)
15. John Mayberry Jr., of, Clinton (Rangers)
16. Justin Sellers, ss, Kane County (Athletics)
17. Eduardo Morlan, rhp, Beloit (Twins)
18. Paul Kelly, ss, Beloit (Twins)
19. Pedro Ciriaco, ss, South Bend (Diamondbacks)
20. Jeff Baisley, 3b, Kane County (Athletics)

## SOUTH ATLANTIC LEAGUE

1. Andrew McCutchen, of, Hickory (Pirates)
2. Jose Tabata, of, Charleston (Yankees)
3. Fernando Martinez, of, Hagerstown (Mets)
4. Elvis Andrus, ss, Rome (Braves)
5. Carlos Carrasco, rhp, Lakewood (Phillies)
6. Chris Volstad, rhp, Greensboro (Marlins)
7. Will Inman, rhp, West Virginia (Brewers)
8. Sean West, lhp, Greensboro (Marlins)
9. Brandon Erbe, rhp, Delmarva (Orioles)
10. Dexter Fowler, of, Asheville (Rockies)
11. Deolis Guerra, rhp, Hagerstown (Mets)
12. John Drennen, of, Lake County (Indians)
13. Clay Buchholz, rhp, Greenville (Red Sox)
14. Lorenzo Cain, of, West Virginia (Brewers)
15. Michael Bowden, rhp, Greenville (Red Sox)

16. Ryan Tucker, rhp, Greensboro (Marlins)
17. Eric Campbell, 3b, Rome (Braves)
18. Aaron Thompson, lhp, Greensboro (Marlins)
19. Matt Maloney, lhp, Lakewood (Phillies)
20. Josh Outman, lhp, Lakewood (Phillies)

## NEW YOUR-PENN LEAGUE

1. Jeremy Hellickson, rhp, Hudson Valley (Devil Rays)
2. Pedro Beato, rhp, Aberdeen (Orioles)
3. Matt McBride, c, Mahoning Valley (Indians)
4. Max Sapp, c, Tri-City (Astros)
5. Kris Johnson, lhp, Lowell (Red Sox)
6. Justin Masterson, rhp, Lowell (Red Sox)
7. Jordan Parraz, of, Tri-City (Astros)
8. Adam Ottavino, rhp, State College (Cardinals)
9. Scott Sizemore, ss/2b, Oneonta (Tigers)
10. Joe Smith, rhp, Brooklyn (Mets)
11. Tim Norton, rhp, Staten Island (Yankees)
12. Mark Hamilton, 1b, State College (Cardinals)
13. Justin Maxwell, of, Vermont (Nationals)
14. Jason Berken, rhp, Aberdeen (Orioles)
15. George Kontos, rhp, Staten Island (Yankees)
16. Chris Vinyard, 1b, Aberdeen (Orioles)
17. Mitch Hilligoss, ss/3b, Staten Island (Yankees)
18. Chris Salamida, lhp, Tri-City (Astros)
19. Wilmer Pino, 2b, Staten Island (Yankees)
20. Neil Wagner, rhp, Mahoning Valley (Indians)

## NORTHWEST LEAGUE

1. Tyler Colvin, of, Boise (Cubs)
2. Shane Lindsay, rhp, Tri-City (Rockies)
3. Matt Sulentic, of, Vancouver (Athletics)
4. Emmanuel Burriss, ss, Salem-Keizer (Giants)
5. Clye Hankerd, of, Yakima (Diamondbacks)
6. Tony Butler, lhp, Everett (Mariners)
7. Kasey Kiker, lhp, Spokane (Rangers)
8. Matt Antonelli, 3b, Eugene (Padres)
9. Mark Pawelek, lhp, Boise (Cubs)
10. Jermaine Mitchell, of, Vancouver (Athletics)
11. Josh Sullivan, rhp, Tri-City (Rockies)
12. Chris Davis, 1b/of, Spokane (Rangers)
13. Chad Tracy, c, Spokane (Rangers)
14. Chad Huffman, of, Eugene (Padres)
15. Daniel Mayora, ss, Tri-City (Rockies)
16. Brooks Brown, rhp, Yakima (Diamondbacks)
17. Andrew Bailey, rhp, Vancouver (Athletics)
18. Scott Deal, rhp, Vancouver (Athletics)
19. Kam Mickolio, rhp, Everett (Mariners)
20. Adam Cowart, rhp, Salem-Keizer (Giants)

## APPALACHIAN LEAGUE

1. Travis Snider, of, Pulaski (Blue Jays)
2. Bill Rowell, 3b, Bluefield (Orioles)
3. Kieron Pope, of, Bluefield (Orioles)
4. Tommy Hanson, rhp, Danville (Braves)
5. Jamie Richmond, rhp, Danville (Braves)
6. Daryl Jones, of, Johnson City (Cardinals)
7. Desmond Jennings, of, Princeton (Devil Rays)
8. Chase Fontaine, ss, Danville (Braves)
9. Jon Edwards, of, Johnson City (Cardinals)
10. Zach Britton, lhp, Bluefield (Orioles)
11. Emmanuel Garcia, ss/2b, Kingsport (Mets)
12. Blake King, rhp, Johnson City (Cardinals)
13. Tyler Herron, rhp, Johnson City (Cardinals)
14. Brian Kirwan, rhp, Elizabethton (Twins)
15. Alex Burnett, rhp, Elizabethton (Twins)
16. Justin Edwards, lhp, Bristol (White Sox)
17. Ronald Ramirez, ss/2b, Greeneville (Astros)
18. Yohermyn Chavez, of, Pulaski (Blue Jays)
19. Nevin Ashley, c, Princeton (Devil Rays)
20. Sergio Sevrino, lhp, Greeneville (Astros)

## PIONEER LEAGUE

1. Bryan Morris, rhp, Ogden (Dodgers)
2. Josh Bell, 3b, Ogden (Dodgers)
3. Hector Gomez, ss/3b, Casper (Rockies)
4. Sean O'Sullivan, rhp, Orem (Angels)
5. Gerardo Parra, of, Missoula (Diamondbacks)
6. Peter Bourjos, of, Orem (Angels)
7. Drew Stubbs, of, Billings (Reds)
8. Andrew Fie, 3b, Missoula (Diamondbacks)
9. Jeremy Haynes, rhp, Orem (Angels)
10. Ryan Mount, ss, Orem (Angels)
11. Cole Gillespie, of, Helena (Brewers)
12. Kenneth Herndon, rhp, Orem (Angels)
13. Chris Valiaka, ss, Billings (Reds)
14. Chris Carter, 1b, Great Falls (White Sox)
15. Steven Johnson, rhp, Ogden (Dodgers)
16. Trevor Bell, rhp, Orem (Angels)
17. Pedro Strop, rhp, Casper (Rockies)
18. Stephen Chapman, of, Helena (Brewers)
19. Brandon Hynick, rhp, Casper (Rockies)
20. Hector Ambriz, rhp, Missoula (Diamondbacks)

## ARIZONA LEAGUE

1. Hank Conger, c, Angels
2. Jeremy Jeffress, rhp, Brewers
3. Cedric Hunter, of, Padres
4. Marcus Lemon, ss, Rangers
5. Brent Fisher, lhp, Royals
6. Matt Sweeney, 3b/1b, Angels
7. Sharlon Schoop, ss, Giants
8. Kyler Burke, of, Padres
9. Jason Taylor, 3b, Royals
10. Vladimir Veras, rhp, Angels
11. Brent Brewer, ss, Brewers
12. Gerardo Avila, 1b, Mariners
13. Luis Durango, of, Padres
14. Jose Ceda, lhp, Cubs
15. Manuel Cabeza, rhp, Giants
16. Derrick Robinson, of, Royals
17. Nick Van Stratten, of, Royals
18. Carlos Peguero, of, Mariners
19. Warner Madrigal, rhp, Angels
20. Felix Carrasco, 3b, Padres

## GULF COAST LEAGUE

1. Clayton Kershaw, lhp, Dodgers
2. Chris Parmelee, of/1b, Twins
3. Gorkys Hernandez, of, Tigers
4. Chris Marrero, of, Nationals
5. Jason Place, of, Red Sox
6. Dellin Betances, rhp, Yankees
7. Adrian Cardenas, ss, Phillies
8. Neftali Feliz, rhp, Braves
9. Jhonny Nunez, rhp, Dodgers
10. Tom Hickman, of, Marlins
11. Preston Mattingly, ss, Dodgers
12. Kyle Drabek, rhp, Phillies
13. Steven Evarts, lhp, Braves
14. Jesus Sanchez, c, Phillies
15. Chad Rodgers, lhp, Braves
16. Josue Calzado, of, Yankees
17. D'Arby Myers, of, Phillies
18. Zach McAllister, rhp, Yankees
19. Carlos Monasterios, rhp, Yankees/Phillies
20. Joe Benson, of, Twins

# INDEX

## A

Abreu, Etanislau (Dodgers) 244
Adams, Ryan (Orioles) 54
Adenhart, Nick (Angels) 227
Albers, Matt (Astros) 195
Aldridge, Richard (Angels) 235
Alexander, Mark (Dodgers) 249
Ambriz, Hector (Diamondbacks) 26
Anderson, Brian (Giants) 409
Anderson, Bryan (Cardinals) 372
Anderson, Josh (Astros) 200
Anderson, Lars (Red Sox) 68
Andino, Robert (Marlins) 186
Andrus, Elvis (Braves) 35
Antonelli, Matt (Padres) 387
Arias, Joaquin (Rangers) 452
Arredondo, Jose (Angels) 231
Atkins, Mitch (Cubs) 93
Avery, James (Reds) 119
Aybar, Erick (Angels) 227

## B

Badenhop, Burke (Tigers) 170
Baez, Sammy (Cubs) 90
Baez, Welinson (Phillies) 346
Bailey, Andrew (Athletics) 333
Bailey, Homer (Reds) 114
Baisley, Jeff (Athletics) 330
Baker, Jeff (Rockies) 149
Balentien, Wladimir (Mariners) 420
Balester, Collin (Nationals) 482
Banks, Josh (Blue Jays) 471
Bankston, Wes (Devil Rays) 442
Bannister, Brian (Royals) 213
Bard, Daniel (Red Sox) 68
Barden, Brian (Diamondbacks) 26
Barratt, Jonathan (Devil Rays) 443
Barthmaier, Jimmy (Astros) 195
Barton, Brian (Indians) 132
Barton, Daric (Athletics) 323
Bates, Aaron (Red Sox) 75
Bauserman, Joe (Pirates) 361
Bayliss, Jonah (Pirates) 360
Beam, T.J. (Yankees) 315
Beato, Pedro (Orioles) 51
Bell, Josh (Dodgers) 245
Bell, Trevor (Angels) 234
Beltre, Engel (Red Sox) 73
Benson, Joe (Twins) 277
Berken, Jason (Orioles) 56
Betances, Dellin (Yankees) 307
Bianchi, Jeff (Royals) 214
Birkins, Kurt (Orioles) 58
Bisenius, Joe (Phillies) 344
Bixler, Brian (Pirates) 357
Blackley, Travis (Mariners) 426
Blanks, Kyle (Padres) 397
Bocock, Brian (Giants) 412
Boesch, Brennan (Tigers) 168
Boggs, Mitchell (Cardinals) 374
Bogusevic, Brian (Astros) 199
Bonifacio, Emilio (Diamondbacks) 23
Boone, James (Pirates) 361
Bostick, Adam (Mets) 295
Botts, Jason (Rangers) 453

Bourjos, Peter (Angels) 230
Bourn, Michael (Phillies) 341
Bourquin, Ronnie (Tigers) 169
Bowden, Michael (Red Sox) 67
Brauer, Dan (Phillies) 346
Braun, Ryan (Brewers) 259
Breit, Aaron (Padres) 390
Bresnehan, Pat (Pirates) 360
Brett Anderson (Diamondbacks) 22
Brewer, Brent (Brewers) 265
Brignac, Reid (Devil Rays) 435
Britton, Zach (Orioles) 55
Broadway, Lance (White Sox) 99
Broadway, Larry (Nationals) 488
Brown, Andrew (Padres) 395
Brown, Brooks (Diamondbacks) 25
Brown, Eric (Mets) 300
Brown, Jordan (Indians) 139
Browning, Barret (Angels) 236
Bruan, Ryan (Royals) 215
Bruce, Jay (Reds) 115
Buchholz, Clay (Red Sox) 67
Buck, Dallas (Diamondbacks) 28
Buck, Travis (Athletics) 322
Buckner, Billy (Royals) 214
Bullington, Brian (Pirates) 359
Burke, Kyler (Padres) 391
Burnett, Alex (Twins) 285
Burns, Greg (Marlins) 188
Burres, Brian (Orioles) 61
Burriss, Emmanuel (Giants) 403
Buschmann, Matt (Padres) 395
Bush, Matt (Padres) 393
Butler, Billy (Royals) 211
Butler, Josh (Devil Rays) 443
Butler, Tony (Mariners) 419

## C

Cabrera, Asdrubal (Indians) 136
Cahill, Trevor (Athletics) 326
Cain, Lorenzo (Brewers) 260
Callaspo, Alberto (Diamondbacks) 19
Calzado, Josue (Yankees) 316
Camacho, Eddie (Mets) 298
Cameron, Kevin (Padres) 393
Campbell, Eric (Braves) 36
Campusano, Edward (Tigers) 168
Campusano, Jose (Marlins) 188
Cannon, Chip (Blue Jays) 476
Cardenas, Adrian (Phillies) 339
Carp, Mike (Mets) 293
Carpenter, Drew (Phillies) 345
Carr, Adam (Nationals) 489
Carrasco, Carlos (Phillies) 338
Carrasco, Felix (Padres) 394
Carrillo, Cesar (Padres) 387
Carroll, Brett (Marlins) 186
Carter, Chris (Diamondbacks) 25
Carter, Chris (White Sox) 102
Carvajal, Yefri (Padres) 391
Casilla, Alexi (Twins) 277
Castillo, Fabio (Rangers) 457
Casto, Kory (Nationals) 483
Castro, Simon (Padres) 397
Cazana-Marti, Amaury 381
Chamberlain, Joba (Yankees) 308

Chapman, Stephen (Brewers) 268
Chavez, Jesse (Pirates) 363
Chavez, Yohermyn (Blue Jays) 474
Chen, Yung-Chi (Mariners) 422
Cheng, Chi-Hung (Blue Jays) 471
Cherry, Rocky (Cubs) 88
Chico, Matt (Nationals) 485
Christensen, Danny (Royals) 219
Christensen, David (Rockies) 157
Ciriaco, Audy (Tigers) 172
Ciriaco, Pedro (Diamondbacks) 27
Clarke, Darren (Rockies) 155
Clay, Caleb (Red Sox) 73
Clemens, Koby (Astros) 203
Clement, Jeff (Mariners) 419
Clevlen, Brent (Tigers) 163
Clippard, Tyler (Yankees) 309
Cobb, Larry (Athletics) 333
Coghlan, Chris (Marlins) 181
Coles, Corey (Mets) 301
Colina, Alvin (Rockies) 155
Colvin, Tyler (Cubs) 83
Conger, Hank (Angels) 228
Conrad, Brooks (Astros) 200
Constanza, Jose (Indians) 140
Copeland, Ben (Giants) 411
Cordier, Erik (Royals) 216
Corley, Brad (Pirates) 357
Coronado, Jose (Mets) 296
Corpas, Manny (Rockies) 150
Correa, Heitor (Phillies) 348
Cortes, Daniel (Royals) 221
Costanzo, Mike (Phillies) 343
Cota, Luis (Royals) 218
Coutlangus, Jon (Reds) 122
Cox, Bryce (Red Sox) 69
Cox, J. Brent (Yankees) 309
Crowe, Trevor (Indians) 131
Cruceta, Francisco (Rangers) 457
Cruz, Luis (Padres) 394
Cueto, Johnny (Reds) 115
Cumberland, Shawn (Devil Rays) 445
Cunningham, Aaron (White Sox) 101
Curtis, Colin (Yankees) 315

## D

Danks, John (Rangers) 450
Davidson, Dave (Pirates) 360
Davis, Chris (Rangers) 454
Davis, Rajai (Pirates) 364
Davis, Wade (Devil Rays) 437
Day, Dewon (White Sox) 106
De la Cruz, Eulogio (Tigers) 164
De la Cruz, Jose (Mariners) 426
Deduno, Samuel (Rockies) 152
DeJesus, Ivan Jr. (Dodgers) 244
Delgado, Jesus (Marlins) 184
Desmond, Ian (Nationals) 486
Devaney, Mike (Mets) 299
Devine, Joey (Braves) 38
DeWitt, Blake (Dodgers) 245
Diamond, Thomas (Rangers) 451
Diaz, Frank (Nationals) 492
Diaz, Robinzon (Blue Jays) 476
Dickerson, Chris (Reds) 119
Dickerson, Joe (Royals) 221

| | | | | | |
|---|---|---|---|---|---|
| Dillard, Tim (Brewers) | 263 | Gamel, Mat (Brewers) | 262 | Henry, C.J. (Phillies) | 346 |
| Donachie, Adam (Orioles) | 61 | Garcia, Anderson (Orioles) | 60 | Henry, Sean (Mets) | 299 |
| Donald, Jason (Phillies) | 348 | Garcia, Chris (Yankees) | 311 | Hernandez, Anderson (Mets) | 294 |
| Doolittle, Todd (Marlins) | 189 | Garcia, Edgar (Phillies) | 339 | Hernandez, Francisco (White Sox) | 107 |
| Dopirak, Brian (Cubs) | 87 | Garcia, Emmanuel (Mets) | 296 | Hernandez, Gaby (Marlins) | 179 |
| Doubront, Felix (Red Sox) | 73 | Garcia, Harvey (Marlins) | 185 | Hernandez, Gorkys (Tigers) | 165 |
| Douglass, Chance (Astros) | 201 | Garcia, Jaime (Cardinals) | 371 | Hernandez, Luis (Orioles) | 58 |
| Dove, Dennis (Cardinals) | 379 | Garcia, Jose (Marlins) | 183 | Herndon, Kenneth (Angels) | 230 |
| Drabek, Kyle (Phillies) | 339 | Garciaparra, Michael (Mariners) | 429 | Herrera, Danny Ray (Rangers) | 461 |
| Drennen, John (Indians) | 132 | Gardner, Brett (Yankees) | 310 | Herrera, Javier (Athletics) | 324 |
| Duensing, Brian (Twins) | 281 | Garrison, Steve (Brewers) | 268 | Herrera, Jonathan (Rockies) | 151 |
| Dukes, Elijah (Devil Rays) | 436 | Garza, Matt (Twins) | 274 | Herrerra, Yoslan (Pirates) | 356 |
| Dumatrait, Phil (Reds) | 120 | Giarratano, Tony (Tigers) | 167 | Herrmann, Frank (Indians) | 141 |
| Duncan, Eric (Yankees) | 311 | Gibson, Glenn (Nationals) | 484 | Herron, Tyler (Cardinals) | 377 |
| Dunlap, Cory (Dodgers) | 249 | Gillespie, Cole (Brewers) | 261 | Hickman, Tom (Marlins) | 186 |
| Durbin, J.D. (Twins) | 278 | Gimenez, Hector (Astros) | 204 | Hill, Shawn (Nationals) | 491 |
| | | Ginley, Kyle (Blue Jays) | 473 | Hinckley, Mike (Nationals) | 493 |

## E

| | | | | | |
|---|---|---|---|---|---|
| | | Godfrey, Graham (Blue Jays) | 473 | Hinton, Robert (Brewers) | 267 |
| | | Godin, Jason (Royals) | 221 | Hirsh, Jason (Rockies) | 147 |
| Edwards, Jon (Cardinals) | 380 | Goleski, Ryan (Athletics) | 329 | Hochevar, Luke (Royals) | 211 |
| Edwards, Justin (White Sox) | 104 | Golson, Greg (Phillies) | 342 | Hodges, Wes (Indians) | 133 |
| Egan, Jon (Red Sox) | 75 | Gomes, Anderson (White Sox) | 107 | Hoey, James (Orioles) | 53 |
| Egbert, Jack (White Sox) | 104 | Gomez, Carlos (Mets) | 291 | Holden, Brandon (Pirates) | 362 |
| Ekstrom, Mike (Padres) | 396 | Gomez, Hector (Rockies) | 152 | Holdzkom, John (Mets) | 300 |
| Elbert, Scott (Dodgers) | 243 | Gonzalez, Alberto (Diamondbacks) | 23 | Holdzkom, Lincoln (Astros) | 202 |
| Ellsbury, Jacoby (Red Sox) | 67 | Gonzalez, Carlos (Diamondbacks) | 19 | Holliman, Mark (Cubs) | 91 |
| Englund, Stephen (Nationals) | 489 | Gonzalez, Esmailyn (Nationals) | 484 | Hollimon, Michael (Tigers) | 167 |
| Erbe, Brandon (Orioles) | 51 | Gonzalez, Gio (White Sox) | 99 | Hoorelbeke, Casey (Dodgers) | 252 |
| Errecart, Chris (Brewers) | 265 | Gonzalez, Rafael (Reds) | 124 | Hopper, Norris (Reds) | 124 |
| Escobar, Alcides (Brewers) | 261 | Gordon, Alex (Royals) | 210 | Horne, Alan (Yankees) | 312 |
| Escobar, Yunel (Braves) | 38 | Green, Nick (Angels) | 234 | Horwitz, Brian (Giants) | 413 |
| Estrada, Marco (Nationals) | 490 | Greene, Tyler (Cardinals) | 376 | House, J.R. (Orioles) | 59 |
| Estrada, Paul (Astros) | 197 | Griffin, Dan (Giants) | 409 | Houser, James (Devil Rays) | 442 |
| Evans, Nick (Mets) | 298 | Guerra, Deolis (Mets) | 292 | Hu, Chin-Lung (Dodgers) | 246 |
| Evans, Terry (Angels) | 233 | Gunderson, Kevin (Braves) | 45 | Huber, Jon (Mariners) | 423 |
| Evarts, Steve (Braves) | 39 | Gutierrez, Juan (Astros) | 196 | Huber, Justin (Royals) | 213 |
| Everts, Clint (Nationals) | 491 | Guzman, Freddy (Rangers) | 459 | Huff, David (Indians) | 134 |
| | | Guzman, Joel (Devil Rays) | 438 | Huffman, Chad (Padres) | 389 |
| | | Gwynn, Tony Jr. (Brewers) | 264 | Hughes, Jared (Pirates) | 365 |
| | | | | Hughes, Philip (Yankees) | 306 |

## F

## H

| | | | | | |
|---|---|---|---|---|---|
| Feierabend, Ryan (Mariners) | 420 | | | Humber, Philip (Mets) | 291 |
| Felix, Mike (Pirates) | 358 | Haeger, Charlie (White Sox) | 100 | Hundley, Nick (Padres) | 389 |
| Feliz, Neftali (Braves) | 41 | Haerther, Cody (Cardinals) | 376 | Hunter, Cedric (Padres) | 386 |
| Fermaint, Charlie (Brewers) | 262 | Haigwood, Daniel (Rangers) | 458 | Hurley, Eric (Rangers) | 451 |
| Fie, Andrew (Diamondbacks) | 26 | Hale, Beau (Orioles) | 58 | Huseby, Chris (Cubs) | 86 |
| Fields, Josh (White Sox) | 99 | Halman, Greg (Mariners) | 427 | Hussey, John (Padres) | 397 |
| Finigan, P.J. (Tigers) | 169 | Hamilton, Josh (Reds) | 125 | Hynick, Brandon (Rockies) | 153 |
| Fiorentino, Jeff (Orioles) | 53 | Hamilton, Mark (Cardinals) | 375 | | |
| Fisher, Brent (Royals) | 214 | Hammel, Jason (Devil Rays) | 439 | | |
| Flores, Jesus (Nationals) | 486 | Hammes, Zach (Dodgers) | 248 | | |

## I

| | | | | | |
|---|---|---|---|---|---|
| Flores, Josh (Astros) | 201 | Hammond, Steve (Brewers) | 260 | Iannetta, Chris (Rockies) | 149 |
| Florimon, Pedro (Orioles) | 59 | Hankerd, Cyle (Diamondbacks) | 24 | Ingram, Jesse (Rangers) | 460 |
| Fontaine, Chase (Braves) | 43 | Hansack, Devern (Red Sox) | 74 | Inman, Will (Brewers) | 259 |
| Fontenot, Mike (Cubs) | 93 | Hansen, Craig (Red Sox) | 69 | Iorg, Eli (Astros) | 199 |
| Ford, Darren (Brewers) | 263 | Hanson, Tommy (Braves) | 41 | Iribarren, Hernan (Brewers) | 266 |
| Ford, Shelby (Pirates) | 362 | Happ, J.A. (Phillies) | 341 | Ishikawa, Travis (Giants) | 406 |
| Fowler, Dexter (Rockies) | 147 | Harman, Brad (Phillies) | 345 | Italiano, Craig (Athletics) | 331 |
| Fowler, Eric (Blue Jays) | 470 | Harper, Brett (Mets) | 295 | Ivany, Devin (Nationals) | 492 |
| Fox, Jake (Cubs) | 91 | Harrell, Lucas (White Sox) | 101 | Iwamura, Akinori (Devil Rays) | 437 |
| Francisco, Juan (Reds) | 124 | Harrison, Ben (Rangers) | 456 | | |
| Frandsen, Kevin (Giants) | 404 | Harrison, Matt (Braves) | 35 | | |
| Frazier, Jeff (Tigers) | 170 | Harvey, Kris (Marlins) | 182 | | |

## J

| | | | | | |
|---|---|---|---|---|---|
| Freese, David (Padres) | 392 | Harvey, Ryan (Cubs) | 85 | Jackson, Austin (Yankees) | 313 |
| Fruto, Emiliano (Nationals) | 487 | Hatch, Anthony (Blue Jays) | 472 | Jackson, Zach (Brewers) | 264 |
| Fuenmayor, Balbino (Blue Jays) | 470 | Hawksworth, Blake (Cardinals) | 371 | Janish, Paul (Reds) | 117 |
| Fuld, Sam (Cubs) | 92 | Hayes, Brett (Marlins) | 187 | Jaramillo, Jason (Phillies) | 347 |
| Furnish, Brad (Cardinals) | 379 | Haynes, Jeremy (Angels) | 232 | Jaso, John (Devil Rays) | 441 |
| | | Head, Stephen (Indians) | 141 | Jay, Jon (Cardinals) | 372 |
| | | Headley, Chase (Padres) | 388 | Jeffress, Jeremy (Brewers) | 259 |

## G

| | | | | | |
|---|---|---|---|---|---|
| | | Hearne, Trey (Cardinals) | 378 | Jennings, Desmond (Devil Rays) | 445 |
| Galarraga, Armando (Rangers) | 456 | Hedrick, Justin (Giants) | 411 | Jeroloman, Brian (Blue Jays) | 477 |
| Gallagher, Sean (Cubs) | 84 | Hellickson, Jeremy (Devil Rays) | 438 | Jimenez, Cesar (Mariners) | 428 |
| Gallardo, Yovani (Brewers) | 258 | | | Jimenez, Ubaldo (Rockies) | 148 |

| | | | | | |
|---|---|---|---|---|---|
| Johnson, Blake (Royals) | 217 | Liotta, Ray (White Sox) | 103 | Meloan, Jonathan (Dodgers) | 245 |
| Johnson, Chris (Astros) | 203 | Lirette, Chase (Blue Jays) | 477 | Menchaca, Pablo (Padres) | 396 |
| Johnson, Cody (Braves) | 45 | Lis, Erik (Twins) | 284 | Mendoza, Tommy (Angels) | 230 |
| Johnson, Elliot (Devil Rays) | 442 | Litsch, Jesse (Blue Jays) | 469 | Mertins, Kurt (Royals) | 220 |
| Johnson, James (Orioles) | 55 | Littleton, Wes (Rangers) | 458 | Mijares, Jose (Twins) | 283 |
| Johnson, Kris (Red Sox) | 70 | Liz, Radhames (Orioles) | 52 | Miller, Adam (Indians) | 130 |
| Johnson, Rob (Mariners) | 424 | Lo, Ching-Lung (Rockies) | 154 | Miller, Andrew (Tigers) | 163 |
| Johnson, Steven (Dodgers) | 248 | Locke, Jeff (Braves) | 41 | Miller, Drew (Padres) | 391 |
| Johnson, Tyler (Cardinals) | 377 | Lofgren, Chuck (Indians) | 131 | Miller, Greg (Dodgers) | 248 |
| Johnston, Andrew (Rockies) | 157 | Logan, Boone (White Sox) | 105 | Miller, Matt (Rockies) | 156 |
| Johnston, Dyland (Cubs) | 89 | Loney, James (Dodgers) | 243 | Mitchell, Jermaine (Athletics) | 324 |
| Jones, Adam (Mariners) | 418 | Long, Matt (White Sox) | 102 | Mitchell, Mike (Athletics) | 331 |
| Jones, Beau (Braves) | 40 | Longoria, Evan (Devil Rays) | 435 | Mock, Garrett (Nationals) | 486 |
| Jones, Brandon (Braves) | 35 | Loo, Milton (Reds) | 117 | Montanez, Luis (Orioles) | 60 |
| Jones, Darryl (Cardinals) | 374 | Lopez, Pedro (White Sox) | 105 | Montero, Jesus (Yankees) | 314 |
| Joyce, Matt (Tigers) | 170 | Lowe, Mark (Mariners) | 421 | Montero, Miguel (Diamondbacks) | 20 |
| Jukich, Ben (Athletics) | 332 | Lowrie, Jed (Red Sox) | 72 | Moore, Scott (Cubs) | 85 |
| Jung, Young-Il (Angels) | 227 | Lubanski, Chris (Royals) | 211 | Morales, Franklin (Rockies) | 147 |
| Jurrjens, Jair (Tigers) | 163 | Lumsden, Tyler (Royals) | 212 | Morillo, Juan (Rockies) | 150 |
| | | Lyman, Jeff (Braves) | 40 | Morlan, Eduardo (Twins) | 282 |
| | | | | Morris, Bryan (Dodgers) | 246 |

# K

| | | | | | |
|---|---|---|---|---|---|
| | | | | Morrow, Brandon (Mariners) | 419 |
| Kaaihue, Kala (Braves) | 38 | | | Morton, Colt (Padres) | 396 |
| Kahn, Stephen (Mariners) | 425 | | | Moses, Matt (Twins) | 279 |
| Kalish, Ryan (Red Sox) | 72 | # M | | Moss, Brandon (Red Sox) | 71 |
| Karstens, Jeff (Yankees) | 316 | MacLane, Evan (Diamondbacks) | 28 | Mount, Ryan (Angels) | 233 |
| Katin, Brendan (Brewers) | 268 | Magee, Brandon (Blue Jays) | 469 | Mujica, Edward (Indians) | 137 |
| Kelly, Paul (Twins) | 277 | Maier, Mitch (Royals) | 212 | Mulvey, Kevin (Mets) | 292 |
| Kendrick, Kyle (Phillies) | 344 | Majewski, Val (Orioles) | 56 | Murphy, David (Red Sox) | 71 |
| Kennedy, Ian (Yankees) | 308 | Maloney, Matt (Phillies) | 342 | Murphy, Tommy (Angels) | 236 |
| Kershaw, Clayton (Dodgers) | 243 | Manship, Jeff (Twins) | 280 | Myers, D'Arby (Phillies) | 342 |
| Kiker, Kasey (Rangers) | 453 | Manzella, Tommy (Astros) | 203 | |
| King, Stephen (Nationals) | 485 | Marceaux, Jacob (Marlins) | 188 | |
| Kinney, Josh (Cardinals) | 373 | Marek, Stephen (Angels) | 228 | # N |
| Kirkland, Kody (Tigers) | 166 | Marquez, Jeff (Yankees) | 311 | |
| Klosterman, Ryan (Blue Jays) | 471 | Marrero, Chris (Nationals) | 483 | Nanita, Ricardo (White Sox) | 109 |
| Komine, Shane (Athletics) | 328 | Marson, Lou (Phillies) | 345 | Narveson, Chris (Cardinals) | 375 |
| Kontos, George (Yankees) | 314 | Martin, Dustin (Mets) | 297 | Natale, Jeff (Red Sox) | 77 |
| Koshansky, Joe (Rockies) | 151 | Martin, J.D. (Indians) | 135 | Navarro, Oswaldo (Mariners) | 429 |
| Kottaras, George (Red Sox) | 70 | Martinez, Edgar (Red Sox) | 76 | Neal, Thomas (Giants) | 410 |
| Kouzmanoff, Kevin (Padres) | 387 | Martinez, Fernando (Mets) | 291 | Negron, Kris (Red Sox) | 77 |
| | | Martinez, Joey (Giants) | 410 | Negrych, Jim (Pirates) | 365 |
| | | Martinez-Esteve, Eddy (Giants) | 406 | Nelson, Chris (Rockies) | 153 |
| # L | | Martis, Shairon (Nationals) | 488 | Neshek, Pat (Twins) | 276 |
| | | Mason, Chris (Devil Rays) | 443 | Newby, Kyler (Diamondbacks) | 28 |
| Laffey, Aaron (Indians) | 138 | Masset, Nick (Rangers) | 453 | Nickeas, Mike (Mets) | 300 |
| LaHair, Bryan (Mariners) | 424 | Masterson, Justin (Red Sox) | 71 | Nickerson, Jonah (Tigers) | 171 |
| Lambert, Chris (Cardinals) | 375 | Mastny, Tom (Indians) | 140 | Nicoll, Chris (Royals) | 218 |
| Lannan, John (Nationals) | 490 | Mateo, Juan (Cubs) | 86 | Niemann, Jeff (Devil Rays) | 435 |
| Lansford, Jared (Athletics) | 328 | Mathieson, Scott (Phillies) | 340 | Niese, Jon (Mets) | 293 |
| Lansford, Josh (Cubs) | 90 | Mathis, Doug (Rangers) | 460 | Nippert, Dustin (Diamondbacks) | 21 |
| Lara, Juan (Indians) | 135 | Mathis, Jeff (Angels) | 228 | Norris, Bud (Astros) | 203 |
| Larish, Jeff (Tigers) | 165 | Matos, Osiris (Giants) | 407 | Norton, Tim (Yankees) | 317 |
| LaRoche, Andy (Dodgers) | 242 | Matsuzaka, Daisuke (Red Sox) | 66 | Nowak, Chris (Devil Rays) | 445 |
| Larrison, Preston (Tigers) | 171 | Mattingly, Preston (Dodgers) | 246 | Nunez, Jhonny (Nationals) | 487 |
| Leach, Brant (Dodgers) | 249 | Maxwell, Justin (Nationals) | 489 | |
| LeBlanc, Wade (Padres) | 392 | Mayberry, John Jr. (Rangers) | 452 | |
| Lebron, Luis (Orioles) | 54 | Maybin, Cameron (Tigers) | 162 | # O |
| LeCure, Sam (Reds) | 118 | Mazzaro, Vin (Athletics) | 329 | |
| Lee, Chad (Athletics) | 333 | McAllister, Zach (Yankees) | 315 | O'Flaherty, Eric (Mariners) | 422 |
| Lemon, Marcus (Rangers) | 455 | McAnulty, Paul (Padres) | 393 | Ohlendorf, Ross (Diamondbacks) | 22 |
| Lerew, Anthony (Braves) | 39 | McBeth, Marcus (Athletics) | 325 | Okajima, Hideki (Red Sox) | 74 |
| Lerud, Steve (Pirates) | 362 | McBride, Matt (Indians) | 136 | Olson, Garrett (Orioles) | 52 |
| Leslie, Myron (Athletics) | 329 | McBryde, Mike (Giants) | 407 | Omogrosso, Brian (White Sox) | 108 |
| Lewis, Fred (Giants) | 405 | McCann, Brad (Marlins) | 189 | Orenduff, Justin (Dodgers) | 247 |
| Lewis, Jensen (Indians) | 139 | McConnell, Chris (Royals) | 220 | Orlando, Paulo (White Sox) | 108 |
| Lewis, Scott (Indians) | 133 | McCormick, Mark (Cardinals) | 373 | Orr, Kyle (Dodgers) | 251 |
| Liddi, Alex (Mariners) | 428 | McCulloch, Kyle (White Sox) | 100 | Ortmeier, Dan (Giants) | 412 |
| Lillibridge, Brent (Pirates) | 355 | McCutchen, Andrew (Pirates) | 354 | Osoria, Franquelis (Pirates) | 363 |
| Lincecum, Tim (Giants) | 402 | McCutchen, Daniel (Yankees) | 317 | O'Sullivan, Sean (Angels) | 229 |
| Lincoln, Brad (Pirates) | 355 | McGee, Jacob (Devil Rays) | 436 | Ottavino, Adam (Cardinals) | 372 |
| Lind, Adam (Blue Jays) | 466 | Medlen, Kris (Braves) | 44 | Outman, Josh (Phillies) | 340 |
| Lindsay, Shane (Rockies) | 153 | Megrew, Mike (Dodgers) | 250 | Overholt, Pat (Phillies) | 347 |
| Lindstrom, Matt (Marlins) | 185 | Melancon, Mark (Yankees) | 312 | Owens, Henry (Marlins) | 183 |
| | | Melillo, Kevin (Athletics) | 327 | Owens, Jerry (White Sox) | 103 |

| | | | | | |
|---|---|---|---|---|---|
| Owings, Micah (Diamondbacks) | 20 | Ramos, Cesar (Padres) | 390 | Sanchez, Romulo (Pirates) | 365 |
| | | Rasmus, Colby (Cardinals) | 370 | Sanders, Marcus (Giants) | 408 |
| **P** | | Rasmus, Cory (Braves) | 40 | Sanfler, Miguel (Dodgers) | 252 |
| | | Rasner, Jacob (Rangers) | 461 | Santana, Carlos (Dodgers) | 251 |
| Parmelee, Chris (Twins) | 275 | Ravin, Josh (Reds) | 119 | Santangelo, Lou (Astros) | 201 |
| Parnell, Bobby (Mets) | 297 | Ray, Jason (Athletics) | 332 | Santos, Sergio (Blue Jays) | 472 |
| Parra, Gerardo (Diamondbacks) | 24 | Raynor, John (Marlins) | 187 | Sapp, Max (Astros) | 197 |
| Parra, Manny (Brewers) | 265 | Recker, Anthony (Athletics) | 331 | Sardinha, Bronson (Yankees) | 316 |
| Parraz, Jordan (Astros) | 202 | Redmond, Todd (Pirates) | 358 | Sarfate, Dennis (Brewers) | 266 |
| Pascual, Rolando (Brewers) | 269 | Reed, Justin (Reds) | 123 | Saunders, Michael (Mariners) | 427 |
| Patterson, Eric (Cubs) | 84 | Reed, Mark (Cubs) | 88 | Schafer, Jordan (Braves) | 44 |
| Patterson, Ryan (Blue Jays) | 467 | Reimold, Nolan (Orioles) | 51 | Schierholtz, Nate (Giants) | 405 |
| Patton, Troy (Astros) | 195 | Reineke, Chad (Astros) | 198 | Schlact, Michael (Rangers) | 459 |
| Paul, Xavier (Dodgers) | 252 | Resop, Chris (Angels) | 235 | Schoop, Sharlon (Giants) | 410 |
| Paulino, Felipe (Astros) | 197 | Reyes, Angel (Yankees) | 312 | Schumaker, Skip (Cardinals) | 381 |
| Pawelek, Mark (Cubs) | 86 | Reyes, Jo-Jo (Braves) | 37 | Segovia, Zach (Phillies) | 343 |
| Peacock, Brian (Nationals) | 491 | Reynolds, Greg (Rockies) | 149 | Seibel, Phil (Angels) | 237 |
| Pearce, Steven (Pirates) | 357 | Reynolds, Mark (Diamondbacks) | 21 | Seidel, R.J. (Brewers) | 267 |
| Pedroia, Dustin (Red Sox) | 68 | Richar, Danny (Diamondbacks) | 27 | Sellers, Justin (Athletics) | 326 |
| Pedroza, Sergio (Devil Rays) | 444 | Richmond, Jamie (Braves) | 43 | Septimo, Leyson (Diamondbacks) | 29 |
| Peguero, Carlos (Mariners) | 428 | Ridgway, Jeff (Devil Rays) | 441 | Severino, Sergio (Astros) | 204 |
| Pelfrey, Mike (Mets) | 290 | Riggans, Shawn (Devil Rays) | 440 | Shafer, David (Reds) | 121 |
| Pelland, Tyler (Reds) | 120 | Rleal, Sendy (Orioles) | 55 | Sharpless, Josh (Pirates) | 356 |
| Pena, Brayan (Braves) | 42 | Robbins, Whit (Twins) | 283 | Shelby, John Jr. (White Sox) | 106 |
| Pena, Francisco (Mets) | 295 | Roberts, Brandon (Twins) | 284 | Shinskie, David (Twins) | 285 |
| Pena, Tony (Diamondbacks) | 22 | Roberts, Ryan (Blue Jays) | 476 | Shoppach, Kelly (Indians) | 137 |
| Pence, Hunter (Astros) | 194 | Robertson, Tyler (Twins) | 283 | Shortslef, Josh (Pirates) | 361 |
| Pennington, Cliff (Athletics) | 327 | Robinson, Chris (Cubs) | 90 | Sillman, Mike (Cardinals) | 380 |
| Pereira, Nick (Giants) | 408 | Robinson, Derrick (Royals) | 218 | Simon, Alfredo (Phillies) | 349 |
| Perez, Chris (Cardinals) | 371 | Robinson, Shane (Cardinals) | 380 | Sinkbeil, Brett (Marlins) | 179 |
| Perez, Fernando (Devil Rays) | 440 | Robnett, Richie (Athletics) | 326 | Sipp, Tony (Indians) | 131 |
| Perez, Miguel (Reds) | 122 | Rodgers, Chad (Braves) | 41 | Sizemore, Scott (Tigers) | 166 |
| Perez, Oneli (White Sox) | 104 | Rodriguez, Aneury (Rockies) | 154 | Slayden, Jeremy (Phillies) | 348 |
| Perez, Rafael (Indians) | 134 | Rodriguez, Josh (Indians) | 139 | Sleeth, Kyle (Tigers) | 173 |
| Perez, Sergio (Astros) | 198 | Rodriguez, Mike (Astros) | 205 | Slocum, Brian (Indians) | 136 |
| Perez, Yohannis (Brewers) | 263 | Rodriguez, Rafael (Angels) | 234 | Slowey, Kevin (Twins) | 275 |
| Perkins, Glen (Twins) | 275 | Rodriguez, Sean (Angels) | 229 | Smit, Alexander (Twins) | 280 |
| Petit, Yusmeiro (Marlins) | 184 | Roe, Chaz (Rockies) | 150 | Smith, Dan (Braves) | 42 |
| Petrick, Billy (Cubs) | 89 | Rogers, Brian (Pirates) | 364 | Smith, Greg (Diamondbacks) | 24 |
| Pettway, Brian (Blue Jays) | 474 | Rogers, Mark (Brewers) | 260 | Smith, Joe (Mets) | 293 |
| Pham, Tommy (Cardinals) | 378 | Rohrbaugh, Robert (Mariners) | 427 | Smith, Jordan (Reds) | 123 |
| Phillips, Heath (White Sox) | 102 | Romak, Jamie (Braves) | 43 | Smith, Matt (Phillies) | 349 |
| Phillips, P.J. (Angels) | 231 | Romero, Alex (Twins) | 285 | Smith, Seth (Rockies) | 152 |
| Phillips, Paul (Blue Jays) | 474 | Romero, Davis (Blue Jays) | 473 | Snider, Travis (Blue Jays) | 467 |
| Pie, Felix (Cubs) | 82 | Romero, Ricky (Blue Jays) | 467 | Snyder, Brad (Indians) | 133 |
| Pimentel, Julio (Royals) | 217 | Roquet, Rocky (Cubs) | 92 | Snyder, Brandon (Orioles) | 53 |
| Pino, Yohan (Twins) | 284 | Rosa, Carlos (Royals) | 217 | Soler, Alay (Mets) | 294 |
| Pinto, Renyel (Marlins) | 182 | Rosario, Francisco (Blue Jays) | 468 | Sonnanstine, Andrew (Devil Rays) | 441 |
| Place, Jason (Red Sox) | 70 | Rottino, Vinny (Brewers) | 269 | Soria, Joakim (Royals) | 215 |
| Plouffe, Trevor (Twins) | 281 | Rowell, Bill (Orioles) | 50 | Sosa, Oswaldo (Twins) | 278 |
| Plummer, Jarod (Royals) | 219 | Ruiz, Carlos (Phillies) | 343 | Soto, Geovany (Cubs) | 89 |
| Pope, Kieron (Orioles) | 54 | Rundle, Drew (Cubs) | 88 | Span, Denard (Twins) | 279 |
| Pope, Van (Braves) | 36 | Rupe, Josh (Rangers) | 454 | Spann, Chad (Red Sox) | 76 |
| Poveda, Omar (Rangers) | 455 | Russell, Adam (White Sox) | 101 | Speigner, Levale (Nationals) | 493 |
| Powell, Landon (Athletics) | 330 | Ryan, Brendan (Cardinals) | 374 | Spoone, Chorye (Orioles) | 59 |
| Privett, Todd (Mets) | 299 | Ryu, Jae-Kuk (Cubs) | 87 | Stammen, Craig (Nationals) | 490 |
| Purcey, David (Blue Jays) | 470 | | | Stange, Daniel (Diamondbacks) | 27 |
| Putnam, Danny (Athletics) | 328 | **S** | | Starling, Wardell (Pirates) | 359 |
| | | | | Statia, Hainley (Angels) | 232 |
| **Q** | | Sadler, Billy (Giants) | 406 | Stavinoha, Nick (Cardinals) | 378 |
| | | Salamida, Chris (Astros) | 205 | Stegall, Daniel (Mets) | 301 |
| Quinowski, David (Giants) | 412 | Salas, Juan (Devil Rays) | 439 | Stern, Adam (Orioles) | 57 |
| | | Salas, Marino (Orioles) | 57 | Stewart, Chris (White Sox) | 107 |
| | | Salmon, Brad (Reds) | 123 | Stewart, Ian (Rockies) | 148 |
| **R** | | Salome, Angel (Brewers) | 262 | Stinson, Josh (Mets) | 297 |
| | | Saltalamacchia, Jarrod (Braves) | 34 | Stokes, Jason (Marlins) | 189 |
| Rabelo, Mike (Tigers) | 169 | Samardzija, Jeff (Cubs) | 83 | Stoner, Tobi (Mets) | 298 |
| Raburn, Ryan (Tigers) | 172 | Sammons, Clint (Braves) | 44 | Strait, Cody (Reds) | 118 |
| Rahl, Chris (Diamondbacks) | 25 | Sampson, Chris (Astros) | 198 | Strop, Pedro (Rockies) | 156 |
| Rainville, Jay (Twins) | 280 | Sanchez, Angel (Royals) | 220 | Stubbs, Drew (Reds) | 116 |
| Ramirez, Ismael (Blue Jays) | 475 | Sanchez, Gaby (Marlins) | 180 | Suarez, Larry (Cubs) | 92 |
| Ramirez, Max (Indians) | 138 | Sanchez, Humberto (Yankees) | 307 | Sulentic, Matt (Athletics) | 324 |
| Ramirez, Ronald (Astros) | 205 | Sanchez, Jonathan (Giants) | 403 | Suzuki, Kurt (Athletics) | 323 |
| Ramirez, Wilkin (Tigers) | 167 | | | | |

Swarzak, Anthony (Twins) 276
Sweeney, Matt (Angels) 232
Sweeney, Ryan (White Sox) 98
Szymanski, B.J. (Reds) 125

# T

Tabata, Jose (Yankees) 307
Talbot, Mitch (Devil Rays) 439
Tankersley, Taylor (Marlins) 180
Tanner, Clayton (Giants) 407
Tata, Jordan (Tigers) 164
Taubenheim, Ty (Blue Jays) 475
Taylor, Jason (Royals) 216
Taylor, Scott (Cubs) 93
Teagarden, Taylor (Rangers) 455
Tejada, Oscar (Red Sox) 74
Thatcher, Joe (Brewers) 267
Thigpen, Curtis (Blue Jays) 468
Thomas, Clete (Tigers) 173
Thomas, Justin (Mariners) 423
Thompson, Aaron (Marlins) 181
Thompson, Daryl (Reds) 121
Thompson, Sean (Padres) 395
Thorman, Scott (Braves) 37
Threets, Erick (Giants) 411
Tillman, Chris (Mariners) 421
Toregas, Wyatt (Indians) 138
Torra, Matt (Diamondbacks) 29
Towles, J.R. (Astros) 196
Townsend, Wade (Devil Rays) 444
Tracey, Sean (White Sox) 108
Tracy, Chad (Rangers) 456
Trahern, Dallas (Tigers) 165
Triunfel, Carlos (Mariners) 422
Troncoso, Ramon (Dodgers) 250
Trumbo, Mark (Angels) 237
Tseng, Sung-Wei (Indians) 134
Tucker, Ryan (Marlins) 181

Tuiasosopo, Matt (Mariners) 425
Tulowitzki, Troy (Rockies) 146

# U

Upton, Justin (Diamondbacks) 18

# V

Valaika, Chris (Reds) 118
Valbuena, Luis (Mariners) 426
Valdez, Jose (Giants) 413
Valdez, Merkin (Giants) 409
Valido, Robert (White Sox) 105
Vallejo, Jose (Rangers) 461
Van Allen, Cory (Nationals) 492
Van Benschoten, John (Pirates) 358
Vanden Hurk, Rick (Marlins) 183
Varvaro, Anthony (Mariners) 425
Vasquez, Sendy (Tigers) 166
Vasquez, Virgil (Tigers) 171
Vazquez, Camilo (Reds) 121
Veal, Donald (Cubs) 83
Vechionacci, Marcos (Yankees) 310
Venable, Will (Padres) 388
Villalona, Angel (Giants) 403
Vinyard, Chris (Orioles) 57
Volquez, Edinson (Rangers) 451
Volstad, Chris (Marlins) 178
Votto, Joey (Reds) 115

# W

Waldrop, Kyle (Twins) 282
Walker, Matt (Devil Rays) 437
Walker, Neil (Pirates) 355
Wall, Josh (Dodgers) 253
Warden, Jim Ed (Phillies) 347
Watson, Sean (Reds) 117

Webb, Ryan (Athletics) 332
Webster, Anthony (Rangers) 459
Weeden, Ty (Red Sox) 76
Wells, Jared (Padres) 390
West, Sean (Marlins) 179
Whelan, Kevin (Yankees) 309
Whisler, Wes (White Sox) 109
White, Cody (Dodgers) 251
White, Steven (Yankees) 314
Whittleman, Johnny (Rangers) 457
Willems, Colton (Nationals) 483
Willits, Reggie (Angels) 236
Wilson, Bobby (Angels) 233
Wilson, Brian (Giants) 404
Wilson, Michael (Mariners) 423
Wimberly, Corey (Rockies) 154
Windsor, Jason (Athletics) 325
Winfree, David (Twins) 281
Winters, Kyle (Marlins) 187
Wood, Blake (Royals) 216
Wood, Brandon (Angels) 226
Wood, Travis (Reds) 116
Worrell, Mark (Cardinals) 379
Wright, Chase (Yankees) 313
Wright, Stephen (Indians) 141
Wright, Wesley (Dodgers) 253

# Y

Yates, Kyle (Blue Jays) 472
Young, Chris (Diamondbacks) 19
Young, Delmon (Devil Rays) 434
Young, Delwyn (Dodgers) 247
Young, Eric Jr. (Rockies) 156

# Z

Zinicola, Zech (Nationals) 484

# Give BA a tryout

**The magazine for baseball insiders**

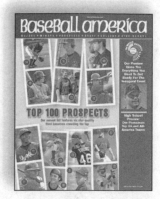

**4 TRIAL ISSUES FOR $4**

With a trial subscription
you'll discover what
makes our readers
so loyal!

**MAJORS
MINORS
PROSPECTS
DRAFT
COLLEGE
HIGH SCHOOL**

# BaseBall america
# PROSPECT
# HANDBOOK
# 2007

Baseball America Inc.
Durham, N.C.